1 MONTH OF
FREE
READING

at

www.ForgottenBooks.com

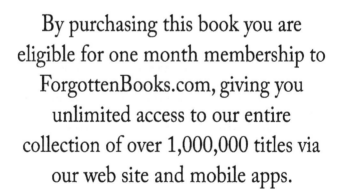

By purchasing this book you are eligible for one month membership to ForgottenBooks.com, giving you unlimited access to our entire collection of over 1,000,000 titles via our web site and mobile apps.

To claim your free month visit:

www.forgottenbooks.com/free923799

ISBN 978-0-260-03646-9
PIBN 10923799

AMERICAN STATE REPORTS,

CONTAINING THE

CASES OF GENERAL VALUE AND AUTHORITY

SUBSEQUENT TO THOSE CONTAINED IN THE "AMERICAN
DECISIONS" AND THE "AMERICAN REPORTS,"

DECIDED IN THE

COURTS OF LAST RESORT

OF THE SEVERAL STATES.

SELECTED, REPORTED, AND ANNOTATED

By A. C. FREEMAN,

AND THE ASSOCIATE EDITORS OF THE "AMERICAN DECISIONS."

Vol. XXXVI.

SAN FRANCISCO:
BANCROFT-WHITNEY COMPANY,
LAW PUBLISHERS AND LAW BOOKSELLERS.
1894.

SAN FRANCISCO:
THE FILMER-ROLLINS ELECTROTYPE COMPANY,
TYPOGRAPHERS AND STEREOTYPERS.

AMERICAN STATE REPORTS.

VOL. XXXVI.

SCHEDULE

showing the original volumes of reports in which the cases herein selected and re-reported may be found, and the pages of this volume devoted to each state.

SCHEDULE

SHOWING IN WHAT VOLUMES OF THIS SERIES THE CASES REPORTED IN THE SEVERAL VOLUMES OF OFFICIAL REPORTS MAY BE FOUND.

State reports are in parentheses, and the numbers of this series in bold-faced figures.

ALABAMA. — (83) **3**; (84) **5**; (85) **7**; (86) **11**; (87) **13**; (88) **16**; (89) **18**; (90, 91) **24**; (92) **25**; (93) **30**; (94) **33**; (95) **36**.

ARKANSAS. — (48) **3**; (49) **4**; (50) **7**; (51) **14**; (52) **20**; (53) **22**; (54) **26**; (55) **29**; (56) **35**.

CALIFORNIA. — (72) **1**; (73) **2**; (74) **5**; (75) **7**; (76) **9**; (77) **11**; (78, 79) **12**; (80) **13**; (81) **15**; (82) **16**; (83) **17**; (84) **18**; (85) **20**; (86) **21**; (87, 88) **22**; (89) **23**; (90, 91) **25**; (92, 93) **27**; (94) **28**; (95) **29**; (96) **31**; (97) **33**; (98) **35**.

COLORADO. — (10) **3**; (11) **7**; (12) **13**; (13) **16**; (14) **20**; (15) **22**; (16) **25**; (17) **31**; (18) **36**.

CONNECTICUT. — (54) **1**; (55) **3**; (56) **7**; (57) **14**; (58) **18**; (59) **21**; (60) **25**; (61) **29**; (62) **36**.

DELAWARE. — (5 Houst.) **1**; (6 Houst.) **22**.

FLORIDA. — (22) **1**; (23) **11**; (24) **12**; (25, 26) **23**; (27) **26**; (28) **29**; (29) **30**; (30) **32**; (31) **34**.

GEORGIA. — (76) **2**; (77) **4**; (78) **6**; (79) **11**; (80, 81) **12**; (82) **14**; (83, 84) **20**; (85) **21**; (86) **22**; (87) **27**; (88) **30**; (89) **32**; (90) **35**.

IDAHO. — (2) **35**.

ILLINOIS. — (121) **2**; (122) **3**; (123) **5**; (124) **7**; (125) **8**; (126) **9**; (127) **11**; (128) **15**; (129) **16**; (130) **17**; (131) **19**; (132) **22**; (133, 134) **23**; (135) **25**; (136) **29**; (137) **31**; (138, 139) **32**; (140, 141) **33**; (142) **34**; (143, 144, 145) **36**.

INDIANA. — (112) **2**; (113) **3**; (114) **5**; (115) **7**; (116) **9**; (117, 118) **10**; (119) **12**; (120, 121) **16**; (122) **17**; (123) **18**; (124) **19**; (125) **21**; (126, 127) **22**; (128) **25**; (129) **28**; (130) **30**; (131) **31**; (132) **32**; (133) **36**.

IOWA. — (72) **2**; (73) **5**; (74) **7**; (75) **9**; (76, 77) **14**; (78) **16**; (79) **18**; (80) **20**; (81) **25**; (82) **31**; (83) **32**; (84) **35**.

KANSAS. — (37) **1**; (38) **5**; (39) **7**; (40) **10**; (41) **13**; (42) **16**; (43) **19**; (44) **21**; (45) **23**; (46) **26**; (47) **27**; (48) **30**; (49) **33**; (50) **34**.

KENTUCKY. — (83, 84) **4**; (85) **7**; (86) **9**; (87) **12**; (88) **21**; (89) **25**; (90) **29**; (91) **34**; (92) **36**.

LOUISIANA. — (39 La. Ann.) **4**; (40 La. Ann.) **8**; (41 La. Ann.) **17**; (42 La. Ann.) **21**; (43 La. Ann.) **26**; (44 La. Ann.) **32**.

MAINE. — (79) **1**; (80) **6**; (81) **10**; (82) **17**; (83) **23**; (84) **30**; (85) **35**.

MARYLAND. — (67) **1**; (68) **6**; (69) **9**; (70) **14**; (71) **17**; (72) **20**; (73) **25**; (74) **28**; (75) **32**; (76) **35**.

MASSACHUSETTS. — (145) **1**; (146) **4**; (147) **9**; (148) **12**; (149) **14**; (150) **15**; (151) **21**; (152) **23**; (153) **25**; (154) **26**; (155) **31**; (156) **32**; (157) **34**; (158) **35**.

MICHIGAN. — (60, 61) **1**; (62) **4**; (63) **6**; (64, 65) **8**; (66, 67) **11**; (68, 69, 75) **13**; (70) **14**; (71, 76) **15**; (72, 73, 74) **16**; (77, 78) **18**; (79) **19**; (80) **20**; (81, 82, 83) **21**; (84) **22**; (85, 86, 87) **24**; (88) **26**; (89) **28**; (90, 91) **30**; (92) **31**; (93) **32**; (94) **34**; (95, 96) **35**.

MINNESOTA. — (36) **1**; (37) **5**; (38) **8**; (39, 40) **12**; (41) **16**; (42) **18**; (43) **19**; (44) **20**; (45) **22**; (46) **24**; (47) **28**; (48) **31**; (49) **32**; (50) **36**.

MISSISSIPPI. — (65) **7**; (66) **14**; (67) **19**; (68) **24**; (69) **30**; (70) **35**.

MISSOURI. — (92) **1**; (93) **3**; (94) **4**; (95) **6**; (96) **9**; (97) **10**; (98) **14**; (99) **17**; (100) **18**; (101) **20**; (102) **22**; (103) **23**; (104, 105) **24**; (106) **27**; (107) **28**; (108, 109) **32**; (110, 111) **33**; (112) **34**; (113, 114) **35**.

MONTANA. — (9) **18**; (10) **24**; (11) **28**; (12) **33**.

NEBRASKA. — (22) **3**; (23, 24) **8**; (25) **13**; (26) **18**; (27) **20**; (28, 29) **26**; (30) **27**; (31) **28**; (32, 33) **29**; (34) **33**.

NEVADA. — (19) **3**; (20) **19**.

NEW HAMPSHIRE. — (64) **10**; (62) **13**; (65) **23**.

NEW JERSEY. — (43 N. J. Eq.) **3**; (44 N. J. Eq.) **6**; (50 N. J. L.) **7**; (51 N. J. L.; 45 N. J. Eq.) **14**; (46 N. J. Eq.; 52 N. J. L.) **19**; (47 N. J. Eq.) **24**; (53 N. J. L.) **26**; (48 N. J. Eq.) **27**; (49 N. J. Eq.) **31**; (54 N. J. L.) **33**; (50 N. J. Eq.) **35**.

NEW YORK. — (107) **1**; (108) **2**; (109) **4**; (110) **6**; (111) **7**; (112) **8**; (113) **10**; (114) **11**; (115) **12**; (116, 117) **15**; (118, 119) **16**; (120) **17**; (121) **18**; (122) **19**; (123) **20**; (124, 125) **21**; (126) **22**; (127) **24**; (128, 129) **26**; (130, 131) **27**; (132, 133) **28**; (134) **30**; (135) **31**; (136) **32**; (137) **33**; (138) **34**; (139) **36**.

NORTH CAROLINA. — (97, 98) **2**; (99, 100) **6**; (101) **9**; (102) **11**; (103) **14**; (104) **17**; (105) **18**; (106) **19**; (107) **22**; (108) **23**; (109) **26**; (110) **28**; (111) **32**; (112) **34**.

NORTH DAKOTA. — (1) **26**; (2) **33**.

OHIO. — (45 Ohio St.) **4**; (46 Ohio St.) **15**; (47 Ohio St.) **21**; (48 Ohio St.) **29**; (49 Ohio St.) **34**.

OREGON. — (15) **3**; (16) **8**; (17) **11**; (18) **17**; (19) **20**; (20) **23**; (21) **28**; (22) **29**.

PENNSYLVANIA. — (115, 116, 117 Pa. St.) **2**; (118, 119 Pa. St.) **4**; (120, 121 Pa. St.) **6**; (122 Pa. St.) **9**; (123, 124 Pa. St.) **10**; (125 Pa. St.) **11**; (126 Pa. St.) **12**; (127 Pa. St.) **14**; (128, 129 Pa. St.) **15**; (130, 131 Pa. St.) **17**; (132, 133, 134 Pa. St.) **19**; (135, 136 Pa. St.) **20**; (137, 138 Pa. St.) **21**; (139, 140, 141 Pa. St.) **23**; (142, 143 Pa. St.) **24**; (144, 145 Pa. St.) **27**; (146 Pa. St.) **28**; (147, 150 Pa. St.) **30**; (151 Pa. St.) **31**; (148 Pa. St.) **33**; (149, 152, 153 Pa. St.) **34**; (154, 155 Pa. St.) **35**; (156 Pa. St.) **36**.

RHODE ISLAND. — (15) **2**; (16) **27**; (17) **33**.

SOUTH CAROLINA. — (26) **4**; (27, 28, 29) **13**; (30) **14**; (31, 32) **17**; (33) **26**; (34) **27**; (35) **28**; (36) **31**; (37) **34**.

SOUTH DAKOTA. — (1) **36**.

TENNESSEE. — (85) **4**; (86) **6**; (87) **10**; (88) **17**; (89) **24**; (90) **25**; (91) **30**; (92) **36**.

TEXAS. — (68) **2**; (69; 24 Tex. App.) **5**; (70; 25, 26 Tex. App.) **8**; (71) **10**; (27 Tex. App.) **11**; (72) **13**; (73, 74) **15**; (75) **16**; (76) **18**; (77; 28 Tex. App.) **19**; (78) **22**; (79) **23**; (29 Tex. App.) **25**; (80, 81) **26**; (82) **27**; (30 Tex. App.) **28**; (83) **29**; (84) **31**; (85) **34**.

VERMONT. — (60) **6**; (61) **15**; (62) **22**; (63) **25**; (64) **33**; (65) **36**.

VIRGINIA. — (82) 3; (83) 5; (84) 10; (85) 17; (86) 19; (87) 24; (88) 29.

WASHINGTON. — (1) 22; (2) 26; (3) 28; (4) 31; (5) 34; (6) 36.

WEST VIRGINIA. — (29) 6; (30) 8; (31) 13; (32, 33) 25; (34) 26; (35) 29; (36) 32.

WISCONSIN. — (69) 2; (70, 71) 5; (72) 7; (73) 9; (74, 75) 17; (76, 77) 20; (78) 23; (79) 24; (80) 27; (81) 29; (82) 33; (83) 35; (84) 36.

WYOMING. — (3) 31.

AMERICAN STATE REPORTS.

VOL. XXXVI.

CASES REPORTED.

AMERICAN STATE REPORTS.

VOL. XXXVI.

CASES

IN THE

SUPREME COURT

OF

PENNSYLVANIA.

FELLOWS v. LOOMIS.

[156 PENNSYLVANIA STATE, 74.]

MORTGAGOR AND MORTGAGEE, FORECLOSURE BY LATTER IN TRUST FOR
FORMER.—If an agreement is made between a mortgagor and mortgagee
that the mortgage shall be foreclosed, the property bid in, a part of it
conveyed to a third person, and the balance to the mortgagor subject
to the mortgage indebtedness, a trust relation is established between the
parties and persons acquiring title under them with notice of the agreement. Therefore an assignee of the judgment of foreclosure who purchased the mortgaged premises thereunder will not be permitted to
repudiate the agreement and to hold the property in violation thereof.

DOWER RIGHTS, AGREEMENT IN FRAUD OF.—An agreement between the
parties to a mortgage that it shall be foreclosed and a sale made for the
purpose of cutting off the dower rights of the wife of the mortgagor in
a part of the premises, and that the balance shall be reconveyed to him,
is not a fraud upon her, depriving a court of equity of the power to enforce the agreement, if the result of the agreement and of the sale is
to free the part left to the mortgagor of a servitude thereon, and to
give to the residue a greater value than was possessed by the whole
tract before the agreement was made. It is not material that the wife
was applied to and refused to release her dower, and that the foreclosure scheme was necessary to counteract her unreasonable obstinacy, if
the result contemplated and realized by her husband was to increase
the value of the property subject to her dower interest.

EJECTMENT. The land in controversy was subject to a mortgage made by its owner, Fellows, in favor of one Brown, between whom an agreement was made that the mortgage should
be foreclosed and a sale had thereunder, that a part of the
premises should be conveyed to a railroad corporation in consideration of an easement existing in its favor
against the remainder of the tract, and the balance was to be

reconveyed to Fellows subject to the mortgage indebtedness.
It was claimed that Loomis was employed as an attorney to
carry out this agreement. After the judgment of foreclosure
was recovered in favor of Brown he transferred it to Loomis who
became the purchaser at the foreclosure sale, and after conveying a part to the railroad company, repudiated the residue
of the agreement and refused to reconvey to Fellows. The
trial court ruled that the agreement was in fraud of the rights
of Mrs. Fellows and that the purpose of the plaintiff with respect to the dower interest of his wife was such that the court
could not give him any relief.

C. Smith and H. A. Knapp, for the appellant.

H. W. Palmer, H. M. Hannah, and S. B. Price, for the appellees.

[81] WILLIAMS, J. There are twenty-two assignments of
error in this case, but they relate to three principal questions.
These grew out of an agreement made between Fellows, then
the owner of the land in controversy, and Brown, who held a
mortgage covering the land. It appears that the tract of land
was subject to an easement or servitude in favor of the Delaware, Lackawanna, and Western Railroad Company, which
gave the company the right to deposit culm upon it. An
arrangement had been made between Fellows and the company for a division of the tract, and a conveyance of about
one-third of it to the company in fee simple in consideration
of the release of the remainder from the servitude. This
would give Fellows an opportunity to subdivide the tract into
city lots, and enable him to sell them for building purposes,
and it would restrict the deposit of culm within fixed and
ascertained limits. In order to carry this arrangement with
the railroad company into effect, it was necessary to relieve
so much of the tract as was to be conveyed to the company
in fee from the lien of Brown's mortgage, and from the right
of dower of Mrs. Fellows, who was living at this time apart
from her husband. She was approached upon [82] the subject
of joining her husband in a conveyance, clearly to the advantage of both of them, of the part of the tract which the railroad company was to accept as the consideration for the
release of the remainder from the right to cover it with culm,
but she refused to join. After her refusal he consulted with
friends, and obtained legal advice, as to the practicability of
carrying out the arrangement without the co-operation of his

wife. As a result of such consultation a plan was devised. The mortgage of Brown was to be used to bring about a judicial sale of the tract, to which Brown or some person to be agreed on should take the title, convey the piece the railroad company was to have, to it, and reinstate Brown's mortgage on the remainder, which was then to belong to Fellows.

The questions arising under this agreement between Brown and Fellows may be stated thus: What was the effect of the agreement upon the parties to it? What was its effect upon the wife of Joseph Fellows? What was its effect upon Loomis, who was the vendee of Brown, and became the purchaser at the sheriff's sale? Proceedings were begun upon the mortgage for the purpose of carrying this agreement into effect while Brown remained the owner of the mortgage. Before the sheriff's sale was effected Loomis purchased the mortgage from Brown, and proceeded to bring the property to sale. He became the purchaser. He carried out the arrangement by making the conveyance to the railroad company, and securing its release or deed for the remainder of the tract, exactly upon the lines of the agreement made by Fellows; but when he was called upon to reconvey, subject to the mortgage debt, he refused to do so, and, claiming to be the absolute owner of the property, denied the right of Fellows to either the land or an account. This action was brought to determine whether the position so taken by Loomis was tenable.

The first point to be determined relates to the legal effect of the contract between Brown and Fellows for the use of the mortgage as a means of making title to the railroad company. The position of the plaintiff is that the proceeding on the mortgage was not adverse, but for the benefit of Fellows; and that in making such use of it he became a trustee under the terms of his agreement with Fellows. The learned judge of the court below took the same view of this question, and in an answer [83] to the first point submitted on the part of the plaintiff instructed the jury that the testimony of Brown and Fellows, corroborated by that of Storrs and by the circumstances disclosed by the evidence, was sufficient to establish a trust relation between mortgagee and mortgagor in relation to the property owned by the mortgagee. He went still farther in his answer to the plaintiff's second point, and told the jury, "If Brown was a trustee, he had no right to transfer the judgment" to Loomis, if the judgment was given to enable Brown to carry out the purpose of his agreement with Fel-

lows, viz., to bring the property to a sheriff's sale. The
instructions left Loomis, the vendee of Brown, in the sa
relation of trust to Fellows that his vendor occupied, unle
he could show himself to be an innocent purchaser witho
notice, actual or constructive, of the trust. The case w
then for the jury upon the credibility of the evidence whi
the learned judge had told the jury would, if credited, crea
the trust relation, and upon the position of Loomis as a pr
chaser at the sheriff's sale. If he bought with notice of t
trust, he took the same title Brown would have taken, a
became a trustee for Fellows under the terms of the origir
agreement.

Notwithstanding this disposition of the first and third
the questions raised, the learned judge withdrew the ca
from the jury under the view taken by him of the secor
He held, as a matter of law, that the contract between Bro
and Fellows was absolutely void, and incapable of enfor
ment in a court of law, because its effect was to divest t
right of dower of Mrs. Fellows, without her consent, from
much of the land as was conveyed to the railroad compar
It did not matter, in the view of the learned judge, that I
refusal to join her husband in the deed left the tract of co
paratively little value to her husband or herself; nor that I
refusal was unreasonable and ill-natured; nor that the
rangement made more than quadrupled the market value
the interest of both her husband and herself in the tra
The mere fact that the arrangement dispensed with her co
sent, by substituting the lawful mode of procedure upor
mortgage to bring the property to a judicial sale, in the pl
of the deed of husband and wife, was held to be a fraud
such flagrant character as to deprive the court of [84]
power to restrain or correct the conduct of a trustee, who v
alleged to be appropriating the entire trust estate.

It was a conceded fact in the cause that the part of
tract that was to be secured by Fellows was of much grea
market value than the entire tract while remaining subjec
the servitude in favor of the railroad company. It is cle
upon the face of the record, that if there is a recovery in
action, the right of dower of Mrs. Fellows in the land so
covered will be worth many times what her right of do
was worth before the arrangement with Brown had b
made by her husband. Unless there is a recovery her r
of dower is absolutely gone.

The logical result of the ruling in the court below is to
punish the husband for divesting his wife's dower interest in
one-third of the land without her consent, by extinguishing
her dower in the other two-thirds. The assignments of error
relating to the second question, the effect of the arrangement
between Brown and Fellows on Mrs. Fellows, are sustained.
This case was improperly taken from the jury. Mrs. Fellows
was not defrauded, but benefited, against her will, if the facts
be as they seem to be conceded to be. As to the effect of the
arrangement with the railroad company on the value of the
two-thirds that remained to Fellows, and the fact that Fellows has increased the value of his wife's dower many times
over, against her will or even in the face of her protest, is no
reason why the doors of a court of justice should be closed
against him, and he refused a hearing upon the merits of his
cause of action. We express no opinion upon the facts, for
they are before us only as they relate to the legal questions
presented. A jury must pass upon them. So far as we can
now see, the question on which this case turned upon the trial
is not an important one. The first and third questions, i. e.,
the relation existing between Brown and Fellows under their
contract to employ Brown's mortgage to make title to the
railroad company, and so secure to Fellows a portion of his
land in a marketable state of the title, and the position of
Loomis as assignee of the mortgage, and the purchaser at
sheriff's sale, are the questions on which this case depends,
and it goes back that it may be tried upon them.

The judgment is reversed, and a venire *facias de novo*
awarded.

————

TRUSTS—FORECLOSURE BY AGREEMENT—CONVEYANCE BY MORTGAGEE TO
MORTGAGOR.—If an agreement is made between a mortgagor and a mortgagee, that for the purpose of clearing the title to the property mortgaged
the mortgage shall be foreclosed and the premises purchased by the mortgagee, and that certain portions shall be by him conveyed to the grantee of
the mortgagor and the residue to the mortgagor himself, and according to
agreement the foreclosure is had and a sale thereunder is made to the mortgagee, who conveys to the grantee of the mortgagee as agreed, and permits
the mortgagor to remain in possession of the other parcels for many years,
but refuses to convey to him, the latter is entitled to a decree of conveyance. The mortgagee, in such a case, is a trustee *ex maleficio* for the mortgagor: *Cutler* v. *Babcock*, 81 Wis. 195; 29 Am. St. Rep. 882, and note. A
judgment creditor agreeing to purchase the debtor's land, and, after satisfying his debt, to reconvey to the debtor, takes the land charged with a trust
in favor of the debtor: *Carter* v. *Gibson*, 29 Neb. 324; 26 Am. St. Rep. 381,
and note.

DOWER RIGHTS—CONVEYANCE IN FRAUD OF.—A conveyance of all of his property, made by a husband shortly before his death, without any valuable consideration, with the intent to defeat his wife's right of dower, is fraudulent as to her, and will be set aside: *Thayer* v. *Thayer*, 14 Vt. 107; 39 Am. Dec. 211, and extended note; *Cranson* v. *Cranson*, 4 Mich. 230; 66 Am. Dec. 534, and note. A deed given by a husband on the eve of his marriage, to his daughter, without consideration, and kept secret until after the marriage, is void as against the dower right of the wife: *Swain* v. *Perine*, 5 Johns. Ch. 482; 9 Am. Dec. 318; but see *Cameron* v. *Cameron*, 10 Smedes & M. 394; 48 Am. Dec. 759.

PEOPLES STREET RAILWAY COMPANY *v.* SPENCER.

[156 PENNSYLVANIA STATE, 85.]

AN OPTION TO PURCHASE REAL PROPERTY IS A SUBSTANTIAL INTEREST IN LAND, and when the option is exercised the purchaser is considered as the owner *ab initio.*

IF AN OPTION IS GIVEN TO PURCHASE REAL PROPERTY UPON WHICH AN INSURANCE AGAINST LOSS BY FIRE exists or is subsequently effected, and the loss occurs, after which the option is exercised and a conveyance of the property made, the purchaser is entitled to the moneys due upon such insurance.

ASSUMPSIT for insurance money. The plaintiff averred that the property insured belonged to it in 1889, when it borrowed of defendant twenty thousand dollars, and gave him a conveyance, and received in return a lease for one year, in which it was stipulated that the plaintiff, at the end of a year, but not afterwards, should have the right to purchase the same property on payment of twenty thousand dollars, with interest; that it was agreed that it should keep the property insured for twelve thousand dollars against loss by fire; that the interest for the first year was paid, and thereupon the loan was continued and the lease renewed for another year; that before the expiration of this year the property was injured by fire, and the sum of ten thousand three hundred and ninety-five dollars was paid by the insurers on account of such injury; that within the year plaintiff exercised its option, paid the sum of twenty thousand dollars, and received from defendant a reconveyance of the property. Both parties claimed to be entitled to the insurance money. The affidavit of defense alleged that the defendant did not loan plaintiff any money whatever, but did purchase the property for twenty thousand dollars; that such purchase was absolute, though it was accompanied with the lease and an option to purchase, and that the insurance moneys were the property of the defendant. Judgment was entered in favor of the plaintiff for want of a sufficient affidavit of defense.

H. M. Hannah and H. W. Palmer, for the appellant.

Jessups and Hand, for the appellee.

[89] Mitchell, J. All the facts appear in the writings set forth in the plaintiff's statement. None of the papers which are merely referred to but not set out in full seems to be essential to the cause of action, and the omission to give them in full is not therefore fatal. The affidavit of defense raises no issue of fact, for it denies no part of the statement except the inferences from the face of the papers. The case was therefore one for the court to decide upon the statement and affidavit.

All the writings constitute parts of one transaction, and the nature of that, beyond question, was a conveyance of the land as security for the repayment of a loan of money. It starts with admitted title in the company appellee, then a conveyance to appellant for twenty thousand dollars, a contemporaneous lease from appellant back to the company, at a nominal rent of one dollar, with no change of possession which remained all the time in the company, and an absolute and exclusive option in favor of the company to repurchase at the end of the year for the same amount, twenty thousand dollars, with interest, that is, to resume its original title on payment of the loan. At the end of the term the arrangement was extended or renewed for another year, during which the option was exercised by the company, the money paid, and the title reconveyed by the appellant. It is unimportant what name we apply to the relation of the parties during the year. Whether technically vendor and vendee, mortgagor and mortgagee, or lessor and lessee, is immaterial. The nature of the relation is incontestable; appellant was the holder of the legal title, subject to an equity in the company. It is strongly argued for appellant that his interest [90] at the time of the fire was an absolute fee simple title. But this is an error, it was not absolute. It was the legal title in fee, but subject to the equitable interest of the company, an interest in the land, capable of being specifically enforced, and good not only against the appellant but all others, creditors, purchasers, or strangers, to whom the recorded deeds and the company's possession gave notice.

The only substantial question in the case is the date at

which the company's equity became complete. The fire took
place during the running of the term, the option to redeem
was exercised after the fire had occurred. Did the company's
interest begin to run only from the exercise of its option, or
did it upon that event relate back for all purposes to the be
ginning of the transaction? We are of opinion that both
principle and authority sustain the latter view.

As already said the transaction was in substance a loan of
money, and appellant's right was to have his money back
with interest at a specified time, or, in default of that, to have
his title become absolute. The insurance was for his protec
tion, not to increase his profit; to keep up the sufficiency of
his security while the loan lasted, or make good the value of
his purchase if it became absolute. For that reason it was to
be kept up by the appellee. If the latter had exercised its
option before the fire there could have been no question that
the insurance money would have belonged to it. But the
date of the fire makes no substantial difference, when, as was
the case, the appellee elected to repay the loan and resumed
its title. On the happening of that contingency the appel
lant got his money with interest, which was all he was enti
tled to, while the appellee got back its land, lessened in value
by the fire, but the loss compensated by the insurance money
The insurance was, in contemplation of law, for the benefit of
whomever should be entitled when the option was exercised
or expired by default, and in fact it was contracted for "as
interest may appear." It stood in place of so much of the
property as was destroyed by the fire, and followed the title
when the equitable and the legal interests united.

The authorittes, so far as we have any analogous cases
lead to the same conclusion. It was held in *Kerr* v. *Day*, 14
Pa. St. 112, 53 Am. Dec. 526, that an option to purchase is
substantial interest in land [91] which may be conveyed to
vendee, and the English chancery cases were reviewed by
Bell, J., with the result that "when the lessee made his op
tion to purchase, he was to be considered as the owner ab
initio. Indeed the determination can only be supported by
attributing to the lessee an equitable estate in the land, under
his covenant for an optional purchase, which passed to his
alienee, vesting him with the right to call for a specific exe
cution on declaring his election." And in *Frick's Appeal*, 10
Pa. St. 485, where the land was sold upon a prior judgment
before payment or conveyance, it was held that the surplus

was the property of the optional vendee. It is true that the
option in that case had been exercised before the levy and
sale, but that circumstance was not of controlling weight,
as the decision was put on the ground that "in equity the
vendee became the owner subject to the payment of the price
stipulated. His right of property therein flows from the contract and exists before any purchase money may have been
paid," citing *Siter's Appeal*, 26 Pa. St. 178. We are of opinion that upon the exercise of its option to redeem, the appellee's equitable title reverted back to the date of the original
agreement, and appellee became the owner of the land as it
was at such date, or of the insurance money which stood *pro
tanto* in its place.

Judgment affirmed. ————

VENDOR AND PURCHASER—OPTION TO PURCHASE—WHETHER INTEREST
IN LAND.—Options for the purchase of land upon unilateral contracts, do
not vest any interest in the vendee, and become binding only by acceptance
or performance of their conditions before the offer is withdrawn: *Gustin* v.
Union School District, 94 Mich. 502, 34 Am. St. Rep. 361, and note. An
option is neither a chose in action nor a transmissible right of property,
but a personal privilege which ceases at the death of the party who has the
right to exercise it: *Newton* v. *Newton*, 11 R. I. 390; 23 Am. Rep. 476. See
further on this subject *Yerkes* v. *Richards*, 153 Pa. St. 646; 34 Am. St. Rep.
721, and note with the cases collected.

————

DOLPH *v.* HAND.

[156 PENNSYLVANIA STATE, 91.]

AN INFANT'S DEED does not bind him, if, upon coming of age, he decides to
disaffirm it. It is not void but voidable, and the right to disaffirm it is
personal to himself.

AN INFANT'S RIGHT TO DISAFFIRM HIS DEED MUST BE EXERCISED WITHIN A
REASONABLE TIME after his coming of age. If, for fifteen years after
attaining his majority, he resides near the property he has conveyed,
and knows of improvements being made upon it and of its use for mining purposes, without objecting and without indicating any intention
of disaffirming his deed, he thereby irrevocably ratifies it.

H. W. Palmer and Charles H. Welles, for the appellants.

W. W. Lathrope and S. B. Price, for the appellee.

96 WILLIAMS, J. This case presents an interesting question upon a state of facts that I do not remember to have met
with in any decided case. The facts are fortunately free
from controversy, so that their legal effect is the only ques-

tion to be determined. It appears from an examination
the evidence that Alexander Dolph was at the time of l
death, in 1860, the owner of a tract of land lying in what
now Lackawanna county, containing seventy acres. He di
intestate leaving eight children to survive him. Edwai
one of his sons, administered [97] on the estate. In 18€
before the final settlement of the estate, Alfred, another s€
died, leaving five children surviving, of whom the plaintiff
this action is one. Some years later Edward undertook
unite in himself the shares of all the heirs at law of his fatl
in this tract of land, by purchase. He agreed upon ter₁
with all his brothers and sisters, and with the heirs at law
his deceased brother Alfred. He paid sixteen hundred d
lars for Alfred's undivided one-eighth part, which was th
held by his five children. A deed was made to him in whi
they joined, James M. Dolph, the plaintiff, being at the ti₁
under the age of twenty-one years. This deed was acknov
edged and delivered on the twenty-ninth day of Decemb₁
1869. The justice of the peace who took the acknowledgme
of the several grantors incorporated into his certificate the f
lowing statement in regard to James: "The said James
Dolph, being a minor, acts with his own will and accord, a₁
agrees to ratify the same when he shall become of full ag₁
James was at the time between seventeen and eighteen ye₁
of age, and reached his majority in August, 1874. This s
was brought to the November term, 1888, without any not
or act of disaffirmance. Upon these conceded facts ought ₁
plaintiff to recover?

Whatever may have been held in earlier times, or in otl
jurisdictions, in regard to sales and conveyances by a min
we understand the fair effect of our own cases to be as follo₁
The deed of James M. Dolph, executed in his minority, ₁
not bind him if, upon coming of age, he decided to disaffi
it. He could affirm or disaffirm at the proper time.]
deed was therefore not void, but voidable; and the right
avoid it was personal to himself. This right ought in j
tice to all the parties, and as a matter of public policy, to
exercised within a reasonable time or be treated as lost
waiver. If one who has this right to elect does not exer₁
it within a reasonable time, but, with full knowledge of
privilege, omits or neglects to assert it, his omission n
fairly be regarded as the equivalent of an act of affirma₁
and as amounting in fact and in law to ratification. ₁

cases hold that a voidable deed may be ratified in many ways.
It may be done by express words, as by a deed of ratification,
a release, a declaration made to one about to become a purchaser, or the like. It may be done by implication [98] from
the acts or declarations of the grantor, showing a recognition
in fact by him of the validity of the title, and an acquiescence
in his previous act of conveyance. It may be done by a neglect to disaffirm, continued for such a length of time, and
under such circumstances, as to make it inequitable for him
to be allowed to disturb the title. The defendant in this case
does not allege an express ratification, but concedes that no
such ratification has been made. He sets up no such acts or
declarations relating to the land or the title thereto as might
be equivalent to an express ratification. What he asserts is
that the voidable deed has been ratified by an implication
fairly arising from the conduct of the grantor, extending
through such a length of time, and having such an unequi-
vocal significance, as to make it as effectual as express words
could be. The circumstances relied on to support this contention may be stated thus: (*a*) Knowledge on the part of
the grantor that his deed was voidable and could be affirmed
or disaffirmed on reaching full age; (*b*) continued residence
near, and most of the time in full view of, the property and the
improvements made upon it; (*c*) his knowledge of the use of
the tract for mining purposes during all these years, and of the
erection of coal-breakers and other improvements thereon by
owners and lessees; (*d*) his failure to disaffirm when he
knew his right to do so fully vested on his arrival at full age;
(*e*) the continued omission for fifteen years after coming of
age, with a full knowledge of all the circumstances affecting
the property, to assert his right to disaffirm.

The case of *Grimes* v. *Urban*, 2 Grant Cas. 96, comes nearer
to this upon its facts than any case in our reports. In that
case there had been a conveyance during the minority of the
grantor and a delay for fourteen years to disaffirm; and it
was held upon the facts of that case that the delay did not
amount to an affirmance. The authority of *Grimes* v. *Urban*
was recognized in *Lenhart* v. *Ream*, 74 Pa. St. 59, but the
case went off on another question raised under the statute of
limitations. *Soullier* v. *Kern*, 69 Pa. St. 16, which was cited
on the argument, did not involve a question of ratification.
The title of the minor was saved in that case by the proviso
to the Act of April 16, 1840, Public Laws, 413, which made

the sale of the property of the minor for taxes irregular and
ineffectual. What shall amount [99] to a ratification of a
voidable instrument generally is a question that has arisen
quite frequently. Thus it has been held that the receipt of
rent falling due upon a lease which the minor might have
avoided, when done with knowledge of the character of the
lease, is sufficient to work a ratification of the lease: *Myers* v
Kingston Coal Co., 126 Pa. St. 582. But such an act will not
operate as a ratification, unless it is done with a knowledge
of the instrument that may be affected by it: *Zoebisch* v
Rauch, 133 Pa. St. 532. Nor will ratification be implied
from mere lapse of time against an express refusal to ratify
Behm v. *Molly*, 133 Pa. St. 614. The retention of a house or
other article purchased by an agent amounts to a ratification
of the unauthorized purchase on the part of the principal
Taking possession and occupying is a ratification of the act
of an agent in buying or leasing property. Retention of the
purchase money for an article sold by another is a ratification
of the act of sale. In the case of an infant vendor, if the
consideration remains in his hands when he comes of age
and he afterwards uses or parts with it, this will ordinarily
amount to a binding ratification of the sale by him. But
when the consideration remains in· his hands after coming of
age, having been used by him, it seems to be agreed on al
sides that one entitled to avoid his deed should make an
signify his election within a reasonable time, or the omissio
so to do may operate as an affirmance. The. difficulty has
been with the application of the rule, and the question
" What is a reasonable time?" has received different answer
in different jurisdictions. In Illinois two years seems to be
regarded as the proper limit of a "reasonable time." I
Iowa three years and eight months have been held to be
unreasonable delay: *Green* v. *Wilding*, 59 Iowa, 679; ·
Am. Rep. 696. In Connecticut thirteen years was held
be unreasonable: *Kline* v. *Beebe*, 6 Conn. 494. In *Urban*
Grimes, 2 Grant Cas. 96, this court held that fourteen yea
was not unreasonable. In this case we have a still long
period of delay, accompanied by retention of the purcha
money, with the fullest knowledge of the voidable charact
of the deed, of his own right to disaffirm, of the occupation
the land by lessees, of the erection of improvements there
and of the steady enhancement in value of the land by r
son of the development of the region in which it was. ·

these considerations were brought daily before him by the circumstance that the land [100] was in full view from his house, or was passed by him in going to and returning from his work for more than eighteen years after the making of deed, and for fifteen years after he came of full age.

We shall not disturb *Grimes* v. *Urban*, 2 Grant Cas. 96, but we are not willing to extend the rule there laid down· On the other hand, when the length of the delay in this case is considered in connection with the circumstances to which ·we have adverted, we conclude that it is unreasonable, and that it should be regarded as amounting to a waiver of the right to disaffirm, and therefore the equivalent of an express ratification. It is inequitable to permit one to wait for fifteen years, with a full knowledge of his rights, and allow him then to disaffirm, when the altered situation of the property and the region in which it is located are so evidently the inducement. Great vigilance in the right to disaffirm ought not to be required of one coming up out of disability. Reasonable opportunity should be given for such an one to become familiar with his situation and his rights. The rule in *Grimes* v. *Urban*, 2 Grant Cas. 96, carries this doctrine of a reasonable opportunity to a great length, beyond which we are not willing to go.

The judgment is reversed.

INFANT'S DEED—RIGHT TO DISAFFIRM.—The deed of an infant is voidable and not void. He can avoid it by disaffirming it within a reasonable time after he becomes of age: *Searcy* v. *Hunter*, 81 Tex. 644; 26 Am. St. Rep. 837, and note with the cases collected; *Vallandingham* v. *Johnson*, 85 Ky. 288; *Ihley* v. *Padgett*, 27 S. C. 300; *Hoffert* v. *Miller*, 86 Ky. 572. See also the extended note to *Craig* v. *Van Bebber*, 18 Am. St. Rep. 582, where the question is fully considered. That the right to disaffirm must be exercised within a reasonable time after the removal of the disabilities, see *Amey* v. *Cockey*, 73 Md. 298, and *Estate of Grindrod*, 140 Pa. St. 161.

CRESWELL IRON WORKS v. O'BRIEN.

[156 PENNSYLVANIA STATE, 172.]

MECHANIC'S LIEN—A SUBCONTRACTOR'S RIGHT TO FILE A LIEN CANNOT BE
DESTROYED except by an express covenant against liens by either the
contractor or subcontractor, or such a covenant so clearly implied that
a mechanic or material-man cannot fail to understand it.

MECHANIC'S LIEN—A SUBCONTRACTOR IS NOT PRECLUDED FROM OBTAINING
A LIEN by a provision in the principal contract that the contractor will
not suffer or permit any lien by any person to be put and remain upon
the building, and that any such lien, until it is removed, shall preclude
any and all claim and demand for any payment under this contract, and
that the last installment shall not be payable unless, in addition to the
architect's certificate, a full release of all claims and liens for all work
done and all materials furnished has been delivered by the contractor.

SUIT to enforce a mechanic's lien. Judgment for the defendant.

Joseph De F. Junkin, for the appellant.

John Dolman, for the appellee.

[173] MITCHELL, J. The learned court below entered judgment for defendant on the point reserved, on the authority of *Benedict v. Hood,* 134 Pa. St. 289; 19 Am. St. Rep. 698. The contracts in that case and in this, so far as relates to the filing of liens, are substantially the same, but there was in that case an additional feature in the fact that the plaintiff, a subcontractor, was surety for the faithful performance by the contractor of his covenants, one of which was that he would not suffer any liens to be filed. The case therefore was rightly decided on the ground of waiver by the plaintiff of his right to any lien, and it is on this ground only that it can be sustained in the face of more recent and fuller adjudications.

By these it has been established clearly that stipulations for a release of liens before final payment of the contractor, or that there shall be no legal or lawful claims against the owner in any manner, from any source whatever, for work or materials [174] furnished, and similar provisions, will not deprive a subcontractor of his right to lien. That result can only be attained by an express covenant against liens by either contractor or subcontractor, or such a covenant so clearly implied that the mechanic or material-man cannot fail to understand it. If the contract is fairly and reasonably susceptible of any other construction it will not debar a lien: *Murphy v. Morton,* 139 Pa. St. 345; *Moore v. Carter,* 146 Pa.

St. 492; *Loyd* v. *Krause*, 147 Pa. St. 402; *Nice* v. *Walker*, 153 Pa. St. 123; 34 Am. St. Rep. 688.

In the present case the covenant is that the contractor "will not suffer or permit any lien . . . . by any person or persons whatsoever, to be put or remain upon the building . . . . and that any such lien . . . . until it is removed shall preclude any and all claim and demand for any payment whatsoever under or by virtue of this contract," and further, "the last installment shall not be payable unless in addition to the architect's certificate, a full release of all claims and liens . . . . for all work done and all materials furnished" has been delivered by the contractor. The contract must be interpreted according to the intention of the parties, and the fair construction of this is that the intention was to protect the owner not by the absolute prohibition of liens, but by providing for their payment by the contractor, and in default of his doing so the stoppage of his own pay. There is no sufficient language in the covenant to indicate that the parties meant, even if they knew of their power, to prevent absolutely the filing of any lien. On the contrary the possible filing of liens is recognized and their validity is not disputed, but a penalty is put upon the contractor for suffering them to remain. The reasoning of our brother Green in *Loyd* v. *Krause*, 147 Pa. St. 402, seems exactly applicable, "as this part of the contract evidently contemplates that liens may be filed, and provides a method by which the owner may protect himself against them, by withholding the money from the builder until they are released, it cannot be contended that it is the necessary meaning of the contract that there were none to be filed in any event."

The contract in this case therefore falls short of the standard established by *Nice* v. *Walker*, 153 Pa. St. 123; 34 Am. St. Rep. 688, the latest case on the subject, in which the rule was maturely considered, and intended to be settled finally. *Benedict* v. *Hood*, 134 Pa. St. 289; 19 Am. St. Rep. 698, as already [175] said, was rightly decided on its own facts, but so far as anything there said conflicts with the views now expressed it is overruled.

Judgment reversed and judgment entered for plaintiff on the verdict.

————

MECHANIC'S LIEN—SUBCONTRACTOR, RIGHT TO FILE LIEN BY HOW LOST. To prevent a contractor or subcontractor from filing a lien against a builder there must be an express covenant against liens, or a covenant resulting as a necessary implication from the language used, and an intended covenant should so clearly appear that a mechanic or material-man can understand it without consulting a lawyer as to its legal effect: *Nice* v. *Walker*, 153 Pa. St. 123; 34 Am. St. Rep. 688.

MECHANIC'S LIEN—SUBCONTRACTOR, HOW AFFECTED BY CONTRACT OF CONTRACTOR.—When a contractor for the construction of a building has stipulated with the owner that no mechanic's lien shall be filed on the building, such a stipulation is binding on subcontractors working for him: *Taylor* v. *Murphy*, 148 Pa. St. 337; 33 Am. St. Rep. 825, and note with the cases collected; *Nice* v. *Walker*, 153 Pa. St. 123; 34 Am. St. Rep. 688; note to *Benedict* v. *Hood*, 19 Am. St. Rep. 699; *Schroeder* v. *Galland*, 134 Pa. St. 277; 19 Am. St. Rep. 691.

COMMONWEALTH *v.* SCHOLLENBERGER.

[156 PENNSYLVANIA STATE, 201.]

INTERSTATE COMMERCE, WHAT IS NOT.—If a nonresident comes into the state to embark in business, his situation is like that of any other resident, and his business done at his store is state, not interstate. It does not matter where he obtains his goods. Men who buy and sell foreign merchandise are not necessarily engaged in interstate commerce.

INTERSTATE COMMERCE, WHAT IS NOT.—One who maintains a store for the purpose of carrying on business in this state is not entitled to immunity as being engaged in interstate commerce on the ground that he is the agent of a nonresident manufacturer of the goods which are kept for sale.

INTERSTATE COMMERCE.—AN ORIGINAL PACKAGE IS SUCH FORM AND SIZE OF PACKAGE as is used by producers or shippers for the purpose of securing both convenience in handling and security of transportation of merchandise between dealers in the ordinary course of actual commerce.

INTERSTATE COMMERCE—OLEOMARGARINE—ORIGINAL PACKAGES.—A sale of oleomargarine, otherwise in violation of a state law, is not protected as a part of interstate commerce by proof that it was made, stamped, and printed in another state for use as an article of food, weighed eighty pounds, and was sold in the form in which the maker put it up at his factory in such other state, and that the person making the sale was his agent in this state, having and maintaining a store here for the purpose of effecting such sales.

ACTION to recover a penalty for the unlawful sale of oleomargarine made by defendant in Philadelphia as agent of a manufacturing company doing business in Rhode Island. The case was submitted upon an agreed statement of facts, from which it appeared that the package sold weighed eighty pounds, was manufactured in Rhode Island, and shipped by the manufacturer to the defendant, who sold and delivered such package unbroken, and which package was marked, printed, and stamped in the manner prescribed by the commissioner of internal revenue, with the approval of the secretary of the treasury. Upon this statement the trial court gave judgment for the defendant.

Luther S. Kauffman, Charles F. Warwick, and Wayne Mac-Veagh, for the appellant.

A. B. Roney for the appellee.

[206] WILLIAMS, J. This case belongs to a rapidly growing class that has already become uncomfortably large and troublesome in this state. The profits to be derived from an unlawful traffic are much larger than those that flow from legitimate trade, provided the unlawful traffic may be pursued without serious interference from the officers of the law. Law-abiding citizens will not embark in a business that is forbidden by the laws of the state in which they live. Timid men are afraid to do so. This kind of operation is left therefore to those who have no respect for law, no interest in the public welfare, and no fear of public opinion. When such men deliberately determine to put money in their pockets by engaging in a business which the state has declared to be injurious to the public morals, the public health, or the public peace, and has therefore forbidden altogether or placed under strict police regulations, they are morally certain to seek immunity for themselves and their unlawful business by immediate flight to the sanctuary of the national constitution, and there laying hold on the horns of the altar of interstate commerce.

The road to this refuge of lawbreakers is well beaten. There are signboards at every crossing on the route, and the intermediate [207] stations for possible rest wear conspicuous signs of invitation. The travelers over it are generally foreigners to the state whose laws they trample upon, and include a motley assortment of traders.

Beginning with the peripatetic swindlers whose worthless wares are transported in tin trunks which they carry in their hands, and who hunt their victims in the secluded villages and along the country roads with an instinct that rarely fails, and running up or down the scale of lawbreakers to the men whose commercial operations extend to the sale of oleomargarine by the pound, and of intoxicating drinks by the pint, there is no man in the procession who is not a conscious and deliberate lawbreaker, and who does not set his possible profits from a forbidden business above his duty to society or the state that protects him. These men seek to pervert a rule of law that has a wide and a beneficial field of operation. They claim to be engaged in interstate commerce and to be entitled to the protection of the general government as against the police laws of the individual states for that reason. In support of their claim they will assert that their "goods," whether consisting of oleomargarine, beer, whisky, paste diamonds, pinchbeck watches, or the like, were made on the other side of the state line, and imported by or for them; or it may be they will claim to be the agents or factors of the makers; or to have received, and to be engaged in selling, "original packages," consisting of a pound of oleomargarine or a pocket flask of whisky, put up expressly for their trade at the still or factory just "over the line." The mischief done and attempted in this manner under the guise of interstate commerce is so great, so open, and so difficult to suppress or punish, that in many states besides this it has become a matter of general and sincere regret that the interstate commerce clause was ever held applicable to trade in any article recognized throughout the civilized world as a proper subject for police regulation and control. We are embarrassed by the difficulties in the way of the enforcement of our police legislation, made in good faith, for the protection of our citizens.

The question involved in this case is therefore one of great practical importance. It is nothing less than whether the police power of the state survives at all or has been absorbed and extinguished by the interstate commerce clause in the national [208] constitution. We recognize the fact that this is a federal question. It has been the subject of many decisions by the supreme court of the United States, and was at one time thought to be well settled in favor of the existence and proper exercise of police powers by the several states. We entertain that opinion still; but the contrary view has been pressed upon us with so much earnestness in the argument that we feel constrained to examine briefly some of the positions taken by the appellant.

It is said that the recent case of *Leisy* v. *Hardin*, 135 U. S. 100, justifies the contention that this state is powerless to interfere with the defendant's traffic. But *Leisy* v. *Hardin*, like all other cases, must be read in the light of its own facts. Leisy was a brewer who made beer in the state of Illinois. Hardin was an officer of the state of Iowa, where the law forbade the sale, and the keeping for sale, of any form of intoxieating drink except for sacramental, medical, or mechanical purposes. Leisy shipped from his brewery in Illinois to his agent in Iowa about three hundred casks and eleven cases of beer sealed in the ordinary manner. These were sent there for sale, and were in the hands of Leisy's agent or employer in Iowa for that purpose. While the entire consignment of beer was yet in the possession of the maker or his agent, with seals unbroken, it was seized by Hardin under the law of Iowa, and taken out of the possession of Leisy's agent. An action of replevin was then brought to recover the casks and cases so taken. Two questions were thus raised: 1. Did Leisy own the packages taken from the possession of his agent; and 2. If he was the owner had he a right to have them in his possession in the state of Iowa? The first question was not controverted. He was the maker and owner of the packages seized. The second question was one of law, and was disposed of upon the interstate commerce clause. The goods being in original packages with seals unbroken, no sales having been made therefrom, it was held that they were not liable to seizure under the police laws of the state into which they had been brought.

This is the single question involved in that case, and beyond this it is not binding as a precedent upon the court that rendered the judgment nor upon us. We shall not question the wisdom of that decision nor abate one jot from its legal force, though we sincerely regret some of its consequences. Standing [209] therefore squarely on the case of *Leisy* v. *Hardin*, 135 U. S. 100, let us proceed to an examination of the question presented on this record.

The defendant Schollenberger is a citizen and resident of this state. For at least two years he has been living under the protection of its laws, and is bound by all the obligations that such residence and protection impose. He is a merchant, with a store in the city of Philadelphia. He sells his goods to customers, as other merchants sell their goods, from his stock in store, open to their examination. The commodity, or one of the commodities, in which he deals is oleomargarine, for the sale of which at his store in Philadelphia he has obtained a license under the internal revenue laws of the United States during the last two years. He sells, not for shipment in original packages to other countries or other states, but to local customers; and in the case now before us to an eating-house keeper near by, for consumption upon his table as an article of food.

Now our statute explicitly forbids the sale, the keeping, and the offering of oleomargarine for sale, as an article of food The identical acts forbidden by the law are thus seen to be the acts which he admits he is engaged in, and which he claims the right to do, notwithstanding his residence in, and the statutes of, the state. This right he claims to derive from the interstate commerce clause in two ways. The first of these rests on the nonresidence of the manufacturer. He asserts that the oleomargarine is made in another state. Because the manufacturer can lawfully make and sell under the laws of the state where the manufactory is located, he contends that the manufacturer can sell his own product anywhere; and for this purpose can establish stores for its sale all over this state, if he chooses to do so. As the manufacturer may do this in person, it is contended that he can do it by an agent, so that he could have as many stores, conducted by as many agents, as there are towns in the commonwealth, and conduct the trade in them all regardless of the police laws of the state. The second line along which he claims to derive immunity is the "original package" doctrine. He says he sells in the packages made up at the factory. He does not divide a roll, a pail or tub of his "goods," but requires the purchaser to take the entire roll, pail [210] or tub, made, filled, or shaped at the factory. We think neither of these positions should avail the defendant.

We do not deny that a nonresident manufacturer may sell his goods and ship them to a buyer in the usual trade packages employed in good faith by manufacturers, without being amenable to the police laws of this state therefor. He may bring them here and hold them in bulk without danger. So much is fairly ruled in *Leisy* v. *Hardin*, 135 U. S. 100. He may sell them to the trade or for shipment to the states in the same unbroken trade packages notwithstanding their unlawful character. This clearly results from the rule in *Leisy* v. *Hardin*, 135 U. S. 100. We might have held, had the question been one for us, that the object of the interstate commerce clause was quite different from what it seems thought to be. We might have thought it intended to prevent the establishment of state custom-houses and taxation along state lines, and to make for the general purposes of legitimate trade all the states open to the manufacturer and merchants of the several states. But for this the states might have intercepted all goods reaching their borders, and weighed, valued, and taxed them, before permitting them to proceed to their destination. The destructive effect upon commerce of such restrictions was clearly foreseen and wisely guarded against by our fathers. But the protection of the lives, the health and morals of citizens was the chief of the duties of government left to the states when the Union was formed. The common-law rights and remedies are to be sought in the courts of the states. For this reason we would have held that the police regulations of the states stood on impregnable ground and that while no state had the right to tax or to burden inter-state commerce, each state had the right to exclude from its territory such articles of food or drink as were injurious in their character and effects upon the health or the morals of the public. But however this may be, it will not be denied that state commerce, that is business conducted within the lines of a state, was left to state control.

It was the intention of the United States to protect the citizens and the productions of one state against unjust discrimination by the other states; but it was, and is, the duty of the state to protect its citizens against each other.

If then the retail of oleomargarine at the defendant's store is [211] to be regarded as in any sense his business, as it would seem to be from the form of the licenses attached to the case stated, and from all the facts, he is clearly liable as an individual to the penalty provided by the law which he had broken. Can the facts that the store is the store of the manufacturer, and that he is their agent, relieve him from liability? The sales are not made from the factory nor under the right which the fact of making confers on the maker. On the contrary the sales are made under a store license, granted, not to an establishment located in another state, but to a store in this state. When a nonresident of Pennsylvania comes into the state to embark in business here, his situation is like that of any other resident, and his business done at his store is state, not interstate. It does not matter where he obtains his goods. Interstate commerce does not necessarily depend on the origin of goods; or rather, all men who buy and sell foreign merchandise are not necessarily engaged in interstate commerce. If it was otherwise, all merchants would be superior to state laws, for all deal to some extent in goods made in other states and in other coun-

tries. It is not simply or mainly the origin of the goods
therefore that is to be considered, but the nature of the business done. One who keeps a stock of goods in store for the
inspection of customers, and sells from this stock to actual
consumers, is a local dealer. His business is intrastate, not
interstate. Our Act of 1885 under which this case arises is
not a trade regulation. It is a police law. This court has so
held repeatedly, and our view of it was expressly affirmed by
the supreme court of the United States in *Powell* v. *Pennsylvania,* 127 U. S. 678, a case which turned upon that single
question. It does not undertake to deal with an importer
from another country or state, but with manufacturers, and
dealers within the state. It prohibits the manufacture of
oleomargarine within the limits of the state. It also prohibits the sale, the offer to sell, and the having in possession
with intent to sell, the same "as an article of food." It lays
its prohibition on those who are fairly subject to its jurisdic-
diction, and on no others. We have then a valid police law,
so declared by the highest tribunal in the land, which prohibits the sale of oleomargarine as an article of food within
the state. We have the proprietor of a store located and
licensed here making sales of the prohibited [212] article to
customers for the prohibited purpose. It does not matter
that the merchant makes his home in another state, or that
he makes his sales by a clerk or agent rather than in person.
He is a local dealer selling in violation of the local law and
liable to its penalty. If the residence of the dealer could
affect the character of his trade then our police laws intended
to protect our own people would operate as a discrimination
against our citizens and in favor of citizens of other states;
and would commit to those having no interests in common
with us a most odious monopoly in every form or kind of
traffic which our state should attempt to regulate or to suppress.

Intrenched behind the interstate commerce clause so construed, citizens of other states could prey upon our people,
trample upon our laws, and make gain out of a traffic forbidden to our citizens, only to be delivered up absolutely and
unconditionally to them. It would require only that such
citizen of another state should establish a local store in some
of our towns or cities, or in all of them, conduct a local business, to meet a local demand, and, when called upon by the
officers of the law, make reply that he made the goods in

some other state, and, as a manufacturer, supplied himself, as a local dealer, with wares of a foreign origin. Neither the foreign origin of the goods sold, nor of the seller nor both together, will convert a business that is local and intrastate into one that is general and interstate within the meaning of the constitution of the United States.

But the defendant's second position is that, admitting the views now stated be correct, he is nevertheless beyond the reach of the state law for another reason, viz., that his sales are made in original packages, and are therefore interstate commerce. We have examined the decisions of the supreme court of the United States for a definition of the term "original package." It does not seem, however, to have received, and perhaps at this time is not capable of, a precise definition that may be applied to it in all cases. The idea for which it stands is, however, not difficult of apprehension or statement. The methods adopted by manufacturers and importers for packing and preparing goods for transportation by sea or land differ with the differences in the character, bulk, and material of the merchandise itself. The general purpose is to adopt that form [213] and size of package best adapted to the safe and convenient transportation and delivery of the particular class of goods to be moved, because the convenience of the trade will be best subserved thereby. Such packages put up with a view to the convenience and security of transportation and handling, in the regular course of trade, are the original packages of commerce. If we look at the meaning of the words employed we are brought to the same conclusion. Original means pertaining to the beginning or origin, the first or primitive form of a thing. Package means a bundle or parcel made up of several smaller parcels combined or bound together in one bale, box, crate, or other form of package. An "original package" is such form and size of package as is used by producers or shippers for the purpose of securing both convenience in handling, and security in transportation, of merchandise between dealers in the ordinary course of actual commerce. Such packages are not always made up by putting smaller packages or bundles together, but may include any form of receptacle that shall hold a fixed quantity; as a barrel of sugar or salt, a bag of coffee, a chest of tea, and the like. The package must not be divided or its unity destroyed. When it is received unbroken from the importer through the custom house, or from the

manufacturer by the ordinary channels of transportation, it
is within the protection of the interstate commerce doctrine,
and the state may not subject it to vexatious delays, appraisement, taxation, or trade restriction. But it has never been
held that the importer might subdivide his package, and
dispose of its several parts in detail. On the contrary in
many cases the United States courts have held that upon
such subdivision or breaking of bulk the original package
ceased to be such, and the goods became mixed with and
indistinguishable from the merchandise already within the
state, and therefore subject to state laws. This assigns to
each jurisdiction its proper powers. The general government
protects the citizens of the several states in the movement of
their commodities across state lines for the purpose of commerce. The state regulates the retail trade conducted within
its own borders, and forbids the sale of such articles to its citizens as it finds to be injurious to them. We are asked in this
case to go a step farther, and hold that any package which a
manufacturer may choose to put up and send [214] to himself
as a merchant or to a customer is necessarily an "original package," because it was put up by a manufacturer outside of the state. We cannot so hold. This question was
brought to our attention recently by the case of the *Commonwealth* v. *Zelt*, 138 Pa. St. 615. In that case a distiller living,
or at least making whisky, just over the state line, established a store or an agency within the state. He put up his
"goods" in bottles ranging in capacity from one quart down
to one-half pint, and packing them in unsealed barrels sent
them to the Pennsylvania store. When they reached the
agent the bottles were taken from the barrels and arranged
upon the shelves and in the windows of the store in the
manner usual in that trade, and sold to customers. The
seller was prosecuted for the sale of intoxicating liquors without a license, such as the laws of the state require. His
defense was the now common one that he was engaged in
interstate commerce. His position was that the bottles sold
by him singly to customers had been filled and corked at the
distillery, which was in another state, and that they were the
"original packages" put up by the maker and transported
across the line to his store for sale. The contention was
seriously and earnestly made that any size or shape of jug or
bottle which the distiller might desire to meet the needs of
the retail sale of drink became, when filled and shipped by

him across a state line, an "original package," within the meaning of that phrase as used by the United States courts in the interstate commerce cases.   The character of the package appears to have been submitted to the jury, who convicted the defendant.   The defendant appealed to this court, and we said, through Paxson, chief justice: "Whether a box or a barrel of beer can be separated and sold in single bottles as original packages will be formally decided when the question squarely arises.   The jury evidently regarded it as a trick and an evasion of our statute."   The judgment was accordingly affirmed.   The question which it was not necessary to decide in *Commonwealth* v. *Zelt*, 138 Pa. St. 615, is fairly involved in this case so far as oleomargarine is concerned.   The case stated concedes that the package was sold by this defendant for consumption as "an article of food," but asserts that it was sold in the form in which the maker put it up at his factory.   It is not said that it was an "original package" [215] in express words, nor that it was in the form usually adopted in the trade for purposes of transportation.   It is reasonable to infer that when the defendant was admitting the sale, and setting up his justification for a violation of the law, he would do this as strongly as the facts would sustain him had he gone into the proof upon a trial before a jury.

What the case stated does tell us is that the defendant sold at his store in Philadelphia, to one John H. Berry, the keeper of a coffee-house at 606 Lombard street, Philadelphia, a package of oleomargarine weighing eighty pounds, made and stamped and branded in Rhode Island, for use as an article of food. This is almost identical with the defense in *Commonwealth* v. *Zelt*, 138 Pa. St. 615, which was that the bottles sold by the defendant were put up and shipped in another state, and sold in the same form in which they were received.   This does not go far enough.   The defendant in this case, as in Zelt's case, was, *prima facie,* a lawbreaker.   It was incumbent on him to show his right to violate the police laws of the state in which he lived, or carried on his store, affirmatively and clearly.   It is not enough to hint or suggest the existence of such a right.   It must be set up, and his ability to escape the penalty of the broken law depends on the sufficiency of the justification.   The fact alleged as a justification is that the package sold was "made, stamped and branded" in Rhode Island.   To enable the defendant to stand on this statement it is necessary for us to go with him to his legal conclusion, viz., Whatever package is put up at a factory outside the state is an "original package" within the meaning of the interstate commerce doctrine. This we distinctly refuse to do. The United States courts have not so held, as we understand the cases, and such a conclusion could not be sustained on principle, as the question presents itself to us. The consequences of such a holding are obvious. In this case the owners of the store in Philadelphia are the owners of the factory in another state. As merchants, they understand the needs of their retail trade, and the forms and sizes of rolls, tubs, or packages, that will best suit the wants of their customers. As manufacturers they can put their product in packages of such size and shape as shall meet their own needs as merchants. They have both ends of the traffic in their hands, and may do, as they undoubtedly are in the habit of doing, whatever their [216] profits as retailers require them to do as manufacturers. A jury would be justified in finding in such a case, as the jury found in Zelt's case, that the mode of putting up the package was not adapted to meet the requirements of actual interstate commerce, but the requirements of an unlawful intrastate retail trade. In this case the facts are found for us as by the parties. We are to determine their legal effect. The defendant is found to have made sales of oleomargarine as an article of food, contrary to the provisions of our statute.

It is also found that he made these sales for a nonresident employer. But the residence or business of the owner, standing alone, is wholly immaterial. Our law deals with the local trade, regardless of the nationality or residence of the trader. It is further found that the sales are made in packages put up by the trader at his factory, and sent to his store in this city for sale. This, as we have said, does not amount to an assertion that the sales are made in the " original packages" of commerce. If it shows anything upon the subject, it shows that they are not so made.

One who plants his feet squarely upon the police laws of this state, and defies its officers to suppress or to punish his unlawful trade, must show a clear legal right to take and maintain his position as a public enemy, or suffer the penalty of the broken law.

To hold otherwise would make it impossible for the people of any state to protect themselves from evils that by common consent throughout the civilized world need to be restrained and removed by suitable legislation. It would also strike a blow of absolutely crushing weight at the existence of the police power in the several states, and render all attempts at its exercise ineffectual and useless.

The judgment of the court below is reversed, and judgment is now entered on the case stated in favor of the plaintiff for the sum of one hundred dollars, for the costs of suit. After judgment is properly entered, let the record be remitted for purposes of execution.

INTERSTATE COMMERCE—WHAT IS NOT.—States may, in the exercise of their police power, enact laws, which, though they affect commerce between the states, are not to be considered regulations of that commerce within the meaning of the constitution of the United States: *Gulf etc. Ry. Co.* v. *Dwyer*, 75 Tex. 572; 16 Am. St. Rep. 926; extended note to *People* v. *Wemple*, 27 Am. St. Rep. 564. A tax on an occupation carried on in a state, or on property therein, is valid unless it discriminates against articles brought from other states, or taxes the sale of such articles in the original package: *State* v. *French*, 109 N. C. 722; 26 Am. St. Rep. 590, and note; *State* v. *Emert*, 103 Mo. 241; 23 Am. St. Rep. 874; *Rash* v. *Farley*, 91 Ky. 344; 34 Am. St. Rep. 233. The negotiation of the sale of goods which are in other states, for the purpose of introducing them into the state in which the negotiation is made, is interstate commerce, and cannot be interfered with by the state in which the negotiation is made: *City of Bloomington* v. *Bouland*, 137 Ill. 534; 31 Am. St. Rep. 382; *McClellan* v. *Pettigrew*, 44 La. Ann. 356. For a full and complete discussion of the subject of interstate commerce, and the constitutionality of state regulations concerning it, see the monographic note to *People* v. *Wemple*, 27 Am. St. Rep. 547–568.

INTERSTATE COMMERCE—ORIGINAL PACKAGE—WHAT IS: See note to *People* v. *Wemple*, 27 Am. St. Rep. 553. A sale is not in the original packages when the purchaser retains the right to examine the goods in such packages and return them if not satisfactory, because under such circumstances the sale cannot be complete until the packages are broken: *Wasserboehr* v. *Boulier*, 84 Me. 165; 30 Am. St. Rep. 344.

HOOVER v. PENNSYLVANIA RAILROAD.

[156 PENNSYLVANIA STATE, 220.]

RAILROAD CORPORATIONS—DISCRIMINATION, WHEN A QUESTION OF LAW. If the facts of an alleged unlawful discrimination are conceded, or are established by undisputed testimony, whether an unreasonable discrimination was made, such as is forbidden by statute, is a question of law for the court.

RAILROAD CORPORATIONS.—A DISCRIMINATION MADE BETWEEN MANUFACTURERS and dealers in coal in charges made for the transportation of such coal is not forbidden by a statute prohibiting discrimination between persons in like conditions and under similar circumstances, if, by reason of the coal so transported for the manufacturers, they produce a larger amount of freight for the carrier, while such a result does not follow the coal carried for the dealers.

RAILWAY CORPORATIONS—DISCRIMINATION.—UNDER A STATUTE PROHIBITING UNREASONABLE PREFERENCE OR ADVANTAGE a railway corporation may lawfully enter into a contract for the carriage of goods for a particular individual or corporation at a lower rate in respect to large quantities of goods and for longer distances than for one who sends them in small quantities or short distances.

RAILWAY CORPORATIONS—DISCRIMINATION IN FAVOR OF A MANUFACTURING CORPORATION, and against retail dealers, in the price charged for shipping coal, though justified on the ground that such corporation is engaged in a business necessarily resulting in an increase of the business of the carrier, must be discontinued if such manufacturer engages in the business of selling coal, and thus becomes a competitor with other dealers in that commodity.

RAILWAY CORPORATIONS.—THE DAMAGES TO A SHIPPER FOR UNJUST DISCRIMINATION between him and other shippers is not necessarily the difference between the prices charged him and them, under a statute giving him treble the amount of injury suffered. The railway corporation has a right to clear and definite proof as to what the actual damage was.

RAILWAY CORPORATIONS.—A DISCRIMINATION IN FAVOR OF A MANUFACTURING CORPORATION, and against a dealer in coal arising from the railway corporation making an agreement in advance of the establishment of the manufacturing corporation to ship coal to it for a specific time and at specified rates, in order to induce such establishment, and increase the railroad's freight and earnings thereby, is not a discrimination between persons in like conditions and under similar circumstances. The railway corporation is not obliged to abandon its agreement, nor, while maintaining it, to carry freight for other shippers on the terms therein stipulated.

David W. Sellers, and W. and J. D. Dorris, for the appellant.

George B. Orlady, for the appellee.

226 GREEN, J. The third section of the seventeenth article of the constitution of 1874 is in the following words:

"SEC. 3. All individuals, associations and corporations shall have equal right to have persons and property transported over railroads and canals, and no undue or unreasonable discrimination shall be made, in charges for, or in facilities for, transportation of freight or passengers, within the state, or coming from, or going to, any other state. Persons and property transported over any railroad shall be delivered at any station, at charges not exceeding the charges for transportation of persons and property of the same class, in the same direction to any more distant station; but excursion and commutation tickets may be issued at special rates."

For the purpose of enforcing the foregoing provision of the constitution the legislature enacted the law of the 4th of June,

1883, Public Laws, 72. The first and second sections are as follows:

"Section 1. That any undue or unreasonable discrimination by any railroad company or other common carrier or any officer, superintendent, manager or agent thereof in charges for or in facilities for the transportation of freight within this state or coming from or going to any other state is hereby declared to be unlawful.

"Sec. 2. No railroad company or other common carrier engaged in the transportation of property shall charge, demand or receive from any person, company or corporation, for the transportation of property, or for any other service, a greater sum than it shall receive from any other person, company or 227 corporation for a like service from the same place upon like conditions and under similar circumstances; and all concessions in rates and drawbacks shall be allowed to all persons, companies or corporations alike, for such transportations and service, upon like conditions, under similar circumstances and during the same period of time. Nor shall any such railroad company or common carrier make any undue or unreasonable discrimination between individuals or between individuals and transportation companies, or the furnishing of facilities for transportation. Any violation of this provision shall make the offending company liable to the party injured for damages treble the amount of injury suffered."

The action in the present case was brought to recover treble damages under the second section of the Act of 1883, for an alleged unjust and unreasonable discrimination against the plaintiffs, in charges for freights on coal shipped from Snow Shoe to Bellefonte within this state, over lines of railroad owned or controlled by the defendant company. The period of time covered by the claim of the plaintiffs was from September, 1889, to April, 1891, and it was alleged that the plaintiffs were overcharged twenty cents per ton on ten thousand six hundred and seven tons carried over the defendant's road during the time named. Substantially the defense set up by the defendant was, that in the year 1881 certain citizens of Bellefonte and vicinity, having in contemplation the erection of a manufacturing plant at Bellefonte, for the manufacture of nails, waited upon the defendant company through Governor A. G. Curtin, who represented them, and endeavored to make, and did make, a special contract, that if the plant was erected the company should not charge them more than thirty

cents per ton for all coal shipped from Snow Shoe to the works
at Bellefonte; that such contract was made and the plant was
then erected and the manufacture of nails thereat was carried
on from 1881 until, and after, the time covered by the plaintiffs' claim; that the plaintiffs were coal-dealers only, who
merely bought and sold coal and returned no freight to the
defendant as the product of any manufacturing operations;
that they did not do any business as coal-dealers, in fact did
not come into existence until the year 1889, eight years after
the nail company was organized and commenced business
and while the defendant company was subject to, and [228] bound
by, the terms of their contract with the nail company; and
that the plaintiffs were not discriminated against at all, because they were charged only the same freights as were
charged to all others who were coal-dealers only. And it was
contended as matter of law, by the defendant, that the discrimination in the rates for freight between the nail company
and the plaintiffs was not, in view of all the circumstances
of the case, an undue or unreasonable discrimination, within
the meaning of the constitutional provision or of the Act of
1883. In reply to points put to the court on the trial on this
subject, the learned judge who tried the cause charged the
jury that the question of unjust discrimination was a question of fact to be determined by them, and he refused the defendant's point on that subject. But he did, nevertheless,
also instruct the jury, as matter of law, that the distinction
between a dealer and a manufacturer set up by the defendant was not a defense, and would not exempt the defendant
from the penalties of the Act of 1883. He said: "The defense claim, as an exemption from the penalty of this act, the
fact that the one may be classed as a manufacturer and the
other simply as a dealer. I do not regard the law as making
that classification. I think that the classification which the
Act of 1883 intended was a classification relating to the carriage and not to the shipper himself. It may charge more for
one kind of freight than for another. It may charge more
for live freight than for wood, coal, iron or ore. It may charge
more for a certain portion of its road than it does for others.
These things are governed largely by the expense to which
the common carrier is subjected. Common carriers may
charge more when they ship but a small quantity than they
do when they ship by wholesale. . . . . But I do not think
the law or the policy of the law permits them to classify the

kind of dealer; that is, that they may make a discrimination
between the character of the consignor or consignee ordinarily. . . . . The evidence here is that each shipment was by
carloads during the same period of time and under like circumstances.   The fact that one party was a manufacturer
and the other party were coal-dealers we think is not material in this case."

The same idea was repeated, and a positive instruction was
given, that upon the facts stated in the plaintiffs' point, "the
service and conditions were alike and the circumstances the
²²⁹ same." We regard this as a binding instruction to the
jury upon the law of the case, which left them no discretion
but to find for the plaintiffs, the only question for them being
the amount of damages to be found.

After a very patient examination of all the testimony and
of all the authorities cited on both sides we find ourselves
unable to agree with the learned court below, either as to their
interpretation of the law or their judgment upon the facts.

So far as the law of the case is concerned, there is no doubt
that the Act of 1883 does not prohibit all discrimination. It
prohibits only discrimination which is undue or unreasonable,
and the prohibited discrimination is further limited by the
consideration that it must be "for a like service, from the
same place, upon like conditions and under similar circumstances." If, therefore, the discrimination, in a given
case, is upon conditions which are not alike, and circumstances which are not similar, the act is inapplicable, and its
penalties are not incurred. Nor can we regard this question
as a question of fact for the jury alone. The ascertainment
of the actual facts of the case, of course, is for them, but where
these are established by undisputed testimony, or are presented by proper points which cover the facts in evidence, the
resulting question is whether the facts established or undisputed, or exhibited in properly drawn points, bring the case
within the operation of the words or necessary meaning of the
statute, and that, of course, is a question of law for the court.
For the question then is one of interpretation. Do the words
of the statute extend to, and embrace, the established facts of
the case, or do they not? If they do not, the statute is not
applicable; if they do, it is, and the court alone, as in all
other similar cases, must determine that question. It is beyond the function of the jury.

Let us now recur to the well-established and the undis-

puted facts of the case, and inquire whether there are any,
and if so, what, differences in the conditions, and in the circumstances which attended the shipping of the coal to the
plaintiffs and to the Bellefonte Iron and Nail Company
respectively.

In the first place we find the undisputed testimony of Governor Curtin to the effect that in 1881, and prior to the erection of the nail works, he called upon the defendant's officials
for the purpose of having them agree to carry the coal for the
prospective [230] works at thirty cents per ton. This testimony is clear, distinct, positive, and entirely uncontradicted,
and it was followed by proof that the contract was carried
out by the defendant after some delay in the adjustment.
Governor Curtin said: "I went to Philadelphia for the purpose of having the arrangement made. I there saw Mr.
Creighton, who was the freight agent of the Pennsylvania
Railroad Company, and after some time in negotiating he
agreed that the freight should be reduced to thirty cents per
ton where the amount consumed per day was twenty tons or
more. He wrote me a letter in which it was settled and fixed
at thirty cents per ton." He then explained the loss of the
letter and his search for it, and said: "but of the contents of
the letter I am perfectly clear in my recollection of it, and it
was one of the inducements which contributed to the erection
of the nail works in this place. There were other parties
in this place engaged in other industries which would have
had a right to the reduction, notably Valentine's Works in
operation, and the glass works, when they used the quantity
indicated."

As the court below charged directly against any effect being
attached to the subject matter of this testimony, the defendant is entitled to have it regarded as proof of an established
fact, and this being so, we have the following differences in
the conditions and circumstances attending the shipments to
the plaintiffs and the nail works, respectively:

1. The defendant, when it began carrying coal for the
plaintiffs, in September, 1889, was bound by the terms of
contract made with the nail works eight years before, and
during all the intervening time the plaintiffs were not even in
existence as a firm, and were doing no coal business whatever.
We know of no reason why that contract was not binding on
the defendant, especially as Governor Curtin testified, without
contradiction, that all the other industries at Bellefonte were

entitled to the benefit of it if they took the requisite quantity of twenty tons daily. This being so, the defendant's hands were tied, and it could not charge the nail works fifty cents a ton if it had desired to do so. This constituted a most material difference in the conditions and circumstances of the shipments. In an action by the nail works to recover the twenty cents a ton higher charge, if it had been made to equalize it with the rate charged [231] to the plaintiffs, it would have been no defense to say that a company of coal-dealers had lately come into existence who were getting coal over the same road from the same point, and therefore the defendant would be obliged to charge fifty cents per ton thereafter.

2. The nail works were bound to take twenty tons every day, while the plaintiffs were under no such obligation.

3. The plaintiffs were dealers in coal merely while the nail company was a manufacturer of fabrics, and itself consumed the coal it received. They were therefore not competitors in the same business, and a lower rate to the manufacturer would not, under the contract, affect the business of the plaintiffs injuriously. It is true there was proof that the nail company did sell some coal to their own workmen, but as it is not shown that the defendant had any knowledge of this fact they cannot be held responsible for it.

4. The business of the plaintiffs paid but one freight to the defendant while the business of the nail company paid not only that freight, to wit., for hauling the coal to the nail works, but also, in addition to that, another and entirely independent freight to the defendant on all the products manufactured by the nail company. This was a most important and vital difference in the conditions and circumstances of the two shipments. The authorities are very clear and strong that where an additional freight is obtained by means of the lower charge, the discrimination is justified both at common law and under the statutes.

The importance of this factor in the discussion is at once manifested by certain testimony given by the plaintiffs through one of their witnesses, L. E. Munson, who was the superintendent of the Bellefonte Iron and Nail Company. On examination by counsel for the plaintiff he was asked: "Q. What did you say the capacity of the nail works was as to outgoing freight? A. About thirty tons a day, thirty to forty tons a day. Q. That would be three hundred kegs,

would it? A. We have a capacity of five hundred kegs. Q.
What was your outgoing freight? A. I suppose part of the
time we made a hundred thousand kegs a year, from seventy-
five to one hundred and twenty-five thousand kegs a year.
Q. Would that mean about one car a day on a three hundred
kegs basis? A. Yes, sir; [232] then we shipped considerable
muck bar. Q. Were you shipping muck bar at the time you
were shipping nails? A. Sometimes; when we were making
nails out of steel rods. Q. Were you making muck bar at
the time you were making nails? A. Yes, sir. Q. Were you
making bar iron and shipping it at the time you were making
nails? A. Yes, sir."

As the foregoing testimony was given by the plaintiffs, and
was not at all contradicted by the defendant, the plaintiffs
are bound by it, and it must be taken as establishing the fact
which it develops, and the fact thus established is of the greatest possible consequence in the case. It entirely destroys, in
our opinion, the fundamental allegation of the plaintiffs that
the shipments of coal to the plaintiffs, and the nail works,
were made "upon like conditions and under similar circumstances." For the shipments of coal to the plaintiffs yielded
but one freight to the defendant, while the shipments to the
nail works yielded not only the same incoming freight on the
coal, of at least twenty tons a day, but an additional outgoing
freight of thirty to forty tons a day of fabrics manufactured
by the nail works. In view of this testimony how can it possibly be said that the conditions of the two shipments are
alike and their circumstances similar? That a railroad company may lawfully secure to itself so important an addition
to its business by making a lower charge to one customer than
to others is fully established by the authorities, as we shall
presently see.

5. The manufacture and sale by the nail works of nails and
muck bar were outside of, and entirely harmless to, the business of the plaintiffs, and hence a lower price for the coal
consumed by the nail works was neither an undue nor an
unreasonable discrimination against the plaintiffs, because it
was an immaterial circumstance as affecting their business.
This is self-evident. The plaintiffs did not deal in nails or
muck bar, and the sale of those commodities by the nail company, necessarily, could have no effect upon the plaintiffs'
business, which was the selling of coal to persons who consumed it.

6. As to all persons who did sell coal at Bellefonte, they were charged the same freights precisely as were charged to the plaintiffs. This is the undisputed testimony.

Let us now see what is the voice of the authorities upon the subject of discriminations in freight charges by carrying companies. [233] The subject is an old one. Prior to any statutes in England, or in this country, the common law had pronounced upon the rights and duties of carriers and freighters, and in the enactment of statutes little more has been done than to embody in them the well-known principles of the common law. It happens, somewhat singularly, that the very question we are now considering, of a discrimination in the rates charged to coal-dealers and to manufacturers who use coal as a fuel does not appear to have arisen. And yet it is very certain that such discrimination does prevail and has prevailed for a long time on all lines of railway and canal. It is highly probable that the absence of litigation upon such discrimination is due to the general sentiment of its fairness and justness. Within the writer's knowledge in the section of the state in which he lives a much greater difference between the rates charged to dealers and those charged to manufacturers by the coal-carrying companies has always existed, and now exists, without any question as to its justness or its legality. It is matter of public history that along the valleys of the Lehigh and Schuylkill there are great numbers of blast furnaces, rolling-mills, rail-mills, foundries, machine-shops and numerous other manufacturing establishments which consume enormous quantities of the coal output of the state, and at the same time in every village, town and city which abound in these regions an immensely large industry in the buying and selling of coal for domestic consumption is also prosecuted. And what is true of the eastern end of the state is without doubt equally true throughout the interior and western portions of the commonwealth, where similar conditions prevail. Yet from no part of our great state has ever yet arisen a litigation which called in question the legality, or the wisdom, or the strict justice of a discrimination favorable to the manufacturing industries as contrasted with the coal-selling industries. This fact can scarcely be accounted for except upon the theory that such discrimination, as has thus far transpired, has not been felt to be undue, or unreasonable, or contrary to legal warrant. In point of fact it is perfectly well known and appreciated, that the output of

freights from the great manufacturing centers upon our lin
of transportation constitutes one of the chief sources of tl
revenues which sustain them financially. Yet no part of th
income is derived [234] from those who are mere buyers ar
sellers of coal. When the freight is paid upon the coal the
buy, the revenue to be derived from that coal is at an en
Not so however with the revenue from the coal that is carrie
to the manufacturers. That coal is consumed on the prer
ises in the creation of an endless variety of products whic
must be put back upon the transporting lines, enhanced :
bulk and weight by the other commodities which enter in
the manufactured product, and is then distributed to the v
rious markets where they are sold. In addition to this,
manufacturing plant requires other commodities besides co
to conduct its operations, whereas a coal-dealer takes nothir
but his coal, and the freight derived by the carrier from tl
transportation of these commodities forms an important a
dition to its traffic and constitutes a condition of the busine
which has no existence in the business of carrying coal
those who are coal-dealers only. Thus a blast furnace requir
great quantities of iron ore, limestone, coke, sand, machi
ery, lumber, fire-bricks, and other materials for the maint
nance of its structures and the conduct of its business, noi
of which are necessary to a mere coal-selling business. The
are some of the leading considerations which establish a rac
cal difference in the conditions and the circumstances whic
are necessarily incident to the two kinds of business we a
considering.

Another important incident which distinguishes them
that the establishment of manufacturing industries and t
conducting of their business necessitates the employment
numbers of workmen and other persons whose services 1
needed, and these, with their families, create settlemei
and new centers of population, resulting in villages, tow
boroughs, and cities, according to the extent and variety
the industries established, and all these in turn furnish n
and additional traffic to the lines of transportation. 1
nothing of this kind results from the mere business of co
.selling. In fact that business is one of the results of
manufacturing business, and is not co-ordinate with it. '
business of the coal-dealer is promoted by the concentrat
of population which results from the establishment of ma
facturing industries, and these two kinds of business are

competitive in their essential characteristics, but naturally proceed together, side by side, the coal-selling increasing as the manufacturing increases in magnitude and extent.

[235] These considerations are generic, and are suggested for the purpose of illustrating the differences between the fundamental conditions and circumstances of the two industries we are considering.

Recurring now to the authorities, we find that the British statute of 17 and 18 Victoria, chapter 31, 1854, is perhaps the earliest instance of direct legislation upon this subject. That statute prohibited "undue or unreasonable preference or advantage" in transportation charges, but lacked the restricting words, "from the same place upon like conditions and under similar circumstances," which appear in our Act of 1883. Yet it was held in the cases of *Ransome* v. *Eastern Counties Ry. Co.*, 1 Com. B., N. S., 437, and *Oxlade* v. *North Eastern Ry. Co.*, 1 Com. B., N. S., 454, that it was competent to a railway company to enter into a special agreement for the carriage of goods for a particular individual or company, at a lower rate in respect of large quantities of goods and longer distances than for one who sends them in small quantities and shorter distances. In Ransome's case it was said by Creswell, J., in delivering the opinion of the court: "After a good deal of consideration, we think that the fair interests of the railway ought to be taken into the account."

In the case of *Nicholson* v. *Great Western Ry. Co.*, 5 Com. B., N. S., 366, the same doctrine was held, and it was also held that the second section of the Railway Traffic Act, 17 and 18 Victoria, chapter 31, was not contravened by a railway company carrying at a lower rate, in consideration of a guaranty of large quantities and full train-loads at regular periods, provided the real object of the company be to obtain thereby a greater remunerative profit, by the diminished cost of carriage, although the effect may be to exclude from the lower rate those persons who cannot give such a guaranty. Crowder, J., said in the opinion: "When the statute speaks of 'undue and unreasonable preference or advantage,' and 'undue or unreasonable prejudice or disadvantage,' it uses language implying that there may be advantage to one person or one class of traffic and prejudice to another, which would not be within the Act of Parliament. The preference and prejudice must be 'undue' or 'unreasonable,' to be within the statute. And although in the case now before

the court it is quite manifest that the Ruabon Coal Compan
have many and important advantages in carrying their ²¹
coal on the Great Western Railroad, as against the complai
ants and other coal-owners in the forest of Dean, still tl
question remains, are they 'undue' or 'unreasonable' adva
tages? This mainly depends upon the adequacy of the co
sideration given in return to the railway company for tl
advantages afforded to the Ruabon Coal Company."

The justice then proceeds to show that it was to the adva
tage and profit of the railway company to carry coals for tl
Ruabon company at a lower rate than for the complainant
and concludes in the language of the *syllabus* above quote
that this was no violation of the act. All of the foregoir
cases recognize the proposition that if the interest of the ra
way company was subserved by charging the lower rate
the one company than to the other the act was not violate
That conclusion was reached in a case where the complai
ant was in the same business with the favored company, ar
was injuriously affected by the discrimination, but the cou
held that this was permissible if the interests of the railwe
company were thereby subserved. With how much great
force can it be said that here, where there is no competiti
in the disposal of the coal of the plaintiffs and the produc
of the nail company, and also where the inducement to t
defendant to make the lower rate for the nail company is
largely increased traffic on the defendant's road, neither t
letter nor the spirit of our Act of 1883 was violated.

The doctrine of the cases above cited was also declared
the case of *In re Baxendale* v. *Great Western Ry. Co.*, 5 C
B., N. S., 353, where Cockburn, J., said: "If an arrangem
were made by a railway company, whereby persons bring
a larger amount of traffic to the railway should have tl
goods carried on more favorable terms than those bringin
less quantity, a court might uphold such an arrangemen
an ordinary incident of commercial economy, provided
same advantage were extended to all persons under the
circumstances." This latter incident would of course
essential where all of the favored class were in the s
business.

In the case of *Messenger* v. *Pennsylvania R. R. Co.*, 37
L. 531, 18 Am. Rep. 754, cited for the appellee, the court
careful to say that, "It must not be inferred that a com
carrier in adjusting his price cannot regard the parti

circumstances of the particular [237] transportation. Many considerations may properly enter into the agreement for carriage or the establishment of rates, such as the quantity carried, its nature, risks, the expense of carriage at different periods of time, and the like; but he has no right to give an exclusive advantage or preference in that respect to some over others for carriage in the course of his business."

In that case there was a very clear preference to one party over all others in the same business, by the railroad company giving him a specific drawback upon freights on hogs carried from the same points, and of course as this was direct preference over all others it was in violation of the law. But that decision has no application to this case.

In the case *Interstate Commerce Commission* v. *Baltimore etc. R. R. Co.*, 145 U. S. 263, it was held that the issue by a railway company engaged in interstate commerce, of a party-rate ticket, for the transportation of ten or more persons at a rate less than that charged to a single individual for a like transportation on the same trip did not make an unjust or unreasonable charge, nor an unjust discrimination, nor give an undue or unreasonable preference or advantage to the purchasers of the party-rate ticket, within the meaning of the several provisions of the Interstate Commerce Act of 1887. There was much discussion of the general subject of the prohibitions of the general statute in the opinion of the supreme court of the United States in this case, from which it will be instructive to present some quotations. The English Traffic Act of 1854, above referred to, was fully considered, and the cases of Oxlade and Ransome, and others hereinbefore cited, were recognized and followed. Amongst other things it was said by Mr. Justice Brown, who delivered the opinion: "It is not all discriminations or preferences that fall within the inhibition of the statute; only such as are unjust and unreasonable. For instance, it would be obviously unjust to charge A a greater sum than B for a single trip from Washington to Pittsburgh; but, if A agrees not only to go but to return by the same route, it is no injustice to B to permit him to do so for a reduced fare, since the services are not alike, nor the circumstances and conditions substantially similar, as required by section 2, to make an unjust discrimination. Indeed the possibility of just discrimination and reasonable [238] preferences is recognized by these sections in declaring what shall be deemed unjust. . . . . In order to constitute an unjust dis-

crimination under section 2, the carrier must charge or receiv
directly from one person a greater or less compensation tha
from another, or must accomplish the same thing indirectl
by a special rate, rebate, or other device; but in either cas
it must be for a 'like and contemporaneous service in th
transportation of a like kind of traffic under substantiall
similar circumstances and conditions.' To bring the presen
case within the words of this section, we must assume tha
the transportation of ten persons on a single ticket is substan
tially identical with the transportation of one, and in view c
the universally accepted fact that a man may buy, contrac
or manufacture on a large scale cheaper proportionally tha
upon a small scale, this is impossible. In this connection w
quote with approval from the opinion of Judge Jackson ir
the court below: 'To come within the inhibition of said sec
tions the differences must be made under like conditions; tha
is, there must be contemporaneous service in the transporta
tion of like kinds of traffic under substantially the same cir
cumstances and conditions. . . . . In short the substance o
all these decisions is that railway companies are only boun<
to give the same terms to all persons alike under the sam
conditions and circumstances, and that any fact which pro
duces an inequality of conditions and a change of circum
stances justifies an inequality of charge. . . . . But in so fa
as relates to the question of "undue preference," it may b
presumed that Congress, in adopting the language of th
English act, had in mind the construction given to thes
words by the English courts and intended to incorporate ther
into the statute: *McDonald* v. *Hovey*, 110 U. S. 619.' "

In the case of *Fitchburg R. R. Co.* v. *Gage*, 12 Gray, 39%
the right to discriminate upon the basis of a carriage for
certain time and in certain quantities was declared. Th
claim of the shipper was for an equality of charge for shi
ments of ice with charges for shipments of bricks, becau
they were of the same class of freight, but the claim was n
allowed. The court said, by way of illustration of the pri
ciple upon which there might be a lawful discrimination
rates upon the same class of goods: " If for special reaso
in isolated cases [239] the carrier sees fit to stipulate for t
carriage of goods or merchandise of any class for individua
for a certain time, or in certain quantities, for less compe
sation than what is the usual, necessary, and reasonable ra
he may undoubtedly do so without entitling all other perso

and parties to the same advantage and relief." And this
court said in the case of *Shipper* v. *Pennsylvania R. R. Co.*, 47
Pa. St. 338: "We are not prepared to say that a railroad company may not discriminate in its rate of tolls in favor of
domestic trade over foreign; in favor of home products over
those which are extraterritorial, especially when the railroad
lies wholly within the state. Ownership may not be a reasonable ground for a distinction, but weight, bulk, value, place
of production, and many other things may be."

These cases are cited as illustrations of various reasons and
principles upon which lawful discriminations may be made,
even in charges for the carriage of the same goods over the
same roads and to be used for the same purposes. But in
the present case where not only a particular quantity must
be furnished to the railroad every day, but the goods at the
point of delivery are to be used for totally different purposes
which do not conflict or compete with each other, the reason
for a discrimination has an infinitely greater force.

In Hutchinson on Carriers, page 353, after a protracted
review of all the cases, and they are very numerous, the writer
sums up the result thus: "Mere inequality in charges does not,
therefore, of itself amount to an unjust discrimination. It
only becomes such when a discrimination is made in the
rates charged for transportation of goods of the same class, of
different shippers, under like circumstances and conditions.
So a mere reduction from the established rate is not necessarily an unjust discrimination. But it becomes such when
it is either intended, or has a natural tendency, to injure
another shipper in his business, and destroy his trade by
giving to the favored shipper a practical monopoly of the
business."

We come now to consider the case of *Borda* v. *Philadelphia
etc. R. R. Co.*, 141 Pa. St. 484. It was an action of case
brought against the Philadelphia and Reading Railroad
Company by the plaintiffs, who were shippers of coal, to
recover damages for alleged illegal discriminations in the
freight charged to the plaintiffs on shipments of coal over the
defendant's road, as against lower rates charged to other [240]
shippers over the same road. The case was by agreement of
the parties referred to Mr. Peter McCall as referee, who made a
most exhaustive and elaborate report, denying the claim of
the plaintiffs, and his report was affirmed by this court. As
the shipments had been made prior to the adoption of our

constitution of 1874 a preliminary question arose, whether it
was the duty of the defendant to carry without discrimination.
The referee held that such was the duty of the defendant,
saying, " I regard it, then, as settled law in this state, that a
railroad company, a common carrier, owes a duty of equality
to every citizen, and I adopt the position taken by Mr. Bullitt
in argument, that railroad companies have no right to make
any undue discrimination or preference in their charges; and
a charge made to one shipper higher than another, for the
same service, under like circumstances, constitutes undue
preference and discrimination, and by consequence renders
the charge unreasonable.   Such is the general rule, and it is
vastly important to the general public that there be no undue
relaxation of this rule; for, exercising, as they practically do,
a monopoly of transportation on their roads, railway managers
have in their hands a tremendous power, by discrimination,
to enrich one man and ruin another.   The equality, however,
which is thus prescribed, is not a strict and literal equality
under all circumstances, however varying and different.   It
is rather an equality in the sense of freedom from unreasonable discrimination.   It is only unjust, undue, or unreasonable discrimination against which the law has set its canon.
Arbitrary discrimination is illegal; so discrimination made
with a view of giving advantage to one person.   But the
truism that circumstances alter cases applies here, and, under
a different state of circumstances, a discrimination may be
reasonable and lawful, which, were the circumstances the
same, would be undue and unreasonable.   In order to render
lawful an inequality of charge, the goods must be carried
under different circumstances, and the question whether the
difference is material or essential arises in each particular
case."

The writer regards the foregoing as the most precise and
the most felicitous expression of the law upon the general
subject under consideration that he has met with, and therefore quotes it entire.

The claim of the plaintiffs was to recover damages to the
241 amount of upwards of sixty thousand dollars for unjust
discrimination in favor of Audenried & Co., rival coal shippers to the plaintiffs, by the payment to Audenried & Co. of
rebates on coal shipped from Port Richmond to points beyond
New Brunswick at the rate of one dollar and sixty-five
cents for steamer coal, and other rates for other grades.   I

was proved that these rebates were paid under agreements between Audenried & Co. and the defendant, made at the beginning of the season, and to continue throughout the season, and the referee was of opinion, and so found, that these contracts for continuous shipments during the whole season at fixed rates constituted such a difference in the conditions and circumstances of the shipments for Audenried & Co. and the plaintiffs respectively, as to justify the discrimination and prevent it from being illegal. In expressing his conclusions the referee says: "The defendant's case denies that the discrimination was willful, and made with any such design as imputed by the plaintiffs. It rests upon the ground that the payment of the drawbacks to Audenried & Co., under an honest and *bona fide* belief that they were entitled to them, under an arrangement by which, in consideration of their having made contracts early in the spring for delivery of coal at fixed prices throughout the season, they were allowed the drawbacks in question. . . . . On the whole, I am of opinion, upon the best consideration I have been able to give the subject, that the defendants did not pay to Audenried & Co. the drawbacks complained of in the first and additional count of the declaration, willfully and with intent to enable them to increase their business at the expense of the plaintiffs, but that it paid the same in good faith under the belief that Audenried & Co. had made contracts in the spring at a fixed price for the delivery of the coal. . . . . I am of opinion therefore that the defendant could legally have allowed the drawbacks to Audenried & Co., which it did allow, if that firm had had contracts made in the early part of the season for delivery of coal in the eastern market at fixed prices. In that case, although the service rendered, to wit, the transportation, would have been the same as that rendered to the plaintiffs, yet the circumstances were different, and the difference of circumstances would have justified the discrimination."

While this court did not review the testimony taken before [242] the referee, because it was not before us, we affirmed the judgment in favor of the defendant, upon the report, conceding the facts to be as found by the referee.

It will be perceived therefore that in that case the circumstance, that the coal was shipped for Audenried & Co. under contracts made at the beginning of the season at fixed prices, and to continue throughout the season, was held a sufficient

reply **to a** charge of unjust discrimination, although the commodity shipped was the same, to wit, anthracite coal, and the
shipments were between the same points, to wit, from Port
Richmond to points east of New Brunswick, and the plaintiffs
were engaged in the same business as Audenried & Co.

Whereas, here, the plaintiffs were not engaged in the same
business as the Bellefonte nail company, there could not be
any competition between them in the products sold, and the
rate at which coal was carried for the nail company was a
matter of absolute indifference to the plaintiffs. We repeat
again that we do not regard the sales of coal by the nail company to its own employees as of any moment in the case: 1.
Because there is no proof that they were made with the
knowledge of the defendant, but there is positive and uncontradicted proof that they were made without such knowledge;
2. Because the defendant is not responsible for such sales by
the nail company; 3. Because the coal carried by the defendant for the nail company was not carried for purposes of sale
at retail, but for the purpose of manufacturing nails and muck
bar; and 4. Because there is no proof that the plaintiffs sustained any damage by reason of the sales of the nail company to their employees.

But it must be understood, and we so decide, that a manufacturing company has no right to engage in the business of
selling coal, even to its own employees, and if it does so, and
the transporting company is notified of such selling, it must
thereupon cease to carry coal to the manufacturing company
at any less rate than it charges to the coal-dealers, or incur
the penalties of unjust discrimination.

The ruling of the court below would require that coal carried to blast furnaces, rolling-mills, rail-mills, foundries and
all other manufacturing enterprises should be carried for the
same price as the coal carried to any retail dealer in the same
locality, though the quantity consumed by the former might
[243] extend to many thousand of tons each year, while the
quantity carried for the latter might be a few hundred tons
only, and although the manufacturing companies gave back
to the carrier many thousands of tons of freight each year,
while the retail dealer gave back none, and although the business of the manufacturer in no wise competes with the business of the dealer, we think the differences in these respects
between these two kinds of business are such as to justify a
discrimination in the rates of freight charged to each, and

the conditions of the two are not alike and their circumstances are not similar within the meaning of our Act of 1883, and therefore there can be no recovery in this case.

The fact that the payment of the rebates was not known to the plaintiffs is of no possible consequence, both because they had no right to know it under our present ruling that the circumstances were not similar and the conditions not alike, and also because if the discriminating charge was lawful, the absence of notice to the plaintiffs would not make it unlawful. The same point was made and ruled in the Borda case. The referee said: "But in point of law I do not think that the duty of giving notice to the world of every special rate rests upon the carrier under penalty of being guilty of unlawful discrimination by his omission to give such notice. How and to whom is such notice to be given?"

It remains only to be added that differences of freight rates on coal to manufacturers and to mere dealers are, and have been for many years, in universal practice, and not a single case other than this has as yet reached the courts of last resort in England or in the United States questioning the entire legality and propriety of such differences, and that circumstance is ample proof that both the professional and the lay mind has assented to the practice.

Speaking upon a similar subject, the difference in passenger rates upon ordinary tickets, and thousand-mile tickets, or go and return tickets, the supreme court of the United States, in the case of *Interstate Commerce Commission* v. *Baltimore etc. R. R. Co.*, 145 U. S. 263, said: "In view of the fact, however, that every railway company issues such tickets; that there is no reported case, state or federal, wherein their legality has been questioned; that there is no such case in England; and that the [244] practice is universally acquiesced in by the public, it would seem that the issuing of such tickets should not be held an unjust discrimination, or an unreasonable preference to the persons traveling upon them."

On the question of damages the court below charged the jury: "If the nail works paid twenty cents less freight per ton on their coal they had that much of an advantage over others; and the law would seem in the mind of the court to fix that excess as the measure of the plaintiffs' damages."

We think this was serious error. The Act of 1883 contains no language justifying an instruction that the party injured can recover three times the amount of the difference in the rates charged. The words of the act are, "any violation of this provision shall make the offending company or common carrier liable to the party injured for damages treble the amount of injury suffered." The "amount of injury suffered" is the measure of the single damages to be allowed. But it does not at all follow that the amount of injury suffered is the difference in the rates charged. It might be, or it might not be, but, in any event, it must be a subject of proof, and there was no proof in the case of the actual damage sustained. How does it follow that because the defendant company paid in 1889 to the nail company a rebate of some six thousand dollars on all the shipments that had been made from 1881, and a few sums thereafter, the plaintiffs suffered damage to any extent? In point of fact the nail company paid the full freight of fifty cents a ton net during all these years, and their claim for rebates was not adjusted until 1889. How then does it appear that damage was suffered by the plaintiffs in consequence of the payment of the rebates to the nail company? It does not appear that the plaintiffs sold their coal for any less than the current market price at any time except when they and the other dealers were engaged in a war of prices and sold it far below the actual cost, in a struggle to capture the market. And it does not appear but that the plaintiffs would have sold their coal at twenty cents less than they did, if they had received the rebate. The natural inference is that that is precisely what they would have done in the contest for the market. But of all this there is not a word of testimony, and yet it is only actual damage that they can recover. The proof for the defendant was that they never cut the market priece to their men, but maintained it even when the coal-dealers [245] of the town were slaughtering each other's trade by selling below cost. As three times the actual damage is the penalty the defendant would have to pay if the judgment were sustained, they have a right to require very clear and definite proof as to what the actual damage was.

When blast furnaces and great iron mills are built they are not placed in cities or towns, but in the open country, where land is abundant and cheap, and of course on the line of a railroad. When they are established there is no population at the place of erection. The railroad companies are very willing to make as favorable terms as possible for freights on all the materials that are brought to the plants and on all products that are carried from them, because they get a largely increased business from such enterprises. When the works are erected, houses are built for the men and officials of the companies. After that come the usual accessories required to supply the wants of the population, to wit, merchants, tradesmen, mechanics, butchers, bakers, grocers, and, amongst others, coal-dealers. But the moment the last of these arrive, if the principles which prevailed in the court below in this case are correct, the whole freight system agreed upon between the transporter and the manufacturer theretofore must be be changed and advanced to the freight rates charged to the retail dealers, or else all the rates charged to such dealers must be lowered to conform to the rates charged to the manufacturer. If this is not done the manufacturer incurs the risk of being visited years afterward with claims for treble damages, which may embrace any period of six years, and as all the dealers have the same right of action in this regard that any one of them has, and every town or city along the line has some or many retail coal-dealers and manufacturing establishments also within its limits, it is easy to see that the aggregate of such claims may soon absorb the entire property and assets of the strongest transporting companies of the state. We do not find anything in the law that renders necessary, or possible, any such results as these, and we think it wiser and better to administer the law so that the rights and interests of all may be conserved within rational and sensible limits.

We sustain the first, second, third, and fifth assignments of error. The fourth and sixth assignments have no merit, and are not sustained.

Judgment reversed.   ———

Railroads—Discrimination—Effect of Dissimilar Conditions —In order to invalidate a contract between a shipper and a carrier, for discrimination, other elements must enter into the contract, so as to make the discrimination unjust and oppressive, and the circumstances of each case must be considered in determining the validity of the contract: *Cleveland etc. Ry. Co.* v. *Closser*, 126 Ind. 348; 22 Am. St. Rep. 593, and note. A railroad company cannot unjustly discriminate between its customers in its charges for carrying freight where the conditions are equal; and what will be an unjust discrimination must be determined from the facts and circumstances of the case: *Root* v. *Long Island R. R. Co.*, 114 N. Y. 300; 11 Am. St. Rep. 643, and extended note; *Cook* v. *Chicago etc. Ry. Co.*, 81 Iowa 551; 25 Am. St. Rep. 512. See the extended notes to the following cases: *Scofield* v. *Railway Co.*, 54 Am. Rep. 862; *Ex parte Benson*, 44 Am. Rep. 568; and *Commonwealth* v. *Power*, 41 Am. Dec. 484.

RAILROADS—LAWFUL DISCRIMINATION—SHIPPING LARGER QUANTITIES, OR FOR LONGER DISTANCES: See extended note to *Root* v. *Long Island R. R. Co.*, 11 Am. St. Rep. 649, 650. In order to secure freight which would otherwise go by a different route, a railroad company may discriminate in rates in favor of persons living at a distance from its route, provided its charges against others similarly situated are reasonable: *Ragan* v. *Aiken*, 9 Lea, 609; 42 Am. Rep. 684, and note; but less rates charged for greater distances only on the ground of the existence of competing lines is an unjust discrimination: *Chicago etc. R. R. Co.* v. *People*, 67 Ill. 11; 16 Am. Rep. 599.

RAILROADS—DISCRIMINATION—REBATE—RECOVERY OF.—A shipper is entitled to recover from a carrier a sum equivalent to the rebate which it allowed other shippers for whom it performed the same kind and extent of services, where it had collected full charges from him and concealed from him the fact that it allowed a rebate to others in his business: *Cook* v. *Chicago etc. Ry. Co.*, 81 Iowa 551; 25 Am. St. Rep. 512, and note.

BRAMBERRY'S APPEAL.

[156 PENNSYLVANIA STATE, 628.]

A TENANCY BY ENTIRETIES ARISES WHENEVER an estate vests in two persons, they then being husband and wife.

A TENANCY BY ENTIRETIES MAY EXIST IN PERSONAL as well as real property, in a chose in action as well as in possession.

TENANCY BY ENTIRETIES IS NOT ABOLISHED by a statute abolishing survivorship among joint tenants, nor by legislation which secures to a wife the enjoyment of her separate estate.

TENANCY BY ENTIRETIES IN A BOND AND MORTGAGE.—If lands purchased by and conveyed to a husband and wife are sold by them and a bond and mortgage are taken by them to secure a portion of the purchase money, they hold such bond and mortgage as tenants by the entireties.

George B. Johnson, for the appellant.

Thomas W. Pierce and E. D. Bingham, for the appellees.

631 McCOLLUM, J.   Assuming that the auditor's findings or deductions of fact were warranted by the evidence before him, we have a purchase by and a conveyance to husband and wife of seventeen acres of land, a payment by the wife from her separate estate of one-half the purchase money, and a payment by the husband of the other half of it. The grantees held the land so purchased and conveyed twenty-five years, when they sold it and took from their vendee his bond and mortgage to secure to them a portion of the purchase money. Ten days after this sale was consummated by a conveyance the wife died, and the question now presented for our determination is whether one-half the sum so secured belongs to her estate or her husband, as survivor, is the owner of the whole of it

The learned auditor's view approved by the learned court be-low was that inasmuch as the wife's money was blended with the husband's in the purchase of the land, one-half the pro-ceeds arising from the sale of it belonged to her estate, al-though the obligation for such proceeds, like the conveyance of the land, was made to the husband and wife. It was also thought by the learned auditor [632] that tenancy by entireties was abolished by the Act of June 3, 1887, relating to the prop-erty of married women and their control of it.

A tenancy by entireties arises whenever an estate vests in two persons, they being, when it so vests, husband and wife. It may exist in personal as well as real property, in a chose in action as well as in a chose in possession: Freeman on Cotenancy and Partition, secs. 63, 68; *Gillan* v. *Dixon*, 65 Pa. St. 395. The common-law rule is that the words which in a conveyance to unmarried persons constitute a joint tenancy, will create, if the grantees are husband and wife, a tenancy by entireties. The tenancy established by a conveyance to hus-band and wife is not destroyed or affected by the Act of March 31, 1812, which abolished survivorship among joint tenants, nor does the rule referred to yield to an express provision in the deed that the grantees shall hold the estate granted as tenants in common: *Stuckey* v. *Keefe*, 26 Pa. St. 397. It has been contended, and in some jurisdictions held, that the legis-lation which secures to the wife the enjoyment of her separate estate is destructive of the legal unity of husband and wife on which tenancies by entireties depend. But the better view is that such tenancies are not destroyed or impaired by it: 9 Am. & Eng. Ency. of Law, 851, and cases cited. In *Diver* v. *Diver*, 56 Pa. St. 106, it was expressly decided that the Act of April 11, 1848, did not in any manner affect the creation and enjoyment of estates by entireties, and Strong, J., in deliver-ing the opinion of the court, said: "To hold it as operating upon the deed conveying land to a wife, making such deed assure a different estate from what it would have assured without the act, is to lose sight of the legislative purpose. Were we to do so it would become in many cases a means of divesting her of her property, instead of an instrument of pro-tection. In the present case, if it has converted the estate granted to Diver and his wife into a tenancy in common, it has taken from her her ownership and enjoyment of the en-tirety during her husband's life and her right of survivorship to the whole. We hold, then, that no such effect is to be given to the Act of 1848 or any of its cognate acts. The legal unity of husband and wife still remains, and consequently Mrs. Diver, on the death of her husband, succeeded to the whole estate granted by [633] the deed." We think this language in reference to the Act of 1848 and tenancy by entirety is applicable to the Act of June 3, 1887, and the case under consideration. The Act of 1887, like the Act of 1848, was "intended to protect the property of the wife from the dominion or control of the husband, but not to change the nature of her estate or to destroy the legal unity of person which characterizes their relations to each other ": *Gillan* v. *Dixon*, 65 Pa. St. 395. *Prima facie* the conveyance of the land in 1865 to H. James Bramberry and Rachael A. Bramberry, they being at the time husband and wife, vested in them an estate by entireties, and when on the sale of the land in 1890 they accepted from their vendee his bond and mortgage to secure to them a portion of the purchase money, they held the sum so secured not as joint tenants or tenants in common, but as tenants by the entirety: Freeman on Cotenancy and Partition, sec. 68, and cases cited. If either had died before the land was sold the survivor would have held it against any claim of the heirs or creditors of the decedent, and no valid reason appears for applying a different rule to the chose in action taken by them in their joint names for a portion of the purchase money. There is certainly nothing on the record to indicate that the parties intended a division of this sum between them, or to repel the presumption arising from the form of the obligations given to secure it. These obligations conform to the ownership established by the conveyance, and we may fairly conclude from them, in the absence of evidence to the contrary, that it was the purpose of the vendors to hold the purchase money as they held the land.

We cannot say that the auditor erred in finding that the husband and wife were joint purchasers of the land, and that the wife paid from her separate estate one-half the sum or price they gave for it. This finding was based on the declarations of the surviving husband, and in a contest between him and the heirs of the wife he ought not to complain that what he said about the purchase was accepted by the auditor as true. The facts so found did not change the character or qualities of the estate granted; they merely showed that the husband and wife were jointly entitled to the land which was conveyed to them. If, as in *Trimble* v. *Reis*, 37 Pa. St. 448, and

Dexter v. *Billings*, 110 Pa. St. 135, the wife alone was entitled to the land, or, as in *McKinney* [634] v. *Hamilton*, 51 Pa. St. 63, the mortgage was for purchase money due on a sale by the wife of land she inherited from her father, a different question would be presented. But a conveyance of land to husband and wife in consummation of their joint purchase of it during coverture vests in them an estate by entireties, and when on a sale of the land so held they take in their joint names an obligation for the purchase money, the presumption is that they intend to hold the latter as they did the former. It follows from these views that the appellant, as survivor, is the owner of the fund secured by the bond and mortgage and that it was error to surcharge him as administrator with one-half thereof, and to award the same to the heirs of the decedent.

Decree reversed at the cost of the appellees, and it is ordered that the record be remitted to the court below, with instructions to enter a decree in accordance with this opinion.

TENANCY BY ENTIRETIES—WHEN ARISES.—Tenancy by the entirety is created by a conveyance of land to a husband and wife which does not state the manner in which they shall hold such land: *Stelz* v. *Shreck*, 128 N. Y. 263; 26 Am. St. Rep. 475, and note; *Appeal of Lewis*, 85 Mich. 340; 24 Am. St. Rep. 94, and note; *Harrison* v. *Ray*, 108 N. C. 215; 23 Am. St. Rep. 57, and note; *Baker* v. *Stewart*, 40 Kan. 442; 10 Am. St. Rep. 213; note to *Enyeart* v. *Kepler*, 10 Am. St. Rep. 99, and note; *Hemingway* v. *Scales*, 42 Miss. 1; 2 Am. Rep. 586; 97 Am. Dec. 425, and note; *Lux* v. *Hoff*, 47 Ill. 425; 95 Am. Dec. 502, and note; *Bennett* v. *Child*, 19 Wis. 362; 88 Am. Dec. 692, and note; *Miner* v. *Brown*, 133 N. Y. 308. See also *Hulett* v. *Inlow*, 57 Ind. 412; 26 Am. Rep. 64, and extended note, and the extended note to *Den* v. *Hardenbergh*, 18 Am. Dec. 377.

TENANCY BY ENTIRETIES IS NOT ABOLISHED by the abolition of joint tenancies: *Marburg* v. *Cole*, 49 Md. 402; 33 Am. Rep. 266, and note; nor by the statutes enabling married women to hold land as single women: *Buttlar* v. *Rosenblath*, 42 N. J. Eq. 651; 59 Am. Rep. 52, and note; *Carver* v. *Smith*, 90 Ind. 222; 46 Am. Rep. 210, and note; *Pray* v. *Stebbins*, 141 Mass. 219; 55 Am. Rep. 462. See also the extended note to *Hulett* v. *Inlow*, 26 Am. Rep. 65.

TENANCY BY ENTIRETIES IN PERSONAL PROPERTY.—See the extended note to *Den* v. *Hardenbergh*, 18 Am. Dec. 382, 383. Tenancy by the entireties can exist only where there is a conveyance of a vested interest in real property. So where a husband and wife contribute equally from their separate estates moneys, which they invest in a bond and mortgage taken in their joint names, they are merely tenants in common thereof: *Matter of Albrecht*, 136 N. Y. 91; 32 Am. St. Rep. 700. This doctrine is in direct conflict with the opinion of the court in the principal case.

CASES

SUPREME COURT

TENNESSEE.

STATE v. PAINT ROCK COAL AND COKE CO.

[92 TENNESSEE, 81.]

CONSTITUTIONAL LAW.—A STATUTE DECLARING THAT ANY PERSONS, FIRMS OR CORPORATIONS REFUSING TO CASH ANY CHECK OR SCRIP presented to them within thirty days of its date of issuance shall be deemed guilty of a misdemeanor is in conflict with the provisions of the constitution prohibiting the legislature from passing any law authorizing imprisonment for debt, and is therefore void.

Attorney-General Pickle, for the state.

Washburn and Templeton, for the company.

81 W. A. HENDERSON, S. J. At the July term, 1891, the grand jurors for Scott county returned an indictment against the Paint Rock Coal and Coke Company, consisting of two counts, in substance as follows:

1. That the said defendant refused "to cash a certain check of its own that was presented it within thirty days of its date of issuance."

82 2. That the said defendant "did unlawfully refuse to redeem, in lawful currency, a certain check of its own which said Paint Rock Coal and Coke Company had issued."

To this indictment the defendant interposed a motion to quash, and set forth the following grounds:

1. Because no criminal offense is alleged in the indictment.

2. Because the Act of 1887, under which this indictment was drawn, is unconstitutional, in that it impairs the obligation of the contract, and attempts to imprison the defendant for refusing to pay a debt.

On the hearing of the questions thus presented his honor, the circuit judge, sustained said motion and quashed said indictment. The state appeals to this court.

Passing over the objections to the form of the indictment, which contains no identification or description of the check complained of, the law of the case is involved in the second ground of the motion to quash.

The Act of March 29, 1887, enacts that from and after the passage of that act it would be unlawful for any person or persons, firms, or corporations or companies to refuse to cash any checks or scrip of their own that may be presented them within thirty days of its date of issuance, and that any such person who should refuse to redeem, in lawful currency, any such [83] checks or scrip would be guilty of a misdemeanor, and, upon conviction, should be fined not less than ten nor more than twenty-five dollars for each offense. In other words, that when any person who owed a debt which was evidenced by check or scrip issued by him did not cash the same within thirty days of its issuance he would be guilty of a misdemeanor, and fined accordingly, which judgment, of course, under the general law, would be liable to be enforced by confinement in the workhouse.

The question is whether or not that act is violative of the fundamental law of the land. If this statute and the indictment under it can be maintained any citizen, corporation, or company drawing a check or giving a written order in good faith in favor of any person, and failing, for any reason, to pay the same, or to redeem it in currency, if presented in thirty days, is guilty of a crime for which he may be punished by imprisonment.

Section 18 of article 1 of the constitution of this state provides: "The legislature shall pass no law authorizing imprisonment for debt in civil cases." The act of the legislature in question, while not directly authorizing imprisonment for debt, does attempt to create a crime for the nonpayment of debts evidenced by check, scrip, or order, and for such crime provides a penalty, which may or may not be followed by imprisonment. In that way and for that reason the act [84] is violative of the spirit, if not the letter, of the constitutional provision above cited. It is an indirect imposition of imprisonment for the nonpayment of debt, and is therefore clearly within the constitutional inhibition.

Affirm the judgment.

A MUNICIPALITY IN ALABAMA ENACTED AN ORDINANCE declaring that any person who should give, sell, barter, or otherwise dispose of spirituous, vinous, or malt liquors, or drugs, or bitters, the basis of which is intoxicating liquor, shall be fined not less than two nor more than twenty-five dollars. The charter of the municipality declared that all persons convicted of violating the ordinances of the municipality who should fail to pay or secure such fines and costs as may be assessed therefor should be placed at hard labor for the town in imprisonment until such fine and costs were paid. A conviction having taken place under the ordinance, an attempt was made to obtain relief from the conviction, on the ground that the municipality had not authority to pass an ordinance prohibiting the sale of whisky therein. The lower court sustained this contention, and released the person convicted. The supreme court, however, while maintaining that the municipality had authority to prohibit the sale of intoxicating liquors, expressed its opinion that the part of the charter authorizing the imprisonment of persons convicted until their fine should be paid was in violation of the constitution of the state prohibiting imprisonment for debt. Upon this subject the court said: "It is to be noted, however, in this connection, that the act does not contemplate hard labor or imprisonment as alternate punishment, or as punishment to be imposed in lieu of the fine, but as means of coercing the payment of the fine; and while it may be that the defendant could be put to hard labor, at a reasonable rate of compensation, for a sufficient length of time for his earnings to equal the fine and cost, we are inclined to the opinion that, in so far as the provision in question undertakes to authorize his imprisonment until the fine and costs are paid, it is inoperative and void. Otherwise the imprisonment might be for a period as indefinite as the duration of the defendant's life, and have much in common with imprisonment for debt, which the organic law inhibits, and hence involve violence to the policy of our jurisprudence": Ex parte Russellville, 95 Ala. 19.

IMPRISONMENT FOR DEBT.—For a discussion of the constitutionality of statutes imprisoning for debt see the extended note to Eikenberry v. Edwards, 56 Am. Rep. 363. It is contrary to the spirit of the constitution and laws of this state to detain in prison any person who is unable, by reason of his poverty, to pay money into court: Ryan v. Kingsbery, 89 Ga. 228. Imprisonment under bail process in an action of trover is not "imprisonment for debt" prohibited by the state constitution: Harris v. Bridges, 5 Ga. 407; 24 Am. Rep. 495. It is such a fraud under the New Jersey constitution as will subject a person to imprisonment for debt if he attempts fraudulently defeat his creditor's recovery of an ordinary debt by the usual process of law: Ex parte Clarke, 1 Spenc. 648; 45 Am. Dec. 394. A statute allowing an arrest in an action for libel does not violate a constitutional provision that "there shall be no imprisonment for debt except in cases of fraud": Moore v. Green, 73 N. C. 394; 21 Am. Rep. 470. See also Frost v. Brisbin, 19 Wend. 11; 32 Am. Dec. 423; and Heath v. Brown, 40 Kan. 33.

MARBLE COMPANY v. HARVEY.

[92 TENNESSEE, 115]

CORPORATIONS.—A CONTRACT FOR THE PURCHASE BY ONE CORPORATION OF THE STOCK OF ANOTHER FOR THE PURPOSE OF ENABLING IT TO CONTROL AND MANAGE the business of the latter, though both corporations are engaged in a similar business, is against public policy, and void. No rights dependent upon such a contract can be enforced in this state.

CORPORATIONS—AGREEMENTS—ULTRA VIRES—ACTIONS IN FURTHERANCE OF.—If an agreement is made whereby the stock of one corporation is to be transferred to a trustee of another, and the purpose of the transfer of stock is to enable the former corporation to obtain the management and control of the latter, and it is part of the agreement that the transferor will assume and discharge any liability that may arise out of certain pending suits against the corporation whose stock is transferred, and the stock is transferred pursuant to such agreement, and the purchase price paid, and thereafter an action is brought by the purchasing corporation to recover for the failure of the transferor to discharge the liability contracted against, such action is in furtherance of the original unlawful and void contract, and cannot be sustained.

CORPORATION—A CONTRACT ULTRA VIRES in the proper sense is wholly void, and cannot be ratified by either party, because it could not have been authorized by either. No performance on either side can give it validity.

Green and Shields, for the Marble Company.

W. C. Kain, for Harvey.

116 LURTON, J. The complainant is an Ohio corporation, and was organized under the general incorporation law of that state, "for the purpose of cutting, dressing, manufacturing, selling, and disposing of marble, stone, slate, granite, and other substances, with such other incidental and necessary powers essential to carry on said business." This company, with its place of business in Cincinnati, Ohio, has acquired the entire issue of shares made by a Tennessee incorporation, engaged in a similar business and under a similar charter, and known as the McMillin Marble Company. Its last acquisition of shares was under a contract with the defendant, who was president of the Tennessee company, and who owned, at the time of the sale, twenty-five shares, being one-half of **117** the entire stock of the company. These shares he conveyed to a trustee, selected by the purchasing corporation, for its use and benefit. The consideration for the sale was the payment of six thousand dollars, the defendant assuming and agreeing to personally pay off and discharge one-half of all liability which might be

fixed upon the McMillin Marble Company as a result of certain suits against that company then pending in the courts of this state.

The bill alleges, and the evidence establishes, that the complainant company has been compelled, in order to protect the property of the McMillin Marble Company, to pay out about the sum of three thousand dollars in settlement and satisfaction of the claims in suit at time of its contract with defendant.

The relief sought is a decree against defendant for onehalf this sum, being the proportion he agreed to pay under his agreement of sale.

The defense is that the contract of sale to the complainant company was unlawful and void; that is to say, that the purchase of these shares was outside the objects of its creation as defined in its charter, and is, therefore, such a contract as is not only voidable, but wholly void, and of no legal effect; that it is not a case of excessive use of a power granted, but that no power whatever was conferred to deal in or hold the shares of another corporation; that the suit is one upon a void contract and in furtherance of it, and that [118] it should not be entertained by a court of law or equity.

"The rule in the United States," says Mr. Green, the American editor of Brice's Ultra Vires, "is that a corporation cannot become a stockholder in another corporation unless by power specifically granted by its charter or necessarily implied in it." Green's Brice's Ultra Vires, 91, note b, and American cases cited.

"A corporation has no implied right to purchase shares in another company for the purpose of controlling its management; nor may a corporation hold shares in another company as an investment, unless this be the usual method of carrying on its own proper business. A corporation must carry on its business by its own agents, and not through the agency of another corporation. It is clear also that a corporation has no implied right to speculate in shares, unless this be the kind of business for which the company was formed ": 1 Morawetz on Corporations, sec. 431.

The evidence shows that the declared purpose of complainant in buying in the shares held by the defendant was to enable it to manage and control the business of the Tennessee company in the interest of the Ohio company.

There is no pretense that it had any express power to pur-

chase shares in another company, and it is too clear to need
argument or further citation of authority, that it had no implied authority to purchase and hold shares, either in its own
[119] name or in that of a trustee, for the purpose of controlling
another corporation. That these corporations were engaged
in a similar business does not help the case. The purpose
and intent in granting a charter is, that the corporation shall
carry on its business through its own agents, and not through
the agency of another corporation. The public policy of this
state will not permit the control of one corporation by another. Especially is this true when a foreign corporation
thus undertakes to control and swallow up a domestic company. Such control of one corporation by another in a like
business is unlawful, as tending to monopoly.

The result is, that this purchase of shares for the express
object of controlling and managing another corporation was
ultra vires, and, therefore, unlawful and void. Being void, it
was of no legal effect, and no rights result from it enforceable
by or through the courts of the state, when such aid is invoked in furtherance of the unlawful agreement.

But it has been insisted very earnestly by the able and
learned counsel for complainant, that where the contract has
been fully executed by the plaintiff, the defendant should not
be permitted to invoke such defense to a suit brought to compel performance; that to permit such a defense would work
injustice, and enable defendant to repudiate his liability while
holding on to the price he has received. There are cases
where, the contract being [120] fully executed on both sides,
the court, in the interest of justice, has refused to aid either in
obtaining a rescission: *Whitney Arms Co.* v. *Barlow*, 63 N. Y.
62, 20 Am. Rep. 504, is one of this class.

So there are cases where the defense of *ultra vires* has not
been entertained when the defect was in the mode of executing the contract or in the power of the agent.

So there are many cases holding the party relying upon the
defense of *ultra vires* to an accountability for the benefits received: Green's Brice's Ultra Vires, 717, and note at end of
chapter.

Again, there are cases where the courts have refused to entertain suits to recover property from corporations which is
held in excess of charter capacity. In such cases the courts
have held that the defect in power could not be set up in a
collateral way, and that the state only could complain of such

violation. To this effect were our own cases of *Barrow* v. *Nashville etc. Turnpike Co.*, 9 Humph. 304, and *Heiskell* v. *Chickasaw Lodge*, 87 Tenn. 668.

The question here is not like any of these. The complainant sues upon its contract, and, in affirmance of it, seeks to have the defendant perform an agreement which sprang from, and was collateral to, it. It has received the shares it purchased, and holds on to them. It simply asks that the defendant be further compelled to perform his contract by contributing, in accordance with his agreement, his proportion of the liability paid off by complainant in protection of the property [121] of the McMillin Marble Company. The suit is clearly in furtherance of the original, unlawful, and void contract. That the contract has been executed by the plaintiff does not make it lawful or entitle it to an enforcement of it.

This proposition was very plainly put in *Pittsburgh etc. Ry. Co.* v. *Keokuk etc. Bridge Co.*, 131 U. S. 389, where it was stated, as a result of all the previous decisions of that court upon this subject, "that a contract made by a corporation, which is unlawful and void because beyond the scope of its corporate powers, does not, by being carried into effect, become lawful and valid; but the proper remedy of the party aggrieved is by disaffirming the contract, and suing to recover, as on a *quantum meruit*, the value of what the defendant has actually received."

The case of *Central Transportation Co.* v. *Pullman Palace Car Co.*, 139 U. S. 24, is an exceedingly interesting case, as it involved a consideration of the circumstances under which a defendant may interpose the defense of *ultra vires*, notwithstanding full performance by the plaintiff.

In that case, the Central Transportation Company had leased and transferred all of its property of every kind to the defendant company, which was engaged in a similar and competitive business. The lessee company undertook to pay all of the debts of the lessor company, and to pay to it annually the sum of two hundred and sixty-four thousand dollars for a term of ninety-nine years. Possession was taken, [12] and the installments paid for a number of years. The suit was for a part of the installment for the last year before suit. The defense of *ultra vires* was interposed, and sustained, the court holding that the sale was unauthorized and in excess of the power of the selling company. It was urged for the plaintiff, as in this case, that, even if the contract was void, because

ultra vires and against public policy, yet that, having been
fully executed on the part of the plaintiff, and the benefits of
it received by the defendant for the period covered by the
declaration, the defendant was estopped to set up the invalidity of the contract as a defense to an action to recover the
compensation agreed on for that period.

After reviewing its own decisions upon this branch of the
case, that court said:

" The view which this court has taken of the question presented by this branch of the case, and the only view which
appears to us consistent with legal principles, is as follows:
A contract of a corporation which is *ultra vires* in the proper
sense—that is to say, outside the object of its creation as defined in the law of its organization, and therefore beyond the
powers conferred upon it by the legislature—is not voidable
only, but wholly void, and of no legal effect. The objection
to the contract is not merely that the corporation ought not to
have made it, but that it could not make it. The contract
cannot be ratified by either party, because it could not have
[123] been authorized by either. No performance on either
side can give the unlawful contract any validity, or be the
foundation of any right of action upon it. When a corporation is acting within the general scope of the powers conferred
upon it by the legislature, the corporation, as well as persons
contracting with it, may be estopped to deny that it has complied with the legal formalities which are prerequisites to its
existence or to its action, because such requisities might in
fact have been complied with. But where the contract is beyond the powers conferred upon it by existing law, neither
the corporation nor the other party to the contract can be estopped, by assenting to it or by acting upon it, to show that
it was prohibited by law.

" A contract *ultra vires* being unlawful and void, not because it is in itself immoral, but because the corporation, by
the law of its creation, is incapable of making it, the courts,
while refusing to maintain any action upon the unlawful contract, have always striven to do justice between the parties, so
far as it could be done consistently with adherence to law, by
permitting property or money, parted with on the faith of
the unlawful contract, to be recovered back, or compensation
to be made for it. In such case, however, the action is not
maintained upon the unlawful contract, nor according to its
terms, but on an implied contract of the defendant to return,

or, failing to do that, to make compensation for property of money which [124] it has no right to retain. To maintain such an action is not to affirm, but to disaffirm, the unlawful contract": *Central Transportation Co. v. Pullman Palace Car Co.* 139 U. S. 60.

This seems to us to fully and clearly state the rule. The passage cited by counsel from *Railway Co. v. McCarthy,* 96 U. S. 267, "that the doctrine of *ultra vires,* when invoked for or against a corporation, should not be allowed to prevail where it would defeat the ends of justice, or work a legal wrong," is misleading; and, if literally construed, would result in an enormous practical extension of the powers of corporations.

We do not understand that a result required by adherence to the law would be either unjust or a legal wrong. The learned judge doubtless intended it to be understood that the defense would be a legal wrong only when the law did not require its consideration by the court.

This passage, and one of similar character in *San Antonio v. Mehaffy,* 96 U. S. 312, was uncalled for in the case in which it was used, and in *Central Transportation Co. v. Pullman Palace Car Co.,* 139 U. S. 60, was characterized as "a mere passing remark."

To sustain this suit, as now presented, would be in affirmance and furtherance of an unlawful and void contract. It is in no sense a suit in disaffirmance.

Whether complainant could tender back the shares received, and maintain a suit to recover the money paid for the shares upon an applied agreement to return money which the defendant had [125] no right to retain, is a question not presented upon this record.

The decree dismissing the bill must, upon the ground herein stated, be, and accordingly is, affirmed.

CORPORATIONS—ULTRA VIRES CONTRACTS ARE VOID.—See the extended note to *Brunswick Gas etc. Co. v. United Gas etc. Co.,* 35 Am. St. Rep. 39 Acts of a corporation done in excess of the power conferred by its chart are void, in that they cannot divest the corporation of any right in or any property belonging to, it: *Franco Texan Land Co. v. McCormick,* 85 Te 416; 34 Am. St. Rep. 815, and note. The *ultra vires* acts of corporatio are void: *Chicago Gas etc. Co. v. Peoples Gas etc. Co.,* 121 Ill. 530; 2 Am. S Rep. 124. See further *Long v. Georgia Pac. Ry. Co.,* 91 Ala. 519; 24 A St. Rep. 931, and note, and *Miners' Ditch Co. v. Zellerbach,* 37 Cal. 543; Am. Dec. 300, where the general rules as to the validity of *ultra vires* co tracts are discussed. The power of one corporation to acquire stock another is discussed in *Denny Hotel Co. v. Schram,* 6 Wash. 134; *post,* 130, and monographic note.

HOLDER *v.* RAILROAD.

[92 TENNESSEE, 141.]

DEATH, COMPROMISE OF CAUSE OF ACTION ARISING OUT OF.—A statute creating a cause of action in favor of a widow, and in case there is no widow, of the children or personal representative of a decedent, for the benefit of his widow and children, against one through whose negligence his death resulted, gives the widow the power to compromise her suit against the objection of the children and without let or hinderance from any one, and such compromise as she may make, either before or after the bringing of the suit, binds all parties having any interest in the cause of action.

WIDOW'S RIGHT TO COMPROMISE CLAIM FOR DAMAGES resulting from the death of her husband includes authority to receive the sum agreed upon, and its payment is a full and complete satisfaction of the claim, and is binding on the children and next of kin of the decedent.

Estill and Alexander, for Holder.

Granbery and Marks, East and Fogg, and J. D. B. De Bow, for the Railroad.

[142] CALDWELL, J. This cause comes up on bill and demurrer.

Complainants allege that W. E. Holder, while in the employment of the Nashville, Chattanooga and St. Louis Railroad Company as an operative on one of its trains, was killed by and through the negligence of said company; that he left surviving him a widow and five children; that before the filing of the bill, the widow, for the sum of twelve hundred and fifty dollars, compromised and settled the statutory cause of action accruing to her and the children against said railroad company for the wrongful killing of the husband and father; that the railroad company [143] had paid the whole of said twelve hundred and fifty dollars to the widow, and no part thereof to the children.

Upon the facts thus alleged complainants further allege, as matter of law, that the widow and children of W. E. Holder were entitled to equal shares of the twelve hundred and fifty dollars, one-sixth each; that the widow was not authorized to receive any part of that sum except her one-sixth; that the railroad company is liable to the children for their respective shares of the twelve hundred and fifty dollars, notwithstanding its payment of the whole sum to the widow.

The bill is filed in the name of the children, by next friend, against the railroad company and the widow; and a recovery is sought against the railroad company in the first instance for five-sixths of twelve hundred and fifty dollars.

The railroad company demurs to the bill, and for cause of demurrer says, in substance, that the widow had full legal power to control the right of action, and that having such power, she also had the power to receive the full sum of twelve hundred and fifty dollars for the parties entitled, and that the payment to her was therefore a full satisfaction of its liability.

The demurrer was sustained and the bill dismissed as to the railroad company. Complainants appealed.

At the common law the widow and children of W. E. Holder would have had no right of action against the railroad company for wrongfully taking his life. The right of action which he had for the injuries negligently inflicted upon his person [144] would have been extinguished by his death but for our statute, which keeps it alive, and provides that it "shall pass to his widow, and in case there is no widow, to his children, or to his personal representative for the benefit of his widow or next of kin": Code (M. & V.), sec. 3130; *East Tennessee etc. Ry. Co.* v. *Lilly*, 90 Tenn. 563; *Louisville etc. R. R. Co.* v. *Pitt*, 91 Tenn. 86.

The action may be instituted by the widow or by the children, if there be no widow, or by the personal representative. The widow has the first right of suit, and the words of the statute which confer upon her the primary right to sue have been held to give her the power to compromise her suit over the objection of the children, and without let or hinderance from anyone: Code, secs. 3130–3132; *Greenlee* v. *East Tennessee etc. Ry. Co.*, 5 Lea, 418; *Stephens* v. *Railway Co.*, 10 Lea, 448; *Webb* v. *Railway Co.*, 88 Tenn. 119; *Knoxville etc. R. R. Co.* v. *Acuff*, 92 Tenn. 26.

The last-named case, though holding that the widow had no power to compromise the suit of the personal representative, distinctly recognizes her right to compromise her own suit.

Having full power to compromise her pending suit, as adjudged in the Greenlee and Stephens cases just cited, the widow, for the same reason, has power to compromise the whole right of action before suit is brought, as is alleged to have been done in the case at bar. If she may compromise [145] her suit after it is brought, she may compromise the right of action before suit is brought. This is too manifest to admit of elaboration.

Complainants concede, on the face of their bill and by the

argument of their counsel, that Mrs. Holder had ample power to make the compromise mentioned in the bill, and that it is binding on all parties concerned. They distinctly recognize the validity of that compromise, and seek to enforce their rights under it; but they contend that her power to represent the children in the matter ceased when an agreement had been reached as to the amount to be paid by the railroad company; that she had no power to receive their part of the money, and that the payment to her was therefore inoperative as to them.

We find no such limitation of her power in the statute.

To our minds it is clear, under the facts alleged in the bill and the authorities herein cited, that Mrs. Holder had the legal right to receive for those entitled the whole of the twelve hundred and fifty dollars, and that its payment to her was a complete satisfaction of all demands against the railroad company. The power to compromise the statutory right of action for all persons concerned carried with it, as a necessary consequence, a right on her part to receive for them the whole sum stipulated in the compromise. If the fact that the statute confers upon the widow the first right to sue authorizes her to fix, by agreement, the aggregate amount to be paid by 146 the wrongdoer to her and the children, it also authorizes her to receive that amount for herself and them. Her *bona fide* compromise binds the children, and her *bona fide* receipt of the money paid under the compromise likewise, and for the same reason, binds them. In the one instance, as in the other, the widow's priority of right to sue justifies her representation of all the beneficiaries, herself and her children.

It is said that to allow the widow to receive the whole of the compromise money is to endanger the interests of the children therein. That may be true; yet we think the statute capable of no other reasonable construction.

The right of the widow to receive the money after compromise is no more perilous to the children than her right to make the compromise agreement in the first instance. If in either respect the legislature has not sufficiently guarded the interests of the children, or has conferred too much power on the widow, the defect is curable by legislative amendment, not by judicial construction.

What the relative and respective interests of the widow and children in the twelve hundred and fifty dollars are cannot properly be determined in the present aspect of this case.

The claim of the children in their bill that each of them i
entitled to an equal share with the widow is not put in issu
by the demurrer; and, besides, the question is one in whic]
the railroad company has no interest.

Affirm, with costs.   ____

The case of *Knoxville etc. R. R. Co.* v. *Acuff*, 92 Tenn. 26, referred to i
the principal case, was an action brought by the administrator of a deaf an
dumb man who, while walking on the track of a railroad company, was ru
over and killed by one of its construction trains. The railroad compan
filed a plea of accord and satisfaction averring that on December 3, 189(
about five weeks after the commencement of the action, the defendant ha
paid to the widow of the decedent one hundred dollars, which she had ac
cepted in full satisfaction of all the claim and demand both of herself an
her children existing against the defendant by reason of the killing of he
husband. The court, while admitting that the widow, had she first brough
an action, had the right to compromise it as she pleased, denied that thi
right continued to exist after the action had been brought by the adminis
trator. The provisions of the code of Tennessee construed in this case an
also in the principal case are sections 3130, 3131, and 3132, which in sub
stance declare that the right of action which a person who dies from injurie
received from another, or from the wrongful action or omission of another
would have had against the wrongdoer in case death had not ensued shal
pass to his widow, and in case there is no widow, to his children, or to hi
personal representative for the benefit of his widow or next of kin, free fron
the claims of creditors; that the action may be instituted by the persona
representative of the decedent, but if he decline it, the widow and childre
may, without his consent, use his name in bringing and prosecuting the suit
or that the action may also be instituted by the widow in her own name, o
if there be no widow, by the children.

DEATH—RELEASE OF RIGHT TO SUE FOR INJURIES RESULTING IN.—
releas- of damages resulting from injuries, given by the party injured, wł
might have maintained an action therefor, precludes any recovery upon h
subsequent death by his personal representatives: *Price* v. *Richmond et
R. R. Co.*, 33 S. C. 556; 26 Am. St. Rep. 700, and note. If a survivir
widow of an intestate fails to bring an action for injuries negligently inflicte
upon her husband by another, causing his death, his administrator may bri
such suit for the benefit of the widow and children: *Webb* v. *Railway Cd
88 Tenn. 119.

JACKSON *v.* BANK.

[92 TENNESSEE, 154.]

BANKING.—ACCEPTANCE BY A BANK OF A CHECK and a promise to pay it according to its terms should be inferred from the receipt and the retention of the check and charging its amount to the account of the drawer, who has sufficient funds on deposit to meet it, if he subsequently recognizes the check in a settlement with the bank, though it was presented to the bank by an unauthorized person and paid to him on his unauthorized indorsement.

A BANK PAYING A CHECK ON A FORGED INDORSEMENT of the names of the payees is answerable to them for the amount thereof.

USAGE OR CUSTOM.—A person cannot by proof establish a usage or custom which, in his own interest, contravenes an established rule of commercial law.

PRINCIPAL AND AGENT—NO AUTHORITY WILL BE IMPLIED FROM AN EXPRESS AUTHORITY.

PRINCIPAL AND AGENT.—AUTHORITY TO INDORSE COMMERCIAL PAPER AS AGENT OF THE OWNER will not be implied from some other express authority unless shown to be strictly necessary to the complete execution of the express power.

PRINCIPAL AND AGENT.—POWER TO INDORSE AND COLLECT A NEGOTIABLE INSTRUMENT is not implied from the possession of such instrument by one claiming to be agent of the payee.

BANK PAYING A CHECK TO PERSON OTHER THAN THE PERSON to whose order it is made payable does so at its peril. It must see that the check is paid to him upon his genuine indorsement.

PRINCIPAL AND AGENT.—AUTHORITY TO RECEIVE CHECKS IN LIEU OF CASH, in payment of bills in the hands of an agent for collection, does not authorize the agent to indorse and collect the checks.

PRINCIPAL AND AGENT.—A DRUMMER OR COMMERCIAL TRAVELER employed to sell and take orders for goods, to collect accounts, and to receive moneys and checks payable to the order of his principal, is not by implication authorized to indorse such principal's name to such checks.

T. C. Lind, and Smith and Dickinson, for the plaintiff.

Murray and Fairbanks, for the defendant.

155 J. H. HOLMAN, S. J. The complainants were wholesale grocery merchants in the city of Nashville, and had in their employ, as a traveling salesman or drummer, one Gibson. Gibson's duty, under his employment, was to travel through the country, take orders from retail merchants for goods, and collect the bills as they became due.

For complainants, Gibson sold a bill of goods, amounting to two hundred and twenty-eight dollars and ninety cents, to J. J. Meadows, of Warren county. On October 12, 1891, before Meadows' bill became due, and while Gibson was still in the service of complainants, he proposed to Meadows that, if he would then pay the bill, he would be allowed a discount

of two per cent. To this Meadows agreed, and gave to Gibson his check on [156] the defendant for two hundred and
twenty-four dollars and thirty-nine cents, payable to the order
of Jackson, Mathews, and Harris. In the face of the check
was inserted the statement that it was "in full of account to
date."

Upon the back of the check Gibson indorsed the names of
complainants, "Jackson, Mathews, and Harris, by Gibson,"
and presented it to the defendant bank, where it was paid to
him by the cashier, and charged against the deposit account
of Meadows. Gibson failed to pay over or account to complainants for this money.

Complainants, having learned that Gibson had collected
other money due them, and failed to account for it, ordered
him in, and discharged him. Gibson absconded. Subsequently, complainants sent to J. J. Meadows a statement of
his account, requesting payment. Meadows replied that he
had paid the account to Gibson by giving him a check on the
defendant bank, and had settled with the bank, and took up
the check. Complainants demanded of defendant payment
to them of the check, which was refused.

Complainants filed their bill to hold the bank liable, and
to recover the amount of the check, alleging that Gibson had
no right to indorse complainants' name, and that the payment of the check to him was unauthorized.

The defendant answered, stating, in substance, that Gibson
was authorized to indorse complainants' name to checks and
secure the money thereon; that, if not expressly empowered,
he was by implication [157] authorized so to do; that Gibson,
while in complainants' service, had frequently received checks
payable to complainants, indorsed complainants' name, and
secured the money thereon, and that these acts of Gibson
were known to and had been ratified by the complainants;
that they were estopped from denying his authority; and that
it was inequitable for complainants to undertake to visit the
consequences of their own negligence and misplaced confidence upon respondent.

The chancellor was of opinion that it would be inequitable
to visit the loss of the Meadows check upon the defendant,
and dismissed the bill. Complainants have appealed.

In the brief of counsel for the defendant it is insisted that
there is no such privity between the complainants and the
defendant as will authorize the bringing of this suit; that

where a check is made payable to the order of one person,
and, upon the faith of a forged indorsement, the bank pays to
another, this is not such an acceptance by the bank as will
make it liable to the payee, because the bank did not accept
the check for the payee, nor promise him to pay it, but, on
the contrary, refused to do so.   To sustain this position, the
case of *First Nat. Bank* v. *Whitman*, 94 U. S. 343, is referred
to.   It is true that the court, in that case, held that a payment to a stranger upon an unauthorized indorsement doe
not operate as an acceptance of the check so as to authorize
an action by the real owner to recover its amount as upon an
accepted [158] check.   But the case of *First Nat. Bank* v. *Whitman*, 94 U. S. 343, on this point, has been expressly dissented
from by this court, and we do not now regard this as an open
question in this state.

In the case of *Pickle* v. *Muse*, 88 Tenn. 380, 17 Am. St. Rep.
900, it was decided, in the opinion of a majority of the court,
that acceptance of a bank check, and promise to pay it in accordance with its directions, will be inferred where the drawee
bank receives and retains the check, and charges it to the
account of the drawer, who had sufficient funds on deposit to
meet it, and subsequently lifted the check on settlement with
the bank, although the check may have been presented to the
bank by, and the money paid on it to, an unauthorized person.

All the members of the complainants' firm testify that Gibson had not been empowered to indorse the firm's name on
checks received in payment for goods.

Several drummers were examined as witnesses for defendant, to prove, and a majority of them say, with some qualification, that it is the usage and custom of traveling salesmen
and drummers who are empowered to collect and receipt bills
and accounts, to indorse the name of their principals to checks
received in payment for goods, and it is insisted that by implication Gibson was authorized to indorse complainants'
name to the check, and receive the money.   We do not think
this usage or custom sufficiently proven, nor do we intimate
an opinion that such a power can be inferred from [159] usage
or by implication.   A person cannot, by proof, establish a
usage or custom which, in his own interest, contravenes the
established commercial law: *Vermilye* v. *Adams Express Co.*,
21 Wall. 139.

No authority will be implied from an express authority.

Whatever powers are strictly necessary to the effectual exercise of the express powers will be conceded to the agent by implication. In order, therefore, that the authority to make or draw, accept and indorse commercial paper as the agent of another may be implied from some other express authority, it must be shown to be strictly necessary to the complete execution of the express power. The rule is strictly enforced that the authority to execute and indorse bills and notes as agent will not be implied from an express authority to transact some other business, unless it is absolutely necessary to the exercise of express authority: Tiedeman on Commercial Paper, sec. 77. Possession of a check payable to order, by one claiming to be agent of the payee, is not *prima facie* proof of authority to demand payment in the name of the true owner: Tiedeman on Commercial Paper, sec. 312. A bank is obliged by custom to honor checks payable to order, and pays them at its peril to any other than the person to whose order they are made payable: Tiedeman on Commercial Paper, sec. 431. It must see that the check is paid to the payee therein named, upon his genuine indorsement, or it will remain responsible: *Pickle* v. *Muse*, 88 Tenn. 380; 17 Am. St. Rep. 900.

[160] An authority to receive checks, in lieu of cash, in payment of bills placed in the hands of an agent for collection does not authorize the agent to indorse and collect the checks: *Graham* v. *United States Sav. Inst.*, 46 Mo. 186; 1 Wait's Actions and Defences, 284; 1 Daniel on Negotiable Instruments, sec. 294.

The indorsement of the check was not a necessary incident to the collection of accounts: *Graham* v. *United States Sav. Inst.*, 46 Mo. 186.

It follows that a drummer or commercial traveler, employed to sell and take orders for goods, to collect accounts, and receive money and checks payable to the order of his principal, is not, by implication, authorized to indorse such principal's name to such checks.

No equitable considerations can be invoked to soften seeming hardships in the enforcement of the laws and rules fixing liability on persons handling commercial paper. These laws are the growth of ages and the result of experience, having their origin in necessity. The inflexibility of these rules may occasionally make them seem severe, but in them is found general security.

The decree of the chancellor is reversed, and a decree in favor of complainants against the defendant will be entered here for the amount of the Meadows check, with interest from date of filing the bill, and the costs.

CUSTOM CANNOT CONTRAVENE AN ESTABLISHED RULE OF LAW: *Columbus etc. Iron Co.* v. *Tucker,* 48 Ohio St. 41; 29 Am. St. Rep. 528, and note with cases collected; *Atkinson* v. *Truesdell,* 127 N. Y. 230.

BANKS—PAYMENT OF FORGED CHECKS BY.—A bank paying a forged check does so at its own peril: *Janin* v. *London etc. Bank,* 92 Cal. 14; 27 Am. St. Rep. 82, and note, and see the extended note to *People's Bank* v. *Franklin Bank,* 17 Am. St. Rep. 889; and *Freeman* v. *Savannah Bank etc. Co.,* 88 Ga. 252.

CHECKS—ACCEPTANCE BY BANK, WHEN IMPLIED.—The acceptance of a bank check and assent to the payment thereof may be inferred from proof of the fact that the bank received and retained it when presented, and subsequently charged the check to the account of the drawer: *Pickle* v. *Muse,* 88 Tenn. 380; 17 Am. St. Rep. 900, and note; *Wasson* v. *Lamb,* 120 Ind. 514; 16 Am. St. Rep. 342, and note; *American Exchange Nat. Bank* v. *Gregg,* 138 Ill. 596; 32 Am. St. Rep. 171, and note.

AGENCY—AUTHORITY TO RECEIVE A CHECK PAYABLE TO ORDER IMPLIES NO AUTHORITY TO INDORSE it in the name of the payee, or to collect it without such indorsement: *Pickle* v. *Muse,* 88 Tenn. 380; 17 Am. St. Rep. 900, and note; note to *Bank* v. *Beirne,* 42 Am. Dec. 561. See also the extended note to *Huntley* v. *Mathias,* 47 Am. Rep. 520.

THOMPSON *v.* BAXTER.

[92 TENNESSEE, 305.]

MECHANIC'S LIEN LAW, CONSTRUCTION OF.—While a mechanic's lien law is favored and the remedial laws for its enforcement should be liberally construed, they should not be so construed as to include persons not enumerated in the statute.

MECHANIC'S LIEN.—A SUPERVISING ARCHITECT employed to draw plans and specifications, solicit bids for, and to supervise the construction of, a building is not entitled to a lien thereon under the statute conferring a right to a lien on all persons doing any portion of the work, or furnishing any portion of the material, in the construction of a house or other building.

Barthell and Keeble, for Thompson.

J. H. Acklen, for Baxter.

H. Parks, for the Insurance Company.

[305] A. D. BRIGHT, S. J.   The defendant, Baxter, the then owner of the lots described in the pleadings, employed plaintiff, Thompson, as supervising architect, to draw plans speci-

fications, solicit bids for, [306] and supervise the constructio
of the building and erection of the house on the same know
as Baxter Court and Baxter Court Hotel. The complainan
alleges he is an architect, residing in Nashville. He now, b
his bill, alleges that he is entitled to a mechanic's lien on sai
house and lot for his services, or compensation for service:
rendered as such supervising architect, under sections 273
and 2740 of the M. and V. compilation of the laws of Tennes
see.

Section 2739 provides: " There shall be a lien upon an
lot of ground or tract of land upon which a house has bee
constructed, built, or repaired, or fixtures or machinery fui
nished or erected, or improvements made by special contrac
with the owner or his agent, in favor of the mechanic or un
dertaker, founder or machinist who does the work, or an;
part of the work, or furnishes the materials, or any part o
the materials, or puts thereon any fixtures, machinery, o
material, either of wood or metal."

Section 2740 provides: " The benefits of section 2739 shal
apply to all persons doing any portion of the work, or furnish
ing any portion of the material for the building contemplatec
in said section."

The mechanic's lien is favored by the legislature, anc
should not be hazarded by niceties in its enforcement: *Burr* v
Graves, 4 Lea, 557.

However, the law is strict in its requirements that th
claimant shall make it to clearly appear that he has a lier
but when that appears, the [307] remedial laws for its enforce
ment are to be liberally construed: *Kay* v. *Smith*, 10 Heisl
43; *Luter* v. *Cobb*, 1 Coldw. 528; *Alley* v. *Lanier*, 1 Cold
541; *McLeod* v. *Capell*, 7 Baxt. 199; *Dunn* v. *McKee*, 5 Snee
658.

This lien is purely statutory, and unknown to the comm
law. Only those enumerated and embraced in the statu
are entitled to the lien. A liberal construction of the n
chanic's lien law does not mean that they shall be liberal
construed in embracing or including others than those enu.
erated in the statutes. It must clearly appear that the clai
ant has a lien. No one is entitled to a lien unless the stat1
includes him or them. They are not to be included
strained construction. Unless the statute gives the lien, '
party has none.

Now, does the statute embrace, include, or give this lien

a supervising architect? Is he a mechanic, undertaker, founder, machinist, or contractor? Has he done any work in building the house? Has he furnished the material, or any part thereof, or has he put in any fixtures, machinery, or material, either of wood or metal? We think not. A supervising architect is not a mechanic, nor is he a contractor in the sense of the statute. He simply draws plans, makes estimates, solicits bids, and supervises the erection of the building. The statute clearly does not embrace or includ_ supervising architects. It makes no provisions for him. It does not give him this lien, and hence the courts cannot.

We have been referred to a number of cases [308] from other states, some holding, under their statutes, that a supervising architect has this lien, others holding the contrary. The weight of authority and the reasoning seems to be that a supervising architect has not this lien. But, be this as it may, we hold that under our statutes he has no lien upon the house or lot as supervising architect. The chancellor decreed differently. In doing so we think he was in error, and the decree declaring and decreeing the lien is reversed, and the attachment discharged.

Complainant insists that in the event that the court should hold that he was not entitled to his lien, that he is entitled to have the deed set aside from Baxter and wife to Baxter Court corporation for fraud, etc., and property sold to satisfy his decree, he having sought, by his bill, an attachment on this ground as well as to enforce mechanic's lien, etc. There was no decree by the chancellor on this feature of the attachment, nor is there any appeal by complainant for his failure to do so, nor is there any proof in 'the record of this fraud etc. The whole case on the attachment seems, by the chancellor and all parties, to have proceeded upon the theory alone as to whether complainant had a lien as supervising architect.

The decree of the chancellor, as modified herein, will be affirmed.

The complainant will pay the costs of the appeal.

[309] LURTON, C. J., dissenting.—I am constrained to dissent. While section 2739 enumerates the persons entitled to the lien, yet section 2740 extends the lien to "all persons doing any part of the work." There is no limitation by enumeration. If the complainant did "any part of the work,"

he is within the extension of the act. Neither is there any limitation to those doing actual manual work, as the laying of brick, the joining of wood, the cutting of stone. The "boss," or "foreman," under a contractor or subcontractor, whose business it was to oversee and direct the labor of others, would be secured as a person "employed by such contractor," etc., and entitled to the benefit of the lien just as much as a carpenter, bricklayer, or hodcarrier, though he did not personally do any of these things. The architect employed to draw plans, and supervise the erection of the building," is a person doing "a part of the work," just as clearly as the laborer whom he supervises. The proof shows that Thompson, personally by day and by night, supervised this work, and I think him within the statute.

MECHANIC'S LIEN—RIGHT OF ARCHITECT TO LIEN.—Under a mechanic's lien law giving a lien to any person who shall perform labor, etc., a supervising architect may enforce a lien: *Stryker* v. *Cassidy*, 76 N. Y. 50; 32 Am. Rep. 262, and extended note; *Gardner* v. *Leek*, supreme court of Minnesota, March 29, 1893. In Illinois the statute gives an architect no lien for keeping books and making settlements with the contractors engaged in the erection of buildings, nor to an architect who supervises the improvement of the grounds and accessories: *Adler* v. *World's etc. Exposition Co.*, 126 Ill. 373.

NASHVILLE *v.* SUTHERLAND AND COMPANY.

[92 TENNESSEE, 335.]

MUNICIPAL CORPORATIONS ARE LIABLE ONLY FOR THE ABSENCE OF REASONABLE CAUTION AND SKILL in the execution of work, and their officers cannot lawfully contract to bind them beyond this without express charter authority. Therefore, so much of a contract purporting to be executed by a city as stipulates that it will have a sewer so constructed with a suitable valve as will prevent, in case of high floods, the flowing back of water from the river through such sewer, is *ultra vires*, and void, because its effect is to make the city answerable as insurer against any damage to result by reason of overflow through this valve and pipe.

IF A MUNICIPAL CORPORATION ENTERS IN A CONTRACT WHICH IS ULTRA VIRES such contract is void.

MUNICIPAL CORPORATION CANNOT ASSUME LIABILITY FOR NEGLIGENCE where none is imposed by law.

J. M. Anderson, for the appellant.

Whitman and Gamble, for the respondent.

335 SNODGRASS, J. The defendant in error, by joint conveyance of its members, William Sutherland and **336** Charles

A. Graves, in deed executed June 15, 1888, conveyed to plaintiff in error a right of way through their lumber-yard for a sewer pipe, to drain into the river a pond lying near the property of Sutherland & Co., for the consideration of one hundred and fifty dollars, and the further consideration expressed in a clause of the deed made by Sutherland and Graves, to be hereinafter quoted, which deed was accepted by the city, the cash consideration paid, and the pipe laid and a valve constructed.

The terms of the contract were expressed in the deed referred to; and while this was signed only by the vendors, it, as stated, was accepted by the city, and is therefore as obligatory as if signed by its authorized officers, to the extent that it is at all binding.

The clause of the contract out of which the present controversy arises is as follows:

"It is further agreed, and the city of Nashville binds itself, to have said sewer so constructed with a suitable valve as will prevent, in case of high rise in the river, the flowing of water from the river back through the said pipe or sewer into the lot or premises of said Sutherland and Graves to their injury or damage."

And its effect, if valid, is to make the city an insurer of the property of the conveyors against injury or damage by reason of overflow through this valve and pipe.

The city laid the pipe and constructed the valve in the fall of 1888. In 1890 an unusually high [337] rise in the river caused an overflow through the valve and pipe, and submerged the property of Sutherland & Co., doing them much damage. The present action was instituted by them to recover damages arising from breach of this contract. The amount claimed was $3,000. There was a verdict for $2,845, $845 of which was remitted, and judgment rendered for $2,000 and costs. The city appealed in error.

The court charged the jury "that if the board of public works and affairs accepted for the city this contract, and in pursuance of it entered upon the plaintiff's premises, and occupied the same by the construction of said sewer or drain, then the city will be bound by all the covenants and stipulations of the contract."

He refused to charge, as requested by plaintiff in error, that "the city is only liable for such negligence as is imposed by law, and the officers of the city cannot bind it to a higher degree of care and skill and diligence than the law imposes. Before the city can be bound by guarantee of its officers, they must have the power, under the charter of the city, to bind the city by such guarantee."

In both respects, his honor, the circuit judge, was in error. It was within the power of the officers of the city to agree to put in any given kind of sewer and valve (had they done so') as part consideration for the grant of right of way; but they could not, in the absence of charter [338] power, bind the city by a guarantee that they or it would put in such pipe or valve as would prevent overflow to the injury or damage of defendants, and thus make the city insurers of property against such injury.

The city is only liable for absence of reasonable care and skill in the execution of such work, and its officers cannot lawfully contract to bind it beyond this without express charter power not claimed or shown in this record to exist.

The first proposition is well settled everywhere, and specially in this state: *Humes* v. *Mayor etc.*, 1 Humph. 403; 34 Am. Dec. 657; *Nashville* v. *Brown*, 9 Heisk. 6; 24 Am. Rep. 289; *Horton* v. *Mayor etc.*, 4 Lea, 49; 40 Am. Rep 1. And the second follows as a matter of course. But this, while not heretofore, as far as we are able to find, expressly adjudged in this state, has been elsewhere settled, and the principle is a sound one.

The theory on which it is founded is thus stated by Mr. Dillon:

" In determining the extent of the power of a municipal corporation to make contracts, and in ascertaining the mode in which the power is to be exercised, the importance of a careful study of the charter or incorporating act and of the general legislation of the state on the subject, if there be any, cannot be too strongly urged. Where there are express provisions on the subject, these will, of course, measure, as far as they extend, the authority of the corporation. The power to make contracts, and to sue and to be sued thereon, [339] is usually conferred in general terms in the incorporating act But where the power is conferred in this manner, it is not to be construed as authorizing the making of contracts of all descriptions, but only such as are necessary and usual, fl and proper, to enable the corporation to secure or to carr' into effect the purposes for which it was created; and th extent of the power will depend upon the other provisions c the charter prescribing the matters in respect of which the corporation is authorized to act. To the extent necessary to execute the special powers and functions with which it is endowed by its charter there is, indeed, an implied or incidental authority to contract obligations, and to sue and be sued in the corporate name": Dillon on Municipal Corporations, sec. 443.

As to the effect of *ultra vires* contracts, the same author adds:

"The general principle of law is settled beyond controversy that the agents, officers, or even city council of a municipal corporation cannot bind the corporation by any contract which is beyond the scope of its powers, or entirely foreign to the purposes of the corporation, or which (not being legislatively authorized) is against public policy. This doctrine grows out of the nature of such institutions, and rests upon reasonable and solid grounds. The inhabitants are the corporators; the officers are but officers or public agents of the corporation. The duties and powers of the officers or [340] public agents of the corporation are prescribed by statute or charter, which all persons not only may know, but are bound to know. The opposite doctrine would be fraught with such danger and accompanied with such abuse that it would soon end in the ruin of municipalities or be legislatively overthrown. These considerations vindicate both the reasonableness and necessity of the rule that the corporation is bound only when its agents or officers—by whom it can alone act, if it acts at all—keep within the limits of the chartered authority of the corporation. The history of the workings of municipal bodies has demonstrated the salutary nature of this principle, and that it is the part of true wisdom to keep the corporate wings clipped down to the lawful standard. It results from this doctrine that contracts not authorized by the charter or by other legislative acts—that is, not within the scope of the powers of the corporation under any circumstances—are void; and, in actions thereon, the corporations may successfully interpose the plea of *ultra vires*, setting up as a defense its own want of power, under its charter or constituent statute, to enter into the contract": Dillon on Municipal Corporations, sec. 457.

In section 458 of same work he says:

"Agreeably to the foregoing principles, a corporation cannot maintain an action on a bond or a contract which is in-

valid; as, where a city, without authority, loaned its bonds
to a private company, and took from it a penal bond, conditioned for [341] the faithful application of the city bonds to
payment for works which the city had no power to construct
or assist in constructing. The remedy in such case must be
in some other form than in an action to enforce the contract.
So, a contract by a city to waive its rights to go on with the
laying out of a street or not, as it might choose, is, it seems,
against public policy; and it is void if it amounts to a surrender of its legislative discretion": Dillon on Municipal Corporations, sec. 458.

See also case of *Vanhorn* v. *Des Moines*, 63 Iowa, 447; 50
Am. Rep. 750. This was a suit brought by the owner of a
certain building, that had been destroyed by fire, against the
city of Des Moines, predicated upon the neglect of Des
Moines Water Works Company to supply sufficient water to
extinguish the fire. It appeared in this case that the water
works company was a private corporation, with which the
city of Des Moines had contracted to furnish its fire department a certain quantity of water, and said water company
further indemnified the city against all damages that might
result to it by reason of the water company's negligence in
the construction and operation of its works.

The court, after discussing the general liabilities of a municipal corporation for its failure to extinguish fires, and
determining that there was no such liability, proceeded to
consider the case with reference to the contract between the
city [342] and the water works, and on this branch of the case
said:

"But it is said that the case at bar is peculiar, in this, that
the city took a contract from the water works company to
protect itself against all actions that might be brought against
it for misfeasance or neglect on the part of the company.
This indemnity, it is claimed, gives a right of action where
otherwise it would not exist; but clearly this is not so. Indemnification against liability must always be regarded as
having reference to existing grounds of liability, and not as
serving to create new ones. Besides, the city could not assume
liability for negligence in cases where the law did not already
impose a liability. The contract, then, must be construed as
covering cases only where an action might be maintained
against the city independent of the contract."

In *Becker* v. *Keokuk Water Works*, 79 Iowa, 419, 18 Am. St.

Rep. 377, the Vanhorn case is cited and approved; and in that case it was held that a city could not assume a liability for negligence where none was imposed by law, and that the contract of indemnity must be regarded as having reference to existing grounds of liability, and not as creating new ones.

Another case involving the same principle is *Black* v. *City of Columbia,* 19 S. C. 412, 45 Am. Rep. 785. This was a suit to recover damages plaintiff had sustained in loss of his house [343] by fire. It was claimed by plaintiff, among other things, that the fire was the result of the defendant's negligence in failing to furnish a sufficient supply of water, as it had contracted and agreed to do. The court said:

"If, however, we consider that there was, as alleged, a distinct, express contract of the officers with the plaintiff, personally undertaken to insure him an adequate supply of water in the pipes at all times for the purposes aforesaid, it does not necessarily follow that the action could be maintained upon such contract. That would involve another question—whether the officers of the corporation have the right to make such a contract. Doubtless there are cases in which a contract by a municipal corporation will be implied from facts. These, however, arise, for the most part, out of transactions in which the corporation itself has in some way received and used property or money which, *ex æquo et bono,* does not belong to it. But in all cases, either of express or implied contract on the part of the corporation, the contract cannot be enforced against the corporation if it is in violation of the charter or beyond the scope of the agency created by it. In such case the principle of *respondeat superior* does not apply, but the alleged contract is *ultra vires,* and void. To this class belongs an alleged contract which restricts the exercise of legislative discretion vested in the municipality or its officers in reference to public duties, and, upon such contract, the corporation [344] cannot be held, either in special or general *assumpsit: Thomas* v. *City of Richmond,* 12 Wall. 349; Dillon on Municipal Corporations, secs. 61, 372, and notes. In the case from Wallace, notes were issued by the city of Richmond to circulate as money, in contravention of law, and it was held that they could not be recovered. The court said: "Municipal corporations represent the public, and are themselves to be protected against the unauthorized acts of their officers when it can be done without injury to third parties. Persons dealing with such officers are chargeable with notice of the powers

which the corporation possesses, and are to be held responsible
accordingly. The issuing of bills by such a corporation,
without authority, is not only contrary to positive law, but,
being *ultra vires*, is an abuse of the public franchise which has
been conferred upon it, and the receiver of the bills, being
chargeable with notice, is in *pari delicto* with the officers, and
should have no remedy against the corporation. . . . . The
protection of public corporations from such unauthorized acts
of their officers is a matter of public. policy, in which the
whole community is concerned,' etc. If, as alleged, there
was, in this case, a contract by the officers of the city insuring to the plaintiff an adequate supply of water at all times
and under all circumstances, we are inclined to the opinion
that it was a contract restricting the discretion of the municipality beyond the scope of the charter, and if actually proved
would not support an action against [345] the corporation."

We add to this case, concluding the citation of authorities
on the point in issue, the admirable comment in argument of
counsel for the city, which concisely and accurately expresses the view of the court:

"As, in this case, it was held as the law itself imposed no
liability on the defendant city for its failure to supply plaintiff with water, no contract that its officers might make
could charge it with such liability; so, in the case at bar, it
should be held that, as the law binds the defendant only to a
careful and skillful exercise of the construction of its sewers,
and does not impose on them the obligation and liability of
an insurer, no contract that its officers might make could impose such liability.

"That a municipal corporation cannot and should not be
bound by an *ultra vires* contract is a proposition that is well
settled by authority and sustained by reason and justice.
To hold otherwise would be to vastly enlarge the authority of
public agents, and permit them to bind a municipal corporation by contracts absolutely prohibited by law, and would
thus expose the public to evils and abuse that the limitations and restrictions thrown around corporate officers are intended to prevent. On the other hand, there is no hardship
in such a doctrine, for these officers are public officers, whose
[346] rights and powers are fixed by law, and he who is ignorant of them is ignorant without excuse."

The Board of Public Works and Affairs could bind the
city by contract so far and no further than it would have

been bound by law, that is, to ordinary skill and care in the execution of the work agreed to be done. So, as is well said in the same argument of counsel:

"If they had undertaken to indemnify Sutherland & Co. against loss resulting from defendant's negligence in the execution of the work, this would have been valid, for this much the city is bound by law, independent of any contract provision; but, instead of limiting the city's obligation, as fixed by law, the board, by contract, attempted to make it liable for what, in the absence of such a contract, it is not pretended it could have been held liable.

"The inhabitants of the city of Nashville—those people who live within the corporate limits—are its corporators. Their liability as well as their rights are fixed by law, and no more can the agents of these corporators increase their liabilities than they can deprive them of their rights.

"The legislature of the state has deemed it a wise policy to charge municipal corporations with a certain liability. All who deal with these corporations are bound to know the extent of this liability; and when the corporation's agents exceed it, they may be guilty of a personal wrong, but [347] cannot subject the corporation they represent to damages on that account."

For the errors indicated, the judgment must be reversed, and the case remanded for a new trial. Defendants in error will pay costs of this court.

MUNICIPAL CORPORATION—ULTRA VIRES ACTS ARE VOID: *Bissell* v. *Kankakee*, 64 Ill. 249; 16 Am. Rep. 554; *Spitzer* v. *Blanchard*, 82 Mich. 235; *Zottman* v. *San Francisco*, 20 Cal. 96; 81 Am. Dec. 96, and extended note; *Clark* v. *Des Moines*, 19 Ia. 199; 87 Am. Dec. 423, and note; *Hasbrouck* v. *Milwaukee*, 13 Wis. 37; 80 Am. Dec. 718, and note. The doctrine of *ultra vires* is applied with greater strictness to municipal bodies than to private corporations, and in general a municipal corporation is not estopped from denying the validity of a contract made by its officers when there has been no authority for making such a contract: *Newbery* v. *Fox*, 37 Minn. 141; 5 Am. St. Rep. 830. A contract made by a municipal corporation, although *ultra vires*, is not illegal if not prohibited by its charter: *St. Louis* v. *Davidson*, 102 Mo. 149; 22 Am. St. Rep. 764, and note.

CITIZENS' BANK *v.* KENDRICK, PETTUS & CO.

[92 TENNESSEE, 437.]

NEGOTIABLE INSTRUMENTS, INSOLVENCY OF MAKER AND INDORSER.—If both the maker and indorser of a negotiable instrument become insolvent and assign their property for the benefit of creditors, the holder of such paper may prove the whole amount thereof against both parties at the same time, and receive from each estate the full *pro rata* of that amount, provided only that the two sums so received shall in no case exceed the true amount of the debt.

ASSIGNMENT FOR THE BENEFIT OF CREDITORS.—An INDORSER for an insolvent debtor is, before the payment of the debt, entitled to prove his claim as such indorser against the estate of the insolvent.

NEGOTIABLE INSTRUMENTS—INDORSER'S RIGHT TO EQUITABLE SETOFF.—Indorser for insolvent maker, being indebted to such maker, may bring the holder of the paper indorsed and the maker before a court of equity and have the indorser's debt to the maker applied to the debt of the holder.

EQUITABLE SETOFF.—The right of an equitable setoff already existing by reason of the insolvency of the creditor cannot be affected by his assignment of his assets.

House and Merritt, for Citizens' Bank.

R. H. Burney, for Kendrick, Pettus & Co.

Leech and Savage, for Franklin Bank.

W. M. Daniel, T. J. Bailey, A. E. Garner, and J. L. Stark, for the creditors of Kendrick, Pettus & Co.

[438] CALDWELL, J.   On December 10, 1890, Kendrick, Pettus & Co. made a general assignment for the benefit of creditors.   The indebtedness aggregated about two hundred and fifty thousand dollars, and the assets were worth about one-fourth that amount.

On the same day, a few hours later, Franklin Bank also made a general assignment for the benefit of creditors.   Its liabilities were over nine hundred thousand dollars, and assets about one-fourth as much.

These bills were filed for the settlement of the two trusts.

Without going much into detail, the legal questions presented on appeal will be considered in order.

1. Franklin Bank was bound as indorser on the paper of Kendrick, Pettus & Co. to the amount of about seventy-five thousand dollars; and that paper was secured in both assignments alike, and in common with other debts of the assignors respectively.

Each holder of the separate pieces of paper making up that

seventy-five thousand dollars claimed the right to prove his debt in full against both debtors, and to receive from each fund a full *pro rata* of his whole debt.

[439] Franklin Bank and its assignees denied that right in the full sense claimed, and contended that the holders of such indorsed paper should first credit their debts by *pro rata* of the fund provided by the principal debtor, and then receive *pro rata* on balance only from the fund of the indorser.

The chancellor was right in sustaining the former contention.

Kendrick, Pettus & Co., the maker of the indorsed paper, secured that paper as it did its other liabilities, giving preference to none. Franklin Bank, the indorser, did the same. That paper, as it then existed, and to its full amount, was provided for in both conveyances; in each as if the other had not been made. Two securities were provided for the holders of that paper, while only one was provided for the other creditors of the respective assignors. Each assignment made equal provision for each beneficiary therein named, without reference to any other security that he might have.

Two trust funds were created, and those entitled to participate in the one or the other were named, and placed upon an equal footing. It was not provided, nor contemplated, that any beneficiary of the one fund should receive a greater or less per.centum of his whole debt from that fund than any other beneficiary thereof should receive. Those who were creditors of both assignors become entitled to share in both funds; having two debtors, they received two securities, one of which they [440] are to share equally with the other creditors of the debtor providing it, and the other of which they are to share equally with the other creditors of the debtor providing it.

In such cases, each trust should be administered separately, and such fund distributed as if the other had not been created, at least up to the point of making full payment of debts entitled to participate in both. Less than that would be unjust to those having two debtors and two securities.

In the present case the most that such creditors can hope for is one-half of their debts—one-fourth under each assignment—while others will receive just half as much on the dollar.

It seems to be well settled that if both maker and indorser of negotiable paper become insolvent, and voluntarily assign their property for the benefit of creditors, as in this case, the holder may prove the full amount of his debt against both estates at the same time, and receive from each a full *pro rata* on that amount, provided only that the two sums so received shall in no case exceed the true amount of the debt. Such is the rule in Kentucky, North Carolina, Michigan, Pennsylvania, Wisconsin, and Massachusetts: *Citizens' Bank* v. *Patterson*, 78 Ky. 291; *Brown* v. *Merchants' etc. Bank*, 79 N. C. 244; *Southern Mich. Nat. Bank* v. *Byles*, 67 Mich. 296; *Miller's Estate*, 82 Pa. St. 113; 22 Am. Rep. 754; *In re Meyer*, 78 Wis. 615, 23 Am. St. Rep. 435; *Sohier* v. *Loring*, 6 Cush. 537.

441 We have been able to find no case holding the contrary upon the precise facts stated. The case of *Bank* v. *Alexander*, 85 N. C. 352, 39 Am. Rep. 702, is not in conflict. It recognizes the authority of *Brown* v. *Merchants' etc. Bank*, 79 N. C. 244, and makes a distinction between the two cases upon their different facts.

The English rule is stated by Mr. Byles as follows: "When accommodation bills are in the hands of a third party, for a valuable consideration, he may prove the whole of each bill upon each of the parties to it, and receive dividends as far as the amount due to him": Byles on Bills, 370.

2. At the time the assignments were made Kendrick, Pettus & Co. had thirty-two thousand dollars on deposit in the Franklin Bank. In its answer and cross-bill, the bank insisted that it was entitled to retain that deposit as indemnity against what it might have to pay as indorser for Kendrick, Pettus & Co. on the seventy-five thousand dollars of commercial paper.

That right was denied by the assignee of Kendrick, Pettus & Co., upon the ground, mainly, that the liability of the bank as indorser had not been ripened into a debt by payment o the paper indorsed.

We think the bank clearly entitled to the indemnity though it has not, in fact, paid any part of the indorsed paper so as to become a creditor of the maker in the full sense Payment is not a prerequisite to the relief sought. Liabilit to **442** pay and insolvency of the principal debtor are suff cient. That, without more, justifies an equitable setoff.

The bank must pay as far as its assets will go—that is i evitable. In fact, it has conveyed its property for that pu pose, and can be protected against certain and irretrievab loss in no other way than that proposed in this case, its pri

-cipal being hopelessly insolvent, and having assigned all of its property for the benefit of general creditors.

An indorser for an insolvent maker, being indebted to that maker by reason of a deposit, or otherwise, may bring the holder of the paper indorsed and the maker before a court of equity, and have the indorser's debt to the maker applied on the debt of the holder.

That is practically what the bank has done in this case.

The fact that the firm of Kendrick, Pettus & Co. assigned its property for the benefit of all its creditors, and that the holders of the paper indorsed by the bank constitute but a small part of those creditors, does not defeat or impair the bank's right to indemnity from the fund in question. In equity, that fund was, at most, an asset of Kendrick, Pettus & Co. only to the extent of any balance thereof that might remain after adjustment of the equities existing between Kendrick, Pettus & Co. and the bank. Being insolvent, the depositor had no power to transfer its claim for the deposit, so as to defeat the bank's right of [443] retention for indemnity. Hence, all that passed by the assignment of the depositor, as against the bank, was what may be left of the thirty-two thousand dollars after the bank shall have been fully reimbursed for all payments made by it on the depositor's paper.

It would be unjust and inequitable in a high degree to compel an indorser, so situated to surrender assets of an insolvent principal before settlement of all liability growing out of the indorsement.

It is worthy of repetition, that the right of equitable setoff existing in favor of the bank by reason of the insolvency of Kendrick, Pettus & Co. was not affected by the latter's assignment of all its assets.

This proposition has unquestioned support in sound reason and justice, and is sustained by authorities directly in point. See *In re Receiver of Middle Dist. Bk.*, 1 Paige, 585; 19 Am Dec. 452; 1 Morse on Banks and Banking, 3d ed., sec. 337.

Our own case of *Nashville Trust Co.* v. *Fourth Nat. Bank*, 91 Tenn. 336, maintains the same doctrine, though involving different facts.

The decree on this point will be modified accordingly.

———

NEGOTIABLE INSTRUMENTS—INSOLVENCY OF BOTH INDORSER AND MAKER—
RIGHT OF HOLDER.—If both the indorser and maker of a promissory note are insolvent, the holder may prove the note for the full amount thereof

against the estate of each, but the amounts received from the two estates will not in any event be permitted to exceed 'in the aggregate the amount of the note: *In re Meyer*, 78 Wis. 615; 23 Am. St. Rep. 435; *Miller's Estate*, 82 Pa. St. 113; 22 Am. Rep. 754. In *Bank* v. *Alexander*, 85 N. C. 352, 39 Am. Rep. 702, it was held that a creditor having received a portion of his claim under a general assignment by his debtor cannot afterwards assert a claim for that portion against a surety for the debt.

SETOFF IS NOT AFFECTED by the appointment of a receiver of a bank, of demands held against the bank when it stopped payment: *In re Middle District Bank*, 1 Paige Ch. 585; 19 Am. Dec. 452, and note. The trustee of an insolvent debtor stands in regard to cross-demands in the same position as the debtor himself: *Krause* v. *Beitel*, 3 Rawle, 199; 23 Am. Dec. 113. See also *First Nat. Bank* v. *Barnum Wire etc. Works*, 58 Mich. 124; 55 Am. Rep. 660, and *Lockwood* v. *Beckwith*, 6 Mich. 168; 72 Am. Dec. 69.

BANK OF JAMAICA *v.* JEFFERSON.

[92 TENNESSEE, 537.]

NEGOTIABLE INSTRUMENTS.—PAROL EVIDENCE IS ADMISSIBLE to prove that persons whose names appear on a note as indorsers signed their names thereon before it was delivered, and are therefore liable as makers.

NEGOTIABLE INSTRUMENTS—PERSONS INDORSING A NEGOTIABLE INSTRUMENT BEFORE ITS DELIVERY must be regarded as joint makers, and liable as such without any demand, protest, or notice of nonpayment.

CORPORATIONS—CORPORATE CAPACITY OF PLAINTIFF WHEN MUST BE PROVED.—Evidence that the plaintiff is a corporation is not required in actions of law under the general issue. If the defendant wishes to put plaintiff's corporate capacity in issue, he must do so by a specific denial. In chancery, on the other hand, every allegation not admitted must be proved. Hence an averment of the corporate capacity of the complainant must be supported by evidence unless expressly admitted

Watson and Hirsch, for the plaintiff.

Gantt and Patterson, and McDowell and McGowan, for the defendants.

538 WILKES, J.   The Bank of Jamaica, claiming in its bill to be a corporation under the laws of New York, brought suit in the chancery court of Shelby county against J. T. Jefferson, C. C. Glover, and Toof, McGowan & Co., to recover note for fifteen hundred dollars and interest.

The note is as follows:

" $1,500.00.   MEMPHIS, TENN., Dec. 4, 1890.

" Four months after date I promise to pay to the order F. W. Dunton fifteen hundred dollars, at Corbin Banking Co., New York, N. Y.   Value received.

                                        "J. T. JEFFERSON."

dorsed as follows:

Without recourse.   F. W. DUNTON,
                          "C. C. GLOVER,
                          "TOOF, MCGOWAN & CO.

[539] "Pay W. H. Porter, Esq., Cashier, or order, for collection account of Bank of Jamaica, Jamaica, Long Island.
                          "WM. S. WOOD, Cashier."

Upon the hearing the chancellor rendered judgment against all the defendants (F. W. Dunton not being sued), and defendants Toof, McGowan & Co. have brought the case to this court on writ of error, and assign as error that the note shows that Toof, McGowan & Co. are only accommodation indorsers on it, and that they are not principals, and that there is no proof in the record that any demand was ever made upon the maker, and that he made default in payment, and that the note was thereupon protested for nonpayment, and especially that no notice was ever given to them of such demand and protest for nonpayment.

The law is plain that to hold an indorser liable upon his indorsement made regularly in the ordinary course of business or for accommodation there must be presentment and demand made of the maker, and protest if payment is not made, and that notice of such demand, failure to pay, and protest must be given to the indorser, and all these facts must affirmatively appear, and the burden of proof is on the party suing upon the note to show such facts: *Rosson* v. *Carroll*, 90 Tenn. 90–130. This is a universal rule in cases where indorsements are made in the regular course of business.

In the case at bar, however, it appears from [540] the testimony of Jefferson, the maker, and Dunton, the payee, which is the only testimony in the case, that the note sued on was made by Jefferson to cover a balance due from him to Dunton; that Dunton lived in New York and Jefferson in Memphis.

Jefferson states that before he sent the note to Dunton he procured Glover and Toof, McGowan & Co. to indorse it for him, and that they did indorse it merely as additional security to Dunton, the payee, for the money that Jefferson owed him, and to enable Dunton to discount it and obtain the money thereon. Dunton states that he received the note by mail with the same understanding, and, inasmuch as the note was payable to him, he indorsed it without recourse, so as to transfer the legal title without legal liability against himself; that it was transferred before due to the Bank of Jamaica, and that by inadvertence the indorsement made by him was placed above the names and indorsements of the other parties.

Under these facts, which are competent to be shown by parol, Toof, McGowan & Co., as well as C. C. Glover, must be regarded as joint makers with Jefferson of the note, and not simply as ordinary indorsers in due course of trade, and they are liable without any demand, protest, or notice being made: *Harding* v. *Heirs of Waters*, 6 Lea, 333, 334; *Rivers* v. *Thomas*, 1 Lea, 649; 27 Am. Rep. 784; *Rey* v. *Simpson*, 22 How. 341; 2 Parsons on Bills and Notes, 120, 121.

541 Again, it is assigned as error that complainant sues as a foreign corporation, and it is insisted that no recovery can be had unless that allegation is sustained by proof, and that no proof was offered on this point in the court below.

On the other hand, it is insisted that this allegation of the bill is not denied in the answer; that the character in which plaintiff sues is not put in issue by the answer; and that, under a general denial, or the general issue, proof of the character in which the suit is brought is not necessary to be made.

This latter contention is unquestionably correct in actions at law, in which actions, if the plaintiff alleges that it is a corporation, even though it be a foreign corporation, that fact need not be proven unless it is put in issue by a specific denial, and the general issue would not be sufficient, and pleading to the merits would be an admission of the character in which the plaintiff sues: 2 Beach on Private Corporations, 867–869; 4 Am. & Eng. Ency. of Law, 285, 286, and notes; *Union Cement Co.* v. *Noble*, 15 Fed. Rep. 502; *Harrison* v. *Martinsville etc. R. R. Co.*, 16 Ind. 505; 79 Am. Dec. 447; *Orono* v. *Wedgewood*, 44 Me. 49; 69 Am. Dec. 81; *West Winsted etc. Assn.* v. *Ford*, 27 Conn. 282; 71 Am. Dec. 66; *McMillan Marble Co.* v. *Black*, 89 Tenn. 118, 121.

We do not think the cases of *Jones* v. *State*, 5 Sneed, 346, 348, *Owen* v *State*, 5 Sneed, 493, 495, and *Augusta Mfg. Co.* v. *Vertrees*, 4 Lea, 75, 78, are in conflict with this ruling. The cases of *Jones* 542 v. *State*, 5 Sneed, 346, and *Owen* v. *State*, 5 Sneed, 493, are criminal prosecutions, in which greater strictness of proof is required, and the case of *Augusta Mfg. Co.* v. *Vertrees*, 4 Lea, 75, was an action of ejectment, in which statute (M. & V. Comp., 3963) it is provided that, under the general plea of not guilty the defendant may avail himself of all legal defenses.

The rule is different in chancery cases. At law every fact alleged in the declaration, and not denied in the plea, is taken as true: Code, sec. 2910; M. & V., sec. 3620. But in chancery every allegation of fact not admitted, whether denied or not, must be proved, the failure to admit or deny being equivalent to a denial: *Hill* v. *Walker*, 6 Cold. 429; 98 Am. Dec. 465; *Hardeman* v. *Burge*, 10 Yerg. 202; *Smith* v. *St. Louis Ins. Co.*, 2 Tenn. Ch. 602; Gibson's Suits in Chancery, sec. 457.

The fact that complainant is a foreign corporation is alleged in the bill, and it is a fact material to the right to recover. It is not admitted in the answer, and there is a general denial of all matters not admitted. It should therefore have been proven; and, for the failure to prove this, we are constrained to reverse the decree of the court below and remand the cause for proof of the corporation, and for further proceedings under the statute: Code, sec. 3170.

The cost of the appeal will be paid one-half by complainants and the other half by defendants.

NEGOTIABLE INSTRUMENTS—PAROL EVIDENCE TO QUALIFY INDORSEMENT. A third person who indorses a note concurrently with its execution, and at or before its delivery to the payee, is presumptively liable only as a second indorser, but may be shown by parol evidence to be liable as a joint maker or guarantor: *Deering* v. *Creighton*, 19 Or. 118; 20 Am. St. Rep. 800, and note with the cases collected. See also, the notes to *Kulenkamp* v. *Groff*, 15 Am. St. Rep. 287, 288; *Jenkins* v. *Bass*, 21 Am. St. Rep. 348; and the extended note to *Drennan* v. *Bunn*, 7 Am. St. Rep. 367. In *Farwell* v. *St. Paul Trust Co.*, 45 Minn. 495, 22 Am. St Rep. 742, it was held that the liability of an indorser cannot be varied by parol.

NEGOTIABLE INSTRUMENTS—INDORSERS, WHEN JOINT MAKERS: See notes to *Temple* v. *Baker*, 11 Am. St. Rep. 931; *Adrian* v. *McCaskill*, 14 Am. St. Rep. 793, 794; and extended note to *Jones* v. *Goodwin*, 2 Am. Rep. 475. The indorsement upon the back of a note prior to its delivery, by one not a party thereto, renders him liable as a joint promisor: *Herbage* v. *McEntee*, 40 Mich. 337; 29 Am. Rep. 536, and note; *Rothschild* v. *Grix*, 31 Mich. 150; 18 Am. Rep. 171; *Ives* v. *Bosley*, 35 Md. 262; 6 Am. Rep. 411; *Killian* v. *Ashley*, 24 Ark. 511; 91 Am. Dec. 519, and note with cases collected; *Good* v. *Martin*, 1 Col. 165; 91 Am. Dec. 706, and note; note to *Riggs* v. *Waldo*, 56 Am. Dec. 358; *Melton* v. *Brown*, 25 Fla. 461.

CORPORATIONS, ACTIONS BY—CAPACITY, WHEN MUST BE PROVED.—When a corporation sues, and the general issue is pleaded, it must prove that it is a corporation: *Bank* v. *Smalley*, 2 Cow. 770; 14 Am. Dec. 526; *Welland Canal Co.* v. *Hathaway*, 8 Wend. 480; 24 Am. Dec. 51, and note; *Phœnix Bank* v. *Curtis*, 14 Conn. 437; 36 Am. Dec. 492, and note; *Lewis* v. *Bank*, 12 Ohio, 132; 40 Am. Dec. 469, and note; *Contra:* Land Mortgage etc. Co. v. *Williams*, 35 S. C. 367; *Prince* v. *Commercial Bank*, 1 Ala. 241; 34 Am. Dec

773; *West Winsted Sav. Bank* v. *Ford,* 27 Conn. 282; 71 Am. Dec. 66, and note. A plea of *non-assumpsit* admits the capacity of the plaintiff corporation to sue: *Alderman* v. *Finley,* 10 Ark. 423; 52 Am. Dec. 244. The corporate existence of the plaintiff is admitted by the defendants pleading the general issue: *Inhabitants* v. *Wedgewood,* 44 Me. 49; 69 Am. Dec. 81, and note; *Harrison* v. *Martinsville etc R. R. Co.,* 16 Ind. 505; 79 Am. Dec. 447, and note.

JOHNSON *v.* JOHNSON.

[92 TENNESSEE, 559.]

A DEVISE OF THE RENTS, PROFITS, AND INCOME OF PROPERTY is in effect a devise of the property itself.

CHARITABLE USES ARE FAVORED IN EQUITY and will be supported when a trust would fail for uncertainty were it not for the charity.

A CHARITABLE DEVISE OR BEQUEST WILL BE UPHELD where it is created in favor of a person having sufficient capacity to take as donee, or if it be not direct to such person, where it is definite in its object, lawful in its creation, and to be executed by trustees.

CHARITABLE BEQUEST.—DESIGNATION OF A TRUSTEE OF A CHARITABLE TRUST is sufficient if the will devises property to the wife and daughter in trust with power to nominate their successors and other associates in trust from the testator's descendants or their Protestant husbands or wives, not exceeding five, who may in turn elect their successors from his descendants, and if there should at any time be not as many as two of his descendants able and willing to take charge of the trust, then it shall revert to a board consisting of the elders of the several Presbyterian churches of the city of M., who shall, with the assistance of the Presbyterian pastors, nominate from the bankers and business men of their body an executive committee, who shall have full power and control to manage the trust.

CHARITABLE TRUSTS.—THE DOCTRINES OF CY PRES AND PARENS PATRIÆ, as recognized in the English law, have never obtained in Tennessee. Only those powers which in England were exercised by the chancellor by virtue of his extraordinary, as distinguished from his specially delegated, jurisdiction exist in the chancery courts of that state.

CHARITABLE TRUSTS—VOID FOR WANT OF BENEFICIARY.—A devise and bequest of property to trustees with power to control and manage the trust so that it shall be productive of the most good to the greatest number, in a will in which the testator expressed his desire that the proceeds of the trust should be devoted to a free female college, but in case the way is not clear to that end, that they should be used for some charitable purpose, preference always being given to something of an educational nature, is void, because under the provisions of the trust there can be no one who can demand of the trustees the benefit of the trust on the ground that he is one of a class for whose benefit it was intended.

H. C. Warriner, for the complainants.

Smith and Trezevant, for the defendants.

560 WILKES, J.   This is a bill to construe the several items of the will of John Cummings Johnson, deceased.

The testator died July 25, 1892, leaving a widow, complainant Mary Mildred Johnson, and seven children by a former marriage, and possessed of quite a large estate of both realty and personalty.

The will was written by the testator, and is somewhat inartificially drawn. It consists of twenty-six items, and purports to convey and dispose of all the property of the testator.

The several items submitted to the chancellor were construed by him, and specific directions were entered in the decree, and a written opinion was filed by him in the court below.

561 The cause has been brought to this court upon writ of error, and it is assigned as error that the chancellor erred in his construction of the eighth, seventeenth, and twenty-fourth items of the will.

We have carefully considered these items and the assignments, and are of opinion that there is no error in the construction placed by the chancellor upon the eighth and twenty-fourth items of the will, and his opinion and decree as to these items is adopted by this court, and need not be more specifically set out.

The main controversy is in regard to the proper construction of the seventeenth item, which is as follows:

" 17. I give and bequeath to my wife, Mary Mildred Johnson, and to my daughter, Lillie W. Johnson, jointly, my 'home lot' of three acres, No. 11, fronting on Poplar street, east of Dunlap, to hold in trust as below cited, with power to lease and sell the same under the terms of this will, and to nominate and elect their successors and other associates in this trust from my descendants or from their Protestant husbands or wives, not exceeding five, who may, in turn, elect their associates and successors from my descendants. If at any time in the future there should not be as many as two of my descendants able and willing to take charge of this trust, then it shall revert to a board, consisting of the elders of the several Presbyterian churches of the city of Memphis, who shall, with the assistance of the Presbyterian **562** pastors, nominate from the bankers or business men of their body an executive committee of five, who, with my descendants, shall have full power and control to manage the trust so it will be productive of most good to the greatest number. It has been my desire to see a grand female college located on this lot, and I hope it may yet be accomplished. If the way be clear to that end, the income may be appropriated in that direction; but if not, then it is my desire and wish that the main income from this property, less the amount needed for repairs, taxes and insurance, shall be used for some charitable purpose, preference always to be given to something of an educational nature, although permissible to appropriate the income in any way it may seem to the trustees to be necessary and most desirable, as they may elect. The property is never to be mortgaged, nor is the income to be pledged for more than three months in advance, and no sale of it shall be made until five years after the termination of the present lease, when it may be sold for reinvestment for some scholastic or charitable purpose."

The question presented is whether this is a valid devise to a charitable purpose, and such as can be upheld under our authorities.

The complainants, who are the executors of the testator's will, are also made, by this item, the original trustees of this charity, and in their bill they allege that the item makes a valid devise to [563] them as trustees of the property in fee, the net rents and income to be applied to charitable purposes which are rendered sufficiently definite to be valid.

The adult defendants answer that they have no desire to obstruct the benevolent and charitable intentions of their father if they can be legally carried out, and they join in the request to the court to construe the item, and determine, as against the minor defendant and devisee, if effect can be given to the devise as a valid charity.

We are of opinion that if the devise is valid, then the item passes the fee in the property for the purposes indicated, the net income from which is to be expended and appropriated by the trustees. While there is no specific devise of the property, yet a devise of the rents and profits and income is in effect a devise of the property itself: *Polk* v. *Faris*, 9 Yerg. 241; 30 Am. Dec. 400; *Morgan* v. *Pope*, 7 Cold. 547; *Davis* v. *Williams*, 85 Tenn. 648; *Pilcher* v. *McHenry*, 14 Lea, 88; 1 Jarman on Wills, 152, note; 3 Washburn on Real Estate, 529, 530; *Spofford, Executrix,* v. *Martin Female College*, Oral Opinion, Tenn., Jan. 1889.

In the case last mentioned Thomas Martin of Giles county

had set apart thirty thousand dollars in bonds of the state of Tennessee, the interest to be applied to the founding and operating of a female school at Pulaski, Tennessee. After ·the school had been founded and successfully operated for a number of years Mrs. O. M. Spofford, his only daughter and [564] residuary legatee, filed a bill claiming that only the interest upon the bonds was devoted by the will of her father to the school, and that when the bonds matured and the interest coupons had all been clipped and exhausted then the bonds or *corpus* of the fund would revert to her as residuary legatee under the will. The court below, as well as this court, held that the gift of the interest of the bonds carried the bonds themselves, and the fund could not be diverted from the charity.

But the question in this case recurs: Is the devise as made in the seventeenth item of the will a valid devise for charitable uses?

Charitable uses are favored in courts of equity, and will be supported when the trust would fail for uncertainty were it not for a charity: *Dickson* v. *Montgomery,* 1 Swan, 348; *Heiskell* v. *Chickasaw Lodge,* 87 Tenn. 668.

This court has no disposition to abridge this rule, or recede from it in any way.

A charity will always be upheld where it is created in favor of a person having sufficient capacity to take as donee; or if it be not direct to such person where it is definite in its object, lawful in its creation, and to be executed by trustees: *Franklin* v. *Armfield,* 2 Sneed, 305; *Gass* v. *Ross,* 3 Sneed, 211; *Cobb* v. *Denton,* 6 Baxt. 235; *Frierson* v. *Presbyterian Church,* 7 Heisk. 683; *Dickson* v. *Montgomery,* 1 Swan, 348.

There is a broad distinction between a gift direct to a charity or charitable institution already [565] established and a gift to a trustee to be by him applied to a charity. In the first case the court has only to give the fund to the charitable institution, which is merely a ministerial or prerogative act; but in the latter case the court has jurisdiction of the trustee, as it has over all trustees, to see that he does not commit a breach of his trust, or apply the funds in bad faith to purposes foreign to the charity: 2 Perry on Trusts, sec. 719.

Hence there must be either:

1. A trustee capable of taking, and a definite, legal purpose declared.

2. A trust so definite and well defined that it can be enforced and executed, if necessary, by a court of chancery.

The chancellor was of opinion that provisions of the will providing for trustees of this charity were sufficient, and in this we think he is well sustained by authority. An executor may act as such trustee: *Cobb* v. *Denton*, 6 Baxt. 236; *Gass* v. *Ross*, 3 Sneed, 211; or third persons may be such trustees: *Dickson* v. *Montgomery*, 1 Swan, 348; *Franklin* v. *Armfield*, 2 Sneed, 346; *State* v. *Smith*, 16 Lea, 665; or the court may appoint a trustee if the trusts are definite and valid: *State* v. *Smith*, 16 Lea, 665; *Vidal* v. *Girard*, 2 How. 126, 128; Perry on Trusts, sec. 722; or a corporation, to be created after the death of the testator, may be such trustee: *Inglis* v. [566] *Sailor's Snug Harbour*, 3 Pet. 99; *Ould* v. *Washington Hospital*, 95 U. S. 303; *Russell* v. *Allen*, 107 U. S. 172; *State ex rel. Duncan* v. *Martin College*, Oral Opinion, Tenn., Jan. 1888.

The real difficulty in the devise is the uncertainty of the beneficiary and the extreme discretion and power vested in the trustees.

Unquestionably under the English law and the law relating to charitable trusts prevailing in many states of our Union which have adopted the doctrines of the English law this trust would be good. The doctrines of *parens patriæ* and *cy pres*, as recognized in the English law, have never obtained in Tennessee. Only those powers which in England were exercised by the chancellor by virtue of his extraordinary, as distinguished from his specially delegated, jurisdiction exist in our chancery court: *Green* v. *Allen*, 5 Humph. 170; *Dickson* v. *Montgomery*, 1 Swan, 348.

Nevertheless the courts will sustain a charity when the plan and scheme for its management is left to the discretion of trustees, and will, if necessary, formulate a scheme for the conduct of the charity, or uphold the plans and schemes which the trustees, in their discretion, may adopt and formulate, and prevent any interference therewith: *State* v. *Smith*, 16 Lea, 670; Perry on Trusts, secs. 700, 744; *Dickson* v. *Montgomery*, 1 Swan, 348; *Gass* v. *Ross*, 3 Sneed, 211; *State ex rel. Duncan* v. *Martin Female College*, Oral Opinion, Tenn., Jan. 1888.

[567] In the case last named a bill was filed in the name of the state of Tennessee on the relation of the Rev. T J. Duncan, a presiding elder in the Methodist Episcopal Church,

South, against the trustees of Martin Female College, an educational charity in successful operation at Pulaski, Tennessee, seeking to set aside the charter of the college, remove its trustees from office, and enjoin the operation of the school, because it had been founded by Thomas Martin, a prominent Methodist layman, and for years had been recognized and patronized by the Tennessee conference, and yet the trustees had not conducted it as a sectarian or denominational school, but had placed in charge of it principals of different tenets of faith. The court held that in the absence of specific instructions in the will of Thomas Martin the trustees had the power and discretion to place in charge of it such persons as they might deem best, and their discretion could not be controlled by any other persons or organizations.

In the case at bar we have a specific and definite property designated and set apart by the testator, and conveyed to trustees whose identity is fixed, and whose succession is provided for. It is apparent also that it was the earnest desire of the testator to devote this property to charitable purposes, and to none other, the principal or *corpus* to be preserved, and the income to be consumed for the purposes of the charity, and in such manner [568] as might be productive of the greatest good to the greatest number.

We think it is also evident that the testator had a primary and a secondary object, the former being to found a charity, and the latter being that (as a matter of preference) the charity should be educational. It is evident also that the testator had the utmost confidence in the trustees selected— to wit, his wife and daughter; and he gave to them unlimited power and discretion, not only as to the kind or character of the charity, but also as the plan for its administration.

In all cases of charities founded by wills broad discretion and ample powers must necessarily be conferred upon the trustees, inasmuch as the testator is attempting to provide for contingencies which will arise after his own death, but at the same time this power and discretion must not go to such extent as that the objects to which the fund is to be devoted, and the kind and character of the charity, will depend, not upon the will and directions of the testator, but upon the choice and preference of the trustee.

In *Read v. Williams,* 125 N. Y. 569, 21 Am. St. Rep. 748, it is said: "That cannot well be said to be a disposition by the testator's will with which the testator has had nothing to do except to create an authority in another to dispose of the property according to the will of the donees of the power."

The important question which primarily arises is whether the object of the trust, and who are [569] to be its beneficiaries, depends upon the will of the testator or the choice of the trustee, and is there any one who could demand of the trustee the benefits of the trust because it was made for his benefit, and others of his class, and, if refused, could compel its performance.

In the case of *Tilden* v. *Green*, 130 N. Y. 29, 27 Am. St. Rep. 487, the devise in trust under the thirty-fifth and thirty-ninth items of the will of Samuel J. Tilden was passed upon.

Under these items property was devised to trustees to be held for two lives in being, with requests that they procure an act of incorporation, to be known as the Tilden Trust, with capacity to establish and maintain a free library and reading-room in the city of New York, and to promote such scientific and educational objects as the trustees might more particularly designate, and authorized them to convey such property to such corporation when formed, and declared that in case it was not formed, or if from any cause or reason they should deem it inexpedient to convey to such corporation, then they were directed to apply it to the use of such charitable, educational, or scientific purposes as, in their judgment, would render such property most widely and substantially beneficial to the interests of mankind.

It was said in that case the devise does not designate any beneficiary, but, on the contrary, leaves [570] it to the discretion of the trustees whether or not they will or will not convey to the corporation. Hence there is not, and cannot be, any person, natural or artificial, who is or will become entitled to the execution of the trust in his favor. The conclusion of the court was that the bequest could not be maintained because of the complete discretion vested in the trustees whether they would give it or not to the beneficiary suggested. A charter was actually obtained, and the property was in fact conveyed by the trustees to the corporation thus created before the suit was brought, but the court held that the invalidity of the trust could not be cured by anything done by the trustees toward its execution.

It is also held in that case that a trust without a beneficiary who can claim its enforcement is void, and this objection is not obviated by the existence in the trustees of a power to select a beneficiary, unless the class of persons in whose favor the power may be exercised has been designated with such certainty that the courts can ascertain who were the objects of the power, and when the beneficiary is not designated in the will, such beneficiary cannot be designated by the trustees in pursuance of a discretion vested in them by the will. It is further said no trust is enforceable unless there is some person or class of persons who have a right to a part or all of the designated fund, and can demand its conveyance to them, and, in [571] case of refusal, can sue the trustees in equity, and compel compliance with the demand.

In the case at bar the power and discretion vested in the trustees is more extensive than in the Tilden will case. Here there is a mere preference expressed for an educational charity by the testator, and a hope that a grand female college may at some time be located on the lot; but absolute power is given to the trustees, at their discretion, to divert the property to any other charitable purpose, even over the preference of the testator himself as expressed in his will. Under this power and discretion, the trustees might at will devote the property to any charity, whether educational, religious, or eleemosynary, and they could at will change and alter the direction in which the charity should flow.

Under this broad discretion and power, the trustees might, instead of a female school, establish a public library or a lecture-room, or a church or woman's home, or any other charity, and if either of these should be selected by these trustees as the object of this devise, certainly it could not be said they had exceeded their powers and discretion, and if either should be established, it would not be because of directions in the will of the testator, but from choice and preference on the part of the trustees. We are constrained to hold that such a charitable devise cannot be enforced, and is invalid: *Reeves* v. *Reeves*, 5 Lea, 644; *Rhodes* v. *Rhodes*, 88 Tenn. 637.

[572] The chancellor decreed that the devise must fail, and the property must pass under the nineteenth clause, which he construed to be the residuary clause of the will. As no point or contest is made upon this part of his decree, we are content to affirm his holding on this point. See also *Reeves* v. *Reeves*, 5 Lea, 650.

The decree of the chancellor is in all things confirmed, and the costs will be paid by complainants out of the estate.

DEVISE OF THE PROFITS OF LAND IS A DEVISE OF THE LAND ITSELF for such time as the profits are devised: *Earl* v. *Rowe*, 35 Me. 414; 58 Am. Dec. 714.

CHARITABLE USES ARE HIGHLY FAVORED BY THE COURTS: *Sanderson* v. *White*, 18 Pick. 328; 29 Am. Dec. 591, and note; extended note to *Howe* v. *Wilson*, 60 Am. Rep. 234. A court of equity will frame a scheme to carry out a charitable trust or bequest upon the death of one to whom property has been left to be disposed of by him for such charitable purposes as he shall see fit: *Minot* v. *Baker*, 147 Mass. 348; 9 Am. St. Rep. 713, and note.

CY PRES—DOCTRINE OF is not applied in carrying out gifts to charitable uses by the courts of New York: *Tilden* v. *Green*, 130 N. Y. 29; 27 Am. St. Rep. 487, and extended note; *Holland* v. *Alcock*, 108 N. Y. 312; 2 Am. St. Rep. 420, and note; *Beekman* v. *Bonsor*, 23 N. Y. 298; 80 Am. Dec. 269, and note. Nor does this doctrine prevail in Pennsylvania or North Carolina: note to *Curling* v. *Curling*, 33 Am. Dec. 479.

TRUSTS WITHOUT BENEFICIARIES WHO CAN CLAIM THEIR ENFORCEMENT are void: *Heidenheimer* v. *Bauman*, 84 Tex. 174; 31 Am. St. Rep. 29; *Tilden* v. *Green*, 130 N. Y. 29; 27 Am. St. Rep. 487, and note; *Read* v. *Williams*, 125 N. Y. 560; 21 Am. St. Rep. 748, and extended note; *Gambell* v. *Trippe*, 75 Md. 252; 32 Am. St. Rep. 388, and note. See also the extended notes to the following cases where the subject is discussed at length: *Howe* v. *Wilson*, 60 Am. Rep. 230; *Bridges* v. *Pleasants*, 44 Am. Dec. 98; *Dashiell* v. *Attorney-General*, 9 Am. Dec. 584.

CAZASSA *v.* CAZASSA.

[92 TENNESSEE, 573.]

DEEDS, DELIVERY OF.—A conveyance from a father to his minor child is inoperative for want of delivery when, though signed and acknowledged by him, it always remained in his possession and was never filed for record, and he never mentioned the fact of making it to his wife or any of his friends, and always during the balance of his life treated as his own the property therein described.

ADVANCEMENTS.—THE PROCEEDS OF AN INSURANCE POLICY taken on his life by a parent in the name of his child, or taken in his name and afterwards transferred to the child, are presumed to be advancements for which the child must account in the settlement of his claims as an heir from his parent's estate.

AN ADVANCEMENT IS a gift by an ancestor of property which, but for the gift, would pass to an heir or distributee on the ancestor's death, or it is something purchased with his funds in the name or for the benefit of the heir.

Malone and Malone, for the complainant.

Julius A. Taylor, for the defendant.

⁵⁷⁴ WILKES, J. This bill is filed by the widow and younger son of Frank Cazassa against the elder son of Frank Cazassa and his guardian. The objects of the bill are:

1. To set aside two deeds made by the father in his life-time to the elder son, upon the ground that they were never delivered, and because they are a fraud upon the rights of the widow to dower and homestead in the lands of her decased husband.

2. To declare certain insurance moneys, amounting to about fourteen thousand dollars, arising from four different life policies, together with the premiums paid thereon, to be an advancement to the elder son, for which he must account upon the settlement of his father's estate. All of these life policies were taken out by the father, one of them [575] being originally payable to his estate, and afterwards transferred to the elder son, and the others taken out originally in the name of and for the benefit of the elder son.

The two deeds were executed by the father on the same day—to wit: May 15, 1889—were written by H. Clay King, then an attorney of the Memphis bar, and acknowledged on the sixteenth day of May, before a notary public. One pur-ports to convey certain property to the elder son, situated on De Soto street, in Memphis, and is an ordinary deed, while the other purports to convey to the same son a lot on Beale street, in Memphis, but provides that "the title to the same is to vest in the donee on a formal future delivery of the deed, no delivery being intended at the present time."

Neither deed was ever registered, but both remained in the father's possession until his death, in November, 1892.

The father continued in the possession of the property em-braced in both deeds until his death, collected the rents, paid the taxes, took out fire insurance, and made leases and rental contracts for the property, in the same way and manner as before the deeds were executed, and always in his own name. The fire policies contained the clause usual in such policies that, if the interest of the assured was less than that of owner in fee, or if he was not sole owner, or if the title was incum-bered, then the policies were to be utterly void.

He never mentioned the fact of having made [576] the deeds to his wife or to any of his friends, nor to the donee, so far as the record shows, and always spoke of the property as his own. It appears, however, that he was quite reticent in re-gard to all his business matters.

The elder son was about twelve years of age, and the younger about nine years of age, when the deeds were made. The former is shown to be a bright, intelligent boy of good memory. He was not examined as a witness, though tendered by the mother for that purpose.

By the mother and two other ladies it is proved that, after his father's death, the elder son stated, in answer to questions by his mother, that his father had never given him any papers, and had never shown him any.

While the father was in his last sickness, and some three or four days before he died, he said to his wife that he had some old papers in his possession with which he was not satisfied; that he did not wish them to stand or remain good, and that he intended to write a will; that he wished to provide well for her, and spoke feelingly of how faithfully she had nursed him.

After the father's death, the two deeds were found in his iron safe, in a separate envelope, tied up, among some old bills and receipts. His fire insurance policies, which seem to have been his only other valuable papers, were in a separate package.

The Beale street property is worth about $15,000, [577] the De Soto street property about $25,000. Besides this, the estate has two farms worth about $5,000, with an encumbrance on one of $2,350. The personal property amounts to $5,000, and the debts against the estate amount to $5,000.

On the trial the chancellor held that both deeds were invalid and inoperative, because never delivered, and set them aside. As to the insurance money, he held that a policy for five thousand dollars in the Mutual Benefit Life Insurance Company was an advancement, but that the other insurance was not an advancement.

This five thousand dollar policy was in what is styled ar "old line company," while the others were certificates in cer tain benevolent orders. The former was paid up, and ha(originally been issued in favor of the father's estate, and sub sequently transferred to the eldest son, while the benefit cer tificates were taken out in the name of the elder son, and fo his benefit. The transfer of the paid-up policy and the issu ance of the benefit certificates were about the same date s the two deeds.

Both parties have appealed from the decision of the chai cellor, and have assigned errors.

For complainants, it is insisted that the court should ha' charged all the insurance and all the premiums paid there(

as an advancement against the elder son, for which he should account in the further settlement of his father's estate.

For defendants, it is insisted that the court should have held the deeds valid and operative, [578] and that the eldest son should not have been charged with any of the money derived from life insurance as an advancement.

The case has been ably argued and very forcibly presented by counsel on both sides.

For defendants it is insisted that the acts done by the father were sufficient to show delivery of the deeds, that both were executed, and, at the same time, that they were acknowledged before a notary public; that a manual delivery was not necessary; that with a child of such tender years such delivery was impracticable. It is further urged that, both deeds being executed at the same time, one providing for future delivery as to the Beale street lot, and the other conveying the De Soto lots, being silent as to delivery, was a convincing fact that, as to the latter in any event, it was intended the deed should take immediate effect, and as to that there was an actual present delivery.

On the other hand, it is urged with great force that no delivery of either deed was ever, in fact, made, nor was there any intention at any time to make an actual present delivery; that if any intention to deliver ever existed in the mind of the father, that he abandoned it; that he continued in the use of the property just as he did before the deeds were made; that he collected rents, made contracts, took out insurance, paid taxes on the property in his own name, and treated the property as his own, and that the deeds, when [579] found, were not among his valuable papers, but among his old bills and receipts.

Many authorities bearing upon the question of delivery are cited by both parties, and the case of *Davis* v. *Garrett*, 91 Tenn. 147, is specially urged by defendants as controlling.

In that case it was held that actual manual delivery to an infant of seven years of age was not absolutely necessary, and a formal delivery, under such circumstances, would have been so extremely formal as to be farcical.

That case, however, differs broadly from this, in that the deed in that case was delivered by the father for registration, was actually registered, and was never again in the father's possession.

Looking at all the facts disclosed in the record, and the

situation and surroundings of the parties, we are of opinic that neither of these deeds was ever delivered, nor was the ever an actual present intent to deliver them.

It would not be reasonable to suppose that the fath intended to make a deed to take effect "*in præsenti*" to tl De Soto property, upon which the residence in which he ar his family were residing was situate, and the deed to the Bea street property provides on its face for future delivery, ar against any vesting of title until such delivery could be mad We can see no evidence of delivery at any date subsequent the making of the deeds, or of any intention to make suc delivery; but the [580] facts, so far as they go, negative tl idea of any delivery.

That the father never mentioned the making of the deec to his wife or to any of his friends; that he continued to u the property as before, paying taxes, making rental contracl and receiving the rents, taking out insurance in his own nam that the deeds, when found, were not among his live ar most valuable papers, but among his old bills and receipts- all these facts negative the idea of any delivery, or of ar present intention to deliver.

As to the insurance money, a new and novel question presented: Whether insurance taken out by the father in tl name of the child, or taken out in his own name and subs quently transferred to a child, shall be treated as an a vancement to that child, for which he must account in t settlement of his father's estate; and, if so treated, then i what amount must such child account?

We have been cited by counsel to but one case beari upon the question, and it is admitted that no other case c be found. The case cited is *Rickenbacker* v. *Zimmerman,* S. C. 110, reported also in 30 Am. Rep. 37; and cited in Am. & Eng. Ency. of Law, 217. In that case it was h(that the value of the insurance at the time the policy v taken out and the first premium paid, together with all p miums subsequently paid, must be treated as an advanceme

[581] In our own books we find nothing directly upon question. We have a general statute providing for absol equality in the division of estates, and for the collatior advancements: M. & V. Code, secs. 3280, 3281.

An advancement is defined to be a gift by a parent (child by anticipation, in whole or in part, of what it is (posed the child will be entitled to on the death of the par

Yancy v. *Yancy*, 5 Heisk. 357; 13 Am. Rep. 5; *House* v. *Woodard*, 5 Cold. 200; *Morris* v. *Morris*, 9 Heisk. 817; *Caw-thon* v. *Coppedge*, 1 Swan, 487; and other cases using sub-stantially the same language.

In the South Carolina case referred to, it is said that it would be a difficult matter to frame such a definition of the meaning of the word "advancement" as would cover every possible case, but that certain elements are absolutely essen-tial—that is, the property given must have been a part of the estate of the ancestor which, but for the gift, would pass to the heir or distributee on his death, or it must be something purchased with the funds of the father in the name of and for the benefit of the child.

While we would not adopt this as a critically correct definition in all cases, we think there is no error in it, as applied to the facts of this case.

Certainly a parent can purchase property, real or personal, and take title to his child if he chooses, with a view and for the purpose of making [582] it an advancement to such child, and it would be no objection to its being so treated that the prop-erty thus advanced had not previously belonged to the estate of the father. Property thus acquired may constitute an ad-vancement as well as property previously owned by the father.

In this case the insurance was purchased by the funds of the father. It was an investment of the money paid as premium by him for the benefit of his son; it was the setting apart and investing of that much of his property, which would otherwise have accumulated in other forms and gone to his distributees just as much as if he had invested the same in some stock or bond for the benefit of his child; and if we add the feature that the father should retain the posses-sion of the bond or stock until his death the analogy would be complete.

It is true the proceeds of a life policy are by statute pro-tected from seizure for the father's debts, but this in nowise bears upon the matter now under consideration.

The premiums being thus invested in the policy, the pro-ceeds of the same are an advancement to the child in the absence of anything showing that the parent intended it to be a gift and not an advancement.

As a matter of course it is competent for the father to give the policy to his child as a gift, and not as an advancement, as it would be for him to give any other property that he

might desire, but in the absence of clear, convincing proof [
the [583] contrary, the property will be treated as an advance
ment, and not as a gift: *Morris* v. *Morris*, 9 Heisk. 817; *John
son* v. *Patterson*, 13 Lea, 626; *Aden* v. *Aden*, 16 Lea, 45[
Williams v. *Williams*, 15 Lea, 438; *Mason* v. *Holman*, 10 Le[
315; *Steele* v. *Frierson*, 85 Tenn. 430.

The mere fact that the policy is taken in the name of th
son is no more evidence that it was intended as a gift instea
of an advancement than would be the placing of title to re[
or personal property in the name of the son. All advance
ments are gifts, but there may be a gift that is not an ad
vancement if not so intended when made by the parent.

The next question presented is at what sum the insuranc
should be charged, treating it as an advancement.

In the South Carolina case cited, it was held that the so
should be charged with the value of the policy at the time [
was taken out and the first premium paid, together with a[
premiums subsequently paid added to that value, but withou
interest. This ruling was, however, based upon the statut
of South Carolina relating to advancements, which provide
that the property advanced shall be estimated at its value a
the ancestor's death, but so that neither the improvement c
real estate nor increase of personal property shall enter int
the computation.

The rule in Tennessee is that advancements shall be charge
at their value when made: *Burton* v. [584] *Dickinson*, 3 Yer
112; *Brown* v. *Dortch*, 12 Heisk. 740; *Andrews* v. *Andrews*,
Heisk. 251; *House* v. *Woodard*, 5 Cold. 200.

Under this rule, we think the property should be charge
at its value at the time it comes into the possession and ben
ficial enjoyment of the child to whom it is given.

The idea is correctly set forth in the case of *Hook* v. *Ho[
13 B. Mon. 528. In that case, a father conveyed to certe
of his children lands and slaves, reserving a life estate in hi
self. The Kentucky statute prescribes the same rule that
recognized in Tennessee, that all advancements shall be
timated at their value when made, and the court constr[
this to mean that the advancement should be deemed to
made at the time it is completed, by the actual possession [
enjoyment of it when the life estate fell in. See also *Cl
v. Wilson*, 27 Md. 693; *Wilks* v. *Greer*, 14 Ala. 443.

Substantially the same idea is held in *Moore* v. *Burrow
Tenn. 104. In that case land was given by parol in 1[

and the donee went into immediate possession. This parol gift was ratified by a conveyance in 1859, and the question was whether the advancement should be valued at the time of the parol gift or when the deed was made, and the court held that the value at the time of the parol gift, and the beneficial enjoyment thereunder, was the proper date. See also *Haynes* v. [585] *Jones*, 2 Head, 373; *O'Neal* v. *Breecheen*, 5 Baxt. 605.

We consider this much the better rule, inasmuch as the child gets no possession or beneficial enjoyment until the father's death. In the mean time, if the policy has been allowed to lapse, the child will not be chargeable with any thing on account of it. Again it is said that if anything is charged as an advancement, it should be simply the amount of premium paid, without interest, but the same rule applied to any other property would make amount paid for the property advanced the criterion of value, instead of what it is actually worth or what may be its real outcome.

We are of opinion, therefore, that the eldest son should be charged, as an advancement, with the net amounts received by him upon all the policies after his father's death. We can see no reason why he should not be charged with the amounts received on the certificates in the beneficial orders as well as that upon the old line policy, nor with the amounts received upon the policies not paid up as well as that paid up in the father's lifetime. The final proceeds and outcome of each is earned by, and is the result of, the premiums invested by the father out of his own means, which would otherwise, upon his death, have gone to his distributees.

The decree of the chancellor as to the real estate is affirmed, and, as to the insurance money, is modified as herein indicated, and the cause is [586] remanded for such further proceedings as may be desired.

The costs of the appeal will be paid by the defendant's guardian out of the trust funds in its hands.

DEEDS—SUFFICIENCY OF DELIVERY TO INFANTS.—When a parent executes a deed to an infant child and in his interest, and manifests by his words and conduct an intention that the deed shall operate at once, a delivery will be presumed and proof of actual delivery is unnecessary, because it is the duty of the parent to preserve the deed for the infant until it becomes of age: *Hayes* v. *Boylan*, 141 Ill. 400; 33 Am. St. Rep. 326, and note.

ADVANCEMENTS—DEFINITION: See the note to *Atkinson, Petitioner*, 27 Am. St. Rep. 748, where the cases defining advancements are collected: also the extended note to *Miller's Appeal*, 80 Am. Dec. 559.

HOPSON v. FOWLKES.

[92 Tennessee, 697.]

A TENANCY BY THE ENTIRETIES, ON THE DIVORCE OF THE HUSBAND AN'
WIFE, is destroyed, and the property which was subject thereto vest
in them as tenants in common.

STATUTE OF LIMITATIONS.—IF AFTER THE DIVORCE OF A HUSBAND AN
WIFE lands which they before held as tenants by the entireties are sol
under an execution against him, and the purchasers take and maintai
possession of the whole thereof, claiming title adversely to the wife, he
right to maintain an action for the recovery of such land is barred b
the statute of limitations of Tennessee, if she has not brought such ac
tion within five years after such adverse possession began.

J. T. Woodson, and Draper and Parks, for Hopson.

Richardson and Hoover, for Fowlkes.

697 McAlister, J. This is an ejectment bill. Complain
ants seek to recover a tract of land, consisting **698** of eigh
hundred acres, situated in Dyer county. Complainant Mar;
E. Hopson was formerly the wife of one James Wilson, t
whom she was married in 1854, and during said marriage
to wit, on September 8, 1856, one William M. Shipp, the fathe
of Mary E., conveyed to her and her then husband, Jame
Wilson, jointly, the tract of land in controverey. The sai
James Wilson died in November, 1886, and complainant
claim that the legal title to said land is vested in the sai
Mary E. by right of survivorship, the land having been owne
by her and her then husband, James Wilson, by entiretie
It should be stated, in this connection, the said Mary E. wa
divorced from the said James Wilson on the 30th of Octobe
1860, and on the 18th of March, 1861, she intermarried wit
W. H. Hopson, her present husband.

It further appears that, on January 4, 1860, the land i
controversy was attached by creditors of the said James Wi
son, and, under proper decrees of the chancery court of Dy
county, it was sold to the defendants, Fowlkes and Ledsinge
The defendants, therefore, claim title to said land as pu
chasers at that judicial sale under the decree of the chance
court vesting title in them, and by continuous adverse pc
session.

Respondents say they are, and all the time have been sin
the date of confirmation of sale, the owners in fee of said tr
of land, holding and claiming the same openly against
persons. Respondents **699** plead the statute of limitation
seven years, and they rely on said adverse claim, title, a

possession of more than seven years as a complete defense to said action.

The chancellor pronounced a decree in favor of defendants, and complainants have appealed.

It appears from the record that the defendant, H. L. Fowlkes, and P. C. Ledsinger, the ancestor of defendant Gilbert Ledsinger, purchased this land at the sale in the case of Ingram and Allen Walker against James Wilson, and that on the 24th of January, 1861, a decree was rendered confirming the sale, divesting title, and vesting the same in the purchasers.

It further appears that said purchasers went into immediate possession of the land, inclosed it with fences, erected improvements thereon, and have remained in continuous and adverse possession of the same up to the institution of the present suit, which was commenced on the 12th of November, 1888—about twenty-six years after the defendants purchased and took possession of said land.

Under the operation of the first section of the Act of 1819, c. 28 (M. & V., sec. 3459), an adverse possession of seven years under a deed, grant, or other title purporting to convey the fee, not only bars the remedy of the party out of possession, but vests the purchaser with a good and indefeasible title in fee to the land described in his assurance of title. Under the second clause of the first section of said act (M. & V., sec. 3460), it is [700] provided, viz: "And, on the other hand, any person, and those claiming under him, neglecting for the said term of seven years to avail themselves of the benefit of any title, legal, or equitable, by action at law or in equity effectually prosecuted against the person in possession, as in the foregoing section, are forever barred." The second section of said Act of 1819 (Code, M. & V., sec. 3461), provides, viz.: " No person, or any one claiming under him, shall have any action, either at law or in equity, for any lands, tenements, or hereditaments, but within seven years after the right of action has accrued." Under the proof in this case, the defendants are protected by each and all of the provisions of the statute, unless it appears that the complainant was laboring under some disability that exempted her from its operation.

It is insisted on behalf of complainant, Mary E., that the defendants, by virtue of their purchase, only acquired such interest as her former husband, James Wilson, had in this land, and that the said James Wilson, having died on the 8th

of November, 1886, the said Mary E. then became entitled
the whole estate by right of survivorship.

It has already been mentioned that the said Mary E. w
divorced from her former husband, the said James Wilsc
on the 13th of October, 1860, but her counsel insist that tl
divorce did not change the nature of her estate in this [7]
land, which she still continued to hold by the entirety wi
the said James Wilson, with the contingent right to the whc
estate in the event she survived him. It is insisted that h
right of possession, and the devolution of the title, did not a
crue until the death of the said James Wilson, and that sl
is not affected by the lapse of time and the statute of limit
tions.

It will be remembered that the decree of divorce was pr
nounced on the 13th of October, 1860, which was prior to tl
purchase by the defendants at the chancery sale, which o
curred on the 24th of January, 1861.

What, then, was the effect of the divorce upon the tenu
of complainant's title to this land?

In the case of *Harrer* v. *Wallner*, 80 Ill. 197, the supren
court of Illinois had occasion to consider the question no
before us. Judge Walker, in delivering the opinion of tl
court, said: "Now, this estate by the entireties is peculia
The possession of one is the possession of both. The esta
is joint for life, and descends to or vests in the survivor abs
lutely, and in fee, and by the destruction of the estate of oi
it inures to the other. Neither can have partition, nor ci
either sell the estate so as to affect the rights of the othe
and when their rights to the property are invaded, a suit f
a recovery for the injury or for the property must be joii
because the property and the right to its enjoyment are joi
during coverture." Then, appellee could not sue for [702] a
recover any interest in the land, without joining her husba
in the action, until the coverture ceased. It is unlike tenar
in common, where either may sue and recover for an inju
to the property, and may use the names of his cotenants.

What effect, then, did the granting of the divorce have
this estate, or the rights of the parties therein? The relati
of husband and wife was thereby terminated, and with it
marital duties. Their interest and duties from thencefor
as related to each other, were as though they never exist
The estate by the entireties is essentially a joint estate,
though it differs in one or two particulars therefrom.

The power to hold jointly arose from the fact that they were married when the conveyance was made. Had the marriage not existed, the parties would have taken as tenants in common.

It was that circumstance, and that alone, which gave to them the joint life estate and the right to joint possession. When the very thing which, by operation of law, gave them a joint estate was destroyed, by operation of the same law the joint estate ceased, and they then became vested with an estate *per my* as tenants in common. They, by that act, and operation of law flowing from it, are not jointly entitled to possession, but, the unity of title and the unity of estate no longer existing with the incidental right of joint possession, it inevitably follows that they then became tenants in common. The termination [703] of the marriage relation having wrought a change in the rights of the parties in the estate, the courts should rather hold that the change is broad enough to convert it into an estate in common, than to hold that, whatever change was made, it left the right of survivorship.

But, on principle, we are satisfied the decree of divorce had the effect to make them tenants in common, and that appellee thereby becomes entitled to partition. See also Bishop on Marriage and Divorce, section 716; Freeman on Cotenancy and Partition, section 76. We are not without authority on the question in this state.

In the case of *Ames v. Norman*, 4 Sneed, 683, 70 Am. Dec. 269, it appeared that Ames and wife were seised of an estate in the land by entireties. Said land was sold at execution sale, in satisfaction of judgment against the husband, and the defendant, Norman, as a creditor of Ames, afterwards redeemed the land from the purchaser at said sale. After Norman's rights had become vested, the wife of Ames, the original judgment debtor, procured a divorce, and the question was whether the interest or title of the purchaser at execution sale was subject to be divested, or in any way affected, by a subsequent divorce *a vinculo matrimonii* to the wife. It was held that the subsequent divorce had no effect whatever upon the rights of such purchaser. It was held that the defendant by his purchase became invested with the right of the husband as [704] it existed at the time of the sale—that is, a right to occupy and enjoy the profits of the land, as owner, during the joint lives of the husband and wife, subject to the contingency that if the complainant survives her former hus-

band his estate will then terminate, but if the husband survives, he will become absolute owner of the whole estate."

The case at bar is to be differentiated from the case of
Ames v. *Norman,* 4 Sneed, 683, 70 Am. Dec. 269, in this important particular, that in the present case it appears that
the wife was divorced prior to the date of defendant's purchase and possession. At that date the wife's status was
that of a *feme sole,* and her estate in this land had, by operation of law, been changed from one by the entirety, to a tenancy in common. That Judge McKinney, who delivered the
opinion of the court in *Ames* v. *Norman,* 4 Sneed, 683, 70 Am.
Dec. 269, recognized this distinction, is apparent from the
following language. We quote from his opinion, viz:

" As one of the necessary results of the unity of person in
husband and wife, it has always been held that where an
estate is conveyed or devised to them jointly, they do
not take in joint tenancy. Constituting one legal person,
they cannot be vested with separate or separable interests.
They are said, therefore, to take by entireties; that is, each
of them is seised of the whole estate, and neither of a part.
If the rights of husband and wife in relation to an estate
held by entireties are not altered by the decree declaring
705 the divorce, what becomes of the joint estate? What
are their respective rights in the future in regard to it? They
are no longer one legal person; the law itself has made them
twain. They are no longer capable of holding by entireties;
the relation upon which that tenancy depends has been destroyed. The one legal person has been resolved, by judgment of law, into two distinct individual persons, having in
the future no relation to each other; and with this change of
their relation must necessarily follow a corresponding change
of the tenancy dependent upon the previous relation. As
they cannot longer hold by a joint seisin, they must hold by
moieties. The law, in destroying the unity of person between
them, has, by necessary consequence, destroyed the unity of
seisin in respect to their joint estate, for, independent of the
matrimonial union, this tenancy cannot exist."

We think these principles are conclusive of this case. The
decree of divorce, while it severed the unity of person of
James and Mary E. Wilson, also severed their unity of estate
in this land, making them tenants in common. That decree
also removed the disability of Mary E. as a married woman,
and left her free to institute proceedings for a partition of

this land, or otherwise to assert her rights therein. She neglected to take any steps, and the bar of the statute was complete when the present suit was instituted. It may be remarked in conclusion that the whole groundwork of complainant's bill is based upon the assumption [706] that complainant, Mary E., was not a party to the original attachment suit, and had no notice of those proceedings. This assumption is earnestly controverted by the defendants. We do not, however, decide that question, as it is wholly immaterial, the title of Mrs. Hopson having been extinguished and her remedy barred by operation of the statute.

The decree of the chancellor is affirmed.

In the case of *Chambers* v. *Chambers*, 92 Tenn. 707, it appeared that a residence and the furniture therein had been conveyed to a husband and wife during the existence of their marital life, and that he thereafter died, leaving her surviving. He was the owner of other real estate at the time of his death, and the commissioners who were appointed to assign a homestead to his widow selected and set aside to her the residence property of which she had been a tenant by the entireties with her husband. The widow insisted that she was entitled to this property as survivor, and therefore could not be required to accept an assignment of the homestead out of it, and was entitled to obtain a homestead in the other property of the husband. The chancellor overruled her contention, but the supreme court very properly declared his action to be erroneous, on the ground that "upon the death of the husband the entire and absolute title to the land vested in the surviving widow," and that "all his interest in said lot ceased with his life, and after his death he had no estate in the lands out of which the widow could be required, or was even entitled, to take dower or homestead."

HUSBAND AND WIFE—ENTIRETIES—EFFECT OF DIVORCE.—Land acquired and held by a husband and wife as tenants by entirety, on their divorce vests in them as tenants in common: *Stelz* v. *Shreck*, 128 N. Y. 263; 26 Am. St. Rep. 475, and note. *Contra:* See *Appeal of Lewis*, 85 Mich. 340; 24 Am. St. Rep. 94, and note. See also the extended note to *Den* v. *Hardenbergh*, 18 Am. Dec. 388.

CASES

SUPREME COURT

OF

WASHINGTON.

WOLFERMAN *v.* BELL.

[6 WASHINGTON, 84.]

NEGOTIABLE INSTRUMENTS—ALTERATIONS.—IT IS PRESUMED that a note was in the same condition when signed as when offered in evidence, and such presumption is not changed by the fact that the note shows upon its face that the orignal draft thereof has been changed.

NEGOTIABLE INSTRUMENTS.—AN ALTERATION AS TO THE DATE OF PAYMENT in a note, in the absence of proof of fraud on the part of the payee or holder, does not prevent a recovery thereon in its original form.

Turner, Graves, and McKinstry, for the appellants.

Feighan, Wells, and Herman, and Patrick H. Winston, for the respondent.

84 DUNBAR, C. J. It would be profitless in this case to undertake to review the authorities, for they are numerous and irreconcilable; some courts holding that an alteration of the face of a writing raises no presumption either way, but that the question is one for the jury. Other courts have held that the alteration raises the presumption that it was made before delivery; others that in such cases the **85** presumption attaches that the change was made after delivery, and that it must be explained before it is received in evidence. Still others, that it raises such a presumption only when it is suspicious. While in California it is held that the change in the printed words of an instrument raises no presumption against the instrument, while a change in the written words does raise such presumption.

The rule that the alteration raises a presumption against

the instrument cannot be indulged without conflicting with
the general proposition that fraud is never presumed, and
with another general proposition that the burden of proof is
upon the party who pleads an affirmative defense. If it is
put in issue by the pleadings, it is a fact in the case to be determined by the jury, subject to the same rule of presumption
as any other fact to be proven in the case.

There is an abundance of authority to sustain this view,
and we think it a reasonable one. As far as this particular
case is concerned, there is no testimony whatever tending to
show fraud on the part of Schneider and those claiming under him. The testimony of Bell and his wife cannot be
considered by this court. They were certainly testifying
concerning a transaction had by them with the deceased
man Schneider, and the testimony falls plainly within the
inhibition in section 1646 of the code. It matters not that
the testimony was not objected to. It is objected to here.
This court is trying the case *de novo*, and it must try it on
legal testimony.

There was no testimony on the subject of the alteration.
The notary simply swore that no change was made in the
instrument in his office at the time it was delivered, but he
did not pretend to testify that the instrument had not been
altered before it was delivered. His testimony amounts to
nothing. But the testimony is abundant that the interlinea-
tion is not in the handwriting of Schneider. An inspection
of the original instrument does not lead us to the same conclusion that it does the attorneys for the appellants. [86] It is
evident, we think, that the added words were not written at
the same time that the note was written and signed by Bell,
or with the same ink or pen. But it seems to us tolerably
plain that they were written with the same ink that was used
by Belle Bell when she signed the notes, and by Harry C.
Bell and Belle Bell when they signed the mortgage; and with
the same pen, which was evidently a heavier and duller pen
than was used in writing the body of the notes; and that the
added words and figures very closely resemble the handwriting
of Bell as shown by the letters introduced in evidence. And
outside of any extrinsic evidence on the subject, we should
be inclined to come to the conclusion that the change was
made when Mrs. Bell signed the notes and mortgage; and
the letters from Bell to Schneider tend to strengthen us in
that view. In such an event the judgment of the court is

more favorable to the appellants than it should be, but it
not complained of here, and will not therefore be disturbed

But the appellants could not prevail here in any eve
They admit the execution of the notes and mortgage, and
the consideration expressed. There is not a syllable of pr
of fraud on the part of respondent. According to their o
version of the transaction, the first note had become due lc
prior to the commencement of the suit. By the terms of 1
contract this matured the second note, and as a matter
fact it was matured by lapse of time without reference to
fault in payment of the first note, before the case was tri
so that the respondent obtained judgment for no more th
he was entitled to, and there is no principle of equity wh.
will justify this court in disturbing it.

The judgment is therefore affirmed.

HOYT, J., concurs.

ANDERS, STILES, and SCOTT, JJ., concur in the result up
the last ground stated. ————

In the subsequent case of *Yakima National Bank* v. *Knipe,* 6 Wash.
the action was brought to recover upon a note executed by the defenc
Knipe to the defendant Dorffel and by him indorsed to the plaintiff.
first-named defendant, by his answer, made certain general denials, and
up, as one of several affirmative defenses, that the note had been alt
after delivery without his consent. This defense was put in issue by
reply, and upon the trial plaintiff offered the note in evidence, the defenc
objecting to its introduction upon several grounds, especially calling th
tention of the court to the fact that the note showed upon its face th
had been altered after it was originally written, and that for that reas
could not be placed in evidence until such alteration had been explai
This objection was overruled, and the note admitted in evidence. This
ing presented the principal question in this appeal from a judgment in 1
of plaintiff; and in considering it the supreme court said: "The que
thus presented is an important one, and the authorities are not harmo:
in regard thereto. It is, however, no longer an open one in this c
Substantially the same question was raised in the case of *Wolferman* v.
6 Wash. 84, 36 Am. St. Rep. 126, and we held that there was a presum
that an instrument in writing was in the same condition when signed
it was when offered in evidence, and that such presumption was not ch
by the fact that the instrument showed upon its face that the original
thereof had been changed. The special concurrence of three of the j
in the opinion would seem to indicate that only a minority of the cou
held as above stated. Such, however, was not the case, as a majority
court concurred in what was thus held, and limited their concurrer
account of what was said upon other questions. Such holding is deci:
the question under consideration, and as we are satisfied with what w
held, it follows that, in our opinion, the note, when received in evi
made a *prima facie* case against the defendant so far as this principa'

tion was concerned. Upon the whole record we find no reversible error, and the judgment must be affirmed."

In the case of *Murray* v. *Peterson*, 6 Wash. 418, the action was brought upon a note which originally contained a provision for an attorney's fee of five per cent upon the amount due in case suit should be instituted to collect the note. The plaintiff admitted that the provision relating to an attorney's fee had been changed from five to fifteen per cent. The first complaint declared upon the note in its changed form, but, with the permission of the court, an amended complaint was filed declaring upon the note as originally executed, and demanding judgment for the amount of the note, together with an attorney's fee of five per cent. The answer filed by the defendants alleged an alteration in the note subsequently to its execution and denied that it was their contract, but did not specifically charge plaintiff with making such alteration. The plaintiff's reply to such answer denied specifically that the alteration in the note was made by him, or by his authority, and alleged affirmatively that it was made without his knowledge or consent, and excused a more definite allegation by stating that he had no knowledge or information as to when or by whom such note was altered. A motion by defendants for judgment on the pleadings was overruled by the court, and the case then went to trial, resulting in judgment for the plaintiff according to the prayer of his complaint.

In considering the case on appeal by the defendants the supreme court said: "There is no question in this case of any presumption as to whethe the alteration was made before or after delivery, for it is admitted that it was made after delivery. Nor do we understand that the rule is contended for by the appellants that a material alteration made in a written instru. ment, whether by a party or a stranger, avoids the instrument. At al events the whole trend of modern authority is opposed to this rule, for while there is no doubt that a willful and material alteration of a written instru. ment made by one of the parties to it, and without the authority of the other party, defeats any rights he would otherwise have under it, the rule that an alteration, although material, cannot invalidate a written instrument when made by a stranger to the contract is just as thoroughly established: 1 Am. & Eng. Ency. of Law, 505, and cases cited.

"And this, in our opinion is a just rule, for while it is true that a party who has the custody of a written instrument should be held to a reasonably strict care of it, and care should be taken to prevent him from declaring on an altered instrument, and then simply curing it if the fraud be discovered, yet more abuses, in our judgment, would occur if, by the spoliation of an instrument by a stranger, the party entitled to it should thereby be deprived of his relief. So that we take it the material and practical question in this case is, does the reply of the plaintiff allege the spoliation? We think it does, and the judgment is therefore affirmed."

ALTERATION OF INSTRUMENTS—PRESUMPTION.—Any alteration found in a written instrument should be presumed to have been made before or co. temporaneously with its execution: *Franklin* v. *Baker*, 48 Ohio St. 296; 29 Am. St. Rep. 547, and note; *Collins* v. *Ball*, 82 Tex. 259; 27 Am. St. Rep. 877; *Stillwell* v. *Patton*, 108 Mo. 352. The burden of proof is on the party alleging that the alteration was made subsequently to the execution: *Hagan* v. *Merchants'* etc. *Ins. Co.*, 81 Iowa, 321; 25 Am. St. Rep. 493, and note. See the extended notes to *Neil* v. *Case*, 37 Am. Rep. 260, and *Woodworth* v. *Bank*, 10 Am. Dec. 273, and also the note to *Beaman* v. *Russell*, 49 Am. Dec. 782.

NEGOTIABLE INSTRUMENT—ALTERATION OF DATE—EFFECT OF.—The alte
ation of the date of a note after its execution and delivery, if done to mal
it conform to the intent of the parties, will not invalidate the note, eve
though the signer had no knowledge of the subsequent alteration: *Duker*
Franz, 7 Bush, 273; 3 Am. Rep. 314. Where the date of the note is imm
terial, its insertion after delivery by the holder does not avoid it: *Inglish*
Breneman, 5 Ark. 377; 41 Am. Dec. 96. If the date of a promissory no
is altered after it passes from the maker, and without his privity and coi
sent, the note is void as to him: *Mitchell* v. *Ringgold,* 3 Har. & J. 159;
Am. Dec. 433; *Bank* v. *McChord,* 4 Dana, 191; 29 Am. Dec. 398, and not
See the extended notes to *Draper* v. *Wood,* 17 Am. Rep. 101; *Woodworth*
Bank, 10 Am. Dec. 268; and *Ames* v. *Colburn,* 71 Am. Dec. 724.

DENNY HOTEL COMPANY *v.* SCHRAM.

[6 WASHINGTON, 184.]

CORPORATIONS—CAPITAL STOCK—LIABILITY OF SUBSCRIBER.—A subscribe
to the stock of a corporation is not liable for the amount of his subscrip
tion, if the corporation fails to obtain subscriptions to the full amoui
of its entire capital stock.

CORPORATIONS—CAPITAL STOCK—LIABILITY OF SUBSCRIBERS.—If the capit;
of a corporation is fixed by its charter, and it has no authority to begi
business until the whole amount of such capital has been subscribed, it
stockholders cannot be required to pay subscriptions until the full cap
tal stock is subscribed.

CORPORATIONS—SUBSCRIPTION TO STOCK IN ANOTHER CORPORATION.—Oi
corporation cannot subscribe to the capital stock of another corporatio

Hawley and Prouty, and Burke, Shepard, and Woods, for th
appellant.

Hughes, Hastings, and Stedman, for the respondent.

[134] DUNBAR, C. J. There are two controlling questions
this case:

1. Is a subscriber to the stock of a corporation in this sta
liable for the amount of his subscription upon the failure
the corporation to obtain subscriptions to the extent of t
full capital stock; or, expressed in other words, is the obtai
ing of the subscription to the extent of the full capital sto
a condition precedent to the liability of the subscriber?

2. Can a corporation under the laws of this state beco:
an incorporator by subscribing for shares in another cor;
ration?

On the first proposition the contention by respondent tl
the subscriber is not liable, we think, is sustained by
overwhelming weight of authority, as well as by ri

reasoning and the plain principles of justice and fair dealing. While it may be a well-recognized principle, as asserted by appellant, that defenses to subscriptions are not
[135] favored by the courts, the principle can only be recognized in its application to inequitable defenses. Contracts of
subscription and capital stock of corporations, like other contracts, are entered into by individuals with reference to the
responsibilities imposed; in this case, no doubt, with reference to the relative responsibilities of the subscribers and the
character and cost of the hotel to be constructed. The inequitable results of holding the subscribers bound in a case
where the whole amount of the stock is not subscribed is set
forth with so much clearness and particularity in *Salem Mill
Dam Corp. v. Ropes*, 6 Pick. 23, a leading case on the subject,
and the arguments and illustrations of the court in that case
are so often repeated and so nearly universally indorsed, that
we will content ourselves with a reference to and an indorsement of the reasoning in that case. Even in the absence of
statutory requirements, such seems to be the prevailing
holding.

"It is an implied part of the contract of subscription that
the contract is to be binding and enforceable against the
subscriber only after the full capital stock of the corporation
has been subscribed. This condition precedent to the liability
of the subscriber need not be expressed in the corporate charter
nor the subscription itself. It arises by implication from the
just and reasonable understanding of a subscriber that he is
to be aided by other subscriptions. This rule is supported
also by public policy, in that corporate creditors have a right
to rely upon a belief that the full capital stock of the corporation has been subscribed": Cook on Stock and Stockholders, 2d ed., sec. 176.

"It is a general principle that the members of a corporation
cannot be required to pay assessments upon their shares until
the company is authorized by law to begin the prosecution of
its enterprise": 1 Morawetz on Private Corporations, sec. 137.

The capital of a corporation being fixed by its charter, the
corporation has no authority to begin business until the whole
amount of such capital has been subscribed. [136] Hence it
follows that the members cannot be required to pay assessments until the full capital stock is subscribed.

"When the capital stock and number of shares are fixed
by the act of incorporation or by vote or by-law, no assess-

ment can be lawfully made on the share of the subscril
until the whole number of shares has been taken": 2 Wat
man on Law of Corporations, sec. 183.

"As a general rule, where, on the organization of a cor]
ration, the number of shares of the capital stock and the su
to be paid for each share are agreed upon and inserted in t
agreement of subscription, the subscribers are not bound
pay their subscriptions until the requisite number of sha
is filled up by subscriptions": Thompson on Liability
Stockholders, sec. 120.

Green's Brice's Ultra Vires, 2d ed., p. 153, after stating t
rule that corporations having the power to raise a defin
capital may begin their business before that capital or a
portion thereof is obtained, says, in note a:

"The American rule seems to be the reverse of that stat
in the text; where the number of shares and the amount
capital is fixed, the whole stock must be subscribed before t
corporation can begin business, unless the constating instr
ments expressly remove this restriction":

The cases cited by these authors fully sustain the text, a
we think the rule, in America at least, is firmly establish
unless a contrary contention appears expressly or by imp
cation, either in the charter or the contract of subscription

But outside of the decisions, on general principles of law a
equity, the statute of our own state, it seems to us, puts t
question beyond a peradventure. Section 1497 of the Gene
Statutes provides, that "no such corporation shall comme
business . . . . until the whole amount of its capital stock
been subscribed." The only object of collecting assessme
from the subscribers is to carry on the business of the cor
ration, and the law prohibiting it [137] from commencing b
ness until the whole amount of its capital stock has b
subscribed, by the strongest implication at least, prohibi
from collecting assessments before that condition is comp
with. We see nothing in the articles of incorporation to t
this case out of the general rule, or that will estop the
scribers from making the defense pleaded herein.

As to the second proposition, a corporation can onl
formed in the manner provided by law and has only a
powers as the law specifically confers upon it. We do
think that a corporation was within the contemplation of
legislature when they used the expression "two or more
sons," in section 1498 of the General Statutes. It is true

section 1709 of the Code of Procedure provides, that the term
"person" may be construed to include the United States, this
state, or any state or territory, or any public or private corporation, as well as an individual.   But it does not follow, by
any means, that the term "person" is always to be construed
as a private corporation any more than it is always to be construed as the United States.

Morawetz on Private Corporations, section 433, says: "A
corporation cannot, in the absence of express statutory authority, become an incorporator by subscribing for shares in a
new corporation; nor can it do this indirectly through persons
acting as its agents or tools": citing *Central R. R. Co.* v. *Pennsylvania R. R. Co.*, 31 N. J. Eq. 475.   The author, continuing,
says: "The right of forming a corporation is conferred by the
incorporation laws only upon persons acting individually, and
not upon associations."

This, it seems to us, for manifest and manifold reasons, is
in accordance with public policy; and we therefore decide
that under the existing laws of this state one corporation cannot subscribe to the capital stock of another corporation.
And, in any event, in this case the amount of the capital
stock of the building company was so exceedingly [138] small
compared with the amount of the liability which it sought to
assume (its subscribed stock being sixty-four thousand dollars and its capital stock only fifty-four thousand dollars),
that there was no apparent ability to pay the amount subscribed; and while it may be true that a party's contract will
not be held void if it is not apparent that he is worth the entire
amount of money necessary to carry it out at the time it is
made, yet the disparity here is too great, and there is not only
not "an apparent ability to pay," but there is an apparent
inability to pay.

We find no error in the proceedings of the court below, and
the judgment is therefore affirmed.

STILES, ANDERS, and SCOTT, JJ., concur.

HOYT, J., disqualified.   ____

CORPORATIONS—SUBSCRIPTION TO STOCK OF CORPORATION TO BE FORMED.
A contract between several persons to form a corporation and subscribe
for stock is incomplete until the contemplated organization is complete:
Marysville Electric Light etc. Co. v. *Johnson*, 93 Cal. 538; 27 Am. St. Rep. 215,
and note; and at any time prior to such organization such subscription may
be withdrawn by the subscriber: *Hudson Real Estate Co.* v. *Tower*, 156 Mass.
82; 32 Am. St. Rep. 434, and note.

Right of One Corporation to Acquire Stock in Another.

Incidental Powers of Corporations.—The execution of an authority, wheth conferred by statutory grant or by personal delegation, may take place an infinite variety of circumstances, and the authority itself may be app ently enlarged or restricted by those circumstances, so that it is rar possible to affirm that under no circumstances is a specific act, otherw lawful, not embraced within the authority conferred as incident, in so contingency, to its proper execution. Every corporation in the lawful ercise of its franchises and powers is pursuing an authority conferred up it either by special statute or by general law, and while pursuing this thority and the objects it may lawfully seek, it necessarily does many a not specially enumerated in its charter, but which are, nevertheless, la fully done because in the lawful pursuit of those objects. To illustrate corporation formed for the purpose of erecting a church and obtaining subscription or other lawful means the funds necessary for that purpo while it may not engage in railroading or in building and operating a th ter, nor subscribe for stock in a corporation formed for either of these p poses, might, nevertheless, as an incident to its power to raise moneys, acc a donation of stock in either corporation, or even take such stock in p ment of a subscription not otherwise collectible. In every instance in wh the purchase or ownership by one corporation of stock in another has be justified or upheld, it will be found, we think, that the decision of the co has been placed upon the ground that the facts of the case were such th the action of the corporation could not be said to be outside of what might properly do as an incident of the pursuit of a power expressly gran to it. Furthermore, as the holding of stock by one corporation in anoth naturally tends to create, or, at least, to aid and encourage, monopolies is not sustainable under any circumstances when it appears that the acq sition of such stock was for the purpose of obtaining the control of anot corporation and thereby enabling a single corporation to possess and e cise the franchises and control the business operations of two or more porations.

Subscriptions to Stock of Other Corporations.—Doubtless there are circ stances in which the business of one corporation may be enlarged or m more profitable, or may be more conveniently conducted, by the organ tion of one or more ancillary corporations. On the other hand, it ma said that no field of fraud has been so fertile as have been the devices thr which, by means of these ancillary or absorbing corporations, the busine the chief corporation has been conducted by, and its profits diverted to conspiring managers. It is not usual for the chief corporation to underta subscribe for stock in the ancillary or absorbing corporation. Its inte therein and its connection therewith are generally concealed. Still t have been instances in which one corporation has undertaken to form other or, at least, to promote its formation by subscribing to its stoc has, after its organization, undertaken to subscribe for such stock, but is not, so far as we are aware, any judicial indorsement of this proce but, rather, judicial condemnation and annulment. A railway corpor by way of counterclaim to an action against it for goods sold and deli to a corporation engaged in the manufacture of iron, alleged that it w the interest of the latter corporation to aid in the construction of the road of the defendant, and that in order to effect a sale of goods man tured by it, the plaintiff corporation had agreed to manufacture iro forgings of the value of two thousand dollars, and to take as pay therefor forty shares of the capital stock of the defendant and that the members and stockholders of the plaintiff assented to such agreement when it was made, and that the goods sued for by plaintiff were manufactured by it under such agreement, and that it carried out all the provisions of the agreement on its part, excepting the delivery of the stock, and it would have made such delivery but for the fact that the plaintiff repudiated the agreement and refused to manufacture any more iron and forgings thereunder. The defendant prayed judgment for the balance due it on the subscription. A demurrer to this counterclaim was sustained by the trial court, and its action was approved by the supreme court on appeal. That court said, "We think it well settled as the result of the decisions in this state, as well as elsewhere, that an incorporated company cannot, unless authorized by statute, make a valid subscription to the capital stock of another; that such subscription is *ultra vires* and void": *Valley R. R. Co.* v. *Lake Erie Iron Co.*, 46 Ohio St. 44. *Central R. R. Co.* v. *Pennsylvania R. R. Co*, 31 N. J. Eq. 475, was an action by one railroad corporation against another to enjoin the latter from constructing a railway. It was alleged that the proposed construction was to be effected by a corporation which had been formed at the instance of the defendant corporation, and that its stock was to be paid for by the latter, though subscribed for in the names of various persons who were friendly to it and who held such stock in trust for its use. In granting the relief asked, the court declared that "A corporation cannot in its own name subscribe for stock or be a corporator under the general railroad law, nor can it do so by a simulated compliance with the provisions of the law through its agents as pretended corporators and subscribers of stock." A savings bank subscribed for a large amount of the capital stock of a manufacturing corporation, and not having on hand the moneys necessary to pay its subscription, procured another corporation to make such payment. Afterwards an action was brought by the latter corporation upon notes given to it for the amount so paid by it at the request of the savings bank. The judgment of the court denying the right to recovery was chiefly founded upon its holding that the banking corporation had no power to purchase property on credit, but it also said, "It would seem on principle, as well as authority, that it is not within the authority of the trustees of a savings bank to invest its funds in the stock of a manufacturing corporation, unless expressly authorized to do so by its charter or the public laws of the state." "If a corporation can purchase any portion of the capital stock of another corporation, it can purchase the whole and invest all its funds in that way and thus be enabled to engage successfully in a business entirely foreign to the purposes for which it was created. A banking corporation could become a manufacturing corporation and a manufacturing corporation could become a banking cortion. This the law will not allow": *Franklin Company* v. *Lewiston Inst.*, 68 Me. 43; 28 Am. Rep. 9. A corporation organized to do business as insurance agents, commission merchants, and brokers applied to a loan association for a loan, and, as a condition of obtaining such loan, subscribed for fifty shares of the stock of the loan corporation, and executed a note for the amount of the loan, including the price of the stock, and secured such loan by a mortgage on real property. In a suit brought to foreclose this mortgage, the power of the officers of the defendant corporation to make this subscription and to impose liability therefor was questioned. This power was denied by the supreme court of errors. "A subscription," said the court, "to the stock of a building association has no legitimate connec-

tion with the business of an insurance agent, commission merchant, or
broker and was not, therefore, authorized by the defendant's articles of
association. It is said that the defendants had power to borrow money,
mortgage their real estate for its security, and, if necessary to obtain a loan,
as in this case, become a stockholder in a building association. We are not
disposed to question the right of the defendants to borrow money and mortgage their real estate for its security. This may be one of the powers incidental to, and necessary in, the prosecution of their business and the
successful management of the same. We are inclined to think the power
is implied in their articles of association. But when the directors of the
company subscribed for stock in a building association, whatever may have
been their motive, whether to obtain a loan of money, or for purposes
of speculation, they transcended the power conferred upon them and de-
parted from the legitimate business of the company, as much so, as if they
had subscribed for stock in a manufacturing company. Such subscription,
in our opinion, is not binding upon the defendants, and any payments made
upon it to the plaintiffs would be money received without consideration":
Mechanics' etc. Mutual Sav. Bank v. Meriden A. Co., 24 Conn. 159.

Purchase Otherwise Than by Subscription.—When we consider the question
of the right of one corporation to acquire stock in another otherwise than
by subscribing to its stock and thereby promoting its formation, we encounter
greater difficulties, because the acquisition of the stock may be so connected
with the authorized business of the corporation, that much doubt may reasonably exist as to whether or not the transaction is defensible, on the
ground that it was incidental to the exercise of some power clearly possessed
by the corporation. Unless the corporation is by its charter or by some
general law, expressly authorized to acquire stock in other corporations, any
transaction, the chief object of which is the acquisition of such stock, is
ultra vires. The abhorrence by the law of all monopolies necessarily insures
its condemnation of every transaction by which one corporation seeks to
obtain the control and management of another, and therefore every attempt
to obtain stock in another corporation for such a purpose is unlawful: *Sumner v. Marcy*, 3 Wood & M. 105. Any stockholder may dissent from any
proposition looking to the use of the funds or credit of the corporation in
which he holds stock, for the acquisition of stock in another corporation,
and it is not an answer to his demand that his corporation keep within the
limits of its powers, that the proposed deviation is to his interest, as well as
to the interest of his corporation. Thus in a suit to enjoin one railroad corporation from purchasing stock in another, and the court said: " We do not
think the profitableness of this contract to the stockholders of the Central
and Southwestern Railroad has anything to do with the matter. These
stockholders have a right, at their pleasure, to stand on their contract.
If the charters do not give to these the right to go into this new enterprise, any one stockholder has a right to object. He is not to be forced
into an enterprise not included in the charter. That it will be to his interest is no excuse; that is for him to judge. By becoming a stockholder he
has contracted that a majority of the stockholders shall manage the affairs
of the company within its proper sphere as a corporation, but no further;
and any attempt to use the funds or pledge the credit of the company not
within the legitimate scope of the charter is a violation of the contract which
the stockholders have made with each other, and of the rights—the contract
rights—of any stockholder who chooses to say, ' I am not willing.' It may
be that it will be to his advantage, but he may not think so, and he has

legal right to insist upon it that the company shall keep within the powers granted to it by the charter": *Central R. R. Co.* v. *Collins*, 40 Ga. 582, 617.

In this case it was insisted that as one of the powers of the railway corporation was to maintain its road, and as for the maintenance of the road it was necessary for the corporation to acquire stock in another corporation, therefore such acquisition was authorized as an incident of the power of maintaining the road. But to this the court answered: "But what does a grant to maintain and sustain a railroad include? Can it in any fair sense be construed to authorize engaging in any enterprise which will extend the business and lessen the rivalries of the company? If this be so, the whole doctrine so frequently and so emphatically stated in the books and decisions is a sham. The maintaining and sustaining of the road has reference to keeping it in repairs, supplying it with machinery, and like acts, and not to projects for extending its business by schemes and enterprises not contemplated or expressed in clear, unambiguous terms by the charter itself." Referring to, and reaffirming, the doctrines of this case, the court, a few years later, declared a similar transaction invalid, saying: "If one railroad company may, at its option, buy the stock of another, it practically undertakes a new enterprise not contemplated by its charter. This it cannot do by any implication. The power so to do must be clear, and that, too, under a rule of construction that a charter is to be strictly construed as against the power. The power granted by the Act of 1860, to hold any kind of property, can only mean any kind of property necessary to carry out the purpose of the franchise, to wit: The building and working of a railroad from Macon to Brunswick. The purchase of this stock would be, and could be, only for the purpose of exercising a new franchise, to wit: the running of a road from Macon to Atlanta. We do not care to go through the arguments we have used in the case referred to. We simply say we can see no reason to change the doctrine there stated": *Hazlehurst* v. *Savannah etc R. R. Co.*, 43 Ga. 13, 58. Many other cases might be cited to the same effect, maintaining that the power of one corporation to purchase the stock of another must be authorized by its charter or by general law, and that while this power may sometimes be incidental to some undisputed authority, its exercise may never be sustained as an incidental power when the object is to obtain the control and management of another corporation: *People* v. *Chicago Gas Trust Co.*, 130 Ill. 268; 17 Am. St. Rep. 319; *Memphis etc. R. R. Co.* v. *Woods*, 88 Ala. 630; 16 Am. St. Rep. 81; *Easun* v. *Buckeye B. B. Co.*, 51 Fed. Rep. 156; *Pearsin* v. *Concord R. R. Co.*, 62 N. H. 537; 13 Am. St. Rep. 590; *Mackintosh* v. *Flint etc. R. R. Co.*, 34 Fed. Rep. 582, 615.

In our judgment, the fact that the object of the purchase of the stock of one corporation by another is not chiefly, or at all, to obtain the control of the former corporation is not sufficient to sustain such a purpose, or to justify the diversion of the corporate funds for the purpose of accomplishing it. The general principle controlling the construction of the charters of corporations and of laws authorizing the formation of corporations is, that they are to be strictly construed in favor of the state and against the corporations, and therefore that they do not authorize the exercise of any authority not expressly conferred unless as an incident to the exercise of the authority so expressed. If the question has reference to the acquisition of stock in another corporation, then the possibility that the power to acquire such stock may lead to the organization of monopolies and to the possession by one corporation of the powers and franchises of several corporations, requires the court to act with great caution, and not to affirm that the power was rightfully exercised in the case in question, unless it clearly appears to have been an innocent and fair exercise of the corporate authority: *Elkins v. Camden & A. R. R. Co.*, 36 N. J. Eq. 5; *Franklin Bank v. Commercial Bank*, 36 Ohio St. 350; 38 Am. Rep. 594; *Marble Co. v. Harvey*, 92 Tenn. 115; *ante*, p. 71; *People v. Chicago Gas T. Co.*, 130 Ill. 268; 17 Am. St. Rep. 319; *Memphis etc. R. R. Co. v. Woods*, 88 Ala. 630, 638; 16 Am. St. Rep. 81; *Milbank v. N. Y. etc. R. R. Co.*, 64 How. Pr. 20; *Franklin Co. v. Lewiston Inst.*, 68 Me. 43; 28 Am. Rep. 9; *Mechanics' Mutual Sav. Bank v. Meriden etc. Co.*, 24 Conn. 159; *Talmage v. Pell*, 7 N. Y. 328. "An incidental power is one that is directly and immediately appropriate to the execution of the specific power granted, and not one that has a slight or remote relation to it": *People v. Chicago Gas T. Co.*, 130 Ill. 283; 17 Am. St. Rep. 319; *Franklin Co. v. Lewiston Inst.* 68 Me. 43; 28 Am. Rep. 9; *Hood v. N. Y. & N. H. R. R.*, 22 Conn. 1.

In England, in a case in which it appeared that a corporation for carrying on the business of broker and scrivener, and making advances, and procuring loans on, and investing in, securities, had by its directors assisted in the construction of another corporation out of an existing banking business, under an agreement by which it should apply for ten thousand shares in the new corporation, but stipulating that of these shares it should not be bound to take more than two-sevenths of what might not be allotted to the public, and that the directors under this agreement took three thousand shares and paid therefor out of the moneys of their corporation, it was held that the whole transaction was *ultra vires*, and that the directors were liable for the moneys so used by them: *Joint Stock Discount Co. v. Brown*, Law R. 8 Eq. Cas. 381. In this case the grounds of the opinion of the court are not stated with sufficient distinctness to enable us to judge whether it intended to assert that the subscription for the shares was in itself *ultra vires*, or was rendered so because of the questionable details of the agreement amounting to a "scheme for bringing out a joint stock company with sham subscriptions for shares and with other arrangements which were to a certain extent sham." In this connection we wish to refer to other English cases which have been cited as authority for the general proposition, that it is perfectly proper, and within the power of an ordinary trading or commercial corporation, to take, or, at least, to purchase, stock in another. The first of these cases was a proceeding against a contract corporation to enforce a liability against it arising out of its alleged ownership of three hundred and sixty-eight shares of a banking corporation. The defendant corporation was by its articles of association authorized "to purchase or accept any obligations, bonds, debentures, notes, or shares in any foreign or English company, and to negotiate the sale of such securities." This contract corporation entered into an arrangement whereby it was to take shares in a projected corporation, and they were applied for in the names of its directors, or of some of them, and subsequently transferred to it. The opinion of the court affirming that the contract corporation was liable did not affirm, as a general proposition, that one corporation could become a stockholder in another, but was based upon the particular provisions of the charter of the corporation before the court. The lord justice said, "The first objection to the order under appeal was that it was *ultra vires* for the contract corporation to take shares in any other trading corporation, and to apply its funds in payment for these shares. Generally speaking, this would be so. It is, at first sight, beyond the province of one trading corporation to become a shareholder in another and to apply its funds for that purpose. But here one of the objects of the trading corporation, as defined by its memorandum of association, was to purchase or accept any obligations, bonds, debentures, notes, and shares of any foreign or English company, and to negotiate the sale of any such securities. It appears to me that in applying for and accepting the shares in the Barned Banking Company, the contract corporations were strictly, and to the letter, complying with and acting within these terms. If it were necessary to make this power still clearer, the forty-seventh clause of the articles of association provides that the directors may invest any of the money of the corporation in such securities (other than the corporation's own shares) as they, the directors, may think desirable, plainly implying that, though they might not invest their money upon the purchase or allotment of their own shares, they might invest them upon an allotment or shares *ejusdem generis* in other companies." The balance of the opinion was, so far as here material, devoted to answering the argument that, although the articles of the contract corporation authorized the transaction in question, yet, that under the English statutes, one trading corporation could not become a member of another trading corporation. These statutes were examined and found not to forbid such ownership. Therefore, a fair summary of this decision asserts no more than that when the articles of incorporation make the acquisition of stock in another corporation one of the purposes of the first corporation, there is nothing in the English statutes, nor at common law, denouncing such purpose as unlawful: *In re Barned's Banking Co.,* Law R. 3 Ch. App. 105. This case was mentioned and its doctrines affirmed in the *Royal Bank of India's Case,* Law R. 4 Ch. 252. That was a proceeding to enforce contribution from the Royal Bank of India, in which its liability rested upon its being a stockholder in another corporation. The bank attempted to escape liability, on the ground that its acts in becoming the apparent owner of the stock in such corporation were *ultra vires.* It was shown, however, that the Bank of India was a general banking corporation, having all the incidental powers properly appertaining to the business of banking; that, in the legitimate transaction of its business, it made a loan and took as security therefore an assignment of a portion of the stock of another corporation, and that afterwards, entertaining some doubts whether the assignment was sufficient for the protection of its rights, it caused these shares to be surrendered and a new certificate of stock to be issued to it and in its name, which it held, however, as collateral security for the payment of the loan made by it, and while so holding the stock, it collected various dividends thereon. The court determined that as it was quite usual in the business of banking to make loans and to take transfers of the stock of corporations as collateral security therefor, neither the loan which had been effected by the Bank of India, nor its subsequent acquisition of the legal title of the stock for the purpose of securing the loan, was *ultra vires.* That the court did not intend to affirm the general proposition that a trading corporation might speculate in the stock of other corporations, or become the owner of such stock, except for a purpose necessarily incidental to the transaction of the corporate business, is clear, for Sir G. M. Gifford, L. J., in his concurring opinion said, "I quite agree that the Royal Bank of India had no authority to speculate in shares, and that if it had gone upon the Stock Exchange and bought shares as a speculation, such a proceeding would have been *ultra vires,* and all that has taken place would not have been enough to constitute the Royal Bank of India shareholders in this bank or prevent them from repudiating these shares."

The illustrations made by the court in its opinion in the case last cited show that it is possible for a corporation, in carrying on its legitimate business, to become interested in other businesses of an entirely different nature, and to be placed in positions where it must necessarily exercise, at least temporarily, functions not directly within the purview of its charter or articles of association. The court pointed out that a banking corporation might properly advance money on a ship and its freight, or upon land secured by a mortgage thereon, and that upon the enforcement of these securities the bank might become both shipowner and landowner, and in the exercise of the privilege of such ownership it might navigate ships or manage and improve lands; for whenever it was proper to make the loan and take the security "it necessarily follows that anything which was a proper and prudent act to do, with a view to obtaining the benefit of such security, was clearly within the scope of their power." An examination of all the well-considered cases sustaining the acquisition by one corporation of stock in another will, we think, show either that the charter or articles of association specially permitted such acquisition, or that it authorized the doing of some business in the doing of which it resulted that the stock came into the hands of the association incidentally, and without any intention on its part, or that of its managers, in entering upon the original transaction that it should result in the ownership of such stock. The designation in the articles of incorporation of the purposes of the corporation necessarily implies that its funds shall be devoted to those purposes, and none other, and that if moneys accumulate in addition to those necessary for such purposes they shall be divided among the stockholders by way of dividends instead of being used in purposes foreign to those specified in the charter.

If a corporation is formed for the purpose of loaning the funds of itself or its stockholders, and is not forbidden to accept corporate stock as security, it may doubtless loan on such security, and, if necessary to its enforcement, may acquire title to the stock; or, if no security was taken, and it becomes necessary to levy upon and sell property in satisfaction of an execution or other writ, the corporation may levy upon the stock of another corporation as well as upon any other species of property, and may purchase such stock at a sale under execution; and if a corporation may by legal proceedings compel a debtor to turn over his stock in another corporation in satisfaction of its debt, it may, doubtless, permit him to do so voluntarily, without the intervention of any hostile proceedings, and accept such stock in payment of his debt. No one will seriously contend that a corporation, whatever its purpose, may not acquire stock as security for, or in payment of, a debt: *Memphis etc. R. R.* v. *Woods*, 88 Ala. 630, 16 Am. St. Rep. 81, 88; *National Bank* v. *Case*, 99 U. S. 628; *Howe* v. *Boston Carpet Co.*, 16 Gray, 493; *First Nat. Bank* v. *National Exchange Bank*, 92 U. S. 128; *Taylor County Court* v. *Baltimore etc. R. R. Co.*, 35 Fed. Rep. 161; *Holmes etc. Mfg. Co.* v. *Holmes etc. Co.*, 127 N. Y. 252; 24 Am. St. Rep. 448. A corporation, having power to dispose of its property, may also, as an incident to the exercise of this power, in some instances at least, determine what shall be accepted in payment, and may be justified in accepting the stock of another corporation for distribution among the stockholders of the first corporation, according to their respective interests therein: *Treadwell* v. *Salisbury Mfg. Co.*, 7 Gray, 393, 405; 66 Am. Dec. 490; *Hodges* v. *New England Screw Co.*, 1 R. I. 312, 347; 53 Am. Dec. 624.

If the purchase by one corporation of stock in another is drawn into question collaterally and there is nothing to show whether the purchase was justifiable or not, it will not be assumed to have been unlawful or *ultra vires: Evans* v. *Bailey*, 66 Cal. 112.

There is one American case the opinion in which cannot be reconciled with the views herein expressed, but it is based upon a misconception and misquotation of the English cases to which we have already referred. This American case affirms that there is nothing in the character of a steam packet corporation or in the nature of its business to prevent its purchasing the shares of another steam packet corporation, and that "having money to loan or invest, there would appear to be no reason why it may not invest in the stock of other corporations as well as in other funds, provided it be done *bona fide* and with no sinister or unlawful purpose": *Booth* v. *Robinson*, 55 Md. 419, 433. This would doubtless be true if the steam packet company were a loan and investment corporation, or were by its articles of incorporation authorized to unite these two businesses, which seem to have no necessary connection or affinity. The case in which this language was used was not one in which the validity of the purchase could have been questioned. Neither the steam packet company whose funds had been used in the purchase of the stock of the steamboat company, nor any of the stockholders of the former corporation had complained of the purchase, nor was it questioned in any way by the state as a usurpation of a franchise which the purchasing corporation was not entitled to exercise.

In some of the states railway corporations have been authorized by statute to consolidate or to purchase stock in connecting lines. Under these statutes the acquisition by one railroad corporation of stock in another is encouraged rather than forbidden and cannot be avoided as *ultra vires: Hill* v. *Nisbet*, 100 Ind. 341; *Atchison etc. R. R. Co.* v. *Cochran*, 43 Kas. 225; 19 Am. St. Rep. 129; *Atchison etc. R. R. Co.* v. *Fletcher*, 35 Kas. 236; *Ryan* v. *Leavenworth etc. Ry. Co.*, 21 Kas. 365.

The arguments usually urged against acquisition by one corporation of stock in another are, that there can be no implication that a corporation is vested with franchises or entitled to exercise powers not enumerated in its charter, that as every franchise must arise from a grant by the state or sovereign, such grant must, like all other grants from the sovereign, be strictly construed as against the grantee, and finally, that the union of the franchises and powers of two or more corporations under one management and control invites and encourages monopolies, and is therefore clearly contrary to public policy: *People* v. *Chicago Gas T. Co.*, 130 Ill. 268; 17 Am. St. Rep. 319. These arguments do not take into consideration the rights of the stockholders in the corporation whose funds are devoted to the acquisition of stock in another corporation. This diversion tends to prevent the declaration of dividends and the realization of those profits which each stockholder must be presumed to seek in acquiring an interest in the corporation. Furthermore, each stockholder has, by virtue of his power to vote his stock at stockholders' meetings and elections, the privilege of contributing to the control of the corporation and determining what course it shall pursue within the limits of its lawful authority, and whether or not he exercises his elective privilege, knows that his liabilities are measured by the debts of his corporation. But if that corporation may organize another or subscribe to the stock of another the latter may be governed by directors in whose selection he can exercise no control, and in addition to being answerable for his proportion of the liabilities of his corporation, he may become indirectly liable, through it, for the debts of another corporation. That corporation may in turn organize or subscribe to stock in another, and these proceedings may go on without end, and every person consenting to become a stockholder in a corporation formed for one purpose may thereby become liable for a portion of the debts of corporations formed for divers purposes, and see the moneys which he was willing to invest in one enterprise diverted to a multiplicity of enterprises, some of which may be of a character never contemplated by him, or, if contemplated, abhorred as improper, or despised as visionary.

STAVER *v.* MISSIMER.

[6 WASHINGTON, 173.]

CONTRACTS—PROMISE TO FORBEAR SUIT—CONSIDERATION.—An order upon a third person for the payment of a debt not due, if accepted, is sufficient consideration for a promise to forbear to sue upon an obligation already due.

CONTRACTS.—A PROMISE TO FORBEAR TO SUE MAY BE PLEADED IN BAR to an action upon the original indebtedness.

ACTION by Staver and Walker against Missimer and Illman to foreclose two mortgages evidenced by four notes dated November 10, 1890, three of which were for $500 each, one due March 10, 1891, one due May 10, 1891, and one due July 10, 1891. The remaining note was for $544, due August 10, 1891.

Defendants admitted the amount claimed to be unpaid, but alleged in defense that prior to October 26, 1891, they were further indebted to the plaintiffs upon two unsecured notes, one for $330, due October 1, 1891, one for $487.97, due November 1, 1891, and also upon an open account, and that on said October 26, 1891, plaintiffs agreed with defendants to take an order for $1,000 on E. J. Blackman and Fannie S. Churchill, to be applied in payment upon said unsecured notes and open account when paid, and that the time of payment on the secured notes should be extended one year from such last-named date. A demurrer to such answer was overruled, and judgment rendered for defendants.

Plaintiffs appealed.

Bell and Austin, and Blaine and De Vries, for the appellants.

Ault and Munns, for the respondents.

[174] DUNBAR, C. J. So far as the testimony in this case is concerned, it is very conflicting; but, considering all the circumstances in the case, especially the fact that appellant received additional security by the arrangement which was

made, and the circumstances under which it was made we do
not feel justified in disturbing the findings of the trial judge
who had the witnesses before him in the trial of the cause.

The legal questions are raised by the demurrer to the
answer, the appellant contending: 1. That the answer failed
to state any consideration for the alleged agreement to forbear
to sue; 2. That a covenant not to sue for a limited time cannot be pleaded as a bar to the action.

As to the first proposition, appellant admits that payment
of a note before the note becomes due is sufficient consideration for a promise or agreement to forbear to sue, but asserts
that an order on a third person, and especially a conditional
order, is not payment and in no way changes the relation of
the parties until payment thereon is made, except to extend
the time of payment until the order is payable. The answer
in this case, however, does not set up a conditional order, but
alleges that an order was given and accepted, and such an
order as was agreed upon by the parties. And so far as the
merits of the case are concerned, the order was paid and respondents given credit for the amount.

[175] The answer also alleges that a portion of the debt was
not due. The fact that it would have been due in a short
time does not change the principle of law. After the acceptance of this order by Blackman and Churchill, appellant
could have maintained an action against them for the amount
accepted, and it can make no difference whether the order
was taken as absolute payment or as security for an unsecured debt. It is certainly sometimes a very great advantage
and benefit to creditors to secure their unsecured accounts,
and the value of the consideration is frequently equal to the
full value of the debt secured.

"A consideration has been well defined as consisting of 'any
act of plaintiff from which the defendant or a stranger derives
a benefit or advantage.' . . . . It is not necessary that a benefit should accrue to the person making the promise; it is sufficient that something valuable flows from the person to whom
it is made, or that he suffers some prejudice or inconvenience,
and that the promise is the inducement to the transaction":
5 Lawson's Rights, Remedies, and Practices, sec. 2244.

It is alleged in the answer that the promise was the inducement to the transaction, and outside of the benefits flowing to
the creditor from the transaction, it is evident that the giving
of this order would be something of an inconvenience to busi-

ness men situated as these respondents were at that ti
We think there was a sufficient consideration to support
agreement to extend the time, and the authorities overwhe]
ingly support this contention.

On the second proposition, it is contended by appell:
that the respondents' remedy for a breach of promise not
sue is a claim for damages, and that the agreement can
be pleaded as a bar to the action. It seems to us that, o
side of the fact that proof could only be made of dama
which had already accrued at the time of the commencem
of the action, and which for that reason would, [176] in a gr
many cases, be an entirely inadequate remedy, it is mark
out a crooked path for litigants to travel, and one that was
nowise contemplated by their contract.

The law, in construing a contract, adopts rules to ascert:
the intention of the parties to the contract, and when t]
intention is ascertained, if it is a contract which the part
had a right to make, the law will simply enforce it so as
make effective such ascertained intention, and will not me
another and a different contract for the parties, and prescr
different remedies and different penalties. In this case
contract was a plain one. The terms were that suit sho\
not be brought for one year. Why should it not be as plai
enforced? If the contract is to be given force at all, it ou
to be given the same force as the original contract. Ther
just as much reason in holding that the defense to an act
on a note before it becomes due on the original contract m
be confined to a claim for damages as there is to hold t
the defense, where the agreement as to time has been chang
must be so restricted. In each instance it is purely and s
ply a question of the maturity of the note. No one wo
have questioned their right under this agreement to take
old notes up and give new ones for the same amounts
one year from date. That was in substance what they
and directness instead of circumlocution in administering
law ought to be the policy of the courts.

We are aware that there is a great conflict of authorit;
this question, some cases holding that the remedy is by d
ages in a separate action, while others, to avoid multifari
ness of suits, have been driven to a more inconsistent prac
of compelling the defendant to allege his damages in
original action; while still others have enforced the cont
that was made by the parties.

The leading case supporting the last practice is *Robinson* v. *Godfrey*, 2 Mich. 408, where it is pointedly held that the [177] promise operates directly upon the original contract and to bar an action brought upon said contract before the time limited expires. The court in that case, in an exhaustive opinion, reviews the authorities and points out the manner in which courts have been misled that have sustained the opposite view; and in referring to the decisions in certain cases sustaining the view that the promise was a bar, viz: *Tatlock* v. *Smith*, 6 Bing. 339; *Stracy* v. *Bank of England*, 6 Bing. 754; *Allies* v. *Probyn*, 2 Cromp. M. & R. 408, says:

" These cases seem to establish the proposition that agreements not to sue, and in the same manner, agreements to extend the credit, operate directly upon the rights and obligations of the parties to the contract, and, as the case may be, destroy or suspend the remedy. Indeed, it seems to us, that the opposite view contended for makes a distinction where none exists, violates all legal analogies, frustrates the real intent of the parties and must make the court an instrument of manifest wrong and injustice."

To the same effect: *Blair* v. *Reid*, 20 Tex. 311, and *Leslie* v. *Conway*, 59 Cal. 442.

In many other cases the right to plead the promise in bar seems to have been unquestioned, the only contention being over the question of consideration. This is a new question in this state, and, being untrammeled by precedent, we feel free to adopt the rule that seems to us to be the most nearly in accord with the general principles of law applied by courts to the construction and enforcement of contracts, and we therefore decide that a promise to forbear to sue for a definite time, where the promise is based upon a sufficient consideration, can be pleaded in bar to the action.

No error appearing, the judgment is affirmed.

STILES and SCOTT, JJ., concur.

HOYT, J., dissents.

ANDERS, J., not sitting.

Forbearance to Sue, Agreements for, Effect of. *

Covenant Never to Sue.—It is everywhere conceded that a promise or covenant by an obligee not to sue an obligor at all amounts in law to a release and may always be pleaded in bar of an action to recover the debt. The

reason for the rule is stated to be that a circuity of action is thus avo
Guard v. *Whiteside*, 13 Ill. 7; *Stebbins* v. *Niles*, 25 Miss. 267; *Cuyler* v. *Ci*
2 Johns. 186; *McAllester* v. *Sprague*, 34 Me. 296–298; *Walker* v. *McCu*
4 Me. 421; *Harvey* v. *Harvey*, 3 Ind. 473; *Reed* v. *Shaw*, 1 Blackf.
Marietta Savings Bank v. *Janes*, 66 Ga. 286; *Jackson* v. *Stackhouse*, 1
122; 13 Am. Dec. 514.

An agreement to forbear to sue in general, without adding any parti
time, is to be understood as a total forbearance, and may be pleaded ii
to an action to recover the debt: *Clark* v. *Russell*, 3 Watts, 213; 27 Am.
348; *Hamaker* v. *Eberly*, 2 Binn. 505; 4 Am. Dec. 477; *Jackson* v. *S*
house, 1 Cow. 122; 13 Am. Dec. 514; *Lane* v. *Owings*, 3 Bibb, 247; *P*
v. *Johnson*, 8 Johns. 54.

Promise Not to Sue for Limited Time.—In some jurisdictions the doc
is maintained that an agreement not to sue for a right resting in contrac
between all the parties to the contract, is never a distinct and indepen
undertaking upon which an action is maintainable, but a mere modifica
or extinguishment, according as it is temporary or perpetual, of the r
and obligations of the contract, and as such may be availed of in defen
an action founded upon it: *Morgan* v. *Butterfield*, 3 Mich. 615; *Robins*
Godfrey, 2 Mich. 408; *Leslie* v. *Conway*, 59 Cal. 442; *Blair* v. *Reid*, 20
311; *Pearl* v. *Wells*, 6 Wend. 291; *Smith* v. *Bibber*, 82 Me. 34; 17 Am
Rep. 464. Thus, when the holder of a note overdue agrees not to su
debtor for a limited time, and, in violation of such agreement, comme
suit on the note before the expiration of the time agreed upon, the rei
of the debtor is to set up such agreement in defense of the action, and
also maintained that the debtor cannot sustain an independent actio
his part for a violation of the agreement: *Pearl* v. *Wells*, 6 Wend. 29
Am. Dec. 328; and to the same effect *White* v. *Dingley*, 4 Mass. 433. *I*
in *Clopper* v. *Union Bank*, 7 Har. & J. 92, 16 Am. Dec. 294, it was
that the rule that a covenant not to sue for a limited period cannot be pl
in suspension of a creditor's action does not extend to actions of assun
and if the holder of a note, in consideration that an accommodation ind
will give him a mortgage to secure its payment, stipulates that he wi
for a definite period sue the maker and then sues before that perio
passed, the promise not to sue may be pleaded in defense of the a
In speaking of the rule that a covenant not to sue for a limited time
pleadable in bar or suspension of an action on the contract Mr. J
Wheeler, in *Blair* v. *Reid*, 20 Tex. 314, said, "by some courts this r
held not to apply to actions of assumpsit, a covenant not to sue for d
certain being there held to be a bar during that time. And so, I appr
it must be held in all cases in our courts, since our practice discounte
circuity of actions, and requires parties to litigate their respective
respecting the subject matter in question in one suit the debtor ma
the covenant not to sue, in suspension of the action": *Blair* v. *Reid*, 2
311–314.

On the other hand, the weight of authority sustains the contrar
trine, that a promise not to sue for a debt for a definite but limited
of time cannot be pleaded in bar of an action to recover the debt befo
time has expired. If the covenant is broken before the expiration of t
limited, the only remedy of the party aggrieved is to bring an actio
cover damages for a breach of the covenant. The cases which sust
rule maintain that a covenant or agreement not to sue within a limit
is not in law a release or suspension of the debtor's right of action, and

be pleaded in bar of an action to recover the debt, for the reason that such covenant, or agreement, is a distinct contract, for the violation of which an action may be maintained: *Winans* v. *Huston*, 6 Wend. 472; *Clopper* v. *Union Bank*, 7 Har. & J. 92; 16 Am. Dec. 294; *Fullam* v. *Valentine*, 11 Pick. 156; *Thurston* v. *James*, 6 R. I. 103; *Guard* v. *Whiteside*, 13 Ill. 7; *Millett* v· *Hayford*, 1 Wis. 401; *Howland* v. *Marvin*, 5 Cal. 501; *Chandler* v. *Herrick*, 19 Johns. 129; *Perkins* v. *Gilman*, 8 Pick. 229; *Ford* v. *Beech*, 11 Q. B. 852; *Webb* v. *Spicer*, 13 Q. B. 886; *Foster* v. *Purdy*, 5 Met. 442; *Gibson* v. *Gibson*, 15 Mass. 106; 8 Am. Dec. 94. In the latter case the reason for the rule was thus stated "if there be a covenant that the obligee shall not put the bond in suit at any time, such covenant is pleadable in bar as a release; because in effect it is so. But where the covenant is, that it shall not be put in suit within a limited time, a breach thereof cannot be pleaded in bar of the bond. And the reason is that the damages for the breach of the latter covenant being uncertain, and not being determined by the amount of the bond, the principle of circuity of action is not applicable. Such covenant, therefore, will not rebut the obligor's action on the bond, although the bringing of the action may be as much as a breach of such covenant as of a perpetual covenant." Again in *Foster* v. *Purdy*, 5 Met. 442–444, the court said: "In *Winans* v. *Huston*, 6 Wend. 472–475, it is said that the reason why a covenant not to sue for a demand within the limited time is not allowed to be pleaded in bar of an action brought contrary to the covenant, is to be ascribed to that principle of law, that if the right of action is once suspended by the act of the party, it is wholly gone. But the more satisfactory reason seems to be, that the damages to be recovered for the breach of a covenant or agreement not to sue for a demand within a limited time may be much less than the demand, and if so, it would be unjust to allow it to bar the whole demand; and thus it is distinguished from a perpetual covenant, which is held to be a bar, to avoid circuity of action, as the damages, if cross-actions were to be brought, would be the same."

We cannot approve the above doctrine on the basis of any of the reasons adduced in its favor. It would seem, from these early cases founded on common-law authority, that the rule that a temporary covenant not to sue would not suspend the remedy originated in the supposed principle that a personal action once suspended is gone forever. Although it was admitted to be the intention of the parties to suspend the action, and although this intention was expressed in words, yet, as it was supposed that the consequence of giving effect to this intention would be to destroy another more important object, namely, the validity of an instrument not designed to be destroyed, the covenant was not allowed to constitute even a temporary bar; but the party injured by its breach was left to his remedy by a cross-action upon it. If there ever was such a principle of law as that assumed by these early cases, and which controlled their determination, it certainly long since has become obsolete; but with that tenacity which characterizes some of the absurd doctrines of the common law it survived long enough to be incorporated into and form the rule of decision in some of the judicial tribunals of this country. The cases cited all agree in this, that a promise not to sue for a right resting in contract is a distinct and independent, or, as it is sometimes expressed, a collateral, undertaking, giving a separate right of action in case of its breach, and not a mere modification of the rights and obligations of the original contract to which it refers. We are confirmed in the opinion that no such principle of law as that assumed as the basis of the reasoning for the establishment of such a rule ever existed.

Some of these cases tacitly concede that an agreement not to su
a limited time is intended by the parties to suspend the remedy, a
cession which implies that it is intended to be a mere modification of
rights and obligations incident to the original contract. But they say
it is a rule of law that a remedy once suspended by the act of the par
gone forever. Hence to construe the agreement as a temporary susper
of the right of action would make it a release, and that, as the parties n
could have intended that it should operate as a release, it is held nc
suspend the remedy at all, but merely to give a right of action for dam
in case of its breach. As has been shown the cases are not agreed i
the ground upon which the proposition referred is to be maintained.
apprehend that it cannot, at this day, be maintained upon any groun
by any train of reasoning; and we agree with the supreme court of M
gan and of other states in saying that "were this question *res integr*
imagine no court would long hesitate as to how it should be determined
seems to us very clear, upon principle, that whenever a creditor ag
with his debtor, upon good consideration, that he will never, or not f
specified time, pursue against him either any or all of the remedies w
the law gives for the enforcement of a particular demand the agreement is
collateral to the original contract of indebtment, giving merely a claim
damages in case of its breach, but operates directly upon the contract,
as the case may be, destroys or modifies the legal rights and obligat
which grow out of it": *Robinson* v. *Godfrey*, 2 Mich. 408, 409.

"A new agreement not to sue for a limited time is a mere modificatio
the original contract, that, under the law that formed a part of it, |
the right to sue immediately on default. It is exactly equivalent in
effects upon the contract to a legislative suspension of the law of the
edy, or an agreement between the parties to extend the time of perform
or payment, which latter agreement is now universally held to be a
change of the original contract. It is manifestly inconsistent and absu
hold that the former of these agreements is independent and the latt
not, that the one modifies the contract and the other does not, and tha
one will suspend the remedy and the other will not, since it is impossib
point out any distinction between them, except in the language used b
parties to express their intentions. So upon these principles an agree
never to sue, in legal sense, destroys the contract. It is exactly equiv
in its effects, as between the parties to an entire and permanent repeal
laws for the enforcement of the contract, or a technical release. It ope
as a release, not as it has often been said, upon the principle of avc
circuity of action, but because in substance and effect it is a release.
principle then, whatever may be the weight of precedent to the con
originating when the source of the rights and obligations of contract
much less perfectly understood than it now is in this country, we th
clear that an agreement not to sue for a right vesting in contract,
between all the parties thereto, is never a distinct and independent u
taking upon which an action is maintainable, but a mere modificat;
extinguishment, according as it is temporary or perpetual, of the righ
obligations of the contract, and as such may be availed of in defense
action founded upon it. No one, we imagine, will carry his legal opt
or his reverence for the sound and venerable maxim of *stare decisis* so
to question that this construction of the agreement is in accordanc
the true intent of the parties": *Morgan* v. *Butterfield*, 3 Mich. 615–6.

Agreement Not to Sue a Joint Obligor.—A covenant or agreement not to sue one of several joint promissors or obligors operates as a discharge of the debt or obligation as to him, and may be set up as a bar to an action brought against him alone for recovery upon the obligation forming the basis of the promise not to sue: *Ellis* v. *Esson*, 50 Wis. 138; 36 Am. Rep. 830; *Sewall* v. *Sparrow*, 16 Mass. 24; *Goodnow* v. *Smith*, 18 Pick. 414; 29 Am. Dec. 600. But a covenant or promise not to sue one of two or more joint or several promissors, while it will discharge the one in whose favor it is made, will not operate as a discharge or release of the other promissors, and it cannot be pleaded as a bar to an action against them to recover on the original obligation. To this effect the authorities are numerous and uniform: *Durell* v. *Wendell*, 8 N. H. 369; *Bank of Chenango* v. *Osgood*, 4 Wend. 607; *Couch* v. *Mills*, 21 Wend. 424; *McLellan* v. *Cumberland Bank*, 24 Me. 566; *Harrison* v. *Close*, 2 Johns. 448; 3 Am. Dec. 444; *Rowley* v. *Stoddard*, 7 Johns. 207; *Tuckerman* v. *Newhall*, 17 Mass. 581; *Shed* v. *Pierce*, 17 Mass. 623; *Walker* v. *McCulloch*, 4 Me. 421; *President etc. Bank of Catskill* v. *Messenger*, 9 Cow. 37; *Carondelet* v. *Desnoyer*, 27 Mo. 36.

WHITTIER *v.* STETSON AND POST MILL COMPANY.

[6 WASHINGTON, 190.]

MECHANIC'S LIEN—NOTICE OF CLAIM.—A notice of a mechanic's lien, describing the property as all of a certain lot except the west twenty feet thereof, is insufficient when the building also occupies a portion of another lot, although it is also described by a certain name and as being located at the northwest corner of two streets.

MECHANIC'S LIENS—NOTICE OF CLAIM—MISTAKE IN.—A mechanic's lien for material used in a building constructed by owners of adjoining lots, under one contract, the material being furnished under the supposition that it is for the entire building as the property of the owner against whom the claim is filed, is not void because it covers some material not used in the part of the building described, but used in the part belonging to the other owner. The claimant has a valid lien for the material furnished for and used in the part of the building described, and may recover therefor against the party named in the claim by remitting for the remainder not used in his part of the building.

MECHANIC'S LIEN—NOTICE OF CLAIM—INSUFFICIENCY OF DESCRIPTION of property in one part of a mechanic's lien claim is cured by a description in correct form in a subsequent part of such claim.

Turner and McCutcheon, Preston, Carr and Preston, and W. R. Bell, for the appellants.

Thompson, Edsen and Humphries, for the respondents.

190 STILES, J. The respondents Brodek and Schlessinger and one Nugent planned the erection of a building upon land at the northwest corner of South Third and Washington streets, in the city of Seattle. The land embraced lot 5, **191** block 9, in D. S. Maynard's plat, which formed the street

corner and fronted 60 feet on South Third street, and 108 f
upon Washington street, and the south half of lot 6, fronti
30 feet on South Third street, and having the same depth
lot 5. The building was thus to be a parallelogram, 90
108 feet in size. Of this area said respondents had a lease
all but the west 20 feet of lot 5—a parallelogram of 20 by
feet—which was the property of Nugent. The buildi
erected was, on the outside, apparently one building, but,
originally planned, partition walls ran up from the baseme
to the roof in such a manner as to completely separate t
two ownerships. While the plans were in this condition ea
owner let a contract with builders, Farnum and others,
the erection of his own portion of the building, but sub
quently, and before the materials furnished by Whittier, F
ler & Co. were supplied, the several owners and the contract
modified their plans so that the separate character of the t
buildings was largely taken away; that is, they removed t
basement partition entirely excepting at the rear of Nugen
part; and instead of a brick party wall between the up
rooms a lath and plaster wall was substituted. To guide t
contractors and to carry out their new understanding, t
owners caused the architect to draw a new set of floor pla
which were signed by all parties, and to be attached to t
original plans and specifications, after which the buildi
progressed to completion.

The appellants filed lien claims for labor and materi
furnished for the Brodek and Schlessinger part of the bui
ing only, and this appeal is prosecuted from a judgment c
missing their several complaints in actions for foreclosu
The nature of the cases requires their separate examinat
and determination.

1. In the matter of the liens of the Stetson Post Mill
and W. C. Stetson, but one point need be noticed.

192 The lien claims of these appellants described the pr
erty as follows:

"All of lot 5 in block 9 of D. S. Maynard's plat of the t
(now city) of Seattle, except the west 20 feet of said lot;
that said building is known as the Brodek-Schlessinger bu
ing, and is on the northwest corner of Third and Washing
streets, in said city, King county, state of Washington."

This claim, it will be observed, located the building
rectly, and it excluded Nugent's part; but it did not incl
within the description of the land sought to be charged

south half of lot 6, which the Brodek-Schlessinger part actually occupied.

The statute requires that the lien claim shall contain a description of the property to be charged with the lien "sufficient for identification": Gen. Stats., sec. 1667. And so far as the claim is concerned, no property could be identified with more certainty to a reader of the record copy. It is lot 5, block 9, Maynard's plat, excepting the west 20 feet of the lot. But the difficulty which the court below found to be insurmountable was, that when the evidence was in it was found that the building covered an additional distinct parcel of land upon which no claim had been filed at all, viz., the south half of lot 6. Appellants see the force of this proposition, and claim to be relieved by the reference to the name of the building and its location at the northwest corner of the two streets. It is said in the lien claim that this building is known as the "Brodek-Schlessinger building," and to such persons as might have seen it and have been familiar with the locality that would undoubtedly be a sufficient identification, although unless they were also acquainted with the separate ownership of Nugent it would not have informed them that under the same roof, and without any apparent distinction of title, there were, in fact, two buildings, upon one of which no [193] lien was claimed. It may be doubted, however, whether a mere private building can be said to be fully identified by giving to it the name of its owners. Private buildings are not generally so identified or spoken of, and particularly when it comes to conveyances, encumbrances, and the like. The name helps to identify, doubtless; but the name does not individualize such property, as names do, in the case of mining claims, for instance, which ordinarily depend upon nothing but their names for identification.

Tredinnick v. *Red Cloud Con. Min. Co.*, 72 Cal. 78, was a case where a lien was properly sustained upon the "Red Cloud Mine, situated in the Bodie mining district, Bodie township, in Mono county." The inception of a mining title is usually by means of a location notice, in which the name is the most prominent feature, and all conveyances follow by the name only. A public record in that case identified the property in the first place; but there is no such record of buildings.

The location at the corner of the streets also helps to identify, and we do not desire to be understood as holding that such a description, without any designation of a lot or block, would not be a sufficient identification if the quantity of land were also identified, as, for example, if the size of the building on the ground were stated.

In *De Witt* v. *Smith*, 63 Mo. 263, the description was of "lots 19 and 20, in block 2, in Ashburn's Addition to Kansas City," and the corner of the street was given. But in fact the block was not block 2, but block 20. Under the facts the clerical error in omitting a figure was held not to invalidate the lien. In *Caldwell* v. *Asbury*, 29 Ind. 451, the case was something like this one, for the description was "house and lot on the southwest corner of Fourth and Oak streets." A foreclosure upon one lot was sustained, although it was held that the claim was not sufficient to [194] sustain a complaint against two lots. It does not appear that the house actually occupied a part of the second lot.

But in *Willamette S. M. Co.* v. *Kremer*, 94 Cal. 205, under a statute like ours, in substance, the description was "lot 6, in block 28, of the Heber tract, at the northeast corner of Hope and Eighth streets"; and although the building extended over on to lot 7 the lien was sustained.

In *De Witt* v. *Smith*, 63 Mo. 263, there was something upon the record which would have served to warn anyone, even though he did not know of the existence of a house, viz., the plat of the addition at a certain street corner on which the building was said to have been erected. Unless in that case blocks 2 and 20 cornered at the same street intersection, it would not be likely that a searcher of the record would be deceived. But in *Willamette S. M. Co.* v. *Kremer*, 94 Cal. 205, the court, upon the theory of liberal construction and that the owner was not misled, and regarding the statute as authorizing a lien upon the "property," which it interpreted to be the house, sustained the lien, although no mention was made in the claim of lot 7.

This court has held that a lien upon a building is ineffectual unless the land, or some interest therein, be included in it: *Kellogg* v. *Littell & Smythe Mfg. Co.*, 1 Wash. 407.

Phillips on Mechanics' Liens says, section 379:

"The best rule to be adopted is, that if there appears enough in the description to enable a party familiar with the locality to identify the premises intended to be described with reasonable certainty, to the exclusion of others, it will be sufficient."

The claim in this case fully meets this requirement, but the trouble with it, and with the rule as applied to it, is, as

we think, that its very exactness tended to mislead the public. [195] The lien claimant is not required to give the owner
any notice whatever; if he were, it would take very little in
any case to satisfy the law. But he is required to make a
record of his claim, and the only purpose of such a record
must be to give constructive notice to third persons, and not
only to those who may have been familiar with the premises
during and since the erection of the building, but also to those
who may never have seen the premises as well as those who
were familiar with them only before the building was erected.
As to all such persons it may be admitted that it would be
entirely sufficient to simply name the Brodek-Schlessinger
building, on the corner of South Third and Washington
streets.

But to the last two classes that description added to the
designation of lot 5, block 9, would be a complete trap in case
they should become purchasers during the life of the lien. A
more sensible and effectual administration of this law could
be had if there were some provision by which a claim in such
a case could be amended where no one could be injured by it;
but we must take the statute as we find it, and in this case
neither the actual building nor the land having been described
the liens must fail.

2. Whittier, Fuller & Co. furnished all the glass for the
building erected by Brodek and Schlessinger and Nugent
jointly. This they did under a subcontract with one Pierson,
who had a subcontract from the principal contractors for all
the glasswork. Their agent was misled into supposing that
the entire building was owned by Brodek and Schlessinger
by hearing it spoken of as the Brodek-Schlessinger building,
and by the fact that Pierson had but one contract for all of
the glasswork. But their counsel, whom they employed to
prepare and file their claim, were aware, through knowledge
acquired otherwise, that the Brodek-Schlessinger building
proper did not include Nugent's part, so that from the mem-
oranda furnished [196] them of glass sold for and used in the
Brodek-Schlessinger building, they prepared, and, after veri-
fication, filed a claim for the whole amount of the glass, which
correctly described the Brodek-Schlessinger building and the
land upon which it stood. Their lien claim, therefore, covered glass which was not used in the part of the building described, but was used in Nugent's part, a fact which was not
discovered until the trial of the action, when the true state of

the matter appeared. Upon this the plaintiffs showed ve
clearly just what glass had, as a matter of fact, been used
the two portions of the building, and asked that they be ;
lowed to remit from their claim the value of the glass used
Nugent's part, and to have a decree for the balance. T
whole claim amounted to fifteen hundred and eighty-ni:
dollars and thirty-nine cents, and the sum proposed to]
remitted was about one hundred and fifty dollars.

The court, upon the ground that the glass used in Nugen'
part of the building was a nonlienable item, refused to allc
the remission, and upon the authority of *Dexter* v. *Sparkma*
2 Wash. 165, and *Dexter* v. *Wiley*, 2 Wash. 171, sustained ;
objection to the claim.

In the first case referred to Kemery filed a claim for a de
due another person and assigned to him, for which he cou
have no lien under the law. Sparkman claimed a lien f
labor on lumber and shingles at wages of three dollars p
day. In the other case liens upon lumber and shingles we
confused in the same way. In none of the shingle cases w
it possible to determine, either from the lien claims or tl
evidence, how much was properly a lien upon the lumbe
The rule laid down in these cases went no further than
declare that a demand for which the law gives no lien cann
be confused with one which is lienable without vitiating t:
whole. The law imputes notice to every one of its terms, ai
when a claim is asserted for a lien to secure a demand f
which no lien is allowed, the act is [197] presumed to be ;
advised attempt to take an unlawful advantage of the statu
But it is not so where mere mistakes or inadvertences cau
items otherwise lienable to be included in a claim. A frau
ulent practice of that kind would render, and many times b
rendered, a claim worthless; but there must be either a gr
excess of demand over just claim or actual fraud to acco
plish that result.

This glass was all lienable. The several owners of {
building, by their conduct in making practically one structi
of it, opened the way to anyone furnishing materials, whi
were distributed about and used indiscriminately by the c
tractors to claim a lien on the whole of it, leaving the own
to settle proportions between themselves. At least it wo:
so seem, although the point is not necessarily in the case
decision. On the other hand, appellants having, as they s
posed, furnished glass for the entire building as the prope

of Brodek and Schlessinger, no less furnished it for the part of the building which actually belonged to Brodek and Schlessinger to the extent they could identify it as having been so used therein.

In the same manner they could have a separate lien upon the Nugent building for the glass which they could identify as having been used in it. Now by the most natural mistake between them and their attorney, when they came to make out their claim, they, without any fraud or attempt to overreach, included the Nugent glass in their claim, a mistake which they voluntarily offered and asked to rectify at the first opportunity after it was discovered. By all means we think they should have been permitted to make the correction.

Upon another ground objection was sustained to this lien claim, viz., insufficiency of description. The land is described twice, and in the first description, on the first page of the claim, it is made to read: "The south one-half [198] of the lot No. 6 of block No. 9, and the easterly eighty-eight (88) of lot No. 5 in said block No. 9." Obviously a clerical error caused the word "feet" to be omitted after the word "eighty-eight," and this was held to make the whole description bad. The lien is a very long one, and it may be that that fact caused both court and counsel to overlook the fact that on the last page the description is repeated with the word "feet" included, which makes it unnecessary to consider the arguments offered upon that point. Other objections we regard as entirely technical and insufficient. Separate notice of each would render this already lengthy opinion much more so.

The judgment is affirmed, except as to the claim of Whittier, Fuller & Co., who will take a reversal. The cause is remanded to the superior court for a retrial of the case as to their claim, in accordance with the law as herein held.

HOYT and ANDERS, JJ., concur.

MR. CHIEF JUSTICE DUNBAR dissented from that part of the opinion involving the claim of Whittier, Fuller & Co., on the ground that "the law will not under any circumstances allow a lien on one man's house for material which goes to another man's house, and such material is as much nonalienable under the statute, for the purposes of this case, as though it were absolutely nonalienable. The fact that the same contractor built the two houses, or that the two houses were built with a joint partition wall, does not affect the case at all. They were two separate contracts, and it devolves upon the material-man when he seeks to charge a third man's property with a debt due from the contractor, to definitely inform himself as to where the material is used."

MECHANIC'S LIEN—NOTICE OF CLAIM—SUFFICIENCY OF DESCRIPTION
PROPERTY: See *White Lake Lumber Co.* v. *Russell,* 22 Neb. 126; 3 Am.
Rep. 262, and note; *Shaw* v. *Barnes,* 5 Pa. St. 18; 47 Am. Dec. 399,
note; *Knabb's Appeal,* 10 Pa. St. 186; 51 Am. Dec. 472, and note. A
chanic's lien will be restricted to the property on which he has the right
lien, though he may assert a claim to a lien on other property: *Lyor
Logan,* 68 Tex. 521; 2 Am. St. Rep. 511, and note; and the fact that a
was claimed on more land than was necessary for the building to which
lien attached will not vitiate the claim: *Derrickson* v. *Edwards,* 29 N. J.
468; 80 Am. Dec. 220.

SEATTLE CROCKERY COMPANY *v.* HALEY.

[6 WASHINGTON, 302.]

ATTACHMENT—RIGHT OF SURETIES TO REQUIRE ACTION ON BOND.—If
principal in an attachment bond is a nonresident, and has no prop
in the state liable to attachment, his sureties cannot require
obligee, by notice in writing, to forthwith institute an action aga
the principal.

ATTACHMENT—ACTION ON BOND—SUFFICIENCY OF COMPLAINT.—A compl
in an action against sureties in an attachment bond which alleges
execution of the bond by the principal, and sets out a copy thereof
the names of the sureties appended, but fails to allege that they joi
in its execution, is insufficient on demurrer.

ATTACHMENT—LIABILITY OF SURETIES ON BOND.—Sureties on an attachn
bond are liable thereon for damages in the first instance, without
demand on the principal, or suit against him to adjudicate the dama
and nonpayment, in the absence of statute to the contrary.

ATTACHMENT—LIABILITY ON BOND—ESTOPPEL.—Persons who have jo
in giving a bond for the attachment of the property of a corporation
not deny its corporate existence.

ATTACHMENT—LIABILITY OF SURETIES—WRONGFUL LEVY—REASON.
CAUSE.—For sureties upon an attachment bond to avoid liability
actual damages for a wrongful levy, reasonable cause for the attach
must exist as a fact, and credible information of facts sufficient to
rant a belief in the existence of reasonable cause tends merely to
prove malice, and thereby to relieve from exemplary damages.

ATTACHMENT—DAMAGES FOR WRONGFUL LEVY—WANT OF REASON
CAUSE.—In an action upon an attachment bond to recover damag
a wrongful levy, the plaintiff in order to recover need only show th
charge of the writ and want of reasonable cause by proof as to the
duct of his affairs and the good faith of his transactions.

ATTACHMENT—LIABILITY ON BOND FOR WRONGFUL LEVY BY AGENT.—
bility upon an attachment bond for a malicious levy accrues if the p
whose direct act caused the writ to be issued was actuated by mal
motives, although the principal for whom he acted as agent knew n
of the transaction, unless it is shown that the agent had no author
attach under any circumstances, and that his act in attaching w
firmatively repudiated as soon as knowledge of it was received.

ATTACHMENT—WRONGFUL LEVY.—LOSS OF BUSINESS CREDIT is not an element of damages in an action on an attachment bond for a wrongful levy.

ATTACHMENT—MALICIOUS LEVY.—EXEMPLARY DAMAGES may be recovered
in an action on an attachment bond, when the writ was maliciously sued
out and levied.

Burke, Shepard and Woods, for the appellants.

Blaine and De Vries, for the respondent.

[303] STILES, J.   Cerf, Schloss & Co., of San Francisco,
brought suit in the United States circuit court against the respondent for the recovery of certain money, a large part of
which was not due.   In aid of their suit an attachment was
issued, in pursuance of which the marshal seized the entire
stock of goods of the respondent, and held them during six
days, until the writ was discharged, on the ground that it had
been improperly issued.   This was an action upon the attachment bond against the sureties only, [304] the principals
being nonresidents, and not appearing, although they were
nominally parties.

1. The first point to be noticed is the action of the court
below in striking out two defenses based upon the Code of Procedure, section 756, which provides that a surety may require a
creditor or obligee, by notice in writing, to forthwith institute
an action upon the contract.   As was said above, the principals on the bond were nonresidents, and it was not made to
appear that they had any property in this state liable to attachment.   For these reasons the statute had no application
to the case: *Phillips* v. *Riley,* 27 Mo. 386; *Conklin* v. *Conklin,*
54 Ind. 289.

2. This was a joint and several statutory bond of indemnity, and the rules in such cases, as to strictness of allegation and proof, were in full force.   But the complaint did not
allege the execution of the bond by the sureties, nor was
there any proof addressed to that point.   The eighth paragraph of the complaint was as follows:

"8. That at the time of filing said (attachment) affidavit
and complaint, to wit, the said seventeenth day of January,
1891, and in compliance with the statute in such case made
and provided, and as a condition upon which the said writ of
attachment should issue, the defendants, Rudolph Cerf and
Benjamin Schloss, made, executed and filed in said circuit
court a bond for attachment in the words and figures following ": . . . .

And the answer admitted the facts stated to be true.
general demurrer, in which the deficiency of the eighth p.
graph was pointed out, was overruled, and on the trial the c₁
treated the case as if the fact that the complaint contain₁
copy of the bond in which Haley and Schram were name₁
sureties, and to which their names were appended, was s·
cient to charge them with the execution of the instrum
and put them to an affirmative denial of that proposit
Citations by counsel for respondent on this point do not ₁
tain him. A late one is *McClellan* [305] *Drydock Co.* v. *Fα*
ers' Alliance Steamboat Line, 43 La. Ann. 258, in which
bond was annexed to the petition, and the prayer as
judgment against the principal and sureties *in solido.*
appearance was for all of the defendants, and the c₁
said:

"The defect of the petition in not alleging specifically ₁
Marston was indebted is cured by the annexing of the b
which was made part of the petition, and which exhib:
his liability, by his answer without exception, and by the
ministration of proof without objection."

If the case at bar had gone through all its stages to
trial, and evidence of the execution of the bond by the s₁
ties had been received, without objection, a different ₁
would be presented.

In *Pefley* v. *Johnson*, 30 Neb. 529, the complaint alle₁
that "plaintiff entered into a contract in writing with
defendant, a copy of which was attached;" and we fin₁
every case of this kind examined some words of allega₁
which show execution of the instrument by the party t₁
charged, upon which the courts, although they do not f₁
that method of pleading, accept the recitals of the ins
ment as allegations of fact as far as they go: *Lambert* v. ₁
kell, 80 Cal. 611.

Clement v. *Hughes* (Ky., October 22, 1891) was an
tion upon a guardian's bond, and it was there said:

"It is necessary, in an action upon a writing, to aver
acts and omissions by the defendant as entitled the pla₁
to relief; and this rule is not complied with in an a
against a surety, unless the petition avers the executi₁
the writing by him, and the substance of his agreement.

But in that case, inasmuch as the petition averred tha₁
guardian executed a bond with the defendants as sur₁
and as the bond was copied into the petition, it was so₁

necessary to allege further the substance of the contract, for
what the sureties covenanted to do was supplied by the copy.
We understand that the rules of pleading go thus far in
favor of exhibits, and no farther.

This holding will necessitate the reversal of the judgment,
but there are other matters to be considered, in view of the
new trial.

3. Appellants claim that the sureties are not liable in the
first instance for the damages, but only after demand on the
principal, or suit against him to adjudicate the damages, and
nonpayment. It is sufficient to say that the statute does not
require a bond conditioned that the plaintiff will pay on demand, or will pay any judgment that may be obtained
against him. Such courts as have held demand, or a judgment in a distinct action, to be prerequisite to recovery on an
attachment bond have based their rulings on their peculiar
statutes: Note to *Burton* v. *Knapp*, 81 Am. Dec. 468; Drake
on Attachments, sec. 166; 2 Wade on Attachments, sec. 298.

4. When it has been established that persons have joined
in giving a bond for the attachment of property of a corporation, they are not in a position to deny its corporate existence; so the alleged errors in proving the corporation in this
case were immaterial.

5. The affidavit for the attachment alleged that the Seattle
Crockery Company was about to dispose of its property with
intent to defraud its creditors, and that it had so disposed of
its property, or a portion thereof. A traverse of these allegations was followed by an order to discharge the attachment,
upon oral proofs of the parties. No findings were made, but
we think, in such a case, it must be taken that the adjudication was final as to the wrongfulness of the attachment.
Now, if the Code of Procedure, section 293, stood alone, it would
seem that the production of the record here would have entitled the respondent to nominal damages, for, by [307] that section, the bond is conditioned that the plaintiff will prosecute
his action without delay, will pay all costs that may be
adjudged to the defendant, and all damages which he may sustain by reason of the attachment should the same be wrongfully, oppressively or maliciously sued out. Nothing is
therein said about reasonable cause. But, when we come to
section 295, we find that recovery upon the bond depends
upon the plaintiff's showing: 1. A wrongful suing out of the
attachment and that there was no reasonable cause to believe

the ground upon which the same was issued to be true, wl
he may recover actual damages and attorney's fees; 2.
malicious suing out of the writ, when he may recover exe
plary damages also.

This looks like a hard statute to comply with, since it
volves the proof of a negative, viz., want of reasonable cau
Appellants maintain that the correct course for the respoi
ent was to begin with the assumption that the attachm(
was wrongful, as appeared from the record of the circ
court, and then to proceed to show that the attaching crec
ors did not have information worthy of credit of facts justi
ing a belief in the existence of the grounds alleged in tb
affidavit; that is, they contend that the reasonable ca\
meant is a state of mind produced in the attaching party,
information which he believes to be true. But the pl\
reading of the statute is not that way. It does not depe
upon the state of mind of anybody, but upon the true facts
the case. It is for the plaintiff in any such case, if there I
been no previous adjudication, to lay before the jury the fa
concerning his affairs sufficiently to show that as they w
known, or might have been known by reasonable inqui
there were no fraudulent transactions on his part, and n(
upon which the ordinary business man would naturally l(
with suspicion; for if one act suspiciously there may be r
sonable cause to justify a belief that a fraud has been, o
about to be, [308] perpetrated, although no fraud be intend
But the facts and acts must exist; mere tale-bearing, althoi
believed in, will not supply their absence. Reasonable
probable cause is a different thing from the information u
which a belief in its existence may be based. To avoid
ability upon the bond for actual damages, the reasonable ca
must exist as a fact; but credible information of facts si
cient to warrant a belief in the existence of reasonable ca
will tend to disprove malice, and thereby to relieve from
emplary damages.

In this matter we are compelled to take issue with
supreme court of Iowa, which has frequently held that
plaintiff in such a case must not only prove that no c\
existed for an attachment, but also that the defendant
no reasonably credible information that such a cause exis
Burton v. *Knapp*, 14 Iowa, 196; 81 Am. Dec. 465; *Vor*
Phillips, 37 Iowa, 428; *Dent* v. *Smith*, 53 Iowa, 262. The 1
named case was decided under a statute as to bonds, and \

upon them, in substance like the statutes of most of the states:
Iowa Stats. 1860; and we think the Iowa supreme court stood
alone in holding that the actual damages were not recoverable
when the attachment was issued without cause existing therefor: *Jerman* v. *Stewart,* 12 Fed. Rep. 271.   The last two cases,
however, were decided under a statute precisely like our own:
Iowa Stats., 1888; and the only one which is like it, in the
section governing recoveries on the bond.   To say that a
debtor may be deprived of the use of his property, not for any
fault of his own, but because his creditor believes that he has
been in fault, is to make his rights depend upon a matter
which the law cannot, and does not pretend to, regulate, viz.,
the nature and condition of the creditor's mind; and is to put
him, upon the trial of his suit for damages, to proof of facts
which he can get positively from no other source but the
creditor himself, which [309] would be entirely unreasonable.
Moreover, different creditors, whose rights to have an attachment are equal when a cause exists, would be placed upon an
entirely different footing if the writ should be discharged for
want of actual cause.   When one creditor attaches, others are
likely to, deeming that the affidavit of the first one on file is
sufficient information to lead a prudent person to act; but in
a suit for damages the first one would escape, under the Iowa
rule, because he had credible information, while the second
would pay the full penalty.   The language of the statute is:
"And that there was no reasonable cause to believe the
ground . . . . to be true."   The "ground" in this case was
that respondent had disposed of its property with intent to
defraud its creditors, and that it was about to do so; but the
"cause" for believing that ground to be true was not the statement of any one that there was a cause, but a fact, or facts;
as, for example, a sham sale of crockery to a third person,
without consideration, with the understanding that he was to
hold it or sell it for the benefit of the respondent, or a plan or
scheme devised for that purpose, but not yet executed.   This
cause the law requires the plaintiff to prove to be non-exist-
ant.

It was competent, therefore, for the respondent to show:
1. The discharge of the writ; 2. The want of reasonable
cause, by proof as to the conduct of its affairs and the good
faith of its transactions; and 3. Under the allegations of the
complaint, the malicious action of the attachment plaintiff.
If at any stage of the case before the cause was submitted to

the jury it abandoned the charge of malice, all evidence u[
that subject, and upon the question of exemplary damag
should have been withdrawn.

What Mr. Carson stated at the hearing in **the circu**it co
we do not think was admissible. He was the collection cl
for the attorneys of Cerf, Schloss & Co., [310] with whom so
conversation was had by one of respondent's officers regardi
the claim of Cerf, Schloss & Co., and it seems to be admit!
that upon that interview and his report of it to Mr. Shepa
who made the affidavit, depends the question whether C
Schloss & Co. had information of any fact which tended
show them that a fraud was threatened. It was sufficie
therefore, for respondent, after showing that no actual cai
existed, to prove the interview with Carson, and stop, J
there being no cause, and, according to its version of the c
versation, nothing said, to lead any one to suspect an int
tion to perpetrate a fraud, it must follow that the attachm
was so recklessly obtained that malice could be argued the
from. From that point it was for the appellants either
dispute the facts in regard to the conversation, or to sh
that Carson had reported it in such a way as to justif
belief that fraud would be attempted if the claim w
pressed, or both; but what Carson reported was only ma
rial in case the charge of malice were pressed. Informat
of such a character from a trusted and confidential emplo
ought to relieve the principal from the charge of malice w
there is no affirmative showing of it, but only a presumpt
from the fact that the attachment was issued without the
istence of reasonable cause therefor.

6. We hold that liability upon the bond for a malici
attachment accrues if the person whose direct act cause!
to be issued was actuated by malicious motives, although
principal for whom he acted as agent knew nothing of
transaction, until it is shown that the agent had no autho
to attach under any circumstances, and that the act of
agent in attaching was affirmatively repudiated as soo!
knowledge of it was received.

7. Some of the evidence in this case was received upon
theory that the respondent might prove damages for lo
business credit, which it alleged it had suffered to [311]
extent of four thousand dollars; and in its charge to the
the court, after stating to them that all question of m
was withdrawn from their consideration, **instructed** as fol

upon the subject of damages for wrongful issuance of an attachment without reasonable cause:

"1. The court further instructs the jury that if they find for the plaintiff, that in the assessment of actual damages they can consider what, if anything, the plaintiff has suffered in its credit as a merchant."

2. A substantial repetition of the foregoing, with limitations taken, as is said, largely from the charge in *Kennedy* v. *Meacham*, 18 Fed. Rep. 312.

"3. The only damages recoverable in this action are the actual damages caused by the attachment, and such damages only include the current expenses of the business during the detention of the store and stock, and the loss of actual net profits, if any, during that time, besides reasonable attorney's fees, to be fixed by the court upon the proper evidence. Actual damages do not include prospective profits of the business, because they are inevitably uncertain and speculative in their nature, and depend on so many remote chances of trade and of subsequent causes."

The third charge was inconsistent with the first two, for it entirely withdrew from the jury the matter of damages to credit. But if that effect was intended by the court it was of no avail, since the jury brought in a verdict of four thousand dollars, more than three-fourths of which must have been allowed for injury to the respondent's credit as a merchant. We conclude that it was not the intention to take this element of credit away from the jury, however, because of the court's refusal to grant a new trial.

Respondent strenuously maintains that injury to the credit of a merchant ought to be allowed in these cases, and some authorities are cited in support of the proposition: *Kennedy* v. *Meacham*, 18 Fed. Rep. 312, is the most outspoken, and *312* follows precedents set in Alabama: *Donnell* v. *Jones*, 13 Ala. 490, 48 Am. Dec. 59.

In *Meyer* v. *Fagan*, 34 Neb. 184, a recovery for loss of credit seems to have been allowed to stand; but the question before the supreme court of Nebraska seems to have been only whether the sum recovered was excessive. No discussion of the subject of damages to credit is in the case. About the same state of things is found in *MacVeagh* v. *Bailey*, 29 Ill. App. 606.

In 7 Lawson's Rights, Remedies, and Practice, sec. 3549, the effect of the attachment upon credit is said to be a proper matter for consideration in assessing damages, the only authority cited being *Kennedy* v. *Meacham*, 18 Fed. Rep. 812, but in section 3551 the contrary doctrine is laid down, and numerous cases are cited.

The general doctrine of the law is that remote, speculative and uncertain damages cannot be recovered for; and injury to credit must necessarily be of the most uncertain value, even when its ascertainment is guarded by the most careful instructions a court can possibly give. What mercantile character and credit are, is clearly defined in *Donnell* v. *Jones,* 13 Ala. 490; 48 Am. Dec. 59.

"By character, in this connection," says the court, "we mean the generally received opinion in the community respecting the solvency of the firm—the probity and punctuality with which it discharged its obligations, and the efficiency with which its affairs are managed. Credit, which is usually the result of those qualities and capacities we have named, may be defined, the ability to borrow money or obtain goods in virtue of the opinion conceived by the lender, or seller, that the party will repay."

While the issuance of an attachment may do injury to this mercantile character and credit of a debtor, it is, in that respect, not different from other judicial proceedings. If the allegations of the affidavit are in the one case libelous, **812** and tend to break down the confidence theretofore reposed in the defendant, they are no more so than would be a complaint in a suit for money obtained by alleged false pretenses. And so this kind of injury may be brought about as effectually where no property at all has been taken under the writ. The commencement of an ordinary suit upon a promissory note has fully as great a tendency to impair credit as any other proceeding, for the presumption is that a business man will take care of his notes at least, if he has any regard for his standing in the commercial world; and, if he cannot take care of them so that he has to be sued, the inference most naturally is that he is weak in resources, and, therefore, not a safe person to credit. But the note may be forged, or not due, or paid, or there may be counterclaims or good defenses so that the suit is totally unjustifiable. But does anyone sue for damages to credit growing out of such proceedings? Not at all, because they are privileged, being proceedings in courts of justice. And so we think this attachment proceeding, and all allegations of fraud made therein, although they may injure the character, reputation or credit of the defendant, are in the same way privileged, and not to be recovered for. All actual damages for the physical taking of property must be compensated under the statute, and when the proceeding is instituted maliciously, exemplary damages can be allowed, at the reasonable discretion of the jury under the evidence. This court in *Spokane Truck etc. Co. v. Hoefer*, 2 Wash. 45, 26 Am. St. Rep. 842, did not undertake to say that, where the statute expressly provided for them, punitive damages could not be recovered.   In such cases, the rules laid down in those jurisdictions where the doctrine of punitive damages is accepted should guide the courts and juries of this state.   The actual damages in this case, under the pleadings, consisted: 1. Of the costs and expenses of the motion to [314] discharge the attachment, including the attorney's fee paid or agreed to be paid therefor, if the same was a reasonable fee; but if a gross fee was paid or promised for the whole case in the circuit court the fee for the motion must be apportioned out of that; and the fee allowed must be no more than a reasonable fee in any event, to be determined by the court without the intervention of the jury; 2. The ascertainable profits of the business while the property was in the possession of the marshal, under a liberal construction of the evidence; 3. Rent and clerk hire during the same time; 4. Actual depreciation of the value of the goods by reason of the marshal's possession and treatment of them, not including, however, any fanciful notion of depreciation because of their having been a "bankrupt stock"; and 5. A reasonable attorney's fee to be fixed by the court for the prosecution of this action for damages, not including the trial already had or the appeal.

We have passed upon this case, not knowing whether the question of malice would be in it upon a retrial or not; and the objections and exceptions to rulings upon evidence and instructions were so numerous and complicated that it was impracticable to review them singly.   We believe what has been said will serve to indicate how this court regards the several matters before it.

The judgment is reversed, and a new trial granted; the respondent having leave to amend its complaint.

DUNBAR, C. J., ANDERS and SCOTT, JJ., concur.

HOYT, J., concurring.   I think that the complaint, when, fairly construed, alleged the execution of the bond by the

sureties as well as the principal.   As to the other questions
discussed, and in the disposition of the case, I concur.

SURETYSHIP—EXHAUSTING REMEDY AGAINST PRINCIPAL.—A surety has
no right to require the creditor to satisfy his demand out of the property of
the principal before proceeding against him: *Morrison* v. *Citizens' Nat. Bank,*
65 N. H. 253; 23 Am. St. Rep. 39, and note; *Abercrombie* v. *Knox,* 3 Ala.
728; 37 Am. Dec. 721, and note; *Martin* v. *Pope,* 6 Ala. 532; 41 Am. Dec.
66.

ATTACHMENT BOND—LIABILITY OF SURETIES—WRONGFUL LEVY—REA-
SONABLE CAUSE.—To sustain an action for a malicious attachment, it must
be shown that the writ was issued maliciously and without probable cause:
Beyersdorf v. *Sump,* 49 Minn. 495; 12 Am. St. Rep. 678, and note; *Calhoun*
v. *Hannan,* 87 Ala. 277.   In an action for wrongful and vexatious attachment the defendant may show that he acted in good faith, in order to disprove malice and avoid exemplary damages, but such a plea is not a bar to
the action: *Donnell* v. *Jones,* 13 Ala. 490; 48 Am. Dec. 59.   See, further, the
extended note to *Burton* v. *Knapp,* 81 Am. Dec. 467.

ATTACHMENT—MALICIOUS LEVY—DAMAGES.—The damages which may be
recovered for a malicious attachment must be restricted to the injury done
by the writ without reference to what it may have caused another creditor
to do: *Goodbar* v. *Lindsley,* 51 Ark. 380; 14 Am. St. Rep. 54, and note; *Reed*
v. *Samuels,* 22 Tex. 114; 73 Am. Dec. 253, and note; *Dickinson* v. *Maynard,*
20 La. Ann. 66; 96 Am. Dec. 379, and note; *McLane* v. *McTighe,* 89 Ala.
411.   For the detention of property wrongfully seized under attachment the
measure of damages is the value of the use of the property while detained:
Turner v. *Younker,* 76 Iowa, 258.   See the extended note to *Burton* v.
Knapp, 81 Am. Dec. 472.

ATTACHMENT—MALICIOUS LEVY—EXEMPLARY DAMAGES.—Where an attachment is maliciously sued out with the intent to injure and harass the
defendant, exemplary damages may be awarded: *Reed* v. *Samuels,* 22 Tex.
114; 73 Am. Dec. 253; *Ellis* v. *Bonner,* 80 Tex. 198; 26 Am. St. Rep. 731,
and note; *Anderson* v. *Harrison,* 38 Mo. 258; 90 Am. Dec. 431, and note;
Chaffe v. *Mackenzie,* 43 La. Ann. 1063.

NEUFELDER *v.* GERMAN AMERICAN INSURANCE CO.

[6 WASHINGTON, 336.]

ATTACHMENT—SERVICE BY PUBLICATION.—If property is attached and the
defendant served by publication only the court has jurisdiction to render
a judgment personal in form, but affecting only the property attached.

ATTACHMENT.—NONRESIDENT IS NOT SUBJECT TO GARNISHMENT unless
when garnished, he has, in the state where the action is pending, and
the attachment is obtained, property of the defendant under his control, or is bound to pay the defendant money, or to deliver to him goods
at some particular place in that state.

INSURANCE POLICY—WHERE ENFORCEABLE.—It is no part or ingredient of
a contract of insurance that it shall be enforced only in conformity to
the law of the place where it is executed.   On the contrary it can gen-

erally be enforced in any state where the company issuing it can be legally served with process.

Garnishment While in the Nature of a Proceeding in Rem is in effect an action by the defendant in the plaintiff's name against the garnishee, the purpose and result of which are to subrogate the plaintiff to the rights of the defendant against the garnishee.

Attachment.—Though Situs of Intangible Personalty may be at the domicile of the creditor for the purpose of taxation or distribution, yet for the purpose of collecting a debt it is ambulatory, accompanying the person of the debtor, and may be attached wherever he may be found.

Garnishment in Another State.—When a foreign insurance company is garnished in one state upon its indebtedness to a citizen of another state, such garnishment is a good defense to an action in the latter state against the company for the same debt.

Strudwick, Peters, and Van Wyck, for the appellant.

Stratton, Lewis, and Gilman, for the respondent.

336 Anders, J. This action was brought by the appellant to recover from the respondent the sum of one thousand dollars alleged to be due upon a policy of fire insurance issued by the respondent to one C. H. Knox, the assignor of the appellant. The respondent is a corporation incorporated and existing under the laws of the state of New York, and, at the time of issuing the policy under consideration, was lawfully authorized to transact business in this state. It also carried on business in Oregon, California, and other states and territories on the Pacific coast, and had a general agent for the management of its business in all of said states and territories, including Washington, whose office was at San Francisco, in the state of California. Its funds for the payment of losses were kept by this general agent, or manager, at San Francisco, and disbursed by him as occasion required, the local agents in the several states having no authority to pay or settle for losses except by his special instructions. On September 11, 1890, the respondent **337** issued a policy of insurance whereby it insured C. H. Knox against loss or damage by fire to the amount of one thousand dollars on a stock of merchandise belonging to him, or in which he was interested, in Seattle, from the eleventh day of September, 1890, to the eleventh day of September, 1891, which policy was duly executed by the respondent through its president and secretary in the state of New York, and countersigned by its duly authorized agent in the city of Seattle, and by said agent there delivered to said Knox. On the nineteenth day of September, 1890, the property so insured was destroyed by fire, and the loss was duly adjusted at the sum of one thousand dollars. On the twenty-fifth day of October, 1890, the assured made a general assignment for the benefit of his creditors, in accordance with the insolvency laws of this state, to the appellant, who accepted the trust and duly qualified as assignee.

After the loss occurred, and prior to the assignment of Knox to the appellant, certain creditors of Knox residing in San Francisco commenced actions in the superior court of the city and county of San Francisco, to recover the amounts due them, and caused the debt due from the respondent to Knox upon the insurance policy to be attached, in accordance with the laws of California, by delivering a copy of the writs of attachment to one Grant, the general agent of the company, together with a notice that the debt owing by respondent to the said Knox was attached in pursuance of said writs. The respondent admits its liability on the policy upon which this action was brought, and does not seek to evade the payment of the sum due, but contends that the levy of the garnishment process in California prior to the time of the assignment to the appellant is a bar to this action. Knox is a resident of this state, and no personal service was made upon him, nor did he enter an appearance in either of the actions in the state ³³⁸ of California in which the attachments were levied. The service of summons was made by publication, in the manner and for the length of time provided by the laws of California. Upon the facts found, concerning which there is no controversy, the court below entered judgment in favor of the respondent, and the question for our determination on this appeal is whether or not the court committed error in so doing.

It is contended by the appellant that the California court never obtained jurisdiction of the debt owing by the respondent to Knox, because the *situs* of the debt was either at the domicile of the creditor or at the domicile of the debtor, and in either event was not within the jurisdiction of the court. And the argument is that the claim of Knox against the insurance company is personal property, and, as such, follows the person of the owner; but that if its *situs* was at the domicile of the debtor, still it was in this state and not in California, for the reason that the policy of insurance was executed here, by a company doing business here, and whose domicile was therefore here for all purposes connected therewith, and especially for the purpose of suit upon the contract.

It is conceded by the respondent that by establishing agencies and doing business here and appointing an agent upon whom service of process should be made, as required by our statute, it became amenable to all the laws of this state concerning foreign corporations, including the liability to be sued for the enforcement of its obligations. And it is not contended by the respondent that the proceedings in the California court are entitled to any faith or credit here if that court had not jurisdiction of the respondent, and of the debt attempted to be garnished there. It is well settled that if a court has neither jurisdiction of the person of the defendant nor of his property, it has nothing [339] before it upon which it can adjudicate, and that any judgment it may render under such circumstances is of no validity whatever: *Pennoyer* v. *Neff*, 95 U. S. 714.

But it is not necessary, in order that a valid judgment may be rendered, that both the person and property of the defendant be within the territorial jurisdiction of the court. If property is attached, and the defendant is not personally served, and does not appear, and publication of the summons is duly and regularly made, the court has jurisdiction to render a judgment personal in form, but which affects only what is attached. But such judgment will not authorize an execution against any other property, nor can it be made the basis of an action against the defendant: Drake on Attachments, 7th ed., sec. 5; *Cooper* v. *Reynolds*, 10 Wall. 308.

The first inquiry therefore is, was the property of Knox attached by the service of the writ and notice upon the respondent at San Francisco? And, there being no question as to the regularity of the garnishment proceedings, the answer must depend upon whether or not the respondent and the debt owing by it to the attachment defendant were within the jurisdiction of the court. There is no question but what the money to pay the debt was in the possession of the respondent at San Francisco, although the particular sum required had not been set apart for that purpose prior to the service of the garnishment process. The laws of California provide that any credit or other personal property in the possession or under the control of any person, or debts owing to the defendant, may be attached in the manner therein prescribed: See Deering's Code of Civil Procedure, secs. 542–544. And under such a statute there is no doubt that a resident may be charged as garnishee in respect of a debt he owes to a nonresident. But a nonresident is not subject to garnishment unless, when garnished, he have, in the state where the action is pending, and the [340] attachment is obtained, property of the defendant under his control, or he be bound to pay the defendant money, or to deliver to him goods at some particular place in that state: Hawes on Jurisdiction of Courts, sec. 253; 2 Drake on Attachments, 7th ed., sec. 474, and cases cited.

But it is claimed by the learned counsel for the appellant that this rule is not applicable in this case for the reason, as already stated, that the respondent cannot be deemed to have a domicile other than in this state, in respect to business transacted here, and for the further reason that the debt sought to be attached is, and always has been, at the domicile of the creditor in this state.

As to the validity of the policy of insurance, if that were in issue, we should say that the contract should be interpreted by the laws of this state: 1 May on Insurance, sec. 66; Wharton on Conflict of Laws, sec. 399; 3 Am. & Eng. Ency. of Law, 551.

But we are not prepared to say that it can only be enforced in our own courts. On the contrary we are of the opinion that the assured himself might have brought an action on his policy in California, or in any other state where the insurance company could be legally served with process.

It is no part or ingredient of the contract of insurance that it shall be enforced only in conformity to the law of the place where it is executed: *Griswold v. Union Mutual Ins. Co.*, 3 Blatchf. 231.

And as, in this instance, Knox could have collected his claim against the respondent in the courts of California it follows that his creditors there had the same right to collect it by process of garnishment, and to apply the proceeds in satisfaction of their demands against him. In fact garnishment, while in the nature of a proceeding *in rem.*, is, in effect, an action by the defendant in the plaintiff's name against the garnishee, the purpose and result of which is to subrogate the plaintiff to the rights of the defendant [341] against the garnishee: 2 Drake on Attachments, 7th ed., sec. 452.

As to the liability of foreign corporations to garnishment we think the law is correctly summarized in 8 Am. & Eng. Ency. of Law, 1131, as follows:

"Except, therefore, in those states where it is held that corporations are in no event subject to garnishment, a foreign corporation may be charged as garnishee in all cases where

an original action might be maintained against it for the recovery of the property or credit in respect to which the garnishment is served."

Although the *situs* of intangible personal property may be
at the domicile of the creditor for the purpose of taxation or
distribution, yet for the purpose of collection a debt is
ambulatory, and accompanies the person of a debtor. We
think this debt was properly attached in California. And
that being so the attachment proceedings there constitute a
defense to this action: *Embree* v. *Hanna*, 5 Johns. 101;
Wheeler v. *Raymond*, 8 Cow. 315, note a; *Andrews* v. *Herriot*,
4 Cow. 521; *Dittenhoefer* v. *Cœur d'Alene Clothing Co.*, 4
Wash. 519.

In the case last above cited this court held that where a
foreign corporation does business in this state, under the laws
prescribed by our legislature, and has an attorney appointed
upon whom service in any proceedings in the courts in this
state may be made, it thereby becomes subject to garnishment here. We have no doubt of the correctness of that
decision, and are therefore bound to recognize the doctrine
therein enunciated when affirmed by courts in other states
which, like California, have statutes substantially like our
own.

The further point is made by the appellant that the plaintiffs in the attachment suits, by filing their claims with the
assignee (appellant), thereby abandoned any rights they [342]
may have had under the attachments. If the objection is at
all available it is certainly not applicable to the action of
Isadore Leviere, in which the amount sued for was two thousand four hundred and thirty-nine dollars and twenty-one
cents, and was made up of various assigned claims, only one
of which was filed with the assignee in this state, and that
only for the sum of two hundred and seventy-nine dollars
and ninety-two cents. The remaining attaching creditors
cannot be affected by the action of those who filed their
claims, and as the amount claimed is largely in excess of the
debt attached the result would be the same to the appellant,
even if we should adopt the rule of law contended for by
him.

The judgment of the court below is affirmed.

Dunbar, C. J., and Scott and Stiles, JJ., concur.

Hoyt, J., dissents.

JURISDICTION—ATTACHMENT.—In attachment suits the property must be within the jurisdiction of the court issuing the process in order to confer jurisdiction: *Douglass* v. *Phenix Ins. Co.*, 138 N. Y. 209; 34 Am. St. Rep. 448, and note. Since property outside of the state cannot be garnished; *Bowen* v. *Pope*, 125 Ill. 28; 8 Am. St. Rep. 330, and note; *Bates* v. *Chicago etc. Ry. Co.*, 60 Wis. 296; 50 Am. Rep. 369.

JURISDICTION TO RENDER A PERSONAL JUDGMENT cannot be obtained against a defendant who does not reside within the state, and upon whom service of process is had only by publication and who does not appear in the action: *Renier* v. *Hurlbut*, 81 Wis. 24; 29 Am. St. Rep. 850, and note. See *Carden* v. *Carden*, 107 N. C. 214; 22 Am. St. Rep. 876, and note, and *McCann* v. *Randall*, 147 Mass. 81; 9 Am. St. Rep. 666, for a further discussion of the subject of attachment against nonresidents.

PORTER v. TULL.

[6 WASHINGTON, 408.]

LANDLORD AND TENANT—DESTRUCTION OF PREMISES—RECOVERY OF RENT PAID IN ADVANCE.—A tenant in possession of premises for which he pays a monthly rental in advance is entitled to recover the amount paid for that part of the month remaining after the total destruction of the premises by fire or otherwise.

Nash and Nash, for the appellant.

Jones, Belt, and Quinn, for the respondent.

408 DUNBAR, C. J. This is an action for the recovery of lease money paid in advance according to the terms of the lease. The respondent, F. M. Tull, the owner and lessor of the leased premises, rented and leased to A. H. Porter and C. F. Jackson certain rooms and portions of the building known as the Tull block, in the city of Spokane. The lessees paid the stipulated rent according to the terms of the lease, monthly in advance, including the month of August, **409** 1889. On the fourth day of August, 1889, the building was destroyed by fire, and Porter for himself, and as the assignee of Jackson. brings this action to recover from Tull the money paid in advance for the remainder of the month of August, 1889.

It is contended by the appellant that the authorities in this country fully sustain the proposition that when there is a total destruction of the subject matter of the lease the rent shall be apportioned, and the tenant is no longer liable on his covenant. This proposition is conceded by the respondent so far as it applies to rent that is due for periods subsequent to

the term for which the rent is paid in advance; but he insists
that a distinction must be made here, and that inasmuch as
the parties have contracted that the money must be paid in
advance, it follows that they have apportioned the risk, or
settled it between them; that the tenant assumes the risk of
losing the rent for the time for which he has paid in advance,
and the landlord assumes the risk of losing subsequent payments, besides the loss of his building.

We are unable to discover any real foundation in logic,
law, or justice for this distinction. The consideration, for
which the lessee pays a monthly rent in advance, is not that
he may be put in possession of the building for a day, or two
days, or a week, but the real consideration is the use and possession of the building for a month. That is the valuable
thing for which he contracts and for which he parts with his
money; and there is an implied contract on the part of the
lessor to furnish him the use of the building for the time for
which he pays for it. It cannot be presumed that because a
lessee pays in advance that he has in contemplation the fixing of a different degree of liability in case of the destruction
of the leased premises by fire; neither is it so intended by
the lessor. It is simply a prudential requirement on his part
to secure the rent, and to [410] protect himself against the
chances of losing it, and the inconvenience and trouble of collecting it. Conceding that the lessee is not liable for the destruction of the leased building for the remainder of the period
for which the building was leased, there must be something
more to warrant the presumption that the parties intended to
establish a different degree of liability than the mere fact that
the money was paid in advance. What difference can there
be in principle, so far as fixing liability is concerned, whether
the contract is to pay the rent monthly in advance or monthly
at the end of the month?

Great stress is placed by respondent on the idea that the
parties have made a positive contract, and that they are
bound by its terms. The contract in one instance is as positive and binding as in the other, and the liability to pay at
the end of the month is as much fixed by such contract as
the liability to pay in advance is fixed by the contract, and
the same reasoning that would prevent the recovery of the
money paid in advance would compel the payment of the
money under the other contract at the end of the month after
the destruction of the building.

We are not cited to any adjudicated cases on this point.
The reason probably is that no one has ever questioned the
right of the lessee to recover money paid for that which he
never received. We think the complaint states a good cause
of action, and that the court erred in sustaining the demurrer.
The judgment is reversed, and the cause remanded, with instructions to overrule the demurrer, and to proceed in accordance with this opinion.

HOYT, ANDERS, and SCOTT, JJ., concur.

STILES, J., dissents.

LANDLORD AND TENANT—EFFECT ON LEASE OF DESTRUCTION OF LEASED
PREMISES.—See the extended notes to *McMillan* v. *Solomon,* 94 Am. Dec.
662, and *Whittaker* v. *Hawley,* 37 Am. Rep. 283. The destruction by fire
of leased premises does not relieve the tenant from his agreement to pay
rent in the absence of a stipulation to the contrary: *Cowell* v. *Lumley,* 39
Cal. 151; 2 Am. Rep. 430; *Womack* v. *McQuarry,* 28 Ind. 103; 92 Am. Dec.
306, and note with the cases collected. See also *Coogan* v. *Parker,* 2 S. C.
255; 16 Am. Rep. 659, where the contrary doctrine was maintained.

WASHINGTON NATIONAL BANK *v.* PIERCE.

[6 WASHINGTON, 491.]

CORPORATIONS—NOTICE TO AGENT AS NOTICE TO.—Notice to the president
of a bank by the maker of a note that it was procured by fraud and
without consideration, and will not be paid, is not notice to the bank,
and will not make it liable for subsequently discounting the note, when
such notice was not given to the president in his official capacity, nor at
the bank, nor with any reference to the bank's business.

NEGOTIABLE INSTRUMENTS—DISCOUNTING BEFORE MATURITY—DUTY TO
MAKE INQUIRY.—When a note payable one year after date has been
discounted by a bank one month before maturity, it can make no possible difference as affecting the right of the bank to recover, whether
or not it is customary for it to make inquiry as to the *bona fides* of all
such paper so discounted by it.

Stevens, Seymour and Sharpstein, for the appellant.

Frank D. Nash, for the respondent.

⁴⁹¹ DUNBAR, C. J. Defendant made his promissory note
in writing, wherein he promised to pay to the order of one
⁴⁹² Cromwell, fifteen hundred dollars one year after date,
with interest at ten per cent until paid. Before the note became due, the plaintiff, a bank, purchased the same from
Cromwell at a discount. After demand and refusal to pay,

the bank brought this action to collect the note from defendant, appellant herein.   The defendant for answer alleged fraud on the part of Cromwell in procuring the note, want of consideration, false representations, etc., and alleged that prior to the time said note came into the possession of plaintiff, that plaintiff well knew, had full knowledge and due notice that the said note was obtained by fraud, and was given without consideration, and that the defendant intended to resist the payment of the same.   Upon the trial of the cause the court instructed the jury to return a verdict for the plaintiff for the amount prayed for.

The view we take of the insufficiency of the notice given to the bank renders unnecessary an examination of the question of want of consideration; for, conceding that the note was fraudulently obtained, we think that the testimony very clearly shows that Ouimette, the president of the bank, did not have such notice as would bind the bank.   It is doubtless true that under certain circumstances notice to the president of a bank is notice to the bank, but we think that no case can be found where notice given under the circumstances testified to in this case is held binding on the bank.   The testimony of appellant concerning this notice was as follows:

" We were at the office of the North Pacific Insurance Company, of which company we were both directors and stockholders, and at that time the matter came up, and I told Mr. Ouimette that this note was procured from me by fraud and misrepresentation, and right-out lying, and that I would not pay it."

But the communication was not made to Ouimette as the president of the bank; it was not made at the bank, or with **493** any reference to the bank's business; the business of another company was being discussed at the time, which was in no way connected with the bank, and, so far as the testimony shows, Ouimette made no response to the remark, and probably cared nothing about it, as it was a matter that did not interest him.   Surely there is nothing in the law that will charge him with the duty of remembering, as president of the bank, such a remark, made under such circumstances, and in such a place, and of communicating such a remark to the cashier of the bank, whose duty it is to conduct transactions of this kind for the bank.

Appellant places considerable stress on the fact that the note, which was due in one year after its execution, was not purchased by the bank until it lacked only one month from being due, and that the court erred in sustaining the objection to the question " Is it customary in that business to discount paper that has run nearly the entire time, long-time paper like this, without some inquiry? " We think the question was entirely irrelevant from any standpoint. The note had not matured, and that was all the inquiry the bank was bound to make. The presumption of the *bona fides* of the transaction was just the same one month before it became due as it was eleven months before it became due. The law fixes the time when the presumption ceases, which is a fixed and definite time.

We have examined the other errors alleged, and think they are untenable. The judgment is therefore affirmed.

SCOTT, STILES, ANDERS, and HOYT, JJ., concur.

CORPORATIONS—NOTICE TO AGENT, WHETHER NOTICE TO CORPORATION: See *Merchants' Nat. Bank* v. *Lovitt*, 114 Mo. 519; 35 Am. St. Rep. 770, and note with the cases collected; also *Koehler* v. *Dodge*, 31 Neb. 328; 28 Am. St. Rep. 518; and the note to *City Nat. Bank* v. *Martin*, 8 Am. St. Rep. 636. The knowledge of an agent of a corporation is imputed to the corporation when the agent is acting in the scope of his employment, and particularly when the corporation receives the benefit of the agent's conduct: *Little Pittsburg etc. Min. Co.* v. *Little Chief etc. Min. Co.*, 11 Col. 223; 7 Am. St. Rep. 226, and note; *Johnson* v. *First Nat. Bank*, 79 Wis. 414; 24 Am. St. Rep. 722, and note. For an extended discussion of this subject see the monographic note to *Bank* v. *Whitehead*. 36 Am. Dec. 188-200.

ABBOTT *v.* WETHERBY.

[6 WASHINGTON, 507.]

HUSBAND AND WIFE—SEPARATE PROPERTY.—Money saved by a wife out of other moneys given her by her husband for household and other community expenses does not thereby become her separate estate, but remains community property, liable for community debts.

HUSBAND AND WIFE—SEPARATE ESTATE BY GIFT.—A declaration by a husband to third persons that his wife has selected certain lots, that she has always worked hard and earned a great deal of money, and that he intends the land for her home, will not create a separate estate therein for her if the land was purchased with community funds, but, on the contrary, it will be deemed community property, liable for community debts.

HUSBAND AND WIFE—EARNINGS OF WIFE DO NOT BECOME HER SEPARATE PROPERTY while she is living with her husband. They can only become such when she lives separate from him.

W. Lair Hill, and Gilliam and Hill, for the appellant.

Fred H. Peterson, for the respondent.

507 DUNBAR, C. J.   Respondent and George F. Abbott were married in the state of Ohio, in 1852, and have ever since lived together as husband and wife until the death of Abbott in the state of Washington, in 1890.   At the time of the marriage respondent had no property, at least the testimony convinces us that she had none worthy of consideration; none which has been the source of any accumulations. **508** As husband and wife, respondent and Abbott lived together in several different states, and with varying fortunes, until in 1883, when Abbott came to Washington, respondent following in due course of time, since which time this state has been her home, and was the home of her husband until he died. They had but little means when they came to Washington. The property in controversy consists of lots 5 and 6 in block 1 of Burke's Second Addition to the city of Seattle.   On July 2, 1883, George F. Abbott took a bond for a deed from Lyman M. Wood for lot 6, and the south half of lot 5, and paid thereon $60, the price agreed to be paid being $275, the remainder of which was paid in small payments.   A deed was executed and delivered to respondent by Lyman M. Wood and wife in pursuance of this bond for a deed on the twenty-eighth day of April, 1887, for the consideration of $450.   The north half of lot 5 was conveyed to George F. Abbott by Lyman M. Wood by deed dated October 11, 1888, expressing a consideration of $250.   August 22, 1889, George F. Abbott and respondent executed and delivered to Cassa Osgood, without consideration, a deed purporting to convey to Mrs. Osgood the last-described tract, under an agreement between Mrs. Abbott and Mrs. Osgood that the latter should reconvey this land to the former without consideration, whenever the former should request it.   In pursuance of this arrangement Mrs. Osgood, on the twenty-ninth day of March, 1890, reconveyed this tract to respondent.   At the time of the delivery of the deed from Mr. and Mrs. Abbott to Mrs. Osgood, Mrs. Abbott furnished Mrs. Osgood $100 to pay Mr. Abbott as a part of the consideration.   After the conveyance of lot 6 to respondent, she and her husband deeded to the First Baptist Church a portion of lot 6.   Afterward they entered into an agreement with the First Baptist Church to exchange for the property in lot 6, deeded to it, lot 1, in block

6, of Jackson Street Addition [509] to the city of Seattle, and did afterwards make such exchange. The property exchanged with the church under said agreement, and which constituted the consideration for said conveyance, stood in the name of George F. Abbott. In July, 1888, the appellant and George F. Abbott entered into a copartnership as contractors and builders, and continued in that relation until about January, 1889. Being unable to agree upon a settlement of their copartnership affairs, they submitted their differences to arbitration, which resulted in a judgment in favor of the appellant and against Mr. Abbott in the sum of $350.63, and $14 costs, a copy of which judgment was filed and recorded in the office of the county auditor of said King county, and this suit was instituted by respondent against the appellant as administrator of the estate of said George F. Abbott, deceased, to prevent him from administering upon the property above described, and to remove the cloud from the title to said land which she alleges the recorded judgment to be; so that it will be seen that it is necessary to determine at the outset, whether the property in dispute is community property or the separate property of the respondent.

The debt upon which the judgment was based was contracted in the ordinary course of the husband's business for the benefit of the community, and is therefore a community debt: *Oregon Improvement Co.* v. *Sagmeister,* 4 Wash. 710. Hence if the property was community property it was properly listed by the administrator, and should be made to respond to the community debt.

We must look to our statutes alone to determine what constitutes separate property. Section 1398 of the General Statutes provides what property is the separate property of the wife, viz., the property and pecuniary rights of every married woman at the time of her marriage and afterwards acquired [510] by gift, devise, or inheritance, with the issues and profits thereof. Section 1399 provides that all other property is community property. As we have already seen, the respondent had none of this property at the time of her marriage; she has not acquired it by devise or inheritance, and it follows that, if she has not acquired it by gift, under the provisions of section 1399 it is community property. We are unable to find anything in the record even tending to support a conclusion that the money with which the payment for this land was made was given to the respondent. The husband was

industrious and so was the wife, the testimony showing that
the labor of both contributed to the fund with which this
property was purchased; that as members of the community
they were both working for the interest of the community.
The respondent's idea of a gift is illustrated by her testimony.
When asked how she obtained certain money which she
claims to have paid for the land, she replied:

" I obtained in this way: He would give me money for the
house, and whatever was over, was mine. He gave me money
to purchase things; I used to spend part of what he gave me,
and the rest of it was mine; and doing that, I very soon
accumulated money."

This surplus, respondent says, she loaned to her husband
when he was in need of a little ready money, and as he did
not pay it back to her she takes credit for the amount which
her husband paid on the purchase price on the land in question. This is, to say the least, a novel and ingenious method
of attempting to convert community property into separate
property. Counsel for the respondent seems to think that
his client is entitled to great credit on account of her economi-
cal habits, and for being able to save something out of the
bountiful provision made by the husband for the household
expenses, and no doubt she should have, if the economy had
been practiced in the interests of the [511] community which
was furnishing the funds; but in this instance the beneficiary
was a stranger to the community; and the encouragement of
a practice working such results might lead to habits of
economy so rigid that the comfort of the community would
be a consideration secondary to that of the thrifty condition
of the separate estate. Ordinarily, it would seem that the
overplus furnished by any particular fund to meet any
expenses should be returned to the fund which furnished it.
We see no good reason for upsetting this well-established
principle in law and morals in this case. So far as the transaction with Mrs. Osgood, in which the record title was transferred from Abbott to his wife, is concerned, the same principle
obtains. It was the community funds which were, through a
deception practiced on Abbott, paid to him, and which it may
be fairly presumed was by him again furnished to his wife to
meet the current expenses of the community. And, according to respondent's own testimony, the whole object of that
transaction was not to change the property from community
to separate property, but to get it into such a condition that

her husband could not dispose of it, which she feared he would do, and by so doing secure it for the use of the community. This is the theory which places the respondent in the most favorable light in her dealings with her husband, and the one on which we believe she acted.

It is true that Abbott stated to Mrs. Woolen and Mrs. Osgood that his wife had selected these lots, and that she had always worked hard and earned a great deal of money, and that he intended the land as a home for her; but such expressions are common with husbands who have not a thought of separate property. Most husbands are considerate enough of their wives to allow them to make a selection of their residence, and to accord to them the credit of having worked hard and helped to accumulate what they possess; but such expressions cannot be construed either as [512] a gift, in the sense of creating a separate estate, or as a payment for money had and received. Indeed, it is hard to tell what the theory of the respondent in this case is, whether her claim is based upon a gift, or upon a debt. If upon a gift, the evidence of a gift must be clear, and it must be apparent that the husband intended to divest the community of all rights, and to set the property apart to the separate use of the wife: *Evans* v. *Covington*, 70 Ala. 440. If upon a debt, that transaction must be as clearly proven.

It is, however, claimed that a large portion of the funds which paid for these lots was earned by the wife, and that such earnings were her separate property under the provisions of the statute. The statute, in addition to the property described in section 1398, provides a way in which a married woman can obtain separate estate. Section 1403 provides that the earnings and accumulations of the wife and of her minor children living with her, or in her custody, while she is living separate from her husband, are the separate property of the wife. It is true that section 1402 provides that the wife may receive the wages of her personal labor; but these sections must be construed together, and thus construed we must conclude that her earnings only become her separate property while she is living separate from her husband. Any other construction would render meaningless section 1403, for if section 1402 created her earnings into a separate estate the enactment of section 1403 would have been absolutely useless, as all its provisions under this construction are embraced in section 1402. And the same reason would apply

to section 480 of the Code of Procedure. While the personal
earnings of a wife are exempt, it must be construed to be a
statute of exemptions, and in no sense defines separate property. The statute seems to definitely distinguish the rights
acquired by wives who are living with their husbands, from
the rights acquired by wives who are living separate from
their husbands.

[513] The case of *Carter* v. *Worthington*, 82 Ala. 334, 60 Am.
Rep. 738, which is cited and relied upon by respondent, is not
a parallel case with the one at bar. In that case a married
woman, who had been conducting a millinery establishment
before her marriage, continued the business for many years
after marriage, with her husband's consent, and took a conveyance of land in payment of an account for goods sold the
grantor. *Held,* That such goods being purchased with the
profits of the business were to be considered as accretions to
her separate estate, which had already accumulated, and that
the land so purchased could not be subjected to the payment
of a judgment against her husband on a debt incurred before
the sale of the goods to the grantor. There is no question of
accretions from respondent's estate here. There was in reality
no conducting of any distinct business, the husband and wife
were both industrious and both no doubt added something by
their labor to the common fund; the wife sometimes kept
boarders, but it appears that the house and supplies were
furnished by money earned by the husband. They were both
doing their share; doing what is common for husbands and
wives to do to prosper and to accumulate a competency for
the community. It is the duty of each spouse to contribute
his or her industry, energy, and intelligence to the community;
and it would encourage a sorry state of affairs in our domestic
relations, if each one of the spouses were allowed, as seems to
us to be attempted in this case, to charge the community with
all the expenses of the living and expenses of the business,
and credit the separate estate with the gross earnings.

Our conclusion is that the property listed by the administrator was properly listed as community property; and the
judgment is, therefore, reversed, and the cause remanded to
the lower court with instructions to dismiss the same at respondent's cost.

HOYT, SCOTT, STILES, and ANDERS, JJ., concur.

HUSBAND AND WIFE—EARNINGS OF WIFE AS HER SEPARATE PROP-
ERTY.—The earnings of a married woman made with the consent of her husband are her separate property: *Coughlin* v. *Ryan*, 43 Mo. 99; 97 Am. Dec.
375, and note; *Bartlett* v. *Umfried*, 94 Mo. 530; *Diefendorff* v. *Hopkins*, 95
Cal. 344. The title to land purchased by a wife with money paid her for
keeping her husband's mother, and realized from keeping boarders when the
husband was out of debt, cannot be questioned by his subsequent creditors:
Hoag v. *Martin*, 80 Iowa, 714. See the note to *Wilder* v. *Abernethy*, 25 Am.
Rep. 736. In *Cramer* v. *Reyford*, 17 N. J. Eq. 367, 90 Am. Dec. 594, and
note, it was held, however, that a wife's earnings during coverture belong to
her husband, and that he cannot as against his creditors give them to her
To bring the wife within the provision of the code of Maryland, which declares that "any married woman who, by her skill, industry, or personal
labor, shall earn any money or other property, real, personal, or mixed, shall
hold the same, and the fruits, increase, and profits thereof to her separate
use," the evidence must be such as to bring her strictly within its meaning,
and to show that she elected to work for herself and independently of her
husband: *Poffenberger* v. *Poffenberger*, 72 Md. 321. See further the extended
note to *Cooke* v. *Bremond*, 86 Am. Dec. 634.

HUSBAND AND WIFE.—INTENTION OF THE HUSBAND that land conveyed to
the wife should be her separate property, and his declarations to that effect
as evidence is extensively treated in the monographic note to *Cooke* v.
Bremond, 86 Am. Dec. 640-643. Where a husband purchased land with his
own money and took the deed as trustee for his wife, he acquired the property for her, and it became her separate estate legally and equitably: *Payton*
v. *Payton*, 86 Ga. 773.

DUGGAN *v.* PACIFIC BOOM COMPANY.

[6 WASHINGTON, 593.]

CORPORATIONS—EFFECT OF UNAUTHORIZED ACTS OF AGENT—ESTOPPEL.
In an action against a corporation on a note signed in its name by its
president, secretary, and treasurer, without express authority from, or
ratification by, the corporation, it is estopped from asserting that such
officers acted outside of their authority, if it appears that all of the business of the corporation, including the kind in question, has universally
been transacted by such officers and informally ratified by the corporation by payments made and otherwise.

PAYMENT BY TAKING NOTE OF THIRD PERSON.—Whether or not the taking of the note of a third person from a debtor without the latter's indorsement is conclusive evidence of payment, depends upon the intent
of the parties, and if it appears that at the time such note was taken it
was not the intent of the parties that it should be received as an absolute
payment, then upon nonpayment of the note, the original indebtedness
can be enforced.

INSTRUCTIONS—REFUSAL TO GIVE WHEN NOT ERROR.—A party is entitled to
have an instruction given for the purpose of making more definite
another instruction given by the court, but when a requested instruction
embodies improper matter, the court may properly refuse to give it as a
whole.

Dunning, Richards, Murray and Pratt, for the appellants.

Million and Houser, and D. H. Hartson, for the respondent.

593 HOYT, J.   This action was brought to cover an amount alleged to be due upon a note purporting to be that of the appellant, the Pacific Boom Company.   It was signed in its name by its president, and secretary, and treasurer.   The defense of the appellant was that the officers of the company who executed the note were not authorized so to do by any formal action on the part of the board of trustees, nor had there been a ratification of their action by the **594** company. And further, that at the time such note was given, the company was not indebted to the plaintiff, and that there was no consideration therefor.

Upon the question as to the authorization of the officers to execute the note, it appeared from the undisputed proofs in the record that there was no express authorization or ratification of such action on the part of the company.   It, however, appeared that all the business of the company, including the making of numerous notes of the kind in question, had been for a long time transacted by said officers, and informally ratified by the company by its action thereon in paying the same, and in other respects.   The record shows that not only had this been occasionally done, but that such was the universal course of business with the company.   From such proofs it appears that to all intents and purposes the business of the company had been transacted by the two officers who signed the note in question, and that, although this course of business had been continued for a long period, no fault had ever been found with the action of these officers in so conducting the business.

Under these circumstances we think that the jury were justified in finding that the company was estopped from asserting the fact that the officers, in executing the note in question, acted outside of their authority as such.   And in our opinion the instruction of the court upon this subject fairly submitted this question to the jury, for while it is true that there seems to be no affirmative proof to justify the court in saying that the company would be estopped under the circumstances shown by the record if the plaintiff relied upon such practice and custom, yet we think that under the circumstances proven there arose from the course of practice a presumption that all who dealt with the company relied thereon, and that for that reason that part of the instruction had a foundation in the proofs, and if it [595] did have, it is conceded by the appellant that the law of the case was fairly expressed therein.

There are two other exceptions which it is necessary to notice, and they may well be considered together.

The court instructed the jury as follows:

"Now, I instruct you, as a matter of law, the taking of a note from a third person, as, in this instance, the taking of the note of Mr. Behrens by Mr. Duggan at the time of delivering up the first note, is not in itself a payment of the debt; but the fact that the plaintiff had a note of the company and delivered that up and took Mr. Behrens' note is a circumstance which you can take into consideration in arriving at the question of whether Mr. Duggan released the boom company and took Mr. Behrens for the debt, and it is for you to determine, gentlemen of the jury, under all the evidence and the instructions given you by the court, whether Mr. Duggan accepted Mr. Behrens, and released the boom company from this obligation. If Mr. Duggan, in accepting the note of Mr. Behrens, did not release the boom company, as I have instructed you before, it is not a payment of the debt, and consequently the boom company would be liable upon the note if you find, under the evidence and the instructions of the court, that this note has been legally executed."

To the giving of this instruction the appellant excepted. The court also refused to give the following instruction asked for by the appellant:

"The taking of Behrens' note and surrendering the company note was presumptive evidence of payment and extinguishment of the original debt between plaintiff and the Pacific Boom Company. If you believe from the evidence that the note sued upon was given in payment or exchange for the private debt of A. Behrens, then you are instructed that such a transaction was unlawful so far as this company was concerned, and your verdict should be for the defendant Pacific Boom Company."

The instruction given, when fairly construed and taken altogther, does not so misstate the law as to lead us to [596] believe that the jury were misled thereby. It is true that the clause, "The taking of the note of Mr. Behrens by Mr. Duggan at the time of delivering up the first note is not in itself a payment of the debt," if unexplained, would be erro-

neous, but such language, when taken in connection with that
of the remainder of the instruction, fairly conveyed to the
jury the idea of the court that such fact alone did not conclusively show a payment of the original debt. And thus
interpreted it stated the law of the case.

There are a few cases going to the extent of holding that
the taking of a note of a third person from a debtor is conclusive evidence of the payment of the debt when such debtor
does not indorse the note of such third person, but the weight
of authority is in favor of the proposition that the intent of
the parties at the time of the transaction must govern, and if
it appears that at the time such note was taken it was not
the intent of the parties that it should be received as an absolute payment of the existing indebtedness, then in case of the
nonpayment of such note the payment of the original indebtedness could be enforced. Taking the whole instruction under
consideration together, we think the jury were sufficiently
informed of this rule of law. If the appellant had desired
that the instruction should be more definite as to any particular point, it should have requested a proper instruction in
regard thereto. This it attempted to do as to one particular
point in the request above set out, and had it been content
with asking the court to give the first clause of such instruction, it would have probably been entitled to have had the
same given to the jury, as the giving thereof would have made
more certain the intention of the court in the instruction
which we have been considering. Appellant, however, saw
fit to couple this clause with another, which, in our opinion,
it was not entitled to have given to the jury, and embody
both clauses in a single instruction, and having [597] done so
it cannot now avail itself of an exception to the refusal of the
court to give such instruction as a whole. The latter part of
the instruction so requested ignores the fact that a proper
consideration might have moved at the time of the execution
of the new note from Behrens to the company, and that for
that reason the note be given not for the accommodation of
Behrens, but for the accommodation of the company, and in
the prosecution of its own business in the manner in which
the proofs show it had been accustomed to do it.

We find no error in the record of sufficient magnitude to
justify a reversal of the judgment, and it must therefore be
affirmed.

Dunbar, C. J., and Stiles, Anders, and Scott, JJ., concur.

PAYMENT—TAKING NOTE OF THIRD PERSON AS.—This question is discussed in *Shepherd* v. *Busch*, 154 Pa. St. 149; 35 Am. St. Rep. 815, and note, where the cases are collected.

CORPORATIONS—EFFECT OF UNAUTHORIZED ACTS OF AGENTS—ESTOPPEL. When the president and secretary of a corporation act openly and publicly as its agents in executing its contracts, with full knowledge and acquiescence of the directors, the corporation cannot escape liability on a contract so executed on the ground that the authority was not conferred by resolution entered on the books of the corporation: *Sherman Center Town Co.* v. *Swigart*, 43 Kan. 292; 19 Am. St. Rep. 137, and note; *Pixley* v. *Western Pac. R. R. Co.*, 33 Cal. 183; 91 Am. Dec. 623, and note. Although the agent of a corporation can convey no legal title to land, unless his authority is in writing, yet the governing body may so act as to estop themselves from denying the existence of such written authority, and thus create an equitable estoppel *in pais*, as where the agent acted openly and notoriously and the corporation for a long time acquiesced in his acts: *Alabama etc. R. R. Co.* v. *South and North etc. R. R. Co.*, 84 Ala. 570; 5 Am. St. Rep. 401. The authority of the agent of a corporation may be proved by the acts of the professed agent acquiesced in by the corporation: *Melledge* v. *Boston Iron Co.*, 5 Cush. 158; 51 Am. Dec. 59, and note. A corporation may ratify the unauthorized acts of its agents without such ratification being expressed by formal resolution: *Washington Sav. Bank* v. *Butchers' etc. Bank*, 107 Mo. 133; 28 Am. St. Rep. 405, and note, with the cases collected; *Leggett* v. *New Jersey Mfg. etc. Co.*, 1 N. J. Eq. 541; 23 Am. Dec. 729, and note. See also on this subject the notes to the following cases: *Simpson* v. *Garland*, 39 Am. Rep. 299; *Farmers' etc. Bank* v. *Butchers' etc. Bank*, 69 Am. Dec. 693; *Blen* v. *Water etc. Co.*, 81 Am. Dec. 137; and *Ward* v. *Williams*, 79 Am. Dec. 387.

CASES

IN THE

SUPREME COURT

OF

ALABAMA.

MATHIS v. CARPENTER.

[95 ALABAMA, 156.]

SHERIFFS—LIABILITY FOR ACTS OF DEPUTY.—A sheriff is liable for the wrongful official acts of a person who, representing himself as a deputy sheriff, acts as such in the presence of, and with the knowledge, consent, and approbation of, such sheriff, although the latter denies the appointment of such deputy, and it appears that his oath of office was irregularly filed.

SHERIFFS—OFFICIAL BONDS OF AS EVIDENCE.—If, in an action against a sheriff and his sureties on two bonds given by him, pleas are filed by the sheriff and his sureties jointly, such bonds are admissible in evidence, although some of the sureties on one bond are not upon the other.

SHERIFFS—LIABILITY FOR FAILURE TO MAKE LEVY—BURDEN OF PROOF.— When a writ of attachment is placed in the hands of a sheriff to be levied, a bond of indemnity given, and property in the possession of defendant apparently subject to levy is pointed out, the sheriff is *prima facie* liable for a failure to make the levy.

Matthews and Whiteside, for the appellant.

Caldwell and Johnston, for the appellee.

157 COLEMAN, J. Appellant as plaintiff moved for a summary judgment against the defendant Carpenter, as sheriff, and his sureties, for failing to levy an attachment. The averments of the motion are, that the writ of attachment was placed in the hands of the sheriff, property pointed out to him as belonging to the defendant in attachment, and that the sheriff was duly indemnified to make the levy. The defendants' pleas were three in number: 1. That the writ was not received by him, or any one authorized to receive it; 2. That defendant had no property subject to levy under the attachment; and 3. The same could not have been executed by the exercise of due diligence.

The proof is ample to show that the sheriff, Carpenter, was liable for the acts of C. F. Porter as his deputy. The testimony of the clerk of the court showed that Porter acted as the deputy sheriff in the presence of the sheriff; that he was in the habit of receiving all kinds of process; that in [158] fact he receipted for executions in the name of the sheriff, by him as deputy, collected money on executions, made due return of the collections in the name of the sheriff, and was generally understood to be the deputy sheriff. To the same effect is the testimony of certain attorneys, who practiced in the court; and in regard to the particular writ of attachment, upon inquiry being made of Caldwell, whom the sheriff acknowledges to have been his regular deputy sheriff, was referred by him to Porter as the officer who had the writ for execution. There is other evidence, also, sufficient to satisfactorily show that Porter was recognized by the sheriff as his deputy.

The pleas are framed jointly for all the defendants, and there is no plea which justified the exclusion of either bond executed by the sheriff, although some of the defendants were sureties upon one bond, who were not sureties upon the other.

Section 3951 of the Penal Code imposes a penalty upon any officer required by law to file an oath of office, who enters upon the duties of his office without first taking and filing such oath in the proper office. The fact that Porter filed his oath of office with the clerk of the court, instead of the probate office, did not relieve the sheriff of his liability for the acts of Porter as his deputy, if the evidence otherwise satisfactorily showed that he, Porter, represented himself as deputy sheriff, and acted as such with the knowledge and consent and approbation of the sheriff; and, if the evidence is credible, there can be but little question of the existence of these facts: *Joseph* v. *Cawthorn*, 74 Ala. 414.

That property in the possession of the defendant, apparently subject to levy, was pointed out, and an indemnifying bond executed to the sheriff, is fully proven. The witness Roberts, the defendant in the attachment suit, testified that in fact the attachment was levied by the deputy sheriff, so far as to take control of the property, and for a consideration of twenty-five dollars paid to the deputy by him the possession was released; but there was no entry of any levy entered on the writ of attachment or elsewhere.

The second and third pleas presented a good defense to the action.

An indemnifying bond is intended for the protection of the officer. Under our statute, no additional duty is imposed upon the officer because he has been indemnified. A bond of indemnity does not devolve upon a sheriff to commit a trespass, or do an illegal act. In no event can it do more than shift the burden on him to show that the property [159] was not subject to levy. The evidence showed that the debt upon which the attachment issued was for rent of a dwelling, and the property pointed out was furniture in the rented house apparently in the possession of the tenant. *Prima facie*, the officer was liable for not making the levy, but he was not absolutely liable. If the property did not belong to the tenant—if it was not subject to levy by attachment—the plaintiff suffered no injury, and sustained no damage. Under the facts proven by the plaintiff, *prima facie* the property was liable, and the burden rested upon the sheriff to prove his defense, by showing that the property was not subject to levy under the attachment: *Mason* v. *Watts*, 7 Ala. 705; *Leavitt* v. *Smith*, 7 Ala. 181; *Minter* v. *Bigelow*, 9 Port. 483; *Smith* v. *Castellow*, 88 Ala. 355; *Abbott* v. *Gillespy*, 75 Ala. 184; *Wilson* v. *Strobach*, 59 Ala. 493; *Governor* v. *Campbell*, 17 Ala. 569. There was no error in admitting such testimony.

Section 12 of the act establishing the city court of Anniston (Acts of 1888, 1889, p. 569) provides that, in cases of appeal, if there be error, the supreme court shall render such judgment as the court below should have rendered, or reverse and remand the same for further proceedings, as shall be deemed right. Although there is proof tending to show that the property pointed out to the sheriff may not have been subject to levy under the attachment, the real contest seems to have been rested upon other grounds. The rulings of the trial court were not in accord with the principles here declared, and we are of opinion that the ends of justice would be better promoted by a reversal of the case.

Reversed and remanded. ___

SHERIFFS—LIABILITY FOR ACTS OF DEPUTIES.—The sheriff's officers, being his known and recognized deputies, he will therefore be held liable civilly for their misconduct in the execution of a writ: *Hazard* v. *Israel*,

1 Binn. 240; **2 Am. Dec.** 438; *King* v. *Chase,* 15 N. H. 9; 41 Am. Dec. **675,** and note; *State* v. *Moore,* 19 Mo. 369; 61 Am. Dec. 563, and note; *Flanagan* v. *Hoyt,* 36 Vt. 565; 86 Am. Dec. 675, and note; *Jamesville etc. R. R. Co.* v. *Fisher,* 109 N. C. 1; *Governor* v. *Vanmeter,* 9 Leigh, 18; 33 Am. Dec. 221, **and note.** See also the extended note to *Campbell* v. *Phelps,* 11 Am. Dec. 145.

SHERIFFS—LIABILITY FOR FAILURE TO MAKE LEVY.—The return of an execution wholly unsatisfied, after a negligent delay by the sheriff in making a levy, establishes *prima facie* his liability for the whole amount of the judgment: *Guiterman* v. *Sharvey,* 46 Minn. 183; 24 Am. St. Rep. 218, and note; *Armour Packing Co.* v. *Richter,* 42 Minn. 188. See further the extended notes to *People* v. *Palmer,* 95 Am. Dec. 423; *Hargrave* v. *Penrod,* 12 Am. Dec. 203, and *Coville* v. *Bentley,* 15 Am. St. Rep. 315, in which this question is thoroughly discussed.

MAXWELL *v.* MOORE.

[95 ALABAMA, 166.]

MORTGAGES—A TENDER OF PAYMENT of a mortgage debt after default, and before the mortgagee has taken or demanded possession, if kept good, operates to discharge the lien of the mortgage, and extinguish the title of the mortgagee. In such case the mortgagor may recover the mortgaged property from a purchaser at a subsequent sale under the mortgage.

ACTION to recover a mule purchased by defendants at a foreclosure sale under a mortgage executed by plaintiff. Defendants filed certain pleas, to which plaintiff interposed replications, and demurrers were filed to these replications. The demurrers were overruled, and judgment rendered for plaintiff. Defendants appealed.

Wood and Mayfield, for the appellants.

Fitts and Somerville, for the appellee.

168 CLOPTON, J. The principal question involved in the special pleas, replications, and demurrers to the replications, is, whether a tender of the amount due on a mortgage of personal property, after condition broken, operates, when kept good, to discharge the lien of the mortgage, and revest the title in the mortgagor, so that he may maintain an action of detinue against the mortgagee, who has taken possession after tender made, sold the property under the mortgage, and purchased at the sale. The contention of appellants is, that, as mortgages are governed in this state by the principles of the common law, a tender cannot effectually extinguish the lien, unless made at the time of payment fixed by the contract of the parties—an offer of strict performance of the condition.

In those states where mortgages are regarded as a mere lien or security for a debt, and the title as remaining in the mortgagor until divested by foreclosure, the rule generally adopted is, that a tender at any time during the continuance of the right of redemption is the equivalent of payment as to things incidental and accessorial to the debt, and extinguishes the lien of the mortgage, though the tender is not kept good. *Kortright* v. *Cady*, 21 N. Y. 343, 78 Am. Dec. 145, though not the first, may be regarded as the leading [169] case holding this view. A qualified and more conservative rule is adopted in those states where a mortgage is considered as immediately transferring the legal title to the mortgagee, subject to be defeated by the payment of the debt at the time and in the manner specified in the mortgage. In a few, the courts hold that an unaccepted tender after default will not, at law, reinvest the mortgagor with the title, and that his only remedy is in equity to redeem; but, in the others, the common-law rule, that after condition broken the title vests absolutely in the mortgagee, has not been applied so strictly, where the mortgage is of personal property, as to hold that a tender after default, when kept good, cannot, under any circumstances, operate the destruction of the lien.

There are *dicta* in some of our early cases, and probably the weight of authority is, that a tender after default, in order to effect the extinguishment of the title of the mortgagee, must be made before he has rightfully and peaceably taken possession for the purposes of foreclosure. This question, however, has never been decided in this state, though directly presented in *Frank* v. *Pickens*, 69 Ala. 369; the disposition of that case not calling for its decision. It is not presented in this case, the replications averring that the tender was made before the mortgagees acquired possession. We shall, therefore, leave it, as it has heretofore been, undecided.

It may be conceded that, by the strict rule of the common law, a tender after failure to perform the condition of the mortgage will not, at law, destroy the title, which has become absolute in the mortgagee by the forfeiture. In equity, however, a mortgage being regarded as incident to, and security for, the debt, the rigor and harshness of the common-law rule has been greatly relieved by holding that the mortgagor has the right to redeem, if not barred by unreasonable delay, by payment, or tendering full payment at any time

before foreclosure. But courts of equity will not enforce the
equity of redemption so as to deprive the mortgagee of his
security by discharging the lien of the mortgage; its enforcement is dependent upon payment of the debt by the mortgagor, or by a sale of the property. In many of the states,
courts of law, while not taking cognizance of the equity of
redemption for the purpose of enforcing the right to redeem,
but acting upon and applying equitable principles, have extended to a tender after default the effect of a tender made
at the time and in the manner specified in the mortgage,
modified so as to prevent the mortgagee's deprivation [170] of
his security without satisfaction of the debt. In *Frank* v.
Pickens, 69 Ala. 369, it was expressly held, that a tender of
payment of the mortgage debt cannot operate to extinguish
the title of the mortgagee, unless the money tendered is kept
ready to be paid to the mortgagee whenever he may manifest
a willingness to receive it; and if the benefit of the tender is
claimed in court, the money must be placed in the custody of
the court, so that, if the tender be adjudged good, it may be
awarded to the mortgagee—otherwise the mortgagor is regarded as having abandoned the tender. Recognizing the
mortgagor's right of redemption, and observing the principles
upon which courts of equity enforce it, the current of the
later decisions is, that an unconditional tender after default,
of the full amount due on the mortgage, if kept good, and
the money brought into court, discharges the lien of the
mortgage. We cite a few of the cases: *Crain* v. *McGoon*, 86
Ill. 43; 29 Am. Rep. 37; *Knox* v. *Williams*, 24 Neb. 630; 8
Am. St. Rep. 220; *Matthews* v. *Lindsay*, 20 Fla. 962; *Musgat*
v. *Pompelly*, 46 Wis. 660; Jones' Chattel Mortgages, sec. 635.

The effect of a plea of tender, accompanied by bringing
the money into court, came incidentally before this court in
the case of *Foster* v. *Napier*, 74 Ala. 393. In that case the
suit was founded on a bond executed by Foster in the institution of a statutory action for the recovery of mules and a
wagon. The record of the proceedings, pleadings and judgment in the action of detinue brought by Foster against Napier was read in evidence. In the action of detinue, Foster
claimed the property under two mortgages, executed by Napier. A special plea was filed by Napier, averring payment
of the mortgages, except one hundred and seventy-five dollars, which, the plea alleged, had been tendered to the mortgagee before action brought; and the money was brought into

court. It is said: "The issues being thus formed, if the defendant proved the truth of his second plea, he was entitled to a verdict; but the money tendered would become the property of the plaintiff. In such case, the issue is confined to the debt, or its payment, for which the mortgage was given as security. . . . . The defense set up in that suit, and the verdict and judgment thereon, taking into the account the pleadings and charge of the court on the trial, settled conclusively that Napier did not, at the commencement of that suit, owe Foster exceeding one hundred and seventy-five dollars on the debts secured by the mortgages, and that before suit was brought he had tendered that sum, and had it in court for Foster." The [171] principle of the decision is that a tender before suit brought by the mortgagee to recover possession, when the money is brought into court, and the truth of the plea of tender is established, is tantamount to, and has the same effect as, actual payment, in extinguishment of the lien and title of the mortgagee—in fact, it was treated as a payment.

Section 1870 of the code declares: "The payment of a mortgage debt, whether the mortgage is of real or personal property, divests the title passing by the mortgage." Under section 2685, a plea of tender of money must be accompanied by a delivery of the money to the clerk of the court. If the money is deposited in court, and the truth of the plea established, the effect is to stop the running of interest from the time of tender. The money became the property of plaintiff, by relation, at the time when the tender was made. That such is the intention and effect of the statute is manifest from the further provision, that if the tender be of personal property, the plea must aver readiness to deliver it to the plaintiff, and judgment for the defendant upon the plea vests the title to the thing tendered in the plaintiff, subject to any claim the defendant may have for his trouble in keeping it. A tender so made, and kept good, and the money brought into court, so as to be the equivalent of payment, if the tender be adjudged sufficient, comes within the spirit, equity and policy of section 1870 of the code. On the foregoing principles, and in line with the current of the decisions of those states where mortgages are governed by the principles of the common law, we adopt as a safe and wholesome rule—conserving the ends of justice, protecting the mortgagor against oppression or undue advantage, and preventing injustice to the mortgagee—that a tender of full payment of the mortgage debt after default, and before the mortgagee has taken or demanded possession for the purpose of foreclosure, if kept good, and the money brought into court, operates to discharge the lien of the mortgage and extinguish the title of the mortgagee.

True, only the first replication avers that the money is brought into court; but the omission of this averment in the others is not assigned as a ground of demurrer. While we have left undecided whether a tender after the mortgagee has taken or demanded possession will be effectual to discharge the lien of the mortgage, we hold that the possession acquired after the tender is made does not affect its operation. The replications not being obnoxious to any of the objections assigned as grounds of demurrer, the demurrers were properly sustained.

Affirmed.

[172] Response to application for rehearing.

Per CURIAM. The court is of the opinion that the replications of the plaintiff to defendant's special pleas are not free from fault. But the demurrers to the replications were properly overruled, because, as framed, they were not directed against the objectionable portions of the replications. We, therefore, adhere to the conclusion reached in the opinion, and overrule the application for rehearing.

MORTGAGES—EFFECT OF TENDER OF MORTGAGE DEBT.—A tender of the money due on a mortgage at any time before foreclosure discharges the lien of the mortgage, though made after the law day, and not kept good: *Kortright* v. *Cady*, 21 N. Y. 343; 78 Am. Dec. 145, and extended note; *Nelson* v. *Loder*, 132 N. Y. 288; *Contra: Perre* v. *Castro*, 14 Cal. 519; 76 Am. Dec. 444, and note. See also *Werner* v. *Tuch*, 127 N. Y. 217; 24 Am. St. Rep. 443, and note; and the note to *Renard* v. *Clink*, 30 Am. St. Rep. 461.

STATE v. HARRUB.

[95 ALABAMA, 176.]

OYSTERS AND OYSTER-BEDS—STATE PROPERTY RIGHTS IN AND CONTROL OF. A state has an absolute property right in its oysters and oyster-beds, and, through its legislature, has the absolute right to dispose of them to its people, and may adopt all precautions and regulations deemed desirable or necessary for the preservation and increased production of its oysters so far as this may be done without obstructing the paramount right of navigation.

INTERSTATE AND DOMESTIC COMMERCE—RIGHT TO REGULATE.—To constitute interstate commerce there must be traffic and interstate intercourse between different states, and the power vested in Congress to regulate interstate commerce does not authorize it to regulate the domestic commerce between the citizens of the same state or different parts thereof. This latter power belongs to the several states alone, exclusive of the power of Congress.

OYSTERS—STATE CONTROL OVER.—A state, through its legislature, may confine the taking and use of its oysters to its own citizens, and regulate their shipment and disposition within its borders for the use of such citizens so as to prevent such oysters from becoming an article of interstate commerce.

OYSTERS—STATE CONTROL OVER.—A state has the right by statute to license its own citizens to catch and take the oysters within its borders, and to deny to citizens of another state the right to take and transport them, and to absolutely prohibit their shipment beyond its borders, and to regulate their sale therein, not imposing any conditions, burdens, or restrictions upon the oyster as a commodity after it has entered another state or after it is legally delivered in the home state for exportation by any of the means by which interstate commerce is effected.

OYSTERS—STATE CONTROL OVER—WHEN BECOME ARTICLE OF INTERSTATE COMMERCE.—A state has the right by statute to limit the exportation of oysters taken within its borders to such as may have been shelled before shipment, and when the statute so provides the oyster cannot become an article of interstate commerce while in the shell.

STATUTES—SUBJECT EXPRESSED IN TITLE.—A statute is not open to the objection that it contains subjects not "clearly" expressed in its title when such subjects are all "referable and cognate" to the subjects expressed in such title.

W. L. Martin, Attorney-General, and Gaylord B. Clark, for the state, appellant.

G. L. and H. T. Smith, and M. D. Wickersham, for the appellees.

[180] COLEMAN, J. The defendants were arrested for a violation of the Act of February 18, 1891, pp. 1072–1084, entitled " An act to regulate the planting and taking of oysters in the waters of this state." Upon *habeas corpus* proceedings the defendants were discharged, the court holding that the act of

the legislature was unconstitutional, and void, as contravening
the third subdivision of the eighth section of article 1 of the
constitution of the United States which provides that Congress shall have power " to regulate commerce with foreign
nations, and among the several states, and with the Indian
tribes."

Sections 1 and 2 of the act of the legislature under consideration read as follows: " SECTION 1. That the title to and
property in all oysters in the waters of this state, whether upon
public reefs or in so-called private beds, or whether the same
be transplanted by riparian proprietors [181] under authority
of law or otherwise, or whether the same be a growth from
natural deposit, is, and shall remain in the state, until such
title shall be divested in manner and form as herein authorized or provided." " SEC. 2. That a license is hereby given
to resident citizens of the state of Alabama, to catch and take
oysters, the property of the state, from the public reefs, or
from private beds planted and owned by them, or in which
they have secured an interest, or permission from the proprietor thereof to take such oysters, upon the terms and
conditions, and subject to the restrictions and regulations
hereinafter set forth and enacted; but no person or persons
not a resident of the state of Alabama is or shall be authorized
to take or transport any such oysters from, in, or through any
of the waters of the state of Alabama; and it is unlawful for
any person, whether a citizen of the state of Alabama, or of
any other state or country, to ship beyond the limits of this
state any oysters taken from the waters of this state, while
the same are in the shells; provided, that between the middle of December and the middle of January, oysters in the
shells may be shipped in barrels by railroad to other states;
and provided further, that such oysters in the shell may be
shipped *bona fide* from any point in the state of Alabama to
any other point in said state, by the lines of transportation
which lie partly within and partly without the state of Alabama; and provided further, that any resident citizen of the
state of Alabama, who shall lawfully take any oysters from
the tide-waters of this state, as in this act authorized, shall
have a qualified interest or property in the oysters so lawfully taken while in the shell, which he may sell and transfer
to any other person within the limits of the state of Alabama;
and after said oysters have been shelled within the state of
Alabama, such lawful taker or his assigns, as the case may

be, shall be vested with all of the state's property and title in
and to said oysters, and shall have the right to sell such
oysters and shells, or to ship the same beyond the limits of
this state, without restriction or reservation; provided further,
that in case of any infringement of the foregoing qualified interest in said taker of oysters, said taker may, in his
own name, maintain an action against the wrongdoer, either
in case or trover, as may be proper; and in case of larceny,
or other public offense concerning such oysters, while in the
hands of a lawful taker, the ownership thereof shall be
averred in such taker or possessor, when by law it shall be
necessary to aver ownership."

We deem it unnecessary to set out the whole act.

¹⁸² The principles of law applicable to the facts of the
cases before us do not call for a discussion or adjudication of
that clause of section 2 which relates to the shipment of
oysters in the barrel by railroad, from the middle of December to the middle of January, or that clause which permits
transportation by lines which lie partly without the state:
Jones v. *Black*, 48 Ala. 540. The agreed facts are, that the
oysters were taken and shipped in the shell, beyond the limits
of the state, by the defendants, in the month of September,
in sailing-vessels; that Harrub was a citizen of Alabama,
and Melvin a citizen of the state of Mississippi; and that
both were guilty of a violation of the statute. The question
involved is as to the constitutionality of the act.

The first question we will consider is as to the extent of
the ownership and control of the state of Alabama in and
over the oyster-beds and oysters within her territorial limits.

In the case of *Martin* v. *Waddell*, 16 Pet. 411, Chief Justice
Taney declares, as a general principle, "When the revolution
took place, the people of each state became themselves sovereign; and in that character hold the absolute right to all
their navigable waters, and the soils under them, for their
own common use, subject only to the rights since surrendered
by the constitution to the general government."

In the case of *Smith* v. *Maryland*, 18 How. 71, the question
was as the constitutionality of an act of the state of Maryland, which was entitled "An act to prevent the destruction
of oysters in the waters of this state." The court laid down
this principle: "But this soil is held by the state not only
subject to, but in some sense in trust for, the enjoyment of
certain public rights, among which is the common liberty of

taking fish, as well shellfish as floating fish. The state holds
the propriety of this soil for the conservation of the public
rights of fishery thereon, and may regulate the modes of that.
enjoyment, so as to prevent the destruction of the fishery. In
other words, it may forbid all such acts as would render the
public right less valuable, or destroy it altogether. This
power results from the ownership of the soil, from the legislative jurisdiction of the state over it, and from its duty to
preserve unimpaired those public uses for which the soil is
held."

In the case of *McCready* v. *Virginia,* 94 U. S. 391, the foregoing principles were reaffirmed, and the court went further
and declared: "The title thus held is subject to the paramount right of navigation, the regulation of which, in respect
to foreign and interstate commerce, has been [183] granted to
the United States. There has been, however, no such grant.
of power over the fisheries. These remain under the exclusive control of the state, which consequently has the right, in
its discretion, to appropriate its tide-waters and their beds to
be used by its people as a common for taking and cultivating
fish, so far as may be done without obstructing navigation.
Such an appropriation is, in effect, nothing more than a regulation of the use by the people of their common property. . . .
It is in fact a property right, and not a mere privilege or
immunity of citizenship. . . . . It does not belong of right to
the citizens of all free governments, but only to the citizens of
Virginia. They, and they alone, owned the property to be
used, and they alone had the power to dispose of it as they saw
fit. . . . . The state may by appropriate legislation confine
the use of the whole to its own people alone."

In the case of *Haney* v. *Compton,* 36 N. J. L. 522, it was
said: "But it cannot with any propriety be said, that a statute which simply prohibits nonresidents on board a vessel
from subverting the soil of the state, and carrying away her
property, or that of her grantees, leaving such vessel to pass
and repass, and go whithersoever those in charge of her may
desire, is a regulation of commerce with foreign nations or
among the states. It is a law for the protection of property
—at most, an internal police regulation, entirely within the
competency of the state to adopt; and it is not perceived that.
it can by possibility interfere with commerce in the sense in
which that word is used in the federal constitution."

In *Manchester* v. *Massachusetts,* 139 U. S. 259, the court reaffirmed the principle declared in the case of *McCready* v. *Virginia*, 94 U. S. 391; and the same principle is announced in *Dunham* v. *Lamphere*, 3 Gray, 268.

We think it clearly established, that the people of Alabama own absolutely the oyster-beds and oysters in question, and that it is a property right as complete and perfect as that held to any other property. As was said by Chief Justice Waite in *McCready* v. *Virginia*, 94 U. S. 391, "the principle is not different from the planting of corn upon dry land." We think it further settled, that the people of Alabama, through its legislature, alone have the power to dispose of their property rights in their oyster-beds and oysters; and if they see proper may dispose of them to their own people only. It is further settled, that the legislature has ample authority to adopt all precautions and regulations deemed desirable or [184] necessary for the preservation and increased production of its fisheries.

That the power of Congress to regulate commerce with foreign nations, among the several states, and with the Indian tribes, is unlimited and exclusive of the power of the state, is settled law. Any statute of a state not authorized by Congress, which in any way obstructs or interrupts free navigation, or restricts or burdens any commodity which is an article of interstate commerce, must be declared null and void: *Tiernan* v. *Rinker*, 102 U. S. 125; *Telegraph Co.* v. *Texas*, 105 U. S. 460; *Brimmer* v. *Rebman*, 138 U. S. 78; *Leisy* v. *Hardin*, 135 U. S. 109.

To constitute commerce, there must be traffic and intercourse, and to constitute interstate commerce, there must be traffic and interstate intercourse—an "intermingling" between different states. As Mr. Chief Justice Marshall says in the case of *Gibbons* v. *Ogden*, 9 Wheat. 1, "Comprehensive as the word 'among' is, it may very properly be restricted to that commerce which concerns more states than one. . . . . The completely internal commerce of a state may be considered as reserved to the state itself." We understand this great case to distinctly recognize the absolute power and control of the state upon subjects within its territorial jurisdiction which are not articles of foreign or interstate commerce.

The case of *Coe* v. *Errol*, 116 U. S. 517, decides an important principle as to the right of the state to tax its products, although the owner may intend them for exportation, and although they may be in process of preparation for exportation at the time of the assessment of the tax; but the case is important in the present connection in determining that "there must be a time when they [the products] ceased to be governed exclusively by the domestic law, and began to be governed and protected by the national law of commercial legislation;" quoting from the case of *The Daniel Ball,* 10 Wall. 565, as follows: "Whenever a commodity has begun to move as an article of trade from one state to another, commerce in that commodity between the states has commenced." But that movement, says the court, "does not begin until the article has been shipped or started for transportation from one state to another." Carrying it from the farm or forest to the depot is only an interior movement of the property, and although it may be for the purpose of exportation, this is no part of the exportion itself.

If the statute of Alabama under consideration militates [185] against any of these well-established principles, in regard to interstate commerce, it must yield to the dominant supremacy of the federal constitution. We do not understand the power vested in Congress to regulate interstate commerce gives it power over domestic commerce, or authorizes it to regulate the commerce between the citizens of the same state, or different parts of the same state. This power belongs to the several states, and is exclusive of the power of Congress. If the state of Alabama should attempt by legislation to tax or burden or restrict the shipment of oysters from the state of Mississippi or other states, such legislation would be unconstitutional; or, if the state of Alabama should attempt to impose similar or other conditions upon the shipment of any articles of interstate commerce from this state to another state, that would be an interference with the law of interstate commerce, which power alone is vested in Congress. To constitute interstate commerce, however, as we have said, there must be an article or commodity the subject of commerce and destined to pass from one state to another.

These authorities do not militate against, but recognize the power of, the state to confine the use of the oyster to its own citizens, and to regulate its shipment and disposition within its borders for their use. This would be domestic commerce, as distinguished from interstate commerce. Neither do we understand the power of Congress to regulate interstate commerce in any way interferes with or restricts the right of the state to prohibit its own property, to which it has an exclusive title, from becoming an article or commodity of interstate commerce.

In the same line may be cited the case of *American Express Co.* v. *People*, 133 Ill. 649; 23 Am. St. Rep. 641. The statute of Illinois for the protection of game permitted the killing of gamebirds for two months in the year. The statute forbade the sale of the game-birds at any time, and made it unlawful, under a penalty, for any carrier or corporation knowingly to receive and transport or convey them beyond the state for sale. Under the act, at the proper time, a person was permitted to kill game for his own use, but not to go upon the market as an article of commerce. The constitutionality of the act was upheld, the court declaring "the ownership was in the people of the state. This being so, it necessarily follows that the legislature had the right to permit persons to kill or take game upon such terms and conditions as its wisdom might dictate, and that the person killing game might have such property interest in it, and such only, as [186] the legislature might confer. The legislature never conferred an absolute property in quail upon the person who might kill the same." It was held that the discretion of the legislature in making rules and regulations for the preservation and protection of the game-birds was not subject to judicial control.

The property rights of the oysters being in the state exclusively, and the legislature having full authority to prohibit it from becoming an article of interstate commerce, and to reserve the oysters for the sole use of its own citizens, and to regulate the sale between its own citizens and between different parts of the state; the question arises, when does the oyster, under the statute, become an article of interstate commerce, and what provision of the statute attempts to burden, restrict, or control it after it has this character. The first section explicitly declares, that "the title and property in all oysters in the waters of this state . . . . shall be divested in manner or form as herein authorized and provided." That this is a valid enactment, under the principles of law declared in many of the foregoing decisions, cannot be questioned. The second section gives a license to resident citizens to catch and take oysters the property of the state, and further enacts that "no person or persons, not a resident of the state of Alabama, is or shall be authorized to take or transport any such oysters from, in or through any of the waters of the state of Alabama; and it is unlawful for any person, whether a citizen of the state of Alabama, or of any other state or country, to ship beyond the limits of this state any oysters taken from the waters of his state while the same are in the shells; provided that, between the middle of December and the middle of January, oysters in the shell may be shipped in barrels by railroad to other states," etc. That the state has the right to license its own citizens to catch and take oysters, and to deny to citizens of another state the right to take and transport them, and absolutely to prohibit the shipment of oysters beyond the limits of the state, and to regulate the sale of them within its own limits, not imposing any conditions or burdens or restriction upon the oyster as a commodity after it has entered another state, or after it may be legally delivered in this state for exportation to a common carrier or ways by which interstate commerce is effected, we think is clearly established by the following authorities: *Haney* v. *Compton*, 36 N. J. L. 522; *The Daniel Ball*, 10 Wall. 557; *Coe* v. *Errol*, 116 U. S. 517: *Gibbons* v. *Ogden*, 9 Wheat. 1; *McCready* v. *Virginia*, 94 U. S. 391; [187] *Kidd* v. *Pearson*, 128 U. S. 1; *Reading etc. R. R. Co.* v. *Pennsylvania*, 15 Wall. 250–252.

If the state has the power to prohibit the exportation of its oysters absolutely, *a fortiori*, it may limit the shipment of such oysters to such as may have been shelled. If the legislature sees proper, as a means to prevent the exhaustion of its oyster-beds, to grant to the takers, who can only be resident citizens of the state, or their grantees within the state, such a qualified property right in the oyster as will permit its exportation only after it is shelled, where is the authority to judicially control this discretion, or what principle of the interstate commerce law is violated by such an enactment? The oyster is the absolute property of the state. The state certainly has the power to prevent its becoming an article of interstate commerce. Until it becomes an article of interstate commerce, Congress has no authority or control in the premises. The state, by the statute itself, expressly retains the title to the oysters, and prohibits their shipment beyond the state until shelled. Only after it is shelled does the state relinquish its title, and the grantee previously having but a qualified interest, becomes the absolute owner, and the oyster may then become an article of interstate commerce. When shelled, and the state has parted with its property rights, the state no longer interferes with the article. The owner ships it wherever he pleases, and by whatsoever transportation he prefers.

The statute nowhere interferes with or obstructs the sailing of the vessels. They can come and go when and whithersoever those in control see proper; but this did not authorize them to subvert the soil of Alabama, and to transport in September oysters in the shells from the reefs of Alabama to other states. The statute expressly prohibited it.

The vice in the argument of the defendant's counsel is in assuming that the oyster in the shell was an article of commerce, when in fact the taker, who could only be a citizen of the state, as we have seen, had but a qualified interest in the oyster, and which he could dispose of only in the state. It would be unsound reasoning to hold that the state could probibit absolutely the taking of its oysters, or confine the use of them exclusively to its own citizens, and yet could not prevent the taker from shipping them beyond the limits of the state. If the statute had undertaken to invest the taker, or his grantee, with a full and absolute property right and title to the oyster in the shell, so as to [188] invest him with the power to convert it into an article of commerce, and had then undertaken to prevent its shipment, or burden its shipment with a tax, a different question might arise. That is not the case here. The state carefully guards against this condition, and it is only after being shelled can it be said that the oyster has become an article of interstate commerce.

These conclusions are fully sustained by the reasonings and principles declared in the case of *Kidd* v. *Pearson*, 128 U. S. 1, in which Mr. Justice Lamar discusses at length and with great clearness the doctrine of interstate commerce, and the application of the principles stated in *Gibbons* v. *Ogden*, 9 Wheat. 1, and *Coe* v. *Errol*, 116 U. S. 517, and other cases cited above.

The policy of the legislature in making provision to keep the shells within the state might be based upon many considerations. However, this court is not called upon to adjudicate upon the policy of the legislature, and we will not consider this view further than to make the following citations from section 5, volume 2, United States Commission of Fish and Fisheries, 564: "Besides, being useful for making roads, streets, filling wharves and lowlands, and making lime, the shells are of great utility as stools for new oyster-beds, as experiments beginning fifty years ago have demonstrated. . . . . These and other minor utilizations are disappearing, however, along the northern coast, through the increased value of the shells to spread on the bottom for the foundation of new colonies, as has been explained; and before long, no doubt, nearly all the shells accumulated will be saved by planters for this purpose, as a better economy than to sell them."

When tested by the rule declared in *Ballentyne* v. *Wickersham*, 75 Ala. 533, the statute is not obnoxious to the objection that it contains subjects not clearly expressed in the title. The rule as there held is, that it is "sufficient if they [the subjects] are all referable and cognate to the subject expressed" in the title.

Our conclusion is that the act is not unconstitutional, and that the court erred in its judgment.

Reversed and remanded. ────

GAME LAWS.—The ownership of game is in the people of the state, and the legislature may withhold from or grant to individuals the right to hunt and kill game, or qualify and restrict that right, as, in its opinion, will best subserve the public welfare: *American Express Co.* v. *People*, 133 Ill. 649; 23 Am. St. Rep. 641, and note with the cases discussing the right of property in animals *feræ naturæ*. For a discussion of the right of property in oysters see the note to *Wheatley* v. *Harris*, 70 Am. Dec. 261.

STATUTES—SUBJECT EXPRESSED IN TITLE.—The title of a statute and the act itself must correspond, not literally, but substantially: *Macon etc. R. R. Co.* v. *Gibson*, 85 Ga. 1; 21 Am. St. Rep. 135, and note. See also *Blair* v. *State*, 90 Ga. 326; 35 Am. St. Rep. 206, and note; note to *Hronek* v. *People*, 23 Am. St. Rep. 663, and the extended note to *Neuendorf* v. *Duryea*, 25 Am. Rep. 239.

INTERSTATE COMMERCE—WHAT IS.—For a thorough discussion of this subject, see the monographic note to *People* v. *Wemple*, 27 Am. St. Rep. 550.

────────

JOHNSON v. OEHMIG AND WIEHL.

[95 ALABAMA, 189.]

SALE OF CHATTELS—FAILURE OF TITLE AS DEFENSE.—The purchaser of personal property in undisturbed possession cannot recover damages in an action on an implied warranty of title, nor set up want of title in his vendor as a defense to an action for the purchase money, although he offers to rescind, in the absence of fraudulent representations made by the vendor in regard to the title.

ACTION to recover two hundred dollars for personal property sold by plaintiffs to defendants. The defendants answered that the sum sued for was the amount unpaid for a stationary engine and mill rocks purchased by them for three hundred dollars, one hundred dollars of which had been paid. The defendants also alleged that subsequently to such pur-

chase and payment, they discovered that plaintiffs had no
title to the engine, but before making this discovery they had
made valuable improvements thereto; that they then offered,
and still offer, to rescind their purchase by returning the
property upon the payment to them of the one hundred dollars and the value of the improvements put on the engine;
that the plaintiffs refused, and still refuse, to accept such
offer, and that they represented that they had a good title to
such engine at the time of the purchase.   A demurrer to the
answer was sustained in the court below, and judgment rendered for the plaintiffs.   The defendants appealed.

Davis and Haralson, for the appellants.

L. A. Dobbs, for the appellees.

¹⁹⁰ WALKER, J.   In *Ogburn* v. *Ogburn,* 3 Port. 126, it was
held that the vendee of personal property cannot, while holding possession thereof, defend against an action for the purchase money by proof of want of title in the vendor.   In the
course of the opinion in that case it was said: "We think no
defense can be made to an action for the purchase money
when the facts relied upon to make it would not, if the parties were changed and the money had been paid, enable the
vendee to recover it back for the breach of the warranty of
title."   The defendants would not be entitled to such recovery on the facts stated in their second plea.   In an action by
a vendee of personal property against his vendor, for a breach
of warranty of title, only damages for actual loss can be recovered.   The plaintiff in such an action must not only establish that his vendor is without title to the property sold, and
that another is the true owner, but also that he has restored
the property to such owner; that it has been taken from him
under compulsory proceedings, or that he has parted with
money or property in consequence of a judgment obtained
against him, or voluntarily in answer to a claim made for
the property: *O'Brien* v. *Jones,* 91 N. Y. 193.   In *Harris* v.
Rowland, 23 Ala. 644, the property sold had been recovered
on the adverse title.   No such state of facts is shown by the
second plea in this case.   It is not averred that the defendants have in any way been disturbed in their possession of
the property.   If that possession remains undisturbed, their
title will be perfected by lapse of time.   If a paramount title
is asserted, the plaintiffs may settle with the adverse claim-

ant, or they will be answerable in damages on their warranty
of title, if the defendants shall be required to deliver up the
property in response to a claim by one who may prove to be
the true owner. So long as the vendee of personal property
remains in undisturbed possession, he cannot recover dam·
ages in an action on an implied warranty of title, or set up
want of title in his vendor as a defense to an action for the
purchase money, unless there were fraudulent representations
made by the vendor in regard to the title. Such a vendee in
peaceable possession has nothing substantial to complain of
in the fact that his vendor was not the true owner of the
property. When nothing more is shown than that he may
suffer loss in the future, in consequence of the outstanding
claim to the property, he must rely upon his warranty, and
he cannot sue [191] thereon until he has suffered damage be
cause of its breach: *Case* v. *Hall*, 24 Wend. 102; 35 Am. Dec.
605, and note; *Sumner* v. *Gray*, 4 Ark. 467; 38 Am. Dec. 39;
Burt v. *Dewey*, 40 N. Y. 282; 100 Am. Dec. 482, and note; 1
Benjamin on Sales (Corbin's ed.), secs. 948 and 1347, and
notes. There was no error in sustaining the demurrer to the
second plea.

Affirmed.

————

Sales—Failure of Title as Defense to Seller's Action for Price
A purchaser of goods cannot set up his vendor's want of title as a defense
to an action for the price, if the true owner has not recovered the property
unless the vendor fraudulently represented himself to be the owner, knowing
such representation to be false: *Case* v. *Hall*, 24 Wend. 102; 35 Am. Dec. 605
and note; *Sumner* v. *Gray*, 4 Ark. 467; 38 Am. Dec. 39. In an action for
the price of goods sold and delivered, the defendant cannot avoid payment
on the ground that the sale was in fraud of the seller's creditors: *Gary* v
Jacobson, 55 Miss. 204; 30 Am. Rep. 514, and extended note. But in such
an action it is a valid defense that the purchaser discovered after the sale
that the vendor had no title; and being threatened with suit by the true
owner, paid him the price, the vendor being insolvent: *Matheny* v. *Mason*
73 Mo. 677; 39 Am. Rep. 541.

TURNER *v.* BERNHEIMER.

[95 ALABAMA, 241.]

HOMESTEADS.—CONVEYANCE OF HOMESTEAD BY HUSBAND TO WIFE, accepted by her, is an alienation of the premises in the sense of passing the legal title to her, but is not an alienation of the homestead exemption, since that does not thereby pass from the husband, the wife, or the family, but the land still remains their homestead in every essential quality and attribute, and cannot be taken under execution, nor again conveyed with out the voluntary consent and signature of both husband and wife.

ACTION by Bernheimer against Turner and wife to recover a house and lot. The plaintiff claimed the land as a purchaser at an execution sale against said Turner. The defendants claimed the premises as their homestead, and Mrs. Turner claimed them as her own by virtue of a deed executed by her husband to her prior to the rendition of the judgment under which such execution sale was had. At the trial defendants offered this deed in evidence, and also offered to show that Turner owned the land and occupied it together with his family as a homestead at the time of the levy of such execution. The court excluded such evidence on objection by plaintiff, and defendants excepted. The court also instructed the jury to find for the plaintiff against the objection and exception of defendants. Judgment for plaintiff, and defendants appealed.

B. B. Boone, for the appellants.

Pillans, Torrey and Hanaw, for the appellee.

243 McCLELLAN, J. The fate of this appeal depends entirely upon whether the husband can convey lands which constitute the family homestead to the wife, the deed to that end being executed by himself alone, but delivered to and accepted by her.

Both the organic and the statute law of Alabama declare that no alienation of the homestead shall be valid without the voluntary signature and assent of the wife to the instrument intended to have that effect. The "Married Woman's Law" of 1887 removed the legal disabilities theretofore existing between husband and wife to the extent, among others, of enabling the husband generally to sell and convey lands to the wife; but it has never been supposed, and is not, we apprehend, the law, that the statute changed in any way pre-existing requirements in respect of the alienation of the homestead, further than this, that if before its passage the husband might have conveyed an equitable title in the homestead to the wife, he may now convey the legal title. So that the question is not really at all affected by the Act of 1887; and it comes back to this: Is such a conveyance an alienation of the homestead within the meaning of section 2, article 10, of the constitution, and section 2508 of the code? If it is, it cannot be effective now any more than before the passage of the Act of 1887; if it is not, it would have been as effectual in equity before that act as it would be now at law. And if the husband may convey land constituting the homestead to the wife, his deed for that purpose cannot be joined in by the wife—that is, her joinder therein would add nothing to its effect, since she cannot be both grantor and grantee in the same instrument: *Trawick* v. *Davis*, 85 Ala. 342.

It is manifest, of course, that the requirement of the wife's voluntary signature and assent to any alienation of the homestead is for the protection of the wife, to secure to her a home of which she cannot be deprived except through her own free act. As is said by Judge Thompson: "The policy of those statutes which restrain the alienation of the homestead without the wife joining in the deed is to protect the wife, and to enable her to protect the family, in the [244] possession and enjoyment of a homestead, after one has been acquired by the husband." It is not perceived how this policy of the law could be in any degree thwarted by upholding the husband's conveyance of the homestead land to the wife. It is still her homestead, and still incapable of passing from her and the family without her voluntary signature and assent to the instrument operating the alienation. She and the family are as fully protected before as after such conveyance, and no violence is done to any purpose of the law respecting her and her children by according validity and giving force to such a conveyance. Not only so, but the premises are still as much the homestead of the husband—he has the same right of occupancy and enjoyment—as before the execution of the conveyance; and this right cannot be taken away from him—the wife cannot convey the land—without his voluntary assent and signature. And this is true whether he be regarded as still having a special property in the land, by reason of its homestead character, or whether it be considered that the land belongs absolutely to the wife; since, even in the latter case, there could be no alienation of it by her without his assent and concurrence, he being *sui juris* and a resident of the state, manifested by his joining in the alienation in the mode prescribed by law for the execution of conveyances of land: Code, sec. 2348. It would seem then in all reason that a conveyance of homestead premises by the husband to the wife, while having effect as an alienation of the land in the sense of passing the legal title to her, is yet not an alienation of the homestead, since that does not thereby pass either from the husband, the wife, or the family, but is still in every essential quality and attribute with respect to possession, enjoyment, and all the rights necessary to its protection as exempted property, the homestead alike of the husband, the wife, and their children. And so it is said further by the eminent author quoted above, that laws requiring the voluntary assent and signature of the wife to an alienation of the homestead, "are not intended to interpose obstacles in the way of a conveyance of the homestead to the wife, or to the wife and children, with the consent and approval of the wife, whatever may be the form of such conveyance": Thompson on Homesteads and Exemptions, sec. 473. And the adjudged cases fully support not only this text, but the conclusion we have arrived at, that such a conveyance is not an alienation of the homestead within the meaning of the constitution and statutes of Alabama, but is valid for the purpose of passing **245** the legal title of the land into the wife, subject to all preexisting homestead rights, without the voluntary signature and assent of the wife: *Harsh* v. *Griffin*, 72 Iowa, 608; *Burkett* v. *Burkett*, 78 Cal. 310; 12 Am. St. Rep. 58; *Riehl* v. *Bingenheimer*, 28 Wis. 84; *Baines* v. *Baker*, 60 Tex. 140; *Ruohs* v. *Hooke*, 3 Lea, 302; 31 Am. Rep. 642; *Spoon* v. *Van Fossen*, 53 Iowa, 494.

The rulings of the trial court to which exceptions were reserved, were made, are attempted to be sustained here, and could be sustained, only on the theory of the invalidity of Turner's deed to his wife. That theory being untenable, each of those rulings, it follows, was erroneous.

The judgment of the circuit court is therefore reversed, and the cause remanded.

————

HOMESTEAD—CONVEYANCE BY HUSBAND TO WIFE.—A husband may convey their homestead to his wife without her joining in the deed, and the conveyance will vest her with title in fee and in severalty to the property, but does not otherwise affect its homestead character: *Burkett* v. *Burkett*, 78 Cal. 310; 12 Am. St. Rep. 58, and note. Where a wife has filed a homestead upon the separate property of the husband, a deed of the land subse-

quently executed by the husband to the wife operates to vest the legal title
in the wife as her separate property, but does not constitute an abandonment of the homestead: *Estate of Lamb,* 95 Cal. 397. A wife does not affect
her homestead right by taking a deed of the homestead from her husband
without consideration, and such conveyance cannot be considered in fraud
of creditors: *Riggs* v. *Sterling,* 60 Mich. 643; 1 Am. St. Rep. 554; *McPhee*
v. *O'Rourke,* 10 Col. 301; 3 Am. St. Rep. 579, and note.

SAINT *v.* WHEELER AND WILSON MFG. COMPANY.

[95 ALABAMA, 362.]

SURETY AND GUARANTOR—DIFFERENCE BETWEEN.—A surety is one who
undertakes to pay at all events if the principal does not; a guarantor
undertakes to pay only if the debtor cannot. The first is an insurer of
the debt; the latter an insurer only of the solvency or ability of the
debtor to pay. A contract of suretyship is the joint and several contract of the principal and surety, while the contract of a guarantor is
his own separate undertaking in which the principal does not join.

SURETYSHIP—JOINT CONTRACT INDICATES.—The joint execution of a contract by a principal and another operates to exclude the idea of a guaranty, and is an index pointing to a contract of suretyship.

SURETYSHIP—CONTRACT OF WHAT CONSTITUTES.—A contract under seal
signed jointly by several persons by which they "guarantee" and
directly obligate themselves, along with one of their number, to pay,
absolutely and wholly, irrespective of his solvency or insolvency, all
damages which may result to the obligee from his default, and by
which they expressly stipulate that the obligee need not exhaust his
remedies against their principal before proceeding against them, is a
contract of suretyship and not of guaranty.

GUARANTY—RIGHT TO REVOKE.—An undertaking of guaranty is primarily
an offer, and does not become a binding obligation until it is accepted,
and notice of acceptance has been given to the guarantor. Such offer
may be recalled at any time before notice of acceptance.

SURETYSHIP—CONTRACT OF WHEN BECOMES BINDING.—A contract of suretyship does not require notice of acceptance, but is complete and binding
on delivery. After delivery one of the obligors cannot revoke it unless
he has expressly reserved the right of revocation.

SURETYSHIP—RELEASE OF ONE SURETY OPERATES TO RELEASE OTHER SURE-
TIES on the same contract or undertaking only to the extent of his aliquot share of the whole liability.

SURETYSHIP—DISCHARGE OF SURETY BY CHANGE IN CONTRACT WITHOUT
HIS CONSENT.—Sureties under a contract for the faithful performance
of certain duties by their principal are not discharged from all liability
by reason of certain parol changes made in the original contract by the
obligee and the principal imposing new and additional duties upon the
latter after the obligors have become sureties, and without their knowledge, consent, or ratification, unless the imposition of these new duties
and their performance by the principal render impossible or materially
hinder, delay or impede the proper and faithful performance of the
service originally undertaken.

SURETYSHIP—DISCHARGE OF SURETY BY CHANGE IN CONTRACT WITHOUT HIS CONSENT.—Sureties are not discharged by a change in the contract between the principal and the obligee as to the amount of compensation of the former, made without the consent or knowledge of the sureties, when the settlement between the parties on which the default of the principal is ascertained is based on the original contract, nor are such sureties discharged by reason of a subsequent parol agreement between principal and obligee, without their knowledge or consent, by which the principal is allowed to retain his compensation out of collections without remitting them to the obligee as required by the original contract.

SURETYSHIP—INDULGENCE TO PRINCIPAL AS DISCHARGE OF SURETY.—Mere indulgence by a creditor or employer to the principal in a contract, or a new agreement to give him further time to pay his debt or make good a default, if not supported by any new consideration, does not discharge the sureties on the original contract.

SURETYSHIP—CONCEALMENT OF PRINCIPAL'S DISHONESTY AS DISCHARGE OF SURETY.—In case of a continuing suretyship for the honesty of a servant, if the master discovers that the servant has been guilty of dishonesty in the service, and if, instead of dismissing him, he continues him in his employ without the consent of the surety, express or implied, the latter is not liable for any loss arising from the dishonesty of the servant during the subsequent service. This rule applies as well to a private corporation as an employer as to an individual, when its agent, in the discharge of his duties, discovers the dishonesty of the servant, and, having authority, fails to give notice of such dishonesty to the surety, and the corporation thereafter retains the servant in its employ.

ACTION by the Wheeler and Wilson Manufacturing Company, a corporation, to recover the sum of eight hundred dollars collected for it by R. F. Saint while employed by it as a collector, which sum he failed to pay on demand. The action was founded on a sealed contract, by which the plaintiff agreed to employ said Saint as its collector, and the defendants R. F. Saint, A. J. Crossthwaite, C. M. Wright, J. F. Hall, and J. R. Spraggins bound themselves in the sum of one thousand dollars for the faithful performance by said Saint of all duties as collector for plaintiff. Judgment for the plaintiff, and the defendants appealed.

Kirk and Almon, for the appellants.

James Jackson, and Roulhac and Nathan, for the appellee.

371 McCLELLAN, J. The contract sued on is not a guaranty, but one of suretyship. Crossthwaite and the other defendants, who undertake that Saint shall faithfully perform his contract with the company, are sureties of Saint, and not guarantors. The distinction between the two classes of undertakings is often shadowy, and often not observed by judges and text-writers; but that there is a substantive distinction, involving not infrequently important consequences, is, of course, not to be doubted. It seems to lie in this: that when the sponsors for another assume a primary and direct liability, whether conditional or not in the sense of being immediate or postponed till some subsequent occurrence, to the creditor, they are sureties; but when this responsibility is secondary and collateral to that of the principal, they are guarantors. Or, as otherwise stated, if they undertake to pay money, or do any other act, in the event their principal fails therein, they are sureties; but, if they assume the performance only in the event the principal is unable to perform, they are guarantors. Or, yet another and more concise statement: a surety is one who undertakes to pay if the debtor do not; a guarantor, if the debtor cannot; the first is sponsor, absolutely and directly, for the principal's acts, the latter only for the principal's ability [372] to do the act: "the one is the insurer of the debt, the other an insurer of the solvency of the debtor." This is the essential distinction. There is another going as well to its form. The contract of suretyship is the joint and several contract of the principal and surety: "The contract of the guarantor in his own separate undertaking, in which the principal does not join." Indeed, it has been held, pretermitting all other considerations, that no contract joined in by the debtor and another can be one of guaranty on the part of the latter (*McMillan* v. *Bull's Head Bank*, 32 Ind. 11; 2 Am. Rep. 323; 10 Am. Law Reg. 435, and notes), though we apprehend that a case might be put involving only secondary liability on the sponsors, though the undertaking be signed also by the principal. However that may be, it is certain that in most cases the joint execution of a contract by the principal and another operates to exclude the idea of a guaranty, and that in all cases such fact is an index pointing to suretyship. See Brandt on Suretyship and Guaranty, secs. 1 and 2; 9 Am. & Eng. Ency. of Law, p. 68; *Marberger* v. *Pott*, 16 Pa. St. 9; 55 Am. Dec. 479; *Allen* v. *Hubert*, 49 Pa. St. 259; *Reigart* v. *White*, 52 Pa. St. 438; *Kramph* v. *Hatz*, 52 Pa. St. 525; *Birdsall* v. *Heacock*, 32 Ohio St. 177; 30 Am. Rep. 572; 18 Am. Law Reg. 751, and notes; *Hartman* v. *First Nat. Bank*, 103 Pa. St. 581; *Courtis* v. *Dennis*, 7 Met. 510; *Kearnes* v. *Montgomery*, 4 W. Va. 29; *Walker* v. *Forbes*, 25 Ala. 139; 60 Am. Dec. 489.

Applying these principals to the bond sued on, the conclusion must be that it is not a guaranty, but a suretyship, on the part of Crossthwaite, Wright, Hall, and Spraggins. It is not their separate undertaking, but the principal also executes it. While they employ the word "guarantee," they directly obligate themselves along with Saint to pay, absolutely and wholly irrespective of Saint's solvency or insolvency, all damages which may result to the obligee from his default. Not only so, but they expressly stipulate that the company need not exhaust its remedies against Saint before proceeding against them. It is, in other words, and in short, a primary undertaking on their part, not secondary and collateral, to pay to the company in the event of Saint's failure, and not an undertaking to pay only in the event of Saint's default and inability to pay. They are sureties of Saint, and not his guarantors, and their rights depend upon the law applicable to the former relation, and not upon the law controlling the latter.

2. One of the important differences in the operation, effect and discharge of the two contracts finds illustration in this case. The undertaking of guaranty in a case like this is [373] primarily an offer, and does not become a binding obligation until it is accepted, and notice of acceptance has been given to the guarantor. Till this has been done, it cannot be said that there has been that meeting of the minds of the parties which is essential to all contracts: *Davis Sewing Machine Co.* v. *Richards*, 115 U. S. 524; *Walker* v. *Forbes*, 25 Ala. 139; 60 Am. Dec. 489. Being thus a mere offer, it may be recalled, as of course, at any time before notice of acceptance. Indeed, there are authorities which hold that, even after acceptance and notice thereof, the guarantor may revoke it by notice that he will be no longer bound, unless he has received a continuing or independent consideration which he does not renounce, or unless the guarantee has acted upon it in such way as that revocation would be inequitable and to his detriment; and, in cases of continuing guaranty, the effect of such revocation is to confine the guarantor's liability to past transactions: 2 Parsons on Contracts, 30; *Allan* v. *Kenning*, 9 Bing. 618; *Offord* v. *Davies*, 12 Com. B., N. S., 748; *Tischler* v. *Hofheimer*, 83 Va. 35.

All this is otherwise with respect to the contract of surety. He is bound originally in all respects upon the same footing as the principal. His is not an offer depending for efficacy upon acceptance, but an absolute contract depending for efficacy upon complete execution, and its execution is completed by delivery. From that moment his liability continues until discharged in accordance with stipulations of the instrument, or by some unauthorized act or omission of the obligee violative of his rights under the instrument, or by a valid release. Nothing that he can do outside of the letter of the bond can free him from the duties and liabilities it imposes. He cannot assert the right to revoke, unless the right is therein nominated. As was said by the English court, "if he desired to have the right to terminate his suretyship on notice, he should have so specified in his contract": *Calvert* v. *Gordon*, 3 Man. & R. 124; Brandt on Suretyship and Guaranty, secs. 113, 114.

3. The evidence here as to the release of Crossthwaite tends to show no more than this: that after the bond had been delivered to plaintiff, and after its officers had advised Saint that they were ready for him to enter on the discharge of his duties under the contract secured by the bond, he, Crossthwaite requested plaintiff to take his name off the paper. No assent to this request is shown, but only an inquiry on the part of plaintiff as to Crossthwaite's reasons for desiring to be released. It would seem that the court itself should have decided that these facts did not release Crossthwaite; but the question [374] appears to have been submitted to the jury. If this submission, or any of the instructions accompanying it, was erroneous, no injury resulted to defendants, since the jury determined the point against the alleged release, as the court should have done, assuming it to have been a question of law. On the other hand, if it were a question for the jury, it is to be presumed they were properly instructed as to the rules of law which should guide them to its solution, as no exceptions were reserved in that regard.

4. The exceptions which were reserved on this part of the case are to charges given, and to the refusal to give charge asked by defendants, declaratory of the effect which the discharge of Crossthwaite, if the jury found he had been discharged, would have upon the liability of his cosureties. As the jury found expressly that he had not been discharged these exceptions present mere abstractions not necessary to be decided. We have no doubt, however, but that the law in this respect was correctly declared by the court to be, that the release of Crossthwaite operated to release the other sureties only to the extent of his aliquot share of the liability

Brandt on Suretyship and Guaranty, sec. 383; Burge on
Suretyship, 386; *Klingensmith* v. *Klingensmith*, 31 Pa. St. 460;
Ex parte Gifford, 6 Ves. 805; *Schock* v. *Miller*, 10 Pa. St. 401;
Currier v. *Baker*, 51 N. H. 613; *Jemison* v. *Governor*, 47 Ala.
390.

5. The sureties of Saint insisted on the trial below that they
were discharged from all liability on the bond by reason of
certain alleged changes made in the original contract between
their principal and the company by the parties thereto, after
they became sureties for its faithful performance, and without
their knowledge, consent, or ratification. It is not pretended
that the paper writing evidencing this contract was ever
altered in any respect, but that its terms were changed by
subsequent parol agreements, in the following respects, among
others to be presently considered: 1. That under this contract, which constituted Saint a collector only for the company, he was instructed and required to take up and resell
sewing-machines, when he found the notes for the purchase
money of the same, and which were in his hands for collection, could not be collected; and, 2. That he was authorized
to discount or sell the notes placed in his hands for collection,
when the same could not be otherwise realized upon. Nothing is claimed in this action on account of Saint's misconduct
in respect of any property thus taken up or resold, or of any
note discounted by him, or with respect to the proceeds of any
such sale or discount. If [375] these duties were such as usually devolved upon a collector for a sewing-machine company
—as to which there is no evidence in this record, and no
necessity for any under the present complaint—it may be
that Saint's sureties would be responsible for their faithful
performance on his part to the same extent as for money collected on notes in his hands: *Detroit Sav. Bank* v. *Ziegler*, 49
Mich. 157; 43 Am. Rep. 456.

However that may be, the fact that they were imposed
upon him, assuming they were not covered by his contract,
and hence were in addition to those assumed by the other
defendants, cannot relieve his sureties from liability with respect to those which were imposed by the contract, unless the
imposition of these new duties and their performance by Saint
rendered impossible, or materially hindered or impeded, the
proper and faithful performance of the service originally undertaken. There is no evidence here that these new and additional duties interfered with the collection of notes placed

in his hands for that purpose; nor is any claim made against his sureties on account of any failure to collect such notes. But the gravamen of the action is, that he 1. Did collect these notes, and converted the proceeds to his own use; or 2. That he failed to deliver such notes to the company on the termination of his employment. We are unable to conceive how the fact that he had other property and funds—machines and the proceeds of discounted notes—in his possession, could have hindered or impeded him in the accounting for funds collected or notes remaining in his hands, or could in any degree have conduced to his conversion of such funds or notes. To the contrary, it would seem, in all reason, that the possession of this other property and these other funds, out of which he might have met the necessities which presumably induced his malversations, would have lessened the chances of misappropriation of the funds and property for which his sureties were responsible, and thus have lessened, instead of increased, their exposure to liability. We are very clear to the conclusion, that the imposition of these new duties not covered by the contract did not discharge the sureties with respect to those embraced in the contract, and as to which no change, in the particulars we are considering, was attempted: *Mayor of New York* v. *Kelly*, 98 N. Y. 467; 50 Am. Rep. 699; *People* v. *Vilas*, 36 N. Y. 459; 93 Am. Dec. 520; *Home Life Ins. Co.* v. *Potter*, 4 Mo. App. 594; *Commonwealth* v. *Holmes*, 25 Gratt. 771; *Home Savings Bank* v. *Traube*, 75 Mo. 199; 42 Am. Rep. 402; *Gaussen* v. *United States*, 97 U. S. 584; *Jones* v. *United States*, 18 Wall. 662; *Ryan* v. *Morton*, 65 Tex. 258; *First Nat. Bank*, v. [376] *Gerke*, 68 Md. 449; 6 Am. St. Rep. 453, and note, 458; *Detroit Sav. Bank* v. *Ziegler*, 49 Mich. 157; 43 Am. Rep. 456.

6. The sureties further defended on the ground that the contract between Saint and the company was changed, without their knowledge or assent, by a subsequent parol agreement entered into by their principal and Walls, representing the company, whereby Saint's compensation was to be reduced from fifty dollars per month to nine dollars per week. There was evidence of such agreement, but none that it was supported by a consideration, or that it was approved by plaintiff. And it appears from other evidence that all of Wall's contracts were subject to approval or rejection by other officers of the corporation, and that plaintiff settled with Saint on a basis as to compensation of fifty dollars per month. We

think, on these facts, this defense is without merit: *Steele* v. *Mills*, 68 Iowa, 406.

Equally untenable, in our opinion, is the defense which proceeds on the ground that the instruction of plaintiff to Saint to retain his salary and expenses out of collections made by him was a material change of that provision of the contract which required him to remit to the company, on the first day of each week, the amount collected up to that day. The contract provided for Saint's compensation and expenses, but was silent as to the manner of payment. The method of payment thus adopted tended to decrease the risks of the sureties, as affording less occasion for conversion by Saint than had payments to him been made only at the end of each month.

7. It is well settled, that mere indulgence of the creditor to the principal, the mere forbearance to take steps to enforce a liability upon default, or even an understanding between them looking to payment of the deficit presently due at some time in the future, which does not, for the want of a consideration to support it, or other infirmity, prevent the creditor from immediately demanding payment, will not discharge the surety. Hence, what took place between Walls and Saint in February, 1888, in regard to allowing the latter further time to make good the sum he had theretofore converted, afforded no defense to the sureties with respect to the sum then due: 3 Brickell's Digest, p. 715, secs. 36–43; 9 Am. & Eng. Ency. of Law, p. 83, n. 4; *Morris Canal etc. Co.* v. *Van Vorst*, 21 N. J. L. 100.

8. The sureties, however, on another aspect of the transaction last above referred to between Saint and Walls, predicate a defense going to the amount of their liability. They insist that Saint was at that time a defaulter by embezzlement; [377] that Walls knew this fact, and, without giving any notice of it to them, he, acting for the company, continued Saint in its employment, and committed other funds to him which were also converted; and that this action of Walls discharged them from all liability for funds thus converted after he knew of Saint's dishonesty. The general principle, here relied on, finds abundant support in the authorities. In the leading case of *Phillips* v. *Foxall*, L. R. 7 Q. B. 666, the proposition in thus stated by Quian, J.: " We think that in a case of continuing guaranty for the honesty of a servant, if the master discovers that the servant has been guilty of acts of

dishonesty in the course of the service to which the guaranty
relates, and if, instead of dismissing the servant, as he may
do at once and without notice, he chooses to continue in his
employ a dishonest servant, without the knowledge and consent of the surety, express or implied, he cannot afterwards
have recourse to the surety to make good any loss which may
arise from the dishonesty of the servant during the subsequent
service." And this proposition is rested upon considerations
which, to our minds, are eminently satisfactory. Premising
that had a default involving dishonesty, and occurring before
the surety became bound, been known to the creditor, and
concealed by him from the surety, the effect would have been
to discharge the surety, a doctrine which appears to be well
established, the court proceeds to declare the same result from
a concealment of dishonesty pending a continuing guaranty,
as follows: " One of the reasons usually given for the holding
that such a concealment [at the time the surety enters into
the obligation] would discharge the surety, is that it is only
reasonable to suppose that such a fact, if known to him, would
necessarily have influenced his judgment as to whether he
would enter into the contract or not; and in the same manner, it seems to us, equally reasonable to suppose that it never
could have entered into the contemplation of the parties that,
after the servant's dishonesty in the service had been discovered, the guaranty should continue to apply to his future
conduct, when the master chose, for his own purposes, to continue the servant in his employ without the knowledge or
assent of the surety. If the obligation of the surety is continuing, we think the obligation of the creditor is equally so,
and that the representation and understanding on which the
contract was originally founded continue to apply to it during its continuance, and until its termination." The citations
directly supporting this conclusion are *quasi dicta* [378] of Lord
Redesdale in *Smith* v. *Bank of Scotland*, 1 Dow. 287, and of
Malins, V. C., in *Burgess* v. *Eve*, 13 L. R. Eq. 450; but the
case was subsequently followed in England and the United
States, and nowhere abstractly doubted. We follow these authorities, and adopt their conclusions as sound in principle:
Sanderson v. *Aston,* L. R. 8 Exch. 73; Brandt on Suretyship
and Guaranty, sec. 368; *Roberts* v. *Donovan,* 70 Cal. 108;
Charlotte etc. R. R. Co. v. *Gow,* 59 Ga. 685; 27 Am. Rep. 403;
Atlantic etc. Tel. Co. v. *Barnes,* 64 N. Y. 385; 21 Am. Rep.
621; *Newark* v. *Stout,* 52 N. J. L. 35.

9. Indeed, the foregoing doctrine is not controverted in this case; but it is contended that it has no application as between a corporation, being the creditor, and the surety of one of its officers or employees. And there are not a few adjudged cases which support this view. The argument upon which this conclusion is reached is, that "corporations can act only by officers and agents. They do not guarantee to the sureties of one officer the fidelity of the others. The fact that there were other unfaithful officers and agents of the corporation, who knew and connived at his (the principal's) infidelity, ought not in reason, and does not in law or equity, relieve the sureties from their responsibility for him. They undertake that he shall be honest, though all around him are rogues. Were the rule different, by a conspiracy between the officers of a bank, or other moneyed institution, all their sureties might be discharged. It is impossible that a doctrine leading to such consequences can be sound": *Pittsburg etc. Ry. Co.* v. *Shaeffer*, 59 Pa. St. 356; *Taylor* v. *Bank of Ky.*, 2 J. J. Marsh. 565; *McShane* v. *Howard Bank*, 73 Md. 135; Brandt on Suretyship and Guaranty, sec. 369.

It is to be noted that these cases—and there may be others which follow them—hold, not only that where there is a conspiracy between officers of a corporation to embezzle its funds, the dereliction of neither officer will discharge the sureties of the other, but also where there is a negligent failure on the part of one such officer to give notice to the sureties of another of his dishonesty, and a continuance of the dishonest servant in the corporate service without the assent of his sureties given with a knowledge of the default, the sureties are not discharged from liability for subsequent deficits, though confessedly they would be were the creditor an individual or copartnership. It may be that the first position stated is sound. It would seem to be immaterial whether an original default results from the dishonesty of the principal alone, or conjointly from his [379] and the dereliction of another corporate employee. The sureties are bound to answer for the results of any form of original dishonesty; that is what they insure against. It may be too, doubtless would be, that no concealment by a conspirator of the fact of the principal's original default, no continuance in the service by an officer of the corporation *in pari delicto* with the principal, would suffice to discharge the surety, since all of this is malversation participated in by the principal, and violative of the contract which the sureties have

undertaken to see faithfully performed. Moreover, the acts
and omissions of one agent of a corporation, in conspiracy
with another to filch their common master, in furtherance of
their nefarious purposes, are, in the nature of things, without
authorization by implication or otherwise, and can in no just
sense be said to be acts of omissions of the corporation.
Upon this idea, it may be that where one officer, though not
originally participating in the default of another, conceals
that default from the sureties of his fellow-officer and from the
company, for sinister purposes of his own, and not as representing his employer, or in his interest, and continues the
defaulting officer in the service, the sureties would not be discharged as to subsequent deficits. Thus far we may go with
the learned courts in which the cases we have cited were
decided.

But even our conversatism in following adjudications of
courts of acknowledged ability and learning can in no degree
constrain us to adopt the second proposition stated above.
We cannot subscribe to the doctrine, that there is the radical
difference insisted on, or any material difference in fact, between the efficacy of acts and omissions of an agent of a
creditor corporation, having authority in the premises, on the
one hand, and the acts and omissions of the agent of an individual creditor, or of the individual himself, on the other,
in respect of condoning the defalcation of an employee, omitting notice to the employee's sureties, and continuing him in
the service, to operate a release of the sureties as to subsequent deficits of the dishonest employee. No doctrine of the
law is more familiar than that notice to an agent, within the
scope of his agency, is notice to the principal; and this doctrine has in no connection been applied more frequently and
uniformly than to corporations and their agents. Indeed,
there is an absolute necessity in all cases for its application
to corporations, since they act and can be dealt with only
through agents. Notice to one agent of a corporation, with
respect to a matter covered by his agency, must be as effica-
cious as to its directors or to its [380] president, since these
also are only agents, with larger powers and duties, it is true,
but not more fully charged with respect to the particular
thing than he whose authority is confined to that one thing.
In the case at bar, Walls had authority to make the contract
with Saint, subject to the approval of another agent of the
corporation. He did in fact make it. This contract contained

a provision for its termination by either party at pleasure.
The evidence was that Walls had full supervision over Saint,
and over all matters embraced in the contract made by Saint.
It was at least a fair inference to be drawn by the jury, that
he could terminate the employment either under the stipulation in the instrument, or for a violation of it by Saint, subject to the approval of the other officer or agent referred to.
There is no ground to doubt but that to have given the sureties notice of Saint's default would have been in the line of
his duty and authority. Equally clear it must be, that their
assent to him to a continuance of Saint's employment would
have bound them for the subsequent defalcation; and, on the
other hand, it must be, that their dissent from such continuance communicated to him would have had the same effect
as had it been given to any other officer of the creditor company. He had notice of the default. He received it as representing the company. In that capacity, he condoned it, made
arrangements with Saint to make it good, continued the employment, and continued Saint's opportunities to embezzle
the company's funds, on the supposed security for its reimbursement afforded by the obligation of the sureties, who had
contracted on the assumption of Saint's honesty, and were
entitled to know of his dishonesty, when it should develop, as
a condition to their subsequent liability. There is no intimation of connivance or conspiracy on the part of Walls with
Saint to defraud either the creditor or the sureties. What he
did was doubtless done in good faith, and for the interest, as
he supposed, of his employer. It was in the line of his employment. If his further duty was to report his action to another
officer of the company, the presumption is that he made such
a report; there is nothing in the record to rebut such presumption. We cannot hesitate to affirm, on this state of the
case, that what he did which ought not to have been done,
and what he failed to do which ought to have been done, were
the acts and omissions of the corporation, involving the same
consequences in all respects as if the corporate entity had
been capable of direct personal action, so to speak, and had
[381] acted as he did, or as if he himself, and not Wheeler and
Wilson Manufacturing Company, had been the creditor.

We suppose it would not be contended in any quarter that
if these sureties had in terms stipulated that, in case of
Saint's default, notice to them and assent on their part should
be a condition precedent to their liability for further defaults,

they could be held without such notice and assent; and yet, under the doctrine announced in the cases cited, such a stipulation would be entirely nugatory, and the failure of every agent and officer, all with knowledge of the stipulation and of the default, to notify the sureties thereof would avail them nothing. Yet it would manifestly be no more the duty of the corporation to give a notice so stipulated for than to give a notice made a part of the contract by the law of the land. And such doctrine, carried to its legitimate results, would defeat all corporate liability growing out of the contracts, acts, and omissions of agents clothed with power and authority in the premises. That it is unsound is demonstrated not only in logic, but upon analogous authority. As we have seen, the English court, in the leading case of *Phillips* v. *Foxall*, L. R. 7 Q. B. 666, which has never been called in question there or in this country, either as to the result or the reasoning upon which it was reached, supported the principle declared upon the same considerations which underlie the doctrine that if an employer have knowledge of the previous dishonesty of a servant, and accept a guaranty for his future honesty without disclosing such knowledge to the surety, this is a fraud upon the latter, and he is not bound. Now suppose an officer of a corporation charged with the duty of finding surety for another officer, knowing of such previous dishonesty on the part of such other officer, takes bond for his faithful and honest performance of the services contracted for without giving the surety notice of the prior dereliction, would not that omission of duty on his part stand upon the same plane before the law, and involve precisely the same consequences, as if the default had occurred after the surety has bound himself, and the officer had then failed to give him notice of it? If the corporation is not prejudiced by the omission in one instance, can it be in the other? If the corporation is responsible for the dereliction of its agent with respect to notice of a previous default, would it not also be responsible for its agent's failure to give notice of the subsequent default? There can, in our opinion, be but one answer to these questions. There can be no possible difference in the duty of the agent [382] and the corporation's liability for its nonperformance in the two cases. And the law is well settled that the failure of the agent of a corporation to give notice of such previous dishonesty avoids the obligation of the sureties for future misconduct. Singularly enough, too, some of the cases holding this doctrine distinctly and broadly were decided by courts, those of Pennsylvania and Kentucky, which hold the contrary view as to notice of after-occurring embezzlement: Brandt on Suretyship and Guaranty, secs. 365–368; *Wayne* v. *Commercial Nat. Bank*, 52 Pa. St. 344; *Graves* v. *Lebanon Nat. Bank*, 10 Bush, 23; 19 Am. Rep. 50; *Franklin Bank* v. *Cooper*, 36 Me. 179; 39 Me. 542.

Our conclusion on this point is further supported by the cases of *Charlotte etc. R. R. Co.* v. *Gow,* 59 Ga. 685, 27 Am. Rep. 403, and *Atlantic etc. Tel. Co.* v. *Barnes*, 64 N. Y. 385, 21 Am. Rep. 621, which, without discussing this point, in effect hold that the omission of an officer of a corporation to notify a surety of the default of his principal in a case like this, and the continuance by such officer of the employment of the principal, will discharge the surety as to all defaults arising during the subsequent service.   And in *Newark* v. *Stout*, 52 N. J. L. 35, the New Jersey court, while adhering generally to the doctrine we have been criticising, yet held that if the default and dishonesty of a municipal officer be brought to the attention of the city council, which is clothed with the power to remove him, and he is allowed to continue in the service without notice to and assent on the part of the surety, the latter will be discharged from liability as to all subsequent defaults.   It does not appear to have been so considered by that court, but it is manifest that this is a radical departure from the doctrine held by the Pennsylvania, Kentucky, Maryland, and other courts, and relied on by appellee here, and goes strongly in support of the contrary rule, which we believe to be the sound one.

It is also to be noticed that much reliance is had by the courts holding that a surety of one officer of a corporation is not discharged by the acts or omissions of another in the particulars under consideration, on cases decided by the supreme court of the United States in respect of sureties of public officers.   Indeed it would seem that this whole doctrine had its inception in this class of cases.   This can but be considered an infirmative circumstance going to the soundness as authority of those cases which involve sureties of corporation officers.   There is a palpable and manifest distinction between the two classes of cases bearing directly upon this question, which, while requiring the application of this rule to public officers, on the grounds of public policy, **383** and that laches should not be imputed to the government, does not require its application to officers of corporations.

We hold that if Walls, while acting for the corporation, and in the capacity of its agent, with respect to the matters and things involved in Saint's contract, received notice of such a conversion of its funds by Saint as amounted to embezzlement, or involved dishonesty, and, without imparting this knowledge to the sureties, and receiving their assent thereto, continued him in the service, that the sureties are not liable for Saint's subsequent defaults. Charges 5, 9, and 7, requested for defendants, when referred to the evidence, were correct expositions of the law, as we understand, in this connection. The refusal of the court to give them involved error which must work a reversal of the case. Most of the other assignments of error are covered by the points considered in the first part of this opinion. Such of the assignments as are not discussed have been considered, and found to be without merit.

The judgment is reversed, and the cause remanded.

SURETY AND GUARANTOR—DIFFERENCE BETWEEN.—A contract of surety ship creates a direct liability to the creditor for the act to be performed by the debtor, but a contract of guaranty creates a liability only for his ability to perform such act. A surety is an insurer of the debt, while a guarantor is only an insurer of the solvency of the debtor: Campbell v. Sherman, 151 Pa. St. 70; 31 Am. St. Rep. 735, and note. A guaranty made by persons acting for an undisclosed principal is an original and not a collateral undertaking, and their liability is not that of sureties but of principals: Kernochan v. Murray, 111 N. Y. 306; 7 Am. St. Rep. 744.

GUARANTY—NECESSITY FOR NOTICE OF ACCEPTANCE.—To bind a guarantor, it must appear that he was notified of the acceptance of the guaranty, and of the reliance upon it: Roberts v. Griswold, 35 Vt. 496; 84 Am. Dec. 641, and note; Walker v. Forbes, 25 Ala. 139; 60 Am. Dec. 498, and note; Bank of Illinois v. Sloo, 16 La. 539; 35 Am. Dec. 223; Wilkins v. Carter, 84 Tex. 438 Johnson v. Bailey, 79 Tex. 516, and see the extended note to Thompson v Glover, 39 Am. Rep. 221.

SURETYSHIP—EFFECT OF ALTERATION OF CONTRACT.—The liability of a surety is limited strictly to the terms of the contract, and any extension of such liability is forbidden: Shreffler v. Nadelhoffer, 133 Ill. 536; 23 Am. St Rep. 626, and note, and any alteration therein without his consent is fatal to his obligation: Anderson v. Bellenger, 87 Ala. 334; 13 Am. St. Rep. 46 This subject is thoroughly discussed in the extended note to First Nat. Ban v. Gerke, 6 Am. St. Rep. 458; Garnett v. Farmers' Nat. Bank, 91 Ky. 614 34 Am. St. Rep. 246, and note, and Shackamaxon Bank v. Yard, 150 Pa. St 351; 30 Am. St. Rep. 807, and note.

SURETYSHIP—RELEASE OF SURETY BY INDULGENCE TO PRINCIPAL.—Se the notes to Campbell v. Sherman, 31 Am. St. Rep. 737, and Okie v. Spence 30 Am. Dec. 257. A mere indulgence to the debtor does not discharge th surety unless there is an agreement upon a sufficient consideration to give time to the principal: *Burke* v. *Cruger*, 8 Tex. 66; 58 Am. Dec. 102, and note; *Martin* v. *Pope*, 6 Ala. 532; 41 Am. Dec. 66; *Brinagar* v. *Phillips*, 1 B. Mon. 283; 36 Am. Dec. 575, and note; *Oberndorf* v. *Union Bank*, 31 Md. 126; 1 Am. Rep. 31.

MANNING v. LOUISVILLE AND NASHVILLE R. R. Co.

[95 ALABAMA, 392.]

RAILROADS—REGULATION AS TO PASSENGERS WITHOUT TICKETS—RIGHT TO EXPEL.—A railroad regulation requiring passengers found on trains without tickets, or with only forfeited tickets, to pay fare, not only for that part of the route to be traveled, but also for the part already passed over, is reasonable, and a passenger may be expelled from the train for a refusal to comply with it without liability on the part of the railroad company.

Bowman and Harsh, for the appellant.

Hewitt, Walker and Porter, for the appellee.

393 STONE, C. J. Plaintiff purchased an excursion ticket to and from New Orleans from defendant's ticket agent at Birmingham. He obtained it at reduced rates, but on certain conditions as to its use, which were printed on the ticket and subscribed by him. Plaintiff testified that he had read the conditions. Among them are the following: "In consideration of the reduced rate at which this ticket is sold, I, the undersigned, agree with the Louisville and Nashville Railroad Company as follows: That on the date of my departure, returning, I will identify myself as the original purchaser of this ticket, by writing my name on the back of this contract, and by other means, if required, in the presence of the ticket agent of the Louisville and Nashville Railroad Company at the point to which this ticket was sold, who will witness the signature, date, and stamp the contract; and that this ticket and coupons shall be good, returning, only for a continuous passage from such date, and in no case later than the date canceled in the margin of this contract."

Plaintiff conformed to all the requirements of this contract until he reached Mobile on his return trip. At that place he stopped off one day. At the end of that time he boarded another train of the railroad at midnight, and took a berth in a sleeping-car. He proceeded unmolested in his homeward trip until he passed Montgomery, and was nearing Calera, less than forty miles from Birmingham. At that stage of his

journey the conductor in charge of the train discovered he
was traveling on a forfeited ticket, but possibly did not learn
he had so traveled before he reached Montgomery. As a condition of his proceeding farther, the conductor exacted of him
that he should pay fare from Montgomery to Birmingham,
or, failing, that he would be put off the train at the next station, which would be Calera. [394] Reaching Calera, plaintiff procured from the ticket agent at that place a ticket to
Birmingham, and upon that ticket sought to continue his
journey on the same train. This the conductor refused to
allow him to do, stating that, under the road's regulations,
he could not permit him to proceed unless he would also pay
the back fare from Montgomery. This he failed to do, and
was ejected from the train. The present action is brought to
recover damages for such ejection. The court gave the general affirmative charge for the defendant.

A regulation by which railroads, when passengers are found
on their trains who have no tickets, or who have only forfeited
tickets, require of such passengers fare, not only for that part
of the route to be traveled, but also for the part already passed
over, is certainly a reasonable one. If persons who are attempting to ride without paying fare can have the past for-
given, and need pay only from the place and time of their
detection, would not this be the offer of a premium for an attempted undue advantage of the railroad? The regulation
needs no argument to uphold its reasonableness.

The authorities are uniform, and very abundant, that the
conductor was authorized to demand fare, not only for the
portion of the road yet to be traveled, but equally for that
part of the road plaintiff had been carried after his ticket had
become *functus* by virtue of his stopover. And the conductor
was fully justified in ejecting Manning from the train on his
refusal to pay the fare as demanded: 3 Wood's Railway Law,
sec. 361, p. 1433; Wheeler's Law of Carriers, 174; Hutchinson
on Carriers, 2d ed., sec. 580 a; *Hill* v. *Syracuse etc. R. R. Co.,*
63 N. Y. 101; *State* v. *Campbell,* 32 N. J. L. 309; *Swan* v. *Manchester etc. R. R. Co.,* 132 Mass. 116; 42 Am. Rep. 432; *Davis*
v. *Kansas City etc. R. R. Co.,* 53 Mo. 317; 14 Am. Rep. 457;
Stone v *C. & N. W. R. Co.,* 47 Iowa, 82; 29 Am. Rep. 458;
Hall v. *Memphis etc. R. R. Co.,* 15 Fed. Rep. 57; *Pennington*
v. *Philadelphia etc. R. R. Co.,* 62 Md. 95; *Pickens* v. *Richmond
etc. R. R. Co.,* 104 N. C. 312; *Atchison etc. R. R. Co.* v. *Gants,*
38 Kan. 608; 5 Am. St. Rep. 780; *Johnson* v. *Concord R. R.*

Corp., 46 N. H. 213; 88 Am. Dec. 199; *Rose* v. *Willmington etc. R. R. Co.*, 106 N. C. 168.

Plaintiff, appellant here, relies on *Ward* v. *New York Cent. etc. R. R. Co.*, 9 N. Y. Supp. 377, 56 Hun, 268, as an authority in his favor. The ticket in that case was an ordinary one, and had no clause or stipulation requiring or looking to continuous passage. The decision is rested on the absence of that provision. It refers to and approves many of the decisions we have referred to above, pronounced [395] on contracts requiring continuous passage. Properly interpreted, that case is an authority against appellant.

In *Alabama etc. R. R. Co.* v. *Carmichael*, 90 Ala. 19, we took occasion to comment on the great importance—the public necessity—of wisely observing regulations in the running of trains on railroads. We need not repeat what we there said.

We hold that in the charge given to the jury the circuit court strictly followed the law.

Affirmed.

————

RAILROADS—REGULATIONS AS TO TICKETS.—Where a passenger has been lawfully ejected from a train for the nonpayment of his fare, he cannot demand to be carried forward on the same train without paying the disputed fare, and his purchase of a ticket at the point of ejectment will not entitle him to readmission to the train: *Stone* v. *Chicago etc. Ry. Co.*, 47 Iowa, 82; 29 Am. Rep. 458, and note; *Pickens* v. *Richmond etc. R. R. Co.*, 104 N. C. 312; *Swan* v. *Manchester etc. R. R.*, 132 Mass. 116; 42 Am. Rep. 432. In *Davis* v. *Kansas City etc. R. R. Co.*, 53 Mo. 317, 14 Am. Rep. 457, the plaintiff bought a ticket from W. to B., but being unable to obtain a seat refused to surrender his ticket, and was ordered to leave the train at F. At that place he secured a seat, and tendered his fare from there to B., but refused to surrender his ticket or to pay his fare from W., whereupon he was ejected. It was held that he could not maintain an action for damages for his ejection.

————

EASTIS *v.* MONTGOMERY.

[95 ALABAMA, 486.]

WILLS—DECLARATIONS AS EVIDENCE.—Declarations by an executor and beneficiary, under a will not made in the presence of the testator, as to the disposition to be made of property, are not admissible either to support or invalidate the will, whether they were made before or after its execution.

WILLS—UNDUE INFLUENCE—EVIDENCE that a son of testatrix, who was her general business agent, signed her name to a bond for title to land sold by her, is inadmissible to show undue influence exercised by him over her.

WILLS—UNDUE INFLUENCE—EVIDENCE.—If a will is contested on the ground of undue influence exercised by the proponent, and evidence is admitted to show that certain grandchildren omitted from the will maintained friendly and affectionate relations with the testatrix, the proponent may prove that such children had some considerable property in their own right.

WILLS—UNDUE INFLUENCE—BURDEN OF PROOF.—Although the proponent of a will is one of the executors and chief beneficiaries named therein, and was the general business agent of the testatrix, his mother, his activity, not of his own motion or prompted by personal motives, but exercised in behalf of the testatrix at her request, and in furtherance of her purposes in assisting her about the execution of the will, does not, combined with such confidential relations, shift the burden of proof as to undue influence upon him.

WILLS—UNDUE INFLUENCE—INSTRUCTIONS.—An instruction that "the conduct of one in vigorous health toward one feeble in body, even though not unsound in mind, may be such as to excite terror or dread, and to make him execute as his will an instrument which, if he had been free from such influence, he would not have executed, imaginary terrors may have been created sufficient to deprive him of his free agency," is properly refused as abstract and argumentative.

WILLS—TESTAMENTARY CAPACITY—BURDEN OF PROOF.—Testamentary incapacity to invalidate a will must exist at the time of its execution. The presumption of capacity is always indulged, and the burden of proof is upon the party contesting the will to show incapacity. This burden can be shifted to the proponent only by showing prior habitual or fixed insanity, or actual insanity, or other incapacity of the testator, at the date of the execution of the will.

WILLS—TESTAMENTARY CAPACITY.—If a testator has mind and memory sufficient to recollect the property he is about to bequeath, the persons to whom he wishes to bequeath it, and the manner in which he wishes it disposed of, and to know and understand the business he is engaged in, then, in contemplation of law, he has a sound and disposing mind; and great age, bodily infirmity, or even an impaired mind, will not vitiate his will.

WILLS—UNDUE INFLUENCE—WHAT SUFFICIENT TO VITIATE WILL.—Unless the will in contest was obtained by moral coercion, or by importunity which could not be resisted by the testator, the will must stand.

INSTRUCTIONS—ERRONEOUS WHEN WILL NOT REVERSE.—A tendency or capacity of instructions to mislead, while it will justify their refusal, is no ground for reversal after they are given, if they in fact assert the law correctly.

CONTEST of the will of Martha Montgomery propounded for probate by her three sons, Jonathan, Felix, and David Montgomery, named as executors, and contested by Mrs. A. C. Eastis, a granddaughter of the testatrix, on the grounds of incapacity, undue influence, and insufficient execution. The due execution of the will was proved by the attesting witnesses thereto, and the court admitted it to probate against the objection and exception of the contestant. The will bequeathed

all of the property of the testatrix to her eight living children, and only five dollars each to the children of her two
deceased daughters, Mrs. Ellard and Mrs. Hawkins. W. W.
Ellard testified on the trial that Mr. Hawkins had property of
very considerable value, and that his own children had valuable land, while he owned two hundred and twenty acres of
land which was not very valuable. This evidence was admitted against the objection and exception of the contestant.
He also testified that Jonathan Montgomery attended to all
of the testatrix's business from 1866 until her death in 1889,
and that he had heard the said Jonathan in 1878 try to persuade the testatrix to deed to him seventy acres of land, and,
upon her refusal, he abused and cursed her. Other witnesses
testified to disrespectful conduct and abusive language used
by the said Jonathan to the testatrix. One of them testified:
"I heard Jonathan say that he was going to see to it that his
mother did not give the Ellard children any of her property,
and that they should have none of it." This evidence was
excluded and the contestant excepted. Mrs. Anderson, a
daughter of the testatrix, was asked, "Were you not present,
and did you not see Jonathan Montgomery sign your mother's
name to the bond for title to W. J. Cameron for the one hundred acres of land?" An objection to this question was sustained, and the contestant excepted. Jonathan Montgomery,
in his own behalf, denied that he had ever abused his mother
by word or act; that she deeded twenty acres of land to each
of the beneficiaries under the will, and had sixty-five acres
remaining; that he signed all the deeds for her, and sold one
hundred acres of her land to Cameron, the purchase money
being loaned to her several children. He was asked on cross-
examination if he had not stated in the presence of Mrs.
Hawkins and her daughter that his mother had executed a
will in which the Ellard children were provided for, and that
he had induced her to destroy that will. An objection to this
question was sustained, and the contestant excepted. The
court refused to give the following instructions requested by
the contestant, and he excepted: 1. "While the existence of
confidential relations between the testator and the beneficiaries is not, in itself. enough to shift the burden of proof upon
the proponents to show that there was not an undue influence
existing upon the mind of the testatrix at the time of the
making of the will, yet the existence of confidential relations
between the testator and the principal or large beneficiary

under the will, coupled with activity on the part of the latter
in and about the preparation and execution of the will, such
as the initiation of proceedings for the preparation, employing the draughtsman, selecting the witnesses, excluding persons from the presence of the testator at or about the time of
the execution, and the like, will raise up a presumption of
undue influence, and cast upon him the burden of showing
that it was not induced by coercion or fraud on his part,
directly or indirectly." 2. If the jury believe from the evidence that Jonathan Montgomery managed and controlled
the affairs of the testatrix for many years before the making
of the will, and up to that time, living in the family with her
and her insane daughter; that he actively participated in and
about the execution of the will, such as procuring the draughtsman, the witnesses, etc., then this is sufficient to cast upon
the proponents the burden of proving that the will was not the
product of undue influence." 3. "The jury is charged that,
in procuring a will to be made by which the testator disposes
of his property in a manner different from what he would
have done, had no improper influence been exercised over
him, is sufficient reason for setting aside the will. 4. "The
conduct of one in vigorous health towards one feeble in body,
even though not unsound in mind, may be such as to excite
terror or dread, and to make him execute as his will an instrument which, if he had been free from such influence, he
would not have executed. Imaginary terrors may have been
created sufficient to deprive him of his free agency." 5. "If
the jury believe from the evidence that Mrs. Montgomery,
from the infirmity of age, or other cause, was reduced to that
condition in which she was under the dominion and control
of Jonathan Montgomery; and that from threats, overpersuasion, putting in fear or dread, or any other improper conduct
on his part, she was induced or influenced to execute this supposed will, contrary to what she otherwise would have done,
then the paper is not a will, and their verdict must be for the
contestants." The substance of the instructions given at the
request of the proponents and excepted to by the contestant
are stated in the opinion, except that one numbered nine
which was as follows: "If the jury believe from the evidence
that Martha Montgomery, at the time she made the will, was
of sound mind, she could make a will; and for her mind to
be sound, it is not necessary that her memory be perfect and
her mind be unimpaired; but if she had mind and memory

enough to recollect the property she was about to bequeath, and
the persons to whom she wished to bequeath it, and the manner in which she wished it to be disposed of, and to know
and understand the business she was engaged in, then, in
contemplation of law, she had a sound and disposing mind,
and her great age and bodily imfirmity, if she was infirm, and
her impaired mind, if her mind was impaired, do not vitiate
a will thus made." Verdict in favor of the will and judgment admitting it to probate. The contestant appealed.

McGuire and Collier, for the appellant.

Hewitt, Walker and Porter, and E. K. Campbell, for the
appellee.

491 McCLELLAN, J. Many of the questions presented by
this record were before this court on a former appeal, and
then determined against the appellants. It was then held
that the error of excluding, when first proposed, evidence as
to the conveyances by the testatrix, after the making of the will,
of seventy acres of land to Jonathan Montgomery, and twenty
acres each to said Montgomery and the other principal beneficiaries, was cured by its subsequent admission, the facts in
this regard being clearly proved, and indeed not controverted;
that the declarations made by **492** Jonathan Montgomery,
then, and now again, offered in evidence, were not competent
either to support or invalidate the will; and that the proposed
testimony as to the transaction between Jonathan Montgomery, representing the testatrix, and W. J. Cameron, involving
a sale and bond for title of and to one hundred acres of land,
was properly excluded. It was also then ruled, that the giving of a charge requested by the proponents, to the effect that
there was no evidence in the case of threats made by Jonathan
Montgomery towards his mother, to 'induce or cause her to
make the will in controversy, involved no reversible error:
Eastis v. *Montgomery*, 93 Ala. 293. And these several rulings
we reaffirm.

This contest is prosecuted by, or in the interest of, grandchildren of the testatrix—the issue of two daughters who had
died before the will was executed—for whom the instrument
makes no substantial provision. One of the two main grounds
of contestation is the alleged undue influence exerted by the
children of the testatrix, or some of them, who **are** equal beneficiaries under it. Evidence was adduced going to show

affectionate relations between the testatrix and these grandchildren. This was, of course, intended to afford an inference
that had the testatrix taken counsel of her affections, and
been allowed to make such dispositions of her property as
they naturally dictated, the grandchildren would not have
been cut off with a penny; and therefore, the argument proceeds, undue influence must have been exerted upon her to
induce this unnatural result. It is manifest that the strength
of this inference depends greatly upon the circumstances and
necessities of the grandchildren. If they, for instance, were
already provided for—if their conditions in life were not such
as to appeal to the bounty of the testatrix—it was much more
reasonable that she should have failed of her own free will to
make additional provision for them in her will, than had they
been in necessitous circumstances. And for the purpose of
showing that this exclusion from any substantial benefits under the will, notwithstanding the affection entertained for
them by the testatrix, was not unnatural, and did not afford
a basis for any inference of undue influence, it was entirely
proper for the proponents to adduce evidence to the effect
that the contestants had property of their own: Schouler on
Wills, sec. 242; *Beaubien* v. *Cicotte,* 12 Mich. 459; *Crocker* v.
Chase, 57 Vt. 413; *Stubbs* v. *Houston,* 33 Ala. 555; *Fountain*
v. *Brown,* 38 Ala. 72.

An objection was made to the introduction of the will in
493 evidence, on the ground that it was not shown to have been
properly executed. We are not advised by counsel in what
respect the preliminary evidence fell short of proving the requisite formality in the execution of the instrument, nor have
we been able to find that anything essential in that regard
was omitted to be done. The objection was without merit.

Charge No. 1 requested by the contestants was well refused
because, to say the least, it is abstract in a sense, and would
have tended to confuse and mislead the jury. Some of it
postulates find no lodgment in any tendency of the evidence.
There is no evidence in this record of any activity on the
part of Jonathan Montgomery in and about the preparation
and execution of the will, except such as was the result of the
wishes and requests of the testatrix, which, so far as the evidence discloses, were entertained and expressed by her of her
own free will, and not themselves induced by any undue influence. Such activity, not of proponent's own motion, or
prompted by personal motives, but in behalf of the testatrix

and in furtherance of her purposes, will not combine with confidential relations to shift the burden of proof as to undue influence upon the proponent. And because of this, the charge
was misleading; the activity shown by the evidence was not
of a character to support the conclusion sought to be drawn
from it. Moreover, there is no evidence whatever that the
proponent excluded persons from the presence of the testatrix
about the time of the execution of the will—a fact which is
made a sub-postulate for the proposition declared in the
charge; and to this extent, at least, the instruction was palpably abstract.

Charge No. 2 refused to contestants is open to the same
objections as those stated to charge 1. There is no evidence
of such procurement of the draughtsman and witnesses, as,
with proof of confidential relations, cast the *onus* of negativing
undue influence on the proponent.

Charge 3 refused to contestants was well calculated to mislead the jury, in that it assumes that the will referred to had
been procured to be made by the exercise of improper influence, and might thereby have led the jury to the conclusion
that, in the opinion of the court, the will in this case had been
so procured. Had this charge directed the jury to the effect
that, if they believed from all the evidence that Martha Montgomery had been induced by improper or undue influence
to execute a will different from the will she would have executed but for such influence, they would be authorized to set
it aside, it would have been unobjectionable; [494] but, as it is
written, it is clearly open to a construction which would have
made it an invasion of the province of the jury, the effect being to deny their right to say, in the first instance, whether
the will propounded had been so procured to be made.

Charge 4 refused to contestants is palpably an argument
throughout. Of course, the conduct of one toward another
may be such as to excite that degree of dread and terror in
the latter as will induce him to execute an instrument purporting to be a will which does not accord with his real wishes
and purposes, and is therefore not a will at all; and this regardless of the respective physical and mental conditions of
the parties. But it is no part of the court's duty, charged
only with the declaring the law to the jury, to enter upon this
kind of disquisition as to the probable or possible effect of the
conduct of one man toward another. This is a matter of fact
and inference for the jury, and one upon which they are

deemed as competent to pass as the presiding judge, and one,
too, upon which the judge is not, and they are, authorized and
required to pass. This charge, moreover, as well as the fifth
instruction requested for contestants, is abstract. There is
no evidence of the excitation of terror and dread in the mind
of the testatrix, nor of any threats, or overpersuasion, or putting in fear on the part of Jonathan Montgomery, in connection with the execution of the will by his mother.

Charges 5, 12, 14, and 15 given at the instance of the proponents, to the effect, or involving the ideas, that testamentary
incapacity is an incapacity existing cotemporaneously with
the execution of the alleged will; that the burden of proof as
to such incapacity is upon the contestants, the original presumption of sanity and capacity being always indulged; and
that this burden can only be discharged or shifted by showing
prior habitual or fixed insanity, or actual insanity, or other incapacity at the date of the instrument, are correct expositions
of the law; as also is charge 9, which defines testamentary
capacity: *Leeper* v. *Taylor*, 47 Ala. 221; *Cotton* v. *Ulmer*, 45
Ala. 378; 6 Am. Rep. 703; *Daniel* v. *Hill*, 52 Ala. 430;
O'Donnell v. *Rodiger*, 76 Ala. 222; 52 Am. Rep. 322; *Kramer*
v. *Weinert*, 81 Ala. 414.

The pleadings presented three issues: 1. Whether the instrument propounded as a will had been efficiently executed;
2. Whether Mrs. Montgomery had testamentary capacity;
and 3. Whether the will propounded was procured to be made
by the exercise of undue influence. Charge 8, "That unless
the evidence shows that the will was obtained [495] by moral
coercion, or by importunity which could not be resisted by
the testatrix, the jury must find the issue in favor of the proponents," had reference to the issue of undue influence *vel non.*
If contestants apprehended that the jury would be misled by
this charge to the conclusion that all three of the issues—the
whole case—should be determined against the contestants, if
they found that no undue influence had been resorted to, they
should have asked an explanatory and limiting charge. This
tendency or capacity to mislead in charges, while it will justify their refusal, is no ground for reversal when they are
given, if they in fact assert the law correctly. And the charge,
abstractly considered, is sound: *Bancroft* v. *Otis*, 91 Ala. 279;
24 Am. St. Rep. 904; *Eastis* v. *Montgomery*, 93 Ala. 293.

Every assignment of error which has not been specifically
discussed is covered, either by what we have said, or by the

opinion of the court on the former appeal; and as the facts
of the case as then and now presented, when brought to the
touch of the principles of law obtaining in the premises, are
substantially the same, we deem it unnecessary to say more
here than that we find no errors in the record.

Affirmed.

WILLS—UNDUE INFLUENCE—EVIDENCE—BURDEN OF PROOF.—For a full
discussion of these questions, see *Haines* v. *Hayden*, 95 Mich. 332; 35 Am.
St. Rep. 566, and note; *Maddox* v. *Maddox*, 114 Mo. 35; 35 Am. St. Rep.
734, and note, and the extended notes to *In re Hess's Will*, 31 Am. St.
Rep. 670; and *Small* v. *Small*, 16 Am. Dec. 257. For a discussion of the presumption of undue influence, see the extended note to *Richmond's Appeal*,
21 Am. St. Rep. 94–104.

WILLS.—TESTAMENTARY CAPACITY—TEST OF—BURDEN OF PROOF: See
Maddox v. *Maddox*, 114 Mo. 35; 35 Am. St. Rep. 734, and note; and *Harrison* v. *Bishop*, 131 Ind. 161; 31 Am. St. Rep. 422, and note, where this
question is discussed at length.

EVIDENCE—WILLS—DECLARATIONS OF REPRESENTATIVE.—The declarations of a sole executor and contingent devisee, representing every interest
under the will, and being a party on record, such declarations being adverse
to the will, and bearing upon the issues raised upon a *caveat* against the probate of it, are admissible in the evidence: *Davis* v. *Calvert*, 5 Gill. & J. 269;
25 Am. Dec. 282, and extended note; *Peeples* v. *Stevens*, 8 Rich. 198; 64
Am. Dec. 750.

KNOX *v.* KNOX.

[95 ALABAMA, 495.]

WILLS—DIFFERENT PAPERS EXECUTED AT DIFFERENT DATES AS ONE WILL.
A testamentary paper executed by a testatrix in execution of a testamentary power conferred on her by her deceased husband is not revoked
by the execution of a later will and codicil containing substantially the
same provisions as the first paper, but without referring to it, and the
two instruments, when taken together, constitute the last will of the
testatrix.

WILLS—TESTAMENTARY CAPACITY—WHAT CONSTITUTES.—If a testator has
mind and memory sufficient to recall and remember the property he is
about to bequeath, the objects of his bounty, the disposition which he
wishes to make, and to know and understand the nature and consequences of the business to be performed, and to discern the simple and
obvious relation of its elements to each other, he has in contemplation
of law a sound mind and testamentary capacity.

WILLS.—UNDUE INFLUENCE SUFFICIENT to avoid a will must amount to
coercion or fraud, and must be an influence tantamount to force or fear,
destroying the free agency of the party, and constraining him to do
what is against his will. Mere persuasion or argument addressed to
the judgment or affections, in which there is no fraud or deceit, does
not constitute undue influence.

WILLS—EVIDENCE OF UNDUE INFLUENCE OR MENTAL INCAPACITY.—When a
will is contested on the ground of mental incapacity or undue influence,
the real issue is as to the condition of the mind, or the operation and
effect of the undue influence, at the particular time of the execution of
the will, but all prior facts and circumstances tending to elucidate the
condition of the mind of the testator at that particular time are admissible in evidence.

WILLS—UNEQUAL BEQUESTS—PRESUMPTION—BURDEN OF PROOF.—Although
a testator may not in his will dispose of his property equally to his next
of kin, that fact alone does not raise a presumption of mental incapacity
or undue influence, but must be considered with other facts in determining that issue. Such fact does not shift the burden of proof upon
the proponent or beneficiaries under the will, and require him to show
a sound mind and freedom of will on the part of the testator at the time
of its execution.

WILLS—UNDUE INFLUENCE—INSTRUCTIONS.—When a will is contested on
the ground of undue influence, an instruction that a controlling agency
exercised by the proponents or beneficiaries under it in procuring its
execution "is a very suspicious circumstance requiring the fullest explanation," requires too high a degree of proof, and is properly refused.
Evidence of any fact sufficient to reasonably satisfy the minds of the
jury is all that is required in civil cases.

CONTEST of the will of Anna O. Knox propounded for probate by William Knox and A. Troy, named therein as executors, and contested by Edward N. Knox, the grandchild of
the testatrix, on the grounds of testamentary incapacity, undue influence, and fraud. Testatrix died June 14, 1890,
when over eighty years of age, and the papers propounded
for probate consisted of a will dated September 16, 1889, and
a codicil dated May 2, 1890. The proponents also asked
probate of another testamentary paper executed by the testatrix on June 28, 1883, which purported to be executed in
execution of testamentary powers conferred on her by her deceased husband by certain deeds and by which she made the
following disposition of the property: "Now, therefore, in
execution of said power, I do hereby, by this my last will,
direct that the said one-half of said property so held in trust
be conveyed to and divided between my daughter Myra and
my son William, to be held by their heirs forever." By the
will of 1889 and codicil thereto of 1890 the testatrix bequeathed the bulk of her property to William Knox and Myra
Semmes the parties above named in the will of 1883, and in
both the contestant was entirely excluded. The contestant
objected to the admission of the will of 1883 to probate, on the
ground that it was revoked by the will of 1889 and the codicil thereto of 1890, but the court below admitted it, and instructed the jury that " as matter of law, said testamentary

paper was not revoked by the subsequent wills." The contestant excepted. On the trial in the probate court one
Falkner testified that he drafted the will of 1889 under the
instructions of the testatrix, and was with her for more than
an hour, during which time her mind seemed bright and clear,
and she seemed to be free from any undue excitement, that
neither William Knox nor Myra Semmes was present when
the will was executed. The codicil to said will was written
by Mrs. Myra Semmes, and a subscribing witness testified
that it was not read over to the testatrix before she signed it.
The proponents proved that the testatrix executed other wills
in 1875 and 1879 in which the contestant's name was not
mentioned. The contestant offered evidence tending to prove
that William Knox exercised great control over the testatrix,
and that she feared him, especially when he was drunk, and
that Mrs. Semmes exercised great influence over the testatrix
during her last illness. The proponents denied the exercise
of undue influence over the testatrix, and offered other evidence in support of their own as to this fact. The contestant excepted to the charges given to the jury upon the request of the
proponents, and also to a refusal to give the following charges
requested by himself. " X. Where a will is unreasonable in
its provisions, and inconsistent with the duties of the testa-
tator or testatrix with reference to his or her family and property, or what is usually denominated an inofficious testament,
and the jury find from the evidence in the cause that the will
or wills and codicil propounded for probate are of such character, this, of itself, will impose upon those claiming under
the instrument the necessity of giving some reasonable explanation of the unnatural character of the will, or at least of
showing that its character is not the offspring of mental defect, obliquity, or perversion. Y. If the jury find from the
evidence that William Knox or Mrs. Myra Semmes exercised
such an influence over the mind and acts of Mrs. A. O. Knox
as to take away from her her free agency, or to substitute
their will for hers then they will be authorized to find against
such will as to the legacies tainted by said undue influence.
Z. If the jury find from the evidence that William Knox or
Mrs. Myra Semmes are largely benefited by the provisions
of the instruments propounded for probate as the will and
testament of Mrs. A. O. Knox, and further find that they had
a controlling agency in procuring their execution, it is universally regarded as a very suspicious circumstance, and re-

quiring the fullest explanation." The jury returned a verdict in favor of the wills, and the probate court rendered judgment admitting them to probate. Contestant appealed to the circuit court, where the judgment was affirmed, and he then appealed to the supreme court.

Charles Wilkinson, for the appellant.

Semple and Gunter, and Tompkins and Troy, for the appellees.

[502] COLEMAN, J. The case comes to this court by appeal from the circuit court, to which court an appeal had been taken from the decree and judgment rendered by the probate court of Montgomery county, on a contest of the validity of the will of Mrs. Anna O. Knox. On June 28, 1883, testatrix executed in due form an instrument purporting to be her last will and testament. One provision of this will was in the following words: "And whereas certain powers were vested in me by two deeds executed by my deceased husband, William Knox, the one to William S. Donnell, trustee, dated May 30, 1853, and the other to Thomas J. Semmes, trustee, dated December 18, 1856, over one-half of the property, real and personal, conveyed by said deeds, and held under the said trusts thereof, to be exercised by last will; now therefore, under the execution of said power, I do hereby by my last will direct," etc., disposing of the property. So much of this instrument as contained the exercise of the power therein specified was offered, in connection with the will and codicil made by testatrix on the sixteenth day of September, 1889, and as a part of testatrix's will which was offered for probate. The bill of exceptions does not undertake to set out all the evidence; in fact there is nothing in the bill of exceptions which indicates that other evidence than that set out was not before the court. Looking at the two instruments together we can not say the one executed in 1883 was not a testamentary exercise of the power authorized by the deeds of trust referred to; and there is certainly nothing in evidence to show that the power thus [503] exercised was subsequently revoked. We find no error in the ruling of the court in this respect.

The grounds of contest were testamentary incapacity, undue influence, and fraud. What constitutes "testamentary capacity," or "sound and disposing mind and memory," as established in this state, is: if the testatrix had mind and

memory sufficient to recall and remember the property she
was about to bequeath, and the objects of her bounty, and the
disposition which she wished to make—to know and understand the nature and consequences of the business to be performed, and to discern the simple and obvious relation of its
elements to each other—she had, in contemplation of law, a
sound mind: *Kramer* v. *Weinart*, 81 Ala. 416; *Taylor* v. *Kelly*,
31 Ala. 59; 68 Am. Dec. 150.

As to undue influence, the rule as declared in *Bancroft* v.
Otis, 91 Ala. 290, 24 Am. St. Rep. 904, is as follows: "The
undue influence which will avoid a will must amount to
coercion or fraud; ideas which involve actual intent to control the testator against his will. The law never presumes
fraud, or the evil intent and unlawful acts essential to the
coercion here contemplated. There must be some proof of
these things. They cannot be considered to have been done,
merely because the proponent had the power to coerce, or to
defraud."

In *Eastis* v. *Montgomery*, 93 Ala. 293, it is said: "The
undue influence which will avoid a will must amount to
coercion or fraud, an influence tantamount to force or fear,
and which destroys the free agency of the party, and con-
strains him to do what is against his will. Mere persuasion
or argument addressed to the judgment or affections, in which
there is no fraud or deceit, does not constitute undue influence."

There was some evidence in the case of *Eastis* v. *Montgomery*,
93 Ala. 293, which tended to show that, on the part of a preferred legatee, he was at times disrespectful, abusive, and ill
treated testatrix, as in the present case; but, as the evidence
failed to show that such conduct operated to influence testatrix at the time of the execution of the will, it was held by a
majority of the court that it was not improper for the court to
instruct the jury, "that there was no evidence in the case of
any threats to induce or cause testatrix to make the will contrary to her intention."

When the probate of a will is contested on the ground of
mental incapacity, or undue influence, the real issue is as to
the condition of the mind, or the operation and effect of undue
influence, at the particular time of the execution of [504] the
will. The condition of the mind of the testate prior to the
execution of the will, and all facts and circumstances which
tend to elucidate its condition, or to show the freedom of the

will, or that it was unduly coerced and influenced at the particular time, although such facts and circumstances may have existed or occurred previous to the time of the execution of the will, are admissible in evidence: *O'Donnell* v. *Rodiger,* 76 Ala. 226; 52 Am. Rep. 322; *Kramer* v. *Weinart,* 81 Ala. 415. Tested by these principles, which have been often adjudicated, and others which are familiar, we find no error in the charges given by the court to the jury.

In charge No. 20 there appears evidently an error in copying. It is conceded by counsel on both sides, that the original charge read "if suffered" instead of "if sufficient," and should be thus corrected. With this correction the charge is free from error.

Charge "X" requested by contestant is objectionable for many reasons. It is misleading. In the next place, the law does not undertake to prescribe the duties of a testator to his family, in regard to the disposition of his property. And again, although a testator might not dispose of his property equally to his next of kin, that fact alone does not raise a presumption of mental incapacity or undue influence. The manner in which a testator disposes of his property is a fact in evidence, to be considered with other facts in determining the issue; but there is no conclusion of law from such a fact as to shift the burden of proof upon proponent, or the beneficiaries under the will, to show a sound mind, or freedom of will, on the part of the testator. It is a mere circumstance to be weighed by the jury: *Eastis* v. *Montgomery,* 93 Ala. 293.

Charge marked "Y" was properly refused. As was previously declared in this opinion, to sustain the contest of the probate of a will on the ground of undue influence, the evidence must show that such undue influence operated at the time of the execution of the will. This principle is not recognized in charge Y. We also think the charge abstract. There is no evidence in the record to show "undue influence," as contemplated by the law.

Charge "Z" was properly refused. It is abstract, and is objectionable for the further reason, that it requires a higher degree of proof than the law demands. When the jury is reasonably satisfied from the evidence of any fact in civil cases, that is all that is required. But, when a charge asserts that any fact requires the "fullest" explanation, we [505] have no legal scales to measure or weigh with any degree of definiteness the testimony necessary to meet this demand.

We find no error in the record, and the judgment is affirmed.

WILLS.—The questions of what is sufficient capacity to execute a will and the test of and burden of proof concerning, as well as the various questions as to undue influence invalidating wills, is discussed in *Eastis* v. *Montgomery,* 95 Ala. 486, *ante* 227, and note, where the notes and cases treating those subjects are collected.

WILLS—CONSTRUING DIFFERENT INSTRUMENTS AS ONE WILL.—All testamentary papers, no matter how numerous, should be proved together as one will: *Pepper's Estate,* 148 Pa. St. 5. A paper may be referred to and made a part of a will, if such paper is then in existence and can be identified: *In re Shillaber,* 74 Cal. 144; 5 Am. St. Rep. 433, and note. Notes made by a testator, payable at his death, folded up in his will and referred to therein, and remaining in his possession at his death, are a part of the will: *Fickle* v. *Snepp,* 97 Ind. 289; 49 Am. Rep. 449, and extended note.

HODGES *v.* WINSTON.
[95 ALABAMA, 514.]

HOMESTEADS IN SEPARATE TRACTS OF LAND.—Two parcels of land, though not contiguous, if occupied and cultivated in connection with each other, and used as a common source of family support, may together constitute a homestead.

HOMESTEADS—CONVEYANCE OF—VALIDITY AS AGAINST CREDITORS.—Simple money judgment creditors and those claiming under them have no right to complain of the conveyance of his homestead by their debtor.

REPUGNANT DEFENSES.—One who for the purpose of maintaining a defense deliberately represents a thing in one aspect is not permitted to contradict his own representation by giving the same thing another aspect in the same case.

HOMESTEADS—REPUGNANT DEFENSES.—A defendant in an action who has obtained a substantial advantage by taking and successfully maintaining the position that the land in controversy is a homestead, is thereby estopped from claiming on the same evidence, and in the same action, that it is not a homestead.

HOMESTEADS—CONVEYANCE OF CERTIFICATE OF ACKNOWLEDGMENT.—A conveyance of a homestead by a husband and wife, without the separate acknowledgment of the wife and certificate thereof as required by the statute is a mere nullity. When such conveyance has been completely executed by delivery and acceptance for record, the officer before whom it was acknowledged has no power to alter or add to the certificate, or make a new one, without a reacknowledgment.

HOMESTEADS—CONVEYANCE OF DEFECTIVE ACKNOWLEDGMENT—LIEN OF EXECUTION.—A conveyance of a homestead by husband and wife, to which the certificate of separate acknowledgment of the wife is not made until after the conveyance has been delivered and recorded, and then without a reacknowledgment and after the lien of an execution has attached, is a mere nullity, and the execution purchaser acquires a good title if the levy and sale were made after the land ceased to be a homestead.

ACTION **by** Winston against Mrs. A. Shubert as tenant in possession to recover two small tracts of land. The plaintiff claimed as a purchaser at sheriff's sale under a judgment and execution in his favor against James G. Coleman. The sheriff's deed to plaintiff was dated November 5, 1885. Hodges intervened as the landlord of Mrs. Shubert, and defended under his own title as a purchaser from said Coleman and wife by deed dated February 20, 1885. Two certificates of acknowledgment were indorsed on this deed taken by the same justice of the peace and dated February 20, 1885, one by the grantor and his wife, and one of separate examination by the wife alone. The deed also recited two indorsements of filing for record, one dated September 1, 1885, the other February 15, 1886. The testimony of the justice of the peace showed that he took both acknowledgments and wrote both certificates, that the certificate of separate acknowledgment of the wife was made on February 20, 1885; that Mrs. Coleman did not again acknowledge the deed before him, and that he did not remember writing a second certificate subsequent to the date of the deed. From the testimony of Coleman it appeared that Mrs. Coleman had a separate examination at the time the deed was executed and acknowledged, the certificate of the grantor and his wife jointly, then being appended, that he discovered the defect in the certificate after the deed was filed for record, and he then procured the justice to make and add the certificate of the separate examination of the wife, and again filed the deed for record. Mrs. Coleman was not present when this was done, and the record copy of the deed as first recorded showed only the joint certificate of the grantor and his wife. Upon these, and the further facts appearing in the opinion, the plaintiff had a verdict and judgment in his favor, and the defendant appealed.

J. E. Brown, for the appellants.

O. D. Street, for the appellee.

516 WALKER, J. The two parcels of land involved in this suit are not contiguous. The house in which James G. Coleman, the judgment debtor, lived with his family was on the forty-acre tract. In connection with this tract he used the other tract containing fifty-five acres, cultivating it every year, and getting from it a support for his family. The aggregate value of the two tracts was less than two thousand dollars. They were occupied and cultivated in connection with each other, and were used as a common source of fami'y support. Together they could constitute a homestead: *Dicus* v. *Hall*, 83 Ala. 159. The facts as to the judgment debtor's occupancy and use of the two parcels together were testified to by the witness Thomas Coleman. After he had testified, evidence offered by the plaintiff to show that the sale of the land by the judgment [517] debtor to Hodges was fraudulent and void as to the former's creditors was objected to by the defendants on the ground that the testimony of the witness Thomas Coleman showed the land sued for to have been the homestead of James G. Coleman at the time of the execution of his deed; and this objection was sustained. Assuming that the lands constituted a homestead, this ruling was correct, as the plaintiffs in a simple money judgment, and those claiming under them, have no right to complain of the disposition of homestead property which could not be subjected to their demand. The testimony of the witness Thomas Coleman as to the judgment debtor's occupancy and use of the two parcels together remained wholly uncontroverted. The defendants, in making the objection on the ground mentioned, precluded themselves from contending that the two parcels together did not constitute a homestead. Having obtained a substantial advantage by taking and successfully maintaining the position that the lands in question constituted a homestead, they estopped themselves from claiming, on the same state of evidence, that they were not a homestead. They could not support one position of defense by claiming that the lands constituted a homestead, and at the same time obtain the advantage of another position which involved a denial of the homestead character of the land. A defendant who, for the purpose of maintaining a defense, has deliberately represented a thing in one aspect, cannot be permitted to contradict his own representation by giving the same thing another aspect in the same case: *Caldwell* v. *Smith*, 77 Ala. 157; *Hill* v. *Huckabee*, 70 Ala. 183; Herman on Estoppel, 4th ed., 687.

James G. Coleman was living on the land as his homestead when he and his wife signed and delivered the deed to the defendant Hodges. Without the separate acknowledgment of the wife and the certificate thereof as required by the statute, that deed was a nullity: Code, sec. 2508. This court, after a full consideration of the question, has decided that when a deed has been delivered to the parties, and has been accepted for record, or as the complete execution of the instrument, the officer before whom the grantors acknowledged it has no power to alter or add to his certificate, or to make a new certificate, without a reacknowledgment: *Griffith* v. *Ventress*, 91 Ala. 366; 24 Am. St. Rep. 918. The reasoning in that case to support the conclusion that the officer taking the acknowledgment is without power is equally applicable whether the officer, when the alteration or addition or the new certificate is made, is holding his office under the same election [518] or appointment under which he held at the time the original acknowledgment was taken, or has gone out of office, or holds office under a new election or appointment. The evidence in the present case shows that the certificate of the separate acknowledgment of the wife was not made until after the conveyance had been delivered and once recorded, and that it was made without reacknowledgment and after the lien of the execution under which the plaintiff purchased had attached. Without the wife's separate acknowledgment and the certificate thereof, the deed to the defendant Hodges was a mere nullity when the lien of the execution attached. The evidence showing, without conflict, a judgment against James G. Coleman, the issue of execution thereon, a levy and sale under the writ, and the sheriff's deed to the plaintiff, all in due form, and that at the time of the levy and sale the land had ceased to be the homestead of the defendant in the judgment and that his attempted conveyance thereof was a mere nullity, the plaintiff was entitled to recover. If there was error in any of the rulings of the court of which the appellants complain, it was error without injury. There was no evidence to support any defense.

Affirmed. ———

HOMESTEAD IN NONCONTIGUOUS TRACTS OF LAND: See note to *Arendt* v. *Mace*, 9 Am. St. Rep. 210, and extended note to *Pryor* v. *Stone*, .9 Am. Dec. 350. A homestead does not include a tract of timber land a mile from the house and farm occupied, not adjoining it, from which fuel was alone derived for the use of the farm: *Walters* v. *People*, 18 Ill. 194; 65 Am. Dec. 730, and note. Different tracts of land which are separated from one another by a distance of several miles cannot be occupied and used together for the purposes of a homestead: *In re Armstrong*, 80 Cal. 71. A homestead must consist of one body of land: *Linn County Bank* v. *Hopkins*, 47 Kan. 580; 27 Am. St. Rep. 309, and note.

HOMESTEAD—CONVEYANCE—VALIDITY OF AS TO CREDITORS.—A convey-ance by a debtor of his homestead not subject to a judgment lien or sale under execution is not fraud as to his creditors: *Bogan* v. *Cleveland*, 52 Ark. 101; 20 Am. St. Rep. 158, and note. A sale of a homestead cannot be fraudulent as to a creditor of the claimant, since such creditor has no inter-est therein which may be taken in the payment of his debts: *McDannell* v. *Ragsdale*, 71 Tex. 23; 10 Am. St. Rep. 729, and note; *McPhee* v. *O'Rourke*, 10 Col. 301; 3 Am. St. Rep. 579, and note; *Dortch* v. *Benton*, 98 N. C. 190; 2 Am. St. Rep. 331, and note; *Campbell* v. *Jones*, 52 Ark. 493; *Schaffer* v. *Beldsmeier*, 107 Mo. 314. See, also, the note to *Pike* v. *Miles*, 99 Am. Dec. 152.

HOMESTEAD—JUDGMENT WHETHER LIEN ON.—A judgment is not a lien on the homestead of the judgment debtor: *Beyer* v. *Thoeming*, 81 Iowa, 517; *Milford Sav. Bank* v. *Ayers*, 48 Kan. 602; *Freiberg* v. *Walzem*, 85 Tex. 264; 34 Am. St. Rep. 808, and note; extended notes to *Vanstory* v. *Thornton*, 34 Am. St. Rep. 496, and *Blue* v. *Blue*, 87 Am. Dec. 278.

HOMESTEAD—CONVEYANCE BY HUSBAND AND WIFE—DEFECTIVE ACKNOWL-EDGMENT.—A deed to the homestead by a husband and wife jointly, without the assent and signature of the wife properly acknowledged by her as the statute requires is a mere nullity: *Smith* v. *Pearce*, 85 Ala. 264; 7 Am. St. Rep. 44; *Gage* v. *Wheeler*, 129 Ill. 197; *Jones* v. *Robbins*, 74 Tex. 615. The homestead can be conveyed only by the joint deed of the husband and wife, the wife being examined apart from her husband, and separate deeds by both spouses conveying such homestead are void: *Poole* v. *Gerrard*, 6 Cal. 71; 65 Am. Dec. 481, and extended note 484.

PLEADING—REPUGNANCY—ESTOPPEL.—Where the complaint sets out in terms the contract sued upon, and also contains an allegation which places a false construction upon the contract, such repugnant allegation may be re-jected as surplusage: *Love* v. *Sierra Nevada Water etc. Co.*, 32 Cal. 639; 91 Am. Dec. 602. A party is estopped by his answer from showing averments therein contained to be true: *Wilcoxson* v. *Burton*, 27 Cal. 228; 87 Am. Dec. 66. A defendant cannot depart from a record under which he avers he claims and relies: *Lowry* v. *Erwin*, 6 Rob. 192; 39 Am. Dec. 556.

YOUNGBLOOD v. BIRMINGHAM TRUST AND SAVINGS COMPANY.

[95 ALABAMA, 521.]

DISCOUNT—DEFINITION OF.—A discount by a bank means a deduction or drawback made upon its advances or loans of money upon negotiable paper, or other evidences of debt payable at a future day which are transferred to the bank. In other words, discount is the interest re-served from the amount loaned at the time the loan is made.

DISCOUNT—WHAT IS.—Every loan made upon evidences of debt when com-pensation for the use of the money till the maturity of the debt is de-ducted from the principal and retained by the lender at the time of making the loan is a discount in the absence of statute to the contrary.

BANKS AND BANKING—DISCOUNT OF NEGOTIABLE PAPER—USURY.—A bank which discounts a draft at a rate of interest equal to twelve per cent per annum in violation of a statute providing that "any banker who discounts any note, bill of exchange, or draft at a higher rate of interest than eight per cent per annum, not including the difference of exchange, is guilty of a misdemeanor," and cannot recover on the draft, as it is void in its hands as being acquired under an unlawful and criminal contract.

CONSTITUTIONAL LAW—VALIDITY OF STATUTE RELATING TO INTEREST.— A statute making it a misdemeanor for any banker to discount any note, bill, or draft at a higher rate of interest than eight per cent per annum not including the difference of exchange applies to all kinds of bankers, and is not invalid as an unlawful exercise of class legislation.

CONTRACTS—VALIDITY OF—RIGHT OF RECOVERY.—No rights can spring from or be rested upon an act in the performance of which a criminal penalty is incurred, and all contracts which are made in violation of a penal statute are absolutely void, and cannot be recovered upon.

Taliaferro and Houghton, for the appellant.

Gillespy and Smyer, for the appellee.

523 McCLELLAN, J. The terms "discount" and "loan" are employed in the books indiscriminately and synonymously in all cases where compensation for the use of money advanced is retained out of the gross sum at the time of the advancement. Thus it is said: "Discounting or loaning money with a deduction of the interest in advance is a part of the general business of banking" etc.: 2 Am. & Eng. Ency. of Law, 92. And a discount is thus defined: "By the language of the commercial world, and the settled practice of banks, a discount by a bank means, *ex vi termini,* a deduction or drawback made upon its advances or loans of money upon negotiable paper, or other evidences of debt, payable at a future day, which are transferred to the bank. The term 'discount,' as a substantive, means the interest reserved from the amount lent, at the time of making the loan; as a verb, it is used to denote the act of giving money for a note or bill of exchange, deducting the interest": 5 Am. & Eng. Ency. of Law, 678, 679. A distinction between discounts and loans is sometimes enforced by the terms of statutes obtaining in the premises; but in the absence of any element of this kind—whenever the words stand alone upon the signification accorded them in the general law—every loan upon evidences of debt, where the compensation for the use of money till the maturity of the debt is deducted from the principal and retained by the lender at the time of making the loan is a discount: *Fleckner v. United States Bank,* 8 Wheat. 351; *National Bank v. Johnson,* 104 U. S. 276; *Saltmarsh v. Planters' etc. Bank,* 14 Ala. 677; *Philadelphia Loan Co. v. Towner,* 13 Conn. 259; *Pape v. Capi-*

tol Bank, 20 Kan. 440; 27 Am. Rep. 183; *Niagara Co. Bank*
v. *Baker*, 15 Ohio St. 85; *Talmage* v. *Pell*, 7 N. Y. 328; *City
Bank* v. *Bruce*, 17 N. Y. 515; *Freeman* v. *Brittin*, 17 N. J. L.
206.

On these principles, we entertain no doubt that the transaction in and by which plaintiff acquired the draft of Swem
and Thomas, which had been accepted by defendant for the
accommodation of the drawers, by advancing to Swem and
Thomas the face value thereof, less a certain per cent thereon
which was retained by plaintiff for the use of the gross sum
so advanced for the time of the paper, was a discounting of
the draft within the usual sense of that term, and hence
within the meaning of the word as employed in section 4140
524 of the code, there being nothing in the context of that section importing a different significance.

The section referred to is as follows: " Any banker who discounts any note, bill of exchange or draft, at a higher rate of
interest than eight per cent per annum, not including the difference of exchange, is guilty of a misdemeanor." It is admitted that the plaintiff discounted the draft in question at a
higher rate of interest than eight per cent per annum; or
rather, it is admitted that the plaintiff, which is a banking corporation, acquired the draft by paying or advancing
thereon the sum nominated therein, less about one per cent,
which was deducted and retained by it as compensation for
the use of the money until maturity of the paper, which was
due and payable at thirty days. This, as we have seen, was
a discounting of the draft within the statute quoted; and the
rate of discount being equal to twelve per cent per annum,
the discount was violative of the statute, and involved a crime
on the part of plaintiff, assuming the constitutionality of the
enactment.

This was section 4435 of the Code of 1876. It was then
directed against individual bankers only. As it then stood
it was adjudged to be unconstitutional by this court in *Carter
Bros.* v. *Coleman*, 84 Ala. 256. The ground of that decision
is not expressly stated, but it was based on authorities (*Smith*
v. *Louisville etc. R. R. Co.*, 75 Ala. 449, and *South etc. R. R.
Co.* v. *Morris*, 65 Ala. 193), a reference to which leaves little
doubt that the statute was held invalid because it did not
apply also to corporations engaged in the business of banking; and this is made manifest by the further statement of
the court: " The statute has since been changed (Code 1886,

sec. 4140), with what effect we need not inquire." The change
here referred to consists in the omission from its last codifica-
tion of the word "individual," the effect being to make it applicable to corporate as well as individual bankers, and to obviate
the infirmity pointed out in *Carter Bros.* v. *Coleman,* 84 Ala.
256. We do not conceive that there could have been any other
objection to the constitutionality of the original enactment;
and, that objection having been eliminated by amendment,
we are clear in the conviction that it is now a valid and effi-
cacious exercise of legislative power. It is quite erroneous to
say that it is class legislation, in a vitiating sense. It does
apply to a class, of course, as do very many other statutes in
our jurisprudence, whose validity has never been, and cannot
be, successfully questioned; as, for instances, statutes regulating railroads, physicians, lawyers, common carriers, warehousemen, etc.; but, [525] like all these, its application is to
all of a number of persons, natural and artificial, whose occupation and business mark the lines of the class to which
they belong, and as members of which they are each and all,
without invidious distinction whatever, amenable to its terms
solely because they pursue an avocation which the lawmaking power conceives should be specially regulated.

The business of banking is well understood and defined.
A chief part of it in most instances consists in the lending of
money, and this is almost always done by discounting evidences of debt. The opportunities and temptations of persons engaged in it to evade or violate laws against usury are
so much greater and more frequent than those of persons not
so engaged as to raise up a necessity for the application of more
stringent measures of repression than are necessary in respect
of other businesses and persons engaged therein. And it is
this consideration which differentiates the business of banking from all others in respect of usury, and furnishes a predicate for such legislation as is embodied in section 4140 for
the regulation of banking and bankers, which does not exist
as to any other occupation; just as the inherent dangers involved in the operation of a railroad differentiates that from
other occupations, and necessitates legislation which would
be entirely unnecessary and innocuous in respect of the business of farming, for instance. And upon this ground statutes
of this character, when made to apply to all persons, whether
individuals or corporations, regulating occupations, have been
uniformly upheld. Judge Cooley, in this connection, says:

"The legislature may also deem it desirable to prescribe particular rules for the several occupations, and to establish distinctions in the rights, obligations, duties, and capacities of citizens. The business of common carriers, for instance, or of bankers, may require special statutory regulations for the general benefit; and it may be matter of public policy to give laborers in one business a specific lien for their wages, when it would be impracticable and impolitic to do the same for persons engaged in some other employments. If the law be otherwise unobjectionable, all that can be required in these cases is that they be general in their application to the class or locality to which they apply; and they are then public in character, and of their propriety and policy the legislature must judge: Cooley's Constitutional Limitations, pp. 480, 481.

In a recent case a statute of Kentucky, which gave a right of action against railroads to the representatives of persons, not in the service of the road, killed through the negligence [526] of railroad employees, came before the supreme court of that state on the question of its constitutionality. The argument was that this was class legislation, in that it applied to railroads alone, and no liability was imposed upon other common carriers. The court, in holding this position to be unsound, among other things, said: "This statute does not single out a particular individual or corporation, and subject him or it to special burdens or peculiar rules. Nor does it do so as to some of those engaged in a particular business, as, for instance, the Chinese in the laundry business, and which the supreme court of the United States condemned in the case of *Soon Hing* v. *Crowley*, 113 U. S. 703, but it subjects all in a particular business to its provisions, just as a law relative to banks and the conduct of banking would subject all in that particular business to its terms. Legislation of like character is to be found upon the statute books of every state": *Louisville Safety Vault etc. Co.* v. *Louisville etc. R. R. Co.* (Ky., Nov. 11, 1891), 14 Lawy. Rep. Ann. C. 579, and notes; and to like effect in principle are the following cases therein cited: *Missouri Pac. Ry. Co.* v. *Mackey*, 127 U. S. 205; *Minneapolis etc. Ry. Co.* v. *Beckwith*, 129 U. S. 27; and so, on the same principle, a statute fixing the rate of interest which may be charged by pawnbrokers is no violation of a constitutional provision for "uniform laws": *Jackson* v. *Shawl*, 29 Cal. 267. And the general power of the legislature to regulate occupations and businesses of all kinds, keeping within the principle that all members of a particular class proposed to be regulated must be equally amenable to the regulations made, has been time and again declared by this court: *Mayor* v. *Yuille*, 3 Ala. 137; 36 Am. Dec. 441; *Ex parte Marshall*, 64 Ala. 266; *Harrison* v. *Jones*, 80 Ala. 412; *Louisville etc. R. R. Co.* v. *Baldwin*, 85 Ala. 619; *McDonald* v. *State*, 81 Ala. 279; 60 Am. Rep. 158. Upon a consideration of the foregoing authorities, and the reasons which underlie them, we are, we repeat, without doubt in the conclusion that section 4140 of the Code of 1886 is a constitutional enactment.

It is equally free from doubt, in our opinion, that the effect of this statute on the transaction, in and by which the plaintiff acquired the draft and acceptance sued on, would vitiate it *in toto*, and avoid and defeat all right on the part of the plaintiff under that contract. The title upon which plaintiff relies is one which he acquired in confessed and palpable violation of a law which denounced his act in that regard as a crime. The doctrine is nowhere more firmly established than in Alabama, that no rights can spring from or be rested upon an act in the performance of which a [527] criminal penalty is incurred, and that all contracts which are made in violation of a penal statute are as absolutely void as if the law had in so many words declared that they should be so: *Moog* v. *Hannon*, 93 Ala. 503, where our cases are collated. And the logical consequence of the doctrine in a case like the present one, involving the acquisition of a note, bill, or draft by criminal means, is that not only is the act of acquisition a crime, and invalid, but the paper itself—the supposed security for money advanced in contravention of the statute—is absolutely void in the hands, at least, of him who comes by it through the commission of a penal offense: *Pennington* v. *Townsend*, 7 Wend. 276; *Bank of United States* v. *Owens*, 2 Pet. 527.

The rulings of the trial court on the pleadings, and its findings and judgment on the facts, are opposed to these views. The judgment is reversed, and the case having been tried without jury below, judgment will be here rendered for the defendant.

Reversed and rendered. ____

DISCOUNT—USURY.—The reserving and receiving in advance of a loan the highest rate of interest is not usurious: *Vahlberg* v. *Keaton*, 51 Ark. 534; 14 Am. St. Rep. 73; *Parker* v. *Cousins*, 2 Gratt. 372; 44 Am. Dec. 388.

Discounting—When Usurious.—If a bank reserves a greater interest than the charter allows, the usury laws apply to the contract, although the rate does not exceed the rate prescribed by such usury law: *Rock River Bank* v. *Sherwood*, 10 Wis. 230; 78 Am. Dec. 669, and note; *Russell* v. *Failor*, 1 Ohio St. 327; 59 Am. Dec. 631, and note; *Planters' Bank* v. *Sharp*, 4 Smedes & M. 75; 43 Am. Dec. 470.

Contract Contravening the Policy of a Statute is void: *Brooks* v. *Cooper*, 50 N. J. Eq. 761; 35 Am. St. Rep. 793, and note with the cases collected; extended notes to *Woods* v. *Armstrong*, 25 Am. Rep. 675, and *De Leon* v. *Trevino*, 30 Am. Rep. 106. A contract in violation of a statute is void, and cannot be enforced: *Ohio etc. Trust Co.* v. *Merchants' etc. Trust Co.*, 11 Humph. 1; 53 Am. Dec. 742, and note; *Linn* v. *State Bank*, 1 Scam. 87; 25 Am. Dec. 71, and note; *Persons* v. *Jones*, 12 Ga. 371; 58 Am. Dec. 476; *Gravier* v. *Carraby*, 17 La. 118; 36 Am. Dec. 608, and note; *Spalding* v. *Preston*, 21 Vt. 9; 50 Am. Dec. 68, and note; *Hooker* v. *Vandewater*, 4 Denio, 349; 47 Am. Dec. 258, and note. *Contra:* See *Lester* v. *Howard Bank*, 33 Md. 558; 3 Am. Rep. 211; *Hammond* v. *Wilcher*, 79 Ga. 421. A contract founded directly on an illegal consideration is void, though the illegal act be prohibited under a penalty only: *Milton* v. *Haden*, 32 Ala. 30; 70 Am. Dec. 523, and note; *Columbia Bank etc. Co.* v. *Haldeman*, 7 Watts & S. 233; 42 Am. Dec. 229, and note; *O'Donnell* v. *Sweeney*, 5 Ala. 467; 39 Am. Dec. 338; *Wilson* v. *Spencer*, 1 Rand. 76; 10 Am. Dec. 491; *Mitchell* v. *Smith*, 1 Binn. 110; 2 Am. Dec. 417.

O'Conner Mining and Manufacturing Company v. Coosa Furnace Company.

[95 Alabama, 614.]

Corporations—Directors as Agents—Power to Bind Corporation.— The directors of a business corporation are its agents, and exercise functions of a fiduciary character disqualifying them from binding the corporation in a transaction in which they are adversely interested, without the full knowledge and free consent or acquiescence of such corporation.

Corporations—Same Directors Acting for Two Corporations—Effect of.—If the same persons as directors of two different corporations represent both in a transaction in which their interests are opposed, such transaction may be avoided by either corporation or at the instance of a stockholder in either, without regard to the question of advantage or detriment to either corporation and no matter how fair and open the transaction may be shown to be.

Corporations—Transactions Between, When Represented by Same Directors.—Dealings between corporations represented by the same persons as directors may be accepted as binding by each corporation and the stockholders thereof. Such dealings are not absolutely void, but are voidable at the election of the respective corporations, or the stockholders thereof, and they become binding if acquiesced in by the corporations and their stockholders.

Corporations—Transactions by Directors of—Right of Creditors to Impeach.—The duty which disqualifies the directors of a corporation from binding it by a transaction in which they have an adverse interest is one owing to the corporation and its stockholders, and does not extend to its creditors in the absence of fraud, and when a disposition of the property of a corporation is assailed by its creditors, they are not clothed with the right of the corporation or of its stockholders to set aside the transaction regardless of its fairness or unfairness on the ground that it was entered into by representatives who had put themselves in a relation antagonistic to the interests of their principal. Corporation creditors can only impeach such transaction upon proof of the insolvency of the corporation at the time of its consummation, or that it was entered into with intent to hinder, delay, or defraud them.

CORPORATIONS—CONVEYANCES BY—RIGHTS OF CREDITORS.—The fact that a corporation in disposing of its property deals with persons who at the same time are charged with the duty of representing its interests, does not of itself render the transaction fraudulent as to its creditors.

CORPORATIONS—TRANSFERS BETWEEN—RIGHTS OF CREDITORS.—When the property of one corporation is transferred to another corporation represented by the same directors the transaction cannot be set aside by corporation creditors except upon proof of fraud, but the fact of such relationship calls for clearer and fuller proof of a valuable and adequate consideration, and of the good faith of the parties, than would be required if the grantee were a stranger.

Dunlap and Dortch, for the appellant.

Aiken and Martin, and Watts and Son, for the appellee.

616 WALKER, J. The bill was filed by the O'Conner Mining and Manufacturing Company as a simple contract creditor of the Coosa Furnace Company, and its principal purpose was to reach and subject to the payment of the debt claimed certain property alleged to have been fraudulently conveyed by the Coosa Furnace Company, first, by a mortgage executed on the seventh day of April, 1884, and again, as to a part of the property, by a deed of absolute conveyance executed on the thirteenth day of July, 1885. The specified ground of attack upon the conveyances in question is, that they were executed for the purpose and with the intent to hinder, delay, or defraud the complainant, and to prevent it from enforcing collection of its just demands; and that the debts the mortgage was given to secure, and also the considerations recited in the deed, were simulated and not real. The execution of the two instruments is alleged in the bill, and is admitted in the answer. The instruments must stand, unless the particular infirmities charged against them are shown by the evidence. There are no allegations to support a contention that their formal execution by the corporation was insufficient in any particular.

The charge that the considerations recited in the two instruments respectively were simulated and not real is not sustained by the proof. The defendants proved, without contradiction, that the debts secured by the mortgage were due from the mortgagor, and represented full value received by it; and, also, that the consideration mentioned in the deed was paid in the discharge of debts which were secured by the mortgage, and that the property conveyed was not at that time worth as much as the amount of the debts in payment of which it was received. We would have to ignore the uncontroverted evidence in the case to arrive at any other conclusion on the subject than that the debts correctly represented money actually advanced to the Coosa Furnace Company and bills contracted by it.

Much stress is laid in the bill, and in the argument of counsel for the appellant, upon the relations existing between the several defendants during the time covered by the transactions which are sought to be impeached. The dealings in question were between the Coosa Furnace Company, on the one side, and the Wabash Iron Company, the Vigo Iron Company, A. L. Crawford, and his two sons, [617] J. P. Crawford and A. J. Crawford, on the other side. It is true that each of the corporations mentioned was controlled and dominated by the Crawfords. The great bulk of the stock in each of them was owned and held by members of the Crawford family. The board of directors in each of the corporations was composed of the Crawfords and their adherents. It thus plainly appears that the transactions were between the Coosa Furnace Company and some of its own stockholders and directors, and also two other corporations having boards of directors composed of the same persons who managed and controlled the first-named company.

The directors of a business corporation are its agents. Though they may not be trustees in the technical sense, yet they exercise functions of a fiduciary character. Their position implies that confidence is reposed in them. The duties which a director assumes to the corporation and to the stockholders thereof disqualify him from binding the corporation in a transaction in which he is adversely interested. He cannot at the same time act for himself and for his principal, without the full knowledge and free consent of the principal. In Morawetz on Private Corporations, section 528, it is said: "A person who is agent for two parties cannot, in the absence of express authority from each, represent them both in a transaction in which they have contrary interests. This rule is based upon the same reason as the rule which prohibits an agent from representing his principal, when his personal interests are opposed to his duty. The principal stipulates for the judgment and skill of his agent, and the latter has no authority to act, when he is not in a position to give the principal the benefits of his best endeavors. It follows, therefore, that the directors, or other agents of a corporation, have no implied authority to bind the company by making a contract with another corporation which they also represent." If the same persons as directors of two different companies represent both companies in a transaction in which their interests are opposed, such transaction may be avoided by either company, or at the instance of a stockholder in either company, without regard to the question of advantage or detriment to either company. Both the corporations are armed with the right to repudiate such a transaction, no matter how fair and open it may be shown to be: *Memphis etc. R. R. Co.* v. *Woods*, 88 Ala. 630, 641; 16 Am. St. Rep. 81.

But the duty which disqualifies the directors from binding the corporation by a transaction in which they have an [618] adverse interest, is one owing to the corporation which they represent, and to the stockholders thereof. A principal may consent to be bound by a contract made for him by an agent who, at the same time, represented an interest adverse to that of the principal. A *cestui que trust* may elect to confirm a transaction which he could have repudiated on the ground that the trustee had an interest in the matter not consistent with his trust relation. In like manner, dealings between corporations, represented by the same persons as directors, may be accepted as binding by each corporation and the stockholders thereof. The general rule is, that such dealings are not absolutely void, but are voidable at the election of the respective corporations, or of the stockholders thereof. They become binding, if acquiesced in by the corporations and their stockholders: *Kelley* v. *Newburyport Horse R. R. Co.*, 141 Mass. 496; *Ashhurst's Appeal*, 60 Pa. St. 290–314; *Buell* v. *Buckingham*, 16 Iowa, 284; 85 Am. Dec. 516; *Manufacturers' Saving Bank* v. *Big Muddy Iron Co.*, 97 Mo. 38; *Alexander* v. *Williams*, 14 Mo. App. 13; *Twin Lick Oil Co.* v. *Marbury*, 91 U. S. 587; *Booth* v. *Robinson*, 55 Md. 419; *United States Rolling Stock Co.* v. *Atlantic etc. R. R. Co.*, 34 Ohio St. 450; 32 Am.

Rep. 380; Taylor on Private Corporations, 2d ed., sec. 630; 1 Beach on Private Corporations, sec. 247.

The directors of a corporation, in the transaction of its business and the disposition of its property, do not stand in any such relation to the general cred*itors of the corporation as they occupy to the corporation itself and to its stockholders. They are not the agents of such creditors, nor can they usually be regarded as trustees acting in their behalf. The creditors are not entitled to disaffirm a transfer of the property of the corporation, made by its directors or other agents, merely because the corporation itself or its stockholders could have done so. When a disposition of the property of a corporation is assailed by its creditors, they are not clothed with the right of the corporation or of its stockholders to set aside the transaction, regardless of its fairness or unfairness, on the ground that it was entered into by representatives of the corporation who had put themselves in a relation antagonistic to the interests of their principal. The right of the creditor to impeach the transaction depends upon its fraudulent character. The question in such case is, Was the transaction which is complained of entered into with the intent to hinder, delay, or defraud creditors? Was the property fraudulently transferred or conveyed? The mere fact that the corporation, in disposing of its property, dealt with persons who at the same time [619] were charged with the duty of representing its interests, does not, by itself, render the transaction fraudulent: *Globe Iron Roofing etc. Co. v. Thacher*, 87 Ala. 458.

Where the property of a corporation is transferred to another corporation represented by the same directors, the fact of such relationship is a circumstance well calculated to arouse suspicion, and calls for a rigid and severe scrutiny in the examination of such transaction when it is assailed by a creditor. When such a relationship is shown to exist between the contracting parties, clearer and fuller proof must be given of a valuable and adequate consideration, and of the good faith of the parties, than would be required if the transferee or grantee had been a stranger. When, however, such examination is made, and such proof is forthcoming, and the result is that no fraud or unfair dealing is shown, and it appears that the transaction was not vitiated by any infirmity of which a creditor has the right to complain, then the transaction must stand, and it is as valid, as against the creditor,

as if the corporation had dealt with a stranger, who was not involved in any way with the corporate representatives.

In the present case, the proof offered by the defendants shows fully, and in great detail, the circumstances connected with the dealings between the defendants, corporations, and individuals. The several witnesses were subjected to rigid examinations. The considerations to support the several debts which figured in the transactions are clearly and distinctly proved. That the mortgage was given to secure debts justly due, and that the deed was executed in *bona fide* and absolute payment of a portion of such debts, in property which was not worth more than the true amount of the debts paid therewith, are facts clearly shown by testimony which is not contradicted in any way. We do feel at liberty to discredit and reject the full and consistent versions of the matters in controversy given by several of the witnesses, merely because these witnesses were the persons in control of the several corporations which were engaged in the dealings in question. There is no prohibition against a corporation dealing with its own stockholders or directors in reference to matters in which such stockholders or directors have interests adverse to those of the corporation; or against several corporations which are controlled by the same persons, dealing with each other. Nor is there anything wrong in a corporation conveying its property as security for, or in absolute satisfaction of, obligations honestly assumed in such dealings, if such transfer involves no fraud [620] upon the rights of other creditors. The evidence in this case fails to show that the conveyances which are assailed were fraudulent as charged.

It is alleged in the amendment to the bill that the Coosa Furnance Company was insolvent at the date of the execution of the mortgage, and has been insolvent ever since that time. Even if it could be conceded that the fact of insolvency, if proved, would create such a change in the relations between the directors and the creditors of the corporation as to take from the directors the right to allow one or more creditors to acquire an advantage over the others in the application of the corporate assets to the payment of debts, yet such concession could have no effect upon the result in this case, because the evidence wholly fails to show that the company was insolvent when the mortgage was made. It plainly appears that the company was insolvent fifteen months after the date of the mortgage. Its property was then worth very much less than it cost. What it was worth at the time the mortgage was executed is not shown. It appears from the evidence that the value of furnace property is very fluctuating. The value of the company's assets at the date of the mortgage is not proved, nor is it shown that they were then worth less than the amount of the company's liabilities at that time. The inference that the company was insolvent at the date of the mortgage does not follow from the proof of insolvency more than a year afterwards. The insolvency of the company at the date of the deed does not affect the validity of that instrument, for the operation of the deed was merely to transfer, in absolute payment of a debt, property which had been conveyed as security therefor at a date when the corporation is not shown to have been insolvent.

The leasehold interest of the Coosa Furnace Company and the income from the leased property are assets of that insolvent corporation. It is shown that the Gadsden Iron Company has been receiving the output from the mines. It is not alleged or proved that the latter company has paid less for the ore than it was worth, and it is not shown that it is chargeable with fraud in the purchase thereof. The complainant, as a simple contract creditor without a lien, is seeking to reach the output from the mines, and to subject it to the payment of its demands. Its claim in this regard is a legal demand which may be enforced by proceeding at law. There is no obstacle to hinder the complainant from reaching this property by legal process. The bill cannot be regarded as a creditor's bill, supported by the equitable [621] demand for a settlement of the affairs of an insolvent corporation, as it is filed in behalf of the complainant alone, and not in behalf of itself and of other creditors, and for an administration of the assets and a ratable distribution among the creditors entitled to share therein. The bill is framed under the statute authorizing a creditor without a lien to file a bill in chancery to subject property fraudulently transferred or conveyed, or attempted to be fraudulently transferred or conveyed: Code, sec. 3544. As, in our opinion, the proof fails to sustain the charge that the transactions which are assailed were fraudulent, the conclusion is that the complainant is not entitled to relief. The decree to that effect must be affirmed.

Affirmed.

CORPORATIONS—DIRECTORS—POWER TO BIND WHERE INTERESTS ARE
ADVERSE: See the extended note to *Beach* v. *Miller*, 17 Am. St. Rep. 298–
308. Directors have no right to represent the corporation in any transaction in which they are personally interested in obtaining any advantage at
the expense of the corporation: *Memphis etc. R. R. Co.* v. *Woods*, 88 Ala.
630; 16 Am. St. Rep, 81; *Ten Eyck* v. *Pontiac etc. R. R. Co.*, 74 Mich. 226;
16 Am. St. Rep. 633, and note; *Trainer* v. *Wolfe*, 140 Pa. St. 279; *Jackson*
v. *McLean*, 100 Mo. 130; *Sargent* v. *Kansas etc. Ry. Co.*, 48 Kan. 672; *Perry*
v. *Tuskaloosa etc. Oil Mill Co.*, 93 Ala. 364; *Schetter* v. *Southern Oregon Co.*,
19 Or. 192. See further the extended note to *Garrett* v. *Burlington Plow Co.*,
59 Am. Rep. 466–471.

CORPORATIONS.—DIRECTORS OF TWO CORPORATIONS cannot act for either
where their interests are opposed or detrimental to a minority of the stockholders: *Memphis etc. R. R. Co.* v. *Woods*, 88 Ala. 630; 16 Am. St. Rep. 81;
note to *Pearson* v. *Concord R. R. Co.*, 13 Am. St. Rep. 607; and see also the
extended note to *Beach* v. *Miller*, 17 Am. St. Rep. 302, 306.

CASES

IN THE

SUPREME COURT

OF

COLORADO.

FORT MORGAN LAND AND CANAL COMPANY *v.* SOUTH PLATTE DITCH COMPANY.

[18 COLORADO, 1.]

WATERS—PROPERTY RIGHTS IN.—The water of every natural stream in Colorado is the property of the public. Private ownership therein is not recognized, but the right to divert water therefrom and apply it to beneficial uses is expressly guaranteed by the constitution.

WATERS—APPROPRIATION OF.—By the diversion and use of the waters of a natural stream, a priority of right to such use may be acquired, and, when so acquired, such priority is a property right, subject to sale and transfer.

WATERS—APPROPRIATION, WHAT CONSTITUTES.—A priority of right to the water of a natural stream can be legally acquired only by the application of such water to a beneficial use. Hence, there must not only be a diversion of the water from the stream, but an actual application of it to the soil, to constitute a constitutional appropriation for irrigation.

WATERS — APPROPRIATION — PRIORITIES.—Awarding priorities to several ditches in excess of the amount of water actually appropriated at the time the decree is rendered is error. A prior diversion and promised future use do not support such decree.

WATERS — APPROPRIATION, WHEN COMPLETE.—An appropriation of the water of a natural stream is complete only when some open, physical demonstration indicates an intent to take, for a valuable or beneficial use, and such intent is followed by taking and applying the water to the use designed.

C. E. Gast and E. A. Reynolds, for the appellant.

H. N. Haynes, J. W. McCreery, and John P. Brockway, for the appellees.

* HAYT, C. J. This is a statutory proceeding instituted for the purpose of procuring an adjudication of priorities of right to the use of water for irrigation, in Water District No. 1, in Weld county. The petition was filed in the month of November, 1886, by the Platte and Beaver Improvement Company.

Upon this petition at the regular November term, 1886, of the district court of Weld county, an order was made appointing one C. A. Bennett referee. By this order the referee was directed to hear and determine such priorities in accordance with the statute regulating the procedure in such cases: Gen. Laws, 1883, c. 57.

The referee having duly qualified soon thereafter proceeded to take testimony, and this being completed he filed his report at the regular May, 1887, term of the court. To this report the appellant, the Fort Morgan Land and Canal Company, filed exceptions. These exceptions were, after argument of counsel, overruled by the court, and judgment was entered in accordance with the report. Twenty-four priorities of appropriation were thus established for the twenty ditches represented at the hearing. Appellant's priority appears as No. 18, and upon this appeal all those adjudged to have senior priorities are joined as appellees.

Under our constitution the water of every natural stream in this state is deemed to be the property of the public. Private ownership of water in the natural streams is not recognized. [3] The right to divert water therefrom and apply the same to beneficial uses is, however, expressly guaranteed. By such diversion and use a priority of right to the use of the water may be acquired. This priority has been declared a property right, and as such subject to sale and transfer: *Strickler* v. *Colorado Syrings*, 16 Col. 61; 25 Am. St. Rep. 245.

From the first this court has recognized and emphasized the idea that a priority could only be legally acquired by the application of the water to some beneficial use. Hence there must be not only a diversion of the water from the natural stream, but an actual application of it to the soil to constitute the constitutional appropriation recognized for irrigation: *Farmers'* etc. *Canal and R. Co.* v. *Southworth*, 13 Col. 111, and cases cited.

This may now be considered as one of the fundamental principles underlying our system of irrigation. It is too well established to be open to controversy. A diversion unaccompanied by an application gives no right. This principle applied to the record in this case is fatal to the decree rendered by the district court.

The capacity of the several ditches enumerated in the decree to convey water seems to have been the criterion by which the court was governed, for although evidence was taken tending to show the amount of water actually used in irrigation, such evidence seems to have had but slight effect upon the final decree. It is apparent that the capacity of the various ditches outweighed all other considerations. Such capacity having once been established, together with proof of diversion and the use of a limited portion of water, with a promise to increase such use up to the limit of the ditch within a reasonable time, was sufficient to procure for the ditch a priority for an amount of water equal to such capacity, such priority dating from the inception of the work of construction upon the ditch.

The decree is not saved by the proviso restricting the ditch-owners from diverting water into their ditches at times when the same is not needed for a beneficial purpose, to the detriment [4] of other later appropriators. This would be the result in the absence of anything in the decree to the contrary. The court erred in awarding priorities to the several ditches in excess of the amount of water actually appropriated at the time the decree was rendered.

For instance: It appears from the testimony in the case that the Platte and Beaver Improvement Company was the owner of more than thirty thousand acres of land adjacent to their ditch. And finding it impracticable to obtain either tenants or purchasers for this land they were about to consummate an arrangement at the time this decree was rendered in the spring of 1887, whereby the same could be divided among its stockholders, with the object in view of accomplishing a more rapid development of the lands, and a more extended application of water to the soil. Counsel say: "It cannot be that under the peculiar circumstances attending this case the court will say that the stockholders of the Platte and Beaver Improvement Company who have, including interest, spent nearly two hundred thousand dollars in the construction of their ditches, have failed to acquire thereby water rights for their lands. Under the circumstances of this case they are entitled to additional time."

In support of this position our attention is directed to the

following paragraph from the opinion of this court in *Larimer County R. Co. v. People*, 8 Col. 614:

"The supreme court of California—*McDonald v. Bear River etc. Co.*, 13 Cal. 220—defines the word 'appropriation' in this connection as follows: 'This appropriation is the intent to take, accompanied by some open, physical demonstration of the intent, and for some valuable use.' We consider these definitions applicable to appropriations of water in this state; that is to say we are of opinion that when the individual, by some open, physical demonstration, indicates an intent to take, for a valuable or beneficial use, and through such demonstration ultimately succeeds in applying the water to the use designed, there is such an appropriation as is contemplated by our constitution and statutes. While a diversion must of necessity take place before the water is actually applied to the irrigation of the soil the appropriation thereof is, in legal contemplation, made when the act evidencing the intent is performed. Of course such initial act must be followed up with reasonable diligence, and the purpose must be consummated without unnecessary delay."

This language was used in a case where the question under consideration related to the right to utilize the bed of a nonnavigable stream for the storage of water that would otherwise have run to waste. This being a preliminary step to the utilization of the water for irrigation, the claim there advanced was that such act was unlawful *per se* without reference to the question as to whether or not the rights of others were injuriously affected thereby. Moreover, the language does not warrant the construction placed upon it by counsel. It expressly states that an appropriation is only consummated in case the water is finally applied to the use designated. No warrant is given for the entry of a decree in advance awarding a priority upon a diversion and promised use, as has been done in this case. To uphold such a decree would necessitate the abandonment of a cardinal principle that has been announced in many carefully considered cases. This principle in the paragraph next preceding the one quoted from the opinion in *Larimer Co. R. Co. v. People*, 8 Col. 614, is stated in this terse language: "The true test of the appropriation of water is the successful application thereof to the beneficial use designed." . . . . The construction contended for by counsel is so radically and palpably wrong that we deem further argument or additional citation of authorities unnecessary to its overthrow.

The decree will be reversed, and the cause remanded, with directions to the district court to allow the parties an opportunity to present further evidence, without prejudice to the evidence already taken.

———

WATERS—PROPERTY RIGHTS IN.—The Colorado constitution dedicates all unappropriated water in the natural streams of the state to the use of the people: *Wheeler* v. *Northern Colorado Irr. Co.*, 10 Col. 582; 3 Am. St. Rep. 603. The use of water in a flowing stream is open to all, subject to the restriction that a person is not permitted to use it to the injury of those through whose land it flows: *Hoy* v. *Sterrett*, 2 Watts, 327; 27 Am. Dec. 313, and note.

WATERS—PROPERTY RIGHTS IN ACQUIRED BY APPROPRIATION.—The prior appropriator's right to the use of the water of a stream is a property right which he may transfer by sale: *Strickler* v. *Colorado Springs*, 16 Col. 61; 25 Am. St. Rep. 245, and note.

WATERS—APPROPRIATION MUST BE TO BENEFICIAL USE.—A diversion of water unless applied to a beneficial use within a reasonable time is not an appropriation thereof: *Combs* v. *Agricultural Ditch Co.*, 17 Col. 146; 31 Am. St. Rep. 275, and note; *Hammond* v. *Rose*, 11 Col. 524; 7 Am. St. Rep. 258; *Wheeler* v. *Northern Colorado Irr. Co.*, 10 Col. 582; 3 Am. St. Rep. 603, and note; *Hindman* v. *Rizor*, 21 Or. 112.

WATERS—APPROPRIATION—How EFFECTED.—There must be an actual diversion of water from its natural channel, by means of a ditch or other structure, to effect a valid appropriation thereof: *Simmons* v. *Winters*, 21 Or. 35; 28 Am. St. Rep. 727.

———

RHODES *v.* JENKINS.

[18 COLORADO, 49.]

NEGOTIABLE INSTRUMENTS—INDORSER'S LIABILITY.—One who indorses commercial paper thereby becomes responsible for its genuineness and that of all previous indorsements.

J. A. Bentley, for the appellant.

Wells, McNeal, and Taylor, for the appellee.

[51] HAYT, C. J. It is admitted that at the time of the transaction which forms the basis of this action, and for many years prior thereto, one John H. Hall was a customer of and depositor with Railey and Brother, bankers, at Weston, Missouri. The draft in question was issued for the balance remaining to the credit of this John H. Hall at this banking house at the time. It was made payable to his order and mailed to his Denver address. This draft did not

reach the party for whom it was intended; on the contrary,
it fell into the hands of another person calling himself John
H. Hall, and this man by the aid of appellant's indorsement
secured payment upon the same. The *bona fides* of the transaction on the part of appellant under these circumstances is
not material. The case may be determined upon the simple
question of the liability of one who indorses a bill of exchange.
It is a well-established principle of commercial law that one
who indorses and delivers commercial paper thereby becomes
responsible for its genuineness and that of all previous indorsements: 1 Daniel [52] on Negotiable Instruments, sec.
669 a; Story on Bills of Exchange, secs. 110–235.

It is not necessary for us to determine the rights of Railey
and Brother, the drawers of this draft, had they paid the
same to an innocent third party upon this forged indorsement.
It is sufficient to say that they did not pay it, are not here
complaining, and are not parties to this action. The draft
was paid to the German National Bank of Denver by the
drawees, Donnell, Lawson, and Simpson of New York, and
the amount so paid turned over to appellant. The drawees
in making this payment had a right to, and undoubtedly did,
rely upon the indorsement of both the Denver bank and that
of appellant. The Denver bank in turn had recourse upon
the indorsement of appellant.

It is evident that the German National Bank in indorsing
this draft was acting upon the guaranty growing out of appellant's indorsement. It is not pretended that its cashier
in indorsing the same was induced to do so by reason of having any knowledge of the handwriting or financial responsibility of the person who indorsed thereon the name of John
H. Hall, other than that derived from the indorsement of
Rhodes. If the facts were otherwise, the liability of appellant by reason of his indorsement would remain the same.
This is not a case of a bank seeking to recover money paid
by it on a forged check against the account of a depositor.
As we have seen, Railey and Brother did not pay this draft,
and although it is well settled that banks are presumed to
know the signatures of their customers, this presumption in
no way aids appellant. There is no principle of law or of
common sense that would extend this presumption to the
officers of banks other than those with which such deposits
are made. Upon the same principle when a drawee pays a
forged bill of exchange to the holder thereof, he cannot re-

cover back the money so paid. The reason upon which this rule is based is the negligence imputed to the drawee, who is supposed to know the handwriting of his correspondent much better than the holder does. This rule has no application to this [53] case. Here, the draft is admittedly genuine, the indorsement of Hall only being spurious. There is no principle upon which the drawee under the circumstances here disclosed can be held to be familiar with the handwriting of the payee. The reason upon which the rule is based failing, the rule cannot be held applicable. While, therefore, Railey and Brother in a proper case might be estopped from setting up the forgery of the signature of one of their depositors to a check paid by them to an innocent third party, the drawees in New York, Donnell, Lawson, and Simpson, with whom Hall is not shown to ever have transacted any business, are not so estopped.

It is contended that the German National Bank was but a mere agent to collect, and having collected the money and paid the same over to appellant, no liability rested upon the bank to refund the amount to the New York institution. This argument is plausible, but not sound. As to the question of the genuineness of the draft, each indorser in receiving and indorsing it was entitled to rely upon the credit of the previous indorsers. Appellant, by his indorsement, guaranteed the genuineness of the indorsement of Hall to him, and upon this guaranty the Denver bank was induced to give the paper the indorsement upon which it was paid by Donnell, Lawson, and Simpson, in New York. Under these circumstances the New York institution had recourse upon the Denver bank, and the latter in turn upon appellant.

The rule of law which makes appellant liable in this case places the loss where it properly belongs. Appellant lent his credit by indorsing the paper to a man confined under a charge of forgery. He transacted the business for him at the bank at a time when such person could not have perpetrated the fraud without assistance. Certainly, as between the Denver bank and appellant, the greater negligence is chargeable upon the latter, he having first received the draft from the person who committed the forgery: *Bank of Commerce* v. *Union Bank*, 3 N. Y. 230.

The judgment of the superior court is right, and must be affirmed.

NEGOTIABLE INSTRUMENTS—LIABILITY OF INDORSERS.—One who indorses a negotiable instrument guarantees the ability to pay and the genuineness of the signatures of all prior parties: *State Bank* v. *Fearing*, 16 Pick. 533; 28 Am. Dec. 265, and note. An indorser guarantees the genuineness of the writing and the validity of the promise: *Willis* v. *French*, 84 Me. 593; 30 Am. St. Rep. 416, and note. See the note to *Temple* v. *Baker*, 11 Am. St. Rep. 930, and the extended note to *Burton* v. *Hansford*, 27 Am. Rep. 580. The first indorser of a negotiable instrument is responsible to every holder and to every person whose name is on the note subsequent to his own, and who has been compelled to pay the amount of the note: *McNeilly* v. *Patchin*, 23 Mo. 40; 66 Am. Dec. 651, and note. An indorser of a promissory note may be considered as the drawer of a bill of exchange upon the maker thereof: *Patterson* v. *Todd*, 18 Pa. St. 426; 57 Am. Dec. 622. Indorsement is equivalent to the drawing of a new bill: *Aymer* v. *Sheldon*, 12 Wend. 439; 27 Am. Dec. 137.

STRUBY-ESTABROOK MERCANTILE CO. *v.* DAVIS.

[18 COLORADO, 93.]

HOMESTEAD ENTRY—WHEN SUBJECT TO EXECUTION.—Lands entered under the United States homestead laws are liable to the satisfaction of debts contracted by the homestead claimant between the date of the final certificate of entry and the date of the patent.

EXEMPTIONS.—CAPITAL STOCK OF DITCH COMPANY is not exempt from levy and sale on the ground that the ditch is used to convey water to land entered under homestead laws.

EXEMPTIONS.—STOCK IN DITCH COMPANY is personal property, and not exempt from execution.

INJUNCTION to restrain a sale under execution. Plaintiffs obtained judgment against defendant for a debt contracted by the latter after the issuance of a final certificate of entry of a homestead to him, and prior to his acquisition of a patent to the land. Plaintiffs then procured an execution, and had it levied on such land as well as on certain ditch stock owned by defendant. On the final hearing, the sale under such levy was perpetually enjoined. Plaintiffs appealed.

Bartels and Blood, for the appellants.

John H. Wells, for the appellee.

94 HAYT, C. J. The following questions are presented by this record:

1. Are lands entered under the United States homestead acts liable to the satisfaction of debts contracted by the homestead claimant between the date of the final certificate and the date of the patent?

2. Is the capital stock of a ditch company exempt from

levy and sale where the ditch is used to convey water to land entered under the homestead act?

The first of these questions is not free from doubt. The debt having been contracted prior to the actual issuance of the patent, the exemption is claimed by the literal terms of the act. On the contrary, plaintiff in error contends that the exemption provided for by section 2296 of the Revised Statutes of the United States applies to the land only prior to the issuance of the receiver's final certificate therefor. That from and after [95] the date of the issuance of such certificate the claimant must be presumed to have complied with all of the conditions of the law necessary to entitle him to a patent therefor, and that when the patent issues it relates back to the date of such final certificate.

A number of cases have been cited in which this section of the United States statute has been under consideration by the courts; in none of these cases, however, has the question now presented been directly before the courts for adjudication. An examination of these cases shows that in nearly all it affirmatively appeared that the debt was contracted prior to the issuance of the receiver's final certificate, and in none of them does the contrary appear: *Seymour* v. *Sanders*, 3 Dill. 437; *Gile* v. *Hallack*, 33 Wis. 523; *Patton* v. *Richmond*, 28 La. Ann. 795; *Miller* v. *Little*, 47 Cal. 348; *Russell* v. *Lowth*, 21 Minn. 167; 18 Am. Rep. 389; *Clark* v. *Bayley*, 5 Or. 343; *Kansas Lumber Co.* v. *Jones*, 32 Kan. 195.

In the case of the *Kansas Lumber Co.* v. *Jones*, 32 Kan. 195, the action was to foreclose a mechanic's lien upon certain real estate. The defense relied upon was the same as here. In that case, however, the final certificate had not been issued at the time the lien was claimed, and the court decided that the lien did not attach, but said: "If the defendant had been entitled to a patent, we think the lien would have attached to the land, for where a person is entitled to a patent—that is, where a patent is already due, the rights and liabilities of the parties are generally the same as though the patent had in fact been issued. But in this case the defendant was not entitled to any patent." Although the views of the court thus declared do not appear to have been necessary to the judgment, they are entitled to weight as an expression of opinion from an able court.

The nature of the title conveyed by the certificate was under investigation. In the case of the *Omaha etc. R. Co.* v. *Tabor*,

13 Col. 41; 16 Am. St. Rep. 185, Mr. Commissioner Reed in an opinion approved by this court said: "The patent does not invest the purchaser with any additional property in the land. [96] It only gives him a better legal evidence of the title which he first acquired by the certificate." It has frequently been held that the final certificate is as binding upon the government as the patent, and that when the patent issues it relates back to the entry. Not only should the patent be treated as mere evidence of title, but it is the settled doctrine of the courts that its issuance is purely a ministerial act: *Blatchley* v. *Coles*, 6 Col. 350; *Poire* v. *Wells*, 6 Col. 406; *Steele* v. *Smelting Co.*, 106 U. S. 447; *Heydenfeldt* v. *Daney Gold etc. Co.*, 93 U. S. 634.

We are of opinion that the exemption provided for only applies up to the time of the divesture of the government title. The title passes with the receiver's certificate. This view finds support from the fact that in nearly all of the states of the union, including Colorado, statutes may be found which authorize and require the listing of real property for taxation from and after the time of the issuance of the receiver's final receipt therefor. In the case of *Carroll* v. *Safford*, 3 How. 459, it was contended that such legislation was not valid under the constitution and laws of the United States, the argument being that it interfered with the disposition of the public domain by congress. In disposing of this question, the court used the following pertinent language:

" But independent of the force of usage, we think the construction is sustainable. When the land was purchased and paid for, it was no longer the property of the United States, but of the purchaser. He held for it a final certificate, which could no more be canceled by the United States than a patent. It is true, if the land had been previously sold by the United States, or reserved from sale, the certificate or patent might be recalled by the United States, as having been issued through mistake. In this respect there is no difference between the certificate holder and the patentee.

"It is said, the fee is not in the purchaser, but in the United States, until the patent shall be issued. This is so, technically, at law, but not in equity. The land in the hands [97] of the purchaser is real estate, descends to his heirs and does not go to his executors or administrators. In every legal and equitable aspect, it is considered as belonging to the realty. Now, why cannot such property be taxed by its proper denom-

ination as real estate?—in the words of the statute 'as lands
owned by nonresidents.' And if the name of the owner could
not be ascertained, the tract was required to be described by
its boundaries or any particular name. We can entertain no
doubt that the construction given to this act by the authorities of Michigan, in regard to the taxation of land sold by the
United States, whether patented or not, carried out the intention of the lawmaking power."

Again, the *Yosemite Valley case*, 15 Wall. 77, is authority
for saying that when a claimant has complied with all the
preliminary acts prescribed by Congress for the acquisition of
title, the power of regulation and disposition conferred upon
Congress by the constitution ceases.

Mr. Washburn, in his work on Real Property, says: "As
soon as the title shall have passed from the United States, it
takes the character of other property within the state, and is
subject to state legislation": 3 Washburn on Real Property,
4th ed., p. 187.

It is the declared policy of the courts, both national and
state, to declare the title in the claimant from the time he
receives the final certificate of entry. When the patent issues
it relates back to the date of such certificate. And the construction of the exemption clause, which holds that the exemption extends only down to the time when a patent should
and would be issued were it not for the delays necessarily
arising from the amount of work before the land department
of the government, is more in harmony with the general
policy of the act, and should be adopted. When a patent is
due, we are of the opinion it should be treated as having been
issued in contemplation of the act, and that the time of the
exemption then ceases: *Aurora Hill Con. M. Co.* v. *85 Mining Co.*, 34 Fed. Rep. 515; *Alta M. & S. Co.* v. *Benson M. & S.
Co.* (Ariz., Feb. 15, 1888).

[98] In this case, therefore, it being conceded that at the
time the defendant contracted the debt, to secure the payment of which the execution in favor of plaintiff was levied,
he was the owner of the land, it follows that it might be lawfully taken in satisfaction of the debt.

2. The conclusion reached upon the first question disposes
of the second. The exemption of the ditch stock is only
claimed on the ground that the ditch was an appurtenant to
the land and was necessary to the full enjoyment thereof.
Having decided that the land was not exempt, of course the

ditch stock is not. Aside from this, by statute in this state, the stock in ditch companies is personal property and subject to execution and sale the same as other personal property. Furthermore, we must not be understood as sanctioning the proposition that the stock of a ditch company is evidence of right appurtenant to the land: Gen. Stats. 1883, sec. 389; *Conway* v. *John*, 14 Col. 30; *Strickler* v. *Colorado Springs*, 16 Col. 61; 25 Am. St. Rep. 245.

The judgment of the district court is reversed and the cause remanded.

———

EXECUTIONS—EXEMPTION—HOMESTEAD IN PUBLIC LAND.—A homestead in public lands, claimed and perfected under the United States statute, is exempt from liability for debts contracted prior to the issuing of the patent therefor: *Faull* v. *Cooke*, 19 Or. 455; 20 Am. St. Rep. 836, and note.

EXECUTION—EXEMPTION—SHARES OF CORPORATE STOCK: See the note to *Princeton Bank* v. *Crozer*, 53 Am. Dec. 258. In *Coombs* v. *Jordan*, 3 Bland, 284, 22 Am. Dec. 236, it was held that the stock of a turnpike or canal company must be considered as realty, and is not subject to sale on execution, or to the lien of a judgment.

———

PEOPLE *v.* MACCABE.

[18 COLORADO, 186.]

ATTORNEYS AT LAW—RIGHT TO ADVERTISE.—The ethics of the legal profession forbid that an attorney should advertise his talents or his skill as a shopkeeper advertises his wares.

ATTORNEYS AT LAW—RETAINER IN DIVORCE.—An attorney at law may properly accept a retainer for the prosecution or defense of an action for divorce when convinced that his client has a good cause, but to invite or encourage such litigation is most reprehensible.

ATTORNEYS AT LAW—ADVERTISEMENT FOR DIVORCE BUSINESS—DISBARMENT. An advertisement published by an attorney at law to the effect that divorces can be legally obtained very quietly which shall be good everywhere is only the more mischievous because anonymous. Such an advertisement is against good morals, public and private, and as it is a false representation and a libel upon the courts of justice, it is ground for the disbarment or suspension from practice of the attorney publishing it.

ATTORNEYS AT LAW—DISBARMENT OF.—A court intrusted with the power to admit and disbar attorneys should be considerate and careful in exercising its jurisdiction; the interests of the attorney must in every case be weighed in the balance against the rights of the public, and the court should endeavor to guard and protect both with fairness and impartiality.

PETITION for the disbarment of an attorney at law for publishing the following advertisement: "Divorces legally obtained very quietly; good everywhere. Box 2344, Denver."

J. H. Maupin, attorney-general, for the petitioners.

Isaac J. MacCabe, pro se.

[188] ELLIOTT, J. The ethics of the legal profession forbid that an attorney should advertise his talents or his skill as a shopkeeper advertises his wares. An attorney may properly accept a retainer for the prosecution or defense of an action for divorce when convinced that his client has a good cause. But for any one to invite or encourage such litigation is most reprehensible. The marriage relation is too sacred; it affects too deeply the happiness of the family; it concerns too intimately the welfare of society; it lies too near the foundation of all good government to be broken up or disturbed for slight or transient causes.

In the present case we are not called upon to deal with a matter of ordinary advertising, but with a peculiar kind of advertising. Respondent did not advertise for business openly, giving his name and office address. His advertisement was anonymous and well calculated to encourage people to make application for divorces who might otherwise have refrained from so doing.

When a lawyer advertises that divorces can be legally obtained very quietly, and that such divorces will be good everywhere, such advertisement is a strong inducement—a powerful temptation—to many persons to apply for divorces who would otherwise be deterred from taking such a step from a wholesome fear of public opinion.

The advertisment published by respondent says in effect: "If you are dissatisfied with your partner in life—if you desire a divorce—communicate with me, and your desire shall be gratified. No one will know it. You see I advertise anonymously. I do not even subject ,myself to criticism. Everything will be done very quietly, and you will be able to sever the disagreeable marriage tie without public scandal, and hence without reproach."

The fear of public opinion is not the highest motive; but it exercises a wholesome influence in many ways. It is undoubtedly [189] potent in preventing many suits for divorce; and, in most of such cases, not only the individuals directly concerned, but the circle of society in which they move, as well as society at large, are greatly benefited by the restraining influence of public opinion.

The advertisement published by respondent, to the effect

that divorces could be legally obtained very quietly which should be good everwhere, was the more mischievous, because anonymous. Such an advertisement is against good morals, public and private; it is a false representation, and a libel upon the courts of justice. Divorces cannot be legally obtained very quietly which shall be good anywhere. To say that divorces can be obtained very quietly is equivalent to saying that they can be obtained without publicity. Every lawyer knows that to obtain a legal divorce a public record must be made of the proceeding; the complaint must be filed; the summons must issue; process must be served upon the defendant either personally or by publication in a public newspaper; proof must also be taken; and a decree must be publicly rendered by the court having jurisdiction of the proceeding. All these public proceedings the statute imperatively requires; and for a lawyer by an advertisement to indicate that such public proceedings can or will be dispensed with by the courts having jurisdiction of such cases is a libel upon the integrity of the judiciary that cannot be overlooked when brought to our notice.

In the case of *People* v. *Brown*, 17 Col. 431, this court said: "When this court grants a license to a person to practice law, the public and every individual coming in contact with the licensee in his professional capacity have a right to expect that he will demean himself with scrupulous propriety, as one commissioned to a high and honorable office. A person enjoying the rights and privileges of an attorney and counselor at law must also respect the duties and obligations of the position."

The case of *People* v. *Goodrich*, 79 Ill. 148, [190] was a disbarment proceeding under statutes from which ours were undoubtedly borrowed. Among other things, the complaint against Goodrich set forth that he had published advertisements without signature, representing that he could procure divorces without publicity, and by such advertisements solicited business of that character by communication through a particular postoffice box. The Goodrich case, though similar to the one before us, was more aggravated in some respects.

Mr. Justice Breese, in delivering the opinion of the court, said: "This court, having power by express law to grant a license to practice law, has an inherent right to see that the license is not abused or perverted to a use not contemplated in the grant. In granting the license, it was on the implied understanding that the party receiving it should at all times demean himself in a proper manner, and if not reflecting honor upon the court appointing him by his professional conduct, he would at least abstain from such practices as could not fail to bring discredit upon himself and the courts. . . . .

"The *morale* of defendant's professional conduct deserves special notice. He makes divorce cases a specialty. How many persons in our broad land weary of the chain that binds them? How many are eager to seize upon the slightest twig that may appear to aid them in escaping from a supposed sea of troubles, in which wedded life has immersed them? How many are fretting under imaginary ills, and what better devises than those practiced by this defendant could be contrived to increase these disquietudes, and stimulate to effort, by perjury, if need be, to free themselves from their supposed unhappy condition? Is it desirable that divorce cases should accumulate in our courts? If so, the defendant is justified in the means he has used and is using to that end. An honorable, high-toned lawyer will always aid a deserving party seeking a divorce, as coming strictly within his professional duties. He will render the aid, not solicit the case; and he will, in all things regarding it, act the man, and respect not only his own professional reputation, but the character of the [191] courts, and discharge the unpleasant duty in all respects as an honorable attorney and counselor should do."

In his answer in this case respondent says in effect that in advertising for divorce business he did it in entire ignorance that it was wrong; that he ceased to so advertise in deference to the court upon the commencement of this proceeding; that if this court shall adjudge such advertising to be wrong or to be malconduct in office as an attorney within the meaning of the statute, he will cheerfully abide by and obey the directions of the court in the premises. In view of these statements in the answer, this being the first case of the kind brought in this court, we do not feel it incumbent upon us to perpetually deprive respondent from pursuing his business as an attorney. A court intrusted with the power to admit and disbar attorneys should be considerate and careful in exercising its jurisdiction; the interests of the respondent must in every case be weighed in the balance against the rights of the public; and the court should endeavor to guard and protect both with fairness and impartiality.

In this connection the words of Chief Justice Marshall in *Ex parte Burr*, 9 Wheat. 529, are particularly appropriate:

" On the one hand, the profession of an attorney is of great importance. to an individual, and the prosperity of his whole life may depend on its exercise. The right to exercise it ought not to be lightly or capriciously taken from him. On the other, it is extremely desirable that the respectability of the bar should be maintained, and that its harmony with the bench should be preserved. For these objects, some controlling power, some discretion, ought to reside in the court. This discretion ought to be exercised with great moderation and judgment; but it must be exercised; and no other tribunal can decide, in a case of removal from the bar, with the same means of information as the court itself."

In view of all the circumstances of this case, the judgment of this court is that respondent McCabe be and is hereby suspended from practice as an attorney and counselor at law for the period of six months from this date, and until the payment of all the costs of this proceeding.

ATTORNEY AND CLIENT—POWER OF COURT TO DISBAR ATTORNEY AND HOW EXERCISED.—A judgment of disbarment should be pronounced only upon clear and convincing evidence: *People* v. *Pendleton*, 17 Col. 544. While the authority of the courts to disbar attorneys should remain unimpaired, protection should be given attorneys against a wrongful exercise of this power, and the supreme court will interfere where a case of wrong or injustice is brought to its attention: *State* v. *Kirke*, 12 Fla. 278; 95 Am. Dec. 314, and extended note 333. That the power of disbarment is a discretionary one; see the extended note to *Burns* v. *Allen*, 2 Am. St. Rep. 848.

PEOPLE *v.* KEEGAN.

[18 COLORADO, 237.]

ATTORNEYS AT LAW—MORAL CHARACTER—DISBARMENT.—A good moral character is one of the essential requisites to admission to the bar, and the tenure of office thereby conferred is during good behavior; and when it appears upon full investigation that an attorney has forfeited his good moral character, and has by his conduct shown himself unworthy of his office, it becomes the duty of the court to revoke the authority it gave him upon his admission.

ATTORNEYS AT LAW—MISCONDUCT—DISBARMENT.—A conspiracy entered into by an attorney at law to cheat and defraud a third person by which a sum of money is obtained is such misconduct as will authorize his disbarment.

PETITION for the disbarment of an attorney at law charging that on December 29, 1887, he entered into a conspiracy with one Crane and one Parrier to cheat and defraud one Bergman, and that in pursuance of such conspiracy procured the latter to execute his note without consideration for one thousand seven hundred and ninety dollars payable to one Fanny Crane. That thereafter the respondent Keegan, in pursuance of such conspiracy, filed a complaint on such note in the county court, procured Bergman to acknowledge service of summons and file an answer prepared by said Keegan. The latter then procured judgment on the pleadings and issued execution thereon. That on January 24, 1888, said Keegan was indicted and thereafter convicted and imprisoned for such fraudulent conspiracy, and served his sentence.

J. H. Maupin, attorney-general, for the petitioners.

C. H. Robinson, for the respondent and John C. Keegan, *pro se.*

238 Per CURIAM. The conviction alleged and admitted might be properly held as *res judicata* of the truth of the facts set forth in the first cause relied on as ground for disbarment. But in view of the fact that respondent has served his sentence thereunder, and realizing the disastrous consequences to him that must necessarily follow from an adverse judgment that will deprive him of his means of livelihood, we have, at counsel's earnest solicitation, concluded to look beyond such conviction, and from a careful investigation of the evidence introduced on the trial in the district court, determine if the facts alleged are fully sustained thereby.

We are satisfied from such investigation that if any doubt can be entertained of his complicity in the concoction of the scheme, no doubt exists as to his procuring the judgment with the knowledge that a fraud was being attempted, and **239** that he procured it for the purpose of assisting Crane to defraud Bergman, or to aid them in defrauding Bergman's creditors. From a letter to C. D. Fornes & Co., a client for whom he held a collection against Bergman, dated December 28, 1887 (the day previous to his active participation in the scheme), it appears that he was aware of the fact that Bergman had consulted Crane as to playing "a smart trick on his creditors."

Without noticing in detail the evidence furnished by the record, it is conclusively shown thereby that the respondent was guilty of conduct highly reprehensible and grossly unprofessional, and that justly brings reproach upon the honorable profession to which he belongs.

The duties imposed upon members of the bar clothe them with important fiduciary responsibilities and make them, amenable to obligations that other members of the community do not share. In no other calling should so strict an adherence to ethical and moral obligations be exacted, or so high a degree of accountability.be enforced.

A good moral character is one of the essential requisites to admission to the bar in this state, and the tenure of office thereby conferred is during good behavior; and when it appears, upon full investigation, that an attorney has forfeited his "good moral character," and has by his conduct shown himself unworthy of his office, it becomes the duty of the court to revoke the authority it gave him upon his admission. ' It is a duty they owe to themselves, the bar and the public, to see that a power which may be wielded for good or for evil is not intrusted to incompetent or dishonest hands": *Mills case*, 1 Mich. 395.

Without determining what weight should be given to the fact of his disbarment in the United States circuit court, we find the facts alleged in the first ground fully sustained, and respondent guilty as therein charged.

The judgment of the court is, that the name of the respondent, John C. Keegan, be stricken from the roll of attorneys.

ATTORNEY AND CLIENT—DISBARMENT OF ATTORNEY—GOOD MORAL CHARACTER.—When an attorney is admitted to the bar the court holds him out to the public as worthy of confidence in all of his professional duties and relations, so that when it comes to the knowledge of the court that he has since become unworthy, it is its duty to withdraw that indorsement by disbarring him: *Dismissal of Serfass*, 116 Pa. St. 455. Good moral character is a condition precedent to admission to the bar and it is a requisite condition for the rightful continuance in practice: *In re O——.*, 73 Wis. 602. For a complete discussion of the disbarment of attorneys for immoral character and dishonest practices see the extended notes to the following cases: *Burns v. Allen*, 2 Am. St. Rep. 850; *Delano's case*, 42 Am. Rep. 557, and *State v. Kirke*, 95 Am. Dec. 335.

HOOK v. FENNER.

[18 COLORADO, 288.]

FILING INSTRUMENT—WHAT CONSTITUTES.—The duty of a party required to file a paper, in the absence of any question as to fees, is discharged when he has placed it in the hands of the proper custodian at the proper time and in the proper place.

FILING INSTRUMENT—WHAT SUFFICIENT.—The placing of a paper in a case as a permanent record in the office of a justice of the peace is a sufficient filing, no matter if he fails to perform the mere clerical act of indorsing it as filed. His failure to so indorse it cannot operate to the prejudice of either party.

FILING INSTRUMENT IN COURT—WHEN COMPLETE.—Filing a paper in court may be complete without the indorsement of such filing. The indorsement is only evidence of the filing, but it is not the exclusive evidence.

REPLEVIN—CERTAINTY IN DESCRIPTION of the property required in actions of replevin is only such as the nature of the property will admit, and when no objection to the description for uncertainty is made in the court below it must be deemed to be waived on appeal.

Charles K. Phillips, and Norris and Howard, for the appellants.

H. M. Jacoway, and Montgomery and Frost, for the appellee.

284 HAYT, C. J. In the county court a motion was made for the first time to dismiss the action for the want of jurisdiction because, as it is alleged, the writ was issued before the filing of any undertaking with the justice. This motion was overruled, and this ruling of the court constitutes the principal ground of error relied upon in this court.

There is an undertaking in the statutory form in the record, but there is a dispute between the parties as to whether it was in fact filed before or after the issuance of the writ by the justice. The plaintiff in error claims that it was not filed until after the writ had been issued and executed. In support of this contention they rely upon the filing indorsement of the justice upon the instrument. This shows that the undertaking was filed upon the eighth day of November— seven days after the date of the writ. The defendant in **285** error claims that this date is manifestly incorrect. To show this, he relies upon the fact that the bond itself bears date the 1st of November, 1889, and also calls attention to the recitals in the writ of replevin, under the hand and seal of the justice, to the effect that the plaintiff having previously given good and sufficient security to prosecute his action, and to make return of the goods and chattels described therein, if return should be awarded, etc.

In the consideration of the question thus raised, it becomes important to determine at the outset what constitutes the filing of a paper. Is it the clerical act of indorsing it as filed, or is it receipt of the paper by the proper custodian, and its lodgment in his office? The duty of a party required to file a paper, in the absence of any question as to fees, would seem to be discharged when he has placed the same in the hands of the proper custodian, at a proper time and in a proper place. If a paper in the case is placed as a permanent record in the office of the justice of the peace this ought to be sufficient, no matter if the justice fails to perform the mere clerical act of indorsing it as filed. If the paper was actually placed in the hands of the justice for filing, before the writ was issued, it is clear that it was his duty to mark the same as filed. Failing to discharge this duty, can it operate to the prejudice of either party to the suit? We are of the opinion that it cannot.

The undertaking as presented by the plaintiff below is in strict accordance with the statute; no question is made upon the responsibility of the sureties. It appears that it was in every way satisfactory to the justice, and the fact that he did not mark it as filed we think is quite immaterial, if, as a matter of fact, it was left with him at his office for filing, within the proper time. It has been repeatedly held that the filing of a paper in court may be complete without the indorsement of such filing: the indorsement being only evidence of the filing, but not the exclusive evidence: *Haines* v. *Lindsey,* 4 Ohio, 88; 19 Am. Dec. 586; *Thompson* [286] v. *Foster,* 6 Ark. 208; *State* v. *Gowen,* 12 Ark. 62; *Bettison* v. *Budd,* 21 Ark. 578.

Was the undertaking in this case filed within the time required by law? That it was executed at the proper time is apparent from the date of the bond; that it was filed before the writ was issued, is certified to by the justice of the peace in the writ itself. When we add to these facts the presumption that must be indulged, in favor of the regularity of the proceedings of all public offices, we think that it sufficiently appears that the bond was filed with the justice of the peace before the writ was issued.

This position receives further support from the fact that none of the papers show a filing indorsement of a date prior to the 8th of November, although it sufficiently appears that the affidavit was made and sworn to before the justice on the

first day of November; and no evidence *aliunde* was offered
to show that either affidavit or bond was not filed upon that
date. Moreover, as no question was raised before the justice
of the peace in regard to the date of the filing of the undertaking, this may be considered as additional evidence that
all parties conceded that the proper preliminary steps had
then been taken to give the justice jurisdiction.

It is contended that the description of the property replev-
ined as given in the writ of replevin is insufficient. The
property is described as follows: "Two thousand pounds of
oats, more or less, now situated in a certain granary, on the
premises now occupied by defendants." The evidence shows
that these oats had been segregated and placed in a certain
bin in a granary owned by the defendants, and that the constable had no difficulty in finding them. The record also
shows that two juries have found the description sufficient.
We think under the circumstances greater minuteness should
not be demanded. While certainty in the description of the
property is required in replevin, this rule does not require
greater certainty of description than the nature of the property will reasonably admit.

Aside from this, as no objection to .the description was
[287] made for uncertainty in the court below, it must be
deemed to be waived. After the defendants have pleaded
that the property is theirs, and have submitted the case to
the jury upon its merits, it is too late to ask that the judgment should be reversed, because of uncertainty in the description: Wells on Replevin, sec. 185.

Some question is raised as to the amount of damages
allowed. This was a question of fact for the jury to determine, under all the evidence in the case, and we see no reason
for interfering with their conclusion in the matter. The judgment is affirmed.

FILING OF INSTRUMENTS—WHAT IS SUFFICIENT.—Papers are properly
filed when delivered to the proper officer, and by him received to be kept on
file: *Beebe* v. *Morrell,* 76 Mich. 114; 15 Am. St. Rep. 288, and extended
note thoroughly discussing the subject. In *Hills* v. *Atlee,* 80 Wis. 219, 27
Am. St. Rep. 32, it was held that under a statute requiring the register of
deeds to keep an index in which the names of grantors should be entered in
their alphabetical order, a tax deed is not regarded as recorded until it is
indexed: See further on the latter point the extended note to *Green* v. *Gar-
rington,* 91 Am. Dec. 109.

REPLEVIN—SUFFICIENCY OF DESCRIPTION.—A writ of replevin should
contain such a description of the goods on its face as would enable the

sheriff, with reasonable certainty, to distinguish them from property of a' like nature: *Stevens* v. *Osman,* 1 Mich. 92; 48 Am. Dec. 696, and extended note thoroughly discussing the subject. Describing an animal in a writ of replevin as a "heifer," and in the certificate of appraisement as a "cow," is no ground for dismissing the writ, particularly where the description in the appraisment directly refers to the writ, and clearly identifies the animal replevied: *Pomeroy* v. *Trimper,* 8 Allen, 398; 85 Am. Dec. 714, and note.

WYATT *v.* LARIMER AND WELD IRRIGATION CO.

[18 COLORADO, 298.]

JURISDICTION OF SUPREME COURT may be invoked upon an appeal from a judgment of the district court or of the court of appeals in actions that relate to a freehold.

ESTATES—FREEHOLD IS ANY ESTATE OF INHERITANCE or for life in either a corporeal or incorporeal hereditament existing in or arising from real property of free tenure.

WATERS—RIGHT TO WHEN A FREEHOLD.—A perpetual right to have a' certain quantity of water flow through an irrigation ditch is an easement therein, and an incorporeal hereditament descendible by inheritance, hence a freehold estate.

WATERS—FREEHOLD IN—JURISDICTION.—An action to enjoin a permanent diminution of a perpetual right to have a certain quantity of water flow through an irrigation ·ditch involves a freehold, and the supreme court has jurisdiction to review the judgment in such action on appeal.

WATERS—STATUS OF IRRIGATION COMPANY.—An irrigation or canal company is not the proprietor of the water diverted by it, but is only an intermediate agency, existing for the purpose of aiding consumers in the exercise of their constitutional rights, as well as a private enterprise prosecuted for the benefit of its owners.

WATERS—VIOLATION OF CONTRACT FOR—SUFFICIENCY OF COMPLAINT FOR INJUNCTION.—A complaint by water-takers from an irrigation ditch to enjoin the ditch company from selling additional water rights, in violation of its contract obligations with them, is sufficient, although it does not allege the cubical dimensions of the ditch, nor the adjudicated priorities in its waters, provided it states the contract, and alleges that the ditch company is violating, or intends to violate, its contract obligations with such water-takers.

WATERS—CONSTRUCTION OF CONTRACT FOR.—The true intent and meaning of a contract between an irrigation company and water-takers must be determined from the terms used, read in the light of surrounding circumstances at the time of its execution, from the subject matter, and the purposes and objects to be accomplished by it.

WATERS—CONSTRUCTION OF CONTRACT FOR.—When an irrigation company, by the terms of its contract with water-takers, having the right to dispose of definite water rights by ambiguous expressions in subsequent provisions of the contract reserves the power to render such rights indefinite and uncertain as to quantity by disposing of water rights in excess of its ability to furnish water, the contract is not only inequitable and unjust, but also illegal, and cannot be enforced.

CONTRACTS—CONSTRUCTION.—If a contract admits of two meanings, one of which will render it unlawful and the other lawful, the latter construction must be adopted, and all doubtful words or provisions must be taken most strongly against the grantor.

CONTRACTS—CONSTRUCTION WHEN TERMS DOUBTFUL.—When doubt exists as to the construction of a contract prepared by one party, upon the faith of which the other party has incurred obligations, or parted with property, that construction most favorable to the latter party will be adopted; and when the contract is susceptible of two constructions, one involving injustice and the other consistent with right, the latter must be adopted.

CONTRACTS—CONSTRUCTION WHEN AMBIGUOUS.—When the language used by parties to a contract is indefinite and ambiguous, the practical interpretation by the parties themselves is entitled to great, if not controlling, influence, in ascertaining their understanding of its terms.

WATERS—CONSTRUCTION OF CONTRACT FOR.—Under a contract between an irrigation ditch company and water-takers by which each taker has the right to a definite amount of water, and providing that the sale of water rights shall terminate when the outstanding rights shall equal the estimated capacity of the ditch, and giving the company the power to distribute the waters flowing through its ditch *pro rata*, among existing water-takers, if from any cause the supply shall become inadequate to furnish an amount equal to then outstanding rights, the company's power to dispose of water rights is limited by the furnishing capacity of the ditch as dependent upon the source of supply or other circumstances and not by its carrying capacity.

ACTION by the plaintiffs by virtue of water-right contracts between them and the defendants to enjoin the latter from selling additional water-rights or entering into further water-right contracts providing for the prorating of waters flowing in the ditch of defendants. The court below sustained a demurrer to the complaint and rendered judgment for the defendants. The plaintiffs appealed.

H. N. Haynes, and Teller and Orahood, for the appellants.

J. W. McCreery and Hugh Butler, for the appellees.

306 GODDARD, J. The right to the relief demanded in this action is predicated upon, and must be determined by, the terms of the contracts entered into by the respective parties; and while those contractual rights are analogous to the rights guaranteed by the constitution to appropriators of water, the action involves only the construction of private contracts between the ditch company and the plaintiffs, and no constitutional question is involved in the decision of the case. The jurisdiction of this court by appeal, therefore, depends solely upon the question whether the action relates to a freehold. It is strenuously insisted by counsel for appellees that an

action must involve a freehold to enable this court to entertain jurisdiction, basing this claim upon the third subdivision
of section four of the act establishing the court of appeals,
above cited.   When construed with other sections of the act,
we think the word "involve," as used in that section, must
be held to be synonymous with·the word "relate," and the
jurisdiction of this court may be invoked upon an appeal
from a judgment of the district court or of the court of appeals in actions that relate to a freehold.   It is therefore
necessary to ascertain and define the nature and kind of property [307] claimed by plaintiffs in the water rights in question,
and whether the nature and extent of their interests therein
constitute freehold estates, and whether this action relates
thereto.   A freehold is defined as "Any estate of inheritance
or for life in either a corporeal or incorporeal hereditament
existing in or arising from real property of free tenure": 2
Blackstone's Commentaries, 104.

An incorporeal hereditament is "Anything, the subject of
property which is inheritable, and not tangible or visible":
2 Wooddeson's Lectures, 4.

"A right issuing out of a thing corporate (whether real or
personal), or concerning or annexed to or exercisable within
the same": 2 Blackstone's Commentaries, 20; 3 Washburn on
Real Property, 401.

"The right of a party to have the water of a stream or
watercourse flow to or from his lands or mill, over the land of
another, is an incorporeal hereditament, and an easement, or
a prædial service, as defined by the civil law": *Cary* v. *Daniels,* 5 Met. 238:

The plaintiffs allege a right to have a certain quantity of
water flow through the irrigation company's ditch.   This right
is an easement in the ditch.   It is a right annexed to realty,
and, being a perpetual right, is an incorporeal hereditament
descendible by inheritance to plaintiff's heirs, and, hence, a
freehold estate.

The subject matter of the action is this estate.   The acts
threatened by defendant's will, if carried out, materially di-
minish this estate and permanently depreciate the value of
the water rights.

The object of the action being to enjoin or prevent such
diminution, or, in other words, to preserve the estate of the
plaintiffs, the necessary result of the decree will be—one party
will gain and the other lose a material portion of such estate.

The action, therefore, relates to a freehold, and this court, under the statutory provisions above cited, has jurisdiction to review the judgment of the court of appeals.

The decision by the court of appeals in this case was rendered by a divided court. We are unable to see wherein the **308** discussion by the learned judge writing the majority opinion touching the constitutional *status* of irrigation companies in this state was essential to the decision of the questions involved in the case. But, inasmuch as the views expressed in that opinion are so at variance with numerous decisions of this court, we feel impelled to express our disapproval thereof, and our adherence to the doctrine heretofore announced by this court in relation to the *status* of canal companies organized for the purpose of carrying water for general purposes of irrigation. We adhere to the doctrine that such a canal company is not the proprietor of the water diVerted by it, but that " it must be regarded as an intermediate agency existing for the purpose of aiding consumers in the exercise of their constitutional rights, as well as a private enterprise prosecuted for the benefit of its owners": *Wheeler* v. *Northern Col. Irrigation Co.*, 10 Col. 582; 3 Am. St. Rep. 603; *Farmers' etc. Canal & R. Co.* v. *Southworth*, 13 Col. 111; *Strickler* v. *City of Colorado Springs*, 16 Col. 61; 25 Am. St. Rep. 245; *Combs* v. *Agricultural Ditch Co.*, 17 Col. 146; 31 Am. St. Rep. 275.

The appellants allege that, by the terms of their contracts, when the company shall have outstanding water-right contracts sufficient to cover the amount of water that the company's canal is able to furnish, the right of the company to enter into further contracts is at an end; and that such limit has been reached.

The company insists that it has the right to dispose of water rights up to the estimated capacity of its canal to carry water. The rights of the respective parties are therefore to be measured and determined by the construction of the contracts in question; and the controversy, as above stated, involves only their contractual rights.

The *status* of the defendant company could in no aspect affect these rights. Its duty to these plaintiffs would be the same whether that duty was to furnish water under their contracts as proprietor or carrier of water.

It is advanced in argument by counsel for appellees, and asserted in the opinion of the court of appeals, that the com-

plaint is obnoxious to demurrer because wanting in certain
309 *data* essential to a fair construction of the questions involved, in this, that it contains no statement of the size, grade,
etc.; in other words, fails to state the cubical dimensions of
defendant's ditch, and also fails to state the adjudicated
priority of such ditch.

It does not appear to us that these matters are essential to
the determination of this controversy, but that the facts alleged fairly present the rights of the respective parties for
adjudication.

It is alleged that by reason of prior appropriations the
water of the Cache la Poudre river, from which the ditch
takes its supply, can furnish water to this ditch in an amount
only equal to the three hundred and sixty-six and one-half
water rights now outstanding and in force for the past two
years; and that the water allotted to those rights has been
required to irrigate the lands they cover; that there is not
sufficient water not otherwise appropriated from the river to
enable defendant company to furnish any more water rights,
and that the company has disposed of, and there is now outstanding, water rights equal to and in excess of its ability to
furnish water.

If, therefore, such conditions limit the right of defendant
company to dispose of further rights, as claimed by appellants, and the company carries out its admitted purpose and
disposes of additional water rights, it would violate its contract obligations, and it is immaterial what the number of its
priority may be, or the size or dimensions of its ditch.

The appellees admit the inability of the irrigation company
to furnish water in excess of the water rights outstanding
during the irrigation season, but insist, notwithstanding that
fact, that it has the right to dispose of water rights up to the
estimated carrying capacity of its ditch. This issue is fairly
presented by the allegations in the complaint.

The vital and controlling question, therefore, and the only
one the decision of which is properly invoked by the issues
presented, is, what is the true intent and meaning of the contracts entered into between the irrigation company and **310**
these plaintiffs? In order to determine this the terms used
must be read in the light of the circumstances surrounding
the parties at the time of their execution, the subject matter
thereof, and the purposes and objects to be accomplished
thereby.

The company is the owner of the canal whereby it proposes to divert water from the Cache la Poudre river for the use of the farmers owning land capable of being irrigated therefrom.

The quantity of water necessary to irrigate a given quantity of land was well understood by the contracting parties. Each water right to be disposed of is defined by the company in its printed forms as "A water right to the use of water flowing through the canal of said company, each water right representing one and forty-four hundredths cubic feet of water flowing through a weir per second."

This quantity of water is necessary to irrigate eighty acres of land. Each consumer, having in view the cultivation of his land, and knowing the quantity of water necessary therefor, contracts for water to that end, and purchases a definite number of such water rights. That this definite quantity may be insured to him, except such diminution as may arise from temporary causes, certain conditions are inserted in the contracts, among which are the sixth, seventh, and eighth conditions set out in the complaint.

The sixth condition provides a limit to the number of such water rights the company may dispose of. It in no way changes or circumscribes the water right as defined in the granting clause. The language used therein pertinent to this inquiry is:

"The company agrees that when it shall have sold, and have outstanding and in force, a number of water rights equal to the estimated capacity of the company's canal to furnish water," it will issue stock, etc.

The controversy arises upon the meaning to be given to the words "estimated capacity to furnish water." Appellees contend that they mean the carrying capacity of the canal. *11 Appellants insist that they plainly import its furnishing capacity—its ability to supply and deliver water. It appears that some element of uncertainty existed that experience was necessary to decide. It certainly did not arise from the want of *data* to determine the physical capacity of the canal. Its cubical capacity was susceptible of definite measurement; its grade was easy of ascertainment, and by mathematical computation its carrying capacity could be determined, and no estimate of that fact was necessary.

But since it appears from the allegations of the complaint that other ditches with earlier appropriations derived their supply from the Cache la Poudre river, it was a matter of un-

certainty how much water could be obtained by the company's canal after their supply had been taken; and the
furnishing capacity of its canal could be ascertained only by
experiment, or estimated, that is, approximated, by taking
into consideration all the factors upon which its ability to
furnish water depended, which necessarily involved taking
into consideration the very material fact, to wit, the probable
amount of water it could obtain.

The seventh condition affords but little aid to this investigation. It is inserted for the purpose of relieving the company from any liability on account of the inability of its canal
to carry and distribute a volume of water equal to its "estimated capacity," in case of unavoidable accident, and when,
by reason of drouth, such volume becomes insufficient.

This would indicate that the company recognized an obligation to deliver a definite amount of water under normal
conditions, and that the capacity of the canal was dependent
upon the water supply.

If, as contended, the rights sold were not definite rights,
and only represented fractional parts of whatever water might
flow in the canal, no liability could accrue under these or any
other conditions, and this provision was useless.

The eighth, or prorating, condition seems to be in harmony
with the construction we have given to the sixth, and recognizes the estimated capacity of the canal as limited by the
312 supply of water to be had under permanent and normal
conditions, and recognizes the water rights outstanding as
rights definite in amount, and in the aggregate equal to such
supply. Its language is: "It is further agreed that if, by
reason of any causes, the supply of water shall be insufficient
to fill and flow through said canal, according to its estimated
capacity, or if from any other cause, as aforesaid, beyond the
control of said company, the supply shall be insufficient to
furnish an amount equal to all the water rights then outstanding, the said company shall have the right to distribute such
water as may flow through its canal to the holders of such
water rights *pro rata*," etc.

If the carrying capacity of the canal was to be the criterion
instead of its furnishing capacity, why use the words "estimated capacity" in this provision? It would have been
enough to say, "If insufficient to fill and flow through said
canal"; but the words "estimated capacity" being used, and
the failure of supply arising from temporary causes, such as

unforeseen accident, drouth, etc., affording the reason for prorating, the supply under normal conditions is the recognized
factor that limits the number of water rights to be sold, and
measures the estimated capacity of the ditch to furnish water.

It is not to be presumed that the consumers of water under
the company's canal, having in view the acquirement of the
use of water for a particular purpose, one that required for its
successful accomplishment a given quantity of water, understood that they were to receive an indefinite fractional part of
the water that might flow through the irrigation company's
canal, instead of the definite quantity specified in the granting
clause of their contracts, unless such understanding is plainly
inferable from the language used by the contracting parties,
and should not be inferred from doubtful or ambiguous terms.

If the company intended to dispose of a definite number of
water rights, regardless of the amount of water it could supply, fair dealing would require it to so specify and define
[313] the rights sold as a fractional part of the water flowing
in its canal.

In the light of the purpose, therefore, to be accomplished,
we think the words "estimated capacity," limited and modified as they are by the words "to furnish," must be construed
as meaning the ability of the canal to supply or deliver water.

With this construction, the contracts in question are fair,
legal, and equitable. If appellees' contention is correct, and
the irrigation company by the terms of these contracts have
the right to dispose of definite water rights, and by ambiguous expressions in subsequent provisions reserve the power
to render them uncertain and indefinite in quantity, by disposing of water rights admittedly in excess of its ability to
furnish water, they are not only inequitable and unfair, but
clearly illegal under the decision of this court in *Farmers' etc.
Canal & R. Co.* v. *Southworth*, 13 Col. 129, wherein it is said:

"A contract to carry more water than has been lawfully
diverted would be unlawful; and to prevent injuries resulting therefrom, or to recover damages in case the injuries are
suffered, ample legal remedies exist."

If the terms of a contract admit of two meanings, one of
which would render the contract unlawful and the other lawful, the latter construction must be adopted: Bishop on Contracts, sec. 392.

If it be conceded that the term "estimated capacity" is, as
used in these contracts, of doubtful meaning, the appellants'

contention **is sustained** by well-settled rules of construction. The printed blanks upon which the contracts are written were prepared and the words therein were selected **by the** company; and, if of doubtful import, must be taken most strongly against it.

"Doubtful words and provisions are to be taken most strongly against the grantor, he being supposed to select the words which are used in the instrument": *Adams* v. *Frothingham*, 3 Mass. 361; 3 Am. Dec. 151.

In *Noonan* v. *Bradley*, 9 Wall. 395, it is said: "Where doubt exists as to the construction of an instrument [314] prepared by one party, upon the faith of which the other party has incurred obligations or parted with his property, that construction should be adopted which will be favorable to the latter party; and where an instrument is susceptible of two constructions—the one working injustice and the other consistent with the right of the case—that one should be favored which upholds the right."

The acts of the company in relation to these contracts are persuasive, if not of controlling weight, in their interpretation. It is alleged in the complaint, "that defendant, The Larimer and Weld Irrigation Company . . . . by reason of the premises, heretofore for two years and more last past has refused to execute any additional water-right contracts, though often requested so to do by divers persons, and except for the wrongful conspiracy hereinafter set forth, has persistently and consistently, through its authorized agents, admitted that it could not dispose of any more water rights without violating its duty to present water-right owners and users."

As announced in *McPhee* v. *Young*, 13 Col. 80, "In the construction of a written contract the intentions of the parties are to be first sought in the instrument itself. If the intent and meaning of the parties is not clearly disclosed by the language therein employed, then competent evidence bearing on the construction of the instrument by the parties themselves, as by their acts and conduct in its performance, may be considered for the purpose of ascertaining their understanding of its terms."

In the case of *Chicayo* v. *Sheldon*, 9 Wall. 54, it is said: "In cases where the language used by the parties to the contract is indefinite or ambiguous, and, hence, of doubtful construction, the practical interpretation by the parties themselves is entitled to great, if not controlling, influence."

In whatever aspect these contracts are considered, whether upon the plain import of the language used or by regarding certain terms as of doubtful meaning, their interpretation must be favorable to the contention of the appellants.

[315] It sufficiently appearing by the allegations of the complaint that appellants have certain well-defined rights that will be materially impaired if defendants do the acts threatened, we think it states a cause of action clearly cognizable by a court of equity.

The demurrer to the complaint should have been overruled. The judgment of the court of appeals is reversed, with directions to reverse the judgment of the district court of Weld county, and remand the cause to that court for further proceedings in accordance with this opinion.

ON PETITION FOR REHEARING.

Per CURIAM.   In support of the petition for a rehearing, counsel for appellees insist that "the subject matter of the action is not an easement or a freehold of any kind or nature," and that to "constitute an easement in freehold it must be inseparably annexed to, or appurtenant to, the estate of complainant." That a valid appropriation of water from a natural stream constitutes an easement in that stream, and that such easement is an incorporeal hereditament, the appropriation being in perpetuity, cannot well be disputed. Washburn in his work on Easements and Servitudes, in discussing the question of property in water, at page 276, says:

"As forming the subject of property, in connection with the realty, water may be viewed in two lights—one as constituting one of the elements of which an estate is composed, and giving, by its qualities and susceptibilities of use, a value to such estate; the other, as being valuable alone for its use, to be enjoyed in connection with the occupation of the soil. In the latter sense, it constitutes an incorporeal hereditament, to which the term 'easement' is applied."

Angell on Water Courses, sec. 141, uses this illustration: "If a miller, or manufacturer, purchases the land itself, over which the water runs, it is evident he would then have a corporeal tenement, and the right which he would possess, in respect to his water course, would be real; but if he [316] should purchase a water privilege, or a portion of water power, without any part of the bed of the river, he, in that case, would gain an incorporeal hereditament, or easement."

The right acquired to water by an appropriator under our system, is of the same character as that defined by the foregoing authorities as an incorporeal hereditament and easement. The consumer under a ditch possesses a like property. He is an appropriator from the natural stream, through the intermediate agency of the ditch, and has a right to have the quantity of water so appropriated flow in the natural stream and through the ditch for his use.

The argument of counsel for appellee seems to us more a criticism upon the use of the word "easement" in this connection, than an answer to the ultimate conclusion we announced as to the nature and extent of complainant's estate or property. They say: "It is not sufficient for the purposes of this action that the complainant be a part owner in the ditch, which of course is real estate, or even to own a right therein of an incorporeal nature; but to constitute such right an easement it must be such an interest as will pass by a conveyance of his farm, as an appurtenant thereto, without further description thereof."

And yet it may be said that a water right does come strictly within the definition given by counsel of an easement, except that its source of supply and place of use may be changed. The natural watercourse, or the ditch, occupies the relation of the servient estate, and the very existence of a water right requires a use which constitutes the dominant estate.

We cannot agree with the proposition that because a water right is susceptible of being changed from one tract of land to another, or its source of supply changed from one point of a natural stream to another, it is any less an easement in the stream, than if it always retained its original point of diversion and place of application. A change of the place of diversion or the place of use does not affect this right either in character or extent.

But the correctness of the conclusions we arrived at depends [317] not so much upon the technical use of terms as upon the substantial right of complainants, which seems to us to be clearly a right incorporeal in its nature, that by its duration constitutes a freehold, and that this action relates to such freehold.

Upon a careful consideration of the other points so forcibly and ably presented by counsel for appellees, we are still of the opinion that our views thereon, as expressed in our former opinion, are correct, and the petition for rehearing is denied.

ESTATES—FREEHOLD—DEFINITION.—A freehold has been defined to be an estate in real property, of inheritance, or for life, or the term by which it is held: *Gage v. Scales*, 100 Ill. 221. A freeholder is one who holds a freehold estate; that is, lands or tenements, in fee simple, fee tail, or for term of life: *Bradford v. State*, 15 Ind. 353.

WATERS—RIPARIAN RIGHTS.—Every riparian owner of land through which streams of water flow has a right to the reasonable use of the running water, which is a private right of property annexed to the freehold, being a real or corporeal hereditament in the nature of an easement: *Ulbricht v. Eufaula Water Co.*, 86 Ala. 587; 11 Am. St. Rep. 72, and note; *Hill v. Newman*, 5 Cal. 445; 63 Am. Dec. 140; *Alta Land etc. Co. v. Hancock*, 85 Cal. 219; 20 Am. St. Rep. 217, and note with the cases collected. See also the extended note to *Davis v. Getchell*, 79 Am. Dec. 638.

WATERS—RIGHTS OF DITCH COMPANIES.—A ditch company as an appropriator does not become the proprietor of the water diverted, the public are entitled to its use upon paying a reasonable compensation therefor: *Wheeler v. Northern Colorado Irr. Co.*, 10 Col. 582; 3 Am. St. Rep. 603, and note; *Combs v. Agricultural Ditch Co.*, 17 Col. 146; 31 Am. St. Rep. 275, and note.

CONTRACTS—CONSTRUCTION OF WHERE CAPABLE OF TWO MEANINGS.—Where a contract is fairly open to two constructions, by one of which it would be lawful and by the other unlawful, the former must be adopted: *Watters v. McGuigan*, 72 Wis. 155, and where one construction would render it void, and the other give it force and effect, the latter is to be adopted: *Shreffler v. Nadelhoffer*, 133 Ill. 536; 23 Am. St. Rep. 626, and note; *Cravens v. Eagle Cotton Mills Co.*, 120 Ind. 6; 16 Am. St. Rep. 298, and note; *Hughes v. Lane*, 11 Ill. 123; 50 Am. Dec. 436, and note; *Thrall v. Newell*, 19 Vt. 202; 47 Am. Dec. 682, and note; *Powers v. Clarke*, 127 N. Y. 417; *Lincoln v. Field*, 54 Ark. 471.

CONTRACTS—IN WHOSE FAVOR CONSTRUED.—In interpreting the words of a contract of which there is an uncertainty, that construction should be adopted which is most beneficial to the covenantee: *Paul v. Travelers' Ins. Co.*, 112 N. Y. 472; 8 Am. St. Rep. 758; *Hoffman v. Ætna etc. Ins. Co.*, 32 N. Y. 405; 88 Am. Dec. 337, and extended note discussing this subject. See also *Evans v. Sanders*, 8 Port. 497; 33 Am. Dec. 297.

CONTRACTS—CONSTRUCTION—ACTS OF PARTIES.—Where the terms of a parol agreement are in doubt the acts of the parties in the execution of it are the best guides for its interpretation: *Robbins v. Kimball*, 55 Ark. 414; 29 Am. St. Rep. 45, and note. The practical construction given to it by the parties to a contract, the meaning of which is capable of two constructions, will be of controlling influence: *Cravens v. Eagle Cotton Mills Co.*, 120 Ind. 6; 16 Am. St. Rep. 298; *Louisville etc. Ry. Co. v. Reynolds*, 118 Ind. 170; *Ellis v. Harrison*, 104 Mo. 270; *Hill v. McKay*, 94 Cal. 5.

CROSS *v.* PEOPLE.

[18 COLORADO, 321.]

LOTTERY—WHAT IS.—A lottery is a scheme by which, on one's paying money or some other thing of value, he obtains the contingent right to have something of greater value, if an appeal to chance, by lot or otherwise, under the direction of the manager of the scheme, should decide in his favor. A valuable consideration must be paid, directly or indirectly, for a chance to draw a prize by lot, to bring the transaction within the class of lotteries or gift enterprises that the law prohibits as criminal.

LOTTERY—WHAT DOES NOT CONSTITUTE.—A gratuitous distribution of property by lot or chance, if not resorted to as a device to evade the law, and no consideration is derived directly or indirectly from the party receiving the chance, does not constitute a lottery prohibited by law.

LOTTERY—WHAT DOES NOT CONSTITUTE.—The gratuitous distribution of business cards to purchasers and nonpurchasers alike which entitle the holders to a chance in a drawing for a piano to be determined as the holders of such chances might elect is not a lottery prohibited by law.

LOTTERY—CONSIDERATION FOR CHANCE.—The fact that chances in a drawing for a piano are gratuitously and indiscriminately given away to induce people to visit a certain store with the expectation that they may purchase goods and thereby increase trade is a benefit too remote to constitute a consideration for the chances and make it a lottery prohibited by law.

Coe and Freeman, and C. E. and F. Herrington, for the appellants.

S. W. Jones, attorney-general, and H. Riddell, for the appellees.

322 GODDARD, J. The principal question, and the only one of practical importance to the people and the plaintiffs in error, is presented by the fourth and fifth assignments of error; and, since it is decisive of the case, it is unnecessary to notice the other errors assigned.

The decision of this case depends upon the meaning to be given to the terms "lottery and gift enterprise" used in section 2196 of the General Statutes, page 677; and whether the facts admitted constitute a violation of that section.

324 The term "lottery" is said to have no technical signification in the law; but to ascertain its meaning we are to consult the common usage of the language. The definition given by Worcester is: "A distribution of prizes and blanks by chance; a game of hazard in which small sums are ventured for the chance of obtaining a larger value."

Bishop defines a lottery as: "A scheme by which, on one's

paying money, or some other thing of value, he obtains the contingent right to have something of greater value; if an appeal to chance, by lot or otherwise, under the direction of the manager of the scheme, should decide in his favor": Bishop on Statutory Crimes, sec. 952.

The accepted doctrine by the court of appeals of New York is that given by Folger, J., in *Hull* v. *Ruggles*, 56 N. Y. 424:

"Where a pecuniary consideration is paid, and it is to be determined by lot or chance, according to some scheme held out to the public, what and how much he who pays the money is to receive for it—that is a lottery."

It may be accepted as the result of the adjudicated cases, that a valuable consideration must be paid, directly or indirectly, for a chance to draw a prize by lot, to bring the transaction within the class of lotteries or gift enterprises that the law prohibits as criminal: *Buckalew* v. *State*, 62 Ala. 334; 34 Am. Rep. 22; *State* v. *Bryant*, 74 N. C. 207; *Commonwealth v. Wright*, 137 Mass. 250; 50 Am. Rep. 306; *State* v. *Clarke*, 33 N. H. 329; 66 Am. Dec. 723; *State* v. *Shorts*, 32 N. J. L. 398; 90 Am. Dec. 668; *Wilkinson* v. *Gill*, 74 N. Y. 63; 30 Am. Rep. 264; *Governors* v. *American Art Union*, 7 N. Y. 228; *State* v. *Mumford*, 73 Mo. 647; 39 Am. Rep. 532; *Hull* v. *Ruggles*, 56 N. Y. 424; *Thomas* v. *People*, 59 Ill. 160; *United States* v. *Olney*, 1 Deady, 461; *Yellowstone Kit* v. *State*, 88 Ala. 196; 16 Am. St. Rep. 38.

The gratuitous distribution of property by lot or chance, if not resorted to as a device to evade the law, and no consideration is derived directly or indirectly from the party receiving the chance, does not constitute the offense. In such case the party receiving the chance is not induced to hazard money with the hope of obtaining a larger value, or to part [325] with his money at all; and the spirit of gambling is in no way cultivated or stimulated, which is the essential evil of lotteries, and which our statute is enacted to prevent.

By the admitted facts it is shown that the plaintiffs in error gave business cards, which entitled the holders to a chance in a piano, to be distributed as the holders of such chances might elect. These tickets, or chances, were given indiscriminately to persons whether they purchased goods of plaintiffs in error or not—to those who registered their names at their shoe store, and to those, who, from a distance, sent the return postage. While it is admitted that Charles Linton purchased goods to the amount of one dollar at their store, and received one of these cards, it is admitted that such purchase, or any purchase of goods, was not a condition upon which the card was delivered.

The fact that such cards or chances were given away to induce persons to visit their store, with the expectation that they might purchase goods and thereby increase their trade, is a benefit too remote to constitute a consideration for the chances.

Persons holding these cards, although not present, were, equally with those visiting their store, entitled to draw the prize. The element of gambling that is necessary to constitute this a lottery within the purview of the statute, to wit, the paying of money directly or indirectly for the chance of drawing the piano, is lacking, and the transaction did not constitute a violation of the statute.

The judgment of conviction is reversed and cause remanded with directions to dismiss the proceeding.

———

LOTTERY—WHAT IS.—Any scheme for the distribution of property by chance among persons who have paid, or agreed to pay, a valuable consideration for the chance is a lottery: *State v. Moren,* 48 Minn. 555; *State v. Boneil,* 42 La. Ann. 1110; 21 Am. St. Rep. 413, and note; *People v. Elliott,* 74 Mich. 264; 16 Am. St. Rep. 640, and note; *Yellowstone Kit v. State,* 88 Ala. 196; 16 Am. St. Rep. 38, and extended note thoroughly discussing the subject. See also *Ballock v. State,* 73 Md. 1; 25 Am. St. Rep. 559, and note, and *Long v. State,* 73 Md. 527; 25 Am. St. Rep. 606, and note.

LOTTERY—WHAT IS NOT.—A vendor of medicine does not maintain a lottery who distributes prizes by lot to parties to whom he has given tickets at various exhibitions which entitles them to a chance in the prizes, but for which they have paid no valuable consideration either directly or indirectly: *Yellowstone Kit v. State,* 88 Ala. 196; 16 Am. St. Rep. 38. A statute which prohibits any person who sells, exchanges, or disposes of any article of food from giving some other article as a prize, premium, or reward, infringes upon the liberty of the seller, and is void: *People v. Gillson,* 109 N. Y. 389; 4 Am. St. Rep. 465; *Long v. State,* 74 Md. 565; 28 Am. St. Rep. 268.

CONNOR *v.* PEOPLE.

[18 COLORADO, 873.]

CONSPIRACY—WHAT IS.—To constitute a criminal conspiracy there must not only be an agreement to co-operate to do a certain act, but that act must also be unlawful.

LARCENY—CONSENT.—TO CONSTITUTE LARCENY there must be a trespass, that is, a taking of property without the consent of the owner, coupled with an intent to steal the property so taken; and the crime is not committed, when, with the consent of the owner, his property is taken, however guilty may be the taker's purpose and intent.

LARCENY—DECOYING INTO CRIME.—Larceny is not committed when property is taken with the consent of the owner, although such consent is given for the purpose of decoying and entrapping the party suspected, and the latter, when taking the property, did not know of the consent which prevented the criminal quality from attaching to the act.

CRIMINAL LAW—RIGHT TO DECOY INTO CRIME.—Officers or detectives have no right to suggest the commission of a crime, and instigate others to take part in its commission, in order to arrest them while in the act, although the purpose may be to capture old offenders. Such conduct on their part is not only reprehensible but criminal, and will not be justified or encouraged by the courts.

EVIDENCE THAT A WITNESS HAS ON OTHER OCCASIONS made statements similar to those to which he has testified is inadmissible. What he has said out of court, and when not under oath, cannot be received to fortify his testimony.

INDICTMENT and conviction of Charles and James Connor, and James Marshall, for a conspiracy to rob.

Rhodes and Carpenter, and Charles Hartzell, for the appellants.

J. H. Maupin, attorney-general, and John G. Taylor, for the appellees.

374 GODDARD, J. We omit the discussion of many of the errors assigned, not because we regard them as without merit, but because those considered are more important, and are decisive of the case.

The vital and important question presented by the record is, whether, under the evidence, any crime is shown to have been committed. The crime charged is a conspiracy entered into by the defendants below, plaintiffs in error here, to rob the Denver and Rio Grande Railroad Company. The statute defines a conspiracy as follows:

"If any two or more persons . . . . shall agree, conspire, or co-operate to do, or aid in doing, any other unlawful act," etc.

To constitute the crime there must be not only an agreement to co-operate to do a certain act, but that act must be
unlawful. The unlawful act to be done in pursuance of the
conspiracy as charged in the indictment was the commission
of a larceny in taking the property of the Denver and Rio
Grande Railroad Company.

The evidence introduced on the trial to sustain the fact of
confederation between the plaintiffs in error was the testimony [375] of the witness Holliday, *alias* Ward, which, in effect is, that he was in the employ of Thiel's Detective Agency,
of St Louis, Missouri, and was sent to Kansas City on a special mission to find out if one James Marshall corresponded
with the police department of Denver, and also to find out if
he knew anything about the First National Bank robbery;
that he met Marshall, and learned from him that the chiefs
and heads of the police department in Denver were his friends,
and would co-operate with him, or anyone he should introduce, in any unlawful scheme, and upon obtaining promise
of a letter of introduction to them from Marshall, he, Holliday, returned to St. Louis, to report to his superiors what he
had done; that his superiors suggested that he devise a
scheme to rob an express company, planning such robbery
like one that had taken place in Missouri. On the ninth day
of April he returned to Kansas City, and on meeting Marshall
again, he told him that he had a friend in New York, who knew
a messenger who run out of Denver, and from whom he could
get a letter to such agent; that he had written for the letter,
and it would be in Denver in a few days; that Marshall expressed a hope that it was on the Denver and Rio Grande;
that he obtained the letter of introduction to James Connor,
and agreed with Marshall to let him know where he was
stopping in Denver, and to wire him before the robbery, so he
could come on and take part. On his arrival in Denver, and
on the 12th of April, he presented his letter of introduction
to James Connor, and stated to him the same in reference to
a letter to an agent; that he, Connor, expressed the hope that
it was over the Denver and Rio Grande; that on the 13th of
April he met Farley, who was then resident manager of
Thiel's Detective Agency in Denver.

"Told Farley I had a talk with Connor. . . . . Up to this
time I had done what I did from instructions from the St.
Louis office. After this I was under instructions from Farley.

"Q. When did you first discuss the plan of the robbery,

376 and with whom did you first talk about the plan of operations to rob this road?

"A. I think it was with Mr. Farley at 31 and Curtis. We
discussed the Denver and Rio Grande road, when I told him
what I had learned from the defendants."

That a letter was prepared in Mr. Farley's office, with the
consent of the officers of the company, purporting to be written by one William S. Buell of New York, to Icon, an express
agent in the employ of the Denver and Rio Grande Express
Company, introducing to him Mr. Holliday as Joe Ward;
that plans were devised between Holliday and Connor to
carry out the robbery.

Mr. Farley testifies that on the night of the 13th of April,
after meeting Holliday, he saw Mr. Gillooly, treasurer of the
Denver and Rio Grande Railroad Company, and told him
what Holliday had said. And it appears from the evidence,
from that time on the company through its officers not only
consented that their property might be taken, but co-operated
with the witness Holliday, through Farley, in perfecting plans
by which such taking might be accomplished.

Mr. Gillooly testifies that: "Holliday was in the employ of
Thiel's Agency; Thiel was in our employ. Whatever Mr.
Holliday did was being done with the full knowledge and
consent of the company. This scheme was being worked for
nearly a month."

To constitute the crime of larceny at common law there
must be a trespass, that is, a taking of property without the
consent of the owner, coupled with an inten.. to steal the
property so taken. It is therefore evident that the crime is
not committed when with the consent of the owner his property is taken, however guilty may be the taker's purpose and
intent. This is the accepted doctrine as laid down by the
various text-writers on criminal law.'

Mr. Bishop, discussing this principle in the fifth edition of
his work on criminal law, section 262, says:

"The cases of greatest difficulty are those in which one,
suspecting crime in another, lays a plan to entrap him; consequently, **377** even if there is a consent, it is not within the
knowledge of him who does the act. Here we see, from
principles already discussed, that, supposing the consent
really to exist, and the case to be one in which, on general
doctrines, the consent will take away the criminal quality of
the act, there is no legal crime committed, though the doer

of the act did not know of the existence of the circumstance
which prevented the criminal quality from attaching ": 2
Archbold's Criminal Practice and Pleading, 1181; 2 Russell on
Crimes, 190; 3 Chitty's Criminal Law, 925; 1 Wharton's
Criminal Law, sec. 914.

To the same effect is the uniform current of the decisions.
In the case of *Regina* v. *Johnson*, 1 Car. & M. 218, 41 Eng.
C. L. R. 123, it was held that where a servant pretended to
concur with two persons who proposed to rob his master's
house, and acting under the advice of the police he opened
the door for them to enter, that there could be no conviction
of burglary.

Of the same purport is the case of *Allen* v. *State*, 40 Ala.
334, 91 Am. Dec. 477, wherein it is said: "Where the proof
showed that the prisoner proposed to a servant a plan for rob-
bing his employer's office by night; that the servant disclosed
the plan to his employer, by whom it was communicated to
the police; that the master, acting under the instruction of the
police, furnished the servant with the keys of his office on the
appointed night; that the servant and the prisoner went
together to the office, where the servant opened the door with
the key and they both entered through the door, and were
arrested in the house by the police, held, that there could be
no conviction of burglary."

In the case of *Speiden* v. *State*, 3 Tex. App. 163, 30 Am. Rep.
126, the defendant was indicted for burglary by breaking into
a bank with intent to commit the theft. The court say:

" In the case at bar the detectives cannot be considered in any
other light than as the servants and agents of the bankers,
Adams and Leonard. They; the detectives, had the legal
occupancy and control of the bank; two of them made arrangements with defendant to enter it; and defendant, when
[378] arrested, had entered the bank at the solicitation of those
detectives, who were rightfully in possession, with the consent
of the owners. This cannot be burglary in contemplation of
law, however much the defendant was guilty in purpose and
intent."

In *Dodge* v. *Brittain*, Meigs, 84, it is said: "Receiving goods,
with the owner's consent, from his servant, is not larceny, it
being of the essence of the offense that the goods be taken
against the will of the owner, *invito domino.*"

Of the same purport are *Kemp* v. *State*, 11 Humph. 320;
State v. *Chambers*, 6 Ala. 855; *Zink* v. *People*, 77 N. Y. 114;

83 Am. Rep. 589; *United States* v. *Whittier*, 5 Dill. 35; *State* v. *Covington*, 2 Bail. 569, and numerous other cases that might be cited.

Counsel for the people concede the soundness of the doctrine as above announced, but seek to escape its application upon the ground that the plaintiffs in error were not prosecuted for stealing from the railway company, and therefore the attitude of the company made no difference. In other words, it is contended that the conspiracy to do an act constitutes a crime, although the act to accomplish which the conspiracy is formed would not be unlawful if committed. To state the proposition is to refute it.

We think the law applicable to this case is clearly and correctly stated. In the case of *Johnson* v. *State*, 3 Tex. App. 593, the court say:

"The fact of such conspiracy once being established, the subsequent consent of the owner (or those acting for him) for the conspirators to enter the building will not affect their guilt in the least, unless the evidence shows that Higgins and Garwood, or the detective employed by them, suggested the offense, or in some way created the original intent or agreement to commit the offense as charged."

In the case of *Saunders* V. *People*, 38 Mich. 218, the defendant was convicted of breaking and entering by night a courtroom, and feloniously taking therefrom certain bonds. **379** The defendant Saunders was a lawyer, and it was shown in evidence that he asked Webb, a policeman, to leave the door of the courtroom unlocked in order that he might get the bonds; and that Webb, after consulting with his superior officer, consented, and then lay in wait, and caught one Moylan removing the papers. The supreme court of Michigan, composed of Judges Campbell, Cooley, Marston, and Graves, reversed the conviction, and severely denounced the conduct of the officers in conniving with persons suspected of criminal designs for the purpose of arresting them in the commission of the offense.

Judge Marston, concurring in a separate opinion, pages 221 and 222, says: "The course pursued by the officers in this case was utterly indefensible. Where a person contemplating the commission of an offense approaches an officer of the law, and asks his assistance, it would seem to be the duty of the latter, according to the plainest principles of duty and justice, to decline to render such assistance, and to take such steps as would be likely to prevent the commission of the offense, and tend to the elevation and improvement of the would-be criminal, rather than to his farther debasement. Some courts have gone a great way in giving encouragement to detectives in some very questionable methods adopted by them to discover the guilt of criminals; but they have not yet gone so far, and I trust never will, as to lend aid or encouragement to officers who may, under a mistaken sense of duty, encourage and assist parties to commit crime, in order that they may arrest and have them punished for so doing. The mere fact that the person contemplating the commission of a crime is supposed to be an old offender can be no excuse, much less a justification, for the course adopted and pursued in this case."

Campbell, C. J., also concurring, at page 223, said: "Assuming that there is not in the record full evidence of such an invitation to enter the clerk's office as would conclusively ³⁸⁰ show there was no breaking, the encouragement of criminals to induce them to commit crimes in order to get up a prosecution against them is scandalous and reprehensible."

We feel warranted in quoting thus fully from these opinions, because the views therein expressed are specially pertinent to the facts in this case, and because of the universally recognized learning and ability of the eminent jurists who announced them.

In the case under consideration, the only evidence of the inception of the scheme to rob the express company is that of Holliday, who states that it was instigated by his superiors at St. Louis, and by him suggested to the plaintiffs in error. It further appears that before the consummation of the conspiracy the officers of the express company were informed of and consented to the scheme. Hence, under the foregoing authorities the prosecution cannot be sustained.

We do not wish to be understood as intimating that the services of a detective cannot be legitimately employed in the discovery of the perpetrators of a crime that has been or is being committed, but we do say that when in their zeal, or under a mistaken sense of duty, detectives suggest the commission of a crime and instigate others to take part in its commission in order to arrest them while in the act, although the purpose may be to capture old offenders, their conduct is not only reprehensible, but criminal, and ought to be rebuked rather than encouraged by the courts. And, accept-

ing the version of the witness Holliday as true, it shows a
state of facts that can have no place in the decent administration of justice.

The witnesses Farley and Newcome were permitted, over
objection, to testify to statements made to them by the witness Holliday, not made in the presence of plaintiffs in error
or either of them. This was hearsay evidence and clearly
inadmissible.

Counsel for the people attempts to justify the admission of
this testimony upon the ground that the testimony of Holliday was attacked on cross-examination and his credibility
[381] questioned, and therefore the people had a right to corroborate him in this manner, asserting that such procedure
was in conformity to well-established authorities. No authority is cited, and upon a full and careful research we feel safe
in asserting that no authority can be found that will sanction
the admission of this evidence. In the language of Buller, J.,
King v. *Parker*, 3 Doug. 242, "It is now settled that what a
witness said, not upon oath, would not be admissible to confirm what he said upon oath."

Greenleaf in his work on Evidence, volume 1, section 469,
says: "But evidence that he has, on other occasions, made
statements similar to what he has testified in the cause, is
not admissible."

In *Robb* v. *Hackley*, 23 Wend. 50, Bronson, J., in a very exhaustive opinion on this subject, says: "But as a general,
and almost universal, rule, evidence of what the witness has
said out of court cannot be received to fortify his testimony.
It violates a first principle in the law of evidence to allow a
party to be affected, either in his person or his property, by
the declarations of a witness made without oath. And, besides, it can be no confirmation of 'what the witness has said
on oath, to show that he has made similar declarations when
under no such solemn obligation to speak the truth. It is no
answer to say, that such evidence will not be likely to gain
credit, and consequently will do no harm. Evidence should
never be given to a jury which they are not at liberty to
believe."

The only exception to this rule as stated by Greenleaf in
the section above cited is: "Where a design to misrepresent
is charged upon the witness in consequence of his relation to
the party or the cause, in which case it seems it may be

proper to show that he made a similar statement before that relation existed."

At the time of the admission of the testimony the plaintiffs in error had made no attempt to impeach the witness Holliday; nor did they at any time do more than to deny his [382] statements, when on the stand as witnesses in their own behalf.

The witnesses Farley and Newcome testified that they had no personal knowledge of the facts stated by Holliday, and were simply repeating the story told by him. The harmfulness of this can be readily seen. The witness Farley was at the time holding an important official position; he was a respectable citizen and possessed the confidence of the community, and the repetition by him of Holliday's story might give it a weight and credibility greater than would have attached to it when told alone by Holliday.

However this may be, the admission of this testimony was so violative of every rule of evidence that in itself it would compel a reversal of the case, and it becomes unnecessary to notice the further objections so fully argued by counsel. For the reasons given the judgment will be reversed.

CONSPIRACY—WHAT IS.—A conspiracy is a combination of two or more persons by some concerted action to accomplish some criminal or unlawful purpose by criminal or unlawful means: *Spies* v. *People*, 122 Ill. 1; 3 Am. St. Rep. 320, and extended note; *State* v. *Setter*, 57 Conn. 461; 14 Am. St. Rep. 121, and note; *Sparks* v. *Commonwealth*, 89 Ky. 644.

LARCENY—CONSENT OF OWNER.—Consent to the commission of a crime, which will relieve the act of its criminal character is something different from mere passive submission without any previous understanding with the criminal: *People* v. *Hanselman*, 76 Cal. 460; 9 Am. St. Rep. 238, and note. Where the owner of a building has previous notice that it is to be burglarized and makes no effort to prevent the crime, but takes steps to secure the burglar, the latter's liability is not thereby changed: *Thompson* v. *State*, 18 Ind. 386; 81 Am. Dec. 364, and extended note; *State* v. *Sneff*, 22 Neb. 481; note to *State* v. *Holnes*, 57 Am. Dec. 271.

CRIMINAL LAW—DECOYING INTO CRIME: See the extended notes to the following cases: *People* v. *Richards*, 2 Am. St. Rep. 387; *Thompson* v. *State*, 81 Am. Dec. 365. Though one assists in the commission of what he believes to be a crime, yet if the person whom he so assists has no such intent and is merely seeking to give others an opportunity to catch his assistant while committing the crime, such assistant is not guilty, unless in the assistance which he rendered, he committed every overt act necessary to constitute the particular crime: *State* v. *Hayes*, 105 Mo. 76; 24 Am. St. Rep. 360; *Speiden* v. *State*, 3 Tex. App. 156; 30 Am. Rep. 126, and extended note. One who has taken active measures to induce another to enter his premises and take his property cannot treat the taking as a crime: *People* v. *McCord*, 76 Mich. 200. Where the defendant proposed to a servant that they should rob the office of the latter's employer, and the servant communicated this fact to his employer, who informed the police, and where the employer, acting under the advice of the police, furnished the servant with a key to his office by means of which on an appointed night the servant opened the office door and together with the defendant entered the room, where they were arrested, the defendant is not guilty of burglary: *Allen* v. *State*, 40 Ala. 334; 91 Am. Dec. 477, and extended note.

LEVY *v.* SPENCER.
[18 COLORADO, 532.]

AGENCY—VOID AGREEMENT AS TO COMMISSIONS.—An agreement between real estate agents by which each is to share in commissions paid by their principals, contingent upon the sale or exchange of the latter's property, is opposed to public policy and void, even though a price is fixed by the principals upon their respective properties.

AGENCY—DUTY OF AGENT TO PRINCIPAL.—Upon an exchange of property, each principal is entitled to the benefit of the unbiased judgment of his agent as to the value to be placed upon the other's property, and to a reasonable effort on the part of such agent to obtain a reduction of the value to be allowed therefor in the exchange. The agents cannot act in each other's interest and antagonistic to the interests of their principals by sharing commissions received upon the completion of the exchange.

ILLEGAL CONTRACTS—ENFORCEMENT.—A claim founded upon and recoverable only through and by virtue of an illegal contract will not be enforced.

ACTION to recover a commission received by defendant on account of an exchange of real estate. Plaintiff was the agent of one Jones and defendant was the agent of one Nix in a transaction involving the exchange of real property belonging to their respective principals. Such agents agreed with each other that in the event of their effecting such exchange and in consideration of that fact and other considerations mentioned, they would each pay to the other, when collected, one-half of all commissions paid to them by their respective principals. Judgment for plaintiff, and defendant appealed.

D. V. Burns, F. C. Goudy, C. M. Campbell, and J. C. Helm, for the appellant.

Long, Johnson, and Given, for the appellee.

[532] GODDARD, J. This record presents but one question that we can properly [537] consider, and one that was fully and fairly presented in the court below by the demurrer, the answer and the objection to the admission of any testimony under the complaint, and that is, whether the complaint states

a cause of action: This is to be determined by the validity or
invalidity of the agreement as therein stated, upon which appellee predicates his right to recover. In our judgment this
agreement comes clearly within that class of contracts that
are inhibited by public policy, and consequently void. By
its terms each agent was to share in the commissions paid by
both principals. The compensation to be jointly shared was
contingent upon the consummation of the trade or sale; and
this would have a tendency to induce them to disregard, if
not to sacrifice, the interests of their principals, if necessary
to effect that result. The fact that a sale price was fixed by
the principals upon their respective properties does not answer
this objection. Each was entitled to the benefit of the unbiased judgment of his agent as to the value to be placed
upon the other's property, and to a reasonable effort on the
part of such agent to obtain a reduction of the value to be
allowed therefor in the exchange. Their pecuniary interest
might have prevented such disinterested action on the part of
these agents; and it appearing from the allegations of the
complaint that they "did effect the trade or sale of the property as between their respective principals," the transaction
is as objectionable as those universally condemned, wherein
one agent acts for both principals without their knowledge or
consent. This objection is not answered by the claim that
the evidence as introduced shows a transaction different from
that pleaded, that their principals negotiated the trade between themselves, and that in fact plaintiff and defendant
acted only as middlemen in bringing Nix and Jones together.
Such evidence was not inadmissible merely because variant
from the allegations of the complaint, but because of the
fundamental vice in the complaint itself in not stating a
cause of action susceptible of proof, or one that would justify
the admission of any testimony or uphold any judgment.

538 The contention of appellee's counsel, that the transaction being completed and money paid, the appellant cannot avail himself of the illegality of the contract to retain it,
cannot be sustained. The cases relied on as upholding the
doctrine that when profits are realized through an illegal
transaction and received by one of the joint owners, they
cannot be retained by him by reason of the illegality of the
transactions through which they are derived, are clearly distinguishable from the case at bar. In this case appellee
asserts a claim against appellant founded upon and recover-

able only through and by virtue of an illegal agreement. It is therefore an action to enforce an illegal executory contract. The well-established rule in such case is as expressed in *Louisville etc. Ry. Co.* v. *Buck*, 116 Ind. 566, 9 Am. St. Rep. 883.

"It is quite true that a plaintiff will in no case be permitted to recover when it is necessary for him to prove his own illegal act or contract as a part of his cause of action, or when an essential element of his cause of action is his own violation of law."

Our conclusion on this question renders a notice of the other errors assigned unnecessary. The judgment therefore will be reversed for the reasons above given.

AGENCY—AGENT'S DUTY TO PRINCIPAL.—This question is discussed in the notes to the following cases: *Potter's Appeal*, 7 Am. St. Rep. 279; *Tyler* v. *Sanborn*, 15 Am. St. Rep. 104; *Winter* v. *McMillan*, 22 Am. St. Rep. 249; *Switzer* v. *Skiles*, 44 Am. Dec. 730; and especially the note to *Walker* v. *Osgood*, 93 Am. Dec. 174.

ILLEGAL CONTRACTS—ENFORCEMENT.—An illegal contract is absolutely void both at law and in equity. It creates no obligation between the parties, and cannot form the basis of judicial proceedings: *Santa Clara etc. Lumber Co.* v. *Hayes*, 76 Cal. 387; 9 Am. St. Rep. 211, and note; *Tatum* v. *Kelley*, 25 Ark. 209; 94 Am. Dec. 717, and note; *Schmidt* v. *Barker*, 17 La. Ann. 261; 87 Am. Dec. 527, and note; *Webb* v. *Fulchire*, 3 Ired. 485; 40 Am. Dec. 419, and note; *Antoine* v. *Smith*, 40 La. Ann. 560. See the extended notes to *Seidenbender* v. *Charles*, 8 Am. Dec. 691; *Tracy* v. *Talmage*, 67 Am. Dec. 153.

PALACIOS *v.* BRASHER.

[18 COLORADO, 593.]

UNDERTAKING—AUTHORITY TO FILL BLANKS IN—ESTOPPEL.—A surety who signs an incomplete undertaking and places it in the hands of another to use for a particular purpose, and with ostensible authority to fill in any needed matter to make it effective, is estopped from controverting its validity to the prejudice of the obligee, after it is accepted by him in its completed form, without negligence on his part.

UNDERTAKING.—AUTHORITY TO COMPLETE AN UNDERTAKING, BY FILLING BLANKS THEREIN after the obligors have signed it, may be implied.

UNDERTAKING—BLANKS IN—LIABILITY OF OBLIGOR.—Sureties who sign an undertaking in blank are bound to know its contents, and that the blanks must be filled to make it accomplish the purpose for which it is intended. They cannot evade liability after it has been completed by filling such blanks, by pleading a want of such knowledge, unless prevented from reading it by some trick or artifice of the obligee.

ACTION on an undertaking in attachment, signed in blank
by B. P. Brasher as principal, and by P. P. Eagan and G. W.
Brown as sureties, and acknowledged by them before E. A.
Clark, a notary public, and attorney for Brasher. Said sureties contend that Clark had no authority from them, express
or implied, to fill the blanks in the undertaking. The following instruction was given by the trial court: "And they [the
defendants] say there was nothing said about anyone filling
out the instrument, and there was no authority given anyone
to fill out that instrument or insert anything else in there but
what was found above their signature. If you should find
that to be true, and that there was no express authority given
to Clark to fill in the blanks in that bond, or if you should
find that these two sureties did not know that there were
blanks in the bond—that they thought it was a complete instrument as they had signed it—then you must find for the
defendants. I do not think there is sufficient evidence in
this case for me to instruct you under any consideration that
there could be any implied authority in Clark to fill out the
bond." Judgment for the defendants, and plaintiffs appealed.

Charles M. Campbell, for the appellants.

E. W. Waybright, for the appellees.

596 GODDARD, J. The only question for our determination
is presented by the assignment of error, predicated upon the
giving of the instruction above quoted.

Counsel for the respective parties have devoted most of
their briefs and argument to the discussion of the question of
the adequacy of an oral authorization to confer the power
597 to fill blanks in a sealed instrument after the same is
signed and before delivery. The pertinency of this contention
to this case is not readily discernible, since the instrument
sued on is not a sealed instrument, but is a parol contract,
and of a class to which the strict and technical doctrine relied on by counsel for appellees is not applicable. The court
below tried the case upon the theory that such authority could
be conferred orally, and admitted evidence upon the question
whether oral authority was given to Clark by Egan and
Brown to fill the blanks with the description and value of
the property attached; and submitted to the jury as the fact
upon which a recovery depended, whether such authority was
expressly given; hence the pertinent inquiry is Was it erro
to take from the jury the consideration and decision of th

question whether, under all the facts and circumstances attending the signing and delivery of the paper to Clark in its then condition, the authority to fill the blanks therein was conferred upon him by implication?

In the case of *South Berwick* v. *Huntress*, 53 Me. 89, 87 Am. Dec. 535, Kent, J., in discussing an instruction embodying in substance the law applicable to this case, said:

"We think that when a party signs a bond and delivers it to another, not stipulating or expecting that the paper will be returned or afterwards exhibited to him, but be delivered to the obligee when perfected, and when he so delivers it there are blanks in it to be filled up before it can be perfected, and he knows the fact, those blanks may be filled out without any further knowledge or assent on his part."

And also on page 96, "It is after all a mere question of assent. Now, consent may be implied as well as expressed, and when fairly and legally inferred it is actual and effective consent, as much so as when direct authority is shown by parol."

The supreme court of the United States has announced the same principle in several cases, notably that of *Drury* v. *Foster*, 2 Wall. 24. Therein the court say:

"We agree that by signing, and acknowledging the deed **598** in blank, and delivering the same to an agent, with an express or implied authority to fill up the blank and perfect the conveyance—its validity could not well be controverted."

In the case of *State* v. *Young*, 23 Minn. 551, the court in discussing the implied authority of the board of county commissioners to fill the penalty in an official bond, no express authority being given, says:

"Such authority may be implied from circumstances. It may be implied from the facts proved, when these facts all taken together and fairly considered justify the inference." See, also, *White* v. *Duggan*, 140 Mass. 18; 54 Am. Rep. 437; *Smith* v. *Crooker*, 5 Mass. 538; *Bank of Commonwealth* v. *McChord*, 4 Dana, 191; 29 Am. Dec. 398; *McCormick* v. *Bay City*, 23 Mich. 457; *Bartlett* v. *Board of Education*, 59 Ill. 364; *City of Chicago* v. *Gage*, 95 Ill. 593; 35 Am. Rep. 182.

Numerous other cases might be cited in support of the rule that authority to fill blanks in such an instrument may be implied, and that when fairly inferable from the conduct of the parties, and circumstances surrounding the transaction, is as effectually given as if expressly conferred. Many of

these decisions are put upon the doctrine of estoppel *in pais*,
ostensible authority being the equivalent of actual authority.
It certainly is consonant with justice and fairness that when
a person as a surety signs an incomplete undertaking, and
places the same in the hands of another to use for a particular purpose, and with ostensible authority to fill in any needed
matter to make the same effective, and the same is accepted
in its completed form by the obligee without negligence on
his part, that such surety ought to be estopped from controverting its validity to the prejudice of such obligee; and we
think that the facts in this case most strongly invoke the
application of this rule. The blank, as presented to Egan
and Brown for their signature, contained a printed condition
that fully advised them of the extent of the obligation they
were assuming: the insertion of the penalty did not affect the
extent of such obligation. The printed recitals in the paper as
presented were to the effect that certain property of their
principal had been attached, and the condition, and essential
599 portion of the contract, in terms provided that in consideration of the releasing of said property they undertook and
promised that if judgment was obtained in the attachment
suit, and the attachment sustained, that on demand they
would redeliver such property, and in default of delivery they
would pay the full value of the property so released. They were
bound to know the contents of the paper they signed, and cannot evade liability by pleading want of such knowledge. To
avail themselves of such a defense it must appear that they
were prevented from reading the paper by some trick or artifice
of the obligee: *Johnston* v. *Patterson*, 114 Pa. St. 398. They
were also bound to know whether there were blanks that must
be filled to accomplish the purpose for which such undertaking was intended. They are presumed to have known the
law, and knew that to accomplish the purpose of their principal it was necessary for him to procure an undertaking in
compliance with the statute. With this knowledge they
signed the undertaking and placed in his agent's hands, as
we have seen, with implied authority to fill the blanks, and
otherwise perfect it for the purpose of releasing the attached
property. Counsel for appellees place stress upon the fact
that Clark, the attorney of Brasher, made the addition, and
that the appellees, by delivering the bond to him when signed,
conferred no authority upon him to do so. This claim is not

tenable. He was their agent as well as the agent of the
principal: *Willis* v. *Rivers*, 80 Ga. 556.

We think the court erred in giving the instruction complained of. The evidence clearly establishes the fact that the
appellees conferred the power upon their principal and upon
his attorney, Clark, to fill in the specific description of the
property attached, and its value, if that was necessary to make
the undertaking effective. It is unnecessary to decide whether
the undertaking as signed was not sufficient before the addi-
tions were made therein. And, since we are of the opinion
that upon the undisputed facts the appellants were entitled
to recover, the judgment is reversed and cause remanded,
with directions to assess damages in favor of appellants.

FILLING IN BLANKS.—The questions relating to this subject, such as the
authority to fill blanks, when is implied and the liabilities of parties who
sign blank instruments, will be found discussed in the cases of *Richards* v.
Day, 137 N. Y. 183; 33 Am. St. Rep. 704; *Market etc. Nat. Bank* v. *Sargent*,
85 Me. 349; 35 Am. St. Rep. 376, and the notes appended thereto where
the cases in this series are collected.

WADSWORTH v. UNION PACIFIC RY. CO.

[18 COLORADO, 600.]

NEW TRIAL—EFFECT OF DENIAL OF.—When a new trial is denied and plaintiff thereupon elects to stand by his case as made, whereupon the court
dismisses the action, an appeal from the judgment of dismissal will be
treated as showing an intention on the part of the parties to treat the
case as though a nonsuit had been granted because of the plaintiff's failure to establish a sufficient case for the jury.

EVIDENCE.—CONFLICT ON A QUESTION OF FACT is presented for the jury under
proper instructions when the evidence is conflicting, or of such character
that different conclusions may be reasonably drawn therefrom.

JUDGMENT OF DISMISSAL MAY BE UPHELD on appeal, though the ground
stated in the judgment order does not warrant it, if the record discloses
other grounds which, as matter of law, show that plaintiff is not entitled
to recover in any event.

JUDICIAL OPINIONS—EFFECT OF GENERAL REMARKS IN.—It is not every remark in a judicial opinion that amounts to a judicial decision. General expressions are to be taken in connection with the case in which
they are used; and if they go beyond the case, may be respected, but
ought not to control the judgment in a subsequent suit, in which the
very point is presented for decision.

CONSTITUTIONAL LAW.—So long as a statute is within the sphere of legislative power and not an encroachment upon the province of some other
department of the government, it will be upheld, unless clearly in conflict with some provision of the constitution of the state or nation, or in
violation of some private right thereby secured.

CONSTITUTIONAL LAW.—THAT STATUTES MAY, in the opinion of the court, be against the spirit of the constitution, or against the policy of the government, is not sufficient to warrant it in declaring them unconstitutional. The courts cannot arrest unwise or oppressive acts of legislation so long as they are within constitutional bounds.

CONSTITUTIONAL LAW—PENAL STATUTES.—A statute cannot be sustained upon the ground that it is penal when it lacks an essential element of a penal statute, in that it permits the penalty to be visited upon a party not guilty of doing anything prohibited, or of violating any duty imposed by law.

CONSTITUTIONAL LAW.—STATUTE CANNOT BE CONSIDERED MERELY REMEDIAL or compensatory which compels a party to pay for property destroyed without allowing him to produce evidence of its value.

CONSTITUTIONAL LAW—EQUAL PROTECTION AND DUE PROCESS OF LAW.—A statute making a railroad company unconditionally liable for damages for any animal killed by it, and fixing a schedule of arbitrary prices for certain animals killed, without allowing proof of their value, though allowing the owner to resort to his common-law action if he so desires, while the company has no alternative if the owner resorts to his statutory action, is unconstitutional, as denying the company the equal protection of the laws, and as depriving it of its property without due process of law.

CONSTITUTIONAL LAW—STATUTES INVALID IN PART.—The invalidity of one provision in a statute, the different parts of which must be construed together as dependent provisions, renders the whole act invalid.

ACTION against a railroad company for killing a horse. The statute upon which the action is based reads as follows in so far as it is necessary to an understanding of the case. "SEC. 13. That every railroad or railway corporation or company operating any line of railroad or railway or any branch thereof, within the limits of this state, which shall damage or kill any horse, mare, gelding, filly, jack, jenny, or mule, or any cow, heifer, bull, ox, steer, or calf, or any other domestic animal, by running any engine or engines, car or cars, over or against any such animal, shall be liable to the owner of such animal for the damage sustained by such owner by reason thereof." "SEC. 14. If the owner of any animal or animals so killed, or his or her authorized agent, shall make affidavit before some officer authorized to administer oaths, that he or she was the owner, or authorized agent of the owner, of the recorded brand found upon the animal or animals so killed or damaged, at the time of such killing or damaging, and such person, shall within six months after such killing or damaging, deliver such affidavit to the agent, or any officer, of such company or corporation, together with a certificate of his or her mark or brand, under official seal of any officer authorized by law to record such mark or brands, or shall

ιake affidavit that the animal killed or damaged, as afore-
aid, had no recorded mark or brand, and that he or she is
he owner of such animal, describing it, and the corporation
r company shall pay to such person delivering such affidavit
nd certificate, or such affidavit last aforesaid, as follows:

"SCHEDULE.

"For American sheep, each, two dollars and fifty cents
($2.50).

" For Mexican sheep and goats, one dollar and fifty cents
($1.50).

" For Texas cattle, yearlings, twelve dollars ($12.00).

" For Texas cattle, two years old, seventeen dollars ($17.00).

" For Texas cattle, three years old, steers and cows, twenty
dollars ($20.00).

" For Texas cattle, four years old, steers or over, twenty-
five dollars ($25.00).

" For American yearlings, fifteen dollars ($15.00).

" For American two years old, twenty dollars ($20.00).

" For American three years old, steers and cows of all ages,
twenty-eight dollars ($28.00).

" For American four years old, steers and over, thirty-four
dollars ($34.00).

" For calves, ten dollars ($10.00).

" The above price, when paid, shall be payment in full; all
Texas and Mexican cattle shall be considered as Texas cattle,
and half-bloods shall be classed as American cattle; thoroughbred cattle, milch cows, high-grade American cattle and grade
bulls shall be paid for at their cash value; thoroughbred sheep
shall be paid for at their cash value; horses, mules, and asses
shall be paid for at their cash value; provided, that no railroad company shall at any time be required to pay more than
the market value of any animal killed or damaged, except as
hereinbefore provided.   In all cases where such railroad company or corporation shall kill any of the stock mentioned.in
this act, and for which no price or sum is fixed, the owner or
agent of such stock shall, after the filing, as aforesaid, of an
affidavit and certificate of brand, or affidavit of ownership,
which affidavit shall contain a statement of class, grade, and
value of such animal or animals, select some disinterested
freeholder of the county where such killing took place, and
shall notify such company or corporation of said selection,
and such company or corporation shall, within three days

thereafter select some suitable person to act with person
so selected, and the two so selected shall select a third, and
the three so selected shall, without delay, proceed to appraise
the value of the stock so killed or damaged, a majority of
which three appraisers shall be sufficient to determine the
same, and shall certify, under oath, such appraisement to an
agent or superintendent of such company or corporation. In
case such railroad or corporation shall refuse or neglect to
appoint such appraiser, it shall be the duty of the justice of
the peace nearest to the place where such stock was so killed
or damaged, to select three disinterested persons as appraisers,
and administer to them an oath to honestly appraise the
value of such stock, which appraisers shall, without delay,
appraise and forward to such justice the result of such
appraisement, which justice shall, within ten days thereafter,
forward to an agent or superintendent of such railroad or
corporation, a certificate of the result of such appraisement
and the costs thereof; and such railroad or corporation shall,
within thirty days after the receipt of such certificate, pay to
the owner of the stock so killed or damaged, or to his or her
authorized agent, the amount of such appraisement, together
with all the costs, as aforesaid; and in all cases where the
value of such stock is established by this act, such company
or corporation shall pay for such stock within thirty days
after the delivery of the affidavit and certificate of ownership
of brand, or affidavit of ownership of said stock, and if any
such company shall so fail to pay for such stock within thirty
days after the delivery of such affidavit and certificate, such
company shall be liable for double the value the appraised
or schedule value of such animal or animals, together with
reasonable attorneys' fees, to be allowed by the court; and all
persons selected or appointed under this section shall receive
the sum of one dollar, to be paid by said railroad company
or corporation, as hereinbefore provided; provided, that any
railroad company having fenced its line of road, or any part
thereof, or who shall hereafter fence its road or any part
thereof, with a good and lawful fence, and put in good and
sufficient cattleguards, and put in gateways upon and across
their said railroad, at the request of persons holding or owning land adjacent to said railroad, for the private use and
accommodation of said adjacent owners or holders of land; said
railroad company shall not be held liable for the killing or
injury of any stock getting through said gateways, belonging

to said party at whose request, and for whose accommodation said gateway was made, unless such killing or injury was occasioned by the fault or negligence of said railway company or its employees." "SEC. 15. Every railroad company shall keep a book at the county-seat of each county through which their road runs; provided, that said road runs, or passes, through the county-seat. If such railroad does not pass through the county-seat, then such book shall be kept at the principal town in the county through which it passes; and it is hereby made the duty of the said company to cause to be entered in said book, within fifteen days after the killing of any animal, a description, as nearly as may be, of such animal, its color, age, marks, and brands, and shall keep said book subject to the inspection of persons claiming to have had animals killed. Should any company fail to keep said book, or to file such notice, in the manner herein provided, or to enter therein such description of any animal killed, for a period of fifteen days thereafter, such company shall be liable to the owner of such animal to an amount twice the full value thereof."

Bailey and Wilkin, for the appellant.

Teller and Orahood, and C. M. Kendall, for the appellee.

605 ELLIOTT, J. The dismissal of the action as shown by the record is assigned for error.

1. The dismissal was somewhat irregular; but it is not difficult to understand its meaning. The cause had been tried by jury resulting in a verdict in plaintiff's favor, finding **606** that the value of the horse killed was two hundred dollars, and assessing plaintiff's damages at four hundred dollars on each of the two causes of action.

Upon consideration of defendant's motion for a new trial, the court was of opinion that it should be allowed, and so announced its conclusion. Thereupon plaintiff declared that he elected to stand by his case as already made, and the district court then and there dismissed the action at plaintiff's costs. The declaration of plaintiff was equivalent to saying that he could not prove any better case, and that he desired to obviate the necessity for another trial.

The bringing of the whole record to this court for review, including the bill of exceptions containing "all the testimony offered, given, or received on the trial," clearly indicates that the intention of the parties was to treat the action of the court as though the court had dismissed the action or granted a nonsuit on the ground that plaintiff had failed to "prove a sufficient case for the jury." That such was the understanding and intention of plaintiff as well as the defendant is confirmed by the fact that the assignments of error and argument of counsel in this court extend to the conclusions of the trial court upon the evidence, the pleadings, and the statutes upon which the action is founded.

2. The Code of Civil Procedure contemplates that the substance and not the mere form of judical proceedings shall be regarded in determining the rights of parties. Hence, we shall review this cause according to the intention of the parties, as above stated, since it is obvious that the ends of justice will be thereby accomplished: Code, sec. 78, also sec. 443; *Denver etc. Ry. Co. v. Chandler,* 8 Col. 376; *Town of Idaho Springs* v. *Filteau,* 10 Col. 105.

3. Upon a careful examination of the evidence, we are of the opinion that the court would not have been justified at the close of the evidence in dismissing the action, or in granting a nonsuit on the ground that there was no evidence tending to prove that defendant's engine or cars ran over or against the plaintiff's horse as stated in the finding of the court. The [607] evidence on that phase of the case was somewhat conflicting, or of such a character that different conclusions might have been reasonably drawn therefrom; and so the evidence did not present a question of law for the court, but one of fact for the jury under proper instructions: 2 Thompson on Trials, sec. 2242 et seq.; *Lord* v. *Pueblo S. & R. Co.,* 12 Col. 394; *Denny* v. *Williams,* 5 Allen, 1–5.

4. But it is contended that, though the grounds for dismissing the action, as stated in the court's finding, are not sufficient in law, yet the judgment of dismissal should be upheld, since the record discloses other facts which, as a matter of law, show that plaintiff was not entitled in any event to recover in the action.

5. The complaint contains two causes of action. Each count is founded upon certain provisions of the statute relating to stock killed by the operation of railroads. The killing occurred in June, 1886. Hence, we must consider the law as it existed at that time: See Gen. Stats. 1883, c. 93, sec. 2804 et seq.; also, acts amendatory thereof, Session Laws, 1885, pp. 304, 338.

Neither count of the complaint alleges any negligence on

the part of the defendant company in respect to the killing of
plaintiff's horse. Prior to the acts of 1885, above cited, it was
provided by statute that any railroad company operating its
road within this state which should damage or kill any
domestic animal by running any of its engines or cars over
or against such animal should be liable to the owner of such
animal for the damages thereby occasioned. The statute contained a fixed schedule of prices to be paid for certain kinds
of animals so killed; it also provided for an appraisement of
the value of animals for which no schedule price was fixed;
but the appraisement was required to be made without any
trial in court; and no proof of negligence on the part of the
railway company was required in order to establish its liability.

By the Act of 1885 an amendment to section 14 was added
relating to fences, cattleguards, and gateways, by which it
⁶⁰⁸ was provided that under certain circumstances a railroad
company should not be held liable for the killing or injury of
any stock, unless such killing or injury was occasioned by
the fault or negligence of the company or its employees. This
peculiar proviso was again amended in 1891 (Session Laws,
p. 281); but the amendment was too late to affect this case.

The first count of the complaint contains an averment to
the effect that defendant's railway line at the place where
plaintiff's horse was killed was not then and there fenced with
a good and lawful fence or with any fence whatever; also, a
further averment, that "said railway line at the point thereon
of said killing was not fenced as by said statute advised.
These averments were not sufficient under the Act of 1885.
According to the terms of that act, before plaintiff could
claim that the defendant company owed him any duty in respect to fencing its railway, it was necessary for him to allege
that he was owner or holder of land adjacent to such railway,
that he had requested defendant to fence its railroad, put in
cattleguards and gateways, and that his horse was killed by
reason of defendant's neglect to comply with such request.
The complaint does not contain such allegations. Moreover,
according to the strict terms of the proviso, the company
could not, even by fencing, putting in cattleguards and gateways, exempt itself from the unconditional liability otherwise
imposed by the statute, except as against the party requesting the gateway to be made.

From the foregoing it follows, that in order to warrant a

recovery for plaintiff under the first count of his complaint, as the statute existed when the first alleged cause of action arose, it must be held, unconditionally, that if any railroad company operating its road in this state should damage or kill a domestic animal by running its engines or cars over or against such animal, the railroad company would be liable therefor, irrespective of any act of negligence on the part of such company. If such statute were valid, then, according to its literal terms, plaintiff's right to recover must be upheld.

609 6. Counsel for plaintiff rely upon the case of *Union Pac. Ry. Co.* v. *De Busk*, 12 Col. 294, 13 Am. St. Rep. 221, as sustaining the stock-killing statute as it existed under the Act of 1885. In that case a statute declaring that every railroad company shall be liable for all damages by fire that is set out or caused by operating its road in this state, was upheld as constitutional, the court holding that "such statutes are not penal, but purely remedial in their nature," and that the liability thus declared "was but the re-enactment, *pro tanto*, of the ancient common law, for the better protection of property exposed to such unusual dangers." The conclusion in the De Busk case was sustained by numerous decisions by courts of last resort in other states having fire statutes similar to our own. As early as 1847, Chief Justice Shaw declared that the design as well as the legal effect of such a statute was to afford indemnity to those suffering damage from fire caused by the use of a dangerous apparatus. This same view was again expressed in 1863 by Chief Justice Bigelow, as follows:

"It is not a penal statute, but purely remedial in its nature; and it is to be interpreted fairly and liberally, so as to secure to parties injured an indemnity from those who reap the advantages and profits arising from the use of a dangerous mode of locomotion, by means of which buildings and other property are destroyed": *Hart* v. *Western R. R. Co.*, 13 Met. 99; 46 Am. Dec. 719; *Lyman* v. *Boston etc. R. R. Co.*, 4 Cush. 288; *Pratt* v. *Atlantic etc. R. R. Co.*, 42 Me. 579; *Smith* v. *Boston etc. R. R. Co.*, 63 N. H. 25; *Ross* v. *Boston etc. R. R. Co.*, 6 Allen, 90; *Rodemacher* v. *Milwaukee etc. R. R. Co.*, 41 Iowa, 297; 20 Am. Rep. 592.

It is true that in *Union Pac. Ry. Co.* v. *De Busk*, 12 Col. 294, 13 Am. St. Rep. 221, various decisions relating to stock-killing statutes were referred to and commented upon by way of analogy or illustration. Such references and comments are not to be taken as sustaining the validity of the stock-killing statute; the question of the validity of such statute was not then before the court. As was said in *Johnson* v. *Bailey*, 17 Col. 69: "It is not every remark in a judicial opinion that amounts to a judicial decision." In [610] *Cohens* v. *Virginia*, 6 Wheat. 264, Chief Justice Marshall said:

"It is a maxim not to be disregarded that general expressions in every opinion are to be taken in connection with the case in which those expressions are used. If they go beyond the case they may be respected, but ought not to control the judgment in a subsequent suit when the very point is presented for decision. The reason of this maxim is obvious. The question actually before the court is investigated with care, and considered in its full extent. Other principles which may serve to illustrate it are considered in their relation to the case decided; but their possible bearing on all other cases is seldom completely investigated."

The decision in *Denver etc. Ry. Co.* v. *Henderson*, 10 Col. 1, cannot be considered as upholding the constitutionality of the stock-killing statute. True, it was remarked in the opinion in that case, that the statute was a cumulative remedy; but the real question decided was that the statute did not repeal or suspend the common-law action for damages occasioned by negligence, and the judgment of the lower court was affirmed upon the ground that the evidence fairly tended to establish negligence. The first point of the *syllabus* in the Henderson case was therefore unwarranted by the decision. In *Atchison etc. R. R. Co.* v. *Lujan*, 6 Col. 338, the decision turned upon a question of pleading. It does not appear that the constitutionality of the stock-killing statute was challenged either in the Lujan case or the Henderson case. The maxim, *stare decisis*, therefore cannot be fairly invoked as sustaining the constitutionality of such statute.

The statute making every railroad company unconditionally liable in case it shall kill or damage a domestic animal by running its trains over or against such animal stands on a footing quite different from the fire statute. Fire is a dangerous element, and, according to the ancient common law, the rule was, as stated in *Union Pac. Ry. Co.* v. *De Busk*, 12 Col. 294, 13 Am. St. Rep. 221, that "a person who makes a fire must see that it does no harm, and must answer for the damage, if it does any." In the case of domestic [611] animals the general rule at common law was that if such animals trespassed upon the lands of others the owner was liable in damages, unless he could show that the lands should have been fenced. Besides, the rule at common law was that a party running coaches or other vehicles could be held liable for damages caused by such vehicles on the ground of negligence or willful misconduct, but not when the damage was the result of pure accident.

Since by the progress of invention vehicles propelled by steam and electricity have come into use as a means of transporting persons and property, the common-law rule of liability on the ground of negligence has been applied to the operation of such vehicles, though a higher degree of diligence has been required on account of the greater liability to injury arising from the use of a more dangerous motive power. But we are not aware that it has ever been held, as a common-law rule, that steam or electric railway companies, lawfully operating their trains, are liable for damages thereby occasioned, in the absence of negligence. By virtue of statutes, however, railway companies have frequently been required to provide additional safeguards against accidents and injuries to persons and property from the operation of their trains; these requirements have been upheld as valid police regulations; and omissions to comply therewith have been held to constitute sufficient ground of liability. For example: It has been held that a statute requiring a railway company to fence its line of railway is a valid police regulation; and in states where such statutes have been adopted, railway companies have been held liable for injuries done to domestic animals where the injury is shown to have been occasioned by the neglect of the company to fence its railway. The element of neglect is the basis of liability in such cases. Perhaps the same rule may apply where the statute gives railway companies the option of fencing their roads on pain of being held liable for injuries caused to animals through neglect to avail themselves of the opportunity of fencing: *Hayes* v. *Michigan Cent. R. R. Co.*, 111 U. S. 228; *Missouri Pac. Ry.* [612] *Co.* v. *Humes*, 115 U. S. 512; *Cairo etc. R. R. Co.* v. *Peoples*, 92 Ill. 97; 34 Am. Rep. 112; *Wilder* v. *Maine Cent. R. R. Co.*, 65 Me. 332; 20 Am. Rep. 698; *Barnett* v. *Atlantic etc. R. R. Co.*, 68 Mo. 56; 30 Am. Rep. 773; *Thorpe* v. *Rutland etc. Co.*, 27 Vt. 140; 62 Am. Dec. 625; *Dacres* v. *Oregon Ry. & Nav. Co.*, 1 Wash. 525.

7. It is earnestly contended that the stock-killing statute as it existed under the Act of 1885 was unconstitutional.

The power of the courts to declare legislative acts unconstitutional should be exercised with that delicacy and consideration which are always due to a co-ordinate department of the government. So long as a legislative act is within the sphere of legislative power, that is, so long as it is not an encroachment upon the province of some other department of the government, it will be upheld, unless clearly in conflict with some provision of the constitution of the state or nation, or in violation of some private right thereby secured. The conflict between the legislative act and some specific provision of the fundamental law must, in general, be clearly apparent, or the act will not be deemed unconstitutional. That a statute may, in the opinion of the court, be against the spirit of the constitution, or against the policy of the government, is not sufficient to warrant the court in declaring it unconstitutional. The courts cannot arrest unwise or oppressive acts of legislation so long as such acts are within constitutional bounds: Cooley on Constitutional Limitations, 6th ed., c. 7.

8. Stock-killing statutes similar to our own have been considered and held unconstitutional in several states. The court of appeals of this state has also expressed a like opinion. These decisions have been placed upon various grounds.

The statute in question was obviously intended to be remedial as well as penal: Sutherland on Statutes, sec. 208, 359. The statute cannot be sustained upon the ground that it is penal; it lacks an essential element of a penal statute, in that it permits the penalty to be visited upon a party not guilty of doing anything prohibited, or of violating any duty imposed by law: Potter's Dwarris, 74. The statute cannot be classed [613] as merely remedial, nor as a statute of indemnity, in that it fixes the amount to be paid for certain kinds of animals by an arbitrary schedule of prices without allowing proof of their actual value; as to other kinds of animals also, it provides for fixing their value by appraisers without allowing proof of their real value, and, in a certain contingency, the value may be fixed by a proceeding wholly *ex parte*. It is no answer to these objections that the schedule of prices may be reasonable, or that railroad companies may join in the appraisement proceedings. A statute cannot be considered merely remedial or compensatory which compels a party to pay for property destroyed without allowing him to produce evidence of its value.

It is true, the statute says, that "no railroad company shall
at any time be required to pay more than the market value
of any animal killed or damaged"; but nowhere in the
statute is there any provision for an ascertainment of such
value by evidence or by the usual mode of hearing and trial,
or by any mode of actual trial. The statute not only makes
a railroad company unconditionally liable for any domestic
animal it may kill or damage, but it deprives the company of
the mode of trial afforded to other litigants in like cases. By
the terms of the statute, when the value of an animal is fixed
by the schedule neither party can vary the same; in the appraisement of other animals neither party can be heard by
witnesses or counsel. This would seem to bear equally
against both parties; but it does not. The remedy of the
statute being cumulative, the owner of animals- killed or
damaged may resort to the statute, or he may rely upon his
common-law action, as was held in *Denver etc. R. R. Co.* v.
Henderson, 10 Col. 1; Sutherland on Statutes, sec. 399. But
when the owner resorts to the statute, there is no alternative
for the railroad company, if the statute be upheld. In these
respects the statute denies to railroad companies "the equal
protection of the laws"; it provides that they may be subjected to liability and to a judgment without opportunity for
hearing or trial according to "the law of the land," and thus,
they may be deprived of their property "without [614] due
process of law." Such a statute cannot be upheld as constitutional.

In this connection the language of Mr. Webster is most
appropriate: "By the law of the land is most clearly intended the general law; a law which hears before it condemns, which proceeds upon inquiry, and renders judgment
only after trial": Const. U. S., art. 14; Const. Col., art. 2,
sec. 25; Cooley's Constitutional Limitations, 6th ed., 431;
East Kingston v. *Towle*, 48 N. H. 65; 97 Am. Dec. 575; 2 Am.
Rep. 174; *San Mateo Co.* v. *Southern Pac. R. R. Co.*, 116 U. S.
138; *Denver etc. Ry. Co.* v. *Outcalt*, 2 Col. App. 395; *Graves* v.
Northern Pac. R. R. Co., 5 Mont. 556; 51 Am. Rep. 81; *Dacres*
v. *Oregon Ry. & Nav. Co.*, 1 Wash. 525.

9. We do not decide that the legislature has not the power
to enact a valid statute making railroad companies liable for
domestic animals killed or damaged by the operation of their
trains, irrespective of the question of negligence. What we
decide is, that as the statute did not require the fencing of

railways, either imperatively or optionally, under such circumstances as are disclosed in this record, there was no basis for a penalty, and that the mode prescribed by the statute for enforcing liability as a matter of indemnity is in violation of constitutional rights.

10. By the second count of the complaint plaintiff seeks to recover twice the full value of the animal killed. This recovery is claimed on account of the alleged failure of the defendant company to keep the book and to file notice therein of the killing of said animal, as required by amended section 15 of the statute. If we were at liberty to ignore amended section 14, the question of the sufficiency of the second count might be somewhat difficult of determination. But we are of the opinion that section 15 must stand or fall with the other sections of the statute considered in this opinion. It evidently was not designed that there should be a trial, as in other civil actions, to ascertain the actual value of the animal killed under section 15, while the schedule price or statutory mode of appraisement as provided by section 14 should [615] be resorted to for other purposes; nor was it, in our opinion, the design of section 15 to give the owner of an animal killed twice the full value thereof in addition to the schedule price or appraised value, or double that sum as provided by section 14. The sections of the statute considered in this opinion must be construed together as dependent and not as independent provisions.

Our conclusion is, that while the reason given for the dismissal of the action by the district court was not warranted, nevertheless, under the law as it then existed, no valid judgment could have been rendered upon the pleadings, and, therefore, the judgment of dismissal must be affirmed.

———

JUDICIAL OPINIONS—WHEN WEIGHT SHOULD BE GIVEN TO.—A distinct expression of opinion by a court is not *obiter dictum* when given in response to a question of equitable jurisdiction, directly involved in the issues of law, and raised by demurrer to the bill, and to which the mind of the court was directly drawn: *Michael* v. *Morey,* 26 Md. 239; 90 Am. Dec. 106.

STATUTES—CONSTITUTIONALITY OF.—Courts will uphold statutes unless they are plainly and palpably in conflict with the constitution: *Burlington etc. Ry. Co.* v. *Dey,* 82 Iowa, 312; 31 Am. St. Rep. 477, and note; *Commonwealth* v. *Erie Ry. Co.,* 62 Pa. St. 286; 1 Am. Rep. 399; *Stewart* v. *Supervisors,* 30 Iowa, 9; 1 Am. Rep. 238; *Davis* v. *Helbig,* 27 Md. 452; 92 Am. Dec. 646, and note; *Mayor etc.* v. *State,* 15 Md. 376; 74 Am. Dec. 572; *Sharpless* v. *Mayor etc.,* 21 Pa. St. 147; 59 Am. Dec. 759; *Lycoming* v. *Union,* 15 Pa. St. 166; 53 Am. Dec. 575, and note; *Flint River Steamboat Co.*

v. Foster, 5 Ga. 194; 48 Am. Dec. 248, and note; *Deal* v. *Mississippi County,* 107 Mo. 464; *Cole Mfg. Co.* v. *Falls,* 90 Tenn. 466; *Sweet* v. *Syracuse,* 129 N. Y. 316; *People* v. *Richmond,* 16 Col. 274.

CONSTITUTIONAL LAW.—Though a statute does not violate any special clause of the constitution, it may be a violation of its essential spirit, purpose, and intent, and contrary to public justice and therefore unconstitutional *City of Janesville* v. *Carpenter,* 77 Wis. 288; 20 Am. St. Rep. 123. Directly contrary to the foregoing expression of law, is the rule laid down in *Sharpless* v. *Mayor etc.,* 21 Pa. St. 147; 59 Am. Dec. 759, and *Stratton* v. *Morris,* 89 Tenn. 497, which latter cases are in accord with the doctrine of the leading case.

STATUTES UNCONSTITUTIONAL IN PART.—The unconstitutionality of one portion of a statute cannot defeat its other portions, unless the nature of the unconstitutional provision is such as to render it of vital importance to the whole statute: *McPherson* v. *Blacker,* 92 Mich. 377; 31 Am. St. Rep. 587, and note with the cases collected: *Lawton* v. *Steele,* 119 N. Y. 226; 16 Am. St. Rep. 813, and note; *State* v. *Blend,* 121 Ind. 514; 16 Am. St. Rep. 411, and note; *State* v. *Gorby,* 122 Ind. 17; *Mathias* v. *Cramer,* 73 Mich. 5.

CASES

IN THE

SUPREME COURT OF ERRORS

OF

CONNECTICUT.

CROMPTON *v.* BEACH.

[62 CONNECTICUT, 25.]

IF BY THE TERMS OF A CONDITIONAL SALE OF CHATTELS, the vendor, on the nonpayment of a note given for the purchase price, is entitled to resume possession of the property sold and to consider all payments made as for the use of the property while in the hands of the vendee, and agrees that the note shall be surrendered and canceled, he cannot, after maintaining a proceeding to collect his note and receiving a dividend by virtue of such proceeding, sustain an action of replevin to recover the property. The vendor has an option either to resume possession of the property and terminate the contract of sale, or to consider it as still subsisting and pursue his remedy on the note, but, having elected to pursue the latter remedy, his election is irrevocable, and precludes any subsequent resort to another.

MORTGAGE OR CONDITIONAL SALE.—An agreement for the conditional sale of chattels whereby the vendor reserves the right, on default in the payment of a note given for the purchase price, to retake the property and to regard all money paid as being paid for its use, and stipulates that, on his doing so, the note shall be canceled, is not a mortgage, and does not invest the vendor with the rights of a mortgagee.

REPLEVIN for machinery. Judgment for the defendant.

F. Chamberlin and *E. S. White,* for the appellant.

H. C. Robinson and *L. F. Robinson,* for the appellee.

32 FENN, J. The present contention grows out of the same contract which was considered by the court in *Beach's Appeal from Commissioners,* 58 Conn. 464, and the facts therein stated are applicable to this case, but need not be repeated here. Under the authority of that decision, the plaintiff, as administratrix of George Crompton, having secured a dividend of

twenty-five per cent from the insolvent estate of the Home
Woolen Mills Company, brought the present action of replevin
for the property against the defendant, who is the trustee in
insolvency of said company; and the sole question for our
decision is the one considered, but not determined, by the
court in the former case, whether the vendor, having elected
to enforce the claim upon the [33] note, could at the same
time retain the right to retake the machinery if the note was
not fully paid. The superior court held that such right could
not be retained, and rendered judgment in favor of the defendant for the return of the property, with damages for the replevin and detention, and the plaintiff appealed.

The contract appears in full in the former case (*Beach's
Appeal from Commissioners*, 58 Conn. 465), but we will repeat
the closing paragraph, which is that upon default the vendor
" shall have the right, at any time, to resume possession of
the machinery, and to enter the premises and remove the
same as his own property; and if any portion of said note, or
renewals thereof, shall remain unpaid, when possession shall
be so taken by the party of the first part or his authorized
agent, then the amount which may have been paid shall be for
the use of said machinery while in possession of the party of
the second part, and said note shall then be canceled and
given up." It is the present claim of the plaintiff that, although by reason of the express stipulation after possession
had been resumed, no further right to recover the purchase
price would exist, yet by resorting to her remedies in the
order in fact taken, both the remedy by collection and that by
resumption were open to her. The argument in favor of such
claim appears to be threefold: 1. That the default of the
vendee did not operate as a rescission of the contract; that
the rights of the vendor survived such default; and that the
rights of the parties thereafter existing were to be determined
not alone by the ordinary methods furnished by the law, but
by those and such other proceedings as were expressly provided in the agreement itself, namely, that until the vendor
exercised his right to resume possession, " the amount which
might have been paid should be for the use of the machinery ";
2. That in this case the remedies provided by the law and the
agreement of the parties are cumulative and collateral and that
each, except as limited in their order by the contract, might be
pursued independently, until full satisfaction resulted; and
3. That the vendor had, under the contract, a lien upon the

property, [34] which was in effect a mortgage, and was entitled
to the same relief as if the title had been transferred and reconveyed for security. We will consider each of these claims
separately. In reference to the first, that the default of the
vendee did not operate as a rescission of the contract, it is
true, and constitutes the basis of the decision in the former
case of *Beach's Appeal from Commissioners,* 58 Conn. 464.
But it must be manifest to anyone who examines that case,
that this court did not then attribute to such facts the consequences which the plaintiff now asserts. Indeed, it is very
evident that while leaving the question now at issue in form
undecided, the mind of both the majority and minority of the
court was strongly opposed to the plaintiff's present position.
This the plaintiff concedes, and a considerable portion of the
brief presented in her behalf, and of the oral arguments based
thereon, was devoted to an effort to explain how this court
was led into its " apparent error," which error is said to have
consisted in " presuming that the case of *Bailey* v. *Hervey,*"
(135 Mass. 172, cited in *Beach's Appeal from Commissioners,*
58 Conn. 480), " was based on a contract similar in effect to
the one under consideration," and therefore, as Judge Loomis
said in the former opinion, "directly in point." The plaintiff
says that, in fact, the contract in *Bailey* v. *Hervey* differed
from the one now under consideration, and was, in effect, the
same as in *Hine* v. *Roberts,* 48 Conn. 267; 40 Am. Rep. 170;
followed by *Loomis* v. *Bragg,* 50 Conn. 228, 47 Am. Rep. 638,
in which the vendor's only remedy was held by this court to
be the retaking of the property. To demonstrate this, since
it does not appear in the reported case, the plaintiff's counsel
have been at the exceptional pains of procuring what is stated
to be an exact copy of the actual contract construed in *Bailey*
v. *Hervey,* 135 Mass. 172, and have caused the same to be
printed in full for our examination at the end of their brief.
The argument is, that such contract would not have been
construed in Connecticut as it was in Massachusetts, as conferring an option upon the vendor; that the assumption on
which the opinion is conditioned is directly negatived by the
law of this court as declared in *Loomis* v. *Bragg,* 50 Conn.
228, 47 Am. Rep. 638, a decision not [35] then published, and
doubtless unknown to Justice Allen "; and that therefore the
case is erroneous, and should have been decided upon other
and better grounds, by which the same result might have

been reached, and should not have been recognized as an authority by this court.

Conceding this, for argument's sake only, we fail to see how it in anywise affects what Judge Loomis declares to be "the clear and cogent reasoning contained in the opinion cited," for the Massachusetts court, having, whether correctly or otherwise, held that the contract was one which did vest an option in the vendor, and was therefore similar to that now before us, the correctness and force of the reasoning upon the premises assumed does not depend in the least upon the truth of the premises themselves. Nor is this court concerned to discover the fidelity to principle, in all its parts, of the case cited from another jurisdiction, but contents itself with so much of the logic of the case as applies clearly and with force to our own. The court there said, in discussing a contract which it at least considered and held to be similar in effect to what we have determined the one before us to be: "When the plaintiff discontinued his payments on account, what was the legal position of the defendants? If it be assumed that they might, at their option, either retain the goods as their own property, without any obligation to account for the proceeds or value to the plaintiff, or that they might collect the price in full, it is plain that they were not entitled to do both. They could not treat the transaction as a valid sale and an invalid one at the same time. If they reclaimed their property, it must be on the ground that they elected to treat the transaction as no sale. If they brought an action for the price, they would thereby affirm it as a sale. Two inconsistent courses being open to them, they must elect which they would pursue, and, electing one, they are debarred from the other. Reclaiming the goods would show an election to forego the right to recover the price. But, instead of reclaiming the goods in the first instance, they brought an action against Bailey for the price, made an attachment of his property by [36] trustee process, and entered their action in court, and he was defaulted." As Judge Loomis has aptly said, "to accept this as good law would be to establish a principle which would, upon the facts found, preclude the appellee from hereafter reclaiming the machinery in question." We do so accept it, because it commends itself to our judgment, and so clearly does this appear that, although, as Judge Loomis further adds, we "are aware that it may receive further support from other decisions to the same effect," we deem their citation uncalled for.

The plaintiff, however, says that she did not exercise any option until she resumed possession; that the provisions of the contract that the amount paid should be for the use of the machinery, applies equally whether such payment, prior to such resumption, was by the voluntary act of the vendee or was coerced by the legal action of the vendor. This claim is, we think, not only opposed to the reasoning which we have quoted and approved, but requires for its support a construction of the contract which must be based upon a presumed intention of the parties, which is neither found expressed in the language of the instrument nor can be conceived of as existing in the mind of its makers. The only thing which, in case of the vendee's default, the contract expressly provides for, is the right of the vendor to retake the property, which is to operate as a discharge of the note. And although we have held that the vendor had the option to enforce payment instead, it cannot reasonably be supposed that the parties ever intended that the vendor, through the exercise of an option not expressly given, could by reversal of the order of procedure, instead of retaking the property and canceling the note, collect the note, and then retake the property. Cases cited by the plaintiff's counsel, which hold that when the option is exercised by retaking the amount already voluntarily paid may be retained and cannot be recovered back by the vendee, are not in point. These are payments made by the vendee in affirmance of a contract which it does not lie in his power to disaffirm, and while the contract remains in force and when [37] the vendor makes default, and it thereby becomes the right of the vendor to elect whether he will affirm or disaffirm, if he does the latter, under a contract similar to the present, the vendor is under no obligation to return to the vendee what he has paid in part performance of a contract which it was his fault that he did not perform altogether.

But while voluntary payments are made by the vendee in affirmance of the contract, involuntary ones can only be coerced after default, and import a like affirmance on the part of the vendor, because upon such default, it being the right of the vendor to elect whether he will affirm or disaffirm, though it may be true that he might defer such election for a considerable time, yet, whenever he brings an action to recover

the contract price, he does affirm it, just as much as he dis-
affirms it when he retakes the property. To say, therefore
that the vendor's option, in the case before us, was not exer
cised until the retaking, is erroneous. It involves a double
election—to affirm the sale to get as much as possible out of
the general assets of the insolvent estate, and then to rescind it
to get as much more as possible out of the property specifically,
which seems to us, it must be said, a fast and loose fingering
of the contract. The plaintiff insists that there is no injustice
in this, since she only seeks to obtain the amount of the purchase price of the property, and cannot get more; that whenever the sum collected equals the debt, the property vests in
the vendee, and whenever such sum less than the debt is
enough to make the balance due below the value of the property, the vendee can obtain title by paying the remainder.
There seems to be an inconsistency in this reasoning. If not
only what is voluntarily paid (in this case nothing was in fact
so paid), but what she collects, may be held as rent, why is
the plaintiff under any obligation to apply it as part payment
upon the note? When she retakes the property it is her duty
under the contract to cancel and give up the note. But the
note being discharged, is she thereupon to return the property? If the sum received is rent merely, why does not the
whole purchase price continue due? If, on the other [38]
hand, she is bound to apply it in part payment, why is it
not because she has elected to treat the obligation as absolute
and not as conditional? We think the plaintiff is mistaken
in her claim.

Coming, then, to the second point in the plaintiff's argument, that the law and the agreement taken together, give to
her cumulative remedies, which she is entitled to pursue separately until they result in satisfaction, the answer to this
claim appears to be clearly embraced in what has already
been said. This is not a question of remedy, but of right.
The contract was conditional. The note should be paid or
the property might be retaken. There was an option. True,
this court has held that such option belonged to the vendor
and not to the vendee. The debt was absolute if the vendor
elected to treat it as such. The plaintiff's intestate, or she as
his administratrix, might therefore upon the vendee's default,
demand and enforce either payment or return. If the latter,
that by the express terms of the instrument inured to discharge

he note. If the former, that equally, though by operation of
aw, transferred and confirmed the title.   Having elected
herefore, to enforce the note, the plaintiff is entitled to all
the remedies which the law or the contract gives her for that
purpose, but not for any other purpose. She could attach
the property. She did in fact attach other property. Insolvency intervening, the claim was presented and the dividend
received. What other remedy for the enforcement of the debt
exists? Not now to retake the property as a means to that
end. A contract of conditional sale imposes no lien upon
property in favor of the vendor, for that or any other purpose.
He does not sell and receive back a pledge. He retains the
title until he elects to part with it, and when he does so elect
the title passes from him; but nothing else thereby springs
up in its place in the nature of a lien or encumbrance upon
the property, inuring to his benefit.

And this brings us directly to the remaining claim of the
plaintiff, that the contract in question is in the nature of a
mortgage. It is not a mortgage. If it had been, it must,
[39] in order to be valid, have been executed with statutory
formalities, which are lacking, and recorded. It would require foreclosure to perfect title, and it ought to have been
considered by the commissioners on the insolvent estate security for the plaintiff's claim upon the property of such estate,
which was not done. It is not, therefore, claimed to be a
mortgage, but that it was in the nature of a mortgage. We
think, however, that it is just as far from the nature of a mortgage as any other conditional sale; no more and no less; and
that to hold that between conditional sales, a class of contracts so often construed and so clearly defined in this state,
and chattel mortgages proper there is an intermediate and
anomalous species of contracts, which the court will regard
as importing in favor of a vendor all the benefits of both a
mortgage and a conditional sale, and against the vendee, the
trustee for the benefit of creditors of the vendee's insolvent
estate and the public generally, to whom such unrecorded and
undisclosed conveyances operate too often disadvantageously,
all—the burdens of both, with none of the advantages of
either—would be opposed to public policy, and cannot be and
is not law.

There is no error in the judgment complained of.

In this opinion the other judges concurred.

CONDITIONAL SALE.—DISTINCTION BETWEEN, AND CHATTEL MORTGAGE, and the rights of the parties thereunder, will be found discussed in the following cases: *Gerow* v. *Castello*, 11 Col. 560; 7 Am. St. Rep. 260, and note; *Bolling* v. *Kirby*, 90 Ala. 215; 24 Am. St. Rep. 789; *Dederick* v. *Wolfe*, 68 Miss. 500; 24 Am. St. Rep. 283, and note; *Tufts* v. *D'Arcambal*, 85 Mich. 185; 24 Am. St. Rep. 79, and note; *Aultman* v. *Olson*, 43 Minn. 409. See further the extended notes to *Turnipseed* v. *Cunningham*, 50 Am. Dec. 195; *Hutzler* v. *Phillips*, 4 Am. St. Rep. 699, and *Palmer* v. *Howard*, 1 Am. St. Rep. 63.

HAVILAND *v.* SAMMIS.

[62 CONNECTICUT, 44.]

STATUTE OF FRAUDS.—IF AN ENTIRE AND INDIVISIBLE CONTRACT IS PARTLY WITHIN THE STATUTE OF FRAUDS, the whole is affected by the statute if part is by parol.

STATUTE OF FRAUDS—COLLATERAL PAROL AGREEMENTS.—If one who has agreed to purchase a lot of land, represented to be one hundred feet wide, on being tendered a conveyance describing the lot as being one hundred feet in width, more or less, refuses to accept such conveyance, and thereupon the vendor, by his agent, agrees by parol that if the vendee will accept the deed, the vendor will pay the difference in value between the tract described in the deed and the tract represented, such agreement is not within the statute of frauds, and may be enforced.

ACTION to recover the difference in value between the land conveyed to plaintiff and that agreed to be conveyed. The defendant demurred to the complaint, and the question presented by the demurrer was reserved for the advice of the appellate court.

M. W. Seymour and *H. H. Knapp*, for the defendant.

R. Frost, for the plaintiff.

[45] ANDREWS, C. J. The complaint alleges in substance that on the twenty-sixth day of June, 1888, the defendants were the owners of a tract of land on West avenue in the city of Norwalk, which they represented to the plaintiff to be one hundred and ten feet wide; that the plaintiff relying on their representation agreed to buy the land, and made on that day a part payment of the purchase money, and on the twenty-ninth day of the same month paid the balance of the purchase price to the defendants; that thereafter the defendants tendered to the plaintiff a deed which described the land to be one hundred and ten feet, more or less, wide on West avenue and eighty-nine feet wide in the rear. Apparently the plaintiff refused to accept the deed, for the complaint avers "that

the said defendants by their said agent agreed by parol with
the plaintiff through her said agent, that if she would accept
said deed they would pay her the difference between the value
of the tract described in the deed and the value of the trac
as represented by them; and that the plaintiff under this
agreement accepted said deed." The complaint alleges the
difference in the value to be seven hundred and fifty dollars,
and that the defendants have refused to pay it. The plaintiff
claims damages to the amount of eight hundred dollars.

The defendants demur to the complaint, "because it appears from the allegations thereof that the agreement upon
which the plaintiff seeks to maintain her action, if any such
was made, was for the sale of real estate, or an interest in or
concerning it, and was by parol and not in writing, as required by the statute of frauds."

The proposition of law maintained by the defendants, "that
when an entire and indivisible contract is partially within the
statute of frauds the whole is avoided by the statute if that
part is by parol," is undoubtedly correct. But this case is
not affected by that proposition. The defendants had contracted to convey to the plaintiff a certain piece of land for
which she had paid them. They proposed to convey a smaller
piece. She refused to accept it. They [46] then say to her—
if you will accept the deed of the smaller piece we will return
to you the difference in value between the piece of land we
agreed to convey to you and the piece of land which in fact
we do convey to you. The promise to return the excess of
money is not affected by any sale of land.

Analyze the transaction between these parties more mi-
nutely and this becomes clear. The defendants had had
negotiations with the plaintiff by which they had contracted
to convey to her a certain piece of land for which she had
paid them. They tender her a deed of a smaller piece which
she refuses to accept. At that moment all contract for the
sale of that piece of land is at an end. Then the parties begin to negotiate for the sale by the defendants to the plaintiff
of a different piece of land—a smaller piece. The plaintiff
consents to take a smaller piece at a smaller price. This is a
new contract. A deed is given and accepted. The price had
been paid. All contracts respecting land or any interest in
or concerning land between these parties were then concluded
—executed on both sides. But the money representing the
difference in price between the piece of land agreed by the

first negotiation to be conveyed, and the price of the land actually conveyed, remained in the hands of the defendants. They had promised to return it to the plaintiff. They have not done so. This action is brought to recover it. "The statute of frauds does not apply to such an action, whether brought on an implied or upon an express agreement. The obligation to repay the money advanced by the plaintiff is independent of the character of the consideration upon which the advance was made. And if an express promise to that effect be separable from the principal agreement to which it is an incident, it may be enforced, although the principal agreement might be avoided. The fact that a certain stipulation is made at the same time and forms a part of an arrangement for the sale of an interest in land, does not prevent an action from being maintained upon it; provided: 1. That the action does not tend to enforce the sale or purchase of the interest in land, and [47] 2. That in other respects the stipulation is susceptible of being separately enforced by action. Such stipulations, collateral to the sale, but contained in the same contract, have been repeatedly enforced": *Wetherbee* v. *Potter*, 99 Mass. 354, 361; *Wilkinson* v. *Scott*, 17 Mass. 249; *Hall* v. *Solomon*, 61 Conn. 476; 29 Am. St. Rep. 218.

The court of common pleas is advised to overrule the demurrer.

In this opinion the other judges concurred.

STATUTE OF FRAUDS—COLLATERAL PAROL AGREEMENTS.—A contract for the sale of land cannot be partly in parol and partly in writing. A modification of a written contract imposing new obligations on one of the parties thereto must be in writing, and upon a sufficient consideration: *Heisley* v. *Swanstrom*, 40 Minn. 196. The alteration of a contract within the statute of frauds by a subsequent verbal agreement is discussed in the monographic note to *Abell* v. *Munson*, 100 Am. Dec. 169-172. A case very similar to the leading one is *Bradley* v. *Blodget*, Kirby, 22, 1 Am. Dec. 11, in which it was held that when lands are sold and conveyed by deed describing the metes and bounds, lines, and supposed quantity, a parol agreement at the same time to pay the grantee for all that it shall fall short on measurement is void, being within the statute of frauds. A memorandum is not sufficient to take a sale out of the statute of frauds, unless it contains substantially the whole agreement and all its material terms and conditions: *Mentz* v. *Newwitter*, 122 N. Y. 491; 19 Am. St. Rep. 514, and note. If part of an agreement is void under the statute of frauds, this does not avoid or annul other parts of the agreement which are separable from it and not founded upon it: *Rand* v. *Mather*, 11 Cush. 1; 59 Am. Dec. 131, and note.

PRIOR *v.* SWARTZ.

[62 CONNECTICUT, 132.]

RIPARIAN PROPRIETOR'S RIGHT TO WHARFAGE.—A proprietor of lands fronting upon navigable waters has the right to connect himself therewith by
means of wharves or channels extending from his uplands out to navigable water, so long as he does nothing to interfere with the free navigation of such water.

NAVIGABLE WATERS—CONFLICT BETWEEN RIGHT TO PLANT OYSTERS AND
THE RIGHT TO CONSTRUCT WHARVES.—The right of a riparian proprietor,
by wharves and channels, to connect his upland with the navigable
water in front thereof is paramount to any right in others to plant or
cultivate oysters on the land covered by such wharves or channels.

SUIT for injunction against the destruction of plaintiff's
oyster-beds. Judgment for defendant. Plaintiff appealed.

J. B. Curtis and H. W. R. Hoyt, for the appellant.

S. Fessenden, for the appellee.

[132] SEYMOUR, J. It will not be necessary to state fully
the finding in this case in order to understand the points
involved.

The defendant owning land adjoining that part of Long
Island sound known as Stamford harbor, and within the
navigable waters of this state, built a wharf opposite and
contiguous to his land from the upland, above high-water
mark, to low-water mark, and thence below low-water mark
out towards the channel of the harbor; and for the purpose of
connecting the end of his wharf with the harbor channel, he
dug a channel between the two, also a channel in front of
and alongside the end of his wharf.

The wharf was built and the channels were dug to enable
steamers and other vessels to receive and discharge passengers and freight to and from the defendant's adjoining upland, and in order that he might use the waters of Long
Island sound opposite and contiguous to his land for the
purposes of navigation.

The plaintiff contends that while it is the law of the state
that the owner of the adjoining upland has the exclusive
right of access to the water over and upon the soil between
high and low water marks, and the exclusive privilege of
wharfing and erecting piers over the same, yet in no case has
it been decided, and the law is not so, that he has a right to
build his wharf below low-water mark.

It is stated in Swift's System, volume 1, chapter 22, page

341, that "all rivers that are navigable, all navigable arms of the sea, and the ocean itself on our coast, may in a certain sense be considered as common, for all the citizens have a common [137] right to their navigation. But all adjoining proprietors on navigable rivers and the ocean have a right to the soil covered with water as far as they can occupy it; that is, to the channel, and have the exclusive privilege of wharfing and erecting piers on the front of their land. . . . . Nor may adjoining proprietors erect wharves, bridges, or dams across navigable rivers so as to obstruct their navigation."

This statement of the law is quoted in the opinion in *East Haven* v. *Hemingway*, 7 Conn. 186, with the suggestion that the court do not understand by it that the adjoining proprietors are seised of the soil covered by water, but that they have a right of occupation, properly termed a franchise. The controversy between the parties regarded the title to the soil, with the wharf and store standing thereon, between high and low water mark on the east side of Dragon river, which is an arm of the sea where the tide ebbs and flows, and was navigable adjoining the premises for large vessels.

That case decided that the proprietor of land ajoining a navigable river has an exclusive right to the soil between high and low water mark, for the purpose of erecting wharves and stores thereon. We do not recall any case in this state in which the precise point made in this case was in issue.

There are, however, expressions in the opinions in several cases which indicate the general views of at least the judges writing the respective opinions. Thus in *Simons* v. *French*, 25 Conn. 345, Judge Storrs says: "In Connecticut it is now settled . . . . that the owner of the upland adjoining such" (adjacent) "flats becomes entitled, by virtue of his ownership of the upland, to the exclusive right of wharfage out over them in front of said upland to the channel of an arm of the sea adjoining such flats."

In *Mather* v. *Chapman*, 40 Conn. 382, 16 Am. Rep. 46, the court says: "It is conceded that by the settled law of Connecticut the title of a riparian proprietor terminates at ordinary high-water mark. It is also conceded that though his title in fee thus terminates, yet he has certain privileges in the adjoining waters. Among the most important of these privileges [138] are: 1. That of access to the deep sea; 2. The right to extend his land into the water by means of wharves, subject to the qualification that he thereby does no injury to the free navigation of the water by the public."

In *State* v. *Sargent*, 45 Conn. 358, the right of owners of land bounded on a harbor to "embark therefrom and go upon the sea" is recognized. And in *New Haven Steamboat Co.* v. *Sargent*, 50 Conn. 199, 47 Am. Rep. 632, the right of a party, owner of the upland, to extend his wharf, if he desires, to the channel of the harbor, in that case some nine hundred feet below low-water mark, is expressly stated, and the words "deep water" and "channel" are used as synonymous.

Aside from these references, the reason ordinarily stated for giving to riparian proprietors the right of wharfage, to wit, to facilitate commerce and the loading and unloading of ships, together with the common sense of the matter, clearly indicates that the right should not be restricted as claimed by the plaintiff unless there are positive decisions to that effect or imperative reasons for so doing.

If, in view of the opinions already quoted, the question is to be regarded as an open one in this state, we see no good reason why it should not be decided in accordance with the convenience of riparian proprietors, and for the encouragement of commerce, so long as there is no counterbalancing injury involved to others. Except in cases where navigability begins at low-water mark, the right to wharf out to low-water mark only would be no privilege to adjoining proprietors nor benefit to commerce.

It is significant that the word "wharf," as ordinarily defined, implies a structure in aid of navigation, and to which vessels have access. This is well stated in *Langdon* v. *Mayor etc.*, 93 N. Y. 151, thus: "A wharf is a structure on the margin of navigable waters, alongside of which vessels can be brought for the sake of being conveniently loaded or unloaded. . . . . Hence water of sufficient depth to float vessels is an essential part of every wharf, a necessary incident thereof or appurtenance thereto, without which there can be no wharf and no wharfage. Indeed, [139] a wharf cannot be defined or conceived except in connection with adjacent navigable water."

It seems to us therefore that a proprietor of land adjoining Stamford harbor, and waters of a like character in this state, has a right to connect himself with navigable water by means of wharves or channels extending from and adjacent to his uplands, so long as he does nothing to interfere with the free navigation of the waters.

The defendant claimed that the legislature had passed an act, which was recited in the finding, which directly authorized the erection of the wharf in question.

The grounds over part of which the wharf was built and the channels dug were designated for the planting and cultivation of oysters by a committee of the town of Stamford in accordance with the statutes. The plaintiff claimed that the defendant had no right to wharf out into said grounds or to dig said channels in the same, the same being situated below low-water mark and within navigable waters of this state; that the plaintiff having acquired his title to.the grounds through original designations of a competent committee appointed for that purpose, his rights therein could not be affected by adjoining landowners, as the rights of such landowners, in contemplation of the statute, only extended to low-water mark; that the statute gave the defendant no right to build a wharf or dig a channel below low-water mark and no right to build any wharf, and that even if it did it gave him such right only as subservient to the plaintiff's right to plant and cultivate oysters, and the right to build such wharf could be exercised only by obtaining the plaintiff's consent so to do.

The court ruled adversely to the claims of the plaintiff, and rendered judgment for the defendant. The view we have taken of the law makes it unnecessary for us to examine the act of the legislature referred to. If, as we hold, the owner of the uplands in question had a right, as incident to such ownership, to connect the same by means of wharves or channels with the navigable water of the harbor, nothing has been done, so far as appears to legally deprive [140] him of that right, and the designation of the grounds for the planting and cultivation of oysters under the terms of the statute (sections 2348 and 2349 of the General Statutes) are ineffectual for that purpose.

There is no error in the judgment appealed from.

In this opinion the other judges concurred.

The doctrine of the principal case is in harmony with that maintained in *Illinois Cent. R. R.* v. *Illinois*, 146 U. S. 387, 464, more commonly known and celebrated by the title of the Chicago Water Front case. In that case the right of the Illinois Central Railroad in and to lands covered by the waters of Lake Michigan, founded upon a grant made by the legislature of Illinois was denied, but the title of the company to certain wharves erected in front of lands owned by it and bordering upon the lake was affirmed, and an inquiry was ordered to be instituted for the purpose of determining whether such wharves extended beyond the point of practical navigability. The court said: "But the decree below, as it respects the pier commenced in 1872, and the piers completed in 1880 and 1881, marked 1, 2, and 3, near Chicago river, and the pier and docks between and in front of Twelfth and Sixteenth streets, is modified so as to direct the court below to order such investigation to be made as may enable it to determine whether those piers erected by the company, by virtue of its riparian proprietorship of lots formerly constituting part of section 10, extend into the lake beyond the point of practical navigability, having reference to the manner in which commerce in vessels is conducted on the lake; and, if it be determined upon such investigation that said piers, or any of them, do not extend beyond such point, then that the title and possession of the railroad company to such piers shall be affirmed by the court; but if it be ascertained and determined that such piers, or any of them, do extend beyond such navigable point, then the said court shall direct the said pier or piers, to the excess ascertained, to be abated and removed, or that other proceedings relating thereto be taken on the application of the state as may be authorized by law; and also to order that similar proceedings be taken to ascertain and determine whether or not the pier and dock, constructed by the railroad company in front of the shore between Twelfth and Sixteenth streets extend beyond the point of navigability, and to affirm the title and possession of the company if they do not extend beyond such point, and, if they do extend beyond such point, to order the abatement and removal of the excess, or that other proceedings relating thereto be taken on application of the state as may be authorized by law."

WHARVES— RIGHT OF RIPARIAN OWNERS TO BUILD ON NAVIGABLE STREAMS: See the extended note to *Miller* v. *Mendenhall*, 19 Am. St. Rep. 231. The right to build and maintain a wharf out to a point in the stream where it is practically navigable, provided it does not interfere with navigation, is a well-established incident to riparian ownership: *Bainbridge* v. *Sherlock*, 29 Ind. 364; 95 Am. Dec. 644, and note; *Jeffersonville* v. *Louisville etc. Ferry Co.*, 27 Ind. 100; 89 Am. Dec. 495; *Sherlock* v. *Bainbridge*, 41 Ind. 35; 13 Am. Rep. 302, and note; *Union Depot etc. Co.* v. *Brunswick*, 31 Minn. 297; 47 Am. Rep. 789; *Rumsey* v. *New York etc. Ry. Co.*, 133 N. Y. 79; 28 Am. St. Rep. 600, and note; *Compton* v. *Hankins*, 90 Ala. 411; 24 Am. St. Rep. 823, and note. See *Dana* v. *Jackson Street Wharf Co.*, 31 Cal. 118; 89 Am. Dec. 164.

HUEBLER *v.* SMITH.

[62 CONNECTICUT, 186.]

EXECUTION SALE, CHANGE OF POSSESSION.—If personal property taken upon execution is sold at public auction *bona fide* and after compliance with all lawful formalities, the rule imperatively requiring a change in the possession of such property as between vendor and vendee and raising, as a matter of law in favor of attaching creditors, from the failure of such change, a conclusive presumption of fraud does not apply.

EXECUTION SALE—RETENTION OF POSSESSION.—If an execution sale is made, and the judgment creditor permits the debtor to remain in possession after the sale, such conduct raises an inference against the validity of the transaction which it is incumbent on such creditor to overcome by proof that his judgment was for an honest debt and that there was no collusion between him and his debtor to cheat or defraud other creditors.

ACTION for possession of chattels. Judgment for plaintiff.

L. E. Stanton and W. J. McConville, for the appellant.

H. O'Flaherty and D. L. Aberdein, for the appellee.

[188] FENN, J. This is an action to recover damages for the taking and carrying away of personal property. It was tried to a jury in the court of common pleas for Hartford county. From the judgment rendered for the plaintiff the defendant has appealed to this court.

The record presents two questions. The first relates to the admission of evidence. The plaintiff claimed to have proved that he recovered judgment against one Alfred Teweles and Clara Teweles his wife, on which execution issued, which was levied on the property in question, which was posted, its sale advertised, and the articles sold upon the premises where situated, being a shop in the rear of No. 66 Asylum street, in Hartford; the sale being made by adjournment from the sign-post, necessitated by the character of the articles; and that the property was purchased by the plaintiff, as the highest bidder therefor. The plaintiff further claimed that the property, at the time of the levy, belonged to and was in the possession of Clara Teweles, and that Alfred Teweles had no interest therein, but was carrying on business for his wife and not for himself. The defendant claimed otherwise; and that he was entitled to hold the property by virtue of a subsequent attachment of [189] it as the property of, and upon a claim against, Alfred Teweles, followed by judgment, levy of execution, and purchase upon execution sale, while the property remained, without change of possession, on the premises in the rear of No. 66 Asylum street.

On the trial the plaintiff offered in evidence a written lease of the premises to Clara Teweles. The defendant objected to its admission as irrelevant and tending to lead the jury to believe that the plaintiff had possession of the premises. The court overruled the objection, and the defendant excepted.

It has not been explained to us, nor do we see, how this evidence tended to create a belief that the plaintiff was in possession of the premises. It certainly was not offered for any such object. Indeed the plaintiff did not make the slightest claim to possession. We think it did tend to show the possession of Clara Teweles, and that it was admissible for that purpose in connection with the other evidence and in support of the plaintiff's contention. The defendant had no claim against her or against the property which she owned and possessed.

But the important question in the case arises upon the charge of the court to the jury, which, overruling the defendant's claims and denying his requests to the contrary effect, was, in substance, that where personal property is taken upon execution, and sold at public auction *bona fide*, and after compliance with all legal formalities, the strict rule of policy imperatively requiring a change of possession of such property as between vendor and vendee, and raising, as matter of law and in favor of attaching creditors, from the failure of such change, a conclusive, irrebuttable presumption of fraud, does not apply.

Was this charge correct? This precise question, and in this form, is now before this court for the first time. And it is one of no small interest and importance, both to the legal profession and to the public generally. It was ably and fully presented in the briefs of counsel on both sides, with ample citation of text-books and decisions. It is evident [190] that the weight of authority, as gathered from the English cases and those of sister state jurisdictions, is in favor of the doctrine as stated by the court below. Yet the reasons given are so various, and sometimes so inconsistent with each other, and the law upon the general subject of the effect of the retention of possession so different in many jurisdictions from our own, that an elaborate examination of such authorities would be as unprofitable as it would be tedious. Indeed this court, by Church, J., said, as early as the case of *Osborne* v. *Tuller*, 14 Conn. 536: " Perhaps there has been no question more frequently discussed, and certainly none discussed with less satisfactory results, than the primary one presented by this motion, namely, how far and in what sense the retention of possession of personal property by the vendor after a sale is evidential of fraud or of a secret trust for his benefit? We have no disposition here to examine all the cases which have been reported upon this prolific subject of controversy. By so doing we should have no hope of reconciling them. Some of them are irreconcilable." We therefore incline to agree with counsel for the appellant who, in asserting that the court below was misled by authorities taken from other jurisdictions, declared that " this question is one relating to a peculiar doctrine of Connecticut law. There is hardly a principle in

respect to which it would be more unsafe to follow the authority of other jurisdictions." Certainly, upon the general subject, we have an abundance of decisions in our own state;
and treating of the present question as of first impression
here, we shall best perform our duty if we square our determination of it to those decisions and the underlying principles
upon which they depend.

In *Hatstat* v. *Blakeslee*, 41 Conn. 302, this court, by Pardee,
J., said: "This rule of law, that the retention of possession of
personal property by the vendor is conclusive evidence of a
colorable sale, is a rule of policy required for the prevention
of fraud, and is to be inflexibly maintained." So also in
Capron v. *Porter*, 43 Conn. 388, this court, by Loomis, J.,
said: "That the retention of possession of [191] personal property by the vendor after a sale raises a presumption of fraud
which cannot be repelled by any evidence that the transaction
was *bona fide* and for valuable consideration, is still adhered
to and enforced by the courts of this state with undiminished
rigor as a most important rule of public policy." And certainly this assertion remains as true now as it was then.

Various reasons for this rule have been stated by this court,
but we think the correct and controlling one is that declared
in *Kirtland* v. *Snow*, 20 Conn. 23, quoted in *Mead* v. *Noyes*,
44 Conn. 490: "The reason of extending it from a mere rule
of evidence, calling it a badge of fraud only, and arbitrarily
declaring, as matter of law, that it renders the sale void as to
creditors, notwithstanding the highest evidence as to the honesty of the sale, is because it has been thought better to take
away the temptation to practice fraud than to incur the danger arising from the facility with which testimony may be
manufactured to show that a sale was honest." We adopt
the foregoing as the true rule and reason therefor. It has
also been said by this court, as in *Capron* v. *Porter*, 43 Conn.
388, by Loomis, J., "that the possessor would obtain by such
continued possession a false credit, to the injury of third persons, if there was no such rule to protect them." This is undoubtedly so, and well states a benefit to be derived from the
existence of the rule. But that it was not given as a reason
for the creation of it, affording warrant for invoking its application in cases whenever possession of property caused the
hazard of false credit, is manifest, and the same judge, in delivering the opinion of this court in *Gilbert* v. *Decker*, 53
Conn. 405, said: "It is said that one reason given for the rule,

making the retention of possession by the vendor fraudulent, is that the possessor thereby may gain a false credit, and that the creditor actually misled ought to be allowed to set aside the transaction. This would require a radical change in our law. The inquiry was not whether the creditor was in fact misled, or when and under what circumstances the debt was contracted, or whether the debt is old or new, but simply whether he attached the property [192] while possession was retained by the vendor." The decisions in *Calkins* v. *Lockwood*, 16 Conn. 276; 41 Am. Dec. 143; *Hall* v. *Gaylor*, 37 Conn. 550, and *Gilbert* v. *Decker*, 53 Conn. 405, which limit the presumption of fraud from retention of possession to attaching creditors and those who stand in their position, it being immaterial whether the debts due such creditors were contracted before or after the sale, and deny it to creditors in general, alike to those who gave credit subsequently and those who gave it prior to such sale, show that this could not have been the reason of the rule and also that the rule is one which has a restricted rather than an extended application, as its very rigor necessarily requires that it should have. The danger of a false credit, desirable as it is to avoid or obviate it when possible, might be as great where there was as where there was not a legal excuse, and is perhaps unfortunately as great as ever in cases of conditional sales, so often supported by our courts.

The rule being inflexible within the scope of its application, and the reason therefore being, as we have seen, a reason analogous to the underlying principle of the statute of frauds, a presumption which avoids the peril of collusion by preventing its accomplishment, let us inquire whether a sheriff's sale on execution is within its letter or its spirit and reason.

That it is not within the letter of the rule is evident, since the retention of possession is not by the vendor, the transfer of title being *in invitum*, and by operation of law. Nor does it seem to us to be any more within the spirit. It is a judicial sale, conducted under and by virtue of a lawful precept by an officer of the court. And while it might, like a judgment, be shown to be collusive and fraudulent in fact, it hardly seems in consonance with the well-established and ordinary presumptions attaching to official proceedings to presume at all, and much less conclusively, as a matter of law, that it is so. Such presumption as there may be ought rather to be favorable to it than otherwise in the first instance. Of course, however, to be so, the levy and sale must be proceeded with in all respects in conformity to the [193] requirements of law. And it is entirely consistent with this view to hold, as we do, that if, as in this case, the execution creditor is himself the purchaser, and if he allow the property to remain in possession of the debtor after the sale on execution, such conduct would raise an inference against the validity of the transaction which it would be incumbent upon him to overcome by proof that his judgment was for an honest debt, and that there was no collusion between him and his debtor to cheat or defraud other creditors of the debtor. And this is what the judge of the court below correctly held, for he said to the jury that it was necessary that the property should be "taken on execution, and sold at public auction, after compliance with all legal formalities"; that the jury must find from the evidence "that the property in question was duly and legally attached by the plaintiff in a suit brought by him against Alfred Teweles and wife; that the plaintiff recovered judgment in the suit against them; that execution was issued in the case, and that the property was sold on execution to the plaintiff, he being the highest bidder, such proceedings being had in good faith," and that "the judgment of the plaintiff against said Alfred Teweles and wife was obtained without fraud, for an honest debt, and the property was honestly and fairly sold to the plaintiff on an execution in said case, having been legally levied upon, posted and advertised."

Indeed, although, as has been stated, this precise question in this precise form has not been passed upon by this court before, it may be determined by the application of the principle stated by Loomis, J., in delivering the opinion of this court in *Pease* v. *Odenkirchen*, 42 Conn. 424. It was there said: "The doctrine of the common law, as held with great rigor in this state, is that continued possession by the vendor after a sale of personal property raises a presumption of fraud, which cannot be repelled by any amount of evidence showing the transaction to be honest and for a valuable consideration. But there may be a legal excuse for retention of possession, and where the facts and circumstances amount to a presumption of law that the retention [194] of possession by the vendor is consistent with the sale, the presumption of fraud is overcome. In *Osborne* v. *Tuller*, 14 Conn. 529, it was held that a valid assignment for the benefit of creditors, under the statute of 1828, was a sufficient legal excuse for the retention of possession by the assignor." And a reference to the case cited (*Osborne* v. *Tuttle*, 14 Conn. 529) and to the case of *Strong* v. *Carrier*, 17 Conn. 319, to the same purport, will more clearly illustrate the meaning of Judge Loomis in the quotation made. In those cases this court all fully established the limitation which we have given, and which the court below distinctly recognized and stated, saying in *Strong* v. *Carrier*, 17 Conn. 319: "If the assignee permitted the assignor to hold himself out to the world as the owner of the assigned estate, so as to furnish evidence that the assignee considered the assignment a mere pretense and not to be followed up, this would be such evidence of fraud as to subject the assignment to the ordinary consequences of ordinary sales in which there had been no change of possession." To use another form of statement, it would be substituting in such cases a rebuttable inference of *mala fides* for the conclusive presumption of fraud which arises in case of ordinary sales unaccompanied by a transfer of possession.

There is no error in the judgment complained of.

In this opinion CARPENTER, SEYMOUR, and J. M. HALL, JJ., concurred.

ANDREWS, C. J., dissented.

EXECUTION SALES—CHANGE OF POSSESSION.—Permitting property sold on execution to remain in the hands of the judgment debtor is of itself no evidence of fraud; but it does not exclude fraud, and may be a circumstance connected with others to show its presence: *McMichael* v. *McDermott*, 17 Pa. St. 353; 55 Am. Dec. 560, and note; *Farr* v. *Sims*, Rich Eq. 122; 24 Am. Dec. 396, and note. It is not necessary that there should be an actual delivery and change of possession of personal property sold under execution to render the sale valid; the publicity of the sale dispenses with the necessity of a delivery: *Greathouse* v. *Brown*, 5 T. B. Mon. 280; 17 Am. Dec. 67. Continued possession of personal property after execution sale by its former owner is presumptive evidence of fraud, and becomes conclusive unless the vendee shows that the sale was made in good faith: *Kuykendall* v. *McDonald*, 15 Mo. 416; 57 Am. Dec. 212, and note with the cases collected; *Stovall* v. *Farmers' etc. Bank*, 8 Smedes & M. 305; 47 Am. Dec. 85. See further the extended note to *Boardman* v. *Keeler*, 15 Am. Dec. 671.

HYNES *v.* WRIGHT.

[62 CONNECTICUT, 823.]

AN AWARD IS IN THE NATURE OF A JUDGMENT from the obligation of which nothing can release the defendant but payment or discharge.

AWARD, REPUDIATION OF.—Though after the making of an award, the party in whose favor it is, declares that he repudiates and will not be bound by it, and his adversary also thereafter gives notice that he will also repudiate and not be bound by it, it is neither paid nor discharged and may be enforced by action.

ACTION upon an award in which a demurrer to the answer sustained and judgment entered for plaintiff.

S. E. Clarke, for the appellant.

T. E. Steele and F. A. Scott, for the appellee.

824 ANDREWS, C. J. This action is brought upon an award of arbitrators to recover the sum which it was awarded the defendant should pay to the plaintiff. The answer of the defendant is in four paragraphs. In the first and second he admits the fact of a submission by the plaintiff and himself to certain arbitrators of a matter in dispute between them, and that the arbitrators heard the parties and published their award, namely, that the defendant should pay to the plaintiff the sum of money named in the complaint. The third and fourth paragraphs of the answer are as follows:

3. At the time of the publication of said award the plaintiff repudiated the same, and refused to abide thereby, and openly refused to accept the same.

4. Afterwards and before the commencement of this action the defendant notified the plaintiff that he, the defendant, repudiated the same, refused to abide thereby, and refused to pay the same.

The plaintiff demurred to these paragraphs of the answer, and the demurrer was sustained by the court.

Upon the admissions in the first two paragraphs of the answer the plaintiff is entitled to have judgment in his favor; unless there is something in the other two paragraphs which avoids that result. The award is in the nature of a judgment—is, in fact, a judgment—from the obligation of which nothing can relieve the defendant but payment or a discharge. If, then, the defendant has not alleged a payment or a discharge of the award, or something that has the effect of the one or the other, he has averred nothing to avoid the effect of his own admissions. Now, it seems almost too plain to need statement that the refusal of the plaintiff to abide by the award is not a discharge of it. [325] Nor does it need anything more than statement to show that the refusal of the defendant to abide by the award is not a payment of it, or to show that the refusal of both plaintiff and defendant, if made, as alleged in the answer, on separate days, without any meeting of their minds and without any consideration, is neither a discharge nor a payment of the award, nor can it be anything else equivalent to either. The award having been lawfully made, the refusal of one or both the parties to abide by it does not in anywise affect its legal validity: Morse on Arbitration, 487; *Curley* v. *Dean*, 4 Conn. 259; 10 Am. Dec. 140; *Hopson* v. *Doolittle*, 13 Conn. 236; *City of Bridgeport* v. *Eisenman*, 47 Conn. 34.

The demurrer to these paragraphs of the answer was properly sustained, and as the defendant alleged nothing else, judgment was necessarily rendered against him.

There is no error in the judgment appealed from.

In this opinion CARPENTER, TORRANCE, and PRENTICE, JJ., concurred. SEYMOUR, J., concurred in the result, but died before the opinion was written.

AWARDS—CONCLUSIVENESS OF: See the notes to the following cases: *Brush* v. *Fisher*, 14 Am. St. Rep. 518; *Nettleton* v. *Gridley*, 56 Am. Dec. 381; and *McGehee* v. *Hill*, 29 Am. Dec. 277. An award is conclusive upon all the facts submitted: *Curley* v. *Dean*, 4 Conn. 259; 10 Am. Dec. 140; *Shackelford* v. *Purket*, 2 A. K. Marsh. 435; 12 Am. Dec. 422, and note; *Johnson* v. *Noble*, 13 N. H. 286; 38 Am. Dec. 485, and note.

DILLS *v.* DOEBLER.

[62 CONNECTICUT, 366.]

INJUNCTION TO RESTRAIN THE BREACH OF A CONTRACT will not be granted unless the injury to be apprehended is not susceptible of adequate damages at law.

INJUNCTION.—IF THE PARTIES TO A CONTRACT STIPULATE FOR THE PAYMENT IN CASES OF ITS BREACH of a specified sum, which is truly liquidated damages, equity will not interfere to prevent such breach, though the party guilty thereof is insolvent.

INJUNCTION WILL NOT ISSUE TO COMPEL THE DEFENDANT NOT TO EXERCISE HIS TRADE OR BUSINESS in a city, or within fifteen miles thereof, he having agreed that he would not so exercise it, and that if he did, he would pay complainant one thousand dollars, and it further appearing that he has not paid such sum, and is insolvent.

G. G. Sill, for the appellant.

T. E. Steele, for the appellee.

366 Andrews, C. J. The plaintiff and defendant in June, 1890, entered into a contract for the lease of certain rooms in the city of Hartford, and the practicing of dentistry therein, the eighth paragraph of which contained these clauses:

"And the said Doebler, in consideration of the premises, does further covenant and agree to and with the said Dills that he, the said Doebler, will not, at any time within ten years after the termination of this contract, engage in or carry on directly or indirectly, within the limits of fifteen miles of said Hartford, the business or profession of a ·dentist, or any branch of the same, either as principal, employee, **367** agent, or partner, or in any manner or form, or in any capacity whatever; provided, and it is hereby understood and agreed by and between the parties hereto, that in the event of the said Dill's failure to retain said rooms for said practice by reason of the said Dills-Hinckley lease, then and in that event this section of the contract becomes void by said Doebler paying to said Dills five hundred dollars, and giving bond in like sum that he, the said Doebler, will not use the term 'Associate Dentists' in connection with announcing or advertising a future practice of dentistry in said Hartford. . . . . And it is further mutually understood and agreed by and between the parties hereto that the said Doebler may be at liberty to practice dentistry in said Hartford at any time after the termination of this contract by the paying to said Dills of one thousand dollars, and giving such bond as is hereinbefore alluded to in reference to the term 'Associate Dentists.' "

The contract was lawfully terminated on the nineteenth day of April, 1892. Since that time the defendant has opened a dentist office in the city of Hartford, and has been engaged in the business of dentistry there on his own account. He has not paid the one thousand dollars, nor any part of it, to the plaintiff, and has refused so to do, nor has he given the bond mentioned in the contract. It did not appear that he had used, or attempted to use, the term "Associate Dentists" in connection with announcing or advertising such business, or that he threatened to do so. The plaintiff complained to the city court in Hartford, praying that the defendant be enjoined, and that court granted an injunction against him, his servants, and agents, commanding him and them that they should not be engaged in or carry on directly or indirectly within the limits of fifteen miles of the city the business or profession of a dentist for the period of ten years from the eighteenth day of April, 1892.

The defendant has appealed to this court, and assigns two reasons of appeal. The first is, in general terms, that the contract is inequitable, unreasonable, and unfair. The second that "the plaintiff had adequate remedy at law in [368] the premises, as said contract specified and fixed upon a sum certain as liquidated damages to be recoverable by the plaintiff from the defendant for the very act complained of by the plaintiff in this case." We consider only the latter reason.

The universal test of the jurisdiction of a court of equity to restrain the breach of a contract is the inadequacy of the legal remedy of damages. An injunction to prevent the breach of a contract is a negative specific enforcement of that contract. And the jurisdiction of equity to grant such an injunction is substantially coincident with its jurisdiction to compel a specific performance by an affirmative decree. In either case a court of equity cannot exercise jurisdiction unless the injury apprehended from a violation of the contract is of such a nature as not to be susceptible of adequate damages at law: Pomeroy's Equity Jurisprudence, sec. 1341; High on Injunctions, sec. 695; *Morris Canal etc. Co.* v. *Society for Manufactures,* 5 N. J. Eq. 203; *Akrill* v. *Selden,* 1 Barb. 316.

When the parties to an agreement have put into it a provision for the payment, in case of a breach, of a certain sum of money, which is truly liquidated damages, and not a penalty; in other words, when the contract stipulates for one of two things in the alternative, or on the one side the doing or the not doing of certain acts, and on the other the payment of a certain sum in money in lieu thereof, equity will not interfere, but will leave the party to his remedy of damages at law: *Shiell* v. *McNitt,* 9 Paige, 101; *Skinner* v. *Dayton,* 2 Johns. Ch. 526, 535; Pomeroy's Equity Jurisprudence, sec. 447. The case turns on the construction to be given to the contract. If the defenlant has agreed not to engage in the business of dentistry in Hartford for the term of ten years under a penalty of one thousand dollars for a breach equity will restrain him; for a penalty is merely a security for the performance of the contract, and is not the price for doing what a man has expressly agreed not to do. But if, on the

other hand, the true interpretation of the agreement is that
the one thousand dollars was intended to be liquidated damages, [369] then the court should not interfere by injunction,
because the plaintiff has his complete remedy at law, and
this mainly on the ground of the nature of the contract. In
determining the question whether, in a given case, the sum
named is a penalty or liquidated damages, courts give but
little weight to the mere form of words, but gather the intent
from the general scope and purport of the contract; and, as
it is difficult to estimate damages from a breach of a contract, the subject matter of which is the carrying on of a
business, the current of authorities is to treat the sum named
as liquidated damages rather than as a penalty: *Ropes v.
Upton*, 125 Mass. 258.

An examination of the agreement between these parties
makes it evident that they were contracting upon the theory
that the defendant was to resume the practice of dentistry in
Hartford upon his own accord when the contract should be
terminated. He was of course to pay for the right so to
resume. The section quoted in its earlier part spoke of a termination of the contract by reason of the failure of the plaintiff's title to the rooms. In such event it is entirely certain
that the defendant would have the right to engage in dentistry
upon paying four hundred dollars, for it is provided that the
section was then to become void. The latter part of the section speaks of the termination of the contract from any other
cause. Then the defendant is required to pay one thousand
dollars in order " to be at liberty to practice dentistry in said
Hartford." In the one case the defendant was to pay four
hundred dollars, in the other one thousand. But in respect
to his liberty to resume business on his own account there is
no distinction. In either case the contract stipulates for damages and not for the removal of competition. The contract
prevents an alternative. It virtually says to the defendant—
" If you enter into the business of dentistry in Hartford after
the termination of this agreement, you must pay to the plaintiff the damages named."

The language used indicates this thought; and there is
nothing in the relation of the parties, or in the business of dentistry, nor in the surrounding circumstances, to indicate [370]
otherwise. Presumably there are many dentists in the city
of Hartford. Lessening their number by one could not benefit the plaintiff in any perceptible degree. Nor would the de-

fendant by practicing there be likely to injure the plaintiff at all seriously. The plaintiff having contracted to take damages must seek his remedy in a court of law.

The brief of the plaintiff's counsel suggests that the defendant is insolvent and that the plaintiff could not collect the damages if he should obtain a judgment therefor. There is no finding to that effect. And if it were so, that fact could not give to a court of equity the right to issue an injunction. It is the contract itself which gives to or takes away from the court its jurisdiction; not the wealth or poverty of the party defendant: *Nessle* v. *Reese,* 19 Abb. Pr. 240; 29 How. Pr. 382.

As the defendant has not attempted to use the term "Associate Dentists," there is no occasion to consider that feature of his contract.

The judgment of the city court is erroneous, and it is reversed.

In this opinion CARPENTER, TORRANCE, and FENN, JJ., concurred; SEYMOUR, J., concurred in the result, but died before the opinion was written.

INJUNCTION TO RESTRAIN BREACH OF CONTRACT.—As a general rule an injunction will not be issued to prevent the violation of a merely personal contract unless it be of such a class or character as to render it capable of being specifically enforced: *Shepherd* v. *Groff,* 34 W. Va. 123. An injunction to prevent the breach of a contract is a negative specific performance and the jurisdiction to grant such an injunction is coincident with the jurisdiction to compel a specific performance: *Chicago Municipal Gas etc. Co.* v. *Town of Lake,* 130 Ill. 42; *Consolidated Coal Co.* v. *Schmisseur,* 135 Ill. 371. An injunction will issue to prevent a breach of contract for personal services which cannot be easily procured or compensated in damages: *Cort* v. *Lassard,* 18 Or. 221; 17 Am. St. Rep. 726, and note. An injunction will issue to prevent the breach of a firm contract by an individual member: *Welsh* v. *Morris,* 81 Tex. 159; 26 Am. St. Rep. 801. See the notes to the following cases: *Burton* v. *Marshall,* 45 Am. Dec. 175, and *Peabody* v. *Norfolk,* 96 Am. Dec. 669, also *Newport* v. *Newport Light Co.,* 84 Ky. 166, and *Graves* v. *Key City Gas Co.,* 83 Iowa, 714.

INJUNCTION—CONTRACTS IN REASONABLE RESTRAINT OF TRADE.—One engaged in business may sell his stock in trade and good-will and make a valid contract with the purchaser that he will not engage in the same business in the same place for a time named, and he may be enjoined and restrained from violating his contract: *Chapin* v. *Brown,* 83 Iowa, 156; 32 Am. St. Rep. 297; *Beard* v. *Dennis,* 6 Ind. 200; 63 Am. Dec. 380, and note; *Guerand* v. *Dandelet,* 32 Md. 561; 3 Am. Rep. 164, and the note to *Frazer* v. *Frazer Lubricator Co.,* 2 Am. St. Rep. 81.

SCOVILL *v.* MCMAHON.

[62 CONNECTICUT, 378.]

CONDITIONS SUBSEQUENT—WAIVER OF.—The right of entry for breach of a condition subsequent may be waived or lost by laches. Therefore, where land was granted on the condition that it should be used as a burying-ground, and that the grantee should build and keep a good and sufficient fence around it, and it was used for a burying-ground for more than forty-five years, but no fence was ever erected around it, and no complaint was ever made of the absence of such fence, it is then too late for the successor in interest of the grantor to enter for condition broken.

CONDITIONS SUBSEQUENT ARE NOT FAVORED and may be created only by express terms or clear implication. The courts will always construe clauses in deeds as covenants rather than as conditions, if they can reasonably do so. Though apt words for the creation of a condition subsequent are employed, yet, in the absence of an express provision for re-entry and forfeiture, the courts, from the nature of the acts to be performed, or prohibited, from the relation and situation of the parties, and from the entire instrument, will determine the real intention of the parties.

CONDITIONS SUBSEQUENT.—If a grant of property to be used as a cemetery contains a condition that a good fence shall be erected and maintained around it, the grantor being then the owner of adjacent lands, the stipulation will be construed to be a covenant and not a condition subsequent, and the grantor is not entitled to re-enter for failure to erect the fence.

CONDITIONS SUBSEQUENT—PERFORMANCE PROHIBITED BY LAW.—If the further performance of a condition subsequent that premises should be used as a cemetery is rendered unlawful by a valid act of the legislature, the condition is thereby discharged and the title of the grantee freed therefrom.

EMINENT DOMAIN—PROPERTY IS NOT TAKEN for a public use within the meaning of the constitution by the enactment and enforcement of a statute forbidding its use in a manner hurtful to the health and comfort of the community. Therefore, though a party had a right of entry for breach of a condition subsequent that lands should be used for a public cemetery, and the land is freed from that condition under a valid act of the legislature forbidding any further interment therein, and requiring the removal therefrom of all bodies and monuments, and authorizing the taking of the property, after such removal, for a public park, upon payment to its owners of the sums decreed by the court, he has no right to any part of the money awarded for such property.

ACTION against the defendant as Roman Catholic bishop to recover money in his hands received by him from the city of Waterbury as compensation for a cemetery taken by it for the purpose of a public park. Judgment for defendant.

L. F. Burpee and G. D. Watrous, for the appellants.

W. W. Hyde and F. E. Hyde, for the appellee.

[285] F. B. HALL, J.—The plaintiffs by this action seek to recover the whole or a part of the sum of twelve thousand five hundred dollars, held by the defendant under a judgment of the superior court. The material facts alleged in the complaint, to which the defendant demurs, are as follows:

The plaintiffs represent the heirs of one J. M. L. Scovill, who, in 1847, by warranty deed with the usual covenants, conveyed to William Tyler, bishop of the Roman Catholic diocese of Hartford, his successors and assigns, in trust for the Roman Catholics of Waterbury, a tract of land in Waterbury containing one acre. The deed contained the following provision; "Provided, and this deed is upon the condition, that the above-described premises are to be used and occupied for the purpose of a burying-ground, and no other purpose; and that the grantee, his successors and assigns, shall at all times maintain, build, and keep a good and sufficient fence around said premises."

Since said date this land has been used and occupied by the grantees as a cemetery for the burial of Roman Catholics, until the removal of all the bodies and monuments by [286] the city of Waterbury under the legislative act hereafter referred to. No interments have been made in this land since 1880. No fence has ever been built around the premises.

In 1882, by a special act of the legislature, the preamble of which recited that this and other old cemeteries within the city of Waterbury had long ceased to be used as places of interment; that they had been in a neglected condition, and that, from the growth of the city and from other causes, they were no longer proper places for cemeteries, it was provided that, from and after the date of the act, it should be unlawful to make any interment in said burying-ground. This act further provided that, upon the petition of the city of Waterbury, the superior court might order the removal by the city of the bodies and monuments from the cemetery; and, after prescribing the manner of ascertaining the owners of the land and the value of their respective interests therein, provided that, upon payment to the owners of the sums decreed by court as the value of their respective interests, the burial-ground should become a public park in the city of Waterbury, and that the same might be used for any suitable public building or other public purpose: 9 Conn. Special Laws, 677.

After a hearing before a committee appointed upon the petition of the city of Waterbury under this act, it was de-

creed by the superior court, January 2, 1891, that when the
city of Waterbury should pay to the defendant the sum of
twelve thousand five hundred dollars, said sum having been
found to be the value of the land in question, and should
remove the remaining bodies and monuments from the burying-ground, the same should become a public part in said city
and be used for any suitable public building or other public
purpose.   By the judgment of the superior court this sum of
twelve thousand five hundred dollars was to be held by
Bishop McMahon "subject to all trusts, claims, and interests
which are or may be found to be created and reserved in the
deed of J. M. L. Scovill."   The heirs of J. M. L. Scovill were
represented at the hearing before said committee, but no claim
was then made in their behalf.

[387] On the 30th of January, 1891, Henry W. Scovill, one
of the plaintiffs, in behalf of said heirs, made entry upon the
land for condition broken.

The city of Waterbury has complied with the requirements
of the act referred to, and, on the 18th of May, 1891, paid to
the defendant the sum of twelve thousand five hundred dollars, which is held by him in conformity to the terms of said
judgment.

By their appeal from the decision of the superior court sustaining the defendant's demurrer to the complaint, the plaintiffs claim that there has been a breach of the condition of
the deed of Scovill to Tyler, by which the title to the land
described in the deed has become forfeited, and that they are
thereby entitled to the whole of the sum in the hands of the
defendant, as that sum represents the value of the land; that
if these facts do not show a breach of the condition of the
deed revesting the title in the plaintiffs, they are still entitled
to some part of the fund in the defendant's hands as a compensation for the loss of the right which they possess to re-
enter upon condition broken, and which right or interest in
the land they say has been taken from them by act of the
legislature without compensation.

Of the alleged breaches of condition there are but two which
we need to consider: 1. That which it is claimed resulted
from the failure to maintain a fence; and 2. That which it
is said was effected by the act of the legislature prohibiting
the use of the land as a place of burial, and by the removal
of the bodies and monuments by the city pursuant to the act.

The alleged right to re-enter for failure to maintain a fence

accrued about forty-five years ago, as the record shows that
the grantees have never built a fence around the premises.
During this period of forty-five years there has apparently
been no demand made, either by the grantor or his heirs, for
the erection of a fence. During this period the grantor and
his heirs have silently permitted interments to be made and
monuments to be erected until this tract was filled with
graves. Indeed, the silence of the grantor and his heirs
respecting their claimed right to re-enter for failure [388] to
erect a fence seems never to have been broken until the sum
of twelve thousand five hundred dollars was placed in the defendant's hands by order of the court.

If the clause in question were to be construed as creating a
condition subsequent, we think, upon these facts, the plaintiffs may be justly held either to have waived their right or
to have lost it by their own laches. A right of entry may be
so waived and lost: 2 Washburn on Real Property, 18; *Guild
v. Richards*, 16 Gray, 309; *Andrews v. Senter*, 32 Me. 394;
Ludlow v. *New York etc. R. R. Co.*, 12 Barb. 440; *Merrifield
v. Cobleigh*, 4 Cush. 178.

But we are not willing to be understood as assenting to
the plaintiff's claim that the provision requiring the erection
of a fence constitutes a condition subsequent. The law is
well established that such conditions are not favored, and
are created only by express terms or by clear implication;
that courts will always construe clauses in deeds as covenants
rather than conditions if they can reasonably do so; that if
it be doubtful whether a clause in a deed imports a condition
or a covenant the latter construction will be adopted; and
that, though apt words for the creation of a condition are employed, yet, in the absence of an express provision for re-entry
or forfeiture, the court, from the nature of the acts to be performed or prohibited by the language of the deed, from the
relation and situation of the parties, and from the entire instrument, will determine the real intention of the parties: 2
Washburn on Real Property, 4 et seq.; *Post v. Weil*, 115 N.Y.
361; 12 Am. St. Rep. 809; *Hoyt v. Kimball*, 49 N.H. 327;
Episcopal City Mission v. Appleton, 117 Mass. 326; *Stanley v.
Colt*, 5 Wall. 119.

As it is clear from the language used in this deed that the
grantor intended the land to be used for a cemetery and for
no other purpose, and as apt words for the creation of a condition are employed, it is a reasonable inference under all the

circumstances that the grantor intended that the property should revert if the grantee failed to use it for the purpose for which it was conveyed; but, in the absence of any express provision for re-entry or forfeiture, we think it [389] is not unreasonable to conclude that the parties did not intend that, while the land was in use as a place of burial and while it was filled with graves and monuments, it should revert to the grantor upon the failure of the grantee to maintain a fence. The description of the property shows that the grantor owned the land on two sides of the lot conveyed. He evidently desired to relieve himself from the burden of maintaining any part of the fence and to impose the duty upon the grantee of building all the fence inclosing the premises. This, we think, was his entire purpose, and that this provision should be construed as a covenant and not as creating a condition subsequent.

Assuming that the provision in the deed that the land should be used for the purpose of a burying-ground and for no other purpose created a condition subsequent, did the act of the legislature forbidding further interments in the place and providing for the removal of the bodies and monuments which remained there, constitute a breach of condition which would work a forfeiture of the defendant's title? If this question is to be answered in the affirmative, the plaintiffs, assuming that they had made the required re-entry, should receive the entire sum in the hands of the defendant, as that sum represents only the value of the land; while the defendant, who, without fault, has not only been deprived of the right to use this land as a place of burial, but has also lost his title to the land itself, will receive no compensation.

If the condition of the deed is broken and the title reverts from the act of the legislature, it would seem, from the claims made by the plaintiffs, that not only should they be reimbursed for the full value of the land taken from them by the city of Waterbury, but that the defendant should be paid the full value of the right and title of which he has been deprived by the state, and which might be equal to the full value of the land.

We think the law is not as contended for by the plaintiffs; and that, the grantee having used the land for a place of burial and for no other purpose, when the state, in the [390] proper and reasonable exercise of its police power, by a valid act of its legislature, rendered the performance of the act

described in the condition subsequent unlawful, the condition
of the deed was thereby destroyed, and the title vested absolutely in the defendant: *Mitchell* v. *Reynolds*, 1 P. Wms. 189;
Doe dem. Marquis of Anglesea v. *Church Wardens of Rugeley*,
6 Q. B. 107; *Brewster* v. *Kitchin*, 1 Ld. Raym. 317; 2 Blackstone's Commentaries, 156; 2 Washburn on Real Property, 8;
4 Kent's Commentaries, 130; 1 Rev. Swift. Dig. 98.

In *Doe dem. Marquis of Anglesea* v. *Church Wardens of
Rugeley*, 6 Q. B. 107, the condition was that the lessees should
use and occupy the premises for the sole use, maintenance,
and support of the poor of Rugeley, and should not convert
the building or the land described to any other use or purpose. For a time the building was used for that purpose,
but afterwards the paupers were removed by order of the
poor law commissioners, and the workhouse closed. Lord
Denman, C. J., in delivering the judgment of the court, said:
" But even if the condition were not performed, it appears to
us that the nonperformance would in this case be excused, as
being by act of law, and involuntary on the part of the
lessee."

If it should be said that the plaintiffs' interests in this
property had been taken from them by the state or by the
city of Waterbury by right of eminent domain, we should
reach the same conclusion upon the question of whether the
condition of the deed had been broken. If the city of Waterbury, by taking this land for a public park, under the valid
act of the legislature, has prevented its use as a burial-place,
it is clear that the performance of the condition of the deed
has been prevented by act of law; and we know of no principle or authority by which the taking of the property under
the right of eminent domain would work a forfeiture which
would require payment both to the plaintiffs of the value of
the land and to the defendant of the value of the estate
forfeited.

If it were true that, by the appropriation of this land to
a public use by right of eminent domain, the plaintiffs had
[391] been deprived of their interest in the property, though
such taking would not work a forfeiture, yet there would be
strong reasons in support of the plaintiffs' claim that the
fund in the defendant's hands should be divided between the
plaintiffs and the defendant in proportion to the value of
their respective interests in the land. And that brings us to
the consideration of the remaining claim of the plaintiffs,

that, even if there has been no breach of the condition of the
deed which would entitle them to recover the entire twelve
thousand five hundred dollars, yet, having, by the act of the
legislature and the subsequent proceedings under it, been
deprived of their interest in the land, that is, of a possibility
of reverter, which, they say, was a valuable estate, they
should receive some part of said fund as a compensation for
their loss.

Upon the facts disclosed by the record this claim cannot
be sustained. Conceding that, by the act of the legislature,
the plaintiff's interest in this property has been destroyed,
and that such interest was one which is susceptible of a valuation in money, it does not follow that they are entitled to
compensation from the fund for the loss of that right or
interest.

Regarding the plaintiff's right to re-enter upon condition
broken as a species of property, that property has neither
been taken nor destroyed by the conversion of this land into
a public park by right of eminent domain. The purpose of
the legislative act was twofold: 1. By prohibiting the use of
this land as a cemetery, to remove a public nuisance; and
2. To permit the city of Waterbury to take the ground for a
public park.   •

The fact is apparent that this old burying-ground, long
since filled with graves, and within the limits of the city of
Waterbury, had become obnoxious to the public, and had
come to be regarded as a public nuisance. The preamble of
the act of the legislature, in effect, declares it to be such.
The language is: "Said old cemeteries have long been in a
neglected condition, and, from the growth of said city around
and from other causes, they are no longer proper places for
cemeteries." The complaint alleges that these cemeteries
were public nuisances, and we think the facts apparent
upon the record fail to show that they had become so by the
fault of the defendant, or that they would have been any the
less a nuisance had they been inclosed by a fence. Evidently,
from the growth of the city and from the location of the cemetery in the city, it had become an unsuitable place for a
burial-ground. Under these circumstances, and with two
distinct objects in view, the act in question was passed, providing: 1. That it should be unlawful to make further interments in the land, and that, upon the petition of the city,
and upon hearing all parties interested, the superior court

might order the removal to other cemeteries of all the remaining bodies and monuments at the expense of the city; and,
2. That upon payment to the owners of the value of the
land, duly assessed as provided by the act, and upon the removal of the bodies and monuments from the cemetery, the
land shall become a public park, etc.

If, because the use of this land as a place of burial was
harmful to the health and welfare of the public, the act had
forbidden further interments to be made in these cemeteries,
and had provided for the removal of the bodies and monuments, without permitting the land to be taken for a public
park, the plaintiffs would have sustained the same injury as
that of which they now complain. The defendant would have
been deprived of his right to the use of this land as a burial-
place without receiving compensation therefor. By the destruction of the condition of the deed the plaintiffs would have
been deprived of their interest, a possibility of reverter, while
the title to the property would have remained absolute in the
grantee.

If the property of the plaintiffs has been taken from them
by the state, it has been taken by the act prohibiting the further use of this land as a place of burial. The provision permitting the city to take the land for public purposes after it
had ceased to be a burial-place, and could no longer be used
for that purpose, did not affect the plaintiffs' rights.

Forbidding the use of this property in a manner hurtful to
the health and comfort of the community is not a taking
[393] of the plaintiffs' property for public use within the meaning of the constitution. It was a proper and valid exercise
of the police power vested in the state, and if, as a necessary
result of the act of the legislature removing a public nuisance,
the plaintiffs have been deprived of the right in question, they
are not thereby entitled to a portion of the money in the defendant's hands: *Raymond* v. *Fish*, 51 Conn. 80; 50 Am. Rep. 3;
Dunham v. *City of New Britain*, 55 Conn. 378; *State* v. *Wordin*,
56 Conn. 216; *Woodruff* v. *New York etc. R. R. Co.*, 59 Conn. 63.

The superior court committed no error in sustaining the
defendant's demurrer to the complaint.

In this opinion the other judges concurred.

DEEDS—CONDITIONS SUBSEQUENT—WAIVER.—A grantor may waive forfeiture for a condition broken by the grantee of land under a deed containing conditions subsequent: *O'Brien* v. *Wagner*, 94 Mo. 93; 4 Am. St. Rep.
362; *Benavides* v. *Hunt*, 79 Tex. 383; *Royal* v. *Aultman etc. Co.*, 116 Ind. 424.

DEEDS.—CONDITIONS SUBSEQUENT ARE NOT FAVORED, and an estate on condition will not be created unless the intent of the grantor to create such an estate is clearly and unequivocally indicated: *Rawson* v. *Inhabitants,* 7 Allen, 125; 83 Am. Dec. 670, and note; *Emerson* v. *Simpson,* 43 N. H. 475; 82 Am. Dec. 168, and note; 80 Am. Dec. 184, and note; *Thompson* v. *Thompson,* 9 Ind. 323; 68 Am. Dec. 638, and note. See the extended note to *Farnham* v. *Thompson,* 57 Am. Rep. 63. An estate upon condition cannot be created by deed except when the terms of the grant will admit of no other reasonable construction: *Raley* v. *Umatilla County,* 15 Or. 172; 3 Am. St. Rep. 142, and note.

DEEDS—CONDITIONS SUBSEQUENT—COVENANTS.—Whether a provision in a deed is a condition subsequent or a covenant depends upon the intent of the parties, and such a provision will, if there is any reasonable doubt, be held to be the latter: *Peden* v. *Chicago etc. Ry. Co.,* 73 Iowa, 328; 5 Am. St. Rep. 680; *Post* v. *Weil,* 115 N. Y. 361; 12 Am. St. Rep. 809, and note.

DEEDS—CONDITIONS SUBSEQUENT PROHIBITED BY LAW.—An estate which has once vested in the grantee cannot be defeated by a condition subsequent which is impossible, illegal, or repugnant to the estate granted: *Ricketts* v. *Louisville etc. Ry. Co.,* 91 Ky. 221; 34 Am. St. Rep. 176, and note; *Taylor* v. *Sutton,* 15 Ga. 103; 60 Am. Dec. 682, and note.

CASES

IN THE

SUPREME COURT

OF

ILLINOIS.

OHIO AND MISSISSIPPI RY. CO. *v.* THILLMAN.

[148 ILLINOIS, 127.]

WATERCOURSES—DUTY OF RAILROAD NOT TO OBSTRUCT.—A railroad company, in constructing its road over watercourses, must make suitable bridges, culverts, or other provisions for carrying off the water as effectually as the stream would if in its natural state, and has no more right than any private owner to turn a stream of water upon land on which it does not naturally flow.

WATERCOURSES—OBSTRUCTION OF BY RAILROAD—COMPENSATION TO LANDOWNER.—Though a railroad company constructs a crossing over a natural watercourse in a thoroughly skillful and proper manner, yet an adjacent landowner is entitled to compensation for any injury which necessarily results to him therefrom.

WATERCOURSES—LIABILITY OF RAILROAD COMPANY FOR NEGLIGENCE IN CONSTRUCTING EMBANKMENT.—Notwithstanding the condemnation of land for a railroad, and the payment of the compensation or damages awarded the landowner, the company is liable to him or his grantee for damages resulting from its negligence in the construction or maintenance of an embankment without proper and sufficient culverts or openings for the passage of a natural watercourse. ,

WATERCOURSES—OBSTRUCTION BY RAILROAD—EACH CONTINUANCE A FRESH INJURY.—Each overflow upon the land of an adjoining owner caused by the negligence or want of skill of a railroad company in its mode of constructing or maintaining a bridge or embankment over a natural running watercourse creates a new cause of action against the company for injury thereby occasioned to the crops upon such land.

WATERCOURSES—OBSTRUCTION BY RAILROAD—FOR WHAT INJURY LIABLE. In case of an obstruction of a natural watercourse by a railroad, if it appears that the injury resulting therefrom arises from causes which might have been foreseen, such as ordinary periodical freshets, the railroad company whose superstructure is the immediate cause of the mischief is liable for the damage; but if the injury is occasioned by an act of Providence, such as an extraordinary flood, which could not have

been anticipated, it cannot be held liable. The company is not liable
for remote and uncertain consequences, but only for the necessary and
proximate effects of the structure.

WATERCOURSES—OBSTRUCTION BY RAILROAD.—DEGREE OF CARE REQUIRED
to be used by a railroad company in constructing a bridge across a natural watercourse is to bring such engineering skill to bear as is ordinarily applied to works of that kind, in view of the size and habits of
the stream, the character of its channel, and the declivity of the circumjacent territory forming the watershed.

WATERCOURSES—OBSTRUCTION BY RAILROAD—DEGREE OF CARE REQUIRED
QUESTION FOR JURY.—A railroad company, in bridging a natural watercourse or building an embankment across it, is bound to exercise such
ordinary care in providing for the free passage of the water as is usually
exercised by men of ordinary prudence in their own affairs; and in the
exercise of such care the company must guard against such freshets or
floods as men of ordinary prudence can foresee, but not against such
extraordinary floods and accidental casualties as cannot reasonably be
anticipated; and whether the flood causing the injury is such as should
have been anticipated and provided against is a question for the jury to
decide.

ACTION to recover damages against a railroad company for
negligently and unlawfully constructing and maintaining a
solid earth embankment across a natural watercourse on
which its railroad track was laid, and which obstructed the
natural flow of water and forced it back upon the adjoining
lands held and cultivated by the plaintiff. On June 20,
1885, and June 16, 1888, a large quantity of rainwater fell
upon said lands as the result of heavy storms, and such water,
which naturally ran into said watercourse and would have
escaped in time of ordinary floods and freshets, without
damage to such land, had the stream remained in its natural
state, was stopped and prevented from running off in its
natural course by reason of such embankment, and by reason
thereof was forced back upon plaintiff's land and flooded it,
damaging it and injuring his crops. Plaintiff had judgment
in the court below, and defendant appealed.

Pollard and Werner, for the appellant.

Turner and Holder, for the appellee.

[132] MAGRUDER, J. The only errors, to which our attention
is called, are those alleged to have been committed by the
giving of three instructions for the plaintiff. The first two of
these instructions are as follows:

"The court instructs the jury, that it is the duty of a railroad company so to construct and maintain its road across

streams and natural watercourses which it intersects as to
inflict no injury upon adjacent lands."

"The court further instructs the jury, that this duty is a
continuing one, and that each overflow caused by the negligence or want of skill of the company creates a new cause of
action for damages to the crops or other property of the rightful possessor of the lands overflowed, although the plaintiff
acquired his interest after the creation of the obstruction; and
if the jury believe, from the evidence, that a portion of the
water of the Little Canteen creek naturally flowed south
across the right of way of defendant prior to the filling up of
the trestle, and would still continue to do so excepting for the
obstruction of the embankment complained of, then they
must find for the plaintiff, giving such damages as the jury
can say, from the evidence, that he has sustained, if they
further believe from the evidence that he has sustained damage by reason [133] of said embankment and partial obstruction of the flow of the water as aforesaid."

If we understand the objection of counsel to the first of
these instructions it is that the language is too broad in stating it to be the duty of the railroad company to so construct
and maintain its road across streams and natural watercourses, which it intersects, as to inflict no injury upon adjacent lands.   It is said that when the company has brought
to the work of building its structure across such a watercourse
a high degree of engineering skill it is not responsible for such
injury as necessarily results from the improvement.

It is settled by all the authorities that it is the right of
each proprietor of land upon a natural watercourse to insist
that the water shall continue to run as it has been accustomed to do, and to insist that no one shall obstruct or change
its course injuriously to him without being liable in damages.
As to running streams a riparian proprietor has no right to
alter their usual flow in any manner injurious to others above
or below him: *Little Rock etc. Ry. Co.* v. *Chapman*, 39 Ark.
463; 43 Am. Rep. 280.   As an individual has no right, in the
improvement of his own land, to turn a stream of water
upon the land of another, so has not a corporation such right
under its charter: *Toledo etc. Ry. Co.* v. *Morrison*, 71 Ill. 616.
A railroad company in constructing its road over watercourses must make suitable bridges, culverts, or other provision for carrying off the water effectually: Angeli on
Watercourses, 7th ed., sec. 465 b.   The duty imposed by

statute upon such company to restore the stream crossed to
its former state, or to so restore it as not to impair its usefulness, exists also in the absence of express statutory requirement: Pierce on Railroads, 203.   The same obligation in such
case rests upon the corporation as rests upon a private owner,
who undertakes to interfere with the watercourse in the same
way: *Chicago etc. R. R. Co.* v. *Moffitt*, 75 Ill. 524.   In *Jacksonville etc. R. R. Co.* v. *Cox*, 91 Ill. 500, we said: "The railroad
[134] company had no right to stop by its embankment the
natural and customary flow of the water. . . . . When it undertook to divert and change the usual and customary flow of
the water it was bound to provide sufficient means to carry
it away from the farm of appellee upon which it had caused
it to accumulate."

In the present case the proof does not show whether the
appellant owns an easement at the point where the obstruction is alleged to exist, or whether it owns the fee, or whether
it made the crossing under special legislative authority, or
whether it acquired its right by condemnation or by purchase.
If where a railroad company constructs a crossing over a
natural watercourse in a skillful and proper manner injury
necessarily results to the adjoining landowner he is entitled
to compensation therefor.   Such necessary injury constitutes
in a certain sense the taking of property; and a man's property cannot be taken without compensation, even though the
damage inflicted is the unavoidable result of a public improvement constructed with the highest degree of care and
skill.   In *Toledo etc. Ry. Co.* v. *Morrison*, 71 Ill. 616, the refusal of the following instruction was held not to be error:
"The law is, that when a railroad company builds its railroad in a proper and skillful manner, and the owner of adjacent land is injured thereby, he cannot recover damages for
such injury; he can only recover where his injury results
from the unskillful or negligent manner of building the
road."   There the case of *Nevins* v. *City of Peoria*, 41 Ill.
502, 89 Am. Dec. 392, was approved.   In the latter case the
constitutional guaranty that private property should not be
taken for public use without just compensation was held to
apply to the act of a city in diverting the natural flow of
water and turning it upon the premises of a private owner
while the city was engaged in grading and draining one of its
streets.   In *Toledo etc. Ry. Co.* v. *Morrison*, 71 Ill. 616, the
railroad company sued for damages was built before adop-

tion of the constitution of 1870, which allows compensation
for property [135] damaged as well as property taken. Where
there is a special remedy provided by statute for fixing the
damages to property not taken as well as the value of property taken, necessary injury resulting from a proper performance of its duty by the railroad company will be presumed
to have been paid for by the amount awarded in such special
proceeding: Pierce on Railroads, 203.

In the case at bar there is no plea of the statute of limitations.

The proof tends to show, that the structure across the watercourse was built before 1870, and that the opening by means
of the trestle was closed up before that date or about that
date. It does not appear, that necessary damages resulting
from a proper construction of the crossing have been awarded
or paid for. Where such necessary damages have been
awarded in a condemnation proceeding, or otherwise paid for,
they cannot be afterwards recovered in an action of tort:
Ohio etc. Ry. Co. v. Wachter, 123 Ill. 440; 5 Am. St. Rep. 532.
Here, the instruction means, of course, that the company
must so construct its road as to inflict no injury which it is
not liable to pay for, and if it is broad enough to include such
necessary injury as is involved in a proper construction of the
crossing, we cannot say under the proofs that compensation
was ever made for such necessary injury.

It is impossible, however, that the jury could have understood this instruction to refer to the damage, which a skillful
construction of the crossing over the watercourse unavoidably
involved. The suit was brought to recover for damages resulting from an improper construction of the road at this
point. Notwithstanding the condemnation of land for a railroad and the payment of the compensation or damages
awarded the landowner, the company will be liable to him
or his grantee for damages resulting from its negligence in
the construction, maintenance, or operation of its road: *Ohio
etc. Ry. Co. v. Wachter*, 123 Ill. 440; 5 Am. St. Rep. 532. The
first instruction must be read [136] in connection with the
language of the second instruction, and with the allegations
of the declaration, and with the proofs in the case, which
all show that it was sought to hold the company liable for
the injury resulting from the negligent and defective construction and maintenance of an embankment without culverts
or openings. The instruction could have conveyed no other

meaning than that it was the duty of the company so to construct and maintain its road as to inflict no injury that could
have been avoided by proper care and skill, or, in other words,
by making sufficient openings for the passage of the water
southward. We are of the opinion, that the defendant has
no good reason to complain of the giving of the first instruction, construed as it must be with reference to the special
facts of this case: *Louisville etc. R. R. Co.* v. *Hays*, 11 Lea, 382;
47 Am. Rep. 291; *Nevins* v. *City of Peoria*, 41 Ill. 502; 89 Am.
Dec. 392; *Gillham* v. *Madison Co. R. R. Co.*, 49 Ill. 484; 95
Am. Dec. 627; *Robinson* v. *New York etc. R. R. Co.*, 27 Barb.
512; *Cott* v. *Lewiston R. R. Co.*, 36 N. Y. 214; *March* v.
Portsmouth etc. R. R., 19 N. H. 372; *Johnson* v. *Atlantic etc.
R. R. Co.*, 35 N. H. 569; 69 Am. Dec. 560; *Eaton* v. *Boston
etc. R. R.*, 51 N. H. 504; 12 Am. Rep. 147; *Hatch* v. *Vermont
Cent. R. R. Co.*, 25 Vt. 49.

We see no objection to the second instruction. It an-
nounces the doctrine that the duty of the railroad in this
regard is a continuing one, and that every continuance of a
nuisance is, in judgment of law, a fresh nuisance. Each
overflow upon the land of an adjoining owner, caused by the
negligence or want of skill of a railroad company in its mode
of constructing or maintaining a bridge or embankment over
a running watercourse, creates a new cause of action against
the company for injury thereby occasioned to the crops upon
such land: *Chicago etc. R. R. Co.* v. *Moffitt*, 75 Ill. 524; *Groff*
v. *Ankenbrandt*, 124 Ill. 51; 7 Am. St. Rep. 342; *Chicago etc.
R. R. Co.* v. *Schaffer*, 124 Ill. 112; *Drake* v. *Chicago etc. Ry. Co.*,
63 Iowa, 302; 50 Am. Rep. 746; *Dorman* v. *Ames*, 12 Minn.
451.

The third instruction given for the plaintiff was as follows:
"The court instructs the jury that floods, which occur as
much [137] as twice in five years, are not in law such extraordinary floods as will prevent a recovery for damages caused
by floods from the person or persons who by negligent or unlawful acts contribute to such overflows."

We are inclined to think that this instruction was erroneous,
and was calculated to mislead the jury. What was an extraordinary flood was a question of fact to be determined by
the jury from the evidence under proper instructions from the
court: *Houston etc. R. R. Co.* v. *Parker*, 50 Tex. 330; *Gray* v.
Harris, 107 Mass. 492; 9 Am. Rep. 61. The suit was brought
to recover damages for floods occurring in June, 1885, and

June, 1888; and there was evidence tending to show that there were extraordinary rainfalls and high water at those dates, but none tending to fix five years as the period within which floods and heavy rains did occur or were likely to occur, nor any tending to show that floods did occur or were likely to occur twice in every period of five years. "Freshets are regarded as ordinary which are well known to occur in the stream occasionally through a period of years although at no regular intervals": Gould on Waters, 2d ed., sec. 211 c. "If, in the case of an obstruction of a public river, it appears that the injury resulting therefrom arose from causes which might have been foreseen, such as ordinary periodical freshets, he, whose superstructure is the immediate cause of the mischief, is liable for the damage. On the other hand, if the injury is occasioned by an act of Providence, which could not have been anticipated, no person can be liable": Angell on Watercourses, 7th ed., sec. 349. In regard to the degree of care to be used by a railroad company in constructing a bridge across a waterway, it may be said, that there should be brought to bear such engineering skill, as is ordinarily applied to works of that kind "in view of the size and habits of the stream, the character of its channel and the declivity of the circumjacent territory forming the watershed": *Illinois Cent. R. R. Co.* v. *Bethel,* 11 Ill. App. 17. The company is not liable for remote and uncertain consequences, [138] but only for the necessary and proximate effects of the structure: *Dorman* v. *Ames,* 12 Minn. 451. It is bound to exercise ordinary care, which is such care as is usually exercised under like circumstances by men of ordinary prudence in their own affairs. In the exercise of ordinary care, it is its duty to guard against such floods or freshets as men of ordinary prudence can foresee, but not against such extraordinary 'floods and accidental casualties, as could not reasonably be anticipated: *Chicago etc. Ry. Co.* v. *Hoag,* 90 Ill. 339; *Houston etc. R. R. Co.* v. *Parker,* 50 Tex. 330. The law is correctly stated in *Gray* v. *Harris,* 107 Mass. 492, 9 Am. Rep. 61, in the following language: "The degree of care, which a party is bound to use in constructing a dam across a stream . . . . must be in proportion to the extent of the injury, which will be likely to result to third persons provided it should prove insufficient, and it is not enough that the dam is sufficient to resist ordinary floods; for, if the stream is occasionally subject to great freshets, those must likewise be guarded against; and the measure of care required in such case must be that which a discreet person would use if the whole risk were his own. . . . . The dam should be sufficient to resist not merely ordinary freshets, but such extraordinary floods as may be reasonably anticipated ": *Ohio etc. Ry. Co.* v. *Ramey*, 139 Ill. 9; 32 Am. St. Rep. 176. Whether the flood causing the injury is such an one, as should have been anticipated and provided against, is a question which should be left to, the jury to decide.

Gould in his treatise on Waters, second edition, section 211 c, says: "The fact that the defendant's dam is not the sole, or even the principal, cause of the damage, if it clearly causes some part of the damage, would not defeat the action, or justify a verdict for merely nominal damages": *Washburn* v. *Gilman*, 64 Me. 163; 18 Am. Rep. 246; *Chicago etc. Ry. Co.* v. *Hoag*, 90 Ill. 339. It was a question of fact for the jury, whether the damage caused in the present case was due wholly to such extraordinary floods as ordinary prudence could not have anticipated, or wholly to [139] the defective construction of the embankment by the defendant, or to both causes. The manner, in which the third instruction placed this matter before the jury, was unfair to the defendant, because the instruction virtually assumes that the company contributed to the overflows by negligent or unlawful acts, instead of leaving it to the jury to determine whether such was the fact or not. For the error in giving the third instruction, the judgment is reversed and the cause is remanded to the circuit court.

RAILROADS—LIABILITY FOR OBSTRUCTING WATERCOURSES.—Where a railway embankment and culverts divert surface-water from its natural and usual course and cause it to flow over a party's land, the company is liable for the damages he may sustain thereby: *Austin etc. Ry. Co.* v. *Anderson*, 79 Tex. 427; 23 Am. St. Rep. 350, and note; *Clark* v. *Dyer*, 81 Tex. 339; *Illinois etc. R. R. Co.* v. *Miller*, 68 Miss. 760; *O'Connell* v. *East Tennessee etc. Ry. Co.*, 87 Ga. 246; 27 Am. St. Rep. 246; *Railway Co.* v. *Mossman*, 90 Tenn. 157; 25 Am. St. Rep. 670, and note; *Payne* v. *Morgan's Louisiana etc. S. S. Co.*, 38 La. Ann. 164; 58 Am. Rep. 174; *Drake* v. *Chicago etc. Ry. Co.*, 63 Iowa, 302; 50 Am. Rep. 746, and note. Though a railroad has a right to build a bridge across a stream it must do so in a proper and skillful manner, so as not to obstruct the flow of the water and cause damage to riparian owners. If they are so damaged the company is liable: *Taylor* v. *Baltimore etc. Ry. Co.*, 33 W. Va. 39; *Peden* v. *Chicago etc. Ry. Co.*, 73 Iowa, 328; 5 Am. St. Rep. 680, and note; *McCleneghan* v. *Omaha etc. R. R. Co.*, 25 Neb. 523; 13 Am. St. Rep. 508, and note.

RAILROADS—OBSTRUCTING WATERCOURSES—LIABILITY IN CASE OF FRESHET. A railroad company is liable in damages for so unskillfully and negligently constructing a culvert as to be insufficient to vent the ordinary high waters of the stream beneath it: *Pittsburg etc. Ry. Co. v. Gilleland*, 56 Pa. St. 445; 94 Am. Dec. 97, and note; *Sullens v. Chicago etc. Ry. Co.*, 74 Iowa, 659; 7 Am. St. Rep. 501, and note; but it is not bound to so construct them as to carry off overflows which result from extraordinary and unusual rainfalls: *Emery v. Raleigh etc. R. R. Co.*, 102 N. C. 209; 11 Am. St. Rep. 727, and note; *Philadelphia etc. R. R. Co. v. Davis*, 68 Md. 281; 6 Am. St. Rep. 440.

Davidson *v.* Burke.

[143 Illinois, 139.]

Joint Debtors—Release of One of Several—Consideration.—An agreement between the holder of a note and one of the joint makers thereof that upon payment of one-half of the note by such maker the holder will probate it against the estate of the other maker to recover the remaining half is void for want of consideration; and a failure to so probate the note is no defense to a suit on a judgment for the balance of the note recovered against such joint maker.

Fraudulent Conveyances—Life Support as Consideration.—A conveyance by a debtor of all his property in consideration of support for life is fraudulent in law, although he acts in good faith under the erroneous supposition that a note for which he is jointly liable has been paid.

Fraudulent Conveyances—Life Support as Consideration.—One cannot transfer all his property in consideration of support for life without first satisfying his existing debts; and without this a fraudulent intent to hinder and delay creditors follows necessarily as a conclusion of law, regardless of what the parties to the transaction in fact intended.

Judgment Liens—When Lost by Neglect.—When statutes prescribe the time during which judgments shall have the force of liens on the land of judgment debtors, one who has neglected to enforce his judgment lien in proper time will not in equity be relieved from the consequences of his neglect.

Judgment Liens—Whether Attach to Lands Fraudulently Conveyed. When a debtor conveys his property in fraud of creditors, before the rendition of judgment against him, by a conveyance valid between the parties to it, such judgment does not create a lien on such property by operation of law.

Creditor's Bill—Lien Created by.—The filing of a creditor's bill and the service of process creates an equitable lien upon lands fraudulently conveyed by the judgment debtor, and when the creditor has no lien on the property sought to be reached it is the filing of the bill in equity after the return of the execution at law which gives him a specific lien. In such case the *lis pendens* is an equitable levy, and creates an equitable lien on the lands, and it is wholly unimportant that the final decree establishing the lien and ordering a sale is not rendered until long after the judgment at law has ceased to be a lien, by force of the statute upon the real estate of the judgment debtor.

Creditor's Bill—Lien Under.—A judgment creditor may have land fraudulently conveyed by his debtor before the rendition of the judgment, sold under a decree establishing an equitable lien thereon in an action

to set the conveyance aside, although at the time of the decree and sale
the judgment at law had ceased to be a lien on the land under the
statute.

PLEADING IN CHANCERY.—RELIEF UNDER GENERAL PRAYER.—Any relief
consistent with, and justified by, facts alleged in a bill in equity, may
be decreed under the prayer for general relief, although not specially
prayed for.

Rinaker and Rinaker, for the appellant.

Palmer and Shutt, for the appellee.

142 BAKER, J. Sarah Davidson is plaintiff in error herein,
and Don A. Burke, surviving executor of Beatty T. Burke, deceased, is defendant in error. On the seventh day of February,
1883, said Burke and his then coexecutor, one John G. Shryer,
who has since ceased to be an executor, filed in the Macoupin
circuit court, against said Davidson and one William Norvell, who died soon after the decree herein was rendered, the
bill in **143** chancery that is found in the record now before
us. The substance of the bill was, that said Burke and said
Shryer, as executors, recovered a judgment on the nineteenth
day of September, 1881, in the said circuit court, against said
William Norvell, for eight hundred and ninety-six dollars and
eighty-one cents damages, and seven dollars and sixty-five
cents costs; that on the third day of November, following, a
writ of *fieri facias* was issued on said judgment, and afterwards returned by the sheriff unsatisfied, no property being
found; that on February 3, 1883, an *alias* execution was
issued, which was yet in the hands of the sheriff· and wholly
unsatisfied; that before the rendition of the judgment said
Norvell was the owner in fee of certain real estate described
in the bill; that on March 10, 1881, it being before the rendition of judgment but after the debt was contracted, said Norvell made a pretended conveyance in fee of said real estate
to said Sarah Davidson, for a pretended consideration of two
thousand dollars; that said conveyance was made with the
intention of defrauding complainants out of their just demands; that no consideration was paid therefor; that when
the conveyance was made Norvell was destitute of any property except said real estate, and was wholly insolvent excepting said land, and retained no property with which to pay his
debts to complainants or other creditors, and that said premises were held by said Davidson in trust for Norvell, and for
his use and benefit, and for the purpose of preventing a levy
and sale; and the bill sought discovery of the circumstances

attending the conveyance, and whether or not the sole consideration therefor was a bond made by said Davidson to said Norvell, whereby said Davidson bound herself to support said Norvell during his natural life.

The answer of the defendants admitted the recovery of the judgment, the issuance of an execution, the return of the same indorsed "no property found," and the conveyance of the land on March 10, 1881, by Norvell to Davidson. It denied that Norvell, at the dates of the deed and the judgment, was justly or in equity indebted to complainants in any sum whatever, [144] and alleged, in substance, that prior to January 29, 1879, said William Norvell and his brother, Spencer Norvell, were indebted, as joint principals, to complainants, upon a promissory note theretofore executed to the testator of the latter; that said Spencer died intestate at the date last mentioned; that thereafter complainants brought suit on the note against said William Norvell; that thereupon an agreement was made between said William and complainants, that if the former would then pay one-half of the amount due on said note, the latter would dismiss said suit and probate said note for the balance due thereon against the estate of said Spencer Norvell; that under said agreement said William paid one-half of the amount then due on the note, and said suit was dismissed without prejudice; that the estate of said Spencer was amply sufficient to pay the remaining one-half of said note and interest, and all other debts and claims against it, and that the two years for filing claims against said estate had not then elapsed, but that complainants neglected to file and prove and have said balance of said note allowed against the estate of said Spencer, and never informed said William of such failure until long after the expiration of the two years allowed for filing claims against said estate. Said answer further alleged that at the time of the execution of the deed to said Davidson it was not suspected by William Norvell that complainants pretended to have any claim against him on account of said note, or otherwise, and that the consideration for said deed was good and valid, and for an honest and legitimate purpose, namely, to provide for the support and maintenance of said William during his declining years.

The cause was submitted to the circuit court upon bill, answer, replication, and proofs, and a decree entered finding that the equities of the case were with the complainant; that

the allegations of the bill were true; that the deed to Davidson was fraudulent and void as to the complainant; that
nine hundred and sixty-five dollars and five cents was due
complainant, and that the same was and is a lien on [145] the
lands described in said deed. The decree ordered payment
of said amount, with interest and costs, and that in default of
payment said lands be sold by the master in chancery, etc.

  It is claimed that the decree was erroneous because William Norvell was not in equity indebted to defendant in error,
and for the reason that by the failure of the latter and his
then coexecutor to probate the note against the estate of
Spencer Norvell, said William Norvell was injured by just
the amount of the judgment recovered on the note, and that
the damages occasioned by such injury must be made good
before relief can be obtained in this case. The time for filing
claims against the estate of Spencer Norvell expired on February 13, 1881, and the suit against William Norvell to recover the amount remaining due and unpaid on the note was
not brought until September 5, 1881, and judgment was not
obtained in said suit until September 19, 1881. If the agreement to probate the note against the estate of Spencer Norvell
could be regarded as a release of William Norvell, then it
should have been interposed as a defense in the suit at law
brought on the note. The judgment at law settled the fact
of the continued existence of the debt, and also the amount
of the indebtedness. When William Norvell paid one-half of
the amount due on the note, and the suit then pending against
him was dismissed, it was expressly stated by the executors
that they could not and would not release him from the note.
Plaintiff in error seems to concede that there was no release
which could have been pleaded in the second suit brought on
the note, but their claim is,that there was a confessed failure
to keep the agreement to probate the note against the estate
of the other maker, whereby an injury was sustained, which
is a complete answer in equity, to the judgment that was
afterwards recovered. We do not clearly understand upon
what principle of equity jurisprudence this contention is
based. But however this may be, the agreement here relied
on as the basis of the supposed right was a mere *nudum pac-
tum,* without any consideration [146] to support it, and therefore of no binding force. William Norvell, it is true, paid
one-half of the amount due as principal and interest on the
note; but that he was already legally bound to do by his

contract, and he was also equally bound to pay the other moiety also, so there was no consideration for the promise to probate.　And William Norvell had no right to rely on the mere naked promise of the executors, and in the exercise of common prudence should have taken the steps necessary to protect his own interests in the premises as against the estate of Spencer Norvell.

It is urged that the fraud charged in the bill of complaint, that the deed was made with the intent to hinder and delay the complainants in the collection of their debt, was absolutely and conclusively disproved by the testimony.　It must be admitted that the evidence seems to show plainly enough that there was no fraud in fact on the part of either William Norvell or plaintiff in error, and that said Norvell, at the time he executed the deed, supposed that the note had been probated against and paid by the estate of his deceased brother, and did not suspect that complainants then had, or pretended to have, any legal demand against him.　But this does not cover the full case made by the bill.　The debt against Norvell in fact existed.　By the deed he conveyed substantially all the property that he owned.　He retained no property with which to pay his debt to complainants.　The only consideration that he received for the land conveyed was the bond of plaintiff in error and her husband to keep, care for, support, and maintain said Norvell during his natural life.　This was a fraud in law, even though no fraud was in fact intended.　One cannot transfer his property in consideration of an obligation for support for life, unless he retains so much as is necessary to satisfy existing debts: *Annis* v. *Bonar*, 86 Ill. 128; *Moore* v. *Wood*, 100 Ill. 451.　In such case the fraudulent intention to hinder and delay creditors in the collection of their debts follows necessarily as a conclusion of law, [147] wholly regardless of what the parties to the transaction in fact intended.

One of the errors assigned on the record is this: That the circuit court erred in declaring and holding that the judgment mentioned in the bill in this cause, and which was rendered on September 19, 1881, was a lien on December 16, 1889, upon the lands described in the decree.　Section 1 of chapter 77 of the Revised Statutes provides that a judgment of a court of record shall be a lien on the real estate of the person against whom it is obtained, situate within the county for which the court is held, from the time the same is rendered

or revived, for the period of seven years, and no longer; and
section 6 of said chapter provides: "No execution shall issue
upon any judgment after the expiration of seven years from
the time the same becomes a lien, except upon the revival of
the same by *scire facias;* but real estate levied upon within
said seven years may be sold upon a *venditio rei exponas,* at
any time within one year after the expiration of said seven
years."

Where statutes prescribe the time during which judgments
shall have the force of liens on the lands of judgment debtors, one who has neglected to enforce his judgment lien in
proper time will not, in equity, be relieved from the consequences of his neglect: Freeman on Judgments, sec. 395.
The judgment against William Norvell was rendered on the
nineteenth day of September, 1881. Execution was issued
thereon on November 3, 1881. The present bill in equity was
exhibited on the seventh day of February, 1883, and the summons issued in the cause served on the defendant on the ninth
day of February, 1883. The statutory lien on the lands of
William Norvell expired in September, 1888, and the decree
herein was not rendered until the sixteenth day of December,
1889. It is manifest that under any theory of the bill of
complaint that can be entertained or suggested it was filed
in due and ample time. The decree, however, was not rendered until more than fifteen [148] months had elapsed after
the lien of the judgment at law had terminated by limitation
of statute, and until more than three months had passed
after the expiration of the time within which the statute permitted a sale to be made upon a levy perfected within the
seven years' limitation. If the bill was properly to be regarded as simply a bill for the enforcement of the statutory
lien of the judgment at law on the lands of the judgment
debtor, then it would be necessary here to determine whether
the failure of defendant in error to obtain a final decree until
more than eight years and three months after the rendition
of said judgment, would preclude him from obtaining a valid
decree for the sale of the lands in satisfaction of said judgment. But in the view we take of the case that question does
not arise.

The statutory lien is on the real estate of or belonging to
the person against whom the judgment is recovered. Here,
William Norvell, some six months prior to the rendition of
the judgment, in consideration of future support and mainte-

nance, conveyed the lands to plaintiff in error by a deed of
conveyance which was valid as between the parties. In *Miller* v. *Sherry*, 2 Wall. 237, Miller had made a fraudulent conveyance of a house and lots to one Williams, and the court
said: "The judgment obtained by Mills and Bliss was the
elder one, but it was subsequent to the conveyance from Miller to Williams. It is not contended that the judgment was
a lien on the premises. The legal title having passed from
the judgment debtor before its rendition, by a deed valid as
between him and his grantee, it could not have that effect by-
operation of law. The questions to be considered arise wholly
out of the chancery proceedings. The filing of a creditor's
bill and the service of process create a lien in equity upon
the effects of the judgment debtor. It has been aptly termed
an equitable levy." In *Lyon* v. *Robbins*, 46 Ill. 276, the matter of the same property was before this court, and it was
there said: "The deed of Miller to Williams was not void,
but only voidable. [149] It vested the title in the grantee subject to be divested by the action of creditors. It was valid as
against Miller, and a conveyance by Williams to an innocent
purchaser, for a valuable consideration, would have been
valid as against all persons. There was then, at the time
these judgments were rendered, no estate in Miller to which
their liens attached in the order of their rendition, and although the judgment of plaintiffs in error was junior in date
to that of the defendants, yet the former having set aside the
title of Williams, subjected the premises to sale and obtained
a master's deed before the defendants made any movement in
this direction, it would now be very inequitable to permit the
defendants to come forward and sweep away the fruits of their
superior diligence." And in *Rappleye* v. *International Bank,*
93 Ill. 396, it was also held by this court that a judgment is
no lien on lands fraudulently conveyed by the debtor before
the judgment was recovered, and that the debtor in such case
has no equitable or legal title upon which a lien can attach.

In a case where the plaintiff has no lien on the property
sought to be reached, it is the filing of the bill in equity, after
the return of the execution at law, which gives to the plaintiff a specific lien: *Edgell* v. *Haywood*, 3 Atk. 352; *Beck* v.
Burdett, 1 Paige, 305; 19 Am. Dec. 436. In *Tilford* v. *Burnham*, 7 Dana, 109, it was held that a suit in chancery being
instituted to subject land fraudulently conveyed to the satisfaction of a judgment, the *lis pendens* is an equitable levy,

and secures a lien to the complainant. And *Miller* v. *Sherry*, 2 Wall. 237, is to like effect.

Although some of the averments contained in the bill at bar seem to indicate a claim on the part of the complainants in the bill that their judgment at law was a lien on the lands described in the bill, yet it fully appears from the facts alleged therein that such claim was not well grounded, and that several months prior to the rendition of the judgment the person against whom it was recovered had sold and conveyed said **150** lands to plaintiff in error by a deed which was valid as between the grantor and grantee. But although defendant in error had no judgment lien on the land by virtue of the statute, yet when he exhibited his bill in chancery to impeach the conveyance that had been made, and obtained service on the defendants to the bill, the *lis pendens* was an equitable levy and created an equitable lien on the lands; and it is wholly unimportant that the final decree establishing the lien and ordering a sale was not rendered until long after the judgment at law had ceased to be a lien, by force of the statute, upon the real estate of the judgment debtor.

The decree directing, in default of payment of the amount found due, a sale by the master in chancery, was not erroneous, because that was not the specific relief asked for in the bill. The bill also contained a prayer for general relief, and under that prayer the court could probably decree any relief that was consistent with and justified by the facts alleged in the bill.

Great reliance is placed by plaintiff in error, in her brief and argument, upon the case of *Newman* v. *Willetts*, 52 Ill. 98. In the late case of *Bennett* v. *Stout*, 98 Ill. 47, this court, in speaking of *Newman* v. *Willetts* said: "In that case there was no execution on the judgment within a year after its rendition, and an execution was issued without reviving the judgment, and it was to aid this unauthorized execution that bill was filed, and all that was there said about a lien was in reference to that state of facts, and was intended to be no more comprehensive. To hold that equity would afford no relief except in cases where the judgment had become a lien on the real estate at the time of the sale, would virtually repeal the statute. But few sales are made to defraud creditors after their claims have become a lien."

We find in the record no sufficient cause for disturbing the decree. It is affirmed.

Joint Liability for the Residue of the Debt Is Unaffected by the fact that payments have been severally made by the persons jointly indebted towards their share of the debt, and receipted for as such, the receipts not being under seal: *Ripley* v. *Crooker*, 47 Me. 370; 74 Am. Dec. 491; *Winslow* v. *Brown*, 7 R. I. 95; 80 Am. Dec. 638, and note with cases collected. See note to *Whittemore* v. *Judd etc. Oil Co.*, 21 Am. St. Rep. 715. A receipt to a codebtor for his part extinguishes the obligation *in solido:* *Baldwin* v. *Gray*, 4 Martin N. S. 192; 16 Am. Dec. 169; *Berry* v. *Gillis*, 17 N. H. 9; 43 Am. Dec. 584, and note.

Fraudulent Conveyances—Consideration—Agreement for Future Support.—An agreement for future support, while it is a valuable consideration, is not sufficient to sustain a conveyance when to do so will operate to the prejudice of the grantor's existing creditors: *Harting* v. *Jockers*, 136 Ill. 627; 29 Am. St. Rep. 341, and note; *Sidensparker* v. *Sidensparker*, 52 Me. 481; 83 Am. Dec. 527, and note.

Judgment Lien—When Not Prolonged.—The lien of a judgment, the time of which is fixed by statute, cannot be prolonged by the court: *McAfee* v. *Reynolds*, 130 Ind. 33; 30 Am. St. Rep. 194, and note; *Wells* v. *Bower*, 126 Ind. 115; 22 Am. St. Rep. 570, and note. See also the note to *Slattery* v. *Jones*, 9 Am. St. Rep. 350.

Judgment Lien, Whether Attaches to Fraudulent Conveyances.— A judgment is not a lien upon lands which the judgment debtor before its entry had conveyed without consideration, and for the purpose of defrauding his creditors, where a judgment is a lien only on lands owned by the debtor at the docketing thereof: *Gilbert* v. *Stockman*, 81 Wis. 602; 29 Am. St. Rep. 922. A judgment against a debtor docketed after an assignment to a receiver, under order of court, of land alleged to have been fraudulently conveyed by such debtor, is not a lien thereon: *Chatauque County Bank* v. *White*, 6 N. Y. 236; 57 Am. Dec. 442. A judgment lien attaches to land bought with the debtor's money, but the title to which is taken in the name of another for the purpose of defrauding the creditors of the judgment debtor: *Slattery* v. *Jones*, 96 Mo. 216; 9 Am. St. Rep. 344, and note. See also the extended note to *Filley* v. *Duncan*, 93 Am. Dec. 350.

Creditor's Bill—Lien of.—The filing of a creditor's bill and the service of process thereon create a lien on the equitable assets of the judgment debtor: *King* v. *Goodwin*, 130 Ill. 102; 17 Am. St. Rep. 277. See the extended note to *Massey* v. *Gorton*, 90 Am. Dec. 288.

Chancery Pleading—Relief Under.—The relief which may be granted in a suit in chancery must be restricted to the issues formed by the pleadings: *Metcalf* v. *Hart*, 3 Wyo. 513; 31 Am. St. Rep. 122, and note with the cases collected.

GIBSON *v.* LEONARD.

[143 ILLINOIS, 182.]

NEGLIGENCE—WHEN ACTIONABLE.—Actionable negligence grows only
of a want of ordinary care and skill in respect to a person to whom
defendant is under obligation or duty to exercise such care and skill

NEGLIGENCE—OWNER'S DUTY TO LICENSEE.—The owner of lands and bui
ings assumes no duty to one who is on his premises by permission or
as a mere licensee, except that he will refrain from willful or affirr
tive injurious acts. Hence a mere licensee who enters without any
ticement, allurement, or inducement being held out to him by
owner or occupant, cannot recover damages caused by obstructions
pitfalls.

LICENSE TO ENTER PREMISES IN CASE OF FIRE.—In case of fire in a buildi
the public authorities, fire-patrol men, or private parties may enter up
adjacent premises, as they may find it necessary or convenient, in th
efforts to extinguish or to arrest the spread of the flames, and thou
they have no permission to enter they have an implied license by law
do so in order to save the property.

LICENSEE—DUTY OF OWNER TO.—A mere naked license or permission to
ter premises, whether implied by law or given by the owner or occupa:
does not impose upon the latter any obligation to provide against
dangers of accident to such licensee.

NEGLIGENCE—DUTY OF OWNER TO FIRE PATROLMAN AS LICENSEE.—T
members of an underwriter's fire patrol who force open and enter a bui
ing to save property from fire, without invitation, permission, or licer
express or implied, from the owner or occupant, are not trespassers,
they enter and remain under a license implied by law; but such owi
or occupant is not liable to one of their number injured by using a
fective elevator and its appliances, especially when such elevator is
tended for freight, and not for passengers.

LICENSE—DUTY OF OWNER TO LICENSEE.—When an entry on premises is
naked license the fact that the licensor has knowledge that the licen
may at some time enter, imposes no duty upon the former in favor
the latter, except to refrain from affirmative or willful acts that work
injury.

NEGLIGENCE MUST BE CAUSE OF INJURY.—When negligence in the bre
of a city ordinance does not cause, or contribute to cause, the inj
complained of no action will lie on account of such breach.

NEGLIGENCE—DUTY OF OWNER OF ELEVATOR TO LICENSEE.—A city o
nance providing that in every structure where machinery is used,
so located as to endanger the lives and limbs of employees, it " shall
far as practicable, be so covered and guarded as to insure against inj
to such employees" protects only the latter and cannot be extended
as to protect or give a right of action to a mere licensee who is inju
through the negligence of the owner of an elevator in failing to hav
properly guarded.

NEGLIGENCE—REMEDY UNDER STATUTE—TO WHOM AVAILABLE.—Wh
statute gives a remedy for negligence in its violation to a certain c
of persons only such persons as are intended to be benefited or prote
by it can rely upon its violation as giving a cause of action.

Brandt and Hoffman, and J. S. Kennard, Jr., for the appellant.

Walker and Eddy, for the appellee.

[187] BAKER, J.   James Leonard, appellee, was owner of the building on West Lake street, in the city of Chicago, which was numbered 47 and 49.   It was constructed of brick, was four stories and a basement high, and was occupied by various tenants for business purposes.   The main floor and basement were leased to one Sues, who carried on therein a wholesale liquor business.   The lease to said Sues was dated May 1, 1888, and at the time of the fire herein mentioned the premises, and the hoist or elevator thereon, were in substantially the same condition that they were in at the date of the demise.   Said elevator ran only from the main floor to the basement, and it consisted of an uninclosed floor or platform about six feet long and four feet wide, with an upright timber at each end and a cross-beam at the top, uniting them, and to the center of the cross-beam a rope was attached.   It is not necessary to state anything further in regard to the construction of the elevator and the mechanism connected with it, except to remark that there was a counter-weight, which consisted of a piece of cast iron three feet long, some fourteen or sixteen inches wide, and three inches thick, and a rope by which said counter-weight was suspended and moved up and down.

Shortly before midnight of May 28, 1888, a fire broke out in the upper stories of the building in question.   Freeborn Gibson, the appellant herein, was a member of the fire insurance patrol.   The company to which he belonged responded to the alarm, but when it got to the scene of the fire the engines were already at work throwing water.   The patrol forced open the door of the main floor and spread waterproof tarpaulins over the goods stored there.   There was an outside pair of stairs that led to the basement, but the door at the foot of the stairs and leading into the basement was locked, and also braced on the inside and barricaded with goods.   There were no stairs inside the building from the main floor to the basement, and the only inside communication from the [188] one to the other was the elevator or hoist.   The platform of the elevator was on the basement floor and two or three barrels of whisky were standing on it.   When the goods on the main floor had been covered with tarpaulins, two of the patrol jumped from the main floor to the heads of the barrels, and then spread a few tarpaulins in the basement. In the mean time the other members of the patrol were sweeping water from the main floor. By the direction of the superintendent of the patrol the two men in the basement then rolled the barrels of whisky from the elevator, and when this was done they were raised, with the elevator, to the main floor, by the superintendent. Shortly afterwards the superintendent ordered six of the patrol to go to the basement, and when they got on the elevator he proceeded to let them down by means of certain ropes forming part of the mechanism. When the elevator was within a very short distance of the basement floor, the rope which held the counter-weight broke, at a distance of about fifteen inches above said weight, and the weight became detached from the post up and down which it traveled, and it fell a distance of about sixteen feet to the bottom of the basement. Gibson, the appellant, was one of the men on the elevator, and the counter-weight fell on one of his legs and drove it through the floor of the elevator, and so injured it as that it had to be amputated above the knee.

It is charged in the declaration that the counter-weight was insecurely fastened in grooves which were insufficient for the purpose, and that it was in a highly unsafe and dangerous condition, without any box or cover around it to prevent it from injuring persons in or about the elevator, when it was easily practicable to have covered, boxed, or guarded it, and also charged that the rope by which the counter-weight was suspended and moved up and down was of insufficient size and old and rotted, and of insufficient strength to hold the weight, and highly dangerous to persons using, operating, or about the elevator.

189 The fundamental inquiry in this case is, whether or not appellee owed a duty to appellant to so construct, keep, and maintain the elevator or hoisting apparatus as that it should be a safe means for his transportation from one story of the building to another. Actionable negligence, or negligence which constitutes a good cause of action, grows out of a want of ordinary care and skill in respect to a person to whom the defendant is under an obligation or duty to use ordinary care and skill. The owner of land and of buildings assumes no duty to one who is on his premises by permission only, and as a mere licensee, except that he will refrain from willful or affirmative acts which are injurious. As was said in *Sweeny* v. *Old Colony etc. R. R. Co.*, 10 Allen, 368, 87 Am.

Dec. 644: "A licensee, who enters on premises by permission
only, without any enticement, allurement, or inducement being
held out to him by the owner or occupant, cannot recover
damages for injuries caused by obstructions or pitfalls. He
goes there at his own risk, and enjoys the license subject to
its concomitant perils."

When, at the time of the fire, the members of the fire patrol
forced open the door and entered the main floor and basement of the building, they were not trespassers, nor did they
enter the premises by virtue of a license, either express or
implied, from either appellee, the owner of the building, or
Sues, his tenant. The facts that the premises were closed for
the night, that the doors were all locked and barred, that no
ingress was possible without using force and violence and
breaking the doors, and that the lawful owners and occupants
were all absent and had no knowledge of either the fire or the
proposed entry, and all the other surrounding circumstances,
preclude any theory of license from the owner or tenant. A
license to enter upon the land and premises of another is not
always based on the permission of the owner—it is sometimes
given by the law. In Cooley on Torts, 313, it is said: "A
third class of licenses comprehends those cases in which the
law gives permission to enter a man's premises. This permission [190] has no necessary connection with the owner's
interest, and is always given on public grounds. An instance
is, where a fire breaks out in a city. Here the public authorities, and even the private individuals, may enter upon adjacent premises, as they may find it necessary or convenient,
in their efforts to extinguish or to arrest the spread of the
flames." In *Proctor* v. *Adams*, 113 Mass. 376, 18 Am. Rep.
500, Gray, C. J., said: "In such a case, though they had no
permission from the plaintiff or any other person, they had
an implied license by law to enter on the breach to save the
property. It is a very ancient rule of the common law, that
an entry upon land to save goods which are in jeopardy of
being lost or destroyed by water, fire, or any like danger, is
not a trespass." So appellant, when he entered the building,
was, by the rules of the common law, a mere naked licensee,
under a license given by the law itself, in no way emanating
from appellee, and by virtue of which he would have had a
right of entry even in the teeth of an express prohibition on
the part of appellee. It is the well-settled doctrine that a
mere naked license or permission to enter premises does not

impose an obligation on the owner or person in possession t
provide against the dangers of accident, and it surely canno
detract from applicability of the rule that the license or pei
mission has its origin in a source other than such owner o
person in possession.

It is provided in section 1 of chapter 142 of the Revise
Statutes that boards of underwriters shall have power to pro
vide a patrol of men, and a competent person to act as supei
intendent, to discover and prevent fires, with suitable apparatu
to save and preserve property or life at and after a fire, an
that the better to enable them so to act with promptness an
efficiency, full power is given such superintendent and sucl
patrol to enter any building on fire, or which may be expose
to or in danger of taking fire from other burning buildingı
subject to the control of the fire marshal of the city, and a
once proceed to protect and endeavor to save the propert
[191] therein, and to remove such property, or any part thereo
from the ruins after a fire. So far as the matter here involve
is concerned, the only effect of said statute was to give in ex
press terms to appellant, as a member of the fire patrol, th
same license and permission of entry that was already give
to him as an individual by the common law. Notwithstand
ing said statute, appellant was a mere licensee under a pei
mission to enter given by the law.

Appellant was not invited or induced by appellee to g
into the building, but he was lawfully there. Both the con
mon law and the statute gave him the right to go there. H
being there lawfully, is there any evidence tending to sho
that appellee invited him to make use of the elevator (
hoist? If appellee had done anything to induce him to con
into the building, then it might possibly be said that he ha
a right to rely on the appellee's keeping the premise
including the elevator, in a safe condition while he was ther
But here there was not even a license from appellee; tl
only license was from the law; and so he had no right to co
clude that there was an assurance from appellee that eith
the premises or the elevator was safe. Besides this, the co
struction of the elevator or hoist was such as to indicate th
it was intended for a freight hoist. It was not at the ma
floor, apparently ready to transport persons to the baseme
but was standing on the basement floor and loaded wi
barrels of whisky, thereby indicating the use it was put
These, surely, were not circumstances of enticement, allu

ment, or invitation.   It may be conceded that it was the duty
of the fire patrol to go down into the basement and cover
with tarpaulins the goods there stored; but at the very first,
two of the men jumped down the elevator shaft to the tops of
the barrels standing on the elevator, and from there to the
basement floor.   No reason is perceived why the other men
could not have reached the basement by the same means.
The two men could readily have removed the brace from the
basement door, and the [192] goods there piled, and thus have
afforded ingress to the basement, and the evidence shows that
this was in fact done just after the accident.   And besides all
this, the patrol had short ladders, with which the basement
could easily be reached by placing them in the elevator
shaft, and this means of ingress and egress was also adopted
after the accident occurred.   The conclusion must be that
there was no invitation to use the elevator, growing out of
either the conduct of the appellee, or the condition in which
the elevator was found, or the necessities of the circumstances
in which the fire patrol was placed.   There is nothing in the
case to indicate an invitation, either express or implied, to
either enter the premises or use the elevator, and there being
no invitation or inducement on the part of appellee, no duty
was imposed upon him to leave the elevator in such condition,
when the building was closed at night, as that it could be
operated with safety.   It is true that appellee might have
anticipated that the fire patrol might at some time have
occasion to enter his building, and go from the main floor
to the basement; but it is equally true in all cases where the
entry is by a naked license, that the licensor has knowledge
that such licensee may at some time enter the premises; and
yet, as we have above stated, the general rule is, that the
licensor assumes no duty to the licensee, except the duty to
refrain from affirmative or willful acts that work an injury.

We have thus far omitted any reference to the ordinances
of the city of Chicago.   Four of said ordinances were pleaded
in the declaration and introduced in evidence.   It is urged
by appellee, that while the power of the legislature is plenary
to create civil rights and duties between citizens, yet that a
municipal corporation cannot create such rights and duties,
and that therefore the breach of a duty required by a city
ordinance will not enable a plaintiff in a civil action to
recover.   For his contention in this behalf he cites as authority the following cases: *Fuchs* v. *Schmidt*, 8 Daly, 317; *Hee-*

ney v. [193] *Sprague*, 11 R. I. 456; 23 Am. Rep. 502; *Van Dyke* v. *Harbeson*, 1 Disn. (Ohio) 532, and *Philadelphia etc. R. R. Co.* v. *Ervin*, 89 Pa. St. 71; 33 Am. Rep. 726. For the purposes of this litigation it is not essential to determine the question thus raised, for in the view we take of said ordinances we may, without detriment to appellee, assume that it is competent for the city to create, by ordinances, new civil liabilities between individuals.

It is a rule of law too well settled to require the citation of authorities, that where the breach of duty alleged is not the cause of the injury received there can be no recovery. Sec tions 1056 and 1057 of the ordinances were here wholly immaterial. The absence of either a fireproof shaft, or of metal doors in the shaft, or of catches or fastenings on the doors which could only be opened on the inside of the shaft, and were entirely under the control of the operator, did not cause or contribute to the personal injury that was received by appellant.

Section 1135 of the ordinances imposes penalties for not having elevators inspected every six months, for not procuring certificates of inspection, and for not framing and posting such certificates. It is manifest that if a person was injured in or by an elevator under circumstances such as would not otherwise impose a liability upon the owner of such elevator, then the mere failure to conform to the requirements of this section would not create a civil liability to the person so injured, for in the nature of things a failure to obtain, frame, or post a certificate of inspection could not be the proximate cause of the injury. It seems plain that said section, also, is immaterial, so far as showing a cause of action herein is concerned.

Section 1074 of the ordinances requires more attention. It reads as follows: "In every factory, workshop, or other place or structure where machinery is employed, the building, shafting, gearing, elevators, and every other thing, when so located as to endanger the lives and limbs of those employed [194] therein while in discharge of their duties, shall be, so far as practicable, so covered or guarded as to insure against any injury to such employees." The claim is that it was a violation of this section not to box or guard with wire, or otherwise protect, the counter-weight. Having in view said section of the ordinances, counsel for appellant places great reliance upon the doctrine announced in *Parker* v. *Barnard*, 135 Mass.

116, 46 Am. Rep. 450. In that case a police officer was acting under a rule of the police commissioners, which made it
his duty to examine, in the night-time, doors and windows,
and see that they were properly secured, and if found open,
give notice to the inmates, or if the building was unoccupied,
make fast the doors and windows. He crossed the threshold
of the elevator entrance of a building, the doors of which were
open, and was precipitated down the well of an elevator, which
was unguarded. The statute of the state that was there involved provided that in any store or building in which there
should exist or be placed any hoistway, elevator, or well-hole,
the openings thereof should be provided with and protected
by good and substantial railings, and with such good and
sufficient trap-doors with which to close the same, as should
be directed and approved by the inspector of buildings, and
that such trap-doors should be kept closed at all times except
when in actual use by the occupant or occupants of the building having the use and control of the same. It was held that
the police officer was a licensee, and that if the entry of a
licensee is permissive only, then there can ordinarily be no
recovery for a neglect properly to guard the premises. The
court then held that, conceding this, still, since it appeared
that the injury proceeded from the neglect of the obligation
imposed by the statute, it was to be determined whether the
protection intended to be afforded by means of the statute
was not for the benefit of all those who were upon the premises in the performance of lawful duties, even if they were but
licensees, as well as for the benefit of those who were there by
inducement [195] or invitation, express or implied, and thus
whether the neglect might not be made the foundation of an
action. The conclusion was, that the statute there in question was intended to provide a protection to all who were in
buildings in the lawful performance of their duties, and that
the policeman, when he entered the building where he was
injured, was in the class of persons so protected. But here,
in section 1074 of the ordinances of Chicago, instead of general language, such as was used in the statute considered in
Parker v. *Barnard*, 135 Mass. 116, 46 Am. Rep. 450, is found
language which shows, in express terms, that the ordinance
was intended only for the protection and benefit of employees
in factories, workshops, and other places or structures where
machinery is employed. It provides that in the places mentioned "the belting, shafting, gearing, elevators, and every

other thing, when so located as to endanger the lives and
limbs of those employed therein while in the discharge of
their duties, shall be, so far as practicable, so covered or
guarded as to insure against any injury to such employees."

In 1 Comyn's Digest, "Action upon Statute, F," it is said:
"In every case where a statute enacts or prohibits a thing for
the benefit of a person, he shall have a remedy upon the same
statute for the thing enacted for his advantage, or for the recompense of the wrong done to him contrary to said law."
And in *O'Donnell* v. *Providence etc. R. R. Co.*, 6 R. I. 211, it
is added, by way of explanation, "confining the remedy to
such things as are enacted for the benefit of the person suing."
In *Ricketts* v. *East etc. Ry. Co.*, 12 Com. B. (3 J. Scott) 160,
an act of parliament provided that the railway company
should make and maintain "fences for separating the land
taken for the use of the railway from the adjoining lands not
taken, and protecting such lands from trespass, or the cattle of
the owners or occupiers from straying thereout by reason of the
railway," and the cattle of Ricketts crossed from his own close
into a close adjoining the railroad, and thence, through some
defect of the fence, to the railroad, and were there killed.
The court held that the company [196] owed no duty to
Ricketts to maintain the fence, and that Ricketts had no
right to recover for the loss of the cattle. It was there said:
"The act of parliament creates no general duty, but only a
duty as between the company and the owners of the adjoining lands, and those in privity with them, and a stranger, as
this plaintiff is, cannot found an action upon an alleged
breach of that duty."

The contention of appellee in this case, that only such
persons as are intended to be benefited or protected by a statute can rely on a violation of that statute as giving a cause
of action, is the established doctrine of the law. That such
is the rule is shown by the decisions of the courts in *Ricketts*
v. *East etc. R. R. Co.*, 12 Com. B. 160; *O'Donnell* v. *Providence
etc. R. R. Co.*, 6 R. I. 211; *Harty* v. *Central R. R. Co.*, 42 N. Y.
468; *Holmes* v. *Central R. R. & B. Co.*, 37 Ga. 593; *Bell* v.
Hannibal etc. R. R. Co., 72 Mo. 50; *Railroad Co.* v. *Feathers*,
10 Lea, 103, and numerous other cases.

Our conclusions in the case at bar are, that appellant was
not, at the time of the accident, within the class or classes of
persons for whose protection ordinance 1074 was passed, and
that he has no right of action against appellee, either at com-

mon law or by virtue of any of the ordinances that were introduced in evidence. Since appellee owed no duty to appellant,
and was under no obligation to him either to keep his buildings and premises in a safe condition, or construct and maintain his hoist or elevator in such manner as that it could be
safely used, it follows that it was not error for the trial court
to instruct and direct the jury to return a verdict in favor of
appellee.

The judgment of the appellate court, in affirmance of the
judgment of the superior court is affirmed.

NEGLIGENCE—WHAT IS ACTIONABLE.—Negligence is the failure to discharge the duty of taking ordinary care, to the injury of one to whom the
duty is due, such failure being the proximate cause of the injury: *Gunn v.
Ohio etc. R. R. Co.*, 36 W. Va. 165; 32 Am. St. Rep. 842, and note; *Montgomery v. Muskegon Booming Co.*, 88 Mich. 633; 26 Am. St. Rep. 308, and
note; *Roddy v. Missouri Pac. Ry. Co.*, 104 Mo. 234; 24 Am. St. Rep. 333,
and note.

REAL PROPERTY—DUTY OF OWNER TO MERE LICENSEE.—This question is
thoroughly discussed in *Plummer v. Dill*, 156 Mass. 426; 32 Am. St. Rep.
463, and the extended note attached thereto.

NEGLIGENCE—BREACH OF CITY ORDINANCE: See the extended note to
Gilson v. Delaware etc. Canal Co., 65 Vt. 213, *post*, 802, and *Clements v. Louisiana Electric Light Co.*, 44 La. Ann. 692; 32 Am. St. Rep. 348, and note with
the cases collected.

NEGLIGENCE—REMEDY UNDER STATUTE—TO WHOM AVAILABLE.—The
right of action for wrongfully or negligently causing the death of a person
is purely statutory, and the action can be maintained only in the name of
the person in whom the right of action is vested by the statutes of the state
where the injuries resulting in death are inflicted: *Usher v. West Jersey R. R.
Co.*, 126 Pa. St. 206; 12 Am. St. Rep. 863, and note; *Oates v. Union Pac. Ry.
Co.*, 104 Mo. 514; 24 Am. St. Rep. 348.

AMERICAN LIVE STOCK COMMISSION COMPANY *v.* CHICAGO LIVE STOCK EXCHANGE.

[143 ILLINOIS, 210.]

CORPORATIONS—RIGHT TO BE ADMITTED TO MEMBERSHIP.—If the by-laws
of a corporation, not for pecuniary profit, provide for admission to
membership on the written application of an applicant indorsed by two
members, approved by seven votes by the board of directors, and upon
payment of an initiation fee, or on presentation of a certificate of unimpaired or unforfeited membership, duly transferred, and by signing
an agreement to abide by the rules, regulations, by-laws, and amendments thereto of the association, the ownership of such certificate does
not constitute the holder a member nor entitle him to any rights as such,
and the only way in which he can avail himself of such certificate is, by

tendering it in lieu of the prescribed initiation fee in case he is admitted to membership, or in case his application is rejected, then by selling it for a consideration to some person who may desire to become a member.

CORPORATIONS—RIGHT TO REGULATE ADMISSION TO MEMBERSHIP.—A corporation, not for pecuniary profit, has a right to adopt rules prescribing the only mode in which membership therein can be maintained; and no one can justly claim to be a member who has not been admitted in the mode thus prescribed, nor has a court of equity any power to compel the corporation to issue a certificate of membership to an applicant who has not complied with such prescribed mode.

CORPORATIONS—STRANGER CANNOT COMPLAIN OF RULES GOVERNING MEMBERSHIP.—A person who is not a member of a corporation, nor entitled, either directly or indirectly, to any of the rights arising from membership therein, cannot complain of any of the rules adopted by it for the government of the conduct of its members, or invoke the aid of a court of equity to restrain their enforcement.

CORPORATIONS—BY-LAWS RELATING TO MEMBERSHIP—RIGHT OF STRANGER TO COMPLAIN OF.—A voluntary association, whether incorporated or not, has, within certain well-defined limits, power to make and enforce by-laws for the government of its members, and such by-laws are ordinarily matters between the association and its members alone, with which strangers have no concern. If it passes by-laws, which are unreasonable, or contrary to law or public policy, and attempts to enforce them against a dissenting or unwilling minority, the latter may, in proper cases, appeal to the courts for relief against their enforcement, but strangers have no right to interfere, as they do not apply to, nor bind, them.

CORPORATIONS—BY-LAWS IN RESTRAINT OF TRADE.—Although the by-laws of a corporation are in restraint of trade, and against public policy in prohibiting its members from dealing with certain other corporations, yet such by-laws are illegal only in the sense that the courts will not enforce them. They are merely void, and the members of the corporation are entitled to protection against such disciplinary consequences as the corporation imposes for disobedience; but such protection cannot be invoked in their behalf by a stranger, nor can they be required to disobey such by-laws except at their own volition.

CONTRACTS IN RESTRAINT OF TRADE—PERFORMANCE OF.—A party to a contract in restraint of trade is not bound to perform it, but he may perform it if he desires, and his doing so exposes him to no legal animadversion.

MARKETS—POWER OF COURTS TO DECLARE THEM TO BE PUBLIC.—If a market has not been established by municipal authority or by virtue of a market franchise by the state such market cannot be deemed merely because of the magnitude of the business carried on therein, to be impressed with a public use, so as to be held by the courts to be a public market in that sense, and subject to the rules of a public policy peculiar to that class of markets.

PRACTICE—DISMISSAL OF BILL ON MOTION TO DISSOLVE INJUNCTION.—When a bill in chancery is in effect a prayer for an injunction only, a motion to dissolve the injunction has the same effect as a demurrer to the bill, and the court on sustaining such motion may properly dismiss the bill.

BILL in chancery by the plaintiff corporation against the defendant corporation, and one H. D. Rogers, for an injunction restraining Rogers from using or disposing of a certificate of membership in the defendant corporation, and to restrain the latter from issuing any certificate in lieu thereof to anyone other than the plaintiff or its authorized manager, and praying that certain rules, by-laws and amendments thereto of the defendant corporation be declared null and void, that it be enjoined from notifying its members not to purchase livestock in the general market or elsewhere from the plaintiff, and that the defendant corporation be restrained from endeavoring to prevent the plaintiff and its agents from selling livestock on the market of the Union Stock Yards, and from endeavoring to maintain an action against the plaintiff for a violation of the rules or by-laws of the defendant corporation; that said injunction be made perpetual, that said Rogers be required to surrender such certificate, that the defendant corporation be required to issue said certificate to the plaintiff, that it be permitted to enjoy its privileges free from any unjust, unreasonable, or illegal restraint, and also a prayer for general relief. A preliminary injunction having been granted, the defendant corporation demurred to the bill, and the demurrer being overruled, it answered and filed a motion to dissolve the injunction. This motion being heard on bill, answer and affidavits was sustained and after hearing the evidence the court awarded the defendant corporation damages and also entered a decree dismissing the bill at plaintiff's costs for want of equity. The plaintiff appealed.

William Brown, for the appellant.

Miller, Starr, and Leman, for the appellee.

[225] BAILEY, C. J. This case so far as it relates to defendant Rogers, having been disposed of in the complainant's favor by a decree from which no appeal has been taken and of which no complaint is made, the only questions now presented are those which relate to the equities which the complainant is seeking to enforce as against the Chicago Live Stock Exchange. Said Live Stock Exchange is a corporation, not for pecuniary profit, organized March 13, 1884, under the laws of this state, the objects for which it was organized, as declared by its articles of incorporation, being: "To establish and maintain a commercial exchange; [226] to promote uniformity in the customs and usages of our merchants; to provide for the speedy adjustment of all disputes between its members; to facilitate the receiving of livestock, as well as provide for

good management and the inspection thereof, thereby guarding against the sale or use of unsound or unhealthy meats; to secure to members a corporation in furtherance of their legitimate purposes." Said corporation has no capital stock, and is itself engaged in no commercial business, but limits its corporate enterprise to furnishing to its members facilities for carrying on, each for himself, the business of buying, selling, and dealing in livestock, meats, and other like commodities, and to adopting and enforcing by-laws, rules, and regulations by which the business of its members shall be conducted and governed.

The location of the Exchange, and the place where its members carry on their business of dealing in livestock under and in subordination to its rules, is the Union Stockyards, Chicago. The Union Stockyards and Transit Company, to which the stockyards belong, is also a private corporation, not itself engaged in the business of buying, selling, or dealing in livestock, but merely owning and furnishing very extensive stockyards, to which livestock is shipped in great quantities from all parts of the West for sale, and where buyers and sellers of livestock, acting either for themselves or as the representatives of others, resort for the purpose of carrying on their business. The Union Stockyards have thus become the place to which nearly all the livestock shipped to Chicago for sale is consigned, and where, as it is said, more livestock is annually bought and sold than in any other market in the world.

No corporate relation exists between the Stockyards and Transit Company and the Chicago Livestock Exchange, the latter corporation being formed merely by an association of commission merchants engaged in selling livestock for others on commission, and parties engaged in the business of buying livestock for themselves, in said market. The evidence shows [227] that the commission merchants and buyers representing much the largest portion of the buisness done at said market are members of the Exchange, though many parties, both sellers and buyers, are not members.

The case sought to be made by the complainant is presented under two aspects: 1. It is claimed that, either by itself or through its general manager, the complainant is, or is entitled to be, admitted a member of the Exchange, and it accordingly prays for an injunction restraining the Exchange from taking any steps to try the complainant for a violation

of its rules, or to impose upon the complainant's privileges as
a member any illegal or unreasonable restraints, and it also
prays that the certificate of membership in Rogers' hands be
issued to the complainant; and 2. It claims that if it is not
a member and entitled to the privileges of membership, the
exchange should be restrained from putting in force certain
rules it has adopted for the government of its own members,
and particularly its amendments to rules 8 and 9.

We are unable to see upon what principle it can be justly
claimed that the complainant is a member of the Exchange
or entitled to the privileges of membership, or that it is in a
position where it can insist upon being admitted to membership as a matter of right. Whatever may have been its rights
while Rogers, its manager, was a member, those rights no
longer exist, as, by its own admission, Rogers is no longer its
manager, and is no longer a member of the Exchange. Nor
can there be any just pretense that the complainant itself is
a member or has ever applied for membership. The Exchange
is a corporation having rules or by-laws determining the qualifications for membership, and prescribing the mode in which
members may be admitted, and there is no pretense that the
complainant has ever brought itself within the terms of said
rules or by-laws so as to be entitled to membership. Rule 8
of the Exchange provides as follows:

[228] "On and after May 1, 1884, any person of good character and credit, and of legal age, whose interests are centered
at the Union Stock Yards, on presenting a written application
indorsed by two members, and stating the name and business
avocation of the applicant, after ten days' notice of such application shall have been posted on the bulletin of the Exchange, may be admitted to membership in the association,
upon approval by at least seven affirmative ballot votes of the
board of directors, and upon payment of an initiation fee of
five hundred dollars, or on presentation of a certificate of
unimpaired or unforfeited membership, duly transferred, and
by signing an agreement to abide by the rules, regulations,
and by-laws of the association, and all amendments that may
in due form be made thereto."

Said association had an undoubted right to adopt this rule,
and as it prescribes the mode and the only mode in which
membership in the Exchange can be obtained, no one can
justly claim to be a member who has not been admitted in
the mode thus prescribed.

It may well be questioned whether, under this rule, a corporation, in its corporate character, can be admitted to membership in the Exchange, as said rule seems to contemplate only the admission of natural persons. But even if that were otherwise, there is no pretense that the complainant itself has ever made application for membership, or that any of the subsequent steps necessary to vest an applicant with the character and rights of membership have been taken, or that they have resulted favorably to the complainant. Nor is it pretended that since Rogers ceased to be the complainant's manager, and thereby ceased to be its representative on the Exchange, any formal application for membership has been made by Titus, its general manager, or by any other person in its behalf, but the evidence, on the other hand, is clear and undisputed that no such application has been made. The fact alleged in the bill, if it be a fact, that the complainant 229 has requested the Exchange to issue the certificate of membership formerly held by Rogers to Titus avails the complainant nothing, as the Exchange is under no obligation to admit a member upon such request, but can, in conformity with its rules, admit to membership only upon formal application duly presented and approved in the manner in said rules prescribed. The equitable or even legal ownership of the unimpaired or unforfeited certificate of membership formerly issued to Rogers and duly transferred to it does not constitute it a member or entitle it to any rights as such. The only way in which the complainant can avail itself of such certificate is by tendering it in lieu of the prescribed initiation fee in case the complainant or its representative, on proper application, shall be admitted to membership, or in case such application should not be granted, then by selling it for a consideration to some other person who may desire to become a member.

It may also be noticed, in immediate connection with the point now under consideration, that a court of chancery has no power to order the Exchange to issue the certificate of membership formerly held by Rogers to the complainant or its general manager, so as to constitute it or him a member. Before an applicant can become a member, his application must, among other things, be indorsed by two members and must receive the approval of at least seven members of the board of directors, voting by ballot. Members and directors of such corporations, in acting upon applications for member-

ship, are necessarily entitled to a freedom which is not subject to judicial compulsion. No two members can be compelled
to indorse an application, nor can any seven members of the
board of directors be compelled to vote in its favor, but both
are entitled to act upon their own judgment and according to
their own choice. In other words, a court of chancery will
not undertake to force upon a corporation of this character, a
member, against the will of those whose duty it is to pass
upon applications for membership.

230 The complainant then not being a member of said Exchange, nor entitled, either directly or indirectly, to any of
the rights arising from membership therein, the question is
presented whether it can complain of any of the rules adopted
by the Exchange for the government of the conduct of its own
members, or invoke the aid of a court of equity to restrain
their enforcement.

The complainant is a joint-stock corporation, organized
May 3, 1889, under the laws of this state, with a capital stock
of one hundred thousand dollars, divided into shares of one
hundred dollars each, the shareholders consisting principally
if not exclusively of persons and firms engaged in the business of shipping livestock to the Union Stock Yards at
Chicago for sale. The principal office of said corporation is
located at the stockyards, and the objects for which said
corporation was formed, as declared by its articles of incorporation, are as follows:

" To engage in the business of buying, selling, and handling
livestock upon commission at the Union Stock Yards, state
of Illinois, and at such other points throughout the United
States as may be deemed advisable, and also to encourage the
stockholders of said corporation to raise, improve, feed, and
ship to market, livestock; and in order to better effectuate
said latter object, it is hereby expressly stipulated and agreed
by and between the parties hereto, that the net earnings of
said corporation shall be distributed among the stockholders
thereof annually in the following manner, to wit: Sixty-five
per cent of said net earnings shall be distributed to said stockholders in the ratio of the number of stock shipped by each
stockholder to the said corporation for sale during the current
year for which said dividend shall be declared, and the remaining thirty-five per cent of said net earnings shall be distributed to the shareholders in said corporation in the ratio of
the amount owned by each shareholder in said corporation.

It is hereby further expressly agreed and stipulated that :
one person shall have the right to subscribe for or own mc
231 than twenty-five shares of stock in said corporation
any time during the existence of said proposed corporation

Said corporation, on being organized, appointed Rogers
its manager, and he applied for admission as a member
the Exchange, and was admitted a member thereof, l
initiation fee being paid by the presentation of an outstan
ing certificate of membership which had been purchased wi
the money of the complainant. The evidence shows, a
upon this point there seems to be no dispute, that wh
Rogers applied for membership, no disclosure was made l
him as to the plan upon which the complainant corporati
was organized, and particularly the obligation which it a
sumed by its articles of incorporation, to distribute annual
among its shareholders sixty-five per cent of its net earning
in the proportion of the number of livestock shipped by ea
to said corporation for sale. Rogers was admitted to mei
bership upon investigation by the Exchange of his own pe
sonal character and credit, and in ignorance of this peculi
feature of the scheme upon which the corporation represent
by him was organized.

The complainant thereupon embarked in the business
receiving consignments of livestock, both from its shareholde
and others, and in selling the same on commission at t
stockyards, the rates of commission charged by it in all ca
being in conformity to the schedule of rates established
the Exchange. Said business was managed by Rogers, w
being a member of the Exchange, was enabled to avail hi
self, in the management of said business, of all the privile
which such membership afforded.

In November, 1889, the complainant having realized a c
siderable sum of money as the net profits of its business
to that time, distributed such net profits to its sharehold
as required by its articles of incorporation, and the Excha
being informed of such distribution, and regarding it as a
tual evasion of its rules establishing minimum rates of c
missions, instituted proceedings against the complainant a
232 its manager for a violation of its rules. Rogers set up
defense of these charges, in substance, that the complain
was not a member of the Exchange nor subject to its ju
diction; that so far as his action as a member of the Excha
was concerned, he had strictly conformed to said rules

charging and collecting the rates of commissions thereby established, and having collected them, he had accounted for and paid the same over to his principal, the complainant, as it was his legal duty to do, and that he had no responsibility for the disposition which the complainant had subsequently seen fit to make of the same. These suggestions seem to have been acquiesced in by the Exchange, as the proceedings against both the complainant and its manager appear to have been thereupon abandoned.

The Exchange, however, for the purpose, as may well be presumed, of protecting itself against similiar evasions of its rules in the future, amended its eighth rule so as to provide, in substance, that no person should be received for membership in the Exchange, who, in any manner acts for or represents any other livestock corporation whose charter, regulations, rules, or by-laws provide for discrimination in rates or charges for commissions between stockholders and other patrons or customers, whether under the guise of dividends, drawbacks, or any other scheme or device whatever, and that no member of the Exchange should act, as agent or otherwise, for any livestock corporation, whose charter, regulations, rules, or by-laws provide for such discrimination, and subjecting a member thus offending to suspension or expulsion. At the same time rule 9 was so amended as to prohibit all members of the Exchange. from buying any livestock, or causing the same to be bought, at the stockyards from any corporation or livestock company which is or may be regularly selling livestock for nonresidents on commission, unless some one or more of the stockholders of such company are members of the Exchange in good standing.

[233] It must be admitted that these amended rules, if enforced by the Exchange and obeyed by its members, will have the effect of debarring the complainant, so long as it adheres to its present policy of distributing its net earnings among its shareholders, from becoming, either by itself or its officer or agent, a member of the Exchange, or entitled to the privileges of membership, and also that the members of the Exchange will refuse to purchase of it or its agents any of the livestock consigned to it for sale at said stockyards. The question then is, whether these facts are sufficient to entitle the complainant to a decree declaring the invalidity or illegality of these rules, and to an injunction restraining their enforcement.

A voluntary association, whether incorporated or not, has, within certain well-defined limits, power to make and enforce by-laws for the government of its members. Such by-laws are ordinarily matters between the association and its members alone, and with which strangers have no concern. If the association, or a majority of its members, pass by-laws which are unreasonable, or contrary to law or public policy, and attempt to enforce them as against a dissenting or unwilling minority, such minority may undoubtedly, in proper cases, appeal to the courts for relief against their enforcement. But mere strangers have ordinarily no right to interfere. As to them, such by-laws are matters of no concern. They do not apply to, and are not binding upon, them.

In the present case, no member of the Exchange is making any complaint of these by-laws, nor is there any suggestion, either in the pleadings or proofs, that these by-laws have been passed, or are likely to be enforced, against the objection of a minority of the members, or against the objection of any one member, of the Exchange. So far then as this proceeding is concerned, it must be assumed that they were adopted with the assent and concurrence of all the members, and are therefore satisfactory to all alike. They are therefore [234] to be regarded as analogous to or in the nature of a unanimous compact or agreement among the members of the Exchange, not to buy livestock of corporations engaged in selling the same on commission, unless one or more of the shareholders thereof are members of the Exchange, and excluding from membership the representatives of the complainant, so long as it persists in its present policy of practically cutting rates of commissions by distributing back a portion of its net earnings to shippers. Or, more specifically stated, said by-laws may be viewed as in the nature of a unanimous compact among the members of the Exchange not to deal with the complainant or its agents, so long as it persists in its said policy.

Two questions arise: 1. Whether such compact or agreement is illegal or contrary to public policy; and, 2. If it is so, whether a court of equity will interpose in behalf of the complainant and set it aside and enjoin its performance. Admitting the right of the complainant to embark in and prosecute the business for which it was organized freely and without improper obstruction, it does not follow that it has a right to deal with parties who are unwilling to so deal, or to

compel those who do not choose to do so to purchase its property. Absolute freedom of commercial intercourse to which
a party may be entitled is not interfered with by the refusal
of another to deal with such party on any terms. The refusal
of any or all of the members of the Exchange to purchase
livestock of the complainant is merely an exercise of their
clear legal prerogative, and if they have a right to so refuse,
it is difficult to see how an agreement, as between themselves,
to abstain from dealing with the complainant, is a matter in
respect to which the complainant is entitled to any species of
equitable relief.

  If it be admitted that said by-laws are so far in restraint
of trade as to be invalid for that reason, we are unable to see
that the position of the complainant is in any respect improved. [235] By-laws or contracts in restraint of trade are
illegal only in the sense that the law will not enforce them.
They are simply void. The law does not prohibit the making
of contracts in restraint of trade; it merely declines, after they
have been made, to recognize their validity: *Mogul Steamboat
Co.* v. *McGregor*, L. R. 23 Q. B. D. 598, 619.

  A party to such contract is not bound to perform it, but he
may perform it if he sees fit, and his doing so exposes him to
no legal animadversion. If the by-laws in question are invalid because of being in improper restraint of trade, they are
merely void, and the members of the Exchange, being under
no obligation to obey them, may perhaps be entitled, at their
own instance, to protection against such disciplinary consequences as the Exchange may see fit to impose in case of disobedience. But such protection cannot be invoked in their
behalf by a stranger, nor can they be required to disobey
such rules except at their own volition. There is no suggestion in the record that they are seeking to disobey said rules,
or desire to do so. The evidence fails to show that the Exchange is taking or contemplates taking any steps for the
enforcement of said rules, or that it will have any occasion so
to do. These rules having been adopted, presumably, with
the approval of the members of the Exchange, there is no reason to suppose that they will not be voluntarily obeyed, and
such voluntary obedience is a matter which the courts have
no power to restrain.

  But the position is taken upon behalf of the complainant
and most strenuously insisted upon, that the livestock market at the Union Stockyards, by reason of its magnitude and

its far-reaching influence upon the commerce of the country,
has become a public market, and therefore impressed with a
public use, and that not only said market, but all those doing
business therein, are brought within the influence of those
rules of public policy which apply to and govern public employments, and which it is the business of the courts to administer and [236] enforce.   After giving this contention our
patient consideration, we are unable to yield to it our assent.
The market itself is established and owned by the Union
Stockyards and Transit Company, a private corporation, not
itself engaged in the business of buying and selling livestock,
but which provides the ground, and has established very extensive stockyards, to which livestock shipped to Chicago for sale
may be consigned, and where buyers and sellers may meet,
either in person or by their agents, and transact the business
of buying and selling such livestock.   The bill alleges, and
the truth of the allegation is not questioned, that the amount
of business annually transacted at said stockyards is such as
to constitute the market thus established the largest livestock
market in the world.

If it be admitted that the magnitude of the business transacted at said market and its influence upon the general commerce of the country are of themselves sufficient to constitute
the stockyards a public market, so as to impress upon it a
public use, it would probably follow that certain public duties
and obligations would thereby be imposed upon the Stockyards Company.   It would doubtless be held bound to keep
its market open alike to all who might desire to do business
therein, and perhaps to make no discrimination between individuals.   But it does not follow that the dealers resorting
to said market for purposes of trade would be subjected to
similar rules of public policy.   They would deal with each
other merely upon the footing of private parties, owing each
other no duties except those which the rules of honesty and
fair dealings impose.   Each would be at liberty to deal or
decline to deal with others precisely as he might see fit.   The
rules of trade would be no different from what they are in
other markets, whether public or private.

Nor can it be seen how combinations between merchants
doing business in such public market, either with a view of
increasing or diminishing competition, or of enhancing or
[237]diminishing prices, would be subjected to any rules different from those which apply to such combinations wherever

made. As individual merchants, they would be subjected,
in their dealings with each other, to no peculiar rules of public policy growing out of the fact that such dealings were in a
public market, and an agreement among any number of them
not to deal with a particular person or class of persons would
not of itself subject them to such rules, but they would be
amenable only to those general rules of law applicable to that
sort of agreements.

But we are not prepared to hold that the mere fact that
the business of a particular market has become very large
gives to the courts any power to declare such markets public
and impressed with a public use, or to apply to them any rules
of public policy peculiar to that class of markets.

It may well be doubted whether the term "public market,"
in the sense in which it is sought to be used here, is one
which is known to our law. Markets overt, such as exist in
England, are unknown here, nor is it usual in this country
to grant to private parties the franchise or liberty of keeping
or holding a fair or market, as is done in England: 2 Blackstone's Commentaries, 37. Our statute in relation to the incorporation of cities and villages authorizes the legislative
authorities of such municipal corporations to establish markets and market-houses, and to provide for the regulation
and use thereof: 1 Starr and Curtis' Statutes, 469. And it
has been held that the power given to a municipal corporation to establish and regulate markets includes power to purchase a site, erect buildings, and provide rules for governing
the same: *Caldwell* v. *City of Alton*, 33 Ill. 416; 85 Am. Dec.
282. But we are not aware that any class of markets in this
country not established by municipal authority, or by virtue
of a market franchise granted by the state, has been held,
merely because of the magnitude of the business carried on
therein, to be impressed with a public use, so as to be held
by the courts to be public markets in that sense.

238 It is not claimed that the keeping or doing business in
a market of this character is one of the employments which
the common law declares to be public, nor is it pretended
that it has been made so by statute. Ordinarily the adoption of new rules of public policy, or the application of existing rules to new subjects, is for the legislature and not for the
courts. Accordingly it may be held to be a general, though
perhaps not an invariable, rule, that the question whether a
particular business which has hitherto been deemed to be

private is public and impressed with a public use is for the
legislature. The doctrine on this subject is stated in *Ladd* v.
Southern Cotton Press Mfg. Co., 53 Tex. 172, where a question
very similar to the one under discussion was before the court,
as follows: "We know of no authority, and none has been
shown us, for saying that a business strictly *juris privati* will
become *juris publici*, merely by reason of its extent. If the
magnitude of a particular business is such, and the persons
affected by it are so numerous, that the interests of society
demand that the rules and principles applicable to public
employments should be applied to it, this would have to be
done by the legislature (if not restrained from doing so by
the constitution) before a demand for such use could be enforced by the courts." The view thus expressed would seem
to be precisely applicable to the present case, and we are inclined to adopt it as a correct statement of the law as it
should be applied to the facts before us. We do not say that
there may not be exceptions to the rule thus stated, but if
there are they are not of such character as to be material
here.

Apart from the consideration that the extension and application of even existing rules of law to subjects not heretofore
within their purview is legislative in its nature, the determination by the courts as to the precise point at which a mere
private business reaches that stage of growth and expansion
which is sufficient to render it *juris publici*, would be sur-
rounded with very great difficulties, and would present questions [239] for which the courts, unaided by legislation, would
be able to find no just or satisfactory criterion or test. But
when the legislature, acting upon a competent state of facts,
has interposed and declared the business to be *juris publici*,
all difficulty is removed.

The views here expressed do not conflict with what was decided in *Munn* v. *Illinois*, 94 U. S. 113. The question raised
and decided in that case was as to the constitutionality of the
act of the legislature of this state, declaring certain grain elevators to be public warehouses, and prescribing rules for their
management, and fixing maximum charges for the storage
and handling of grain. There the legislative department had
interposed and declared the public use, and the court, in holding the act constitutional, held merely that the legislative
power had been properly exercised. This was the only question, having any relevancy here, presented in that case or

which the court undertook to decide, and the discussion of the evidence showing that the business carried on in said grain elevators was of such character that it had in fact become impressed with a public use, was only for the purpose of showing that a condition of things existed which justified the legislature in passing the statute then under consideration.

The case of *Stock Exchange v. Board of Trade*, 127 Ill. 153, 11 Am. St. Rep. 107, is clearly distinguishable from the one now before us. There the board of trade had for a series of years, voluntarily engaged in the business of compiling market quotations, showing the fluctuations of the prices of commodities bought and sold on the board, and of furnishing the same, for a consideration, by telegraph, to all members of the public who desired to obtain them. By this means, the business of buying and selling agricultural products throughout the entire country had been brought under the control of the market prices fixed and determined on said board. It was held that these quotations were property, and that the board, by its own act, had so far impressed upon them a public interest, that it should [240] be required, so long as it compiled and furnished them to anyone, to furnish them to all without discrimination. This conclusion was reached upon the theory that the board had, for a series of years, voluntarily and intentionally, devoted its property to a use in which the public had an interest, and had, in effect, granted to the public an interest in that use, and that it must therefore, so far as it dealt in that species of property at all, submit to be controlled by the public for the common good, to the extent of the interest it had thus created.

The determining elements present in that case are wanting here. The business which is here sought to be subjected to a public use was, at its commencement, confessedly private and private only, and the public use is sought to be impressed upon it, not by virtue of any voluntary grant to the public, but simply because, by mere process of growth and expansion, the business has reached such magnitude as to affect public interests because of its magnitude alone. These facts would doubtless be sufficient to warrant the legislature, in the exercise of its legislative discretion, in declaring a public use, and placing said business under legal control and supervision, but such power, in our opinion, does not rest with the courts.

The point is made that it was error for the court on sustaining the defendant's motion to dissolve the injunction, to also enter a decree dismissing the bill for want of equity, the contention being, that the bill should have been retained for final hearing on pleadings and proofs, according to the usual practice in chancery. We are of the opinion that the bill was properly dismissed. It was, in substance, at least as against the Exchange, a bill for an injunction only. Its prayer, as against Rogers, having been granted by a prior decree, that portion of the relief sought is not to be considered, and as against the Exchange, nothing is prayed for but an injunction, except that the Exchange be required to issue the certificate of membership formerly held by Rogers to the complainant. Under no possible view of the case, even if the bill had been [241] retained for a further hearing, could this latter relief have been granted. The dissolution of the injunction was, in effect, a disposition of the entire case. Besides the bill, upon its face, as we think sufficiently appears from what has been said, is without merit, and when that is the case, a motion to dissolve an injunction, the bill being in effect for an injunction only, has the same effect as a demurrer to the bill, and the court, on sustaining such motion, may properly dismiss the bill: *Titus* v. *Mabee*, 25 Ill. 257; *Weaver* v. *Poyer*, 70 Ill. 567; *Prout* v. *Lomer*, 79 Ill. 331.

What we have said renders it unnecessary for us to consider the effect upon the *status* of the complainant of the fact, about which there seems to be no dispute, of its failure to record its certificate of incorporation, until after the commencement of the present suit.

It is contended that the decree in favor of the defendant corporation awarding damages on dissolution of the injunction is not sustained by the evidence, and is therefore erroneous. We have duly considered the evidence, applicable to that question, and are of the opinion that it supports the decree. The only damages proved are for solicitors' and counsel fees incurred in obtaining a dissolution of the injunction. It appears to us to be a fair conclusion from all the evidence that the sum awarded, viz., twelve hundred and fifty dollars, is no more than is fairly chargeable for the services rendered by solicitors and counsel in the mere matter of obtaining a dissolution of the injunction.

We find no material error in the record, and the judgment of the appellate court will be affirmed.

MAGRUDER, J. I do not concur in this decision.

VOLUNTARY ASSOCIATIONS—RIGHT TO BE ADMITTED TO MEMBERSHIP — Membership in a voluntary association of individuals, organized without charter, but regulated as to their action by a constitution and by-laws, is a privilege, which may be accorded or withheld, and is not a right which can be gained independently and then enforced: *McKane* v. *Adams*, 123 N. Y. 609; 20 Am. St. Rep. 785. The decisions of voluntary societies in admitting members, suspending, disciplining and expelling them will not be interfered with by the courts except to see that the proceeding was according to the rules of the society, in good faith, and not in violation of the law of the land: *Connelly* v. *Masonic etc. Benefit Assn.*, 58 Conn. 552; 18 Am. St. Rep. 296, and extended note. See the extended notes to *Otto* v. *Journeyman Tailors' etc. Union*, 7 Am. St. Rep. 162, and *Hiss* v. *Bartlett*, 63 Am. Dec. 776.

BY-LAWS OF VOLUNTARY ASSOCIATIONS IN RESTRAINT OF TRADE, if not unreasonable, are not void, and may be enforced: *Mathews* v. *Associated Press*, 136 N. Y. 333; 32 Am. St. Rep. 741, and note.

MARKETS.—The establishment and regulation of, will be found thoroughly discussed in the extended notes to the following cases: *Jacksonville* v. *Ledwith*, 23 Am. St. Rep. 581; *Henkel* v. *Detroit*, 43 Am. Rep. 473; *Ex parte Canto*, 57 Am. Rep. 611, and *Caldwell* v. *City of Alton*, 85 Am. Dec. 286.

ELMORE *v.* JOHNSON.

[143 ILLINOIS, 513.]

ATTORNEY AND CLIENT—TRANSACTIONS BETWEEN, HOW REGARDED.—In view of the confidential relations existing between attorney and client, transactions between them are often declared to be voidable which would be deemed to be unobjectionable between other parties.

ATTORNEY AND CLIENT—CONTRACTS BETWEEN AS TO FEES.—Before an attorney undertakes the business of a client he may contract with reference to compensation for his services, as no confidential relation then exists and the parties deal with each other at arm's length. The same rule applies with regard to dealings between them after the relation of attorney and client has been dissolved.

ATTORNEY AND CLIENT—RIGHT TO RECOVER COMPENSATION.—When the amount of compensation is not fixed by any contract under which an attorney is employed, he is entitled to recover such reasonable fee under an implied contract as his services are worth, or as has been usually paid to others for similar services.

ATTORNEY AND CLIENT—CONTRACTS BETWEEN, WHEN VOIDABLE.—If the title to property is so involved in litigation that the value of the property depends upon the decision as to such title, a contract between attorney and client made during the pendency of the litigation to compensate the attorney for his legal services with part of the property involved, is voidable at the election of the client, irrespective of the fairness or unfairness of the contract, provided such election is exercised within a reasonable time.

ATTORNEY AND CLIENT—PURCHASE BY ATTORNEY—PRESUMPTION—BURDEN OF PROOF.—In case of a purchase of all or a part of the subject matter in litigation during the pendency of the suit by an attorney from

his client, the transaction is presumably fraudulent, and the burden is
on the attorney to show affirmatively the most perfect good faith,
the absence of undue influence, a fair price, knowledge, intention,
and freedom of action by the client, and also that he gave him full information and disinterested advice.

SALES OF REAL ESTATE—EVIDENCE OF VALUE.—Actual sales of property in
the vicinity and near the time are competent, and the most satisfactory,
evidence of value as far as they go, yet, they are only one of the modes
of proving value, and not the only mode. Sales made in one year are
not an exact criterion of values in the same vicinity five years later.

ATTORNEY AND CLIENT—CONTRACT AND DEED BETWEEN—WHEN MAY BE
AVOIDED.—A contract for compensation between attorney and client
and a deed made in pursuance thereof, executed during the existence or
the relation of attorney and client securing a larger compensation to
the former for his legal services than those services are really worth,
may be set aside by the client by a suit commenced within a reasonable
time. What is such reasonable time is to be determined by the court
under all the circumstances of the case.

ATTORNEY AND CLIENT—VOIDABLE CONVEYANCE BETWEEN—LACHES.—In
case of a voidable conveyance of land between attorney and client, the
latter who is entitled to set the transaction aside, cannot be charged
with delay, or with acquiescence, or confirmation, unless there has been
full knowledge on his part of all the facts, and perfect freedom of action. Acts which might appear to be acts of acquiescence, are not
deemed to be such if the client is ignorant of the circumstances, or
under the control of the original influence, or otherwise so situated as
not to be free to enforce his rights.

ATTORNEY AND CLIENT—LACHES IN AVOIDING DEED BETWEEN.—When a
client, during the pendency of his suit, conveys to his attorney part of
the property in litigation as payment for his legal services, with full
knowledge that the part conveyed is of greater value than such services, a delay of seven years before seeking to set the deed aside, during all of which time both parties treated the land as belonging to the
attorney, is such laches on the part of the client as will bar his right of
action.

BILL in chancery to set aside a deed executed by the plaintiff to the defendant in payment of his services to her as her
attorney. The court below rendered a decree dismissing
the bill for want of equity, and the plaintiff appealed.

Alexander S. Bradley, for the appellant.

James E. Munroe, for the appellee.

523 MAGRUDER, J. Appellee testifies, that the deed made
to him by appellant, conveying to him the west half of the
lots in controversy, was executed by her in pursuance of a
previous contract, which she had made with him, in reference
to payment for his legal services. He swears, that, by the
terms of this contract, she was to pay all the costs and he
was to have a contingent fee of one-half of what should be

recovered both in the suit for alimony, and in the chancery suit in regard to the lots.

The evidence shows, that this contract was made during the pendency of the legal proceedings which the appellee was [524] conducting for the appellant. It was not entered into before, or at the time of, his original employment, which took place on February 15, 1882, nor did it exist when he · filed the bill on February 23, 1882. His answer states, that " early in the spring or summer of 1882 . . . . it was . . . . mutually agreed that this defendant should have and receive as a contingent fee for his services one-half." He testifies, that he cannot fix the date of the agreement, but that, to the best of his recollection, " it was in March, or April, possibly in May, after I discovered I had a pretty good sized job on hand, and a good deal of work to do, and had done a good deal of work. . . . . She claimed to have no money early in the proceedings, and could not pay my fees in money, and that was why I subsequently made a different arrangement with her."

Appellant swears that she never made an agreement with the appellee to give him one-half of the money, or of the land, to be recovered.

The deed to appellee was also executed while the relation of attorney and client existed between himself and the appellant. That deed was made on January 17, 1884, and he concedes that he did not cease to be appellant's solicitor until some time thereafter.

In England " it is a settled doctrine of equity that an attorney cannot, while the business is unfinished in which he has been employed, receive any gift from his client, or bind his client in any mode to make him greater compensation for his services than he would have a right to demand if no contract should be made during the relation ": Weeks on Attorneys at Law, 2d ed., sec. 364. More than fifty years ago, the English doctrine was adopted by the supreme court of Alabama in an able opinion in the case of *Lecatt* v. *Sallee*, 3 Port. 115, 29 Am. Dec. 249, where it was held, that " an agreement made by a client with his counsel after the latter has been employed in a particular business, by which the original contract is varied, [525] and greater compensation is secured to the counsel, than may have been agreed upon, when he was first retained, is invalid, and cannot be enforced."

The reason for the doctrine is to be found in the nature of

the relation, which exists between attorney and client. That relation is one of confidence, and gives the attorney great influence over the actions and interests of the client. In view of this confidential relation, transactions between attorney and client are often declared to be voidable, which would be held to be unobjectionable between other parties. The law is thus strict, "not so much on account of hardship in the particular case, as for the sake of preventing what might otherwise become a public mischief": *Lewis* **v.** *J. A.*, 4 Edw. Ch. 599. "No single circumstance has done more to debase the practice of the law in the popular estimation, and even to lower the lofty standard of professional ethics and self-respect among members of the legal profession itself in large portions of our country, than the nature of the transactions, often in the highest degree champertous, between attorney and client, which are permitted, and which have received judicial sanction. It sometimes would seem, that the fiduciary relation and the opportunity for undue influence, instead of being the grounds for invalidating such agreements, are practically regarded rather as their excuse and justification": 3 Pomeroy's Equity Jurisprudence, sec. 960, note 1. Before the attorney undertakes the business of the client, he may contract with reference to his services, because no confidential relation then exists and the parties deal with each other at arm's length. The same is true in regard to dealings which take place after the relation has been dissolved: 1 Story's Equity Jurisprudence, 13th ed., secs. 310–313. But the law watches with unusual jealousy over all transactions between the parties, which occur while the relation exists.

In the case at bar, it does not appear that any definite contract in regard to fees existed between appellant and appellee [526] prior to the spring of 1882. But inasmuch as he undertook to manage her legal interests before that time, there was an implied contract, created by operation of law, which entitled him to receive such reasonable compensation as his services might be worth: "If the amount of compensation be not fixed by the terms of the contract, by which an attorney or solicitor was employed, he would be entitled to be paid such reasonable fees, as have been usually paid to others for similar services": *Lecatt* v. *Sallee*, 3 Port. 115; 29 Am. Dec. 249.

The question then arises, what was a reasonable compensation for the services rendered by the appellee to the appellant. He has introduced no independent evidence upon this subject. His only witness is an office companion, who says, that, in his opinion, appellee's legal services were worth $30 per day, but does not claim to have full knowledge of the services rendered in the matters herein involved. Appellee is unable to state, except approximately, the time spent by him in attending to appellant's matters, but he says: "I believe that in the whole matters . . . . I spent at least forty days." Forty days' services at $30 per day would be $1,200.

We do not think, however, that the proof establishes $1,200 as the value of the services. Mr. W. I. Culver swears, that the customary and usual charge for all the work done by appellee in the divorce, attachment, and "resulting trust" cases would be $250 in money. Mr. B. F. Richolson, the attorney for Pratt, swore that appellee's services in the chancery, or "trust," suit in regard to the land were reasonably worth, from $300 to $350, and he made the following statement: "If the fee was contingent upon success, I think he would be justified in charging somewhat more; I hardly think double that, because I think the success was so reasonably assured there was not very much doubt."

What was the value of the lots, of which appellee was to have one-half? In the affidavit f'ed by appellant in the divorce proceeding on March 6, 1882, she swore that she had been [327] informed that the lots were then worth $3,000, and were encumbered for $540 only. This affidavit was drawn by appellee, and was presented to the court upon an application to set aside the agreement of settlement for $500. We cannot suppose, that the value of the lots was exaggerated, in order to induce the court to believe that Pratt was not too poor to pay more than $500. Taking $3,000 as the estimated value of the lots on March 6, 1882, then, by appellee's agreement for fees, he was to get property worth $1,500 less $270 of encumbrance, amounting to $1,230. This amount exceeded the reasonable compensation to which appellee would have been entitled under the implied contract, under which he began his services for appellee.

We have recently held in *Morrison* v. *Smith*, 130 Ill. 304, that a sale by a client to an attorney will be sustained, if it is fair and honest, and in no manner tainted with fraud, undue influence, or corruption, and that the law does not go so far as to hold such a sale voidable at the election of the client. In that case the subject matter of the purchase by the attorney from the client was a judgment obtained by the former

for the latter. The judgment debtor was insolvent except as
to his ownership of an undivided interest in land, which was
subject to a life estate. The doctrine of that case is the law
of this court as applied to such a purchase by an attorney
from a client as is there described. The litigation had reached
the point where judgment had been obtained; the judgment
was a lien upon a reversionary interest in land; its value
could therefore be easily ascertained by ascertaining the value
of the interest in the land subject to the life estate. But
there is a manifest distinction between a purchase by an attorney from a client and a contract, made during the pendency
of a litigation, for the conveyance or transfer by the client to
the attorney of a part of the property involved in the litigation as a compensation for his legal services therein. Where
a purchase is proposed the seller is always, to a certain extent, [528] put on his guard. He knows that it is for the interest of the buyer to get the property as cheaply as possible.
He has every motive to inquire into and learn the value of
the thing to be sold. But in the case of the contract above
indicated the client is at a great disadvantage. The value of
the property in litigation depends upon the result of the litigation, and, being unable to understand the legal aspects of
the case, he is unable to foresee what such result will be.
He must rely, not upon his own judgment, but upon the
judgment and statements of his attorney. Moreover he is
unable to judge as to the value of his attorney's services, because he cannot know what legal steps are necessary to be
taken in the conduct of the case. The advantage is overwhelmingly on the side of the attorney where such a contract
is made. Whatever may be the rule as to a purchase by an
attorney from a client we think that where the title to property is so involved in litigation that the value of the property
depends upon the decision as to such title a contract made
during the pendency of the litigation to compensate the attorney for his legal services with a part of the property involved therein should be held to be voidable at the election
of the client, irrespective of the fairness or unfairness of the
contract, provided such election is exercised within a reasonable time. Such a rule as this is demanded by public
policy, and in the interests of a wholesome administration
of justice. The distinction here noted is pointed out in
Berrien v. *McLane*, 1 Hoff. Ch. 421, where it is said: "A
voluntary gift made while the connection of attorney and

client subsists is absolutely void, and the property transferred
by it can only be held as security for those charges which the
attorney can legally make.   Next, ... a transfer of property made upon an ostensibly valuable consideration, such as
a lease or sale, is presumptively void; the client has the ad-
Vantage of driving the attorney to produce evidence to prove
its fairness, and to show that the price or terms were as beneficial as could have been obtained from a [529] stranger.   And
lastly, ... a transfer of a part of the property actually in
litigation, or a contract to transfer a part, is . . . . void;
illegal . . . . because of the existing relation of the parties;
. . . . such a contract will not be enforced on the application
of the attorney, and, if the client applies, will be canceled on
equitable terms.

The above passage from the Berrien case is quoted for the
purpose of showing, that a distinction is recognized between
a sale and a transfer of a part of the property in litigation in
payment of fees, or a contract to transfer the same, but we
do not go so far as to hold with the learned vice-chancellor
in that case, that such a contract or transfer is absolutely
Void, but that it is voidable at the option of the client.   The
view here expressed is supported by the following authorities:
Rogers v. *Marshall*, 3 McCrary, 76, and note to first opinion
and cases cited in note; 4 Kent's Commentaries, 12th ed., p.
449, note b; *Wallis* v. *Loubat*, 2 Denio, 607; *Lecatt* v. *Sallee*,
3 Port. 115; 29 Am. Dec. 249; *Pearson* v. *Benson*, 28 Beav.
598; *Newman* v. *Payne*, 2 Ves. Jr. 199; *Wood* v. *Downes*, 18
Ves. Jr. 120; *Lewis* v. *J. A.*, 4 Edw. Ch. 599; *Starr* v. *Vander-
heyden*, 9 Johns. 253; 6 Am. Rep. 275; *West* v. *Raymond*, 21
Ind. 305; *Simpson* v. *Lamb*, 40 Eng. L. & Eq. 59; *Hall* v.
Hallett, 1 Cox, 134; *Hawley* v. *Cramer*, 4 Cow. 717; Weeks
on Attorneys at Law, 2d ed., sec. 273; *Armstrong* v. *Huston*, 8
Ohio, 552; *Gray* v. *Emmons*, 7 Mich. 533; *Merritt* v. *Lambert*,
10 Paige, 352; *Bolton* v. *Daily*, 48 Iowa, 348; 1 Perry on
Trusts, 3d ed., sec. 202.

But even if the rule, which applies to a purchase by an attorney from his client, should be held to be applicable in the
present case, the contract and the deed made in pursuance
thereof must be subjected to a rigid test.   In case of such a
purchase, the transaction is presumptively fraudulent, and
the burden is on the attorney to show "fairness, adequacy,
and equity": *Lewis* v. *J. A.*, 4 Edw. Ch. 599.   He must
remove the presumption against the validity of the transac-

tion "by showing affirmatively the most perfect good faith, the absence of undue [530] influence, a fair price, knowledge, intention and freedom of action by the client, and also that he gave his client full information and disinterested advice": 2 Pomeroy's Equity Jurisprudence, sec. 960.

In order to sustain the deed made to appellee on January 17, 1884, it must appear that the consideration received by appellant was "adequate," and that the appellee paid "a fair price." This involves the determination of the question whether the services rendered to the appellant were worth what the property was worth on the day of the delivery of the deed. Counsel on both sides have presented this as one of the material issues in the case, and have introduced testimony to show the value of the lots in January, 1884. Of appellant's witnesses three swore that the lots were then worth $3,200; two, that they were worth $4,000; and two, that they were worth $4,800. Of appellee's witnesses two placed the value of the lots at that time at about $900, one at from $1,000 to $1,400, one at $1,200, and one at from $1,950 to $2,400.

It is claimed by counsel for appellee, that the valuations of his witnesses are based upon actual sales, while the valuations proven by appellant are matters of opinion formed from a general knowledge of values. It has been well said, that "there is no more important factor in determining the-value of particular property than the sales of similar property in the same neighborhood at about the time in question": Lewis on Eminent Domain, sec. 443. We have held, that "actual sales of property, in the vicinity and near the time, are competent evidence, as far as they go": *Culbertson etc. Provision Co. v. City of Chicago.* 111 Ill. 651. But, while such sales may be the most satisfactory evidence of value, yet they are only one of the modes of proving value, and not the only mode: *St. Louis etc. R. R. Co. v. Haller,* 82 Ill. 208. It is true that the witnesses of appellant do not testify to actual knowledge of sales, made in the neighborhood where these lots are located in the year 1884, or about that time, and that some of the witnesses of appellee do refer to sales. Purchases made in [531] 1879 are not an exact criterion of values in 1884. Nor are forced sales under trust deeds and foreclosure decrees always a correct indication of value. After making allowance for the difference thus indicated between the testimony produced by appellee and that produced by appellant we are unable to reach the conclusion, that the value of the services rendered to the appellant was equal to the value of the lots conveyed to appellee in January, 1884.

We cannot say, however, after a careful review of the evidence, that the contract for compensation and the deed made in pursuance thereof are liable to any other objections than these two: 1. They were executed during the existence of the relation of attorney and client; 2. They secured a larger compensation for legal services than those services were really worth. We see no evidence of any undue influence exercised by the appellee over the appellant, except perhaps in the matter of obtaining from her a renewal of the contract. In the fall of 1882 appellee seemed to fear that appellant would make a settlement with Pratt without consulting him or upon a basis not approved by him; and on November 24, 1882, he wrote her a letter in which, after referring to her previously expressed desire that he should conduct her business "upon a contingent fee of fifty per cent of the amount recovered," he said: "A definite understanding is therefore necessary before any further action is taken." He says that after this date she renewed the contract for one-half of what should be recovered; and thereafter, in March, 1883, as the record shows, he amended the bill by praying that Pratt be declared a trustee, etc. It was said in *Bolton* v. *Daily*, 48 Iowa, 348: "We think that where an attorney sets up an express agreement to pay more than an ordinary fee exacted of a client when the work was two-thirds done, under a threat of withdrawing from the case if the agreement was not made, nothing but the best of reasons would be sufficient to uphold the agreement." Here, however, the implied threat to take no further action without a definite [532] understanding had reference to reaffirming a contract already made rather than to the making of a contract for the first time. Appellee had perhaps good reasons for asking for a definite understanding. The appellant had thrown out intimations of a settlement of her litigation. She had shown herself to be changeable in her humor, and had already employed two attorneys besides appellee in her lawsuits. She had repudiated the agreement of settlement entered into with her second husband. She had made some incorrect statements to her counsel; for example, she had charged that the note to Eimers and the trust deed to Thornton had been obtained by fraud, when the evidence overwhelmingly established the fact that those securities rep-

resented a *bona fide* loan, and that she herself had voluntarily
united in the execution of the trust deed.

Aside from the haste with which appellee secured his deed
on January 17, 1884, we are satisfied that the action of appellant in the execution of that deed was free and voluntary.
She admits that she was pleased with the result reached in
getting a decree for the lots. The proof does not sustain her
in the claim which she now makes, that she thought she was
conveying to appellee an undivided one-half of the lots, so
that as cotenant she would have the benefit of his services in
the future management of the property. On the contrary, the
proof shows that the deed was fully explained to her, and
that she well understood it to be a conveyance of the west
half of the lots, and that she chose the east half in preference
to the west half upon being given her choice.

We think the proof also shows that appellant was fully advised of all the steps taken in the suit. She was acquainted
with the value of the lots, and received information in relation
thereto from the beginning of her troubles, having accepted a
trust deed thereon in 1879, and having executed a trust deed
thereon in 1880. In 1882 she had made an affidavit as to
the value of the lots. Afterwards she is shown to have talked
with a number of persons in regard to the future outcome of
[533] the property. She was a shrewd, capable business woman;
had been engaged in business before she married Pratt; and
though without much ready money, owned a house and two
lots in a suburb called Melrose.

If appellant had filed her bill within a reasonable time, we
are of the opinion that she would have been entitled to have
the deed to appellee set aside, either upon the ground that
both the deed and the contract which preceded it were obtained from her while the relation of client and attorney existed between herself and appellee, or upon the ground that
the property, agreed to be given and subsequently conveyed
to appellee as compensation for his legal services, was worth
more than the reasonable and customary value of those services. But inasmuch as the contract, which appellee could
not have enforced, was fully completed and executed by the
conveyance to him of one-half the property, the question
arises whether or not appellant has been guilty of laches in
not sooner filing her bill to have the deed set aside. From
January, 1884, when the deed was made, to December, 1890,
when the present bill was filed, a period of almost seven years

elapsed. In connection with the question of laches it is a fair subject of inquiry, under the facts of this case, whether the conduct of the appellant does not show acquiescence, if not confirmation, on her part.

Where bills are filed to set aside contracts or deeds between parties standing in a confidential relation to each other, the defense of laches is not usually regarded with favor. It has been said that "length of time weighs less in such a case than in any other," and that it is "extremely difficult for a confidential agent to set up an available defense grounded on the laches of his employer": *Wood* v. *Downes*, 18 Ves. Jr. 130, note 1. But even in cases where it has been held, that such contracts and sales, without reference to their fairness or honesty, will be set aside upon the application of the party in interest, it has at the same time been held, that such application [534] must be made within a reasonable time to be judged of by the court under all the circumstances of the case: *Hawley* v. *Cramer*, 4 Cow. 717; *Smith* v. *Thompson*, 7 B. Mon. 310; *Fox* v. *Mackreath*, 1 Lead. Cas. Eq., pt. 1; White and Tudor, 4th Am. ed., p. 188, sec. 115 and page 257; *McCormack* v. *Malin*, 5 Blackf. 509; *Williams* v. *Reed*, 3 Mason, 405. What is a reasonable time cannot well be defined, but must be left, in large measure, to the determination of the court in view of the facts presented. Equity does not always follow the period of limitation fixed by statute and enforced in courts of law. Parties will be required to assert their rights within a shorter time in states where the values of real estate increase rapidly, and greater temptations are thereby afforded for speculative litigation: *Burr* v. *Borden*, 61 Ill. 389. But the party, who is entitled to set the transaction aside, cannot be charged with delay, or with acquiescence, or confirmation, unless there has been full knowledge of all the facts, and perfect freedom of action. Acts which might appear to be acts of acquiescence will not be held to be such, if the client or *cestui que trust* is ignorant of the circumstances, or under the control of the original influence, or otherwise so situated as not to be free to enforce his rights: *Rogers* v. *Marshall*, 3 McCrary, 76; *Hawley*, v. *Cramer*, 4 Cow. 717. Confirmation may be evidenced by long acquiescence, "as by standing by and allowing the purchaser to lay out money in the firm belief that his title would not be contested": *Pearson* v. *Benson*, 28 Beav. 598.

Let us see how the appellant stood relative to the two objections, heretofore pointed out, on January 17, 1884, and for nearly seven years thereafter. She must be held to have known that the property which she conveyed to appellee was worth more than his services. She alleges in her bill in this case, that she agreed to pay him $400, and, while that allegation is not sustained by the proof, she must be held to be bound by it. In her testimony, after stating that appellee [535] introduced the subject of his fees after Pratt's arrest, she says: "I asked him . . . . what would be his fees for attending to all my business and making everything perfectly clear and straight for me. . . . . He said there was a great deal of work about the case and would probably be a great deal more, and he would have to have $400." She swears that she thus knew the value of his services as fixed by himself. On January 17, 1884, with knowledge, according to her own evidence, that his services were estimated by himself to be worth only $400, she conveyed to him one-half of property which she had sworn to be worth $3,000 in March, 1882, and which was of greater value in 1884.

With admitted knowledge as to the disparity between the value of the land and the value of the services, she permitted the appellee to deal with the west half of the land as his own, and recognized him as the owner thereof, for six years and eleven months, without giving any intimation that she intended to disturb his title. In December, 1884, he paid off one-half of the encumbrance held by Eimers, and she not only permitted him thus to spend his own money on the property, but furnished him with the money to pay off the other half of the encumbrance for herself. From June 30, 1884, down to the time of filing the present bill, she paid taxes on the east half of the property, and suffered him to pay taxes on the west half, sometimes taking the money over to the treasurer's office for him, and paying his taxes for him on the west half. A little more than a month before filing the bill she paid $83.35 for an outstanding tax title against the east half, and he at the same time with her consent paid the same amount for a tax deed to himself of the same outstanding title against the west half. In 1888 and 1889 she made efforts not only to sell her own lots in the east half, but also to sell for him the lots in the west half which she had conveyed to him. She went out to the property in 1885, and employed a man to plant trees for her on the east half, telling him that appellee owned [536] the west half. In 1886 she had some negotiations with one Whittemore about selling one of her lots in the east half to him, and spoke of Johnson as the owner of the west half by deed from herself for services. At another time she was present when appellee offered to sell his lots in the west half for $75 a lot, and talked to the same party about buying her own lots in the east half. In 1887 she occupied a part of the office of a real estate agent named Hopson, and proposed to him that he should sell her lots, referring to appellee as the owner of the adjoining lots, and as being willing to sell them.

The evidence shows that between January, 1884, and December, 1890, a belt line railroad was built to the west of these lots, and the Wisconsin Railroad Company laid its tracks in the neighborhood, and certain locomotive works were located in that vicinity. On account of these improvements the lots, which had been bought for $600 in 1879, had become worth $16,000 in 1890.

It appears from the evidence that the defendant went into the office of the appellee as a typewriter in 1883, and did the business of a typewriter for several years. The appellee and two other attorneys had each a private room, and a large reception or waiting room. The appellant was permitted to use a typewriter belonging to appellee, occupying the reception-room for that purpose. She was allowed the use of the room and of the typewriter without charge, and, in consideration thereof, she did for appellee such typewriting as he required. We cannot see that the appellee owed her anything for work done under this arrangement. While she was in his office she seems to have done a profitable business as a typewriter for outside parties. When she procured a typewriter of her own and took another office in the same building, he paid her for the services which she rendered.

Upon the grounds of laches and acquiescence we think that the court below properly dismissed the bill.

The decree of the superior court of Cook county is affirmed.

In the case of *Story v. Hull*, 143 Ill. 506, it appeared that C. J. Hull died February 12, 1889, possessed of a valuable estate, both real and personal, leaving as his surviving heirs at law six nephews, two nieces, the daughter of a deceased niece, and five children of a deceased nephew, five of such heirs being minors, and these heirs at law were the appellees in the present case. Hull by his last will bequeathed the whole of his estate to one Helen Culver, his cousin, therein designating her as executrix. At the time of the admission of the will to probate the adult appellees elected to contest the will, and secured the services of A. C. Story, the appellant, as their attorney. For about two months thereafter Story devoted a considerable portion

of his time to the matters connected with the estate, examining authorities
and performing various other services. In the mean time several offers of
compromise were made, and at last an offer of $212,500 was accepted by the
heirs in full settlement, but several of such heirs being minors, chancery proceedings were instituted in order to render the compromise effective. Upon
the termination of these proceedings, Story by leave of court filed an intervening petition, based on a claim that he entered into an agreement with
such heirs, whereby they agreed that he was to receive "an heir's share,"
or "one-tenth" of whatever might be recovered as the price of his legal services; that under such agreement he is entitled to $21,250, and that the
agreement operates as an equitable assignment of such sum. The heirs
denied entering into any such agreement, and alleged that they only agreed
to pay appellant a reasonable compensation for his services. The court below found the facts in favor of the contention of the heirs, and rendered a
decree dismissing the intervening petition on the ground that a court of
equity had no jurisdiction. The plaintiff appealed, and the supreme court
in passing upon the questions presented and affirming the judgment of the
lower court, said:

"The evidence seems to show that it was the understanding of the parties
that the reasonable compensation to appellant, except such reasonable advances as might be made pending litigation, should be paid out of the proceeds of 'the proposed litigation. It is urged by appellant that it is not
essential that a specific sum or fixed proportion of the proceeds should be
agreed upon in order to constitute a valid equitable assignment, but that it
is sufficient for that purpose if, by the agreement, the reasonable compensation did not depend upon the mere personal responsibility of the heirs, but
was to come out of the proceeds. An equitable assignment is such an assignment as gives the assignee a title which, though not cognizable at law,
equity will recognize and protect: Abbott's Law Dict.; 6 Am. & Eng. Ency.
of Law, 656. It is not perceived how there can be an appropriation of a
part of a fund, and a transfer of title thereto, when there is no ascertainment
of the part or proportion in respect to which the agreement is to operate as
an appropriation and transfer, in equity, of title. It would seem that such
a supposed assignment would necessarily be void for uncertainty, for there
must be an actual appropriation of the fund, or of some designated part,
proportion, or per cent of it. Appellant wholly ignores the distinction,
which is clearly pointed out in *Wyman* v. *Snyder*, 112 Ill. 99, and also in
Trist v. *Child*, 21 Wall. 441, between an actual assignment of a part of a
debt or claim or fund, and a mere promise or agreement to pay a part of
such debt or claim when collected or recovered, or pay out of such fund.
Here the agreement that the compensation of appellant should come out of
the proceeds of the proposed litigation was simply a promise by the heirs
that they would pay such compensation out of such proceeds, and depended
for its performance upon the mere personal responsibility of such heirs.

"Some of the authorities which appellant cites in connection with the particular claim now under consideration, we do not consider here applicable.
They might be in point if the $212,500 was a fund which was in charge of
the chancery court, and which said court was administering upon. But
such was not here the case. Here the minor heirs were unable to bind themselves by the compromise that had been made, and in the principal suit the
chancery court merely approved of the compromise, and made provision for
carrying the same into effect by the payment of the $212,500 to the heirs
and the guardians of such of them as were minors, and the execution of

necessary and proper receipts, releases, and discharges. The $21,250 was brought into court merely by agreement of parties, and with the express stipulation, made in open court and entered of record, 'that all legal and equitable rights, as between the complainants and the said Story, including the right to question the jurisdiction of the court, are reserved for future determination, with a reservation to the complainants, severally and respectively, and to said Story, of all legal and equitable rights to the same, in all respects as if a deposit in court of moneys had not been provided for as aforesaid.'

"The case, then, stands upon this footing: Appellees promised to pay appellant a reasonable compensation for his services, and promised to pay it out of the proceeds of the contemplated litigation. The question, What is a reasonable compensation? is purely a question of fact, upon which appellees have a constitutional right to take the verdict of a jury; and the only remedy is an action at law for a breach of the promise to pay: *Wright* v. *Ellison*, 1 Wall. 16; *Trist* v. *Child*, 21 Wall. 441.

"It is, perhaps, hardly necessary to add that in this state, and in the absence of an express contract out of which an equitable assignment arises, an attorney at law has no lien for his compensation upon the judgment or decree rendered in a suit prosecuted by him, or upon the real estate, moneys, funds, or other property recovered by means of his exertions and labors: *Humphrey* v. *Browning*, 46 Ill. 476; 95 Am. Dec. 446; *Forsythe* v. *Beveridge*, 52 Ill. 268; 4 Am. Rep. 612; *La Framboise* v. *Grow*, 56 Ill. 197; *Nichols* v. *Pool*, 89 Ill. 491."

ATTORNEY AND CLIENT—TRANSACTIONS BETWEEN, HOW REGARDED.—An attorney is required to exercise the utmost good faith in his dealings with his client, and he cannot retain an advantage over his client which his position enabled him to acquire: *Taylor* v. *Barker*, 30 S. C. 238; *Cooper* v. *Lee*, 75 Tex. 114; *Powell* v. *Willamette Valley R. R. Co.*, 15 Or. 393; *Darlington's Estate*, 147 Pa. St. 624; 30 Am. St. Rep. 776, and note with the cases collected.

ATTORNEY AND CLIENT.—TRANSACTIONS BETWEEN, BURDEN OF PROOF AS TO FAIRNESS: See the note to *Darlington's Estate*, 30 Am. St. Rep. 785. In dealings between an attorney and his client, the burden of proving their fairness is upon the attorney: *Morrison* v. *Smith*, 130 Ill. 304; *Felton* v. *Le Breton*, 92 Cal. 457; *Bingham* v. *Salene*, 15 Or. 208; 3 Am. St. Rep. 152; *Kisling* v. *Shaw*, 33 Cal. 425; 91 Am. Dec. 645, and note; *Miles* v. *Ervin*, 1 McCord Ch. 524; 16 Am. Dec. 623.

ATTORNEY AND CLIENT.—AN AGREEMENT FOR A LARGER COMPENSATION than that originally agreed upon is invalid: *Lecatt* v. *Sallee*, 3 Port. 115; 29 Am. Dec. 249.

ATTORNEY AND CLIENT.—CONTRACTS BETWEEN entered into before the relation existed, but not made obligatory until after the establishment of such relation, will be sustained if they are fair and the consideration ample: *Bingham* v. *Salene*, 15 Or. 208; 3 Am. St. Rep. 152.

ATTORNEY AND CLIENT—PURCHASE BY ATTORNEY OF SUBJECT MATTER OF LITIGATION.—The law will not permit an attorney to take advantage of his relations with his client to make a contract in reference to the property in litigation to the latter's disadvantage: *Miles* v. *Ervin*, 1 McCord's Ch. 524; 16 Am. Dec. 623; *Burnham* v. *Heselton*, 82 Me. 495; *Cunningham* v. *Jones*, 37 Kan. 477; 1 Am. St. Rep. 257, and note; *Henry* v. *Raiman*, 25 Pa. St. 354; 64 Am. Dec. 703, and note.

Attorney and Client.—Attorney's Right to Recover a Reasonable
Fee: See *Horton* v. *Long*, 2 Wash. 435; 26 Am. St. Rep. 867; *International
etc. Ry. Co.* v. *Clark*, 81 Tex. 48.

Real Estate—Evidence as to Value.—Evidence of the price paid on
sales of other land in the neighborhood is competent on an inquiry as to the
value of lands taken for railroad purposes when there is a similarity between
the properties: *Laing* v. *United New Jersey R. R. etc. Co.*, 54 N. J. L. 576; 33
Am. St. Rep. 682, and note.

Kozel *v.* Dearlove.

[144 Illinois, 23.]

Statute of Frauds.—An Oral Approval by a Principal of a sale of
lands made by an agent who had written authority to make the sale,
but on different terms than those upon which it was made, is unavailing. To sell upon different terms requires a new and further authority,
and such authority, to be valid under the statute of frauds, must
itself have been in writing, signed by the principal.

Goldzier and Rodgers, for the appellant.

[23] BAILEY, C. J. This was a proceeding by petition, under
the provisions of chapter 29 of the Revised Statutes, entitled
"Contracts," to compel George Manlove and Edwin D. Mes-
singer, the executors of the last will and testament of Richard
Manlove, deceased, to execute and deliver to the petitioner a
deed conveying to him certain real estate, in performance of
a contract for such conveyance entered into by Richard Manlove, in his lifetime. The contract thus sought to be enforced
purports to have been executed by Asa W. Clark as agent
for Richard Dearlove to Anthony Kozel, and appears to have
been assigned, prior to the filing of the original petition, by
Kozel to Frank C. Layer. The petition was accordingly filed
by Layer, but the contract having [24] been subsequently re-
assigned by him to Kozel, the latter intervened and, by leave
of the court, filed his supplemental petition, and the proceeding was thereafter prosecuted in his name.

It appears that on the first day of October, 1889, Richard
Dearlove executed an instrument in writing, in which he
placed certain prices on each of forty lots in Dearborn's addition, etc., in Cook county, and authorized Asa W. Clark to
sell said lots at an advance of not less than sixteen per cent
upon the prices thus fixed, one-third of the purchase money
to be paid in cash, and the residue on or before the expiration
of three years, with six per cent annual interest, "unless a
less amount in cash or more favorable terms be agreed to by

said Dearlove." On the nineteenth day of June, 1890, Clark executed a memorandum of the contract in question, by which he agreed to sell and convey to Kozel a portion of the lots at prices and upon terms which are conceded to have been more favorable to the purchaser than those fixed by the written authority given to Clark by Dearlove. The evidence tends to show that, before the memorandum of the contract was signed, Clark communicated the proposed terms to Dearlove, who was then sick, and that Dearlove assented to them, and orally instructed Clark to close the transaction on those terms.

The petition alleges the performance by the petitioner of the contract on his part, that is to say, by the payment of the cash required to be paid at the execution of the contract, and by being willing and ready to pay to the executors the install-ment payable by the terms of the contract upon the execution of the conveyance, and to secure the deferred payments in the manner in the contract provided, and by having tendered such performance to the executors. It is also alleged that Dear-love, by his will, devised the lots covered by the contract to George M. Dearlove, who was also one of his heirs at law. The petition made the executors, the devisee and the heirs of Dearlove parties defendant, and prayed for a decree compell-ing the executors to execute to the petitioner a good and suf-ficient warranty [25] deed conveying said lots to the petitioner, upon payment by him of the amount required by the contract to be paid upon the execution of the conveyance, and upon execution by him of the notes and mortgage for the deferred payments provided for by the contract.

The executors answered admitting the allegations of the petition, and alleging that the interests of the estate of the tes-tator demand that the purchase of the premises in question should be completed at the earliest practicable date, and they therefore ask that the prayer of the petition be granted.

The devisee and certain of the heirs of Dearlove answered, denying that the petitioner has any interest, either legal or equitable, in the premises in the petition described, or that Dearlove, ever, by his agent duly authorized in writing, entered into a written contract for the conveyance of said premises to the petitioner upon the terms in the petition set forth. They also denied performance by the petitioner of the terms of the alleged contract as alleged in the petition.

The cause being heard on pleadings and proof, a decree was entered finding that the petitioner was not entitled to the relief prayed for by the petition, and dismissing the petition, at the petitioner's costs, for want of equity. To reverse this decree, the petitioner now brings the record to this court by writ of error.

The only question presented by the record which we need consider is, whether Clark was authorized to sign the contract sought to be enforced, or a note or memorandum thereof, by any written instrument signed by Dearlove, as required by the second section of the statute of frauds. That he had competent written authority to sell the lots in question at certain specified prices and upon certain prescribed terms is not disputed. But the written instrument gave him no authority to sell at lower prices or upon different terms. No one, we presume, would claim that, if he had undertaken to do so without consulting his principal, his act would have had any legal [26] validity, or have been enforceable against the principal. The agent was just as powerless to make such sale as he would have been if no written authority had existed. To sell upon different terms required a new and further authority, and such new authority, to be valid under the statute of frauds, must itself have been in writing and signed by the principal.

It is of no avail to show that the modified terms were communicated to Dearlove and were assented to by him, and that he directed the execution of the contract on those terms. The authority thus given to the agent was not in writing, and so was not a compliance with the requirements of the statute. We think the petition was properly dismissed, and the decree will therefore be affirmed.

———

AGENCY TO SELL LAND—APPOINTMENT BY PAROL.—Under the Alabama statute of frauds, no legal title to lands will pass by a contract made with an agent, unless he has written authority: *Alabama etc. R. R. Co.* v. *South etc. Alabama R. R. Co.*, 84 Ala. 570; 5 Am. St. Rep. 401. The same rule is maintained in *Toan* v. *Pline*, 60 Mich. 385. In other states an agent authorized by parol may execute a contract for the sale of land: *Worrall* v. *Munn*, 5 N. Y. 229; 55 Am. Dec. 330, and note; *Despatch Line* v. *Bellamy Mfg. Co.*, 12 N. H. 205; 37 Am. Dec. 203. The statute of frauds does not require an authority to sell lands to be in writing: *Talbot* v. *Bowen*, 1 A. K. Marsh 436; 10 Am. Dec. 747, and note; *Malone* v. *McCullough*, 15 Col. 460; *Jackson* v. *Murray*, 5 T. B. Mon. 184; 17 Am. Dec. 53, and extended note. An agent may sign a memorandum of contract in the name of the principal, so as to comply with the statute of frauds, though not authorized thereunto in writing: *Blacknall* v. *Parish*, 6 Jones' Eq. 70; 78 Am. Dec. 239, and note; *Curtis* v. *Blair*, 26 Miss. 309; 59 Am. Dec. 257.

ARNOLD *v.* BOURNIQUE.

[144 ILLINOIS, 132.]

BUILDING CONTRACTS, ARCHITECT'S CERTIFICATE.—If, by the terms of a building contract, it is provided that payment shall be only upon the certificate of the architect, such certificate is a condition precedent to payment, and no action can be sustained upon the contract in the absence of such certificate, unless it has been demanded from the architect and fraudulently withheld.

BUILDING CONTRACT—PRESENTATION OF ARCHITECT'S CERTIFICATE, WHEN EXCUSED.—If, by the terms of a contract, the builders were to be paid on the presentation of a certificate signed by the architect, and such architect adjusts the account between the parties and gives the builders a certificate showing the amount found due them, which by them is handed back to the architect because not satisfactory, after which he refuses either to return the certificate or to make any other, the builders may recover the amount specified in such certificate, though they have not presented and cannot present it to the defendant. Presentation of the certificate is not one of the substantial requirements of the contract.

Albion Cate, for the appellants.

George W. Brandt, for the appellees.

[134] CRAIG, J. This was an action of assumpsit brought by Arnold and Taggart, appellants, against Augustus E. Bournique to recover [135] a balance claimed to be due on a building contract, executed by the parties on the first day of March, 1883. On the trial in the circuit court, after the plaintiffs had closed their testimony, on motion of the defendant, the court instructed the jury to find for the defendant. Under the instruction a verdict was returned for defendant, upon which the court entered a judgment which, on appeal, was affirmed in the appellate court. In order to determine whether the court erred in the instruction to the jury, it will be necessary to refer briefly to the testimony introduced by the plaintiff. Under the contract executed by the parties, and read in evidence, plaintiff's carpenters agreed to do all the carpenter work and furnish the material therefor for defendant's dancing academy and dwelling-house on Twenty-third street, Chicago, in consideration of which defendant agreed to pay plaintiffs, "upon the presentation of certificates signed by the said Burnham and Root (who were the architects named in contract), the sum of eleven thousand two hundred and fifty-four dollars and thirty cents . . . . ; damages for delay, as mentioned in the specifications, shall be deducted from the contract price as liquidated; and further-

more, fifteen per centum of the value of all work done and
materials furnished shall be held back until this contract is
declared by said Burnham and Root completed; or, if the
contract is completed at specified time or times, said fifteen
per cent kept back shall then be paid forty days after the
work of this contract is declared by architects finished, provided said work and materials are free and discharged from
all claims, liens, and charges." The contract also contained
the following clause: "And in case the parties shall fail to
agree as to the time, value of extra or deducted work, or the
amount of extra time, the decision of the architects shall be
final and binding; the same in case of any disagreement between the parties relating to the performance of any covenant
or agreement herein contained."

The plaintiffs, after reading the contract in evidence, introduced evidence tending to prove that, after the contract was
[186] executed, the plaintiffs proceeded with the work under
the contract, and fully completed their contract, as they
claimed, about the last day of October, 1883. As the work
progressed, the defendant paid, on certificates issued by the
architects, eight thousand eight hundred dollars. In November, 1883, plaintiffs called on Burnham and Root for a final
certificate of the balance due under the contract, claiming
also for extras. On the twenty-second day of November,
Burnham and Root adjusted the accounts of the plaintiffs,
allowing a certain amount for extras, and deducting certain
amounts for work left off, and as showing the conclusion
reached on the amount for extra work claimed, and as respects
the deductions they gave plaintiffs two papers as follows:

"Deduction for work left off and defective workmanship
done by Taggart and Arnold, %c A. E. Bournique:

    Total................ ....$238 91
    Also, extras."

                 "CHICAGO, November 22, 1883.

Items allowed Taggart and Arnold on Bournique:

    Total........ ....$281 75."

These two papers were delivered as the final decision of the
architects on the two questions embraced therein. A few days
after the above papers were delivered, the architects, Burnham
and Root, made out and delivered plaintiffs or one of them a
final certificate for seventeen hundred and forty-seven dollars,
the balance due from the defendant to plaintiffs under the
contract, and for extras, after allowing for deductions in favor

of defendant. This final certificate was executed by the architects and delivered to one of the plaintiffs, who, being dissatisfied with the amount, handed it back to Burnham and Root. Some time after the certificate was handed back, plaintiffs called on Burnham for the certificate, but they failed to get it, Burnham informing them that he had made out one certificate and would not make another.

The theory upon which the circuit court instructed the jury to find for the defendant, as we understand from the [137] record, was that the plaintiff could not recover unless he had first obtained a certificate from the architects of the balance due, and presented that certificate to the defendant; that the presentation of a certificate under the contract was a condition precedent to a recovery.

Where, by the terms of a contract under which materials are furnished and labor is performed in the erection of a building, it is provided that payment shall only be made upon the certificate of an architect, the law is well settled that the obtaining of such certificate is a condition precedent to the payment of the money, and an action cannot, as a general rule, be maintained to recover the money until the certificate has been obtained from the architect: *Packard* v. *Schoick*, 58 Ill. 79; *Coey* v. *Lehman*, 79 Ill. 176; *Barney* v. *Giles*, 120 Ill. 154.

If, however, the materials have been furnished and the work completed according to the contract, and a certificate has been demanded from the architect and fraudulently withheld by him, the contractor will be relieved from the necessity of procuring the architect's certificate: *Michaelis* v. *Wolf*, 136 Ill. 68.

In the first count of the declaration it was averred that the defendant had fraudulently prevented the architects from issuing a certificate, and that they, the architects, had wrongfully and fraudulently neglected and refused to issue a certificate; and on the first trial of the cause the plaintiffs undertook to establish the averments of the declaration. In this, however, they did not succeed. Subsequently, and on October 27, 1888, an additional count to the declaration was filed, in which the plaintiffs, after setting out the building contract, averred that as to deductions and extras Burnham and Root were to decide, and their decision was to be final, as well as to all payments to plaintiffs and all other matters growing out of and pertaining to the performance of all of said work and prom-

ises, and that defendant promised to pay plaintiffs such sums
as Burnham and Root should adjudge due them.

138 That after the completion of said work, on, to wit, November 1, 1883, said architects made a full and final adjudication in writing, which they signed, of the final amount and
balance due plaintiffs for said work and material, and passed
upon all deductions and extras, in which writing they found
that there was due from defendant to plaintiffs a balance of
seventeen hundred and forty-seven dollars. That by means
of the premises defendant became indebted to pay plaintiffs
the said sum of seventeen hundred and forty-seven dollars
when requested, yet, although often requested, hath hitherto
refused.

The evidence of the plaintiff in regard to the adjustment of
the accounts of the parties by the architects, and the execution and delivery of a final certificate showing the balance
due the plaintiffs, was introduced for the purpose of sustaining the averments of the additional count of the declaration,
and we are inclined to the opinion that the court erred in
taking the case from the jury by the instruction.

By the terms of the contract itself the parties had agreed
that in case of disagreement relating to extra work, or work
to be deducted, or in regard to the performance of any covenant of the contract, the decision of the architects should be
final. Under this provision of the contract, after the labor
and materials had been furnished and the job completed, the
plaintiffs had the right to prove that their accounts for labor
and material had been adjusted by the architects, and that
the amount due had been determined, and a final certificate
made and delivered to them, showing the amount then due.
The execution and delivery of the certificate by the architects
was final and conclusive upon both the plaintiffs and the
defendant, unless fraud or mistake was shown, which is not
pretended on either side: *McAuley* v. *Carter*, 22 Ill. 53; *Korf*
v. *Lull*, 70 Ill. 420; *Lull* v. *Korf*, 84 Ill. 225. When the architects had adjusted the accounts, determined the amount due,
and executed and delivered to plaintiffs a final certificate, the
rights of the parties became fixed. The fact that the plaintiffs
did not keep the final certificate, but handed it back to the
architects, did **139** not change the relation or rights of the
parties, nor did such act affect the validity of the certificate;
its validity remained the same after it was returned as it was
when in plaintiffs' hands.

It is, however, claimed that the defendant could only be made liable to pay upon the presentation of the certificate to him by the plaintiffs, and as the plaintiffs failed to present the certificate, they could not recover. We do not concur in this view. A recovery may be had on a promissory note payable on demand, although no demand has been made. So also an action may be maintained on a certificate of deposit which provides that it is payable on return of the certificate properly indorsed, although no return of the certificate has been made: *Hunt* v. *Divine*, 37 Ill. 137. We perceive no reason why a different rule should be applied to a certificate of this character. Suppose plaintiffs had lost their final certificate after it was issued, and it had been destroyed so that it never could be presented to defendant, would they be precluded of a recovery? A rule of that character would be unjust, and might in many cases result injuriously to parties. The presentation of the certificate was not one of the substantial requirements of the contract. As has been substantially said before, the decision of the architects, reduced to writing and signed by them, was the substantial act which determined the right of plaintiffs to the money, and determined the obligation of the defendant to pay. From what has been said it follows that the instruction of the court was erroneous. The judgment of appellate and circuit courts will be reversed and the cause remanded to the circuit court.

BUILDING CONTRACTS—ARCHITECTS' CERTIFICATES.—An agreement in a building contract that there shall be no liability for the work except upon the architects' certificate is valid; but if such certificate is arbitrarily or fraudulently withheld, the failure to obtain it will not bar a recovery by the contractor who may recover on showing the fact that he has performed the contract according to its terms: *Crouch* v. *Gutmann*, 134 N. Y. 45; 30 Am. St. Rep. 608, and note with the cases collected. See also the extended note to *Campbell* v. *American etc. Ins. Co.*, 29 Am. Rep. 602.

DAY v. WALLACE.

[144 ILLINOIS, 256.]

WILL, CONSTRUCTION OF.—IF THE SAME TRACT OF LAND IS DEVISED IN
Two DIFFERENT CLAUSES of a will to different persons, such clauses are
not regarded as repugnant, but are treated as manifesting an intention
that the devisees shall hold as cotenants.

Patton and Hamilton, for the appellants.

Ricks and Creighton, and Drennan and Hogan, for the appellee.

256 WILKIN, J. By the eighth clause of the last will of
George Gregory, deceased, he devised to appellants two tracts of
land, one of twenty acres, and the other of eighty acres. By the
ninth clause of the same will, he devised to appellee two tracts
also; one of twenty acres, and the other of eighty acres. The
eighty-acre tract in both clauses is the same. By her certain
cross-bill in the court below, appellee alleged that the two
clauses, in so far as they attempt to devise the same land, are
irreconcilably repugnant to each other, and, therefore, the
last must prevail, and she asked the court to decree her the
said eighty-acre tract to the exclusion of appellants, and
the prayer of her bill was granted. From that decree this
appeal is prosecuted.

Appellants do not deny that said eighty-acre tract was devised twice, in the manner alleged in the bill, but they deny
that the two clauses of said will are thereby rendered wholly
and irreconcilably repugnant, within the meaning of the rule
which gives effect to the later clause to the exclusion of the
former, and insist that the rule of construction in such case
is to give the land to the devisees in both clauses concurrently as tenants in common.

The authorities are not uniform on the subject, but the later
and more generally approved rule seems to be as contended
by appellants. In Jarman on Wills, volume 2, page 44, it is
said:

"Sometimes it happens that the testator has, in several
parts of his will, given the same lands to different persons in
fee. At first sight this seems to be a case of incurable repugnancy, and, as such, calling for the application of the rule,
which sacrifices the prior of two irreconcilable clauses, as the
only **257** mode of escaping from the conclusion that both are
void. Even here, however, a reconciling construction has

been devised; the rule being in such cases, according to the
better opinion, that the devisees take concurrently. The contrary, indeed, is laid down by Lord Coke, and other early
writers, who say that the last devise shall take effect; and a
similar opinion seems to have been entertained by Lord Hardwicke, though he admitted that, latterly, a different construction had prevailed. The point underwent much discussion in
Sherrat **v.** *Bentley*, 2 Mylne & K. 149, already stated; and
Lord Brougham, after reviewing the authorities and fully
recognizing the general doctrine, which upholds the latter
part of a will by the sacrifice of the former, to which it was
repugnant, considered that, consistently with this rule, it
might be held, that, where there are two devises in fee of the
same property, the devisees take concurrently. 'If, in one
part of a will,' he said, 'an estate is given to A, and afterward the same testator gives the same estate to B, adding
words of exclusion, as 'not to A,' the repugnance would be
complete, and the rule would apply. But if the same thing
be given first to A, and then to B, unless it be some indivisible chattel, as in the case which Lord Hardwicke puts in
Ulrich v. *Litchfield*, 2 Atk. 372, the two legatees may take together without any violence to the construction.' It seems,
therefore, by no means inconsistent with the rule, as laid
down by Lord Coke and recognized by the authorities, that a
subsequent gift, entirely and irreconcilably repugnant to a
former gift of the same thing, shall abrogate and revoke it, if
it be also held that where the same thing is given to two
different persons in different parts of the same instrument,
each may take a moiety; though, had the second gift been in
a subsequent will, it would, I apprehend, work a revocation."

Redfield, speaking on the same subject, says: "The more
rational, and perhaps the general, opinion at the present day
is that, where the same thing is given in the same will to two
different persons, they shall take jointly, either as joint tenants [260] or tenants in common, according to the terms of the
devise or bequest." After referring to what was said by Lord
Brougham in *Sherrat* v. *Bentley*, 2 Mylne & K. 149, quoted
by Jarman as above, he adds: "We fully concur in his lord-
ship's suggestions here, as every one must, we think, in regard
to the reasonableness of the latter rule of construction, when
it can be applied, as in the case of the devise of the same
estate to different devisees, and we have no doubt it will generally be recognized as the true rule, and the one established

by the authorities for the government of cases of this character. But, as well observed by the learned chancellor, in an after portion of his opinion, that is not a case of clear and irreconcilable repugnancy. But the testator having given the same estate to two persons, in different portions of his will, it is the same as if all the names had been united in one gift of the same estate": 1 Redfield on Wills, 443. The case of *McGuire* v. *Evans*, 5 Ired. Eq. 269, goes to the full extent of holding this doctrine, even as applied to a double bequest of indivisible property.

On the contrary, as said by Jarman, *supra*, authorities are not wanting holding the contrary construction: *Hollins* v. *Coonan*, 9 Gill, 62; *Covert* v. *Sebern*, 73 Iowa, 564.

The case is one of first impression in this state, and in the conflict of authority on this subject we are left free to adopt that rule which to us seems most reasonable and best calculated to effectuate the intention of the testator. Taking into consideration all the facts of this case proper to be considered, it is manifest that whatever presumption might otherwise arise in favor of the latter clause expressing that intention rather than the former, is rebutted. In the first place it is clear from the two clauses that he intended to give appellants one hundred acres of land, and a like quantity to appellee. He owned at the time of making his will, and when he died, some two hundred and forty acres of land not disposed of by the will. Eighty acres of this undisposed of land was in the same section [261] as the eighty in question. It is, therefore, clear that, instead of changing his mind after making the first devise of the eighty-acre tract described in the will, either he or the person who wrote his will made a mistake in the description in one of the clauses. It is impossible to tell in which clause that mistake occurred. We know of no rule by which we are allowed to say it was made in the first, rather than in the last. We can conceive of no good reason why the consequences of such a mistake should be wholly visited upon appellants.

While it is true that an application of the rule laid down by the above-named authors will not fully carry out the intention of the testator, it will come nearer accomplishing that purpose than the one insisted upon by appellee, and adopted by the court below. Certainly it does justice between the parties. Appellants and appellee should take said real estate as ten-

ants in common, appellants taking one undivided half thereof
and appellee the other.

We are of the opinion that the decree below is erroneous,
and should be reversed, and the judgment of this court will
be entered accordingly, and the cause will be remanded to
the circuit court with directions to enter another decree con-
forming to the views herein expressed.

WILLS—CONSTRUCTION.—Where there is a general devise of property in one
part of a will, and a specific disposition of it in another part, these are to be
regarded, generally, as excepted out of the general devise: *Dickison* v. *Dickison*, 138 Ill. 541; 32 Am. St. Rep. 163, and note on the construction of wills.
To the same effect see *Babbidge* v. *Vittum*, 156 Mass. 38. See also the note
to *Estate of Hunt*, 19 Am. St. Rep. 644, on the construction of wills containing repugnant clauses.

JACKSON v. JACKSON.

[144 ILLINOIS, 274.]

BILLS OF REVIEW.—If there has been an erroneous application of facts found
   by a decree, a court of equity may revise or reverse the decree by a bill
   of review.

BILLS OF REVIEW MUST BE PROSECUTED WITHIN THE TIME FOR PROSECUTING
   WRITS OF ERROR where there is no statute specifying the time within
   which such bills may be prosecuted.

FINAL DECREE—BILL OF REVIEW—TIME FOR PROSECUTING.—If a decree of
   partition determines the interests of the respective parties and directs
   partition to be made accordingly, the time within which a bill of review
   may be prosecuted must be computed from the date of such decree and
   not from the date of a subsequent order or decree dismissing the action.

AN ESTATE AS TENANT BY THE CURTESY VESTS IN a husband if his wife dies
   seised of an estate of inheritance, having had issue born alive and which
   might have inherited it as her heir, and she thereafter dies in the lifetime of her husband.

CONSTITUTIONAL LAW—IF AN ESTATE AS TENANT BY THE CURTESY HAS
   VESTED in a husband it cannot be divested by subsequent legislative
   action.

CONSTITUTIONAL LAW.—If by the statute in force when land is acquired by
   a married woman she is declared to remain during coverture the sole
   owner thereof as her separate estate to be held, possessed, and enjoyed
   by her the same as though she were unmarried, the legislature may, as
   to such lands, abolish the estate by the curtesy at any time prior to her
   death, because until then, her husband has no vested estate therein.

M. A. Fuller and V. G. Fuller, for the plaintiffs in error.

M. Shallenberger and Allen P. Miller, for the defendants in
error.

278 CRAIG, J. This was a bill of review brought by William A. and John M. Jackson against John Jackson and others on the twentieth day of August, 1890, in which the complainants sought to review and vacate a decree in a partition proceeding rendered on the sixth day of April, 1883, in the circuit court of Stark county.

279 The facts out of which the litigation arose may be briefly stated.

John Jackson and Paulina A. Jackson were married on the fourteenth day of October, 1858, and the following named children were born to them: Lydia E. Jackson, born June 15, 1859; Laura B. Jackson, born October 24, 1860; William A. Jackson, born October 23, 1862; Ursula A. Jackson, born October 7, 1864; John M. Jackson, born August 25, 1866. On the thirteenth day of March, 1860, Paulina A. Jackson became seised in fee of the west half of the northeast one-quarter of section 2, 12 N., 5 E., in Stark county, and on the fourth day of January, 1873, she became seised of forty acres, part of the northwest one-quarter of section 2, in the same township, more particularly described in the petition for partition.

On the twenty-ninth day of November, 1875, Mrs. Jackson died, leaving her husband, John Jackson, and her four children surviving her. On the 31st of August, 1882, the two daughters, Laura B. and Lydia, together with their husbands and William A. Jackson, who was then a minor, filed a petition for partition of the premises involved against John Jackson and the other two heirs. John Jackson answered the bill claiming an estate of tenancy by the curtesy in the premises.

On the hearing at the March term, 1883, of the court, the court found: That John Jackson had an estate in curtesy in all of said premises, and was in possession thereof. That the foregoing named children of Paulina A. Jackson are "the owners in common of said premises, subject to life estate by the curtesy of John Jackson."

A decree was rendered, ordering partition of the premises subject to the life estate, and Samuel M. Adams, Benjamin R. Brown and Charles Potter were appointed to make such partition, **280** and if not subject to division, to appraise and report the same.

The case was continued from term to term without further action until the March term, 1888, when said commissioners reported:

That they had examined the premises and find that they are not susceptible of division without prejudice to parties, and appraise the west one-half N. E. 2, at sixty dollars per acre, and the forty-acre tract at fifty-five dollars, both, however, subject to the life estate of John Jackson.

At the March term, 1889, the cause was dismissed.

It is first contended by appellee that there is no such error appearing on the face of the decree as will authorize a court of equity to interfere by bill of review. If there has been an erroneous application of the facts found by the decree a court of equity may revise or reverse the decree by bill of review: *Evans* v. *Clement,* 14 Ill. 208. The facts upon which the court found that John Jackson was entitled to hold the premises as tenant by curtesy all appear on the face of the decree.

The date of the purchase of the lands by Paulina A. Jackson, with their description, date of her marriage, date of the birth of her children, and date of her death, all appear on the face of the decree. If, therefore, the decree, under the facts as found, was erroneous it could be corrected. The next question presented is, whether the complainants, or either of them, have lost their right to bring this bill, by lapse of time. As has been seen, the decree was rendered on the sixth day of April, 1883, and this bill was brought on the twentieth day of August, 1890. No time has been prescribed by statute within which a bill of review must be brought, but writs of error are required to be sued out within five years from the time a judgment or decree has been rendered; and in analogy to the time prescribed for prosecuting writs of error, it has been held that a bill of this character should be brought within the time allowed for suing out a writ of error: *Lyon* v. *Robbins,* 46 Ill. 278. In [281] case of writ of error, section 86, chapter 110, of our Practice Act, prescribes, that a writ of error shall not be brought after the expiration of five years from the rendition of the decree or judgment, but if the party entitled to the writ was an infant when the judgment was entered, the time of minority shall be excluded from the five years.

Applying this rule to the present case, which we think should be done, John M. Jackson, one of the complainants, as found by the court in its decree, was born August 25, 1866, he would not, therefore, be of age until August 25, 1887, and, excluding his minority, he would have until August 25, 1892, to bring his bill, and the bill was filed two years before the time expired. So far, therefore, as John M. Jackson is concerned, his bill was brought in apt time. As respects the other complainant, he occupies a different position; he, as appears, became of age in October, 1883, and hence would be barred in October, 1888. It is, however, said that the time did not begin to run until the suit was finally disposed of in March, 1889. We do not concur in that view. The rights of all the parties as to their title and interest in the premises were fully and definitely determined and settled by the decree of April 6, 1883. That was a final decree and as to all persons who were parties to the proceeding, and under no disability, the decree could not be reviewed by writ of error or bill of review after five years, and the fact that the cause remained on the docket until 1889, and was then stricken from the docket, does not materially affect the question. The decree of April 6, 1883, was the only one ever entered in the case, and there was nothing to prevent a writ of error from being prosecuted to review the decree at any time after it was rendered, for the period of five years.

We now come to a consideration of what may be regarded the merits of the case. That is, whether John Jackson was entitled to an estate of tenant by the curtesy in the premises. At common law, "When a man marries a woman seised at any [282] time during coverture of an estate of inheritance, ... and hath issue by her, born alive, and which might by possibility inherit the same estate as heir to the wife, and the wife dies in the lifetime of the husband, he holds the land during his life by the curtesy of England ": 4 Kent, page 27; *Shortall* v. *Hinckley*, 31 Ill. 219. There are four things necessary to constitute the tenancy by the curtesy: marriage, seisin of the wife, issue, and death of the wife. Here all of these facts existed, and it is plain at common law John Jackson would have an estate by the curtesy in the lands. It may also be remarked in this connection that, under the common law, there were two interests which, under the marriage relation, a husband might acquire in the lands of the wife. 1. By virtue of the marriage alone the husband possessed the right to occupy the lands of which the wife was seised and receive the rents and profits during coverture; and 2. Upon the birth of a child capable of inheriting, the husband became invested with an estate in the lands which, during the life of the wife, was denominated initiate and upon her death it became consummate. There is, however, but little or no dispute between counsel in regard to the rules of the common law on the subject, but the question in dispute is how far and to what extent the common law has been changed and modified by our statute. In 1861 the legislature passed an act known as the "Married Woman's Act," which provides, "That all the property, both real and personal, belonging to any married woman as her sole and separate property, or which any woman hereafter married owns at the time of her marriage, or which any married woman during coverture acquires in good faith from any person, other than her husband, by descent, devise, or otherwise, together with all the rents, issues, increase and profits thereof, shall, notwithstanding her marriage, be and remain during coverture her sole and separate property, under her sole control, and be held, owned, possessed, and enjoyed by her the same as though she was sole and unmarried.

[283] In 1874 the legislature passed an act to revise the law in relation to dower, the first section of which provides as follows: "That the estate of curtesy is hereby abolished, and the surviving husband or wife shall be endowed of the third part of all the lands whereof the deceased husband or wife was seised," etc. Under the Act of 1861 and the Dower Act of 1874, it is claimed that Jackson was only entitled to dower in the lands. It will be observed that Paulina A. Jackson acquired the eighty-acre tract of land in 1860, before the Act of 1861 was passed; that she was married in 1858, issue born capable of inheriting in 1859, and also in 1860. As to this tract of land, Jackson had an estate as tenant by the curtesy initiate before the Act of 1861 was passed. This was a vested estate, one which Jackson, had he desired, might have conveyed, and one, too, which might have been sold on execution against him: *Shortall* v. *Hinckley*, 31 Ill. 219; *Mettler* v. *Miller,* 129 Ill. 640. As the estate of Jackson was a vested estate before the Act of 1861 was passed, it was not within the power of the legislature to destroy it or deprive him of it by any act that might be passed for that purpose: *Rose* v. *Sanderson*, 38 Ill. 247. As to the eighty-acre tract of land, we think the decision of the court was correct.

The forty-acre tract stands upon a different footing. That tract was acquired by Mrs. Jackson in 1873, when the Act of 1861 was in full force. Under that act Jackson was precluded from acquiring any estate whatever in the land during coverture. It was, during coverture, the sole and separate property of the wife, and she alone was entitled to the rents, issues, and profits thereof: *Cole* v. *Van Riper*, 44 Ill. 64. As Jackson, therefore, in 1874, his wife being still alive, had no vested estate in the land, the legislature had the undoubted right to abolish the estate of curtesy, as to him and all others who were alike situated, and provide, as it did, that a surviving husband or wife shall only be entitled to dower. This view is fully sustained by the late case of *McNeer* v. *McNeer*, 142 Ill. **284** 388. There is nothing in *Cole* v. *Van Riper*, 44 Ill. 64, holding that the husband has any vested estate in the lands of the wife acquired after the passage of the Act of 1861, before the death of the wife. Before the death of the wife he has no estate by curtesy, either initiate or consummate. The fact that the husband might, after the death of the wife, become vested with an estate as tenant by the curtesy, did not stand in the way of the legislature abolishing that estate at any time before the estate became vested. As to the eighty-acre tract, the decree of the circuit court will be affirmed, but as to the forty-acre tract, the decree will be reversed, and the cause remanded.

Appellants will recover costs.

BILLS OF REVIEW—NATURE AND SCOPE OF.—See the extended notes to *Brewer* v. *Bowman*, 20 Am. Dec. 160-175, and *Duggen* v. *McGruder*, 12 Am. Dec. 529-537, where they are fully discussed.

ESTATES BY THE CURTESY—WHEN EXIST: See *Jackson* v. *Johnson*, 5 Cow. 74; 15 Am. Dec. 433, and extended note; *Malone* v. *McLaurin*, 40 Miss. 161; 90 Am. Dec. 320, and note with the cases collected, and the note to *Haight* v. *Hall*, 17 Am. St. Rep. 124.

SCHULTZE *v.* SCHULTZE.

[144 ILLINOIS, 290.]

TREATIES—CONSTRUCTION OF.—IF A TREATY ADMITS OF TWO CONSTRUCTIONS, one restrictive of the rights that may be claimed under it and the other liberal, the latter is to prevail.

TREATIES—INHERITANCE BY NONRESIDENT ALIENS.—A treaty stipulating that the citizens of the contracting parties shall have power to dispose of their personal goods by testament or otherwise, and their representatives, being citizens of either party, shall succeed to such goods, and if in the case of real estate, the said heirs would be prevented from entering into the possession of the inheritance on account of their character as aliens, there shall be granted to them three years to dispose of the same, gives nonresident aliens who would be heirs but for their alienage, three years within which to dispose of their share of the lands of their ancestor, and to remove the proceeds. The estate which they acquire is a fee, determinable by the nonexercise of the power of sale within the three years.

PARTITION—WHO MAY SUE FOR.—A nonresident alien, whose interests in the property will terminate unless he exercises, within three years, his power to sell it, can maintain a suit in partition to have his interest set aside in severalty.

IF A NONRESIDENT ALIEN DOES NOT SELL PROPERTY INHERITED BY HIM within the time stipulated in the treaty between the United States and the sovereignty of which he is a subject, the state law comes into force, and controls the disposition to be made of such property.

IF THE NEXT OF KIN OF A DECEDENT IS A NONRESIDENT ALIEN, NOT CAPABLE OF INHERITING under the laws of the state, but there are other kindred who are residents of the state, the property does not escheat, but vests in the kindred who have capacity to inherit in the same manner as if the person incapable of inheriting by the laws of the state had never existed.

Arthur Schroeder, for the appellant.

William Vocke and Julian W. Mack, for the appellees.

295 MAGRUDER, J.   The main questions involved in this case are settled by the opinion filed at this term in the case of *Wunderle* v. *Wunderle*, 144 Ill. 40.   In that case, the nonresident aliens claiming to take lands by descent in Illinois were held to be incapable of inheriting under the Act of 1887, there being no treaty, permitting them to acquire or hold lands in this country, between the Grand Duchy of Baden of which they were subjects, and the United States of America. Here, however, the appellees, who are nonresident aliens, are citizens of the Hanseatic Republic of Bremen, between which republic and the United States a convention or treaty was concluded on December 20, 1827, and afterwards ratified and proclaimed.   Article 7 of said treaty is as follows: "The citizens of each of the contracting parties shall have power to dispose of their personal goods, within the jurisdiction of the other, by sale, donation, testament, or otherwise; and their representatives, being citizens of the other party, shall succeed to their said personal goods, whether by testament or *ab intestato*, and they may take possession thereof, either by themselves or others acting for them, and dispose of the same at their will, paying such duties only as the inhabitants of the country, wherein said goods are, shall be subject to pay in like cases; and if, in the case of real estate, the said heirs would be prevented from entering into the possession of the inheritance on account of their character of aliens, there shall be granted to them the term of three years to dispose **296** of the same, as they may think proper, and to withdraw the proceeds without molestation and exempt from all duties of detraction on the part of the governments of the respective states."

The language of this article is not as clear in its meaning as the provision quoted in *Wunderle* v. *Wunderle*, 144 Ill. 40, which allows a reasonable time to sell and remove the proceeds " where on the death of any person holding real estate within the territories of the one party, such real estate would, by the laws of the land, descend on a citizen or subject of the other were he not disqualified by alienage," etc. But the rule laid down by the supreme court of the United States is that, " where a treaty admits of two constructions, one restrictive as to the rights that may be claimed under it, and the other liberal, the latter is to be preferred": *Hauenstein* v. *Lynham*, 100 U. S. 483. If the language of article seven be given a liberal construction, it may be held to mean, that, where a citizen of the United States dies intestate owning land and leaving nonresident alien kindred, residing in and citizens of Bremen, who would be his heirs but for their alienage, there will be granted to such kindred the term of three years within which they may dispose of such lands and remove the proceeds. The word, " representatives" in the second clause of the article must refer to all who take by will or descent, including devisees and heirs, as well as executors and administrators; otherwise, there would be no antecedent, to which the word " said " before the word " heirs" in the third clause could be made to refer. The second clause can be construed to mean, that the representatives or heirs of American citizens being citizens of Bremen shall succeed to personal goods. It follows that, by the terms of the third clause, the heirs of American citizens who are citizens of Bremen shall have the prescribed term of three years to dispose of real estate, etc.

The appellees are, therefore, entitled, under said article seven of the treaty, to the privilege of selling the interests in the land [297] in controversy, which they would have inherited from the deceased George Ludwig Schultze under the laws of Illinois but for their alienage, and of removing such proceeds of sale, provided they do so within three years. The question then arises: what interest in the land is vested in nonresident aliens by the grant to them of a term of three years within which they can sell such land and remove the proceeds?

It would seem, that, in such case, the alien heirs take a fee

determinable by the nonexercise of the power of sale within
three years: *Kull* v. *Kull*, 37 Hun, 476. By the terms of the
treaty the power to dispose of the land and appropriate its
proceeds is granted in positive terms. Such a power to sell
cannot be exercised unless the donee is vested with the fee,
or, in other words the complete ownership. It has been said
that, "it is an affront to common sense to say that a man has
no property in that which he may sell when he chooses, and
dispose of the proceeds at his pleasure": *Kull* v. *Kull*, 37
Hun, 476. In the case of *Kull* v. *Kull*, 37 Hun, 476, where
the proceeding, like the present one, was for partition, the
precise question now under consideration was involved, and
it was there held, that the fee vested in the nonresident alien;
that the treaty intended to confer upon him the rights of
ownership in the property and the advantages of its use and
possession for the purpose of making the sale; that, under
the provisions of the treaty, the alien heir was clothed, for the
period granted for the purpose of making the sale, with the
same rights he would enjoy if he were a resident heir, being
subject simply to the obligation to sell and convey the fee to
some other party capable of holding.

It follows, that the nonresident aliens, thus vested with the
power of sale under the treaty, can bring a partition suit for
the purpose of having their interests set apart in severalty.
The right to bring such a suit is involved in the ownership of
the determinable fee; and the partition of the property will
make it easier to dispose of it in accordance with the permission [298] granted by the treaty. An undivided interest in
land is always less salable than a definite portion thereof as
fixed by a division.

The effect of the treaty is to suspend, during the period of
three years, the operation of the alien law of this state which
makes the nonresident aliens incapable of taking land by
descent. The rights of the resident heirs, or the heirs capable of taking under the state law and the right of the state
or county to take the land by escheat in default of heirs capable of holding the same, are also suspended during the term
of three years named in the treaty: *Kull* v. *Kull*, 37 Hun,
476. If, at the end of the three years, no sale is made by the
nonresident aliens, the state law again comes into force and
directs the disposition of the property: Laws of 1887, p. 5.

In the case at bar, upon the showing made by the present
record, the land could not escheat to the state or the county,

because appellant, the brother of the deceased, is a citizen of
the United States and a resident of Illinois, and, therefore,
capable of inheriting according to the views expressed in
Wunderle v. *Wunderle*, 144 Ill. 40. By clause second of section 1 of the Statute of Descents in this state, it is provided,
that estates shall descend, "when there is no child of the intestate, nor descendant of such child, and no widow or surviving husband, then to the parents, brothers, and sisters of
the deceased," etc.: Rev. Stats. c. 39, sec. 1. It being alleged
in the bill and also in the plea that the widow, Louisa H. A.
Schultze, one of the appellees herein, is a citizen of Bremen,
no question as to the effect of the citizenship of her deceased
husband upon her alleged alienage is presented in this case.
The statute evidently refers to cases where the surviving
widow or husband is capable of taking, and not to cases where
there is incapacity by reason of alienage. Hence, it is manifest that appellant would take the whole of the land under
the state law if the treaty were not in the way. As the appellant is a party to the partition proceeding, he will be bound
by it. As it is not [299] shown that the land will escheat for
failure of heirs capable of inheriting, it cannot be said that
the state or county is a necessary party.

For the reasons here stated, we think that the plea of the
appellant was not sufficient to bar the right to the relief prayed
for in the bill.

Accordingly, the decree of the circuit court is affirmed.

————

The case of *Wunderle* v. *Wunderle*, 144 Ill. 40, referred to in the foregoing
opinion was a suit for partition, in which the complainants alleged themselves to be brother and sister of Alexander Wunderle, that he died intestate in January, 1891, leaving as his only heirs at law the complainants and
the defendant Catharine, the surviving widow of the decedent, that he was
at the time of his death seised of a tract of land of which, by such death,
such widow became seised of the undivided one-half and the complainants
the remaining one-half, subject to the widow's right of dower. The defendant answered that the decedent, when he acquired the property and also at
the time of his death, was a citizen and resident of the United States, but
that the complainants were, and had always been, nonresident aliens, resident in the Grand Duchy of Baden and subjects of the German Empire, and
that by the act of the legislature of the state of Illinois, approved January
16, 1887, they were not capable of acquiring title to or holding real estate
by descent, etc. This answer, having been adjudged sufficient by the trial
court, an appeal was taken to the supreme court. In disposing of the appeal and the questions presented by it, that court determined: 1. That the
act pleaded by the defendant, if constitutional and not in conflict with any
existing treaty, excluded the complainants from participation in their
brother's estate; 2. That the title of aliens to lands within the limits of the

several states is a matter of state regulation, and the right of foreigners to
hold title to real estate is dependent upon the laws of the state in which the
land is situate, but that all state regulations upon this subject are subordinate to the provisions of any treaty made between the national government and the sovereignty of which the alien is a subject; 3. That there was
no treaty with the Grand Duchy of Baden, nor with the German Empire,
conferring upon plaintiffs any right or capacity to inherit lands in the
United States; 4. That the Act of 1887 was not unconstitutional because it
made exceptions in favor of certain nonresident aliens therein enumerated;
5. That at the common law, aliens had no inheritable blood and were incapable of taking by inheritance, and that the Act of 1887 was not unconstitutional, the sole effect of that act, so far as the case before the court was
concerned, being to repeal pre-existing statutes and leave aliens in a condition not less favorable to them than was the common law, and that the legislature had the power to change the course of descent, and such change
would operate instantly upon all estates which might subsequently descend,
and an expectancy or property in the future is not a vested right, and hence
the rules of descent are subject to change in their application to all estates
not already passed to an heir by the death of an ancestor, and neither citizens nor aliens have any vested rights in the estates of their living kindred;
6. That the complainants did not take any interest which they could hold
until the state, by a direct proceeding, assailed their title, and that there was
no necessity of any proceeding or inquest of office to determine their want
of capacity to acquire lands; 7. That if a citizen dies, leaving as his next of
kin, an alien who cannot inherit, such alien cannot interrupt the descent to
others, and the inheritance descends to the next of kin who is competent to
take in like manner as if such alien had never existed, and finally, as the
defendant was a resident competent to inherit from her deceased husband
and entitled to take the whole of his estate if he left no surviving kindred,
he must, from the fact that no other of his kindred were residents of the
United States, be regarded as dying without any kindred, save his wife, who
is therefore entitled to the whole of his estate.

TREATIES—CONSTRUCTION OF.—Where a treaty invests aliens with an interest in lands in certain cases, provided it is asserted within three years
after the right accrues, their right is inviolable during such time, but after
this the state may deny such right to that class of persons: *Yeaker v. Yeaker*,
4 Met. (Ky.) 33; 81 Am. Dec. 530, and extended note, where the effect of
treaties as laws, and the power to annul them by hostile legislation, is fully
discussed.

ALIENS—POWER TO INHERIT AND HOLD LANDS: See the extended note to
Elmondorff v. Carmichael, 14 Am. Dec. 97. An alien cannot inherit land in
South Carolina: *McClenaghan v. McClenaghan*, 1 Strob. Eq. 295; 47 Am.
Dec. 532, and note; nor in Kentucky: *Yeaker v. Yeaker*, 4 Met. (Ky.) 33;
81 Am. Dec. 530; but in Louisiana they may inherit: *Duke of Richmond v.
Milne*, 17 La. 312; 36 Am. Dec. 613, and note. See, further, the extended
note to *Commonwealth v. Hite*, 29 Am. Dec. 232.

ALIENS—RIGHT TO SUE: See the extended note to *Molyneux v. Seymour*, 76
Am. Dec. 667. The objection to a partition suit that one of the parties is
an alien is in abatement only, and must be made before issue is joined: *Scanlan v. Wright*, 13 Pick. 523; 25 Am. Dec. 344.

STEVENS *v.* ST. MARY'S TRAINING SCHOOL.

[144 ILLINOIS, 336.]

MUNICIPAL CORPORATIONS.—COURTS OF EQUITY will not attempt to control discretionary or legislative powers vested by law in municipal corporations.

COUNTIES ARE MUNICIPAL CORPORATIONS created for the purpose of convenient local government, and possess only such powers as are conferred upon them by law. They may be called *quasi* municipal corporations, and their corporate powers are more limited than those of incorporated cities and towns.

MUNICIPAL CORPORATIONS.—A COURT OF EQUITY, at the instance of a taxpayer, may restrain municipal corporations and their officers from making unauthorized appropriations of the corporate funds, and. from making payments of illegal claims.

MUNICIPAL CORPORATIONS—VOID ORDINANCES—RESTRAINING ENACTMENT OF.—The enactment of void ordinances will not ordinarily be enjoined. The restrictive powers of the courts should be directed against the enforcement rather than against the passage of such ordinances. Therefore, an injunction will not issue to prevent county commissioners from entering into a contract with a corporation controlled by the Roman Catholic Church for the payment to it of moneys for the instruction of boys committed to its care, though such contract is prohibited by the state constitution, and will be void if made. A court of chancery cannot assume in advance that the commissioners will ignore the real facts and violate the fundamental law of the state by making an illegal contract, and, if they should make such contract, the county will not be estopped from taking advantage of its incapacity to make it.

BILL in equity by and on behalf of the taxpayers of the city of Chicago against St. Mary's Training School and its officers, and the board of commissioners of Cook county and its members, and the treasurer of such county, to enjoin such school and its officers from prosecuting any claim against the city for compensation for the instruction of the inmates of the school, and to enjoin the board from approving or ordering any claim paid, and from making any contract for such payment. The bill was dismissed on demurrer, and the complainants appealed.

Francis C. Russell, for the plaintiffs in error.

George W. Smith, for the defendants in error.

342 MAGRUDER, J. The bill in this case was demurred to, and therefore its statements must be assumed to be true. It alleges that the defendant in error, the Saint Mary's Training School, is a corporation which is controlled by the Roman Catholic Church, and that the board of commissioners of Cook county has made contracts with said corporation for

the payment to it out of the funds of the county of certain
moneys for the instruction and training of boys committed to
its care.   That such contracts are void and such payments
illegal is settled by the decision of this court in *Cook Co.* v.
Industrial School for Girls, [343] 125 Ill. 540, 8 Am. St. Rep.
386.   It was there held that county boards in this state have
no power to appropriate county funds in aid or support of
sectarian schools, or of any school controlled by a church.
The constitution of Illinois is very emphatic upon this subject, and the language, in which its meaning is expressed, is
too plain to be misunderstood.   Section 3 of article 8 of that
instrument is as follows: "Neither the general assembly nor
any county, city, town, township, school district, or other
public corporation, shall ever make any appropriation or pay
from any public fund whatever anything in aid of any church
or sectarian purpose, or to help support or sustain any school,
academy, seminary, college, university, or other literary or
scientific institution controlled by any church or sectarian
denomination whatever; nor shall any grant or donation of
land, money, or other personal property ever be made by the
state or any such public corporation to any church or for any
sectarian purpose."

But the question presented by the record is, whether a court
of chancery has power to enjoin a board of county commissioners from passing a resolution that an illegal contract be
made by the county, and from making an order that an illegal
claim be allowed against the county.   The bill prays, that the
county board may be enjoined from making contracts with
the training school in the future, and also from ordering the
payment to said school of a balance due for the quarter ending December 31, 1888, upon a contract already existing
between the board and the school.   Has equity the power to
enjoin the passage of ordinances, by-laws, resolutions and
orders by municipal corporations, or is its power confined to
the issuance of injunctions against the enforcement and execution of such ordinances, by-laws, resolutions and orders
after the same have been passed?

It is well settled, that courts of equity will not attempt to
control the discretionary or legislative powers vested by law
in municipal corporations: 2 Dillon on Municipal Corporations, 4th ed., secs. 94, 475, 908; 2 High on Injunctions, 3d
ed., secs. 1240, 1246. [344] Counties are corporations created
for the purpose of convenient local government and possess

only such powers as are conferred upon them by law: *Harney* v. *Indianapolis etc. R. R. Co.*, 32 Ind. 244. They have been called *quasi*-municipal corporations; and their corporate powers are more limited than those of incorporated cities and towns: 1 Dillon on Municipal Corporations, 4th ed., sec. 25; *Symonds* v. *Clay County*, 71 Ill. 355. In the exercise of such discretionary or legislative powers as are conferred upon them by law, counties are as much beyond judicial control as other municipal corporations: *Fitzgerald* v. *Harms*, 92 Ill 372.

The board of commissioners of Cook county can exercise the same powers as boards of supervisors in other counties: *McCord* v. *Pike*, 121 Ill. 288; 2 Am. St. Rep. 85. Each county has power to make all contracts and do all other acts in relation to the property and concerns of the county necessary to the exercise of its corporate powers; and each county board has power to manage the county funds and county business, and to examine and settle all accounts against the county: *Fitzgerald* v. *Harms*, 92 Ill. 372. Where county boards are acting within the boundaries of their discretionary or legislative powers, the courts will not only refrain from interfering with the passage of resolutions and orders by them, but will also refuse to enjoin the enforcement of such resolutions and orders, except in certain cases where they are unreasonable. In *Fitzgerald* v. *Harms*, 92 Ill. 372, where we refused to sustain an injunction against the county clerk from issuing an order upon the county treasurer for the amount of a claim previously allowed by the county board and against the county treasurer from paying the same, we placed such refusal solely upon the ground that the board was acting within the bounds of the powers conferred upon it by law, and said: " a court of equity cannot interfere with the deliberations or the action of the board of commissioners over a matter which the law has entrusted to them, unless fraud be shown, or they have undertaken to allow a claim which was not of a character [345] to be paid by the county." Literally interpreted the language here used might be construed to mean, that a court of equity could interfere with the deliberations of the board, if its members were undertaking to allow a claim which was not of a character to be paid by the county. But the case cannot be regarded as so deciding. because the question of the power of a court of equity to enjoin the board from making an order by a vote of its members for the payment of a claim, as distinguished from its power to enjoin the clerk or auditor from drawing a warrant and the treasurer from paying the amount of the claim after the order of allowance had been made, was not involved nor in any way suggested.

It is correctly announced by the text-writers in general terms, that taxpayers and property holders may resort to equity to restrain municipal corporations and their officers from making unauthorized appropriations of the corporate funds, and from misapplying the moneys of the corporation, and from making payment of illegal claims: 2 Dillon on Municipal Corporations, 4th ed., secs. 914, 919; Cooley on Taxation, 2d ed., p. 764; 2 High on Injunctions, 3d ed., secs. 1237–1239; 1 Pomeroy's Equity Jurisprudence, sec. 260; 10 Am. & Eng. Ency. of Law, p. 959. It is also correctly laid down as a general proposition, that the restrictions upon the right of a court of equity to interfere with the action of municipal bodies do not extend to cases where those bodies are exceeding their lawful powers: 2 High on Injunctions, 3d ed., sec. 1241.

But some of the adjudged cases, which are referred to as sustaining these general doctrines, are not in harmony with each other, and others of them are not definite and decided in their conclusions, upon the question whether equity will confine its restraining power to the instrumentalities which undertake to carry out and execute the unauthorized resolutions and ordinances of municipal corporations, or whether it will enjoin such corporations, acting in their corporate capacity, from adopting resolutions and ordinances which are in excess of their [346] legal or constitutional authority. There are cases, which hold, or seem to hold, that, where a municipal corporation is about to pass a resolution or ordinance which is void as being *ultra vires*, a court of chancery will enjoin it from so doing. Among such cases may be mentioned the following: *Davis* v. *Mayor etc.*, 1 Duer, 451; *People* v. *Sturtevant*, 9 N. Y. 263; 59 Am. Dec. 536; *Davis* v. *Mayor, etc.*, 14 N. Y. 506; 67 Am. Dec. 186; *Spring Valley Water Works* v. *Bartlett*, 16 Fed. Rep. 615; *Town of Jacksonport* v. *Watson*, 33 Ark. 704; *State* v. *Commissioners*, 39 Ohio St. 58; *Page* v. *Allen*, 58 Pa. St. 338; 98 Am. Dec. 272; *Follmer* v. *Nuckolls Co.*, 6 Neb. 204; *Peter* v. *Prettyman*, 62 Md. 566; *Patton* v. *Stephens*, 14 Bush, 324; *Board of Education* v. *Arnold*, 112 Ill. 11; *Spilman* v. *Parkersburg*, 35 W. Va. 605; *City of Valparaiso* v. *Gardner*, 97 Ind. 1; 49 Am. Rep. 416; *City of*

Springfield v. *Edwards,* 84 Ill. 626; *Howell* v. *City of Peoria,* 90 Ill. 104.

In none of the cases last above cited, except the first four, was the question now under consideration expressly passed upon, but the facts stated in the opinions seem to warrant the conclusion, that injunctions were sustained against the corporate action of the municipalities, as distinguished from the action of agents or officers proceeding under their orders.

In the New York cases it was held that a court of chancery could enjoin the board of aldermen of a city from passing an ordinance to construct a·railway in one of the streets; that municipal corporations are creatures of limited powers in the appropriation of the funds of the people; that, when they attempt to appropriate such funds to purposes not authorized by their charters or by positive law, whether it be done by resolution, ordinance, or under the form of legislation, their acts are void, and that, while courts will not attempt to control their discretion, yet, if, under pretense of exercising such discretion, they threaten, or are about to do, what amounts to a gross abuse of power to the injury and in fraud of the rights of individuals and the public, the courts will interfere to prevent [347] the threatened injury. But later decisions in New York, some of which are referred to hereafter, have taken a different view, refusing to follow the earlier cases above mentioned as going too far in the direction of subjecting the legislative and political powers of municipal bodies to the control of the courts: *Alpers* v. *San Francisco,* 12 Sawy. 631. In *Spring Valley Water Works* v. *Bartlett,* 16 Fed. Rep. 615, an injunction against the mayor and supervisors of San Francisco, restraining them from passing an ordinance to fix the price of water furnished to the city, was sustained over the objection that the defendants were a "legislative body endowed with legislative powers, to be exercised with absolute discretion"; and it was held that the board of supervisors of a municipal corporation will be enjoined from passing an ordinance which is not within the scope of their powers, where its passage will work an irreparable injury. The Bartlett case, however, seems to have been overruled by the later case of *Alpers* v. *San Francisco,* 12 Sawy. 631.

The last four cases above cited, to wit, *Spilman* v. *Parkersburg,* 35 W. Va. 605, *City of Valparaiso* v. *Gardner,* 97 Ind. 1, 49 Am. Rep. 416, *City of Springfield* v. *Edwards,* 84 Ill. 626, and *Howell* v. *City of Peoria,* 90 Ill. 104, are cases where cities were enjoined from incurring indebtedness in excess of the constitutional limit, or from entering into contracts that would involve such excess of indebtedness.   But in these cases the point to which attention was more especially directed, was the meaning of the word "indebtedness," and what constituted a "debt" within the meaning of the constitution; and it is not altogether clear, that "incurring indebtedness" does not refer as well to the enforcement as to the passage of corporate resolutions.

A large number of the decisions, which uphold the right of equity to interfere with the action of municipal corporations where such action is in excess of their legal powers, will be found, on examination, to be based upon facts which show that the injunctions were issued against the officers or agents ³⁴⁸ attempting to execute or enforce corporate resolutions, ordinances, by-laws, or orders, as will be seen by reference to the following cases: *New London v. Brainard*, 22 Conn. 553; *Webster v. Town of Harwinton*, 32 Conn. 131; *Bayle v. New Orleans*, 23 Fed. Rep. 843; *Harney v. Indianapolis etc. R. R. Co.*, 32 Ind. 244; *Davenport v. Kleinschmidt*, 6 Mont. 502; *Willard v. Comstock*, 58 Wis. 565; 46 Am. Rep. 657; *Lynch v. Eastern etc. Ry. Co.*, 57 Wis. 430; *Place v. City of Providence*, 12 R. I. 1; *Austin v. Coggeshall*, 12 R. I. 329; 34 Am. Rep. 648; *Sherman v. Carr*, 8 R. I. 431; *Newmeyer v. Missouri etc. R. R. Co.*, 52 Mo. 81; 14 Am. Rep. 394; *Osterhout v. Hyland*, 27 Hun, 167; *Mayor v. Gill*, 31 Md. 375; *Merrill v. Plainfield*, 45 N. H. 126; *Hospers v. Wyatt*, 63 Iowa, 264; *Roberts v. Mayor*, 5 Abb. Pr. 41; *Schumm v. Seymour*, 24 N. J. Eq. 143; *List v. Wheeling*, 7 W. Va. 501; *Rutz v. Calhoun*, 100 Ill. 392; *McCord v. Pike*, 121 Ill. 288; 2 Am. St. Rep. 85; *English v. Smock*, 34 Ind. 115; 7 Am. Rep. 215; *City of Madison v. Smith*, 83 Ind. 502; *Sackett v. City of New Albany*, 88 Ind. 473; 45 Am. Rep. 467; *Wright v. Bishop*, 88 Ill. 302; *Sherlock v. Village of Winnetka*, 59 Ill. 389; *Crampton v. Zabriskie*, 101 U. S. 601.

In the case of *Crampton v. Zabriskie*, 101 U. S. 601, which may be regarded as a leading case upon this general subject, Mr. Justice Field uses the following language: "Of the right of resident taxpayers to invoke the interposition of a court of equity to prevent an equal disposition of the moneys of the county, or the illegal creation of a debt, which they in common with other property holders of the county may otherwise be compelled to pay, there is at this day no serious ques-

tion. . . . . From the nature of the powers exercised by
municipal corporations, the great danger of their abuse, and
the necessity of prompt action to prevent immediate injuries,
it would seem eminently proper for courts of equity to interfere
upon the application of the taxpayers of a county to prevent
the consummation of a wrong, when the officers of those corporations assume, in excess of their powers, to create burdens
upon property holders"; [349] but the facts of the case, in the
decision of which this language was used, show that the legislative action of the county board had already been put forth
in all essential respects before the injunction was asked for;
there, the board of chosen freeholders of a county in New
Jersey had purchased certain lands without legal authority to
do so, and had issued bonds in payment for the same; and
the object of the injunction, as is stated in the opinion of the
court, was "to enjoin the prosecution of the action to enforce
their payment" by the holder of the bonds.

In *Colton* v. *Hanchett*, 13 Ill. 615, it was held that the board
of supervisors of a county had no authority to appropriate the
county funds to aid a private individual in the construction
of a toll-bridge, and that an injunction would issue at the suit
of a taxpayer to restrain the board from granting a sum of
money to a private individual for such purpose; but it appears from the statement of the facts in the case, that the
board had previously passed a resolution directing that an
order should be drawn upon the county treasurer for the
money, to wit: $1,000, in favor of such individual, upon his
completion of the bridge, and upon his conveying to the
county a right of way over the bridge for certain of its
officers.

In *Perry County* v. *Kinnear*, 42 Ill. 160, the county board
made an appropriation to pay to a judge of the circuit court
money in addition to the salary allowed him by law; and it
was held that such appropriation of the money of the citizens was illegal and would be enjoined by a court of equity
at the suit of taxpayers; but, before the injunction was applied for, the board had passed a resolution ordering the
county clerk to issue an order on the treasurer in favor of
the judge, and the injunction was against the county clerk
from issuing the order and the county treasurer from paying
it. In *Beauchamp* v. *Kankakee Co.*, 45 Ill. 274, the facts were
similar to those in the Perry county case, and the ruling was
the same.

In *Carter* v. *City of Chicago*, 57 Ill. 283, where the question was whether a city could be enjoined from so constructing a [350] roadway as to include in it the portion of land set apart in the plat for sidewalks on either side of the roadway, it was held that the city held the fee of the streets in trust for the public, and would be enjoined from a violation of such trust by such an abuse of its powers as to injure the property of individuals; but the injunction there issued was against the enforcement of an ordinance which had already been passed.

In *Sherlock* v. *Village of Winnetka*, 59 Ill. 389, where it was held that, although a municipal corporation was vested with the largest discretion in the exercise of its public and political powers, yet it must be regarded as the depositary of a trust in reference to the corporate property, and, if guilty of a breach of such trust, would not be exempt from judicial interference merely because the forms of legislation were used; it appears that the injunction was mainly directed against the collection of a tax, the levy of which had been ordered in an ordinance theretofore passed by the village council: *Milhau* v. *Sharp*, 15 Barb. 193.

But we are not limited, in the investigation of this subject, to an examination of the facts of the cases, which, while sustaining the general power of equity to restrain the action of municipal bodies, do not make any special reference to the mode of exercising such power. There are many decisions which hold, in express and definite terms, that "the courts will not enjoin the passage of unauthorized ordinances, and will ordinarily act only when steps are taken to make them available": 1 Dillon on Municipal Corporations, 4th ed., sec. 308, note on page 387. There may be instances where this restriction upon the power of the courts will sometimes be disregarded, as where municipal corporations are exercising mere business or ministerial, rather than legislative, powers (*City of Valparaiso* v. *Gardner*, 97 Ind. 1; 49 Am. Rep. 416; 1 Dillon on Municipal Corporations, 4th ed., secs. 473, 474, 927, 1048); or are wrongfully disposing of property held by them as trustees for the public (*Milhau* v. *Sharp*, 15 Barb. 193; *Sherlock* v. *Village of Winnetka*, 59 Ill. 389); or [351] are attempting to act upon matters not by their charters or by the law subject to their jurisdiction (*Alpers* v. *San Francisco*, 12 Sawy. 631); or where it appears that the mere voting on and formal passage of a resolution or ordinance will instantly, without any action or attempt to enforce any right or privi-

lege under it, effect an irremediable private injury: *Whitney*
v. *Mayor etc.*, 28 Barb. 233.

The weight of authority and the tendency of the more recent decisions are in favor of the position that the restraining
power of the courts should be directed against the enforcement, rather than the passage, of unauthorized orders and
resolutions, or ordinances, by municipal corporations.   To
this effect are the following authorities: *Des Moines Gas Co.*
v. *City of Des Moines*, 44 Iowa, 505; 24 Am. Rep. 756; *Linden*
v. *Case*, 46 Cal. 171; *Merriam* v. *Board of Supervisors*, 72 Cal.
517; *City of Chicago* v. *Evans*, 24 Ill. 52; *Whitney* v. *Mayor*,
28 Barb. 233; *People* v. *Mayor*, 32 Barb. 35; *People* v. *Mayor*,
9 Abb. Pr. 253; *Cincinnati Street R. R. Co.* v. *Smith*, 29 Ohio
St. 291; *Harrison* v. *City of New Orleans*, 33 La. Ann. 222; 39
Am. Rep. 272; *Alpers* v. *San Francisco*, 12 Saw. 631; 2 High
on Injunctions, 3d ed., sec. 1243.

In *Alpers* v. *San Francisco*, 12 Saw. 631, Mr. Justice Field,
who wrote the opinion in *Crampton* v. *Zabriskie*, 101 U. S.
601, says: "If by either body, the legislature or the board of
supervisors, an unconstitutional act be passed, its enforcement may be arrested.   The parties seeking to execute the
invalid act can be reached by the courts, while the legislative body of the state or of the municipality in the exercise
of its legislative discretion is beyond their jurisdiction.   The
fact that in either case the legislative action threatened may
be in disregard of constitutional restraints, and impair the
obligation of a contract, ... does not affect the question.
It is legislative discretion which is exercised, and that discretion, whether rightfully or wrongfully exercised, is not subject to interference by the judiciary. . . . . The principle
that the exercise of legislative [352] power by a municipal
body is beyond judicial control is too important in our institutions to be weakened by occasional decisions in disregard
of it."

In *Des Moines Gas Co.* v. *City of Des Moines*, 44 Iowa, 505,
24 Am. Rep. 756, where the city of Des Moines had chartered
a gas company with certain exclusive privileges, and attempted by a subsequent ordinance to repeal said charter
and grant the same privileges to another company, it was
sought to enjoin the passage of the repealing ordinance, on
the ground that it would be a violation of the contract created by the charter, and therefore unconstitutional; but it
was held that the court had no power to issue the injunction

under the circumstances, and **it is** there said: "The general
assembly is a co-ordinate branch of the state government,
and so is the law-making power of public municipal corporations within the prescribed limits.   It is no more competent for the judiciary to interfere with the legislative acts of
the one than the other.   But the unconstitutional acts of either
may be annulled.   Certainly the passage of an unconstitutional law by the general assembly could not be enjoined.
If so, under the pretense that any proposed law was of that
character, the judiciary could arrest the wheels of legislation.
. . . . After its passage the judiciary may declare the law
unconstitutional: *Piqua etc. Bank* v. *Knoop,* 16 How. 369;
Dodge v. *Woolsey*, 18 How. 331; but previous to that time
judicial powers cannot be invoked. . . . . A void law is no
law, and this without doubt is true as to an ordinance. . . . .
While it is not the province of the judiciary to interfere and
arrest the passage of the ordinance, yet the doors are open for
the purpose of testing its legality."

In *Linden* v. *Case*, 46 Cal. 171, it was held that an injunction will not be granted to restrain a board of supervisors
from contracting a liability, which is not a legal charge
against the county, or "from allowing any accounts against
the county thereon," the supreme court of California saying:
"No order made by a board of supervisors is valid or binding [353] unless it is authorized by law.   No claim against
a county can be allowed, unless it be legally chargeable to
the county; and if claims not legally chargeable to the
county are allowed, neither the allowance nor the warrants
drawn therefor create any legal liabilities. . . . . If illegal
claims are allowed by the board against the county, it will
be the duty of the auditor to refuse to draw warrants therefor; and if warrants are drawn, it will be the duty of the
treasurer to refuse to pay them.   The presumption is that
these officers will faithfully discharge their duty in the
premises."

In the more recent case of *Merriam* v. *Board of Supervisors*,
72 Cal. 517, decided in 1887, it was held that an injunction
would not lie at the instance of a taxpayer to restrain the
board of supervisors of a county from ordering certain claims
to be paid on the ground **that** they were not proper or valid
demands against the county, and it was there said: "The
members of the board would themselves be individually
responsible for moneys willfully paid out without authority

of law. They are trustees of the funds for certain specified purposes, and cannot, except by violating their oaths, allow them to be applied to other purposes. They act judicially, it is true, and will not be held accountable for mere errors, but they will not be excused on the ground that they have acted honestly merely because they do not steal the funds. If they willfully appropriate moneys for a purpose not authorized by positive law, they are liable civilly and criminally."

In *City of Chicago* v. *Evans*, 24 Ill. 52, a bill was filed to enjoin the common council of Chicago from passing an ordinance, granting to the North Chicago City Railway Company the right to construct a railway across the Clark Street bridge, etc., and we said in that case: "The procuring the adoption of this ordinance is not such an illegal and unwarranted act as can produce injury, and until they act under it as their only warrant, no reason is perceived why they should be stayed in their action. The passage of ordinances which confer no [354] rights or authority, are harmless until steps are taken to make them available."

Our survey of the authorities leads us to the conclusion that, in the case at bar, the application for an injunction was premature. If the board of commissioners had passed a resolution to make a new contract with the appellee, or had made an order directing the payment of the balance due on the old contract, and the appellants had filed a bill to prevent the mandates of the board from being carried into effect by enjoining the clerk or auditor of the board from drawing a warrant on the county treasurer and by enjoining the county treasurer from paying such warrant, or by enjoining such other steps as might be taken to enforce the action of the board, then a very different case would have been presented for our consideration.

The direction, that no county shall appropriate or pay any of the public funds to a school controlled by a church involves the ascertainment of a fact. It must be ascertained by the county board, whether the school applying for the appropriation or payment is or is not controlled by a church. A court of chancery cannot assume in advance, that the board of county commissioners will ignore the real facts, and violate the fundamental law of the state by making illegal contracts, or illegal appropriations. It is time enough for equity to stretch forth its preventive arm, when some attempt is made to enforce the unconstitutional act. A municipal corporation, which has entered into a void contract, cannot be estopped from taking advantage of its own incapacity when suit is brought upon such contract, or other efforts are made to secure its execution: *Austin* v. *Coggeshall*, 12 R. I. 329, 34 Am. Rep. 648; *Schumm* v. *Seymour*, 24 N. J. Eq. 143.

There is nothing in the bill to show that there would have been any haste in drawing a warrant upon the county treasurer, or in obtaining payment from him, if the order allowing appellee's claim had been made by the board. It does not appear that the remedy of appellants would not have been as effective [355] against the instrumentalities attempting to carry out the mandate of the board as against the corporate body itself. While the legislative power, which has been delegated to municipal corporations, is of a limited and subordinate character, it yet remains true, that judicial interference with it is fraught with serious consequences, and cannot be too carefully avoided.

The decree of the circuit court is affirmed.

The case of *Roberts* v. *City of Louisville*, 92 Ky. 95, is perhaps not altogether consistent with the principal case in the disposition of the question made respecting the power of courts of equity to enjoin the enactment of void municipal ordinances. There was introduced into the general council of the city of Louisville an ordinance directing the mayor to convey to the commissioners of the sinking fund of that city all the real property fronting on the Ohio river and held by the city for wharf purposes, upon trust, that the commissioners would hold it for the same purposes as it had hitherto been held by the city. While this ordinance was pending before the general council, certain residents and owners of the property subject to municipal taxation thereon filed their bill in equity, alleging that the ordinance in question would be at once passed and would be followed by an immediate transfer of the property, unless an injunction should be granted by the court. No answer was filed on behalf of the mayor or any member of the common council, save one, who denied that he was in favor of the passage of the ordinance, but did not deny that it would be enacted if an injunction did not issue. The city on its part answered, alleging, in effect, that it had power to make the transfer contemplated by the ordinance, and the commissioners of the sinking fund by their answer also claimed the existence of the power of the city to make the transfer to them. The court of appeals first considered the question, whether it was within the power of the municipality to make the transfer in question, and reached the conclusion, that the wharf property was held in trust, and that the trust involved certain duties and obligations in their nature inalienable, and therefore, that the ordinance if enacted, must be invalid; secondly, the court considered whether the plaintiffs occupied such a position that they were entitled to call into question the action of the municipality, and decided that, because they were engaged in buying and selling stone coal, for sale and delivery, which had to be landed

at the city wharves, they would consequently suffer special and peculiar injury distinct from that of the public in case of either excessive wharfage or
obstruction of the free use of public property, and therefore, that the interest
of the plaintiffs was such as to entitle them to be heard: Lastly, the court
determined, under the circumstances of the case, it was proper for a court
of equity to interpose to prevent the enactment of the alleged illegal ordinance, upon this subject saying: "But it is contended in argument and
seems to have been the ground for dismissing the action, that a court of
equity will not enjoin passage by a municipal body of an ordinance or resolution. In High on Injunctions, section 1243, relied on by counsel, it is
said: 'It is unquestionably true that purely legislative acts, such as the
passage of resolutions, or the adoption of ordinances by a municipal body,
even though alleged to be unconstitutional and void, will not be enjoined,
since it is not the province of a court of equity to interfere with the proceedings of municipal bodies in matters resting within their jurisdiction, or
to control in any manner the exercise of their discretion. A distinction,
however, is properly drawn between the case of restraining an alleged act
attempted under the authority and sanction of a municipal body and restraining the corporation itself from granting such authority.' But in the
same section it is conceded that 'the question of equitable interference by
injunction with the legislative action of municipal bodies has given rise to
some apparent conflict of authority and is not wholly free from doubt.'

"It is said by Dillon, section 308, 'to be settled that it is competent for
the legislature to delegate to municipal corporations the power to make by-
laws and ordinances with appropriate sanctions which, when authorized,
have the force, in favor of the municipality and against persons bound
thereby, of laws passed by the legislature of the state.' And, in a note,
cases are cited in which is stated the general proposition that courts will not
enjoin the passage of unauthorized ordinances and will ordinarily act only
when steps are taken to make them available.

"Of course if every municipal ordinance has the quality and force of a law
of the state legislature, courts of equity would be without power to enjoin
or otherwise interfere with passage of any, because, on account of the peculiar structure of the state government, each of the three departments thereof
is distinct and acts in its own sphere independent of the others. But the
power delegated to a municipality to legislate is not, as to all subjects, absolute, even within corporate limits. On the contrary, it is not only restricted
by statute but also subordinate to settled principles of law and equity, in
view of which it is presumed to be delegated; for such a corporation is created
for a double purpose, and consequently has a dual character—one governmental or public, the other private or proprietary. As said in *Oliver* v.
Worcester, 102 Mass. 489, 3 Am. Rep. 485, 'the distinction is well established between the responsibilities of towns and cities for acts done in their
public capacity in the discharge of duties imposed on them by the legislature
for their public benefit, and for acts done in what may be called their private
character, in the management of property and rights voluntarily held by
them for their own immediate profit and advantage as a corporation, although
inuring, of course, ultimately for the benefit of the public.'

"It was in reference to its govermental or public character that it was, in
the case of the *City of Louisville* v. *Commonwealth*, 1 Duv. 295, 85 Am. Dec.
624, held that a city or town in this state, 'to the extent of the jurisdiction
delegated to it by its charter, is but an effluence from the sovereignty of
Kentucky, governs for Kentucky, and its authorized legislation and local

administration of law are legislation and administration by Kentucky, through the agency of that municipality.' But a municipal corporation, when holding in its private or proprietary character property or funds in trust for taxpayers and inhabitants within its limits, occupies toward them a relation like that of a purely private corporation to its *cestuis que trust*, who are its shareholders; for in each case the corporation, or its governing body, is a trustee; and if creditors, or shareholders, may maintain an action against the board of directors, the governing body, of a private corporation, to prevent or avoid an illegal and wrongful act, as unquestionably they can do, why may not taxable inhabitants maintain one against a municipal corporation and its governing body, the city council or board of trustees, to prevent as well as avoid an act illegal and wrongful, done, or about to be done, in relation to property or funds held in trust?

"In High on Injunctions, section 1241, is this language: 'The restrictions thus placed upon equitable interference with the action of municipal corporations do not extend to cases where the act sought to be enjoined is in excess of the corporate power, but are limited to cases of a conceded jurisdiction, within the bounds of which the municipal power is acting. And while it is thus shown equity will not enjoin the action of municipal corporations while proceeding within limits of their well-defined powers as fixed by law, it has undoubted jurisdiction to restrain them from acting in excess of their authority and from the commission of acts *ultra vires*.' Though it is not quite clear from the language used whether the test of jurisdiction is meant to apply to acts of municipal corporations done as well in their public as private character, it is manifest such restraining power, to be effectual, must operate upon the general council of a city or board of trustees of a town; for acts done in excess of authority, or *ultra vires*, cannot be committed by a corporation except by its governing body or head. And such must have been intended to be the meaning and scope of the proposition, for several leading cases in England are cited in which the power of a court of equity to enjoin passage of an illegal ordinance is distinctly recognized.

"The case of *Des Moines Gas Co.* v. *The City of Des Moines*, 44 Iowa, 505; 24 Am. Rep. 756, cited by counsel, was as to the power of equity to enjoin passage of an ordinance repealing a former one under which a contract had been made with the plaintiff. It was held by the court that the municipal council had in reference to the matter discretionary power and was acting within the scope of it, and was neither violating a trust nor doing an irreparable injury to the plaintiff. And though it was there said in general terms that the ordinance in question had the force of an act of the legislature and could not be enjoined, it was still conceded that one creating a public nuisance might be, because it could not be a rightful subject of legislation, and the mischief therefrom might be irreparable, which was in effect a concession of the power in every case of like conditions.

"In the *People* v. *Dwyer*, 90 N. Y. 402, it was, upon principle and authority of previous decisions in that state, held that while equity will not ordinarily interfere with matters resting largely in the discretion of municipal authorities, when the threatened action will produce irreparable injury, and consists in an illegal grant, or the disposition of property, by devoting it in whole or in part to the use of a private corporation, or where an illegal grant is threatened, or the action attempted is corrupt and fraudulent and an abuse of trust, the court may interfere by injunction to restrain passage of an ordinance for the purpose.

"In our opinion, the general proposition that a court of equity may not enjoin passage of a municipal ordinance, must be confined in its application to subjects over which the corporation in its governmental or public character has discretionary authority. And if it be conceded taxable inhabitants have a right to resort to equity, at all, to restrain a municipal corporation and its officers from making an illegal or wrongful disposition of corporate property, whereby the plaintiffs will be injuriously affected, it reasonably follows the power exists to enjoin passage of the ordinance authorizing the act whenever irreparable injury will be done to the plaintiffs, and they have no adequate remedy at law; for, from its nature, a preventive remedy may be applied at the inception of a wrongful act; in fact, when it is about to be done or is threatened.

"There may, however, be subjects in relation to which the municipal corporation has discretionary power to legislate, and with which courts of equity upon grounds of expediency and policy will not interfere in the absence of fraud or breach of trust. But this is not such a case; for the plain legal duty is imposed upon the general council to hold, control and manage the wharf property for use of the public, which can not be evaded by transfer of it or otherwise. Yet, passage of the ordinance in question might have been, if it was not actually intended to be, followed so soon by transfer of the property as to put it out of the power of the plaintiffs and all other parties aggrieved to prevent consummation of the wrongful act.

"We think the court of equity has not only the power to restrain passage of an ordinance authorizing an illegal or wrongful disposition of property acquired and held, as is the case of the wharf property, but, if needful, compel the general council to perform the duty of preserving, protecting and maintaining it for the purpose intended, though, of course, leaving it to the discretion of that body as to the manner of discharging its trust.

"It is stated, in the answer, that the ordinance was withdrawn after commencement of the action, and was not before the general council when the trial was had. But as the plaintiffs had a cause of action, withdrawal of the ordinance did not have effect to defeat their right to the relief sought, especially as another ordinance of the same character may be hereafter introduced and passed, unless the right to do so be perpetually enjoined. The judgment dismissing the action, being as already indicated erroneous, is reversed and cause remanded for proceedings consistent with this opinion."

COUNTIES—DEFINITION.—Counties are political subdivisions of the states created by the sovereign power for the exercise of the functions of local government: *Fry* v. *County of Albemarle*, 86 Va. 195; 19 Am. St. Rep. 879. A county is a corporation within the meaning of the article of the constitution of Pennsylvania providing that municipal and other corporations exercising the right of eminent domain shall make just compensation: *County of Chester* v. *Brower*, 117 Pa. St. 647; 2 Am. St. Rep. 713. Counties are political, aggregate corporations, capable of exercising such power as they may be vested with by the legislature, and are sometimes called *quasi* corporations: *Louisville etc. R. R. Co* v. *County Court*, 1 Sneed, 637; 62 Am. Dec. 424, and note. Counties are public corporations, subject to complete legislative control: *Coles* v. *County of Madison*, Breese, 154; 12 Am. Dec. 161. A county is not a corporation for municipal purposes, so far as they are to be considered corporations at all, they are political corporations: *People* v. *McFadden*, 81 Cal. 489; 15 Am. St. Rep. 66. See also the extended note on counties to *Gilman* v. *County of Contra Costa*, 68 Am. Dec. 291.

INJUNCTION TO RESTRAIN THE DISCRETIONARY POWERS of officers will not be issued: *McWhorter* v. *Pensacola etc. R. R. Co.*, 24 Fla. 417; 12 Am. St. Rep. 220, and note.

CITY OF JOLIET *v.* SHUFELDT.

[144 ILLINOIS, 403.]

NEGLIGENCE—PROXIMATE CAUSE.—IF A PERSON IS INJURED BY THE CONJOINT RESULT of an accident and of the negligence of a city, and but for such negligence the injury would not have occurred, the city is liable. Therefore, if, without the fault of the driver of a horse attached to a buggy, the bridle broke, and the horse became unmanageable, and ran away, and turned into a public street, and there, because of the defective condition and want of repair of the street, the buggy was thrown against a wall, and an injury inflicted on the driver, which he would not have suffered had the street been in proper repair, the municipality is answerable.

ACTION to recover damages for injuries suffered by the plaintiff, Mary A. Shufeldt, while she was driving along a street in the city of Joliet. It was found "that the bit had broken at the connection of the mouthpiece with one ring, and the bridle was pulled back off from the horse's head upon his neck, and he was freed from any kind of restraint." He ran down Broadway street, and turned into Exchange street, at which point the buggy struck a stone wall, about five feet in height, and was turned over into a lower roadway, and the plaintiff fell upon the wall, and thence into the lower roadway, broke her arm, lacerating her hand, and sustaining injuries from which she was paralyzed, and became utterly helpless, with no prospect of recovery. The wall causing this damage had been erected and maintained by the city for the purpose of separating the two roadways constructed in Exchange street, leaving one of them very much higher than the other. Judgment for the plaintiff.

J. W. Downey, city attorney, and *J. L. O'Donnell*, for the appellant.

George S. House, and *Shuman and Defrees*, for the appellee.

407 SHOPE, J. The principal point urged for reversal arises upon the second instruction given on behalf of plaintiff; whereby the jury were in effect told, that if the plaintiff with a companion who was driving, was riding in a buggy drawn

by a horse along and upon one of the public streets of the city,
and that without the fault of the plaintiff, or her companion,
they being in the exercise of ordinary care and prudence, the
bit of the bridle, on the horse, became loosened so that control of the horse was lost, [408] and thereby the horse became
and was unmanageable and ran away, without negligence on
the part of plaintiff or said driver, and turned from said street
into another public street of said city; and the loosening of
the bit, and loss of control of the horse was a pure accident,
which common prudence and sagacity could not have foreseen
and provided against, and that said street into which the
horse turned was so out of repair, or defective, that the same
was not reasonably safe or secure to guard against ordinary
accidents likely to occur thereon to persons using the same
without fault, and in the exercise of ordinary care and prudence, and that by reason of the unsafe and defective condition and repair of said street, the said buggy was thrown
against a wall there existing, with such force as to throw the
plaintiff out of the buggy, and cause the injury complained
of, and the city had actual notice of such defects in the street,
etc., the city would be liable for the injuries thus sustained.

It is insisted with great force that conceding the negligence
of the defendant, such negligence was not the proximate cause
of the injury; and that in any event the running away of the
horse concurring in producing the injury, the defendant is,
therefore, not liable. We are referred to a number of Massachusetts cases, and some others may be found, which sustain
the views of counsel. In this state, however, those cases have
not been followed. In *Joliet* v. *Verley*, 35 Ill. 58, 85 Am.
Dec. 342, we held that if a plaintiff, while observing due
care for his personal safety, was injured by the combined result of an accident, and the negligence of a city, or village,
and without such negligence the injury would not have oc-
cured, the city or village will be held liable, although the
accident be the primary cause of the injury, if the consequences could with common prudence and sagacity have been
foreseen and provided against. This doctrine has received
express approval in many subsequent cases, among which
may be mentioned *Bloomington* v. *Bay*, 42 Ill. 503; *City of
Lacon* v. *Page*, 48 Ill. 499; *Village of* [409] *Carterville* v. *Cook*,
129 Ill. 152; 16 Am. St. Rep. 248. In *City of Lacon* v. *Page*,
48 Ill. 499, the doctrine was applied to a case like the present,
where the accident concurring with negligence of the city in

producing the injury, was the running away of the plaintiff's horses, without fault on his part. There the city having constructed a drain under one of its streets, allowed it to so get out of repair, that a hole a foot wide, two feet long, and eight inches deep had been made in the street. The plaintiff was driving his horses to a lumber-wagon, when they ran away, one wheel of the wagon going into this hole; in the rebound plaintiff was violently thrown to the ground and injured. We there said, after approving the rule in the case of *Joliet* v. *Verley*, 35 Ill. 58, 85 Am. Dec. 342, and holding it applicable: "One great reason for requiring a corporation to keep its streets in repair is to reduce, as far as possible, the injuries that may result from the accidents so liable to occur in crowded thoroughfares. If the accident would not have caused the injury but for the defect in the street, and that defect is the result of carelessness on the part of the city, and the plaintiff has used ordinary care, the city must be held liable."

The same doctrine has been announced in many decided cases elsewhere: See *Ring* v. *City of Cohoes*, 77 N. Y. 83; 33 Am. Rep. 574; *Baldwin* v. *Greenwoods Turnpike Co.*, 40 Conn. 238; 16 Am. Rep. 33; *Hull* v. *Kansas City*, 54 Mo. 601; 14 Am. Rep. 487; *Hunt* v. *Town of Pownal*, 9 Vt. 411; *Winship* v. *Enfield*, 42 N. H. 197; *Hey* v. *Philadelphia*, 81 Pa. St. 44; 22 Am. Rep. 733; *Sherwood* v. *City of Hamilton*, 37 U. C. Q. B. 410; *Palmer* v. *Andover*, 2 Cush. 600; *Kelsey* v. *Glover*, 15 Vt. 708.

In *Baldwin* v. *Greenwoods Turnpike Co.*, 40 Conn. 238, 16 Am. Rep. 33, it is said: "If the plaintiff is in the exercise of ordinary care and prudence, and the injury is attributable to the negligence of the defendants combined with some accidental cause to which the plaintiff has not negligently contributed, the defendants are liable. Nor will the fact that the horse of the plaintiff was uncontrollable for some distance before the injury occurred in any way affect **410** the liability of the defendants." And the court held the loss should be charged upon the party guilty of the first and only negligence. In *Ring* v. *City of Cohoes*, 77 N. Y. 83, 16 Am. Rep. 33, after reviewing the authorities upon this subject, it is said: "When, without any fault of the driver, a horse becomes uncontrollable or runs away, it is regarded as an incidental occurrence, for which the driver is not responsible; and the rule, as laid down in the cases cited, may be formulated thus: When two causes combine to produce an injury upon a traveler upon a highway, both of which are in their nature proximate—the one being a culpable defect in the highway, and the other some occurrence for which neither party is responsible—the municipality is liable, provided the injury would not have been sustained but for such defect. This appears to us to be the reasonable rule." And after noting the care and diligence required of municipalities the court adds: "They are not bound to furnish roads upon which it will be safe for horses to run away, but they are bound to furnish reasonably safe roads; and if they do not, and a traveler is injured by culpable defects in the roads, it is no defense that his horse was at the time running away, or was beyond his control."

We are aware that the courts of Massachusetts, Maine, Wisconsin, and perhaps others have adopted the contrary rule, but we regard the doctrine to which this court is committed as the better and more reasonable one, and must decline to depart from it. No additional duty or obligation is imposed thereby upon the municipality. It is only required to use reasonable diligence and care in making its streets safe for the public use in view of those accidents which may, in the exercise of common prudence, be anticipated and guarded against. The general doctrine is, that it is no defense, in actions for injuries resulting from negligence, that the negligence of third persons, or an inevitable accident, or that an inanimate thing contributed to cause the injury to the plaintiff, if the negligence of the defendant was an efficient [411] cause, without which the injury would not have occurred: *Wabash etc. Ry. Co.* v. *Shacklet*, 105 Ill. 364; 44 Am. Rep. 791; *Union etc. Transit Co.* v. *Shacklet*, 119 Ill. 232; *Consolidated Ice Mach. Co.* v. *Keifer*, 134 Ill. 481; 23 Am. St. Rep. 688; *Pullman Palace Car Co.* v. *Laack*, 143 Ill. 242; *Peoria* v. *Simpson*, 110 Ill. 301; 51 Am. Rep. 683; sec. 16 Am. & Eng. Ency. of Law, 440, 443, and notes; 2 Thompson on Negligence, 1085. This being the general rule, we are unable to perceive in what way the intervention of the mere brute force or will of the horse, at liberty without fault or negligence of the plaintiff, and for which neither party is responsible, can be different in its effects or consequences from the intervention of the act of a third person or of an accident having a like effect, provided the injury would not have occurred but for the negligence of the defendant. In such case neither the running away of the horse nor the defects in the street are alone sufficient to produce the injury, but it is produced by the combination of both, and they become, therefore, in combination, the efficient and proximate cause. The causal relation is direct between the defective street, occasioned by the negligence or omission of duty by the defendant, and the injury to the plaintiff, and without any intervening efficient cause.

The verdict of the jury in this case was general, and might have been predicated on either of the charges contained in the declaration. They may have found that the negligence consisted in not raising the wall a sufficient height to prevent the plaintiff from being precipitated seventeen feet upon the stones at the bottom of the cut, or that the road was left too narrow, or because of its sloping toward the wall. The horse had already run down the declivity upon Broadway, and upon reaching the intersection with Exchange street made the turn into this narrow twelve-foot street with a descent of about nine feet in one hundred to the east, or lengthwise of the street, and descending also to the south, or toward the wall separating this roadway from the other cut by the city, and the natural result, the road, as stated by counsel for appellant, being smooth, [412] would be to give the buggy a violent lateral motion in the direction of the wall, which would be accelerated by the declivity of the road, and which might have been avoided had the road been level, or the outer edge of the segment of the circle described by the horse in turning been higher than the inner, or had the road sloped from, instead of to, the wall. The evidence shows that the horse did not come in contact with the wall, and the jury would be justified in finding that if the street had been of reasonable width, or had been so constructed that the buggy would not have been thrown against the wall, the injury would not have occurred. If they found that the injury resulted from either of said causes, and that the city was negligent therein, they would also be justified in finding that such negligence was the proximate cause of the injury. It is, however, urged that the court in this instruction assumed that the accident by which the horse became uncontrollable was an ordinary accident likely to occur, and that being a question of fact proper to be passed upon by the jury, it was error. Without pausing to discuss or determine whether the instruction is susceptible of that interpretation, if the point be conceded, it is not prejudicial error. The requirement of the instruction before the

jury could find the defendant guilty was, that they should
believe from the evidence "that said Exchange street was so
out of repair or defective that the same was not reasonably
safe or secure to guard against ordinary accidents likely to
occur thereon to persons using the same," in the exercise of
ordinary care and prudence. By another instruction given
by the court, at its own instance, the jury were told that the
defendant was not liable for the injury if they believed from
the evidence that the wall in question was of sufficient height
to be safe for persons who were exercising reasonable care, etc.,
and sufficiently high to prevent horses, carriages, and persons
from tipping or falling over the same "in case of accidents,
ordinarily likely to occur, while so driving on said street at
that point, and that the street at said point was otherwise,
[413] as to its condition of repair, in a reasonably safe condition for persons driving thereon," etc. Taking these instructions together, it seems impossible that the jury could have
understood the court as assuming the fact stated. But if
this was otherwise, it would form no just ground for reversal.
The breaking of bridles and harness, and of vehicles, are of
constant occurrence. That horses, otherwise tractable and
gentle, are liable to and do run away when thus freed from
restraint, is a common and ordinary experience, against
which every reasonable and prudent man takes precaution.
There was nothing extraordinary in this horse running away,
and it might reasonably have been anticipated. No one
would think it necessary to prove that it was an accident
likely to occur; it is a matter of common knowledge and
experience. And if the case were sent back for another trial,
and the question submitted as one of fact, the finding could
by no possibility be different, as to the accident being one
ordinarily likely to occur. Other objections were interposed
which we have carefully examined, but deem without merit.
Finding no prejudicial error, the judgment of the appellate
court will be affirmed.

———

NEGLIGENCE—PROXIMATE CAUSE. —This question will be found thoroughly
discussed in the lengthy note to *Gilson* v. *Delaware etc. Canal Co..*, 65 Vt.
213, *post*, 802, in which the leading case is cited and discussed.

GOODRICH v. TENNEY.

[144 ILLINOIS, 422.]

CONTRACTS ARE ILLEGAL WHEN FOUNDED ON A CONSIDERATION CONTRA BONOS MORES, or against the principles of sound public policy, or affected with fraud, or in contravention of the provisions of some statute. Instances of illegal contracts are those stipulating to pay money for influencing legislation, for violating public trust or office, for performance by public officers of their duties, for procuring public offices, for stifling criminal prosecutions, for procuring testimony to prove designated facts.

AN AGREEMENT TO PROCURE THE AFFIDAVITS OF DESIGNATED WITNESSES stating that no consideration was paid at a sale alleged to be fraudulent, and that the vendee knew of the vendor's insolvency, such affidavit to be used on motion for a new trial, and to procure the testimony of such witnesses of like tenor to be used upon the trial, in consideration that the party furnishing such affidavits and witnesses should be given one-fourth of all moneys and property realized on certain claims, and that the fraudulent transferrer whose testimony was to be procured should not be prosecuted, is against public policy and void, and no suit can be sustained for any relief thereon, or for any portion of the money or property realized in consequence thereof.

CONTRACTS, ILLEGAL.—COURTS OF JUSTICE WILL NOT ENFORCE the execution of an illegal contract, nor aid in the division of the profits of an illegal transaction between associates.

SUIT to have a contract declared to remain in force, and to compel an accounting of profits received by defendant by virtue thereof. Smith, an insolvent debtor, transferred a large amount of property to Lowey. Suits were brought by Smith's creditors to have this transfer set aside as a fraud upon them. In one of these suits a decree was entered in favor of the defendant. While a motion for a new trial was pending, the complainant Goodrich and the agents of sundry creditors entered into an agreement by which the complainant was to procure an affidavit on the part of Smith and two other persons, to the effect that in the sale made by Smith no consideration had been paid, and that the purchaser, Lowey, knew that Smith was insolvent, and if a new trial was granted, then complainant was to procure these witnesses to testify to the facts stated in the affidavits, and in consideration of his services complainant was to receive one-fourth of all money recovered by the creditors, and Smith was to be released by the creditors from any right they might have to arrest him for making the fraudulent transfer. The affidavits were procured and a new trial granted thereon, and when the case was again tried, the witnesses again testified to the facts stated in the affidavits, decrees were entered declaring the trans-

fer fraudulent void, and as a result of which the defendant
Tenney recovered about one hundred and twenty thousand
dollars, but he refused to share any portion thereof with the
complainant. Judgment was entered in favor of defendant
on demurrer to the bill.

H. T. and L. Helm, for the appellant.

William E. Church, for the appellees.

427 Shope, J. It is probable that the demurrer was properly sustained upon the ground, that if the complainant had
a right of recovery, his remedy was complete at law, and possibly also upon the ground of laches, but we will consider the
single question of the validity of the contract sought to be
enforced.

No good purpose can be served by a consideration of the
allegations of this bill, setting up the confederacy and fraud
by which appellant was induced to surrender the written contract to Tenney. It is alleged that it was expressly agreed,
that the surrender of the writing should not abrogate the contract, or make any difference as to the rights of appellant
thereunder, but that his interest should remain the same. If
the allegations of the bill are true, the surrender was made to
destroy the written evidence of appellant's interest, because
of the pretended fear that his interest under such a contract,
if known, would prejudice Tenney's case against Lowey, and
to enable the attorney to more safely, but falsely, testify, if
called therein, that no such contract existed. So with those
allegations, which are explanatory of why appellant, himself,
falsely denied that there was any such contract, or that he
had any interest in the litigation against Lowey, as it is
alleged he did, when called and examined in said creditor's
bill proceeding. And the same is true of the allegations setting up the fraudulent and oppressive acts and conduct, by
which, after the rendition of the decree against Lowey, appellant was induced to execute and **428** deliver to Tenney an
absolute release and acquittance of all claim or right whatsoever, to the money derived under said decree. If the utmost
that can be claimed in respect of such allegations be conceded,
they amount to no more than that, because of the fraud practiced, the surrender was ineffectual to abrogate or destroy the
contract; that appellant should not be estopped from now
asserting his rights under said contract by his false denial of
its existence; and that said release is, as between appellant

and appellees, fraudulent, and should be set aside, and the
contract as originally made be held to be in full force and
effect. The specific prayer of this bill is, "that the said contract so delivered to said defendants may be restored to your
orator, and the rights in and under the same may be established and confirmed, and the said release so fraudulently ex-
torted from your orator be cancelled and annulled and for
naught held, and the said defendants may be required to pay
to your orator the amount that shall be found due and owing
. . . . under and pursuant to the terms of said agreement,"
etc. The right of recovery, if it exists, is, therefore, predicated
solely upon and involves the enforcement of the contract set
up in the bill. It is under and by virtue of that contract
alone, that it is sought to establish appellant's right to the
money, and there is nothing, except said agreement, that
would give him any right, either at law or in equity, to demand the payment of the twenty-five per cent of the amount
collected of Lowey.

The English reports, as well as American, abound with
cases holding that contracts are illegal when founded upon a
consideration, *contra bonos mores*, or against the principles of
sound public policy, or founded in fraud, or in contravention
of the provisions of some statute (2 Kent's Commentaries,
466); and we need not review the cases illustrating the application of the rule. Thus, contracts to pay money to influence
legislation (*Marshall* v. *Baltimore etc. R. R. Co.*, 16 How. 314;
Mills v. *Mills*, 40 N. Y. 543; 100 Am. Dec. 535; *McBratney* v.
Chandler, 22 Kan. 692; 31 Am. Rep. 213; [429] *Bryan* v. *Reynolds*, 5 Wis. 200; 68 Am. Dec. 55; *Powers* v. *Skinner*, 34 Vt.
274; 80 Am. Dec. 677); agreements founded upon violations
of public trust or confidence· (*Cooth* v. *Jackson*, 6 Ves. 12–35);
contracts to pay public officers for the performance of official
duty (*Odineal* v. *Barry*, 24 Miss. 9); contracts for the buying,
selling or procuring of public office (*Chesterfield* v. *Janssen*,
1 Atk. 352; *Boynton* v. *Hubbard*, 7 Mass. 119; *Waldo* v. *Martin*, 4 Barn. & C. 319); agreements for the purpose of stifling
criminal prosecutions (*Gorham* v. *Keyes*, 137 Mass. 583; *Henderson* v. *Palmer*, 71 Ill. 579; 22 Am. Rep. 117; *Ricketts* v.
Harvey, 106 Ind. 564; *McMahon* v. *Smith*, 47 Conn. 221; 36
Am. Rep. 67; *Roll* v. *Raguet*, 4 Ohio, 400; 22 Am. Dec. 759);
agreements relating to civil proceedings involving anything
inconsistent with the full and impartial course of justice
therein (*Dawkins* v. *Gill*, 10 Ala. 206); or that tend to per-

vert the course of justice or its pure administration by the courts (*Gillett* v. *Board of Supervisors*, 67 Ill. 256; *Patterson* v. *Donner*, 48 Cal. 369), and many others, are justly deemed contracts of turpitude, contrary to sound public policy and void: 1 Story's Equity Jurisprudence, secs. 293–300; 3 Am. & Eng. Ency. of Law, 875–881, and notes.

In *Gillett* v. *Board of Supervisors*, 67 Ill. 256, the contracts were to pay for procuring testimony showing that a certain number of votes cast at an election were illegal, and we said that: "On account of their corrupting tendency we must hold them to be void as inconsistent with public policy." It was also there said, in effect, that such contracts created a powerful inducement to make use of improper means to procure the testimony contracted for, to secure the desired result; that they led to the subornation of witnesses, to taint with corruption the atmosphere of courts and to pervert the course of justice. In *Patterson* v. *Donner*, 48 Cal. 369, it was agreed among other things that a certain sum of money should be paid, etc., provided the party procured "two witnesses to testify that they had seen what purported to be a genuine grant" of the land mentioned, etc., and it was held that the stipulation was immoral, against public policy and void.

430 Courts of justice will not enforce the execution of illegal contracts, nor aid in the division of the profits of an illegal transaction between associates: *Neustadt* v. *Hall*, 58 Ill. 172. It is there said: "In the language of Lord Ellenborough in *Edgar* v. *Fowler*, 3 East, 222, 'we will not assist an illegal transaction in any respect; we leave the matter as we find it and then the maxim applies, *melior est conditio possidentis.*'" It may be insisted that it is unjust as between the parties for Tenney to raise the question, and very dishonest toward appellant for him to take advantage of it, but the contract being illegal no rights can be enforced under it. As said by Lord Mansfield, in *Holman* v. *Johnson*, Cowp. 341, "no court will lend its aid to a man who founds his cause of action upon an illegal or immoral act." The maxim *ex turpi contractu non oritur actio* applies in all such cases, and neither party, if *in pari delicto*, can have assistance from courts of justice in enforcing the contract. And the objection may be made by a party *in pari delicto*, for the offense is not allowed because the party raising the objection is entitled to the relief, but upon principles of public policy and to conserve the public welfare.

No better illustration can perhaps be found of the soundness and wisdom of the rule, and the dangers to be apprehended from its relaxation, than is shown in this case. It is apparent that Lowey was in equal peril of recovery against him, whether he had paid full and honest value upon purchase of the goods from Smith, or had taken them in fraud of the rights of the creditors. Smith, a dishonest debtor, after cheating his creditors, absconded. The appellant, as alleged, in consideration of the agreement of Tenney to pay him twenty-five per cent, practically, of whatever should be collected from Lowey, undertook and agreed to procure the affidavit of said Smith, of one Fuller with an *alias*, and one Moies "of the facts of the sale by Smith to Lowey, showing clearly that no consideration was paid by Lowey, and that he knew of Smith's insolvency," "and that [431] the testimony of said witnesses, either in person or by deposition, should be given of like tenor," etc.

Copies of the affidavits alleged to have been furnished, and which, it is alleged, were received as a satisfactory fulfillment of appellant's contract in that regard, are attached to the bill as exhibits, and show that the witnesses testified up to the high mark set by the contract. Smith was brought back from Canada, secured immunity from arrest for his fraud, his debts canceled, if he would testify as required, and it is apparent from the bill that he at least claimed a portion of the money, and was actually paid fourteen thousand dollars; and this under the direction and control, if the bill be true, of an attorney who deliberately laid the foundation for the commission of perjury with safety by himself, if called to testify, and advised the commission of perjury by appellant, and framed the language in which he should commit it. And the testimony was procured by appellant, who, after planning with the attorney as to the wording of his false testimony, deliberately gave it, for no other reason, than that he was led to believe that his telling the truth would endanger the chances of success in the litigation against Lowey. If transactions of this kind should receive sanction, and contracts based upon them be enforced, the suborner of perjury would become a potent, if not a necessary, factor in litigation. The fact that purchase was made in good faith would be no protection to the buyer; premium would be offered to the dishonest and unscrupulous, and would result in the perversion of justice and bringing its administration into deserved disrepute. It

is not enough that the parties may have intended no wrong,
or that the testimony produced in the case may have been
true, it is the tendency of such contracts to the perversion of
justice, that renders them illegal. It is perhaps a singular
fact, however, though unimportant, that this bill nowhere
alleges that either the attorney or appellant believed, or had
any reason to believe, the testimony of Smith was in fact true.
That, so far as this bill goes, seemed to have been a matter
not considered.

432 That this contract falls directly within the maxim
before quoted is unquestionable; and by all the authorities
the courts can do nothing to enforce it by either party.

But it is said that Tenney having received the money must
account for it to appellant. And, we are referred by counsel
to a line of cases, holding that although the money may have
been realized in an illegal transaction, yet where the liability
of the defendant to pay it to the plaintiff arises upon some
new or independent consideration, unaffected with illegality,
and the enforcement of the illegal contract is not involved,
there may be a recovery. None of the cases referred to have
any application to the case at bar. As said in *Dent* v. *Ferguson*, 132 U. S. 50, in commenting upon this line of cases:
" In all those cases the court was careful to distinguish and
sever the new contract from the original illegal contract.
Whether in the application of this principle some of them do
not trench upon the line which separates the cases of contracts
void in consequence of their illegality, from new and subsequent contracts arising out of the accomplishment of the illegal object, is not the subject of inquiry here." It is to be
remembered, the contract was, as alleged, with the defendant
D. K. Tenney, and signed by him, and who collected the
money of Lowey as trustee for the creditors of Smith. If the
money had been paid to a third person for the use of appellant, or there were collateral circumstances, disconnected
with the illegal contract, out of which an implied promise to
pay the money to appellant would arise, the cases referred to
would apply. But the fact that Tenney received the money
upon the decree against Lowey would, independently of the
contract, raise no implied *assumpsit* in appellant's favor.

The controversy here arises between the parties to the illegal agreement, and appellant must, if at all, assert his claim
to the money in Tenney's hands through and under that contract. Treat that as void, as if never made, and there is

nothing upon which appellant can base a claim to the money. The case [433] principally relied upon by appellant, as sustaining his contention is *McBlair* v. *Gibbes*, 17 How. 232.

In that case one Goodwin had an interest in a claim held by the Baltimore Company, for supplies furnished in fitting out a military expedition against dominions of the Spanish government, under a contract in violation of the neutrality laws of the United States, and therefore illegal: *Gill* v. *Oliver*, 11 How. 529. In 1829 Goodwin, for an independent valuable consideration, assigned his right and interest in the claim to one Oliver. Under the convention of 1839 "for the adjustment of claims of citizens of the United States against the Mexican Republic," the illegality of the contract was waived and the claim paid. The question at issue was, whether the assignment to Oliver was valid. The court found that in determining that question, the illegality of the contract with the Mexican general, Mina, upon which the claim against Mexico was based, was not involved; its illegality had been waived by the Mexican government, and payment of the claim made. The court finding that the assignment was made for a valuable consideration paid by Oliver, and was in itself untainted with illegality, after review of the authorities, held that it passed whatever rights Goodwin had, which might be nothing if the illegality of the contract was interposed, or all that was claimed if the promisor saw fit to waive it. It seems clear that this case in principle can have no application to the case at bar, and is clearly distinguishable from a case where it is sought to enforce the illegal contract, or to enforce one made in aid or furtherance of a contract so infected. Appellant also relies on *Willson* v. *Owen*, 30 Mich. 474. There the defendant received money as treasurer of a horse-fair association for entrance fees, stock subscriptions and commissions on pools sold, which he refused to pay over. It was conceded that the business in which the money was earned was unlawful. The plaintiffs, who had organized the association, brought an action for money had and received. It was held, that the defendant having in fact received the money for the plaintiffs' [434] use, he could not appropriate it to himself but must account for it. The plaintiff's case was made out, when they showed that the defendant had received the money for their use. And the court distinguished the case from that of *Bronson etc. Assn.* v. *Ramsdell*, 24 Mich. 441, where the attempt was to collect money earned by illegal

means, and where the recovery must be had, if at all, in furtherance of the illegal transaction. In *Tenant* v. *Elliott*, 1
Bos. & P. 3, a broker procured illegal insurance; upon loss
the insurance company paid the money to the broker, who
refused to pay it over to the insured, setting up the illegality
of the insurance. The plaintiff was held entitled to recover,
upon the ground that the implied promise of the defendant,
arising from the receipt by him of the money, was a new undertaking unaffected by the illegality of the insurance. So in
Sharp v. *Taylor*, 2 Phill. Ch. 801, a bill was filed to recover a
moiety of freight money earned by a vessel engaged in trade in
violation of the navigation laws and illegal, which money had
come into the hands of one of the joint owners. The illegality
of the trade was set up as a defense, but it was answered by
the lord chancellor that the plaintiff was not seeking the
enforcement of an illegal agreement, or compensation, for the
performance of an illegal voyage, but was seeking his share
of the profits realized, and in the hands of the defendant joint
owner. It there required no enforcement of an illegal contract
or agreement, to hold the defendant liable to account to the
other joint owner. The liability arose from the receipt of the
money as the agent of the plaintiff in respect of his moiety.

The cases of *Tenant* v. *Elliott*, 1 Bos. & P. 3, and *Farmer* v.
Russell, 1 Bos. & P. 296, are referred to as sustaining the distinction in this case. A further reference to this line of cases
will not be necessary. The distinction between the enforcement of the illegal contract, and asserting title to money
arising therefrom, where there is an express contract to pay
upon sufficient consideration, or where the collateral circumstances are such as to raise an implied promise to pay to the
[435] plaintiff, is recognized and carefully made, in practically
all of the cases.

In the case of *Thomson* v. *Thomson*, 7 Ves. 470, Sir William
Grant, master of the rolls, drew the distinction with great
clearness. A sale of the command of an East India Company ship was made to the defendant, who agreed to pay
therefor an annuity of two hundred pounds. Under regulations adopted by the company to prevent such sales, the defendant subsequently relinquished the command, and was
allowed three thousand five hundred pounds; two thousand
and forty pounds of which was delivered to an agent of the
defendant. A bill was filed by the annuitant for the purpose
of procuring a decree declaring the value of the annuity, and

enforcing its payment out of the allowance to the defendant.
The master of the rolls found the agreement for the payment
of the annuity to be illegal, and admitting there existed an
equity against the fund, if it could be reached through a legal
agreement, said: "You have no claim to this money, except
through the medium of an illegal agreement, which, according to the determinations, you cannot support. I should have
no difficulty in following the fund, provided you could recover against the party himself." And after citing *Tenant* v.
Elliott, 1 Bos. & P. 3, as authority for the position that, if the
company had paid the money into the hands of a third person for the use of the plaintiff, he might have recovered, further observed: "But in this instance it is paid to the party —
for there can be no difference as to the payment to his agent
—then how are you to get at it, except through this agreement? There is nothing collateral, in respect of which, the
agreement being out of the question, a collateral demand
arises. Here you cannot stir a step but through the illegal
agreement, and it is impossible for the court to enforce it."
So here, the right of appellant to recover of appellees depends
solely upon the contract, the provisions of which cannot be
enforced in a court of justice.

The unfortunate delay of appellant in disclosing the fact
alleged, for more than three years after the facts occurred,
will [436] probably prevent their investigation where they could
receive that attention their merit demands, and the bill not
being verified, forms no basis for further investigation in this
court.

The bill was properly dismissed, and the judgment of the
appellate court will be affirmed.

CONTRACTS—ILLEGALITY.—A contract is illegal when it violates good
morals, or is opposed to public policy, or is affected with fraud, or violates
the provisions of a public statute: *Ohio etc. Trust Co.* v. *Merchants' etc. Trust
Co.*, 11 Humph. 1; 53 Am. Dec. 742, and note; *City Bank* v. *Perkins*, 29
N. Y. 554; 86 Am. Dec. 332, and note; *Schmidt* v. *Barker*, 17 La. Ann. 261;
87 Am. Dec. 527, and note; *Bowman* v. *Gonegal*, 19 La. Ann. 328; 92 Am.
Dec. 537, and note; *Tatum* v. *Kelley*, 25 Ark. 209; 94 Am. Dec. 717, and
note; *Mahood* v. *Tealza*, 26 La. Ann. 108; 21 Am. Rep. 546; *Hubbard* v.
Moore, 24 La. Ann. 591; 13 Am. Rep. 128. See the extended notes to *Lemon*
v. *Grosskopf*, 99 Am. Dec. 61–68; and *Bowman* v. *Phillips*, 13 Am. St. Rep.
297.

CONTRACTS—ILLEGAL—ENFORCEMENT OF.—An illegal contract is void, it
creates no obligation between the parties, and cannot form the basis of
judicial action: *Santa Clara Valley Mill etc. Co.* v. *Hayes*, 76 Cal. 387; 9

Am. St. Rep. 211, and note; *Comstock* v. *Draper*, 1 Mich. 481; 53 Am. Dec. 78; *Howell* v. *Fountain*, 3 Ga. 176; 46 Am. Dec. 415, and note; *Webb* v. *Fulchire*, 3 Ired. 485; 40 Am. Dec. 419, and note; *Bowman* v. *Phillips*, 41 Kan. 364; 13 Am. St. Rep. 292; *Leonard* v. *Poole*, 114 N. Y. 371; 11 Am. St. Rep. 667. See the extended notes to *Tracy* v. *Talmage*, 67 Am. Dec. 153; and *Seidenbender* v. *Charles*, 8 Am. Dec. 691.

RHOADS *v.* CITY OF METROPOLIS.

[144 ILLINOIS, 580.]

RES JUDICATA—WHERE SEVERAL DEFENSES ARE PLEADED, upon all of which evidence is given, a general verdict in favor of the defendant followed by a judgment thereon, is at least *prima facie* evidence that all the issues were found in his favor. Therefore if in an action of trespass *quare clausum fregit* against a city for removing soil from an alleged street, the defendant pleaded 1, that the *locus in quo* is a public highway; 2, the statute of limitations; 3, that the *locus in quo* is the property of the defendant, and evidence was offered by both parties on all the issues, and a general verdict entered in favor of the defendant, such verdict is in a subsequent action between the same parties, *prima facie* evidence that all the issues were found in favor of the defendant.

C. L. V. Mulkey, for the plaintiff in error.

Courtney and Helm, for the defendant in error.

[583] BAILEY, J. The city of Metropolis brought against Solomon J. Rhoads, before a police magistrate, for a violation of a city [584] ordinance, such violation consisting, as is alleged, in erecting two fences across a certain public street, of said city, thereby obstructing said street. The police magistrate imposed upon the defendant a fine of ten dollars and rendered judgment against him for that sum and costs, and the defendant thereupon removed the cause to the circuit court by appeal. In that court a jury was waived, and a trial *de novo* was had before the court upon the following stipulation as to the facts:

"It is agreed and stipulated by and between the parties to the above-entitled suit, which is a prosecution for the recovery of a penalty for the violation of a city ordinance in obstructing a street within said city, that the same shall be tried upon the following agreed state of facts:

"It is agreed that, in the year 1885, the above-named defendant brought an action of trespass *quare clausum fregit* against the city of Metropolis for removing the soil from the alleged street and grading the same. To this action of trespass the city pleaded: 1. The general issue with notice that evidence would be offered under the general issue to prove that the *locus in quo* was a public highway within the corporate limits of the city; 2. The statute of limitations; and 3. That the *locus in quo* was the property of the city. Issue was taken on all the pleas. Evidence was offered by both parties on all the issues made by the pleadings, and also evidence was offered by both parties under the notice that the *locus in quo* was a public highway within said city. That is to say, under the notice evidence was given to the jury by the city that the *locus in quo* was a public highway within the city, and that the acts done were in repairing the same. Rhoads gave evidence to the jury that the *locus in quo* was not a public highway. But no evidence was offered by the city under the general issue. The plaintiff Rhoads offered evidence to prove the allegations in his declaration. The jury found the defendant in that suit not guilty, and at the April term, 1887, of said court, a judgment was rendered for the defendant on the general verdict of not guilty.

[585] "Now if the above verdict and judgment thereon concludes and estops Rhoads from offering evidence in the present suit to prove that the *locus in quo* or the alleged street, which is the same identical property in controversy in the trespass suit, is not a public highway, or estops him from proving the property to be the property of himself, then the court is to render a judgment for the city of Metropolis, and assess a penalty against Rhoads, under the ordinance, for ten dollars and costs. But if such judgment does not operate as an estoppel as above set forth then, and in that event, the court shall render a judgment in this suit in favor of Rhoads, and assess costs thereon against the city of Metropolis."

The foregoing stipulation was all the evidence offered on said trial, and on said stipulation the court found the defendant guilty, and rendered judgment against him for a fine of ten dollars and costs. The defendant having excepted to said finding and judgment, appealed to the appellate court, where said judgment was affirmed, and he now brings the record to this court by writ of error to the appellate court.

The only contention made here is, that the courts below erred in holding that the verdict and judgment in the action of trespass *quare clausum fregit*, mentioned in said stipulation, should have the effect of an estoppel upon the defendant in this suit to deny that the *locus in quo* of the alleged obstructions is a public highway, within the corporate limits of and the property of said city. In that action, as the stipulation shows, the plaintiff, who is the defendant here, charged the city with trespass in breaking and entering his close, which is the *locus in quo* of the present controversy, and digging up and removing the soil therefrom. The city, by its pleadings, set up three distinct defenses: 1. That presented by the plea of not guilty, which in that form of action constituted merely a denial of the acts of trespass complained of; 2. That raised by the notice filed with the general issue that the city would prove on the trial that said *locus in quo* was a public highway [586] within and the property of the city, thus presenting in substance the defense of *liberum tenementum;* and 3. The statute of limitations. It is admitted that evidence applicable to all of these defenses was introduced at the trial, except that the city gave no evidence in support of its plea of not guilty. The verdict of the jury was not guilty, which, as must be admitted, was in form at least, if not in substance and effect, a general verdict in favor of the defendant upon all the issues submitted, and on such verdict judgment was rendered in favor of the city.

The plaintiff in error insists that as there were several distinct defenses presented by the pleadings, either of which, if sustained by the evidence, justified a verdict of not guilty, it cannot now be determined upon which of said defenses the jury in fact based their verdict. It is therefore argued that the verdict and judgment are not inconsistent with the theory that the city may have failed to prove its title, but succeeded in proving that the trespasses with which it was charged were committed at such time that an action therefor was barred by the statute, and consequently that no conclusive presumption arises that the defense of *liberum tenementum* was sustained.

The decisions of the courts of the different states are not altogether uniform as to the effect, as an estoppel, of a verdict and judgment in favor of a defendant, in a case where several distinct and separate defenses are presented by the pleadings; but in our opinion the preponderance of authority sustains what seems to us to be the better and more reasonable rule, that where evidence upon all the issues is heard a general verdict in favor of the defendant is at least *prima facie* evidence that all the issues presented by the pleadings were

found in his favor. *White* v. *Simonds*, 33 Vt. 178, 78 Am.
Dec. 620, is quite in point. That was an action of *assumpsit*
on three promissory notes, and the defendants relied for their
defense upon a judgment in their favor in the state of Massachusetts in a suit on the same notes, in which two issues
were tried, one denying the merits of the plaintiff's claim,
and the other only presenting a temporary [587] bar to the
plaintiff's recovery. It appeared that upon the trial of that
case evidence was introduced by the defendants on both
issues, and that a general verdict was returned in their favor,
on which a general judgment was rendered. Such former
verdict and judgment were held to be conclusive of the issue
denying the merits, the court saying: "When a case is
submitted to the jury, involving two or more issues, with
evidence tending to sustain them all, and a general verdict
is rendered, such verdict is *prima facie* evidence that all the
issues were found in favor of the party for whom the verdict
is rendered. And when, as in this case, a judgment on such
verdict is presented by the defendants to defeat a recovery
in a subsequent suit, brought on the same cause of action,
the burden of showing that the verdict in the first suit was
rendered upon an issue presenting only a temporary bar, and
that such bar has since been removed, or has ceased to operate, is thrown upon the plaintiff."

In *Day* v. *Vallette*, 25 Ind. 42; 87 Am. Dec. 353, a general
verdict and judgment in favor of the defendants was pleaded
in bar, and it appeared that the issues joined in the former
suit involved the same questions presented in the suit on trial,
but that there were also other issues in the former suit, which
if found for the same party would have produced the same
result, even though the issues involved in the suit on trial
had been decided the other way, and it was held that while
the former verdict and judgment were not necessarily a conclusive bar to the second suit, they were so *prima facie*.

In *Sheldon* v. *Edwards*, 35 N. Y. 279, the defendant in a
former suit, had, under the provisions of the New York code,
joined in his answer what amounted to a plea in abatement
with a plea to the merits in bar, and it was held that a general verdict and judgment in favor of the defendant in such
former suit was a bar in his favor in a subsequent suit, as to
both defenses.

In *Merchants' International Steamboat Line* v. *Lyon*, 12 Fed.
Rep. 63, the trial court charged the jury, that where two

588 defenses are set up in an answer, and evidence is submitted to a jury upon the trial of the action tending to support both defenses, and a general verdict is rendered for the defendant, such verdict and judgment is a bar in another action upon the same demand. On motion for a new trial heard by both the circuit and district judges it was held that said charge was correct: See Freeman on Judgments, sec. 276.

It should be observed that in the case at bar there is no attempt to rebut the presumption arising from the verdict and judgment, and it is therefore unnecessary for us to consider whether said presumption is anything more than *prima facie*, or whether it is subject to be rebutted by proof that the jury in fact found but one of the issues in the former suit in favor of the city. It is difficult, however, to see how a party, after admitting that evidence in support of both defenses was submitted to the jury, could show *aliunde* that the verdict was found upon one and not both defenses, without inquiring into the secret deliberations of the jury-room, and that is seldom if ever admissible.

We are of the opinion that the circuit and appellate courts adopted the correct rule in the premises, and the judgment of the appellate court will therefore be affirmed.

JUDGMENTS—RES JUDICATA.—A former judgment is conclusive only as to the matters which were directly in issue in the former suit: Note to *King v. Chase,* 41 Am. Dec. 682. A judgment for the plaintiff sweeps away every defense which should have been raised against the action: *Graham v. Culver,* 3 Wyo. 639; 31 Am. St. Rep. 105, and note. A judgment rendered on its merits is conclusive as to all the matters directly at issue in the pleadings which the defeated party might have litigated: *Lorillard v. Clyde,* 122 N. Y. 41; 19 Am. St. Rep. 470, and note; *Huntley v. Halt,* 59 Conn. 102; 21 Am. St. Rep. 71, and note; *Day v. Vallette,* 25 Ind. 42; 87 Am. Dec. 353, and note. See the extended notes to the following cases: *Gayer v. Parker,* 8 Am. St. Rep. 229; *Lea v. Lea,* 96 Am. Dec. 775, and *Borngesser v. Harrison,* 78 Am. Dec. 760.

SPEYER v. DESJARDINS.

[144 ILLINOIS, 641.]

STATUTE OF FRAUDS—PLEADING.—Compliance with the statute of frauds need not be pleaded either at law or in equity, because it is presumed.

STATUTE OF FRAUDS—PLEADING—THE BENEFIT OF THE STATUTE OF FRAUDS AS A DEFENSE cannot be taken by demurrer, unless when it affirmatively appears by the bill and complaint that the demurrer relied upon was not evidenced by a writing duly signed. If the agreement is alleged to have been made between the parties, it will be presumed to have been in writing and signed, when such signature and writing are necessary to its validity.

STATUTE OF FRAUDS—AN ORAL AGREEMENT BETWEEN TWO OR MORE PERSONS TO PURCHASE REAL ESTATE for their joint benefit is within the statute of frauds.

STATUTE OF FRAUDS—A PARTNERSHIP FOR BUYING AND SELLING LANDS FOR PROFIT may be created by parol. The existence of such partnership and the respective interests of the several parties therein may also be established by parol.

BILL in chancery alleging that the complainant Speyer and defendant Desjardins entered into an agreement to purchase certain land in Cook county, Illinois, and to erect six buildings thereon according to plans drawn by complainant; that the purchase of the lands and the erection of the buildings were with a view to selling the property and dividing the profits between the parties; that it was agreed that each should furnish one-half of the money required and should be entitled to one-half of the profits realized; that the lands were purchased for three thousand seven hundred and fifty dollars, and the title taken in the name of the defendant, and a loan was effected for the sum of twelve thousand dollars, secured by deed of trust on the same property; that the purchase price was paid out of the moneys raised by the deed of trust, and the residue of the moneys borrowed was used to erect the buildings; that on these buildings complainant performed the duties of architect and superintendent, and the defendant gave his services as a carpenter; that after the buildings were completed, defendant refused to account with complainant, and took and held exclusive possession and claimed to be the sole owner of the property. The bill contained other allegations tending to show the amounts advanced by each party and the sum which should be awarded each upon an accounting. A demurrer to the bill for want of equity was interposed and sustained, and complainant appealed.

Duncan and Gilbert, W. J. Hynes, and E. F. Dunne, for the appellant.

Henry Meiselbar, for the appellees.

647 BAKER, J. Appellees assume that, since the bill of complaint fails to affirmatively allege that the contract between appellant and Desjardins was in writing, therefore, under the primary rule of pleading that allegations must be taken most strongly against the pleader, it is to be regarded as sufficiently appearing upon the face of the bill that said agreement was not in writing, and rested entirely in parol. Appellees are wrong in this assumption. While in England, prior to recent changes by acts of Parliament, the presumption, that prevails in actions at law, that the statute of frauds has been complied with, did not obtain in suits in equity, and the complainants in such suits were bound either to aver compliance with its provisions, or allege facts that took the case out of the statute, yet, in this country, the doctrine is, both at law and in equity, that compliance with the statute is presumed, and the party plaintiff is not required to set out compliance in his declaration or bill. In Indiana and Iowa, and possibly in a few other states, special statutory requirements change or modify that which may be regarded as the American rule, but no such statute is in force in this state. See 8 Am. & Eng. Ency. of Law, p. 745, and cases cited in note 7.

The rule then is, that the benefit of the statute, as a defense, can be taken by demurrer only when it affirmatively appears from the bill that the agreement relied on was not evidenced by a writing duly signed. Here the allegation simply is, that the complainant and Desjardins "entered into an agreement to purchase" certain designated lots and real estate, and "to erect thereon" certain specified buildings. It must be presumed from these averments that the agreement was in writing and properly signed by the parties. This being so, and there being no question but that the bill, if based on an agreement made in conformity with the requirements of the statute, states a case for equitable relief clearly within the jurisdiction of **648** a court of equity, it necessarily follows that it was error to sustain the demurrer, and dismiss the bill for want of equity.

To simply reverse the decree and remand the cause for the error stated, without any expression of opinion in regard to

the principal matter of contention between the parties, would
be unadvisable. It would likely be of little benefit in the
future progress of the cause upon the remandment, that the
decree was reversed on a point which only incidently arose,
that which is evidently the real controversy being ignored.

The theory of the bill is that there is a partnership between
appellant and Desjardins, and that the lots and the buildings
erected thereon are partnership property; and the claim of
appellant is that the statute of frauds has no application to
such a case.

It is well settled that an oral contract by two or more persons to purchase real estate for their joint benefit is within the
statute. But it has been a mooted question whether a partnership can be created by parol for the purpose of buying and
selling lands for profit. There is a very considerable conflict
in the cases upon that question, but the decided weight of
authority seems to have answered it in the affirmative. That
an agreement for a partnership, for the purpose of dealing and
trading in lands for profit, is not within the statute, and that
the fact of the existence of the partnership, and the extent of
each party's interest, may be shown by parol is now quite
generally accepted as the established doctrine: *Dale* v. *Hamilton*, 5 Hare, 369; *Essex* v. *Essex*, 20 Beav. 449; *Holmes* v.
McCray, 51 Ind. 358; 19 Am. Rep. 735; *Richards* v. *Grinnell*,
63 Iowa, 44; 50 Am. Rep. 727; *Chester* v. *Dickerson*, 54 N. Y.
1; 13 Am. Rep. 550; *Black* v. *Black*, 15 Ga. 449; *Fall River
Whaling Co.* v. *Borden*, 10 Cush. 458; *Bunnel* v. *Taintor*, 4
Conn. 568; *Pennybacker* v. *Leary*, 65 Iowa, 220; *Gibbons* v.
Bell, 45 Tex. 417; *Personette* v. *Pryme*, 34 N. J. Eq. 26.

It is useless to restate the arguments *pro* and *con* bearing on
the point under consideration; and it is hardly probable [649]
that we could now make any suggestion that has not already
been fully considered. The leading and more important cases
are discussed or referred to in Browne on the Statute of
Frauds, 4th ed., section 259 et seq. and notes, and are also
cited in notes to pages 700 to 704 of volume eight of American
and English Encyclopedia of Law.

- The cases we have cited, and many others, proceed upon the
theory that the real estate of a partnership is treated and administered in equity, as between partners and for all the purposes of the partnership, as personal property and partnership
assets. From its *status* in equity of being stock in trade and
partnership assets, it is readily deducible that it is immaterial

whether the legal title to the partnership land is in all the partners, or in one, or in some number less than the whole; that it is not material whether the partnership was already established and engaged in its business when the land was acquired and brought into the partnership stock, or whether the partnership was established and the land acquired and put in contemporaneously, or whether the partnership was established for the express and special purpose of dealing in and making profit out of the very land itself which is in question; and that the facts of the existence of the partnership and that the lands were acquired and used for partnership purposes, being shown by parol, it is immaterial whether such partnership was formed by written articles or by parol: Browne's Statute of Frauds, sec. 261 a.

The doctrine of the cases we have cited, so far as it involves the provisions of the statute of frauds, seems to proceed upon the ground of a trust implied from the relation of copartnership.

The matter here at issue is a close question and beset with difficulties whichever view is taken. It seems difficult to demonstrate to a certainty that the doctrine above stated should prevail and take partnership agreements and partnership property out of the statute, and equally difficult to satisfactorily [650] demonstrate that such agreements are within the statute, as held in *Smith* v. *Burnham*, 3 Sum. 437, *Bird* v. *Morrison*, 12 Wis. 138, and other cases. Upon the whole, we are inclined to follow the view which seems to obtain in England and in most of the states of the Union, that partnership agreements and partnership lands, as between the partners and for all partnership purposes, are not within the statute.

The bill in the case at bar shows that the parties agreed to purchase the five lots and erect buildings thereon, each party contributing one-half of the money necessary for the enterprise, the lots and buildings then to be sold, and the profit or loss arising from the enterprise to be divided equally between them. This was manifestly a partnership agreement. The bill then shows that the parties purchased the lots "in pursuance of the agreement," and that at the same time and as a part of the same transaction, money was raised by placing mortgages on the lots and the purchase price of the lots paid with such money. Whose money, then, was it that was applied in payment of the lots? It is admitted that, by the terms of the partnership agreement, all liabilities that the partners,

or either of them, should create in furtherance of the enterprise, were to be, as between the partners, treated and considered as joint liabilities to be met and shared by them in equal
shares. This would seem to stamp the money that was received on the mortgages and paid on the lots as partnership
money. Since, then, the money, by force of the agreement,
was partnership money, it follows that when three thousand
seven hundred and fifty dollars of it was, at the time of the
purchase, paid as the purchase money of the lots, a resulting
trust at once arose by operation of law, out of the transaction,
in favor of the partnership: See *Wallace* v. *Carpenter*, 85 Ill.
590.

Our conclusion, therefore, is, that, without regard to the
question whether or not the partnership agreement mentioned
in the bill of complaint was in writing, a proper case for the
[651] interposition of a court of chancery was stated in the bill,
and it was error to sustain the demurrer and dismiss said bill.

The decree is reversed and the cause is remanded, with
directions to overrule the demurrer.

STATUTE OF FRAUDS--NECESSITY FOR PLEADING.—The statute of frauds is
not waived because it is not specially pleaded: *Feeney* v. *Howard*, 79 Cal.
525; 12 Am. St. Rep. 162, and note with the cases collected. A denial by
the defendant in his answer of the making of the contract is sufficient to
enable him to avail himself of the statute of frauds: *Fontaine* v. *Bush*, 40
Minn. 141, 12 Am. St. Rep. 722. That the statute of frauds must be pleaded
in order to constitute it a defense is maintained in *Osborne* v. *Endicott*, 6 Cal.
149; 65 Am. Dec. 498; and *Switzer* v. *Skiles*, 3 Gilm. 529; 44 Am. Dec. 723,
and note. For a thorough discussion of this subject, see the extended note
to *Hotchkiss* v. *Ladd*, 86 Am. Dec. 684, and the note to *Wentworth* v. *Wentworth*, 72 Am. Dec. 102.

STATUTE OF FRAUDS—WHETHER RAISED BY DEMURRER.—The defense of
the statute of frauds may be taken advantage of by demurrer, if the complaint states that the alleged express trust upon which the plaintiff relies
rests in a parol agreement to reconvey: *Barr* v. *O'Donnell*, 76 Cal. 469, 9 Am.
St. Rep. 242. To make the statute of frauds available as a defense to be
raised by demurrer in equity, the bill must show affirmatively that the contract declared on was not in writing: *Manning* v. *Pippen*, 86 Ala. 357; 11 Am.
St. Rep. 46. The statute of frauds cannot be relied on by demurrer, unless
the objection appears on the face of the complainant's bill: *Switzer* v. *Skiles*,
3 Gilm. 529; 44 Am. Dec. 723.

A PARTNERSHIP FOR DEALING IN LANDS MAY BE FORMED WITHOUT A
WRITING: *Bates* v. *Babcock*, 95 Cal. 479; 29 Am. St. Rep. 133, and note.
See the extended notes to *McCormick's Appeal*, 98 Am. Dec. 197, and *Greene*
v. *Greene*, 13 Am. Dec. 646.

METCALFE *v.* BRADSHAW.

[145 ILLINOIS, 124.]

PARTNERSHIP TO PRACTICE LAW—FIRM PROFITS, WHAT ARE NOT.—Commis. sions received by one member of a law firm while acting as an executor or administrator for the estate of a third person, without objection or with the assent of the other members of the partnership, are not firm profits or earnings for which he must account to the partnership.

ATTORNEYS—PRACTICE OF LAW.—EXECUTION OF TRUSTS, such as accepting appointments as executor or administrator, and acting as such, is not part of the duties peculiarly pertaining to the legal profession, and does not constitute what is ordinarily understood as the practice of law.

PARTNERSHIP—CONTINUATION AFTER EXPIRATION OF TERM.—If a partner. ship is continued after the expiration of the term fixed by the articles of copartnership, without the adoption of new articles or new arrange-ments, it is continued in all respects subject to the original articles, ex-cept that either partner may terminate it at pleasure.

PARTNERSHIP TO PRACTICE LAW—FIRM PROFITS.—If a partner in a law firm carries on a business not connected with nor competing with that of the firm, such as acting as an executor or administrator, his partners have no right to the profits he thereby makes, though he has agreed not to carry on any separate business.

PARTNERSHIP TO PRACTICE LAW—FIRM PROFITS, WHAT ARE NOT.—- Though a partner in a law firm has agreed to give his time, talents and strength to the prosecution of the firm business, he does not by becom-ing an executor or administrator with the consent and approval of his copartners, engage in a business or enterprise in competition with his firm, or which involves the use, for his own advantage, of anything be-longing thereto. The commissions received by him as such executor or administrator are not firm assets, and he is entitled to retain them as his own.

John G. Irwin, for the appellant.

Wise and McNulty, for the appellee.

[129] BAILEY, C. J.   This was a bill in chancery, brought by Andrew W. Metcalfe against William P. Bradshaw, for an accounting. [130] On the twenty-sixth day of August, 1874, the complainant and defendant formed a copartnership for the practice of the law, and for that purpose executed the following copartnership articles:

"Articles of Agreement signed and agreed upon between Andrew W. Metcalfe and William P. Bradshaw, this twenty-sixth day of August, A. D. 1874:

"1st. Reposing in each other mutual confidence and trust, do hereby associate ourselves together for the purpose of prac-ticing the law, firm to be known by the name of Metcalfe & Bradshaw, and to continue for five years from this date, un-less sooner dissolved by mutual consent.

" 2d. Terms.—First year said Metcalfe to take two-thirds and said Bradshaw one-third; second year said Metcalfe to take three-fifths and said Bradshaw two-fifths of the receipts of said firm, and from the end of the second year until the dissolution of said partnership, each to share equally in the receipts of said firm.

" 3d. The expenses of said office and firm to be paid by each partner in proportion to his share of the receipts of the firm.

" 4th. We, and each of us, pledge ourselves to each other not to become a candidate for any political office, so as to become involved in politics, during the continuance of said firm, unless by mutual consent.

" 5th. We, and each of us, do promise and agree to give our time, our talents, and our strength, to the prosecution of the interests of the firm.

" 6th. Any omission to keep and observe the promises and agreements herein named and agreed upon, by either of the parties hereto, will justify the other in a dissolution of the partnership.

"7th. An account is to be taken between the parties hereto at the end of each six months, if either party shall so desire it. This agreement shall not prevent the parties [131] hereto from adopting any rules for the control and government of the office.

"Witness of names: A. W. Metcalfe,
        Wm. P. Bradshaw."

The copartnership thus formed continued until December 15, 1885, when it was dissolved. The bill which was filed October 8, 1889, alleges the formation of the copartnership, and sets forth the copartnership articles *in extenso*, and alleges the dissolution of the firm by mutual consent December 15, 1885, and also, that during its continuance, business to a large amount was done by the firm for various parties on credit, and that the business still remains unsettled; that no settlement has ever been made between the copartners; that since the dissolution, the complainant has well hoped that the defendant would adjust and settle the partnership accounts, and has frequently applied to him for that purpose, but that the defendant has declined so to do; that the defendant has collected a large amount due and owing to the firm, under the copartnership articles, of moneys earned by members of the firm and belonging thereto, and had failed to

enter the same in the partnership books of account, and
wholly refuses to render to the complainant an account
thereof; that upon a full and true statement of the accounts
of the firm business, it will appear that there is a large balance due from the defendant to the complainant in respect
thereto.

The defendant's answer admits the formation of the partnership, the execution of the copartnership articles and the
dissolution as alleged, and that no actual settlement by an
account taken was then had, the parties agreeing, by a tacit
understanding, to a dissolution as matters then stood pecuni-
arily, defendant then believing that an account stated would
show a balance largely in his favor, but being willing, for the
sake of peace and a dissolution, to consider that each had
received what he was entitled to under the articles. The
answer admits that many debts were due [132] the firm at the
time of the dissolution, and alleges that the defendant expects
to share in such outstanding debts, but that the complainant
carried off and retains all evidence of such indebtedness, and
has collected much of it. It denies that the defendant has
collected any part of the outstanding indebtedness, or received any portion of that collected by the complainant; that
the complainant, since the dissolution, had ever called for a
settlement or pretended that the defendant was indebted to
him on account of copartnership matters, until shortly before
the bill was filed, when he spoke about it for the first time;
that the only claim then set up by him was, that the defendant, during the partnership, had, as executor of the wills of
Charles R. Bennett and John Neudecker, received commissions, and although not legally liable therefor to the complainant, yet as such commissions were received during the
existence of the partnership, the defendant ought to share
them with the complainant.

A replication was filed, and the parties thereupon entered
into and filed the following stipulation: "It is stipulated and
agreed by and between counsel, that the matters contended
for by the complainant in this case are limited to the commissions involved in three certain cases, namely, Charles R.
Bennett's estate, Theodore Emmett's estate, and John Neudecker's estate, with the understanding that everything outside of these estates, in the partnership, has been settled by
and between them." The cause was then heard upon pleadings and proofs, and the stipulation, and the court found that

the commissions received by the defendant from those estates were not, and were not by the parties considered and treated, as profits of or belonging to the firm, and that the complainant was not entitled to have an account thereof from the defendant. A decree was thereupon entered dismissing the bill at the complainant's costs for want of equity. On appeal by the complainant to the appellate court, the decree was affirmed, and the present appeal is from the judgment of affirmance.

133 It appears that on the twenty-fifth day of May, 1878, the defendant was appointed one of two joint executors of the last will and testament of Charles R. Bennett, deceased, and served in that capacity until September 17, 1881, when the estate was settled. The evidence tends to show that the commissions to which he became entitled as executor and which he received amounted to seven hundred and eighty-four dollars and forty-two cents. During the progress of the administration, the complainant was employed by the executors to render certain legal services, for which, according to the testimony of the defendant, he was paid, for his individual use, and not as a part of the earnings of the partnership, the sum of six hundred dollars. The complainant, on the other hand, testifies, that he in fact received nothing for his legal services, and that whatever he did was a part of the law business of the firm, and was done on firm account. It seems, however, that he made no charges for his services on the firm books, and gave no credit on the books for the money received by him, if he in fact received any. So far as the testimony of these witnesses is at variance, all we need say is, that the court saw them and heard them testify, and from all the evidence found the equities of the case to be with the defendant. That finding, so far as we can see, is entitled to the credit which is ordinarily given to the finding of a court of chancery, where the evidence is given orally in open court, and on appeal, it must be accepted as conclusive, unless it clearly appears to be against the weight of the evidence. There is nothing in the record from which we can say that such is the case here, and we must therefore assume, not only that the issues of fact thus raised by the witnesses in their testimony, so far as they have any bearing upon the correctness of the decree, were found by the court in favor of the defendant, but also that such finding, for all the purposes of this appeal, must be accepted as the true one.

On the fifth day of June, 1882, the defendant was appointed administrator of the estate of William T. Emmett, [134] deceased, and continued to act as such administrator until June 4, 1887, when the estate was settled, and he was discharged. The complainant was also employed by him to render legal services for that estate, and both agree that for such services the complainant received the sum of one hundred and twenty-five dollars. There is the same disagreement between them, however, as to whether this sum was paid him for his individual use, or as a part of the earnings of the firm. The commissions to which the defendant became entitled as administrator of that estate seem to have been something over five hundred. dollars, but he testifies, and in this he does not seem to be contradicted, that having paid a portion of the claims against the estate in full in ignorance of the existence of a claim that was afterwards presented, and which more than exhausted the remaining assets in his hands, he was compelled to use the money due him for commissions and more, to make good to the new claimant what he had paid to other creditors, and that he therefore in fact retained nothing on account of commissions.

On the twelfth day of September, 1883, the defendant was appointed executor of the last will and testament of John Neudecker, deceased. The Neudecker estate was large, and consisted principally of personal property. The administration involved no controversies, and was conducted without litigation, the bulk of the assets, consisting of moneys and securities, being distributed within two months of the date of the appointment of the executor. This estate was finally settled December 21, 1885, six days after the dissolution of the partnership between the complainant and defendant. The commissions received by the defendant, according to his own testimony, were a little less than six thousand dollars.

Whether the administration of these estates is to be regarded as firm business, and the commissions received by the defendant therefor as a part of the proceeds or earnings of the business, must depend chiefly if not wholly [135] upon the construction to be placed upon the partnership articles. By those articles the complainant and defendant associated themselves together "for the purpose of practicing law," and they mutually promised to give their time, talents, and strength "to the prosecution of the interest of the firm." Each pledged himself not to become a candidate for any political office, so as to become involved in politics, during the continuance of the firm, except by mutual consent, and it was agreed that any omission to keep and observe these promises and agreements by either party should justify the other in dissolving the partnership.

We think it too plain for argument, that accepting an appointment as executor or administrator of a deceased person, and acting as such, does not, as the term is ordinarily understood, pertain to the practice of the law. Persons accepting and performing the duties of trusts of that character need not be lawyers, and, as is well known, those who are appointed as executors or administrators are, in the great majority of cases, men who do not belong to the profession. Their duties are usually of a business rather than of a professional character. True, the administration of estates frequently requires legal advice, and often involves more or less of litigation, but substantially the same may be said of all other business pursuits, and especially of all positions involving the executions of trusts. But men are ordinarily appointed to execute trusts because of the confidence of the donor of the trust has in the honor, integrity, and business capacity of the appointee, rather than because of his knowledge of legal principles or his ability to carry on litigation with success. At all events the execution of trusts is not and never has been regarded as a part of the duties peculiarly pertaining to the legal profession, or as constituting a part of what is ordinarily understood as "the practice of the law."

It cannot, therefore, with any propriety be claimed, that the business transacted by the defendant in his trust capacity [136] as executor or administrator of the estates in question, was a part of the firm business, within the contemplation of the copartnership articles, or that the commissions realized by him from the execution of such trusts constituted a part of the earnings or profits of the firm. It seems to be admitted that, although the copartnership was continued for several years after the expiration of the term fixed by the articles, no new articles were adopted and no new arrangement was made, and it therefore follows, as a legal conclusion, that it was continued as a partnership at will, but subject in all respects, except as to the right of either partner to terminate it at pleasure, to the terms of the copartnership articles.

If there had been an agreement, either express or to be implied from the circumstances, that the commissions to be received by the defendant for his services as executor or administrator should be regarded and treated as partnership earnings, a different result would probably follow. But upon a careful examination of the record, we are unable to find that such agreement is established by either direct or circumstantial evidence. The fair conclusion from all the evidence is, that the defendant accepted and executed these trusts without objection, and even with the express approval of the complainant, but without any agreement or understanding, express or implied, that the compensation to be received by him should be turned over to the firm as firm profits.

We are not unmindful of the well-settled rule, that a partner will not ordinarily be permitted, for his own profit, to enter into business in competition with his firm. Thus, he cannot, without the consent of his copartners, embark in a business that will manifestly conflict with the interest of his firm. Nor can he clandestinely use the partnership property or funds in speculations for his own private advantage, without being required to account to his copartners for the property and funds thus used, and for the profits. [137] The general rule being that each partner shall devote his time, labor and skill for the benefit of the firm, he cannot purchase, for his own use and for the purpose of private speculation and profit, articles in which the firm deals, and if he does so, the profits arising therefrom may be claimed by the copartners as belonging to the firm: 5 Wait's Actions and Defenses, 125.

Thus, as said in 1 Bates on Partnership, section 306: "If a partner speculate with the firm funds or credit, he must account to his copartners for the profits, and bear the whole losses of such unauthorized adventures himself. And if he go into competing business, depriving the firm of the skill, time, and diligence or fidelity he owes to it, so he must account to the firm for the profits made in it; and a managing partner will be enjoined from carrying on the same business for his own benefit." But the same author says a little further on that a partner may traffic outside of the scope of the business for his own benefit. So also in Lindley on Partnership, 312, the rule is laid down as follows: "Where a partner carries on a business not connected with or competing with that of the firm, his partners have no right to the profits he thereby makes, even if he has agreed not to carry on any separate business."

Applying these principles to the case before us, we see no ground for sustaining the complainant's bill. The defendant, by becoming executor or administrator, engaged in no business or enterprise which can be regarded as in any sense in competition with his firm, or which involved the use for his own advantage of anything belonging to the firm. True, by the copartnership articles he agreed to give his time, talents, and strength to the prosecution of the firm business, but it does not appear that he failed, by reason of the acceptance of those trusts, in the performance of his agreement in that respect. It is not shown that any firm business suffered for lack of attention on his part by reason of his performance of the duties of executor or [138] administrator. Nor did he accept either of these trusts clandestinely or without the consent or approval of his copartner. As to the Neudecker executorship, the complainant takes pains to prove that the will of Neudecker was drafted by himself, and that the defendant was named therein as executor at his suggestion, and as the result of some importunity on his part, and that he subsequently became the defendant's surety on the bond given by him as executor. The complainant's consent to the defendant's acceptance of the trust could not be more clearly shown. It cannot be seen how the acceptance of these trusts, under the circumstances thus appearing, was in any sense a fraud on the partnership, or in contravention of the defendant's duties as partner, so as to call for an application of the rules arising in such cases, as stated above.

In view of all the evidence, we are disposed to hold that the only proper result is the one reached by the circuit court in its decree, and the judgment of the appellate court affirming the decree will be affirmed.

PARTNERSHIP—CONTINUING AFTER TIME LIMITED IN ARTICLES.—When partners commence business under an agreement that it is to last for a definite term, and without any new agreement they continue the business for a longer period, the business of subsequent years must be considered as conducted under the terms and conditions of the original agreement: *Bradley* v. *Chamberlain*, 16 Vt. 613; *Stephens* v. *Orman*, 10 Fla. 9; *Frederick* v. *Cooper*, 3 Iowa, 171; *Sangston* v. *Hack*, 52 Md. 173.

PARTNERSHIP—FIDUCIARY RELATIONS.—Every partner occupies a fiduciary position with respect to his copartners and the funds of the firm, and he will not be permitted to make a personal profit out of them: *Holmes* v. *Gilman*, 138 N. Y. 369; 34 Am. St. Rep. 463, and note with the cases collected; *Goldsmith* v. *Eichold*, 94 Ala. 116; 33 Am. St. Rep. 97.

WILLIAMS v. VANDERBILT.

[145 ILLINOIS, 238.]

MECHANIC'S LIEN ON LEASEHOLD.—A material-man's lien for making, altering, or repairing a building under a contract made with the lessee of the premises extends to the leasehold interest only.

MECHANIC'S LIEN—TO WHAT INTEREST ATTACHES.—The party with whom the contract is made by a person furnishing labor or materials, is regarded as the owner of the premises only to the extent of his interest, and that interest only is subject to a mechanic's lien. Hence a tenant for life or years cannot, by contract, create a lien upon the fee, on the contrary he can create a lien only to the extent of his right and interest in the premises.

MECHANIC'S LIEN LAW—CONSTRUCTION OF.—A statute creating a right to a mechanic's lien is in derogation of the common law, and must receive a strict construction. It must not be applied to cases which do not fall within its provisions. If they are not broad enough, it is the province of the legislature to extend them.

MECHANIC'S LIEN ATTACHING TO LEASEHOLD ESTATE is subject to all conditions of the lease, and may be defeated by a forfeiture under the express conditions thereof.

MECHANIC'S LIEN ON LEASEHOLD—SUBJECT TO ARREARS OF RENT.—When a lease for years has been forfeited for nonpayment of rent under the express conditions of the lease, a holder of a mechanic's lien upon the premises must pay all arrears of rent to the lessor before he can acquire the rights of the lessee thereunder, even by purchase.

LANDLORD AND TENANT—FORFEITURE OF LEASEHOLD INTEREST IN LAND is not implied, nor favored in law.

LANDLORD AND TENANT—SURRENDER OF written lease may be made by parol, by abandonment of the premises by the tenant and entry by the landlord, or by an executed agreement to surrender.

LANDLORD AND TENANT—SURRENDER OF LEASED PREMISES operates from the execution of a new lease with the tenant's consent to another person who enters thereunder and pays rent, or from an agreement, either express or implied, to release the original lessee and accept a new tenant, or from an actual and continued change of possession by the mutual consent of the parties.

LANDLORD AND TENANT.—One lessee cannot destroy rights of his co-lessees nor extinguish their title by conveying to his lessor.

LANDLORD AND TENANT—FORFEITURE OF LEASE—A DEMAND FOR RENT on the day it falls due is not necessary in order to cause a forfeiture of the lease. The lessor may declare a forfeiture on some subsequent day.

MECHANIC'S LIEN ON LEASEHOLD—REPAIRS—CONSTRUCTION OF STATUTE.—A statute conferring a mechanic's lien upon a leasehold interest in land, must be construed with reference to the common-law rule, that the burden of repairs is cast upon the tenant, and that the landlord is under no implied obligation to make them.

LANDLORD AND TENANT—WAIVER OF FORFEITURE OF LEASE—EFFECT ON MECHANIC'S LIEN.—Although generally any act done by a landlord knowing of a cause of forfeiture by his tenant, affirming the existence of the lease and recognizing the lessee as his tenant, is a waiver of such forfeiture, yet a landlord with such knowledge and also knowledge that the premises are undergoing repairs under the direction of the lessee, but with no reason to believe that the latter is not able to pay his debts, is not obliged to assume that the employees will not receive their money from the lessee, and declare an immediate forfeiture to save himself from liability under a mechanic's lien.

IMPROVEMENTS BY PERSON NOT OWNER—REIMBURSEMENT.—Improvements of a permanent character made upon land and attached thereto without the consent of the owner of the fee, by one having no title or interest, become a part of the realty and vest in the owner of the fee without reimbursement from him.

IMPROVEMENTS ON LAND—EQUITABLE LIEN FOR REIMBURSEMENT.—In equity when one has made improvements innocently, or through mistake, upon the land of another, he will not ordinarily be allowed to enforce a claim for reimbursement as an actor; but when the true owner seeks relief in equity he may be required to make compensation for the improvements. Even in such case compensation is not allowed for the increased value caused by the improvements, nor will the courts sustain a bill to recover for such enhanced value after the true owner has recovered the premises at law.

IMPROVEMENTS ON LAND—RIGHT TO RECOVER FOR.—To entitle one making improvements on the land of another innocently, or through mistake to recover the value thereof in proceedings instituted by the true owner, he must show that he made the improvements under a claim of title which proved defective, or, under some mistake concerning his rights, or because he was induced to incur the expenditure through the fraud or deception of the owner.

IMPROVEMENTS—EQUITABLE LIEN FOR AFTER FORFEITURE OF LEASE.—A party who repairs buildings on leased premises under a contract with the tenant, but without authority or contract express or implied from the landlord to pay therefor, is not entitled to an equitable lien on the premises for the value of the improvements, if the lease is declared forfeited for nonpayment of rent as provided for therein, subsequently to the time when the improvements are completed.

BILL to enforce a mechanic's lien for work done and materials furnished upon a building and lot. The defendant, Vanderbilt, being the owner of the property leased it to Bartels, Crelly, and Luits, for five years at a certain monthly rental payable in advance under a lease providing that upon default of the payment of the rent for any month the landlord might, at his election, without notice, declare the term ended, and re-enter the premises. The lessees paid the first month's rent from July 21 to August 21, 1889. And on August 2, 1889, Bartels entered into a written contract with the plaintiff, Williams, by which the latter agreed to make the repairs for which this lien is sought to be enforced. The lessees failed to pay the rent falling due August 21, 1889, and the landlord, through his agent, declared a forfeiture of the lease on September 13, 1889, and then re-entered and took possession. The superior court rendered judgment for the

plaintiff and on appeal to the appellate court the judgment
of the lower court was reversed and the bill dismissed. The
plaintiff then appealed from the judgment of the appellate
court.

Oliver and Showalter, for the appellant.

Robert Mather and William E. Foster, for the appellee.

243 MAGRUDER, J. Appellant's contract for doing the
work and furnishing the material, in altering and repairing
the building, was with the lessee or lessees of the premises.
Therefore whatever lien he had under the contract extended
to the leasehold interest only. Section 1 of the Lien Law
provides "that any person who shall by contract . . . . with
the owner of any lot or piece of land furnish labor or materials . . . . in building, altering, repairing, or ornamenting
any house, or other building or appurtenance thereto, on such
lot, ... shall have a lien upon the **244** whole of such tract
of land or lot, and upon such house or building and appurtenance, for the amount due to him for such labor, material, or
services." Section 2 provides that said lien "shall extend to
an estate in fee, for life, for years, or any other estate, or any
right of redemption or other interest which such owner may
have in the lot or land at the time of making the contract":
2 Starr & Cur., Ann. Stat., c. 82, pp. 1512–1515. The party
with whom the contract is made by the person furnishing the
labor or materials is only regarded as owner, within the
meaning of the law, to the extent of the interest which he
owns. It is that interest which is subjected to the lien:
Hickox v. *Greenwood*, 94 Ill. 266. A tenant for life or years
cannot, by contract, create a lien upon the fee; he may, by
contract, create a lien to the extent of his right and interest
in the premises, but no further: *McCarty* v. *Carter*, 49 Ill.
53; 95 Am. Dec. 572; *Judson* v. *Stephens*, 75 Ill. 255. As
appellant's lien extended to the leasehold estate only, it did
not take effect upon appellee's legal title. The statute which
gives a mechanic a lien is in derogation of the common law,
and must receive a strict construction: *Belanger* v. *Hersey*,
90 Ill. 70. It will not be applied by the courts to cases
which do not fall within its provisions. If those provisions
are not broad enough it is the province of the legislature to
extend them: *Stephens* v. *Holmes*, 64 Ill. 336; *Huntington* v.
Barton, 64 Ill. 502.

A mechanic's lien which attaches to a leasehold estate is

subject to all the conditions of the lease: Phillips on Mechanics' Liens, sec. 192; 2 Jones on Liens, sec. 1273; 15 Am. &
Eng. Ency. of Law, 21.   Here one of the conditions of the lease
was that, in case of default in the payment of the rent, the
landlord could, without notice, declare the term ended, and
re-enter the premises.   A forfeiture will not be implied, nor
is it favored by the rules of law: 2 Jones on Liens, sec. 1273.
But in the present case there seems to be no question as to
the right of the appellee [245] to forfeit the lease under its
terms, nor do we see that there can be any question as to the
effectiveness of the forfeiture which actually took place.

The month's rent, which was payable in advance on August
21, 1889, was not paid.   When Bartels, one of the lessees,
was called upon to pay the rent in the early part of September, 1889, he stated to appellee's agent that he could not pay
it, and that his co-lessees, Crelly and Luits, were irresponsible,
and unable to pay.   Appellant knew that Bartels had nothing but a lease of the premises before he did any work upon
the building.   He also knew early in September, that default
had been made by the lessees in the payment of the rent due
on August 21st.   He, and the architect who was superintend-
ing his work, had an interview with the appellee's agent on
September 10th, in which it was conceded, that the lessees
were unable to pay either the rent, or the amount due for said
work.   Appellant was then informed by the agent, that the
lease would be canceled or forfeited within a few days on
account of the nonpayment of the rent due, but he made no
offer to pay the rent so as to keep the lease alive, and made
no opposition to the threatened forfeiture of the lease.   The
appellee re-entered the premises, in pursuance of the terms of
the lease, on September 13th, and took possession of the same,
and at once notified appellant that he had done so.   On September 14th, appellant had another interview with appellee's
agent, but made no tender of the rent due, nor any offer to
pay it, nor any complaint that the forfeiture of the lease had
not been regular and valid.   If the lease has been forfeited,
the holder of the lien must pay all arrears of rent to the lessor
before he can acquire the rights of the lessee thereunder, even
by purchase: 2 Jones on Liens, sec. 1273; *Rothe* v. *Bellin-
grath*, 71 Ala. 55.

Counsel for appellant invoke the doctrine that, where the
landlord elects to accept a surrender of the lease, he takes
back the premises subject to liens existing at the time [246]

against the estate of the lessee. It was said by this court in *Dobschuetz* v. *Holliday*, 82 Ill. 371, that the voluntary surrender of the lease to the owner of the fee cannot affect the lien upon the estate of the lessee which attached during the existence of the lease, and that the merger of the estate of the lessee with that of the owners of the fee would not destroy the previous lien: *Gaskill* v. *Trainer*, 3 Cal. 334; Phillips on Mechanics' Liens, sec. 192; 2 Jones on Liens, sec. 1273; 15 Am. & Eng. Ency. of Law, p. 21. But in the case at bar, there was a forfeiture of the lease, and not a voluntary surrender of it. It is true, that Bartels, one of the lessees, expressed his willingness to have the lease canceled in order to get rid of Crelly and Luits, and have a new lease in which he should have an interest, made out to the appellant; and the latter desired a new lease to himself when the old one should be forfeited.

There may be a parol surrender of a written lease: *Baker* v. *Pratt*, 15 Ill. 568. There may be a surrender by an abandonment of the premises by the tenant and an entry into them by the landlord: 2 Wood's Landlord and Tenant, sec. 494, pp. 1169–1173. An executed agreement to surrender may be operative as a surrender: 2 Wood's Landlord and Tenant, p. 1169. Execution of a new lease, with the tenant's consent, to another person, who enters thereunder and pays rent, will amount to a surrender: *Stobie* v. *Dills*, 62 Ill. 432. An agreement, either express or inferable from the conduct of the parties, to release the original lessee and accept a new tenant, may operate as a surrender: *Fry* v. *Patridge*, 73 Ill. 51. An actual and continued change of possession, by the mutual consent of the parties, will amount to a surrender by operation of law: *Dills* v. *Stobie*, 81 Ill. 202. But we do not think that an application of these definitions to the conduct of the parties herein will establish a voluntary surrender of the demised premises. Crelly and Luits were regarded as being averse to a forfeiture of the lease, and were not spoken to or consulted [247] about it. Indeed, it was feared that a suit might be necessary to extinguish their interest. Even if Bartels' willingness to have the lease forfeited could be construed as a surrender on his part, this would not affect the rights of Crelly and Luits. One lessee cannot destroy the rights of his co-lessees, nor extinguish their title by conveying to his lessor: *Baker* v. *Pratt*, 15 Ill. 568.

It is furthermore claimed on behalf of appellant, that the

appellee waived his right to forfeit the lease. It is said, that, after appellee's right to forfeit the lease accrued on August 21, 1889, he waited until the thirteenth day of September thereafter before taking any steps towards forfeiture, and in the mean time permitted appellant to do work upon the building. At common law, where a lease contained a condition for re-entry for nonpayment of rent, the law required a demand of the precise amount of the rent due, and that it be made upon precisely the day when due and payable by the terms of the lease. Under this strict rule, it may be that the appellee, in order to work a forfeiture of the lease, would have been obliged to make a demand for the rent on the twenty-first day of August. But we have held in a number of cases, that the common-law rule, making it necessary to demand the rent on the day it falls due in order to cause a forfeiture, was abrogated by section 2 of the Act of 1865, which is now section 9 of the act in regard to landlord and tenant: 2 Starr & Cur. Ann. Stat., c. 80, p. 1494; *Chadwick* v. *Parker*, 44 Ill. 326; *Dodge* v. *Wright*, 48 Ill. 382; *Chapman* v. *Kirby*, 49 Ill. 211; *Leary* v. *Pattison*, 66 Ill. 203; *Burt* v. *French*, 70 Ill. 254; *Woodward* v. *Cone*, 73 Ill. 241. The mere fact, that the landlord did not forfeit the lease on the very day on which the monthly installment of rent fell due did not deprive him of the right to declare a forfeiture on some subsequent day.

But it is said the appellee knew, that the lessees were making repairs and improvements upon the property [248] during the period from August 21st to September 13th, and that, by suffering them to do so without attempting to forfeit the lease, there was thereby a waiver of his right of forfeiture as against appellant. A statute, which confers a lien upon the leasehold interest, must be construed with reference to the common-law rule, that the burden of repairs is cast upon the tenant, and that the landlord is under no implied obligation to make them: 2 Jones on Liens, sec. 1276. The estate of the lessor cannot be subjected to a lien for work done or materials furnished under a contract with the lessee, unless the agreement or consent of the lessor is shown, or unless he has done some act to make his estate liable: 15 Am. & Eng. Ency. of Law, p. 19, and cases cited in notes; 2 Jones on Liens, sec. 1276. Where a lessor agrees to pay to the lessee a gross sum towards the erection of a house on the demised premises, the estate of the lessor is bound by the mechanic's lien: *Leiby* v. *Wilson*, 40 Pa. St. 63; *Boteler* v. *Espen*, 99 Pa. St. 313. We

have recently held in *Henderson* v. *Connelly*, 123 Ill. 98, 5
Am. St. Rep. 490, that, where a contract of sale of land did
not authorize or in any manner empower the purchaser to
erect a building on the premises, or to incur any liability for
the improvement thereof, and the vendor was in no manner
connected with the building the purchaser erected on the
premises, but merely sold the lot leaving the purchaser to
improve it or not as he pleased, under such circumstances
the lien of the mechanic would only attach to such title as
the purchaser had; but that, if the vendor in the contract
authorizes and empowers the purchaser to erect a building
on the premises and advances money to aid him in the improvement, the mechanic, who has furnished labor and
materials before the termination of the contract by notice,
will be entitled to subject the vendor's legal title to the lien.

In the present case the lease does not provide for making
any improvements, and contains no provisions, which connect [249] the lessor in any way with any improvements to be
made by lessees. Nor does the lease show that the lessor
gave his consent to the making of any improvements, or
agreed to make, or to aid in making them. The proof is not
clear, that the appellee had knowledge of the labor and
materials furnished by appellant during the progress of the
work. Appellee's agent, who negotiated the lease and received payment of the first installment of the rent, was absent
from the city of Chicago from August 8th until the seventh
or eighth day of September.

The general rule is, that "any act done by a landlord knowing of a cause of forfeiture by his tenant, affirming the existence of the lease, and recognizing the lessee as his tenant, is
a waiver of such forfeiture": *Webster* v. *Nichols*, 104 Ill. 160.
We fail to discover any such act done by the appellee between
August 21st and the forfeiture of the lease on September 13th.
Beyond the mere fact that the second installment of rent was
not promptly paid, there is no evidence that appellee had any
knowledge, until a few days before his re-entry, of the inability of the lessees to pay for the repairs ordered by them.
Although a lessor may be aware, that the premises are undergoing repairs under the direction of the lessee, yet, if he has
no reason to believe that such lessee is not able to pay his
debts, he is not obliged to assume that the persons employed
to do the work will not receive their money from the lessee,
and that an immediate forfeiture is necessary to save himself

from liability. The proof tends to show, that appellee did not know of the contract between Bartels and appellant until about the tenth day of September.

Counsel for appellant refer us to a large number of cases, holding that a grantor entitled to re-enter or forfeit an estate on breach of condition, who does not exercise this right when facts within his knowledge occur that would entitle him to do so, has waived his right; but the facts in these cases show, that there were long continued acts or [250] declarations in recognition of the estate sought to be forfeited; and it was held that the grantor was estopped from exercising his right of forfeiture, because, by his failure to assert the right after breach of condition, he induced the grantee to believe that he would not do so, and to continue in the prosecution of an enterprise requiring the expenditure of large sums of money. We find no fault with the doctrine of these cases, but think that they have no application here, where the lessees and the holder of the lien were given an opportunity to avoid the forfeiture, and were fully advised in due time of the lessor's intention to exercise the right of forfeiture.

It is further claimed, however, that, if appellant was not entitled to a mechanic's lien, he is entitled to the enforcement of an equitable lien against appellee's legal title to the property. This seems to have been the theory upon which the decree of the court below was based. An equitable lien is sought to be sustained upon the alleged ground, that appellant was induced to believe, by the agent of appellee, that a new lease of the premises would be executed to him after the old lease to Bartels, Crelly, and Luits should be forfeited. Upon the question of fact whether appellee's agent made a promise to give a new lease, or held out any representations that he would give a new lease, upon which appellant was authorized to rely, we are inclined, after a careful re-examination of the evidence, to adhere to the conclusion announced upon the former hearing. We are not satisfied that any such promise was made, or that any such representations were held out. The agent denies positively, that he said or did anything to induce appellant to complete the performance of his contract with the lessees, or to induce him to believe that the premises would be relet to him. Appellant himself admits, that the agent declined to make any promises, but stated that he intended to cancel the lease, and, after he had done that, he

would then determine whether he would make another lease
or not.

251 Counsel for appellant say in their brief, that this suit
is not brought to declare and enforce a vendor's lien, nor a
lien created by estoppel, but they claim that an equitable lien
was created by the acts of the parties. They furthermore say:
"It is not claimed that appellee fraudulently acquiesced in
the work during its progress, but that appellee was guilty of
fraud after its completion, making it inequitable for appellant
to hold the property free from the equitable lien asked for."

The theory of equitable liens has its ultimate foundation
in contracts, express or implied, which deal with, or in some
manner relate to, specific property. (3 Pomeroy's Equity
Jurisprudence, sec. 1234.) There was here no express contract between appellant and appellee, nor do we think that
there is any implied contract to pay for the repairs or
improvements. As a general rule, improvements of a permanent character, made upon real estate, and attached thereto,
without the consent of the owner of the fee, by one having no
title or interest, become a part of the realty and vest in the
owner of the fee: *Mathes* v *Dobschuetz*, 72 Ill. 438. In equity,
where one makes improvements innocently, or through mistake, upon the land of another, he will not ordinarily be
allowed to enforce a claim for reimbursement, as an actor;
but when the true owner seeks relief in equity, as, for instance,
to set aside a sale of the land on which the improvements
have been made, or to obtain an accounting for rents and
profits, he may be required to make compensation for the
improvements upon the principle, that he who seeks equity
must do equity: *Ebelmesser* v. *Ebelmesser*, 99 Ill. 541; 3 Pomeroy's Equity Jurisprudence, sec. 1241, and note. Even in
such case, compensation will only be allowed for the increased
value caused by the improvements: *Ebelmesser* v. *Ebelmesser*,
99 Ill. 541. Courts of equity will not grant active relief, and
sustain a bill to recover for such enhanced value, after the
true owner has recovered the premises at law: 2 Jones on
Liens, sec. 1136. In proceedings instituted by the **252** real
owner, it must appear, that the party making the improvements did so under a claim of title which turned out to be
defective, or under some mistake concerning his rights, or
because he was induced to incur the expenditures through
the fraud or deception of the owner, 3 Pomeroy's Equity
Jurisprudence, sec. 1241, note 1. Here, the repairs were

made for a party known to be the owner of only a leasehold
estate, presumably in reliance upon the statutory mechanic's
lien, and not through confidence in a defective title, or
through mistake, or through the fraud of the owner of
the fee.

Counsel have called our attention to the case of *Perry v·
Board of Missions*, 102 N. Y. 99. In that case there was a
special agreement embodied in the resolution of a corporate
body to pay the moneys advanced for the repairs. It is
there announced as a general doctrine of equity, that a lien
will be given when the plaintiff's right can be secured in no
other way. This is carrying the doctrine of equitable liens
farther than the courts of the other states have gone in that
direction: *Crane v. Caldwell*, 14 Ill. 468; *Dewey v. Eckert*, 62
Ill. 218. It appears, however, in the Perry case, as it does
not appear here, that the owner of the property expressly
authorized the party making the repairs to proceed with
them, directed a mortgage to be executed to raise money
to pay for them, approved of them after they were made, accepted them "not as a gratuity, but as services for which
compensation should be given"; and that the party, in whose
favor the equitable lien was enforced advanced his own
money to pay the bills incurred for the improvements at the
request of the officials of the corporate body; and that his
right to remuneration was clear. We do not regard the
decision in that case as a precedent which should control the
disposition of the case at bar. The judgment of the appellate
court is affirmed.

MECHANIC'S LIEN ON LESSEE'S INTEREST: See the extended notes to *Lyon
v. McGuffey*, 45 Am. Dec. 678, and *Loonie v. Hogan*, 61 Am. Dec. 697, also
the case of *Evans v. Young*, 10 Col. 316; 3 Am. St. Rep. 583.

MECHANIC'S LIEN—WHAT INTEREST BOUND BY.—A mechanic's lien will
bind only such title as the person making the contract has and no more:
Taylor v. Murphy, 148 Pa. St. 337; 33 Am. St. Rep. 825, and note; *Henderson v. Connelly*, 123 Ill. 98; 5 Am. St. Rep. 490, and note; *Monroe v. West*,
12 Iowa, 119; 79 Am. Dec. 524, and note; *Lyon v. McGuffey*, 4 Pa. St. 126;
45 Am. Dec. 675, and extended note.

MECHANIC'S LIEN—CONSTRUCTION OF STATUTE.—Statutes giving liens for
materials used in making improvements on land are remedial and should be
liberally construed: *Dugan Cut Stone Co. v. Gray*, 114 Mo. 497; 35 Am. St.
Rep. 767, and note with the cases collected; note to *Harrison v. Homeopathic
Assn.*, 19 Am. St. Rep. 717.

FORFEITURES ARE NOT FAVORED: *Murray v. Home Benefit etc. Assn.*, 90
Cal. 402; 25 Am. St. Rep. 133; *Phœnix Ins. Co. v. Tomlinson*, 125 Ind. 84;
21 Am. St. Rep. 203, and note.

LEASES—FORFEITURE AND SURRENDER OF—HOW MANIFESTED: See the extended note to *Guffy* v. *Hukill*, 26 Am. St. Rep. 910. To effect a surrender of an existing lease by operation of law, there must be a new lease, valid in law, to pass an interest according to the contract and intention of the parties: *Smith* v. *Kerr*, 108 N. Y. 31; 2 Am. St. Rep. 362; *Welcome* v. *Hess*, 90 Cal. 507; 25 Am. St. Rep. 145, and note with the cases collected.

IMPROVEMENTS ON LAND—REIMBURSEMENT TO ONE MAKING: See the extended note to *Pitt* v. *Moore*, 6 Am. St. Rep. 496; *Stewart* v. *Stewart*, 83 Wis. 364; 35 Am. St. Rep. 67. The value of improvements made by a life tenant while in possession of land cannot be recovered as a setoff in an equitable action by the remainder-man to enforce the payment of a debt which such life tenant owes him: *Sparks* v. *Ball*, 91 Ky. 502; 34 Am. St. Rep. 236, and note. A mortgagee in possession of land is not entitled to compensation for improvements made upon the mortgaged premises further than is necessary to keep them in repair: *Robertson* v. *Reed*, 52 Ark. 381; 20 Am. St. Rep. 188, and note. As to when parties making improvements on land are entitled to be reimbursed therefor, see the following cases: *Barrett* v. *Stradl*, 73 Wis. 385; 9 Am. St. Rep. 795, and extended note; *Ferris* v. *Montgomery Land etc. Co.*, 94 Ala. 557; 33 Am. St. Rep. 146; *Metcalf* v. *Hart*, 3 Wyo. 513; 31 Am. St. Rep. 122.

GREGSTEN v. CITY OF CHICAGO.

[145 ILLINOIS, 451.]

MUNICIPAL CORPORATIONS—USE OF STREETS FOR PRIVATE PURPOSES.—A city, acting under special as well as general authority in granting a permit to a private person to construct vaults under its streets or alleys, and requiring compensation therefor, acts in its private corporate capacity, as distinguished from its public and political or governmental capacity, and the rules applicable to the exercise of its public political powers do not apply.

MUNICIPAL CORPORATIONS—PERMIT FOR PRIVATE USE OF STREET WHEN CONSTITUTES CONTRACT.—A city, acting under special as well as general authority in granting a permit for, and regulating the construction of, vaults under its streets and alleys not inconsistent with their use by the public, and requiring compensation therefor, acts in its private corporate capacity, and when such permit is accepted and acted upon by the holder, by making costly improvements required, it constitutes a contract between the parties, irrevocable at the mere will of the city.

MUNICIPAL CORPORATIONS—USE OF STREETS FOR PRIVATE PURPOSE—APPROVAL OF PERMIT.—The approval by the city council of a permit granted by the city's agents to a person to construct a vault under a street or alley is presumed from the acts of the permit holder in constructing the vault at great expense, and its use and occupation by him for twenty years without objection on the part of the city, especially when such occupation inures to the benefit of the city, which it receives with knowledge of the right claimed by the occupant.

MUNICIPAL CORPORATIONS—WHEN BOUND BY CONTRACT.—A city, when acting in its private capacity as contradistinguished from its governmental capacity, is bound by its contracts, and may be estopped by the conduct of its proper officers when acting within the lawful scope of their powers.

MUNICIPAL CORPORATIONS—PERMIT FOR PRIVATE USE OF STREET—RIGHT OF CITY TO REVOKE.—When a person constructs and maintains a costly vault under an alley or street by authority of a permit regularly given by a city, providing that he is not to be taxed as rent for the vault in excess of the tax on similar vaults, and that the vault will not be removed unless public convenience or necessity requires it, and under a bond executed by himself that he will keep such street or alley forever in repair, and save and keep the city harmless from all loss or damage by reason of its being out of repair, the permit and bond together constitute a contract between the parties founded upon a sufficient consideration, securing rights mutually advantageous to both, and is not revocable by the city unless the public interest or convenience demands it, or the holder of the permit fails to perform his covenants or some one of them, and the city cannot, at will, revoke such permit for the benefit of some other person who is sought to be invested with a similar permit.

BILL by Gregsten and others to enjoin the city of Chicago and its officers from bringing suits to recover possession of a certain alley in said city, and from evicting plaintiffs therefrom. The court below rendered judgment dismissing the bill, and plaintiffs appealed.

Knight and Brown, for the appellants.

John S. Miller, and Condee and Rose, for the appellees.

[460] SHOPE, J. By the amendment to the charter of the city of Chicago, passed in 1863, the board of public works was given the power " to regulate the placing or building of vaults under the streets, alleys, and sidewalks, and require such compensation for the privilege as they shall deem reasonable and just, subject to the approval of the common council.' Under the authority thus conferred, as well as in execution of the power of exclusive control over the streets and alleys of the city by the city authorities, the board of public works executed a permit to appellant, Gregsten, to excavate for and construct a vault under the alley running north and south through block 142, school section addition to said city, in the rear of and adjoining lot 16 in said block, and to maintain and use such vault "in connection with the building erected, or to be erected, upon said lot," etc. As will be seen from the foregoing statement, said permit is, by its terms, subject to all the restrictions, limitations, and [461] conditions of the bond of said Gregsten, of even date, executed to the city.

The question sharply presented in this record is, whether the permit, construed in connection with the bond, so far as it relates to matters not affecting the public use of the alley,

constitutes a contract, irrevocable by the city at will. "It is
the general doctrine that municipalities, under the power of
exclusive control of their streets, may allow any use of them
consistent with the public objects for which they are held":
Nelson v. *Godfrey*, 12 Ill. 20; *City of Quincy* v. *Bull*, 106 Ill.
337; *Gridley* v. *Bloomington*, 68 Ill. 47; *Chicago etc. Ry. Co.* v.
People, 91 Ill. 251; *Chicago Mun. Gas L. Co.* v. *Town of Lake*,
130 Ill. 42; Dillon on Municipal Corporations, 541–551.

In this case, however, special power had been conferred, by
the act amendatory of the charter, to make the grant, upon
such consideration as the city authorities might deem reasonable and just. (Sec. 12, Act 1863.)   Upon looking into the
bond, it is seen that appellant was required, as part consideration for the grant, to so construct his vault and cover the
same that the alley should, at the grade established by
the city, be at all times open, and in safe repair and condition for the passage over it of all persons, animals and
vehicles.   Beneath the surface, the city reserved the right of
entry, at all times, for all purposes affecting the public interest.   The water, gas, and sewer pipes, etc., of the city, might
be constructed, enlarged, and repaired, at all times, through
and under said vault and the walls thereof, in the discretion
of the city authorities.   The permit, it is apparent, relates
solely to such use of the alley as was in no wise inconsistent
with its full enjoyment for all public uses and purposes.
Moreover, as will be seen, it is expressly stipulated, that
whenever the public interests shall demand it, the rights
under the permit shall cease.   The city, through its constituted authorities, in granting the permit upon the covenants,
conditions, and [462] limitations contained in the bond taken
by the city from Gregsten, was, therefore, acting in its private
corporate capacity, as distinguished from its public and
political, or governmental capacity, and the doctrine applicable to the exercise of its public political powers does not
apply: *Bailey* v. *Mayor, etc.*, 3 Hill, 539; 38 Am. Dec. 669;
De Voss v. *City of Richmond*, 18 Gratt. 338; 98 Am. Dec. 646;
Quincy v. *Bull*, 106 Ill. 337.   The public, except in so far as
it might be benefited, had no interest in the subject matter of
the grant.

It is insisted, however, that the permit was void, because
no approval thereof by the city council is shown.   It is alleged
and proved, that upon receiving the permit Gregsten exca-
vated the vault, built, and covered it, as required by the con-

dition of his bond, at large expense to himself. That he entered into occupancy of it, placing therein boilers and apparatus, using it as appurtenant to his building located on said lot 16. That the building having been destroyed by the great fire of October, 1871, he rebuilt upon said lot, and again putting said alleyway in like condition as before, maintained the vault, as an appurtenance to his said building, to the filing of this bill, a period of practically twenty years. During all that time, with knowledge of the construction and use of the vault by the city authorities, as admitted in the answer, he kept the alley in repair; and, for this time, the city was saved all expense of the maintenance and repair of the surface of the alley, in the rear of and abutting said lot 16.

In *Gridley* v. *Bloomington*, 68 Ill. 47, we said: "Although no license from the city to make the vault is shown, on the other hand no objection by the city is shown either to the making of the vault, the mode of its construction, or the state of repair in which it has been kept; and situated as it is under the sidewalk, in a public street, and for so great a length of time, we cannot presume that those having charge of the streets were ignorant of its existence, or of the respective rights and duties of the city, and the [463] owners of the property in relation to it. We regard this acquiescence as a sufficient recognition by the city of authority to construct and maintain the vault in a prudent and careful manner." So, in the previous case of *Nelson* v. *Godfrey*, 12 Ill. 20, it is held that, as the privilege of excavating under sidewalks, etc., for vaults is of great convenience, and may with proper care be exercised with little or no inconvenience to the public, authority to make the same will be inferred in the absence of any action of the corporate authorities to the contrary, they having knowledge of the progress of the work: See, also, Dillon on Municipal Corporations, sec. 554. So, in this case, the approval of the city council may be inferred from its long acquiescence in the use of the alley, for the purpose for which the permit was granted. And especially will this be so, when it is shown, as it is here, that the occupancy under the permit inured to the benefit of the city, which it received with knowledge of the right claimed by complainant.

As we have seen, the city authorities were authorized to regulate the placing of vaults under sidewalks, streets, and alleys of the city, and require compensation for the same. A reference to the condition of the bond will show, that the con-

sideration fixed and agreed upon between Gregsten and the
city was, that he should bring the alley to the grade established by the city, make approaches of easy slope thereto
covering the vault, so as to render it safe and secure as a way
for public use and travel, and to forever keep and maintain
said alley in such condition and repair. The said Gregsten
was required to covenant for himself, his heirs, executors,
administrators, and assigns, to forever keep and maintain
said alley in said condition, and to renew and repair the same
whenever required so to do by the city authorities. By the
express terms of the permit he is granted the right to build,
maintain, and use the vault in connection with his buildings
erected, or to be erected, on said lot 16. It seems clear,
that the parties [464] had in contemplation, at the time of entering into the arrangement, that Gregsten, his heirs and
assigns, should have the right to build and maintain a vault
under said alley, as appurtenant to the building upon lot
16, and be bound to maintain the same in suitable repair
and condition for the public use and convenience perpetually,
unless the public convenience or necessity required the removal of the vault from the alley. He and his representatives are required to forever keep and maintain said alley in
repair, and to save and keep harmless the city from all loss
or damage by reason of its, at any time, being out of repair.
It was also in contemplation of the parties that, in addition
to the liability of the grantee in the permit, his heirs and
assigns, to keep said alley in repair, and thereby save the city
the cost and expense of paving, maintaining, and repairing
the same, and from all loss by reason of its being out of repair, he or they might be subject to a further tax as rent, as
the city in the exercise of reasonable discretion might determine. It is expressly stipulated in the bond, "that said
Samuel Gregsten shall not be subject to any tax upon the
same" (the vault) "as rent, beyond what shall be charged for
similar vaults." The objection, therefore, that the contract
was without consideration, is without merit. By the arrangement thus made the municipality in its private corporate
capacity made the grant upon a sufficient consideration,
securing rights mutually advantageous to the parties, and in
no wise conflicting with or infringing upon any public interest. And the permit having been granted upon the express
conditions and stipulations to be kept and performed by Gregsten, the two instruments constituted a contract mutually

binding upon the parties: 15 Am. & Eng. Ency. of Law, 1106, note 3. The city, when acting in its private capacity, is contradistinguished from its governmental capacity, is bound by its contracts, and may be estopped by the conduct of its proper officers when acting within the scope of their lawful power: *Chicago etc. R. R. Co.* v. [465] *Joliet*, 79 Ill. 39; *Board of Supervisors* v. *Lincoln*, 81 Ill. 156; *Martel* v. *East St. Louis*, 94 Ill. 67; *Chicago* v. *Sexton*, 115 Ill. 230.

We are of opinion that the permit and bond, forming parts of the same transaction, constituted a contract between the parties, not revocable by the city, unless the public interest or convenience demanded it, or for some other cause for which the contract, by its terms, might be revoked. By the terms of the bond the city reserved the right to revoke the permit and re-enter whenever the public interest should require it, and also, upon the failure of Gregsten, his heirs, executors or assigns, to keep and perform the covenants and conditions in the condition of his bond mentioned, and upon the termination of the permit, it was stipulated that Gregsten should remove and fill up the vault, thereby restoring the alley to its former condition. It is not pretended that the interests of the public demand, or its convenience requires, the removal by Gregsten from the vault, or its abandonment, and a resumption by the city of absolute control over the alley. We have already seen that for all public purposes the municipal authorities had and retained under the contract absolute control of the same. In addition, by reference to the conditions of the bond, it will be seen that Gregsten, his representatives and assigns, were bound to renew and repair the surface of the alley whenever and in such manner as should be ordered by the city council or board of public works of the city. It is admitted in the answer, and if it were not it is abundantly shown, that the attempt to oust the present occupants of the vault is not demanded in the public interest, or to serve a public purpose, but is solely to enable the abutting owner, upon the east of the alley, to occupy one-half of the alley space in the rear of said lot 16 for private uses. The answer admits that a permit had been given to one McVicker, to occupy and improve the east half of that part of said alley abutting on complainants' [466] lot, and that it is the intent and purpose to put said McVicker in possession of such right under said permit. No such right is reserved in and by the contract, and such purpose is, therefore, unlawful. The city is without power to deprive the complainants of their rights, under its contract with Gregsten, for the benefit of private individuals, or to subserve private purposes and ends.

The bill alleges, and the proof sustains the allegation, as we think, that the grantee in the permit put the surface of the alley in the condition required by the contract, and kept and maintained the same in safe repair and condition for the passage and travel over and across the same of all persons, animals, and vehicles, as required in and by his bond. It is true, the answer sets up that the surface of said alley over said vault had been permitted to become out of repair, and was in a dangerous condition, etc., and that there was, therefore, a right of revocation of the permit under the terms of the contract. There is some evidence tending to show that the surface was depressed in the middle of the alley, and that some boards were broken. That the alley over the vault was in a dangerous condition, or unsafe or insecure for the passage of all persons or vehicles, is clearly rebutted. The beams holding the covering were of oak, and sound, on which there was first laid three-inch plank and on top of these a layer of two-inch plank, which had been renewed practically within two years. Up to the filing of this bill it would seem that no complaint had been made, knowledge of which was carried home to complainants, at least, that the surface of the alley was in any wise out of repair. Mr. Hirsch, of the engineering department of the city, upon his examination of it shortly before the service of notice upon complainants to remove from the vault, is shown to have pronounced it safe, etc. We are not unmindful that the commissioner of public works says, in effect, that he gave the notice, and was proceeding against complainants because the surface of the alley was in a dangerous [467] condition.

Without criticism of this statement, it may be said that it is abundantly shown that such was not its condition, and that as early as December, 1889, without any complaint that the alley was out of repair, and without any notice to complainants, a permit to occupy the east half of the alley, then in possession of the complainants, was given to McVicker. There is not a scintilla of evidence tending to show that the alley was then in any way out of repair; and the avowed purpose of the city and commissioner of public works in their answers is, as we have seen, to permit McVicker to occupy under the permit to her. Moreover it appears, and is not controverted, that immediately upon receiving notice that it was claimed that the alley was out of repair, etc., and being the first notice complainants had of any intention on the part of the city or its officers to require them to give up the alley, or any part of it, complainants went to the commissioner of public works and demanded of him that if he claimed said alley was not properly planked or paved, that he give them specifications showing in what manner and in what material it was required they should plank or pave the same; and then offered, if the commissioner required it, "to put iron beams across said alley space, and to place over the same concrete, stone blocks, wood blocks, or any other kind of pavement said commissioner might require"; and practically the same offer is made in and by complainants' bill.

By an ordinance of the city passed April 17, 1885, in reference to the improvement of alleys in the district of the city in which this alley is located, it is (section 3) provided that: "The commissioner of public works shall furnish the proper grades for all work done under this ordinance, and all improvements so made shall be done under the direction of said officer and as he shall direct, and in no other manner." It is shown that the commissioner, although repeatedly requested so to do, declined to give complainants any direction whatever in respect of the manner ⁴⁶⁸ in which the alley should be repaired or improved, or to direct them in respect thereof. If the alley was out of repair, and the public interest alone was to be considered, every duty to the public would have been subserved by the performance of the duty required by said ordinance of said commissioner. It is clear from this record that the complainants were not only ready, able, and willing, but offered to put the surface of said alley in such condition and repair, and use such material, as said commissioner might require. It is impossible to consider this record, as it seems to us, and not find that the decided preponderance of the evidence is against the contention, not only that the surface of the alley was out of repair, but also that the proceedings against the complainants were instituted for that reason. It is true that there is, and must necessarily be, vested in city authorities a large discretion to determine when the public streets and alleys of the city are in suitable repair to insure safety to the public. If the commissioner of public works had condemned the covering to the vault and required its renewal, or had deemed it necessary for the public con-

venience or safety that the vault should be more securely
covered or differently paved, and complainants had neglected
or refused to keep their covenant, and repair or renew, a
different question would have been presented by the record,
which it is unnecessary for us here to discuss or determine.

We are of opinion that the court erred in sustaining the
motion to dissolve the injunction and in dismissing the bill.
The decree and the judgment of the appellate court affirming
the same is reversed, and the cause remanded to the circuit
court for further proceeding not inconsistent with this opinion.

MUNICIPAL CORPORATIONS—RIGHT TO USE OF STREET, WHEN CONTRACT.
Where a right to use a street is acquired pursuant to a statute and under
license from the municipality, it is, in the nature of a contract right, and
the municipality cannot destroy or materially alter it: *Williams* v. *Citizens'
Ry. Co.*, 130 Ind. 71; 30 Am. St. Rep. 201, and note. A franchise to operate
a street railway is not a mere license or privilege revocable at the will of the
state; it is indestructible by legislative authority, and is property in the
highest sense of the term: *People* v. *O'Brien*, 111 N. Y. 1; 7 Am. St. Rep.
684, and extended note at page 721. Where a city has stood by and seen a
gas company make a large outlay of money in the exercise of their rights
under their charter, without intimating to them that objection would be
made to the use of the streets for the purposes authorized, without the use
of which enterprises would not have been undertaken, and they would lose
their entire outlay, the city will be estopped from refusing to allow the laying of the pipes: *Atlanta* v. *Gate City Gas Light Co.*, 71 Ga. 106, cited in the
extended note to *Guffey* v. *O'Reiley*, 57 Am. Rep. 431.

MUNICIPAL CORPORATIONS—RATIFICATION OF ACTS OF AGENTS.—Mere
silence or acquiescence on the part of a municipal corporation will not
amount to a ratification of the unauthorized acts of its agents; there must
be some affirmative action in that respect, or an action from which ratification can be inferred: *Murphy* v. *City of Albina*, 22 Or. 106; 29 Am. St. Rep.
578; *Mayor* v. *Reynolds*, 20 Md. 1; 83 Am. Dec. 535, and note. See further
the extended note to *Hilsdorf* v. *St. Louis*, 100 Am. Dec. 358; and note to
Zottman v. *San Francisco*, 81 Am. Dec. 108.

TAUSSIG *v.* REID.

[145 ILLINOIS, 488.]

GUARANTY—DEMAND AND NOTICE OF NONPERFOMANCE.—In case of an
absolute guaranty, the guarantor is not entitled to demand or notice of
nonperformance, but when the undertaking is collateral, notice must
be given within a reasonable time, unless circumstances exist which excuse want of notice or the guarantor is not prejudiced thereby.
If the principal is insolvent when the debt becomes due, or default is
made, so that no benefit could be derived by the guarantor from the receipt of notice, none is required.

GUARANTY—NEGOTIABLE INSTRUMENTS—DEMAND AND NOTICE OF NON-
PAYMENT.—When the payee of an unconditional promissory note, or

a third party, executes a contract on the back thereof for the payment of
the money at a specified time, in which he guarantees the payment of the
note at maturity, the holder thereof is under no obligation to demand
payment of the maker, and, on default of payment, notify the guarantor.

GUARANTY—NECESSITY FOR NOTICE OF ACCEPTANCE.—In case of a written
guarantee for a debt yet to be created and uncertain in amount, the
guarantor must be given notice within a reasonable time that the guaranty is accepted, and that credit has been given upon the faith of it.

GUARANTY—NOTICE OF DEFAULT IN PAYMENT.—In case of a collateral continuing guaranty, as for the payment of goods to be thereafter purchased, reasonable notice of the default of payment on the part of the
principal debtor must be given to the guarantor, and he will be discharged from payment, so far as he has sustained loss or damage resulting from a failure of the creditor to give him notice.

GUARANTY—INSOLVENCY OF PRINCIPAL—EFFECT OF FAILURE TO NOTIFY
GUARANTOR OF DEFAULT.—When notice of default by the principal
debtor can result in no benefit to the guarantor, as when the principal
is insolvent when the guaranty is made, and so remains, a failure to
give notice of his default in payment is not a defense to an action on
the guaranty.

GUARANTY—COLLATERAL AND CONTINUING CONSTRUCTION.—A written
guaranty for the prompt payment of the price of goods purchased or to
be thereafter purchased to the amount of a certain sum named, is a
collateral continuing guaranty, and the amount stated is a limitation
upon the liability of the guarantor and not upon the credit to be extended to the principal debtor.

GUARANTY—CONSTRUCTION OF CONTRACT.—A collateral continuing guaranty is to be construed as favorably in favor of the creditor, and as
strongly against the guarantor, as the sense of the words of the contract will permit.

GUARANTY.—LIABILITY OF GUARANTOR IS NOT AFFECTED by the previous
condition of the debtor's account with that of the creditor, as to any
sum from the payment of which the guarantor is not discharged by the
failure of the creditor to give notice within a reasonable time, of nonpayment by the principal debtor.

GUARANTY—LIABILITY WHEN ATTACHES.—Under a guaranty that the purchaser will promptly pay a debt at maturity, the liability of the
guarantor does not attach until the expiration of the term of credit
given the principal debtor.

GUARANTY—NOTICE OF DEFAULT BY DEBTOR.—Reasonable time is allowed
to the creditor in which to give notice to a guarantor of the default of
the principal debtor to make payment, and what is such reasonable
time depends upon the circumstances of each particular case.

Kraus, Mayer, and Stein, for the appellants.

Hofheimer and Zeisler, for the appellees.

489 CRAIG, J. This was an action brought by Reid, Murdoch, and Fischer against E. Kohn and Wm. Taussig, on the
following written instrument:

" REID, MURDOCH, AND FISCHER, *Chicago:*

" CHICAGO, January 14, 1887.

" For value received, I hereby guarantee the prompt pay

ment at maturity of any indebtedness owing to Reid, Murdoch, [490] and Fischer, by Mrs. Mathilde Zuckerman, of 370 State street, and 214 and 216 North Clark street, Chicago, for goods purchased, or which may be purchased hereafter, of them, to the amount of fifteen hundred dollars ($1,500.00), with interest on all the above indebtedness, according to the tenor and effect thereof, at the rate of eight per cent per annum, and I agree to pay all costs or expenses paid or incurred in collecting the same.

" Signed at Chicago, this fourteenth day of January, 1887.

" Witness: Jos. Zuckerman. [SIGNED] E. KOHN.

[SIGNED] WM. TAUSSIG."

In the circuit court the plaintiffs recovered a judgment for $1,680.34, the amount named in the instrument, and interest thereon from the time the action was brought. The judgment, on appeal, was affirmed in the appellate court, and for the purpose of reversing the latter judgment this appeal was taken. It appears from the record that, immediately upon the execution and delivery of the writing, Reid, Murdoch, and Fischer commenced selling goods to Mrs. Zuckerman on credit, and continued the sales until November 23, 1887. Her indebtedness to the firm varied in amount from time to time. On the first day of June, 1887, she was indebted in the sum of $1,762.30. On the 1st of July, 1887, $1,958.39. On the 1st of August, 1887, $1,925.98. On the 1st of September, $2,112.68. On the 1st of October, 1887, $2,342.80. On the 1st of November, 1887, $2,389.51. On November 23, 1887, when the account was closed, $2,714.96.

Mrs. Zuckerman failed on the twenty-fourth day of November, 1887, and this action was brought on the guaranty December 9th following. No notice was given the defendants by Reid, Murdoch, and Fischer of the failure of Mrs. Zuckerman to pay for the goods which she purchased, and it was insisted on the trial that her insolvency, and the failure of Reid, Murdoch, and Fischer to give notice of her [491] default in payment, relieved the guarantors from liability on the guaranty. But the court held otherwise, and in the first instruction on behalf of plaintiffs the jury were authorized to find for the plaintiffs, although demand and notice of nonpayment had not been established, and the soundness of this ruling is the principal, and indeed the only, question of any importance presented by the record.

Whether notice of the default of a principal debtor is required in order to fix the liability of a guarantor on a contract like the one involved, is a question upon which the authorities are conflicting. We shall not attempt to review the authorities at length, nor shall we attempt to harmonize the various decisions bearing up the question, but we shall content ourselves by stating what we understand to be the law on the subject, as established by the weight of authority.

Story on Contracts, volume 2, section 1133, in the discussion of the question, says: "Whenever the undertaking by a guarantor is absolute, notice is unnecessary, but where it is collateral merely, notice must be given within a reasonable time, otherwise the guarantor will be discharged, unless he is not prejudiced by the want of notice." In Baylies on Sureties and Guarantors, 202, the author says: "It may be laid down as a general rule that in case of an absolute guaranty the guarantor is not entitled to demand or notice of nonperformance, but where the undertaking is collateral, and not absolute, notice must be given within a reasonable time, unless circumstances exist which will excuse the want of notice. If the principal is insolvent when the debt becomes due or default is made, so that no benefit could be derived by the guarantor from the receipt of notice, no notice is required."

Where the payee of a promissory note or third parties execute a contract written on the back of an unconditional promissory note for the payment of money at a specified time, in which they guarantee the payment of the promissory ⁴⁹² note at maturity, the holder of the note is under no obligation to demand payment of the maker, and, on default of payment, notify the guarantors. The reason is obvious. The contract of the guarantors is absolute and unconditional, and it requires payment by the guarantors upon maturity of the note. This rule is clearly laid down in *Gage* v. *Mechanics' Nat. Bank*, 79 Ill. 62, and is well sustained by authority. The principle upon which this doctrine rests is that the contract is absolute, and not conditional or collateral. But does the contract upon which this action is brought rest upon the same principle, or is it to be governed by a different rule? Is the contract in question an absolute contract, or is it collateral or conditional? By the terms of the agreement the appellants guaranteed appellees payment to the amount of $1,500 for goods purchased, or for goods which might thereafter be purchased, of them, by Mathilde Zuckerman.

It is not claimed that any liability exists on account of

goods purchased before the execution of the guarantee, so
that the words embraced in the guaranty, "for goods purchased," has no special bearing in construing the agreement.
It will be observed that the amount of the goods which might
be purchased, nor the time during which the deal between
Mrs. Zuckerman and appellees should continue, was not
mentioned or determined. The contract did not compel
Mrs. Zuckerman to purchase or appellees to sell a dollar's
worth of goods. They could deal with each other as much
or as little as they might desire, or as they might see proper.
After the guaranty was executed, if appellees chose not to
sell Mrs. Zuckerman any goods, it could not be claimed that
an absolute guaranty existed, because there was no debt upon
which it could operate. How can a guaranty be absolute
where it is uncertain whether a debt will ever exist to which
it could apply? We think it is manifest that the guaranty
was not an absolute undertaking, but, on the other hand, the
contract in question was a continuing guaranty of a debt
[493] to be created in the future, of an indefinite amount, depending entirely upon the will of appellees and Mrs. Zuckerman.

In *Douglass* v. *Reynolds*, 7 Pet. 113, where an action was
brought on a guaranty of eight thousand dollars, on account
of the advancement of cash or acceptance or indorsement of
the principal's paper to assist him in business, it was held
that demand of payment and notice to the guarantors were
required. It is there said: "By the very terms of this guarantee, as well as by the general principles of law, the guarantors are only collaterally liable upon the failure of the
principal debtor to pay the debt. . . . . The creditors are not
indeed bound to institute any legal proceedings against the
debtor, but they are required to use reasonable diligence, to
make demand and to give notice of the nonpayment." In
McDougal v. *Calef*, 34 N. H. 534, in an action on a guaranty
for goods purchased, it was held that where the undertaking
was absolute, notice is unnecessary; but where it is collateral
merely, notice must be given within a reasonable time, otherwise the guarantor will be discharged, unless he be not prejudiced by the want of notice. In *Smith* v. *Bainbridge*, 6 Blackf.
12, in an action against a guarantor for goods sold to another,
the contract was held to be collateral. It is there said:
"Letters of credit . . . . frequently state, in express terms,
that if the third party do not pay, the writer will. But the

insertion or omission of such statement is not the test by which to determine the character of the contract. If the writer states that he will guarantee the payment of the goods to be afterwards sold to another, or that he will see the goods paid for, or that he will be security for their payment, the promise is only collateral. In the same case it was also held that demand of payment from the principal and notice of nonpayment to the guarantor was required. In *Babcock* v. *Bryant*, 12 Pick. 133, where an action was brought on an agreement, which read as follows: "New Bedford, November 20, 1826. This is to certify that I, [494] the subscriber, do hereby agree to be responsible and pay Messrs. Babcock and Allen for whatever goods have been or may be delivered to Thomas C. Case." In passing upon the obligation of the parties to the contract, the court said "the question is whether the promise is to be considered as an original or a collateral undertaking. We think it is the latter. . . . . The claim of the plaintiffs is for goods delivered after the making of the promise, for which Case gave to them his negotiable note. If he were not the principal debtor, it is difficult to account for the plaintiffs having taken the note of him. They must have understood that he was liable in the first instance. It would follow, that the meaning of the parties to the contract now in question was that the defendant was to be liable to pay if the principal debtor did not, and if the defendant should have reasonable notice of the default of the principal."

In *Mussey* v. *Rayner*, 22 Pick. 223, which was an action on a guaranty, it is said: The general rule of law on this subject seems now to be well settled, requiring that in cases of a written guaranty for a debt yet to be created and uncertain in its amount, the guarantor should have notice in a reasonable time that the guaranty is accepted and that credit has been given upon the faith of it. See also *Allen* v. *Pike*, 3 Cush. 238; *Norton* v. *Eastman*, 4 Greenl. 521; *Howe* v. *Nickels*, 22 Me. 175; 2 Parsons on Contracts, 28.

Here the appellants were apprised when they executed the guaranty that it was accepted by appellees; no further notice of acceptance was, therefore, required. But while the testimony disclosed that Mrs. Zuckerman became insolvent on the twenty-fourth day of November, 1887, no notice of her default in payment was furnished to appellants before her failure. We think that the decided weight of authority establishes the rule, that in case of a collateral continuing guaranty, like the

one in question, reasonable notice of the default of payment
on the part of the principal debtor should be given to the
guarantor. And the guarantor will [495] be discharged from
payment, so far as he has sustained loss or damage, resulting from a failure of the creditor to give him such notice:
Tiedeman on Commercial Paper, 421. Cases may arise where
notice would result in no benefit whatever to the guarantor;
for example, where the principal debtor was insolvent when
the guaranty was executed and remained in that condition.
In such cases the failure to give notice could result in no loss
to the guarantor, and could not be relied upon as a defense
to an action on the guaranty. But where the guarantor may
be able to protect himself, notice of default in payment imposes no unreasonable hardship on the creditor, and every
principle of commercial usage requires that it should be given.

Subsequently, on petition for rehearing, the following additional opinion was filed:

Per CURIAM. Upon the filing of the foregoing opinion,
judgment was entered reversing and remanding the cause for
a new trial. Upon petition for rehearing points were made
to which our attention had not been directed, and we have
again considered the case. Counsel for appellees, conceding
the correctness of the views expressed, insist that a reversal
should not be had because of the error in giving said instruction, for the reason that at the time Mrs. Zuckerman became
insolvent, November 24, 1887, there was more than $1,500 of
the indebtedness to plaintiff not due, and in respect of which
there had been no default of payment; and the rule being
that in case of insolvency, notice of nonpayment in such case
being without avail, and not required to be given, the guarantors were not released from liability in respect of such
indebtedness. It is conceded that over $1,500 of the indebt-
edness from Mrs. Zuckerman to plaintiffs had not matured at
the date she became insolvent. It is, therefore, said that if
the instruction is erroneous, as applied to the facts of this
case, it was not prejudicial error. It would follow from the
principles before announced, if the amount of $1,500 was due
when this suit [496] was brought, which was not due on the
24th of November, 1887, notice of nonpayment thereof would
have been unavailing to the guarantors.

It is insisted, however, that although there was over $1,500
not due from Mrs. Zuckerman when she became insolvent,
the guarantors were discharged from liability, because after

the execution of the guaranty she made default in payments
in excess of $1,500, of which no notice was given to the guar-
antors. It is shown that, commencing in February, 1887,
considerable balances remained unpaid, and on the 18th of
April, 1887, she was in default in payment of over $1,800,
and that a note or notes were taken in settlement of the
amount then due; that subsequently to that date she was in
default in payment of various sums, aggregating October 24,
1887, something over $1,100.

As this cause must be again submitted for trial, we have
deemed it proper to notice this insistence. The position of
appellants is untenable. They guaranteed the prompt payment at maturity of any indebtedness owing by Mrs. Zuckerman to the plaintiffs for goods purchased, or thereafter to be
purchased, of them, to the amount of $1,500. This amount
stated in the guaranty was a limitation upon the liability of
the guarantors, and not a limitation upon the credit to be
extended to Mrs. Zuckerman. It was, as we have seen, a
continuing guaranty, and plainly contemplated that payments made, or indebtedness otherwise settled by Mrs. Zuckerman, should not in any wise affect their liability for
indebtedness incurred by her for goods purchased and not
paid for at maturity. The contract of guaranty looked to a
future course of dealing for an indefinite time, that is, a succession of credits was to be extended, and the guarantors
undertook to be liable to the extent of $1,500 for any indebt-
edness contracted in the course of such dealings, and not
paid by Mrs. Zuckerman at maturity. Without extending
this opinion by citation from the authorities, it will be found
that the position taken is supported by *Bent* v. [497] *Hartshorn*,
1 Met. 24; *Douglass* v. *Reynolds*, 7 Pet. 113; *Hatch* v. *Hobbs*,
12 Gray, 447; *Gates* v. *McKee*, 13 N. Y. 232; 64 Am. Dec.
545; *Rindge* v. *Judson*, 24 N. Y. 64; *Grant* v. *Ridsdale*, 2 Har.
& J. 186; *Mason* v. *Pritchard*, 12 East, 227; *Rapelye* v. *Bailey*,
5 Conn. 149; 13 Am. Dec. 49; *Hargreave* v. *Smee*, 6 Bing. 244;
Martin v. *Wright*, 6 Adol. & El., N. S., 917; *Crittenden* v. *Fiske*,
46 Mich. 70; 41 Am. Rep. 146, and other cases.

It cannot be said that the cases are entirely harmonious as
to the principles which govern in the construction of this class
of instruments. But the weight of authority seems to be in
favor of construing them by rules at least as favorable to the
creditor as those applied to other written contracts, notwithstanding the guarantor is, in a sense, to be regarded as a

surety. In *Mason* v. *Pritchard*, 12 East, 227, it is held, that
the words are to be taken as strongly against the party giving the guaranty as the sense of them will admit. The same
general principle is held, more or less directly, in *Drummond*
v. *Prestman*, 12 Wheat. 515; *Douglass* v. *Reynolds*, 7 Pet. 113;
Lawrence v. *McCalmont*, 2 How. 426; *Bell* v. *Bruen*, 1 How.
169; *Dobbin* v. *Bradley*, 17 Wend. 422; *Mayer* v. *Isaac*, 6
Mees. & W. 605.

Taking the language of this instrument, and construing it
in the light of the circumstances surrounding, it seems clear
that it was intended that Mrs. Zuckerman should have credit
with the plaintiffs, and that appellants would be liable for
any balance that might remain unpaid at maturity at any
time during the continuance of the guaranty. That is, that
it was intended to give her credit with the plaintiffs to the
amount of $1,500, until the guaranty should be revoked. We
are of opinion, that the previous condition of her account with
the plaintiffs in no wise affected the liability of the guarantors for any sum owing by Mrs. Zuckerman, from which they
had not been discharged by the failure of the plaintiffs to
give notice, within a reasonable time, of nonpayment.

[498] It will, however, be observed that the contract of the
guarantors is, that Mrs.' Zuckerman would pay promptly " at
maturity" any indebtedness, etc. Counsel for appellees show
conclusively, that at least $578.18 of the indebtedness of Mrs.
Zuckerman was not due until after the fifteenth day of December, 1887. After giving the items of sales of goods by
plaintiffs to Mrs. Zuckerman, from the 15th to the 23d of
November, counsel say: "The earliest of these sales was
made on November 15th, and therefore, the credit on the
same did not expire until December 15th, and those following
became due at a correspondingly later period." It was conceded, and is shown by the record, the amount sold on each
day was treated as a separate transaction, and the indebtedness for the day's sales would mature at the end of the credit
given. That is, the credit being thirty days, the indebtedness contracted on the 15th of November would become due
December 15th, and that contracted on subsequent days at
corresponding dates in December. The same is true of the
goods purchased on the ninth, tenth, eleventh, twelfth, and
fourteenth days of November, as shown by the record, and
amounting in the aggregate to several hundred dollars. It
is apparent, therefore, that on December 9, 1887, these several

amounts had not matured, and the liability of appellants, for their prompt payment at maturity, had not attached. Counsel for appellees are correct in their contention that the record shows that these goods were mainly, at least, sold upon thirty days' time, and there is nothing shown by which the credit could, at the option of the plaintiffs, be shortened. This suit was brought December 9, 1887, and it is clear that the liability of the guarantors in respect of such sales had not attached. If suit had been brought against Mrs. Zuckerman at that time, a complete defense as to these items of indebtedness would have existed, because they had not matured at the time the suit was brought. The indebtedness not having matured, there was no liability upon the guaranty therefor.

[499] A casual examination of the accounts will show that if reasonable time of giving notice of nonpayment be allowed, and for this purpose the accounts maturing on or before the 18th of November only be excluded because of failure to give notice of nonpayment, it will be found that much less than $1,500 of the indebtedness of Mrs. Zuckerman to the plaintiffs had matured on the 9th of December, 1887. It cannot be presumed that there was included in the judgment, which was for the full amount of the guaranty, indebtedness not matured, and it is, therefore, clear that the instruction complained of must have led the jury into the error of taking into consideration, in determining the amount for which appellants were liable, the indebtedness of Mrs. Zuckerman that had matured before the 18th of November, and in respect of which appellants' liability as guarantors had been discharged.

What will be reasonable time in which to give notice must depend upon the circumstances in each particular case (*Dickerson* v. *Derrickson*, 39 Ill. 574; 2 Parsons on Contracts, 174), and while it is not necessary to determine the question, it would seem, from the facts here shown, that five days' time would at least be reasonable within which to give notice of nonpayment.

Other errors are assigned, which will undoubtedly be corrected upon another trial, and need not be considered. We are of opinion that the judgment heretofore entered, reversing the judgments of the appellate and circuit courts, and remanding the cause, was correct, and the same judgment will be again entered.

GUARANTY—INSOLVENCY OF PRINCIPAL—NOTICE OF NONPAYMENT.— Notice to the guarantor is unnecessary where the debtor is insolvent when the debt matures: *Skofield* v. *Haley*, 22 Me. 164; 38 Am. Dec. 307, and note; *Beebe* v. *Dudley*, 26 N. H. 249; 59 Am. Dec. 341; *Jones* v. *Scott*, 59 Pa. St. 178; 98 Am. Dec. 328, and note; *Gibbs* v. *Cannon*, 9 Serg. & R. 198; 11 Am. Dec. 699, and note.

GUARANTY—NECESSITY FOR NOTICE OF NONPAYMENT GENERALLY.— Guarantors are liable immediately upon the default of their principals, without notice, unless they are in effect indorsers: *Chafoin* v. *Rich*, 77 Cal. 476; or the undertaking is a collateral one: *Beebe* v. *Dudley*, 26 N. H. 249; 59 Am. Dec. 341, and note; *Bonebrake* v. *King*, 49 Kan. 296. See, also, the extended note to *Gibbs* v. *Cannon*, 11 Am. Dec. 703.

GUARANTY—NECESSITY FOR NOTICE OF ACCEPTANCE.—This question is fully discussed in *Saint* v. *Wheeler etc. Mfg. Co.*, 95 Ala. 362; *ante* p. 210, and note with the cases collected. See, also, the notes to the following cases: *Kincheloe* v. *Holmes*, 45 Am. Dec. 47; *Union Bank* v. *Coster*, 53 Am. Dec. 289; *Menard* v. *Scudder*, 56 Am. Dec. 618, and the extended note to *Thompson* v. *Glover*, 39 Am. Rep. 221–227.

GUARANTY—CONSTRUCTION OF CONTRACT OF.—A guarantor is bound by the precise terms of the contract guaranteed: *Staver* v. *Locke*, 22 Or. 519; 29 Am. St. Rep. 621, and note; *Glassell* v. *Coleman*, 94 Cal. 260; *Kepley* v. *Carter*, 49 Kan. 72.

GUARANTY—CONTINUING—WHAT IS LIABILITY ON.—A guaranty to pay for goods sold "from time to time," not exceeding a specified sum, continues until the amount unpaid reaches that limit: *Crittenden* v. *Fiske*, 46 Mich. 70; 41 Am. Rep. 146; *Mathews* v. *Phelps*, 61 Mich. 327; 1 Am. St. Rep. 581, and note. See the notes to the following cases: *Fellows* v. *Prentiss*, 45 Am. Dec. 492; *Menard* v. *Scudder*, 56 Am. Dec. 619; *Columbus Sewer-Pipe Co.* v. *Ganser*, 55 Am. Rep. 701–703, and *Gard* v. *Stevens*, 86 Am. Dec. 53.

PEOPLE *v.* WILLIAMS.

[145 ILLINOIS, 573.]

OFFICE AND OFFICERS.—MANDAMUS WILL LIE TO COMPEL ACCEPTANCE of a municipal office by one who, possessing the requisite qualifications, refuses to accept the office after he has been duly elected or appointed thereto.

OFFICE AND OFFICERS—DUTY TO ACCEPT OFFICE.—It is the duty of every person having the requisite qualifications, when elected or appointed to a public municipal office, to accept it. The refusal to do so is a crime, punishable as such under the principles of the common law.

OFFICE AND OFFICERS—MANDAMUS TO COMPEL ACCEPTANCE OF OFFICE.— One elected to an office owes a duty to the public to qualify himself therefor, and to enter upon the discharge of his duties, and upon a refusal so to do he may be compelled by *mandamus* to assume the office and take upon himself the duties thereof, although he is also subject to indictment or fine for a failure to do so.

OFFICE AND OFFICERS—POWER TO RESIGN.—A person holding a public office has no power of his own motion to resign it, and his resignation does not become effective to discharge him from the performance of the duties of such office, until accepted by lawful and competent authority·

OFFICE AND OFFICERS—MANDAMUS TO COMPEL ACCEPTANCE OF OFFICE.—A person duly elected or appointed to a public municipal office who refuses to qualify and assume the duties of such office upon notice of his election or appointment, may be compelled to do so by writ of *mandamus*, without any formal demand upon him to accept the office, notwithstanding the fact that a statute provides a penalty for his refusal to accept.

PROCEEDING by *mandamus* to compel the respondent, T. C. Williams, to accept, assume, and perform the duties of town clerk of the town of Mount Morris, and to take and subscribe the oath of office, and file a bond as required by law.

J. A. Crain, for the relator.

Rector C. Hitt, for the respondent.

576 SHOPE, J.   The principal question presented is, whether *mandamus* will lie to compel acceptance of a municipal office by one who, possessing the requisite qualifications, has been duly elected or appointed to the same.

It is stated by textwriters, that no case has arisen in this country involving this precise question (Merrill on Mandamus, sec. 145; Dillon on Municipal Corporations, sec. 162), and in the researches of counsel, and our own examination, none have been found.   There are, however, a number of cases where analogous questions, involving the same principle, have been elaborately discussed and determined in the state and federal courts.   Very many English cases are found, in which it has been held that it was a common-law offense to refuse to serve in a public office, to which one had been elected or appointed under competent authority; and that *mandamus* will lie in such case to compel the taking of the official oath, and entering upon the discharge of the public duty.   It is objected that these cases do not show that *mandamus* would lie for the refusal to accept public office, prior to the fourth year of James the First.   If the contention be true, it is unimportant whether the particular remedy was by *mandamus*, by the ancient common law, or not.   The important subject of inquiry is, whether it was a common-law duty to accept and discharge the duties of a public municipal office.   **577** The writ of *mandamus* was in use as early as the 14th and 15th centuries: *Rex v. Cambridge University,* Fortes. 202; *Rex v. Dr. Gower,* 3 Salk. 230.   It appears from *Dr. Widdrington's case* (A. D. 1673), 1 Lev. 23, that *mandamus*

had been in use as early as in the times of Edward II. and
Edward III., between 1307 and 1377.

Originally it was a letter missive from the sovereign
power commanding the party to whom it was addressed to
perform the act or duty imposed.   Later it obtained sanction
as an original writ, emanating from the king's bench, where,
by fiction of law, the king was always present.   But it does
not seem to have been frequently used, nor adopted, as the
remedy to compel the acceptance of office until late in the
17th century.   In modern times the uses of the writ, and
the purposes to which it will be applied, have been greatly
enlarged, and it has come into general use wherever there is
a legal duty imposed, and no other remedy is provided by law
for a failure to discharge it, and in many other cases against
those exercising an office or franchise, where there may be
another remedy, but it is less direct and effective.   In this
state, as in most, if not all, the states of the union, the proceeding is regulated by statute: Rev. Stats., c. 87.

The common law of England, so far as the same is applicable and of a general nature, and all statutes or acts of the
British Parliament made in aid of and to supply the defects
of the common law prior to the fourth year of James I. (excepting certain statutes), and which are of a general nature
and not local to that kingdom, are, by our statutes, made the
rule of decision until repealed by the legislature.   Thereby
the great body of the English common law became, so far as
applicable, in force in this state.

It is held in numerous English cases that by the common
law it was the duty of every person having the requisite
qualification, elected or appointed to a public municipal
[578] office, to accept the same, and that a refusal to accept
such office was punishable at common law.

The case of *Rex* v. *Lone,* 2 Strange, 920, was an indictment
for refusing to execute the office of constable by one who had
been chosen to it, and it was held that he was indictable by
the common law.   *Rex* v. *Jones,* 2 Strange, 1146, was an indictment for not taking upon himself the office of overseer of
the poor; it was held that the offense was indictable upon
the principles of the common law: See *Rex* v. *Burder,* 4 Term
Rep. 778.

Rex v. *Larwood* (A. D. 1695), 4 Mod. 270, was an information against the defendant for his refusal to take the office of
sheriff, to which he had been duly appointed; the defense

was that the defendant had not taken sacrament within a
year before he was chosen, he being a dissenter, and so the
appointment was void under 25 Car. I., c. 2, and 30 Car. I., c.
1, disabling papists, etc. It was held that it was the fault of
the defendant not to have received the sacrament, and that
his neglect of duty was no excuse, and that he was liable,
etc.

In *Vanacker's case* (A. D. 1700), 1 Ld. Raym. 496, it was
held that the city of London, a municipal corporation, of
common right possessed authority, by by-law of the corporation, to impose penalties for refusal to accept office, Lord
Holt remarking that "if a franchise be granted to a corporation it is under a trust that the corporation shall manage it
well. . . . . The acceptance of the charter obliges the body
politic to perform the terms upon which it was granted, and,
as every citizen is capable of the benefit of the franchise, so
he ought to submit to the charge also. . . . . And therefore,
as they have advantage by some franchises, so they ought to
submit to the charges of others. . . . . Therefore it is necessary that they should have coercive power to compel persons
to take the office upon them, and that without any custom;
otherwise this office might be lost to the city": *King v.
Raines*, 3 Salk. 162.

579 About the beginning of the 18th century the English courts adopted *mandamus* as an appropriate remedy
in such cases, as it would seem, and the practice has been
since followed. *Rex v. Hungerford*, decided in 1708 (11 Mod.
142), was an information in the nature of *quo warranto*
against a common councilman of Bristol, for refusing to take
upon himself the office, etc. The remedy was denied, but it
was said "if they had applied to the court for *mandamus* they
should have had it." *King v. Bower*, 1 Barn. & C. 585, was
mandamus to compel the defendant to'take the oath, and to
take upon himself and execute the office of common councilman of the borough and town of Lancaster. The court said:
"It is an offense at common law to refuse to serve an office
when duly elected," and refused to hold that the payment of
a fine, imposed by by-law of the corporation, discharged the
obligation to accept and serve in the office, and a peremptory
writ was awarded: See *Rex v. Corporation of Bedford*, 1 East.
79; *Rex v. Mayor etc. of Fowey*, 2 Barn. & C. 584; *Clarke v.
Bishop of Sarum*, 2 Strange, 1082; *Barber Surgeons v. Pelson,*
2 Lev. 252; *Vintners Co. v. Passey*, 1 Burr. 239; *Rex v. Grosve-*

nor, 1 Wils. 18; *Rex* v. *Whitwell,* 5 Term Rep. 86; *Rex* v. *Ley-land,* 3 Maule & S. 184.

Further citation from cases will not be necessary; so uniformly has the doctrine been maintained, that there is a legal duty to accept an office when duly elected or appointed, in a public or municipal corporation, at common law, and that *mandamus* is an appropriate remedy in cases of refusal, that it is accepted by all the textwriters.

Thus Mr. Grant (Law of Corporations, 230) states the rule: " On the other hand, when not being exempt or disqualified, a man is duly elected to an office, the court, if the corporation is a public one, and the office of a sufficiently important nature to justify its interference, and in all cases where the office is connected with the administration of local jurisdiction vested in the corporation, or the administration of ⁵⁸⁰ justice, will interfere by *mandamus* to compel him to take upon him and serve the office."

To the same effect, see Wilcocks, 128; Mechem on Offices, sec. 243; High on Extraordinary Legal Remedies, sec. 334; Shortt on Information, 324–328; Tapping on Mandamus, 189.

In Merrill on Mandamus it is said: "A party who has been elected to an office owes a duty to the public to qualify himself therefor, and to enter upon the discharge of his duties. Such duty being incumbent on him by law, he may be compelled by the writ of *mandamus* to assume the office, and take upon himself the duties thereof. Though he may be subject to an indictment or fine for failure to do so, still the writ of *mandamus* will be granted, because neither the indictment nor the fine is an adequate remedy in the premises, since it does not fill the office and prevent a failure of the discharge of the public duties": Sec. 145.

It follows, necessarily, that if to refuse the office is a common-law offense, and punishable as such, then a legal duty attaches to the person to take upon himself the office, which may now be enforced by *mandamus.*

While offices of this class, in England, were accepted as a burden, they have not been generally so regarded in this country. Under our system of local government, even the smallest offices are generally accepted, either because they are supposed to lead to those which bring higher honors and greater emoluments, or because of a sense of duty. To this fact, and perhaps to the prevalent but mistaken idea that one holding a public office may resign at will, may be attributed

the want of decision in this country upon the precise question
at issue. The cases bearing upon this question, in this country, have ordinarily arisen where the incumbent has sought
to resign from public office. And it has been uniformly held
that the power to resign did not exist, or resignation become
effective to discharge the officer from the public duty, until
accepted by lawful and competent authority. In *Edwards v.*
United States, 103 [581] U. S. 471, Edwards had been elected
supervisor of the town of St. Josephs, Berrien county, Michigan, on April 3, 1876, and entered upon the duties of his
office, and on the 7th of June following, resigned, in writing,
and filed the same with the town clerk. No action was alleged to have been taken by the township authorities, and the
question was: "Was the resignation complete without an acceptance of it, or something tantamount thereto, such as the
appointment of a successor?" The court holds that it was
not, and says: "In England, a person elected to a municipal
office was obliged to accept it, and perform its duties, and he
subjected himself to a penalty by a refusal. An office was
regarded as a burden, which the appointee was bound, in the
interest of the community and good government, to bear."
And it is said that it followed from this, as a matter of course,
that after the office was assumed it could not be laid down at
will. And that court holding that the common-law rule prevailed in Michigan, the judgment awarding a peremptory
writ, compelling the performance of the duty as a supervisor,
etc., was affirmed.

In the case of *Hoke* v. *Henderson*, 4 Dev. 1, 25 Am. Dec. 677,
it is said, in passing upon the question there at issue: "An
officer may certainly resign, but without acceptance his
resignation is nothing, and he remains in office. It is not
true that an office is held at the will of either party. It is
held at the will of both." And after saying that the acceptance of resignations, in respect of lucrative offices, has been
so much a matter of course that it has become the common
understanding that to resign is a matter of right, but the law
is otherwise, it is said: "The public has a right to the service
of all the citizens, and may demand them in all civil departments as well as the military." In *State* v. *Ferguson*, 31 N. J. L.
107, the question was, whether the respondent, at the time of
the service of the writ of *mandamus*, was an overseer of highways, etc. The respondent proved that before the service of the
mandamus [582] he had sent in his resignation of said office,

on which certain of the township committee had indorsed acceptance. It was insisted that the officer had a right to resign at will, and that the mere notification of the proper officers, of the fact, relieves him from performance of the official duty. The chief justice, after reviewing the common-law authorities, says: "I think it undeniable, therefore, that upon general principles of law, as contained in judicial decisions of the highest authority, the refusal of an office" of the class to which the one under consideration belongs, was an offense punishable by a proceeding in behalf of the public. Regarding, then, the doctrine of the law as established, it seems to be an unavoidable sequence that the party elected, and who is thus compelled by force of the sanction of the criminal law to accept the office, cannot afterwards resign it *ex mero motu.* If his recusancy to accept can be punished, it cannot be that he can accept, and immediately afterwards, at his pleasure, lay down the office. The same principle has been more or less directly announced in *Van Orsdall* v. *Hazard,* 3 Hill, 243; *London* v. *Headen,* 76 N. C. 72; *Winnegar* v. *Roe,* 1 Cow. 258; *People* v. *Supervisors Barnett Tp.,* 100 Ill. 332; *Badger* v. *United States,* 93 U. S. 599.

The reason assigned in *Rex* v. *Larwood,* 1 Salk. 168, for the public duty is, "that the king hath an interest in every subject and a right to his service, and no man can be exempt from the office of sheriff but by Act of Parliament or letters patent." Under our form of government, the principle applies with even greater force than under a monarchy. In a republic the power rests in the people, to be expressed only in the forms of law. And if the duty, preservative of the common welfare, is disregarded, society may suffer great inconvenience and loss, before, through the methods of legislation, the evil can be corrected. Upon a refusal of officers to perform their functions, effective government, *pro tanto,* ceases. All citizens owe the duty of [583] aiding in carrying on the civil departments of government. In civilized and enlightened society men are not absolutely free. The burden of government must be borne as a contribution by the citizen in return for the protection afforded. The sovereign, subject only to self-imposed restrictions and limitations, may, in right of eminent domain, take the property of the citizen for public use. He is required to serve on juries, to attend as witness, and, without compensation, is required to join the *posse comitatus* at the command of the representative of the sovereign power. He

may be required to do military service at the will of the
sovereign power. These are examples where private right
and convenience must yield to the public welfare and necessity. It is essential to the public welfare, necessary to the
preservation of government, that public affairs be properly
administered; and for this purpose civil officers are chosen,
and their duties prescribed by law. A political organization
must necessarily be defective, which provides no adequate
means to compel the observance of the obvious duty of the
citizen, chosen to office, to enter upon and discharge the public duty imposed by its laws, and necessary to the exercise of
the functions of government.

It is admitted by the demurrer that the respondent was legally appointed town clerk of the town of Mount Morris. The
office is connected with, and necessary to, the levy of taxes to
carry on the municipal concerns of the town and administration of its local jurisdiction. It is shown that there was a public
necessity, as well as that relators had a private interest in the
performance of the duties of that office.   No election had
been held in the town since the annual town meeting of 1891.
Numerous persons had been appointed to said office, but it
remained vacant, and the duties, consequently, undischarged.
It is admitted by the demurrer, also, that claims against the
town, in favor of the relator, to a large amount, had been
[584] audited by the board of town auditors of said town, and
allowed, and certificate thereof duly made, as provided by
law, but that the same could not be delivered to or filed with
the town clerk, because of such vacancy in said office, nor
could the aggregate amount thereof be certified to the county
clerk of said county, to be levied and collected as other town
taxes. It is conceded that the respondent was eligible to the
office; that a vacancy therein existed; that he was appointed
conformably to the law, and duly notified thereof: Secs. 1, 2, 3,
art. 10, c. 139, Rev. Stats. The statute provides that every
person appointed to the office of town clerk, before he enters
upon the duties of his office, and within ten days after he shall
be notified of his appointment, shall take and subscribe, before
some justice of the peace, etc., the oath or affirmation of office
prescribed by the constitution, and within eight days thereafter file the same in the office of the town clerk: Sec. 2, art. 9,
c. 139, Rev. Stats.   Section 3 of the same article provides that
if any person elected or appointed to said office shall neglect to
take and subscribe the oath, and cause the same to be filed

as aforesaid, such neglect shall be deemed a refusal to serve.
And section 7 of the same article provides: "If any person,
elected to the office of . . . . town clerk shall refuse to serve,
he shall forfeit to the town the sum of twenty-five dollars."
One of the special duties enjoined upon a town clerk is: "He
shall annually, at the time required by law, certify to the
county clerk the amount of taxes required to be raised for all
town purposes": Sec. 4, art. 12, c. 129, Rev. Stats. Sections 127
and 128 of chapter 120 of the Revised Statutes provide that
the county clerk shall determine the rate per cent, upon the
valuation of the property of towns, etc., that will produce not
less than the net amount of the sums certified to them according to law, to be extended by the county clerk upon the
equalized valuation of property in such town, etc. The only
mode provided by law by which a tax can be levied upon the
property of a town for the [585] payment of its debts or current expenses, is by the certificate of the town clerk of the
town to the county clerk, as thus prescribed. It is apparent,
therefore, that a public necessity exists for the discharge of
the public duty.

It is insisted, that the legislature having provided a penalty
for the refusal to accept the office, that that remedy is exclusive, and that a payment of the penalty imposed was intended
to be in lieu of the service. We cannot concur in this view.
The purpose of imposing the penalty, was to enforce the acceptance of the office and performance of its duties, and the
statute cannot be construed as intending that the person
chosen should be discharged from the duty by payment of the
penalty, and thereby the purposes of the creation of the office
frustrated, and the public duty remain unperformed. Authorities *supra.* It is to be presumed that, had the legislature intended that the payment of the fine should be in lieu
of the service, they would have so enacted, and not having
done so, the duty remains, nothwithstanding the imposition
of the fine or penalty: High on Extraordinary Legal Remedies, 334, and *supra.*

It is also insisted, that the demurrer should be sustained
for the reason that no demand is averred to have been made
upon respondent to accept the office and perform its duties.
It is alleged that he was duly forthwith notified of his appointment by the board authorized by law to make the same (sec.
3, art. 10, c. 139, Rev. Stats.), and that he refused and neglected to accept the office. Upon being notified, it was his

duty by law to take and subscribe the oath of office, and file the same, and enter upon the discharge of the duties.

Relator was not alone interested, nor did the failure of respondent to qualify affect its interest only. On the contrary, the duty, the performance of which is sought to be enforced, is a public duty, commanded by public law. The case is, therefore, clearly distinguishable from one in which the act sought to be enforced is for the benefit of some [586] private party. In cases of this class no formal demand was necessary as preliminary to the application for *mandamus*: *People v. Board of Education*, 127 Ill. 624.

We are of opinion that the respondent ought to be required to accept the office of town clerk of said town, to which he has been duly and legally appointed, to take and file the oath as such town clerk, as provided by law, and to discharge the duties of said office, and a peremptory writ of *mandamus* is awarded accordingly. ___

OFFICE—OBLIGATION TO ACCEPT.—The doctrine of the common law that a person duly elected or appointed to a public office, and qualified to fill it, is under obligation to accept it and perform the duties connected therewith, is so fully and correctly stated in the principal case that any attempt to enlarge upon it here would be a mere waste of words. Hence we shall only state that the refusal of a person duly elected or appointed to a public office to which he is eligible is an offense at common law indictable and punishable as such: *Rex* v. *Lone*, 2 Strange, 920; *Rex* v. *Jones*, 2 Strange, 1145; *King* v. *Burder*, 4 Term Rep. 778. Although such refusal to accept it and to discharge its duties is punishable by fine or otherwise, yet *mandamus* will lie to compel him to qualify for and enter upon the discharge of the duties of such office: *King* v. *Bower*, 1 Barn. & C. 585; *Edwards* v. *United States*, 103 U. S. 471.

A person elected to an office owes a duty to the public to qualify himself therefor, and to enter upon the discharge of his duties. Such duty being incumbent by law, he may be compelled by the writ of *mandamus* to assume the office and take upon himself the duties thereof, and though he may be subject to indictment or fine for a failure to qualify for and accept the office, yet *mandamus* will be granted, for the reason that neither the indictment nor the fine is an adequate remedy in the premises, because it does not fill the office and prevent a failure of the discharge of public duties. This is the rule uniformly laid down by the few existing cases on the subject, and it has universally been accepted by textwriters as the true exposition of the law: Mechem's Public Officers, secs. 240–245; High on Extraordinary Legal Remedies, sec. 334; Grant on Corporations, sec. 230; Topping on Mandamus, 189; Merrill on Mandamus, sec. 145.

A penalty may be imposed by statute upon the person elected to a public office for his neglect to accept and his refusal to serve. Such penalty attaches against the party elected if he omits to signify his acceptance of the office, and the authorities are thereby compelled to proceed to a new election: *Winnegar* v. *Roe*, 1 Cow. 258.

The rule that the acceptance of a public office is a duty enforceable by *mandamus* is of little practical utility if, as some of the cases imply, the acceptance cannot be enforced if a salary or other compensation for the services to be rendered has not been guaranteed by law. For certainly if the person selected to fill an official station has the right to be compensated at all, he must have the right to be adequately compensated; and the right of the public to his services is likely to be defeated by interposing an issue as to the adequacy of the compensation allowed by statute for such services. In Illinois it has been said that "no man can be compelled to give his time and labor, any more than his tangible property, to the public without compensation, and since there is no mode by which policemen appointed by the commissioners can be compensated, it follows that no one, even after accepting their appointment, can be compelled to perform any police duties": *Hinze* v. *People,* 92 Ill. 406, 424.

A man cannot be compelled to accept a second office while he is in possession of, and discharging the duties of, one to which he has been chosen. Thus when a citizen is elected to the office of constable, but refuses to serve, and an action is brought against him for the statutory penalty provided for such refusal, and he answers alleging that at the same election he was elected to the office of supervisor, that he accepted the latter office, and entered upon the discharge of the duties connected therewith, such answer discloses a sufficient defense to the action. A citizen will not in such case be compelled to accept both offices: *Township of Hartford* v. *Bennett,* 10 Ohio St. 441. When a person has been elected or appointed to a judicial office with his consent and knowledge, the holding of which renders him, during the term of such office ineligible to any office of trust or profit other than a judicial office, he may without accepting such office be afterwards elected to and hold an office not judicial, the term of which will run during the judicial term to which he has been elected or appointed: *Smith* v. *Moore,* 90 Ind. 294.

OFFICE—RIGHT OF OFFICER TO RESIGN AND EFFECT OF RESIGNATION.—A person elected or appointed to, and in the possession of, any public office, and performing the duties connected therewith, may tender his resignation at pleasure. Before he can resign, however, he must have accepted the office, as acceptance is necessary to the full possession and responsibility of an office: *Smith* v. *Moore,* 90 Ind. 294–306. Hence one who has been elected to an office cannot resign it until the time has arrived when he is entitled by law to possess it, has taken the oath, given the required bond, and entered upon the discharge of its duties. Every attempt to resign an office before the officer has qualified and entered upon the discharge of its duties is abortive and ineffectual: *Miller* v. *Board of Supervisors,* 25 Cal. 94.

To constitute a complete and operative resignation there must be an intention to relinquish a portion of the term of the office, accompanied by the act of relinquishment: *Biddle* v. *Willard,* 10 Ind. 62. When by law a resignation is required to be made in any particular form it must be substantially complied with, but if no such form is prescribed by statute the resignation may be made in any method indicative of a purpose to resign. It may be by parol, unless required to be in writing under the statute: *Van Orsdall* v. *Hazard,* 3 Hill, 243. The statute usually prescribes to whom the resignation of a public officer is to be made, and in the absence of such provision it should be made to such officer or body as is by law authorized to act upon it by appointing a successor, or by calling an election to fill the vacancy: *Edwards* v. *United States,* 103 U. S. 471.

Resignation, Whether Must Be Accepted.—There is a line of cases maintaining the proposition that when an unconditional resignation of a public officer is transmitted to the proper officer or body with the intention that it shall operate as such, it amounts, so far as the resigning officer is concerned, to a complete resignation, so as to vacate the office, and relieve such officer from longer performing the duties connected therewith, and so also as to relieve him from all further responsibility or liability in connection with the office from which he has resigned. In other words, the resignation is effectual to relieve the officer without its acceptance by the appointing power, and regardless of the fact as to whether such resignation is accepted or not: *People* v. *Porter*, 6 Cal. 26; *State* v. *Clarke*, 3 Nev. 566; *State* v. *Fitts*, 49 Ala. 402; *Bunting* v. *Willis*, 27 Gratt. 144; 21 Am. Rep. 338. Under this view of the law it has been maintained that the tendering of his resignation by a public officer, in writing, to the officer authorized by law to receive it, and the filing of the resignation by such officer, without objection, operates to vacate the office resigned according to the tenor of such resignation: *Gates* v. *Delaware County*, 12 Iowa, 405; that a civil officer has a right at any time to resign his office, and after his resignation has been received at the proper department his surety is not bound for the faithful performance of the duties of the office by his principal: *United States* v. *Wright*, 1 McLean, 509; that a drainage commissioner appointed by statute has a right to resign, and his resignation is complete when it is received by the county judge; no formal acceptance by the latter is needed to give it effect; and after such resignation the person resigning cannot legally act in the office from which he has resigned: *Olmstead* v. *Dennis*, 77 N. Y. 378; that the acceptance of a resignation of a municipal office by the authorities to whom it is tendered is not necessary in order to make it effective: *State* v. *Mayor of Lincoln*, 4 Neb. 260. These cases are not susceptible of reconciliation with the principle hereinbefore stated, that the acceptance of a public office is an enforceable duty; for certainly it would be a vain and idiotic procedure to compel the acceptance of a public office if the officer could by immediate resignation exonerate himself from the performance of the duties assumed under compulsion.

Therefore, on the other hand, the doctrine was maintained at common law and now prevails in a great number of the states of the American union that the resignation of a public officer is not complete so far as the public is concerned until it is duly accepted by the proper authorities. In the absence of statute this rule is supported by the better reasoning as well as by a major part of the authorities, and it has been adopted by the supreme court of the United States in the case of *Edwards* v. *United States*, 103 U. S. 471, to the effect that the resignation of a public officer is not complete until the proper authority accepts it, or does something tantamount thereto, such as to appoint a successor. In this case Mr. Justice Bradley, in delivering the opinion of the court, said: "As civil officers are appointed for the purpose of exercising the functions and carrying on the operations of government and maintaining public order, a political organization would seem to be imperfect which should allow the depositaries of its power to throw off their responsibilities at their own pleasure. This certainly was not the doctrine of the common law. In England a person elected to a municipal office was obliged to accept it and perform its duties, and he subjected himself to a penalty by refusal. An office was regarded as a burden which the appointee was bound, in the interest of the community and of good government, to bear. And from this it followed, of course, that after an office was conferred and assumed, it could not be laid down without the consent of the appointing power. This was required in order that the public interests might suffer no inconvenience for the want of public servants to execute the laws. . . . . In view of the manifest spirit and intent of the laws above cited it seems to us apparent that the common law requirement, namely, that a resignation must be accepted before it can be regarded as complete, was not intended to be abrogated. To hold it to be abrogated would enable every office-holder to throw off his official character at will, and leave the community unprotected. We do not think that this was the intent of the law."

Chief Justice Ruffin in *Hoke* v. *Henderson*, 4 Dev. 1, 25 Am. Dec. 677, said: "It is not true that an office is held at the will of either party. It is held at the will of both. Generally resignations are accepted, and that has been so much a matter of course with respect to lucrative offices, as to have grown into a common notion that to resign is a matter of right, But it is otherwise. The public has a right to the services of all the citizens, and may demand them in all civil departments as well as in the military. Hence there are on our statute books several acts to compel men to serve in offices. Every man is obliged, upon a general principle, upon entering upon his office, to discharge the duties of it while he continues in office, and he cannot lay it down until the public, or those to whom the authority is confided, are satisfied that the office is in a proper state to be left, and the officer discharged. The obligation is therefore strictly mutual, and neither party can forcibly violate it." "The rule in relation to the resignations of officers is, that such resignations take effect on their acceptance by the officer or officers authorized to fill the vacancy, and until accepted they are simply offers to resign": *Rogers* v. *Slonaker*, 32 Kan. 191. In *State* v. *Clayton*, 27 Kan. 442, 41 Am. Rep. 418, it was held that the acceptance of the resignation of a public officer is necessary to render it effective, and that when such resignation is accepted to take effect upon the appointment of a successor, the resignation is not complete, nor the office vacant, until such successor is appointed.

The following cases also maintain the rule that public officers cannot, at their pleasure, lay aside their offices by merely resigning, but that in order to make their offices vacant by resignation, such resignation must be accepted by competent authority, and that until the resignation is so accepted, it is inoperative and the officers remain in office: *Coleman* v. *Sands*, 87 Va. 689; overruling *Bunting* v. *Willis*, 27 Gratt. 144; 21 Am. Rep. 338; *State* v. *Ferguson*, 31 N. J. L. 107; *Van Orsdall* v. *Hazard*, 3 Hill, 243. An officer's resignation is virtually accepted when it is tendered by him, taken by the proper authority and placed on file in court. It is not necessary to enter an order of court upon the records accepting the resignation in form: *Pace* v. *People*, 50 Ill. 432.

After a public officer has resigned his office, and before his resignation has been accepted by the proper authority or his successor appointed, *mandamus* will lie to compel him to perform the duties pertaining to such office: *Edwards* v. *United States*, 103 U. S. 471.

In those states having a statute which provides that a person elected to office shall serve therein until his successor is elected or appointed, and qualified an officer although his resignation is tendered to and accepted by the proper authority, continues in office and is not relieved from his duties or responsibilities as such officer until his successor has qualified. During the interval between the acceptance of his resignation and the qualification and induction of his successor into office, the resigning officer may be compelled by *mandamus* to perform any of the duties which pertain to the office from which he has resigned: *Badger* v. *United States*, **93 U. S.** 599; *United States* v. *Justices*, 10 Fed. Rep. 460; *People* v. *Supervisors of Barnett Tp.*, 100 Ill 332; *Jones* v. *City of Jefferson*, 66 Tex. 576. Of course this is not true where the doctrine prevails that the mere tendering of a resignation of the office renders it vacant and relieves the officer resigning of further duties or responsibilities in relation thereto: *Olmstead* v. *Dennis*, 77 N. Y. 378, but as we have said, the latter rule is not supported by reason or the weight of current authority.

RIGHT TO WITHDRAW RESIGNATION.—As an officer has a right to tender his resignation at any time, so a prospective resignation by a public officer may be withdrawn at any time before it it is finally accepted: *Bunting* v. *Willis*, 27 Gratt. 144, 21 Am. Rep. 338; *Biddle* v. *Willard*, 10 Ind. 62. Thus the resignation of a person as coroner takes effect on its acceptance by the proper authority, and until so accepted it is merely an offer to resign, and may be withdrawn: *Rogers* v. *Slonaker*, 32 Kan. 191.

It has been decided that a prospective resignation may be withdrawn by the consent of the authority accepting, if no new rights have intervened: *Biddle* v. *Willard*, 10 Ind. 62; *Bunting* v. *Willis*, 27 Gratt. 144; 21 Am. Rep. 338. But if after the resignation has become complete and new rights have intervened, it cannot be withdrawn even with the consent of the appointing power: *Bunting* v. *Willis*, 27 Gratt. 144; 21 Am. Rep. 338. Although it has been decided that when a county clerk resigns by tendering his resignation to take effect at a future date, and then withdraws it before the date when it is to take effect, he is still entitled to hold the office notwithstanding that in the mean time, against his express wishes and without his consent, such resignation has been forwarded to the appointing power and by him approved and another person appointed clerk: *State* v. *Van Buskirk*, 56 Mo. 17.

When an officer has transmitted his written resignation of an office to, and it has been received and accepted by, the officer or an authority appointed by law to receive it, he cannot withdraw it even with the consent of the appointing power, if it is not so worded as to take immediate effect, as there is then a vacancy in the office to be filled by the proper authority: *State* v. *Hauss*, 43 Ind. 105; 13 Am. Rep. 384; *Pace* v. *People*, 50 Ill. 432; *Gates* v. *Delaware County*, 12 Iowa 405; *State* v. *Clarke*, 3 Nev. 566; *Queen* v. *Mayor*, L. R. 14 Q. B. Div. 908. Thus when a county officer transmits an unconditional resignation of his office, with the intention that it shall be delivered to the officer or authority entitled to receive it, the resignation thereby becomes complete and effectual and cannot afterwards be withdrawn: *State* v. *Fitts*, 49 Ala. 402.

CASES

IN THE

SUPREME COURT

OF

INDIANA.

BOARD OF COMMISSIONERS OF CARROLL COUNTY *v.* JUSTICE.

[138 INDIANA, 89.]

HIGHWAYS—FALSE INDUCEMENTS TO SIGN PETITION FOR—REMEDY.—When a free gravel highway is sought to be established, and certain petitioners therefor are harmed by false inducements held out to influence them to sign the petition, their remedy is by objection made before the sufficiency of the petition is established by the board of commissioners, and failing to do so they are precluded by the judgment if the latter is regular and effectual.

HIGHWAYS—MINISTERIAL ACT IN APPROVING BOND FOR COSTS OF ESTABLISHING.—The act of a board of commissioners in approving a bond to secure the expense of a preliminary survey and report in establishing a free gravel road, is merely ministerial and the fact that one of the commissioners is an interested party does not affect the action of the board.

JUDGMENT BY DISQUALIFIED JUDGE—COLLATERAL ATTACK.—The act of a board of commissioners in passing upon the sufficiency of a petition and appointing viewers and a surveyor for the establishment of a free gravel road is judicial in its nature, and the participation therein by a commissioner disqualified to act by reason of interest or otherwise renders the judgment of the board voidable by appropriate proceeding, but when the board has acquired jurisdiction of the subject matter and of the person by giving the required statutory notice, and an opportunity by appeal is given of having a trial by an impartial tribunal, such voidable act by the board is not subject to collateral attack by injunction or otherwise.

JUDGMENT BY DISQUALIFIED JUDGE.—In an action to declare a judgment participated in by a disqualified and interested judge a nullity, the fact that the major portion of the members of the court were disinterested, and that a large number of parties litigant, other than such disqualified judge, were interested in, and would be affected by, such judgment is not without weight.

W. C. Smith, J. H. Gould, and G. R. Eldridge, for the appellant.

D. C. Justice, Q. A. Myers, and J. C. Nelson, for the appellees.

[90] MILLER, J. This action was brought by the appellees in the Carroll circuit court, to declare void the proceedings of the board of commissioners of that county for the establishment of a free gravel road, and to enjoin the placing of assessments against their lands for its construction.

The improvement sought to be enjoined was being made under the Act of March 3, 1877: Rev. Stats. 1881, sec. 5091, et seq.

The complaint proceeds upon two grounds:

1. That some of the landowners who signed the petition for the making of the improvement were induced to do so by false representations and false promises as to the amount which would be assessed against their lands, and by promises by one John G. Cornell that he would pay all that their lands were assessed above a fixed amount.

2. That the proceedings before the board of county commissioners are void, because John G. Cornell, one of the county commissioners, was one of the petitioners, owned lands within two miles of the proposed road, which were subject to assessment for its construction, [91] and was, also, related by blood and marriage to certain other named petitioners and interested parties; and, being so disqualified, acted with the board of commissioners in certain proceedings relating to the making of the improvement.

Taking these questions in their order, if it be admitted that the appellees were harmed by the inducements held out to influence other landowners to sign the petition, they should have made the objection before the sufficiency of the petition was established by the adjudication of the board of commissioners. Not having done so, if that adjudication was effectual, they are precluded by that judgment: *Osborn v. Sutton,* 108 Ind. 443; *Million v. Board etc.,* 89 Ind. 5; *White v. Fleming,* 114 Ind. 560; *Loesnitz v. Seelinger,* 127 Ind. 422.

The other proposition presents a question of more difficulty.

The complaint charges that Cornell and others filed their petition with the auditor of the county for the construction of the gravel road, together with a bond payable to the board of commissioners, by which they agreed to pay the costs and expenses of the preliminary survey and report, in case the proposed road was not finally ordered by the board; that at the June term of the commissioners' court the bond was accepted and approved, Cornell acting with the other commissioners; that on the succeeding day of the term, Cornell again acting with them, the board of commissioners heard proofs upon the petition, and made findings of fact thereon, appointed three viewers and an engineer to view, examine, and lay out the proposed free gravel road, to make assessments of damages, and to determine upon the public utility thereof, and to ascertain the lands which were liable to be assessed for the improvements. The auditor was also ordered to give the viewers and surveyor notice of the time and place fixed for their meeting, as well as the notice required [92] by publication in some newspaper; that afterwards the viewers and surveyor made their report, and the board of commissioners, at their December term, Cornell being absent and not acting, approved the report, and made an order declaring the improvement to be of public utility, and appointing three disinterested freeholders to make an assessment upon the lands for the amount of the estimated cost thereof; that afterwards the assessors made their report to the county auditor, who gave notice, by publication, of the time when the commissioners would meet at his office to hear the same; that on the day named the board met, Cornell acting with them, heard the report, confirmed the assessment, and ordered it put upon the duplicate for collection.

Taking up the questions presented by the action of the board of commissioners, in the order of their occurrence, we find that the first action complained of was the approval of the bond of the freeholders, securing the expense of the preliminary survey and report. The condition of the bond being fixed by statute, and no action being required to fix the amount of penalty, nothing remained to be determined but the sufficiency of the obligors. This was a ministerial act, such as a clerk or sheriff, possessing no judicial functions, may perform: *Gregory v. State,* 94 Ind. 384; 48 Am. Rep. 162; *Gulick v. New,* 14 Ind. 93; 77 Am. Dec. 49; *Votaw v. State,* 12 Ind. 497; *State v. Winninger,* 81 Ind. 51.

While it would have been proper for the member of the board of commissioners interested in the matter before them to have absented himself when action was taken upon the approval of the bond, it was not error to remain and act.

The next action taken by the board was entertaining the petition, and making the order appointing the viewers and surveyor. In construing this section 5092, this court, in *Million* v. *Board etc.* 89 Ind. 5, said:

"The presentation of this petition called into exercise [93] the jurisdiction of the county board, and required the board to determine the question of the sufficiency of the petition, in form and substance, and whether or not such petition was signed by the requisite number of landholders, whose lands would be assessed for the cost of the proposed improvement, and every other fact, precedent or concurrent necessary to the granting of the prayer of the petition." To the same effect we cite *Stoddard* v. *Johnson*, 75 Ind. 20; *McEneney* v. *Town of Sullivan*, 125 Ind. 407; *Loesnitz* v. *Seelinger*, 127 Ind. 422.

The conclusion seems irresistible that action of the board was judicial, and not merely ministerial.

The maxim that no man should be a judge in his own case is so well established, both in reason and by authority, that it needs neither argument nor the citation of adjudged cases in its support. The effect to be given an adjudication rendered by a disqualified tribunal is another and a more troublesome question.

A judgment rendered by a court where the judge is disqualified must necessarily be either void or voidable. If void, it may be disregarded and treated as if it had never been rendered. It would be no protection to officers acting under it. If, on the contrary, such a judgment is not void, but merely voidable, it will protect persons lawfully acting under it, and will be given full force and effect as a valid and subsisting judgment until reversed or set aside on appeal, or other appropriate method of direct attack.

The decided weight of authority seems to establish the proposition that, at common law, the acts of a disqualified judge are not mere nullities; they are liable to be avoided or reversed on proper application, but cannot be impeached collaterally: *Dimes* v. *Grand Junction Canal*, 3 H. L. Cas. 759 (785); *State* v. *Crane*, 36 N. J. L. 394; *Fowler* v. *Brooks*, 64 N. H. 423; 10 Am. St. Rep. 425; *Trawick* v. *Trawick's Admrs.*, 67 Ala. 271; *Moses* v. [94] *Julian*, 45 N. H. 52; 84 Am. Dec. 114; *Rogers* v. *Felker*, 77 Ga. 46; *Hine* v. *Hussey*, 45 Ala. 496 (513); 1 Black on Judgments, sec. 174; Freeman on Judgments, sec. 145; Wells on Jurisdiction, sec. 172.

In many of the cases cited as sustaining the proposition that judgments rendered by a disqualified tribunal are void, it will be found, upon examination, that the judgments so rendered were attacked on appeal, and the language must be construed as applicable to the case before the court: *Peninsular Ry. Co.* v. *Howard,* 20 Mich. 18; *Gregory* v. *Cleveland etc. R. R. Co.,* 4 Ohio St. 675. In many states statutes have been passed which prohibit judges disqualified by interest or relationship from acting in certain cases. Under these statutes it has usually been held that judgments rendered in contravention of statute are not simply voidable, but void: Black on Judgments, sec. 174, and cases cited; *Templeton* v. *Giddings,* Tex. Dec. 6, 1889; *Frevert* v. *Swift,* 19 Nev. 363.

We do not hold that a case might not arise where a judgment rendered by a sole judge might not be absolutely void; such, for instance, as one granting himself a divorce from his wife.

While it has been held that if incompetent magistrates or judges composing a court sat at the hearing, a judgment rendered by the court should be quashed or set aside: *Peninsular Ry. Co.* v. *Howard,* 20 Mich. 18; *Queen* v. *Justices etc.,* 6 Q. B. 753. We are of the opinion that in an action brought to declare such judgment a nullity, the fact that the major portion of the members of the court were disinterested is not without weight, and also the fact that a large number of parties litigant, other than such disqualified judge, were interested in and would be affected by such judgment.

It will be presumed in a collateral attack such as this, and especially in the absence of an averment to the contrary, that the county auditor gave the notice required by section 5092 of the Revised Statutes of 1881 of the time and place of meeting of the viewers: *White* v. *Fleming,* 114 Ind. 560; and it appears from an exhibit of the complaint that the notice required by section 5096 of the Revised Statutes of 1881 was given. This gave the appellees and all other landowners interested an opportunity to appeal to the circuit court in which the proceedings taken before the board of commissioners might have been reviewed before a duly constituted and impartial tribunal: *White* v. *Fleming,* 114 Ind. 560; *Markley* v. *Rudy,* 115 Ind. 533; *Fleming* v. *Hight,* 101 Ind. 466; *Wilkinson* v. *Lemasters,* 122 Ind. 82; *Board etc.* v. *Fullen,* 118 Ind. 158.

If no provision had been made in the statute for notice to

the landowners affected at some stage of the proceedings, or opportunity given by appeal of having their causes tried by a duly constituted and impartial tribunal, the remedy by injunction would doubtless be open to the appellees: *McEneney* v. *Town of Sullivan*, 125 Ind. 407; *Bass* v. *City of Fort Wayne*, 121 Ind. 389; *Updegraff* v. *Palmer*, 107 Ind. 181; *Forsythe* v. *Kreuter*, 100 Ind. 27. In *Osborn* v. *Sutton*, 108 Ind. 443, it was held that an objection to the competency of an assessment committee must be made at the time the committee is appointed, or within a reasonable time thereafter.

In *Bradley* v. *City of Frankfort*, 99 Ind. 417, a commissioner to assess damages to property affected by the opening of a street was related to one who was financially interested in having it opened. It was held that one served with notice of the meeting of the commissioners before the assessment against his property, and of the incompetency of the commissioner, must then and there make the objection, or it will be deemed waived.

The general rule to be deduced from these and similar cases is that where the board of county commissioners has jurisdiction of the subject matter, and has acquired **96** jurisdiction of the person by giving the required notice, and an opportunity by appeal is given of having a trial by an impartial tribunal, the proceedings are not subject to a collateral attack by injunction or otherwise.

This being a joint action by several landowners, the complaint is not aided by section 5102. In *Stoddard* v. *Johnson*, 75 Ind. 20, it was held that was only applicable to suits brought by single individuals, or by individuals having a single interest, where a judgment could be rendered "without affecting the rights or liabilities of other parties in interest."

We are satisfied that the court erred in overruling the demurrer to the complaint.

A demurrer was sustained to an answer which set forth the supsequent proceedings taken by the board in relation to this improvement. What we have said in discussing the ruling of the court on the demurrer to the complaint renders it unnecessary to set out the answer. The same principles of law require us to hold that the court erred in sustaining the demurrer to the answer.

Judgment reversed.

HIGHWAYS.—ROAD COMMISSIONERS, IN ADJUDICATING UPON THE NECESSITY OF A ROAD, and in locating and making assessments for the same, act judicially: *Longfellow* v. *Quimby*, 29 Me. 196; 48 Am. Dec. 525.

JUDGMENTS BY A DISQUALIFIED JUDGE ARE VOID: Extended note to *Moses* v. *Julian*, 84 Am. Dec. 126–130; note to *Sigourney* v. *Sibley*, 32 Am. Dec. 251; *Horton* v. *Howard*, 79 Mich. 642; 19 Am. St. Rep. 198, and note; *Chicago etc. Ry. Co.* v. *Summers*, 113 Ind. 10; 3 Am. St. Rep. 616, and note; *Newcome* v. *Light*, 58 Tex. 141; 44 Am. Rep. 604.

A DISQUALIFIED JUDGE MAY PERFORM MERELY MINISTERIAL ACTS: See extended note to *Moses* v. *Julian*, 84 Am. Dec. 131.

SPAULDING *v.* SPAULDING.

[183 INDIANA, 122.]

DIVORCE—ALIMONY—LEWD LIFE AS BAR TO.—A wife who leads a lewd life, yielding her person to the embraces of different men, has no claim upon her husband for support and maintenance or alimony when divorce is granted to the husband on account of her misconduct. A court abuses its discretion in granting the wife alimony in such a case.

E. R. Wilson and *J. J. Todd*, for the appellant.

A. L. Sharpe and *F. L. Burgan*, for the appellee.

[122] ELLIOTT, J. The appellant petitioned for a divorce from the appellee, charging her with adultery, and the court found that the charge was true. A decree of divorce was granted the appellant, and an allowance of nine hundred dollars, as alimony, was made in favor of the appellee. The question as to the correctness of the part of the decree awarding alimony is well made, and properly saved, and it is the important question in the case.

The evidence shows that the appellee was guilty of many adulterous acts, with many men. Her conduct was that of a woman who had surrendered her person to promiscuous intercourse with men, and who yielded to her passion without restraint, and in utter disregard of her duty to her husband. This is not the case of a single act of adultery, nor the case of continued acts with one man, but it is the case of a woman indulging in repeated and flagrant violations of her wifely vows and duties; nor was there any misconduct on the part of the husband [123] which excused the wife's life of shame; on the contrary, he seems to have borne with her with unusual patience, and to have treated her with kindness. The evidence also shows desertion, and that the appellee left the appellant to live with a paramour. The appellant has property of the probable value of fifteen thousand dollars, but he is in debt to a considerable sum, and his property is encumbered.

In our judgment, the trial court abused its discretion in allowing the appellee alimony. We are satisfied that a wife who lives a life of shame, yielding her person to the embraces of different men, has no claim upon the husband she has disgraced to support or maintenance. Her course of life forfeits all claim to the rights of a wife. We do not regard the decision in the case of *Cox* v. *Cox*, 25 Ind. 303, as opposed to the conclusion we have stated. A woman who lives a lewd life occupies a very different position from one who retains her chastity, but treats her husband with cruelty. We agree to the doctrine of *Hedrick* v. *Hedrick*, 28 Ind. 291, that the allowance of alimony "is not yet controlled by definite rules, and the determination of each case must, therefore, depend upon its own circumstances and an enlightened sense of justice and public policy." We cannot agree, however, that the doctrine lends support to the appellee's cause. It would be against public policy, and contrary to justice, to compel a husband to contribute to the support of a wife who had deserted him for another, and who had brought shame upon him by lascivious conduct so gross as to bring her down among courtesans. The doctrine of the case of *Stock* v. *Stock*, 11 Phil. 324, applies here with controlling force. In speaking of a defendant, who occupied much the same position as that occupied by the defendant in this case, the court said: "By such a course she throws off alike her allegiance to her husband and to the law, and forfeits the right to demand support from the former, or assistance [124] from the latter to compel him to render it. This is a conclusion supported alike by law, good morals, and public policy." Our statute sanctions this general doctrine, for it denies to an adulterous wife any share of her deceased husband's estate. Our own court has recognized the doctrine, as the decision in *Conner* v. *Conner*, 29 Ind. 48, attests. In that case it was said: "The question, then, is almost purely whether a wife's thrice repeated and promiscuous adultery—the gravest of all possible crimes against the institution of marriage, and against the husband's honor and happiness, and against society—shall receive from our courts the same tender pecuniary consideration which the laws of the state bestow upon honest and virtuous widowhood. To state the question ought to be enough." Other courts have asserted similiar conclusions: *Osgood* v. *Osgood*, 2 Paige, 621; *Whitsell* v. *Whitsell*, 8 B. Mon. 50; *Bray* v. *Bray*, 6 N. J. Eq. 27; *Goldsmith* v. *Goldsmith*, 6 Mich. 285; *Latham* v. *Latham*, 80 Gratt. 307; *Harris* v. *Harris*, 31 Gratt. 13; *Spitler* v. *Spitler*, 108 Ill. 120. In the case last named the court, in speaking of a statutory provision similar to ours, said: "On the other hand, because alimony may, under special circumstances, be decreed to the wife, where the divorce has been granted to the husband for her misconduct, it does not follow that such an order would be warranted where the conduct of the wife, as in the present case, has been grossly improper." It was also said: "It was manifestly not the intention of the legislature, in adopting the provisions of the statute above cited, to abrogate the general principles or policy of the law relating to the subject of alimony; but rather to clothe the courts with power to mitigate occasional hardships that would otherwise occur on account of the inflexible rule that the wife is not entitled to alimony where the divorce is granted to the husband on account of her misconduct."

Under the rule declared in *Cox* v. *Cox*, 25 Ind. 303, and *Hedrick* [125] v. *Hedrick*, 28 Ind. 291, we feel bound to adjudge that there was no such abuse of discretion in allowing counsel's fees, or in taxing costs against the appellant as will justify our interference.

Judgment reversed, with instructions to sustain the appellant's motion to modify so much of the decree as awards alimony, and to vacate and annul that allowance; as to all other matters, the decree is affirmed.

———

MARRIAGE AND DIVORCE—ALIMONY—BAD CONDUCT OF WIFE AS AFFECTING ALLOWANCE OF.—See the extended note to *Methvin* v. *Methvin*, 60 Am. Dec. 671, 672. After a divorce has been granted and alimony allowed, the subsequent immoral conduct of either party is not a ground for an increase or decrease of such allowance: *Cole* v. *Cole*, 142 Ill. 19; 34 Am. St. Rep. 56.

HUTCHINSON *v.* FIRST NATIONAL BANK OF MICHIGAN CITY.

[133 INDIANA, 271.]

ASSIGNMENT OF MORTGAGED PREMISES FOR BENEFIT OF CREDITORS—FORECLOSURE OF MORTGAGE—RIGHTS OF ASSIGNEE.—If mortgaged premises are assigned by the mortgagor in trust for the benefit of creditors, the assignee is a necessary party defendant in a suit to foreclose the mortgage, because the legal title to the property is in him, and it is his duty on behalf of creditors to protect their rights in the foreclosure suit. If he represents any creditor, who, if the assignment had not been made, would have had a standing in court to question the validity of the mortgage, the assignee may, as the representative of that creditor, assail such conveyance.

ASSIGNMENT OF MORTGAGE FOR BENEFIT OF CREDITORS—FORECLOSURE OF MORTGAGE—DUTY OF ASSIGNEE.—If the creditors of a mortgagor, who has assigned the mortgage in trust for the benefit of his creditors, are not in a position to successfully assail its validity on foreclosure, it is not the duty of the assignee to assail it.

UNRECORDED MORTGAGES—EFFECT OF ON CREDITORS.—When by statute unrecorded mortgages are to be deemed, as an inference of law, fraudulent and void as to "subsequent purchasers, lessees, or mortgagees," the terms of the statute will not be extended so as to include and protect the general creditors of the mortgagor.

UNRECORDED MORTGAGES—EFFECT OF ON CREDITORS OF MORTGAGOR.—In the absence of express fraud, the mere failure of a mortgagee to record his mortgage within the time fixed by statute does not as against the creditors of the mortgagor, either prior or subsequent, render it invalid.

FRAUD—WHEN MUST BE FOUND AS FACT.—If by statute the question of fraud is made one of fact, and fraud is essential to the cause of action, it must be found as a fact, and not left to be inferred as matter of law.

FRAUDULENT CONVEYANCES—FRAUD MUST BE ALLEGED AND FOUND.—Not only must fraud be found as an ultimate fact, in order to avoid a conveyance as being fraudulently executed to hinder and delay creditors, when the statute makes fraud a question of fact, but the complaint in such action must also expressly allege that the instrument was executed with a fraudulent intent.

FRAUDULENT CONVEYANCES—FRAUDULENT INTENT MUST BE ALLEGED.— In an action brought by, or for the benefit of, subsequent creditors, the complaint must aver that the instrument to be avoided was executed with intent to defraud subsequent as well as existing creditors.

MORTGAGES.—MERE FAILURE TO RECORD a mortgage within the time fixed by statute, whether such failure is in pursuance of a previous contract, or by mere neglect, is not sufficient of itself to enable the mortgagor's creditors to avoid such instrument. In such cases the known insolvency of the mortgagor, active misrepresentation of his financial condition, or other *indicia* of fraud, must enter into the transaction in order to render it void as to creditors.

MORTGAGES—EFFECT OF FAILURE TO RECORD UPON CREDITORS.—Withholding a mortgage from record in order to maintain the credit of the mortgagor is not of itself sufficient to justify a court in holding, as matter of law, that such mortgage is fraudulent and void as to creditors of the

mortgagor, either existing or subsequent, but it is a badge of fraud to
be considered with all the facts and circumstances surrounding the
transaction, in determining whether or not there was, in fact, a fraudulent intent in so withholding the mortgage from record.

RECEIVER—WHEN SHOULD NOT BE APPOINTED IN ACTION TO FORECLOSE
MORTGAGE.—When, in an action to foreclose a mortgage against a mortgagor and his assignee, the mortgagee asks that a receiver be appointed
without notice, for the reason, as he alleges, that his security will be
impaired because such assignee will not prevent a sale of buildings and
machinery on the mortgaged premises under a pretended chattel mortgage, the application for the appointment of the receiver should be denied, when the assignee avers in his answer that he has refused to allow,
and has obtained an injunction against, such sale, and has instituted suit
to have the chattel mortgage declared void.

*H. B. Tuthill, H. A. Schwager, J. S. Duncan, and C. W.
Smith,* for the appellant.

J. H. Orr, M. Nye, and J. H. Bradley, for the appellee.

272 MILLER, J.   The appellee brought this action against
the Hopper Lumber and Manufacturing Company and William B. Hutchinson, its assignee, to foreclose a mortgage executed by the company prior to its assignment.

In addition to the foreclosure, the complaint charged that
there was situate upon the mortgaged premises certain buildings and machinery used in the business of the company,
which one James S. Hopper had advertised for sale under a
pretended chattel mortgage held by the Sutton Manufacturing Company of Detroit, Michigan; that the **273** assignee of
the Hopper Lumber and Manufacturing Company permitted
said Hopper to take possession of the property, and will allow
him to dispose of it; that the mortgaged property, including
the machinery, is of less value, by six thousand dollars, than
the amount due the plaintiff; that unless a receiver is appointed without notice, the mortgaged machinery, or part of
it, will be removed, and the plaintiff's security will be materially impaired.

In accordance with this prayer, a receiver was appointed.

No question is made as to the regularity of the proceedings
in making the appointment of the receiver.

This suit was commenced, and the receiver appointed, on
the eleventh day of August, 1891, in vacation.

On the tenth day of September an answer, in two paragraphs, was filed, which are as follows:

"Paragraph 1. The defendant, William B. Hutchinson,
assignee of the Hopper Lumber and Manufacturing Com-

pany, for a partial answer to so much of the complaint herein
as prays for the foreclosure of the mortgage in the complaint
mentioned and described, says that he admits that on the
sixth day of January, 1891, the defendant, the Hopper Lumber and Manufacturing Company, executed to the plaintiff
the several notes and the mortgage in the complaint mentioned and described, and therewith exhibited. But he says
that the plaintiff is not entitle to the decree of this court for
the foreclosure of said mortgage, and ordering the sale of said
real estate to pay the notes aforesaid, for the reasons following, that is to say: That said notes were executed to secure a
pre-existing indebtedness; that at the time of the execution
of said notes and mortgage, the defendant, the Hopper Lumber and Manufacturing Company, was engaged, and expected
to continue, in the business of buying and selling lumber and
the manufacture and sale of certain refrigerators, and the
manufacture and sale of certain furniture specialties, and
that said [274] corporation was then in good credit; that said
corporation was then indebted in large amounts to persons
other than the plaintiff herein, to wit, in the sum of more
than seventy-five thousand dollars, which indebtedness would
mature at various dates within ninety days next succeeding
the sixth day of January, 1891, which indebtedness said Hopper Lumber and Manufacturing Company expected and intended to continue by renewals and extensions thereof by its
creditors; and such renewals and extensions were necessary
in order for it to continue in business; that said Hopper Lumber and Manufacturing Company, at said date, also expected
and intended to purchase very large amounts of lumber and
other material necessary for its use in the prosecution of its
said business; all of which facts were at the time fully known
to the plaintiff herein; that at said time it was also well known,
both to the plaintiff and said lumber manufacturing company,
that if said Hopper Lumber Manufacturing Company should
execute to the plaintiff the mortgage in the complaint mentioned and described, the credit of said Hopper Lumber and
Manufacturing Company would be utterly destroyed, and it
would be wholly unable either to procure renewals, or extension, of its then existing indebtedness, or to purchase lumber,
or other material, needed by it in the prosecution of said business upon credit; that said corporation defendant, being so
indebted to the plaintiff, the latter demanded from it the execution of the mortgage in the complaint mentioned and de-

scribed, and therewith exhibited, to secure said indebtedness;
that upon such demand being so made, the defendant corporation called the attention of the plaintiff to the foregoing facts,
and to its intention to renew its then existing indebtedness,
and to purchase lumber and other material upon credit, and
that it was necessary for it to be able so to do, and said defendant corporation wholly refused to execute said mortgage
to the plaintiff except upon the condition that the fact of the
execution [275] of such mortgage and its existence should be
concealed from the public, and that the same should not be
recorded, to the end that it might continue in good credit,
and be enabled thereby to renew said indebtedness, and to
make such purchases upon credit; that said plaintiff, with a
full knowledge of all of the foregoing facts, and that knowledge of the execution of said mortgage would destroy the
credit of said defendant corporation, and render it impossible
to renew such debts and make such purchases; and well
knowing that certain agencies, well known in the mercantile
and business world as mercantile agencies, exist, whose business it is to keep constant watch over the credit of all persons
engaged in business, and particularly to keep close watch over
the records of mortgages, and at once, if on the record of mortgages, to publish such fact to all persons engaged in business;
and well knowing that if such mortgage should be put upon
record the fact would be published to the persons to whom
said defendant corporation was indebted, and from whom it
expected to purchase such lumber and other material; and
well knowing that thereby said defendant corporation would
be precluded from renewing said indebtedness then existing,
as well, also, as from making such purchases of lumber and
other material upon credit; and well knowing that if the existence of such mortgage, and the fact of its execution, were
concealed, and it withheld from record, said corporation would
be able to make such renewals, and such purchases, and
would in point of fact do so; and calculating and intending
to enable it to do so, and to maintain its credit, said plaintiff
did agree with said corporation defendant that it would conceal the fact of the execution of said mortgage and its existence, and would withhold the same from record; and thereupon,
upon said agreement and condition, said defendant corporation did execute said mortgage in the complaint mentioned
and described, and therewith exhibited; and said plaintiff

did, in accordance [276] with its said agreement, withhold said mortgage from record, and did conceal its existence.

"And said defendant further says that said defendant thereafter, proceeding according to its said intentions as hereinbefore set out, and as it was intended by the plaintiff that it should, did proceed to renew its then existing indebtedness, the creditors holding the same consenting to do so in ignorance of the existence of said mortgage, when they would not have done so had they known of its existence; of which debts so renewed there now exists unpaid the sum of more than twenty-five thousand dollars, and more than the full value of said mortgaged property; and said corporation defendant further proceeded according to its said intention, and as was intended by plaintiff it should, to purchase large amounts of lumber and other material needed by it on credit, the sellers thereof relying upon the credit had by said defendant, and ignorant of the existence of said mortgage, when they would not have sold said lumber and other material to said defendant corporation had they known of the existence of said mortgage; that of said indebtedness for such lumber and material so purchased there now remains unpaid the sum of twenty-five thousand dollars.

"And the defendant further shows that thereafter, to wit, on the twenty-fifth day of July, 1891, said defendant, being insolvent and unable to pay its debts, and owing the various sums above set forth, did, under the provisions of the statute of the state of Indiana in such cases made and provided, execute to this defendant its indenture of assignment of all of its property for the benefit of all of its *bona fide* creditors, which indenture of assignment was duly recorded in the recorder's office of Laporte county, on the said twenty-fifth day of July, and delivered all of said property, including that in the said mortgage mentioned and described, to this defendant, and that this defendant accepted said trust, and within fifteen days thereafter filed with the [277] clerk of the circuit court of Laporte county his affidavit that said property had actually been delivered to him for the purposes declared in said indenture, and as to the probable value thereof, and did execute and file with said clerk his written undertaking in double the amount of the value of said property, with surety to the acceptance and approval of said clerk, conditioned that he would faithfully execute the duties of his trust, and did also file with said clerk an oath, duly subscribed by him, that he would faithfully execute the duties of his trust, and thereupon he entered upon the execution of said duties, and thenceforward, hitherto, until now, he had been, and yet continues in the execution thereof; and that thereafter, on the 27th of July, 1891, the plaintiff caused said mortgage to be recorded in the recorder's office of Laporte county; that the total value of the assets of said Hopper Lumber and Manufacturing Company included in said indenture of said assignment, and so coming into his possession, will not exceed the sum of sixty thousand dollars; that the *bona fide* indebtedness of said corporation will exceed the sum of one hundred and five thousand dollars; that by the means aforesaid, and in the manner aforesaid, the plaintiff gave, and intended to give, the said Hopper Lumber and Manufacturing Company a credit to which it was not entitled, and to which plaintiff well knew it was not entitled; and the plaintiff well knew and intended that its conduct would result, as it did result, in the then existing creditors making such renewals, and in many persons selling said Hopper Lumber and Manufacturing Company goods upon credit.

"Wherefore, this defendant says that the plaintiff cannot now take advantage of its own wrongful conduct, and claim that it has any priority over the other creditors of said defendant corporation, who by such conduct it has induced to renew such indebtedness, and to make such sales to said defendant corporation. He, therefore, prays the [278] judgment of this court that the plaintiff is not entitled to a foreclosure of said mortgage.

"Paragraph 2. And for a partial answer to so much of said complaint as asked for the appointment of a receiver herein, the defendant, William B. Hutchinson, assignee of the Hopper Lumber and Manufacturing Company, says that he admits the execution of the mortgage to the plaintiff, set out and exhibited with the complaint; and that James S. Hopper, president of said Hopper Lumber and Manufacturing Company, pretended to execute what purported to be a chattel mortgage to the Sutton Manufacturing Company, upon a large amount of personal property belonging to said defendant corporation, including the machinery in said complaint mentioned and described; and that said Sutton Manufacturing Company gave notice that it intended to sell said personal property under said pretended chattel mortgage; but he denies that he has ever permitted or intended to permit said

Sutton Manufacturing Company, or any person acting in its
behalf, to take possession of any of the property claimed by
the plaintiff under its mortgage, or that he ever intended to
permit said Sutton Manufacturing Company, or any person
acting in its behalf, to sell or dispose of said property; but,
on the contrary, he avers the fact to be, that before the application of the plaintiff for the appointment of the receiver
herein, he had refused to permit said Sutton Manufacturing
Company to take possession of any portion of the property
under said chattel mortgage, which fact would have been
made known to the plaintiff upon inquiry.

"And this defendant further shows that as such assignee
he has filed his certain suit in equity in the United States
circuit court for the district of Indiana against said Sutton
Manufacturing Company to have said pretended chattel
mortgage decreed null and void, and has procured from said
court a restraining order enjoining and restraining said Sutton Manufacturing Company from proceeding [279] with said
proposed sale; that, at all times since his acceptance of said
trust, he has retained possession and control of all the property of every nature and description which has come into his
hands as such trustee under such assignment, and he intends
to continue to retain the possession thereof, and the same to
dispose of and administer for the benefit of all of the *bona fide*
creditors of said Hopper Lumber and Manufacturing Company according to their several and respective rights therein,
as they may be decreed and determined by the proper courts
having jurisdiction thereof, and at all times subject to the
direction of this honorable court in the premises.

"Wherefore, he says that there was no just ground for the
application to this court for the appointment of a receiver
herein; and such receiver having been appointed without
notice to him, or opportunity afforded to him to make any
showing why such receiver should not be appointed, said receiver ought now to be discharged, and all costs made upon
said application, and growing out of said appointment, ought
to be taxed against the plaintiff, and he prays the judgment
of this court accordingly."

A demurrer was filed to each of these paragraphs of answer,
and was sustained by the court. To these rulings the appellant at the time excepted, and elected to abide by his answers,
and thereupon judgment was rendered in favor of appellee
against the Hopper Lumber and Manufacturing Company for

the full amount of the mortgage indebtedness, and there was a decree of foreclosure and order of sale of the mortgaged realty for the payment of the judgment.

The only errors assigned in this court are, that the court below erred in each of its rulings in sustaining demurrers to the answers.

So that the only question to be considered by this court is as to the sufficiency of each of the partial answers, for [280] the purposes and to the extent to which they were respectively pleaded.

The mortgaged premises having been conveyed by the mortgagor to the appellant Hutchinson, in trust for the benefit of its creditors, he was a necessary party defendant in the suit to foreclose the mortgage. The legal title to the mortgaged premises rested in him, and it became his duty, on behalf of the creditors, to protect their rights in the foreclosure suit. He was made a defendant in the action in order that he might defend. An assignee may not only defend actions to foreclose mortgages which he deems fraudulent, but, ordinarily, is the only one who can institute actions to set aside mortgages or conveyances executed by the assignor, prior to the assignment, for fraud: *Voorhees* v. *Carpenter*, 127 Ind. 300; *Cooper* v. *Perdue*, 114 Ind. 207; *Seibert* v. *Milligan*, 110 Ind. 106; *Wright* v. *Mack*, 95 Ind. 332; *Lockwood* v. *Slevin*, 26 Ind. 124; *Barker* v. *Barker's Assignee*, 2 Wood. 87; *In re Leland*, 10 Blatchf. 503; *Hildeburn* v. *Brown*, 17 B. Mon. (Ky.) 779.

The fact that the rights of the creditors, among themselves, to the property or fund sought to be protected or recovered are not the same, is not a matter that concerns the adverse party. If the assignee represents any creditor who, if the assignment had not been made, would have had a standing in court to question the conveyance, such assignee may, as the representative of that creditor, assail such conveyance. The distribution of the proceeds recovered in such action is a matter between the assignee and the creditors he represents, to be determined by the court having jurisdiction of the trust according to the rules of equity.

It follows, that if any of the several classes of creditors mentioned in the first paragraph of answer could, if the assignment had not been executed, have successfully defended the action on account of the matter pleaded in the answer, then the demurrer should have been overruled, [281] although such assignee may represent other creditors who would have been unable to make such defense.

We are satisfied that the creditors who did not alter their condition, after the execution of the mortgage sought to be foreclosed, do not occupy such a position as to enable them to successfully complain of its execution, or of the failure of the bank to record it within the time allowed by law. It remains to determine whether the creditors who gave credit upon new purchases, or renewed obligations, since the execution of the mortgage, occupy a more advantageous position.

The section of the statute regulating the recording of deeds and mortgages of real estate reads as follows.

Section 2931, Revised Statutes, 1881: "Every conveyance or mortgage of lands, or of any interest therein, and every lease for more than three years, shall be recorded in the recorder's office of the county where such lands shall be situated; and every conveyance or lease, not so recorded in forty-five days from the execution thereof, shall be fraudulent and void as against any subsequent purchaser, lessee, or mortgagee in good faith and for a valuable consideration": *Kirkpatrick v. Caldwell's Admrs.*, 32 Ind. 299.

None of the creditors whose claims are represented by the assignee are either "subsequent purchasers, lessees or mortgagees," and are, therefore, not within the classes against whom the instrument is, by statute, declared to be fraudulent and void: *Runyan v. McClellan*, 24 Ind. 165; *Kirkpatrick v. Caldwell's Admrs.*, 32 Ind. 299; *Shirk v. Thomas*, 121 Ind. 147; 16 Am. St. Rep. 381; *Mann v. State*, 116 Ind. 383; *Evans v. Pence*, 78 Ind. 439.

We cannot extend the terms of the statute so as to include general creditors in the classes of persons, against whom unrecorded mortgages are to be deemed, as an inference of law, fraudulent and void, for that would be legislation.

It may be, and doubtless is, the policy of the law to encourage [282] the prompt recording of instruments affecting the title of real estate, and to discourage their withholding from record. The legislature has stated the consequences which result, as a matter of law, from the failure to so record them, and we can only ascertain and enforce its mandates.

It follows, that in the absence of express fraud, the mere failure of the appellee to record the mortgage in suit within the time fixed in the recording act will not, as against the

creditors of the mortgagor, either prior or subsequent, render
it invalid.

We are then to determine whether the failure to record the
mortgage will, when taken in connection with the agreement
to withhold the same from record, and the other facts stated
in the answer, make such a showing of fraud as to either invalidate the mortgage or postpone its lien to the claims of
some of the creditors represented by the assignee.

In pursuing this investigation, the fact must constantly be
kept in view, that, in this state, it is provided by statute that
in deeds and mortgages claimed to have been executed in
fraud of creditors, the question of fraudulent intent shall be
deemed a question of fact. In construing this section of the
statute this court, in *Cicero Township* v. *Picken*, 122 Ind. 260,
said:

"In this state there is no such thing as constructive fraud;
by statute the question of fraud is made a question of fact.
Section 4924, Revised Statutes, 1881; *Rose* v. *Colter*, 76 Ind.
590; *Leasure* v. *Coburn*, 57 Ind. 274; *Bentley* v. *Dunkle*, 57
Ind. 374."

This may be, when applied to a state of facts not pertinent
to this case, an overstatement of the law, but as a general
statement it is correct. In *Phelps* v. *Smith*, 116 Ind. 387, it
was said:

"By our statute the question of fraud is made one of fact,
and where fraud is essential to the existence of a [383] cause
of action it must be found as a fact, and not left to be inferred
as a matter of law."

To the same effect we cite: *Farmers' Loan and Trust Co.* v.
Canada etc. R. R. Co., 127 Ind. 250; *Fletcher* v. *Martin*, 126
Ind. 55; *Cicero Township* v. *Picken*, 122 Ind. 260; *Kirkpatrick*
v. *Reeves*, 121 Ind. 280; *Sickman* v. *Wilhelm*, 130 Ind. 480.

Not only must fraud be found as the ultimate fact, in order
to avoid a conveyance as being fraudulently executed, but the
complaint in such action must expressly charge that the instrument was executed with a fraudulent intent: *Plunkett* v.
Plunkett, 114 Ind. 484; *Bentley* v. *Dunkle*, 57 Ind. 374.

The section of our statute under consideration seems to
have been copied from the statute of New York. In construing the section from which ours is copied, the court, in *Smith*
v. *Long*, 9 Daly, 429 (436), said:

"Under the law of this state, fraud is a mixed question of
law and fact, and in order to support a finding of fraud as a

conclusion of law, in the findings of a court or referee, it is well settled that the existence of fraud must be found as a fact. Whatever is necessary to be found to sustain a conclusion of law must be alleged; consequently, to raise an issue of fraud under our code, fraud, as a fact, must be alleged." In the late case of *Threlkel* v. *Scott*, 89 Cal. 351, the court said:

"Nor will such fraudulent intent, which is itself a question of fact, be inferred from the facts stated in the complaint, either for that or any other purpose, for the further reason that a voluntary conveyance by an insolvent debtor is not necessarily fraudulent and void as to creditors: *Jamison* v. *King*, 50 Cal. 136; *McFadden* v. *Mitchell*, 54 Cal. 628; *Bull* v. *Bray*, 89 Cal. 286. Hence it follows that the fraudulent intent is a fact necessary to be alleged in the complaint."

This position is sustained by many cases, from which we [284] cite *Beardsley Scythe Co.* v. *Foster*, 36 N. Y. 561; *National Union Bank* v. *Reed*, 27 Abb. N. C. 5; same case on subsequent appeal, 12 N. Y. Sup. 920; *Martin* v. *Fox*, 40 Mo. App. 664.

In an action brought by, or for the benefit of, subsequent creditors, the complaint should aver that the instrument to be avoided was executed with intent to defraud subsequent as well as existing creditors: *Barrow* v. *Barrow*, 108 Ind. 345; *Stumph* v. *Bruner*, 89 Ind. 556; *Stevens* v. *Works*, 81 Ind. 445; *Lynch* v. *Raleigh*, 3 Ind. 273.

The paragraph of answer under consideration does not aver, or charge, that the mortgage was either executed, or kept off the record after its execution, with intent to defraud existing or subsequent creditors.

We have examined the cases cited by counsel of the appellants in their exhaustive brief, but are of the opinion that they are not in conflict with the views we have expressed.

In *Barker* v. *Barker's Assignee*, 2 Wood, 87, the deed of conveyance was not executed with intent to defraud creditors, but having been kept from record for many years, it was held invalid as against an assignee in bankruptcy. The case went off on the ground that an unregistered act of alienation was, under the code of Louisiana, of no effect as against *bona fide* purchasers or creditors. The fact that the code of Louisiana includes creditors, among those as against whom an unrecorded instrument is to be deemed fraudulent and void, destroys the effect of this case as an authority in this state.

where it would only be invalid as against subsequent purchasers, lessees, or mortgagees.

In re Leland, 10 Blatchf. 503, a chattel mortgage was not filed in the county where the mortgagor resided, as required by statute, and was held invalid under the statute of New York, which declared that a mortgage of chattels should, [285] as against creditors, be void unless filed in the town in which the mortgagor resides.

In *Hildeburn* v. *Brown*, 17 B. Mon. 779, an unrecorded mortgage was held invalid, because it had not been acknowledged, or legally proved and lodged for record, as required by a statute of Kentucky, in order to be valid as against purchasers or creditors.

In *Putnam* v. *Reynolds*, 44 Mich. 113, the court held that the statute made the chattel mortgage void against creditors for failure to have it recorded. The language of the statute, as set out in the opinion, is that such unrecorded mortgage should be "absolutely void as against the creditors of the mortgagor."

The case of *Hilliard* v. *Cagle*, 46 Miss. 309, tends to support the position assumed by the appellants. That was a case where the keeping of a trust deed from record was held, when aided by some evidence that the beneficiaries actively promoted the sale of goods to the grantor, after the execution of the deed, and before it was recorded, sufficient to avoid the deed as against creditors.

In *Blennerhassett* v. *Sherman*, 105 U. S. 100, the case came before the court on the evidence. The court held that keeping a mortgage from record in pursuance of an agreement made at the time of its execution, coupled with the fact that the mortgagee knowing that the mortgagor was insolvent, concealed the mortgage and misrepresented the financial condition of the mortgagor, was sufficient to avoid the mortgage.

In the case of the *Stock-Growers' Bank* v. *Newton*, 13 Col. 245, the withholding of a mortgage from the record for a considerable time, in pursuance of an agreement not to record it, was held to be a badge of fraud, which, with some other evidence of concealment and misrepresentation, was sufficient to avoid the instrument.

In reading the foregoing cases and others cited by counsel for appellants, we have been impressed with the weight [286] and influence upon the minds of the various courts of the

withholding of instruments from record in pursuance of agreements, or understandings to that effect, when considered as
an element of fraud.

In none of the cases cited by counsel has the mere failure
to record an instrument within the time fixed by statute,
whether such failure was in pursuance of a previous contract,
or by mere neglect, been held sufficient, of itself, to avoid such
instrument. In each of the cases the element of the known
insolvency of the mortgagor, active misrepresentation of his
financial condition, or other *indicia* of fraud entered into the
transaction.

We are satisfied that an arrangement for the withholding
of a mortgage from record is not of itself sufficient to justify
a court in holding, as a matter of law, such mortgage fraudulent and void as to creditors, either existing or subsequent;
but that it is a badge of fraud to be considered with all the
other facts and circumstances surrounding the transaction in
determining whether or not there was, in fact, a fraudulent
intent.

In *Folsom* v. *Clemence*, 111 Mass. 273, the court, in disposing of this question, said:

"The judge rightly ruled, also, that the arrangement or
understanding in regard to withholding the mortgages from
record, unless the mortgagors should have trouble, did not
render them void, but was 'a matter entitled to consideration
by the jury in passing upon the question' of fraud at the
common law.

This case was cited with approval and followed in *Stewart*
v. *Hopkins*, 30 Ohio St. 502 (530).

In standard works, concealment and failure to record instruments are classified and discussed in the chapters under
the head of "Badges of Fraud" or "*Indicia* or Badges of
Fraud": Bump on Fraudulent Conveyances, chapter 4; Waite
on Fraudalent Conveyances, etc., chapter 16.

The answer under consideration states no facts from [287]
which an inference of fraud can arise, other than the agreement relating to the keeping of the mortgage from record.
It is not alleged that the mortgagor was at the time of the execution of the mortgage insolvent; or, if an inference of its
insolvency arises from the facts averred, it is not charged that
the mortgagee knew of such insolvency.

We are of the opinion that the court did not err in sustaining the demurrer to the first paragraph of answer.

The second paragraph of answer, which is addressed to so much of the complaint as asked for the appointment of a receiver, fully meets the allegations contained in the complaint relating to that subject. The question is before us on this appeal, nothwithstanding the appellant might have appealed within ten days; from the order making the appointment: Rev. Stats. 1881, sec. 1231; *Buchanan* v. *Berkshire Life Ins. Co.*, 96 Ind. 510 (528).

The judgment of the court sustaining the demurrer to the first paragraph of answer is affirmed; and, in sustaining the demurrer to the second paragraph of answer is reversed.

ASSIGNMENT FOR THE BENEFIT OF CREDITORS—ASSIGNEE AS PARTY TO SUIT TO FORECLOSE MORTGAGE.—An assignee for the benefit of creditors may avoid transfers and mortgages of the assignor which the latter's creditors could avoid: *Merrill* v. *Ressler*, 37 Minn. 82; 5 Am. St. Rep. 822, and note.

FRAUDULENT CONVEYANCES—EFFECT OF UNRECORDED MORTGAGE ON CREDITORS: See *Springfield Homestead Assn.* v. *Roll*, 137 Ill. 205; 31 Am. St. Rep. 358, and note. An unrecorded mortgage does not operate upon creditors who became such before the conveyance was executed: *Brown* v. *Babb*, 67 Mich. 17; 11 Am. St. Rep. 549.

FRAUD—PLEADING.—A complaint in an action for fraud must charge the fraud in positive terms: *Bartholomew* v. *Bentley*, 15 Ohio, 659; 45 Am. Dec. 596, and note. In an action for fraud, the plaintiff must allege the facts constituting the fraud: *People* v. *Healy*, 128 Ill. 9; 15 Am. St. Rep. 90, and note; *Albertoli* v. *Branham*, 80 Cal. 631; 13 Am. St. Rep. 200, and note; *Feeney* v. *Howard*, 79 Cal. 525; 12 Am. St. Rep. 162, and note. Fraud must be specially pleaded: *De Votie* v. *McGerr*, 15 Col. 467; 22 Am. St. Rep. 426. See further the extended note to *Huston* v. *Williams*, 25 Am. Dec. 95.

FRAUDULENT CONVEYANCES—FRAUD IN, IS A QUESTION FOR THE JURY. See *State* v. *Mason*, 112 Mo. 374; 34 Am. St. Rep. 390, and extended note.

CLEVELAND, CINCINNATI, CHICAGO, AND ST. LOUIS RAILWAY COMPANY *v.* KETCHAM.

[133 INDIANA, 346.]

RAILROADS—POSTAL CLERK AS PASSENGER—LIABILITY TO FOR NEGLIGENCE.—A United States railway postal clerk on a railway train, entitled to ride free while on duty or going to or returning therefrom, is a passenger, and may recover for an injury inflicted by the negligence of the railway company.

RAILROADS—POSTAL CLERK WHEN PASSENGER.—A United States railway postal clerk, entitled to ride free on trains while on duty, or going to or returning from duty, is a passenger entitled to protection as such while returning home and doing extra work in a postal-car handling mail, although he is not on his regular run and has not paid, nor offered to pay, fare or exhibited his commission or notified the conductor of his presence. In such case he may recover for an injury inflicted by the negligence of the railroad company.

RAILROADS—To WHOM LIABLE AS PASSENGERS.—A railroad company is liable to persons whom it accepts for transportation over its line, and from whom it demands no fare, to the same extent that it is liable to passengers who pay fare.

RAILROADS—LIABILITY TO PASSENGER FOR NEGLIGENCE.—The liability of a railroad company to a passenger for damages resulting from negligence of its employees is the same, whether he is in one car of the train or another, provided he has a lawful right to be in the car he occupies at the time the injury is negligently inflicted.

RAILROADS—FELLOW-SERVANTS WHO ARE NOT.—A railway postal clerk upon a train as an employee of the United States is not a fellow-servant with the men employed by the railway company.

RAILROADS—POSTAL CLERK AS PASSENGER, WHILE ON EXTRA DUTY—LIABILITY FOR NEGLIGENCE TO.—A United States postal clerk while doing extra work on a train, and not on his regular run, is not a trespasser, nor deprived of the protection due to a passenger. He may recover for the negligence of the railway company or its employees in injuring him.

RAILROADS—POSTAL CLERK WHEN RIGHTFULLY ON TRAIN.—If a railway company has continuously recognized the right of a United States postal clerk to free transportation on its trains, he has a right to assume that he will be carried free, and to enter the cars as is his custom without looking up the conductor and informing him of his presence and presenting his commission. It is the duty of the conductor to look the clerk up and demand to see his commission, or the payment of fare, if fare is claimed for his transportation.

J. T. Dye, for the appellant.

W. A. Ketcham, for the appellee.

346 OLDS, J. The appellee was a railway postal clerk and received injuries in a collision on the appellant's railroad, **347** and he brings this action to recover damages resulting from the injuries sustained, which are alleged to have occurred on account of the negligence of the appellant and its employees, and without fault on the part of the appellee.

There was a trial and a special verdict returned, and judgment on the verdict in favor of the appellee. As appears from the facts found in the special verdict, the appellee, at the time of receiving the alleged injuries, was a regularly appointed and acting railway postal clerk in the employment of the United States. At the time of his appointment, he received from the United States government a photograph commission appointing him a railway postal clerk, requesting the railway company to extend to him the facilities of free travel when on duty, and when traveling to and from duty, and assigning him to duty between Chicago, Illinois, and **Cincinnati,** Ohio. His photograph was attached, and the commission contained directions to the appellee that if fare was charged to take receipt, and stated that the same was only good between Chicago, Illinois, and Cincinnati, Ohio. This commission was signed by the general superintendent of the railway mail service and by the postmaster-general of the United States; that appellee, at the time of his appointment, and on, up to, and after, the injury, resided at the city of Indianapolis, on the line of the appellant's railroad; that appellee, after his said appointment, was assigned to duty between Cincinnati and Chicago, the run beginning and terminating at Cincinnati; that, after appellee's appointment and before the alleged injury, by consolidation appellant became the owner of the whole line of road over which appellee traveled, between Cincinnati and Chicago; after the consolidation, no new photograph commission was issued, but at all times thereafter the appellant, its officers and conductors, recognized the request in the commission relating to transportation, as if [348] made to them specifically; that the appellant, in consideration of a payment to be made by the United States government to it for the furnishing of mail-cars and carrying the mails, recognized and acceded to the requests contained in the photograph commission held by clerks running over the line of its railroad, and suffered and permitted all of the clerks holding such photograph commissions, when on duty and when returning from duty, to ride over the lines of their railroad, without exacting the payment of fare or the purchase of tickets, and, at all times, conceded and admitted the right of postal clerks holding such photograph commissions to ride over the lines of its said railroad, without demanding or exacting the payment of fare, or the presentation of tickets, or other evidences of their right to ride than said photograph commission, and suffered, permitted, recognized, and conceded the right of such clerks to ride either in the postal-car or in the ordinary passenger coaches.

On the day previous to the alleged injury, appellee had finished his regular run, ending at Cincinnati, and on the following evening, July 18, 1889, he entered the car of the appellant at Cincinnati as a passenger for Indianapolis; that he entered the postal-car, and being requested by the clerk in charge thereof to assist in handling the mail (the same being on that evening unusually heavy), acceded to said request, and remained in said postal-car to assist in handling said mail, and did not enter or take passage in any of the passenger coaches of the appellant on said train, although he knew that such passenger coaches were attached thereto. Facts are found showing that a collision occurred through the negligence of the appellant and its servants, and, through no fault of the appellee, he was injured. It is further found that at the time of such collision the appellee, as such passenger, was in said postal-car, as aforesaid, assisting in the handling of said mail, while returning to his home.

[349] Appellant contends that, under the facts found, appellee was not a passenger at the time of the injury, and, therefore, cannot recover. It is urged that the appellee was not a passenger for very many reasons; that he did not enter a car provided for the carriage of passengers; that he had not purchased a ticket; that he had not paid his fare; that he did not intend to pay his fare; that it does not appear that he had notified the conductor of his presence on the train, or that he was on the train with the knowledge or assent of the conductor; that there is no contract existing between the appellee and appellant for transportation upon which to base the right of action.

Section 4000 of the United States Revised Statutes makes it the duty of railway companies carrying the mails to "carry on any train which may run over its road, and without extra charge therefor, all mailable matter directed to be carried thereon, with the person in charge of the same."

The findings of fact in this case take from the case all question in regard to compensation for the carrying of the appellee, for it is found, as a fact, that "in consideration of a payment to be made by the United States government to them for the furnishing of mail-cars and carrying the mails [the appellant company], recognized and acceded to the requests contained in the photograph commissions held by clerks running over the line of their railroad, and suffered and permitted all the clerks holding such photograph commissions, when on duty and when returning from duty, to ride over their lines, without exacting the payment of fare," etc.

This finding is to the effect that, as a part of the contract for carrying the mails, and as a part consideration received for carrying the mails by the appellant, it was likewise to carry all mail clerks handling the mails, while on duty or returning from duty; so that, whether the appellee be regarded on duty or off duty, and returning home from duty, his fare was provided for and paid by the [350] United States government; and, certainly, the liability is the same whether the fare be paid by the passenger himself, or by some third person, or by the United States government, even if payment of fare was necessary to create a liability. But a carrier is liable to persons whom it accepts for transportation over its line, and from whom it demands no fare, to the same extent that it is liable to passengers who pay fare: 2 Am. & Eng. Ency. of Law, p. 744, and authorities there cited.

Under the findings of facts and the United States statute, the appellee, we think, must be regarded as being upon the train as of right, without paying or offering to pay any fare. He was upon the train as an employee of the United States government; and, by a contract with the government, appellant was required to carry him, and received compensation for doing so. By a construction placed upon the contract with the government, and the photograph commission held by the appellee, by the appellant itself, it recognized the right of the appellee to ride upon the train exempt from the payment of fare, and he had a right to treat it in the same manner, and enter upon the train as he had theretofore been accustomed to do.

It may be pertinent to inquire what relation the appellee bore to the appellant, if not that of a passenger. Having, as we think, a lawful right upon the train, he certainly is not an intruder or a trespasser, and we think he certainly does not occupy the same relation as an employee of the appellant, to whom it would not be liable for an injury resulting from the negligence of a co-employee, and he certainly could not be held to be a co-employee with the employees running and operating the train. He is not employed by the appellant. It has no control over him, nor does he take any part in the business of the railway company. The company is under contract to carry both the mail and the mail agent who has charge of and [351] handles the mail. He is employed and paid by the government. He is, in our opinion, a passenger having the same rights in relation to the recovery of damages for injuries sustained on account of the negligence of the railway company as any other passenger.

The fact that he may ride in a postal-car can make no difference with his right of recovery of damages for an injury sustained by reason of a collision resulting on account of the negligence of the railway company. The postal-car, the smoking-car, the ladies-car, and the parlor-car, may all constitute one train. All are upon the train for the purpose of carrying passengers. The railway mail clerk, while on duty, necessarily rides in the postal-car, for there his duty calls him. It is there he performs his labor. They are constructed purposely for work upon the railway. The mail clerks are as helpless, in so far as avoiding danger which is the result of the negligence of the railway employees, as are any other passengers. They have no more connection with or control over the movements of trains than has any other passenger.

It is suggested on behalf of the appellant, that the danger is enhanced by riding in the postal-car, and that, in this case, had the appellee been in the smoking-car or other cars provided for passengers only, he would not have been injured. The suggestion, we think, can have but little force. It very often occurs, no doubt, that if one receiving an injury had been in another car than the one in which he was at the time of the collision he would not have been injured, and *vice versa*. One pays extra for the privilege of riding in a palace-car, and yet, having done so, if he choose to go out of it and for a time ride in the smoking-car, and while there receives an injury resulting from the negligence of the railway company, the liability is the same as if he had received a like injury while in the palace-car. The liability of a railway company to a passenger for damages resulting from negligence [552] of its employees is the same, whether he be in one car or another, so he has a lawful right to be in the car he occupies.

A complete, and, we think, a legitimate answer to the proposition that the passenger would not have been injured had he been in another car than that in which he was riding at the time of the injury, is that he would not have been injured at all had it not been for the negligence of the railway employees, which caused the collision.

We regard it immaterial whether the appellee was or was not on duty at the time, but under the facts found, we think, notwithstanding the appellee had finished his regular run and was returning home, he was in fact on duty and legitimately in the car for that purpose at the time the injury occurred. It would be impossible for mail clerks to remain constantly on duty during their time of service. They must have rest and sleep, and for the benefit of the service—to facilitate the transportation and distribution of mail matter—regular runs are provided for the mail clerks, sufficient time for rest intervening between each. The fact that a clerk may be requested to, and does, perform extra duty on board a train does not make him a trespasser, or render him any the less a passenger, while performing such extra labor, than if he were upon his regular run. The fact that he may have availed himself of the opportunity for rest in returning from his home in Cincinnati, and have ridden in a car intended to be occupied by passengers only, did not exonerate the railway company from liability for injuries resulting solely from its negligence, because the appellee did not choose to avail himself of his privilege to rest while returning to his home.

The principal reason urged for a reversal of the judgment is that the appellee did not occupy the relation of passenger, and we are cited to the case of the *Pennsylvania R. R. Co. v. Price*, 96 Pa. St. 256, and *Bricker* v. *Philadelphia R. R. Co.*, 132 Pa. St. 1; 19 Am. St. Rep. 585. But these decisions are [353] based upon a statute of Pennsylvania placing mail agents upon the same footing as employees of the company. We think, independently of any statute, the current of authority is almost unanimously to the effect that mail agents are passengers and occupy the same relation to the company as any other passengers. In *Seybolt* v. *New York etc. R. R. Co.*, 95 N. Y. 562, 47 Am. Rep. 75, it is held that a railroad corporation owes the same degree of care to mail agents riding in postal-cars, in charge of the mails, as they do to passengers.

In *Blair* v. *Erie R. W. Co.*, 66 N. Y. 313 (318); 23 Am. Rep. 55, the court say: "Without an express exemption provided by contract, the defendant is liable for the consequences of its negligence, or that of its servants, to all persons traveling and carried upon its trains, as messengers or agents of the express company, to the same extent as to other passengers." In that case, by agreement, the express messenger was being carried free of charge. The party injured was not, at the time of the injury, a regular, acting messenger, but had formerly been, and on that day, at the request of the regular messenger, he took his place, and was acting as a messenger. As in this case, the appellee, at the request of the mail agent in charge of the postal-car, was assisting him in the work upon the train, and was at the time a regular mail agent in the employ of the government.

In *Mellor* v. *Missouri Pacific Ry. Co.*, 105 Mo. 455, the supreme court of Missouri held that a postal clerk in the service of the United States, and doing his duty in a mail-car of a train, is a passenger. In that case the court say: "Plaintiff was riding upon defendant's train, by virtue of some contract or arrangement between defendant and the federal government touching the carriage and care of the United States mail, was clearly established by the testimony. Defendant's contention [354] that in such a situation, he should be regarded as its servant, we consider too untenable for serious discussion. There was neither allegation nor proof on defendant's part that plaintiff was in its employ in any capacity, and certainly no such inference fairly arises from any of the facts in evidence. This being so, there is no foundation on which to predicate a defense that plaintiff's injury arose from any negligence of fellow-servants. The train operatives were clearly not such as to him. Defendant's duty to him, so far as concerned safe transportation, was as a passenger": *Baltimore etc. R. R. Co.* v. *State*, 72 Md. 36; 20 Am. St. Rep. 454; *Gleeson* v. *Virginia Midland R. R. Co.*, 140 U. S. 435. The same rule was held by this court in *Ohio etc. R. W. Co.* v. *Voight*, 122 Ind. 288.

The appellee in this case was a passenger to whom the company owed the same duty as to any other passenger. He had the right to enter upon the train, as he was accustomed to do, and to be carried. If the appellant company had adopted a rule by which it was declining to honor the request in the commission for free transportation, and so notified the appellee, and demanded payment of fare, and he had refused to pay, a different question would be presented; but it is not claimed that any such thing was done. Having, therefore, continuously recognized his right to free transportation under its contract with the government, the appellee had the right to assume that he would be transported without payment of fare, and enter the car, as was his custom, without looking up the conductor and informing him that he was upon the train, and presenting his photograph commission. It was the duty of the conductor to look up the appellee, and demand of him to see his commission, or to demand the payment of fare, if the appellant company claimed fare for his transportation.

There is no error in the record. Judgment is affirmed.

RAILROADS—POSTAL CLERK AS PASSENGER.—A United States postal agent riding on a railway train, in the discharge of his duties under a contract between the government and the company, will be regarded as a pas-

senger so far as the company's liability for its negligence is concerned:
Mellor v. *Missouri Pac. Ry. Co.*, 105 Mo. 455; *Seybolt* v. *New York etc. R. R. Co.*, 95 N. Y, 562; 47 Am. Rep. 75, and note; *Gulf etc. Ry. Co.* v. *Wilson*, 79 Tex. 371; 23 Am. St. Rep. 345, and note; *Magoffin* v. *Missouri Pac. Ry. Co.*, 102 Mo. 540; 22 Am. St. Rep. 798, and note on the liability of railroad companies to express messengers. See, also, *Baltimore etc. R. R. Co.* v. *State*, 72 Md. 36; 20 Am. St. Rep. 454.

McClure v. Raben.

[133 Indiana, 507.]

Expectancies—Conveyance of—What Necessary to Sustain—Insanity of Testator.—A contract for the conveyance of an expectant interest in an ancestor's estate cannot be enforced until it is shown that there was neither fraud nor oppression, and that the ancestor had knowledge of and consented to such contract; and the fact that he was incapable of consenting because of his insanity does not constitute an exception to the rule requiring his assent.

Expectancies—Conveyance of Against Public Policy.—Contracts for the conveyance of expectant interests in ancestor's estates, without the knowledge and consent of the latter, are illegal as being contrary to public policy.

W. Loudon and F. P. Leonard, for the appellant.

G. V. Menzies, for the appellee.

[507] Coffey, C. J. This case is in this court for the second time: *McClure* v. *Raben*, 125 Ind. 139.

The cross-complaint of the appellee, which was adjudged insufficient, is fully set forth in the opinion in that case, and sets up, among other things, that Samuel D. McReynolds purchased from the appellant, during the lifetime of his mother, his expectant interest in the land described in such cross-complaint; that McReynolds paid the full value of such interest, and received from the appellant a quitclaim deed for such land; that the contract by which the appellant sold and conveyed to McReynolds his expectant interest in said land was *bona fide*, and without any fraud practiced on Leah McClure, the mother of the appellant, who was then the owner of such land, and who was then insane.

The cross-complaint further alleged that McReynolds had conveyed his interest in the land in controversy to the appellee.

[508] Upon a return of this cause to the Posey circuit court the appellee filed an amended cross-complaint against the appellant, in which he alleged that "heretofore, to wit, on the

thirtieth day of March, 1853, Leah McClure, the mother of said Joseph McClure, was a widow, and was the owner in fee simple and in possession of all the lands described in the deed hereinafter mentioned, containing about three hundred and eighteen acres, more or less.

"That for a long time prior to said date, at said date, and continuously therefrom till the date of her death, to wit, the first day of March, 1886, said Leah McClure was a person of unsound mind, incapable of managing her own estate, or making or ratifying contracts of her own, or affirming or consenting to contracts made by her children of and concerning her, the said Leah's, estate.

"That on the first day of March, 1886, said Leah died, in Posey county, Indiana, intestate, leaving as her only heirs in law the defendant, Joseph McClure, and six other persons whose names are unknown.

"That on the date first above mentioned, the thirtieth day of March, 1853, the defendant, Joseph McClure, was of the age of twenty-one years, and an heir expectant or presumptive of his mother, the said Leah McClure, and as such expectant or presumptive heir expected to inherit in fee simple one-seventh in value of said land, about thirty-nine and three quarter acres of the same.

"That the actual, full, and fair market value of said land, valued as an absolute vested estate per acre on the thirtieth day of March, 1853, was seven dollars per acre, making the actual, full, and fair market value of the entire interest of said Joseph McClure valued at that date as an absolute and vested estate, the sum of two hundred and seventy-eight dollars and twenty-five cents.

"That on said date, March 30, 1853, the defendant, Joseph McClure, by his quitclaim deed, a copy of which is filed herewith as a part of this paragraph, marked exhibit [509] "A," conveyed to one Samuel D. McReynolds his interest in the land therein described as heir presumptive of his mother, the said Leah McClure, in consideration of the sum of three hundred dollars, that sum being at that date in excess of the actual, full, and fair market value of an undivided one-seventh part in value of said land, valued at that time as an absolute and vested estate in fee simple.

"That said sum of three hundred dollars was paid by said McReynolds to the defendant, Joseph McClure, in good faith, said McReynolds and said defendant Joseph McClure each

knowing and believing at the date of the execution of the
conveyance aforesaid that the said Leah McClure was and forever would remain hopelessly insane and incapable of managing her estate, and that the only event which could defeat the
defendant, Joseph McClure, from subsequently becoming the
owner of an absolute estate in fee simple, of an undivided one-
seventh in value of said lands, was the death of said Joseph
McClure before his mother, Leah McClure.

"That at or near the time of the conveyance aforesaid several of the children and presumptive heirs of Leah McClure,
knowing that said Leah was hopelessly insane, and believing
that such insanity would continue without a lucid interval,
sold and conveyed, as heirs presumptive of said Leah, their
interests in said lands for the actual, full, and fair market
value of the same at the date of such conveyance as absolute
estates in fee simple.

"That in the selling of his said interest by the defendant,
Joseph McClure, and the buying of the same by said McReynolds, there was neither fraud, concealment, catch-bargaining,
nor overreaching by the one upon the other, nor upon the said
Leah McClure, but said sale and conveyance was made *bona
fide* for the actual, full, and fair market value of an undivided
one-seventh part in value of said land valued at the time as
an absolute estate in fee simple. That afterwards, to wit, on
the first day of June, 1865, [510] said McReynolds sold and
conveyed to the defendant, Anthony Raben, all his right, title,
and interest in the lands aforesaid purchased by him from
the defendant, Joseph McClure.

"That said defendant, Joseph McClure, claims to be the
owner in fee simple of one-seventh part in value of said lands,
as an heir at law of said Leah McClure, in derogation of and
adversely to the title of this defendant, thereby casting a
cloud upon his title to an undivided one-seventh part in
value of said lands. Wherefore, this defendant prays judgment that the defendant, Joseph McClure, and those claiming under him may be forever inhibited and enjoined from
setting up any right, title, or interest to and unto said land,
adverse to the right, title, or interest of the defendant, and
that this defendant be decreed, as against said Joseph McClure
and those claiming under him, to be the owner in fee simple
of an undivided one-seventh part in value of said lands, and
for all proper relief."

The rules of law applied to this case, as it is reported in

McClure v. *Raben*, 125 Ind. 139, must remain the law of the case throughout all its subsequent stages: *Pittsburgh etc. R. W. Co.* v. *Hixon*, 110 Ind. 225; *Forgerson* v. *Smith*, 104 Ind. 246; *Hawley* v. *Smith*, 45 Ind. 183; *Test* v. *Larsh*, 76 Ind. 452; *Dodge* v. *Gaylord*, 53 Ind. 365; *Braden* v. *Graves*, 85 Ind. 92; *Kress* v. *State*, 65 Ind. 106.

In this case, it was said, in substance, that where no estoppel had intervened, it must be made to appear, in order that a contract such as we are considering would be adjudged of binding force, that the ancestor holding the estate should be informed of such contract, and should give his or her assent to the same. It was further held that, in the absence of such information and consent, the conveyance would be regarded by the court as against public policy. This is the rule by which this case must be governed.

[511] After giving the authorities another careful consideration, we feel warranted in saying that the rule here announced is the true one. All such contracts are regarded by the law with disfavor, and are presumed to be founded in fraud or oppression, so much so that one who attempts the enforcement of such a contract must allege and prove that there was neither fraud nor oppression before he is entitled to any consideration.

Many reasons are given for this rule, among which is that in a case where the ancestor has no knowledge of the contract, he may permit his property to go under the law of descents, believing that his son, or next of kin, will receive the benefit, when, in truth, it goes to an entire stranger, if the contract is to be enforced. This he might not be willing to do if he was informed of the facts. By keeping him ignorant of the facts he is induced to leave his property to a stranger, without his knowledge or consent. This is a fraud upon him. As to the manner in which such contracts may affect the public, we adopt the language of Chief Justice Parsons, in the case of *Boynton* v. *Hubbard*, 7 Mass. 112, in which he said:

"Heirs who ought to be under the reasonable advice and direction of their ancestor, who has no other influence over them than what arises from a fear of his displeasure, from which fear the heirs may be induced to live industriously, virtuously and prudently, are, with the aid of money speculators, let loose from this statutory control, and may indulge in prodigality, idleness, and vice, and taking care by hypocritically preserving appearances not to alarm their ancestor, may go on trafficking with his expected bounty, making it a fund to supply the wastes of dissipation and extravagance. Certainly the policy of the law will not sanction a transaction of this kind, from a regard to the moral habits of its citizens."

Much more might be said as to the objectionable character of the class of contracts now under consideration, but [512] we think it sufficient to say that where such a contract is not made known to the ancestor it is illegal as being contrary to public policy.

, The ancient rule of the courts of chancery, to the effect that a man may bind himself to do anything which is not in itself impossible, and that he ought to perform his obligations, is subject to many exceptions, among which is that he should not be compelled to perform a contract which is against public policy.

Inasmuch as the ancestor of the appellant in this case was insane, and incapable of consenting to this contract, it is contended the reason for the rule does not apply, and that, therefore, we should hold that such consent was not necessary. In other words, it is contended we should hold that where the ancestor is not competent to assent, an exception to the rule requiring such assent exists.

We know of no precedent for such an exception, and without such precedent we could not so hold without extending the rule. In a class of contracts so much in disfavor as the class to which this belongs, we do not think the rules should be extended beyond that required by the authorities.

The court erred, in our opinion, in overruling the demurrer to the cross-complaint of the appellee set out in this opinion.

Judgment reversed, with directions to the circuit court to sustain the demurrer of the appellant to the cross-complaint of the appellee.

EXPECTANCIES—CONVEYANCE OF.—See the extended notes to *Trull* v. *Eastman*, 37 Am. Dec. 128–130, and *Butler* v. *Duncan*, 41 Am. Rep. 713. A child has no interest in his parent's estate during the lifetime of the parent that can be sold or devised: *Wheeler* v. *Wheeler*, 2 Met. (Ky.) 474; 74 Am. Dec. 421; *Needles* v. *Needles*, 7 Ohio St. 432; 70 Am. Dec. 85, and note. As to whether expectancies can be assigned, see the note to *Stott* v. *Franey*, 23 Am. St. Rep. 135, and the case of *Watson* v. *Smith*, 110 N. C. 6; 28 Am. St. Rep. 665, and note. Whether a mere expectancy can be mortgaged is discussed in the extended note to *Moody* v. *Wright*, 46 Am. Dec. 713.

CITY OF BEDFORD *v.* WILLARD.

[133 INDIANA, 562.]

STATUTE OF LIMITATIONS—WHEN WILL RUN AGAINST MUNICIPALITIES.—The statute of limitations runs against municipal corporations such as cities, towns, or counties, except as to the property devoted to a public use, or held upon a public trust, and contracts and rights of a public nature.

STATUTE OF LIMITATIONS—WHEN RUNS AGAINST LAND OWNED BY MUNICIPALITY.—When land is held by a county in its private capacity, subject to sale by it to private individuals, and is by it conveyed to a city, the statute of limitations runs against both county and city in favor of an adverse holder for the statutory period.

M. F. Dunn and R. N. Palmer, for the appellant.

N. Crooke, M. Owen, and J. H. Wallace, for the appellee.

563 OLDS, J.   The appellee brought this action against the appellant, in the court below, to recover possession of, and to quiet the title to, a certain piece or parcel of land in the complaint described.   The complaint is in two paragraphs.   One paragraph seeks to have the title quieted, and the other is for the possession of the real estate.   Issue was joined by the answer of general denial.   On proper request, the court made a special finding of facts, and stated its conclusions of law.

By the finding of facts, it appears, that in 1826 there was conveyed to one Robert M. Carlton, agent for Lawrence county, by one Robert Kilgore, in consideration of the relocation of the seat of justice of Lawrence county, and that a part of the town be located thereon, and for the sole use of, and benefit of, Lawrence county, a certain tract of land described in the finding, which includes the tract in controversy; that immediately after receiving said conveyance, said agent platted and recorded said real estate, with other lands, and on which was located the town, now city, of Bedford, in said Lawrence county, which, with the streets, alleys, squares, and lots, as thus platted, are now a part of said city.

It is further found, that in laying out and platting said town, all of said real estate was not platted; that giving to all streets, alleys, squares, and lots their full width, there remained a strip on the south side of the plat, and off the south side of the tract so conveyed to said agent, thirty-two feet in width, which has been inclosed by the appellee and his grantors, and possessed by them continuously and **564** uninterruptedly, and used by them uninterruptedly for a period of thirty years prior to March, 1890, and prior to the commencement of this action; that in March, 1890, the mayor and common council, by a resolution, ordered that all streets and alleys in said original plat in the town be opened, and, also, the thirty-two feet of ground in controversy, and in pursuance of said order, by direction of the city authorities, the fences inclosing the same were taken down by the officers; that on the eighth day of March, 1890, the board of commissioners of said county conveyed said strip to the city of Bedford, the same being sold and conveyed at private sale, without notice, in consideration of one dollar.

Conclusions of law were stated in favor of the appellee.

The sole question presented and discussed by counsel for appellants is that the statute of limitations did not run against the city or county, and, hence, no title could be acquired by possession.

It is contended that the finding of facts shows that the land was conveyed to the agent of the county, for the sole use of the county, to be platted with other lands as a town to be the county-seat of the county, and that the land was thereby conveyed for a public use, and the statute of limitations would not run either against the city or county. In support of this position we are cited: *Sims* v. *City of Frankfort,* 79 Ind. 446.

The case to which we are cited related to the use and occupancy of a public street, by an adjacent lot-owner encroaching upon the street with his fences and improvements, and presents an entirely different question from the one in this case. In this case the property was conveyed to the county for its own use. The only part to be devoted to public use was the portion dedicated to the purposes of streets and alleys, or possibly for public squares or parks. The portion not so dedicated to the use of the ⁵⁶⁵ public remained the property of the county, to be disposed of by contract and sale, the title passing to individuals.

In the quotation in the case of *Sims* v. *City of Frankfort,* 79 Ind. 446, from Judge Dillon's work on Municipal Corporations, he expressly recognizes the doctrine that as to property not held for public use the statute of limitation runs. He says: "As respects property not held for public use or upon public trusts, and as respects contracts and rights of a private nature, there is no reason why such corporations should not fall within limitation statutes and be affected by them."

It is further said: "But such a corporation does not own and cannot alien public streets or places, and no laches on its part or on that of its officers can defeat the right of the public thereto."

The real estate in controversy was held by the county in a private capacity, subject to be sold by it, and the title to the same passed to an individual purchaser; and as to such property, the recognized rule is that the statute of limitation runs.

In the case of *St. Charles Co.* v. *Powell*, 22 Mo. 525, 66 Am. Dec. 637, it is held that the statute of limitation runs against a county. In that case the court recognizes the doctrine that at common law the statute did not run against the government, and says that: "The immunity, however, it seems was even at common law an attribute of sovereignty only, and did not belong to the municipal corporations or other local authorities established to manage the affairs of the political subdivision of the state."

In the case of *City of Pella* v. *Scholte*, 24 Iowa, 283, 95 Am. Dec. 729, the same doctrine is recognized. In that case the court says: **566** "Of course it is well understood that statutes of limitation do not constructively apply to the state or sovereignty; but the principle has not, so far as we know, been extended to municipal or public corporations. On the contrary, it has been expressly held that these corporations are within the statute of limitations the same as natural persons": *Lessee of City of Cincinnati* v. *First Presbyterian Church*, 8 Ohio, 298; 32 Am. Dec. 718.

Wood on Limitation of Actions, 93, states that the doctrine that the statute of limitations does not run against the sovereign power has no application to municipal corporations deriving their powers from the sovereign, although their powers, in a limited sense, are governmental, and that the statute runs against towns and cities, also for and against counties.

In *Sims* v. *City of Frankfort*, 79 Ind. 446, it is said: "The fee in the street does not vest in the municipal corporation, but it does take a right to the street as the trustee of the public, of which it cannot be divested except by the paramount law. The corporation cannot extinguish the public use in the streets"; but as to the real estate in controversy, the fee did vest in the county.

The conclusion we reach is, that the statute of limitation did run as to this real estate, both against the county and city, and the appellee gained a title in fee by possession, and was entitled to recover. There is no error in the record.

Judgment affirmed.

STATUTE OF LIMITATIONS—WHEN WILL RUN AGAINST MUNICIPAL COR-
PORATIONS.—The statute will run against a city in cases involving property
or contracts which do not pertain to the authority of the state which is exercised through it, but against the exercise of such authority the statute
does not run: *Waterloo* v. *Union Mill Co.*, 72 Iowa, 437. The maxim, "Lapse
of time does not bar the state," applies only in favor of the sovereign power,
and does not apply to municipal corporations deriving their powers from the
sovereign: *May* v. *School District*, 22 Neb. 205; 3 Am. St. Rep. 266, and
note; *County of St. Charles* v. *Powell*, 22 Mo. 525; 66 Am. Dec. 637, and note;
City of Pella v. *Scholte*, 24 Iowa, 283; 95 Am. Dec. 729, and note. The statute
of limitations runs against cities, towns, and school districts: *State* v. *School
District*, 30 Neb. 520; 27 Am. St. Rep. 420, and note with the cases collected.
See further the extended notes to *Fort Smith* v. *McKibben*, 48 Am. Rep. 24,
and *Cincinnati* v. *First Presbyterian Church*, 32 Am. Dec. 719.

O'BRIEN v. MOFFITT.
[133 INDIANA, 660.]

MORTGAGE FORECLOSURE—PARTIES—CONCLUSIVENESS OF JUDGMENT BY
DEFAULT.—All persons claiming an interest in mortgaged premises are
proper, if not necessary, parties to a suit in foreclosure, and when made
parties, a judgment by default is conclusive upon the judgment defendants as to every matter admitted by the default and adjudicated by the
judgment.

MORTGAGE FORECLOSURE—DEFAULT.—If one is made a party to a suit to
foreclose a mortgage in which it is alleged that he claims some interest
in the property, and the relief sought against him is to foreclose his
equity of redemption, if he have such interest, he is required thereby to
assert his interest, and failing to do so, he is precluded by the decree of
foreclosure against him.

MORTGAGE FORECLOSURE BY ONE OF SEVERAL MORTGAGEES—EFFECT OF.
A suit by one of several mortgagees to foreclose, as to his separate note
secured by the same mortgage, does not merge the claims of the other
mortgagees, nor preclude them from foreclosing and selling; and the
mortgagors' rights of redemption as to each mortgagee cannot be lost
by several foreclosures as to each mortgagee instead of a united foreclosure of all the mortgages.

JUDGMENT—FORMER DECISION WHEN NOT RES JUDICATA.—It will not be
presumed that the supreme court adjudicated a question not before it
in a former case, not affecting the rights of the same parties, and collateral thereto, so as to make that decision a rule of the case upon new
questions thereafter arising between other parties.

MORTGAGE FORECLOSURE—REDEMPTION—RIGHT OF AGAINST ASSIGNEE OF
PURCHASER.—The assignee of a certificate of purchase to land on which
a mortgage has been foreclosed occupies no better position in relation
to the property than his assignor, and if a right of redemption exists
against the latter, it exists against the former.

MORTGAGES—FORECLOSURE—FORFEITURE OF PRIMARY SECURITY—EFFECT
ON SECONDARY SECURITY.—If the holder of a mortgage secured by
primary security forfeits his right to foreclose it by permitting an ad-

judication which estops him from pursuing it, he is also estopped from enforcing the mortgage against secondary security held by him.

MORTGAGES—FORFEITURE OF LIEN—KNOWLEDGE OF THIRD PARTIES AS AFFECTING.—Knowledge of third parties interested in mortgaged property that others have forfeited their mortgage lien thereon, cannot increase or give new equities to the latter.

B. M. Cobb and *B. F. Ibach*, for the appellants.

W. H. Trammel, J. B. Kenner, and *U. S. Lesh*, for the appellees.

661 HACKNEY, J.   In June, 1887, John Roche instituted proceedings in the Huntington circuit court to foreclose a mortgage for three hundred dollars, balance of the purchase price for a house and lot in Huntington, executed by Ann R. Moffitt and Patrick W. Moffitt.

To the suit by Roche the mortgagees were defendants and the appellants were made parties to answer as to their interests.   The appellants, in January, 1884, after the cause had returned from the supreme court (as reported in 77 Ind. 48), filed three separate and substituted amended cross-complaints against the appellees.   Upon issues on said cross-complaints there was a trial by the court, a special finding, and a judgment for the appellees.   There are numerous assignments of error, but we will consider only such as present the question of the correctness of the conclusions of law upon the special findings of facts by the court, some of the assignments being waived by the failure to present them in argument, and others being lost by the absence of the evidence from the record.

The following is a summary of the special finding:

1. January 6, 1862, Ann R. and Patrick W. Moffitt executed to John Roche a purchase-money mortgage for $300 on a house and lot.

2. July 12, 1869, Moffitt and wife, McCurdy and wife, and Gotshall and wife gave a mortgage on foundry property, to secure nine notes of the same date, due in five **662** years, as follows: To John Roche, $1,000; William Ewing, $500; Ewing Brothers, $500; Enos T. Taylor, $500; Frederick Dick, $500; Patrick O'Brien, $500; Abram Michler, $500; John Michler, $500, and Jacob Weber, $250.

Gotshall conveyed his interest to Patrick Moffitt, and McCurdy conveyed to Thomas Roche.

3. July 12, 1869, Ann R. and Patrick Moffitt executed a mortgage on said house and lot as secondary security for said several notes, in finding two above.

4. Abram Michler assigned his note to John Lawler, and Ewing Brothers assigned their note to Cyrus Meely.

5. October 8, 1875, Lawler sued to foreclose against the foundry property, making defendants the mortgagees, the mortgagors, Mcely and Thomas Roche and wife.

There were judgments for Lawler, Dick, Taylor, Weber, and Meely against Patrick Moffitt and Thomas Roche, and a foreclosure in their favor against all other defendants. Upon these judgments such payments were made as that $1,100 remained due April 7, 1877.

6. There was a decree and sale of foundry property to John Roche April 7, 1877.

7. There was no redemption, and a deed was made by the sheriff to John Roche, April 7, 1878.

8. May 19, 1877, John Roche sued to foreclose his purchase-money mortgage on the house and lot, making the Moffitts and John Michler, William Ewing and Patrick O'Brien defendants. Michler, Ewing, and O'Brien cross-complained against the Moffitts. Roche recovered judgment against the Moffitts for $309.35, and a foreclosure against all the defendants. Michler, Ewing, and O'Brien recovered judgment against the Moffitts, foreclosing the "secondary security" mortgage on the house and lot. The Moffitts appealed from the judgments and the Roche judgment was affirmed, while the judgment as to O'Brien et al. was reversed.

9. May 21, 1877, John Roche sued to foreclose **663** the foundry mortgage as to his $1,000 note. He made defendants the Moffitts, Thomas Roche, Hannah Roche, his wife, Ewing, O'Brien, and Michler. There was personal judgment against Patrick Moffitt and Thomas Roche, and foreclosure against all of the defendants. The Moffitts appealed, and the judgment was affirmed.

10. In 1883, on decree, the foundry was sold to John Roche under the foreclosure (9) for $2,180, the full value of the property, and there was no redemption.

11. March 6, 1883, on decree, the house and lot was sold to John Roche, under foreclosure (8) of purchase-money mortgage.

12. March 1, 1884, John Roche transferred certificate of purchase for house and lot to Ewing, O'Brien, and Michler.

13. March 1, 1884, the Moffitts executed a mortgage on the house and lot to Trammel to secure a pre-existing debt of $1,500. March 5, 1884, Trammel redeemed said house and lot from sale of March 6, 1883, by paying the necessary amount to the clerk, which amount John Roche received, said Trammel not knowing of the transfer of the certificate to Ewing et al.

14. March 6, 1884, Trammel brought suit against the Moffitts to foreclose the mortgage of the house and lot given March 1, 1884, and obtained judgment for $1,658, a foreclosure of the mortgage and a decree maintaining a lien on the property for the redemption money so paid.

There was an order of sale in the nature of a *venditioni exponas*, and there was a sale to Enos T. Taylor for $2,154.59, a deed was made to Taylor, and a subsequent sale by him to Welsey W. Hawley.

15. During the pendency of said action and cross-action, Trammel was the active attorney for the Moffitts, and had actual knowledge of the equities of O'Brien, Ewing, and Michler.

664 16. When Taylor purchased, and when Hawely purchased, both knew of the action by O'Brien, Ewing, and Michler, and of their equities.

17. The notes of O'Brien, Ewing, and Michler are not paid, and there is due upon each $1,285.11.

CONCLUSIONS OF LAW.

1. John Roche owns in fee the foundry property, and his title should be quieted.

2. Hawley owns in fee the house and lot, and his title should be quieted.

3. O'Brien, Ewing, and Michler should each recover from Patrick Moffitt and Thomas Roche $1,285.11.

The brief for the appellants is illegible, contains words having no proper place in the sentences to which they are assigned, omits many words necessary to the comprehension of the sentences from which they are omitted, and fails to make citations to the record and of authority, when they would seem to be important. However, we gather from it that the appellants contend that the first and second conclusions of the court are not authorized by the facts found: 1. Because the adjudication, sale, and deed, shown by the fifth, sixth, and seventh findings of facts constitute no bar to the proceeding by the several cross-complaints in this cause, as to the foundry property, under the mortgage found in the second finding of facts; that this position has been adjudicated in their favor, in this cause, by this court, and, there-

fore, becomes the law of the case throughout all of its stages;
and that it is further contended that the title of Hawley to
the house and lot, through the Roche foreclosure in the eighth
finding, sale under the eleventh finding, redemption under
the thirteenth finding, and through the mortgage, foreclosure,
redemption money lien, sale and subsequent transfers as
shown by findings thirteen and fourteen, is not superior to
the rights and equities of the appellants.

665 Under the issues it became necessary for the court to
determine whether, in the Lawler foreclosure, the defendants
thereto, O'Brien, Ewing, and Michler, who were adjudged to
have no interest in the mortgaged premises, were estopped to
foreclose for their benefit, the same mortgage, in a subsequent
suit. The finding recites that it was alleged, as to them, that
they claimed some interest in the premises mortgaged. It
does not appear whether they were defaulted or filed pleadings setting up their claims. The most favorable view of the
findings, as to the appellants is that they were defaulted, for
if they made an affirmative issue there could be no doubt that
they were precluded by the decree.

They were mortgagees holding separate claims secured by
the same mortgage securing the claim of Lawler, and were
proper parties defendant to the proceeding of Lawler to foreclose: *Goodall* v. *Mopley*, 45 Ind. 355; *Cain* v. *Hanna*, 63 Ind.
408; *Minor* v. *Hill*, 58 Ind. 176, 26 Am. Rep. 71.

If they were not actually made parties, the decree would,
of course, not preclude them as held by the cases just cited
and in effect by the case of *Moffitt* v. *Roche*, 76 Ind. 75. All
persons claiming an interest in the mortgaged premises are
proper parties, if not always necessary parties. When made
parties it is often important to ascertain what interest is, expressly or by necessary implication, sought to be adjudged
against them, and when ascertained, it has been held by a
long line of decisions in this state, to that extent, that they
are precluded by a default or by failure to set up their real
interests. A judgment by default is as conclusive upon the
judgment defendant as to any matter admitted by the default
and adjudicated by the judgment which ensues, as any other
form of judgment: *Barton* v. *Anderson*, 104 Ind. 578; Freeman on Judgments, secs. 248, 330.

In the last case cited it was said: "As applicable, however,
to a suit to foreclose a mortgage, and other kindred **666** suits,
in the nature of a proceeding *in rem*, where a party is made

a defendant to answer as to his supposed or possible, but unknown or undefined, interest in the property, we think that,
as against him, a default ought to be construed as an admission, that, at the time he failed to appear as required, he had
no interest in the property in question, and hence as conclusive of any prior claim of interest or title adverse to the plaintiff. Any less rigid rule of construction might, and in many
cases doubtless would, defeat the very object properly had in
view in making the party a defendant to answer as to his
supposed or possible interest in the property involved, to the
end that all claims to or against such property might be adjusted by the final judgment or decree, and further litigation
thereby avoided." Citing authorities.

In *Craighead* v. *Dalton*, 105 Ind. 72, the rule and the reason
for it are stated with clearness and precision as follows:
"Since the adoption of the code it has been the rule in this
state that where parties are brought into court upon a complaint to foreclose a mortgage and are challenged to assert
such interest or title in the land as they may have, a decree
adjudging that they have no title or interest will conclude
them. One of the leading purposes of a suit to foreclose a
mortgage is to secure such a decree as will enable the plaintiff to sell all the right and title that his mortgage covers,
and enable a purchaser at the sale to ascertain what title it
is that he buys. To attain this end it is necessary that all
the claims held against the mortgaged premises should be
adjusted in one suit. This the spirit of our code requires, for
it makes ample provision for bringing all the interested parties into court and for adjusting all conflicting claims and
equities. The rule is a salutary one, it tends to repress litigation, gives confidence in public records, secures respect for
judgments and decrees, and invests sheriffs' sales with strength
and certainty **667** that do much to promote the interests of
both debtor and creditor."

We cite the following cases to the general proposition that
one made a party to a suit to foreclose a mortgage, where it
is alleged that he claims some interest in the property, and
the relief sought against him is to foreclose his equity of
redemption, if he have such an interest, he is required
thereby to assert his interest, and failing to do so he is precluded by the judgment and decree of foreclosure against
him: *Elwood* v. *Beymer*, 100 Ind. 504; *Crane* v. *Kimmer*, 77
Ind. 215; *Parker* v. *Wright*, 62 Ind. 398; *Newcome* v. *Wiggins,*

Rec., 78 Ind. 306; *Indiana etc. Ry. Co.* v. *Allen*, 113 Ind.
581; *Hoes* v. *Boyer*, 108 Ind. 494; *De Haven* v. *Musselman*,
123 Ind. 62; *Koons* v. *Carney*, 87 Ind. 34; *Bowen* v. *Wood*, 85
Ind. 268; *Buchanan* v. *Berkshire Life Ins. Co.*, 96 Ind. 510;
Porter v. *Reid*,-81 Ind. 569; *Greenup* v. *Crooks*, 50 Ind. 410;
Davenport v. *Barnett*, 51 Ind. 329, and the cases from which
we have quoted.

We have no case to the contrary, and we know of no case
where such right is not lost, unless expressly reserved or excluded from the operation of the decree.

The case of *Moffitt* v. *Roche*, 76 Ind. 75, is urged upon us
as not only at variance with the rule we have found, but as
establishing, for the purposes of this proceeding, a rule, however erroneous, nevertheless the law of the case. That was
an appeal by the Moffitts and Thomas Roche and wife, from a
judgment in favor of John Roche, foreclosing said foundry
mortgage as to his note for $1,000. The foreclosure was de-
creed not only against the Moffitts and Thomas Roche and
wife, but also as to O'Brien, Ewing, and Michler, as we learn
from the ninth finding in this case. The appellants there
urged no question of former adjudication; only two questions
were made, namely: the sufficiency of the plaintiff's second
paragraph of complaint, and the first paragraph of the defendant's answer. [668] The character of the answer is not disclosed, but the court said it was not error to sustain a
demurrer to it, as it at most only affected questions of cost.
The second paragraph of complaint there reviewed is, in substance, set out in the opinion. It discloses the Lawler foreclosure and sale, but does not disclose the adjudication in
that foreclosure against O'Brien, Ewing, and Michler, or even
that they were parties. The effect of the point against the
paragraph of complaint, and of the decision upon it, is that
a suit by one of several mortgagees to foreclose, as to his separate note, secured by the same mortgage securing others, does
not merge the claims of the other mortgagees, and does not
preclude them from foreclosing and selling, and the mortgagors' rights of redemption, as to each mortgagee, could not
be lost to the mortgagors simply by several foreclosures as to
each mortgagee instead of the united foreclosure of all the
mortgagees.

We will not presume that this court adjudicated a question
not before it, in a case not affecting the rights of these appellants, so as to make that decision a rule of the case upon new

questions arising thereafter between other parties, although possibly in proceedings collateral to such case.

We find in the record no error as to the appellee Roche.

The title of the appellee Hawley to the house and lot, through the redemption from the Roche sale, as found in the thirteenth and fourteenth special findings, is attacked for an alleged irregularity in the payment of the redemption money to the clerk of the circuit court instead of the appellants, who held, as assignees of Roche, the certificate of purchase. The Revised Statutes of 1881, section 768, provides the right and the manner of redemption by the owner of lands sold; sections 771 and 772 provide the right and the manner of redemption by judgment creditors, and section 774 provides the right of redemption by lienholders other than judgment creditors, "upon the same terms [669] and conditions as (therein) herein before required in cases of redemption by judgment creditors."

The "terms and condition,' taking together all of these sections with the fact that section 774 does not provide the manner of making the redemption, mean the manner of redemption provided as to judgment creditors.

This manner was pursued by Trammel, as found by the court, and the subsequent sale and title under section 773, Revised Statutes, 1881, by *venditioni exponas*, seem to be regular, as found by the court below: See *Hervey* v. *Krost*, 116 Ind. 268.

If the appellants held any enforceable interest in the house and lot at the time of the redemption, it was by and through the Roche certificate of purchase transferred to them. By the assignment of the certificate they occupied no better relation to the property than Roche occupied before the transfer. It cannot be maintained that Trammel could not have redeemed from Roche, and if not, why not from his assignees, the appellants? The appellants desire to treat their purchaser of the certificate from Roche as a redemption by them from the sale in his behalf, and they cite *Westerfield* v. *Kimmer*, 82 Ind. 365, in support of this proposition.

· In that case it was held that a title acquired under sheriff's sale in 1872 was strengthened by the purchase of the decree of 1876; that such purchase operated not as a redemption or assignment, but as a cancellation. There is no analogy between the two positions.

O'Brien, Ewing, and Michler had no recourse upon the

house and lot under their mortgage as secondary security, until they had exhausted the foundry property held as primary security. This was expressly held against them in *Moffitt v. Roche*, 77 Ind. 48. When, as we have here held, they forfeited their remedy against the primary property by permitting an adjudication which estopped them to pursue it, the circumstances were such as to release [670] their lien against the house and lot, the secondary security.

In this view of the question the appellants were entitled to no foreclosure of either of the mortgages sought in their cross-complaints to be foreclosed. The knowledge of Trammel, Taylor, and Hawley, as found by the court in the fifteenth and sixteenth special findings, that the appellants had lost their lien on the house and lot, did not increase the equities of O'Brien, Ewing, and Michler, nor give them new equities.

We find no error in the record.

The judgment is in all things affirmed.

MORTGAGES—FORECLOSURE—PARTIES DEFENDANT.—When a suit is instituted to foreclose a mortgage lien, all persons interested in the estate should be made parties: *Whitney v. Higgins*, 10 Cal. 547; 70 Am. Dec. 748, and note; *San Francisco v. Lawton*, 18 Cal. 465; 79 Am. Dec. 187, and note; *Jones v. Vert*, 121 Ind. 140; 16 Am. St. Rep. 379, and note; extended note to *Berlack v. Halle*, 1 Am. St. Rep. 189; notes to *Childs v. Childs*, 75 Am. Dec. 517, and *Goodenow v. Ewer*, 76 Am. Dec. 550.

MORTGAGES—FORECLOSURE—RES JUDICATA.—After the foreclosure of a mortgage the defendant is precluded from showing its prior payment: *Rigg v. Cook*, 4 Gilm. 336; 46 Am. Dec. 462; *Doyle v. Reilly*, 18 Iowa, 108; 85 Am. Dec. 582. But see *Millspaugh v. McBride*, 7 Paige, 509; 34 Am. Dec. 360, and note, as to when a decree of foreclosure will be opened to let in defenses.

MORTGAGES—REDEMPTION FROM FORECLOSURE.—This question is thoroughly discussed in the extended note to *Horn v. Indianapolis Nat. Bank*, 21 Am. St. Rep. 245.

APPEAL—LAW OF THE CASE.—The decision of the supreme court upon a former appeal in a case is as to every point presented and decided on such appeal the law of the case: *Murphy v. Albina*, 22 Or. 106; 29 Am. St. Rep. 578; note to *More v. Calkins*, 29 Am. St. Rep. 133.

CASES

IN THE

COURT OF APPEALS

OF

KENTUCKY.

STULTS *v.* SALE.

[92 KENTUCKY, 5.]

HOMESTEAD, CONDITIONS ESSENTIAL TO ENJOYMENT OF.—A homestead right cannot be acquired by one who has no family, but after the right has once vested, the loss of the family by death or marriage will not divest it.

A. C. Rucker and C. B. Seymour, for the appellant.

Abbott and Rutledge, for the appellee.

[5] HOLT, C. J. This appeal presents a single, but hitherto undecided, question by this court.

When the appellee, H. H. Sale, in 1864, first came into the occupancy of the property in contest, and in which [6] he had a life estate, he was undoubtedly a *bona fide* housekeeper with a family. It then consisted of a wife and five children; and that he then acquired a homestead right in the property is beyond question.

He has occupied it as a housekeeper ever since. In 1883, when this suit was brought upon a return of *nulla bona* to subject whatever property he had to the payment of the appellant's debt, his family had narrowed to one daughter, an invalid brother, and his mother-in-law; and since October, 1887, although a housekeeper in the property, he has, by reason of death and marriage, had no family whatever, within the legal meaning of that term, living with him: *Brooks etc.* v. *Collins,* 11 Bush, 622. It is therefore claimed that it is not now exempt to him as a homestead, but is liable to the appellant's debt.

Our statute exempts to the debtor as a homestead, land worth not over one thousand dollars, if he be a *bona fide* housekeeper, with a family of this commonwealth. The nature of this right is not fixed by the statute by name. He. may sell the property, but is divested of the right to it, if he permanently abandons it as his home. It may, perhaps, be said to be a qualified estate. It continues after his death for his widow during her occupancy of it, though there be no children: *Gay* v. *Hanks*, 81 Ky. 552.

The husband has the like right in the homestead of the deceased wife. This court has decided that where the right is thus derivative, the having of a family is not necessary to its continuance. It is to the creation of the right at the outset in the husband or wife but not to the continuance of it in the survivor: *Ellis* v. *Davis*, 90 Ky. 183.

In this case, however, there is no derivative right of [7] homestead. The property belongs to the husband, who is the debtor, and is claiming it as exempt to him as a homestead. Undoubtedly the having of a family was necessary to the creation of the right in him, but is it necessary to the continuance of it? While essential to its coming into existence, yet when it has once vested in the debtor, does he lose it by death or the marriage of his children, leaving him alone, but still a housekeeper in the occupancy of the property?

The statute makes no express mention in this respect. We must, therefore, look to its general scope and spirit for guidance, the right being the creature of it.

It is urged with force that the homestead exemption is for the benefit of the family, and, therefore, where this family relation does not exist, there is no homestead exemption. In other words, the reason for the rule ceasing, the rule ceases. This is true as to the coming into existence of the homestead right; and it is no doubt also true that the primary object of the statute was the protection of families from want, and the giving to them a shelter; yet the fact that the statute gives the homestead of the deceased wife to the husband during his occupancy of it, although he has no family, shows that it was not intended to provide for the wife and children alone. He, in such a case, does not become homeless.

Can it well be supposed that the legislature intended that in the event of the death of the wife owning the homestead, the benefit of it should continue to the husband during his occupancy, although he has no family, and yet that if he be

the owner of it, and his wife or children die, or the latter marry
and leave him, his right to the exemption ceases? If so, it is
a singular state of [9] case; and if so, it is equally true of the
wife, where she owns the homestead. In the event of the
husband's death owning the homestead, she takes it as survivor so long as she occupies it, although she has no family;
but if she owns it, and her husband dies, there being no longer
any family, her homestead right ceases.

Why should not the original owner have a right equal to
the survivor, and why should not the law favor the latter
equally at least with the former? Is the party to be worsted
because he owns the property? Can any reason be given why
the same right should not exist as to his own property as is
given to him in his wife's property after her death? Ought
not his claim to a homestead in his own property, as against
his own creditors, to be as much regarded as his claim to one
in her property after her death?

The construction here contended for by the creditor should
not be given to a statute which was enacted from a spirit of
liberality toward the debtor. The Massachusetts statute of
1855 limited the homestead exemption to a "householder
having a family." It continued it to the widow and children
after his death, but contained no provision for its continuance
to the husband after the death of his wife and the departure
of his children; but the supreme court of that state held that
his right was not thereby lost so long as he continued to
occupy the property as his home, saying: "Any other construction would render a husband, who had been deprived of
his family by accident or disease, or by their desertion, without any fault of his, liable to be instantly turned out of his
homestead by his creditors": *Silloway* v. *Brown*, 12 Allen, 30.

[9] This case and other somewhat kindred ones, are cited in
section 72 of Thompson on Homesteads with apparent approval; and while the Massachusetts statute, as well as that
of Illinois, denominates the right as "an estate of homestead,"
while our own merely exempts land worth one thousand dollars as a homestead, yet the case last cited, as well as *Kimbrel*
v. *Willis*, 97 Ill. 494, and *Kessler* v. *Draub*, 52 Texas, 575, 36
Am. Rep. 727, are so far kindred to this one as to merit citation. True, the question is one of statutory construction, and
the decisions in other states are of value only so far as their
statutes are like our own; but considering the entire act, and
the spirit which led to its enactment, it seems to us its only

reasonable construction is that while the having of a family
is necessary to the creation of the homestead right, that this
is not necessary to its continuance. It is not necessary to
inquire why this was made a necessary condition to its creation. The statute, in substance, says so; but it does not
provide that it is necessary to its continuance; and in order
to harmonize and render consistent and reasonable its other
provisions, it should not, in our opinion, be so construed.

Here the debtor was invested with the right; it existed
when this suit was brought; he has done nothing to release
or forfeit it, and, in our opinion, is still entitled to it, being
yet a housekeeper in the property, although by misfortune he
no longer has a family.

Judgment affirmed.

HOMESTEAD—TERMINATION IN GENERAL.—A homestead is not lost by the
death of the wife of the owner, so long as he continues to make it his residence with his servants and family, if he have any, and without them, if he
have none: *Taylor* v. *Boulware*, 17 Tex. 74; 67 Am. Dec. 642, and note.
The homestead exemption ceases when the claimant ceases to be the head of
a family: *Revalk* v. *Kraemer*, 8 Cal. 66; 68 Am. Dec. 304, and especially
note. The homestead is secure to the use of the family so long as the family continues to exist and the head thereof to occupy the homestead: *Lieff-
man* v. *Neuhaus*, 30 Tex. 633; 98 Am. Dec. 492. The question as to whether
the head of a family is divested of his homestead upon the death or marriage
of the members of his family is discussed in the extended note to *Kessler* v.
Draub, 36 Am. Rep. 728–730. As against creditors a homestead held by a
widow in her deceased husband's estate does not terminate until her death:
Holloway v. *Holloway*, 86 Ga. 576; 22 Am. St. Rep. 484. The death of one of
the spouses does not in any way alter the estate or character of the homestead: *Estate of Ackerman*, 80 Cal. 208; 13 Am. St. Rep. 116. See further
the extended note to *Sanders* v. *Russell*, 21 Am. St. Rep. 29.

COMMONWEALTH *v.* SMITH. COMMONWEALTH *v.* UNITED STATES EXPRESS CO.

[92 KENTUCKY, 38.]

INTERSTATE COMMERCE, INVALIDITY OF TAX ON AGENCIES OF.—A tax may
be levied by a state upon the property of a foreign corporation within
its boundaries, although that corporation is an agency of interstate
commerce, but a statute imposing a tax which is essentially a burden
upon the business of such a corporation is an attempted exercise of a
power belonging to the national government, and must be held invalid.

INTERSTATE COMMERCE, LICENSE TAX, WHEN DEEMED ATTEMPTED REGU-
LATION OF.—A statute providing that "all express companies doing
business in this state shall be required to pay a license-tax of five hundred dollars per annum where the distance over which the lines of such

companies operate or extend in this state is less than one hundred miles, and the annual sum of one thousand dollars where the distance is more than one hundred miles," imposes a tax upon the privilege of transacting business within the state, and, as regards express companies operating between this and other states, is invalid as an attempt to regulate interstate commerce.

INTERSTATE COMMERCE, TAX ON PROPERTY OF TELEGRAPH COMPANIES, WHEN DEEMED AN ATTEMPTED REGULATION OF.—A revenue law providing that, at a certain time in each year, the managing officer of "any telegraph company, working, operating, or controlling any telegraph line in this state," shall "pay into the treasury a tax equal to one dollar per mile for the line of poles and first wire, and fifty cents per mile for each additional wire," imposes a tax on the business, not on the property, of the companies affected, and if those companies are agencies of interstate commerce, the law is invalid as being an attempted exercise of a power belonging exclusively to the federal legislature.

Helm and Bruce, for the appellant.

Rozel Weissinger, for the appellee Smith.

Harmon, Colston, Goldsmith, and Hoadly, for the appellee express company.

[41] PRYOR, J.   These two cases involve the validity of a tax imposed upon the two appellees, both being foreign corporations, and resisting its payment upon the ground that the statute imposing the burden is in violation of the federal constitution.

The exercise of the power is claimed to be derived from two sections of the statute, the one applying to the United States Express Company, and the other to Charles Smith, an agent of the Western Union Telegraph Company.   The cases were argued as one by counsel for the state, and will be disposed of in the one opinion.

The section of the statute with reference to express companies provides: "That all express companies doing business in this state shall be required to pay a license tax of five hundred dollars per annum, where the distance over which the line of such companies operate or extend in this state is less than one hundred miles, and the annual sum of one thousand dollars where the distance is more than one hundred miles; and neither the company nor agent of any company which has paid the license tax required to be paid by this section shall be required to pay any other license or tax to any county, city, or municipality in this state; provided such company shall pay [42] ad valorem taxes for county and municipal purposes upon all horses, wagons, furniture, real estate, and other property at the same rate of taxation as is

collected upon other property in this commonwealth": Gen.
Stats., c. 92, art. 4, sec. 6.

The appellee, the express company, insists that this statute
is in violation of that provision of the federal constitution
giving to Congress the power "to regulate commerce with•
foreign nations and among the several states, and with the
Indian tribes": Fed. Const., art. 1, sec. 8, subsec. 3.

In this action by the state to recover the license tax, a proceeding authorized by statute, the appellee has filed an answer alleging the payment of all taxes assessed against it by
the state, whether state, county, or municipal, and then proceeds to deny the right of the state to impose a burden upon
it for the privilege of conducting a business that is in aid of,
or as a carrier of, commerce between the several states; that
it transmits goods, etc., over its lines for commercial and
business purposes between points within the state of Kentucky, and from points within the state to points in all the
other states, its lines affording business relations in the way
of transportation between the several states and territories,
and between the United States and foreign countries.

The only question presented is, does this statute amount to
a regulation of commerce, as settled in cases of a kindred
character by the supreme court? The case of *Crutcher* v.
Kentucky, 141 U. S. 47, recently decided on an appeal from
this court, where a license fee of five dollars was required to be
paid by every agent of an express company before engaging
in such business, was [43] held to be an exaction in respect of
commerce; and the reasons given by this court for sustaining
the validity of the act upon the idea that it was passed to protect its citizens against irresponsible corporations, and not to
interfere with interstate commerce, was held not to be a sufficient response to the defense, because the effect of the act
was to impose conditions as to the manner of conducting interstate commerce that could not be sustained. This is a
stronger case for the corporation than that of Crutcher.

It is plain that this tax is imposed upon the business, or
upon the privilege of transacting business within the state, and
if such a right, when given, can be taxed as contended by
counsel for the state, it would be conceding to the state government the right to prohibit any express company in another
state from doing business here by reason of the heavy burdens placed upon it by state legislation. If the regulation
of commerce belongs alone to the national government, and

·of this there is no question, then it is apparent the state has no power to impose such burdens. Nor is it material that the ·burden imposed may not likely affect interstate business or -commerce. It may not amount to a prohibition, still, if the -attempt or the effect of the legislation is to regulate interstate traffic the statute is invalid. Such is the decision of the ·supreme court in several cases: *Lyng* v. *Michigan*, 135 U. S. 161; *Crutcher* v. *Kentucky*, 141 U. S. 47. "All express com·panies doing business in the state shall pay a license tax," -and this being exacted for the right to do business, the act must be held to be invalid.

In the case of the *Commonwealth* against *Charles Smith* the appellee questions the validity of the revenue [44] law taxing telegraph companies, Smith being an agent of the Western Union Telegraph Company, and as such liable for the tax imposed and for the penalty for nonpayment. The provision of the revenue law is as follows:

"It shall be the duty of the president, treasurer, secretary, or manager of any telegraph company or association working. operating, or controlling any telegraph line in this state, to report, under oath, to the auditor of public accounts, on or before the 1st of July in every year, a full and complete state-' ment of each line, and the whole number of miles of wire worked, or under their control and management in this state; and shall pay into the treasury, on or before the 10th of July, in each year, a tax equal to one dollar per mile for the line of poles and first wire, and fifty cents per mile for each additional wire": Gen. Stats., c. 92, art. 4, sec. 4.

This corporation has tangible property within the state, and this property, as is conceded, is subject to taxation under its laws, nor is it denied that it does an extensive business within the state as well as out of it, and it is admitted, as has been already determined in more than one case, that this company is an agent of interstate commerce: *Telegraph Co.* v. *Texas*, 105 U. S. 460; *Pensacola Tel. Co.* v. *Western Union Tel. Co.*, ·96 U. S. 1. The lines of this company cross the boundary of the state at Louisville, and all the principal cities bordering on the Ohio river. The penalty for failing to pay this tax, and to which the agent is subjected, is a fine of five hundred ·dollars.

It is contended by the defense that the tax imposed is a mere arbitrary sum fixed by the state without regard to the value of the property owned by the company, or [45] even the income derived from it, and, in addition, that specific taxation is not a tax on property, but must necessarily be a tax on the occupation or business of the person sought to be taxed; while, on the other hand, it is claimed that the legislature must judge whether the tax shall be *ad valorem* or specific, and when uniform, it must be held valid.

In this state the power of the legislature to determine the mode of taxation, and to classify the property to be taxed, is not an open question. It may be termed a specific tax as to corporate property, and an *ad valorem* tax as to property that is ordinarily the subject of taxation. A railroad company may be taxed at a certain valuation for each mile, and if termed a specific tax, it is a taxation based on value, or the franchise itself granted by the state may be the subject of taxation without reference to the tangible property it owns: *Cincinnati etc. R. R. Co.* v. *Commonwealth*, 81 Ky., 492. The right of a state to tax the property of its citizens, when uniformity and equality exist in imposing the burden, can not well be doubted, and if this were the question presented in this case, we would have no difficulty in sustaining the tax. If this is a tax on the property of the corporation within the state, the statute imposing the burden must be enforced, but if a tax on the business of the corporation, and that corporation an agent of interstate commerce, it is then an exercise of power belonging to the national government and must be held invalid. As said by Mr. Justice Strong, in *Railroad Co.* v. *Peniston*, 18 Wall. 5: " It is, therefore, manifest that exemption of federal agencies from state taxation is dependent not upon the nature of the agent or upon the mode of their constitution, or upon [46] the fact that they are agents, but upon the effect of the tax, that is, upon the question whether the tax does in truth deprive them of power to serve the government as they were intended to serve it, or does it hinder the efficient exercise of their power. A tax upon their property has no such necessary effect. It leaves them free to discharge the duties they have undertaken to perform. A tax upon their operations is a direct obstruction to the exercise of federal power."

In this case the amount of the taxes alleged to be due the state for the year ending in July, 1888, is four thousand and twenty-four dollars and forty-five cents, with a fine of five hundred dollars for the failure of the corporation or its agent to pay it. It may be difficult to estimate the value of the

telegraph poles and the strands of wire necessary to the conduct of the business, but it becomes apparent from the act
itself, connected with the burden imposed on the corporation,
that it is its occupation and business that have been taxed,
without regard to the value of the property it actually owns
within the state, and, with the heavy penalty imposed, it may
directly interfere with the regulation of interstate commerce
and cannot be sustained. Mr. Justice Field, in *Gloucester
Ferry Co.* v. *Pennsylvania,* 114 U. S. 196, says: "While it is
conceded that the property in a state, belonging to a foreign
corporation engaged in foreign or interstate commerce, may
be taxed equally with like property of a domestic corporation
engaged in that business, we are clear that a tax or other
burden imposed on the property of either corporation because
it is used to carry on that commerce, or upon the transportation of persons or property, or for the navigation of public
waters over which the transportation is made, is invalid and
void as an [47] interference with and an obstruction of the
power of carriers in the regulation of such commerce." And
in the case of *Le Loup* v. *Mobile,* 127 U. S. 640, the court,
through Mr. Justice Bradley, says: "The fairest and most
just construction of the constitution leads to the conclusion
that no state has a right to lay a tax on interstate commerce
in any form, whether by way of duties laid on the transportation of the subjects of commerce, or on the receipts derived
from that transportation or on the occupation or business of
carrying it on, and the reason is that such taxation is a
burden on that commerce, and amounts to a regulation of it
that belongs solely to Congress." There is no limitation to
the power within the state to tax, except such as virtually
amounts to a confiscation of one's property; but there is not
only a limitation, but a prohibition, on the power of the state
to impose a tax on the business of corporations or other
agencies of interstate commerce that in effect regulates interstate traffic.

In both of the cases under consideration, mere arbitrary
sums are fixed without reference to value, and evidently, as
is to some extent conceded, on the business of each, and
whether under the guise of a specific or an *ad valorem* tax, it
is manifest that the object and effect of each section of the
statute is to impose burdens on the transportation or business
of both corporations, and not upon the property within the
state. The amount of the tax, and the penalties annexed for

enforcing payment, is, in effect, a prohibition of the exercise of the legitimate business of each of the appellees without first complying with the conditions of the statute. In view of the authorities cited, and the mode of enforcing this specific tax, it must [48] be held that the two sections of the statute are in violation of subsection 3 of section 8, article 1, of the federal constitution.

Judgment affirmed in both cases.

INTERSTATE COMMERCE—TAX FOR PRIVILEGE OF DOING BUSINESS.—A statute imposing a tax upon corporations created in another state, the basis of which is the amount of their capital in use in this state in the transaction of their ordinary business, is not in conflict with the provision of the constitution of the United States conferring upon Congress the power to regulate commerce between the states: *People* v. *Wemple*, 131 N. Y. 64; 27 Am. St. Rep. 542, and see the extended note to this case at page 563, where the subject of license fees exacted of interstate commerce is thoroughly discussed. On the same subject see *Bloomington* v. *Bourland*, 137 Ill. 534; 31 Am. St. Rep. 382 and *State* v. *French*, 109 N. O. 722; 26 Am. St. Rep. 590, and note.

INTERSTATE COMMERCE—TELEPHONE AND TELEGRAPH MESSAGES AS.— See *Matter of Pennsylvania Telephone Co.*, 48 N. J. Eq. 91; 27 Am. St. Rep. 462, and note. See also the extended note to *People* v. *Wemple*, 27 Am. St. Rep. 559.

FLETCHER *v.* TYLER.

[92 KENTUCKY, 145.]

DEEDS CONSTRUCTION OF.—A CONVEYANCE TO A MARRIED WOMAN AND THE HEIRS OF HER BODY by a specified husband, from whom the consideration moves, passes only a life estate to the woman herself, and her children, whether born before or after the execution of the deed, take a vested estate in the remainder.

J. A. Dean, for the appellants.

R. W. Slack, of counsel on the same side.

Wilfred Carrico, for the appellee.

[145] BENNETT, J. This action was brought by the appellees against the appellants to subject the supposed interest of the appellant, Woodson Fletcher, in a house and lot in the city of Owensboro to the satisfaction of their judgment against him

The granting clause of the deed, by which said lot is held, is as follows: "This indenture, made and entered into this, the twenty-eighth day of May, 1851, by and between O. F. Stirman of one part and Chloe Ann Fletcher and the heirs of her body by Woodson Fletcher upon her begotten, for and in consideration," etc. (naming the consideration), "do hereby sell and convey to Chloe Ann Fletcher and the heirs of her body aforesaid," etc.

It is a fact that the appellant, Woodson Fletcher, husband of Chloe Ann Fletcher, and the father of the then born children of her body, and of her children thereafter [147] born, bought and paid for said house and lot for the benefit of his said wife and children. It is also a fact that the purchase thus made, he not being indebted at the time, was not a fraud upon his creditors, nor was it intended to be a fraud upon them. Chloe Ann Fletcher, the wife, and some of the children who were living at the time of the conveyance, and some of those that were born after the conveyance, having died, and the lower court having decided that said wife and the then living children took a present joint estate in fee in said land, and that the appellant, Woodson Fletcher, having inherited the interests of those that had died, etc., said interests were subject to the appellee's demand, etc., the appellants have appealed from that judgment.

The sole question necessary to be determined is, what estate did Chloe Ann Fletcher and the heirs of her body take by said deed? The lower court thought that the case of *Tucker* v. *Tucker*, 78 Ky. 503, controlled the case; hence, it held that Chloe Ann Fletcher took a joint estate in fee with said living children. The appellants contend that Chloe Ann Fletcher took a life estate only, and all of said children took an estate in remainder. We concur in the latter contention.

In the case of *Smith* v. *Upton*, 12 Ky. Rep. 27, the conveyance was made "to Mrs. Smith and her children" by Upton, the consideration moving from Mrs. Smith's husband. It was held in that case that, as the consideration moved from the husband, the deed, for the purpose of construction, should be regarded as having been made by him; that the intention of the parties is gathered from the language of the deed, as such language is explained by the attendant circumstances and the relation of the [148] parties, and must control. Hence, it was held that it was evidently the intention of the husband to give the whole estate to his wife and their children, for whom he was under equal obligation to provide; that this could be certainly done by giving to the wife a life estate, remainder to their children. Whereas, to construe the instrument as giving to the wife and children a joint estate in fee might defeat this intention by the wife's interest passing to her children by a second marriage, who would be strangers to his blood and for whom he was under no legal or moral obligation to provide. Also, the court's construction that the wife and children took a joint present interest in fee, and that, consequently, none but those living at the time could take directly as grantees, clearly defeated the intention of the grantor.

In the line above indicated is the well-considered case of *Davis* v. *Hardin*, 80 Ky. 672; also, the case of *Bodine's Admr.* v. *Arthur*, 91 Ky. 53; 34 Am. St. Rep. 162. In the latter case it was held that, as the estate was confined to the heirs of the body in the *habendum* and not in the granting clause, they could not take a present estate as grantees, but they could take an estate in remainder. But the case also gives and adheres to the reasons given in the other cases.

The judgment is reversed, and the case is remanded, with direction for further proceedings consistently with this opinion.

DEEDS—CONSTRUCTION—ESTATE GRANTED.—A deed to a woman and her children begotten by a specified husband, forever, conveys a life estate to the wife with a remainder to her children begotten by the designated husband: *Bodine* v. *Arthur*, 91 Ky. 53; 34 Am. St. Rep. 162. Where one conveys land to his daughter and the lawful heirs of her body, "to hold to her, her natural life, and her children," she takes a life estate and her children a remainder in fee: *Jarvis* v. *Davis*, 99 N. C. 37. A deed of gift to J. B. during his natural life and then to return to the male children lawfully begotten of his body, vests a life estate in J. B. with a remainder in fee to his sons: *Brown* v. *Ward*, 103 N. C. 173. A conveyance of land to a daughter for life, and to descend to the children equally, creates a life estate in the daughter and a remainder to such of her children as are living at the date of her death: *Irvin* v. *Clark*, 98 N. C. 437; *Jackson* v. *Jackson*, 127 Ind. 346.

PREWITT *v.* TRIMBLE.

[92 KENTUCKY, 176.]

FRAUD, ACTUAL KNOWLEDGE OF FALSITY OF STATEMENT, WHEN NOT ESSENTIAL.—When a person is in a situation to know, and it is his duty to know, whether a statement, upon the faith of which another has been induced to enter into a contract, is true or false, the law imputes such knowledge to him, and the statement, if untrue, is held to be fraudulent as regards the person who relied upon it.

FRAUD—INNOCENT MISREPRESENTATION NO ONE PERMITTED TO RETAIN FRUITS OF.—Though one who brings about a contract by misrepresentation commits no fraud, because his representation was, when made, innocent in the ordinary sense, yet if, after ascertaining its falsity, he refuses to relinquish the advantage derived therefrom, upon receiving

an offer of reciprocal relinquishment from the injured party, he is guilty
of constructive fraud, and the contract is subject to rescission by a court
of equity.

FRAUD—FALSE STATEMENT AS TO CONDITION OF BANK—PRESIDENT CANNOT
PROFIT BY.—A statement signed by the president and directors of a
bank, which is circulated with and refers with approval to a statement
in which the cashier sets forth the resources and liabilities of the bank,
is a deliberate affirmation of the truth of the latter statement, and
equivalent to a report of the affairs of the bank made by the president
and directors themselves. Under such circumstances, if the cashier's
statement proves to be false, one who has been induced by it to purchase bank shares from the president at a price exceeding their real
value may maintain an action against his vendor to recover damages for
misrepresentation or to procure the rescission of the sale.

Edward C. O'Rear and Z. Taylor Young, for the appellant.

Wood and Day, for the appellee

[178] LEWIS, J. January 19, 1888, appellee, then president
of the Exchange Bank of Kentucky, at Mt. Sterling, sold and
transferred to appellant twenty shares of stock in that bank
at the price of one hundred and twenty dollars per share, and
twenty-one shares in the Mt. Sterling National Bank at one
hundred and twenty dollars per share for twenty shares and
one hundred and eighteen dollars for the remaining one, payment for which was then made, partly in notes assigned to
and received by appellee at their face value, and partly in
money.

May 14, 1888, appellant brought this action for rescission
of the contract and restoration of the notes, or, if collected,
payment of amount thereof, and the money received by appellee and interest on the whole; it being alleged and not
denied, a tender and offer to retransfer the stock and demand
of repayment of the purchase price had been made by appellant and refused by appellee.

It appears that December 31, 1887, a statement of resources
and liabilities of the Exchange Bank of Kentucky, signed by
the cashier, was published in the newspapers of Mt. Sterling,
and by printed cards which were generally distributed; there
being at foot of the statement [179] an announcement the bank
had declared its usual semi-annual four per cent dividend.
There was printed on the same card a statement signed by
the president and directors, in which the cashier's statement
was referred to as evidence of the prosperous condition and
increasing business of the bank.

According to that statement the resources of the bank,

having a capital of $100,000, amounted to $329,380.42, of
which $245,790 were loans and discounts and $13,338.68
overdrafts, while the undivided profits were $15,851.41.
But no mention was made of any insolvent debts being part
of the aggregate of either loans or overdrafts.

In respect to the statement it is alleged and appears that
of the total amount of loans and discounts more than $30,000
consisted of stale and worthless demands, and of overdrafts
at least $7,000 were likewise worthless, the drawers being
insolvent; and that after charging off such worthless demands
there would be left in the bank no undivided profits at all.
It is further alleged and proved that the books of the bank
showed, at date of the statement, about $7,600 more due to
depositors, and consequently that much more liabilities than
disclosed by it.

The evidence places beyond question that when the statement was published and circulated the real value of stock in
the Exchange Bank of Kentucky, calculated and determined
by the actual condition of its resources and liabilities, was
not over $70 per share. It is also satisfactorily shown that
when he made the purchase appellant did not know, nor
have any other means of knowing, the true condition of that
bank's affairs than such information as was afforded by the
cashier's statement, [180] and that given directly to him by
appellee, and that he believed and acted on that information.

There is discrepancy in the testimony of the parties as to
what occurred between them when the contract was made.
But that of another person present at the time is substantially
that appellee said, if not directly to, in hearing of, appellant,
that the notes held by the Exchange Bank of Kentucky were
worth dollar for dollar, and being asked about value of the
stock, took in his hands the card upon which was printed the
cashier's statement, one of which he had, on a previous
occasion, in person, given to appellant, and referring to it
explained that the capital being $100,000, the surplus of
$15,000 made the stock worth $115 per share, and more, as
an investment, and that it was going at $120.

But independent of what occurred between the parties at
the time of the contract, it is manifest the cashier's statement
was published and circulated by authority of the president
and directors for the purpose and in expectation of it being
accepted and treated by the public as in all respects true and
reliable: thereby not only increasing business of the bank, but

keeping up or enhancing market value of the stock in which each of them had a personal interest. And as their own accompanying statement was obviously intended to be, it should be regarded a deliberate affirmation of the truth of that of the cashier, and as equivalent to a report of the affairs of the bank made directly by them. And if so, upon both principle and authority no other relation or privity between the parties to this action need · be shown than the act of appellee, as president, indorsing and authorizing [181] publication and circulation of the cashier's statement, and the resulting injury to appellant, who was within the class designed to be influenced by the statement: Cook on Stock and Stockholders, secs. 353, 354, and cases cited.

Whether they published and gave currency to the statement, knowing it to be materially untrue, and for the fraudulent purpose of deceiving the public as charged in the petition, we need not inquire, for it was not, in order to maintain this action, indispensable that appellee be shown to have known the statement was false. For it is elementary doctrine that a false representation may, in contemplation of law, be made with knowledge of its falsity, that is, made *scienter*, so as to afford a right of action in damages, and, *a fortiori*, ground for equitable proceedings: 1 Without actual knowledge of either its truth or falsity, as when the party has affirmed his knowledge by a positive statement which implies knowledge; 2. When made under circumstances in which the party ought to have known, if he did not know, of its falsity; as when having "special means of knowledge," it is his duty to know: Bigelow on Fraud, 509, 516.

In Story's Equity, sec. 193, it is laid down that "affirmation of a material fact that one does not know or believe to be true, is, equally in morals and law, as unjustifiable as the affirmation of what is known to be positively false. And even if the party innocently misrepresents a material fact by mistake, it is equally conclusive, for it operates as surprise and imposition on the other."

Representations by a party having means of knowledge in regard to a matter, not possessed generally, are apt to be believed and acted upon, especially if he is in a [182] situation where he owes a duty to the public to deal honestly and intelligently. Therefore, something more than use of ordinary diligence to know the condition of a bank should be required of the president in order to exempt him from liability to a person who has suffered loss by a false statement or report of its affairs officially made or affirmed by him, especially when he has been thereby personally benefited.

In Cook on Stock and Stockholders, section 145, it is said on authority of numerous cases cited, that any statement by the authorized agents of a corporation in regard to the *status* of the corporation, or material matters connected therewith, whereby subscriptions of stock are obtained, is a fraudulent representation, for which a person sustaining loss thereby may hold such agents personally liable, or have the contract rescinded. This is upon the principle and for the reason that such agents have exceptional means of knowledge, and owe a duty to speak the truth, or not at all, about the matter. But as observed by the author, "in all these cases, the distinction between statements relative to the prospects and capabilities of the enterprise, and statements specially specifying what does or does not exist, must be carefully borne in mind."

In this case not the bank, but appellee personally, profited by the bargain appellant was induced by the false report or statement of its condition to make with him; and, therefore, it would be contrary to reason and justice for him to be permitted to enjoy the benefits of it at the expense of appellant, upon the flimsy ground of ignorance about the material matters in reference to which he made the deliberate and positive representation. For leaving out of view the question whether he did in [183] fact, know the statement was untrue, being in a situation to know and where it was his duty to know, he, in contemplation of law, did know it, and, consequently, such statement is to be held fraudulent; and appellant has a remedy for the loss sustained, either by action in damages, or for rescission. For it is a settled rule, that even when one who brings about a contract by misrepresentation commits no fraud, because his representation was, when made, innocent in the ordinary sense, still, if when the fact of its falsity becomes known he refuses to relinquish the advantage, upon offer of reciprocal relinquishment received by the injured party, it would make him guilty of constructive fraud, and the contract subject to rescission by a court of equity.

In our opinion appellant, as the record stands, was entitled to a rescission of the contract, as prayed for in his petition, and the court had jurisdiction to grant it.

Wherefore the judgment is reversed, and cause remanded for judgment in favor of appellant.

Judge Holt not sitting. ____

FRAUD—INNOCENT MISREPRESENTATIONS.—Whether representations are made innocently or knowingly, they operate equally as a fraud upon a party who relies upon them in ignorance of the facts, provided they are false, and are made as of the party's own knowledge: *Bullit* v. *Farrar*, 42 Minn. 8; 18 Am. St. Rep. 485; *Mooney* v. *Davis*, 75 Mich. 188; 13 Am. St. Rep. 425, and note; *Converse* v. *Blumrich*, 14 Mich. 109; 90 Am. Dec. 230, and note; *Gould* v. *York County etc. Ins. Co.*, 47 Me. 403; 74 Am. Dec. 494, and note; *Tyson* v. *Passmore*, 2 Pa. St. 122; 44 Am. Dec. 181, and note, with the cases collected; *Sears* v. *Hicklin*, 13 Col. 143; *Ripley* v. *Case*, 86 Mich. 261; *Totten* v. *Burhans*, 91 Mich. 495. The following line of cases hold that representations must be shown to have been made with knowledge of their falsity, before one who acts upon them can recover on the ground of fraud: *Pryor* v. *Foster*, 130 N. Y. 171; *High* v. *Berret*, 148 Pa. St. 261; *Lewark* v. *Carter*, 117 Ind. 206; 10 Am. St. Rep. 40, and note; *Smith* v; *Mariner*, 5 Wis. 551; 68 Am. Dec. 73, and note, at page 88; *Campbell* v. *Hillman*, 15 B. Mon. 508; 61 Am. Dec. 195, and note; *Miller* v. *Howell*, 1 Scam. 499; 32 Am. Dec. 36, and note. See the extended note to *Cottrill* v. *Krum*, 18 Am. St. Rep. 555.

FRAUD—KNOWLEDGE IMPUTED.—One's title may be postponed without fraud by positive acts for whose consequences he is civilly liable, without regard to his ignorance or knowledge, because a loss which must fall on one of two innocent persons should be borne by him whose act has occasioned it: *Robinson* v. *Justice*, 2 Pen. & W. 19; 21 Am. Dec. 407, and note. A person will be presumed to know of the existence or nonexistence of a fact which he undertakes to warrant: *Hexter* v. *Bast*, 125 Pa. St. 52; 11 Am. St. Rep. 874; to the same effect see *Griswold* v. *Gebbie*, 126 Pa. St. 353; 12 Am. St. Rep. 878, and note.

HOWES *v.* PERRY.

[92 KENTUCKY, 260.]

OFFICES—REQUISITES OF A VALID ELECTION.—No person can be regarded as duly elected to an office unless he receives a majority of the votes, when there are two candidates, or a plurality of the votes, when there are more than two.

OFFICES—DEATH OF ONE OF TWO CANDIDATES BEFORE THE CLOSE OF THE POLL, EFFECT OF.—A candidate for an elective office who receives a smaller number of votes than the only other competitor therefor, is not entitled to be declared elected because it appears that the latter died before all the votes were cast. Such a candidate cannot show that he was the choice of a majority or a plurality of those voting at the election, and is therefore incapable of establishing his right to be installed in the office which he claims.

R. T. Burns, for the appellant.

Stewart and Stewart, for the appellee.

[261] LEWIS, J. It appears from the petition of appellant, a general demurrer to which was sustained, that on the first Monday in August, 1890, he and S. T. Bayes were opposing candidates for election by the qualified voters of Johnson county to the office of county court clerk; that said Bayes died about 3 o'clock P. M. on the day of election, leaving appellant the only candidate or person to be thereafter voted for; but that, nevertheless, the board of officers empowered and required by law to examine the poll-books and give certificates of election refused to give [262] to appellant such certificate; and that afterwards the judge of the Johnson county court wrongfully declared the office of county court clerk vacant and appointed appellee to fill such vacancy.

As to the regularity of appellee's appointment and qualifications for the office in question we need not inquire, because to recover, which is the object of this action, it was incumbent upon appellant to show his title to it. He alleges that he received four hundred and ninety-eight votes, but at the same time admits that there were cast and recorded on the poll-books for S. T. Bayes, the opposing candidate, a greater number of votes than for himself, which fact, in our opinion, is decisive against his right to the office.

It is a principle of free elections by the people, firmly fixed and understood, that no person is or can be regarded duly elected to an office unless, when only two persons are voted for, he receives a majority of the votes cast for them, or receives a plurality in case there are more than two voted for. Any other rule would be subversive of the fundamental idea of elections by the people under our form of government, which is, that only that person shall be entitled to hold an elective office who appears, from the record of votes cast, to have been the choice of a majority or plurality of those voting in such election. There is no means of ascertaining whether S. T. Bayes had, at the time of his death, received more votes than the whole number given to appellant, nor is it necessary to inquire, for it is admitted by appellant he was not the choice of a majority of the qualified voters, whose votes were cast in good faith and recorded in that election, and that is enough to decide the contest against [263] him. And such is the well-settled rule, nowhere plainer than in section 2, article 5, chapter 33 of the General Statutes, where it is made the duty of the comparing board to give certificates of election to those who have respectively received the highest number of votes for any office within the gift of the particular county.

As, in our opinion, it is manifest from the statements of appellant's petition, he is not entitled to the office sued for, the demurrer was properly sustained.

The judgment must be affirmed.

ELECTIONS.—DISQUALIFICATION OF THE PERSON RECEIVING THE HIGHEST NUMBER OF VOTES does not entitle the one receiving the next highest number to the office: *Commonwealth* v. *Cluley*, 56 Pa. St. 270; 94 Am. Dec. 75, and extended note; *Barnum* v. *Gilpin*, 27 Minn. 466; 38 Am. Rep. 304; *Sublett* v. *Bedwell*, 47 Miss. 266; 12 Am. Rep. 338, and note; *People* v. *Clute*, 50 N. Y. 451; 10 Am. Rep. 508; *State* v. *Giles*, 2 Pinn. 166; 1 Chand. 112; 52 Am. Dec. 149, and extended note in which the question as to whether the death of the party receiving the highest number of votes would entitle the candidate receiving the next highest number to the office. See also the extended note to *People* v. *Pease*, 84 Am. Dec. 268, where the rule is laid down that a majority of the legal votes must elect.

ABERNATHY *v.* WHEELER.

[92 KENTUCKY, 320.]

WAREHOUSEMEN SELLING GOODS ON COMMISSION, LIABILITY OF.—A mortgagee of goods cannot maintain an action for conversion against a public warehouseman who receives a portion of those goods from the apparent owner, in the usual way and without any notice, either actual or constructive, of an adverse claim, and sells them on commission at a public sale in the regular course of business, without asserting any interest or right hostile to such mortgagee.

Petree and Downer, and D. L Johnson, for the appellants.

H. J. Stites, for the appellees.

321 BENNETT, J.   C. S. Anderson agreed to do farm-work in Christian county for J. S. Anderson during the year 1888. He was to receive as compensation for his work his board and lodging and one hundred and fifty dollars, and any balance that might be due him at the end of the year on account of his wages; he was to have tobacco enough raised on the farm in 1888 to pay said balance. At the close of said year J. S. Anderson was indebted to C. S. Anderson, on account of said contract, in the sum of one hundred and thirty-five dollars. On the respective dates of July 21 and the 19th of September, 1888, J. S. Anderson executed a mortgage on said crop of tobacco to Wheeler, Mills & Co., tobacco warehousemen in the city of Hopkinsville, Kentucky, which mortgage was duly recorded, etc.

In 1889, said balance being unpaid, and J. S. Anderson having died, C. S. Anderson caused two hogsheads of said tobacco to be prized and sent in the name of G. S. Anderson to the tobacco warehouse of the appellants, in the city of Hopkinsville, for sale. The appellants, as such warehousemen, sold said tobacco at public sale, and placed the net proceeds of sale in bank to the credit of said sale, and thinking that C. S. Anderson was G. S. Anderson, [322] they gave him a check for the net proceeds of said tobacco. Wheeler, Mills & Co., mortgagees, sued Abernathy and Long and C. S. Anderson, etc., for the price of said tobacco. It is admitted that Ahernathy and Long received and sold said tobacco as public tobacco warehousemen, in the usual course of business, and paid the proceeds of sale to C. S. Anderson without actual notice of the existence of appellees' mortgage. Are Abernathy and Long responsible for the sum for which the tobacco was sold? We think not. They were public warehousemen for the purpose of receiving the tobacco of the producer and selling it at public auction in consideration of receiving pay for storage and certain commissions on the sales. They assumed the obligation of serving the entire public in the matter of receiving and selling the tobacco of the producer, and they had no right to select their customers and to refuse others, provided they conformed to the reasonable rules and regulations of the house: See *Nash* v. *Page*, 80 Ky. 539; 44 Am. Rep. 490.

It is not contended that the warehousemen had any interest in the tobacco whatever; they were only entitled to a commission for making the sale and to be reimbursed for their other expenses and trouble in receiving and handling the tobacco.

So the question is, Are they responsible to the mortgagees of the tobacco as for a conversion of it? That question seems to be settled in principle in *Newcomb-Buchanan Co.* v. *Baskett*, 14 Bush, 658. It is there settled that a public warehouseman receiving, stowing, and selling goods, in his line of duty, on commission, and having no property interest in the goods, and having no notice of an adverse claim to them, is not guilty of a conversion of [323] them by the mere sale of them on account of the person that consigns them to his house for sale. In such case the warehouseman asserts no interest in the goods or right to them hostile to the mortgagee or true owner; he simply acts as the custodian and mouthpiece of the apparent owner. No one would contend that had C. S. Anderson employed the appellants, as auctioneers, to sell the tobacco at auction on the streets of Hopkinsville, they receiving a compensation for their services only, and having no property right in the tobacco, they would have been liable to the appellees as for a conversion of the tobacco. Why? Because they asserted no right or interest hostile to the appellees, but acted simply as the intermediaries or indifferent parties between the apparent owner of the tobacco and the bidders for it. So here they act as public intermediaries in receiving and selling the tobacco, not having any interest therein, but for compensation merely, and when the tobacco is presented to them for public storage and sale by the apparent owner in the usual way, and they having no knowledge or information that others had an adverse interest in the tobacco, and there being no fact or circumstance attending the transaction that should put them, as persons of ordinary prudence, upon inquiry as to the rights of others in reference to the tobacco, it would not be in the interest of trade to require them to institute inquiry and investigation before sale as to the true condition of the title of the tobacco.

The judgment is reversed as to Abernathy and Long, and affirmed as to C. S. Anderson.

WAREHOUSEMEN—LIABILITY FOR CONVERSION.—The principle involved in the leading case is analogous to the liability of an auctioneer for the selling of goods delivered to him to be sold by one other than the true owner. The latter proposition is discussed in *Robinson* v. *Bird*, 158 Mass. 357; 35 Am. St. Rep. 495, and note. See also the extended note to *Velsian* v. *Lewis*, 3 Am. St. Rep. 201.

STANDARD OIL CO. *v.* TIERNEY.

[92 KENTUCKY, 367.]

NEGLIGENCE—DUTY OF SHIPPER OF DANGEROUS GOODS.—If the shipper of an explosive or dangerous substance fails to notify the carrier or his agent of the danger which attends the handling of it, while in course of transportation, and an injury results to the employees of the carrier, the shipper is liable for the injury thus sustained; but when the carrier is notified whether by a mark upon the parcel or otherwise, that the article shipped is of a dangerous character, and one of the carrier's employee's is injured by handling the article, the mere fact that no knowledge of its real nature was brought home to the employee will not render the shipper liable.

NEGLIGENCE—CARRIAGE OF DANGEROUS ARTICLES—DUTY OF SHIPPER AND CARRIER.—Where a dangerous article is delivered to a carrier for transportation, it is the duty both of the shipper and the carrier to notify those who handle it of its dangerous character, and no arrangement between the shipper and the carrier, though made in the best of faith, by which the article is to be shipped under a name which does not indicate its true nature, will excuse the shipper for the nonperformance of that duty on his part.

NEGLIGENCE.—THE SHIPPER'S DUTY TO MARK DANGEROUS ARTICLES delivered to a carrier for transportation in such a way that the carrier's employees may have due notice of the real character of those articles is not sufficiently performed when a substance so extremely dangerous as naphtha is described on the freight-bill as carbon oil, and merely branded, "unsafe for illuminating purposes."

NEGLIGENCE—DAMAGES.—EVIDENCE that the plaintiff in an action to recover damages for personal injuries has a wife and child should not be admitted.

NEGLIGENCE—DANGEROUS ARTICLE SHIPPED UNDER A FICTITIOUS NAME. Where the employee of a carrier is suing a shipper to recover damages for injuries sustained by an explosion of naphtha which was described in the bill of lading as carbon oil, it is not error to refuse evidence going to show that the carrier had been informed of the real meaning of the words used in the bill of lading.

NEGLIGENCE.—EVIDENCE that the defendant in an action to recover damages for personal injuries has adopted, since the occurrence of the accident, certain precautions calculated to prevent a repetition thereof is not admissible.

DAMAGES, MEASURE OF.—A plaintiff prevailing in an action to recover damages for personal injuries is entitled to be awarded such an amount as, in the opinion of the jury, will fairly compensate him for any suffering, mental or physical, theretofore experienced by him, directly resulting from the injury, and for any suffering or disability that may be believed from the testimony to be reasonably certain to be experienced by him in the future, and for any reduction in his power to earn money during the remainder of his life, if such reduction there be directly resulting from the injury.

DAMAGES FOR PERSONAL INJURIES, WHEN DEEMED EXCESSIVE.—Where the conductor of a train, a vigorous man of about thirty years of age, and a laborious and useful employee, is so badly burnt about the face, as to be disfigured for life, suffers much pain and anguish for several months, and loses the use of his left arm, and to some extent of his right also, a verdict for twenty-five thousand dollars is excessive.

Humphrey and Davie, for the appellant.

Willson and Thum, for the appellee.

William Lindsay, of counsel on the same side.

372 PRYOR, J. In April, of the year 1888, the Standard Oil Company, at its place of business in the city of Louisville, loaded two cars belonging to the Louisville and Nashville Railroad Company with oil. One of the cars contained sixty-five barrels, thirty-five of those barrels being naphtha oil and the remainder the ordinary illuminating oil. This car was loaded by the company, the car being on a side-track near its

warehouse, belonging to the Louisville and Nashville Railroad, and was intended to be shipped south. The testimony
shows that the cars were known as cattle-cars with open lat-
tices, and that offered by the defense shows that the oil was
in barrels that had been carefully inspected, and such barrels
as were generally used in shipping naphtha or other products
of petroleum, and the barrels containing naphtha branded, as
they maintain, as required by the statute, "unsafe for illuminating purposes." The head of the barrel was painted
white with this brand in black letters in the center. The
cars were taken from this switch by the Louisville and Nashville road by its freight engine or train in charge of the appellee, who was the conductor. After leaving Louisville,
when some twenty or thirty miles from the city, the appellee
discovered that oil was leaking from some one of the barrels,
and after passing one or two depots he directed one of the
employees to ascertain where the [373] leak was. There is a
window about two feet square at the end of the car which the
employee climbed into with his lantern and passing through
this window into the car discovered the barrel that was leaking. The appellee being informed by the employee of the
condition of the barrel, the two, with a lamp each, passed
through this window into the car, and finding that they could
not handle the barrel the appellee called for another employee who passed through this window with his lamp. They
set their lamps on the heads of the barrels and proceeded to
raise the leaking barrel from the floor when, by the motion
of the barrel or its peculiar position when being moved, the
naphtha spouted out in a stream as large as a pencil, took
fire from the burning lamp and seriously injured the appellee.

Whether the liquid was thrown on the lamp or the explosion took place from the vapor produced by the naphtha
is a mooted question. The appellee was badly burned, and
instituted this action against the appellant to recover damages for the injury, alleging that this naphtha was shipped
as carbon oil, and that he had no notice whatever of the inflammable character of the fluid. He claimed damages to
the amount of twenty-five thousand dollars, and that sum the
jury awarded him. He was badly burned about the face, so
much so as to disfigure him for life; suffered much pain and
anguish for several months; lost the use of his left arm, and
his right hand is to some extent injured; his feet were also
badly burned, but the principal injury after his recovery con-

sists in the loss of the use of his left arm and the disfigure-
ment of his face.

The defense relies upon various grounds for a reversal: 1.
That it took all the necessary care and precaution in [374]
shipping the oil; that it marked it unsafe for illuminating
purposes; that the carrier knew the car contained barrels of
naphtha and that the entire product of petroleum had been
shipped and was being shipped as carbon oil under an agreement to that effect with the railroad company, and that it
was the duty of that company to have notified its employees
of the danger; 2. That the court erred in admitting incompetent testimony and in denying to the defendant the right
to introduce testimony that was competent; 3. In giving
erroneous instructions to the jury and in refusing to give defendant's instructions, and 4. The damages are excessive.

There were numerous instructions asked by the plaintiff
and the defendant, all of which were refused, and the instructions prepared and given by the trial judge. In determining the questions raised by the instructions it will be
necessary to notice the testimony for the defense that was excluded, as this testimony, if admitted, must have an important bearing on the issue in establishing at least good faith
on the part of the appellant in delivering this naphtha to the
carrier. It was offered by way of defense on the part of the
appellant that the railroad company, whose agent and employee the conductor was at the time of the injury, knew that
this car contained naphtha, and if not, that under an agreement with the company, through its officials, it had been
shipping on its cars barrels of naphtha for a long period
branded in the manner specified, with bills of lading, under
the general designation of carbon oil, the railroad company
knowing that the term embraced naphtha, and took it with
that understanding, charging the same freight and shipping
it as any other oil. The court refused to permit this testimony [375] to go to the jury, and this is one of the errors complained of.

It is evident that if the owner, when shipping explosive or
combustible substances, fails to notify the carrier or his agent
of the danger attending its use, when transporting it, and an
injury results to the employees of the carrier, the owner is
liable for the injury sustained; but when the carrier is notified of the dangerous article or product (and there is none
more so than naphtha when coming in contact with a burn-

ing lamp or with fire), and there is marked on the head of
the barrel that which must necessarily apprise the carrier of
its dangerous nature, and the carrier in his ordinary line
of business undertakes to transport it and an injury occurs to
one of its employees, the question then arises, Is the shipper
liable because knowledge was not brought home to its employee? We think not.

This, however, is not the question arising in this case. It
is the mode of shipping and branding this naphtha adopted
by both parties under an agreement or implied understanding, at least, between them, from which this liability to the
employee springs, if any exists. The railroad company had
been in the habit of receiving and shipping this naphtha as
carbon oil under an arrangement with the appellant, with a
brand placed on the head of each barrel: "Unsafe for illuminating purposes."

There was an implied, if not a positive, duty on the part of
both corporations to notify those who handled this substance
of its dangerous character, and no arrangement between them,
although made in the best of faith, by which dynamite was to
be shipped as powder or naphtha as carbon oil should protect
the appellant from a violation [376] of this duty it owed to the
hands or employees whose duty it was to keep it secure and
to handle it when necessary. The freight bill or paper by
which this plaintiff was guided showed that it was oil or
carbon oil, and it seems to us the only question for the jury
to decide is: Was the brand on these barrels sufficient notice
to the appellant of the dangerous substance within them?
The dangerous quality of naphtha requires more vigilance
and care in shipping and handling it than almost any other
explosive substance, and as a means of great precaution it
would be prudent to give other warning than the mere name
of the substance.

As an explosive it is said the danger is ten times greater
than that of gunpowder; it ignites as soon as the blaze is applied to it and becomes explosive when the vapor from it
mingles with the atmosphere in which there happens to be a
burning lamp or other light. The conductor might not have
known the danger if the word "naphtha" had been placed on
these barrels; still, it would doubtless have put him on inquiry, and that it was not carbon oil, and at the same time
removed all question of negligence from the door of the appellant. The contention by counsel is that the brand "Unsafe

for illuminating purposes" was intended by the statute as the
warning to be given those who handle naphtha.   Whether
this provision of the statute applies to naphtha or to the production from petroleum, less dangerous and known as oil, is
uncertain; and it is manifest that the car purporting to be
loaded with carbon oil from the freight-bill did not apprise
the appellee of the danger.   While the testimony of the agreement between the two corporations as to the manner of shipping should have gone to the jury to show an absence [377] of
bad faith on the part of the appellant, still it was its duty,
looking to the very great danger connected with the movement of such a substance on trains, to have so branded the
barrels as to have informed the conductor of the inflammable
character of the substance they contained; and unless they
were so marked as that one exercising ordinary care and prudence with reference to his own personal safety and whose
duty it was to handle the barrels should have ascertained the
danger the appellant is liable.   The converse of the proposition being that if so branded as that one of ordinary care
and prudence should have discovered the danger, the verdict
should be for the defendant.   While the instructions given
by the court below embrace this view of the case this is the
issue to be tried.

The appellee had to deal with and deliver this naphtha,
and he should have been informed in some way that the barrels contained it.

There are other questions raised as to the admission and
rejection of testimony.   It was shown that the appellee had a
wife and child over the objections of the appellant.   While
this fact may not have influenced the finding, it should not
have been admitted.

The defense offered to prove that the Louisville and Nashville Railroad Company, whose conductor the plaintiff was,
had been informed that the words "carbon oil," contained
in the bill of lading, meant naphtha.   This was refused, and
properly, because an employee of even more than ordinary
intelligence would not have attached such a meaning to this
bill of lading.   The court, however, should have admitted the
testimony showing that wooden barrels were safe, and that
naphtha was ordinarily shipped in that way by prudent business men.

[378] Another error complained of by the appellant is in the
trial court permitting the appellee to prove that after this ac-

cident both corporations changed the manner of branding the barrels and labeling the cars. There seems to be some diversity of opinion on this point, the weight of authority being opposed to the admission of this character of testimony as a means of showing neglect on the part of the defendant. The Minnesota court, in *Morse* v. *Minneapolis etc. R. R. Co.*, 30 Minn. 465, said: "We think such a rule puts an unfair interpretation upon human conduct, and virtually holds out an inducement for continued negligence."

In *Lang* v. *Sanger*, 76 Wis. 71, in an action for an injury sustained by reason of defective machinery, the court held that it was erroneous to show that the defects were repaired after the accident.

In *Terre Haute R. R. Co.* v. *Clem*, 123 Ind. 15, 18 Am. St. Rep. 303, it is said: "To declare such evidence competent is to offer an inducement to omit the use of such care as new information may suggest, and to deter persons from doing what the new experience informs them may be done to prevent the possibility of future accidents."

Other cases determine that such evidence is open to the objection that it raises distinct and independent issues for the consideration of the jury: *Nalley* v. *Hartford Carpet Co.*, 51 Conn. 524; 50 Am. Rep. 47; *Payne* v. *Troy etc. R. R. Co.*, 9 Hun, 526; *Ely* v. *St. Louis etc. Ry. Co.*, 77 Mo. 34; *Reed* v. *New York etc. R. R. Co.*, 45 N. Y. 574.

There is still another question in this case that every court of final resort appproaches with reluctance, and that is the one of excessive damages. The verdict in this case is for twenty-five thousand dollars, the entire sum claimed [379] in the petition. As said by Mr. Sedgwick, in his work on the Measure of Damages: "It is one thing for a court to administer its own measure of damages in a case properly before it, and quite another thing to set aside the verdict of a jury merely because it exceeds that measure." There must, says he, "be some mistake of the principles upon which the damages have been estimated, or some improper motives or feelings or bias influencing the jury": sec. 1320.

It is not for this court to determine the amount the plaintiff is entitled to recover in this character of action, and the verdict in every case for an injury to the person must depend upon the facts and circumstances connected with the commission of the wrong in the particular case, the verdict and judg-

ment in no one case being a criterion by which the court and
jury are to be controlled in all cases of a similar character.

It was the province of the jury to fix the compensation to
which the appellee was entitled, and the court in the instructions given placed properly before them the mode of ascertaining the damages if, from the evidence, the appellee was
entitled to recover. The jury reached the conclusion that the
appellant was guilty of such an omission of duty as entitled
the appellee to a verdict, but was not authorized to increase
the amount of recovery by reason of any willful design on the
part of the appellant to injure the appellee. The mode of
ascertaining the compensation to which the plaintiff was entitled is found in instruction No. 11 given by the court. The
jury was told that if they find for the plaintiff they will give
him such damages as they believe from the evidence will
fairly compensate him for any suffering, mental or [380] physical, heretofore experienced by him directly resulting from the
injuries complained of, and for any suffering or disability that
they may believe from the testimony is reasonably certain he
will experience in the future as the direct and necessary result
of said injuries, and for any reduction in his power to earn
money in the future, if such reduction there be, directly resulting from the injury, not exceeding twenty-five thousand
dollars claimed in the petition."

The appellee at the time of the injury was about thirty
years of age, was a vigorous man and a laborious and useful
conductor. His conduct at the time of the burning, as described by the witnesses, deserved the admiration of, and
created a sympathy with, both judge and jury. His appearance before the jury after the injury, with a disfigured face
and limbs, as described in the testimony, doubtless excited a
feeling with every juror, however honest, that drove them to
fix the verdict beyond the proper limit of compensation.

We are to judge of this question by the light of the cases
before us involving verdicts where compensation was the
measure of damages, or even verdicts based upon the willful
neglect of the defendant, and where punitive damages were
sought and recovered. It is by comparison with verdict after
verdict in this state, where more flagrant wrongs were committed and punitive damages claimed in which juries composed of men, as we have the right to assume, of like intelligence, passion, and feeling, have made their findings for a
much less amount; and without enumerating the cases it will

be found that ten thousand dollars is the extent to which a verdict has been sustained by this court. Besides, in the case of [381] *Louisville etc. R. R. Co.* v. *Fox*, 11 Bush, 495, where the verdict was for thirty thousand dollars, and set aside as excessive, most of the cases are referred to. While we do not pretend to adjudge that no verdict would or ought to be sustained for a larger amount than ten thousand dollars, we do say that some moderation should be indulged in when arriving at verdicts in this class of cases. As said by the court in *Heddles* v. *Chicago etc. Ry. Co.*, 74 Wis. 239, where the injury resulted in the amputation of both legs of the plaintiff, and a verdict of thirty thousand dollars was set aside: "No rational being would change places with the injured man for an amount of gold that would fill the room of the court, yet no lawyer would contend that such is the legal measure of damages. Courts and juries must deal with such questions in a deliberate and practical sense." In our opinion the verdict in this case is excessive, and it is therefore reversed and cause remanded, with directions to set it aside and for proceedings consistent with this opinion.

NEGLIGENCE—EVIDENCE OF SUBSEQUENT ACTS.—When an accident has happened through the alleged negligence of a person, his subsequent acts in taking additional precautions to prevent other accidents are not admissible in evidence against him for the purpose of showing that such precautions were needed at the time of the accident: *Shinners* v. *Proprietors etc.*, 154 Mass. 168; 26 Am. St. Rep. 226, and note, with the cases collected. *Contra:* see *St. Louis etc. Ry. Co.*, v. *Weaver*, 35 Kan. 412; 57 Am. Rep. 176, and extended note. Evidence that soon after the happening of an accident to a traveler at a railroad crossing the company put it in good repair is admissible as tending to show that the railway company was under obligations to keep it in repair: *Hinkle* v. *Richmond etc. R. R. Co.*, 109 N. C. 472; 26 Am. St. Rep. 581, and note.

DAMAGES—EVIDENCE THAT PARTY INJURED HAD A WIFE AND CHILDREN: See *Central etc. Ry. Co.* v. *Kuhn*, 86 Ky. 578; 9 Am. St. Rep. 309; *Stephens* v. *Hannibal etc. R. R. Co.*, 96 Mo. 207; 9 Am. St. Rep. 336, and note; *Dayharsh* v. *Hannibal etc. R. R. Co.*, 103 Mo. 570; 23 Am. St. Rep. 900.

DAMAGES—MEASURE OF.—Where one has been injured by the negligence of another, the jury in estimating the damages may take into account his physical and mental suffering, his medical expenses, his loss of wages for the time he was prevented from working, and proper compensation for his being deprived by the injuries from following such calling as he could have otherwise followed: *Richmond etc. Ry. Co.* v. *Norment*, 84 Va. 167; 10 Am. St. Rep. 827, and note; *Heddles* v. *Chicago etc. Ry. Co.*, 77 Wis. 228; 20 Am. St. Rep. 106, and note; *Stephens* v. *Hannibal etc. R. R. Co.*, 96 Mo. 207; 9 Am. St. Rep. 336, and note.

WEAVER *v.* WEAVER.

[92 KENTUCKY, 491.]

WILLS—DEVISE TO WIFE AND CHILDREN.—Under a devise by a husband directly to his wife and children the wife takes a life estate only, unless there is some other provision in the will showing a contrary intention.

WILLS—DEVISE TO WIFE WITH DIRECTIONS TO MANAGE FOR BENEFIT OF CHILDREN.—Where a testator directs his executor to "take possession of his estate, both real and personal," and, after paying his debts, "deliver the remainder to his wife, who is requested and expected to manage the same to the best advantage in caring for and educating the children and supporting herself," the will is to be construed as giving to the widow a life estate in all the property, both real and personal, and the children take merely an estate in remainder expectant upon the decease of their mother.

George S. Fulton, for the appellant.

Nat. W. Halstead, for the appellee Shields.

491 LEWIS, J. The only question in this case is whether under the will of William T. Weaver his widow is entitled to an estate for life in the real and personal property devised, **492** remainder to his two children; or, as adjudged by the chancellor, each of the three persons take absolutely one-third thereof. The will is as follows: "I desire that John W. Shields takes possession of all my estate, both real and personal, including a policy of insurance on my life of three thousand dollars ($3,000.00), as executor of this my last will and testament and manage and dispose of same to the best possible advantage, that is so much thereof as may be necessary to pay all my just debts and personal expenses, and deliver the remainder to my wife, Mary Eliza Weaver, who is requested and expected to manage same to the best advantage in caring for and educating the children and supporting herself."

It seems to us the language of the testator makes his intention to give to his widow a life estate in all the property left after paying debts so plain that there is no need of resorting to rules of construction. He directs the executor to deliver to her not a part but all the remainder of his estate, the possession and control of which he manifestly intended she should have during her life. No provision is made for either division of the real or distribution of personal property, which would have to take place if she and the two children are each entitled absolutely and presently to one-third. Nor can it be inferred from the language used or any existing condition, that he intended her to be restricted to the possession and use of less than the whole estate left after payment of debts and delivered to her by the executor.

In the case of *Frank* v. *Unz*, 91 Ky. 621, the language of the will was: "The rest and residue of my estate, real, personal, and mixed, I give to my dear wife, Ann Maria Frank, for her own use and the benefit of our [493] children forever." He also appointed his wife executrix and guardian of the minor children, and requested she be allowed to qualify without security.

In that case, after examining and referring to numerous cases, the opinion was rendered that the widow took under the will a life estate, remainder to the children, this language being used: "It may be regarded as settled law in cases where the devise is by the husband directly to his wife and children that the wife takes a life estate only, unless there is something else in the will showing a contrary intention."

That case we regard as decisive of the question here presented. Indeed, the intention of the testator to give to his widow a life estate is more clearly indicated in this than in that case. For here, unlike that, the estate does not go into possession of the widow as executrix, but what is left after paying debts by an executor appointed for the purpose is directed to be delivered to her; nor is any provision made for a guardian of the infants to take possession of their share of the estate.

It seems to us, both the language of the testator in this case, and settled rules of construction applicable to it, require the will to be construed as giving to the widow a life estate in all the property, real and personal, and therefore the judgment is reversed for proceedings consistent with this opinion.

————

DEVISE TO WIDOW AND CHILDREN—WHAT WORDS WILL CONVEY A LIFE ESTATE ONLY TO FORMER.—This question is discussed in the notes to *Carpenter* v. *Van Olinder*, 11 Am. St. Rep. 99, and *Larsen* v. *Johnson*, 23 Am. St. Rep. 410, where the cases are collected.

SEWELL *v.* SEWELL.

[92 KENTUCKY, 500.]

INFANTS—AVOIDANCE OF DEEDS BY—ESTOPPEL.—The mere fact that a married woman who executed a deed while still a minor appeared to be of full age, and that the grantee, when he made his purchase, believed her to be of full age, will not estop her to avoid the deed, after she reaches her majority.

INFANTS—POWER OF TO SELL LAND—WHEN NOT IMPLIED.—A conveyance of land to an infant, in which no power to sell such land during his minority is conferred in express terms, implies merely the right to sell, when the disability of infancy is removed, and the law enables him to make a good title to the property. The existence of such a power cannot be inferred where a deed, by which a father conveys land to an infant married daughter, contains a clause which provides that "nothing is to prevent her selling the land, if she so desire, by her husband uniting with her."

INFANTS—DECREE CANCELING DEED OF INFANT MARRIED WOMAN—PROPER FORM OF.—When a married woman, during her minority, executed a deed of her land, by uniting with her husband, who had a contingent estate therein, dependent upon his surviving his wife, and brought suit, after becoming of full age, to avoid the conveyance, and it appeared that the grantee had made valuable improvements on the land, but not exceeding the value of the rent, no account should be taken of the rents and improvements, and the decree should merely require the petitioner to account for whatever part of the purchase money she may have received, with interest from the date of the deed, and leave to the grantee such title as her husband has.

William Lindsay, for the appellant.

J. B. White, Riddell and Son, and Thomas H. Hines, for the appellees.

501 PRYOR, J.   In October of the year 1881, Thomas Sewell, who was the grandfather of Thomas Sewell, Jr., the latter being the husband of the appellant, conveyed to the appellant a large tract of land lying in the county of Breathitt. The consideration was five hundred dollars paid, and that of love and affection.

502 It was provided by the deed that in the event the appellant, the wife, did not dispose of the land, it was to pass or descend to her husband at her death, with the further proviso: "But nothing is to prevent her selling said land if she so desire, and by her husband uniting with her."

On the 24th of February, 1882, about five months after the land had been conveyed to the appellant, the wife of Thomas Sewell, Jr., her husband sold it to William Day for one thousand nine hundred dollars.   Five hundred dollars was paid in cash, and notes executed to the husband for the balance, and those notes he sold and appropriated the proceeds to his own use.

The husband of the appellant was a lawless man, and had been convicted of manslaughter, and his confinement fixed in the state prison for ten years. The grantee in the deed was the surety of the husband of the appellant on his bail bond. The verdict of manslaughter was set aside and the husband left to convert the property of the wife to his own use, and this he seems to have done. It appears that the wife received but little, if any, benefit from the proceeds of sale.

It is evident that the reckless character of the husband of appellant induced the grandfather to make this conveyance to the wife, in order that she might have a support for herself and children. The condition of the husband and the circumstances surrounding the family was a sufficient inducement to the grandfather to secure something to this appellant and her children. She swears that she was compelled by her husband to execute the deed to Day, and while this does not affect the question involved, there is but little doubt that such was the case.

This petition was filed against the heirs of Day, who are appellees here, alleging this fraudulent conduct on the part of the husband, and that at the date of the deed to Day she was only nineteen years of age, and therefore incapacitated from executing the conveyance. Her petition was dismissed. There is no question as to the infancy of Mrs. Sewell when she signed the conveyance, and the only question presented is: Has she the right to rely on her infancy as a ground for canceling the deed? Of this we have no doubt. She made no representation as to her age, but when in the coercive power of her husband was compelled to execute it. If, however, she voluntarily signed the conveyance, still her infancy authorized the chancellor to cancel it. She was at the time a *feme covert* with two children, and her marital relation and condition might have authorized the ancestor of the appellees to believe that she was of full age, but if such a defense is availing the plea of infancy could scarcely be interposed as a defense. She is not estopped by the fact that she appeared of full age, and the grantee labored under this belief when he purchased the land.

It was held in *Buchanan* v. *Hubbard*, 96 Ind. 1, that a married woman laboring under the disabilities of both infancy

and coverture might at any time during coverture disaffirm
the deed made when an infant, and that her coverture, with
her appearance indicating that she had arrived at majority,
constituted no defense.

But it is said the clause in the deed giving the wife the
right to sell, by the husband uniting with her, conferred on
the wife the power to convey, although an infant, and in the
exercise of this power the deed was signed by the wife and
delivered. That an infant may have the power [504] conferred
on him by a grant to convey will not be doubted, but where
the infant is invested with the title by a plain deed the power
to sell, if conferred, implies only the right to sell when the
law enables him to make title, and that can be done when
the disability is removed. We know of no rule of law where
an absolute conveyance to the infant of the estate and the title
will authorize the grantor to remove the disability of infancy
and authorize the infant to trade as an adult.

In this case the conveyance is to a married woman, but it
provides that nothing shall prevent her from selling by the
husband uniting with her. This provision does not remove
the disability of either infancy or coverture, and she could
convey only in the same manner as if that provision in the
deed had been omitted. We have a statute authorizing and
designating the manner in which married women shall convey land, but it will not be insisted that the disability of infancy is removed because the grantor was a married woman
and the statute authorized married women to convey. This
clause in the deed by the grandfather was not intended to
enlarge the capacity of the wife to convey, but left her as the
deed found her, laboring under the disability of infancy, and
any conveyance made by her while an infant she can disaffirm. The conveyance should therefore be set aside on
equitable grounds in so far as it affects the appellant, but as
to the husband, who is a defendant to the action, his title,
although contingent upon his surviving his wife, passes by
the conveyance. It is not the question of the alleged fraud
on the part of the grantee that induces the chancellor to
grant the relief, but it arises from the inability of the married
woman, who was an infant, to dispose of her estate. It appears [505] that the appellant received but little, if any, benefit
from the sale of the land.

Her pleadings in the first instance, admitted five hundred
dollars, and this she should be held to account for, with the

interest. The appellees, or their ancestor, have made valuable improvements on the land, but not exceeding the value of the rent, and if they did the chancellor could not make the appellant account exceeding the rental value of the land. This, we think, is the equity of this case. The land is liable for the five hundred dollars with the interest from the date of the deed, but for no more. There will be no account taken of rents and improvements, but a judgment entered restoring to the appellant the possession, leaving the appellees as heirs at law of Day, the title that the husband of the appellant has. If he survives the wife they get the land, as his right is purely contingent.

Judgment reversed and remanded for proceedings consistent with this opinion.

INFANTS—DISAFFIRMANCE OF DEEDS BY.—When an infant wife joins her husband in the execution of a deed to her lands, in the absence of any act on her part sufficient to ratify the same, she may disaffirm it at any time during coverture: Stull v. Harris, 51 Ark. 294. For a full discussion of this subject see Searcy v. Hunter, 81 Tex. 644; 26 Am.St. Rep, 837, and note; and the monographic note to Craig v. Van Bebber, 18 Am. St. Rep. 584.

INFANTS—CONCEALMENT OR MISREPRESENTATION AS TO AGE.—ESTOPPEL BY: See extended note to Craig v. Van Bebber, 18 Am. St. Rep. 633.

COMMONWEALTH v. SCHWARTZ.

[92 KENTUCKY, 510.]

FALSE PRETENSES—WHAT CONSTITUTE.—If a person obtains a loan of money by a false pretense of an existing fact, although he intends to repay such money, he is guilty of the crime of obtaining money by false pretenses.

FALSE PRETENSES—DELIVERY OF PROPERTY, HOW FAR ESSENTIAL.—If the possession of goods has been delivered to the defendant, but the right of property has not passed, and after such delivery he obtains the title by false pretenses, he is guilty under the statute of obtaining the goods by false pretenses.

FALSE PRETENSES—DELIVERY—BAILEE, WHEN GUILTY OF CRIME.—If a banker collects money on commercial paper, and has possession of it as agent, and when the owner demands it induces him by false representations as to the solvency of the bank, to part with his title and lend the money to the bank, there is a complete transfer of property without delivery, and therefore it is not necessary in order to make out the offense against the statute to prove false pretenses relating to the delivery of the money.

W. J. Hendrick, attorney-general, and R. Reid Rogers, for the appellant.

Abbott and Rutledge, and O'Neal, Phelps, and Pryor, for the appellee.

[511] BENNETT, J. On the trial of the appellee, under an indictment for obtaining money by false pretenses, the court instructed **[512]** the jury absolutely to find for him. The commonweath appeals from the judgment acquitting the appellee under that instruction.

Are the indictment and the evidence sufficient to have authorized the jury to pass upon the question of the guilt or innocence of the appellee?

The indictment charges that the appellee obtained by false pretenses, and with the intention to defraud Maria Buchholtz, twenty-five hundred dollars; that he was a banker, and had a safe place to invest the money; that his bank was solvent and safe and able to repay her money at any time upon thirty days' notice; that the laws of the state did not allow him to pay her but four per cent interest, but he would give her six per cent interest, but would enter only four per cent on her book, if she would leave her money with him; that she relied upon said representation, and let him have the money, but his said representations were false and fraudulent, but made with a design to deceive her, and did deceive her, whereby he obtained the said twenty-five hundred dollars and appropriated the same to his own use, and she was permanently deprived of it, etc. The testimony of said Maria Buchholtz is in substance that on the twenty-fourth day of February, 1891, she took a note and mortgage which she held on some Chicago parties for twenty-five hundred dollars to the banking house of the appellee in the city of Louisville and employed him at the price of ten dollars to take charge of said papers and collect the money. He agreed to do so promptly and to notify her when the money was collected; that not hearing anything from the appellee, on the 9th of March, which was Monday, she again visited his banking house and inquired after the collection; **[513]** that the appellee told her that he had collected the money on Saturday previous, but too late to notify her. She then expressed a desire to have the money, and he replied that if she did not need the money to let it remain there, that he had a solid, safe place for it; that the bank was good and able to pay, or he was able to pay, and he would pay her four per cent for the money, and repay the money itself at any time after thirty days' notice. She declined to take four per cent. He then, after consulting with one of his partners, said that he would give her six per cent for the use of the money, but would make a memorandum of the transaction in her book showing only four per cent, as the law did not allow him, or that he was not allowed, to pay over four per cent. She then consented to let him have the money upon said terms, saying that if she should lose it she would be turned into the street, as that was all she had and no one to help her; and he replying, "Oh, we are able to pay."

The witness being a German and not speaking or understanding our language well there is some confusion and apparent contradiction in her evidence, but the foregoing is a fair synopsis of it. It was also in evidence that at the time mentioned the appellee and his bank were hopelessly insolvent, amounting to about four hundred and twenty thousand dollars net, and the jury would have been authorized to infer that the appellee knew it.

Article 13, section 2, chapter 29, General Statutes, provides: "If any person by false pretense, statement, or token, with intent to commit a fraud, obtain from another money, property, or other thing which may be the subject of larceny . . . . he shall be confined in the penitentiary," etc.

[514] If the appellee was enabled to borrow said money from Mrs. Buchholtz by falsely pretending that his bank was solvent when he knew or had reason to believe that it was not, is he guilty of the crime denounced by the statute *supra?* Upon that subject the rule is well settled that if a person obtains a loan of money from another by a false pretense of an existing fact, although he intended to repay it, he is guilty of the crime of obtaining money by false pretenses: See 7 Am. & Eng. Ency. of Law, pp. 752, 753, and notes. Also upon the subject that the false pretense must be of an existing fact, see *Glackan v. Commonwealth,* 3 Met. (Ky.) 232.

The false pretense of an existing fact in this case, if any false pretense there was, consists in the false representation that the appellee's bank was solvent and the loan was safe, when he knew or had reason to believe that it was insolvent and unable to pay, and which induced her to make the loan, or if he induced her to loan the money by false pretense that he had a safe place to invest it upon which she would realize six per cent, intending at the time to appropriate the money to his own use, to wit: that of the bank, knowing or having reason to believe that the bank was insolvent, although he intended to repay her, such false pretenses, if made as indicated, were sufficient to authorize the case to go to the jury.

But it is contended that, as the appellee, at the time he obtained the loan of the money, had it in his possession, the statutory offense of receiving money by false pretenses was not made out because, under the statute, the offense is not made out unless both possession and title are obtained by the false pretense, and as the appellee did not [515] obtain the possession by the false pretense, the offense was not made out.

The counsel for the appellee refer to many cases that sustain that proposition, and we concur with the general principle therein announced; but we think that principle does not apply to this case. For that principle only applies where it takes the delivery of the possession to complete the transfer of the title to the property. The statute reads, "obtain from another money or property." So, according to all the authorities, if it takes the delivery of the property to deprive the owner of dominion over it, the defendant must have obtained the delivery as well as the title before he can be made liable under the statute *supra*.

Mr. Wharton in the second volume of his work on Criminal Law, section 1227, 9th edition, correctly sums up the meaning of all the cases upon the subject in the following language: "A delivery of the property must be averred, as the result of false pretenses, in all cases in which the prosecution rests upon such delivery." Of course, as said, if the delivery is necessary to complete the transfer of the property, the prosecution in that case "rests" upon such delivery. To illustrate the rule: Suppose A, by false pretenses, buys a horse from B, but B does not deliver the horse to A; in such case it cannot be said that A has, in the sense of the statute, obtained B's property by false pretense, because, as yet, B has the property; he has not parted with it, and by reason of the fraud, he is not bound to part with it; hence he has not parted with his property by the false pretenses of A. But if the property is so situated that B can make a complete transfer of the property to A without delivering the [516] possession to him, and such transfer is obtained by false pretenses, then there is an offense against the statute. The rule is illustrated by the following authorities: 2 Bishop on Criminal Law, section 465, 7th edition, says: "If, after goods are delivered, the vendor becomes suspicious of the solvency of the purchaser, and expresses his intention to reclaim them, whereupon the latter, by false pretenses, induces him to relinquish his purpose, there is no offense against the statute, the sale having been completed before the false pretenses were made; and, though the right of stoppage *in transitu* may remain, the rule appears to be the same, the relinquishment of right not being deemed a parting with the goods. But, where the sale is on condition subsequent and a delivery thereupon, and afterwards the vendor is induced by false pretenses to give up his property in the goods, this is probably within the statute."

In the case of *People* v. *Haynes*, 11 Wend. 557, it was held by the supreme court that, where goods were delivered to a person, but the title did not pass to him except upon condition, and, after the delivery, the purchaser obtained the title by false pretenses, he was guilty of obtaining the goods by false pretenses. Upon appeal to the court of appeals that court approved of the principle announced, but reversed the case on the ground that the sale was absolute.

In the case of *Commonwealth* v. *Hutchison*, 114 Mass. 327, it was held, under a statute that provided if any person obtained, by false pretenses, the signature of another to a writing that would be forgery at common law, he should be punished, etc., that if it was necessary that the writing should be delivered in order to [517] complete the crime of forgery, and it was not delivered, an offense against the statute was not made out; but if the instrument was obligatory upon the signer without delivery, the offense against the statute was made out.

In the case of *Commonwealth* v. *Devlin*, 141 Mass. 423, it was held where there was a delivery of sheep to a purchaser, the title not to pass until the sheep were paid for, and the purchaser obtained the title by false pretenses, he was guilty, etc.

These cases establish the doctrine that it is only in case the delivery of the property is necessary in order to completely deprive the owner of it, that the false pretense must relate to such delivery. But if the delivery is not necessary to a complete transfer, the false pretenses need not relate to the delivery in order to make out the offense against the statute. And if the possession has been delivered to the party, but not the right of property, and he, after such delivery, obtains the title by false pretenses, he is guilty under the statute of obtaining goods, etc., by false pretenses. In this case the appellee had collected the woman's money, as her collecting agent, and had the possession of it as such agent; and when she demanded-it, he, recognizing her right and the character of his possession, induced her to part with her title to him. In such case, it is clear that the prosecution does not rest upon delivery, as there was a complete transfer of property without the delivery. The case is ordered to be certified, etc.

FALSE PRETENSES.—What constitutes the crime and the various other questions relating thereto will be found thoroughly discussed in the extended notes to *Barton* v. *People*, 25 Am. St. Rep. 378–392; *Perkins* v. *State*, 33 Am. Rep. 94, 95, and *Bowen* v. *State*, 40 Am. Rep. 75–80. To render one guilty of the crime of obtaining money under false pretenses, he must be shown to have made a representation which he knew was false, calculated and intended to deceive, and which did deceive the person from whom the money was obtained, and upon which such person reasonably relied at the time of the taking: *State* v. *Moore*, 111 N. C. 667.

CARR'S ADMINISTRATOR *v.* CARR.
[92 KENTUCKY, 552.]

DOWER—A DECREE OF DIVORCE BARS ALL CLAIM TO DOWER.

JUDGMENTS UPON CONSTRUCTIVE SERVICE OF PROCESS—WARNING ORDER, REQUISITES OF.—The omission of the name of the defendant's postoffice in the affidavit upon which the warning order is made will not invalidate a judgment rendered upon constructive service of process.

JUDGMENTS UPON CONSTRUCTIVE SERVICE OF PROCESS.—THE PREMATURE HEARING of an action commenced by publication of summons will not invalidate the judgment rendered therein.

JUDGMENT OF DIVORCE, WHEN WILL NOT BE VACATED ON PETITION. When a woman who has been divorced on the ground of desertion brings suit after her husband's death to recover a widow's part of his estate, averring that the decree of divorce is a nullity for the reason that she had no notice of the proceedings against her, and that, although she abandoned her husband, she was forced to do so by his cruel treatment, and, issue having been joined on these averments, it appears not only that she had actual knowledge of the pendency of the proceedings, but that, if she had made her defense, her husband would have been entitled to a decree in his favor, the equity of the case is against her, and the judgment of divorce, even if erroneous, cannot be reopened and vacated upon a petition in a court of chancery.

Fenton Sims and R. A. Burnett, for the appellants.

James B. Garnett, for the appellee.

552 HOLT, C. J. November 12, 1888, J. M. Carr, living in Trigg county, sued his wife, the appellee, Rhoda J. Carr,

then living but two or three miles from him, but in the state
of Tennessee, in the circuit court of his county for a divorce
upon the ground of abandonment without cause.

Being a nonresident a warning order was made against her
to appear at the next term of the court, beginning more than
sixty days thereafter, to wit: on February 11, 1889, and an
attorney was appointed to defend for her. He filed a report,
and the evidence for the plaintiff having been taken the cause
was submitted on February 19, 1889, resulting in a judgment
of absolute divorce to the husband. He died in July, 1889.
Although the appellee knew of the pendency of the suit she
remained silent until August 23, 1889, when she brought this
action against his administrator and heirs, claiming that the
judgment of divorce was void, and that she was therefore entitled to share in his estate as his widow. The lower court so
held.

By our statute a divorce bars all claim to dower: Gen.
Stats., c. 52, art. 4, sec. 14.

If, however, the judgment was void it would not, of course,
affect the marital rights of the appellee. She claims that she
was compelled to the abandonment by the cruel treatment of
J. M. Carr; that she was not before the court upon even constructive notice, because the affidavit upon which the warning order was made was substantially defective, and therefore
the order of warning [554] was void; and, if this be not true,
yet that the judgment of divorce was prematurely rendered.

If the court granting the divorce had no jurisdiction, then,
of course, its action is void. What facts constitute a want of
jurisdiction is, however, often a troublesome question.

The Civil Code, section 60, provides that the warning order
and appointment of an attorney to defend is a constructive
service.

Section 58 provides, however, that the clerk of the court
shall not make the warning order except upon an affidavit of
the plaintiff stating the nonresidence of the defendant, and
in what country he resides or may be found, and the name
of the place wherein a postoffice is kept nearest to the place
where he resides or may be found; or stating the affiant's
ignorance of these matters so far as they are unknown to
him.

The affidavit upon which the warning order was made stated
that the appellee resided in Stewart county, Tennessee, and
was then absent from this state, but the name of her post-

office was left blank.   Did this omission render the judgment void for want of jurisdiction?

An action against a nonresident upon construction service is of an *ex parte* nature.   The right to it is based altogether upon the statute.   It has, therefore, very properly been held by this court that in such a proceeding the statute must be so far strictly followed as to show a substantial compliance with it.   A decree in such a cause may, however, be void or merely erroneous.   If it be had without any warning order and the appointment of an attorney to defend for the nonresident it is of course void.   There is then no construotive service.

[555] The judgment now in question, however, is that of a court of general jurisdiction, rendered upon a warning order, entered in proper form, and after the filing of the report of the attorney appointed to defend.   A warning order under the present practice takes the place of an order of publication under the old mode of procedure.

An act of our legislature of 1815 authorized proceedings against unknown heirs, but provided that before an order of publication should be made the complainant should file in the clerk's office with his bill an affidavit stating that the names of the heirs were unknown to him.

In *Hynes* v. *Oldham*, 3 T. B. Mon. 266, it was held, however, that the failure to do so rendered the decree merely erroneous, and not void.

This case was followed in the subsequent one of *Benningfield* v. *Reed*, 8 B. Mon. 102, and both are cited with approval in *Newcomb* v. *Newcomb*, 13 Bush, 544; 26 Am. Rep. 222.   In analogy to these cases we think the failure to give the name of the postoffice in the affidavit did not render the decree void, nor was it a nullity even if the action was prematurely heard.

The appellee, after the death of her former husband, brings her suit to recover a widow's part of his estate.   She avers that while she abandoned him, yet she was forced to do so by his cruel treatment of her.   Issue is joined as to it, and the evidence being taken and case fully prepared it is perfectly manifest the decreee in the divorce suit was correct. She fails altogether to show any ill-treatment of her by the husband.   It follows that if she had appeared and made defense to the divorce suit her husband would have been entitled to the decree.   The result would not have been changed.

Not only therefore [556] does it appear that she knew of the pendency of the suit, but that if she had defended it the result would have been the same. The equity of the case is against her, and now, upon a rehearing of the matter involved in the former suit, and in which she claims she was prejudiced by want of proper notice of its pendency, it appears nothing more was therein granted to the complainant than he was entitled to in equity and good conscience.

Under these circumstances the judgment of divorce should not be reopened and vacated upon petition as erroneous even if this be allowable in such a character of action. Its correctness has again had full and fair investigation; the appellee has had her day in court, and it now appears to have been a proper judgment.

It follows that the appellee has no right in the estate of her former husband, and the judgment is reversed, with directions to dismiss her petition.

DOWER—WHETHER BARRED BY DIVORCE.—A wife is not entitled to dower, nor to any part of her husband's estate, so long as a decree of divorce in favor of the husband for the fault of the wife remains in force, of the pendency of the application for which she had personal service: *McCraney* v. *McCraney*, 5 Iowa, 232; 68 Am. Dec. 702, and note. In a state where divorce allows both parties to remarry, a decree in favor of a wife with permanent alimony bars dower: *Tatro* v. *Tatro*, 18 Neb. 395; 53 Am. Rep. 820. A wife's right of dower, which is vested in her prior to divorce, is not divested thereby, unless the statute has expressly so declared: *Van Cleaf* v. *Burns*, 118 N. Y. 549; 16 Am. St. Rep. 782, and note. See also the notes to *Adams* v. *Storey*, 25 Am. St. Rep. 396, and *Boykin* v. *Rain*, 65 Am. Dec. 358.

MARRIAGE AND DIVORCE—VACATING DECREES OF DIVORCE.—See the extended note to *Greene* v. *Greene*, 61 Am. Dec. 459–468. Equity will annul, at the suit of the widow, a judgment of divorce obtained by her husband in his lifetime on the ground of desertion, where it appears that the separation was voluntary, and that the husband by false representations, obtained service of process by publication when personal service could have been had: *Johnson* v. *Coleman*, 23 Wis. 452; 99 Am. Dec. 193. Equity will set aside a decree of divorce which was fraudulently obtained: *Morton* v. *Morton*, 16 Col. 358; *Edson* v. *Edson*, 108 Mass. 590; 11 Am. Rep. 393; *Adams* v. *Adams*, 51 N. H. 388; 12 Am. Rep. 134; *Rush* v. *Rush*, 46 Iowa, 648; 26 Am. Rep. 179; *Brown* v. *Grove*, 116 Ind. 84; 9 Am. Rep. 823, and note. A judgment of divorce from bed and board should not be set aside on the ground that the defendant supposed it to be a divorce from the bond of matrimony, where his motion for such relief was made more than a year after he had notice of the judgment: *Jones* v. *Jones*, 78 Wis. 446.

BRYANT'S ADMINISTRATOR *v.* DUNGAN.

[92 KENTUCKY, 626.]

WILLS—CONDITION SUBSEQUENT—NONCOMPLIANCE WITH WITHOUT FAULY.
A devisee who takes a vested remainder subject to the performance of a
condition subsequent does not forfeit his interest by noncompliance with
that condition, if such noncompliance is not the result of his own fault.

O. H. Waddle, for the appellants.

Will C. Curd, for the appellee.

[626] BENNETT, J.   William Bryant, in a codicil to his will,
gave his wife one hundred acres of land, to be taken from the
homestead place.   The appellee, his grandson, who was living
with him, and whom he had raised, is provided for in the
codicil as follows: "The remainder of said farm to be sold
and divided as in my former will, except E. L. Dungan, who
I will and devise the above one hundred acres of land willed
to my wife, Sarah, to go to my grandson, E. L. Dungan, at
the death of his grandma, Sarah Bryant, upon the condition
that he stays with her and supports her and cares for her
until her death, then he is to have her part of said farm and
homestead; otherwise to be void if he shall fail to perform my
will."

The testator having died, his wife renounced the provisions
of the will in her favor, and notwithstanding the appellee was
ready, willing, and proffered to comply with the conditions of
the will, and who was nowise in fault or remiss in his treatment of his grandmother, she refused to live with him on the
place and to allow him to support and care for her; but she
went to live with one of her daughters, with whom she is now
living.

The appellants contend that the conditions of the will requiring the appellee to live with his grandmother, and support and care for her, were conditions preceding the investiture
of title to the one hundred acres of land in him; and the precedent condition not having been complied with, though without fault on his part, no estate passed to him.   On the other
hand, the appellee contends that his title was that of a vested
remainder, and the support, care, etc., required of him by the
will were conditions subsequent, a failure to comply with
which would [629] not operate as a forfeiture of his remainder
interest, unless such failure was the result of his fault.   The
language of the will is: "Except E. L. Dungan, who I will

and devise the above one hundred acres of land willed to my wife, Sarah." The language quoted clearly conveys to the appellee an immediate title to the one hundred acres of land, which, taken in connection with the life estate devised to his grandmother, is a vested remainder. And the subsequent expression: "To go to my grandson, E. L. Dungan, at the death of his grandmother, Sarah Bryant, then he is to have her part of said farm and homestead," evidently relate to the time that the appellee was to enjoy the estate. The will also provides: "Otherwise, to be void if he shall fail to perform my will."

If the conditions mentioned in the will were conditions procedent, the last clause quoted would be unnecessary; but the devisor evidently understood that he had devised to the appellee a vested remainder, and he meant by the clause to make the devise void if he failed to comply with the conditions. From what has been said, it is evident the appellee took a vested remainder; and the conditions imposed were conditions subsequent; and it follows that the noncompliance with those conditions did not divest him of his estate, unless the noncompliance was the result of his fault, which was not the case here, because he was ready and willing to comply, and proffered to comply, but his grandmother refused.

The case of *Irvine* v. *Irvine*, 12 Ky. Law Rep. 827, is not like this case. In that case no title passed to the devisee until the death of the life tenant, and then the title did not pass, unless the devisee had complied with certain [630] conditions. But here, as said, there was a vested remainder, and the conditions were conditions subsequent.

The judgment is affirmed.

DEVISE—CONDITIONS SUBSEQUENT IN: See extended note to *Coppage* v. *Alexander*, 38 Am. Dec. 160. A devise of an estate to the sons of the testator, "they jointly and severally paying" to his daughters a certain sum within a specified time, is strictly conditional upon the payment of the money within the time limited: *Wheeler* v. *Walker*, 2 Conn. 196; 7 Am. Dec. 264, and note; to the same effect, see *Thomas* v. *Kelly*, 3 S. C. 214; 16 Am. Rep. 716. A devise of property on condition that the devisee shall provide for the son of the testator until he shall become of age is a gift on a condition subsequent, and if the son die during the life of the testator the devisee will take an absolute title to the property: *Morse* v. *Hayden*, 82 Me. 227, see also *Phillips* v. *Wood*, 16 R. I. 274. Where a condition subsequent in a devise is bad, the estate devised is discharged of the condition and is absolute in the first taker: *Den* v. *Gibbons*, 22 N. J. L. 117; 51 Am. Dec. 253, and note; *Moore* v. *Sanders*, 15 S. C. 440; 40 Am. Rep. 703.

CASES

SUPREME COURT

OF

MINNESOTA.

STATE v. ASLESEN.

[50 MINNESOTA, 5.]

CONSTITUTIONAL LAW.—STATUTE REGULATING MANUFACTURE AND SALE OF LARD SUBSTITUTES and compounds, and of food prepared therefrom, requiring the seller to disclose to the purchaser, by label or card, the nature and ingredients of the article offered for sale, is valid as a legitimate exercise of the police power.

CONSTITUTIONAL LAW—REGULATION OF SALE OF FOOD COMPOUNDS.—No man has a constitutional right to keep secret the composition of substances which he sells to the public as articles of food. Therefore, a statute requiring the seller of "lard substitutes" to give notice of that fact to the purchaser, by labeling the article with a quantitative analysis of its ingredients, does not deprive the seller of his property without due process of law, but is a valid exercise of police power.

C. M. Hertig and Oliver and Showalter, for the appellants.

R. D. Russell, L. A. Dunn, Ace P. Abell, J. F. McGee, and Moses E. Clapp, attorney-general, for the respondent.

* MITCHELL, J. Each of the defendants was convicted of a violation of the provisions of the Laws of 1891, chapter 12, regulating the manufacture and sale of lard, and of lard compounds and substitutes, and of foods prepared therefrom. Defendant Aslesen was convicted of selling a "lard substitute" called "cottoline," consisting of a mixture of beef stearine and refined cotton-seed oil, without affixing to the package containing the same a label containing the words "lard substitute," together with "the names and approximate proportions of the several constituents contained in the mixture or compound." The defendant Bassett was convicted of selling certain articles of food prepared with this same "lard

substitute," without furnishing the purchaser with a card containing the required notice of that fact.

Upon the trials each of the defendants offered to prove that "cottoline was a wholesome, palatable, and nutritious article of food; also that it does not resemble lard in appearance, and has never been ᵗ sold as lard." This evidence the trial court excluded on the ground that, under the provisions of the act, the facts sought to be proved were immaterial. The court's construction of the act was clearly correct. It is evident from its language that its provisions are not confined to articles "made in the semblance of lard, or as an imitation of lard," or which so resemble lard that they are liable to be sold and passed off on the public as lard, and which, for the sake of brevity, we may call "simulated articles." The act applies as well to any substance made as "a substitute for lard, and which is designed to take the place of lard," and which consists of any mixture or compound of animal or vegetable oils or fats other than hog fat in the form of lard, whether such substance resembles lard in appearance or not. Neither is the act limited in its application to substances that are unwholesome. It applies alike to all "lard substitutes" consisting of the specified mixture or compound, regardless of their appearance or actual hygienic qualities. The cases therefore come down to the question whether the act, as thus construed, is valid as a legitimate exercise of the police power of the state.

Had the act absolutely prohibited the manufacture and sale of all such articles, its validity might well be questioned. The doctrine of *Butler* v. *Chambers*, 36 Minn. 71, 1 Am. St. Rep. 638, does not go far enough to sustain such an act; for in that case we construed the "oleomargarine" act as applying to and aimed at those compounds resembling butter in appearance and flavor, and which for that reason were liable to deceive and mislead purchasers and consumers as to the real nature of the product; and the act was sustained upon the theory that if, in the reasonable opinion of the legislature, this fraud or imposition on the public could not be effectually prevented, except by prohibiting the sale and manufacture of the "simulated articles" altogether, it was competent for them to do so.

But the act now under consideration is one of regulation, merely. It does not prohibit the sale of these "lard substitutes," or of articles of food prepared with them, but simply

requires that the seller shall disclose to the purchaser, by
label or card, the nature and ingredients of the article which
he offers for sale, so that the purchaser may be fully advised
as to just what he is buying. As applied to [8] such articles
of food, we are unable to see why such regulations are not
valid, as a legitimate exercise of the police power. We think
the case is not distinguishable in principle from *Stolz* v.
Thompson, 44 Minn. 271, in which we sustained the validity
of a similar regulation with reference to the sale of baking-
powders containing alum. It is a matter of common knowledge that substitutes for old and well-known articles of food
are becoming quite common at the present day. Being com-
paratively new on the market, their qualities and ingredients
are not usually a matter of common knowledge. The nature
of the ingredients of these compounds is usually not discernible by the appearance of the article, and the means of ascertaining what these ingredients are, are not available to the
mass of the people. Many of them, like cottoline, may be
entirely wholesome, but, in this day of the common adultera-
tion of articles of food, others may be composed of deleterious
ingredients. And what may be wholesome for one person
may be unwholesome for another. Moreover it is also a
matter of common knowledge that whether well founded or
not, there is a popular prejudice against certain ingredients
as an article of food. This is so, for example, with cotton-
seed oil. Many would not purchase or use a lard substitute
of which that oil was an ingredient, or any article of food prepared with it. In view of all these facts, the legislature has
seen fit to require the seller of these lard substitutes to label
the article which he sells with what, for convenience, we may
call a quantitative analysis of its ingredients, and to require
the seller of any article of food prepared with such lard substitute to give notice of the fact to the purchaser, so that he
may know just what he is buying. This certainly does not
deprive the seller of his property without due process of law.
No man has a constitutional right to keep secret the composition of substances which he sells to the public as articles of
food. Such regulations do certainly have some real or substantial relation to the objects aimed at, to wit, as expressed
in the title of the act, "to prevent fraud, and to preserve the
public health." They do not impair any fundamental rights
of life, liberty, or property. Under such circumstances, we
cannot say that the legislature has exceeded the legitimate

exercise of the police power of the state. If the legislation
is unwise or inexpedient, the only appeal is to "the ultimate
tribunal of the public judgment, exercised either in the pressure of public opinion, or by means of the suffrage."

Judgments affirmed, and causes remanded, with directions
to carry the sentences into execution.

CONSTITUTIONAL LAW—STATE OR MUNICIPAL REGULATION OF SALE OF
ARTICLES OF FOOD: See the extended note to *State* v. *Goodwill*, 25 Am.
St. Rep. 888. Laws providing for the detection and prevention of imposition and fraud, in the manufacture and sale of articles of food are free from
constitutional objection: *People* v. *Wagner*, 86 Mich. 594; 24 Am. St. Rep.
141, and note; *State* v. *Campbell*, 64 N. H. 402; 10 Am. St. Rep. 419; and
extended note; *Butler* v. *Chambers*, 36 Minn. 69; 1 Am. St. Rep. 638, and
extended note.

LUND v. WHEATON ROLLER MILL COMPANY.

[50 MINNESOTA, 36.]

CORPORATIONS.—UNREGISTERED SALE AND TRANSFER OF CORPORATE STOCK,
which either by statute or charter is declared to be transferable only on
the books of the corporation, is effectual to pass the title to the property as against subsequent attaching creditors of the vendor, who have
notice of the transfer before any sale is made under their writ.

Thomas O'Hair, and Ferguson and Kneeland, for the appellants.

J. W. Reynolds and W. H. Townsend, for the respondents.

[37] DICKINSON, J. The defendant, the Wheaton Roller Mill
Company, is a corporation created under 1878 General
Statutes, chapter 34, title 2. In June, 1890, one Howell
owned and held forty shares of the stock of the corporation,
certificates for which had been issued to him. At that time
he, in good faith and for a valuable consideration, sold and
assigned such stock to the intervenor, the Grant County Bank,
but no entry of such transfer was made in the books of the
mill company.

In November of the same year, in an action prosecuted by
the plaintiffs against Howell—who appeared on the books
of the corporation as being still the owner of the stock—the
stock was levied upon by virtue of a writ of attachment. The
plaintiffs then had no notice or knowledge that the stock had
been transferred by Howell. Afterwards the plaintiffs recovered judgment in the action against Howell, and under execu-

tion issued thereon, in December, 1890, the stock was levied
on and sold, the plaintiffs being the purchasers. The
plaintiffs had notice of the intervenor's claim when the levy
was made under the execution. The sole question to which
attention will be directed is whether by force of the statute
the sale and assignment of the stock to the bank by Howell
was ineffectual as to attaching creditors of the assignor, by
reason of the fact that no entry of the transfer had been made
in the books of the corporation.

The statute referred to is 1878 General Statutes, chapter 34,
section 8, which, by force of section 110 of the same chapter
(1866 General Statutes, chapter 34, section 46), is made
applicable with respect to corporations organized under title
2. It is in terms as follows: "The transfer of shares is not
valid, except as between the parties thereto, until it is
regularly entered on the books of the company, so far as to
show the names of the persons [88] by and to whom transferred,
the numbers or other designation of the shares, and the date
of the transfer. . . . . The books of the company shall be so
kept as to show intelligibly the original stockholders their
respective interests, the amount which has been paid in on
their shares, and all transfers thereof; and such books, or a
correct copy thereof, so far as the items mentioned in this section are concerned, shall be subject to the inspection of any
person desiring the same."

It is also provided by 1878 General Statutes, chapter 34,
section 114 (1866 General Statutes, chapter 34, section 49),
that "the stock of any such corporation shall be deemed
personal property, and be transferable only on the books
of such corporation, in such form as the directors prescribe. . . . . "

The law cannot be said to be generally settled and uniform
as to whether an unregistered sale and transfer of stock,
which either by statute or charter is declared to be transferable only on the books of the corporation, is effectual to pass
the property as against subsequent attaching creditors of the
vendor. The decisions are contradictory. But we do not
feel ourselves at liberty to now treat the question as a new
one in this state. As early as May, 1879, in the case of *Baldwin* v. *Canfield*, 26 Minn. 43; it was held that an unregistered
transfer of stock in pledge to secure indebtedness of the
pledgor was effectual. This decision was cited and followed
in *Joslyn* v. *St. Paul Distilling Co.*, 44 Minn, 183. The court

in *Baldwin* v. *Canfield*, 26 Minn. 43, referring to the above-cited 1866 General Statutes, chapter 34, section 49, said: "Provisions of this kind are intended solely for the protection and benefit of the corporation; they do not incapacitate a shareholder from transferring his stock without any entry upon the corporation books [citing authorities]. Except as against the corporation, the owner and holder of shares of stock may, as an incident of his right of property, transfer the same as any other personal property of which he is the owner." It is true that the court made no reference to section 8 of that chapter, which by force of 1866 General Statutes, chapter 34, section 46, became a part of the law concerning corporations created under title 2. An examination of the briefs in that case shows that the latter section was not referred to, and it seems probable that the attention of the court was [39] not directed to it.

When the structure of the statute is observed, it will be seen that both counsel and court might naturally fail to discover the applicability to title 2 of this section 8, found in title 1, and relating to a subject specifically treated of in section 49 of title 2. However that may be, and even if a consideration of the provisions of section 8 might possibly have led to a different conclusion as to the validity of the pledge, that decision, made nearly thirteen years ago, and hitherto unquestioned, should now be deemed decisive of the question. It has probably been generally so regarded, and it is believed that transfers of stocks in pledge and by sale have been extensively made, without having the transactions entered on the books of the corporations. The rule of *stare decisis* should deter us from now declaring the statute law to be different from what it has heretofore been pronounced to be. We therefore follow former decisions, without entering upon a consideration of the construction which might be given to section 8 of the statute if the question were 'a new one. In deciding the case in this way, we would not be understood as expressing the opinion that a proper construction of the statute would lead to a different conclusion. The tendency of many decisions is in accordance with the rule heretofore announced in this court and now followed: See *Robinson* v. *National Bank*, 95 N. Y. 637; *McNeil* v. *Tenth Nat. Bank*, 46 N. Y. 325, 331; 7 Am. Rep. 341, and cases cited; *Finney's Appeal*, 59 Pa. St. 398; *Telford & F. Turnpike Co.* v. *Gerhab* (Pa., March 19, 1888), 13 Atl. Rep. 90; *Broadway Bank* v. *McElrath*, 13 N. J. Eq.

24; *Hunterdon County Bank* v. *Nassau Bank,* 17 N. J. Eq. 496; *Thurber* v. *Crump,* 86 Ky. 408; *Continental Nat. Bank* v. *Eliot Nat. Bank,* 7 Fed. Rep. 369; Cook on Stocks, sec. 487.

Judgment affirmed.

CORPORATIONS—VALIDITY OF TRANSFERS OF STOCK NOT ENTERED ON THE BOOKS.—A by-law of a corporation prohibiting the transfer of the stock of the corporation, except by a formal transfer on its books, does not, in the absence of a constitutional or statutory prohibition, render invalid a transfer of its stock by a transfer of the certificate thereof. Such a transfer is good against an execution creditor of the stockholder, who did not have notice of the transfer when the execution was levied, but was notified of it before he purchased the stock at a sale under the execution: *Wilson* v. *St. Louis etc. Ry. Co.,* 108 Mo. 588; 32 Am. St. Rep. 624, and note with the cases collected. See also the notes to the following cases where this subject is thoroughly discussed: *Jennings* v. *Bank,* 12 Am. St. Rep. 152; *Nicollet Nat. Bank* v. *City Bank,* 8 Am. St. Rep. 647, and the extended note to *Dickinson* v. *Central Nat. Bank,* 37 Am. Rep. 353-356.

MERCHANTS' INSURANCE COMPANY *v.* PRINCE.

[50 MINNESOTA, 53.]

CUSTOM AS TO INSURANCE—WHEN UNREASONABLE.—A local custom that insurance agents, after their agency has terminated, may cancel policies issued through them within a certain period, so that they may turn over the insurance represented by such policies to some other company of which they may have the agency, is unreasonable and void as being opposed to established rules of law governing the relation of principal and agent.

CUSTOM—WHEN UNREASONABLE AS BETWEEN PRINCIPAL AND AGENT.—A custom that an agent, as soon as his agency is terminated, may at once for his own advantage undo, so far as it can be undone, all the business that he has done for his principal, is unreasonable, opposed to the policy of the law, and void.

Morphy, Gilbert and Morphy, and H. C. Eller, for the appellants.

Morris and Williams, for the respondents.

[53] GILFILLAN, C. J. This is an action by an insurance company against its agents for premiums alleged to have been received by them on policies issued by it through them as its local agents in St. Paul. It is conceded that the authority of the defendants as agents was terminated by plaintiff in the spring of 1890, though there seems some question as to the exact date of the withdrawal of authority. They had been its local agents some ten years. The real controversy in the

case is upon the claim of defendants to a right, after their
agency was terminated, to cancel policies issued by it through
them within a certain period, say since the date of their last
report to the company; not to cancel them for the benefit of
the company, or because its interest might require it, but to
do so in their own interest, and so that they might turn over
the insurance represented by the policies to some other company of which they [56] might have the agency.   There was
no attempt to prove any express contract between the plaintiff and defendants to continue the authority of the latter to
cancel policies after the termination of their agency generally.
But that right or authority is claimed by reason of an alleged
custom in the insurance business in St. Paul.   Evidence to
prove such a custom was introduced by defendants.

The plaintiff makes the point that the evidence was not
sufficient to establish such a custom.   We will not, however,
consider that point, but come to the question presented by an
instruction to the jury pursuant to the defendants' fifth request, as follows: " If you find from the evidence that it was
a common, recognized custom in St. Paul at the time here in
question that, upon the change of agency, the retiring agent
canceled and took up all policies already paid for if he saw
fit, as a part of the closing of the agency, you will find for the
defendants as to those policies."   The custom referred to is
characterized in defendants' fourth request, likewise given
and excepted to, thus: "That agents, in case of change in
agency, considered the business worked up and secured by
them belonged to them, to the extent that, at least, took up
all policies issued or delivered since the making of the last
correct report pending the change of agency."   As one of the
witnesses for the defendants testified, the agent generally con-
siders the business he works up as his own, and does with
it as he sees fit.   The proposition that any part of the business
done by an agent for his principal, and for doing which the
principal pays him, belongs to the agent, rather upsets our
notions of the rights growing out of the relation of principal
and agent.   Is such a local custom valid?   Is it reasonable?
For, if unreasonable in the legal sense, it is not valid.   While
a custom may not be reasonable merely because it is not contrary to any established rule of law, there is a uniform concurrence of authorities that, in the legal sense, it is to be
deemed unreasonable if it be opposed to the policy of the law,
as where it tends to unsettle well-established rules of law,

established for the protection of the rights of parties. Thus of a usage that a factor may pledge the goods of his principal (*Newbold* v. *Wright,* 4 Rawle, 195); that the master of a vessel may sell the cargo without necessity (*Bryant* v. *Commonwealth Ins. Co.,* 6 Pick. 131); to charge [57] interest where the statute provides none shall be charged (*Henry* v. *Risk,* 1 Dall. 265); authorizing a landlord to re-enter for a forfeiture in a manner different from that provided by law (*Stoever* v. *Whitman,* 6 Binn. 417); requiring two thousand two hundred and forty pounds for a ton when the statute provides two thousand pounds shall be a ton, unless otherwise specified in the contract (*Evans* v. *Myers,* 25 Pa. St. 114; *Green* v. *Moffett,* 22 Mo. 529); that when a seller of goods receives the consignee's note without the buyer's indorsement, the latter is discharged, and the maker of the note alone is responsible (*Prescott* v. *Hubbell,* 1 McCord, 94); so of a usage contrary to the rule *caveat emptor: Barnard* v. *Kellogg,* 10 Wall. 383; *Dickinson* v. *Gay,* 7 Allen, 29; 83 Am. Dec. 656. The cases of *Johnson* v. *Gilfillan,* 8 Minn. 395, and *Globe Milling Co.* v. *Minneapolis Elevator Co.,* 44 Minn. 153, are in the same line.

These are but a few of the cases that might be cited to the same effect. But where the rule of law is established, not merely to define the rights of parties under particular circumstances, but to protect those rights by enforcing good faith and fair dealing between them, the reason for excluding local usage to the contrary of the rule is still stronger. The requirement of good faith is the basis of the rules of law governing the duties of an agent to his principal. The agent is held to the utmost good faith in the business of his principal, and, to secure this, he is not permitted to place himself in a position antagonistic to the interest of his principal, nor to secure any advantage to himself from the business without the full and free consent of the principal. It was because such a usage would tend to subvert this principle of the law of agency it was held in *Farnsworth* v. *Hemmer,* 1 Allen, 494, 79 Am. Dec. 756, and *Raisin* v. *Clark,* 41 Md. 158, 20 Am. Rep. 66, that a usage permitting an agent employed to sell or exchange property to take commissions from both seller and buyer was void.

There could be no question that, pending his agency, an agent of an insurance company authorized to issue policies cannot, without the consent of the company, treat the business represented by policies issued through him as in any sense his business, or the business of any one but his principal; and, if he has authority to cancel policies, he could only exercise it for the benefit of his principal. [58] A usage that he might cancel policies for his own advantage would be so subversive of all the principles underlying the rules of the law of agency as to be void. Defendants do not claim otherwise. Their claim amounts really to this: that by the usage, upon the revocation by the company of the revocable authority conferred on the agent, a part of the business, conceded to be that of the company up to that time, becomes the business of the agent, so that he may do with it what he pleases, and that as to that part of the business the revocation clothes him with power that he did not have before. The proposition would justify a custom that any agent, as soon as his authority should be withdrawn, might at once, for his own advantage, undo, so far as it could be undone, all the business that he had done for his principal.

The rules of law established to secure and enforce good faith in fiduciary relations are so necessary and so salutary that no local custom to the contrary can be sustained.

Order reversed.

A CUSTOM OR USAGE, NOT ACCORDING TO LAW, cannot be set up to control the law: *Columbus etc. Iron Co.* v. *Tucker*, 48 Ohio St. 41; 29 Am. St. Rep. 528, and note, and such a custom cannot be held good: *Missouri Pac. R. R. Co.* v. *Fagan*, 72 Tex. 127; 13 Am. St. Rep. 776; *Hopper* v. *Sage*, 112 N. Y. 530; 8 Am. St. Rep. 771 and note. See also the extended notes to *Smith* v. *Clews*, 11 Am. St. Rep. 632, 633; and *Governor* v. *Withers*, 50 Am. Dec. 103-105.

SLIPP v. HARTLEY.

[50 MINNESOTA, 118.]

PARTNERSHIP—INDORSEMENT BY MEMBER OF FIRM—WHO BOUND BY. When notes are indorsed by a member of a firm, not on account of any partnership liability or transaction, but solely for accommodation purposes, a substitute note given to take up the prior notes, in the hands of a third person having knowledge of the facts is not enforceable against the firm, nor the members thereof, except as against the one so indorsing without affirmative evidence of prior authority to execute, or subsequent ratification of such execution by the other partners.

PARTNERSHIP—DECLARATIONS OF PARTNER WHEN EVIDENCE AGAINST FIRM.—Admissions or declarations of a partner made during the existence of the partnership while engaged in transacting its legitimate business, or relating to matters within the scope of the partnership, are admissible against the firm.

PARTNERSHIP—DECLARATIONS OF PARTNER WHEN NOT EVIDENCE AGAINST
FIRM.—A partner's declarations or admissions do not bind his associates in concerns and transactions foreign to the partnership, and he
cannot, by such declarations or admissions, bring a transaction within
the scope of the partnership business, when in fact it had no connection
therewith.

W. W. Billson and Leon E. Lum, for the appellant.

W. H. Mantor and A. Y. Merrill, for the respondent.

120 COLLINS, J. This was an action upon a promissory
note signed by the firm of Witt, Hartley & Co., payable to
the order of D. E. Slipp, by whom it was indorsed to plaintiff,
his brother, after maturity. Before delivery to the payee it
was indorsed by Mr. Leland, and by the firm of Hartley
Brothers and Dewar. The appellant, G. G. Hartley, was the
only answering defendant, and at the time of the making and
delivery of this paper he was a member of both firms before
mentioned. There was no contention over his claim upon
the trial **121** that the note sued upon was only given as a
substitute and to take up two past-due notes made payable to
one Mrs. Pangborn, one signed by Mr. Leland, the other by
the firm of Witt and Leland, of which he was a member, both
indorsed before delivery by D. E. Slipp and the firm of Hartley Brothers and Dewar, solely for the accommodation of their
respective makers. It was also undisputed that these two
notes, as well as the one sued upon, were signed and indorsed
by B. F. Hartley, a member of both firms, without the
knowledge or consent of appellant. As the Pangborn notes
were not indorsed on account of any firm liability or partnership transaction, but, admittedly and solely, for accommodation purposes, and the note in litigation was simply a
substitute, given to take up the Pangborn paper, which had
gotten into the hands of D. E. Slipp with knowledge of the
facts, it was not enforceable against either firm, or against the
individual members of either firm, except the one who signed
or indorsed the same, without affirmative evidence of prior
authority to execute, or a subsequent ratification of such
execution by the other partners, the burden of proof being
upon the plaintiff: Van Dyke v. Seelye, 49 Minn. 557, and
cases cited.

The only affirmative proof offered by the plaintiff or received by the court on this point, or which connected the appellant or either firm in any manner with the note now under
consideration, was in the nature of admissions or statements

made by B. F. Hartley to D. E. Slipp after the maturity of
the Pangborn notes, and before the execution of the note in
suit, to the effect that one or both of the firms of which he
was a member had assumed and were to pay the indebtedness
represented by the notes first mentioned. These admissions
or statements were not made in the course of a business transaction with either firm, but in a conversation had between
these two persons at a time when the liability of both, Slipp
as an indorser before delivery, and B. F. Hartley by means
of his unauthorized use of the firm name of Hartley Brothers
and Dewar as an indorser of the paper, had become fixed and
certain. To this class of testimony appellant very strenuously objected, but without avail. All that was said on this
occasion by B. P. Hartley in regard to an assumption of the
amount due on the Pangborn notes by one or both of his firms
was [122] allowed to go to the jury, and on this testimony alone
the verdict against appellant must have been predicated.
We say on this testimony alone advisedly, because it is not
contended that there was anything of importance in the conversation detailed by D. E. Slipp as having been held with
appellant after the indorsement of the Pangborn notes.

It was clearly error to receive in evidence these statements
or declarations of B. F. Hartley made after his own liability
on the notes had become fixed through the unauthorized and
unlawful use of the firm name by him. The effect of it was
to recognize the power of one partner to unload upon the firm
an individual liability and indebtedness, and to establish the
authority of one member of a firm to bind his associates by
verbal declarations where he could not bind them by a physical act, such, for instance, as signing the firm name to a
promissory note in a transaction outside of the partnership
business, and at a time when his interests were adverse to
those of his associates, as was well known to the person to
whom the declarations were made, and who thereafter became
the payee of the note in suit.

While it may be well settled that the admissions or declarations of a partner, during the existence of the partnership,
while engaged in transacting its legitimate business or relating
to matters within the scope of the partnership, are admissible
in evidence against the firm, the admissions or declarations
in question were not within that rule. They were made after
the Pangborn notes matured, and prior to the execution of
the note on which this action was brought, in the course of a

casual conversation with Mr. Slipp in relation to a transaction which he well knew, when entered into, was not within
the scope of the partnership business, and, as he also well
knew, a fraud.upon the other partners, unless authorized by
them. A partner's declarations or admissions may, as will
his acts, bind his associates in partnership matters, but not
in concerns and transactions foreign to the partnership; and
he cannot, by such declarations or admissions, bring a transaction within the scope of the partnership business when in
fact it has no connection. To sanction such a proceeding
would be to enable a partner at [133] any time to turn all his
individual liabilities upon the partnership and to render it
helpless, as against his unlawful and fraudulent acts performed in the name of the firm: *Heffron* v. *Hanaford*, 40 Mich.
305; *Kaiser* v. *Fendrick*, 98 Pa. St. 528; *Boor* v. *Lowrey*, 103
Ind. 478; 53 Am. Rep. 519; *Uhler* v. *Browning*, 28 N. J. L. 79;
Thorn v. *Smith*, 21 Wend. 365. See also *Osborne* v. *Stone*, 30
Minn. 25, and *Wells* v. *Turner*, 16 Md. 133.

We need not consider the appellant's third assignment of
error.

Order reversed.   ———

PARTNERSHIP—INDORSEMENT BY ONE PARTNER.—The power of partners
to bind one another by commercial paper does not extend to indorsements
or other contracts for the accommodation of a third party. The rule is well
settled that when one member of a partnership uses the firm name as accommodation maker or indorser, without the assent, express or implied, or the
subsequent ratification of his copartners, the paper cannot be enforced
against them or the firm by a holder who takes it with knowledge of its
accommodation character. Extended note to *Altoona etc. Nat. Bank* v. *Dunn*,
31 Am. St. Rep. 754, where the cases are collected, and the subject thoroughly discussed.

PARTNERSHIP—DECLARATIONS OF PARTNER, WHETHER BINDING ON FIRM:
A partner's declarations are binding upon the firm in an action against the
latter on a partnership liability: *Fickett* v. *Swift*, 41 Me. 65; 66 Am. Dec.
214, and note; *Griswold* v. *Haven*, 25 N. Y. 595; 82 Am. Dec. 380, and note
with the cases collected; *Baker* v. *Stackpoole*, 9 Cow. 420; 18 Am. Dec. 508.
An acknowledgment of a debt by one partner amounts to a promise binding
on the firm: *Burgan* v. *Lyell*, 2 Mich. 102; 55 Am. Dec. 53. An admission
of one partner upon a process of garnishment, where both parties have been
served, binds the other: *Anderson* v. *Wanzer*, 5 How. 587; 37 Am. Dec. 170.
But declarations of a partner engaged in transactions in his own name do
not bind the partnership: *Lockwood* v. *Beckwith*, 6 Mich. 168; 72 Am. Dec.
69. Declarations of a partner that a note made and indorsed in the firm's
name was accommodation paper, and was transferred by him for his personal benefit, is not evidence against the indorsees: *Bank of St. Albans* v.
Gilliland, 23 Wend. 311; 35 Am. Dec. 566. See also *Williams* v. *Lewis*, 115
Ind. 45; 7 Am. St. Rep. 403, and especially note.

BAXTER v. CHUTE.

[50 MINNESOTA, 164.]

JUDGMENT—VACATING FOR—ATTORNEY'S MISTAKE.—If a defendant having a meritorious defense, relying upon the erroneous advice of his attorney, allows a judgment by default to be rendered against him, his failure to answer in time may be excused, and the judgment set aside so as to allow him to answer, when he acts promptly, and none of the parties are prejudiced by reopening the judgment.

A. D. Polk, for the appellant.

Brooks and Hendrix, for the respondent.

[165] DICKINSON, J.   This action is prosecuted to recover upon several promissory notes executed to the plaintiff by the defendants Chute, and across the back of which also the defendant Cooley wrote his name before the delivery of the notes, for the accommodation of the defendants Chute, as may be considered for the purposes of this appeal.   As to the plaintiff, Cooley thereby assumed the liability of a maker, while as to the other defendants he occupied the position of a surety.   The defendants Chute interposed an answer setting up [166] the defense of usury.   The defendant Cooley had previously consulted an attorney, by whom he was advised that if the other defendants should answer it would not be necessary for him (Cooley) to do so, and that the plaintiff could not take judgment against him for a greater amount than should be recovered against his codefendants.   Relying on this advice, and learning that his codefendants had interposed the defense of usury, Cooley did not defend, and judgment was entered against him for default of an answer.   Learning this fact Cooley moved promptly, within some six days after the expiration of the time for answering, to have the judgment set aside, and that he be allowed to interpose by answer the same defense which had been made by his codefendants.   This motion was denied, and Cooley took this appeal from the order refusing such relief.   The action had not been tried against the other defendants when this appellant sought such relief from his default, and indeed issue was not joined therein until some days thereafter, when the plaintiff pleaded in reply to the answer.

As we understand the case the plaintiff must be regarded as having waived on the hearing of the motion all defects in the motion papers, including the fact that the answer of the defendants Chute setting forth the defense which this appel-

lant sought leave to interpose was not embraced in such
papers. It seems to be apparent that the only question submitted for the decision of the district court was as to whether,
assuming that the appellant showed that he had a defense
on the merits, his failure to plead it in time was excused.
The court seems to have considered that he was not entitled
to relief, because his neglect to answer was induced solely by
a mistake of law. In this we think that the court put too
narrow a construction upon the statute authorizing the court
to relieve a party from a judgment taken against him through
his "mistake . . . . or excusable neglect." A mistake of
law may afford ground for relief as well as a mistake of fact.
The default in *Brown* v. *Brown*, 37 Minn. 128, was suffered
under a mistake of the law, yet relief was afforded. See also
Jorgensen v. *Boehmer*, 9 Minn. 181; *Wicke* v. *Lake*, 21 Wis.
410; 94 Am. Dec. 552; *Whereatt* v. *Ellis*, 70 Wis. 207; 5 Am.
St. Rep. 164.

[167] Of course all mistakes, whether of fact or of law, and
whether committed by a party to an action or by his attorney,
are not subject to relief. But this case was such that the
discretion of the court might properly have been exercised in
favor of the appellant. There was no apparent reason for
doubt as to the facts. The appellant was not personally at
fault. As must be considered for the purposes of the motion
he had a good defense, which was the same as that made by
the other defendants to whom he stood in the relation of a
surety. He seasonably pursued the proper course, with a
a view to defending, by consulting an attorney, the same attorney through whom the other defendants answered. It was
only by reason of the mistaken advice of the attorney that
the appellant suffered default. The time for answering had
only recently expired, and the cause was not yet at issue as
to the other defendants when this relief was sought. The
granting of it would not have delayed the trial of the cause,
nor have prejudiced the plaintiff in any other way than by
requiring her to try her case on the merits, as to this appellant, as she was to do as to his codefendants, and, as it would
seem, too, upon precisely the same issue. The relation of the
appellant to the other defendants affords an additional inducement to the exercise of discretion in his favor. His
rights as a surety to recover against his principals, in case he
is compelled to pay their debt, would become complicated, if
not prejudiced, by the fact that he had suffered a recovery

without having interposed a known defense. On the other
hand, the only reason opposed to granting such relief to the
appellant is the fact that his attorney ignorantly advised
him erroneously, in a matter concerning which the party
was justified in trusting to and acting upon the advice of
the attorney.

Order reversed.

————

JUDGMENTS BY DEFAULT—ATTORNEY'S MISTAKE—RELIEF AGAINST.—A
default incurred by following in good faith the advice of counsel should be
relieved against where a meritorious defense exists: *Whereatt* v. *Ellis*, 70
Wis. 207; 5 Am. St. Rep. 164, and note; *Brown* v. *Brown*, 37 Minn. 128;
Douglass v. *Todd*, 96 Cal. 655; 31 Am. St. Rep. 247. A judgment by default is properly set aside on the ground of surprise and excusable neglect,
when it was entered through the failure of counsel to act, after being engaged by defendant to enter a plea for him, and left in attendance upon the
court: *Taylor* v. *Pope*, 106 N. C. 267; 19 Am. St. Rep. 530, and note with
the cases collected. But see *McDaniel* v. *McLendon*, 85 Ga. 614, and *Dusy*
v. *Prudom*, 95 Cal. 646, where the clients were refused relief from default
judgment rendered against them on account of the neglect of their counsel.

————

PANTON *v.* DULUTH GAS AND WATER COMPANY.

[50 MINNESOTA, 175.]

DURESS—PAYMENT FOR WATER UNDER.—Payment under protest by a property owner employing a large number of persons of an excessive charge
for necessary water in order to prevent the threatened shutting off of the
only available water supply is compulsory and made under duress, and
an action lies to recover the excess so paid.

Cotton and Dibell, for the appellants.

Draper, Davis, and Hollister, for the respondent.

[176] DICKINSON, J. The defendant is a corporation owning
and operating the waterworks by which the city of Duluth is
supplied with water, and authorized by law to charge for
water supplied to the inhabitants at specified rates, measured
by the quantity supplied.

The plaintiffs occupy a building in the city for mercantile
purposes, and keep in their service therein some forty or fifty
employees. The only water supply for the premises is that
afforded by the defendant. There are three water-closets in
the building, and faucets elsewhere for drawing water, these
all being supplied with water in the usual manner. The
water thus supplied is used for the closets, for sprinkling,

washing floors and windows, for drinking, and for the ordinary daily use of the persons in the building, but not for
culinary purposes. The defendant made a demand on plaintiffs for payment of a specified sum for use of water during a
particular period. The plaintiffs refused to pay that sum,
claiming that the water meter on the premises, put in by the
defendant, did not correctly measure the amount of water
passing through it, and that the amount of water for which
the charge was made was much in excess of the amount
actually used. The ·defendant was about to shut off the
water supply from the building because of such refusal, as
it assumed the right to do, when the plaintiffs, in order to
prevent the water being shut off, paid the sum charged, under
protest, and now prosecute this action to recover back the
amount of the alleged overcharge.

1. Upon the question of fact as to the water meter having
erroneously indicated the amount of water passing through
it, the jury found in favor of the plaintiffs. The court, considering that the evidence did not justify the verdict, granted
a new trial. Upon this point the case of *Hicks* v. *Stone*, 13
Minn. 434, and the numerous decisions in which the rule
there announced has been reaffirmed and applied, is conclusive. The evidence was such as to justify the order.

2. The question is presented, and may be expected to again
arise upon a second trial, whether the circumstances under
which the plaintiffs made the payment were such that the
payment may be regarded as having been so far compulsory
or necessary that an action will lie to recover it back. We
are of the opinion that it is to be [177] so regarded. In buildings as now constructed in populous cities, where there is an
adequate supply of water, and especially in buildings occupied by so many persons as are shown to have been employed
in the plaintiffs' store, water-closets may well be regarded as
reasonably necessary. The closets provided for use on these
premises, and comprising a part of the building, would have
been useless unless supplied with water; and there was no
other practicable source of supply save that afforded by the
defendant. The defendant was under legal obligation to supply water at the proper price. It was the plaintiffs' right to
have it thus supplied. The defendant of its own will merely,
and without any legal determination as to the disputed fact
upon which the exercise of such a power depended, was about
to cut off the whole water supply from these premises. This

was a kind of execution in advance of judgment. The plaintiffs would be compelled to submit to being deprived of the
use of water on their premises until, by such legal proceedings as they might institute for that purpose, they could
legally establish the fact that the charge was excessive.
Their only alternative was to pay what was demanded of
them.   We think that such a case falls within the class in
respect to which it may be said that the payment is virtually
compulsory, and not voluntary, in the sense that the party is
concluded by it.   What was said upon the law of duress in
the recent decision in *Joannin* v. *Ogilvie*, 49 Minn. 564, 32 Am.
St. Rep. 581, renders unnecessary any more full discussion
of the subject.

   Order affirmed.   ____

DURESS—RECOVERY OF MONEY PAID UNDER: See the extended notes to
Mayor v. *Lefferman*, 45 Am. Dec. 153–171, and *Peters* v. *Railroad Co.*, 51
Am. Rep. 820–833; also *Joannin* v. *Ogilvie*, 49 Minn. 564; 32 Am. St. Rep.
581, and note with cases collected.

BUCKLEY *v.* HUMASON.
[50 MINNESOTA, 195.]

CONTRACT FOR COMMISSIONS EARNED IN VIOLATION OF LAW.—When a city
ordinance duly enacted prohibits unlicensed real estate brokers from
transacting business within the city limits, a real estate agent negotiating a sale or exchange of city real estate without procuring a license
cannot recover commissions for his services.

CONTRACTS—WHEN INVALID.—Business transactions in violation of law cannot be made the foundation of a valid contract.

CONTRACTS IN VIOLATION OF LAW—LICENSES.—If a statute or ordinance
makes a particular business unlawful generally or for unlicensed persons,
any contract made in such business by one not authorized is void.

CONTRACTS VOID WHERE MADE and to be performed cannot be enforced
in another state.

   Stevens, O'Brien, and Glenn, and Armand Albrecht, for the
appellant.

   Otis and Godfrey, for the respondents.

   197 VANDERBURGH, J.   This action is brought by plaintiff
to recover commissions for services as a real estate agent or
broker in procuring a purchaser for certain real estate in
Chicago.   The cause of action is stated as follows in the complaint: " During the year 1890 the plaintiff, at the special

instance and request of the defendants, performed services for
said defendants in the city of Chicago, in the state of Illinois,
in and about procuring a purchaser for certain property in
the state of Illinois, which said services were then and there
of the reasonable value of four thousand three hundred and
seventy-five dollars, and which said sum the defendants agreed
and promised to pay plaintiff therefor."

The plaintiff testified that at the time of the alleged services he resided in the city of Chicago. The transactions referred to occurred there, and the negotiations were there
concluded, and the contract [198] and purchase were consummated in that city, and the plaintiff claims to be entitled to
the usual commissions charged and received in Chicago for
such services. He also testified that he had been previously
engaged in the real estate business in Chicago, as an agent,
and sold and exchanged property for others on commission,
and the transaction in question appears clearly enough to
have been in the line of his regular business as a real estate
agent or broker. In this connection we must observe that it
is admitted in the pleadings that during the year 1890, and
prior thereto, an ordinance of the city of Chicago, enacted in
pursuance of a statute of the state, was in force, which provided that it should not be lawful for any person to exercise
within that city the business of real estate broker, without a
license therefor, and defined a "real estate broker" as a person who, for commissions or other compensation, is engaged
in the selling of, or in negotiating sales of, real estate belonging to others. A license fee of twenty-five dollars per annum
is required to be paid by such broker, and any person violating the provisions of the ordinance is subject to a penalty of
not less than twenty-five dollars, and to the same penalty for
every subsequent violation thereof.

The testimony shows that the plaintiff was using and exercising the business of a real estate broker in the city of Chicago during the time in question, and in performing the
services for which a recovery is sought in this action. It was
made unlawful for him to do so by the terms of the ordinance
referred to. It was not at all material that the parties for
whom he negotiated a sale agreed to take property in St. Paul
in payment or exchange for the Chicago property of which
plaintiff negotiated a sale, and for which he found a purchaser.
The ordinance, which is set out in full in the answer, was
valid, and the case as presented by the evidence clearly falls

within it: *Braun* v. *City of Chicago*, 110 Ill. 187.   It has the force of law within the city of Chicago: *Bott* v. *Pratt*, 33 Minn. 323; 53 Am Rep. 47.

The particular transaction in question was therefore in violation of law, unless he was duly licensed, which was not shown.   On the contrary, the answer alleges, and it stands admitted, for want of a reply, that the plaintiff was not duly licensed as a broker.   The [199] plaintiff cannot, therefore, recover his commissions: *Hustis* v. *Pickands*, 27 Ill. App. 270; *Johnson* v. *Hulings*, 103 Pa. St. 501; 49 Am. Rep. 131; *Holt* v. *Green*, 73 Pa. St. 198; 13 Am. Rep. 737.

Business transactions, in violation of law, cannot be made the foundation of a valid contract; and the general rule is that where a statute makes a particular business unlawful generally, or for unlicensed persons, any contract made in such business by one not authorized is void: Bishop on Contracts, secs. 471, 547; 1 Pomeroy's Equity Jurisprudence, sec. 402.

And the contract, being void where it was made and to be performed, will be so held here: Bishop on Contracts, sec. 1383.

The case was properly dismissed upon the evidence.

Order affirmed.

————

CONFLICT OF LAWS—VALIDITY OF CONTRACTS IS TO BE DETERMINED BY THE PLACE WHERE THEY ARE TO BE PERFORMED: *Waverly Nat. Bank* v. *Hall*, 150 Pa. St. 466; 30 Am. St. Rep. 823, and note with the cases collected; *Baum* v. *Birchall*, 150 Pa. St. 164; 30 Am. St. Rep. 797, and note. A contract void by reason of the laws of the state where it was made and is to be performed is generally void elsewhere: *Bank of Commerce* v. *Fuqua*, 11 Mont. 285; 28 Am. St. Rep. 461, and note; *Tredway* v. *Riley*, 32 Neb. 495; 29 Am. St. Rep. 447, and note.

CONTRACTS IN VIOLATION OF LAW.—See *Brooks* v. *Cooper*, 50 N. J. Eq. 761; 35 Am. St. Rep. 793, and note.

GROFF *v.* STATE BANK.

[50 MINNESOTA, 234.]

NOTICE FROM POSSESSION—CREDITORS MAY BE POSTPONED OR DEFEATED by notice of claims of third parties to property, the record and title of which is in their debtor, and possession may be notice to them, as well as to a purchaser, so as to preclude them from obtaining a lien on the estate or interest of the occupant.

NOTICE FROM POSSESSION OF GRANTOR.—Possession by a grantor after the delivery of his deed is as effectual as notice of his interest in the granted premises as against the creditors of the grantee, as is the possession by a stranger to the record title.

Fletcher, Rockwood, and Dawson, for the appellant.

S. A. Reed, for the respondent.

[236] MITCHELL, J. The undisputed facts in this case are that Benjamin B. Groff and Hugh A. Gilson, being the owners as tenants in common of certain real estate, on May 4, 1887, without consideration, [237] conveyed it to one William H. Groff for the sole purpose of effecting a partition of the premises between them by having William H. Groff convey one-half in severalty to each. This conveyance was recorded July 13, 1887. In pursuance and execution of this arrangement, William H. Groff conveyed one-half in severalty to Gilson, but made no conveyance at that time of the other half (the premises in dispute) to Benjamin B. Groff; but the latter immediately (June 18, 1887) went into the actual, open, and exclusive possession and occupancy of it, and so continued until it was conveyed to the plaintiff, as hereinafter stated. While Benjamin B. Groff was thus in the actual possession and occupancy of the premises, but the title of record in William H. Groff, the defendant, on May 10, 1888, obtained and docketed a judgment against William H. Groff. On September 10, 1889, William H. Groff, at the request of Benjamin B. Groff, conveyed the premises to plaintiff, who immediately entered into the actual possession and occupancy of the same, and has ever since so continued. This action is brought to remove the cloud on plaintiff's title caused by the apparent lien of defendant's judgment on the premises.

1. It is not important whether or not the trust under which William H. Groff held the title for the benefit of Benjamin B. Groff was enforceable while still executory. It was entirely competent and lawful for him to recognize and execute the trust, although not enforceable, and he has done so: *Randall v. Constans,* 33 Minn. 334.

2. Creditors may be postponed or defeated by notice of claims of third parties to property the record and title of which is in their debtor; and possession may be notice to them, as well as to a purchaser, so as to preclude them from obtaining a lien on the estate or interest of the occupant: *Lamberton* v. *Merchants' Nat. Bank,* 24 Minn. 281. The general rule is that possession of land is notice to a purchaser of the possessor's title.

The only question in this case is whether this rule applies where the grantor remains, after the delivery of his deed, in possession of the granted premises. This is a question upon which the authorities are not agreed.

238 Some cases hold that the deed is conclusive that the vendor has reserved no interest in the land; that having, in effect, so declared by his conveyance, he is estopped from setting up any secret arrangement by which his grant is impaired; that, although he remains in possession, a person seeking to obtain an interest in the premises has a right to assume, without inquiry, that he is in possession merely for a temporary purpose, as tenant at sufferance of his grantee. But it seems to us that, inasmuch as the law allows possession to have the effect of notice, there is no good reason for making a distinction between possession by a stranger to the record title and possession by the grantor after delivery of his deed. In either case the possession is a fact inconsistent with the record title, and, if possession by the stranger is sufficient to make it obligatory upon a purchaser to ascertain his right, possession by the grantor is a circumstance entitled to equal consideration. An absolute deed divests the grantor of the right of possession as well as of the legal title, and when he is found in possession after delivery of his deed it is a fact inconsistent with the legal effect of the deed, and is suggestive that he still retains some interest in the premises. Under such circumstances, a purchaser has no right "to give controlling prominence to the legal effect of the deed," in disregard of the other "notorious antagonistic fact," that the grantor remains in possession just as if he had not conveyed. To say that the grantor is estopped by his deed is begging the question; for, if his possession is notice to third parties of his rights, there is no principle of estoppel that would prevent him from asserting against purchasers or creditors any claim to the premises which he might assert against his grantee. This view is abundantly sustained by authority: See Devlin

on Deeds, secs. 761-765; note to *Le Neve* v. *Le Neve*, **2 Lead.**
Cas. Eq., pt. 1, p. 180 et seq; *Pell* v. *McElroy*, 36 Cal. 268.

In fact this court has already adopted it in *New* v. *Wheaton*,
24 Minn. 406. This disposes of the only questions in this
case, and the result is that the judgment is affirmed.

NOTICE FROM POSSESSION.—Possession by a grantor after conveyance is
notice of his rights and equities in the granted premises: *Turman* v. *Bell*,
54 Ark. 273; 26 Am. St. Rep. 35, and note. The general rule is, that the
purchaser of realty is chargeable with notice of the equities of one in possession, but in Iowa possession by a grantor after full conveyance is not constructive notice of any right reserved in the land by the grantor: *May* v.
Sturdivant, 75 Iowa, 116; 9 Am. St. Rep. 463, and note in which the cases
in the series are collected.

ANDERSON *v.* MAY.

[50 MINNESOTA, 280.]

CONTRACTS—EXCUSE FOR NONPERFORMANCE.—Under a contract to grow,
sell, and deliver certain quantities of specified kinds of beans, a failure
to deliver the entire quantity is not excused by an early unexpected
frost destroying or injuring the crop to such an extent that the grower
is unable to deliver the entire quantity from beans grown by him.

CONTRACTS—NONPERFORMANCE—EXCUSE FOR.—If one contracts to do a
thing which is possible in itself, or when it is conditioned on any event
which happens, the promisor is liable for a breach thereof, notwithstanding it is beyond his power to perform it. An exception to this rule exists when the contract is made on the assumed continued existence of a
particular person or thing, and such person or thing ceases to exist.

CONTRACTS—NONPERFORMANCE—EXCUSE.—Performance of an agreement to
produce, by manufacture or otherwise, a particular thing, such performance being possible in the nature of things, is not excused by the
destruction, before completion or delivery of the thing, from whatever
cause, except the act of the other party.

ACTION to recover the value of one hundred and fifty-two
bushels of beans delivered by plaintiff to defendant in part
performance of a contract between them. Plaintiff recovered
judgment in the court below, and defendant appealed.

H. J. and E. A. Horn, for the appellant.

J. C. and W. H. Michael, for the respondent.

282 GILFILLAN, C. J. The defendant having alleged as a
counterclaim a contract in June, 1890, between him and
plaintiff, whereby the latter agreed to sell and deliver to the
former, on or before November 15th, certain quantities of
specified kinds of beans, and that he failed so to do except

as to a part thereof, the plaintiff in his reply alleged in substance that the contract was to deliver the beans from the crop that he should raise that year from his market gardening farm near Red Wing. Upon the trial the contract was proved by letters passing between the parties. From these it fairly appears that the beans to be delivered were to be grown by plaintiff, though it cannot be gathered from them that he was to grow the beans on any particular land. They contain no restriction in that respect. There can be no question that if grown by him, and of the kinds and quality specified, defendant would have been obliged to accept the beans, though not grown on any land previously cultivated by plaintiff. The contract, therefore, was in effect to raise and sell and deliver the quantities, kinds, and quality of beans specified— a contract in its nature possible of performance.

As an excuse for not delivering the entire quantity contracted for, the plaintiff relies on proof of the fact that an early unexpected frost destroyed or injured his crop to such an extent that he was unable to deliver the entire quantity.

What, in the way of subsequently arising impossibility for the party to perform, will suffice as excuse for nonperformance of a contract is well settled in the decisions; the only apparent difference in them arising from the application of the rules to particular circumstances. The general rule is as well stated as anywhere in 2 Chitty on Contracts, 1074, thus: "Where the contract is to do a thing which is possible in itself, or where it is conditioned on any event which happens, the promisor will be liable for a breach thereof, notwithstanding it was beyond his power to perform it; for it was his own fault to run the risk of undertaking to perform an impossibility, when he might have provided against it by his contract. And [283] therefore, in such cases, the performance is not excused by the occurrence of an inevitable accident or other contingency, although it was not foreseen by or within the control of the party."

An application of this rule is furnished by *Cowley* v. *Davidson*, 13 Minn. 92. What is sometimes called an "exception to the rule" is where the contract is implied to be made on the assumed continued existence of a particular person or thing, and the person or thing ceases to exist, as, where it is for personal service, and the person dies, or it is for repairs upon a particular ship or building, and the ship or building is destroyed. An agreement to sell and deliver at a future time a specific chattel existing when the agreement is made would come under this exception. The exception was extended further than in any other case we have found in *Howell* v. *Coupland,* L. R. 9 Q. B. 462. That was a contract to sell and deliver a certain quantity from a crop to be raised on a particular piece of land, and the entire crop was destroyed by blight. The court held the contract to be to deliver part of a specific thing, to wit, of the crop to be grown on a given piece of land, and held it to come within the rule that, where the obligation depends on the assumed existence of a specific thing, performance is excused by the destruction of the thing without the parties' fault. Without intimating whether we would follow that decision in a similar case, we will say that the case is unlike this, in that in this case the plaintiff was not limited or restricted to any particular land. It was not an undertaking to sell and deliver part of a specific crop, but a general undertaking to raise, sell, and deliver the specified quantity of beans. We have been cited to and found no case holding that, where one agrees generally to produce, by manufacture or otherwise, a particular thing, performance being possible in the nature of things, he may be excused from performance by the destruction, before completion or delivery, of the thing, from whatever cause, except the act of the other party. Applications of the general rule, where the thing agreed to be produced was, before completion, destroyed without the party's fault, are furnished in *Adams* v. *Nichols,* 19 Pick. 275, 279; 31 Am. Dec. 137; *School District* v. *Dauchy,* 25 Conn. 530; 68 Am. Dec. 371; and *Superintendent etc.* v. *Bennett,* 27 N. J. L. 513; 72 Am. Dec. 373, approved and followed [284] in *Stees* v. *Leonard,* 20 Minn. 494. Where such causes may intervene to prevent a party performing, he should guard against them in his contract.

Order reversed.

———

CONTRACTS.—EXCUSE FOR NONPERFORMANCE OF.—An accident against which a party might have stipulated in his contract, but omitted to do so, does not excuse the nonperformance thereof: *Adams* v. *Nichols,* 19 Pick. 275; 31 Am. Dec. 137, and especially note; extended note to *Harmony* v. *Bingham,* 62 Am. Dec. 151; note to *Tompkins* v. *Dudley,* 82 Am. Dec. 355.

CONTRACTS.—EFFECT OF DESTRUCTION OF THING AGREED TO BE PRODUCED is discussed in the following cases: *Galyon* v. *Ketchen,* 85 Tenn. 55; *Tompkins* v. *Dudley,* 25 N. Y. 272; 82 Am. Dec. 349; *Superintendent etc.* v. *Bennett,* 27 N. J. L. 513; 72 Am. Dec. 373, and note; *School District* v. *Dauchy,* 25 Conn. 530; 68 Am. Dec. 371, and note; *Fildew* v. *Besley,* 42 Mich. 100; 36 Am. Rep. 433, and note.

KERWIN *v.* SABIN.

[50 MINNESOTA, 320.]

STATUTE OF LIMITATIONS—RESIDENCE OUT OF STATE.—A Congressman who
leaves his home in the occupancy of servants during sessions of Congress
and then resides with his family in rented premises at the national capital, returning to and occupying his permanent home during congressional recesses, without intending to change his place of residence, does
not at any time reside out of the state so as to interrupt the running of
the statute of limitations.

STATUTE OF LIMITATIONS—RESIDENCE OUT OF STATE.—When one has an
established residence within the state he can only "depart from and
reside outside the state" by changing his residence and taking up an
actual residence elsewhere, as distinguished from a temporary sojourn,
and the fact that he departs from and remains out of the state for some
considerable time without changing his permanent place of residence
does not interrupt the running of the statute of limitations.

C. D. and T. D. O'Brien, for the appellant.

Clapp and McCartney, for the respondent.

[321] DICKINSON, J.   This is an action to recover for an alleged conversion of corporate stock belonging to the plaintiff.
The plaintiff discovered the fact complained of in May, 1884,
but the action was not commenced until August, 1890, more
than six years thereafter.   Upon the facts disclosed at the
trial, and now presented by a bill of exceptions, the court dismissed the action without submitting it to the jury, for the
reason that it was considered that the action was barred by
the statute of limitations.   The evidence upon which the applicability of the statute of limitations is to be determined
consisted only of the testimony of the defendant, by which
the facts were shown without controversy.   They may be thus
stated:

About the time the cause of action accrued, the defendant
was elected to represent the state of Minnesota as one of its
senators in the Senate of the United States.   For many years
he had resided at Stillwater, in this state, owning the house
which constituted his homestead.   Upon his election to the
Senate he rented a house in Washington, and during the
greater part of the sessions of Congress he kept house with
his family in such rented premises, but returning with his
family and resuming the occupancy of his homestead during
the intervals between the sittings of Congress.   The furniture
[322] was not removed from his house in Stillwater, but during
such absence of the family therefrom servants were left in

occupancy of it. Such absences of the defendant and his
family from the state extended over about one-half of each
year. Only to that extent, and under such circumstances,
does there appear to have been any interruption of his residence with his family in their former home. The defendant
always voted here, and had no intention of changing his residence; and it was only because his duties in Congress required
him to be in Washington while Congress was in session that
he had his family there, living in the manner stated.

The statute, the applicability of which is in question (General
Statutes of 1878, chapter 66, section 15), provides that if after
the cause of action accrues, the debtor "departs from and resides out of the state, the time of his absence is not part of
the time limited for the commencement of the action." The
question before us is whether the defendant could be deemed
to have resided out of this state, within the meaning of this
statute, while he was thus living with his family in Washington.

The case would not have justified the conclusion that the
defendant's residence was in Washington, and not in Minnesota, within the meaning of the statute, and hence the ruling
of the court was right. Prior to his going to Congress the
defendant's residence, in every sense of the term, was in this
state. His established, permanent home and abiding place
and his legal domicile were here. To suspend the running of
the statute of limitations it would not be enough that the
debtor, thus resident here, should depart from and remain for
some time out of the state. "Departs from and resides out
of the state" is the language of the statute. This necessarily
imports, in the case of one having an established residence
here, a change of residence, and the taking up of an actual
residence, as distinguished from a temporary sojourn elsewhere: *Venable* v. *Paulding*, 19 Minn. 488, and cases cited.
The defendant cannot fairly be said to have ceased to reside
in Minnesota, or to have made Washington his place of residence, under the circumstances stated. Had he boarded with
his family at an hotel or elsewhere in Washington during the
sessions of Congress, his home here being left as it was, and
his actual occupancy of it being maintained [323] during the
rest of the time, as was done, there could have been but little
reason for a claim of a change of residence. But in view of
the uncontradicted facts as to the reason of his being in Washington, and as to the continued maintenance and the occu-

pancy of his former home here, the fact of his keeping house with his family in rented premises in Washington during the sittings of Congress is of little significance as respects the question involved. His residence here, in the ordinary sense of the term, was not relinquished, and a new residence acquired in Washington. His former home continued to be "the house of his usual abode," and by the terms of our statute (General Statutes of 1878, chapter 66, section 59), under the circumstances shown by the evidence, a summons might have been served by leaving a copy there, and an action be thereby effectually commenced against him. He resided there each year, with his family, except when, during the sessions of Congress, his duties as a representative of this state required him to be in Washington. These absences were not permanent or continuous, but rather temporary, and reasonably incident to the discharge of public duties to this state, which unquestionably continued to be his domicile. While the periods of absence were somewhat extended, they were no more so than his representative duties to the state of his legal domicile required, and he habitually returned to and occupied his home here when such duties did not require him to be in Washington. There was no intention to discontinue his residence here or to acquire one elsewhere; and it is clear, from the unquestioned facts, that he cannot be deemed to have done so.

Order affirmed.   ——

LIMITATIONS OF ACTIONS.—ABSENCE FROM STATE TO SUSPEND RUNNING OF STATUTE: See the extended notes to the following cases: *Moore* v. *Armstrong*, 36 Am. Dec. 72-77; *Stanley* v. *Stanley*, 21 Am. St. Rep. 809; *Langdon* v. *Doud*, 83 Am. Dec. 644; *McCann* v. *Randall*, 9 Am. St. Rep. 675; and the note to *Cook* v. *Holmes*, 77 Am. Dec. 550. Domicile remains, notwithstanding absences from the state for special purposes and definite periods, so long as the intention to return remains; and such absences do not stop the running of the statute of limitations: *Bucknam* v. *Thompson*, 38 Me. 171; 61 Am. Dec. 237: *Sage* v. *Hawley*, 16 Conn. 106; 41 Am. Dec. 128, and note; *Garth* v. *Robards*, 20 Mo. 523; 64 Am. Dec. 203, and note.

CRONFELDT v. ARROL.

[50 MINNESOTA, 827.]

EXEMPTIONS—TOOLS.—TWO SEWING-MACHINES KEPT AND PERSONALLY USED BY A TAILOR for the purpose of carrying on his trade, if reasonably necessary therefor, are exempt from attachment or execution as tools and instruments used in carrying on a trade.

EXEMPTIONS—TOOLS.—GENERAL EXEMPTION OF ONE SEWING-MACHINE from attachment or execution has no reference to the occupation of the owner, and in no way qualifies or restricts a specific exemption of the tools and instruments of a person used in carrying on his trade. A tailor who necessarily uses two sewing-machines in carrying on his trade is entitled to the exemption as to both of them.

APPELLATE PRACTICE—EVIDENCE NOT PREJUDICIAL NOT GROUND FOR REVERSAL.—The admission of immaterial evidence, when not prejudicial, is not reversible error.

EVIDENCE—OBJECTION TO WHEN WAIVED.—A specific objection to the admissibility of evidence not presented to the trial court cannot be presented on appeal, but must be deemed to have been waived.

EXEMPTIONS—EXEMPLARY DAMAGES FOR WRONGFUL SEIZURE.—Exemplary damages may be recovered for a seizure of exempt property under attachment with knowledge of the exemption, and in culpable disregard of the debtor's rights.

E. M. Card, for the appellants.

B. H. Schriber, for the respondent.

[329] DICKINSON, J. The defendant Farrell, a constable, under a writ of attachment issued in an action prosecuted by the defendant Arrol against the plaintiff, seized two sewing-machines owned by the plaintiff. This is an action to recover damages for the taking of the property. The question to be considered is whether, under the circumstances shown by the evidence, the two machines may be deemed to have been exempt from attachment or execution by reason of their being within the General Statutes of 1878, chapter 66, section 310, subdivision 8, which exempts "the tools and instruments of any mechanic, miner, or other person, used and kept for the purpose of carrying on his trade."

The plaintiff is a tailor, and was personally engaged in that trade in a small shop in the city of St. Paul, in which these machines were [330] when they were levied upon. One was an old machine, designed especially for the use of tailors; the other was a lighter machine, designed for general use. The evidence showed that the plaintiff kept and used both machines in carrying on his trade, and it was submitted to the jury to determine whether it was reasonably necessary for him to use

both. The evidence justified the conclusion of the jury in
favor of the plaintiff in this particular. Such being the case,
both machines were exempt under the statute recited above,
and the plaintiff was entitled to recover. Subdivision 9 of
the same section specifies "one sewing-machine" as exempt.
This was added to the statute subsequent to the enacting of
the law exempting the tools and instruments of mechanics,
above recited. This general exemption of a sewing-machine
has no reference to the occupation of the owner, and in no
way qualifies or restricts the specific exemption of the tools
and instruments of mechanics and others used in the carrying
on of their trades.

The evidence of the witness Nemerovsky as to his brother's
statement to him on the occasion of the taking was objectionable, but we conclude, after some hesitation, that it can have
done no harm. It otherwise appeared that when the property
was taken, on the second day of April, the defendant Arrol,
in whose favor the attachment was issued, was claiming rent
from the plaintiff for the entire month of April, but that the
plaintiff, who had occupied the premises only one or two days
of that month, and had either removed or was about to do so,
claimed that he should only be required to pay for the time
of actual occupancy. The objectionable testimony went to
show in an improper way the fact which had already been
shown without objection, and was not controverted, that the
property was being taken upon a claim for rent. It was quite
immaterial in this action whether the plaintiff was owing rent
for the full month or only for a part of the month. That was
not tried or determined. The real issue submitted to the jury
was as to whether the property taken was exempt. In view
of the facts which were before the jury without objection, and
of the clearly defined issue plainly presented to the jury, it
seems impossible that the verdict of the jury, either as to the
fact of exemption [331] or as to the amount of the damages,
can have been influenced by proof that a bystander had made
the statement to the witness that the machines were being
taken "for one day's rent."

The plaintiff claimed and recovered exemplary damages.
In the trial the plaintiff called the defendant Arrol to testify
to his financial standing, or the value of his property. The
objection was made that such proof was "incompetent and
immaterial." It is now urged that such evidence was not
admissible to affect Farrell, who was a joint defendant with

Arrol. It is too late now to present that objection. The point was not suggested to the trial court by the objection there made. If it were not for the joinder of Farrell, the evidence would have been admissible: *McCarthy* v. *Niskern*, 22 Minn. 90, and it may be doubted whether the joinder of several defendants for the same wrong would make any difference. But, if so, the objection to the evidence should be such as to direct attention to that feature of the case.

The court should be sustained in the conclusion that the witness Forrestal was not competent to prove the value of the machine which he purchased.

The evidence was such that it was within the province of the jury to award exemplary damages, and the amount of the same—about one hundred and thirty-eight dollars in excess of what may have been deemed to be the value of the machines—was not beyond the limits of reasonable discretion. The evidence was such that it may have been considered by the jury that the plaintiff asserted his right of exemption when the levy was made; that the defendants knew that one of the machines at least was exempt, and that the levy was made under the express direction of the defendant Arrol, oppressively, and in culpable disregard of the rights of the plaintiff. As respects the power of the jury to award exemplary damages, the case is governed by the decision of this court in *Lynd* v. *Picket*, 7 Minn. 184; 82 Am. Dec. 79.

Order affirmed.

EXEMPTIONS.—TOOLS OF TRADE: See the extended notes to the following cases: *Richards* v. *Hubbard*, 47 Am. Rep. 190; *Baker* v. *Willis*, 25 Am. Rep. 63, and *Kilburn* v. *Demming*, 21 Am. Dec. 545.

EXEMPT PROPERTY.—EXEMPLARY DAMAGES FOR LEVYING ON: See the extended notes to *Burton* v. *Knapp*, 81 Am. Dec. 474, and *Van Dresor* v. *King*, 75 Am. Dec. 653. In an action to recover damages for a wrongful attachment, exemplary damages are not recoverable, if the plaintiff in attachment believed that the property attached was subject to the payment of his debt, and there was no malice or oppression: *Ellis* v. *Bonner*, 80 Tex. 198; 26 Am. St. Rep. 731, and note; note to *Reed* v. *Samuels*, 73 Am. Dec. 255.

APPEAL—ADMISSION OF NONPREJUDICIAL EVIDENCE IS NOT REVERSIBLE ERROR: *State* v. *Woodruff*, 47 Kan. 151; 27 Am. St. Rep. 285; *Empire Mill Co.* v. *Lovell*, 77 Iowa. 100; 14 Am. St. Rep. 272; *Stutz* v. *Chicago etc. Ry. Co.*, 73 Wis. 147; 9 Am. St. Rep. 769, and note; *Menk* v. *Home Ins. Co.*, 76 Cal. 51; 9 Am. St. Rep. 158; *Parkhurst* v. *Berdell*, 110 N. Y. 386; 6 Am. St. Rep. 384; *Oshkosh Gas etc. Co.* v. *Germania etc. Ins. Co.*, 71 Wis. 454; 5 Am. St. Rep. 233, and note; *Mathews* v. *Phelps*, 61 Mich. 327; 1 Am. St. Rep. 581; *State* v. *Houx*, 109 Mo. 654; 32 Am. St. Rep. 686.

STATE *v.* BROWN.

[50 MINNESOTA, 853.]

CONSTITUTIONAL LAW—REFORM SCHOOLS.—A statute authorizing and empowering justices of the peace to commit infants to the care and guardianship of the board of managers of a reform school in consequence of incorrigibly vicious conduct, though for a time exceeding the criminal jurisdiction of such justices, is a valid exercise of legislative power.

REFORM SCHOOLS—CONSTITUTIONAL LAW.—A person committed by a justice of the peace to the care and custody of a board of managers of a reform school is not punished or imprisoned in the ordinary meaning of those words. Hence a constitutional provision regulating and limiting the jurisdiction of justices of the peace in criminal matters has no application in the premises.

REFORM SCHOOLS—JURISDICTION OF COMMITTING MAGISTRATE—CONSTITUTIONAL LAW.—When committing an infant to the care and custody of the board of managers of a reform school, a justice of the peace is not appointing a guardian for him, nor does such magistrate or the board of managers assume any control over his estate. Hence the committing magistrate does not violate a constitutional provision conferring jurisdiction in matters of guardianship solely upon probate courts.

REFORM SCHOOLS—JURISDICTION TO COMMIT TO—CONSTITUTIONAL LAW.—An infant committed by a justice of the peace to a reform school is not punished or imprisoned in the ordinary meaning of those words, hence he is not deprived of his constitutional right to a jury trial.

REFORM SCHOOLS—PROCEEDING TO COMMIT TO—PARTIES.—In a proceeding to commit a minor to a reform school his natural or legal guardian should be made a party.

Sawyer, Abbott, and *Sawyer,* for the appellant.

Moses E. Clapp, attorney-general, and *H. W. Childs,* for the respondent.

856 COLLINS, J.   Appeal from an order dismissing a *habeas corpus* proceeding wherein the writ was directed to the superintendent of the state reform school, commanding that he produce one Oscar E. Olson, a minor son of the relator, said to be unlawfully restrained at said school. Young Olson and one Connolly were brought before the municipal court of the city of Waseca on the charge of incorrigibly vicious conduct, and were committed to the guardianship of the board of managers of the reform school at the same time and on the same testimony. The proceedings had in the municipal court, and as they were certified to the district judge, in so far as we were then advised, fully appear in a statement found in *State v. Brown,* 47 Minn. 472.

But the technical points upon which the latter case was decided and the relator released from the reform school do not now arise; for the record in this case, as we view it, affirmatively shows that all the evidence introduced before the municipal court was reduced to writing, and transmitted to the judge of the district court, who approved the commitment. The additional evidence upon this hearing in the district court was competent, and in no way tended to impeach the record of the municipal court. There is nothing in the point that the municipal judge did not reduce to writing the questions propounded to the witness, but simply took the testimony in a narrative form. Neither is there anything in the point that he transmitted a typewritten copy of the evidence to the district judge, instead of the original.

In proceedings to commit infants to the care and guardianship of the board of managers of the reform school, the right of the municipal court in question is derived through the statute under which it was organized, conferring upon it the authority, powers, and rights of a justice of the peace, under the general laws of the state. It follows that, if a justice has no power to commit to the reform school, the municipal court for the city of Waseca has not, and the claim [357] is made by the relator that the statute by which this power is given to justices is unconstitutional and void. We are therefore obliged to consider the relator's contention that the legislation of this state, whereby justices are authorized and empowered to commit infants to the care and guardianship of the board of managers of the reform school in consequence of incorrigibly vicious conduct, and for a time exceeding three months, is not a valid exercise of legislative power, under the constitution of this state. Two propositions are laid down in support of this contention: 1. That the authority is conferred upon a justice of the peace to punish a criminal by imprisonment for a period exceeding three months, contrary to the constitution, article 6, section 8; and 2. That jurisdiction in the matter of "persons under guardianship" has been conferred on such justices, contrary to the provisions of section 7 of the same article, by which jurisdiction over such persons is granted unto another constitutional tribunal, the probate court.

The questions raised by the first of these propositions have often been discussed by the judicial tribunals of this country. Legislation which, brushing aside and disregarding the views, wishes, or supposed rights of natural guardians, has had for its object the future welfare of the minor children of incapable and unworthy parents, or the care, custody, and proper train-

ing of incorrigible and vicious youth by the state, has occasionally been denounced with great vigor by the courts. A
notable example of this species of denunciation may be found
in the opinion in *People* v. *Turner,* 55 Ill. 281, 8 Am. Rep.
645, written by Mr. Justice Thornton. But legislation of this
character has been adopted in nearly all of the northern
states, and its validity has often been upheld. We do not
propose to add to the very many pages which, in the reports
and text-books, have been devoted to the support of the
position, now taken almost universally by the courts, that a
person committed to the care and custody of a board in
charge of an institution of the character of the Minnesota
state reform school is not "punished," nor is he "imprisoned," in the ordinary meaning of those words. Hence, the
constitutional provision which regulates and limits the jurisdiction of justices of the peace in criminal matters has no
application. We can do no better than [358] to call attention
to some of the leading authorities on this subject, and to quote
from the case first cited the clear language used therein by
the late Chief Justice Ryan: *Milwaukee Industrial School* v.
Supervisors, 40 Wis. 328; 22 Am. Rep. 702; *Farnham* v. *Pierce,*
141 Mass. 203; 55 Am. Rep. 452; *Prescott* v. *State,* 19 Ohio St.
184; 2 Am. Rep. 388; *Cincinnati House of Refuge* v. *Ryan,* 37
Ohio St. 197; *Roth* v. *House of Refuge,* 31 Md. 329; *Ex parte
Crouse,* 4 Whart. 9; *In re Ferrier,* 103 Ill. 367; 42 Am. Rep.
10; *McLean Co.* v. *Humphreys,* 104 Ill. 378; Tiedeman's Limitation of Police Power, c. 33. In the Wisconsin case, commencing on page 337, Judge Ryan thus expressed his views:
" And, in the first place, we cannot understand that the detention of the child at one of these schools should be considered
as imprisonment, any more than its detention in the poor-
house—any more than the detention of any child at any
boarding-school, standing, for the time, *in loco parentis* to the
child. Parental authority implies restraint, not imprisonment. And every school must necessarily exercise some
measure of parental power of restraint over children committed to it. And when the state, as *parens patrix,* is
compelled, by the misfortune of a child, to assume for it parental duty, and to charge itself with its nurture, it is compelled also to assume parental authority over it. This
authority must necessarily be delegated to those to whom the
state delegates the nurture and education of the child. The
state does not, indeed we might say could not, intrude this

assumption of authority between parent and child standing in no need of it. It assumes it only upon the destitution and necessity of the child, arising from want or default of parents. And, in exercising a wholesome parental restraint over the child, it can be properly said to imprison the child no more than the tenderest parent exercising like power of restraint over children. This seems too plain to need authority; but the cases cited for the respondent, and other cases, amply sustain our view."

We pass to an examination of the claim that, under the constitution, a justice has no power to place a person under the guardianship of this board of managers, because jurisdiction has been conferred solely upon the probate courts in all matters of guardianship.

[359] When committing an infant to the care and custody of the board of managers of the reform school the magistrate is not appointing a guardian for him, nor does such officer or the board of managers assume any control over his estate, if he has one. A proceeding of this nature would not stand in the way of, nor would it be prevented by, the appointment of a statutory or testamentary guardian—the only guardian coming within the purview of the constitution. It is no more a violation of the fundamental law for the magistrate to commit a child to the guardianship of the managers of an institution of this kind than it would be for a competent court to appoint a guardian *ad litem* for him. The language of the constitution does not apply where the state acts as the common guardian of the community, exercising its power whenever the welfare of an infant demands it, or where the state acts in the legitimate exercise of its police power. Therefore the lawmakers were not prohibited from conferring jurisdiction in such cases upon any of the judicial officers of the state.

The mode and method of procedure, as fixed by statute and followed in this case, are also attacked by relator's counsel. The proceeding is wholly statutory, and the party proceeded against is not punished or imprisoned. What has been said heretofore in regard to the nature of the proceedings, as well as the views expressed in *City of Mankato* v. *Arnold*, 36 Minn. 62, *State* v. *Harris*, 50 Minn. 128, disposes of the claim that Olson was deprived of his constitutional right to a jury trial.

It is not necessary for us to pass upon a further claim made by the relator that in all such cases the parent or guardian or next friend must be made a party, and that because such parent or guardian or next friend stands charged in the complaint (General Statutes of 1878, chapter 35, section 44, subdivision 2) with moral depravity, or of being incapable or of unwillingness to care for and discipline the infant, the justice has no right to proceed until he had obtained jurisdiction over the parent or the guardian or the next friend, as the case may be.

There may be a stronger reason than the one suggested why the natural or legal guardian of the infant should be made a party to the proceeding in question, but the statute does not seem to contemplate it, and it is possible that it is not necessary: *Milwaukee Industrial* [360] *School* v. *Supervisors*, 40 Wis. 328; 22 Am. Rep. 702; *Fitzgerald* v. *Commonwealth*, 5 Allen, 509. But from the record in this case it affirmatively appears that the relator herein, the only living parent of the boy, did appear in his behalf in the municipal court, and did take part in the proceedings which resulted in his commitment. She has no cause for complaint on that score.

This disposes of such of the assignments of error as are of importance, and our conclusion is that Olson is not improperly held at the reform school.

Order affirmed. ____

CONSTITUTIONALITY OF STATUTES CONCERNING INDUSTRIAL SCHOOLS.—In the following cases, statutes providing that children under a certain age, who have been abandoned by their parents, and are growing up under circumstances exposing them to lead idle or dissolute lives, should be committed to reform or industrial schools were held not unconstitutional as authorizing imprisonment without due process of law: *Farnham* v. *Pierce*, 141 Mass. 203; 55 Am. Rep. 452, and extended note thoroughly discussing the subject: *Milwaukee Industrial School* v. *Supervisors*, 40 Wis. 328; 22 Am. Rep. 702; *Prescott* v. *State*, 19 Ohio St. 184; 2 Am. Rep. 388; *Petition of Ferrier*, 103 Ill. 367; 42 Am. Rep. 10. The contrary doctrine is maintained in *People* v. *Turner*, 55 Ill. 280; 8 Am. Rep. 645. See also *Doyle, Petitioner*, 16 R. I. 537; 27 Am. St. Rep. 759, and note, and *Portland* v. *Bangor*, 65 Me. 120; 20 Am. Rep. 681.

STATE v. LOCKERBY.

[50 MINNESOTA, 363.]

SEDUCTION—BURDEN OF PROOF AS TO CHASTITY—CORROBORATION OF PROS-
ECUTRIX.—In a prosecution for seduction under promise of marriage the
burden of proof is upon the prosecution to prove the previous chaste
character of the prosecutrix, and her testimony must be corroborated
by other evidence, but only such corroborative evidence is required as,
in the nature of the case, is obtainable, and when produced, though circumstantial and slight in its character, a case is made for the jury to
determine.

SEDUCTION—EVIDENCE OF GENERAL REPUTATION FOR CHASTITY.—In a
prosecution for seduction under promise of marriage, evidence of the
general reputation of the prosecutrix for chastity is admissible in corroboration of her own testimony.

J. C. McClure, for the appellant.

Moses E. Clapp, attorney-general, and *S. J. Nelson*, county
attorney, for the respondent.

363 VANDERBURGH, J. Indictment for seduction under
. promise of marriage. The principal question in this case
arises upon the introduction of evidence in corroboration of
the complaining witness to prove her previous chaste character. In several of the states, under similar statutes, the
courts hold that, the natural presumption being in favor of
the chastity of the female, this supplies the place of evidence
in the first instance, and no proof is required of her previous
364 chaste character until it is assailed. The courts of other
states, including our own, adopt the opposite rule; and this
seems supported by the better reason. The presumption in
favor of her chastity is overcome by the presumption of the
innocence of the defendant, and the burden rests upon the
state to prove the averment in the indictment: *West v. State*,
1 Wis. 209; *Commonwealth v. Whittaker*, 131 Mass. 224; *State
v. Zabriskie*, 43 N. J. L. 369; *People v. Roderigas*, 49 Cal. 9·
State v. Timmens, 4 Minn. 325; *State v. Wenz*, 41 Minn. 197
1 Bishop's Criminal Procedure, sec. 1106; Bishop's Statutory
Crimes, 2d ed., sec. 648. The state is then obliged to produce
some evidence in support of the previous chaste character
the prosecuting witness. But only such corroborative ev
dence is required as in the nature of the case is obtainable-
such proof as the fact is susceptible of: *People v. Kearne*
110 N. Y. 193; *Armstrong v. People*, 70 N. Y. 44; and where
there is some evidence given by corroborating witnesses which
supports the prosecutrix the case is for the jury.

It must be so submitted, though it be circumstantial and apparently slight in its character: *Crandall* v. *People*, 2 Lans. 311. In the case last cited the fact that the prosecutrix went in good society was held proper evidence that she was of previous chaste character. In *State* v. *Timmens*, 4 Minn. 333, prosecutrix was shown to have been a constant inmate in her father's house, and was during the time sought in marriage by another man. And in *State* v. *Brinkhaus*, 34 Minn. 287, the girl went into such society as the neighborhood afforded, of the social rank of the family, and neighbors had never seen anything improper in her conduct.

A similar line of inquiry was pursued in this case, and a stronger case, based on such evidence, was made for the jury than in the cases cited. The evidence of the witness Hathaway, for whom the prosecutrix worked for a year previous to her seduction, shows that he knew her reputation for chastity in the community, and that he had never heard anything affecting the reputation or character of the girl except the matter on trial, and had never seen anything improper in her conduct. Other evidence of a similar character was received. In addition to this, the same and other witnesses were permitted and **365** did testify that her general reputation for chastity in the community where she resided was good. The admission of this evidence of her general reputation is specially assigned as error.

I have a good deal of doubt whether the evidence was competent, for the reason that the fact to be proved is not the repute of the person for chastity, but actual personal virtue; hence it is said that the question being whether she is chaste in fact and from principle, and not whether she is reputed to be so, evidence of reputation for chastity is not competent: *State* v. *Prizer*, 49 Iowa, 531; 31 Am. Rep. 155; *Kauffman* v. *People*, 11 Hun, 87.

In the leading case of *Kenyon* v. *People*, 26 N. Y. 203, 84 Am. Dec. 177, evidence of the general bad reputation of the prosecutrix was held properly rejected on the ground above stated; and in *Kauffman* v. *People*, 11 Hun, 87, a case where the prosecution was held bound to prove the previous chaste character of the prosecuting witness, the court decided that the rule must be the same, as it affects both sides of the question.

The general rule is that the state cannot offer evidence to prove the reputation of witnesses produced by it, for the purpose of corroborating or strengthening their testimony, unless the defense shall have first attacked their character: *People* v. *Hulse*, 3 Hill, 309. I think it has not been the usual practice to resort to such evidence in prosecutions of this kind in this state, and this is the first case which has come before us in which it has been attempted.

But my brethren are of the opinion that the evidence was proper, and the following considerations may be urged in support of the rulings of the trial court. As was said by that court in its charge to the jury, unchastity in a female is much more likely to attract attention and be talked about in a community than chastity; and if the jury believe from the evidence in the case that the conduct and deportment of the complaining witness in the village where she lived was correct and proper, and that up to the date of the alleged seduction by the defendant she was not talked about with regard to chastity or unchastity, that is a circumstance which they were entitled to consider in corroboration of the witness. That is to say, the evidence in such cases must necessarily be chiefly negative in its character, and hard to distinguish from that which is allowed to [366] prove general reputation: *State* v. *Lee*, 22 Minn. 409; 21 Am. Rep. 769. In *State* v. *Hill*, 91 Mo. 427, it is suggested that the difference in the language of statutes—"female of good repute" and of " previous chaste character"—was not such as to call for any variation of the rules of evidence; and in *West* v. *State*, 1 Wis. 217, the court say that the very fact that her chastity has never been questioned would perhaps establish it.

Where a witness is acquainted with the prosecutrix in the community where she resides, and has never heard anything to her prejudice, the fact ought to be evidence in her favor, though it would be negative testimony of her general reputation in the community; and that would naturally be the character of the testimony in such cases. The shifting of the natural order or burden of proof, by reason of the nature of the offense as defined in the statute, substantially places her in the same position as if her character had already been assailed, in which case it is well settled she may introduce evidence of general reputation.

In *State* v. *Prizer*, 49 Iowa, 533, 31 Am. Rep. 155, it is said a pure character may not be shown by reputation, but evidence of particular lewd conduct may be rebutted by proof of good reputation. This is the rule theoretically stated, but

ignores the effect of the statute in removing the presumption
of innocence; and it is difficult to see any practical difference
between evidence of the indefinite or negative character ordinarily given and evidence of reputation, as, for instance,
that the prosecutrix was received in good society, or had good
social standing. From the nature of the case general reputation must be regarded as having some relation to actual character, and goes directly to the question of the probability of her
being chaste. As the law assumes all characters to be good,
they must be first assailed before they can be proved to be good.
But in a case of this kind the character of the prosecutrix is
already impeached by the fact of seduction. It is true, under
the general rule as established, if the defendant attempts to
assail her character in the first instance he is put upon the
proof of specific facts tending to show unchaste character, but
these facts are susceptible of proof by affirmative evidence;
and the distinction, if not exactly logical, is nevertheless
grounded upon [367] practical reasons. The court, therefore,
holds that the evidence was properly received.

There was no error in rejecting evidence of subsequent
offers of marriage by defendant. It was clearly immaterial,
and did not tend to support any defense: *Cook* v. *People*, 2
Thomp. & C. 404.

The other assignments we do not deem necessary to be considered.

Order affirmed.　　——

SEDUCTION—BURDEN OF PROOF AS TO CHASTITY.—In prosecutions for seduction, the state has the burden of proving the good repute of the prosecutrix: *State* v. *Eckler*, 106 Mo. 585; 27 Am. St. Rep. 372, and note; *Zabriskie*
v. *State*, 43 N. J. Eq. 640; 39 Am. Rep. 610; *Oliver* v. *Commonwealth*, 101
Pa. St. 215; 47 Am. Rep. 704; *Polk* v. *State*, 40 Ark. 482; 48 Am. Rep. 17;
note to *People* v. *De'Fore*, 8 Am. St. Rep. 872, and extended note to *State* v.
Carrón, 87 Am. Dec. 406.

SEDUCTION—EVIDENCE OF GENERAL REPUTATION FOR CHASTITY.—In a
prosecution for seduction evidence of general reputation is not admissible
upon the issue of character, but only to impeach or corroborate testimony
regarding particular acts of unchastity: *State* v. *Prizer*, 49 Iowa, 531; 31
Am. Rep. 155; *Kenyon* v. *People*, 26 N. Y. 203; 84 Am. Dec. 177, and note.
See further on this subject, the notes to *State* v. *Reeves*, 10 Am. St. Rep. 356;
People v. *De Fore*, 8 Am. St. Rep. 871, and *State* v. *Carron*, 87 Am. Dec. 407.

MAGIE *v.* HERMAN.

[50 MINNESOTA, 424.]

EVIDENCE—CONTENTS OF TELEGRAM.—When one commences correspondence with another by telegraph he makes the telegraph company his agent for the transmission and delivery of his communication, and the transmitted message actually delivered is primary evidence of the transaction. If such message is lost or destroyed, its contents may be proved by parol.

ACTION by plaintiff, a physician and surgeon, to recover the value of professional services rendered two laborers injured in a sawmill owned by defendant Herman and others. On the trial plaintiff offered to prove by parol the contents of a lost telegram sent him by direction of the defendants employing him in the matter in dispute. This evidence was rejected under an objection to its competency. The defendants recovered judgment, and the plaintiff appealed.

Ellsworth Benham, for the appellant.

R. R. Briggs, for the respondents.

910 GILFILLAN, C. J. There was evidence tending to show that the telegram, the contents of which plaintiff offered to prove by parol, was sent by direction of Herman, one of the defendants, and it had been lost or destroyed. When one commences a correspondence with another by telegraph he makes the telegraph company his agent for the transmission and delivery of his communication, and the transcribed message actually delivered is primary evidence: *Wilson v. Minneapolis etc. R. R. Co,* 31 Minn. 481.

Every other evidence of its contents is secondary, and, as to its admissibility, stands on the same footing. One kind of secondary evidence—as, for instance, a written copy—may be more satisfactory than another, but it is no more admissible than any other secondary evidence.

The court below therefore erred in excluding the parol evidence of the contents of the telegram on the grounds stated in the objection, which went only to its competency.

If we could see that this error did not prejudice the plaintiff, if we could see that the telegram, if proved, would not tend to establish anything material to the case, a reversal because of the error might be avoided. But confining the objection to the question of competency must be taken as a concession that, if competent, the evidence is admissible as against any other objection, including any that might go to its materiality. It is a concession that, if competent, the evidence is material. Judgment reversed, and new trial ordered.

———

TELEGRAMS AS EVIDENCE.—A telegram delivered by the transmitting company, is admissible evidence where the original and the office from which it was sent are beyond the jurisdiction of the court: *Whilden* v. *Merchants' etc. Nat. Bank,* 64 Ala. 1; 38 Am. Rep. 1. Telegraphic messages are evidence against a party of his declarations, and also to show communications with the person addressed, if proved to be in his handwriting, and to have been received at the telegraph office, and sent over the wires properly directed to a person who was then living at the place of their destination: *Commonwealth* v. *Jeffries,* 7 Allen, 548; 83 Am. Dec. 712. See also *Rees* v. *Jackson,* 64 Pa. St. 486; 3 Am. Rep. 608, and the extended note to *State* v. *Davis,* 32 Am. St. Rep. 648.

———

SMITH v. HURD.

[50 MINNESOTA, 503.]

PROCESS—CONSTRUCTIVE SERVICE—CONSTITUTIONAL LAW.—A statute providing for service of process by publication in actions to foreclose liens on real estate against both residents and nonresidents, without making any distinction between them, if void as to residents is also void as to nonresidents.

PROCESS—SERVICE ON OWNER AS SERVICE ON LIENHOLDER.—There is no unity of interest between the legal owner of real estate and one claiming a lien on it through him, either by mortgage, mechanic's lien, or otherwise, such as makes either the representative of the other in an action, so that service of summons on one is equivalent to service on the other.

PROCESS—SERVICE AS COMMENCEMENT OF ACTION.—As to each defendant in any action it is commenced and pending against him only from the time of service of summons on him, or of his appearance without service, and, when each may object that the action was not commenced within the time limited by statute, its commencement as against his objection is to be determined solely by the time of service on him, and not by the time of service on some other defendant.

PROCESS—SERVICE AS COMMENCEMENT OF ACTION TO FORECLOSE MECHANIC'S LIEN.—One entitled to defend against a mechanic's lien may show that it is not a lien against his interest because the lien has expired or the remedy upon it has been lost by lapse of time before the action was commenced as to him.

PROCESS—SERVICE AS COMMENCEMENT OF ACTION TO PRESERVE LIEN.—In an action to enforce a mechanic's lien service of summons on the owner, of the premises within two years, as prescribed by statute, will not preserve the lien as against other defendant lienholders, not served with summons until after the expiration of the two years.

Ueland and Holt, for the appellants.

Charles J. Bartleson, for the respondents.

506 GILFILLAN, C. J.   Action to foreclose a mechanic's lien.
According to the findings of fact and the settled case, defendant Knight was, March 30, 1889, the owner of the premises
consisting of two lots (eleven and twelve).   Defendant Hurd
was the contractor to construct the buildings, and plaintiffs·
sold to him the materials, the last item of which was furnished July 17, 1889.   June 3, 1889, Knight executed a mortgage on one of the lots to defendant Doten, and on the other
to defendant Lovell.   January 17, 1890, plaintiffs filed the
lien statement.   June 2, 1890, each of the mortgages was
foreclosed, the mortgagee in each instance being the purchaser, and there was no redemption.   June 17, 1890, the
complaint in the action and a notice of *lis pendens* were filed,
and July 28, 1890, the summons was served on defendants
Knight and Hurd.   No attempt was made to serve on the defendants Doten and Lovell, except that, without any affidavit
of nonresidence or return on the summons by the sheriff that
said defendants were not found, the plaintiffs, under the supposition that the case came within the General Statutes of 1878,
chapter 81, section 28, caused the summons to be published
for six successive weeks; the first publication being July 19,
1890, and the last August 25, 1890.   Those defendants were
nonresidents, and have not been within this state since the
filing of the complaint, and no attempt to serve on them under
the General Statutes of 1878, chapter 66, was made till July
30, 1891.

But there was an attempt at service by publication under
the General Statutes of 1878, chapter 81, section 28.

We think that section was wholly void under the decision
in *Bardwell* v. *Collins*, 44 Minn. 97; 20 Am. St. Rep. 547.   It
is true that decision was on the ground that it is incompetent
for the legislature to provide that mode of service on resident
defendants, and the defendant in that case was a resident.
But the section makes no distinction between residents and
nonresidents.   In terms, it applies equally to both.   There is
no reason to suppose the legislature would have enacted the
section for the cases of nonresidents alone.   On the **507** contrary, there is every reason to suppose it would not have done
so had it known the section could not take effect as to residents, for there was already ample provision in chapter 66 for
substituted service in such cases on nonresidents, and no need
of further provision, so far as they were concerned.

There is no unity of interest between the legal owner of real estate and one claiming a lien on it through him, either by mortgage, mechanic's lien, or otherwise, such as makes either the representative of the other in an action, so that service on one is equivalent to service on the other.

As to each defendant in an action, the action is commenced and is pending only from the time of service of the summons on him or of his appearance without service; and where each may object that the action was not commenced within the time limited by statute, its commencement as to his objection is to be determined by the time of service on him, and not by the time of service on some other defendant. This is a rule applicable to every action, and applies as well to actions to enforce mechanics' liens as to any others. And anyone who may defend against such a lien, who may show that for any reason it is not a lien as against his interest, may object that the lien had expired or the remedy upon it been lost by lapse of time, before the action was commenced against him. This also is a rule applicable to every action. It amounts to just this: that when an action is commenced as to any defendant, there must be an existing cause of action against him and the right to a remedy upon it.

The General Statutes of 1878, chapter 90, section 7, was not an ordinary statute of limitations limiting the time for commencing an action, but it put a limit to the life and duration of the lien, and it contains no exception to its operation, either because of nonresidence or for any other reason.

Order affirmed.

STATUTES VOID IN PART—CONSTITUTIONALITY OF.—If a statute contains provisions, some of which are void and others are not, the general rule requires the court to sustain the valid and reject the invalid if they can be separated: *Lawton* v. *Steele*, 119 N. Y. 226; 16 Am. St. Rep. 813, and note; *State* v. *Blend*, 121 Ind. 514; 16 Am. St. Rep. 411, and note; *People* v. *Squire*, 107 N. Y. 593; 1 Am. St. Rep. 893; *East Kingston* v. *Towle*, 48 N. H. 57; 97 Am. Dec. 575, and note; *Brown* v. *Beatty*, 34 Miss. 227; 69 Am. Dec. 389; *Regents etc.* v. *Williams*, 9 Gill. & J. 365; 31 Am. Dec. 72. See also the notes to *State* v. *Deal*, 12 Am. St. Rep. 218, 219, and *Wellington et al., Petitioners*, 26 Am. Dec. 645.

ACTIONS.—WHEN COMMENCED: See *Montague* v. *Stelts*, 37 S. C. 200; 34 Am. St. Rep. 736, and note with the cases collected, also the extended note to *Ross* v. *Luther*, 15 Am. Dec. 345–347.

CASES

IN THE

COURT OF APPEALS

OF

NEW YORK.

SPEIR *v.* CITY OF BROOKLYN.

[139 NEW YORK, 6.]

NUISANCE.—THE DISCHARGE OF FIREWORKS at the junction of two narrow streets of a large city, completely built upon, and where any misadventure is likely to result in injury to persons or property when the display is of considerable magnitude, and the explosives heavily charged, and the discharge is managed by private persons, not under any official responsibility, is an unreasonable and unlawful use of the streets, and constitutes a public nuisance.

A MUNICIPAL CORPORATION MAY COMMIT AN ACTIONABLE WRONG and become liable for a tort.

A MUNICIPAL CORPORATION DIRECTING OR AUTHORIZING THE DISCHARGE OF FIREWORKS in the public streets under such circumstances as to create a public nuisance is liable to any person who, without any fault on his part, is injured thereby.

A MUNICIPAL CORPORATION FOR A MISTAKE IN THE EXERCISE OF ITS POWERS, OR FOR ACTING IN EXCESS of its powers upon any subject within its jurisdiction, is answerable to a third person injured thereby.

A MUNICIPAL CORPORATION IS ANSWERABLE FOR INJURIES TO PROPERTY FROM A DISPLAY OF FIREWORKS in the public streets of a densely populated part of the city, if such display was sanctioned by permit from the mayor, purporting to be authorized by one of its ordinances, though the ordinance may have transcended the powers of the common council, or may not have sanctioned the permit granted, if it had been generally understood and acted upon as if authorizing such permit.

ACTION to recover damages for injuries inflicted upon plaintiff's property by the explosion of a rocket, which explosion was part of an exhibition of fireworks at the intersection of Montague and Clinton streets in the city of Brooklyn. A permit for such fireworks was issued by the mayor of the city. A municipal ordinance upon the subject forbade the discharge of any cannon or gun, or the explosion of any fireworks, un-

less authorized by a permit from the mayor to exhibit the
same for public amusement. This ordinance had been
usually understood as authorizing the granting of permits
for the exhibition of fireworks. Judgment for plaintiff.

Almet F. Jenks, for the appellant.

William C. De Witt, for the respondent.

[10] ANDREWS, C. J. The finding of the trial judge that the
use of the street for the discharge of fireworks constituted a
public nuisance is amply justified in view of the circumstances. [11] It has been decided in some cases that the discharge of fireworks in the streets of a city or village is a
nuisance *per se,* and subjects persons engaged in the transaction to responsibility for any injury to person or property
resulting therefrom: *Jenne* v. *Sutton,* 43 N. J. L. 257; 39 Am.
Rep. 578; *Conklin* v. *Thompson,* 29 Barb. 218. It may be
doubted whether the doctrine in its full breadth can be maintained. The practice of making the display of fireworks a
part of the entertainment furnished by municipalities on
occasions of the celebration of holidays, or the commemora-
tion of important public events, is almost universal in cities
and villages, and we are not prepared to say that this may
not be done, and that streets and public places may not be
used for this purpose, under the supervision of municipal authorities, due care being used both as to the place selected,
and in the management of the display, without subjecting
the municipality to the charge of sanctioning a nuisance and
the responsibility of wrongdoers.

But the circumstances in the present case do not take the
transaction in question out of the category of nuisances, or
relieve the parties who conducted or promoted the affair from
liability for the injury occasioned. The discharge of fireworks in a city under any circumstances is attended with
danger. In the present case the danger was greatly enhanced by the location. It was at the junction of two narrow
streets of a large city, completely built upon, and where any
misadventure in managing the discharge would be likely to
result in injury to persons or property. The display was of
considerable magnitude and the explosives, especially **the**
rockets, were heavily charged, and, when exploded, were carried with immense velocity. It was managed by private persons under no official responsibility, and no municipal or
public interest was concerned. Under the circumstances, in

view of the place, the danger involved and the occasion, the
transaction was an unreasonable, unwarranted, and unlawful
use of the streets, exposing persons and property to injury,
and was properly found to constitute a public nuisance.

The judgment below adjudges that the city of Brooklyn is
[12] liable for the injury sustained by the plaintiff, and this is
the only question in the case.   That a municipal corporation
may commit an actionable wrong and become liable for a
tort is now beyond dispute.   If the city directed or authorized
the discharge of the fireworks which resulted in the injury
complained of it is, we think, liable.   The inquiry is whether
the city of Brooklyn did anything which as to this plaintiff
placed it in the attitude of a principal in carrying on the display.   The mayor of the city, its chief executive officer, expressly authorized it, assuming to act under an ordinance of
the common council.   In so doing and in construing the ordinance as authorizing him to grant a permit to private persons
to use the public streets for the discharge of fireworks, he was
following the practice which had long prevailed, and so far
as appears no question had been raised that such permits
were not within the ordinance.   The permit when given and
communicated to the police was understood as preventing
any police interference with the act permitted, and it had
that effect in the case in question.   The city had power to
prohibit or regulate the use of fireworks within the city and
to enact ordinances upon the subject.   The ordinances passed
were not *ultra vires* in the sense that it was not within the
power or authority of the corporation to act in reference to
the subject under any circumstances: See Dillon on Municipal Corporations, sec. 963 et seq.   It is the settled doctrine
of the courts that a municipality is not bound merely by the
assent of its executive officers to wrongful acts of third persons, nor could the mayor bind the city by a permit, for the
granting of which he had no color of authority from the common council, and which was not within the general scope of
his authority: *Thayer* v. *City of Boston*, 19 Pick. 511; 81 Am.
Dec. 157.   If the permit was in fact authorized by the ordinance the city would, as we conceive, be liable, although the
particular act authorized was wrongful.   For a mistake in
the exercise of its powers, or by acting in excess of its powers
upon a subject within its jurisdiction, whereby third persons sustain an injury, there seems to be no reason in justice
which should deny the injured party reparation.   The com-

mon [13] council is the governing body. It represents the corporation, and its acts are the acts of the corporation when they relate to subjects over which the corporation has jurisdiction. It is true that the power to pass ordinances and to regulate the use of fireworks did not embrace a power to authorize or legalize nuisances. But if the ordinance transcended the power of the common council in this respect, the misconstruction of the common council of the extent of its powers in dealing with the subject, which was concededly within its power of regulation, does not, we think, within any just view of municipal exemption from the consequences of unauthorized and wrongful acts of the governing body, exempt the city from liability: See *Cohen* v. *Mayor etc.*, 113 N. Y. 532; 10 Am. St. Rep. 506. But it is claimed that the ordinance did not by its true construction authorize the mayor to grant permits to use the streets for the discharge of fireworks. The contention is that there is an implied limitation that the permit should extend only to proper and suitable places other than the public streets. But there is no such limitation in terms in the ordinances, and the streets are not excepted from the power granted, and the case shows that the ordinance has been acted upon for many years, and has never been construed as now claimed. We are not prepared to say that the legal construction of the ordinance is not that which is now claimed by the counsel for the city, or that there is not to be read into it the limitation claimed. But the ordinance is at least indefinite and ambiguous. It might well be construed by laymen as it has been construed by the executive officers of the city. The ordinance was in fact the reason for the granting of the permit in this case. We think that as to the plaintiff, who has suffered the injury, the city is bound by the construction of the ordinance placed upon it by the mayor, and upon which for years the mayor had acted.

We think the judgment is sustainable, and it should, therefore, be affirmed.

All concur.

Judgment affirmed.

———

MUNICIPAL CORPORATION—LIABILITY FOR TORTS.—For a full discussion of this subject see the monographic note to *Goddard* v. *Inhabitants etc.*, 30 Am. St. Rep. 405–411. Municipal corporations are liable for injuries caused by their tortious conduct: *Elmore* v. *Drainage Commissioners*, 135 Ill. 269; 25 Am. St. Rep. 363, and note; extended notes to *Orr* v. *Bank of United*

States, 13 Am. Dec. 597, and *Williams* v. *Planters' Ins. Co.*, 57 Miss. 759; 34 Am. Rep. 494.

MUNICIPAL CORPORATIONS—LIABILITY FOR ACTS OF LICENSEE.—A city having an ordinance prohibiting the use of powder, but allowing the mayor to grant permission to use it on certain occasions, is not liable for injury caused by a licensee, in the absence of proof that the authorized act was intrinsically dangerous: *Wheeler* v. *Plymouth,* 116 Ind. 158; 9 Am. St. Rep. 837. *Lincoln* v. *Boston,* 148 Mass. 578; 12 Am. St. Rep. 601, and note, is an illustration of the foregoing rule. As to the liability of municipal corporations for authorizing third persons to maintain a nuisance, see the extended note to *Fort Worth* v. *Crawford,* 15 Am. St. Rep. 845. A city permitting "coasting" on its public streets will be held liable to one injured thereby for maintaining a nuisance: Note to *Robinson* v. *Greenville,* 51 Am. Rep. 860. But if the city designates a particular street for coasting, it will not be liable for injury to passersby caused thereby: *Burford* v. *Grand Rapids,* 53 Mich. 98; 51 Am. Rep. 105. See also the note to *Schultz* v. *Milwaukee,* 35 Am Rep. 781. The question as to the liability of a municipal corporation for authorizing a nuisance is further discussed in the extended note to *Orlando* v. *Pragg,* 34 Am. St. Rep. 27.

FIREWORKS—DISCHARGE OF, WHETHER A NUISANCE.—The discharge of fireworks at suitable places is not unlawful, when not prohibited by statute or ordinance, but the circumstances may be such as to make it culpable negligence: *Dowell* v. *Guthrie,* 99 Mo. 653; 17 Am. St. Rep. 598. See also *Jenne* v. *Sutton,* 43 N. J. L. 257; 39 Am. Rep. 578.

People *v.* Cannon.

[139 New York, 32.]

STATUTE—CONSTRUCTION AND CONSTITUTIONALITY OF.—A STATUTE FOR THE PROTECTION OF OWNERS OF BOTTLES used in the sale of soda waters and like beverages, making it unlawful for anyone to fill any bottle marked by a trademark, or to deface or obliterate such mark, or to sell or otherwise dispose of such bottles, unless purchased from the person whose mark is on the bottle, or sanctioned by his written consent, does not prohibit one who has purchased the beverage in such bottles from reselling it while in the same bottles in which he bought it, nor does the statute unnecessarily destroy or unlawfully decrease the trade in empty bottles; therefore it is not unconstitutional. One purchasing or coming into the possession of a bottle with such a mark upon it is charged with the duty of ascertaining, at his peril, whether the person whose name or mark is upon it has parted with his ownership in it or given written permission to any one to refill it.

CONSTITUTIONAL LAW.—THE LEGISLATURE POSSESSES THE WHOLE LEGISLATIVE POWER of the people, except so far as such power may be limited by the constitution.

CONSTITUTIONAL LAW—EVIDENCE.—A statute providing that any junk-dealer or dealer in second-hand articles, having possession of certain kinds of bottles having on them the mark or name of a person, without his written consent, shall be presumed to be in the unlawful use, purchase, or traffic in such bottles, is not unconstitutional.　Such presumption may be made applicable to criminal prosecutions.　Notwithstanding the presumption, the jury should refuse to convict unless satisfied from the whole evidence, beyond a reasonable doubt, of the guilt of the accused.

EVIDENCE.—STATUTE MAY MAKE THE EXISTENCE OF CERTAIN FACTS PRIMA FACIE EVIDENCE OF THE COMMISSION OF A CRIME, though the explanation of the facts from which the presumption arises is not peculiarly within the knowledge of the person accused.

SALE—WHAT IS.—If a person engaged in the manufacture and sale of soda waters delivers them in bottles to a customer, and takes a deposit from him, with the understanding that he may return the bottles and take back his deposit, or keep the bottles and regard it as payment, as he may elect, such transaction constitutes a sale of the bottles at the election of the customer, and a prosecution against a dealer in second-hand bottles for having such bottles unlawfully in his possession without the consent of such manufacturer cannot be sustained.

PROSECUTIONS for violation of the Bottling Act of 1887 as amended in 1888.　The defendants were dealers in second-hand bottles, of which they had several hundred thousand in their possession when their premises were visited by the police, and a small number of registered bottles were found therein.　The defendants' purchases were made in many different parts of the country and were shipped to them by rail and in vessels, and the character of the bottles could not be ascertained by them until they were unpacked and sorted. The statute upon which the prosecutions were based, so far as material, was as follows: "SECTION 1.　Any and all persons and corporations engaged in manufacturing, bottling, or selling soda waters, mineral or aerated waters, porter, ale, beer, cider, ginger ale, milk, cream, small beer, lager beer, weiss beer, white beer, or other beverages, or medicines, medical preparations, perfumery, compounds or mixtures, in bottles, siphons, tins, or kegs, with his, her, its, or their name or names or other marks or devices branded, stamped or engraved, etched, blown, impressed, or otherwise produced upon such bottles, siphons, tins, or kegs, or the boxes used by him, her, it, or them, may file in the office of the clerk of the county in which his, her, its, or their, principal place of business is situated, and also in the office of the secretary of state, a description of the name or names, marks or devices so used by him, her, it, or them, respectively, and cause such description to be printed once in each week for three weeks successively, in a newspaper published in the county in which said notice may have been filed as aforesaid, except that in the city and county of New York and the city of Brooklyn, in the county

of Kings, such publication shall be made for three weeks successively in two daily newspapers published in the cities of
New York and Brooklyn, respectively. "SEC. 2. It is hereby
declared to be unlawful for any person or persons, corporation
or corporations, to fill with soda waters, mineral or aerated
waters, porter, ale, cider, ginger ale, milk, cream, beer, small
beer, lager beer, weiss beer, white beer, or other beverages, or
with medicine, medical preparations, perfumery, compounds
or mixtures, any bottle, box, siphon, tin, or keg, so marked or
distinguished as aforesaid, with or by any name, mark or
device, of which a description shall have been filed and published, as provided in section one of this act, or to deface,
erase or obliterate, cover up or otherwise remove, or conceal,
any such name, mark, or device thereon, or to sell, buy, give,
take, or otherwise dispose of or traffic in the same without
the written consent of, or unless the same shall have been
purchased from, the person or persons, corporation or corporations whose mark or device shall be or shall have been in
or upon the bottle, box, siphon, tin, or keg so filled, trafficked
in, used or handled as aforesaid.   Any person or persons or
corporations offending against the provisions of this section
shall be deemed guilty of a misdemeanor, and shall be punished for the first offense by imprisonment not less than ten
days nor more than one year, or by a fine of fifty cents for
each and every such bottle, box, siphon, tin, or keg so filled,
sold, used, disposed of, bought or trafficked in, or by both
such fine and imprisonment, and for each subsequent offense
by imprisonment, not less than twenty days nor more than
one year; or by a fine of not less than one dollar nor more than
five dollars for each and every bottle, box, siphon, tin, and
keg so filled, sold, used, disposed of, bought or trafficked in,
or by both such fine and imprisonment in the discretion of
the magistrate before whom the offense shall be tried."   " SEC.
3. The use by any person other than the person or persons,
corporation or corporations, whose device, name, or mark
shall be or shall have been upon the same, without such
written consent or purchase as aforesaid, of any such marked
or distinguished bottle, box, siphon, tin, or keg, a description
of the name, mark, or device whereon shall have been filed
and published as herein provided, for the sale therein of soda
waters, mineral or aerated waters, porter, ale, cider, ginger ale,
milk, cream, beer, small beer, lager beer, weiss beer, white
beer, or other beverages, or of any articles of merchandise,

medicines, medical preparations, perfumery, compounds, mixtures or preparations, or for the furnishing of such or similar beverages to customers, or the buying, selling, using, disposing of or trafficking in any such bottles, boxes, siphons, tins, or kegs by any person other than said persons or corporations having a name, mark, or device thereon, or such owner without such written consent, or the having by any junk dealer or dealers in second-hand articles possession of any such bottles, boxes, siphons, tins, or kegs, a description of the marks, names or devices wherein shall have been so filed and published as aforesaid, without such written consent, shall and is hereby declared to be presumptive evidence of the said unlawful use, purchase, and traffic in of such bottles, boxes, siphons, tins, or kegs."

Judgment of conviction was entered in each case.

Everett P. Wheeler and Wm. J. Gaynor, for the appellants.

William Travers Jerome, for the respondent.

[88] PECKHAM, J. These prosecutions have been instituted for the purpose of obtaining a decision in regard to the validity of the law under which the convictions have been secured. Counsel for both parties have so stated, and the courts below have distinctly ruled upon the various propositions raised, so that the constitutionality of the statute might be fairly tested.

It is claimed that the act deprives all persons other than the manufacturers of the right to traffic in or give away sparkling or aerated liquors or beer, which have ever been placed in a trademark bottle. It is said that if the manufacturer refuses to sell the bottle, he in effect prohibits the sale or gift of that which is contained in it, except over the counter, and it is urged that the legislature cannot grant to the manufacturer such a monopoly.

It is needless to speculate as to the powers of the legislature upon this subject, because we are of the opinion the statute is not susceptible of any such construction.

It is made unlawful for any one to fill up with soda waters, etc., any bottle marked and distinguished as in the first section of the act is provided, or to deface, erase, or obliterate any such mark on such bottle, or to sell, etc., or to otherwise dispose [89] of, or traffic in, the same, without the written consent of, or unless the same have been purchased from the person whose mark is on the bottle. This provision of the act

refers to the use of these empty bottles by some one other
than the owner of the marks thereon, and after the original
contents of such bottles have been taken out, and then unlawfully using or trafficking in the empty bottles.

After the retail dealer or any one else has purchased the
soda water or beer from the manufacturer, and the same has
been delivered to him packed in the bottles thus marked, he
is not prevented by anything in the statute from himself selling such soda water or beer and delivering the same to the
purchaser packed in the same bottles in which it was delivered to him from the manufacturers. This process may be
continued indefinitely. The act is not aimed at the sale and
delivery of the water or beer packed in the original bottles as
it came from the manufacturer, but it is aimed at an unlawful dealing in empty bottles that have been marked, and
after their original contents have been used. If otherwise, it
is clear that an enormous amount of the business of the manufacturers would be curtailed. It is a fact that every one
knows, that large amounts of the liquors originally put up in
these bottles are sold by the manufacturers to the retail
dealers, who sell them to the customers, who take them away
in the original bottles in which the manufacturers delivered
them to the retail dealers, and it cannot be contended with
any degree of plausibility, as it seems to us, that there is anything in the language of the statute, properly construed, which
prohibits such a dealing in and delivery of the liquors by any
one into whose possession and ownership they have lawfully
come.

Nor is there any just foundation for the assertion that the
act necessarily destroys or unlawfully decreases the trade in
empty bottles, which is a fair trade and one entitled to the
equal protection of the law. The act contains no provision
in regard to empty bottles in general. It forbids the use or
traffic in certain kinds of bottles without the written consent
of the owners of the marks on them, or unless they have
themselves [40] once sold the bottles. It is not necessary that
they should have sold to the person using them. A sale of
the bottles to any one thereafter precludes the application of
the provisions of the statute. A bottle that has been marked
as described in the first section, and has thereafter been used
by the owner of the marks for the purpose of identifying in
the market the particular goods manufactured by him and
put up in such bottles, ought not to be used for other purposes;

against the will of the manufacturer, so long as he has not
sold the bottles to any one, nor authorized any one to use or
traffic in them; in other language, so long as he continues the
owner of the bottles.

And this kind of use or traffic the law is intended to prevent.

Under the broadest definition of the term "liberty," as used
in the constitution, it is not probable that any one would contend that it covers, or ought to cover, the liberty of dealing in
property which the original owner has not sold to any one or
authorized any one else to deal in. And yet the claim that
the act destroys the trade in second-hand bottles would lead
to this result if it were allowed. Because the act prohibits
the dealing in the property of a third person without his consent, it may be that the business of the second-hand bottle
dealer is affected so far as to necessitate further precautions
in regard to making purchases, than would otherwise be necessary. Before purchasing second-hand bottles he must be
assured that the person selling has the right to sell them, and
that he, the dealer, has the right to buy them. This may require more of an inspection of the kinds of bottles purchased
than the dealer has heretofore been accustomed to give, but
there is nothing improper in such obligation, and if he fail to
perform it he must omit it at his peril. The act in question
has a tendency to prevent frauds upon the public in the way
of filling these bottles with articles of the same nature as
originally put in them, but not manufactured by the owners
of the marks. Even though there may already be a section
or sections of the Penal Code which cover such a subject, that
does not render the further enactment of the legislature upon
the same subject [41] void.

If naturally there may be trouble in showing that the person of whom the second-hand dealer purchased had himself
obtained the bottles of some one who had purchased them
from the manufacturers, or who had their written consent to
deal in, use or traffic in them, such fact is only an additional
reason for not purchasing such bottles until it is clear that
they may be lawfully purchased. The act does, undoubtedly,
in this respect seriously hamper any one dealing in these
kinds of empty bottles. I can, however, see no constitutional
objection to the enactment based on that ground. A mere
possessor of one of these empty bottles may wish to fill it
without using the trademark. It is true he is prohibited
from effacing the trademark or erasing it, and this, it is said,

de-troys all property in the bottle, because the person who possesses it can make no earthly use of it. But in the case to which the act is applicable, the person who has the bottle in his possession has no property right in it, and never did have. The consequence may be that he has no right to use the bottle himself, and that he does not stand in a position with regard to the person from whom he procured the bottle and contents, to require such person to take it back and give him its value, or an agreed sum, after the contents have been used. This may be his misfortune, but it does not create any right. As he never owned the bottle, or had any property right in it of that nature, that fact does not and cannot affect him.

I fail to find any constitutional defect in this statute so far as its general features under review in these cases are concerned.

There is a ground of invalidity now to be noticed that has been urged in regard to that portion of the act which relates to matters of evidence. That portion of section three of the act which provides that the having by any junk dealer or dealers in second-hand articles, possession of these kinds of marked bottles, or kegs, without the written consent of the owner of such marks, shall be presumptive evidence of the unlawful use, purchase and traffic in such bottles, is asserted to be unconstitutional as an invasion by the legislature of the domain of the judicial branch of the government.

[43] It is said the legislature can create and define a crime, but it cannot declare what shall be *prima facie* evidence of its commission. Whether the crime as defined by the legislature has been committed by an accused is a question for the court and jury, and it is claimed that no direction to the court or jury as to what shall be considered *prima facie* proof can be given by the legislature. It may be remarked at the outset that this question does not arise in the case of Cannon. The defendant in that case agreed upon a state of facts upon which the judgment of the court and jury was requested, and in the statement it was agreed that the corporation which owned the marks and bottles in question had never granted any written or oral consent that the bottles should be used or trafficked in and had never sold or given away any such bottle.

In the other two cases the question is fairly up, and must be decided.

The legislature of this state possesses the whole legislative

power of the people, except so far as such power may be
limited by our constitution: *Bank of Chenango* v. *Brown*, 26
N. Y. 467. The power to enact such a provision as that
under discussion is founded upon the jurisdiction of the
legislature over rules of evidence, both in civil and criminal
cases. This court has lately had the question before it:
Board of Commrs. v. *Merchant*, 103 N. Y. 143; 57 Am. Rep.
705. The act in that case provided that whenever any person was seen to drink in a shop, etc., spirituous liquors which
were forbidden to be drank therein, it should be *prima facie*
evidence that such liquors were sold by the occupant of the
premises or his agent with the intent that the same should be
drank therein. The defendant was an occupant of premises
where liquor could not be legally sold to be drank there, and
he was prosecuted for selling the same in violation of the act.
The only evidence of a sale by the accused occupant was the
fact that a person was seen to drink liquor upon the premises,
and a conviction was asked for under the provisions of the
act quoted. The defendant was convicted, and his counsel
urged that the act was unconstitutional on the ground that it
[43] violated the constitutional guarantees of due process of
law and trial by jury. It was held the claim was unfounded
and that the general power of the legislature to prescribe rules
of evidence and methods of proof was undoubted and had not
been illegally exercised in that case. It is true it was a case
for the recovery of a penalty and was brought by the commissioners of excise and a civil judgment for damages was
recovered. It was, however, treated as a *quasi* criminal case
and criminal prosecutions were cited in support of the principle decided in it.

It cannot be disputed that the courts of this and other
states are committed to the general principle that even in
criminal prosecutions the legislature may with some limitations enact that when certain facts have been proved they
shall be *prima facie* evidence of the existence of the main fact
in question. (See cases cited in *Board of Commrs.* v. *Merchant*, 103 N. Y. 143; 57 Am. Rep. 705.) The limitations
are that the fact upon which the presumption is to rest must
have some fair relation to, or natural connection with, the
main fact. The inference of the existence of the main fact,
because of the existence of the fact actually proved, must
not be merely and purely arbitrary, or wholly unreasonable,
unnatural or extraordinary, and the accused must have

in each case a fair opportunity to make his defense, and
to submit the whole case to the jury, to be decided by it
after it has weighed all the evidence and given such weight
to the presumption as to it shall seem proper. A provision of this kind does not take away or impair the right
of trial by jury. It does not in reality and finally change
the burden of proof. The people must at all times sustain the burden of proving the guilt of the accused beyond
a reasonable doubt. It, in substance, enacts that, certain
facts being proved, the jury may regard them, if believed, as
sufficient to convict, in the absence of explanation or contradiction. Even in that case, the court could not legally direct
a conviction. It cannot do so in any criminal case. That is
solely for the jury, and it could have the right, after a survey
of the whole case, to refuse to convict unless satisfied beyond
a reasonable doubt of [44] the guilt of the accused, even though
the statutory *prima facie* evidence were uncontradicted. The
case of *Commonwealth* v. *Williams*, 6 Gray, 1, supports this
view.

Without the aid of the statute, the presumption provided
for therein might not arise from the facts proved, although
the statute says they shall be sufficient to authorize such presumption. The legislature has the power to make these facts
sufficient to authorize the presumption (*State* v. *Mellor*, 13
R. I. 669), and the jury has the power, in the absence of all
other evidence, to base its verdict thereon, if satisfied that the
defendant is guilty. But the jury must in all cases be satisfied of guilt beyond a reasonable doubt, and the enactment in
regard to the presumption merely permits, but cannot in
effect direct, the jury to convict under any circumstances.
The dissenting opinion of Mr. Justice Thomas, delivered in
Commonwealth v. *Williams*, 6 Gray, 1, contains all that can
be said against the validity of this kind of legislation.

It is argued, however, that assuming the validity of the
provision in cases of excise sales and kindred cases, such as
having in possession game out of season (*Phelps* v. *Racey*, 60
N. Y. 10; 19 Am. Rep. 140), and in civil cases, such as providing that the comptroller's deed upon a sale of land for
taxes affords a presumption of the regularity of all prior proceedings (*Howard* v. *Moot*, 64 N. Y. 262; *Colman* v. *Shuttuck,*
62 N. Y. 348), yet the principle does not apply to a case like
this. The reason alleged is that the fact which is to be regarded as *prima facie* evidence of guilt, viz: The possession

of the bottles by a dealer in second-hand bottles without the written consent of the owner, was not one sufficiently identified in ordinary circumstances with guilt to make it the foundation of such a presumption.

The case of *People* v. *Lyon*, 27 Hun, 180, was a prosecution under the same section of the statute as that in *Board of Commrs.* v. *Merchant*, 103 N. Y. 143; 57 Am. Rep. 705. One of the judges at the general term in illustration of his meaning that the fact from which the inference of guilt may be drawn should have some kind of natural reference to, or bearing [45] upon, the main fact, said that if the legislature could provide for such a presumption, it could enact that the drinking of liquors a mile distant from such premises should be *prima facie* evidence of a sale on the premises with intent that the liquors should be drank there. Or it might enact that if a dead body were found in any house, it should be *prima facie* evidence that the occupier of the house had murdered the deceased.

The learned judge thought the act in question was entirely arbitrary and had no regard to the connection or want of connection between the fact from which the presumption was to flow and the guilt of the accused. Yet this particular enactment, thus condemned by the supreme court, was upheld by this court in *Board of Commrs.* v. *Merchant*, 103 N. Y. 143; 57 Am. Rep. 705. The cases cited by way of illustration by the learned judge in his opinion in the supreme court are, in our view, far beyond the mark, and contain nothing in common with the enactment here under review. In the cases supposed there would be, as the learned judge said, no kind of connection between the fact proved and the main fact in controversy. Such an enactment would be purely arbitrary. In this case, however, we think such connection exists. Of course the fact from which the presumption is to be drawn may exist without the existence of the main fact. That is true in all cases. In other words, the two facts are not necessarily inseparable. But in this case the fact of the possession of these kinds of bottles by a dealer in second-hand articles without the written consent of the owner, while it may be innocent, yet the presumption of an unlawful use or traffic in them is not so forced or so extraordinary as to be regarded by sensible and unprejudiced men as unreasonable or unnatural. It is some evidence of the main fact, and the strength of it is properly a matter for legislative enactment in the first instance, subject to its

submission **to the** jury for its deliberation and determination.
So the presumption from the possession of certain birds out
of season that they were unlawfully killed or taken in the
state is not a certain presumption in any sense. A person
might of course have the birds and have procured [46] them
in another state, and therefore not be guilty of a violation of
the game law. Yet the presumption of a violation of the
statute is not such a forced and unnatural one that the legislature may not enact that it shall be made, and thus leave the
defendant to explain it: *Commonwealth* v. *Williams*, 6 Gray,
6, in opinion of Shaw, C. J.

Nor can it be successfully maintained that this species of
legislation is to be confined to those cases where the explanation of the fact from which the presumption is to arise is
peculiarly within the knowledge of the party who is accused.
There are many cases in the books (and they are cited in the
cases already alluded to) where the principle is held that the
burden of proving the existence of a fact peculiarly within
the knowledge of the accused is at common law placed upon
him: *Potter* v. *Deyo*, 19 Wend. 361; *People* v. *Nyce*, 34 Hun,
298. If legislation were confined to such cases, it is plain
that it would be entirely unnecessary and would accomplish
nothing, as the law would place the burden of explanation
upon the defendant without the aid of the statute. Within
the limitations already alluded to and described, the statute
may provide for the presumption, and call upon the defendant
to explain the fact. In prosecutions for the sale of liquor
without a license the supreme court of Massachusetts held
that under the old act the prosecution must prove by proper
evidence that the accused had no license, and no presumption
that he had none could arise from the fact of selling: *Commonwealth* v. *Thurlow*, 24 Pick. 374. Thereupon the legislature passed an act that in all prosecutions for selling liquors,
the legal presumption should be that the defendant had not
been licensed, thus reversing what had been held to be the
common-law rule in *Commonwealth* v. *Thurlow*, 24 Pick. 374.
This was held to be within the power of the legislature: *Commonwealth* v. *Kelly*, 10 Cush. 69, 70; *Commonwealth* v. *Williams*,
6 Gray, 1. It is true the fact of having a license is one peculiarly within the knowledge of the party licensed. Yet the
validity of legislation is recognized in these cases, although
it enacts [47] that a presumption shall be made from certain
facts which at common law would not give rise to any such

presumption. I do not know of any constitutional principle
which, while permitting the legislature to enact that the legal
presumption arising from the sale of liquor shall be that the
person selling had no license, yet at the same time prevents
the enactment of a provision like the one in the statute under
discussion. If the legislature have the power in the first instance, I think it follows that it must have the power in the
other. I can see no solid ground for distinction between the
two cases. That it has the power in the first case is substantially conceded by all. The inference of guilt, under the provision in question here, is quite as strong as in many other
cases that arise under statutory enactments, and we think it
is sufficiently reasonable and natural to warrant a legislature
in passing such an act. The opinion of this court upon the
question of the policy of this kind of legislation is not at all
material, and will not, therefore, be stated.

The effect of the presumption is to call upon the accused
for some explanation. If none be given, the jury may, as I
have said, still refuse to convict; but, if they convict, the
verdict may be upheld as founded upon sufficient evidence.
The provision fills all the requirements of an act of this
nature, for it leaves an accused a fair opportunity to relieve
himself from the presumption, to explain the circumstances
under which the bottles came into his possession, and that
they were of such a nature as to show him innocent of an unlawful use, purchase, or traffic therein.

A dealer in second-hand bottles intending to obey the law
would fairly be open to no danger of unjust conviction.
While not giving personal supervision to the receipt of bottles coming by railroad or vessel, or brought to him for sale,
he may direct his agents to receive none of the kind mentioned, and when they come from abroad he may so far con-
ditionally receive them as to open their coverings and see
what they are, and reject those which he cannot lawfully buy
or deal in. Such a momentary or conditional possession,
fairly [48] explained and believed by the jury, or in regard to
which they were doubtful, would rebut the statutory presumption and call for an acquittal. Proof that the bottles in
question had been sold, or written authority to deal in them
had been given by the owners to some one else, would also be
a defense. It might be difficult of proof, it is said, and this
may sometimes be true. If difficult of proof, the defendant

should think of that before he purchases or deals in them, and decides to run the risk.

The Rhode Island supreme court has held an act unconstitutional which in substance provided that the notorious character of the premises, or the notoriously bad or intemperate character of the persons frequenting the same, or the keeping of implements or appurtenances usually appertaining to a grog shop where liquors are sold, should be *prima facie* evidence that the liquors were kept on the premises for the purpose of sale within the state: *State* v. *Beswick*, 13 R. I. 211; 43 Am. Rep. 26; *State* v. *Kartz*, 13 R. I. 528. The same court, and in the same volume of its reports, held that a statute providing that evidence of the sale or keeping of intoxicating liquors for sale in any building should be *prima facie* evidence that the sale or keeping was illegal, and that the premises were nuisances, was constitutional: *State* v. *Higgins*, 13 R. I. 330; *State* v. *Mellor*, 13 R. I. 666.

In *State* v. *Kartz*, 13 R. I. 528, the court said that the introduction in the law of the principle that a person could be punished for what other people said about him, was to render all constitutional provisions unavailing for his protection. The distinction is plain, I think, between the two classes of cases, and the statute under review here does not come within the principle which the Rhode Island court held to be a violation of constitutional rights.

We conclude that the provision in question cannot be assailed upon any constitutional ground.

The statute, however, is so framed that if the proprietors or owners of these marked bottles have once sold them, no matter to whom, the bottles may thereafter be freely dealt in.

[49] In the Bartholf case the evidence shows, as I think, a conditional sale of the bottles, at the option of the party who deposits the money as a security for their return. It does not show an agreement to return the bottles. The evidence is that the drivers of the beer or soda water carts who take out the liquors for the owners or manufacturers, take them in these bottles, and that they deliver the beer, soda water, or other liquor in the bottles to the customers. They (the drivers) then give a receipt to the customers for the deposit given by the customers to the drivers for the safe return of the bottles. This deposit is taken to the manufacturers and they credit the customer with its amount, keeping what is termed a separate deposit account, and when they return the

bottles, the manufacturers refund the money, and if the bottles
are not returned the manufacturers keep the money.   That a
deposit was given as security for the safe return of the bottles
does not prove there was an agreement to return them.   The
evidence here shows, as it seems to us, the existence of an
understanding that the party may return the bottles and get
back his money, or keep the bottles and regard the deposit
as a payment, just as he might elect.   This construction is
strengthened by proof of the fact that the manufacturer acted
on the theory that if the bottles were not returned he was to
keep the money.   The case is barren of any evidence proving
an obligation to return the bottles.   The book-keeper said he
did not know of any sales of bottles, but the above evidence
is all there is on the subject of the delivery of bottles by the
manufacturers, and whether it constitutes a sale thereof at
the election of the persons receiving them and upon the condition of the deposit operating as a payment for the bottles, is
a question of law.

The taking of security for the return of the bottles from the
party to whom they were delivered, so long as there is no evidence of an agreement and the party is under no legal obligation to return them, he having the right to retain them if he
choose to leave the money deposited as a payment for the
bottles, amounts in law to a sale of them at the election of the
party to whom they are delivered.   We think the evidence
in this case of Bartholf, at least, shows just such a state of
facts.

The case of *Westcott* v. *Thompson*, 18 N. Y. 363, is unlike
this.   An express agreement to return the barrels was there
proved, and the agreement to thereafter pay two dollars for
such barrels as were not returned was intended by the parties,
as the court held upon a view of all the facts, to mean that
the manufacturers should have all the barrels after the ale
was drawn, but they contemplated the possibility of the loss
or destruction of some, and the consequent inability of the
purchaser of the ale to return them, and they intended to fix
by the agreement a price to be paid as the value of each barrel which should not, for the above reason, be redelivered to
the manufacturers.

Here no such agreement to return the bottles is proved, but,
on the contrary, the evidence shows that the right to retain
the bottles was with the party receiving them from the manufacturer of the beer or soda water, subject, however, in that

case, to the payment of the deposit made for the purpose. This may not be the actual truth of the case. The evidence is quite loose and somewhat unsatisfactory on this branch, The receipts given by the driver are nowhere put in evidence, and whether they contain anything further in the way of an actual agreement to return the bottles cannot be known from this record.

Another trial may show the whole case more fully and accurately.

The Quinn case is not as specific in the offers and exceptions as the Bartholf case. Yet it is seen that even in the former case there was some attempt made to show the facts as to the deposit, and seemingly a ruling of the judge that it was immaterial, or that the court would take notice of such custom. We are not disposed to be technical in such a case, where the subject seems to have been presented to the mind of the court and definitely ruled on by it, and when we think that possible injustice might result from a refusal to notice a point which was in reality raised by counsel and actually passed upon by the trial court.

[51] We think the judgment in the Cannon case must be affirmed, and in the other cases the judgments must be reversed and a new trial ordered.

All concur.

Judgment affirmed in Cannon case and reversed in the others.

———

LEGISLATURE—POWER OF.—The power of the legislature to enact laws is limited only by the constitution: *In re Madera Irr. District*, 92 Cal. 296; 27 Am. St. Rep. 106; *People* v. *Seymour*, 16 Cal. 332; 76 Am. Dec. 521, and note; *Thorpe* v. *Rutland etc. R. P Co.*, 27 Vt. 140; 62 Am. Dec. 625, and extended note.

SALES—DEPOSIT WITH OPTION TO RETURN PROPERTY.—EFFECT OF: See note to *Chase* v. *Washburn*, 59 Am. Dec. 630.

EVIDENCE, VALIDITY OF STATUTES CREATING PRESUMPTIONS—REBUT-TABLE PRESUMPTIONS.—In civil cases there can remain no doubt that it is within the power of the legislature to determine on which party the burden of proof shall rest, and, having made such determination, it may change it from time to time and thus shift the burden as in its discretion shall seem proper: *Gage* v. *Caraher*, 125 Ill. 447. This result, instead of being accomplished by a formal declaration that such burden shall be assumed by one party rather than by the other, may be attained by declaring that evidence proving one fact shall of itself be *prima facie* evidence of another and entirely different fact, and, at least in civil cases, it does not appear to be necessary that there shall be any logical connection between the two facts, or that the fact presumed shall be a probable consequence of the fact proved.

An act of the legislature of the state of New York authorized the perpetuation of testimony in certain cases under the direction of the court of chancery, and made the testimony so perpetuated *prima facie* evidence of the facts set forth in the examination of the witnesses. Testimony so perpetuated having been offered and received in evidence, the action of the court and the validity of the statute were sustained by the court of appeals in an opinion from which we make the following extract: "But two objections were taken to this evidence upon the trial: 1. That the legislature had no power to authorize the testimony to be taken *de bene esse* without giving any adverse party the right of cross-examination; and 2. That the testimony as given in the depositions was mere hearsay and upon points upon which hearsay evidence was incompetent. While the legislature can not take from parties vested rights without compensation, the remedies by which rights are to be enforced or defended are within the absolute control of that branch of the government. The rules of evidence are not an exception to the doctrine that all rules and regulations affecting remedies are, at all times, subject to modification and control by the legislature. The changes which are enacted from time to time may be made applicable to existing causes of action, as the law thus changed would only prescribe the rule for future controversies. It may be conceded for all the purposes of this power that a law that should make evidence conclusive which was not so necessarily in and of itself and thus preclude the adverse party from showing the truth, would be void as indirectly working a confiscation of property or a destruction of vested rights. But such is not the effect of declaring any circumstance or any evidence, however slight, *prima facie* proof of a fact to be established, leaving the adverse party at liberty to rebut and overcome it by contradictory and better evidence. That this may be done is well settled by authority: *Hand* v. *Ballou,* 12 N. Y. 541; *Hickox* v. *Tallman,* 38 Barb. 608; *Commonwealth* v. *Williams,* 6 Gray, 1; Cooley's Constitutional Limitations, 367, and cases cited. The Act of 1821 was not in excess of the legislative power. The objection that the testimony taken under it was hearsay is not tenable. It was not all hearsay. Some of the facts stated by the witnesses were within their own knowledge. But if it were otherwise, the legislature made the chancellor the final arbiter to determine what should be good *prima facie* evidence of the facts stated; and such evidence, whether resting wholly upon hearsay, or otherwise, is, under the act and within the authorities cited, conclusive in the absence of any evidence to controvert it, or suggestion that it is untrue or mistaken. Perhaps some of the facts stated were susceptible of better proof, and the evidence might not have been admissible under the application of strict rules upon the trial; but upon reading the whole evidence, there was clearly sufficient to justify the chancellor in certifying that it was good *prima facie* evidence of the facts stated, those facts relating to the death of some parties and the succession and inheritance by the claimants of the large tract of land of which the *locus in quo* is a part. If, however, the evidence was slight and unsatisfactory, it would have been more easy to meet and overcome it before the jury. It is enough that it was competent; its effect was for the jury": *Howard* v. *Moot,* 64 N. Y. 262.

In Support of Tax Titles and of other proceedings taken for the collection of taxes, the statutes of a majority of the states have made the assessment and delinquent assessment rolls *prima facie* evidence of the existence and regularity of all proceedings necessary to a valid assessment and tax deeds executed by proper officers evidence of the regularity and sufficiency of all proceedings up to and including the sale. The validity of these statutes, though often questioned, has never been denied, and is now beyond controversy: *Pillow* v. *Roberts*, 13 How. 472–476; *Callahan* v. *Hurley*, 93 U. S. 387; *Hand* v. *Ballou*, 12 N. Y. 541; *Delaplaine* v. *Cook*, 7 Wis. 44; *Allen* v. *Armstrong*, 16 Iowa, 508; *Lacey* v. *Davis*, 4 Mich. 140; 66 Am. Dec. 524; *Wright* v. *Dunham*, 13 Mich. 414; *Groesbeck* v. *Seeley*, 13 Mich. 329; *Lumsden* v. *Cross*, 10 Wis. 282; *Abbott* v. *Lindenhower*, 42 Mo. 162; *McDonald* v. *Conniff*, 99 Cal. 390; *Rollins* v. *Wright*, 93 Cal. 395; *Colman* v. *Shattuck*, 62 N. Y. 348.   On the other hand, the legislature may, after adopting a statute making tax deeds *prima facie* evidence of title, repeal such statute and require one claiming under a tax deed to prove the existence of all steps essential to its validity: *Gage* v. *Caraker*, 125 Ill. 447.

Prosecutions for Unlawful Sales of Liquor.—The difficulty of obtaining direct evidence of the violation of statutes forbidding or regulating the sale of intoxicating liquors has resulted in various enactments making the possession or delivery of such liquors *prima facie* evidence of their unlawful sale, and in some instances going still farther and making evidence of the reputation of the house as being one in which liquors were unlawfully sold *prima facie* evidence of the guilt of the person keeping it.   These enactments have, with a single exception, been sustained, though the cases to which they applied were criminal prosecutions: *Board of Commissioners etc.* v. *Merchant*, 103 N. Y. 143; 57 Am. Rep. 705; *Edwards* v. *State*, 121 Ind. 450; *State* v. *Morgan*, 40 Conn. 44; *Lincoln* v. *Smith*, 27 Vt. 328; *State* v. *Cunningham*, 25 Conn. 195.   There is no doubt that the delivery of liquor to a person may be made *prima facie* evidence that it was unlawfully sold to him: *Howard* v. *Moot*, 64 N. Y. 262; *State* v. *Hurley*, 54 Me. 562; *Commonwealth* v. *Williams*, 6 Gray, 1; *Commonwealth* v. *Wallace*, 7 Gray, 222; *Commonwealth* v. *Mahoney*, 14 Gray, 46; or that the drinking of liquor on defendant's premises may be evidence that it was sold with the intent that it should be drunk there: *Board of Commissioners etc.* v. *Merchant*, 103 N. Y. 143; 57 Am. Rep. 705; and the reputation of defendant's place of business may by statute be made material and cast upon him the burden of proof: *State* v. *Thomas*, 47 Conn. 546; 36 Am. Rep. 98.   Upon this subject the decisions are not entirely harmonious.   The statute of Connecticut under consideration in the case last cited forbade an unlicensed person to keep liquors with intent to sell them, and declared that every person keeping a place in which it is reputed that intoxicating liquors are kept for sale, without having a license therefor, should be deemed guilty of violating the law.   The constitutionality of this statute was affirmed on the ground that it was applicable only to those places which had a reputation, founded on proof of actual sales of liquor therein.   A statute of Rhode Island, in effect, made it the duty of a jury to convict a defendant of unlawfully keeping liquors for sale upon proof that his place was frequented by persons of notoriously bad, or intemperate character, or upon proof that he had there the implements and appurtenances of a grog or tippling shop, in the absence of rebutting testimony. The supreme court of that state regarded this statute as in conflict with the presumption of innocence to which every accused person was entitled, and as depriving the defendant of the judgment of his peers as to his actual guilt, and of due process of law: *State* v. *Beswick*, 13 R. I. 211; 43 Am. Rep. 26. The courts of that state, however, conceded that when the sale of liquor is unlawful unless licensed, the sale or keeping liquor for sale may be made *prima facie* evidence that such sale or keeping is illegal, which defendant must rebut by producing his license: *State* v. *Higgins*, 13 R. I. 330; *State* v. *Mellor*, 13 R. I. 666.

The Protest of Any Foreign or Inland Bill of Exchange or promissory note certified by a notary public may be made legal evidence of the facts stated in such protest, and the statute giving it that effect is constitutional, and is not restricted to protests made before its enactment: *Fales* v. *Wadsworth*, 23 Me. 553.

Auditor's Reports.—A statute authorizing the appointment of an auditor in actions of account for the purpose of stating the account between the parties, and of making a report to the court, which report may, under the direction of the court, be given in evidence to the jury, may have the effect of changing the burden of proof, because the report must be assumed *prima facie* to be correct. The statute is nevertheless valid and free from constitutional objection: *Holmes* v. *Hunt*, 122 Mass. 505; 23 Am. Rep. 381; *Allen* v. *Hawks*, 11 Pick. 359; *Morgan* v. *Morse*, 13 Gray, 150.

Gambling Cases.—A statute of Florida declared that if any of the implements, devices, or appurtenances actually used in games of chance usually played in gambling-houses or by gamblers are found in any house, room, booth, shelter, or other place, it shall be *prima facie* evidence that such house, room, or place, where the same are found is kept for gambling; and a statute of Indiana enacting that it shall be sufficient evidence that any building or other place was rented for the purpose of gaming, if such gaming was actually carried on, and the owner or lessor thereof knew, or had reason to believe, that the lessee suffered any gaming therein, and such owner or lessor took no sufficient means to prevent or restrain the same. These statutes were assailed on the ground that they deprived the accused of due process of law and usurped the functions of the jury. Each was determined to be within the constitutional power of the legislature, and the general authority of the legislature to establish rules of evidence was affirmed: *Wooten* v. *State*, 24 Fla. 335; *Morgan* v. *State*, 117 Ind. 569. In the case last cited the court said: "As incident to the power of defining crimes and misdemeanors and of declaring what shall constitute a criminal offense, our legislature has always assumed to determine what shall in certain cases be deemed sufficient evidence of the commission of an offense or of some criminal act necessary to be proven in a criminal prosecution, and this assumption has never, as we believe, been either questioned or antagonized by the courts. That body has so assumed to determine what shall be sufficient evidence in cases of rape, seduction, receiving stolen goods, obstructing highways, and other cases which might be enumerated."

In Criminal Prosecutions.—The cases already cited arising out of prosecutions for the unlawful sale of intoxicating liquors, or for keeping or renting places for the purpose of gambling therein, sufficiently establish that in criminal, as well as in civil cases, the legislature may declare that the proof of certain facts shall be *prima facie* evidence of the existence of a crime or of some other act constituting an essential ingredient of a crime. So far as we are aware, there is no decision denying that this legislative power is as applicable to criminal prosecutions as to civil cases. The opinions in the criminal cases, however, are more cautiously expressed, and seem to imply that the power is not unlimited and that the fact which is made *prima facie* evidence of some other fact necessary to sustain a conviction, must be one from which the existence of the latter may be reasonably inferred: *Voght* v. *State*, 124 Ind. 358. In *Board of Commissioners etc.* v. *Merchant*, 103 N. Y. 143, 148; 57 Am. Rep. 705, it was said: "The general power of the legislature to prescribe rules of evidence and methods of proof is undoubted. While the power has its constitutional limitations, it is not easy to define precisely what they are.

A law which would practically shut out the evidence of a party, and thus deny him the opportunity for a trial, would substantially deprive him of due process of law. It would not be possible to uphold a law which made an act *prima facie* evidence of a crime over which the party charged had no control and with which he had no connection, or which made that *prima facie* evidence of a crime which had no relation to a criminal act, and no tendency whatever, by itself, to prove a criminal act. But so long as the legislature, in prescribing rules of evidence, in either criminal or civil cases, leaves a party a fair opportunity to make his defense and to submit all the facts to the jury, to be weighed by them, upon evidence legitimately bearing upon them, it is difficult to perceive how its acts can be assailed upon constitutional grounds." So in the principal case, the court evidently was not prepared to admit that the power of the legislature, in criminal cases, with respect to creating presumptions of crime, was unlimited, for it said: "The limitations are, that the fact upon which the presumption is to rest must have some fair relation to, or natural connection with, the main fact. The inference of the existence of the main fact, because of the existence of the fact actually proved, must not be merely and purely arbitrary, or wholly unreasonable, unnatural, or extraordinary, and the accused must have in each case a fair opportunity to make his defense, and to submit the whole case to the jury, to be decided by it after it has weighed all the evidence and given such weight to the presumption as to it shall seem proper." There is beyond controversy a reason for imposing limitations in criminal prosecutions which has no existence in civil cases. One accused of a criminal act is presumed to be innocent, in the absence of any evidence of his guilt, and we apprehend that this presumption is one protected by the fundamental law of each state from legislative destruction. If so, the courts must not permit it to be indirectly destroyed by declaring certain facts to be *prima facie* evidence of guilt, when those facts are neither criminal in themselves nor indicative of the existence of any criminal act or intent. While this is true, the courts may often experience difficulty in determining judicially that an act which, in the judgment of the legislature, tends to prove another criminal act, has, in fact, no such tendency; and in all cases in which reasonable doubt exists, we assume that the legislative determination will not be regarded as beyond the legislative power. In civil cases there is probably no inhibition in any state constitution, express or implied, against the legislature imposing the burden of proof upon one rather than upon another party litigant. Hence it is not probable that any contingency will ever arise in which the judiciary will declare that a statute, applicable to civil cases only, is unconstitutional because it declares proof or evidence of a particular act or condition shall be *prima facie* evidence of some other act, or shall relieve the party in whose favor the presumption is created from the necessity of offering further evidence in its support, in the absence of rebutting evidence on the part of his adversary.

Conclusive Presumptions.—Statutes have also frequently been enacted purporting to make one fact conclusive evidence of another, when, as a matter of fact, the existence of the former is not necessarily connected with the existence of the latter. The effect of such a statute, if constitutional, is to create a liability or cause of action or of defense where the presumed fact, but for the existence of the statute, might be disproved. If, therefore, the fact is one which, in the nature of things, is an essential part of the cause of action or of the right claimed, the statute must be unconstitutional; otherwise the power of the legislature to dispense with an essential fact and to create a cause of action where none otherwise exists must be affirmed, and to affirm this would be to place the rights of all persons within the abso. lute control of the legislature.   Probably the most familiar instances of constitutional statutes making one fact conclusive evidence of another, when it is clear that there is no necessary connection between the two, are those statutes which make a tax deed or an assessment roll evidence of the regularity of certain proceedings directed by a statute to be taken in the assessment of property or in advertising and selling it for delinquent taxes.   The rule upon this subject is as follows: If the legislature has prescribed any step to be taken which it might have omitted to prescribe without affecting the validity of the proceedings, then it may declare that the tax deed or the assessment roll shall be conclusive evidence of the taking of such step, at the proper time and in the proper manner, though the roll may have been made in due form or the deed executed without such step being taken at all, and though neither the roll nor the deed affirms in direct terms that the step has been taken.

Such a statute is constitutional, because it cannot, in any event, do more than deprive the party of the right to have something done which has not been guaranteed to him by any provision of the constitution, and which the legislature might have in the first instance failed to require.   Hence, if property has been assessed and equalized, and is subject to taxation, and taxes thereon have not been paid, the other steps required by statute to be taken may be regarded as directory merely, and the legislature may create a conclusive presumption of their existence: *Phelps* v. *Meade*, 41 Iowa, 470; *De Treville* v. *Smalls*, 98 U. S. 525; *Smith* v. *Cleveland*, 17 Wis. 556; *Ensign* v. *Barse*, 107 N. Y. 329; *Matter of Lake*, 40 La. Ann. 142.   Thus, referring to a statute making a tax deed *prima facie* evidence of the assessment and equalization of the property, of the levy and nonpayment of taxes, of the regularity of the sale, of the nonredemption therefrom, and that the proper officer executed the deed, and conclusive evidence of all other proceedings from the assessment by the assessor inclusive, up to the execution of the deed, the court said: "We see no valid objections to these provisions. If the property owner held property which was liable to taxation, which had been properly assessed, for a tax duly levied, which had not been paid, but allowed to become delinquent, and the property had been sold as required by law and not redeemed, there is no hardship in providing that he shall not take advantage of mere irregularities which did not affect his substantial rights, to avoid the effect of his delinquency.   The matters which he is expressly authorized to dispute enable him to raise every point essential to a just defense. Justice does not require that he should be entitled to interpose pure technicalities": *Rollins* v. *Wright*, 93 Cal. 397.   The legislature may provide for the sale of property for delinquent taxes without requiring any notice of such sale, and therefore it may declare that a tax deed shall be conclusive evidence of the giving of such notice as the statute has prescribed: *Allen* v. *Armstrong*, 16 Iowa, 508, 513; *Abbott* v. *Lindenbower*, 42 Mo. 162.   On the other hand, it has been said that, "Due and reasonable notice of the sale of property for delinquent taxes is necessary to the validity of the sale," and therefore that a tax deed cannot be made conclusive evidence of such notice: *Marx* v. *Hanthorn*, 30 Fed. Rep. 585.   Further instances in which it has been held that a statute may make tax deeds conclusive evidence, and thus shut out testimony to the contrary, are that the sale was made in a lawful manner: *Gould* v. *Thompson,* 45 Iowa, 450; *McCready* v. *Sexton,* 29 Iowa, 356; 4 Am. Rep. 214; *Callahan* v. *Hurley,* 93 U. S. 387, and, at the proper time, *Shawler* v. *Johnson,* 52 Iowa, 472; *Clark* v. *Thompson,* 37 Iowa, 536, 541.

However the courts may differ as to what is an indispensable essential to a tax sale, they agree that the property holder cannot be deprived of his property where such essential does exist, by declaring that the deed or assessment shall be conclusive evidence of it. "We state the principle which must be legally and logically true in this wise: If any given step or matter in the exercise of the power to tax (as, for example, the fact of a levy by proper authority), is so indispensable that without its performance no tax can be raised, then that step or matter, whatever it may be, cannot be dispensed with, and with respect to that the owner cannot be concluded from showing the truth by a mere legislative declaration to that effect": *Allen* v. *Armstrong,* 16 Iowa, 513. "The true rule on the subject seems to be that the legislature may make a tax deed conclusive evidence of the regularity of the prior proceedings as to all nonessentials or matters of routine which rest in mere expediency—acts which need not have been required in the first place, as an affidavit of the sheriff to the delinquent list—and which the legislature may, by a curative act, excuse when omitted. But the owner of property cannot be precluded from showing the invalidity of a tax deed thereto by proving the omission of any act essential to the due assessment of the same, or levy of the taxes thereon and sale thereof on that account. As to the performance of these acts and the facts necessary to constitute them, the deed can only be made *prima facie* evidence": *Marx* v. *Hanthorn,* 30 Fed. Rep. 585. "It would doubtless be a wholesome and safe rule to establish that the legislature has power to declare that the neglect to perform any act relating to the assessment and collection of taxes that it had the right to dispense with in the outset, should not defeat the sale of the property for nonpayment thereof; but to attempt to dispense with the assessment of the property or levy of the tax and allow an enforcement of a pretended tax would be sanctioning an arbitrary exaction. It would not be a tax levied in pursuance of law as provided, in effect, by the constitution of the state": *Strode* v. *Washer,* 17 Or. 53. It is therefore clear that where the constitution of a state requires an assessment and equalization of property, the legislature cannot make a tax deed conclusive evidence of such assessment or equalization: *Davis* v. *Vanarsdale,* 59 Miss. 367; *Strode* v. *Washer,* 17 Or. 53; *Sharpleigh* v. *Surdam,* 1 Flip. 472; *Immegart* v. *Gorgas,* 41 Iowa, 439; *Cairo etc. R. R. Co.* v. *Parks,* 32 Ark. 131, 142; *Allen* v. *Armstrong,* 16 Iowa, 508, 514; *Stoudenmire* v. *Brown,* 48 Ala. 699; 57 Ala. 482. The dicta all agree that the owner cannot be precluded from showing a want of a valid levy of the tax, but we have not discovered any case in which the question was necessarily involved. Where a warrant is required to issue to authorize some officer to proceed to sell property delinquent for taxes, it may be that it is a "material and fundamental step in the sale, and the rightfulness of any sale must rest upon the fact of such warrant, and it is not competent for the legislature to create a presumption which shall override the fact or estop the party proving the truth": *Corbin* v. *Hill,* 21 Iowa, 72.

Conclusive Presumptions in Other Cases.—We have referred at some length to the rules here under consideration as applied to tax cases. The decisions applicable to these cases are more numerous than elsewhere, and the principles applicable to them may by analogy be applied to other cases concerning which the courts have not had occasion to speak so frequently or clearly.

The legislature by creating a conclusive presumption cannot deprive a party of a vested right. In criminal prosecutions, we apprehend that under no circumstances can the legislature create a conclusive presumption of guilt, nor deprive the accused of the right to offer proof of his innocence, nor require the jury to disregard such proof, nor to give effect to any presumption of the truth of which they are not satisfied: *Voght* v. *State*, 124 Ind. 358; *State* v. *Beswick*, 13 R. I. 211; 43 Am. Rep. 26. In civil cases, though we have met no direct adjudication on the subject, we think it safe to assert that where a party would be able to establish his cause of action and of defense, were he permitted to prove the truth, and such cause or defense does not consist of a mere irregularity or technicality, he cannot be precluded from offering such proof by a statute creating a conclusive presumption against him: *L. R. etc. R. R. Co.* v. *Payne*, 33 Ark. 816; 34 Am. Rep. 55; *Cairo etc. R. R. Co.* v. *Parks*, 32 Ark. 131, unless such presumption is a mere enforcement against him of the doctrines of estoppel, or a mere application of a statute of limitation under which he is prevented from asserting some cause of action or of defense because he had not acted within the time allowed him by law. Perhaps the decision in *Webb* v. *Den*, 17 How. 576, cannot be reconciled with what we have here said. The legislature of the state of Tennessee enacted that whenever a deed has been registered "twenty years or more, the same shall be presumed to be upon lawful authority, and the probate shall be good and effectual, though the certificate on which the same has been registered has not been transferred to the register's books, and no matter what has been the form of the certificate of probate or acknowledgment." In an action of ejectment a copy of the registry of a deed was offered in evidence, to the admission of which the defendants objected, because it was not proved, acknowledged, or authenticated, so as to entitle it to registration, and there was no proof of its acknowledgment or of the privy acknowledgment of Mary Stiff, a *feme covert*, party thereto. The objection was overruled, and the copy read in evidence. In sustaining the action of the trial court, the supreme court of the United States, after referring to the fact that the deed was registered in 1809, and that some of the grantees had been in possession under it ever since, added: "After such a length of time the law presumes it to have been registered on lawful authority, without regard to the form of certificate of probate or acknowledgment. As a legal presumption it is conclusive that the deed was properly acknowledged, although the contrary may appear on the face of the papers." This language, standing alone and disconnected from the circumstances of the case in which it was used, might imply that the statute which the court was interpreting had created a conclusive presumption of the execution of the deed, and that such statute was nevertheless constitutional and valid. There was not, however, in the case, any offer to prove that the instrument as it appeared on record had not been executed by the grantors, and the only effect of the decision of the trial court was to cast upon those disputing the deed the burden of proving its nonexecution. This, taking into consideration the possession maintained under it, and the length of time for which it had appeared upon the registry, was unquestionably within the power of the legislature.

PEOPLE v. SHELDON.

[139 NEW YORK, 251.]

CONSPIRACIES INJURIOUS TO TRADE AND COMMERCE.—An agreement between dealers, made for the purpose of controlling the price and managing the business of the sale of coal, so as to prevent competition in
price between the parties to the agreement, is illegal, and if the price
of coal was raised in pursuance of the agreement and to effect its objects the crime of conspiracy was committed, and is punishable, under
a statute making it a misdemeanor for two or more persons to conspire
to commit any act injurious to trade and commerce; nor can the guilty
parties escape conviction by proving that the object of the agreement
was to prevent ruinous rivalry between dealers in the same commodity,
and that it had not resulted in raising the price beyond its nominal and
reasonable value.

CONSPIRACIES—OVERT ACT.—If an unlawful agreement to raise the price
of coal was entered into between dealers therein, the raising of the
price in pursuance of such agreement, and to accomplish its purpose,
is an overt act sufficient to sustain a conviction for conspiracy.

PROSECUTION for conspiracy. The defendant and others,
constituting all but one of the retail dealers in coal in the
city of Lockport, entered into an agreement to organize a
coal exchange for such city. The agreement was in writing,
purporting to be the constitution and by-laws of such coal
exchange. The objects of the Exchange were stated to be the
fostering of trade and commerce in coal, wood, and other
products, the protection from unjust and unlawful exactions,
the production of uniformity and certainty in the customs
and usages of the trade, the establishing of such rules
and regulations as might be proper and necessary for the
mutual co-operation, interest, and protection of the retail
dealers in coal and wood in the city of Lockport, and it was
made the duty of all members to strictly obey all the provisions of the constitution, by-laws, and resolutions of the
Exchange, and to permit the secretary the free exercise of the
duties imposed upon him in enforcing them. Officers and
committees of the Exchange were provided for; one of such
officers was its secretary, who, it was agreed, should be permitted to see any portion of the books of any member, when
in pursuit of wrongdoing, and to demand an affidavit when
he thinks it necessary to refute or sustain any specific
charge. Any member charged with violating any provision
of the by-laws, or any rule or resolution of the Exchange, or
of being guilty of conduct unbecoming a member or prejudicial to its interests, or of giving short weight or over-

weight, was liable to be summoned before the secretary, and
if the charge were regarded as sustained by the secretary
the member was considered to be "in default" until five-
sixths of all the members should vote to reinstate him.
A member in default forfeited all rights to any moneys or
property held by the Exchange as its own or in trust,
and all rights of membership, unless reinstated, and could
not be reinstated except by a vote of five-sixths of the
members, and depositing with the treasurer one hundred
dollars as a fee for renewal of membership. A member
accused by the secretary of having violated any provision of
the constitution or by-laws, or of any resolution, though there
was no evidence upon the subject, was required to make an
affidavit "that he has in no instance sold or delivered coal
for which he has not received the full price at which the
majority of the other members were selling coal of the same
size at the same time, and that he has not directly or indirectly given any rebate, commission, or other concession
equivalent to cash, thereby actually reducing the established
market price made by the Lockport Coal Exchange, and that
not less than two thousand and not more two thousand
pounds had of his knowledge been sold by himself, his partner, or any employees, and delivered as a ton." The agreement further declared that the price of coal in retail should,
as far as practicable, be kept uniform; that it should require a five-sixths vote of all members of the Exchange to
advance or reduce the price of coal; and "no price shall be
made at any time which amounts to more than a fair and
reasonable advance over wholesale rates, or is higher than
the current prices of exchanges at Rochester or Buffalo,
figured upon corresponding freight tariff, but at no time shall
the price of coal at retail exceed one dollar above the cost of
the same at wholesale, except by the unanimous vote of all
the members of the Exchange"; that the sale of coal should
be through the nominal channels of the trade; that soliciting
should be discouraged, and no club orders to associated
buyers to reduce prices should be considered or accepted;
that no member should employ any person to solicit orders,
nor display any sign indicating that orders for coal would be
taken at outside places. The indictment averred that this
agreement constituted an unlawful conspiracy to increase the
price of coal at retail in the city of Lockport, and that in
pursuance of it the defendants and other members of the

Exchange elected officers, and by resolutions fixed and established the rate and price of coal at various sums, which were seventy-five cents per ton higher than the previous market price of coal of like quality at retail in the same city. The evidence left no doubt of the execution of the agreement, the organization of the Exchange, and the fixing of the advanced price of coal as charged in the indictment.

E. M. Ashley, for the appellants.

P. F. King, for the respondent.

[261] ANDREWS, C. J. Section 168 of the Penal Code makes it a misdemeanor for two or more persons to conspire (subd. 6) " to commit any act injurious to the public health, to public morals, or to trade or commerce, or for the perversion or obstruction of public justice, or of the due administration of the law." The Revised Statutes contained a similar provision: 2 Rev. Stats., 692, sec. 8, subd. 6.

The fact that the defendants subscribed the constitution and by-laws of the "Lockport Coal Exchange," and participated in its management was not controverted on the trial. Nor is it denied that the object of the organization was to prevent competition in the price of coal among the retail dealers, acting as the "Lockport Coal Exchange," by constituting the Exchange the sole authority to fix the price which should be charged by the members for coal sold by them, and there is no dispute that in pursuance of the plan the [262] Exchange did proceed to fix the price of coal, and that the parties to the agreement were thereafter governed thereby in making sales to their customers. It is not questioned that the price first established was seventy-five cents in advance of the then market price, and that there was afterwards a still further advance. The defendants gave evidence tending to show (and of this there was no contradiction), that before and at the time of the organization of the Exchange the excessive competition between the dealers in coal in Lockport had reduced the price below the actual cost of the coal and the expense of handling, and that the business was carried on at a loss. It was not shown that the prices of coal, fixed from time to time by the Exchange, were excessive or oppressive, or were more than sufficient to afford a fair remuneration to the dealers. The trial judge submitted the case to the jury upon the proposition that if the defendants entered into the organization agreement for the purpose of controlling the price of coal and managing the business of the sale of coal, so as to prevent competition in price between the members of the Exchange, the agreement was illegal, and that if the jury found that this was their intent, and that the price of coal was raised in pursuance of the agreement to effect its object, the crime of conspiracy was established. The correctness of this proposition is the main question in the case. If a combination between independent dealers, to prevent competition between themselves in the sale of an article of prime necessity, is, in the contemplation of the law, an act inimical to trade or commerce, whatever may be done under and in pursuance of it, and although the object of the combination is merely the due protection of the parties to it against ruinous rivalry, and no attempt is made to charge undue or excessive prices, then the indictment was sustained by proof. On the other hand, if the validity of an agreement, having for its object the prevention of competition between dealers in the same commodity, depends upon what may be done under the agreement, and it is to be adjudged valid or invalid according to the fact whether it is made the means for raising the price of a commodity beyond its normal and [263] reasonable value, then it would be difficult to sustain this conviction, for it affirmatively appears that the price fixed for coal by the Exchange did not exceed what would afford a reasonable profit to the dealers. The obtaining by dealers of a fair and reasonable price for what they sell does not seem to contravene public policy, or to work an injury to individuals. On the contrary, the general interests are promoted by activity in trade, which cannot permanently exist without reasonable encouragement to those engaged in it. Producers, consumers, and laborers are alike benefited by healthful conditions of business.

But the question here does not, we think, turn on the point whether the agreement between the retail dealers in coal did, as matter of fact, result in injury to the public or to the community in Lockport. The question is, was the agreement, in view of what might have been done under it and the fact that it was an agreement the effect of which was to prevent competition among the coal-dealers, one upon which the law affixes the brand of condemnation. It has hitherto been an accepted maxim in political economy that " competition is the life of trade." The courts have acted upon and adopted this maxim in passing upon the validity of agreements, the design

of which was to prevent competition in trade, and have held
such agreements to be invalid. It is to be noticed that the
organization of the "Exchange" was of the most formal character. The articles bound all who became members to conform to the regulations. The observance of such regulations
by the members was enforced by penalties and forfeitures.
A member accused by the secretary of having violated any
provision of the constitution or by-laws was required to purge
himself by affidavit, although evidence to sustain the charge
should be lacking. The shippers of coal were to be notified
in case of persistent default by the member, that "he is not
entitled to the privileges of the membership in the Exchange."
No member was permitted to sell coal at less than the price
fixed by the Exchange. The organization was a carefully devised scheme to prevent competition in the price of coal
[264] among the retail dealers, and the moral and material
power of the combination afforded a reasonable guaranty that
others would not engage in the business in Lockport except
in conformity with the rules of the Exchange.

The cases of *Hooker* v. *Vandewater*, 4 Denio, 349; 47 Am.
Dec. 258, and *Stanton* v. *Allen*, 5 Denio, 434, 49 Am. Dec. 282,
are, we think, decisive authorities in support of the judgment
in this case. They were cases of combinations between transportation lines on the canals, to maintain rates for the carriage
of goods and passengers, and the court, in those cases, held
that the agreements were void, on the ground that they were
agreements to prevent competition, and the doctrine was
affirmed that agreements having that purpose, made between
independent lines of transportation, were, in law, agreements
injurious to trade. In those cases it was not shown that the
rates fixed were excessive. In the case in 5 Denio, the judge
delivering the opinion referred to the effect of the agreement
upon the public revenue from the canals. This was an added
circumstance, tending to show the injury which might result
from agreements to raise prices or prevent competition. See
also, *People* v. *Fisher*, 14 Wend. 10; 28 Am. Dec. 501; *Arnot*
v. *Pittston etc. Coal Co.*, 68 N. Y. 558; 23 Am. Rep. 190. The
gravamen of the offense of conspiracy is the combination.
Agreements to prevent competition in trade are in contemplation of law injurious to trade, because they are liable to be
injuriously used. The present case may be used as an illustration. The price of coal now fixed by the exchange may
be reasonable in view of the interests both of dealers and

consumers, but the organization may not always be guided
by the principle of absolute justice. There are some limitations in the constitution of the Exchange, but these may be
changed and the price of coal may be unreasonably advanced.
It is manifest that the Exchange is acting in sympathy with
the producers and shippers of coal. Some of the shippers
were present when the plan of organization was considered,
and it was indicated on the trial that the producers had a
similar organization between themselves. If agreements and
combinations to prevent competition in prices are or may be
hurtful to [265] trade, the only sure remedy is to prohibit all
agreements of that character. If the validity of such an
agreement was made to depend upon actual proof of public
prejudice or injury, it would be very difficult in any case to
establish the invalidity, although the moral evidence might
be very convincing. We are of the opinion that the principle
upon which the case was submitted to the jury is sanctioned
by the decisions in this state, and that the jury were properly
instructed that if the purpose of the agreement was to prevent
competition in the price of coal between the retail dealers, it
was illegal and justified the conviction of the defendants.

There is a single remaining question. The trial judge was
requested by the defendants' counsel, in substance, to charge
that the overt act required to be proved to sustain a conviction for conspiracy, must be one which might injuriously affect
the public, and that the act of the defendants in raising the
price of coal was of itself not such an overt act as was required. The request was, we think, properly refused. The
offense of conspiracy was complete at common law on proof
of the unlawful agreement. It was not necessary to allege or
prove any overt act in pursuance of the agreement: 3 Ch.
Cur. Laws, 142; *O'Connell* v. *Reg.*, 11 Clark & F. 155. In
this state this rule of the common law was changed by the
revised statutes, and, with certain exceptions, it was provided
that no agreement should be deemed a conspiracy "unless
some act beside such agreement be done to effect the object
thereof by one or more of the parties to such agreement":
2 Rev. Stats, 692, sec. 10. And this principle was re-enacted
in the Penal Code, sec. 171. The object of the statute was to
require something more than a mere agreement to constitute
a criminal conspiracy. There must be some act in pursuance
thereof and done to effect its object, before the crime is consummated. A mere agreement, followed by no act, is insuf-

ficient. The overt act charged in the indictment and proved, was the raising of the price of coal. The raising of the price of coal by a dealer connected with any conspiracy is not unlawful, but if there is a conspiracy to regulate the [266] price, and that conspiracy is unlawful, then raising the price is an act done to effect its object, whether the price fixed is reasonable or excessive. The object of the statute is accomplished when it is shown that the parties have proceeded to act upon the agreement.

We think there is no error in the record, and the conviction should, therefore, be affirmed.

All concur.

Judgment affirmed.

CONSPIRACIES INJURIOUS TO COMMERCE AND TRADE: See the extended notes to *People* v. *Fisher*, 28 Am. Dec. 512, and *People* v. *Richards*, 51 Am. Dec. 92. A conspiracy or combination to injure one in his trade or occupation is indictable: *Crump* v. *Commonwealth*, 84 Va. 927; 10 Am. St. Rep. 895, and note.

COMBINATIONS IN RESTRAINT OF TRADE.—All combinations, whether of capitalists or workmen for the purpose of influencing trade in their favor by raising or reducing prices, are so far illegal that the agreements to combine cannot be enforced by the courts: *More* v. *Bennett*, 140 Ill. 69; 33 Am. St. Rep. 216, and note. Combinations of individuals, formed for the purpose of stifling competition in trade, are against public policy and void: *Texas etc. Oil Co.* v. *Adoue*, 83 Tex. 650; 29 Am. St. Rep. 690, and note. Combinations creating monopolies are void: *Pacific Factor Co.* v. *Adler*, 90 Cal. 110; 25 Am. St. Rep. 102, and note; *Chapin* v. *Brown*, 83 Iowa, 156; 32 Am. St. Rep. 297, and note.

FARMERS' LOAN AND TRUST COMPANY *v.* WILSON.
[139 NEW YORK, 284.]

PRINCIPAL AND AGENT.—ON THE DEATH OF A PRINCIPAL the power of his agent to collect and receive rents terminates, unless the agent had a power coupled with an interest. A payment made to the agent after such death does not bind the estate of the principal, though neither the agent nor the person making the payment had notice of such death.

PRINCIPAL AND AGENT—POWER COUPLED WITH AN INTEREST, WHAT IS NOT.—The fact that an agent is entitled to commission on moneys collected by him does not give him a power coupled with an interest so as to support a payment made to him after the death of his principal. The interest which can protect the power from the death of the person by whom it was created must be an interest in the thing itself.

Hugo Hirsh, for the appellant.

Turner, McClure, and Rolston, for the respondent.

285 O'BRIEN, J. The plaintiff, as general guardian of infants, heirs, and devisees of one William Maden, has recovered judgment against the defendant for rent claimed to be due under a lease of certain real estate executed in the lifetime of the testator. Maden died in Cuba on the 6th of August, 1884, having by will devised the real estate in Brooklyn, the rent of which was claimed in this action, to his infant children, who are represented by the plaintiff. He had been for many years before his death a resident of Cuba, and the owner of the real estate in question. The will was duly proved and established under the laws of that country on the 27th of August, 1884, **286** and such proceedings were afterwards had here that it was admitted to record in the office of the surrogate of New York on the 10th of June, 1885, and the plaintiff was appointed guardian December 19, 1888. The real estate had been for many years managed and rented by an agent of the owner, who acted under a verbal authority. The judgment was for rent accruing under the lease subsequent to the death of the owner, from the month of September, 1884, to and including the month of May, 1885. It is undisputed that the defendant paid all the rent claimed to the agent subsequent to the death of his principal, but as it does not appear that the agent ever accounted for the same, the sole question presented by this appeal is whether the defendant is protected by such payment in this action. On the 8th of April, 1884, the testator, by his agent, and the defendant executed the lease which appears to be under seal, acknowledged, and recorded. By this instrument Maden, who is described as " of Cortenas, Island of Cuba," demised to the defendant for the term of five years from May 1st thereafter the buildings in respect to which the rent is claimed to have accrued, at the yearly rent of three thousand five hundred dollars, payable monthly in advance. The lease contains a provision for renewal for five years, at four thousand dollars per year, payable in like manner. The defendant, on his part, covenanted to pay the rent as stipulated, and to surrender the premises at the expiration of the term. The defendant had, during the four years prior to the execution of this lease, occupied the premises as tenant under agreement with the agent, and had paid the rent to him, and it appears that the defendant never had any personal dealing with the owner, though he knew he was in fact the landlord and where he resided. At the time that the defendant paid the rent in question to the agent neither of them had any knowledge or information in regard to the death of the owner.

The rule is well settled by authority that the power of an agent to collect and receive payment of rents falling due to his principal, when such power is not coupled with an interest, terminates and ceases upon the death of the principal, and [287] that payment made thereafter to the agent does not bind the estate of the principal, though the payment be made in ignorance of the principal's death: *Weber* v. *Bridgman*, 113 N. Y. 600.

The rule seems to have originated in the presumption that those who deal with an agent knowingly assume the risk that his authority may be terminated by death without notice to them. The case of an agency coupled with an interest is made an exception to the rule: *Grapel* v. *Hodges*, 112 N. Y. 419; *Hunt* v. *Rousmanier*, 8 Wheat. 204. It is urged that the exception applies to this case for the reason that the agent was entitled to commissions upon the rents collected, and to be allowed his disbursements for repairs, insurance, and taxes. The trial court refused to find that he had such an interest as would prevent the revocation of the power upon the death of the principal. There was no proof to show that the agent, at the time of the death, had any claim on account of repairs, insurance, or taxes, and, therefore, it is needless to inquire how far, if at all, these elements, if shown to exist, would change the case. It may be assumed that the agent was entitled to compensation for his services, in the form of commissions, upon the money collected, while the agency was in force. But this would not give him such an interest as would continue his power after his principal's death. Agents are quite frequently paid by commissions upon sales of property, or upon moneys collected, and to hold that this constitutes such an interest as would save the power from revocation by the death of the principal, would be, in effect, to abrogate the rule in most cases. The interest which can protect a power after the death of the person by whom it was created must be an interest in the thing itself. The power must be ingrafted upon some estate or interest in the thing to which it relates: *Hunt* v. *Rousmanier*, 8 Wheat. 204. Here the agent had no estate or interest in the property nor in the rents as such. The most that can be said is that he was entitled to commissions upon what was to be produced by the exercise of the power, and hence it cannot be said that the power and

the interest are united in the same person at the time of their
289 creation.   It cannot, we think, be claimed for a moment
that the principal, in the creation of the power, conferred
upon the agent any interest in the subject to which it was
intended to relate.   At no time could the agent act except in
the name of his principal, and a power thus limited must
necessarily cease with the death of the person in whose name
it is to be exercised.   The learned counsel for the defendant,
in an interesting and ingenious argument, has attempted to
take this case out of the operation of the general rule, but,
while much impressed with the equity of his position, we have
not been able to make any satisfactory distinction between
the facts as they appear in the record and those that appeared
in the cases to which reference has been made.   The result
which we feel constrained to reach will illustrate how a rule
or principle of law will operate harshly and produce what
might seem to be injustice in a particular case.   This conclusion must, however, be modified when we consider that
either the defendant or the infant children of the deceased
must bear the loss which has occurred by the default of the
agent.   The defendant could have foreseen what has happened
and protected himself against loss by insisting upon payment
to the owners alone, or by proper stipulations in the lease.
There can be no doubt that a party may, by his contract, estop his personal representatives or his estate from recovering
money paid to his agent in good faith, after his death, under
such circumstances as appear in this case, but we see no
reasonable way that the children of the owner, who are the
real plaintiffs in this case, could have avoided the result.   The
presumption that every man knows the law implies that they
will act with reasonable caution and vigilance in their business affairs, and that in entering upon contracts or carrying
them out they will become informed by competent advice of
the risks and dangers that beset them.   When a man knowingly deals with the agent of a principal who resides in a foreign country, it must be assumed that he will guard against
the perils that the transaction necessarily involves, and while
courts are disposed to exercise all their power to relieve parties who have acted in **289** good faith, from the result of their
neglect to provide, in the first instance, against accidents
which might have been foreseen, there seems to be no way
open for such a result in this case, without disregarding **or**
refining away an important rule of law.   This would **practi-**

cally be judicial legislation. We feel bound to follow the current of authority, and to leave the work of reforming the law on this question, if reform be necessary or desirable, to the legislature.

There would seem to be an incongruity in the law of agency with respect to the effect of a revocation of the agent's powers by the act of the principal himself and a revocation produced by his death. In the former case, the revocation does not affect third parties, dealing with the agent in good faith, without notice: *Claflin* v. *Lenheim*, 66 N. Y. 301; *Williams* v. *Birbeck*, Hoff. Ch. 359; *Blake* v. *Garwood*, 42 N. J. Eq. 276; Wharton on Agency, secs. 99–104; Story on Agency, sec. 470. While in the latter, as we have seen, the revocation operates upon all parties, without notice, unless the power is coupled with an interest, in which case the agent may execute it in his own name, notwithstanding the death of the principal. The civil law protected third parties who dealt in good faith with the agent without notice in all cases, whether the power was revoked by the act of the principal or his death, but as Chancellor Kent has observed this equitable principle does not prevail in the English law (2 Kent's Commentaries, 13th ed. 646), from which the rule that obtains in this state was derived, though in other jurisdictions, and perhaps in England, the harshness of the common law has been modified by statute: *Weber* v. *Bridgman*, 113 N. Y. 602. The common-law rule has become too firmly established in this state to be disturbed by judicial action, though a change by the law-making power would be in harmony with more enlightened views and would promote the interests of justice.

The judgment must, therefore, be affirmed, with costs.

All concur.

Judgment affirmed.

———

AGENCY.—TERMINATION OF BY DEATH OF PRINCIPAL: See the extended note to *Cassiday* v. *McKenzie*, 39 Am. Dec. 81, and the note to *Spitler* v. *James*, 2 Am. Rep. 341, also *Rigs* v. *Cage*, 2 Humph. 350; 38 Am. Dec. 559, and note.

POWER COUPLED WITH AN INTEREST IS NOT TERMINATED BY THE DEATH OF THE DONOR: *Cleveland* v. *Williams*, 29 Tex. 204; 94 Am. Dec. 274, and note; *Staples* v. *Bradbury*, 8 Greenl. 181; 23 Am. Dec. 494, and note; *Norton* v. *Whitehead*, 84 Cal. 263; 18 Am. St. Rep. 172, and note; *Knapp* v. *Alvord*, 10 Paige, 205; 40 Am. Dec. 241, and note; *Mansfield* v. *Mansfield*, 6 Conn. 559; 16 Am. Dec. 76; *Bergen* v. *Bennett*, 1 Caines Cas. 1; 2 Am. Dec. 281, and note; *Benneson* v. *Savage*, 130 Ill. 352; *Krumdick* v. *White*, 92 Cal. 143. See also the extended note to *Cassiday* v. *McKenzie*, 39 Am. Dec. 83.

FAIRCHILD *v.* MCMAHON.

[139 NEW YORK, 290.]

FALSE REPRESENTATIONS AS TO THE PRICE WHICH HAD BEEN PAID FOR THE PROPERTY when bought about a month previously is a sufficient basis to predicate a finding of fraud upon, when such representation is deliberately made by the holder of such property or his agent then seeking to sell it, and is relied upon by the party to whom it was made, and was intended to influence him.

PRINCIPAL AND AGENT.—IF FALSE REPRESENTATIONS ARE MADE BY AN AGENT employed to sell property as to the price paid for it by his principal, they must be regarded as made by the principal if he accepts their fruits. He cannot accept the property secured by means of such representations and then disclaim responsibility for the fraud through which the property was procured.

SUIT to foreclose a mortgage.   Judgment for defendant.

Payson Merrill, for the appellant.

Denis McMahon, for the respondent.

291 O'BRIEN, J.   The plaintiff sought to foreclose a mortgage assigned to her, before the commencement of the action, executed and delivered by the defendant, upon certain real estate of which she was the owner, subject to other mortgage liens, and bearing date April 30, 1890, for fifteen hundred dollars, payable one year from date, with semi-annual interest.   The mortgage was given to one Joseph H. Cain, with whom the negotiations **292** and transactions which resulted in its execution and delivery were had, or with agents acting for him or in his interest.   The defense is fraud practiced upon the defendant, by means of which she was induced to make and deliver the mortgage and the accompanying bond. The facts to sustain this defense are stated with considerable detail, the substance of which, in brief, is as follows:

On the 9th of April, prior to the execution of the mortgage, the defendant, through her husband acting for her, entered into an agreement with Cain to exchange real estate.   Each owned a house and lot encumbered by mortgage, the equity of redemption in which was to be conveyed to the other, and the agreement was actually carried out by the execution and delivery of proper conveyances.   The mortgage in question was executed and delivered in pursuance of this agreement. It is alleged in substance that one Yoran, the plaintiff's son, was the principal actor in the transaction and the real party to be benefited.   That though the record title to the real es-

tate to be conveyed to the defendant was in Cain, yet his title
was nominal, as his name was simply used by Yoran in the
purchase of the property and in the negotiations for its sale
to the defendant and in the conveyance. It is then charged
in substance that Yoran, Cain, and their broker, and another
broker employed by and acting for the defendant's husband,
her agent, conspired together to cheat and defraud the defendant by false and fraudulent representations concerning
the value and condition of the house which the defendant by
the agreement was to receive in exchange for her property
and which she subsequently conveyed, and that, in reliance
upon the truth of the statements, she, through her husband,
entered into and executed the agreement and made the exchange. It is further averred that upon discovery of the
fraud the defendant offered to rescind the whole transaction.
The courts below have sustained the defense, and the charges
of fraud and other facts alleged by the defendant are found
by the learned trial judge to be substantially true. The testimony upon the issues of fact was very conflicting, but [293]
after considering it with all the circumstances we are unable
to say that any of the findings, material to the defense, and
challenged by exception, are without support, and, therefore,
feel concluded by them as to the facts.

There are one or two questions of law, however, that should
be noticed. One of the false representations made by Yoran
and his broker to the defendant's husband, as appeared from
the findings, which was relied upon, and which influenced her
.action in making the exchange and giving the bond and mortgage in suit, and upon which the finding of fraud is based,
was that the house and lot transferred to the defendant in the
exchange was worth $15,000; that Cain had just purchased
it at the price of $12,000 from the executors of the deceased
owners, who were compelled to sell at a price below the real
value, and that such was the consideration expressed in the
deed to him from the executors, as would appear from the
record in the county clerk's office.

It is further found that the defendant's husband, before
entering into the transaction, did examine the deed in the
clerk's office under which Cain took the title, and that it
appeared from the same that the consideration was $12,000,
and that the defendant and her husband believed the statement; that while it was true that the consideration stated in
the deed was $12,000, it was not true that the real considera-

tion paid was that sum, but, on the contrary, the fact was that about twenty-four days before the transaction Yoran had purchased the property for $7,000, which was its true value, and had taken the deed in the name of Cain, expressing a fictitious consideration, for the purpose of deceiving investors, and that the defendant had procured the consideration to be falsely stated in the deed.　This finding raises the question whether a false statement, deliberately made, by a party about to sell property, to the party about to purchase it, with respect to the price which he had paid for it to a former owner, is a sufficient basis upon which to predicate a finding of fraud, when the statement is relied upon by the party to whom made.

It has been held that a false statement by a vendor to [294] a vendee concerning the value of property about to be sold will not sustain an action for fraud, but the vendee, in such cases, must rely on his own judgment: *Ellis* v. *Andrews*, 56 N. Y. 83; 15 Am. Rep. 379.

It may be that the rule in such cases would be different if the purchaser was prevented by any act or artifice of the seller from exercising his judgment in ascertaining the value.

But the question here is not one arising out of a representation as to value.　The representation was with respect to a fact which might, in the ordinary course of business, influence the action and control the judgment of the purchaser, namely, the price paid for the property about to be sold by the vendor within less than a month prior to the transaction; and so, we think, that a false statement with respect to the price paid under such circumstances, which is intended to influence the purchaser, and does influence him, constitutes a sufficient basis for a finding of fraud.

It was so held in *Sandford* v. *Handy*, 23 Wend. 260, where a new trial was granted to the plaintiff in an action of this character on the ground that proof of such representations was improperly excluded at the trial.'　Chief Justice Nelson, delivering the opinion of the court, page 269, said:

" I am also inclined to think that any misrepresentation as to the actual cost of the property is a material fact, and naturally calculated to mislead the purchaser. . . . . Misrepresentation as to the cost of an article stands somewhat on the same footing.　It is a material fact, which not only tends to enhance the value, but gives to it a firmness and effect beyond the force of mere opinion.

"The vendor is not bound to speak on the subject, but if he does, I think he should speak the truth."

The same principle received the sanction of the court in *Van Epps* v. *Harrison*, 5 Hill, 63, 40 Am. Dec. 314, and is apparently recognized in *Smith* v. *Countryman*, 30 N. Y. 655, *Hammond* v. *Pennock*, 61 N. Y. 151, and *Goldenbergh* v. *Hoffman*, 69 N. Y. 326.

There is another question in the case as to how far these statements as to the cost of the property made by a broker [295] employed by Yoran can bind the plaintiff or Cain, her assignor; but it sufficiently appears that Yoran used Cain's name in the transactions with his consent, and that he also employed the broker to sell the property or negotiate the agreement for an exchange. All persons who acted for or in the name of Cain, or with his consent, in bringing about the transaction must now be deemed to be his agents, and as he accepted the fruits of their efforts in this regard and took the title to the bond and mortgage, which was a part of the result of their negotiations, and transferred them to the plaintiff, all the methods employed by either Yoran or his broker to procure the agreement for an exchange and the mortgage in suit are imputable to the person in whose name they acted, and who voluntarily received the securities thus procured. He could not, even though innocent, receive a mortgage thus procured, and at the same time disclaim responsibility for the fraud, by means of which the defendant was induced to deliver it: *Krumm* v. *Beach*, 96 N. Y. 398. The findings imply that the broker was the general agent of Cain, and as such his statements bound his principal, and those findings are sustained by the evidence.

The plaintiff took no other or different title to the bond and mortgage than Cain had. The record discloses no estoppel or other principle of equity which can protect the plaintiff against any defense which might have been urged if the securities had remained in the hands of the original parties.

We have examined the other exceptions in the case, and as they do not present any question requiring discussion, or any error that affects the judgment, it should be affirmed, with costs.

All concur.

Judgment affirmed.

AGENCY—PRINCIPAL'S LIABILITY FOR FALSE REPRESENTATIONS OF AGENT. A principal is liable to third persons in a civil suit for the frauds, deceits, concealments, misrepresentations, torts, negligences, and other malfeasances or misfeasances and omissions of duty of his agent in the course of his employment, although the principal did not authorize or justify the same, or even know of such misconduct: *Fifth Avenue Bank* v. *Forty-second Street etc. Ry. Co.*, 137 N. Y. 231; 33 Am. St. Rep. 712, and note with the cases collected discussing a principal's liability for the false representations of his agent.

SALE OF LAND INDUCED BY FALSE REPRESENTATIONS: See *Roberts* v. *French*, 153 Mass. 60; 25 Am. St. Rep. 611, and note; notes to *Williams* v. *McFadden*, 11 Am. St. Rep. 350, and *Lewark* v. *Carter*, 10 Am. St. Rep. 45. The question as to the effect of the false representations of a vendor as to the value of his property will be found fully discussed in the extended note to *Cottrill* v. *Krum*, 18 Am. St. Rep. 556.

CASCO NATIONAL BANK *v.* CLARK.

[139 NEW YORK, 307.]

NEGOTIABLE INSTRUMENTS SIGNED BY OFFICERS OF A CORPORATION.—If a negotiable promissory note is given in payment of the debt of a corporation but the language of the promise does not disclose a corporate obligation, and the signatures are the names of individuals, a holder taking *bona fide* and without notice of the circumstances of the making of the note is entitled to hold and enforce it as the personal obligation of the signers, though they affixed to their names the titles of their offices. Unless the note creates, or fairly implies, an undertaking of the corporation, if the purpose is equivocal the obligation is that of the apparent makers.

NEGOTIABLE INSTRUMENT.—APPEARANCE ON THE MARGIN OF A NEGOTIABLE INSTRUMENT OF THE NAME "RIDGEWOOD ICE CO." does not create any presumption that such paper was, or was intended to be, the paper of that company.

CORPORATIONS.—AN OFFICER'S KNOWLEDGE DERIVED AS AN INDIVIDUAL, and not while acting officially for the corporation, cannot operate to its prejudice. Hence, if a note is executed which appears to be the note of certain persons, but which was in fact intended to be the note of a corporation of which they were officers, and such note is negotiated to a banking corporation, the latter is not chargeable with notice that the note was intended to be the note of the former corporation from the fact that one of its directors was also a director of the banking corporation. The directors did not owe any duty to parties executing the instrument appearing to contain their individual promise to explain that the note was not intended to be the obligation of the persons so signing it, but of the corporation of which they were officers.

ACTION upon a promissory note. Judgment in favor of the plaintiff.

Henry Daily, Jr., for the appellant.

Edward B. Merrill, for the respondent.

³¹⁰ GRAY, J.   The action is upon a promissory note in the following form, viz:

	BROOKLYN, N. Y., Aug. 2, 1890.

Ridgewood Ice Co.

$7,500.   Three months after date we promise to pay to the order of Clark & Chaplin Ice Company seventy-five hundred dollars at Mechanics' Bank.   Value received.

JOHN CLARK, Prest.

E. H. CLOSE, Treas.

. It was delivered in payment for ice sold by the payee company to the Ridgewood Ice Company, under a contract between those companies, and was discounted by the plaintiff for the payee before its maturity.   The appellants, Clark and Close, appearing as makers upon the note, the one describing himself as " Prest." and the other as " Treas.," were made individually defendants.   They defended on the ground that they had made the note as officers of the Ridgewood Ice Company, and did not become personally liable thereby for the debt represented.

Where a negotiable promissory note has been given for the payment of a debt contracted by a corporation, and the language of the promise does not disclose the corporate obligation, and the signatures to the paper are in the names of individuals, a holder, taking *bona fide* and without notice of the circumstances of its making, is entitled to hold the note as the personal undertaking of its signers, notwithstanding they affix to their names the title of an office.   Such an affix will be regarded as descriptive of the persons and not of the character **³¹¹** of the liability.   Unless the promise purports to be by the corporation, it is that of the persons who subscribe to it; and the fact of adding to their names an abbreviation of some official title has no legal signification as qualifying their obligation, and imposes no obligation upon the corporation whose officers they may be.   This must be regarded as the long and well-settled rule: Byles on Bills, secs. 36, 37, 71; *Pentz* v. *Stanton,* 10 Wend. 271; 25 Am. Dec. 558; *Taft* v. *Brewster,* 9 Johns. 334; 6 Am. Dec. 280; *Hills* v. *Bannister,* 8 Cow. 31; *Moss* v. *Livingston,* 4 N. Y. 208; *De Witt* v. *Walton,* 9 N. Y. 571; *Bottomley* v. *Fisher,* 1 Hurl. & C. 211.   It is founded in the general principle that in a contract every material thing must be definitely expressed, and not left to conjecture.   Unless the language creates, or fairly implies, the undertaking of the corporation, if the purpose is equivocal, the obligation is that of its apparent makers.

It was said in *Briggs* v. *Partridge*, 64 N. Y. 357, 363, 21 Am. Rep. 617, that persons taking negotiable instruments are presumed to take them on the credit of the parties whose names appear upon them, and a person not a party cannot be charged, upon proof that 'the ostensible party signed, or indorsed, as his agent. It may be perfectly true, if there is proof that the holder of negotiable paper was aware, when he received it, of the facts and circumstances connected with its making, and knew that it was intended and delivered as a corporate obligation only, that the persons signing it in this manner could not be held individually liable. Such knowledge might be imputable from the language of the paper, in connection with other circumstances; as in the case of *Mott* v. *Hicks*, 1 Cow. 513, 13 Am. Dec. 550, where the note read, "the president and directors promise to pay," and was subscribed by the defendant as "president." The court held that that was sufficient to distinguish the case from *Taft* v. *Brewster*, 9 Johns. 334, 6 Am. Dec. 280, and made it evident that no personal engagement was entered into or intended. Much stress was placed in that case upon the proof that the plaintiff was intimately acquainted with the transaction out of which arose the giving of the corporate obligation.

[312] In the case of *Bank of Genesee* v. *Patchin Bank*, 19 N. Y. 312, referred to by the appellants' counsel, the action was against the defendant to hold it as the indorser of a bill of exchange, drawn to the order of "S. B. Stokes, Cas.," and indorsed in the same words. The plaintiff bank was advised, at the time of discounting the bill, by the president of the Patchin Bank, that Stokes was its cashier, and that he had been directed to send it in for discount, and Stokes forwarded it in an official way to the plaintiff. It was held that the Patchin Bank was liable, because the agency of the cashier in the matter was communicated to the knowledge of the plaintiff as well as apparent.

Incidentally, it was said that the same strictness is not required in the execution of commercial paper as between banks, that is, in other respects, between individuals.

In the absence of competent evidence showing or charging knowledge in the holder of negotiable paper as to the character of the obligation, the established and safe rule must be regarded to be that it is the agreement of its ostensible maker and not of some other party, neither disclosed by the language, nor in the manner of execution. In this case the language is "we promise to pay," and the signatures by the defendants Clark and Close are perfectly consistent with an assumption by them of the company's debt.

The appearance upon the margin of the paper of the printed name "Ridgewood Ice Company" was not a fact carrying any presumption that the note was, or was intended to be, one by that company.

It was competent for its officers to obligate themselves personally, for any reason satisfactory to themselves, and, apparently to the world, they did so by the language of the note; which the mere use of a blank form of note, having upon its margin the name of their company, was insufficient to negative.

In order to obviate the effect of the rule we have discussed, the appellants proved that Winslow, a director of the payee company, was also a director in the plaintiff bank, at the time when the note was discounted, and it was argued that the [313] knowledge chargeable to him, as director of the former company, was imputable to the plaintiff. But that fact is insufficient to charge the plaintiff with knowledge of the character of the obligation. He in no sense represented, or acted for the bank in the transaction, and whatever his knowledge respecting the note, it will not be imputable to the bank: *National Bank* v. *Norton,* 1 Hill, 572, 578; *Mayor etc.* v. *Tenth National Bank,* 111 N. Y. 446, 457; *Farmers' etc. Bank* v. *Payne,* 25 Conn. 444; 68 Am. Dec. 362. He was but one of the plaintiffs' directors, who could only act as a board: *National Bank* v. *Norton,* 1 Hill, 572. If he knew the fact that these were not individual but corporate notes, we cannot presume that he communicated that knowledge to the board. An officer's knowledge, derived as an individual, and not while acting officially for the bank, cannot operate to the prejudice of the latter: *Bank of United States* v. *Davis,* 2 Hill, 451. The knowledge with which the bank as his principal would be deemed chargeable, so as to affect it, would be where as one of the board of directors and participating in the discount of the paper, he had acted affirmatively, or fraudulently, with respect to it; as in the case of *Bank* v. *Davis,* 2 Hill, 451, by a fraudulent perversion of the bills from the object for which drawn; or as in *Holden* v. *New York & Erie Bank,* 72 N. Y. 286, where the president of the bank, who represented it in all the transactions, was engaged in a fraudulent scheme of conversion. It was said in the latter case that the knowledge of the president, as an individual or as an executor, was not imputable to the bank merely because he was the president, but because, when it acted through him as president, in any transaction where that knowledge was material and applicable, it acted through an agent.

The rule may be stated, generally, to be that where a director or an officer has knowledge of material facts respecting a proposed transaction, which his relations to it, as representing the bank, have given him, then, as it becomes his official duty to communicate that knowledge to the bank, he will be presumed to have done so, and his knowledge will then [314] be imputed to the bank. But no such duty can be deemed to have existed in this case, where the appellants have made and delivered a promissory note, purporting to be their individual promise. If one of the plaintiff's officers did have knowledge, whether individully or as a director of the Clark and Chaplin Company is not material, that the paper was made and intended as a corporate note, his failure to so state to the bank could not prejudice it. It was in no sense incumbent upon him, assuming that he actually participated in the discount (a fact not shown), to explain that the note was the obligation of the Ridgewood Company and not of the persons who appeared as its makers. He was under no duty to these persons to explain their acts, and the law would not imply any. At most, it would be merely a case of knowledge, acquired by a director, of facts not material to the transaction of discount by the plaintiff, and which he was under no obligation to communicate. No other questions require discussion, and the judgment rendered below should be affirmed, with costs.

All concur.

Judgment affirmed.

___

Corporations—When Not Chargeable With Knowledge of Agents. Knowledge casually obtained by a corporate agent is not imputed to the corporation, unless the corporation acts through such agent in a matter in which the information possessed by him is pertinent: *Willard* v. *Denise*, 50 N. J. Eq. 482; 35 Am. St. Rep. 788, and note. See also *Merchants' Nat. Bank* v. *Lovitt*, 114 Mo. 519; 35 Am. St. Rep. 770, and note.

Corporation—Liability on Negotiable Instruments Executed by Officers of.—A note by which the directors of a corporation promise to pay a certain sum, and signed by them without official designation, must be regarded as the undertaking of the parties whose names appear to it as obli-

gors, and not that of the corporation: *McKensey* v. *Edwards*, 88 Ky. 272;
21 Am. St. Rep. 339, and note; *McClure* v. *Bennett*, 1 Blackf. 189; 12 Am.
Dec. 223; note to *Hodges* v. *New England Screw Co.*, 53 Am. Dec. 649. A
note signed by the president of a corportion in his own name with nothing
to indicate that he is acting as the agent of the corporation in the execution
of the instrument, is his note: *Sparks* v. *Dispatch Transfer Co.*, 104 Mo. 531;
24 Am. St. Rep. 351, and note; *Barker* v. *Mechanics' etc. Ins. Co.*, 3 Wend.
94; 20 Am. Dec. 664. This question is fully discussed in *Kline* v. *Bank*, 50
Kan. 91; 34 Am. St. Rep. 107, and note with the cases collected.

MERCHANTS' NATIONAL BANK *v.* CLARK.

[139 NEW YORK, 314.]

A CORPORATION IS NOT CHARGEABLE WITH THE KNOWLEDGE OF ITS
PRESIDENT OR OTHER OFFICER unless it is shown that such knowledge
was acquired by the officer, not casually and through his individual relations to other parties, but in an official capacity, and because of the
necessity for him to inquire and know the facts with knowledge of which
it is sought to charge the corporation. Hence, if he is the president of
a banking corporation and a note is offered to it for discount purporting
to be the individual promise of the persons signing it, he is under no
obligation to state what his opinion is as to the liability of the persons
appearing as makers of the note.

CORPORATIONS—EVIDENCE.—ADMISSIONS AND DECLARATIONS OF THE OF-
FICERS of a corporation made after it has discounted a note are not
admissible to prove knowledge on the part of the bank that such note,
though apparently the note of the signers thereof, was intended to be
the note of a corporation of which they were officers. An agent has no
authority to bind his principal by statements as to bygone transactions.

ACTION upon a promissory note payable to the Clark and
Chaplin Ice Company and in other respects in the same form
as the note set out in the opinion in the preceding case. The
note was given in payment of an indebtedness of the Ridgewood Ice Company, a corporation, of which the defendants
Clark and Close were respectively the president and treasurer.
Judgment for plaintiff.

Henry Daily, Jr., for the appellant.

Edward B. Merrill, for the respondent.

314 GRAY, J. The promissory notes sued upon in this case
were in the same form as was the note in the case of the
Casco National Bank against the same defendants, decided
at this term, 139 N. Y. 307, *ante*, p. 705. The reasons given for
the affirmance of the judgment in that case apply to the
present. These appellants, however, claim that there was
error committed by the trial court, in the exclusion of evi-

dence offered for the purpose of showing that the plaintiff knew, at the time it discounted the notes, that they were the notes of the Ridgewood Ice Company and not the notes of these defendants.

It appears that at that time Dennis, who was a director of the Clark and Chaplin Ice Company, the payee in the notes, and which procured them to be discounted, was also the president of the plaintiff. The notes were handed to him in the company's office. He was not examined, and it was not shown that he was conversant with the transaction out of which the note arose, or how it was made; but, assuming that he was, his knowledge was not attributable to the plaintiff. When it is sought to prove that the plaintiff took the note, knowing it to be the promise of the Ridgewood Company, and not that of the appellants, it is essential that the knowledge to be attributed to the plaintiff should have been acquired by its officer, not casually and through his individual relations to the other parties, but in an official capacity, and because of a necessity for him to inquire and to know the facts in behalf of the bank. That was not this case. Dennis, receiving these notes from the company of which he was a director, to be offered for discount by the board of his bank, was under no obligation to state to the board what his opinion was as to the liability of the parties appearing [319] as makers upon the notes. The questions, which were put for the purpose of showing a knowledge by plaintiff that these were the notes of the Ridgewood company, were addressed to the defendant Close, and related to conversations had with Dennis, or with any other officer of the plaintiff, before the commencement of the suit, with regard to the notes. The inquiry was whether, in any of these conversations, the witness had been told that at the time the plaintiff received the notes, it knew they were the notes of the Ridgewood company. The exclusion of such evidence was perfectly proper. A party to a promissory note should not be permitted to invalidate his written agreement by any testimony of that hearsay nature. If the statements sought to be elicited in the testimony had been made to Close they would have been quite incompetent to prejudice the rights of the bank. While evidence to show what took place at the time when the notes were offered and received for discount, in order to prove knowledge by the bank of the facts, might be proper, subsequent admissions and declarations by individual directors, or

other officers, would be of no effect to bind the bank. What
they may have said, not being under oath, cannot be evidence
against the bank; and upon that principle, as because the
statements were not made in strict relation to any agency for
the bank, such evidence is inadmissible. The principle of
the exclusion is the same as obtains in the ordinary relation
of principal and agent. The statements of the latter are
inadmissible to affect the former, unless in respect to a transaction in which he is authorized to appear for the principal,
and he has no authority to bind his principal by any statements as to bygone transactions. Hearsay evidence of this
character is only permissible when it relates to statements by
the agent, which he was authorized by his principal to make,
or to statements by him which constitute part of the transaction which is at issue between the parties: 1 Morawetz on
Private Corporations, sec. 540 a.

The judgment should be affirmed, with costs.

All concur.

Judgment affirmed.

CORPORATIONS.—AN OFFICER'S KNOWLEDGE DERIVED AS AN INDIVIDUAL
and not while acting officially for the corporation cannot operate to its
prejudice: *Casco Nat. Bank v. Clark,* 139 N. Y. 307, *ante,* p. 705, and note.

EVIDENCE.--THE DECLARATIONS AND ADMISSIONS OF AN AGENT as to past
transactions do not bind his principal, and are not admissible as evidence
against him: *Terry v. Birmingham Nat. Bank,* 93 Ala. 599; 30 Am. St. Rep.
87, and note with the cases collected.

NEWHALL *v.* WYATT.
[139 NEW YORK, 452.]

PAYMENT MADE WITH FUNDS NOT BELONGING TO THE PAYER.—The payment of money to a creditor who receives it in discharge of an existing
debt innocently and without knowledge, or means of knowledge, that
the debtor had no rightful ownership in the funds received, is good and
effectual, and does not subject the creditor to a recovery by the true
owner of such funds.

James Byrne, for the appellant.

L. Laflin Kellogg, for the respondent.

454 FINCH, J. In an action brought by the plaintiff for a
dissolution of the partnership of C. A. Wyatt & Co., a receiver was appointed, who advertised for the presentation of
claims against the firm, as preliminary to the winding up

of its [455] affairs. James R. Clark appeared as one of the
creditors, and presented a claim for something over thirty-
three thousand dollars. Upon the application of the receiver,
a referee was appointed to take evidence and pass upon this
claim, and his report, awarding the creditor only about three
thousand dollars, has been confirmed by the court and approved by the general term on appeal. The creditor comes
to this court complaining of the result, and insisting that his
claim has been improperly reduced.

Most of the conclusions reached by the referee seem to us
justified by the facts, but one of them, involving a serious
amount, we deem erroneous and an injustice to the creditor.
That error consists in charging Clark with the amount of
five drafts drawn by him, amounting to nearly seven thousand dollars, on the theory that he was debtor in that amount
to the firm, and should allow it by way of setoff against his
own demand. The facts underlying the question raised are,
in substance, the following:

There were two firms bearing the same name of C. A.
Wyatt & Co. The first consisted of Wyatt alone, no one else
having an interest with him. The second, formed later, was
composed of Wyatt and the plaintiff, Newhall, as special
partner. Clark was a creditor of each firm, which we may
distinguish as the old and the new. Before the formation of
the latter, he drew five drafts upon the old firm for sums which
were concededly due to him, payable to the order of Conway,
Gordon, and Garnett, bankers, which were accepted by C. A.
Wyatt & Co., and discounted by the bankers, Clark remaining contingently liable as drawer, and receiving the proceeds.
All this occurred before the formation of the new firm, and
was, in every respect, a regular, usual, and proper business
transaction These acceptances, the referee finds, were paid
by Wyatt out of the funds of the new firm. The appellant
criticises the finding, mainly because the bank account of the
new firm was a continuation of that of the old, without break
or change; but the proof so far warrants the finding, as to
make it conclusive upon this appeal. The payees of the draft
had no reason to suspect the real source [456] from which the
money came. They had no knowledge of the existence of
the second firm, and necessarily believed, as they had a right
to believe, that the payment was made by the real debtors
out of their own funds. They accepted the payment, surrendered up the drafts, and of course canceled and extin-

guished the contingent liability of the drawer. And yet, upon
this payment, the referee grounds his conclusion that Clark
thus became a debtor to the new firm, and that the amount of
the drafts which, through the discount, went to his benefit,
should be applied as a setoff against an equal portion of the
debt due him from the new firm.

It is undoubtedly the rule that one partner may not appropriate the property or money of the firm to the payment of
his own debt without the consent of his copartners, and that
if he does so the property misapplied may be followed and
recovered until it reaches the hands of a *bona fide* purchaser
for value. But I think it is equally well settled that the payment of money to a creditor, who receives it in discharge of
an existing debt innocently and without knowledge or means
of knowledge that the debtor paying had no rightful ownership of the fund, is good and effectual, and does not subject
the recipient to a recovery by the true owner. That doctrine
was very explicitly asserted in *Stephens* v. *Board of Education*, 79 N. Y. 187; 35 Am. Rep. 511. In that case one Gill,
who was a member of the board of education of the city of
Brooklyn, had converted to his own use the money of the
board, and so became indebted to it for the amount abstracted.
In order to procure the means of payment, Gill forged a mortgage upon the land of another and sold it to the plaintiff, receiving from him the proceeds and depositing them to his
own credit. He then drew a check for the amount of his
debt to the board, and with it paid that debt in full, the board
receiving the money and expending it in its own business.
When the plaintiff discovered the forgery and fraud he sought
to follow his own money into the hands of the board and recover it back, as in this case the new firm seeks to regain its
money misappropriated by Wyatt from the hands of Clark
as the [457] beneficial recipient.

This court held that there could be no such recovery. In
the case cited the plaintiff contended that his money had
been virtually stolen and could be followed and regained
until it reached the hands of an innocent party giving at the
time a valuable consideration therefor, and that the discharge
of a precedent debt was insufficient to afford protection against
the true owner. This court refused to accede to that doctrine, arguing that money has no earmark; that while the
purchaser of a chattel or chose in action may generally ascertain the title of his vendor, that is not so as to money, the

title to which in the possessor cannot usually be traced to its source; and that no case had been referred to in which the doctrine that an antecedent debt is not a sufficient consideration to cut off certain equities had been applied to money received in good faith and the ordinary course of business in payment of a debt; and that such a rule would obviously introduce confusion and danger into all commercial dealings. This general doctrine was further illustrated and approved upon another condition of the facts in *Southwick* v. *First Nat. Bank*, 84 N. Y. 434, 435, and seems to me well founded both in justice and the necessities of business.

We may treat the case, therefore, irrespective of the fact that the money could not have been collected back from the bankers, who gave up their drafts, and never fixed the liability of the drawer on the faith of the payment made, and treat the case as if the money had been paid directly to Clark, upon the debt due him from the old firm. His good faith cannot be questioned. He did not even know that a new firm had been formed, or that there could be any possible question as to the ownership of the moneys paid, and he may hold the payment made. A contrary rule would do him great injustice, and without the excuse of fault or negligence on his part. If his drafts had been unpaid, and his debt against the old firm had remained as desperate and valueless, he would not have extended further credit and suffered an added debt of a large amount to have accumulated. He cannot be restored to his [458] original position. There is no proof that the new firm was insolvent when the drafts were paid, and we fail to discover any ground on which the setoff can be properly allowed.

The order of the general term should be reversed, and the report of the referee and its confirmation by the special term be set aside, and the account restated, with costs of this appeal in this court and the general term.

All concur.

Order reversed.

———

PAYMENT WITH FUNDS NOT BELONGING TO PAYER.—One cannot receive money for one purpose and apply it to another without the consent of the party to whom it belongs: *Longworth* v. *Aslin*, 106 Mo. 155. A corporation can recover moneys misappropriated by one of its officers and used in liquidating his debts to another corporation: *Atlantic Mills* v. *Indian Orchard Mills*, 147 Mass. 268; 9 Am. St. Rep. 698. See, also, on this point, *Stephens* v. *Board of Education*, 79 N. Y. 187; 35 Am. Rep. 511.

CRONER *v.* COWDREY.

[139 NEW YORK, 471.]

MORTGAGEE IN POSSESSION.—One who enters into the possession of property under a mortgage foreclosure, defective in not making the owner of the fee a party thereto, is entitled to the rights of a mortgagee in possession, and cannot be ousted by an action of ejectment brought by the owner of the fee whose title is subject to such mortgage. His remedy is by a suit to foreclose his equity of redemption by an equitable action to redeem from the mortgage.

TAX SALE OF PROPERTY ESCHEATED TO THE STATE.—If persons are in possession of land claiming to own it, and having the rights of mortgagees in possession, and it is assessed to them for delinquent taxes, they cannot defeat an action of ejectment by the purchaser by proving that the property had escheated to the state, and was therefore not subject to taxation. They are not in a position to dispute the plaintiff's title. The state, because it cannot do so without paying off the mortgage, may choose never to enforce its right to escheat.

Ira L. Bamberger and W. J. Gaynor, for the appellant.

F. H. Cowdrey, for the respondent.

474 EARL, J. This is an action of ejectment to recover a lot of land situate in the city of Brooklyn, known as No. 116 Prospect street. The facts of the case are quite complicated, and we must first endeavor to set them forth with accuracy.

Paul Pontau, being the owner in fee of the lot, on April 27, 1854, executed a mortgage thereon to George B. Meade and Halsey R. Meade to secure the payment of three thousand three hundred dollars, with interest, on the twenty-eighth day of April, 1857, and that mortgage was duly recorded. Pontau died without heirs about the year 1865 seised of the lot. He left a will by which he devised the lot to his wife Nannette for life, with remainder to his **475** adopted son, Anthony N. Pontau, in fee. Anthony died before the testator, unmarried and without issue. Nannette, the widow, about 1867, married James E. Johnson. In 1871, by chapter 558 of the laws of that year, the legislature released to her all the interest of the state in the lot, and thus she became seised of the lot in fee. Her husband Johnson died in January, 1871, and in September, 1871, being at the time a widow, she made a will devising the lot to James M. Johnson, the son of her second husband.

In March, 1873, she married James Harrison. He died before his wife, and she died in 1878 without heirs. The Meades assigned the mortgage executed to them by Paul

. Pontau to James M. Johnson in November, 1869, and he assigned it to Henry W. Bates in November, 1879. In 1880, Bates foreclosed the mortgage by action, making parties defendant "Ann Le Court, John Doe, Richard Roe, Jane Styles, Thomas Nookes, Rebecca Johnson, Edward Styles, and Mary I. Blackwell, whose names are unknown to the plaintiff, unknown heirs at law and next of kin of Paul Pontau, late of the city and county of New York, deceased." Neither the state nor the heirs or devisees of Nannette, Pontau's widow, were made parties to that action. The referee, in pursuance of the judgment of foreclosure, sold the lot and conveyed it to Alexander B. Crane and Louise E. Bates by deed bearing date July 23, 1880. Subsequently, in May, 1881, Crane conveyed his interest in the lot to Mrs. Bates. In February, 1885, Mr. and Mrs. Bates united in a mortgage of the lot to Emily Golder for two thousand five hundred dollars, and in the same month Mrs. Bates executed and delivered a deed of the lot to Frances A. Denike. Thereafter, Emily Golder commenced an action for the foreclosure of her mortgage, and under the judgment in that action the defendant, Samuel F. Cowdrey, became the purchaser of the lot and received a deed thereof on the fourteenth day of October, 1889. Neither James M. Johnson nor the state was made a party defendant in the last foreclosure action. During all these years the lot was possessed as follows: By Paul Pontau from April 27, **476** 1854, to April 12, 1855; then by Nannette, his widow, to June 6, 1878; then by James M. Johnson to July 23, 1880; then by Alexander B. Crane and Louise E. Bates to May 10, 1881; then by Mrs. Bates to February 11, 1885; then by Frances A. Denike to October 14, 1889, and then by the defendant, Samuel F. Cowdrey, to the present time. All the persons thus successively in the possession of the lot claimed title thereto.

Nannette's will was made prior to her marriage with Harrison, and by that marriage the will was revoked, and thus she died intestate: 2 Rev. Stats. 64, sec. 44; *Brown* v. *Clark,* 77 N. Y. 369. As she died without heirs, whatever interest in real estate she possessed at her death at once escheated to the state, and the title thereto immediately vested in the state by operation of law: 1 Rev. Stats. 718; 4 Kent's Commentaries, 425; *McCaughal* v. *Ryan,* 27 Barb. 376; *Ettenheimer* v. *Heffernan,* 66 Barb. 374. But the mortgage executed by Paul Pontau in his lifetime being valid, the title of the state by

escheat was subject thereto, and if the state had been made
a party to the foreclosure of that mortgage the title acquired
under the foreclosure sale would have been perfect. But the
persons who entered into possession under the foreclosure, defective as to the state because it was not made a party, became mortgagees in possession, and we think this defendant
is in a position to claim the rights of a mortgagee in possession under the Pontau mortgage: *Townshend* v. *Thomson,* 139
N. Y. 152. Therefore, the state could not maintain an action
of ejectment based upon its title by escheat against the defendant to recover the possession of the lot, and the only right
it has is to enforce its equity of redemption by an equitable
action to redeem from the mortgage. It has never yet asserted its right of redemption or taken any steps whatever to
redeem from the Pontau mortgage.

The facts thus far stated show the title and relation of the
defendant to the lot.

In 1885 and 1886 the lot was assessed for general taxation,
and it is not questioned that the assessment was regular and
legal in form against the parties then in possession of the lot.
[477] The taxes imposed under those assessments not having
been paid, the lot was sold at public auction in the year 1888
by the registrar of arrears, for the nonpayment of the taxes,
to the plaintiff, and he claims title to the lot by virtue of a
conveyance to him in pursuance of that sale. He was defeated in the courts below on the sole ground that, upon the
death of Nannette Harrison in 1878, intestate and without
heirs, the title to the lot became vested in the state, and that
the lot was, therefore, not legally taxable. So we have the
defendant in the possession of the land and claiming title
thereto, setting up title in the state by escheat to defeat the
title of the plaintiff, based upon a sale for the nonpayment of
taxes regularly imposed upon this lot, unless they were illegal
and void for the reason stated.

We do not think this defense is available to the defendant.
Where taxes are regularly assessed against parties in the
possession of land and claiming title thereto and the right of
possession, and the land is subsequently sold for the nonpayment of the taxes thus imposed, the purchaser at the sale gets
a good title as against such persons in possession and all persons claiming under them. The plaintiff's title may not be
perfect as against the state; but the defendant is not in a
position to dispute it. The state may never enforce the

escheat and may never redeem the land from the Pontau mortgage. The amount due upon that mortgage may be more than the value of the land. And we know of no rule of law which will permit the defendant under such circumstances to retain possession of the land and refuse to pay any taxes thereon upon the ground that it is state land, and, therefore, not taxable.

We have assumed that the defendant could establish the escheat in this action, and that his evidence was sufficient for that purpose, But it may well be doubted whether an escheat of land can be enforced or established by anyone but the state, through its attorney-general, in the mode prescribed in statutes carefully framed to protect the rights of heirs at the time unknown or undisclosed: Code, secs. 1977, et seq. It [479] would be quite extraordinary to allow a party to establish an escheat in an action where there are no allegations or issues as to the escheat, by methods not allowed to the state, for the purpose of defeating a title good as against the whole world except the possible right of the state to enforce the escheat.

The learned counsel for the defendant also claims that the deed executed to the plaintiff by the registrar of arrears under section 6 of chapter 405 of the Laws of 1885 is invalid because he had not given the notice of sale required by that section. A careful scrutiny of the notice served shows that it is in substantial compliance with the statute, and its service was properly proved. This objection is, therefore, unfounded.

The judgment should be reversed, and a new trial granted, costs to abide event.

All concur.

Judgment reversed.

MORTGAGES—RIGHTS OF PURCHASERS UNDER FORECLOSURE.—A purchaser at a foreclosure sale succeeds to all the rights of the holder of the mortgage foreclosed: *Turman* v. *Bell*, 54 Ark. 273; 26 Am. St. Rep. 35, and note; *Champion* v. *Hinkle*, 45 N. J. Eq. 162; notes to *Berthold* v. *Holman*, 93 Am. Dec. 239; *Berlack* v. *Halle*, 1 Am. St. Rep. 189, 190.

CASES

SUPREME COURT

SOUTH DAKOTA:

GREELEY *v.* WINSOR.

[1 SOUTH DAKOTA, 117.]

CHATTEL MORTGAGE IN LEASE—VALIDITY OF.—A lease executed and recorded as required by the law relating to chattel mortgages, providing that the "rents, whether due or to become due, shall be a perpetual lien on any and all goods, merchandise, furniture, and fixtures now contained, or which may at any time during the continuance of the lease be contained in the building, except such goods as are sold in the usual course of retail trade," must be treated as a chattel mortgage, and because it gives permission to the mortgagor to sell part of the mortgaged property for his own benefit, is presumptively fraudulent as to his other creditors.

CHATTEL MORTGAGE—FRAUDULENT IN PART.—A lease which is in legal effect a chattel mortgage, if presumptively fraudulent as to part of the goods therein described, is presumptively fraudulent as to all.

Winsor and Kittredge, for the appellants.

Wynn and Nock, for the respondent.

¹¹⁹ KELLAM, J. On the third day of October, 1883, respondent, who was then the owner of a store-building in the city of Sioux Falls, leased the same, by a written contract, to Waxman & Co. for the term of five years, which lease was duly filed for record October 12, 1883, in the office of the register of deeds of the proper county, and "was duly entered upon the chattel-mortgage calendar of said office." The lease contained the following provision: "That said rents, whether due or to become due, shall be a perpetual lien on any and all goods and merchandise, furniture, and fixtures now contained, or which may at any time during the continuance of this lease be contained, in the building, except such goods as

are sold in the usual course of retail trade." Afterwards the
lessees, Waxman & Co., gave several chattel mortgages, to
secure different creditors, upon the stock of merchandise, furniture, and fixtures contained in the said leased store-building, being the same personal property described and referred
to in the provision of said lease above quoted. Afterwards
the appellants, Winsor and Swezey, as the attorneys and
agents of the several mortgagees, undertook to foreclose said
chattel mortgages, and to that end took possession of said
mortgaged property, and advertised the same. Greeley, the
lessor, and respondent herein, then commenced an action
against said Winsor and Swezey to restrain such foreclosure
sale. At this time, by an arrangement between the parties,
the respondent dismissed the said action and released his
claim [120] upon said goods, furniture, and fixtures in consideration of a bond from said appellants to secure him against
loss of rent on said lease to an amount therein named, the
condition of the bond being, "that if the said Charles A.
Greeley shall and does sustain any damages from the loss or
decrease of rents during said four years, and had at the time
of the commencement of his said action a valid and subsisting
lien, legal or equitable, upon or against said property, or any
part thereof, as security for said rents according to the terms
of said lease, and the undersigned shall pay or cause to be
paid," etc., "then this obligation," etc. Upon this obligation
respondent Greeley brought this action against appellants,
obligors therein named. To the complaint, setting out the
history of the bond and a copy of the lease, appellants demurred for insufficiency. The demurrer was overruled, and
from such decision this appeal is taken.

The controversy is over the force and effect of the provision
in the lease for a lien for rent. If, as against the mortgage
creditors represented by appellants, respondent had "a valid
and subsisting lien" upon the property taken by them under
their mortgages, then the condition of the bond is met under
which appellants' liability as obligors should attach, and the
complaint would state a cause of action against them. If
such a provision is effectual at all as against creditors, it is
plain it must be as a chattel mortgage. The rents were to be
a "perpetual lien." The possession of the property did not
change, and no lien except that of a chattel mortgage is tol-
erated by our statute, unless accompanied by possession in
the lienor. It seems to have all the requisites of a chattel

mortgage, both as to its construction and its execution, and
the statutory requirements as to filing as a chattel mortgage
were fully complied with.

The pivotal question, then, is, What was the legal value of
respondent's chattel mortgage upon his lessee's stock of goods,
furniture, and fixtures, "except such goods as are sold in the
usual course of retail trade?" for the answer to this question
must determine whether or not respondent held a "valid and
subsisting lien" upon such property, or any part of it. While
121 there is here no express and affirmative reservation in the
lessee and mortgagor of a power to sell any of the mortgaged
property, such power is so specifically recognized and provided for as to be tantamount to express authority; and the
immediate question before us is, What effect has such a reservation of an unqualified power of sale upon an otherwise
valid mortgage?

In the absence of any provision indicating directly or
indirectly any intention of the parties, or either of them, that
the proceeds of sales, or any part thereof, should be used,
applied, or appropriated in any other manner, or to any other
purpose, than as the interest and pleasure of the mortgagor
might dictate, the instrument at once attaches itself to that
class of chattel mortgages in which is reserved to the mortgagor a power of sale for his own benefit, and is subject to
the law governing such mortgages. Chattel mortgages are
authorized by our statutes, and are recognized by and in all
departments of business as a legitimate means of security,
useful alike to debtor and creditor. They have become and
are an important factor in the transaction of business in the
state, and the courts should adopt and be governed by such
principles and rules in the construction and effect given to
these instruments, in the different forms, and with the various qualifying provisions, with which they are presented,
as will be most likely to conserve the rights and interests of
all parties interested in the mortgaged property, whether
mortgagor, mortgagee, or general creditor. In this case the
mortgagor was permitted by the terms of the mortgage to
make sales from the mortgaged property, in the usual course
of retail trade, for his own use and benefit. The right to
appropriate the proceeds of sales was unlimited. It was not
even qualified by any undertaking, express or implied, that
such proceeds, or any part of the same, should be reinvested
in goods, that the security might thus be kept intact. It was

a plenary license to possess, manage, and sell the mortgaged property, subject only to the condition that the sales should be **made in** the usual course of retail trade, allowing the entire proceeds to be diverted to purposes hostile to the interests of the unpreferred creditors, if the mortgagor should be so disposed. The [122] mortgagee had agreed in advance that the mortgagor might dispose of the property which apparently constituted his security—retain, spend, or give away the proceeds, as he saw fit; and thus his entire stock might be dissipated and melt away without diminishing the aggregate of indebtedness a dollar, and this might all occur in exact pursuance of the terms of this mortgage. Every debtor is, in a sense, trustee of his property for the benefit of his creditors; and every creditor has a right to have the trust so administered as not to unfairly predjudice his interests, or jeopardize his chances for the collection of his debt. Without further argument, it is sufficient to say that such mortgages are held to be at least presumptively fraudulent in most of the states of the union, and in many of them conclusively so. It is needless to fortify this proposition with authorities. Whether in this state the presumption is a rebuttable one, it is not now necessary to consider or determine.

The question is before us on demurrer to the complaint. The complaint presents this mortgage as showing respondent's right to the property which the bond of appellants represents. If the mortgage on its face is presumptively fraudulent, then the complaint would state no cause of action, because, if presumptively fraudulent it is presumptively void; and no facts are stated in the complaint tending to negative or rebut such presumption. The bond was only to be operative in case the respondent had a valid and subsisting lien upon the property, and the complaint offers the mortgage clause of the lease as showing such lien.

A more troublesome question occurs when we come to consider the effect of the power of sale upon the property in the mortgage not covered by nor included in such power of sale. The mortgage was upon "goods, merchandise, furniture, and fixtures." The permission to sell covered only "such goods as are sold in the usual course of retail trade." Is the mortgage *prima facie* fraudulent *in toto*, or is it good as to the furniture and fixtures; they evidently not being included in the permission to sell? The law condemns such a mortgage as this, not because its terms prove any fraudulent or corrupt motive on [123] the part of those who made or those who took it, but because such a mortgage furnishes such easy facilities for fraud, and is so well adapted to accomplish unfair and fraudulent results, as to put it under the ban of suspicion. It is condemned not because the transaction was inspired by a bad intent, but because it naturally leads to bad results. If it were the actual, proved intent of the parties which fixed the character of this instrument as fraudulent, it would hardly be contended that because they intended to and did reserve the furniture and fixtures from the operation of this vicious power of sale the mortgage ought to be held good as to them; but upon the familiar principle that every man must be presumed to have intended the natural and legitimate results of his acts the law substitutes the effect for the intent, and, as it has found that the effect of such provisions is ordinarily bad, it assumes that the intent is ordinarily, or, in other words, presumptively, bad.

There are other reasons for applying this rule to the entire mortgage provision in this case. The mortgagee, while claiming to have security upon all this property, has stipulated and consented that the mortgagor might gradually, by retail sales, deplete and consume the bulk of his security, leaving the burden of the debt, not upon the entire property which he pretends to hold under, and which he protects by, his mortgage, but upon the furniture and fixtures, which alone, of all the mortgaged property, is to remain under the lien of his mortgage, and must constitute his real security. It is very evident that all the real security respondent could have under his mortgage was the property that the mortgagor had no right to sell. Power to sell the goods was power to annul and destroy the lien of the mortgage upon them; and this respondent had agreed might be done, and that without any diminution of the debt as the result of such sales. If respondent were content with security upon the furniture and fixtures only—and such conclusion the facts clearly argue—he ought not to be allowed to encumber by the same instrument a large amount of other property from which he expected no benefit or advantage. To the creditors of the mortgagor respondent said by this mortgage: "I hold a mortgage [124] upon this entire stock and furniture and fixtures to secure five years' rent at thirteen hundred dollars per year; and if you desire to proceed against any of this property for

the collection of your claims you must pay off my mortgage
as provided in the statute." But to the mortgagor he said:
"You may pay no attention to my mortgage, so far as the
goods are concerned. You may sell them as though I had no
mortgage, but the furniture and fixtures must remain and be
bound by my mortgage, and, as between us, I will depend
upon them for my security." Such a mortgage would allow
a mortgagee, if so disposed, without risk or danger to his own
security, unless an actual fraudulent intent could be proved,
to shelter under his mortgage property, which he never expected to subject to his apparent lien, and in the interest of
the mortgagor exhibit his mortgage on the record, and thus,
with entire safety to his own security, experiment with the
chances of driving away approaching creditors. We think
creditors have a right to complain of a chattel mortgage susceptible of such uses, and that it is at least *prima facie* void
as to all the property covered by it. The rulings of the
courts have not been uniform upon this question; but this
view is fully sustained in the following cases: *Russell* v.
Winne, 37 N. Y. 591; 97 Am. Dec. 755; *Horton* v. *Williams,*
21 Minn. 187; *Wilson* v. *Voight,* 9 Col. 614; *Harman* v. *Hos-
kins,* 56 Miss. 142.

It follows that the demurrer should have been sustained.
The judgment of the court below overruling the demurrer is
reversed, all the judges concurring.

CORSON, P. J. I am of the opinion that the court should
go further and hold that the mortgage or agreement in this
case is not only at least presumptively fraudulent, but absolutely fraudulent, as to the creditors of the mortgagor. A
chattel mortgage in which the mortgagor is permitted by the
terms of the mortgage to sell all or any part of the property
embraced in the mortgage, and apply the proceeds to his own
use and benefit, is, in my opinion, fraudulent in law, without
regard to the intent of the parties. It is evident that as to
the property so permitted to be sold for the benefit of the
mortgagor the mortgagee has no real interest in or lien upon
it, [125] and that the effect of such a mortgage will necessarily
be to aid the mortgagor in withholding his property so covered by the mortgage from his creditors. The agreement is
necessarily fraudulent, because it operates, of necessity, to
hinder, delay, and defraud the creditors by securing to the
debtor the use and benefit of his property and its proceeds,

while it protects it from levy and sale for the payment of his debts. Honesty and good faith are necessary to render a chattel mortgage valid, and whenever it appears that one object was, or the effect is, to hinder and delay the creditors to any extent the entire instrument is, in judgment of law, fraudulent and void.

REPORTER. A rehearing was granted in this case, but after such rehearing the court reaffirmed the original opinion.

CHATTEL MORTGAGES—LEASE.—A lien for rent created by a lease, and claimed on property left in the posession of the tenant, is in the nature of a mortgage rather than a pledge, and is governed by the rules of law applicable to chattel mortgages: *Borden v. Croak,* 131 Ill. 68; 19 Am. St. Rep. 23; note to *Almand v. Scott,* 12 Am. St. Rep. 243. As to the right of a landlord to reserve a lien on the crops to be raised by his tenant, see the extended note to *De Vaughn v. Howell,* 14 Am. St. Rep. 166-168.

A CHATTEL MORTGAGE VOID IN PART for fraud against creditors is void as to the whole: *Russell v. Winne,* 37 N. Y. 591; 97 Am. Dec. 755.

THOMAS *v.* PENDLETON.

[1 SOUTH DAKOTA, 150.]

JUDGMENTS OF SISTER STATES—COMPLAINT IN ACTION ON.—A complaint upon a judgment recovered in another state containing a copy of a note and power of attorney upon which the judgment was rendered before the maturity of the note is insufficient in the absence of any allegation of law authorizing the rendition of such judgment, to sustain an attachment issued upon an affidavit stating no ground of claim except by reference to such complaint.

JUDGMENTS OF SISTER SATES—BURDEN OF PROOF IN ACTION ON.—If a judgment of another state is offered in evidence, the burden of proof is upon the party who relies upon it, to show that it is valid according to the laws of the state within whose jurisdiction it was pronounced.

LAWS OF SISTER STATE—PRESUMPTION.—In the absence of allegation and proof, the laws of another state are presumed to be the same as the laws of the state in which action is brought.

Henry Hoffman, for the appellant.

Loring E. Gaffy, for the respondent.

152 CORSON, P. J. This is an appeal from an order of the court vacating and setting aside attachment proceedings in this action. The warrant of attachment was issued upon an affidavit, the part of which material to a determination of the question involved in this case is as follows: "That a cause of action exists in favor of said plaintiff and against said de-

fendants, the grounds of which are fully set forth in the complaint hereto annexed, which is on file in this action, the
statements contained in which are true; that the defendants
are not residents of this territory." A motion was made by
defendant Pendleton to vacate and set aside the attachment
upon the following grounds: "Because the same was irregularly issued in this: 1. The grounds of the cause of action,
if any there be, are not stated and set forth, as by law required, in the affidavit for attachment; 2. The affidavit does
not state that this is an action on contract for the payment
of money only; and 3. The attachment was improvidently
issued in this, that defendant Henry F. Pendleton is not and
was not a nonresident of this territory. This motion is made
upon all the papers filed in this case, and upon the affidavit
of Henry F. Pendleton, served herein." It will be observed
that the amount of plaintiff's claim is stated in his affidavit,
but not the grounds thereof, except by reference to the complaint annexed thereto. It therefore becomes necessary to
examine the complaint, to ascertain the grounds of plaintiff's
claim, and the sufficiency of the same.

The action is founded upon an alleged judgment in the
[153] court of common pleas of Crawford county, in the state of
Pennsylvania.

Although the complaint sets out the note and warrant of
attorney upon which the alleged judgment is founded, it is
clear that there is only one cause of action set out, and that
is upon the judgment: *Krower* v. *Reynolds*, 99 N. Y. 248.
In the complaint the judgment is alleged to have been rendered on the eighth day of May, 1889, upon a note bearing
date March 12, 1889, payable ninety days after its date. It
therefore appears upon the face of the complaint that the
alleged judgment was rendered more than thirty days before
the note, by its terms, became due and payable. No law of
the state of Pennsylvania is set out or pleaded authorizing a
judgment to be entered upon a note before its maturity. In
the absence of any allegation as to what the laws of Pennsylvania are on this subject, the court will presume they are
the same as our own. The authorities are conflicting on this
question, when applied to a judgment purporting to have been
rendered by a court of general jurisdiction in another state,
but we think the weight of authority is in favor of the rule
as stated. Mr. Freeman, in his work on Judgments, section
571, says: "A judgment of another state, when offered in evi-

dence ought to be shown to be valid. If it would not be valid if rendered in the state where it is offered in evidence the party who relies upon it must show that it is valid according to the laws of the state within whose jurisdiction it was pronounced": *Crafts* v. *Clark*, 31 Iowa, 77; *Pelton* v. *Platner*, 13 Ohio, 209, 42 Am. Dec. 197; *Draggoo* v. *Graham*, 9 Ind. 212; *Rape* v. *Heaton*, 9 Wis. 328; 76 Am. Dec. 269; *Taylor* v. *Barron*, 30 N. H. 78; 64 Am. Dec. 281; *Hill* v. *Grigsby*, 32 Cal. 55; *Norris* v. *Harris*, 15 Cal. 226. And in the late case of *Teel* v. *Yost*, 5 N. Y. Supp. 5 (decided in 1889) this was substantially held to be the law as applied to that case. The complaint in this case, tested by the law in force in this state, is clearly insufficient. It shows upon its face that the alleged judgment, if rendered by our own court, would not be a valid judgment Under our statute, there is only one class of cases in which a judgment may be rendered on a debt before its maturity, and that is on confession of judgment under sections 5537–5539, [154] of the Compiled Laws. But the proceeding is purely statutory, and the provisions of the statute must be strictly complied with. There are no facts alleged in this complaint that can sustain this alleged judgment as one coming within the provisions of the sections above referred to.

On the hearing of the motion to vacate the attachment, the plaintiff introduced in evidence an exemplified copy of the record from the court of common pleas of Crawford county, state of Pennsylvania. This record is as follows:

"Copy of continuous docket entry, February term, 1889. [Title.] By virtue of a power of attorney, C. W. Tyler, Esq., appears for defts., and confesses judgment against them, in favor of plff., for the sum of five hundred and seventy-seven and 50-100 dollars, with costs of suit, release of errors, and waiving exemptions and inquisition. Debt, $577.50. Interest from June 11, 1889. Judgment. A. B. Edson, Pro. Due June 11, 1889. Filed and entered May 8, 1889. A. B. Edson, Pro."

This with the declaration and judgment docket entry of the names of the parties, date and amount of judgment, constitutes the entire record as certified to by the prothonotary. There is no record of any process or plea; no record of any service or appearance by the defendants, or either of them; and, at the time of the entry of this alleged judgment, nothing was due upon the note. It had over a month yet to run before its maturity. Neither is there an adjudication of any court that defendants should pay anything, or that plaintiff should have execution or process of any kind to enforce collection of any sum. There was no evidence adduced on the hearing of any law of Pennsylvania that would authorize a judgment on a note before it becomes due by its terms, or that in any way explains the meaning of this record. It does not appear from this record that there was any judgment in favor of the plaintiff and against the defendants for any sum of money that would justify the presumption that any question was adjudicated between the parties. The essential elements of a judgment are wanting. A judgment is defined to be "the conclusion of law upon facts found or admitted by the parties. or upon their default in the course [155] of the suit; the decision or sentence of the law, given by a court of justice or other competent tribunal, as the result of proceedings instituted therein for the redress of an injury": Bouvier's Law Dictionary, 760. In *Teel* v. *Yost*, 5 N. Y. Supp. 5, which was a case in which a judgment on a similar note before its maturity, and record from the state of Pennsylvania, was sought to be enforced in the state of New York, the court says: "In the absence of the process to bring the defendant before the court, and of an order or decree which is an adjudication, and with no proof of the law or practice in Pennsylvania which provided that such a record was in effect an adjudication, the evidence was insufficient to prove that the plaintiff had recovered a judgment against the defendant. I think, therefore, that plaintiff failed to prove the cause of action set forth in the complaint, and that the complaint should have been dismissed." If the proof offered would not sustain an action on the trial, it will not be sufficient to show that the grounds of the claim as stated are sufficient to sustain the attachment. We think, therefore, the court was right in vacating and setting aside the attachment on the first ground stated in the motion; and without passing upon the second and third grounds of the motion, we think the order of the court should be affirmed, and it is so ordered.

EVIDENCE—PRESUMPTION AS TO LAWS OF OTHER STATES.—The laws of another state are presumed to be the same as the laws of this state: *Hill* v. *Wilker*, 41 Ga. 449; 5 Am. Rep. 540; *Peterson* v. *Chemical Bank*, 32 N. Y. 21; 88 Am. Dec. 298; *Brimhall* v. *Van Camper*, 8 Minn. 13; 82 Am. Dec. 118, and note; *Commonwealth* v. *Graham*. 157 Mass. 73; 34 Am. St. Rep. 255, and note.

JUDGMENTS OF SISTER STATES—SUFFICIENCY OF COMPLAINT IN ACTIONS ON—JURISDICTION.—A complaint on a judgment of a sister state need not aver that the court pronouncing the judgment had jurisdiction: *Williams* v. *Preston*, 3 J. J. Marsh, 600; 20 Am. Dec. 179, and note; *Specklemeyer* v. *Dailey*, 23 Neb. 101; 8 Am. St. Rep. 119, and note; *Gunn* v. *Peakes*, 36 Minn. 177; 1 Am. St. Rep. 661, and note; *Butcher* v. *Bank*, 2 Kan. 70; 83 Am. Dec. 446, and note; *Weller* v. *Dickinson*, 93 Cal. 108. An averment of liability and breach must be made in actions on the case upon judgments of a sister state: *Spencer* v. *Brockway*, 1 Ohio, 259; 13 Am. Dec. 615. A complaint on the judgment of a court of a sister state was held to be bad because it did not in any manner disclose what was the cause of the action or the subject of the controversy: *Ashley* v. *Laird*, 14 Ind. 222; 77 Am. Dec. 67, and note. This decision was erroneous. The complaint need not contain any averments as to the subject matter of the jurisdiction or the steps taken to acquire jurisdiction over the defendant: Freeman on Judgments, sec. 453, and cases cited above.

JUDGMENTS OF SISTER STATES.—CONCLUSIVENESS OF: See *Ambler* v. *Whipple*, 139 Ill. 311; 32 Am. St. Rep. 202, and note.

HALL *v.* HARRIS.

[1 SOUTH DAKOTA, 279.]

NEW TRIAL.—NOTICE OF INTENTION to move for a new trial is not rendered uncertain by a statement that the motion will be made on the minutes of the court and a bill of exceptions.

RES JUDICATA—DECISION OF MOTION.—An order discharging a writ of attachment after a full hearing is appealable either before or after judgment upon the main issue in the case. Such order is conclusive of all matters adjudicated thereby.

RES JUDICATA—DECISION OF MOTION TO DISCHARGE ATTACHMENT.—An action by defendant in attachment to recover the value of property claimed as exempt, against a sheriff who holds the property under an attachment, and under an order of court denying a motion to dissolve the attachment on the ground, among others, that the debt for which it was issued was incurred for property obtained under false pretenses, is barred by the order denying the motion to discharge the attachment.

Charles H. Burke and Walter C. Fawcett, for the appellant. ·

Crawford and De Land, for the respondent.

[280] CORSON, P. J. This is an action brought by the plaintiff against the defendant, as sheriff of Hughes county, to recover the value of certain personal property, alleged to have been wrongfully taken and converted by the defendant, claimed by plaintiff as exempt property under the provisions of the statute [281] providing for additional exemptions. The defendant justified his taking and detention of the property under and by virtue of a warrant of attachment issued out of

the district court of said Hughes county, in an action wherein
William E. Sawyer et al. are plaintiffs, and James Hall
(the plaintiff herein) is defendant; and also under and by
virtue of a decision and order of the district court made in
said action denying defendant's motion to discharge the said
attachment. A trial was had in the district court, resulting
in a verdict and judgment for the plaintiff. On motion, a
new trial was granted in the court below, and a second trial
had, resulting in a verdict and judgment for defendant; and
from this judgment the plaintiff appeals to this court, for a
review, not only of the errors in law alleged to have occurred
on the second trial, but a review also of the order granting a
new trial.

The action of *Sawyer* v. *Hall,* which we shall hereafter
designate as the "attachment suit," was commenced on the
seventh day of September, 1886, and the property in controversy in this action was seized under the warrant of attachment issued in that action about the 9th of that month. One
of the grounds for the attachment set forth in the affidavit for
the same was that the debt on which the attachment suit was
brought was incurred for property obtained under false pretenses, and this allegation in the affidavit was recited in the
warrant of attachment as one of the grounds on which the
warrant was issued. Hall, through his agent, took the proper
proceedings to obtain out of the property attached his additional exemptions under the statute, but the sheriff refused
either to have the property appraised or to deliver it up.
Hall thereupon gave notice of a motion to discharge the attachment, which was heard by the court and denied, but with
leave to renew the motion. Subsequently, in October, 1886,
a new motion to vacate, discharge, and dissolve the attachment was given, and the second ground on which the motion
was based, as stated therein, was as follows: "That each and
every allegation contained in said affidavit, except the allegation of indebtedness therein contained, are false." On this
motion a hearing [282] was had before the court in which a
large mass of evidence, in the form of documentary evidence
and affidavits, was presented by the respective parties, and
the court, after a full consideration of the motion, decided it
against the defendant Hall, and on December 10, 1886, made
an order in which, after various recitals, is the following: "It
is hereby ordered and adjudged that said motion be, and the
same is, hereby denied, and said attachment is hereby sus-

tained on the grounds: 1. That the defendant has assigned
and disposed of his property with intent to defraud his creditors, and on the further ground that the debt herein sued on
was incurred for property obtained under false pretenses."
Subsequently, to the above-mentioned hearing and order, the
plaintiff herein (Hall) again demanded an appraisement and
the setting apart of his additional exemptions, which being
refused by the sheriff, he commenced this action before the
issuance of an execution in the attachment suit, and while
the sheriff still held the property under his warrant of attachment. On the first trial of this action the court refused to
admit in evidence the order of the court of December 10th, a
part of which is above given, denying the motion to discharge
the attachment; and this refusal was the ground mainly relied on in the motion for a new trial and the ground upon
which the new trial was granted. On the second trial the
court not only admitted this order in evidence, but held it
conclusive of the fact that the debt on which the warrant of
attachment was issued was incurred for property obtained
under false pretenses, and a bar to plaintiff's action, and
directed the jury to render a verdict for the defendant.

Section 5139 of the Compiled Laws, in relation to exemptions, is as follows: "No exemptions, except the absolute exemptions, shall be allowed any person against an execution
or other process issued upon a debt incurred for property obtained under false pretenses." The assignment of errors is
as follows: "1. The court below erred in entertaining and in
refusing to dismiss defendant's motion for a new trial, inasmuch as the defendant's notice of intention to make said
motion failed to specify whether the same would be made
upon the minutes of [283] the court, a bill of exceptions, or a
statement of the case; 2. The court below erred in allowing
defendant's motion for a new trial, inasmuch as the same was
allowed upon the ground of error of law occurring at the trial
of said action, and excepted to by the party moving for a new
trial, and no such error appears from the record; 3. The court
below erred in allowing defendant's motion for a new trial on
the ground that there was error of law by the court below in
excluding the order made by the Hon. Louis K. Church, J.,
on the tenth day of December, 1886, sustaining the attachment proceedings under which the defendant seized the property in controversy, the court below having correctly decided
in excluding said order; 4. The court below erred upon the

second trial of this action in admitting as evidence the order
mentioned in the last assignment; 5. The court below erred
upon the second trial of said action in holding that the order
mentioned in the last two assignments was a conclusive bar
to this action and upon this ground in directing the jury to
find a verdict for the defendant; and 6. That the judgment of
the court below should have been for the plaintiff and against
the defendant, according to the law of the land."

· On the hearing in the court below of the motion for a new
trial, the appellant moved to dismiss the motion, upon the
ground that, in the notice of intention to move for a new trial,
the moving party specified that the motion would be based
" upon the minutes of the court, and upon a bill of exceptions,
to be thereafter settled in the case," which motion to dismiss
was denied.   The learned counsel for appellant contend that
such a motion was insufficient, and that the moving party
must specify whether the motion will be based upon the
minutes of the court, or a bill of exceptions, or a statement;
and that a conjunctive statement left the appellant in as
much doubt as would a disjunctive one.   Section 5090 of the
Compiled Laws provides that "the party intending to move
for a new trial must, within twenty days, ... serve upon
the adverse party a notice of his intention, designating the
statutory grounds upon which the motion will be made, and
whether the same will be made [284] upon affidavits, or the
minutes of the court, or bill of exceptions, or a statement of
the case."   The learned counsel for the respondent contend
that only the first clause relating to the time within which the
notice must be given is mandatory, and that the latter clause
is directory only, and that the notice given was, in form, a
substantial compliance with the statute.   We think the counsel are correct.   The appellant had full notice that all the
statutory methods of proceeding to obtain a new trial would
be relied on, and when respondent elected which of the two
methods he would pursue, such an election was an abandonment of the other method specified in his notice.   We fail to
see how the appellant could in any manner be prejudiced by
such notice and election under it.   It frequently happens, as
in this case, that the notice is given before the bill of exceptions or statement is settled, and the moving party may be
uncertain whether or not the bill of exceptions or statement
can be settled before the motion for a new trial can be heard.
If it cannot, for any reason, be settled before the motion is

heard, he may be compelled to rely upon the minutes of the court. If settled, he would, naturally, rely upon his statement, or bill of exceptions, on the hearing. This question under a similar if not a statute identical with our own, was before the supreme court of California, in *Hart* v. *Kimball,* 72 Cal. 284, in which the court says: "The respondent contends that the appeal from the order first mentioned should not be considered, for the reason, as he alleges, that the notice of motion for a new trial specified that such motion would be made, not only upon the minutes of the court, but also upon a bill of exceptions and a statement of the case, and that therefore the statement upon which the motion was heard by the trial court should have been disregarded, since the moving party relied upon that method of procedure, and did not file any affidavit or use the minutes of the court. We do not concur in this view of the law, for the respondent had full notice that all the statutory methods of procedure to obtain a new trial would be adopted by the appellants; and, when they elected which of such methods they would pursue, such election was their privilege, [285] and did not prejudice, in any way, the rights of the respondent, the other methods being thereby abandoned." The same question was also before the supreme court of Montana in a late case, also under a similar statute, *Gamer* v. *Glenn,* 8 Mont. 371, in which the court says: "Particular stress is laid upon the use of the words, 'option of the moving party,' and the disjunctive word 'or,' connecting the several grounds upon which the motion may be made. We do not think this construction tenable. While the appellant may select any one ground given by the statute, and rely upon it alone, he certainly is not precluded from relying upon two or more, or all of them, if, in his judgment, the necessities of his case require it. And if he sees fit to rely upon one ground, and abandon the others, when he comes to file, his motion for a new trial, he can then elect to do so. To notify the respondent that he intends to rely on all of them cannot prejudice his rights in any manner that we can see. If he were to put his notice in the alternative, and thus leave it uncertain which of the grounds he relied on, this would be objectionable." We are of the opinion, therefore, that the court committed no error in denying appellant's motion.

This brings us to a consideration of the main question in this case, and that is whether or not the court erred in granting the new trial, and in holding on the second trial that the

órder of December 10th was admissible in evidence, and a bar
to this suit. All the assignments of error on this branch of
the case will be considered together, as they really present
but the one question. It is earnestly contended by the learned
counsel for the appellant that such an order and decision of
the district court, made upon a motion to discharge the attachment, cannot be a bar to this action, because upon the
question of plaintiff's additional exemptions, under the law,
he had the con⁻titutional right of a jury trial, and that the
effect of the decision of the district court in this case would
be to deprive him of that right; and, further, that it is only
judgments rendered in an action that can have the effect of
res adjudicata, and be pleaded in bar to an action. While
the appellant would, undoubtedly [286] have had the right to
a jury trial in case he had sought his remedy in a different
proceeding, and at the proper time, he could waive his right,
either in an action commenced in the proper court or by a
proceeding in which he seeks to have an adjudication by the
court of the question, without the intervention of a jury.
Such, we think, was the case here. Appellant made his
motion to vacate the attachment proceedings before the court,
and on that motion presented, and had determined, the question, as to whether or not the debt for which the attachment
was issued " was incurred for property obtained under false
pretenses," and the court, having heard all the evidence adduced by the respective parties, and the arguments of counsel,
determined that question against the appellant, the defendant in that action. The motion and hearing by the court for
the discharge of the attachment was a proceeding authorized
by the statute, and the determination of the motion was an
adjudication by the court of a matter within its jurisdiction
where the duty of hearing and deciding the questions presented by the motion was by law imposed upon the court.
By section 5011 of the Compiled Laws, it is provided that,
"in all cases, the defendant . . . . may move to discharge
the attachment; if the motion be made upon affidavits on the
part of the defendant, ... but not otherwise, the plaintiff
may oppose the same by affidavits or other proof in addition
to the affidavit on which the attachment was granted, and in
such case the defendant . . . . may sustain the motion by
affidavits or other proof in rebuttal of the affidavits or other
proof offered and submitted on the part of the plaintiff to
approve the motion." It will thus be seen that a full and

thorough investigation of the facts is provided for on the
hearing of the motion. Affidavits, documentary and oral evidence, may be given on either side. In addition to a full
hearing in the court below, an appeal to this court is provided
for. In *Quebec Bank* v. *Carroll,* 1 S. D. 1, this court held that
an order discharging, continuing, refusing, or modifying an
attachment is appealable, and that an appeal may be taken
from such an order before judgment upon the main issue in
the original [287] cause of action. In that case, the court,
speaking through Mr. Justice Bennett, says: "The primary
object of the act was to give the right of appeal from all orders
granting, refusing, continuing, or modifying a provisional
remedy, or setting aside or dismissing a writ of attachment
for irregularity. The words 'granting,' 'refusing,' 'continuing,' or 'modifying,' taken collectively, may embrace, and
without doubt were intended to cover, all the proceedings
that might be instituted in any provisional remedy; that is,
anything which pertains to the granting of an attachment, it
being a provisional remedy, or the refusing to grant it, or to
any proceeding or order which after its issuance continued
its life or existence, or that in any way modified or discharged
it." The decision of the court, then, on that motion, being
made upon a full hearing of the motion, and from which an
appeal could have been taken, had the appellant so desired,
should we think, be held conclusive of the matters adjudicated, upon all parties in that action, at least during its
pendency.

What could have been the object the lawmakers had in
view in specifically providing for this motion to discharge the
attachment, if the decision of the motion when made was not
to be regarded as an adjudication of the matters submitted to
the court, upon the motion? This court had occasion to consider the effect of an appealable order in the case of *Weber* v.
Tschetter, 1 S. D. 205, in which the court, speaking through
Mr. Justice Kellam, says: " We think that where an issue of
fact is distinctly and formally presented to the court for determination, as a means of fixing the legal rights of the
parties, the supporting evidence of both sides duly considered,
and from which determination either party may appeal, the
decision of the court upon such issue ought to be held conclusive and final, without regard to the form in which such issue
is presented, whether by action or motion, the important
matter being that the issue be well defined, so as to preclude

doubt as to what question was before the court; that it be
fully heard and litigated, each side having an opportunity to
be heard; and that the court should judicially pass upon and
decide it. This being done, [288] the determination as to the
facts and rights involved should be final. In *Board of
Commrs.* v. *McIntosh*, 30 Kan. 234, the court (Brewer, J.)
says: "We think there is a growing disposition to enlarge the
scope of the doctrine of *res adjudicata*, and to place more
regard on the substance of the decision than on the form of
the proceedings. One thing which indicates this is the increased facility of review in the appellate courts. . . . . Now,
that the decision of a motion can be preserved in a separate
record, and taken up by itself, presupposes a full and careful
consideration in both the trial and appellate courts; and,
when that is had, it would seem that the question thus
separately and carefully considered should be finally disposed
of, and not be thrown back for further litigation at the mere
caprice of either party." In *Mabry* v. *Henry*, 83 N. C. 298, it
is said: "The principle of *res adjudicata* does not extend to
ordinary motions incidental to the progress of a cause, ...
but it does apply to decisions affecting a substantial right
subject to review in an appellate court." In *Dwight* v. *St.
John*, 25 N. Y. 203, the order of the court denying a motion
to cancel a judgment entered by confession, being appealable
as effecting a substantial right, was held conclusive between
the parties as to all matters actually involved and tried.
"The reasons assigned for investing courts with a discretionary power in rehearing matters decided upon motion, are
applicable only to those proceedings from which no redress
can be obtained by appeal": Freeman on Judgments, sec. 325;
McCullough v. *Clark*, 41 Cal. 298.

In this case, at the time the action was commenced, the
defendant, as sheriff, was holding this property, not only
under his warrant of attachment by which he was informed
that this property was not exempt, because the debt had been
incurred for property obtained under false pretenses, but
under the order and decision of the court, out of which his
writ had issued, adjudicating that such was the fact. If an
officer cannot be protected under such circumstances there
must be a defect in the law; for, being advised both by his
warrant of attachment and the decision and order of the court
that the property could [289] not be claimed as exempt prop-

erty, he certainly could not have proceeded to have it appraised or deliver it up to the defendant.

We think the law is not chargeable with such injustice, and must hold that, in this case, the order of the court protected him. What effect we would give the order had the plaintiff waited until an execution had been issued in the attachment suit, and had claimed his exemptions under the execution, we do not here decide, leaving that question to be determined when it properly arises. The case of *Bennett* v. *Denny*, 33 Minn. 530, decided by the supreme court of Minnesota, and by the supreme court of the United States on writ of error: 128 U. S. 498, is confidently relied on by the learned counsel for appellant, as sustaining the appellant's view in this case. We think, however, that, on a careful examination of that case, it will be found that it is materially different from the case at bar, and that the principle upon which it was decided has no application to this case. That was a case where a United States marshal had levied upon property under a writ of attachment issued out of the United States circuit court. The property was claimed by an assignee, under an assignment made under the state laws of Minnesota. In deciding the motion, Justice Nelson, of the United States district court, says: "It is by virtue of this seizure that the marshal holds the property. On this statement of the facts, I shall not decide on this motion who has the better title and right to the possession of the property taken. . . . . The writ of attachment properly issued in this suit against the debtor, and if the marshal has seized the property which belonged to Bennett, he is certainly liable in an action of trespass for the damages thereby sustained." The question, therefore, of the right of the assignee to the property, as between himself and the marshal, was not adjudicated, and the court did not intend to pass upon or determine that question, but intended to do as it did do—leave it to be adjudicated in the proper suit beween the marshal and assignee. In the case at bar the court does determine and adjudicate the rights of the party to the exemption by determining [290] that the debt for which the property was held was incurred for property obtained under false pretenses, which, as we have seen by section 5139 of the Compiled Laws, precludes a party from claiming additional exemptions under the statute. The order of the court would be a bar to any new motion to discharge the attachment, and must be equally a bar to a suit brought against the officer while he still holds the property under his warrant of attachment, which the court had refused to discharge, because the property was not exempt property. We are of the opinion, therefore, that the court committed no error in granting the new trial or in holding the order of December 10th a bar to this action. The judgment must therefore be affirmed, and it is so ordered. All the judges concurring.

APPEAL.—JUDGMENTS OR ORDERS FROM WHICH AN APPEAL WILL LIE are those which either terminate the action itself or operate to divest some right in such a manner as to put it out the power of the court making the order to place the parties in their original condition after the expiration of the term: *Harrison* v. *Lebanon Water Works*, 91 Ky. 255; 34 Am. St. Rep. 180, and note; *Davie* v. *Davie*, 52 Ark. 221; 20 Am. St. Rep. 170, and extended note with the cases collected.

FARMERS AND TRADERS' BANK *v.* KIMBALL MILLING COMPANY.

[1 SOUTH DAKOTA, 388.]

RESULTING TRUSTS.—INTENTION IS AN ESSENTIAL ELEMENT in a resulting trust, and though not expressed in words, the law presumes the intent from the facts and circumstances accompanying the transaction and the payment of the consideration for the whole or a definite or aliquot part of the property sought to be impressed with the trust.

RESULTING TRUSTS.—FRAUD DOES NOT EXIST in a resulting or implied trust, but the conveyance is made or taken with the knowledge and consent, express or implied, of the person who has paid the consideration. If he seeks to enforce the trust he must show that he is entitled to a definite or aliquot part of the property.

CONSTRUCTIVE TRUST—WHAT CONSTITUTES.—When one takes a conveyance secretly, contrary to the wishes of and in violation of his duty to the beneficiary, and in fraud of his rights, the trust is not resulting, but constructive or involuntary.

INVOLUNTARY OR CONSTRUCTIVE TRUSTS INCLUDE all instances in which a trust is raised by the doctrines of equity for the purpose of working out justice when there is no intention of the parties to create a trust relation, and a contrary intent exists on the part of the holder of the legal title. These trusts may usually be referred to fraud, either actual or constructive, as an essential element.

CONSTRUCTIVE TRUSTS—JURISDICTION IN EQUITY TO FOLLOW PROPERTY.—Equity in enforcing a constructive trust can follow the real owner's property and preserve his ownership, into whatever form it may be changed or transmuted, even into the hands of third parties, so long as the property or fund into which it has been converted can be traced, until it goes into the hands of an innocent purchaser for value and without notice. The rule applies to both real and personal property.

CONSTRUCTIVE TRUSTS—LIABILITY OF CORPORATION FOR PROPERTY ACQUIRED
UNDER.—When the officers of a bank fraudulently divert its funds and
assets, and invest them in the property of a corporation in which they
are also officers, the latter corporation holds such property impressed
with a trust in favor of the bank to the extent of bank funds that can
be traced into such corporate property, unless the corporation can show
that it is an innocent purchaser for a valuable consideration without
notice.

CORPORATION HAS PRESUMPTIVE NOTICE OF FRAUDULENT ACTS OF ITS OFFI-
CERS who are also the officers of a bank, and who have misappropriated
the funds of the bank and invested them in the property of such corporation.

CONSTRUCTIVE TRUSTS.—GAINS AND PROFITS arising from property impressed
with a constructive trust inure to the benefit of the real owner, and
should be impressed with a like trust in his favor.

CONSTRUCTIVE TRUSTS—RIGHT TO ENFORCE—TRACING PROPERTY.—A party
claiming under a constructive trust for funds fraudulently obtained and
invested in the property of another need not show that his funds paid for
any definite or aliquot part of the purchased property, but is entitled to
have the trust impressed upon such property to the extent of his funds
invested, together with the profits thereof which he can trace into the
property.

CONSTRUCTIVE TRUSTS—RIGHT TO TRACE PROPERTY.—One whose funds
have been fraudulently obtained and invested by the parties so obtaining them in the property of a corporation, and stock of such corporation
received therefor, is not compelled to follow the stock, but has the right
at his option to pursue the property itself, when it is alleged that substantially the entire property has been created with, and the business
of the company almost entirely conducted on, such funds, and that the
entire capital stock of such corporation is held by the original wrongdoers or those who have purchased with full notice of the facts.

CONSTRUCTIVE TRUSTS—PLEADING TO ENFORCE.—NOTICE OF FRAUD need not
be alleged in a complaint in an original action to enforce a constructive
trust in property acquired from funds fraudulently diverted and invested. Want of notice, payment of a valuable consideration, and good
faith are affirmative matters to be pleaded and proved by the defendant.

CONSTRUCTIVE TRUSTS—PLEADING—COMPLAINT IN AN ACTION TO ENFORCE.
A constructive trust which alleges that a specific amount of funds has
been fraudulently diverted and invested in corporation property, and
that the entire property sought to be charged has been created from the
funds fraudulently obtained, except a specified amount thereof, is sufficient on general demurrer as a definite statement of amount.

W. A. Porter, for the appellant.

G. L. McKay and W. S. Farmer, for the respondent.

391 CORSON, P. J.—This is an action brought by plaintiff to
enforce a trust against the defendant, for an accounting, and
for an injunction. A general demurrer was interposed to the
complaint on the ground that it does not state facts sufficient
to constitute a cause of action. The demurrer was overruled,

and defendant appeals from the order.   The complaint alleges, in substance, that plaintiff and defendant are corporations; that on the incorporation and organization of the plaintiff, in August, 1884, one Gates was made its president, and one Foote its cashier, and that said Gates and Foote were intrusted with the custody and control of plaintiff's business; that upon the incorporation and organization of the defendant, in November, 1886, said Gates was elected president, and the said Foote secretary; that, immediately upon his entry upon his employment as cashier, [392] of the plaintiff's bank, said Foote began to and did misappropriate and convert the money, assets, and funds of the bank to his own use and benefit, and that with the money, assets, and funds of the said bank, so misappropriated and converted, he purchased certain mill machinery and fixtures, which, upon the organization of the said milling company, he subscribed and contributed to and merged into the property and assets of the said milling company as representing and in payment of a part of its capital stock; that the citizens of the city of Kimball raised and paid over to said Foote about $1,250 in money, notes, and assets, as a bonus to assist in the construction of a mill, and that said Foote obtained and received said bonus by reason of his possession of said mill machinery and fixtures so purchased with the money and assets so diverted and fraudulently obtained by him from plaintiff's said bank; that, upon the incorporation and organization of the said milling company, said Gates and Foote, still being officers of said bank and of said milling company, began and continued to divert and misappropriate the funds, assets, and credit of said bank to the use and benefit of said milling company in the construction of its mill, the purchase of mill machinery, fixtures, real estate, and appurtenances, and that the amount so wrongfully obtained from said bank and diverted to the use and benefit of said milling company was about $10,000; that while such officers of said bank and said milling company they used and traded upon the credit and responsibility of said bank to aid the said milling company in carrying on its milling business, and in obtaining its mill machinery, fixtures, real estate, and appurtenances, etc., and that they neglected the business of said bank, and gave their time and attention to the business of said milling company; that said milling company began its business without other capital than that so fraudulently obtained from said bank by said Gates and Foote, except about $2,500 contributed by one

Hayden, and that the value of the milling company's property is about $15,000, all of which was purchased and created by the money, funds, and assets of said bank, so fraudulently misappropriated and diverted by said Gates and Foote; that **393** said Gates and Foote hold the stock of said milling company, except that held by parties to whom it has been transferred, with full knowledge of all the facts, and that said milling company has been a profitablé and successful institution, and has done a large and lucrative business since its organization.

Before proceeding to examine the complaint and the objections made to it by counsel for appellant, it may be proper to consider the different classes of trusts, and the provisions of our statutes relating to them, as well as the general principles of equity governing cases of this character. Trusts, under section 3911 of the Compiled Laws, are divided into voluntary and involuntary, and by section 3913 an involuntary trust is declared to be created by operation of law. It is further defined in sections 3919 and 3920, which are as follows: "Sec. 3919. One who wrongfully detains a thing is an involuntary trustee thereof for the benefit of the owner. "Sec. 3920. One who gains a thing by fraud, accident, mistake, undue influence, the violation of a trust, or other wrongful act is, unless he has some other and better right thereto, an involuntary trustee of the thing gained for the benefit of the person who would otherwise have had it." And by section 3933 it is provided: "Every one to whom property is transferred in violation of a trust holds the same as an involuntary trustee under such trust, unless he purchased it in good faith, and for a valuable consideration." These sections are evidently intended to include that class of trusts known, in equity jurisprudence, as "constructive trusts," as a resulting trust is defined in section 2796, and the effect of a transfer of the trust property under that section is provided for in section 2797. These sections are as follows: "Sec. 2796. When a transfer of real property is made to one person, and the consideration therefor is paid by or for another, a trust is presumed to result in favor of the person by or for whom such payment is made. "Sec. 2797. No implied or resulting trust can prejudice the rights of a purchaser or encumbrancer of real property for value, and without notice of the trust."

In a resulting trust intention is an essential element, although that intention is never expressed by words of direct

[394] creation. The law, however, presumes the intent from the facts and circumstances accompanying the transaction, and the payment of the consideration for the whole or a definite or aliquot part of the property sought to be impressed with the trust. There is usually no element of fraud in a resulting or implied trust, but the conveyance is made or taken with the knowledge and consent, express or implied, of the person who has paid the consideration. When one, therefore, takes a conveyance secretly, contrary to the wishes of, and in violation of his duty to, the beneficiary, and in fraud of his rights, the trust is not a resulting but a constructive or involuntary trust. In resulting trusts, the principle that the party seeking to enforce the trust must show that he is entitled to a definite or aliquot part of the property applies, and is well illustrated in the cases cited by appellant's counsel: *White* v. *Carpenter*, 2 Paige, 217; *Sayre* v. *Townsend*, 15 Wend. 650; *Olcott* v. *Bynum*, 17 Wall. 44. See also *Dyer* v. *Dyer*, 2 Cox, 92; 1 Lead. Cas. Eq. 314; *Crop* v. *Norton*, 2 Atk. 74; Pomeroy's Equity Jurisprudence, sec. 1038. But as it is quite apparent that the complaint in this case was drawn by the pleader, not upon the theory of an implied or resulting trust, but upon that of a constructive trust or involuntary trust as defined in section 3920, it will not be necessary to refer further to this class of trusts.

Involuntary or constructive trusts embrace a much larger class of cases, and include all those instances in which a trust is raised by the doctrines of equity for the purpose of working out justice in the most efficient manner, when there is no intention of the parties to create a trust relation, and contrary to the intention of the one holding the legal title. This class of trusts may be usually referred to fraud, either actual or constructive, as an essential element. This extension of the fundamental principles of trusts enables courts of equity to wield a remedial power of great efficacy in protecting the rights of property. They can follow the real owner's property, and preserve his real ownership, into whatever form it may be changed or transmuted, even into the hands of third parties, so long as the property or fund into which it has been converted can be traced, [395] until it goes into the hands of an innocent purchaser for value, and without notice; and the rule applies to either real or personal property.

And these principles of the courts of equity seem to have been embodied in sections 3919, 3920, and 3933, above cited:

Fox **v.** *Mackreth,* 2 Cox, 320; 1 Lead. Cas. Eq. 188; *Swinburne* v. *Swinburne,* 28 N. Y. 568; *Newton* v. *Porter,* 69 N. Y. 133; 25 Am. Rep. 152; *Van Alen* v. *American Nat. Bank,* 52 N. Y. 1; *People* v. *City Bank,* 96 N. Y. 33; *Farmers' etc. Bank* v. *King,* 57 Pa. St. 202; 98 Am. Dec. 215; *Third Nat. Bank* v. *Stillwater Gas Co.,* 36 Minn. 75; *Peak* v. *Ellicot,* 30 Kan. 156; 46 Am. Rep. 90; *National Bank* v. *Insurance Co.,* 104 U. S. 54; *Pennell* v. *Deffell,* 4 De Gex, M. & G. 372; *McLeod* v. *Evans,* 66 Wis. 401; 57 Am. Rep. 287; Pomeroy's Equity Jurisprudence, sec. 1044; *In re Hallett's Estate,* L. R. 13 Ch. Div. 696. This doctrine has been usually applied to cases of conventional trustees or to persons holding some fiduciary position; but, in order that this species of trust may arise, it is not indispensable that a trust relation exists or even any fiduciary relation between the wrongdoer and the beneficiary, and it would seem, under the provisions of our statute, no such distinction exists, except in case of the violation of a trust, specified in the section. The language of section 3920 is that "one who gains a thing by fraud . . . . or other wrongful act . . . . is an involuntary trustee of one who would otherwise have had it." The omission from this section of any reference to a conventional trustee, except in one class of cases, or one holding some fiduciary position, is important as showing the intention of the lawmakers to eliminate from the law in this state the distinction usually made by courts of equity between wrongdoers who do not and persons who do hold a trust or fiduciary position. It would seem, then, that, under the provisions of our statute we are now considering, a person who acquires property by fraud or any other wrongful act holds the property as the trustee for the rightful owner, and that such owner can follow not only the identical property so fraudulently or wrongfully obtained, but any property into which such property has been converted or transmuted, so long as he can identify [396] the same as acquired with the fraudulently or wrongfully obtained funds; and if the property so obtained has been used with funds of his own by the wrongdoer in the purchase of other property, such property is impressed and chargeable with a trust in favor of the beneficiary to the extent of the fund traceable into the property. And a person into whose hands such property may come in its original or changed condition, charged with notice, though he may not be guilty of any fraud or wrong, nevertheless holds the property subject to the trust,

precisely as the wrongdoer would hold it. In other words,
under section 3920, all persons who have acquired property,
as provided by that section, without regard to whether or not
they hold any trust or fiduciary position, are chargeable as
trustees, and persons not *bona fide* purchasers, into whose
hands or possession the property may come, also hold the
property as trustee of the beneficiary, so long as the funds
belonging to the beneficiary can be identified, into whatever
form it has been transmuted or changed.

The doctrine of courts of equity applicable to trust property in its original or transmuted form is clearly stated *In re
Hallett's Estate*, L. R. 13 Ch. Div. 696, a late and leading
English case, substantially as follows: That the modern doctrine of equity as regards property disposed of by persons in
a fiduciary position is that, whether the disposition be rightful or wrongful, the beneficial owner is entitled to the proceeds, whatever be their form, provided only he can identify
them. If they cannot be identified by reason of the trust
money being mingled with that of the trustee, then the *cestui
que trust* is entitled to a charge upon the new investment to
the extent of the trust money traceable into it; that there is
no distinction between an express trustee, or an agent, bailee,
or collector of rents, or anybody else in a fiduciary position,
and that there is no difference between investments in the
purchase of lands or chattels, or bonds, or loans, or money deposited in a bank account. The master of the rolls in that
case adopts the principle of Lord Ellenborough's statement
Taylor v. *Plumer*, 3 Maule & S. 562, in which he says: " It
makes no difference in reason or law into **397** what other
form different from the original the change may have been
made, whether it be into that of promissory notes for the
security of money which was produced by a sale of the goods
of the principal, as in *Scott* v. *Surman*, Willes, 400, or into
other merchandise, as in *Whitecomb* v. *Jacob*, 1 Salk. 161; for
the product or substitute for the original thing still follows
the nature of the thing itself as long as it can be ascertained
to be such, and the right only ceases when the means of ascertainment fail ": *National Bank* v. *Insurance Co.*, 104 U. S.
54. And in *Pennell* v. *Deffell*, 4 De Gex, M. & G. 372, Lord
Justice Turner said: " It is, I apprehend an undoubted principle of this court that as between *cestui que trust* and trustee,
and all parties claiming under the trustee otherwise than by
purchase for valuable consideration without notice, all prop-

erty belonging to a trust, however much it may be changed
or altered in its nature or character, and all the fruits of such
property, whether in its original or altered state, continue to
be subject to or affected by the trust."

With these preliminary observations, we proceed to examine the complaint in this action. It is quite apparent from
an inspection of it, as before stated, that it was drawn, or
intended to be drawn, upon the theory that the trust sought
to be impressed upon the property held by the defendant is
one coming under the head of a constructive or involuntary
trust, to be enforced by a court of equity, not in accordance
with any presumed intention of the parties, but to subserve
the ends of justice by "subjecting the substituted property to
the purposes of indemnity and recompense" to the plaintiff
for its moneys alleged to have been embezzled and fraudulently used in the purchase and creation of the milling
property. It appears from the complaint that Foote, while
cashier of the bank, and intrusted, in connection with Gates,
president, with its management, fraudulently diverted and
misapplied the funds of the bank to his own use and benefit,
and with the funds so fraudulently obtained from the bank
purchased certain mill machinery and fixtures which he subsequently, on the organization of the mill company, of which
he [398] was made secretary at the time of its organization,
contributed, as a part of the capital stock of said mill company. Such machinery and fixtures, though purchased in
the name of said Foote, but with the funds fraudulently obtained from the bank, was impressed with a trust in favor of
the bank in his hands, and was, in equity, the property of the
bank. It is insisted by appellant's counsel that this allegation is defective in not stating the amount so diverted by
Foote, and expended in the purchase of the mill machinery
and fixtures. Perhaps, considered as an independent allegation, the objection would be good; but it must be considered
in connection with the other allegations of the complaint,
and was inserted for the purpose, doubtless, of showing that
the $1,250 donated by the citizens of Kimball belonged to the
bank, as it is subsequently alleged that, by means of the apparent ownership and possession of said mill machinery and
fixtures, said Foote obtained a bonus from the citizens of
Kimball of about $1,250 in notes, money, and assets, which
was also contributed to the capital stock of the mill company.
As Foote held the mill machinery and fixtures as trustee of

the bank, all gains or profits arising from the apparent ownership and possession of the mill machinery and fixtures, so in
equity the property of the bank inured to the benefit of the
bank, and should be impressed with a like trust in favor of
the bank: *Colburn* v. *Morton*, 5 Abb. Pr., N. S., 308; *Ackerman* v. *Emott*, 4 Barb. 649.

It is further alleged that upon the organization of the mill
company, of which Gates was made president, and Foote
secretary, they fraudulently diverted the funds of said bank
to the use and benefit of said mill company to the extent of
about $10,000, and that the mill company began its business
without other capital than that wrongfully and fraudulently
obtained from the bank, except about $2,500 contributed by
one·Hayden. It is further alleged that the value of the mill
property is about $15,000, all of which has been created by
plaintiff's said money, assets, and credit so fraudulently
diverted and misappropriated by said Gates and Foote, except the $2,500 contributed by Hayden. It is clear, then,
from these allegations of [399] the complaint, that this entire
milling property was created with the funds, assets, and credit
of the bank so fraudulently diverted and misappropriated by
said Foote and Gates, except the $2,500 contributed by
Hayden. Assuming this to be true, which the demurrer
admits, the property in the name and possession of the milling company should be impressed with a trust in favor of the
bank to the extent of the funds and assets of the bank so
fraudulently diverted and misappropriated by said Foote and
Gates that can be traced into the mill property, with the
profits arising therefrom, unless the milling company can
show that it acquired said property in good faith, for a valuable consideration, and without notice of the fraudulent acts
of said Foote and Gates, in obtaining said bank funds. If
Foote and Gates had purchased and were still holding the
mill property in their own name, no one would question, we
apprehend, the right of the bank to hold them as trustees, or
the right of the bank to have impressed upon the property a
trust in its favor to the extent of its funds and assets fraudulently diverted and invested in the property. The mill company being chargeable with notice is in no better position
than Foote and Gates would be if they held the property in
their own name.

Appellant contends that the plaintiff should have alleged
that the milling company had obtained the property or funds

and assets of the bank with notice of the fraudulent acts of
Foote and Gates. There are two answers to this proposition,
and they are: 1. That it is alleged that Foote and Gates were
general officers of the milling company from its organization,
and that they gave their time and attention to the business
of the milling company; therefore, there was no time when
they could have transferred property or assets to the milling
company when they were not officers of said company. No
conveyance of property can be made to an incorporated com -
pany until it is incorporated, and therefore the knowledge of
Foote and Gates was, presumptively at least, the knowledge
of the company; and 2. It was not incumbent upon the plaintiff to allege notice, as want of notice, the payment of a valu-
ble **400** consideration, and good faith are affirmative matters,
to be pleaded and proved by the defendant: 1 Daniell's Chancery Practice, 702, 703; *Boone* v. *Chiles*, 10 Pet. 177; *Vattier*
v. *Hinde*, 7 Pet. 252; *Tompkins* v. *Anthon*, 4 Sand. Ch. 97;
Balcom v. *New York etc. Ins. & T. Co.*, 11 Paige, 454; *Baynard*
v. *Norris*, 5 Gill, 468; 46 Am. Dec. 647; Pomeroy's Equity
Jurisprudence, sec. 785.

It is also contended by appellant that no sufficient facts are
stated in the complaint to require defendant to account to the
plaintiff. We think otherwise. If defendant has this property, purchased and created with funds and assets so wrongfully obtained from the bank by Foote and Gates, and so
holds it that it is chargeable as a trustee, it should, undoubtedly, be compelled to account to the bank not only for the
property it has received, impressed with a trust upon it, but
for all the profits received therefrom. Again, if the milling
property, standing or held in the name of the company, in
equity belongs to the bank, subject to the rights of Hayden
for his proportionate amount advanced by him, an accounting
will not only be proper, but perhaps necessary for the protection of Hayden's interest; and if it should appear that defendant has contributed any part of the funds creating said milling property, such an accounting might be necessary for its
own protection.

It is also contended that the plaintiff, by its own showing,
has no claim against the defendant, because it has affirmatively alleged that Gates and Foote have received in payment
for the funds and property advanced to the defendant stock
of the company, and therefore plaintiff should follow the stock
so received by them. This is a question that has caused us

some embarrassment, but we are of the opinion that one whose
property, money, or assets has been fraudulently obtained,
and invested by the parties so obtaining it in the property of
a corporation, and stock of the company received therefor,
ought not to be compelled to follow the stock, but should
have the right, at his option, to pursue the property itself,
when, as in this case, it is alleged that substantially the
entire property has been created with, and the business of the
company almost entirely conducted on, the moneys, assets,
and credits of the bank, and [401] when it is alleged, as in this
case, that the entire capital stock of the corporation is held
by the original wrongdoers, or those who have purchased it
with full notice of all the facts.

It is contended that the plaintiff has not stated definitely
the amount of its money, funds, and assets that have been
fraudulently diverted by Gates and Foote, and invested in the
milling company's property. The plaintiff, in its complaint,
states, perhaps, as definitely as it is able to do, the amount
misappropriated and diverted by Gates and Foote of the
funds and assets of the bank, when it alleges that the amount
so diverted and appropriated to the use and benefit of the defendant is about $10,000, with the other allegations of the
bonus of $1,250. In addition to these is the allegation that
the entire milling property was created by the fraudulently
misappropriated and diverted funds, assets, and credit of the
bank, except the sum of $2,500. We are of the opinion that
the complaint is sufficient, in this respect, on general demurrer. We have not attempted to follow the order of the able
briefs of counsel, but have, we believe, considered all the
points raised. The order overruling the demurrer is affirmed.
All the judges concurring. ____

RESULTING TRUSTS.—HOW CREATED: See the extended note to *Neill* v.
Keese, 51 Am. Dec. 751-760. If real property is bought and a conveyance
taken in the name of one person while the purchase money is paid by another, a resulting trust arises in favor of the person thus paying the purchase price: *Champlin* v. *Champlin*, 136 Ill. 309; 29 Am. St. Rep. 323, and
note; *Peek* v. *Peek*, 77 Cal. 106; 11 Am. St. Rep. 244; *Reynolds* v. *Sumner*,
126 Ill. 58; 9 Am. St. Rep. 523, and note.

CONSTRUCTIVE TRUSTS—WHEN ARISE—FRAUD.—Persons acquiring the
title to property by fraud are trustees of the injured party: *Lewis* v. *Lewis*,
9 Mo. 182; 43 Am. Dec. 540; *Coleman* v. *Cocke*, 6 Rand. 618; 18 Am. Dec.
757; *Larmon* v. *Knight*, 140 Ill. 232; 33 Am. St. Rep. 229, and note; *Cutler*
v. *Babcock*, 81 Wis. 195; 29 Am. St. Rep. 882, and note; *Ragsdale* v. *Ragsdale*, 68 Miss. 92; 24 Am. St. Rep. 256, and note. See also the notes to

Salsbury v. *Black*, 4 Am. St. Rep. 634, and *Piper* v. *Hoard*, 1 Am. St. Rep. 797.

TRUSTS.—EQUITY WILL FOLLOW A TRUST FUND so long as its identity exists, or when it can be shown to be the product of the original trust property: *Lathrop* v. *Bampton*, 31 Cal. 17; 89 Am. Dec. 141, and note; *Farmers'* etc. *Nat. Bank* v. *King*, 57 Pa. St. 202; 98 Am. Dec. 215; *Dolliver* v. *Dolliver*, 94 Cal. 642; *Johns* v. *Williams*, 66 Miss. 350; *Holmes* v. *Gilman*, 138 N. Y. 369; 34 Am. St. Rep. 463, and note. See the extended note to *Union Nat. Bank* v. *Goetz*, 32 Am. St. Rep. 125-130, where the subject is thoroughly discussed.

TOWN OF WAYNE *v.* CALDWELL.

[1 SOUTH DAKOTA, 488.]

JURISDICTION—WAIVER OF BY STIPULATION. —Mere irrregularities in judicial proceedings may be waived by stipulation, but no such waiver can confer jurisdiction on any tribunal having no jurisdiction of the subject-matter of the action.

JURISDICTION—EFFECT OF.—When judicial tribunals have no jurisdiction of the subject matter on which they assume to act, their proceedings are absolutely void, but when they have jurisdiction of the subject matter, irregularity, or illegality in their proceedings does not render them void, but merely voidable.

JURISDICTION—RIGHT OF COURT TO DETERMINE.—A court which is competent to decide on its own jurisdiction in a given case can determine that question at any time in the proceedings, whenever that fact is made to appear to its satisfaction, either before or after judgment.

HIGHWAYS—COMPLIANCE WITH STATUTE IN ALTERING OR LAYING OUT.— The altering and laying out of roads for the use of the public is a taking of private property for a public use, and every substantial requirement of the statute must be complied with by the supervisors or road officers. Otherwise their proceedings are void.

HIGHWAYS—WAIVER OF STATUTORY PROVISIONS CONCERNING.—In proceedings to lay out or alter a public highway statutory requirements relating solely to private persons may be waived by the parties interested, but provisions in which the public have a general interest must be strictly followed or the proceedings are void.

JURISDICTION—WHEN NOT ACQUIRED.—An appellate court acquires no jurisdiction of a question of damages to be awarded in laying out a public highway, when such highway is illegally laid out, on the ground that the proceeding of the lower tribunal in establishing such road are void for a failure to comply with statutory requirements.

HIGHWAYS—LAYING OUT, ALTERING, OR DISCONTINUING a public highway is an exercise of arbitrary power conferred upon supervisors or road officers for the good and necessity of the general public, and the exercise of this power must be made a matter of public record by them, so that private and public rights may be clearly defined.

HIGHWAYS—OPENING, AND LAYING OUT—FAILURE TO COMPLY WITH STATUTE.—When a statute provides that if the board of supervisors does not file an order describing a hi·hway within twenty days after an application for the establishment thereof, it shall be deemed to have decided

against the application, any proceeding by the board thereafter, and
after a failure to file such order for record, is of no force and effect, and
the parties thereto stand in the same position as if no application had
been made.

Bailey, Davis, and *Lyon,* for the appellant.

Palmer and *Rogde,* for the respondent.

[484] BENNETT, J.   This is an appeal from an order of the
circuit court setting aside a verdict, and vacating a judgment
rendered in a matter of damages arising by reason of the
board of supervisors of the town of Wayne laying out and
establishing a [485] road across the land of appellant.   The
bill of exceptions shows that the cause was submitted to the
court below upon a stipulation entered into and agreed to by
both the town of Wayne and the appellant.   The stipulation
is as follows: "Whereas it appears from the papers on appeal
in the above-entitled action that certain irregularities exist
concerning the proceedings of the board of supervisors of said
Wayne township in their attempt to lay out and establish a
new road or highway across the land of the said Ann A. Caldwell and Elias Wiser, appellants herein.   Now, in the interest
of a speedy trial and determination of these cases on their
merits, it is hereby stipulated and agreed, by and between the
attorneys in said action, that all irregularities of said board
of supervisors are hereby waived, and that said trial shall be
had, and proceed to determine the actual damages sustained
by appellants herein, the same as if all proceedings on the
part of said board of supervisors had been regular, and according to law; it being the purpose of the parties to this
stipulation to submit to and determine in this court the
amount of damages which each of these appellants have or
shall sustain, by reason of the establishment of a highway
in controversy in this action."   A trial was had; verdict and
judgment for the appellant for two hundred and twenty-five
dollars damages.   Afterwards, the town of Wayne served a
notice on the appellant, to show cause why this verdict should
not be set aside and vacated, and the proceedings dismissed,
for want of jurisdiction of the court.   The motion was based
upon the affidavits of C. S. Palmer, O. Brandenburg, and John
Alguire.   The court, upon hearing the motion, made an order
setting aside the verdict, vacated the judgment, and dismissed
the proceedings for want of jurisdiction.   From this order the
appeal is taken.   The appellant contends that the question of

jurisdiction cannot be raised by motion and affidavits after trial and judgment, and especially after the filing of a stipulation signed by both appellant and respondent, waiving all irregularities in the proceedings had before the town supervisors. This contention, no doubt, would be correct if the waiver only went to irregularities, but no waiver by stipulation can confer [486] jurisdiction on any tribunal to hear and try a cause that has not jurisdiction of the subject matter of the action. When judicial tribunals have no jurisdiction of the subject matter on which they assume to act, their proceedings are absolutely void in the strictest sense of that term; but when they have jurisdiction of the subject matter, irregularity or illegality in their proceedings does not render them absolutely void, though they may be avoided by timely and proper objection. A court which is competent by its own constitution to decide on its jurisdiction in a given case can determine that question at any time in the proceedings of the cause, whenever that fact is made to appear to its satisfaction, either before or after judgment. A void proceeding is a nullity.

The case at bar was brought to the circuit court by an appeal from the action of the board of supervisors of Wayne township in assessing damages in laying out a road across the land of appellant. The action of the board of supervisors was based upon sections 1296–1305 of the Compiled Laws, inclusive, relating to altering, discontinuing, and laying out roads. The altering and laying out of roads for the use of the public is taking private property for public use, and every substantial requirement of the statute must be complied with by the supervisors of a town; otherwise their proceedings will be void.

The sections above enumerated provide, with great particularity, the mode and manner of procedure. Some of the requirements pertain to private individuals alone, and as to them, the manner of procedure may be waived by the parties interested, but that portion of the statute in which the public have a general interest must be strictly followed in order to be valid. The face of the proceedings had before the board of supervisors, as disclosed by the affidavits of one of the town supervisors and the town clerk, shows clearly that the supervisors failed to proceed in the manner prescribed by the statute. It is not necessary to examine or point out more than one of these irregularities and omissions to comply with the statute upon the part of the town supervisors, as that is fatal to this appeal.

[487] By the affidavits of Brandenburg, the town clerk, and of Alguire, one of the town supervisors, it will be seen that no order was ever made by the board of supervisors, or signed by them, in any manner describing the said highway, and that no order of any description or character was ever made or filed with the town clerk by said board of supervisors, as contemplated by section 1300 of the Compiled Laws. This section provides that, "whenever the supervisors shall lay out, alter, or discontinue any highway, they shall cause a survey thereof to be made when necessary, and they shall make out an accurate description of the highway so altered, discontinued, or laid out, and incorporate the same in an order to be signed by them, and shall cause such order, together with all the petitions and affidavits of service of notice, to be filed in the office of the town clerk, who shall note the time of filing the same. . . . All orders, petitions, and affidavits, together with the award of damages, shall be made out and filed within five days after the date of the order for laying out, altering, or discontinuing such highway. But the town clerk shall not record such order within thirty days, nor until a final decision is had, and not then unless such order is confirmed, and after such order is confirmed, and such order, together with the award, has been recorded by such town clerk, the same shall be sent by him to the county auditor, or county clerk, who shall file and preserve all such papers thus transmitted to him, and in case the board of supervisors shall fail to fill such order within twenty days, they shall be deemed to have decided against such application." In the case at bar, the twenty days having elapsed, and no final order being filed with the town clerk laying out the road, and the statutory requirement not being fulfilled, all of the proceedings of the board in relation to this road fell, and their decision was against the application to lay out and vacate this road, by operation of law.

This being the case, there was nothing for the appellant to appeal from to the circuit court. The action of the board in relation to assessing damages to the appellant was of no force or effect. A highway is not legally laid out unless the board of [488] supervisors, within the time required by the statute, file with the town clerk this order describing such highway. This was an omission of a very important matter. Independent of the fact that it is the command of the statute, and must be performed, there is abundant reason why it should be done, if it were not required by law. The laying out, altering, or discontinuing a public highway, is an exercise of an arbitrary power conferred upon the board of supervisors for the good and necessity of the general public, and the exercise of this power should be made a matter of public record, so that private and public rights may be clearly defined.

The making and filing this order is the final culmination of the proceedings. Without the order, no conclusion has been arrived at by the board, and, without the record of it, no publication to the public has been made that a road has been established, as called for by the petition. If no road has been laid out, or land taken belonging to appellant, for public use, she has no claim for damages, and there is nothing from which she could appeal. It is the notice of appeal which gives the appellate court jurisdiction, and from this it appears that there has never been any filing of the order- laying out said road, in the office of the town clerk. This failure leaves the parties in the same condition they were in before any proceedings were had in relation to laying out the road in question. There being nothing to appeal from, the circuit court took jurisdiction of nothing, and could determine nothing. Judgment affirmed. All the judges concurring.

———

Jurisdiction Cannot Be Conferred by Consent where it does not exist at law: Bent v. Graves, 3 McCord, 280; 15 Am. Dec. 632; Block v. Henderson, 82 Ga. 23; 14 Am. St. Rep. 138, and note. See also the notes to Keeler v. Stead, 7 Am. St. Rep. 323; Alley v. Cospari, 6 Am. St. Rep. 180, and Roy v. Horsley, 25 Am. Rep. 539–541.

Jurisdictions, Effect of Want of.—Judgments of a court acting without jurisdiction are mere nullities: Cockey v. Cole, 28 Md. 276; 92 Am. Dec. 683, and note. Any act, judicial in its nature, is void when attempted to be exercised by a court or other tribunal having no jurisdiction: Carron v. Martin, 26 N. J. L. 594; 69 Am. Dec. 584, and note; Gray v. Fox, 1 N. J. Eq. 259; 22 Am. Dec. 508; Two Rivers Mfg. Co. v. Beyer, 74 Wis. 210; 17 Am. St. Rep. 131, and note. Want of jurisdiction makes an act void, but a mistake or error makes it erroneous only: Miller v. Brinkerhoff, 4 Denio, 118; 47 Am. Dec. 242, and note.

Jurisdiction.—Objection to May Be Made at Any Time: Durant v. Comegys, 2 Idaho, 809; 35 Am. St. Rep. 267, and note with cases collected.

Highways.—Whether Condemnation of Land For Is a Taking For Public Use see the extended note to Vanderlip v. Grand Rapids, 16 Am. St. Rep. 614, and the note to Wild v. Deig, 13 Am. Rep. 401.

SIMMONS HARDWARE COMPANY *v.* WAIBEL.

[1 SOUTH DAKOTA, 488.]

RECEIVERS—APPOINTMENT—DISCRETION OF COURT.—Appointing or refusing a receiver is within the sound judicial discretion of the court to which application is made. The exercise of such discretion will not be interfered with on appeal when the evidence is conflicting unless such discretion has been clearly abused, but when such abuse is shown and the evidence is not conflicting the judgment of the lower court will be reversed or modified.

TRADE SECRETS—INJUNCTION AND RECEIVER TO PROTECT.—The inventor and owner of a secret code or system of letters, figures, or characters showing the cost and selling price of goods for the use of himself and his traveling salesmen has a property therein which, when the remedy at law is inadequate, will be protected in equity by granting a temporary injunction and appointing a receiver in order to prevent irreparable injury *pendente lite.* If a copy of such code and of the key thereto is wrongfully and fraudulently in the possession of a third person the court should, upon proper application, take such copy into its possession through a receiver and retain it during the pendency of the action. The refusal of the court to do so is an abuse of discretion which will be corrected on appeal.

Mouser and Vollrath, for the appellants.

A. B. Melville and E. H. Aplin, for the respondents.

490 CORSON, P. J.   On March 1, 1889, the plaintiff filed its verified complaint in the district court, in which it is alleged, in substance, that it is engaged in the wholesale and retail hardware business in the city of St. Louis; that it has a large amount of capital invested in its said business, several hundred clerks and about ninety traveling salesmen engaged in selling its wares and merchandise in nearly all the states and territories; that it has prepared and published, at great expense, an illustrated and printed catalogue containing about fifteen hundred pages, for distribution among its customers; that it has invented and prepared, at a cost of many thousand dollars, a secret code or system, represented by letters, figures, and characters, showing the cost and selling price of its many articles of merchandise, which is marked in such of its catalogues as are intended for use in its said business by its traveling salesmen, and which said secret code or system is not marked in the catalogues distributed to its customers; that in January, 1887, it employed one Frank Meech as one of its traveling salesman, and intrusted to him, as such, one of its catalogues containing its said secret code or system of letters, figures, and characters marked therein, with the key thereto; that in his business as such traveling salesman, said Meech frequently visited the city of Huron, in Dakota, and made sales of goods to the defendants, who were customers of plaintiff, and engaged in the hardware business; that during the year 1888 the defendants, in collusion with said Meech, who still continued in the employment of. plaintiff as such traveling salesman, wrongfully and fraudulently obtained from said Meech the said privately marked catalogue, containing its secret code or system of letters, figures, [491] and characters, showing the cost and selling price of its said wares and merchandise, with the key thereto, and copied the same therefrom into one of plaintiff's catalogues that had been furnished to defendants as customers of plaintiff, and that defendants thereby wrongfully and fraudulently became possessed of a knowledge of plaintiff's said secret code or system, and a copy of the same; that plaintiff, upon ascertaining said fact, demanded of defendants the said copy of its secret catalogue so wrongfully and fraudulently made by them, and that on or about February 19, 1889, defendants returned to plaintiff said marked copy, but before doing so they fraudulently and wrongfully copied said secret code or system into one of plaintiff's said catalogues it had furnished to Shefler Brothers, also customers of plaintiff from whom defendants had obtained it, and that said defendants now retain said last-mentioned or Shefler copy, refuse to return same to plaintiff, and threaten to make known said secret code or system, with the key thereto, to customers of plaintiff, to the great damage and injury of plaintiff; that to invent and prepare a new code or system will cost the plaintiff several thousand dollars and require at least six months' time, and that during such change of system plaintiff will be greatly embarrassed in the transaction of its business. An injunction, receiver, etc., are prayed for.

On filing the complaint, and two supporting affidavits, the court granted *ex parte* a temporary injunction, and appointed a receiver, to whom defendants were required to deliver said (Shefler) copy of the catalogue alleged to have been copied by them from the former copy returned to plaintiff. On April 18th the defendants moved the court, upon the affidavit of defendant Donaldson, pleadings, proceedings, etc., in the case, to vacate said order made March 1st. The court on the bearing refused to vacate said order, but made an order modifying it by directing that receiver to return said (Shefler) copy of

catalogue to defendants. From so much of said order of
April 18th as required the receiver to return said copy of catalogue to defendants, plaintiff appeals to this court, and assigns
such modification of the original order as error.

492 The appointing or refusing a receiver is within the
sound judicial discretion of the court to which application is
made, and this court will not interfere with the exercise of
this discretion by the lower court when the evidence is conflicting, unless this court is satisfied such lower court has
abused its discretion: *Mays* v. *Rose*, Freem. (Miss.) 703;
Chicago etc. M. Co. v. *United States P. Co.*, 57 Pa. St. 83;
Whelpley v. *Erie R. R. Co.*, 6 Blatchf. 271; Story's Equity
Jurisprudence, secs. 831, 832; High on Receivers, secs. 7–25;
Pomeroy's Equity Jurisprudence, sec. 1331. Was there, then,
a substantial conflict in the evidence upon the material facts
in this case? and, if there was such conflict, was there an
abuse of discretion by the court? The respondents contend
that the affidavit of Donaldson denies all the equities of the
bill relating to the Shefler catalogue, and invoke the rule of
the courts of equity applicable to injunctions, that, when the
equities of the bill are denied by the answer, the injunction
will be denied: *Anderson* v. *Reed*, 11 Iowa, 177; *Stevens* v.
Myers, 11 Iowa, 184. But that rule does not apply to this
case, for the reason that the receiver was appointed, not upon
the complaint alone, but on the complaint and supporting
affidavits, and upon the hearing additional affidavits were
read on the part of the plaintiff; and the rule itself is subject
to many qualifications and exceptions not necessary now to
be noticed. This affidavit will therefore be considered as the
other affidavits in the case.

The only evidence introduced on the part of the defendants
on the hearing was the affidavit of defendant Donaldson, before referred to. This affidavit, while it denies each and
every allegation in the complaint in general terms, does not
deny the various allegations of the complaint and supporting
affidavits in that clear and specific manner that entitles it to
much weight in a court of equity. It is evasive and unsatisfactory, and leaves upon the mind the impression that, while
there is an attempt to deny the allegations of the complaint
and supporting affidavits, there is a want of good faith on the
part of Donaldson, and an effort on his part to conceal the
real facts in the case. All the material facts stated in
the complaint were fully sustained by affidavits introduced

and read in evidence on the [493] part of the plaintiff. That defendant Donaldson did, in collusion with Meech, plaintiff's traveling salesman, wrongfully and fraudulently obtain from said Meech the secret, catalogue intrusted to him by the plaintiff, and make a copy of the same, and that they did in the same manner obtain the key to the same, and did thereby become possessed of a knowledge of plaintiff's secret code or system to which he was not entitled, is proved by too clear and satisfactory evidence to admit of any doubt. That he did return to plaintiff the first copy so made is admitted.

The only question remaining is, did Donaldson, before returning the said marked copy, make a second copy therefrom in the Shefler catalogue now in controversy? After a careful examination of the evidence we think there cannot be much doubt upon this question. It may be true that there were some slight changes made in the letters, figures, and characters used by plaintiff to represent the cost and selling prices of plaintiff in the Shefler copy; but we think it is equally true that in the changes made, if any, defendant Donaldson had so arranged them that he preserved in substance the plaintiff's system. H. P. Huckins says in his affidavit that he is one of the traveling salesmen of plaintiff, and is fully acquainted with the private and secret code of plaintiff, represented by letters, figures, and characters showing the cost and selling prices of plaintiff's goods, and the key thereto, and that he had examined the Shefler catalogue in the hands of the receiver, and that the basis of the prices marked therein is throughout the said cost price to plaintiff, and that it would have been impossible for any one to have marked the said Shefler catalogue with the prices marked, and the explanatory remarks therein contained, unless the person who so marked the same had access to and copied from one of plaintiff's private catalogues. In connection with this testimony are to be considered the efforts made by Donaldson to obtain one of plaintiff's catalogues from some one of plaintiff's customers before he returned to it his own marked copy. After efforts by himself and through his confederate Meech he obtained one from George C. Shefler, who says, in his affidavit, that he first loaned to Donaldson his [494] catalogue on February 15, 1889, and that when, soon after, he requested Donaldson to return it he replied: "I have marked the price of my goods in the catalogue, but am expecting a catalogue from the Simmons Hardware Company

every day, and as quick as it comes I will express it to you."
It is true he couples the admission that he had marked the
Shefler catalogue with the qualification that he had marked
the price of his own goods in it; but this is not inconsistent
with the fact that he had marked the prices contained in plaintiff's secret catalogue, as he was a customer of plaintiff, and
was then in possession of a copy made from one of plaintiff's
catalogues intrusted to Meech, and he subsequently took
great pains to obtain a bill of sale of this catalogue from
Shefler. Why these efforts and this haste to get another
catalogue before he returned the first copy marked by him if
he did not require it in which to make another copy? We
are of the opinion that there is no substantial conflict in the
evidence, and that upon the facts the court below should have
retained the catalogue in question in the hands of the receiver.

It is contended on the part of respondents that the catalogue in controversy was the absolute property of defendants,
and that the court, under the established rules of equity, was
not authorized to take it from them, and place in the hands
of a receiver. It may be conceded, as claimed, that the Shefler catalogue in its original condition was the absolute property of defendants; but the catalogue in controversy had
been changed from its original condition by the defendants
by incoporating therein the private code or system invented
and prepared at great expense by the plaintiff. The original
catalogue was of itself of but trifling value, but with the
private code or system of plaintiff marked therein it was of
great value. That such a code or system as was invented
and used by plaintiff in its business, and described in its
complaint, was its property is well settled both at common
law and under our own code: Comp. Laws, sec. 2676. It was
the product of the skill and labors of the plaintiff, and, as
such, is property, and is entitled to the protection of the law;
and when the injury threatened would [495] be irreparable, and
the remedy at law is inadequate, a court of equity will interfere to prevent a party who has wrongfully obtained possession of the secret from using it or disclosing it to others.

And when, as in this case, a party has not only obtained
knowledge of the secret code or system, but has wrongfully
made a copy of the secret system, a court of equity will, in
furtherance of justice and to prevent the party from fraudulently making a disclosure of the secret, not only enjoin him,

but will, we apprehend, take into its possession, by means of
a receiver, who is an officer of the court, such copy, so wrongfully made, to prevent fraud; and if on the trial the facts alleged are established, the court will be authorized to place
such copy in the hands of the plaintiff, or at least see that
plaintiff's secret marks therein shall be erased or canceled.
This accords with the spirit, if not with the letter, of our code:
See Comp. Laws, secs. 3213–3221.   These sections embody
the rules of the civil law upon the doctrine of accessions to
personal property, except perhaps section 3219, which is a
rule of the common law: *Silsbury* v. *McCoon*, 3 N. Y. 379, 53
Am. Dec. 307.   That courts do not hesitate to grant injunctions in such cases is well settled by the adjudged cases.   In
Yovatt v. *Winyard*, 1 Jacob & W. 394, the court granted an
injunction against one who had obtained a knowledge of a
secret by a breach of trust.   In *Morison* v. *Moat*, 9 Hare, 241,
the court restrained the defendants from using a secret in
compounding a medicine, surreptitiously obtained.   In *Peabody* v. *Norfolk*, 98 Mass. 452, 96 Am. Dec. 664, the court held
that an injunction to restrain a party from communicating a
secret imparted to him in the court, of his business, was
proper: See 2 Story's Equity Jurisprudence, sec. 952.   The
court was therefore clearly right in granting and continuing
the tempory injunction, and this being so, we are unable to
see any legal reason why the court should not have retained
in the hands of the receiver the marked catalogue in controversy in this action.   The powers of courts of equity over
property, the title to which is involved in litigation, is broad
and comprehensive, and its power to take into its possession,
through its receiver, any property that is the subject of litigation, is ample and unquestioned.

496 The contention of defendants that, as they were the
owners of the catalogue of trifling value, into which they have
copied plaintiff's valuable secret code or system, it cannot be
taken into its possession by a court of equity, through its receiver, and held *pendente lite* we cannot assent to.   One of the
grounds upon which a receiver will be appointed is that there
is no other adequate remedy.   In this case the remedy by injunction is not adequate to accomplish the ends of justice.
The plaintiff, by its complaint and affidavits, shows that its
business extends over a large number of states and territories,
in which it has many customers.   Enjoining a party, therefore, from using or communicating the plaintiff's secret code

or system, while effective so long as the defendants are within
the jurisdiction of the court, would yet be of little efficacy in
case defendants should go beyond the jurisdiction of the
court, and take with them the copy, where they might use
this secret by communicating it to plaintiff's customers, to
the irreparable injury of the plaintiff.   The flexible nature of
the equitable jurisdiction of courts of equity enables that
court to so mould and administer its remedies as to prevent
such fraudulent and wrongful use of the catalogue in question,
by at once placing it within the control of the court, and thus
placing it beyond the power of the defendants to make any
improper disposition of it pending the suit, by taking it beyond
the jurisdiction of the court.   We are clearly of the opinion
that under the established jurisdiction of courts of equity the
power exists in that court to take into its possession this catalogue, and we think under the evidence it was clearly the
duty of the court to do so, and that its modification of its order
of March 1st was an abuse of its judicial discretion.   The
modified order, so far as it directed the return of the catalogue
to defendants, is reversed.   All the judges concurring.

RECEIVERS.—DISCRETION OF COURT IN APPOINTING: See the extended
note to *Cortleyeu* v. *Hathaway*, 64 Am. Dec. 482.

INJUNCTION TO RESTRAIN INFRINGMENT OF TRADEMARK: See the notes
to *Liggitt etc. Tobacco Co.* v *Reid Tobacco Co.*, 24 Am. St. Rep. 316.   One
who by unfair means discovers the mode of manufacturing an article or the
formula for compounding a medicine will be enjoined from using it himself
or imparting it to others to the injury of the proprietor: *Tabor* v. *Hoffman,*
118 N. Y. 30; 16 Am. St. Rep. 740, and note; *Peabody* v. *Norfolk,* 98 Mass.
452; 96 Am. Dec. 664, and note.

GRISWOLD LINSEED OIL CO. *v.* LEE.

[1 SOUTH DAKOTA, 531.]

JUDGMENTS—VACATING DEFAULTS—EVIDENCE.—On the hearing of an application to set aside a judgment rendered by default, and for leave to
answer, the evidence is confined to the question whether or not the
judgment has been taken through the inadvertence, mistake, surprise,
or excusable neglect of the defendant. He is not required to make
more than such a *prima facie* showing on the merits as arises from his
own affidavits; and evidence to controvert the merits of his defense is
irrelevant to the issue, and inadmissible.

JUDGMENTS—VACATING DEFAULTS—RELIEF WHEN GRANTED.—A judgment
by default should be opened and leave given to answer upon prompt
application therefor, and a good and sufficient showing of mistake, inad-

vertence, surprise, or excusable neglect, together with an affidavit of merits stating that the applicant *prima facie* has a good defense and makes the application in good faith.

JUDGMENTS—VACATING DEFAULTS—DISCRETION OF COURT.—The granting of applications for relief from judgments by default is entirely within the discretion of the court to which application is made.

JUDGMENTS—VACATING DEFAULTS—IMPOSING TERMS.—A court may, upon opening a judgment rendered by default, impose, in addition to costs as terms, that the judgment stand as security for any judgment finally recovered, in the absence of a good and sufficient bond for the payment of such final judgment.

JUDGMENTS—VACATING DEFAULTS—IMPOSING TERMS.—A court can modify a default judgment by depriving it of its ordinary character as *res judicata* and leave it in full force as a lien, or collateral security, for any judgment finally recovered.

Keith, Bates, Winsor, and Kittridge, for the appellant.

McMartin and Carland, for the respondent.

[533] CORSON, P. J. This action was instituted by the plaintiff to recover the sum of seven hundred and fifty-nine dollars and fifteen cents, alleged to be due from defendant for money advanced under a certain contract entered into between plaintiff and defendant on July 13, 1887, and for the sum of four thousand three hundred and seventy-two dollars and fifty-eight cents, for profits received by defendant on resale of flaxseed alleged to have been purchased by defendant for account of plaintiff, interest, etc., under the terms of said contract. The summons and complaint were personally served upon the [534] defendant in Minnehaha county on the twenty-fifth day of March, 1890, and, defendant failing to serve an answer within the thirty days allowed by law, judgment was entered against him April 26, 1890, for the sum of four thousand six hundred and forty-three dollars and twenty cents, an execution was issued thereon, and a levy made thereunder on the property of the defendant. On May 6, 1890, the defendant obtained from the court below an order requiring plaintiff to show cause why the judgment should not be vacated and set aside, the execution and levy set aside, and the defendant have leave to serve an answer in the action. This order was made upon the affidavit, affidavit of merits, and proposed verified answer of defendant, and the pleadings and proceedings had in the action. The grounds upon which the application was based were inadvertence, surprise and excusable neglect on the part of the defendant. On May 9th a hearing was had, an order made discharging the order to show cause, and the application of defendant

denied. From this order and the judgment entered in the action, the defendant appeals to this court.

Appellant assigns several errors, which may be condensed and briefly stated as follows: 1. That the court erred in discharging the order to show cause, and denying to defendant the relief applied for; and 2. That the court erred in entering judgment for the plaintiff, said judgment not being supported by the allegations of plaintiff's complaint. Preliminary to the discussion of the first assignment of error is a question as to the relevancy and admissibility of certain evidence. On the hearing of the order to show cause, in the court below, the respondent introduced and read in evidence the affidavits of Mr. Carland, Mr. McMartin, and several letters written by defendant to the law firm of McMartin and Carland, tending to controvert the affidavit and proposed answer of defendant as to the merits of his defense, and also tending to show that the defendant's failure to answer in time was not excusable, and that his application was not made in good faith. Counsel for appellant contend that the evidence controverting the merits of defendant's defense was not admissible, and that such evidence should not have been considered by the court below. [535] But, as no objection was taken to this evidence in that court, counsel for respondent insist that it is now too late to make the objection in this court, and cites *Warder etc. Co. v. Ingli*, 1 S. D. 155 (decided by this court), as authority for their position.

We held in that case that, where incompetent but relevant evidence was admitted in the court below without objection, an objection to it could not be taken in this court, but this opinion went no further. On the hearing in the court below the only issue properly before the court was whether or not there was inadvertence, surprise, or excusable neglect on the part of the defendant in failing to serve his answer in time; and evidence to controvert the merits of defendant's defense was entirely irrelevant to the issue. Mr. Freeman, in his work on Judgments, in section 109, states the rule of evidence applicable to such a hearing as follows: "The hearing of evidence is confined to the question whether the judgment has been taken through the inadvertence, mistake, surprise, or excusable neglect of the defendant. The applicant is not required to make more than such a *prima facie* showing on the merits as arises from his own affidavits. The code did not intend that there should be two trials on the merits.

Therefore the defendant is not required to prove his defense as he would on the trial, nor can his affidavit of merits be controverted": *Gracier* v. *Weir*, 45 Cal. 53; *Francis* v. *Cox*, 33 Cal. 323; *Hill* v. *Crump*, 24 Ind. 291; *Buck* v. *Havens*, 40 Ind. 221; *Joerns* v. *La Nicca*, 75 Iowa, 705; *Hanford* v. *Mc-Nair*, 2 Wend. 286. We are of the opinion that the appellant's contention is correct, and that the counter-affidavits and exhibits, so far as they tended to controvert the merits of the defendant's defense, were clearly irrelevant and inadmissible, and should have been disregarded by the court below.

Did the court err in discharging the order to show cause, and denying to defendant the relief sought by him? The affidavit of the defendant on which the order to show cause was issues denies all indebtedness to plaintiff, and states fully the facts on which he relies to show inadvertence, surprise, and excusable neglect. This affidavit also contained an affidavit [536] of merits, and was accompanied by a proposed verified answer. The defendant, among other things, states in his affidavit "that he did not understand it was necessary for him to put in an answer to protect his rights, but thought that the matter could be settled up without suit; . . . . that he was never sued before, and did not understand that plaintiff's attorneys could enter judgment against him without further notice; and that, to his great surprise and astonishment, the next day [after his conversation with Mr. McMartin, hereinafter stated] the sheriff came to him with an execution, claiming that plaintiff's attorneys had taken judgment against him for about four thousand six hundred dollars." He also states that in a conversation with Mr. McMartin, one of plaintiff's attorneys, about the time judgment was taken in the case, "he understood him to say that he [defendant] could have thirty days more time in which to make a settlement with plaintiff." Mr. McMartin, in his affidavit, denies that he gave defendant further time, but this does not disprove defendant's statement that he so understood him. While these matters stated by defendant as reasons why he did not answer in time are not of the most satisfactory character, yet, taken in connection with the circumstances surrounding the case, they make, we think, a case entitling defendant to relief. It appears from the affidavit of Mr. Carland, and letters of defendant written by him to the law firm of McMartin and Carland, that he was exceedingly apprehensive of the effect of litigation upon his business, and that he was continually appealing to plaintiff's attorneys for further time in which to make a settlement of his matters with plaintiff; many of the letters being written after the summons and complaint were served upon him. So great appears to have been his anxiety upon the subject of this litigation, that he seems to have had a confused idea of the nature and object of the proceedings taken against him, and of the duties of a defendant to protect himself against such proceedings by retaining counsel and acting under his advice, as a prudent business man would have done. The section of our code conferring upon courts the power to grant relief in such cases, is section 4939, which is as follows: " The court [537] may likewise, in its discretion and upon such terms as may be just, allow an answer or reply to be made, or other act to be done, after the time limited by this code, or, by an order, enlarge such time; and may also, in its discretion, and upon such terms as may be just, at any time within one year after notice thereof, relieve a party from a judgment, order, or other proceeding taken against him through his mistake, inadvertence, surprise, or excusable neglect, and may supply an omission in any proceeding; and whenever any proceeding taken by a party fails to conform in any respect to the provisions of this code, the court may, in like manner, and upon like terms, permit an amendment of such proceedings, so as to make it conformable thereto."

The provisions of this section are exceedingly liberal in their terms, remedial in their character, and were evidently designed to afford parties a simple, speedy, and efficient relief in a most worthy class of cases. The power thus conferred upon courts to relieve parties from judgments taken against them by reason of their mistake, inadvertence, surprise, or excusable neglect should be exercised by them in the same liberal spirit in which the section was designed, in furtherance of justice and in order that cases may be tried and disposed of upon their merits. When, therefore, a party makes a showing of such mistake, inadvertence, surprise, or excusable neglect, applies promptly for relief, after he has notice of the judgment, shows by his affidavit of merits that *prima facie* he has a defense, and that he makes the application in good faith, a court could not hesitate to set aside the default and allow him to serve an answer upon such terms as may be just under all the circumstances of the case: 3 Wait's Practice, 665, 666; *Security Bank* v. *Bank of Commonwealth*, 2 Hun, 287; *Com-*

missioners v. *Hollister*, 2 Hilt. 588; *Hill* v. *Crump*, 24 Ind. 291;
Bertline v. *Bauer*, 25 Wis. 486; *Stafford* v. *McMillan*, 25 Wis.
566; *Lynde* v. *Verity*, 3 How. Pr. 350; *Davenport* v. *Ferris*, 6
Johns. 131; *Tallmadge* v. *Stockholm*, 14 Johns. 342; *Packard*
v. *Hill*, 4 Cow. 55; *Wieland* v. *Shillock*, 24 Minn. 345. See
also *Gracier* v. *Weir*, 45 Cal. 53; *Francis* v. *Cox*, 33 Cal. 323;
and *Joerns* v. *La Nicca*, 75 Iowa, 705, before [538] cited. Counsel for respondent have cited a number of cases f.om the
earlier reports of California, in which the courts of that state
held the rule against setting aside defaults quite strictly, but
the later cases of *Gracier* v. *Weir*, 45 Cal. 53, and *Francis* v.
Cox, 33 Cal. 323, show that a much more liberal rule has since
prevailed in that state, and that the rule as laid down in those
earlier cases has been very materially modified. We recognize the rule that, on applications for relief under this section,
much must be left to the sound judicial discretion of the court
to which application is made, but we are of the opinion that
in the case at bar the defendant was entitled to relief, and
that the court below should have granted it. The facts should
have been taken into consideration by the court that the judgment is for quite a large amount, and that it is principally
for profits alleged to have been received by defendant on re-
sales of flaxseed, claimed by.plaintiff to have been purchased
by defendant for his account. Such a case should be heard
upon its merits. But the setting aside the default and permitting defendant to serve an answer in such a case should
be, upon the terms, in addition to costs, that the judgment
stand as security for any judgment that may be recovered,
or, in lieu thereof, a good and sufficient bond should be given,
conditioned for the payment of any judgment that may be
recovered on a trial of the action, such judgment, pending the
final disposition of the case, to have no other effect than as a
security. In pursuance of the authority conferred by the provisions of section 4939 of the Compiled Laws, as well as by
its general powers, a court may modify a judgment by depriving it of its ordinary character as *res adjudicata*, and leaving
it in full force as a lien or collateral security: *Mott* v. *Union
Bank*, 38 N. Y. 18; 35 How. Pr. 332; *Anonymous*, 6 Cow. 390;
Wilson v. *White*, 7 Cow. 477. The order of the court below
discharging the order to show cause, and denying the defendant leave to serve an answer is reversed, and the court is
directed to enter an order granting defendant leave to serve
an answer upon such terms as may be just and as will secure

to plaintiff the payment of any judgment it may recover in the action. All the judges concurring.

JUDGMENTS BY DEFAULT—GROUNDS FOR VACATING.—If a defendant fails to make his defense to an action because, after consulting with an attorney, he is advised that his defense is not good in law, and he relies on that advice, he may on motion be relieved from a judgment subsequently entered against him by default: *Douglass* v. *Todd*, 96 Cal. 655; 31 Am. St. Rep. 247; *Whereat* v. *Ellis*, 70 Wis. 207; 5 Am. St. Rep. 164, and note. A judgment by default is properly set aside on the ground of surprise or excusable neglect when such judgment was entered through the failure of counsel to act after being engaged by the defendant to enter a plea for him: *Taylor* v. *Pope*, 106 N. C. 267; 19 Am. St. Rep. 530, and note. A judgment by default may be set aside upon sufficient showing, even though it was caused by a mistake which related to a matter concerning which the party is charged with notice by law: *Jean* v. *Hennessy*, 74 Iowa, 348; 7 Am. St. Rep. 486, and note. See also the notes to the following cases, *Ratliff* v. *Baldwin*, 92 Am. Dec. 332, and *Burnham* v. *Hays*, 58 Am. Dec. 397.

BOARD OF EDUCATION OF RAPID CITY *v.* SWEENEY.

[1 SOUTH DAKOTA, 642.]

OFFICIAL BONDS—LIABILITY OF SURETY.—An official bond in which the officer is named as principal, but which is not executed by him, is *prima facie* invalid, and not binding upon the sureties named therein.

William Gardner, Schrader and Lewis, and W. H. Mitchell, for the appellants.

John W. Nowlin, for the respondents.

642 CORSON, P. J. This was an action on the official bond of Bentley B. Benedict, probate judge of Pennington county. A **643** trial was had before a jury, and a verdict and judgment rendered for plaintiff. A motion for a new trial was made, and overruled, and the defendants appeal from the judgment· and order overruling the motion for a new trial. The bond upon which the action was based is as follows:

"OFFICIAL BOND AND OATH FOR COUNTY OFFICERS.

"Know all men by these presents that we, Bentley B. Benedict, as principal, and Francis J. McMahon, Joseph B. Gossage, Abram Boland, Thomas Sweeney, Joseph B. Gossage, P. B. McCarthy, Charles Roberts, Louis Volin, and Herbert S. Hall, as sureties, of the county of Pennington and territory of Dakota, are held and firmly bound unto the county of Pennington, in the territory of Dakota, in the penal sum of five

thousand dollars, lawful money of the United States, to
paid to the **said** county of Pennington, for which paym
well and truly **to** be made we bind ourselves, our execut(
and administrators, jointly and severally, by these preser
Sealed with our seals and dated this ninth day of Janus
A. D. 1883. The condition of the above obligation .is st
that whereas, the said Bentley B. Benedict has been elec
to the office of probate judge within and for the count;
Pennington, Dakota territory: Now, therefore, if the s
Bentley B. Benedict shall faithfully and impartially discha
the duties of his said office of probate judge, and render a t
account of all moneys, verdicts, accounts, and property of s
kind that shall come into his hands as such officer, and t
over and deliver the same according to law, then the ab,
obligation to be void; otherwise to remain in full force s
virtue.   "FRANCIS J. McMAHON,   [SEAL.
                  "JOSEPH B. GOSSAGE,   [SEAL.
                  "ABE BOLAND,   [SEAL.
                  "THOMAS SWEENEY,
                  "CHARLES ROBERTS,   [SEAL.
                  "P. B. McCARTHY,
                  "LOUIS VOLIN,
                  "HERBERT S. HALL,·
  "CHAS. ROBERTS.
  "Signed in the presence of J. F. Schrader.
  644 Territory of Dakota, County of Pennington—ss.:
Bentley B. Benedict, having been elected to the office of t
bate judge within and for the county of Pennington,
solemnly swear that I will support the constitution of
United States, and the act organizing this territory, and
I will faithfully and impartially, to the best of my knowle
and ability, perform all the duties of my said office of prot
judge, as provided by the condition of my official bond wri
within.   BENTLEY B. BENEDIC
  "Subscribed and sworn to before me this ninth da;
January, A. D. 1883.   J. S. GANTZ, County Clerk,
                       By A. P. STERLING, Deputy,
  The bond was filed January 9, 1883, and approved Fe
ary 15, 1883.
  The appellants rely for a reversal of the judgment t
four propositions, which are stated in their brief as follow
This is **no** bond because not executed by principal; 2. It
not **given to** cover the duties of trustee of **the townsite;** :

given to cover duties of trustee of the townsite, the duties of such trustee were materially changed, and his responsibility increased after the giving of the bond; and 4. The school board is not a party to the contract, and cannot sue upon the bond.

It will be observed that while the name of Bentley B. Benedict is inserted in the body of the bond as principal, it was not executed by him. The first proposition of counsel for appellants presents the important question as to the liability of sureties upon an official bond when the name of the officer appears upon the face of the bond as principal, but the bond is not signed by him. The authorities upon this question are irreconcilably conflicting, and it therefore becomes the duty of the court to follow that line of decisions best calculated to subserve the ends of justice, and carry out the intention of the lawmakers in providing for such official bonds. Section 1371 of the Compiled Laws provides that "all civil officers elected by the people . . . . shall, before entering upon duty, give bond [645] conditioned that they will faithfully and impartially discharge the duties of their office. . . . ." Section 1375 provides that "every official bond shall be given with at least two sureties." These sections were in force as sections 2 and 7, chapter 5, of the Political Code of 1877.

The fair import of the expression " give bond " would seem to be that the officer giving bond should be a party to the instrument itself; and this is emphasized by the fact that such bond shall be given " with at least two sureties." The term " sureties " contemplates a principal for whom there are to be sureties, and a bond not signed by any person as principal can hardly be said to be given with sureties, in the strict sense of that term; for without the signature of the principal the persons who execute it nominally as sureties are really principals, as they are the only'parties primarily liable upon the bond. The expression " give bond," as used in reference to official bonds, imports a very different meaning from the expression " give an undertaking," as used in the sections of the statute relating to undertakings in provisional remedies, appeals, etc., which are usually executed by sureties only. And there is much reason for this distinction. In the case of the giving of an official bond, the officer, being required to " subscribe his official oath on the bond," is presumed to be present when the bond is given, and acting in person in giving the bond, while undertakings in the class of cases referred to are frequently, if not generally, given by agents or personal friends, in the absence of the real principal. We think, therefore, the expression "give bond," as used in section 1381, was intended by the legislature to require the officer giving the bond to be a party to it by executing it.

But, without placing our decision upon this construction of our statute, we proceed to examine the authorities bearing upon this question in other states. This question was fully considered in *Johnston* v. *Kimball Tp.*, 39 Mich. 187, 33 Am. Rep. 372, in which Mr. Justice Campbell, speaking for the court, says: "Our statutes plainly contemplate that the treasurer shall himself be a party to his own official bond; . . . . and while we are not prepared to hold that a bond knowingly and intentionally given, [646] without his concurrent liability, will not bind the obligors, we are of opinion that when he purports to be obligor, and does not sign the bond, there must be positive evidence that the sureties intended to be bound without requiring his signature, before they can be held responsible. The obligation of a surety cannot fairly be extended beyond the scope of his written contract, inasmuch as under the statute of frauds his agreement must be in writing; and we think that presumptively, at least when the contract which he signs calls for the signature of other parties, the instrument is to be deemed inchoate and imperfect until they sign it." Again he says: "When several names are written as co-obligors, and one of them is called upon to sign it, he does so upon an implied understanding that he can, in case of being held responsible, not only have his right of contribution, but a further right to have it capable of proof and enforcement according to the terms of the contract as it purports to be drawn up." See, also, *Hall* v. *Parker*, 39 Mich. 287; *Green* v. *Kindy*, 43 Mich. 279. In *Wells* v. *Dill*, 1 Mart., N. S., 592, the court says: "The contract is incomplete until all the parties contemplated to join in its execution affix their names to it, and while in this state cannot be enforced against any of them. The law presumes that the party signing did so upon the condition that the obligors named in the instrument should also sign it, and the failure to comply with their agreement gives him a right to retract." In *Russell* v. *Annable*, 109 Mass. 72; 12 Am. Rep. 665, the court says: "The instrument is incomplete without the signature of each partner, or proof that the signature affixed [firm name] had the assent and sanction of each of them. The sureties on a bond are not holden if the instrument is not executed by the person whose name is stated as principal therein. It should be executed by all the intended parties." And the court cites *Bean* v. *Parker,* 17 Mass. 591, and *Wood* v. *Washburn,* 2 Pick. 24.   See, also, *Bunn* v. *Jetmore,* 70 Mo. 228; 35 Am. Rep. 425; *Ferry* v. *Burchard,* 21 Conn. 602; *Wild Cat Branch* v. *Ball,* 45 Ind. 213; *Fletcher* v. *Austin,* 11 Vt. 447; 34 Am. Dec. 698; *Johnson* v. *Erskine,* 9 Tex. 1; *Sacramento* v. *Dunlap,* 14 Cal. 421; *People* v. *Hartley,* **647** 21 Cal. 585; 82 Am. Dec. 758. In the case of *Sacramento* v. *Dunlap,* 14 Cal. 421, the court, speaking through Mr. Justice Field, says: "The liability of the sureties is conditional to that of the principal. They are bound if he is bound, and not otherwise. The very nature of the contract implies this.

"The fact that their signatures were placed to the instrument can make no difference in its effect. It purports on its face to be the bond of the three. Some one must have written his signature first, but it is to be presumed upon the understanding that the others named as obligors would add theirs. Not having done so, it was incomplete, and without binding obligation upon either." It is true the bond in that case was a joint bond. Judge Field, in referring to the case of *State* v. *Bowman,* 10 Ohio, 445, and some other cases holding a contrary doctrine, intimates that, as the bonds in those cases were joint and several, a distinction might be drawn between a joint and a joint and several bond; but in *People* v. *Hartley,* 21 Cal. 585; 82 Am. Dec. 758, Mr. Justice Field, while holding that the bond in that case was joint, and quoting from his former opinion, cites *Bean* v. *Parker,* 17 Mass. 591, and *Wood* v. *Washburn,* 2 Pick. 24, with other cases as authority. The bonds, however, in *Bunn* v. *Jetmore,* 70 Mo., 228; 35 Am. Rep. 425, and *Russell* v. *Annable,* 109 Mass. 72; 12 Am. Rep. 665, were joint and several; and in the Michigan and several other cases cited this distinction is not referred to, but the decisions are placed upon the broad doctrine that the instrument, as delivered, is an incomplete and imperfect instrument, and is not the contract contemplated by the parties, or that the sureties understood they were making when they affixed their signatures to the instrument. To hold that a surety who signs an official bond with the name of the officer named therein as principal intends to be bound, though such named principal may not sign it, is to hold directly in opposition to the probable actual intention of such surety; and to further hold that he must be bound by this incomplete and imperfect instrument, on the presumption that because he did not place it in escrow until executed by the principal, as is held in some of the cases, is to do violence to all reasonable presumptions as to the actual intention of the sureties in such cases. No necessity exists for such [648] a rule. The obligee always has it in his power to protect himself by requiring the principal to complete and perfect the bond before he accepts it, and thereby protect the sureties as well as himself. If the obligee does not do this, he has no right to complain if his incomplete instrument is not held good. The leading cases opposed to this doctrine are *State* v. *Peck*, 53 Me. 284; *State* v. *Bowman*, 10 Ohio, 445; *Loew* v. *Stocker*, 68 Pa. St. 226; *Trustees etc.* v. *Sheik*, 119 Ill. 579; 59 Am. Rep. 830. The last case cited was decided in 1888, and while the court very fairly reviews the decisions in support of the doctrine laid down in the Michigan, Massachusetts and Missouri cases, it finally concludes that the doctrine as laid down in the Ohio and Pennsylvania cases enunciates the correct rule. The reasoning of the court in coming to such a conclusion is not satisfactory to us, and as the doctrine relied on is well stated in that case, we will examine it at some length.

The court says: "If the sureties saw proper to bind themselves without the principal executing the bond and becoming bound, we think they may do so, and their undertaking is one that may be enforced in the court by an appropriate remedy. It may be true that if sureties see proper to bind themselves absolutely without the signature of the principal, though named as such in the instrument, they may do so; but when signing an official bond, with the name of the officer inserted as principal, have the sureties not the right to presume that before the bond is delivered it will be signed by the principal? For what purpose is the name of the officer inserted as a principal in the bond, if he is not expected to sign it? Is there not an implied understanding in such a case that the principal shall execute the bond before its delivery? We think there is, and that the failure to sign the bond on the part of the principal is a fraud upon the sureties. If the obligee seeks to enforce a bond against the sureties which appears upon its face should have been signed by the principal to make it a complete instrument according to its purport, it devolves upon the obligee to show by evidence that the sureties intended to be bound by this incomplete and imperfect instrument, without [649] the signature of the principal, and that until such proof is made the sureties may stand upon their contract as it is made, and the implied agreement of the principal to complete the instrument by his signature.

The insertion of the name of the principal in the bond, and his failure or neglect to sign it is notice that the bond is incomplete and imperfect, and puts the obligees upon inquiry as to the cause of this omission of the principal's signature, and if the obligee accepts it in this condition he does so with full knowledge that he is accepting an incomplete and imperfect instrument. No doubt the rule is that if the bond is perfect on its face when delivered, no secret understanding between the sureties and the principal that other persons should sign will avail as a defense, unless actual notice of such an agreement is brought home to the obligee; but when the instrument itself shows that to be completed and perfected other parties must sign it, this is notice to the obligee that puts him upon inquiry: *Wild Cat Branch* v. *Ball*, 45 Ind. 213; *Dair* v. *United States*, 16 Wall. 1. Again, the court in that case says: "The fact that the principal obligor in the case failed to sign the bond was a mere technicality, which ought not to affect the rights of any of the parties concerned." We cannot assent to this proposition, as we think the failure of a principal to sign an official bond and become bound in the instrument is a matter that does affect the rights of the sureties in many important respects. The sureties may have a right against the officer to be reimbursed the amount they are compelled to pay, whether he signs the bond or not, but, as said by the court in *Johnston* v. *Kimball Tp.*, 39 Mich. 187, 33 Am. Rep. 372: "This may be true, but, if he had signed the bond, he would not only have been estopped by the judgment from contesting his liability, but the sureties could require recourse to his property to satisfy the execution before seizure of theirs. These are not barren advantages." They are not only not barren advantages, but oftentimes of the very greatest importance to sureties. It affords a surety but little comfort to assure him that he can collect money he has been compelled to pay for a principal by the process of long and expensive litigation, when this [650] could have been avoided by requiring the principal to do what he virtually contracted to do by inserting his name as principal in the instrument, and by requiring the obligee to see that it is done—see that the instrument he accepts is complete by being executed by all the parties named as such therein. The case of *Bollman* v. *Pasewalk*, 22 Neb. 761, cited by counsel for respondent, seems to have been decided upon the facts peculiar to that case, as the court in its opinion says: "Where the statute requires a bond to be signed by the principal, or a bond is incomplete on its face when delivered, it is probable that the sureties might insist on a failure to perfect the instrument before delivering it to the obligee; but that question is not before the court, and will not be decided." After a careful review of the authorities, and the reasoning upon which they are based, we think the better rule is that an official bond in which the officer is named as principal, but which is not executed by him, is *prima facie* invalid, and not binding upon the sureties. As this view necessitates a reversal of the judgment, we do not deem it necessary to consider the other questions presented. Judgment reversed, and the cause remanded to the court below for such further proceedings as counsel may be advised, consistent with this opinion. All the judges concurring.

OFFICIAL BONDS—LIABILITY OF SURETY.—The signature of the principal is essential to the validity of a bond which is the joint, and not the joint and several bond of him and his sureties, and without his signature it has no binding force upon his sureties: *People* v. *Hartley*, 21 Cal. 585; 82 Am. Dec. 758, and extended note. A surety is not bound by an official bond not signed by the principal named therein, but delivered without the surety's consent or knowledge: *Johnson* v. *Kimball Tp.*, 39 Mich. 187; 33 Am. Rep. 372, and note; *Bunn* v. *Jetmore*, 70 Mo. 228; 35 Am. Rep. 425; *Russell* v. *Annable*, 109 Mass. 72; 12 Am. Rep. 665.

CASES

SUPREME COURT

VERMONT.

STATE *v.* BURPEE.

[65 VERMONT, 1.]

EVIDENCE SHOWING A MOTIVE OF A WITNESS TO TESTIFY FALSELY SHOULD NOT BE EXCLUDED.—Hence in a trial for larceny, it is error to refuse to permit the defendant to prove that an important witness for the prosecution has himself been arrested on a charge of stealing the property named in the indictment.

WITNESSES—VERACITY—EVIDENCE IS ADMISSIBLE TO SHOW the reputation of a witness for truth and veracity.

APPEAL—A JUDGMENT WILL NOT BE REVERSED because an improper question is asked, if the witness refuses to answer the question, and it is not insisted upon.

TRIAL—FUNCTIONS OF COURT AND JURY.—In criminal cases the jury are not judges of the law as well as of the facts.

INDICTMENT for larceny.

Gibert A. Davis and Frank H. Clark, for the respondent.

W. W. Stickney, state's attorney, for the state.

⁴ THOMPSON, J. The witness Potter was an important witness for the prosecution. He had slaughtered the cattle named in the indictment.. He testified that he bought them of respondent. The respondent claimed this testimony to be untrue, and as showing a motive on the part of Potter to falsify in this respect, offered to prove that Potter had been arrested on the charge of stealing the cattle in question. The evidence offered was excluded. In this there was error. If Potter had a motive to testify falsely, it rendered the proof of the claim that he had done so more probable. If he was under suspicion of having committed the identical crime in question, and had been arrested for it, he was testifying as it

775

were with a rope about his neck, and might naturally desire
and seek to screen himself in the account he gave as to how
the cattle came into his possession. It has been repeatedly
held by this court, that "All facts and circumstances upon
which any reasonable inference or presumption can be
founded as to the truth or falsity of the issue or of a disputed
fact are admissible in evidence ": *Richardson* v. *Royalton etc.*
Turnpike Co., 6 Vt. 496; *Randall* v. *Preston,* 52 Vt. 198;
Beckley v. *Jarvis,* 55 Vt. 348; *Aiken* v. [5] *Kennison,* 58 Vt. 665;
Tufts v. *Town of Chester,* 62 Vt. 356; *Armstrong* v. *Noble,* 55
Vt. 428; *Tenney* v. *Harvey,* 63 Vt. 520.

2. The evidence of Warren Bailey tended to prove that his
general knowledge of respondent's witness, Clark Spaulding,
was such as to include a knowledge of his reputation for truth
and veracity, and it was not error to allow Bailey to state what
Spaulding's reputation was in that respect.

3. The state's attorney put a question to respondent's witness,
Mary Poor, which the court ruled she might answer, to which
ruling the respondent excepted. Upon the refusal of the witness to answer the question, it was not insisted upon, and was
not answered. It is not necessary to decide whether the question was proper or not. Were it assumed to be improper, the
defendant's exception cannot avail him. A judgment will
not be reversed because an improper question is asked, if no
inadmissible evidence is obtained in answer to it: *Randolph*
v. *Woodstock,* 35 Vt. 291; *Carpenter* v. *Corinth,* 58 Vt. 214;
Smith v. *Niagara F. Ins. Co.,* 60 Vt. 682; 6 Am. St. Rep. 144.

4. The respondent requested the court below to charge the
jury that "in a criminal case the jury are judges of the law
applicable to the case upon the testimony given in court, and
that the jury have a right to adopt their own theory of the
law, instead of the law as laid down by the court." The refusal of the court to charge as requested raises the question
whether, in criminal cases, the jurors are paramount judges
of the law as well as of the fact.

In 1829 this question was incidently before this court in
State v. *Wilkinson,* 2 Vt. 480, 21 Am. Dec. 560, but no authorities were cited in the opinion of the court on this question,
and the charge of the court below was so construed as not to
raise it for decision.

In 1849 in the case of *State* v. *Croteau,* 23 Vt. 14, 54 Am.
Dec. 90, the [6] question was raised for decision, and a majority
of the court held that in all criminal cases the jury are, by

the common law, the paramount judges both of the law and the facts. The court consisted of Royce, C. J., and Bennett, Kellogg, and Hall, JJ. Bennett, J., dissented from the holding of the majority, in an opinion both able and vigorous.

In 1850 the case of *State* v. *Woodward*, 23 Vt. 97, was decided. Royce, C. J., and Redfield and Kellogg, JJ., constituted the court. In this case, the respondent was indicted for a nuisance by inclosing a portion of a public common in the town of Westford. The respondent contended that it was for the jury to say whether the act complained of constituted a nuisance. On this point the court said: "It is argued that the question, whether the act charged upon the respondent was a nuisance, should have been submitted to the jury, and in support of it several cases are cited, which are claimed as sustaining the proposition. Whether, in cases of this kind, the question should be put to the jury must depend upon the character of the nuisance charged in the indictment. If the act complained of does not divest the property, or any part of it, from the use of the public, or in any manner impair the public use and enjoyment of it, but the act was done for the purpose of making the use more beneficial to the public, there would seem to be a manifest propriety in submitting the same to the jury. And the cases which we have examined, where the question has been submitted to the jury, seem to have been of this character. But where the act complained of is the taking of property dedicated to the use of the public, and appropriating it to private use, thereby wholly excluding the public from the enjoyment of it, we are not aware of any rule of law, that requires such an act to be submitted to the jury, to say whether it is a nuisance. Such is the character of the act with which the respondent is charged; and in the judgment of the court, it is *ipso facto*, in law, a nuisance, [7] for the commission of which there can be no justification. It is difficult to see how this holding can be reconciled with the doctrine adopted without reservation or exception in *State* v. *Croteau*, 23 Vt. 14, 54 Am. Dec. 90.

In *State* v. *Paddock*, 24 Vt. 312, heard in 1852, and which was a prosecution for selling spirituous liquors, the court below "directed the jury to return a verdict of guilty, for each act of selling," to which the respondent excepted. In passing upon this exception this court say: "It is argued that the jury, in cases of this character, are judges of the law and fact, and that under this charge that right was taken from

the jury. In criminal cases it is the duty of the court to aid
and instruct the jury, and decide upon the law arising in the
case. But the jury are the ultimate judges of both the law
and the fact, and this right cannot be taken from them. . . . .
If it appeared that the court were requested to charge or inform the jury that they were the judges of the law and the
fact, and the court neglected or refused so to do, and directed
them as to the verdict they were to bring in, the exceptions
would have been well taken. But as the matter now rests,
that direction in the choice of the court must be considered
as an expression simply of his opinion of the law in the case,
and which it was his duty to give, and as informing the jury
that it was their duty to return such a verdict, without in
any way controverting their ultimate right of exercising their
own judgment in the case. For the want of positive error,
affirmatively appearing in the exceptions, this objection is
overruled." If the jury had the legal right to ignore the
instructions of the court, and substitute their own judgment
as to the law for that of the court, it could not have been
their legal duty to return such a verdict as the court directed.
Hence, the court in this case is left in the position of holding
that it is not error for the court below to charge the jury that
it is their duty to do a thing, although it is not their legal
duty to [8] do it. Again, it is not easy to reconcile the reasoning in this case with the well-settled rule in this state,
that "it is the duty of the court to charge fully upon all the
points of law in the case," without being requested to do so:
State v. *Hopkins*, 56 Vt. 250.

In *State* v. *McDonnell*, 32 Vt. 491, decided in January, A. D.
1860, and which was an indictment for murder, the court
below instructed the jury that they were the judges of the law
and the facts under the law of this state, but that it was "a
most nonsensical and absurd theory," and that the jury "would
be amply and fully justified in relying upon the court for the
law that should govern the case, and holding them accountable for that." This was urged as error, in this court, but
the objection was not sustained. In passing upon this exception the court said: "We see no objection, where the interference of a jury is directly invoked in a criminal case, to the
judge stating to the jury, in his own way, that this rule is not
intended for ordinary criminal cases; that it is a matter of
favor to the defendant, and should not be acted upon by the
jury, except after the most thorough conviction of its neces-

sity and propriety; that any departure by the jury from the law laid down by the court must be taken solely upon their own responsibility; and that the safer, and better, and fairer way, in ordinary criminal cases, is to take the law from the court, and they are always justified in doing so. This is substantially what was done by the court below, and we see no just ground of exception to the mode in which it was done."

In *State* v. *Haynes,* 36 Vt. 667, while the rule laid down in *State* v. *Croteau,* 23 Vt. 14, 54 Am. Dec. 90, was recognized, it was held that records of former convictions, to enhance the penalty, need not be offered to the jury, as the law then stood, but might be introduced after verdict to affect the sentence only. Poland, C. J., in delivering the opinion of the court said: "To say that the defendants must have an opportunity to ⁹ have this question of law submitted to the jury, so as to have the benefit of the chance of their deciding it contrary to law, seems to us a very great absurdity."

In *State* v. *Barron,* 37 Vt. 57, decided in 1864, the court said: "We think the rule is now settled in this state that in criminal cases the jury are judges of the law. It is the duty of the court, however, to instruct the jury as to the law applicable to the case on trial, and if the jury disregard the instructions or mistake the law, and render a verdict that is clearly in violation of law, the court may for that reason set aside the verdict, if the respondent is convicted." The court thus in effect held that jurors are judges of the law to acquit, but not, in the discretion of the trial court, to convict.

In *State* v. *Hopkins,* 56 Vt. 263, decided in 1883, this court affirmed the ruling of the court below, denying to respondent's counsel the right and privilege of reading to the jury authorities in support of the rule of law for which he contended. In passing upon this question the court say: "It does not follow that because the jury are judges of the law, that counsel can read what they please to them. This rule, that the jury are judges of the law, does not affect the course or order of procedure of the trial in the least; it is the result of the power of the jury rather than of any abstract inherent right, and the trial should be conducted in the usual course of proceedings."

In *State* v. *Meyer,* 58 Vt. 457, heard in January, 1886, and which was an indictment for murder, the court below instructed the jury that they had the right to adopt their theory of the law instead of that of the court, with the qualification

that they must not adopt a rule of law more prejudicial **to the** respondent than the law laid down by the court. In passing upon this point this court say: "The charge was clearly more favorable to the respondent than the request or the law, and he cannot complain.

"There is no qualification of the right of the jury, in a [10] criminal cause, to disregard the law, as given them by the court, and adopt their own theory; and they may, in the exercise of this power, with the same propriety, adopt a rule of law more prejudicial to the respondent as well as one less prejudicial."

In *State* v. *Freeman*, 63 Vt. 496, heard in May, 1891, which was a complaint for profane swearing, based upon the Revised Laws, section 4254, the respondent claimed in the trial below, that it should be submitted to the jury to say, as a matter of law, whether the words used by him were profane curses or not, and it was so submitted to the jury, and they found the respondent guilty. In this court he contended that the jury made a mistake as to the law. Upon this contention the court say: "The respondent evidently was not satisfied with the judgment of the court in respect to the law, but insisted that the jury should pass upon both law and fact, and they were permitted to do so; if they judged correctly, he is not harmed, if erroneously, as it was a matter of his own seeking, he should not now be permitted 'to unravel the whole proceedings,' to be relieved from a misfortune which he has brought upon himself. If he was erroneously convicted it is only another instance of 'the engineer hoist with his own petard.'"

The views expressed in *State* v. *Meyer*, 58 Vt. 457, and *State* v. *Freeman*, 63 Vt. 496, are in accord with the opinion of the court delivered by Barrett, J., in *State* v. *Clark*, 37 Vt. 471, although that case cannot be considered an authority, as it was held that it was not properly before the court.

These are all the cases in this state in which the question whether jurors, in criminal cases, are judges of the law and the fact, has been passed upon, and they all substantially follow the doctrine laid down in *State* v. *Croteau*, 23 Vt. 14, 54 Am. Dec. 90, and are based upon it, with the exception of *State* v. *Woodward*, 23 Vt. 97. It will be observed, however, that in the later cases there has been a tendency to give this rule such [11] effect, even to its extreme, logical results **as to** discourage and perhaps deter respondents from invoking it in their behalf.

Neither the constitution of this state nor its statutes confer, in express terms, this power upon jurors, if they possess it.

Revised Laws, section 689, provides that "so much of the common law of England as is applicable to the local situation and circumstances, and is not repugnant to the constitution or laws, shall be law in this state."

Therefore, in this state, jurors do not possess the legal right to judge of the law as well as of fact, unless jurors had such right at common law. If such right existed at common law, but is repugnant to the constitution and laws of this state, then the common law does not confer such right. In other words, to establish that jurors have such right, it must appear that it existed at common law, and that it is not repugnant to our constitution and laws.

The decisions of the courts of justice contain the most certain and authoritative evidence of what the rules of the common law are: 1 Blackstone's Commentaries, 69–73; 1 Kent's Commentaries, 473. That respondents on trial have claimed jurors to be judges of the law, or that jurors in some instances have returned verdicts apparently contrary to the law as laid down by the court, affords no evidence of what the common law is on this subject.

In *State* v. *Croteau*, 23 Vt. 14, 54 Am. Dec. 90, the majority opinion does not cite a single English decision which supports the rule laid down. De Lolme on the English constitution is there cited in support of the doctrine. This work, strictly speaking, was only an essay. It has been well said that its author "must be regarded simply as a learned foreigner, and sometimes showing that want of thoroughness and precision which even a learned man may display when writing [12] on subjects which his previous education had not fitted him to appreciate, and especially when discussing such a subject as the common law of England." He cites no authority in support of what he says in regard to jury trials in criminal cases.

The court, in *State* v. *Croteau*, also rely upon the Statutes of Westminster, 2, chapter 30, 13 Edward I. (A. D. 1285) as showing that the common law is as stated in the majority opinion. It is difficult to see how it can be said to be an authority for the doctrine there declared to be the common law. This statute, so far as it relates to this subject, is as follows:

"The justices assigned to take assizes shall **not** compel **the** jurors to say precisely whether it be disseisin or not, so that they do show the truth of the fact, and require aid of the justices; but if they, of their own accord, are willing to say that **it** is disseisin or not, their verdict shall be admitted **at their** own peril": 2 Coke's Institutes, 421, 422.

In commenting upon this statute. the court in *Pierce* **v.** *State*, 13 N. H. 536, well say: "Now in giving construction to this act, Lord Coke says that the first question was, whether in case of assize, if the issue were joined upon **a** collateral matter out of the point of the assize, upon this special issue, the jury might give a special verdict. And it was resolved that in all actions the jury might find the special matter of fact pertinent, and pray the direction of the court for the law: 2 Inst. 425. If any collateral matter, distinct from the general issue of *nul disseisin*, etc., were pleaded, then the assize was turned into a jury, instead of a separate recognition to try the fact: Glanville, lib. 13, c. 20, 21. The collateral matter was determined by the same recognition *in modum jurator*. The jury were therefore limited to the collateral matter of fact out of the point of assize. But Glanville says that the assize could not decide upon the law connected with disseisin. He states that if the demandant object to put himself upon the grand assize, he [13] must show some cause why the assize should not proceed. If the objection be admitted, the assize itself shall thereby cease, so that the matter shall be verbally pleaded and determined in court, because it is then a question of law, etc. If the assize could not determine questions of law it would be most groundless assumption to say that they could be determined by the jury, who were to find only collateral facts out of the points of assize.

"The citation from Glanville is a strong authority against the right of the jury to decide the law upon the general issue involving law and fact. The implication from the latter part of the clause cited from Statutes of Westminster, 2, is a strong argument against it. If the jury 'of their accord, are willing to say that it is disseisin or not, their verdict shall be admitted at their own peril.' But what peril could they incur if, by deciding the law, they simply exercised **a** right given to them by the statute? This phraseology is most singular, if the statute was intended to submit the law to them. The reasonable construction of it is, that if the jury will undertake to decide the law, they shall be subject to

such penalty as may be imposed upon them for exceeding
their jurisdiction. If they should incur a penalty, the act
for doing which the penalty is imposed must be illegal, for
nothing is better settled than that a penalty attached to the
performance of an act makes the act itself unlawful."

In his great argument in support of a motion for a new
trial in the case of *King* v. *Dean of St. Asaph*, 3 Term Rep.
428, note a; 1 Erskine's Speeches (ed. 1870) 170, Lord Erskine contended that, from the words of this statute, the right of
the jury to decide the law upon the general issue was vested
in them by the English constitution. But notwithstanding
all the learning and genius with which he sought to maintain
this proposition, he does not cite a single adjudged case in
support of it.

The court, in *State* v. *Croteau*, 23 Vt. 14; 54 Am. Dec. 90,
also cite Littleton's Tenures, sec. 368, [14] and Coke on Littleton, 228 b, as supporting their holding. After speaking of
giving a general verdict in an assize, Littleton, in section 368,
says: "In such case, where the inquest may give their verdict at large, if they will take upon themselves the knowledge
of the law, they may give their verdict generally, as is put in
their charge: as in the case aforesaid, they may well say
the lessor did not disseise the lessee, if they will."

The comments of the court in *Pierce* v. *State*, 13 N. H. 536,
upon this passage from Littleton are so sound that we quote
them. The court say: "Now it is to be remembered that
Littleton, in the section cited, was not examining the rights
or powers of juries. He was discussing matters very different. The passage was introduced in explaining the pleadings
in real actions relative to estates upon condition. His remarks are, in brief, that after an estate tail is determined for
default of issue, the donor may enter by force of the condition.
But in the pleadings he must vouch a record, or show a writing under seal, proving the condition; but though no writing
was ever made of the condition, a man may be aided upon
such condition by a verdict taken at large upon an assize of
novel disseisin, for as well as the jury may have conusance
of the lease, they also as well may have conusance of the
condition which was declared and rehearsed upon the lease.
And in all actions where the justices will take the verdict at
large, there the manner of the whole entry is put in issue.
He then adds: 'If they will take upon them the knowledge
of the law upon the matter, they may give their verdict

generally, as put in their charge.' An extended examination of the rights of juries would have been foreign to the
particular matter in hand, and it was necessary for him
merely to state the effect of a general verdict relative to
estates upon condition. Littleton's treatise was written in
the reign of Edward IV., between the years 1461 and 1483,
and his remark is nothing more than a cursory statement of
[15] the provision of the Statutes of Westminster, 2. It is
plain from Lord Coke's Commentary, that he did not understand Littleton as laying down the limits of the duties of
jurors, or meaning to go any further than to allude to this
statute. Coke says: 'Although the juries, if they will take
upon them (as Littleton here saith) the knowledge of the law,
may give a general verdict, yet it is dangerous for them so to
do, for if they doe mistake the law, they runne into the
danger of an attaint': Co. Litt. 228 a. This by no means
admits, but substantially denies, the right of juries to decide
the law. If they may settle the law, their conclusion is the
law, and they cannot 'runne into the danger of attaint.' "

We do not think the authorities support the decision in
State v. *Croteau*, 23 Vt. 14; 54 Am. Dec. 90.

In *State* v. *Croteau*, after citing several early English cases
in which jurors had been fined or imprisoned for disregarding the instructions of the judges as to the law, the court
cite *Bushell's Case*, Vaughn, 135 (6 State Trials, 999), as the
final vindication of the claim that jurors, at common law,
are judges of the law in criminal cases. This was not the
ground of the decision in that case. That case arose in this
way: William Penn and William Mead were tried together
at the Old Bailey before a court of oyer and terminer, for a
breach of the peace in being concerned in a tumultuous and
unlawful assembly. The proof tended to show that two or
three hundred persons had quietly and peaceably met in
Grace street, London, and listened to the preaching of Penn.
Penn contended that there had been no breach of the peace.
The court charged against the prisoners, but disregarding
the charge, the jury returned a verdict of not guilty. The
court thereupon fined them forty marks each, and committed
them to Newgate. Bushell, one of the jurors, brought his
writ of *habeas corpus* to the court of common pleas. The return upon the writ was that Bushell, being one of the jury,
had acquitted Penn and [16] Mead against evidence, and
"that the jury did acquit against the direction of the court

in matter of law." The court put its decision upon the narrow, though, for the case, conclusive, ground, that the general issue, embracing fact as well as law, it can never be proved that the jury believed the testimony on which the fact depended, and in reference to which the direction was given, and so they cannot be shown to be guilty of any legal misdemeanor in returning a verdict, though apparently against the direction of the court in matter of law. The relator was accordingly discharged, and it has been the settled law from that day to this in England and this country that jurors cannot be called to account for their verdict. This, however, is far from saying that it is their legal province to override the law laid down by the court, and to declare it for themselves.

We think such a rule contrary to the fundamental maxims of the common law, and to adjudged cases in England and the uniform practice of its highest courts.

In his able work on Trial by Jury, Mr. Forsyth says: "It was early provided that the jury should not entangle themselves with questions of law, but confine themselves simply and exclusively to facts. This rule was afterwards expressed by the well-known maxim called 'that *decantatum* in our books,' '*ad quæstionem facti non respondent judices, ad quæstionem juris non respondent juratores*'—it is the office of the judge to instruct the jury in points of law—of the jury to decide on matters of fact: Broom's Legal Maxims, 6th Am. ed., 80. "An invaluable principle of jurisprudence, which more than anything else has upheld the character and maintained the efficiency of English juries as tribunals for the judicial investigation of truth": Forsyth's Jury Trials, Morgan's ed., 216. In further discussing the claims of some writers that "the jury are entitled in all cases, where no special pleas have been put on the record, to give a general verdict according to their own views of the law, in [17] criminal as well as civil cases," he says (pp. 217–219): "But it is impossible to uphold the doctrine. It is founded on a confusion between the ideas of power and right. . . . . Although juries have undoubtedly the power in such cases to take the law into their own hands, and so, it may be, defeat the ends of justice, or do what they believe to be substantially justice, they do so at a sacrifice of conscience and duty. The law cannot depend upon a verdict of a jury, whose office is simply to find the truth of disputed facts; and yet such must be the result if they may decide contrary to what the judge, the

authorized expounder of the law, lays down for their guidance. This would introduce the most miserable uncertainty
as to our rights and liberties, the *misera servitus* of *vagum jus*,
and be the most fatal blow that could be struck at the existence of trial by jury. Can it for a moment be contended
that twelve men in a jury-box are to determine that not to be
an offense which the law, under a penalty, forbids? May
they pronounce that to be manslaughter or justifiable homicide
which the law declares to be murder? If so, then they may
by their verdict abrogate, by rendering ineffective every enactment of the legislature, and they become a court of appeal
from the solemn decision of parliament and the crown. That
they can do so is not disputed, but so can the judges give
judgments contrary to law, if they choose to disregard their
oaths and yield to the influence of corrupt motives. In both
cases the law presumes that men will act according to their
duties.

"Indeed, it is difficult to understand how anyone acquainted with the principles and settled practice of the
English law, can assert that it sanctions the doctrine which
is here combated."

Mr. Forsyth, after showing that juries became unpopular
and fell into disuse in Scandinavia and Germany, for the
reason that they there were invested with the whole judicial
power, the right to determine the law as well as the fact, ·
says [18] (pages 9, 10): "Far otherwise has been the case in
England. Here the jury never usurped the functions of the
judge. They were originally called to aid the court with information upon questions of fact, in order that the law might
be properly applied; and this has continued to be their province to the present day. The utility of such an office is felt
in the most refined, as well in the simplest, state of jurisprudence. . . . . Hence it is that the English jury flourishes still
in all its pristine vigor, while what are improperly called the
old juries of the continent have either sunk into decay or
been totally abolished."

In *Townsend's Case*, 1 Plow. 111, decided about A. D. 1554, the
jury undertook to decide a point of law as to a remitter, and
the finding was held void, because it was not the duty of the
jury to judge what the law is. The case of *Willion* v. *Berkley*,
1 Plow. 223, is express upon the same point. The court
there said: "At the beginning of our law it was ordained that
matters of fact should be tried by twelve men of the country

where the matter arises, and matters of law by twelve judges
of the law, for which purpose there were six judges here
and six in the king's bench, who, upon matters of law, used
to assemble, together in a certain place, in order to discuss
what the law was therein, so that if a traverse should be
here taken, it would be to make twelve ignorant men of the
country try that whereof they are not judges, and which does
not belong to them to try." The case of *Grendon* v. *Bishop of
Lincoln*, 2 Plow. 493, is also to the same effect.

In 1649 John Lilburne was tried for treason. At his trial
he retorted upon the judges by saying: "You that call your-
selves judges of the law are no more but Norman intruders;
and in deed and in truth, if the jury please, are no more but
cyphers to pronounce their verdict," a doctrine which caused
Jermin, J., to exclaim, "Was there ever such a damnable,
blasphemous heresy as this is, to call the judges of the law
[19] cyphers?" The jury were instructed that they were not
judges of the law, and that they "ought to take notice of it,
that the judges, who are twelve in number, and who are
sworn, have ever been the judges of the law, from the first
time that we can ever read or hear that the law was truly expressed in England, and the jury only judges of matter of
fact": 2 Hargrave's State Trials, 19, 70; Forsyth's Trial by
Jury, 220.

In *Algernon Sidney's Case*, 3 Harg. St. Tr. 818, tried in
1683, and in *Rex* v. *Oneby*, 2 Strange, 766, tried in 1727, the
jury were instructed to the same effect.

In *King* v. *Poole*, Hardw. 28, determined in 1734, and
which was a criminal information in the nature of a *quo warranto* to try the validity of an election to a corporate office,
and which had been submitted to a jury, a motion was made
to set aside the verdict as against law. In passing upon this
motion Lord Hardwicke said: "The thing that governs
greatly in this determination is that points of law are not to
be determined by juries; juries have a power by law to determine matters of fact only; and it is of the greatest consequence
to the law of England, and to the subject, that these powers
of the judge and jury are kept distinct; that the judge determine the law and the jury the fact; and if they ever come to
be confounded, it will prove the confusion and destruction of
the law of England."

The case of *Rex* v. *Dean of St. Asaph*, 3 Term Rep. 428, note
a, was determined in 1784, and was an indictment for libel.

Mr. Erskine defended him, and insisted that the jury had the
right to pass upon the whole issue, including the law as well
as the fact.   But Buller, J., instructed the jury that the judges
were appointed to decide the law, the jury to decide the fact,
and that whether the publication charged in the indictment
was a libel or not was merely a question of law, with which
the jury had nothing to do: 1 Erskine's Speeches, ed. 1870),
132.   Erskine moved for a new trial on the ground of misdi-
rection, [20] and in support of the motion is said to have made
one of the most captivating arguments ever listened to in
Westminster Hall.   But the judges unanimously sustained
the ruling of the court below.   In delivering his opinion in
this case, Lord Mansfield, who had been chief justice of the
king's bench for twenty-eight years, said: "The fundamental
definition of trial by jury depends upon a universal maxim
that is without an exception.   Though a definition or maxim
without an exception, it is said, is hardly to be found, yet
this I take to be a maxim without an exception: *Ad quæstionem juris non respondent juratores; ad quæstionem facti non
respondent judices.*

"Where a question can be severed by the form of pleading,
the distinction is preserved upon the face of the record, and
the jury cannot encroach upon the jurisdiction of the court;
when, by the form of the pleading, the two questions are
blended together and cannot be separated upon the face of
the record, the distinction is preserved by the honesty of the
jury.   The constitution trusts that under the direction of a
judge they will not usurp a jurisdiction which is not in their
province.   They do not know, and are not presumed to know,
the law; they are not sworn to decide the law; they are not
required to decide the law. . . . . But further, upon the reason of the thing and the eternal principles of justice, the jury
ought not to assume the jurisdiction of the law.   As I said
before, they do not know, and are not presumed to know,
anything of the matter. . . . . It is the duty of the judge, in
all cases upon general issues, to tell the jury how to do right,
though they have it in their power to do wrong, which is a
matter between God and their own consciences.

"To be free is to live under a government of law. . . . .
Miserable is the condition of individuals, dangerous is the
condition of the state, if there is no certain law, or which is
the same thing, no certain administration of law, to protect
individuals or to guard the state."

[21] We have been unable to find any English case since the
Dean of St. Asaph's case holding that that case was not
decided in accordance with the common law and the uniform
course of decision.

The controversy in England over the question whether
jurors are judges of the law originated largely from the course
of procedure in prosecutions for libel. Under the law as it
stood at the time of the Dean of St. Asaph's case, and for
some years after, if the respondent made no attempt at justification on trial, the only questions submitted to the jury
were whether the respondent was guilty of publishing the
alleged libel, and whether the innuendoes were true as charged.
The judges in such cases were accustomed to direct the jury
to return a verdict of guilty upon proof of publication and
the truth of the innuendoes, without instructing them as to
whether the paper, if they so found, was or was not a libel.
The question of the malicious intent charged in the indictment was not submitted to the jury. If the verdict was
guilty, whether the publication was libelous, was determined
by the court, and, if held to be libelous, then malicious intent was applied as a matter of law, and need not be proved.
The respondent was thus put to the trouble and expense of
moving in arrest of judgment, or suing out a writ of error, if
he thought the publication innocent. The doctrine of implied malice, which, when applied to homicides, has been
questioned by some of the ablest jurors in this country and
in England, was very obnoxious to respondents when thus
applied to libels. It was strenuously contended that the
intent with which an alleged criminal act was done was not
a question of law, but one of fact, to be determined by the
jury, and that the jury should be permitted to pass upon
the malicious intent in libel cases the same as in other criminal cases. After a discussion of this question in the courts
and Parliament for over half a century in England it was
finally settled in A. D. 1792, by statutes 32, [22] George III.,
chapter 60, known as "Fox's Libel Act," which provides that
in prosecutions for libel the jury may give a general verdict of
guilty or not guilty upon the whole matter put in issue, and
they shall not be required or directed by the court to find the
respondent guilty merely on proof of publication and of the
truth of the innuendoes. This act further provides that on
every such trial the court shall, according to their discretion,
give their opinion and direction to the jury on the matter in

issue, in like manner as in other criminal cases; that nothing
in the act shall prevent jurors from finding a special verdict
in their discretion, as in other criminal cases, and that in
case the respondent is found guilty by the jury he may move
an arrest of judgment on such ground and in such manner as
by law he might have done before the passage of the act.

It has been claimed that this act made jurors, at least in
libel cases, judges of the law, and declared such to be the
common law. But such is not the construction given to it
in England. In *Rex* v. *Burdett*, 4 Barn. & Ald. 131, 6 E. C. L.
Rep. 420, Best, J., says: "The judge is the judge of the law
in libel as in all other cases": *Regina* v. *Parish*, 8 Car. & P.
94; 34 E. C. L. Rep. 628; *Parmiter* v. *Coupland*, 6 Mees & W.
105; *Levi* v. *Milne*, 4 Bing. 195; *Forsyth's Trial by Jury*
(Morgan's ed.), 233.

After a careful examination of the authorities Judge Curtis,
in *United States* v. *Morris*, 1 Curt. 53, says: "Considering the
intense interest excited, the talent and learning employed,
and consequently the careful researches made in England
near the close of the last century, when the law of libel was
under discussion in the courts and in Parliament, it cannot
be doubted that if any decision having the least weight could
have been produced in support of the general proposition that
juries are judges of the law in criminal cases it would then
have been brought forward. I am not aware that any such
was produced. And the decision [23] of the king's bench in
Rex v. *Dean of St. Asaph*, 3 Term Rep. 428, note, and the answers of the twelve judges to the questions propounded to
them by the House of Lords, assume, as a necessary postu-
late, what Lord Mansfield so clearly declares in terms, that
by the law of England juries cannot rightfully decide a question of law.

Passing over what was asserted by ardent partisans and
eloquent counsel, it will be found that the great contest concerning what is know in history as Mr. Fox's Libel bill, was
carried on upon quite a different ground by its leading friends;
a ground which, while it admits that the jury are not to decide the law, denies that the libellous intent is matter of law;
and asserts that it is so mixed with the fact that, under the
general issue, it is for the jury to find it as fact: 34 Annual
Register, p. 180; 29 Parliamentary History Debates in the
House of Lords, and particularly Lord Camden's speeches.
Such I understand to be the effect of that great famous de-

claratory law: Statutes 32, Geo. III., c. 60. The defendant's counsel argued that this law had declared that on trials for libel the jury should be allowed to pass on law and fact, as in other criminal cases. But this is erroneous. Language somewhat like this occurs in the statute, but in quite a different connection, and, as I think, with just the opposite meaning.

The court or judge before whom such indictment or information shall be tried shall, according to their or his discretion, give their or his opinion and directions to the jury, on the matter in issue between the king and the defendant, in like manner as in other criminal cases. This seems to me to carry the clearest implication that in this and all other criminal cases the jury may be directed by the judge; and that while the object of the statute was to declare that there was other matter of fact besides publication and the innuendoes to be decided by the jury, it was not intended to interfere with the proper province of the judge, to decide all matters of law.

[24] In 1 Russell on Crimes, 8th Am. ed., sec. 263, it is said: "In criminal cases the judge is to define the crime, and the jury are to find whether the party has committed that offense. This act made it the same in cases of libel, the practice having been otherwise before. It has been the course for a long time for the judge, in cases of libel, as in other cases of a criminal nature, first to give a legal definition of the offense, and then leave it to the jury to say whether the facts necessary to constitute that offense are proved to their satisfaction, and that whether the libel is the subject of a criminal prosecution or a civil action."

The old common-law oath of jurors would seem to indicate that they were not the judges of the law. By it they are sworn "a true verdict to give according to the evidence": 4 Blackstone's Commentaries, 355. This must mean that they are to decide the facts according to the evidence. If they may decide the law, they may act as to that without the obligation of an oath. The law is not given in evidence.

˜ It has been urged that because jurors have the power, therefore they have the legal right to ignore the law as laid down by the court, and to decide it according to their own notion. This argument proves too much, and is based upon a confusion of the idea of physical power to do a thing, as distinguished from the moral and legal right to do it. A judge has

the power to render a judgment which is corrupt and contrary
to law, but when he does so he goes beyond his legal right as
judge, and violates his oath of office.   No one claims that in
civil cases jurors are judges of the law, yet they have the
same power in an action of trespass or trover to return a verdict contrary to the instructions of the court as to the law, that
they have in a criminal case.   If the physical power to do a
thing makes them judges of the law in the one case, it is not
apparent why it should not have the same effect in the other,
and therefore make them paramount judges of the law in all
cases, civil and criminal.

  25 If, at the common law, jurors are the paramount judges
of the law in criminal cases, the respondent must have the
legal right to have such supreme judges pass upon the law of
his case when he puts himself upon his country for trial.   By
the common law, however, jurors in such a case may, if they
so elect, return a special verdict setting forth the facts which
they find, and leave it for the court to pass upon and apply
the law: 4 Blackstone's Commentaries, sec. 361.

  Notwithstanding the doctrine laid down in *State v. Croteau,*
23 Vt. 14, 54 Am. Dec. 90, we have seen that under the
decisions of this court, cited, it is not error for the trial court
to attempt to persuade jurors not to act as judges of the law,
thus without doubt, in a great majority of cases actually
depriving the accused of his right to have them pass upon
the law as well as the facts of his case, if they are the paramount judges of the law.

  Again, if jurors are the judges of the law, if in them is
vested the right and supreme power by the law to declare
what the law is which shall govern and decide each case as
it comes before them, it seems inconsistent and absurd to
hold, as do the courts in this and other states, that the court
may direct a verdict of acquittal, when in its opinion the
evidence will not justify a conviction, and may also set aside
a verdict convicting the accused, if it thinks the verdict is
contrary to law or not warranted by the evidence.

  As before suggested, this practice in effect makes jurors
paramount judges of the law only in case they acquit, as in
that event the court cannot set aside the verdict, nor can the
accused be again put upon trial for the same offense.   But
the doctrine of *autrefois acquit* is in no wise dependent on
jurors being judges of the law.   A verdict of acquittal in a
criminal case is final, "not because the jury have a right

finally to decide the law, but because of the rule *ne bis idem*, familiar to all jurisprudence, that no man is to be tried for [26] an offense of which he has been acquitted": 1 Crim. Law Mag. 54.

In the opinion of the court in *State* v. *Croteau*, 23 Vt. 14, 54 Am. Dec. 90, considerable stress is laid upon the idea that in the past jurors have been the palladium of the liberties of the subject against the encroachments of the government, and the usurpation of unjust judges in its behalf, and that the mutation of time may bring in a day when our judges will become corrupt and the tools of tyranny in high places, and that then the rule that jurors are judges of the law will prove to be the conservator of the rights of individuals. When examined in the light of facts, this argument is without weight. This is a "government of the people, by the people, for the people." In this state the making of constitutions and the enacting of laws is vested in the people. However elected or appointed, our judges are the servants of the people, to administer justice according to law and equity, and it would be sufficient to say that they have never been recreant to the trust imposed upon them. Whenever a rule of law as administered by the courts becomes obnoxious to the people, or they think it detrimental to their best interests, they have only to exercise their power to abolish or modify it to rid themselves of it.

In times of public commotion or excitement, a respondent charged with the commission of crime often has just cause to fear popular passion and predjudice, which may be represented more or less by the jury, more than anything else in the case against him, and it is then that he has occasion to rely upon the court to protect him from the *vox populi*, and to see that he is tried and judged according to the law, and not by the passions or caprice of a jury.

The theory that jurors have always proved a protection to the individual against the corruption and oppression of those of influence and of those in power is not sustained by the facts of history.

[27] In Queen Elizabeth's time, trial by jury was not much in favor among the middle and lower classes on account of the corruption of juries and their subserviency to the upper classes: 1 Brodie's Constitutional History of England, 227. Says Wharton (1 Criminal Law Magazine, 54): "The despotism of which William Penn complained was exercised not

through courts, but through juries. . . . . In England, not only during the Stuarts, but for many years after the Stuart dynasty ceased, it was the rule that after a conviction by a jury there could be no new trial. Convictions were thus assimilated to acquittals. A verdict, when rendered in a criminal case, could not be disturbed. . . . . But who were the juries? . . . . They were virtually the appointees of the crown. 'The juries,' says Macaulay (4 History of England, 135, Harper's ed.), 'carefully selected by sheriffs whom the crown had named, were men animated by the fiercest party spirit—men who had as little tenderness for an Exclusionist or a Dissenter as for a mad dog.' Quakers, of course, being among the maddest of mad dogs, were convicted under such a system on the most frivolous evidence and in defiance of law, and when appeal was made to the court, the answer was, 'Verdicts in criminal cases are final.' It was to this rule that many infamous convictions in the reign of Charles II. and James II. are to be charged."

The doctrine that jurors are judges of the law is contrary to a great preponderance of authority in this country. Among the more important authorities against it are: Proffatt's Jury Trials, secs. 373 et seq.; Cooley's Constitutional Limitations, 4th ed., 397–402; 2 Thompson on Trials, secs. 2132 et seq.; 3 Greenleaf on Evidence, 8th ed., sec. 179; Walker's American Law, 5th ed., 696; 3 Wharton's Criminal Law, 6th ed., secs. 3094 et seq.; 1 Benn. & H. Crim. Cas., 2d ed., 428; note to *State* v. *Croteau*, 23 Vt. 14; 54 Am. Dec. 90; *State* v. *Wright*, 53 Me. 328; *Pierce* v. *State*, 13 N. H. 536; *Lord* v. *State*, 16 N. H. 325; 41 Am. Dec. 729; *Commonwealth* v. *Porter*, 10 Met. 263; *Commonwealth* v. *Anthes*, 5 Gray, 185; 12 Gray, 29; *Commonwealth* v. *Rock*, 10 Gray, 4; [28] *Commonwealth* v. *Thorniley*, 6 Allen, 445; Dorr's Trial, 121; *People* v. *Pine*, 2 Barb. 566; *Carpenter* v. *People*, 8 Barb. 610; *Safford* v. *People*, 1 Park. 474; *Duffy* v. *People*, 26 N. Y. 588; *Pennsylvania* v. *Bell*, Addis. 156; 1 Am. Dec. 298; *Nicholson* v. *Commonwealth*, 96 Pa. St. 503; *State* v. *Jeandell*, 5 Harr. (Del.) 475; *Davenport* v. *Commonwealth*, 1 Leigh, 588; *Commonwealth* v. *Garth*, 3 Leigh, 761; *Dejarnette* v. *Commonwealth*, 75 Va. 867; *State* v. *Peace*, 1 Jones, 251; *State* v. *Drawdy*, 14 Rich. 87; *State* v. *Syphrett*, 27 S. C. 29; 13 Am. St. Rep. 616, and note; *Ridenhour* v. *State*, 75 Ga. 382; *Danforth* v. *State*, 75 Ga. 614; 58 Am. Rep. 480; *Pierson* v. *State*, 12 Ala. 153; *Batre* v. *State*, 18 Ala. 119; *Washington* v. *State*, 63 Ala. 135; 35 Am. Rep. 8; *Williams* v. *State*, 32

Miss. 389; 66 Am. Dec. 615; *Nels* v. *State*, 2 Tex. 280; *Mc-Gowan* v. *State*, 9 Yerg. 184; *Montee* v. *Commonwealth*, 3 J. J. Marsh. 149; *Commonwealth* v. *Van Tuyl*, 1 Met. (Ky.) 1; 71 Am. Dec. 455; *Pleasant* v. *State*, 13 Ark. 360; *Sweeney* v. *State*, 35 Ark. 585; *Montgomery* v. *State*, 11 Ohio, 424; *Robbins* v. *State*, 8 Ohio St. 131; *Adams* v. *State*, 29 Ohio St. 412; *Hamilton* v. *People*, 29 Mich. 173; *Hardy* v. *State*, 7 Mo. 607; *State* v. *Jaeger*, 66 Mo. 173; *State* v. *Hosmer*, 85 Mo. 553; *Parrish* v. *State*, 14 Neb. 60; *People* v. *Anderson*, 44 Cal. 65; *People* v. *Ivey*, 49 Cal. 56; *State* v. *Ford*, 37 La. Ann. 443, 465; *State* v. *Hannibal*, 37 La. Ann. 619; *State* v. *Miller*, 53 Iowa, 156.

In the federal courts the doctrine is denied in *United States* v. *Shive*, 1 Bald. 512: *United States* v. *Battiste*, 2 Sumn. 243; *United States* v. *Fenwick*, 4 Cranch C. C. 675; *Stettinius* v. *United States*, 5 Cranch C. C. 573; *United States* v. *Morris*, 1 Curt. 53; *United States* v. *Riley*, 5 Blatchf. 204; *United States* v. *Greathouse*, 4 Saw. 457; and *United States* v. *Anthony*, 11 Blatchf. 204.

For an able discussion of this question and for a vigorous statement of reasons against the rule adopted in *State* v. *Croteau*, 23 Vt. 14, 54 Am. Dec. 90, also see an article by Wade, C. J., of Montana, [29] in 3 Criminal Law Magazine, 484, and a criticism in 1 Criminal Law Magazine, 51, by Francis Wharton, of the opinion of Sharswood, C. J., in the case of *Kane* v. *Commonwealth*, 89 Pa. St. 522, 33 Am. Rep. 787, which opinion and decision is explained in *Nicholson* v. *Commonwealth*, 96 Pa. St. 503.

In the trial of a criminal case in the United States circuit court in the city of New York, Thompson, J., was requested to instruct the jury that they were the judges of the law as well as of the fact, which he refused to do, in the terse but not ambiguous language. "I shan't; they ain't": 2 Wharton on Criminal Law, sec. 3100.

We are not able to learn that this question has been before the supreme court of the United States, but Baldwin, Curtis, Field, Story, and Thompson, judges of that court and eminent jurists, have emphatically denied the right of jurors to determine the law in civil or criminal cases.

Maryland, Louisiana, Illinois, Indiana, and Georgia have an express constitutional provision by which jurors are declared to be judges of the law in criminal cases. Yet in some of these states the supreme court has held that it is not error to charge the jury that it is their duty to take the law from the court: See *State* v. *Ford*, 37 La. Ann. 443; *State* v. *Hannibal*, 37 La. Ann. 619; *Ridenhour* v. *State*, 75 Ga. 382; *Danforth* v. *State*, 75 Ga. 614; 58 Am. Rep. 480; 1 Crim. Law Mag. 52.

Under a provision of the constitution of Maryland, the language of which was: "In the trial of all criminal cases the jury shall be judges of the law as well as fact," it was held in *Franklin* v. *State*, 12 Md. 236, that this language did not authorize the jury to judge of the constitutionality of an act of the assembly, and that counsel for the respondent had no right to argue that question to them. It is difficult to see the logic of this limitation, or to understand why jurors may not pass upon the fundamental law embodied in the constitution, and on the statute and common law, as occasion may require, if they are the paramount judges of the law.

[30] By statute in Connecticut jurors are made judges of the law in criminal cases: *State* v. *Buckley*, 40 Conn. 247.

By an examination of the authorities above cited, it appears that every American case cited by the court in *State* v. *Croteau*, 23 Vt. 14, 54 Am. Dec. 90, not turning upon a statutory or constitutional provision, has since been, expressly or in effect, overruled.

While a jury are out deliberating upon a criminal case, it is reversible error for the court to furnish them with the statutes of the state that they may read certain sections designated by the court touching the case under consideration. In such a case the rule is the same if the jury attempt to enlighten themselves as to the law by reading the statutes or other law books, whether they do so with or without the knowledge or consent of the court: *State* v. *Patterson*, 45 Vt. 316; 12 Am. Rep. 200; *State* v. *Smith*, 6 R. I. 33.

The doctrine that jurors are judges of the law in criminal cases is repugnant to article 4 and article 10 of chapter 1 of the constitution of Vermont, which guarantee to every person within this state "a certain remedy" for all wrongs conformably to the laws, and that he shall not be "deprived of his liberty except by the laws of the land."

In *United States* v. *Battiste*, 2 Sum. 243, Mr. Justice Story said: "If the jury were at liberty to settle the law for themselves, the effect would be not only that the law itself would be most uncertain, from the different views which juries might take of it, but, in case of error, there would be no remedy or redress of the injured party; for the court would not have any right to review the law, as it had been settled by the jury. Indeed, it would be almost impracticable to ascertain what the law, as settled by the jury, actually was. On the contrary, if the court should err in laying down the law to the jury, there is an adequate remedy for the injured party by a motion for a new trial or a writ of error, as the nature of the jurisdiction of the particular court may require. Every person accused as a criminal has a [31] right to be tried according to the law of the land—the fixed law of the land—and not by the law as a jury may understand it or choose, from wantonness or ignorance or accidental mistake, to interpret it."

With great force and clearness, Justice Campbell, in *Hamilton v. People*, 29 Mich. 173, on this subject says: "It is necessary for public and private safety that the law shall be known and certain, and shall not depend on each jury that tries a cause; and the interpretation of the law can have no permanency and uniformity, and cannot become generally known except through the action of the courts. . . . . If the court is to have no voice in laying down these rules, it is obvious that there can be no security whatever, either that the innocent may not be condemned, or that society will have any defence against the guilty. A jury may disregard a statute just as freely as any other rule. A fair trial in time of excitement would be almost impossible. All the mischief of *ex post facto* laws would be done by tribunals and authorities wholly irresponsible, and there would be no method of enforcing with effect many of our most important and legal safeguards against injustice. Parties charged with crime need the protection of the laws against unjust convictions quite as often as the public needs it against groundless acquittals. Neither can be safe without having the rules of law defined and preserved, and beyond the mere discretion of any one."

Chief Justice Wade strikingly sums up this phase of this question. He says: "The end of all good governments is the honest and uniform administration of good laws. Safety comes to a people, and life, liberty, and property are secure when no one can be deprived thereof except by 'due process of law,' and when, in the adjudication of public and private rights, judicial authority speaks the pure voice of the law—'the law of the land.' The doctrine that jurors are judges of the law in criminal cases abolishes the sacred 'law of the [32] land,' which, since the days of King John and *Magna Charta*, has been the birthright of all English speaking people, and

tends to the exercise of irresponsible arbitrary power. They
are judges whose decision cannot be reviewed. Their decrees
are irrevocable and final. If they set aside a constitution or
a statute, their act cannot be questioned. If in the jury-room
they legislate and enact a law for the case in hand, it never
sees the light of day; it is a mystery and a myth; no one can
lay his hands upon it; no one can construe or interpret it; it
affords no guide for the future, for it vanishes into nonenity
the moment the verdict is returned, and the verdict makes no
sign; the decision and the judges quickly disappear.

> 'The showman and the show,
> Themselves but shadows, into shadows go.'"

3 Crim. Law Mag. 497.

Wharton says: "We must hold, to enable us to avoid the
inconsistency, that, subject to the qualification that all acquittals are final, the law in criminal cases is to be determined
by the court. In this way we have our liberties and rights
determined, not by an irresponsible, but by a responsible,
tribunal; not by a tribunal ignorant of the law, but by a
tribunal trained to and discip'ined by the law; not by an
irreversible tribunal, but by a reversible tribunal; not by a
tribunal which makes its own law, but by a tribunal that
obeys the law as made. In this way we maintain two fundamental maxims. The first is, that while to facts answer
juries, to the law answers the court. The second, which is
still more important, is ' *nullum crimen, nulla pæna, sine lege.*'
Unless there be a violation of law preannounced, and this by
a constant and responsible tribunal, there is no crime, and
can be no punishment": 1 Crim. Law Mag., 56.

In *Commonwealth* v. *Anthes*, 5 Gray, 195, that able judge
and profound jurist, Chief Justice Shaw, said: "It is a fundamental principle of the common law that the adjudication of
the highest [33] tribunal, or court of last resort, in matters of
law, shall stand as rules of law in all similar cases, which
makes it necessary, in every system of jurisprudence following the common law, that all decisions in matters of law made
by subordinate courts and judges, shall in some mode be re-
examinable, and in some form be brought before the court of
last resort, to one tribunal, one judicial mind and judgment,
whether vested in one or many persons, in order that the rules
of law may be uniform throughout the whole extent of territory subject to the same government, that all the inhabitants

alike owing allegiance shall stand equal before the law, alike
entitled to its protection and benefits, and alike amenable
and punishable for its violation."

   This principle is recognized in our system of jurisprudence,
and is embodied in Revised Laws, sections 1699 and 1700,
which provide that after a verdict of guilty in a criminal case
all questions of law arising therein, decided by the county
court, shall, upon motion of the respondent, be allowed and
placed upon the record, and that the same shall thereupon
pass to the supreme court for a final decision.

   The doctrine that jurors are the paramount judges of the
law is repugnant to these provisions of our statute law.

   Juries are usually composed of honest men, who desire to
perform their duties to the best of their abilities, but they are
usually unlearned in the law. For the sake of illustration we
will assume that a criminal case is on trial, in which the jury
think the court has erred in its statement of the law, and they
set about to correct it. The case is submitted to them. What
follows? Under our procedure they are put in charge of an
officer, and are not allowed to separate until they have agreed
upon a verdict and delivered it in court, or have been discharged from a further consideration of the case, nor are
they allowed to speak to anyone about the case but to
their fellow-jurors, nor is anyone permitted to speak to them
about it. Debarred from access to law books of [34] authority,
from which they might hope to obtain some light to aid them,
not even permitted to read the statutes which perchance they
are attempting to construe, unaided by precedent, and utterly
ignorant of the law of the case, they are left to evolve it from
their "inner consciousness." When thus evolved and applied
by them to the case, their decision as to the law cannot be
placed upon the record pursuant to the requirements of the
statute, for it can never be known, except by inference or conjecture, what they held the law to be.

   Article 6 of the constitution of the United States makes it,
and all laws and treaties made in pursuance thereof, the
supreme law of the land, and declares that judges in every
state shall be bound thereby, notwithstanding anything in the
constitution or laws of any state to the contrary. The judges
of the supreme court of the United States are the final arbiters
to adjudicate and determine all questions of law arising under
this supreme law of the land: 1 Sto. Const., Cool. ed., sec. 375
et seq.

In *State* v. *Wright*, 53 Me. 328, the court well said: "**To allow**
juries to revise, and, if they think proper, overrule, those adjudications would deprive them of their final and authoritative character, and thus destroy the constitutional functions
of the court." On this ground the court in that case, and in
Pierce v. *State*, 13 N. H. 536, held that the doctrine that jurors
are the paramount judges of the law is in contravention of
the constitution of the United States, and therefore unconstitutional. We think this view is sound. These courts support
it by reasoning which, so far as we are able to find, remains
unanswered.

We are thus led to the conclusion that the doctrine that
jurors are the judges of the law in criminal cases is untenable;
that it is contrary to the fundamental maxims of the common
law from which it is claimed to take its origin; contrary to
the uniform practice and decisions of the courts [35] of Great
Britain, where our jury system had its beginning and where
it matured; contrary to the great weight of authority in this
country; contrary to the spirit and meaning of the constitution of the United States; repugnant to the constitution of
this state; repugnant to our statute relative to the reservation
of questions of law in criminal cases, and passing the same to
the supreme court for final decision; and, as was said by
Walton, J., in *State* v. *Wright*, 53 Me. 328, "Contrary to reason and fitness, in withdrawing the interpretation of the laws
from those who make it the business and the study of their
lives to understand them, and committing it to a class of men
who, being drawn from nonprofessional life for occasional and
temporary service only, possess no such qualification, and
whose decision would be certain to be conflicting in all doubtful cases, and would therefore lead to endless confusion and
perpetual uncertainty."

It is the province and duty of the court in the trial of a
criminal cause to decide all questions of law which arise, and
if there is a verdict of guilty to place them upon the record,
and pass them to the supreme court for final decision on motion of the respondent. If the question of law touches matters affecting the course of the trial, such as the competency
of witnesses, the admissibility of evidence and the like, the
jury receive no direction concerning it; it affects the materials out of which they are to form their verdict, but they
have no more to do with it than they would have had if it
had arisen in some other trial. The presiding judge is to

instruct the jury as to the law and its ultimate application to the facts of the case, if proved to their satisfaction beyond a reasonable doubt by the evidence submitted to them, and they are legally and morally bound to consider that they are correctly told the law by the judge. That law they are to apply to the facts which they find, and from both frame their verdict of guilty or not guilty.

36 Thus trial by jury is seen to be as so aptly described by Chief Justice Shaw, when he said: "In my judgment the true glory and excellence of the trial by jury is this, that the power of deciding fact and law is wisely divided; that the authority to decide questions of law is placed in a body well qualified, by a suitable course of training, to decide all questions of law; and another body, well qualified for the duty, is charged with deciding all questions of fact, definitely; and whilst each, within its own sphere, performs the duty entrusted to it, such a trial affords the best possible security for a safe administration of justice, and the security of public and private rights."

We, therefore, have no hesitation in holding that it was not error for the court below to refuse the instruction requested, although in so doing, we, on this question, overrule *State* v. *Croteau*, 23 Vt. 14; 54 Am. Dec. 90, and the cases in this state which have followed it.

For the error indicated the exceptions are sustained, judgment reversed, verdict set aside, and cause remanded for trial.

WITNESSES—EVIDENCE TO SHOW INTEREST.—The motives, interest, or animus of a witness may be shown and considered by the jury in estimating his credibility: *Eldridge* v. *State*, 27 Fla. 162; *Cincinnati etc. R. R.* v. *Nettles*, 77 Ga. 576; *Joy* v. *Diefendorf*, 130 N. Y. 6; 27 Am. St. Rep. 484; *New Orleans etc. R. R. Co.* v. *Allbritton*, 38 Miss. 242; 75 Am. Dec. 98. See also the extended note to *Dunn* v. *People*, 86 Am. Dec. 329.

WITNESSES—BY WHOM MAY BE IMPEACHED.—To impeach a witness by proof that another witness would not believe the former on oath, the latter must first testify that he knows the former's reputation among his neighbors for truth and veracity, and that it is bad: *Spies* v. *People*, 122 Ill. 1; 3 Am. St. Rep. 320; *Benesch* v. *Waggner*, 12 Col. 534; 13 Am. St. Rep. 254, and note; *Stanton* v. *Parker*, 5 Rob. (La.) 108; 39 Am. Dec. 528, and note; *Holmes* v. *State*, 88 Ala. 26; 16 Am. St. Rep. 17, and note. See further *Montgomery* v. *Crossthwait*, 90 Ala. 553; 24 Am. St. Rep. 832, and note, and the extended note to *Blue* v. *Kirby*, 15 Am. Dec. 96.

APPEAL—NONREVERSIBLE ERROR.—A question, though improper, if not shown to have been answered by the witness to whom it was put is not ground for reversal: *Smith* v. *Niagara etc. Ins. Co.*, 60 Vt. 682; 6 Am. St. Rep. 144.

THE JURY ARE NOT JUDGES OF THE LAW; it is the province of the judge to expound and explain the law, and the province of the jury to determine the facts: *McCorry* v *King*, 3 Humph. 267; 39 Am. Dec. 165; *Roth* v. *Buffalo etc. R. R. Co.*, 34 N. Y. 548; 90 Am. Dec. 736, and note; *Manhattan Co. v. Lydig*, 4 Johns. 377; 4 Am. Dec. 289; *Lord* v. *State*, 16 N. H. 325; 41 Am. Dec. 729; *Washington* v. *State*, 63 Ala. 135; 35 Am. Rep. 8. In the following cases it is held that in a criminal case the jury may disregard the law as given them by the court and render a verdict of not guilty: *State* v. *Croteau*, 23 Vt. 14; 54 Am. Dec. 90, and note; *Commonwealth* v. *Van Tuyl*, 1 Met. (Ky.) 1; 71 Am. Dec. 455, and note; *Kane* v. *Commonwealth*, 89 Pa. St. 522; 33 Am. Rep. 787, and note, and the note to *Mitchell* v. *State*, 68 Am. Dec. 501.

GILSON *v.* DELAWARE AND HUDSON CANAL CO.

[65 VERMONT, 213.]

NEGLIGENCE—PROXIMATE AND REMOTE CAUSE—DIVERSION OF WATER-COURSE.—A railroad company which, for purposes of its own, wrongfully turns a stream from its natural channel, is bound to see that no harm is thereby done, and cannot avoid its liability for the flooding of a neighboring quarry through the escape of unusual quantities of water accumulated, as the result of such wrongful act, in another quarry, between the one injured and the company's embankment, by showing that, at some previous time, the plaintiff's ancestors, in working the quarry, had encroached on the land of the adjoining proprietor, and thus weakened the barrier which separated it from the one in which the flood-waters gathered. Such weakening of the barrier cannot be deemed the proximate cause of the injury.

CONTRIBUTORY NEGLIGENCE IS PREDICABLE ONLY OF CASES in which the plaintiff owes the defendant the duty of being careful in respect to the act or omission which is alleged to constitute such negligence. Therefore the fact that the ancestors of the plaintiff, in an action to recover damages for the flooding of a quarry caused by the accumulation of waters which have been wrongfully diverted by a railroad company, encroached at some previous time upon the premises of an adjoining land-owner, while they were working the quarry, and thus weakened the barrier through which the flood-waters made their way, is not such contributory negligence as will deprive the plaintiff of his right to compensation from the railroad company.

ACTION on the case for damages caused by the flooding of the plaintiff's quarry by the diversion of an ancient watercourse. The defendant's road had been constructed on a steep hillside above the quarry, crossing by an embankment the watercourse in question, which received the drainage of a considerable area during the wet season, but was for a large part of the year entirely dry. No provision had been made in the construction of the road for the passage of the water in this watercourse under the embankment. The land between the plaintiff's quarry and the road belonged to the Vermont Marble Company, and upon it were two abandoned quarries. The lower one adjoined the plaintiff's quarry, being separated therefrom by an apparently solid wall of rock, which was of such a height that water accumulating in the abandoned quarry would flow over the defendant's track before it ran over into the plaintiff's quarry. The water in the watercourse, being deflected by the embankment, ran down alongside it into the higher of these abandoned quarries, out of which it was conducted under the track by a culvert, which, in ordinary seasons, was sufficient to carry off all the water that accumulated. In 1888, however, an extraordinarily heavy freshet occurred, and the culvert being inadequate to dispose of the flood-waters, they overflowed into the lower of the abandoned quarries, and burst through the dividing wall which separated it from the plaintiff's quarry, inflicting the damage complained of. At some time before the building of the railroad the ancestors of the plaintiff, while working the quarry, had carried their excavations several feet over the boundary line of the lands of the Vermont Marble Company, and the defendant's testimony went to show that if the dividing wall had not been thus weakened, it would have withstood the pressure of the water. The defendant accordingly asked the court to instruct the jury that if the plaintiff's ancestors had thus trespassed on the adjoining premises, and by so doing had caused that weakening of the dividing wall which led to the injury complained of, the plaintiff could not recover. The court refused to give this instruction, and charged the jury that for the determination of the defendant's liability it was immaterial whether there had or had not been such an encroachment, and that, if there had been, the fact would not be available as a defense in the action. To this charge the defendant excepted.

C. A. Prouty, for the defendant.

F. G. Swinington, for the plaintiff.

216 ROWELL, J. It is a maxim of the law that the immediate, not the remote, cause of an event is regarded. In the application of this maxim the law rejects, as not constituting ground for an action, damage not flowing proximately from the act complained of. In other words, the law always refers the damage to the proximate, not to the remote, cause.

It is laid down in many cases and by leading textwriters,

that in order to warrant a finding that negligence or an act
not amounting to wanton wrong is the proximate cause of an
injury, it must appear that the injury was the natural and
probable sequence of the negligence **or** the wrongful act, [217]
and that it was such as might, or ought to, have been foreseen
in the light of the attending circumstances. But this rule is
no test in cases where no intervening efficient cause is found
between the original wrongful act and the injurious consequences complained of, and in which such consequences, although not probable, have actually flowed in unbroken
sequence from the original wrongful act. This is well illustrated by *Stevens* v. *Dudley*, 56 Vt. 158, which was this: Defendant was a marshal at a fair, and in clearing the track
for a race he turned off a man's team so negligently that the
man was thrown from his wagon, his horse broke loose and
ran against plaintiff's wagon and injured him. The court
below charged that defendant was not liable unless he might
reasonably have expected plaintiff's injury to result from
his act. Held error, and that the court should have charged
that if the defendant negligently turned the team off the
track, and thereby the team was deprived of the control of
a driver and became frightened and ran over plaintiff's team
and caused the injury, without any superior uncontrollable
force, or without the negligence of a responsible agent having
intervened, the defendant would be liable, although he did
not anticipate, and might not have anticipated, such consequences from his negligent act. In other words, that the
court should have charged that if defendant's act was negligent, and in the natural order of cause and effect the
plaintiff was injured thereby, the defendant was liable:
Smith v. *London etc. Ry. Co.*, L. R. 6 Com. P. 14, in the exchequer chamber, is to the same effect. There the company's workmen, after cutting the grass and trimming the
hedges bordering the railway, placed the trimmings in heaps
between the hedge and the line, and allowed them to remain
therefor several days during very dry weather, which had continued for some weeks. A fire broke out between the hedge
and the rails and burnt some of the heaps of trimmings [218]
and the hedge, and spread to a stubble field beyond, and was
thence carried by a high wind across the stubble field and
over a road, and burnt plaintiff's cottage two hundred yards
away from where the fire began. There was evidence that
an engine had passed the spot shortly before the fire was first

seen, but no evidence that it had emitted sparks, nor any further evidence that the fire originated from the engine, nor was there any evidence that the fire began in the heaps of trimmings and not on the parched ground around them. The court below held that the plaintiff could not recover, because no reasonable man would have foreseen that the fire would consume the hedge and pass across a stubble field, and so get to plaintiff's cottage at a distance of two hundred yards from the railway, crossing a road in its passage. In the exchequer chamber, Chief Baron Kelley said that he felt pressed at first by this view, because he then and still thought that any reasonable man might well have failed to anticipate such a concurrence of circumstances as the case presented; but that on consideration he thought that was not the true test of defendant's liability; that it might be that defendant did not anticipate, and was not bound to anticipate, that plaintiff's cottage would be burnt as the result of its negligence; but yet, if it was aware that the heaps were lying by the side of the rails, and that it was a dry season, and that therefore by being left there the heaps were likely to catch fire, defendant was bound to provide against all circumstances that might result from this, and was responsible for all natural consequences of it. And with this agreed all the judges. Channell, B., said that where there is no direct evidence of negligence, the question what a reasonable man might forsee is of importance in considering whether there is evidence for the jury of negligence or not. And Mr. Justice Blackburn said that what the defendant might reasonably anticipate was material only with reference to the question whether it was [219] negligent or not, but could not alter its liability if it was negligent.

In *Rylands* v. *Fletcher*, L. R. 3 H. L. 332, in the House of Lords, Lord Cranworth says that in considering whether a defendant is liable to a plaintiff for damage that the latter has sustained, the question in general is, not whether the defendant has acted with due care and caution, but whether his acts occasioned the damage; that this is all well explained in the old case of *Lambert* v. *Bessey*, T. Raym. 421; that the doctrine is founded in good sense; for where one, in managing his own affairs, causes, however innocently, damage to another, it is obviously only just that he should be the party to suffer; that he is bound so to use his own as not to injure another.

In *Smith* v. *Fletcher*, L. R. 7 Ex. 305, defendants' mines adjoined and communicated with plaintiff's mines, and on the surface of defendants' land were certain hollows and openings, partly caused by defendants' workings, and partly made to facilitate them. Across the surface of defendants' land there ran a brook, which they had diverted from its original course into an artificial channel they had made, and which by reason of exceptionally heavy rains overflowed its banks, and quantities of water poured from it into said hollows and openings, where already the rains had caused an unusual amount of water to collect, and thence, through fissures and cracks, water passed into defendants' mine, and so into plaintiff's mine. If the land had been in its natural condition, the water would have spread over the surface and done no harm. The defendants tendered evidence to show that they had taken every reasonable precaution to guard against ordinary emergencies. and that they had, by diverting and improving the watercourse and otherwise, greatly lessened the chance of water escaping from the surface of the land into their own mines, and thence into the plaintiff's mine; and contended [220] that they were not liable for the consequences of an exceptional flood. It was conceded that they had not been guilty of any personal negligence. But the court ruled that they were absolutely liable for the consequences, and rejected the evidence, and a verdict was taken for the plaintiff, which was allowed to stand. Baron Bramwell, in disposing of the case *in banc,* said that the defendants, for their own purposes, and without providing the means of its getting away without hurt, brought the water to the place whence it escaped and did the mischief, and that that made a case against them calling for an answer, and that they answered: "We brought the water there, indeed, and did not provide a sufficient outlet for it, but had we not altered the original course of the stream, it would have escaped in greater quantities and done more mischief," which, he said, was no answer: See *Cahill* v. *Eastman,* 18 Minn. 324; 10 Am. Rep. 184.

In the case at bar, the defendant, for purposes of its own, wrongfully turned the brook from its natural channel, and let it flow towards plaintiff's quarry, not knowing what would happen, whereby large and unusual quantities of water were brought to and accumulated in the Marble Company's abandoned quarries, and it was the duty of the defendants to see that no damage was thereby done; and the fact that it did not know and had no reason to suspect that the plaintiff's predecessors had worked their quarry out of bounds and thereby weakened the wall between it and the adjacent quarry, makes no difference, unless such fact constitutes contributory negligence imputable to the plaintiff.

Now, an act or omission of a party injured, or of those for whose acts and omissions he is responsible, in order to constitute contributory negligence, must have related to something in respect of which he or they owed to the defendant, or to those in whose place he stands, the duty of being careful, and have been negligent, and in the production [221] of the injury have operated as a proximate cause, or as one of the proximate causes, and not have been merely a condition. It follows, therefore, that when there is no duty there can be no negligence.

In working their quarry the plaintiff's predecessors did not know, and could not possibly anticipate, the then nonexistent circumstances, that years afterwards the defendant would build a new road where it did in 1884, and wrongfully turn the brook into the quarries above, whereby their quarry would be endangered if they weakened the wall by working out of bounds. Their act in this respect was not wrongful as to the defendant, and they owed the defendant no duty concerning it, and therefore negligence is not predicable of it, even though it was wrongful as to the Marble Company, with the rights of which the defendant in no way connects itself. The state of the wall, legally considered, was not a proximate cause of the injury, but was merely a condition that made the injury possible.

Judgment affirmed. ____

Proximate and Remote Cause.[*]

1. The legal theory of causal connection is that which is briefly set forth in Lord Bacon's oft-cited gloss upon the maxim *In jure non remota causa sed proxima spectatur*—"It were infinite for the law to consider the cause of causes and their impulsions one of another; therefore it contenteth itself with the immediate cause, and judgeth of acts by that, without looking for any further degree." Mr. Wharton (Negligence, sec. 73), by comparing with this passage the classification of causes in another of the great philosopher's works, shows it to be very probable that the "proximate cause" of the maxim was regarded by him as synonymous with "efficient cause." Whether this inference is correct or not, there is no doubt that, in the practical appli

[*]REFERENCE TO MONOGRAPHIC NOTES.

Contributory negligence must be proximate cause of injury to excuse defendant: Note to *Freer* v. *Cameron*, 55 Am. Dec. 668–670.

Defect in highway, when proximate cause of injuries to traveler: Note to *Morse* v. *Town of Richmond*, 98 Am. Dec. 608–612.

Concurrent liability: Note to *Village of Carterville* v. *Cook*, 16 Am. St. Rep. 250–257.

cation of the maxim by the courts, this convertibility of these terms is always assumed. "The proximate cause is the efficient cause, the one that necessarily sets the others in motion": *Insurance Co.* v. *Boon*, 95 U. S. 117.

The principle embodied in the maxim has been found useful in the solution of two distinct classes of cases: 1. Those which require the determination of the responsibility for a wrongful act, whether a tort or a breach of contract; and 2. Those in which it is necessary to ascertain whether a catastrophe involving the loss of property, life, or bodily capacity has been caused by a peril, the consequences of which have been assumed by an insurer. The fundamental difference between these classes is that in the latter, the investigation ceases when the nearest cause adequate to produce the result in question has been discovered, while in the former, the object is to connect the circumstance which is the subject of the action with a responsible human will. These two classes of cases will be discussed separately in this note.

Proximate and Remote Cause in Cases Involving Wrongful Acts.

2. In every action in which redress for an injury is sought, two principal questions are raised: 1. Who is responsible for the injury? and 2. What compensation is to be awarded? The determination of the latter point may require an examination of various subsidiary injuries springing from the one which forms the subject of the action, and it is therefore evident that the maxim, in its most comprehensive sense, applies to cases involving merely the measure of damages, which are granted or not, according as they are proximate or remote. Properly speaking, however, the award of compensation involves a determination of the extent of the injury, and not its authorship, and, as the form in which the maxim is couched comtemplates rather a retrospective than a prospective view of the chain of causation, it seems preferable to confine its application to cases in which the question raised is strictly one of responsibility for the failure of duty alleged. This test will exclude all cases of breach of contract, inasmuch as the authorship of the wrong is, in such cases, never in doubt. An exception, however, may properly be made in regard to the cases in which the circumstances give the plaintiff the option of suing in tort or in contract— that is, where the facts show both a common-law duty and an obligation to perform a contract: *Rich* v. *New York Cent. etc. R. R. Co.*, 87 N. Y. 382. That large class of cases involving the negligence of carriers is the most striking instance of this double remedy: *Eaton* v. *Boston etc. R. Co.*, 11 Allen, 500; 87 Am. Dec. 730; *Warren* v. *Fitchburg R. R. Co.*, 8 Allen, 227; 85 Am. Dec. 700; *McElroy* v. *Nashua etc. R. R. Co.*, 4 Cush. 400; 50 Am. Dec. 794; *Sullivan* v. *Philadelphia etc. R. R. Co.*, 30 Pa. St. 234; 72 Am. Dec. 698. In these cases the rule of duty is said to be the same, whether the plaintiff sues in tort or in contract, but, as will be pointed out later, this principle has not been universally acted upon.

The subject of proximate and remote damages in actions for breaches of contract was treated in the notes to *Sutton* v. *MacDonald*, 60 Am. Rep. 488–496; *Griffin* v. *Colver*, 69 Am. Dec. 724–727; *McKinnon* v. *McEwan*, 42 Am. Rep. 461–465; *Masterton* v. *Mayor of Brooklyn*, 42 Am. Dec. 48–51; *Western Union Tel. Co.* v. *Cooper*, 10 Am. St. Rep. 778–790.

3. STATEMENTS OF THE RULE AS TO PROXIMATE AND REMOTE CAUSE.— (a) *Generally.*—"The *proxima causa* was originally the same as the *causa causans*, or cause necessarily producing the result. But the practical construction of 'proximate cause' by the courts has come to be the cause which

naturally led to, and which might have been expected to be directly instru. mental in producing, the result": *State* v. *Manchester etc. R. R. Co.*, 52 N. H. 552; *Topsham* v. *Lisbon*, 65 Me. 449; *Ins. Co.* v. *Boon*, 95 U. S. 117. "By 'proximate cause' is intended an act which directly produced, or concurred directly in producing, the injury. By 'remote cause' is intended that which may have happened, and yet no injury have occurred, notwithstanding that no injury could have occurred if it had not happened": *Baltimore etc. R. R. Co.* v. *Trainer*, 33 Md. 542; adopted in *Troy* v. *Cape Fear R. R. Co.*, 99 N. C. 298; 6 Am. St. Rep. 521. "A proximate cause is one without which the accident would not have occurred": *Taylor* v. *Baldwin*, 78 Cal. 517.

Proximate Cause is One of Which the Injury is a Natural and Probable Consequence.—The necessity for connecting an injury with a responsible agent before compensation can be awarded has led to the identification of the rule embodied in the maxim with another legal principle which bears more directly upon the question of accountability, viz., that "every man must be taken to contemplate the probable consequences of the act he does": *Townsend* v. *Wathen*, 9 East, 277. In other words, the construction now generally accepted for the maxim, so far at least as it applies to negligent acts, is that, "in determining what is the proximate cause, the true rule is that the injury must be the natural and probable consequence of the negligence: *Hoag* v. *Lake Shore etc. Ry. Co.*, 85 Pa. St. 293; 27 Am. Rep. 653; *Pennsylvania R. R. Co.* v. *Kerr*, 62 Pa. St. 353; 1 Am. Rep. 431; *West Mahonoy Tp.* v. *Wagner*, 116 Pa. St. 344; 2 Am. St. Rep. 604; *Milwaukee etc. Ry. Co.* v. *Kellogg*, 94 U. S. 469; *Putnam* v. *Broadway etc. R. R. Co.*, 55 N. Y. 108; 14 Am. Rep. 190; *Sharp* v. *Powell*, L. R. 7 Com. P. 253. The reasoning by which this identification of the two principles is effected is thus clearly expressed in Addison on Torts, sec. 6: "If the wrong and the resulting damage are not known by common experience to be naturally and usually in sequence, and the damage does not, according to the usual course of events, follow from the wrong, then the wrong and the damage are not sufficiently conjoined or concatenated as cause and effect to support an action." (Cited with approval in Cooley on Torts, 69.)

(*b*) *Various Forms of the General Expression.*—A few expressions in the reports may be quoted to show the various shades of meaning attached by the courts to the rule. Thus a liability arises if the result of the act is "direct and natural": *Topeka* v. *Tuttle*, 5 Kan. 311; or if it is "such as might probably ensue in the natural and ordinary course of events": *East Tennessee etc. R. R. Co.* v. *Hesters*, 79 Ala. 315; *Gerhard* v. *Bates*, 2 El. & B. 490; or "ordinary and natural": *Henry* v. *Southern Pac. R. R. Co.*, 50 Cal. 176; or "such as according to common experience is likely to result": *Smethurst* v. *Congregational Church*, 148 Mass. 261; 12 Am. St. Rep. 550; or "such as, according to common experience and the usual course of events, might reasonably be anticipated": *Hoadley* v. *Transportation Co.*, 115 Mass. 304; 15 Am. Rep. 106; *Derry* v. *Flitner*, 118 Mass. 131; or such as are known by common experience to be usually in sequence": *Hoey* v. *Felton*, 11 Com. B., N. S., 143; or such as follow according to the usual experience of mankind: *Lane* v. *Atlantic Works*, 111 Mass. 136; or such as are "legal and natural": *Vicars* v. *Wilcocks*, 8 East, 1, a phrase which, in view of the later decisions, seems somewhat tautological, since an act is not legally connected with the injury unless the connection is natural. In *Smith* v. *Green*, L. R. 1 C. P. D. 92, Justice Grove was of opinion that the expression "natural" was unsatisfactory, and remarked that "normal, or likely or probable of occurrence in the ordinary course of things" would perhaps be preferable. In

Burton v. *Pinkerton,* L. R. 2 Ex. 340, Justice Bramwell remarked that damages to be recoverable "must inevitably flow from the tortious act of the defendant," but this *dictum* seems to be scarcely warranted by the authorities, and is directly contradicted by *Miller* v. *St. Louis etc. Ry. Co.,* 90 Mo. 389, where the court said that it was not necessary that the result should be inevitable, if it was natural."

(c) *Test; That the Result Might Have Been Foreseen.*—Many cases make the test of liability the fact that the consequence of the act was "such as, under the surrounding circumstances of the case, might and ought to have been foreseen by the wrongdoer as likely to flow from his acts": *Pennsylvania R. R. Co.* v. *Hope,* 80 Pa. St. 373; 21 Am. Rep. 100; *Atchison etc. R. R. C* v. *Stanford,* 12 Kan. 354; 15 Am. Rep. 362; *Poeppers* v. *Missouri Pac. Ry. Co.,* 67 Mo. 715; 29 Am. Rep. 518; *Maher* v. *Winona etc. R. R. Co.,* 31 Minn. 401; *Pennsylvania R. R. Co.* v. *Kerr,* 62 Pa. St. 353; 1 Am. Rep. 431; *Morrison* v. *Davis,* 20 Pa. St. 171; 57 Am. Dec. 695; *Lynch* v. *Knight,* 9 H. L. Cas. 577; *Crater* v. *Binninger,* 33 N. J. L. 513; 97 Am. Dec. 737; *McGrew* v. *Stone,* 53 Pa. St. 436; *Henry* v. *Southern Pac. R. R. Co.,* 50 Cal. 176; *Doggett* v. *Richmond etc. R. R. Co.,* 78 N. C. 305; *Stanley* v. *Union Depot R. R. Co.,* 114 Mo. 606; *Weick* v. *Lander,* 75 Ill. 93; *Daniels* v. *Ballentine,* 23 Ohio St. 532; 13 Am. Rep. 264; *Fent* v. *Toledo etc. Ry. Co.,* 59 Ill. 349; 14 Am. Rep. 13; *Greenland* v. *Chaplin,* 5 Ex. 243. In *Atkinson* v. *Goodrich etc. Co.,* 60 Wis. 141; 50 Am. Rep. 352, the full extension was given to this principle. "It is not enough to show that the injury is the natural consequence of the defendant's act. It must appear that, under all the circumstances, it might reasonably have been expected by a man of ordinary intelligence and prudence that such injury would result."

(d) *Precise Form of Injury Need Not Have Been Foreseen to Raise a Liability.* On the other hand it appears to be an accepted principle that the liability of the defendant does not depend upon whether, by the exercise of ordinary prudence, he could or could not have foreseen the precise form in which the injury actually resulted, and that he may be held for anything which, after the injury is complete, appears to have been a natural and probable consequence of his act: *Hill* v. *New River Co.,* 9 Best & S. 303; *Hill* v. *Winsor,* 118 Mass. 251; *Lane* v. *Atlantic Works,* 111 Mass. 136; *Bunting* v. *Hoggsett,* 139 Pa. St. 363; 23 Am. St. Rep. 192; *Oil City Gas Co.* v. *Robinson,* 99 Pa. St. 1; *Higgins* v. *Dewey,* 107 Mass. 494; 9 Am. Rep. 63; *Smith* v. *London & Southwestern Ry. Co.,* L. R. 6 Com. P. 14; 5 Com. P. 98; *Louisville etc. Ry. Co.* v. *Wood,* 113 Ind. 544; *Alabama etc. R. R. Co.* v. *Chapman,* 80 Ala. 615; *Quigley* v. *Delaware etc. Canal Co.,* 142 Pa. St. 388; 24 Am. St. Rep. 504; *Pullman Palace Car Co.* v. *Laack,* 143 Ill. 242; *Galveston* v. *Posnainsky,* 62 Tex. 118; 50 Am. Rep. 517. The reasoning upon which this rule is founded is that the law regards only the general character of the act: *Louisville etc. Ry. Co.* v. *Wood,* 113 Ind. 544; for, as was remarked in *West* v. *Ward,* 77 Iowa, 323; 14 Am. St. Rep. 284, "when there is danger of a particular injury which actually occurs, we must surely say that is the usual, ordinary, natural, and probable result of the act exposing the person or thing injured to the danger." If we combine this principle with the one stated in the preceding paragraph, the result seems to be that, when the act complained of was such that, in view of all the circumstances, it might not improbably cause damage of some kind the doer of the act cannot shelter himself under the defense, that the actual consequence was one which rarely follows from that particular act.

(e) Time or Distance Not a Decisive Test of Proximity of Cause.—It seems to be very generally agreed that the "proximate cause" of the maxim has no necessary connection with time or distance. It means "closeness of causal relation, not nearness in time or distance": *Delaware etc. R. R. Co. v. Salmon*, 39 N. J. L. 299; 23 Am. Rep. 214; *Pullman Palace Car Co. v. Laack*, 143 Ill. 242; *Pennsylvania R. R. Co. v. Kerr*, 62 Pa. St. 353; 1 Am. Rep. 431; *Hoag v. Lake Shore etc. Ry. Co.*, 85 Pa. St. 293; 27 Am. Rep. 653; *Haverly v. State Line etc. R. R. Co.*, 135 Pa. St. 50; 20 Am. St. Rep. 848. At the same time it may be presumed that both time and distance may be important as bearing upon the question of improbability. In *Sneesby v. Lancashire etc. Ry. Co.*, L. R. 9 Q. B. 263, Justice Grove remarked that lapse of time may make a cause remote, and it will be seen in a succeeding section that in determining responsibility for damage done by fires, some courts have ascribed a decisive importance to the intervention of space.

(f) Defendant Not Liable for all Possible Consequences of Wrongful Act.—In *Greenland v. Chaplin*, 5 Ex. 243, decided in 1850, Chief Baron Pollock said that he "entertained considerable doubt, whether a person who is guilty of negligence is responsible for all the consequences which may under any circumstances arise, and in respect of mischief which could by no possibility have been foreseen, and which no reasonable person would have anticipated," this expression of doubt being a statement of his own views and not that of the rest of the court, and in *Rigby v. Hewitt*, 5 Ex. 240, the same learned judge used similar language. The modern development of the law of negligence has, we think, settled any doubt of this kind in favor of the defendant. Thus it was said in *Belding v. Johnson*, 86 Ga. 177, with reference to the Georgia code, which excludes "possible or imaginary" dangers, that this provision was merely declaratory of the common law. Indeed, if language has any definite meaning, it is difficult to see how it could ever have been a matter of doubt whether a liability for "probable" consequences could have been deemed equivalent to a liability for "all possible" consequences. See, however, the cases illustrating the exception to this principle where goods are wrongfully intermeddled with or there is a deviation by a carrier: Secs. 8, 26 (c) *post*.

3. VAGUENESS OF THE GENERAL RULES PROPOSED.—From a review of the foregoing summary of the attempted generalizations of principles, it will be seen that the courts have not as yet succeeded in formulating any rule expressed in terminology scientifically exact. The words used have no meaning except such as they acquire from a reference to considerations by which that rather shadowy personage, the man of ordinary caution and prudence, is supposed to regulate his conduct. This unsatisfactory condition of the law of causal connection has frequently been commented on by the courts. Thus, it has been said by an eminent English judge, that the task of the courts is "something like having to draw a line between night and day": *Hobbs v. London etc. Ry. Co.*, L. R. 10 Q. B. 111. Compare the remarks of Chief Justice Thompson in *Pennsylvania R. R. Co. v. Kerr*, 62 Pa. St. 353; 1 Am. Rep. 431. In *Willey v. Belfast*, 61 Me. 575, it was said that "much depends on the common sense of the thing," and in a case of the very highest authority the court declared that, after all, each case must be "decided largely on the special facts belonging to it, and often on the very nicest discriminations": *Insurance Co. v. Tweed*, 7 Wall. 52; *Page v. Bucksport*, 64 Me. 53; 18 Am. Rep. 239. "The law looks to a practical rule, adapted to the rights and duties of all persons in society, in the common and ordinary concerns of actual and real life": *Marble v. City of Worcester*, 4 Gray, 395.

(Per Shaw, C. J.) "The law regards practical distinctions, rather than those which are merely theoretical": *Metallic etc. Co.* v. *Fitchburg R. R. Co.*, 109 Mass. 277; 12 Am. Rep. 689. (Per Chapman, C. J.) "The terms 'proximate' and 'remote' are really used by the courts in their ordinary and popular sense": *Atchison etc. R. R. Co.* v. *Stanford*, 12 Kan. 354; 15 Am. Rep. 362.

In fact, after all the efforts of the most learned judges and text-writers in England and the United States, it seems impossible not to admit the justice of the following remarks of Mr. Justice Earl in *Ehrgott* v. *Mayor etc. of New York*, 96 N. Y. 264, 48 Am. Rep. 622: "It is sometimes said that a party charged with a tort, or with breach of contract, is liable for such damages as may reasonably be supposed to have been in the contemplation of both parties at the time, or with such damages as may reasonably be expected to result under ordinary circumstances from the misconduct, or with such damages as ought to have been foreseen or expected in the light of the surrounding circumstances, or in the ordinary course of things. These various modes of stating the rule are all apt to be misleading, and in most cases are absolutely worthless as guides to the jury. . . . The true rule, broadly stated, is, that a wrongdoer is responsible for the damages caused by his misconduct. But this rule must be practicable and reasonable, and hence its limitations."

4. General Principles Stated.—Under these circumstances it is believed that the method of generalization which is likely to give the clearest idea of the present state of the law of proximate and remote cause will be to analyze the meaning of the term "natural consequences" so as to indicate, with as much precision as the circumstances admit, the proper standpoint from which to examine each of the great groups under which the cases naturally fall.

The rule that a wrongdoer is liable for the "natural and probable consequences" of his misconduct involves the following propositions:

1. Everyone is presumed to know that inorganic matter is governed by certain fixed laws, and that no portion of that matter can be made the subject of human activity without the production of results, the character of which is determined by the character of the particular portion of matter affected.

2. Everyone is presumed to know that the bodies of all animals, including human beings, are so constituted that they may be injured in many ways by external violence, and that if exposed to certain unhealthy conditions are reasonably certain to become diseased.

3. Everyone is presumed to know that all animals, including human beings, are controlled more or less strongly by various appetites, impulses, instincts, feelings and emotions, each of which, if worked upon in a certain manner, will be likely to induce a certain kind of conduct. Where the lower animals are concerned this presumption is carried to its logical conclusions with as much strictness as where the laws regulating inorganic matter have to be reckoned with. In the case of human beings the problems introduced by the fact that those appetites, etc., are to some extent under the control of an intelligent mind, capable of distinguishing between right and wrong, raise questions of great difficulty to which the cases do not furnish a consistent or satisfactory answer.

The following note will be a discussion of the extent to which the courts have given effect to the three foregoing presumptions.

Before entering upon the general treatment of the subject, however, it is necessary to notice two cases in which, although the act of the defendant is in a very real sense the cause of the plaintiff's injury, the latter is nevertheless not allowed to recover damages in a court of justice. A plaintiff may fail to make good his case; (1) If he is not the person in whose favor the duty, alleged to have been violated, is imposed upon the defendant; (2) If the duty imposed upon the defendant is not a duty to refrain from inflicting the particular damage of which the plaintiff complains. In both these cases the legal connection is not established, although it may be perfectly clear that the injury would not have occurred but for the defendant's act.

5. ACTION FOR TORT NOT MAINTAINABLE UNLESS DEFENDANT OWES A DUTY TO PLAINTIFF.—In the first class of cases an injury may be proximately and directly caused by a wrongful act, but the plaintiff cannot recover damages, because the defendant owes him no duty, whether contractual or inferred from the relations of the parties. The leading case on this point is *Winterbottom* v. *Wright*, 10 Mees. & W. 109. There A contracted with the postmaster-general to provide a mail coach to carry the mails, and B and others also contracted to furnish the horses for the coach. B and his cc-contractors hired C to drive the coach. *Held*, That C could not maintain an action against A for an injury sustained by him, while driving the coach, from its breaking down, owing to latent defects in its construction. Among other things Lord Abinger said: "There is no privity of contract between these parties; and if the plaintiff can sue, every passenger, or even any person passing along the road, who was injured by the upsetting of the coach might bring a similar action. Unless we confine the operation of such contracts to the parties who entered into them, the most absurd and outrageous consequences, to which I can see no limit, would ensue." Referring to the allegation in the declaration that the defendant was under a "duty" to keep the coach in a safe condition, Rolfe, B., pointed out that the only duty arising from the contract was a duty to the postmaster-general, and that the case was one of those "in which there was certainly *damnum*, but *damnum absque injuria*. The mere fact that the postmaster general could not be made liable was no reason for allowing an action to be maintained, and thus breaking in upon the general rule. The principles enunciated in this case have frequently been recognized. "Contractors and manufacturers do not owe a duty to the whole world that their productions or works shall have no hidden defect": *Curtin* v. *Somerset*, 140 Pa. St. 70; 23 Am. St. Rep. 220. See *Collis* v. *Selden*, L. R. 3 Com. P. 495; *Loop* v. *Litchfield*, 42 N. Y. 351; 1 Am. Rep. 543; *Cosulich* v. *Standard Oil Co.*, 122 N. Y. 118; 19 Am. St. Rep. 475; *Hofnagle* v. *New York Cent. R. R. Co.*, 55 N. Y. 608; *Heizer* v. *Kingsland etc. Mfg. Co.*, 110 Mo. 605; 33 Am. St. Rep. 482, and cases cited in note. *A fortiori*, if one do a lawful act on one's own premises, he cannot be held responsible for injurious consequences resulting therefrom, unless the act is so done as to constitute negligence. Thus there is no liability to a neighbor injured by the bursting of a steam boiler: *Spencer* v. *Campbell*, 9 Watts & S. 32; *Losee* v. *Clute*, 51 N. Y. 494; 10 Am. Rep. 638; *Losee* v. *Buchanan*, 51 N. Y. 476; 10 Am. Rep. 623. But Judge Thompson (Negligence, 233) thinks, with considerable reason, that steam boilers should properly be placed in the list of dangerous articles. (See next section.) See also *Rockwood* v. *Wilson*, 11 Cush. 221, sustaining the same general principle. On analogous grounds no breach of duty is shown where a tax-collector exhibits to an intending purchaser a receipt for a check for the amount of the taxes, and the purchaser, after paying a price based on the supposition that the taxes have

been satisfied, finds that the check is worthless, and is compelled to pay the
taxes himself. The sole duty of the collector, it was remarked, was to give
acquittances to the taxpayers. Nor can A recover damages from B, who
has assaulted one of the paupers of a town whom A has contracted to
support in health and sickness, and thereby put A to increased expense:
Anthony v. *Sluid*, 11 Met. 290. Nor can an insurance company, unless by
being subrogated to the rights of the insured, maintain an action against one
who has caused a loss which is covered by a policy issued by such company:
Insurance Co. v. *Brame*, 95 U. S. 754; *Rockingham Mut. Fire Ins. Co.* v.
Bosher, 39 Me. 253; 63 Am. Dec. 618; *Connecticut Mut. Life Ins. Co.* v. *New
Haven etc. R. R. Co.*, 25 Conn. 265; 65 Am. Dec. 571. Nor is the failure of
a railroad company to furnish cars, in pursuance of a contract with a com-
press company—the result being that the cotton accumulates on the premises of the latter company—the juridical cause of damage done to the
property of a neighbor by a fire communicated from one which broke out
among the cotton from some unknown source: *Martin* v. *St. Louis etc. Ry.
Co.*, 55 Ark. 510. And when cotton was destroyed under circumstances
similar to those just mentioned, it was held that there was no liability on
the part of the railroad company for the loss, and therefore no ground for
applying the principle of subrogation in favor of an insurance company
which had indemnified the owners of the cotton: *St. Louis etc. Ry. Co.* v.
Commercial U. Ins. Co., 139 U. S. 223, the court saying that the loss by fire
was not proximately caused by the carrier's breach of contract.

6. MODIFICATION OF THIS PRINCIPLE IN THE CASE OF DANGEROUS ARTI-
CLES.—In many instances, on the other hand, the law raises a liability which
is independent of privity of contract. The most striking illustration of this
is furnished by the rule that "a person who negligently uses a dangerous instrument or article, or causes or authorizes its use by another person, in such
a manner or under such circumstances that he has reason to know that it is
likely to produce injury, is responsible for the natural and probable consequences of his act to the person injured, who is not himself in fault": *Carter*
v. *Towne*, 98 Mass. 567; 96 Am. Dec. 682, per Gray, J., who relies principally on the English case of *Dixon* v. *Bell*, 5 Maule & S. 198, where the defendant was held liable for intrusting a loaded gun to an unfit person, the
result being that the plaintiff's son was severely wounded by its discharge. A leading decision in the United States is *Thomas* v. *Winchester*,
6 N. Y. 397, 57 Am. Dec. 455, where the defendant, a wholesale druggist, sold
as an innocent drug a deadly poison which, by the negligence of the vendor's
servant, had been wrongly labeled. The vendee, a retail druggist sold the
drug to a country practitioner, who administered it to a patient, and the
latter became seriously ill in consequence. The wholesale druggist was held
liable to the consumer. The same principle was applied in *Norton* v. *Sewall*,
106 Mass. 143; 8 Am. Rep. 298; *Wellington* v. *Downer Kerosene Oil Co.*, 104
Mass. 64; *Elkins* v. *McKean*, 79 Pa. St. 493; *Binford* v. *Johnston*, 82 Ind. 426;
42 Am. Rep. 508; *George* v. *Skivington*, L. R. 5 Ex. 1; *Longmeid* v. *Holliday*,
L. R. 6 Ex. 761; *Rippin* v. *Sheppard*, 11 Price, 400. In *Davidson* v. *Nichols*,
11 Allen, 514, a distinction was taken in a case where A sold a chemical innocent in itself, erroneously supposing it to be another chemical equally
innocent, and his vendee sold it to B, who, assuming it to be what it purported to be, mixed it with another substance and thus produced a dangerous
explosive, which subsequently injured him. It was held that B could not
recover against A. Compare, for other applications of the rule, *Bird* v. *Hol-
brook*, 4 Bing. 628, where a landowner who set spring guns without giving

notice was held liable for injuries resulting to a trespasser, and the cases cited in *Carter* v. *Towne*, 98 Mass. 567, 96 Am. Dec. 682, affirming the liability of persons who deliver dangerous articles to carriers. A later case is *Boston etc. R. R. Co.* v. *Shanly*, 107 Mass. 568, where two manufacturers shipped dangerous explosives by the same carrier to a customer, neither of them being aware of the other's consignment. The articles exploded, and the manufacturers were held responsible. *Langridge* v. *Levy*, 2 Mees. & W. 519, was decided on the ground of fraudulent misrepresentation rather than careless handling of a dangerous article. There a defective gun was sold to the plaintiff's father for the use of the plaintiff, the result being that the latter was injured by its explosion, and the vendor was held liable; but in the masterly judgment of Brett, M. R., in the recent case of *Heaven* v. *Pender*, L. R. 11 Q. B. Div. 503, it is classed with other cases in which a duty is implied independently of privity of contract. This judgment contains the clearest discussion yet given of the question, "What is the proper definition of the relation of two persons, other than the relation established by contract or fraud, which imposes on the one of them a duty towards the other to observe, with regard to the person or property of such other, such ordinary care or skill as may be necessary to prevent injury to his person or property." The reasoning of the learned judge is too lengthy to quote at large, but the proposition which he deemed deducible from the cases was, that "whenever one person is by circumstances placed in such a position with regard to another, that everyone of ordinary sense would at once recognize that, if he did not use ordinary care and skill in his own conduct with regard to those circumstances, he would cause danger of injury to the person or property of the other a duty arises to use ordinary care and skill to avoid such injury." The other justices of appeal declined to concur in such an extended principle, and Mr. Pollock thinks that, so far as the judgment of the master of the rolls purported to exhibit the rules defining the duties of the occupiers of real property, this dissent was well founded: Pollock on Torts, p. 354, note. But with this limitation, there is probably no good reason to question the correctness of the principle announced: Shearman and Redfield on Negligence, sec. 116.

7. NECESSARY CONNECTION BETWEEN DEFENDANT'S ACT AND PLAINTIFF'S INJURY—(a) *Generally.*—It is well established that, although the defendant may have been negligent, and the plaintiff may have suffered an injury, the latter must fail in an action against the former unless the connection between the negligence and the injury can be made out: *Holmes* v. *City of Fond du Lac*, 42 Wis. 282; *Adkins* v. *Atlanta etc. Ry. Co.*, 27 S. C. 71; *Daniel* v. *Metropolitan Ry. Co.* 3 C. P. 215: *Williams* v. *Great Western Ry. Co.*, L. R. 9 Ex. 157, and the cases cited in the following paragraphs. The test of such a connection is either that the wrongful act must have been the *causa sine qua non* of the injury, a cause without the existence of which the injury would not have been suffered: *Walker* v. *Goe*, 3 Hurl. & N. 395; 4 Hurl. & N. 350; *Hayes* v. *Michigan Cent. R. R. Co.*, 111 U. S. 228; or that the injury is one of those which it was the purpose of the law to prevent, when it imposed upon the defendant the duty which he is charged with having infringed. Thus the negligence of a railway company in allowing a train to be overcrowded is not the proximate cause of the crushing of the thumb of a passenger, who was trying to keep out intruders, and leaning upon the door-lintel, when a porter suddenly closed the door and caught his hand. It was an accident which might no less have happened, if the car had not been overcrowded at all: *Metropolitan Ry. Co.* v. *Jackson*, 3 App. Cas. 193. Nor is

the wrongful expulsion of the plaintiff from a railway car without unnecessary violence the proximate cause of the loss of a pair of field glasses which the plaintiff left behind him: *Glover* v. *London etc. Ry. Co.,* L. R. 3 Q. B. 25. There is no connection between the omission of a conductor to give an expected signal regarding the movement of a train and an injury to the engineer, who, in leaning out of his engine for the purpose of watching for the signal, was struck by a water-crane: *Gould* v. *Chicago etc. R. R. Co.,* 66 Iowa, 590; nor between an omission to fence a right of way and an injury to an animal which got upon the track and injured itself by putting its foot in a very small hole, since such an accident might have occurred anywhere: *Nelson* v. *Chicago etc. R. R. Co.,* 30 Minn. 74; nor between a carrier's want of skill, or a defect in his vessel, and a loss caused by a sudden squall, unless those conditions actually contributed to the loss: *Hart* v. *Allen,* 2 Watts, 114; nor between the omission of an engineer to sound a whistle and slacken the speed of the train, upon discovering an animal on the track, and the running over of the animal, if it appears that the accident would have happened, even if those precautions had been observed: *Flattes* v. *Chicago etc. R. R. Co.,* 35 Iowa, 191; nor between the omission of the engineer of a gravel train to give a starting signal, and an injury to a laborer, who steps outside the track to avoid the train, and is forced underneath the wheels by the weight of a mass of sand which suddenly falls from the side of the pit: *Handelun* v. *Burlington etc. Ry. Co.,* 72 Iowa, 709, nor between the derailment of a train and the negligent leaving of piles of snow between the rails, when the evidence shows that something outside the track must have caused the accident: *McClurney* v. *Chicago etc. R. R. Co.,* 80 Wis. 277; nor between the obstruction of a highway by a train, and an injury received in attempting to pass over the track at a place where there is no regular crossing: *Jackson* v. *Railway Co.,* 13 Lea, 491; 49 Am. Rep. 663; *Pittsburgh etc. R. R. Co.* v. *Staley,* 41 Ohio St. 118; 52 Am. Rep. 74; nor between the negligence of the plaintiff in standing on the platform of a car and an injury received by him after alighting, by reason of the negligent backing of another train without a signal: *Gadsden* v. *Cansler* (Ala. Sup. Ct. Feb. 2, 1893. Compare *Henry* v. *St. Louis etc. Ry. Co.,* 76 Mo. 288; 43 Am. Rep. 762); nor between the negligence of a railroad company, in allowing moving cars to separate, and an injury to a person walking on the track, who had stepped aside to allow the train to pass, and, not observing its separation into two parts, went on to the track after the first had passed and was run over by the second: *Patton* v. *East Tenn. etc. R. R. Co.,* 89 Tenn. 370; *Galveston etc. R. R. Co.* v. *Chambers,* 73 Tex. 296; nor between the omission of a street-car company to expel a drunken passenger, and an assault committed by him on another passenger, after they had both left the car: *Putnam* v. *Broadway etc. R. R. Co.,* 55 N. Y. 108; 14 Am. Rep. 190. The question of proximate cause was left to the jury, where an engineer broke his arm in reversing the lever of a locomotive, for the purpose of saving a train which had been derailed by a defective track: *Knapp* v. *Sioux City etc. R. R. Co.,* 65 Iowa, 91; 54 Am. Rep. 1, and also where a horse escaped through the barbed-wire fence of a right of way, and was so scared by a hand-car that he ran into the fence: *Savage* v. *Chicago etc. Ry. Co.,* 31 Minn. 419, though it would seem that, in the former case, decisive weight should have been given to the fact, that the injury was received in an attempt to save life and property, and that in the latter the likelihood of the horse's being frightened by some moving object on the track was sufficiently strong to justify the

court in saying, as a matter of law, that the non-repair of the fence was
the cause of the accident.

(*b*) *Breach of Statutory Duty.*—The general rule is that, if a breach of a
statute is relied upon by the plaintiff as a cause of action he must show
not only that he is one of the class for whose benefit the statute created a
duty, *Gibson* v. *Leonard*, 143 Ill. 182; 36 Am. St. Rep. 376 (citing several
cases), but, also, that the breach of the statute is the proximate cause of the
injury: *Laflin etc. Powder Co.* v. *Tearney*, 131 Ill. 322; 19 Am. St. Rep. 34.
"The question is, was the breach a *causa sine qua non*, a cause which, if it
had not existed, the injury would not have taken place": *Hayes* v. *Michigan
Cent. R. R. Co.*, 111 U. S. 228. To the same general effect, see *Couch* v.
Steel, 3 El. & B. 402; *Galena etc. R. Co.* v. *Loomis*, 13 Ill. 548; 56 Am. Dec.
471; *Holman* v. *C. R. I. etc. R. R. Co.*, 62 Mo. 564; *Wallace* v. *St. Louis etc.
R. R. Co.*, 74 Mo. 597; *Powell* v. *Missouri Pac. R. R. Co.*, 76 Mo. 82; *Brax-
ton* v. *Hannibal etc. R. R. Co.*, 77 Mo. 457; *Pennsylvania Co.* v. *Hensil*, 70 Ind.
569; 36 Am. Rep. 188. The doctrine held in some early cases, that a
breach of statutory duty was evidence not only of negligence, but also that
such negligence caused the injury complained of, is now abandoned: Shearman and Redfield on Negligence, section 27. The question of natural consequence does not, it would seem, arise in this class of cases, the only
condition of recovery being proof that the breach of the statute was the
efficient cause of the injury. For this reason it is difficult to admit the
soundness of the ruling in *Poland* v. *Earhart*, 70 Iowa, 285, where the defendant sold a revolver to a minor, in contravention of a law making such
sales a misdemeanor, and the vendee, in using the weapon, shot himself in the
hand. The court held that there could be no recovery unless there was something in the minor's disposition or want of experience from which the defendant might reasonably have anticipated that such an accident would
happen. It seems to us that the accident was precisely one of those which
the statute was designed to prevent.

(*c*) *Omission by Railroad Companies to Give Signals at Crossings.*—The general rule has been often applied to cases of omission on the part of the servants of railroad companies to give signals on approaching crossings: *Jackson*
v. *Chicago etc. Ry. Co.*, 36 Iowa, 451; *Indianapolis etc. R. R. Co.* v. *Blackman*, 63 Ill. 117; *Stoneman* v. *Atlantic etc. R. R. Co.*, 58 Mo. 503; *Holman* v.
Chicago etc. R. R. Co., 62 Mo. 564; *Chicago etc. R. R. Co.* v. *Henderson*, 66
Ill. 494; *Illinois Cent. R. R. Co.* v. *Phelps*, 29 Ill. 447; *Rockford etc. R. R. Co.*
v. *Linn*, 67 Ill. 109; *Quincy etc. R. R. Co.* v. *Wellhoener*, 72 Ill. 60. This
breach of duty may be taken advantage of even by one who has passed a
crossing, and whose horses are startled by the unexpected sound of a warning whistle within the prescribed distance, so that they run away and strike
the train: *Wakefield* v. *Connecticut etc. R. R. Co.*, 37 Vt. 330; 86 Am. Dec.
711, but not by a trespasser on the track: *Parker* v. *Wilmington etc. R. R.
Co.*, 86 N. C. 221; *Roden* v. *Chicago etc. Ry. Co.*, 133 Ill. 72; 23 Am. St. Rep.
585. Where the question of the connection is doubtful, it should be submitted to the jury: *Chicago etc. R. R. Co.* v. *McDaniels*, 63 Ill. 122; and a
general finding for the plaintiff will be construed as a finding that the necessary connection exists: *Orcutt* v. *Pacific Coast Ry. Co.*, 85 Cal. 291.

(*d*) *The Obstruction of a Highway by a Train*, in contravention of an ordinance or other statutory provision, will not render the company liable for
the fright of horses, caused by the appearance of the cars themselves, that
result not being the one which the statute was designed to obviate: *Cleveland etc. Ry. Co.* v. *Wynant*, 114 Ind. 525; 5 Am. St. Rep. 644; nor for

fright caused by noises proceeding from another train: *Stanton* v. *Louisville etc. Ry. Co.*, 91 Ala. 382; *Selleck* v. *Lake Shore etc. Ry. Co.*, 58 Mich. 195; though, on the other hand, if the noise proceeds from the obstructing train itself, the frightening of a team is actionable, if the obstruction has continued an unreasonable length of time: *Andrews* v. *Mason City etc. R. R. Co.*, 77 Iowa, 669. Nor is such an obstruction the proximate cause of an injury to a person who, in running to go round the train, after it begins to move, stumbles and falls underneath the cars: *Barkley* v. *Missouri Pac. Ry. Co.*, 96 Mo. 367; nor of an injury to one who tries to pass between the cars: *Hudson* v. *Wabash etc. R. R. Co.*, 101 Mo. 13. In another case the question of proximate cause was, under similar circumstances, said to be one for the jury: *Pennsylvania R. R. Co.* v. *Kelly*, 31 Pa. St. 377.

(e) *Unlawful Speed of Trains.*—Similar rules are applied where the injury is alleged to have occurred on account of the unlawful speed of the train: *Philadelphia etc. R. R. Co.* v. *Stebbing*, 62 Md. 504; *Plaster* v. *Illinois Cent. R. R. Co.*, 35 Iowa, 449; *Evans etc. Brick Co.* v. *St. Louis etc. R. R. Co.*, 17 Mo. App. 624; *Story* v. *Chicago etc. Ry. Co.*, 79 Iowa, 402; *Western Ry. Co. of Alabama* v. *Match* (Ala. Sup. Ct., Dec. 1, 1892); *Winstanley* v. *Chicago etc. Ry. Co.*, 72 Wis. 375; *Crowley* v. *Burlington etc. R. R. Co.*, 65 Iowa, 658.

(f) *Other Breaches of Statutory Duty.*—The same principles are illustrated in many other cases, such as a failure to fence a right of way: *Maher* v. *Winona etc. R. R. Co.*, 31 Minn. 401; or to fence in stock: *Orcutt* v. *Pacific Coast Ry. Co.*, 85 Cal. 291; or to maintain a gate at a railroad crossing: *Williams* v. *Great Western Ry. Co.*, L. R. 9 Ex. 157; or to put a street in good condition after laying a track for street-cars: *McCandless* v. *Chicago etc. Ry. Co.*, 71 Wis. 41; or to fasten horses properly in a town: *Siemers* v. *Eisen*, 54 Cal. 418.

(g) *Violation of Law by Plaintiff.*—Whether the plaintiff's breach of a statute is in such a sense the proximate cause of his injury as to disable him from recovery is a question upon which there is much conflict of authority. That the plaintiff is so disabled, if he is obliged to lay the foundation of his action in his own violation of the law, is on all hands admitted: *Gregg* v. *Wyman*, 4 Cush. 322; *Way* v. *Foster*, 1 Allen, 408; *Morrison* v. *General Steam Nav. Co.*, 8 Ex. 733; *Heland* v. *Lowell*, 3 Allen, 407; 81 Am. Dec. 670; *Thorp* v. *Hammond*, 12 Wall. 408; nor is the converse of this proposition open to dispute, viz: that the mere fact that he is engaged in an unlawful act is not enough to bar his action unless the transgression of the law has contributed to the accident: *Steele* v. *Burkhardt*, 104 Mass. 59; 6 Am. Rep. 191; *Klipper* v. *Coffey*, 44 Md. 117; *Welch* v. *Wesson*, 6 Gray, 805; *Baker* v. *Portland*, 58 Me. 199; 4 Am. Rep. 274; *Spofford* v. *Harlow*, 3 Allen, 176; *Kearns* v. *Sowden*, 104 Mass. 63 n.; *Norris* v. *Litchfield*, 35 N. H. 271; 69 Am. Dec. 546; *Damon* v. *Scituate*, 119 Mass. 66; 20 Am. Rep. 315; *Blanchard* v. *Ely*, 21 Wend. 342; 34 Am. Dec. 250 (citing *Hoffmann* v. *Union Ferry Co.*, 47 N. Y. 176; 7 Am. Rep. 435); *The Farragut*, 10 Wall. 334; *Smith* v. *Conway*, 121 Mass. 216; *Wrinn* v. *Jones*, 111 Mass. 360; *Kidder* v. *Dunstable*, 11 Gray, 342; *Tuttle* v. *Lawrence*, 119 Mass. 276; *Gale* v. *Lisbon*, 52 N. H. 174; *Flagg* v. *Hudson*, 142 Mass. 280; 56 Am. Rep. 674. Where a breach of statutory duty is shown, the burden of proving that it did not contribute to the injury is on the plaintiff: *The Pennsylvania*, 19 Wall. 125.

To violations of the Sunday law the courts have applied these general principles with different results in different states. Thus in some jurisdictions the mere fact that the plaintiff, at the time he was injured, was transgressing that law by traveling is sufficient to deprive him of his right of action for an injury sustained through a defect in the highway: *Johnson* v. *Irasburgh*, 47 Vt. 28; 19 Am. Rep. 111; *Jones* v. *Andover*, 10 Allen, 19; *Hinckley* v. *Penobscot*, 42 Me. 89; *Connolly* v. *Boston*, 117 Mass. 64; 19 Am. Rep. 396; *Hamilton* v. *Boston*, 14 Allen, 475. And this disability to maintain an action has been extended, even to cases where the plaintiff was traveling on a street-car: *Stanton* v. *Metropolitan R. R. Co.*, 14 Allen, 485; or working in the wheel-pit of a mill: *McGrath* v. *Merwin*, 112 Mass. 467; 17 Am. Rep. 129; or is hurt while crossing a railroad through the negligence of the company's servants: *Smith* v. *Boston etc. R. R. Co.*, 120 Mass. 490; 21 Am. Rep. 538; or seeks to recover for an injury to his horse, which was hitched at the side of the road and run into by a team: *Lyons* v. *Desotelle*, 124 Mass. 387. The Massachusetts and other courts which have carried this doctrine to such an extreme do not deny that a breach of the Sunday law stands on the same footing as other breaches of statute, where the plaintiff is not obliged to aid his case by showing his illegal act. Thus in *Hall* v. *Corcoran*, 107 Mass. 251; 9 Am. Rep. 30, it was held, after an elaborate review of the authorities, that the owner of a horse from whom it is hired on a Sunday to drive to a particular place may sue the bailee for conversion, if he drives the animal to another place. In several other courts the Massachusetts doctrine, as it may be called, has been emphatically repudiated: *Mohney* v. *Cook*, 26 Pa. St. 342; 67 Am. Dec. 419, approved in *Philadelphia etc. Ry. Co.* v. *Philadelphia etc. Towboat Co.*, 23 How. 209; *Sutton* v. *Wauwatosa*, 29 Wis. 21; 9 Am. Rep. 534; *McArthur* v. *Canal Co.*, 34 Wis. 139; *Dutton* v. *Weare*, 17 N. H. 34; 43 Am. Dec. 590. In these courts, there is of course no difficulty in holding a defendant liable under a state of facts like that in *Hall* v. *Corcoran*, 107 Mass, 251; 9 Am. Rep. 30; see *Woodman* v. *Hubbard*, 25 N. H. 67; 57 Am. Dec. 310.

8. UNLAWFUL AND NEGLIGENT ACTS, WHETHER MEASURE OF LIABILITY DIFFERS IN REGARD TO.—Some cases seem to countenance the theory that one who willfully commits an unlawful act is liable even for remote and unlikely consequences. The strongest instance is *Salisbury* v. *Hirchenroder*, 106 Mass. 458; 8 Am. Rep. 354, in which the defendant had suspended a heavy sign in a street, thereby contravening a city ordinance, and it was blown down during a gale of extraordinary violence, inflicting the injuries complained of. The court, after remarking that if the defendant had merely been negligent he could not have been held liable, decided against him on the ground that his act was illegal, and that this circumstance prevented him taking advantage of the abnormal nature of the agency by which the damage was ultimately done. The two cases chiefly relied on are *Dickinson* v. *Boyle*, 17 Pick. 78, 28 Am. Dec. 281, and *Woodward* v. *Aborn*, 35 Me. 271, 58 Am. Dec. 699. The former was a case where the defendant broke into a neighbor's close and dug away a portion of a river-bank near a dam—(the facts are incorrectly stated in the opinion in *Salisbury* v. *Hirehenroder*, 106 Mass. 458, 8 Am. Rep. 354)—the consequence being that a flood which occurred three weeks afterwards forced a passage round the end of the dam and damaged the plaintiff's property. The only point raised was whether the fact that the damage done was not actually consummated till the three weeks elapsed disabled the plaintiff from suing in trespass *vi et armis*, and it was held that it did not. Nothing was said about the abnormal nature of the agency, nor is there anything in the statement of the case to show that the flood was at all out of the common. In *Woodward* v. *Aborn*, 35 Me. 271, 58 Am. Dec. 699, the gist of the action was negligence, and the very brief opinion of Chief Justice Shepley concludes with the remark that "a person should not place,

or negligently allow, a deterious substance to remain where the useful waters of another may be corrupted either by the ordinary or extraordinary, yet not very uncommon, action of the elements." In fact it is not easy to see that the circumstances in *Salisbury* v. *Hirchenroder*, 106 Mass. 458, 8 Am. Rep. 354, require the application of any broader doctrine than that one who maintains a nuisance is liable for all the consequences which flow directly therefrom, and are of the kind which it was the intention to prevent by declaring the act in question to be a nuisance; and such a doctrine is plainly a corollary of the ordinary principle, that the question of care is not involved in an action for injuries resulting from a nuisance: See cases cited in *Laflin etc. Powder Co.* v. *Tearney*, 131 Ill. 322; 19 Am. St. Rep. 34. If a municipal corporation forbids the suspension of a dangerous object in a position where it will be likely, in the long run, to harm travelers, it is reasonable to suppose that high winds were among the perils against which it was designed to guard. The ordinary laws of probability then become immaterial, for the authorities having expressly declared that the violent action of the elements is sufficiently within the range of practical possibilities to be taken into account, the courts, in passing upon such a case, are absolutely bound by such declaration as a rule of evidence.

On the other hand, the cases assuming that the liability for unlawful acts involves the question whether the results complained of are natural and probable are numerous: *City of Allegheny* v. *Zimmermann*, 95 Pa. St. 287; 40 Am. Rep. 649; *State* v. *Rankin*, 3 S. C. 438; 16 Am. Rep. 737. So in *Derry* v. *Flitner*, 118 Mass. 131, it was said, in a case where the owner of a vessel had unlawfully taken possession of a place of shelter, and so caused the wreck of the vessels of another person who had received permission to occupy it, that "one who commits a tortious act is liable for any injury which is the natural and probable consequence of his misconduct." In *Brown* v. *Chicago etc. Ry. Co.*, 54 Wis. 342, 41 Am. Rep. 41, the liability for a trespass was stated to be that "legitimately flowing" from it, and in *The E. D. Holton*, 55 Fed. Rep. 1010, "reasonable anticipation" was mentioned as the test. Such, too, seems to be the principle of *Renner* v. *Canfield*, 36 Minn. 90; 1 Am. St. Rep. 654, where it was held that the shooting of a dog on a highway, though an unlawful act, was not the proximate cause of the illness of a woman who was terrified by the report. A still stronger case is *Sharp* v. *Powell*, Law R. 7 Com. P. 253, where the defendant, contrary to the provisions of a police statute, caused his van to be washed in a public street. The water ran down a gutter, and, but for a hard frost which prevailed, would have flowed harmlessly through a grating into a sewer; but, as the grating happened to be frozen over, the water spread out and froze into a sheet of ice, on which the plaintiff's led horse slipped and injured himself. In holding that the defendant was not liable, the court used such expressions as that the damage was not "within the ordinary consequences" of such an act, nor "one which the defendant could fairly be expected to anticipate as likely to ensue from his act," and laid stress upon the fact that the "water would accumulate and freeze at the spot where the accident happened." This standard of liability Mr. Pollock believes to be the right one (Torts, page 43), and states that, in his opinion, the observations of the court in the later case of *Clark* v. *Chambers*, L. R. 3 Q. B. D. 327 (the facts of which will be given in a subsequent section), are opposed to the general weight of authority, so far as they countenance the principle, that the liability of a wrongdoer may extend even to remote and unlikely consequences, where the original wrong is a willful trespass. Such a principle, however, was not necessary for the decision of this case, which may fairly be rested, as will be seen (sec. 28, *post*), on other grounds, and was not, in fact, made to turn entirely on that principle. The ruling in *Sharp* v. *Powell*, is strongly supported in *Regina* v. *Bennett*, 4 Jur., N. S., 1088. The defendant was engaged in manufacturing fireworks, contrary to statute. By the negligence of his servants, a fire broke out which caused an explosion of the fireworks, and a rocket flying across the street ignited a house, the result being that a person was burned to death. Under these facts, the defendant was held not guilty of man. slaughter. (For cases in which the connection between the unlawful act and the injury is involved rather than the measure of the liability, see sec. tion 7, *ante*.)

The above summary of the cases seems to justify the conclusion that there is no essential difference between the measure of liability for willful and negligent torts, and that in both cases the injury complained of must be a natural and direct result. To this rule there is, however, an important ex. ception in those cases in which the willful tort consists in the unlawful as. sumption of dominion over another's property. If A intermeddles with or appropriates what belongs to B he clearly does so at his peril, and, being liable for the full value of the goods, is precluded from raising the question whether the loss, whether total or partial, which ensues while they are under his control was or was not due to an extraordinary or even irresist. ible force. Such seems to be the doctrine deducible from *Harrison* v. *Berk. ley*, 1 Stroh. 525, 47 Am. Dec. 578, cited approvingly in *King* v. *Shanks*, 12 B. Mon. 410; *Wilhite* v. *Speakman*, 79 Ala. 400; *Eten* v. *Luyster*, 60 N. Y. 253. By an analogous principle a carrier who deviates from his route is liable, absolutely and in all events, for a loss of goods during such devia. tion, irrespective of any exceptions in the bill of lading: *Phillips* v. *Brig. ham*, 26 Ga. 617; 71 Am. Dec. 227; *Powers* v. *Davenport*, 7 Blackf. 497; 43 Am. Dec. 100; *Crosby* v. *Fitch*, 12 Conn. 410; 31 Am. Dec. 745; *Hand* v. *Baynes*, 4 Whart. 204; 33 Am. Dec. 54; *Davis* v. *Garrett*, 6 Bing. 716; *Williams* v. *Grant*, 1 Conn. 487; 7 Am. Dec. 235; *Railroad Co.* *O'Donnell*, 49 Ohio St. 489; 34 Am. St. Rep. 579.

The general rule seems to be subject to the limitation that the loss in. curred by the misappropriation is suffered in regard to the goods them. selves. Thus in *Vedder* v. *Hildreth*, 2 Wis. 427: A unlawfully took possession of B's wagon and horses while he was on his way to settle in an. other state. At the time of the taking the roads were hard with frost and in a good condition for traveling; but during the detention a thaw came, and B was consequently unable to proceed, and lost his opportunity for put. ting in a crop. It was held that this was too remote a consequence of the original trespass, the change of weather not being an occurrence which A was bound to anticipate.

9. LIABILITY AS DETERMINED BY THE OPERATION OF NORMAL PHYSICAL LAWS.—The general principle is thus succinctly stated in *Jordan* v. *Wyatt*, 4 Gratt. 151, 47 Am. Dec. 720: "He who gives a mischievous impulse to matter is the actor, by whatever instrument or agent he acts, and whether he uses muscular strength or mechanical force, or even moral power, as if he commands or procures another to do the act; or whether he excites or in. flames into action some dormant quality or property of a substance, natural or artificial, animate or inanimate." Thus everyone must take notice at his peril of such ordinary results of the operation of physical laws as the effect of rain upon earth newly replaced in an excavation: *Johnson* v. *Friel*, 50 N. Y. 679; the falling of the tide: *Bohannan* v. *Hammond*, 42 Cal. 227; the

possible silting up of a river as the result of diverting its waters: *Cheeves* v. *Danielly*, 80 Ga. 114; the possibility of damage to riparian property as the result of the removal of gravel from the bed of a stream: *Dickinson* v. *Boyle*, 17 Pick. 78; 28 Am. Dec. 281; the flooding of land by the obstruction of a river: *Hines* v. *Jarrett*, 26 S. C. 480; the possible aggravation of the ill results of such obstruction, in consequence of the more rapid denudation of the soil above by a wider cultivation thereof: *Mississippi etc. R. R. Co.* v. *Archibald*, 67 Miss. 38; the action of water in carrying substances of a certain specific gravity: *Woodward* v. *Aborn*, 35 Me. 271; 58 Am. Dec. 699; the destructive effects of letting loose water which has been dammed up: *Pollett* v. *Long*, 56 N. Y. 200; the increased percolation of water which may follow an alteration of the surface of ground: *Hindman* v. *North Eastern Ry. Co.*, L. R. 3 C. B. D. 168; or from the collection of the water in a reservoir, so as to augment the pressure: *Wilson* v. *City of New Bedford*, 108 Mass. 261; 11 Am. Rep. 352; the possibility that a dam may be formed by the breaking up of ice upon which a quantity of logs have been negligently left: *George* v. *Fisk*, 32 N. H. 32; the possibility that the accumulation of snow upon an awning may break it down: *Day* v. *Milford*, 5 Allen, 98; the effect of water of a certain temperature in melting ice; *Union Ice Co.* v. *Crowell*, 55 Fed. Rep. 87 (Ct. of App.); the ordinary effect of a thaw is causing masses of snow to slip from the roofs of houses: *Smethurst* v. *Congregational Church*, 148 Mass. 261; 12 Am. St. Rep. 550; the fact that the freezing of water in a pipe frequently breaks it: *Siordet* v. *Hall*, 4 Bing. 607; the dangerous properties of electricity passing along a wire: *Ahern* v. *Oregon Telephone Co.* (Oregon Supreme Court, June, 1893); the certainty that a hard substance striking against another will rebound: *Hartvig* v. *North Pacific Logging Co.*, 19 Or. 522; the probability that a boat turned adrift without anyone to control it will damage itself by stranding or otherwise: *Heaney* v. *Heaney*, 2 Den. C. C., 625; the certainty that gas under pressure will escape from a defective pipe, and produce a dangerous explosive, when mixed with the air: *Burrows* v. *March Gas etc. Co.*, L. R. 5 Ex. 67; 7 Ex. 96. In *Chamberlain* v. *Oshkosh*, 84 Wis. 289, 36 Am. St. Rep. *post*, a city was held not liable for personal injuries, caused by stepping on ice formed in a depression on a sidewalk, but it is difficult to see how such a ruling can be sustained on general principles, or how the causal connection can be broken by the accumulation of water in a hole and the consequent formation of a dangerously smooth surface by the normal action of frost. The case is directly opposed to *Atchison* v. *King*, 9 Kan. 550, and probably depends on the peculiar doctrine adopted in Wisconsin regarding liability for defects in streets: See *Ring* v. *Cohoes*, 77 N. Y. 83; 33 Am. Rep. 574. A similar remark may be made in regard to *Brandon* v. *Manufacturing Co.*, 51 Tex. 121. There the plaintiff's cotton was wetted by the defendants' negligence, and in this condition shipped to New York. On the way the water in the cotton froze and the latter was damaged. The court said that the cold weather was the proximate cause of the loss, and that the defendant was therefore not liable. In *Alabama etc. R. R. Co.* v. *Chapman*, 80 Ala. 615, a locomotive struck a cow and threw her against the plaintiff. The defendant was held liable (subject to proof that the collision was due to negligence), on the general principle that injuries produced by instrumentalities put in operation by negligent acts are proximate consequences of such acts. In *McAfee* v. *Crofford*, 13 How. 447, the defendant abducted several of the plaintiff's slaves, and the rest were so frightened that they ran away and hid themselves. As a part of his damages the plaintiff was allowed to show that a river running past his plantation was swollen by heavy rains, while his slaves were thus missing, and carried away or spoilt a large quantity of firewood; and also that by reason of the plantation being thus left unguarded, droves of cattle broke in and destroyed a portion of his corn crop. This is criticised as an extreme case in *Scott* v. *Hunter*, 46 Pa. St. 192, 84 Am. Dec. 542; but, although the court does not state the grounds of its decision, there seems no difficulty in saying that the defendant was fairly chargeable with knowledge, that the action of the elements may at any time raise a river, and that animals are accustomed to stray and to seek their food without any regard to the rights of property. Cases based on the latter propensity will be found in another section, and that the flood and its consequences were something reasonably to be anticipated seems clear from the cases just cited. This principle that, if a person deprives another of the means of protecting his property, he must respond in damages for any injury which that property suffers in conse. quence of the normal operation of natural forces was also exemplified in *The George and Richard*, L. R., 3 Adm. 466, where a ship lost her masts by a collision which occurred through the defendant's negligence and was afterwards wrecked while in that helpless condition. So, too, where the defendant supplied a chain-cable, warranted to last two years, and it broke within that time, and an anchor affixed thereto was lost, it was held that the value of the anchor, as well as of the cable, might be recovered: *Borra. daile* v. *Brunton*, 8 Taunt. 535. Compare *Pittsburg* v. *Grier*, 22 Pa. St. 54; 60 Am. Dec. 65.

10. THE GROWTH OF VEGETATION in places where its presence may cause injury to person or property may also raise a liability, as where a railroad allows weeds to grow so high at a crossing as to obstruct the view along the track, and, as a result, a train runs over stock: *Indianapolis etc. R. R. Co.* v. *Smith*, 78 Ill. 112. Compare *Eames* v. *Texas etc. R. R. Co.*, 63 Tex. 660.

11. SPREAD OF FIRES.—(a) *General Principles.*—The theory of causal con. nection, where natural forces are concerned, has been discussed most fre. quently in determining the limits of liability for injuries by fire. *Prima facie* it would appear that decisions based upon the well-known phenomena of combustion should be entirely harmonious. Fire will spread as long as it finds any aliment in its path, and since the intervals over which it will leap depend upon such ordinary considerations as the heat of the flame, the dry. ness of the weather, the strength of the wind, and the like, there does not seem to be much room for difference of opinion. Logically, the originator of the fire should have no defense except the occurrence of some abnormal event, like an explosion or the prevalence of a wind so strong as to amount to *vis major.* Perhaps the weight of authority is in favor of this view, but many courts have shrunk from the consequences of carrying out this theory consistently, and have put forth decisions which seem to have no support but the supposed expediency of not imposing too severe a penalty upon the wrongful actor, though it is not very apparent upon what principle a tort-feasor should be thus favored. If any extraneous consideration is to be re-garded, it would seem that the innocent person who loses by the wrongful act has a decidedly stronger claim upon the bounty of the law than the per-son who has caused the loss: See *Hoyt* v. *Jeffers*, 30 Mich. 181.

Up to a certain point the cases are in harmony. If a fire is started on the plaintiff's premises by the defendant's negligent use of his property, or if the fire starts on the defendant's premises and spreads directly to the plain-tiff's, the defendant's liability is not disputed even in the states which have confined that liability within the narrowest limits: *Webb* v. *Rome etc. R. R.*

Co., 49 N. Y. 420; 10 Am. Rep. 389; *Woodruff's Case*, 4 Md. 242; 59 Am.
Dec. 72; *Baltimore etc. R. R. Co.* v. *Dorsey*, 37 Md. 19; *Annapolis etc. R. R.
Co.* v. *Gantt*, 39 Md. 116; *Ryan* v. *Gross*, 68 Md. 377; *Philadelphia etc. R. R.
Co.* v. *Constable*, 39 Md. 149; *Baltimore etc. R. R. Co.* v. *Shipley*, 39 Md. 251;
Kellogg v. *Chicago etc. R. R. Co.*, 26 Wis. 223; 7 Am. Rep. 69; *Oil Creek etc.
R. R. Co.* v. *Keighron*, 74 Pa. St. 320; *Henry* v. *Southern Pac. R. R. Co.*, 50
Cal. 176. The fact that the fire dies away and smolders for two days, and
then starts afresh, does not show any break of causation: *Krippner* v. *Biebl*,
28 Minn. 139; nor is the defendant less liable because the fire does not spread
immediately after breaking out: *Haverly* v. *State Line etc. R. R. Co.*, 135 Pa.
St. 50; 20 Am. St. Rep. 848; nor is it material that the defendant did not
anticipate that the fire would be communicated in the particular direction
in which it actually spread: *Higgins* v. *Dewey*, 107 Mass. 494; 9 Am. Rep. 63.

(*b*) *Intervention of Space, Diversity of Ownership, etc.*—The rule most consistent with principle is that stated in *Cincinnati etc. R. R. Co.* v. *Barker* (Ky.
Ct. of App. Feb. 16, 1893): "If the fire spreads from the matter first ignited,
the intervention of considerable space, diversity of ownership, or various
physical objects, does not preclude recovery." To the same effect see *Perley*
v. *Eastern R. R. Co.*, 98 Mass. 414; 96 Am. Dec. 645; *Jordan* v. *Wyatt*, 4
Gratt. 151; 47 Am. Dec. 720; *Clemens* v. *Hannibal etc. Ry. Co.*, 53 Mo. 366;
14 Am. Rep. 460 (space of fifty yards); *Hooksett* v. *Concord R. R. Co.*, 38
N. H. 242 (space of fifty feet); *Atchison etc. R. R. Co.* v. *Bales*, 16 Kan. 252;
Atchison etc. R. R. Co. v. *Stanford*, 12 Kan. 354; 15 Am. Rep. 362; *Adams*
v. *Young*, 44 Ohio St. 80; 58 Am. Rep. 789; *Quigley* v. *Stockbridge etc. R. R.
Co.*, 8 Allen, 438; *Grand Trunk R. R. Co.* v. *Richardson*, 91 U. S. 454; *Delaware etc. Ry.* v. *Salmon*, 39 N. J. L. 299; 23 Am. Rep. 214; *Crandall* v. *Goodrich Transportation Co.*, 16 Fed. Rep. 75; *Ingersoll* v. *Stockbridge etc. R. R.
Co.*, 8 Allen, 438; *Louisville etc. Ry. Co.* v. *Krinning*, 87 Ind. 351; *Jacksonville
etc. Ry. Co.* v. *Peninsular Land etc. Co.*, 27 Fla. 1; *Smith* v. *London etc. Ry.
Co.*, L. R. 5 Com. P. 98; 6 Com. P. 14. Other cases hold that where the fire
is communicated indirectly to the plaintiff's property it should be left to the
jury to say whether the connection of cause and effect is made out: *Perry* v.
Southern Pac. R. R. Co., 50 Cal. 578; *Henry* v. *Southern Pac. R. R. Co.*, 50
Cal. 183; *Green Ridge R. R. Co.* v. *Brinkman*, 64 Md. 52; 54 Am. Rep. 755;
especially when the distance is great: *Atkinson* v. *Goodrich etc. Co.*, 60 Wis.
141; 56 Am. Rep. 352.

(*c*) *Wind, Whether Breaks Causation.*—Some authorities adopt the logical
doctrine that no wind, unless it be an extraordinary one, is an intervening
cause sufficient to excuse the defendant: *Insurance Co.* v. *Tweed*, 7 Wall. 52;
East Tennessee Ry. Co. v. *Hesters*, 90 Ga. 11; *Chicago etc. R. R. Co.* v. *Williams*,
131 Ind. 30, overruling the earlier case, *Pennsylvania Co.* v. *Whitlock*, 99 Ind.
16; 50 Am. Rep. 71; *Allison* v. *Corn Exchange Ins. Co.*, 57 N. Y. 87; *Louisville etc. R. R. Co.* v. *Nitsche*, 126 Ind. 229; 22 Am. St. Rep. 582. In other
cases a more qualified liability is laid down. Thus in *Marvin* v. *Chicago etc.
R. R. Co.*, 79 Wis. 140, it was held that a heavy wind suddenly arising and
carrying a burning brand a considerable distance is an intervening cause
which will relieve the defendant. In *Pennsylvania etc. R. R. Co.* v. *Lacey*,
89 Pa. St. 459, it was said that under such circumstances the question should
be left to the jury; and such seems to be the effect of *Toledo etc. Ry. Co.* v.
Pindar, 53 Ill. 447; 5 Am. Rep. 57. But in *Toledo etc. Ry. Co.* v. *Muthers-
baugh*, 71 Ill. 572, the court took stronger ground, and adopting an illustration used in the earlier case, *Fent* v. *Toledo etc. Ry. Co.*, 59 Ill. 349, 14 Am.
Rep. 13, set aside a verdict for the plaintiff where the evidence showed that

a strong wind had carried burning brands a distance of one hundred rods over a space in which there was no combustible matter.

The fact that the wind drops and then rises again does not break the causation: *Poeppers* v. *Missouri etc. R. R. Co.*, 67 Mo. 715; 29 Am. Rep. 518; *Haverly* v. *State Line etc. R. R. Co.*, 135 Pa. St. 50; 20 Am. St. Rep. 848, the latter case holding that such a circumstance was merely one to be considered by the jury. In *Northern Pac. R. R. Co.* v. *Lewis*, 51 Fed. Rep. 658 (Ct. of App., 9th Circuit), a change of wind was said not to break the causation, while *Gram* v. *Northern Pac. R. R. Co.*, 1 N. Dak. 252, makes such a circumstance merely a portion of the evidence for the jury.

(d) *Rulings in New York and Pennsylvania.*—Two courts whose authority is second to none in the union have gone very far in regard to intervening agencies. In the following cases the doctrine was announced that, if the fire started by the defendant passes through the premises of one or more parties before reaching the property of the plaintiff, the chain of causation is broken: *Ryan* v. *New York Cent. R. R. Co.*, 35 N. Y. 210; 91 Am. Dec. 49; *Read* v. *Nichols*, 118 N. Y. 224; *Pennsylvania R. R. Co.* v. *Kerr*, 62 Pa. St. 353; 1 Am. Rep. 431. In the later case *Pennsylvania R. R. Co.* v. *Hope*, 80 Pa. St. 373; 21 Am. Rep. 100, the court referred with some temper to the criticisms leveled at *Pennsylvania R. R. Co.* v. *Kerr*, 62 Pa. St. 353; 1 Am. Rep. 431, and asserted that it was not intended to lay down the broad rule deduced from it, the decision merely being that, where the court was asked to say, on a question reserved, whether the burning of the second building was a "direct and necessary" consequence of the ignition of the first, no other answer could be given than it was not such a consequence. Since however *Ryan* v. *New York Cent. R. R. Co.*, 35 N. Y. 210, 91 Am. Dec. 49, was expressly approved in *Pennsylvania R. R. Co.* v. *Kerr*, 62 Pa. St. 353; 1 Am. Rep. 431, it seems little less than certain that the case turned on something more substantial than a verbal distinction, and that the inference drawn in other states as to the purport of the decision was the correct one: *Pennsylvania R. R. Co.* v. *Hope*, 80 Pa. St. 373; 21 Am. Rep. 100, therefore, is principally noteworthy as showing that the extreme doctrine of the earlier case is no longer law in the court from which it emanated. The influence of that case is still traceable in *Hoag* v. *Lake Shore etc. R. R. Co*, 85 Pa. St. 293, 27 Am. Rep. 653, in which a train was derailed by a collision with a suddenly developed landslide. The oil tanks in the train burst and the oil, having taken fire, was carried down stream to the plaintiff's property and burnt it. The court held the water be an intervening agency which broke the chain of causation. This ruling is, on general principles, only justifiable, if the fact that the intervening agency is of a somewhat unusual kind absolves the defendant, a position which would probably not be admitted in states which adopt the more logical doctrine. Thus in *Kuhn* v. *Jewett*, 32 N. J. Eq. 647, the defendant was held liable under a precisely similar state of facts.

The decisions in New York and Pennsylvania have been very generally condemned as contrary to sound principle (see, for example, in *Perley* v. *Eastern R. R. Co.*, 98 Mass, 414; 96 Am. Rep. 645, a succinct and apparently unanswerable criticism of *Ryan* v. *New York Cent. R. R. Co.*, 35 N. Y. 210; 91 Am. Dec. 49), but have found a strong advocate in Mr. Wharton, who has even attempted the difficult feat of reconciling the two cases last cited. The learned commentator adopts the view that, when "the damage is not a probable or ordinary result of the negligence, causal connection ceases when there is interposed between the negligence and the damage an object which, if due care had been taken, would have prevented the damage," and states, as an illustration, that "if a house is properly built, if it is properly watched, if a proper fire apparatus is in operation, it can be prevented, when a fire approaches from a neighboring detached house, from catching fire." He also refers to negligence in leaving combustible matter on premises near the track, as being sufficient to break the causal connection. As for the first illustration it is not apparent why A should be subjected to loss, because no sufficient fire apparatus has been supplied to prevent the burning of B's house. It would be hard to find any support for the theory that one failure of duty can be excused by another, under such circumstances: See the next subdivision. If the negligence of the intervening person is actionable, the case seems to be plainly one of concurrent liability. If it is not actionable, it cannot affect the responsibility either way. The illustration of combustible matter left near the track of a railroad is not a happy one, for it will be seen in the following section that such an act is not deemed to be negligent. Mr. Wharton's arguments have, however, been adopted in *Doggett* v. *Richmond etc. R. R. Co.*, 78 N. C. 305. There the defendant was held not liable, where the fire passed along a continuous line of fence belonging to four owners, the plaintiff being the last. The court placed its decision on the ground that the fire had been checked, and was supposed to have been extinguished by those who had been contending with it, and afterwards broke out afresh. It was said that "if they did not contemplate a renewed outbreak of the fire, upon no reasonable hypothesis could it be assumed that the defendant contemplated it as a necessary or probable result of the first cause." We doubt if any authority can be found for the view that the opinion of those engaged in a transaction is binding on the court or jury to this extent. The theory of Mr. Wharton as to the effect of intervening negligence was also referred to with approval, and the linking together of the four fences, instead of having them "disconnected, each surrounding the land of its own proprietor, as the defendant had a right to expect," made the spread of the fire to the land of the plaintiff a sufficiently improbable consequence to absolve the defendant. For what reason the defendant had a right to expect that the fences should be so disconnected we are not informed. Certainly not, it would seem, on the ground of the prevalence of such a usage. We think the case an unsound one as regards both the reasons assigned for it, and that it shows very plainly the difficulties to which Mr. Wharton's principles must lead.

(e) *Acts of Landowners and Others.*—As a landowner has a right to do what he pleases on his own premises so long as he does not inflict some positive injury upon his neighbor, it is not negligence in such landowner to place combustible materials near a railroad track or other place, from which a fire is likely to start. The position of the combustible matter is merely a condition, not the proximate cause of the fire: *Fitch* v. *Pacific R. R. Co.*, 45 Mo. 322; *Johnson* v. *Chicago etc. R. R. Co.*, 31 Minn. 57; *Delaware etc. Ry. Co.* v. *Salmon*, 39 N. J. L. 299; 23 Am. Rep. 214; *Jacksonville etc. Ry. Co.* v. *Peninsular Land etc. Co.*, 27 Fla. 1. In Pennsylvania such a circumstance makes the question of proximate cause one for the jury: *Lehigh Valley R. R. Co.* v. *McKeen*, 90 Pa. St. 122; 35 Am. Rep. 644. Nor is the failure, though culpable, of a third party owning the intervening premises to extinguish the fire an independent cause: *Wiley* v. *West Jersey R. R. Co.*, 44 N. J. L. 247; *Small* v. *Chicago etc. R. R. Co.*, 55 Iowa, 582. If the defendant accedes to the request of a third person to allow the fire to burn, such request will not relieve him from liability for damage to another's premises by a subsequent spread of the fire: *Simmonds* v. *New York Cent. R. R. Co.*, 52 Conn. 264; 52

Am. Rep 587. Back fires, if swallowed up in the advancing flame, do not break the causal connection: *Perley* v. *Eastern etc. R. R. Co.*, 98 Mass. 414; 96 Am. Dec. 645. The setting of such fires merely raises a necessity for clearer evidence of the connection between the act of the defendant and the damage done: *Marvin* v. *Chicago etc. R. R. Co.*, 79 Wis. 140.

(*f*) *Insurable Interest of Railroad Companies in Property Adjacent to the track.*—In view of the circumstance that in a large majority of the cases in which the liability for negligent fires comes in question railroad companies have been the defendants, the legislatures in some states have conceded to those companies the right to secure partial protection by insuring property adjacent to their lines. Laws for the purpose have been passed in Massachusetts, New Hampshire, Connecticut, Maine, and perhaps in other states: *Perley* v. *Eastern etc. R. R. Co.*, 98 Mass. Dec. 645; 96 Am. Dec. 645; *Hooksett* v. *Concord R. R. Co.*, 38 N. H. 242; *Simmonds* v. *New York Cent. R. R. Co.*, 52 Conn. 264; 52 Am. Rep. 587; *Chapman* v. *Atlantic etc. R. R. Co.*, 37 Me. 92. Since these statutes do not limit the distance within which property may be insured, it has been held that the ordinary rules as to casual connection are not thereby affected: *Perley* v. *Eastern R. R. Co.*, 98 Mass. 413; 96 Am. Dec. 645.

(*g*) *Lability for Preventing the Extinguishment of Fires.*—In *Metallic Compression Casting Co.* v. *Fitchburg R. R. Co.*, 109 Mass. 277, 12 Am. Rep. 689, a railroad company was held liable for negligently cutting in two a fire hose, which had been laid across its track, and thus causing the destruction of the plaintiff's building. In *Bosch* v. *Burlington etc. R. R. Co.*, 44 Iowa, 402; 24 Am. Rep. 754, on the other hand, where a railroad company had illegally taken possession of a street on a river-bank, and by filling out into the channel created an obstruction which prevented the firemen from reaching the water so as to play with their hose upon the plaintiff's house, it was held that the company was not liable for the consequent destruction of the house, the occupation of the streets being an independent act, not connected with the fire. This case seems to discountenance the doctrine already discussed that the commission of an illegal act involved a larger measure of liability than mere negligence. The Massachusetts case was followed in *White* v. *Colorado Cent. R. R. Co.*, 5 Dill. 429, where a railroad company's negligence in storing gunpowder in a building with other goods was held to be the proximate cause of the loss of the goods by fire, on the ground that the firemen were thereby deterred from approaching the building.

12. ACTION OF MACHINERY.—Principles analogous to those which determine the limits of responsibility where purely natural forces are concerned, are applied in cases where those forces have been subjected to the use of man by mechanical devices. In other words, if machinery acts as it might be expected to do, the person who made it potent for mischief, or does something which deprives it of its usefulness at a time when its services are needed, is responsible for the resulting damage. The first branch of the rule is illustrated in *Bunting* v. *Hogsett*, 139 Pa. St. 363, 23 Am. St. Rep. 192, where the engineer of a donkey engine, running on a track which crossed a railroad, saw that a collision with a train was imminent, closed the throttle, and leaped from the engine to save his life. The throttle was reopened by the shock, and the donkey engine started round the railroad track in the opposite direction and collided a second time with the train a' another crossing, doing the damage complained of. *Held*, That the engineer's negligence in causing the first collision was the natural, primary, and proximate cause of the occurrence. The other branch of the rule is illustrated by

King v. *Ohio etc. R. R. Co.,* 25 Fed. Rep. 799, where it was held that the breakdown of a part of the machinery of a steamer, owing to the sudden necessity for a change of course, caused by the negligence of the defendant in not opening a drawbridge, as the master had a right to anticipate, is not such an intervening cause as will excuse for the injury caused by a collision of the disabled steamer with a bridge-pier.

13. SICKNESS OR OTHER PHYSICAL INCAPACITY RESULTING FROM WRONG-FUL ACTS.—The general principle is that ill health and the various kinds of mental or physical disability which follow the negligent exposure of the plaintiff to insalubrious surrouudings or the infliction of a direct bodily injury, are such natural and probable consequences of the injury as the tort-feasor must answer for: *Bradshaw* v. *Lancashire etc. Ry. Co.,* L. R. 10 Com. P. 189; *Williams* v. *Vanderbilt,* 28 N. Y. 217; 84 Am. Dec. 333; *Wade* v. *Leroy,* 20 How. 34; *Nebraska City* v. *Campbell,* 2 Black, 590; *Ballou* v. *Farnum,* 11 Allen, 72; *New Jersey Exp. Co.* v. *Nichols,* 33 N. J. L. 434; 97 Am. Dec. 722; *Smith* v. *St. Paul etc. Ry. Co.,* 30 Minn. 169; *Hatchell* v. *Kimbrough,* 4 Jones, 163; *Blake* v. *Lord,* 16 Gray, 387; *Clifford* v. *Denver etc. R. Co.* 9 Col. 333; *Baltimore Pass. Ry. Co.* v. *Kemp,* 61 Md. 619; 48 Am. Rep. 134; *Dickson* v. *Hollister,* 123 Pa. St. 421; 10 Am. St. Rep 533; *Stewart* v. *City of Ripon,* 38 Wis. 594; *Oliver* v. *Town of La Ville,* 36 Wis. 592. The liability of the defendant does not depend upon whether the particular form which the actual disease assumed was such as might be contemplated or foreseen: *Sloan* v. *Edwards,* 61 Md. 89, where the victim of an assault became subject to convulsions and fits; nor is it material that the effect of the original injury does not appear until after a considerable interval: *Schmidt* v. *Pfeil,* 24 Wis. 452; *Delic* v. *Chicago etc. R. R. Co.,* 51 Wis. 400. Under the statutes allow-ing recovery of damages by the representatives of a person negligently killed, the defendant is responsible although an illness intervenes between the original injury and the death of the victim, provided that such illness is of a kind that may reasonably be expected to follow the injury: *Jucker* v. *Chicago etc. Ry. Co.,* 52 Wis. 151; and the same rule prevails in criminal cases: *Kelley* v. *State,* 53 Ind. 311. That physical injury resulting from a nervous shock is a sufficiently probable consequence upon which to found a claim for damages has been affirmed in *Bell* v. *Great Northern Ry. Co.,* 26 L. R. Ir. 428, following an earlier case *Byrne* v. *Great Southern etc. Ry. Co.* (not reported), and in *Purcell* v. *St. Paul City Ry. Co.,* 48 Minn. 134; but denied in *Victorian Ry. Commrs.* v. *Coultas,* 13 App. Cas. 222. The miscar-riage of a woman is not a natural and reasonable consequence of the defend-ant's conduct in quarreling and abusing her husband, she not being present and the defendant having no knowledge that she was within hearing or was pregnant. This case can only be sustained on the ground that the defend-ant did not know that he was overheard, for it seems certain, on principle as well as authority, that if he had acted in the presence of the woman so as to frighten her, he would have been liable: See *Barber* v. *Reese,* 60 Miss. 906. Where a similar consequence resulted from alarming a woman by the imprisonment of her husband, it was held that no damages were recoverable, when it was ascertained that, owing to the husband's being imprisoned in a county different from that in which he was arrested, the imprisonment was technically illegal: *Ellis* v. *Cleveland,* 55 Vt. 358. If a person negligently injures another he is bound to be reasonably prudent to secure the injured person from further hurt. Thus where a passenger was thrown off a train owing to its being negligently started while he was alighting, and the serv-

ants of the company knowing that he has been so dazed by the shock as to be incapable of helping himself, left him on the track where he was afterwards run over, the company was held liable for his death: *Cincinnati etc. Ry. Co.* v. *Cooper*, 120 Ind. 469; 16 Am. St. Rep. 334. A similiar obligation exists when a person to whom the defendant owes a duty is, though not actually injured, so paralyzed by fear as to be incapable of caring for himself: *Smith* v. *British etc. S. S. Co.*, 86 N. Y. 408, where a female passenger on a steamer was so terrified by the fall of a tier of berths that she became incapable of taking care of herself, and the defendant's servants neglected to put her in a place of safety, the result being that she was thrown down by the motion of the steamer and seriously injured.

14. NEGLIGENT TREATMENT OF DRUNKEN MEN.—The principles illustrated by the decisions cited at the end of the preceding paragraph are to some extent applicable when the person to whom the duty is owed is in a peculiarly helpless condition through his own fault, as by intoxication. In several cases of the expulsion of drunken men from trains, who were afterwards run over, the question has been discussed, how far the original act is to be considered the proximate cause of the resulting injury. Of course, if the man is so drunk as to be incapable of taking care of himself there must be a clear liability for putting him in a dangerous position: *Louisville etc. R. R. Co.* v. *Sullivan*, 81 Ky. 624; 50 Am. Rep. 186. Otherwise there is no liability: *Louisville etc. R. R Co.* v. *Johnson*, 92 Ala. 204; 25 Am. St. Rep. 35, citing *Railway Co.* v. *Valleley*, 32 Ohio St. 345; 30 Am. Rep. 601, especially if he is placed at a safe distance from the track, and it is apparent that he must put himself in danger by afterwards wandering back to it: *McClelland* v. *Louisville etc. Ry. Co.*, 94 Ind. 276. Even if he was left in a dangerous place, the company cannot be declared negligent, as a matter of law, where the evidence shows that he was run over half a mile from the spot where he was put off. The question should then be given to the jury under proper instructions: *Haley* v. *Chicago etc. R. R. Co.*, 21 Iowa, 15. See further on this subject the note to *Louisville etc. Ry. Co.* v. *Johnson*, 25 Am. St. Rep. 40–43.

15. PREDISPOSITION TO DISEASE NO DEFENSE.—Wherever sickness or other bodily incapacity is produced by a wrongful act, it is no defense that the injured person is in a feeble state of health temporarily, or is weaker and more susceptible to disease than the average human being, whether constitutionally or by reason of a previous injury, or that he has a predisposition to the particular disease which actually results from the injury, and it is immaterial whether the condition of such person was known to the defendant or not: *Brown* v. *Chicago etc. Ry. Co.*, 54 Wis. 342; 41 Am. Rep. 41; *Owens* v. *Kansas City etc. R. R. Co.*, 95 Mo. 169; 6 Am. St. Rep. 39; *Tice* v. *Munn*, 94 N. Y. 621; *McNamara* v. *Clintonville*, 60 Wis. 207; 51 Am. Rep. 722; *Louisville etc. Ry. Co.* v. *Falvey*, 104 Ind. 409; *Jeffersonville etc. Ry. Co.* v. *Riley*, 39 Ind. 568; *Louisville etc. R. R. Co.* v. *Jones*, 83 Ala. 376; *Lapleine* v. *Morgan etc. S. S. Co.*, 40 La. Ann. 661; *Terre Haute etc. R. R. Co.* v. *Buck*, 96 Ind. 346; 49 Am. Rep. 168; *East Tenn. etc. R. R. Co.* v. *Lockhart*, 79 Ala. 315; *Allison* v. *Chicago etc. Ry. Co.*, 42 Iowa, 274; *Driess* v. *Frederich*, 73 Tex. 460; *Ohio etc. R. R. Co.* v. *Hecht*, 115 Ind. 443; *Louisville etc. R. R. Co.* v. *Northington*, 91 Tenn. 56. The only case opposed to these is *Pullman Palace Car Co.* v. *Barker*, 4 Col. 344, 34 Am. Rep. 92, which seems to have never been cited except with disapproval. Nor is the causal connection broken merely by reason of the fact, that the injured person contracts an illness which is not directly due to the original injury, but to the weakly state of bodily health produced by the sickness which followed the injury: *Beachamp* v. *Saginaw Min. Co.*, 50 Mich. 163; 45 Am. Rep. 30. The condition of the plaintiff's health may be proved in aggravation of the damages, without being specially alleged: *Heim* v. *McCaughan*, 32 Miss. 17; 66 Am. Dec. 588. Similar principles are applicable where the wrongful act raises a criminal liability: *Commonwealth* v. *Fox*, 7 Gray, 585. Nor is the defendant absolved, because the sickness which follows the infliction of a wound and thus produces death might have been avoided by care: *McAllister* v. *State*, 17 Ala. 434; 52 Am. Dec. 180, citing 1 Hale's Pleas of the Crown, 428; 1 Russell on Crimes, 529. In *Scheffer* v. *Railroad Co.*, 105 U. S. 249, however, an important limitation was put upon the liability for consequential damages incurred by one who inflicts bodily injuries upon another. There the plaintiff, by reason of the sufferings he endured as a result of a railroad accident, became insane, and committed suicide. It was held that the company was not liable to his representatives for his death.

16. MEASURE OF CARRIER'S LIABILITY FOR CAUSING SICKNESS UNDER DIFFERENT FORMS OF ACTION.—In *Murdock* v. *Boston etc. R. R. Co.*, 133 Mass. 15; 43 Am. Rep 480, it was held, on the authority of *Hobbs* v. *London etc. Ry. Co.*, L. R. 10 Q. B. 111, that when a passenger is wrongfully arrested by a carrier and detained in prison, where he becomes sick, this sickness cannot be proved as an element of damages in an action for breach of contract. As the English case has been virtually overruled in *MacMahon* v. *Field*, L. R. 7 Q. B. D. 591, and the form of action under such circumstances would, on general principles, seem to be immaterial (see section 2, *ante*), the distinction here taken by the Massachusetts court is probably not sustainable.

17. LIABILITY FOR CAUSING BODILY INCAPACITY BY SUPPLYING INTOXICATING LIQUORS.—By the statutes giving a right of action for injuries arising from the sale of intoxicating liquors, an act which at common law could not, with some rare exceptions noticed below, be made the basis of a claim for damages, has been converted into a tort, for which compensation may be obtained whenever the injury is the natural and probable consequence of reducing the plaintiff, or the person in whose name the plaintiff sues, to a state of intoxication: *Dunlap* v. *Wagner*, 85 Ind. 529; 44 Am. Rep. 42. At common law the only cases in which an action of this kind seems to have been sustained are one in which a slave was made drunk, and, being unable to take care of himself, died from exposure to inclement weather: *Harrison* v. *Berkley*, 1 Strob. 525; 47 Am. Dec. 578 (a decision evidently depending on the principle that the act complained of was an injury to property); and a late case in Pennsylvania, where an intoxicated person attached a piece of burning paper to the clothes of a companion also intoxicated, and the latter was severely burned. The proprietor of the saloon where the incident occurred was held liable on the ground that he owed a duty to all his customers to protect them against such assaults: *Rommel* v. *Schambacher*, 120 Pa. St. 579. For the decisions under the statutes, which can only be of interest to the citizens of states where the innovation in the law has been made, reference must be made to the reports of the several states. The following cases will show how they have been applied under various circumstances. The general tendency has been to give them a very liberal construction: *Belding* v. *Johnson*, 86 Ga. 177; *Schroeder* v. *Crawford*, 94 Ill. 357; 34 Am. Rep. 236; *Collier* v. *Early*, 54 Ind. 559; *Mulcahey* v. *Givens*, 115 Ind. 286; *Backes* v. *Dant*, 55 Ind. 181; *Krach* v. *Heilman*, 53 Ind. 517; *English* v.

Beard, 51 Ind. 489; *Schlosser* v. *State*, 55 Ind. 82; *Swinfin* v. *Lowry*, 37 Minn.
345; *King* v. *Haley*, 86 Ill. 106; 29 Am. Rep. 14; *Bertholf* v. *O'Reilly*, 74
N. Y. 509; 30 Am. Rep. 322; *Mulford* v. *Clewell*, 21 Ohio St. 191; *Duroy* v.
Blinn, 11 Ohio St. 331; *Barnaby* v. *Wood*, 50 Ind. 405: *Woolheather* v. *Risley*,
38 Iowa, 486; *Hemmens* v. *Bentley*, 32 Mich. 89; *Shugart* v. *Eagan*, 85 Ill.
56; 25 Am. Rep. 359; *Schmidt* v. *Mitchell*, 84 Ill. 195; 23 Am. Rep. 446;
Davis v. *Justice*, 31 Ohio St. 359; 57 Am. Rep. 514; see also note to *Shugart*
v. *Eagan*, 25 Am. Rep. 362.

18. CAUSING THE SPREAD OF DISEASE.—The principle is well-established
that the person, by whose fault animals suffering from a contagious disease
are placed in a position where they will, in the natural course of things,
communicate the disease to other animals, must respond in damages to the
owner of the latter, if he is on his part free from negligence. This principle
is frequently illustrated by the cases where there has been a sale of diseased
animals to a vendee, who is not informed of their condition, or to whom they
are represented as being sound: *Faris* v. *Lewis*, 2 B. Mon. 375; *Jeffrey* v.
Bigelow, 13 Wend. 518; 28 Am. Dec. 478; *Joy* v. *Bitzer*, 77 Iowa, 73; *Wintz*
v. *Morrison*, 17 Tex. 372; 67 Am. Dec. 658; *Fultz* v. *Wycoff*, 25 Ind. 321;
Routh v. *Caron*, 64 Tex. 289; *Mullett* v. *Mason*, L. R. 1 Com. P. 559; *Smith*
v. *Green*, L. R. 1 C. P. D. 92; *Knowles* v. *Nunns*, 14 L. T. R. 592; *Wheeler*
v. *Randall*, 48 Ill. 182; *Sherrod* v. *Langdon*, 21 Iowa, 518; *Broquet* v. *Tripp*,
36 Kan. 700; *Bradley* v. *Rea*, 14 Allen, 20; *Long* v. *Clapp*, 15 Neb. 417;
Packard v. *Slack*, 32 Vt. 9. A similar rule holds, where A's diseased sheep
trespass on B's field, and there infect B's sheep: *Barnum* v. *Vandusen*, 16
Conn. 200.

19. DETERIORATION IN THE VALUE OF ANIMALS may also be recovered
for on the same principles as those which have been above illustrated in the
case of injuries to human beings. Thus where a horse is injured by the defendant's wrongful act, and is rendered timid, unsound, and unkind, these
effects are proximate results of the wrongful act: *Whiteley* v. *China*, 61 Me.
199. So also is the non-thriving of cattle in consequence of the construction
of a railroad through their pasture: *Baltimore etc. R. R. Co.* v. *Thompson*, 10
Md. 76; and the depreciation of the value of horses caused by their exposure
to inclement weather through being turned out of a stable, for the use of
which the plaintiff had contracted with the defendant, the expulsion being
the act of a third person, to whom the defendant had let the same stable,
and of a servant of the defendant: *MacMahon* v. *Field*, L. R. 7 Q. B. D. 591.
Compare with this case *Lange* v. *Wagner*, 52 Md. 310; 36 Am. Rep. 380,
where an injunction prevented the erection of a stable, and it was held that
the plaintiff, in an action on the injunction bond, might recover for the consequent exposure of his cow to inclement weather, and the diminution of
her milk.

20. ANIMALS—PROXIMITY OF CAUSE AS DETERMINED BY THE HABITS,
INSTINCTS, ETC., OF.—The principle underlying the cases in which injuries
are caused by, or inflicted on, animals, is, that for the purpose of preventing
them from doing harm to themselves, or to the persons or property of other
citizens, they are kept under more or less complete control by their owners,
and therefore anyone through whose fault they escape from that control,
and are enabled to follow the promptings of their instincts and appetites,
is liable for all the consequences which naturally result up to the time when
they are again brought under control. Thus, if they are enabled to indulge
their propensity to stray, the person who gives them their freedom is an-

swerable, as a general rule, for the damage which they may do to themselves: *Rooth* v. *Wilson*, 1 Barn. & Ald. 59; *West* v. *Ward*, 77 Iowa, 323; 14 Am. St. Rep. 284; *Powell* v. *Salisbury*, 2 Younge & J. 391; *Gilman* v. *European etc. R. R. Co.*, 60 Me. 235; or to property, such as crops, or other things which they are capable of damaging, and not unlikely to damage: *Miller* v. *St. Louis etc. R. R. Co.*, 90 Mo. 389 (fire from locomotive destroyed the plaintiff's fences, and stock broke into his field); *Bridgers* v. *Dill*, 97 N. C. 222; *Henly* v. *Neal*, 2 Humph. 551; *Richardson* v. *Northrup*, 66 Barb. 85; *Keenan* v. *Cavanagh*, 44 Vt. 268 (trespassing cattle destroyed trees, and this was held an actionable injury, though not the kind which cattle are prone to do). On the other hand, in *Berry* v. *San Francisco etc. R. R. Co.*, 50 Cal. 435, where the defendant had torn down fences in making surveys, evidence that hogs had thereafter invaded the plaintiff's land and destroyed his crops was held inadmissible. This case is directly opposed to *Miller* v. *St. Louis etc. R. R. Co.*, 90 Mo. 389, cited above, and seems impossible to sustain on general principles. In *Singleton* v. *Williamson*, 7 Hurl. and N. 410, it was held that a person into whose field cattle have strayed, owing to a defect in fences which he was bound to keep in repair, cannot distrain them damage feasant in another field into which they have made their way by breaking through a hedge which he had kept in good repair. In such a case, his own negligence is the original cause of the mischief. So, too, a railroad company is liable if a horse gets upon the right of way where it should have been fenced, and, being frightened by a train, runs against a barbed-wire fence, either near the right of way (*Missouri Pac. Ry. Co.* v. *Eckel*, 49 Kan. 794), or crossing it: *Missouri Pac. Ry. Co.* v. *Gill*, 49 Kan. 441. A similar liability arises if the animal, under such circumstances, runs along the track and jumps upon a bridge: *Atchison etc. R. R. Co.* v. *Jones*, 20 Kan. 527. So, too, if a train is derailed by running into a drove of hogs which start so suddenly out of a clump of bushes, which the company negligently allows to remain close to the track, that the engineer has no time to stop the locomotive, injuries suffered by a passenger from the derailment are not too remote: *Eames* v. *Texas etc. R. R. Co.*, 63 Tex. 660. The propensity of animals to return to a place to which they have been accustomed was made the ground for recovery in *St. Louis etc. R. R. Co.* v. *McKinsey*, 78 Tex. 298, 22 Am. St. Rep. 54, where fences had been wrongfully destroyed, and the fact that the animals had been brought from a great distance was held to be no excuse.

21. CONSEQUENCES OF FRIGHTENING ANIMALS.—There are a large number of cases in the books illustrating the principle that a person who wantonly or negligently alarms an animal so that he is deprived of the guidance which he ordinarily receives from his own instincts and habits, or is taken out of the control of his owner, must respond in damages for such injuries as follow in regular and natural sequence from the original act. The extent to which such a liability is carried is well illustrated in *Harris* v. *Mobbs*, L. R. 3 Ex. D. 268. There the defendant negligently left a house-van on a highway, and the mare of the plaintiff's testator shied at it while passing, and galloped, kicking continually, about a hundred and fifty yards, when she got her leg over the shafts, fell, and kicked her driver as he rolled out of the cart. The plaintiff was held entitled to recover. Denman, J., referring to the contention of the defendant's counsel that the *causa proxima* of the injury was the kicking of the mare, which was not a necessary or a natural consequence of the running away, and that, although it might be true, in some sense, that the van and plough being there led to the accident, it was

not true that their being there was material to the accident or caused it, in such a sense, as to make the defendant responsible, said: "Looking at the undisputed facts in the case, I think it is clear that though the immediate cause of the accident was the kicking of the mare, still the unauthorized and dangerous appearance of the van and plough on the side of the highway was, within the meaning of the law, the proximate cause of the accident. . . . . Was the kicking which caused the death a natural and necessary consequence of the act complained of? I think, upon the whole, that it was. The van was there, and in fact frightened the deceased's mare so that she swerved to run away, and having got one wheel on the footpath kicked violently, and within a hundred and fifty yards fell, and injured the deceased so that he died. The whole transaction is within a few seconds, and originates in the fright of the mare caused by the van. . . . . It cannot be laid down as the right of the defendant to assume that no nervous or runaway or kicking horse would come along the highway. It is only in the case of horses liable to be frightened that any danger exists; and where a horse has once been frightened by a dangerous apparition, unlawfully placed on the highway, running away and kicking can hardly be considered to be unusual or unnatural consequences of the fright." If a team is frightened by a negligent collision with a vehicle it is attached to, and runs away, and throws the occupant out, fatally injuring him, the person responsible for the collision may be held in a civil or criminal action: Leame v. Bray, 3 East, 593; Belk v. People, 125 Ill. 584. So where a runaway horse comes into collision with another horse, or with a traveler on the highway, the person who caused the runaway is liable for the injury: McDonald v. Snelling, 14 Allen, 290; 92 Am. Dec. 768; Billman v. Indianapolis etc. R. R. Co., 76 Ind. 166; 40 Am. Rep. 230; Lee v. Union R. R. Co., 12 R. I. 383; 34 Am. Rep. 668; Wasmer v. Delaware etc. R. R. Co., 80 N. Y. 212; 36 Am. Rep. 608; Childress v. Yourie, Meigs, 561; Forney v. Geldmacher, 75 Mo. 113; 42 Am. Rep. 388; Pennsylvania R. R. Co. v. Barnett, 59 Pa. St. 259; 98 Am. Dec. 346; Gibbon v. Pepper, 2 Salk. 637. In such a case, the act of the driver in trying to control the horse does not break the causal connection between the original act and the injury: Lowery v. Manhattan R. R. Co., 99 N. Y. 158; 52 Am. Rep. 12; Sherman v. Favour, 1 Allen, 191; nor is the connection broken by the fact that the runaway team collides with a second team, which thereupon runs away, and does the damage complained of: Griggs v. Fleckenstein, 14 Minn. 81; 100 Am. Rep. 199.

In Lynch v. Northern Pac. R. R. Co., 84 Wis. 348, there was held to be no liability where a train frightened a horse on a highway which ran nearly parallel to the track, but finally approached and crossed it, and the horse, having reached the crossing before the train, leaped over a cattle-guard, and, running along the track, became entangled in a bridge. This case is clearly distinguishable from those cited in the preceding subdivision, in which the failure to maintain a fence enabled the frightened animals to get on the right of way.

In Sneesby v. Lancashire etc. Ry. Co., L. R. 9 Q. B. 263, the negligence of the defendant's servants caused some cattle to break away from the drovers at a crossing. They ran down a neighboring road, made their way into an orchard, and thence broke through to a hedge on to the defendants' track, where they were run over by a train. It was held that the defendant was liable for the loss of the cattle. Blackburn, J., saying that he thought the case might be treated as if the cattle had been killed on another line of railway instead of the defendants', said: "In a case like the present this much is clear, that, so long as the want of control over the cattle remains without any fault of the owner, the *causa proxima* (of the loss) is that which caused the escape, for the consequences of which he who caused the escape is responsible. . . . . It is the most natural consequence of cattle being frightened that they go galloping about and get into a dangerous position, and, being in the neighborhood of railways, should get on the line and be run over by a passing train, whether that of the defendants or not is immaterial. When once it is established that the cattle were driven out of the control of the plaintiff by the defendants' negligence, and that the control could not be recovered until they were killed, which was the natural consequence of their being uncontrolled, the liability of the defendants is beyond dispute."

In *West Mahanoy Township* v. *Watson,* 116 Pa. St. 344, 2 Am. St. Rep. 604, a case which seems to involve precisely the same principle, the original tort feasor was held not liable. There a team was frightened by an ash-heap on a highway and ran away. Making their way on to a railroad track the horses were struck by a train, and turning round continued their flight in the opposite direction until they were run over by another train. The court based its decision upon the two facts, that the course of the team was entirely changed by the stroke received from the first engine, and that the actual and immediate cause of the destruction of the plaintiff's property was its collision with the second engine. The former fact was held to be an intervening cause sufficient to break the connection. The influence of the former rulings of the court on the subject of the spread of fires is distinctly traceable in this decision, and, indeed, these are the only authorities cited. No allusion was made to the precedents in England and the other states which have been controlled by the general principle that, as Mr. Justice Blackburn remarked in the passage above quoted, "it is the most natural consequence of cattle being frightened that they go galloping about and get into a dangerous position." It is not easy to see why the chance stroke of the first engine should interrupt the chain of causation, any more than a turn in the road or any kind of obstruction which compelled or induced them to change their course. On the whole we think the soundness of this case is fairly open to question.

In *Gilbertson* v. *Richardson,* 5 Com. B. 502, A's carriage was driven against the wheel of B's chaise. C, an occupant of the chaise, was thrown by the shock of the collision against the dashboard of the chaise, which fell on the horse's back and caused him to kick and damage the chaise. *Held,* That B might recover in trespass for the whole injury as an immediate consequence of the act, Maule, J., remarking that "the effect of the collision was to induce that which the horse might be expected to do." This case is an excellent illustration of the general rule already referred to, that the liability of the defendant depends rather upon the general character of the act than upon the particular form in which the injury finally results.

For the liability of towns and cities for frightening teams by defects in highways, see cases cited in section 25, *post.*

22. ATTACKS BY ANIMALS ON HUMAN BEINGS OR OTHER ANIMALS.—The cases in which the owners of vicious or dangerous animals are held liable for injuries inflicted by them have been treated in various notes in this series: See especially the note to *Knowles* v. *Mulder,* 16 Am. St. Rep. 631. The cases where the owners have been held to answer on the simple principle that the attack was the ordinary consequence of the animal's being

allowed to escape from control are fewer in number, but rest on the principle that some attacks are natural and some are not. Thus one who turns a horse loose in a highway where he can kick another horse is liable if an injury results from his negligence: *Barnes* v. *Chapin,* 4 Allen, 444; 81 Am. Dec. 710; *Lee* v. *Riley,* 18 Com. B., N. S., 722; *Ellis* v. *Loftus Iron Co.,* L. R. 10 Com. B. 10; but it is held not to be an ordinary consequence of a horse's escape from control that he should kick a human being: *Cox* v. *Burbidge,* 13 Com. P., N. S., 430. Whether the goring of horses by a bull making his way, through the defendant's negligence, into their pasture, is a question for the jury: *Saxton* v. *Bacon,* 31 Vt. 540.

23. INJURIES ARISING FROM THE PROPENSITY OF ANIMALS TO SEEK THEIR FOOD WHEREVER OBTAINABLE.—Where the defendant was bound to maintain a fence, and a breach was negligently made therein by one who had purchased the right to fell timber on the land, the defendant was held liable for the loss of cows which strayed through the fence and ate the poisonous leaves of a yew-tree: *Lawrence* v. *Jenkins,* L. R. 8 Q. B. 274. So also the defendant is liable if he kills dogs by attracting them into traps by the scent of meat put therein as a bait for vermin: *Townsend* v. *Wathen,* 9 East, 277; or allows a wire fence to decay so that portions thereof fall on an adjoining field, and are swallowed, with fatal results, by cattle: *Firth* v. *Bowling Iron Co.,* L. R. 3 C. P. D. 254.

24. LIABILITY FOR INJURIES RECEIVED BY CHILDREN.—In *Mangan* v. *Atterton,* 1 L. R. Ex. 239, the defendant was held not liable for leaving a machine with dangerous cog-wheels unguarded in a public place, the consequence being that two children set it in motion, and one was injured by crushing his hand in the cogs. But this case was overruled in *Clark* v. *Chambers,* L. R. 3 Q. B. D. 327; and the principle now generally accepted, where children are concerned, is that, to use the words of an earlier English case—*Lynch* v. *Nurdin,* 1 Q. B. 29—where a person leaves a dangerous article where he "knows it to be extremely probable that it will be unjustifiably set in motion to the injury of another, the injured person may recover damages against the former." As it was tersely put in *Binford* v. *Johnston,* 82 Ind. 426; 42 Am. Rep. 508: "One who deals with children must anticipate the ordinary behavior of children." This rule has been applied to charge with liability one who puts in a position, where children are likely to be attracted by them for the purposes of play, such articles as a swing-gate: *Bire* v. *Gardiner,* 19 Conn. 507; 50 Am. Dec. 261; a truck loaded with iron: *Lane* v. *Atlantic Works,* 111 Mass. 138; a signal torpedo: *Harriman* v. *Pittsburg etc. Ry. Co.,* 45 Ohio St. 11; 4 Am. St. Rep. 507 (in this case the children had implied permission to pass along the railroad track); a detonator: *Powers* v. *Harlow,* 53 Mich. 507; 51 Am. Rep. 154 (in this case also the children were technically trespassers, but accustomed to play in the place where the detonator was found); a railroad turntable: *Gulf etc. Ry. Co.* v. *McWhirter,* 77 Tex. 357; 19 Am. St. Rep. 755; *Keffe* v. *Milwaukee etc. Ry Co.,* 21 Minn. 207; 18 Am. Rep. 393; *Koons* v. *St. Louis etc. Ry. Co.,* 65 Mo. 592; *Nagel* v. *Missouri Pac. Ry. Co.,* 75 Mo. 653; 42 Am. Rep. 418; *Railroad Co.* v. *Stout,* 17 Wall. 657. The general rule, however, is subject to the limitation that the object which injures the child must be such as is likely to produce that result. Thus, where a child, in trying to clamber on to a heavy counter left on a broad sidewalk out of the ordinary line of travel, pulled it down on himself, it was held that the city was not liable for the injuries received: *Chicago* v. *Starr,* 42 Ill. 174; 89 Am. Dec. 422.

Nor is the principle that "one who deals with children must anticipate ordinary behavior of children" confined to cases like the above. Thus, in *Drake* v. *Kiely*, 93 Pa. St. 492, it was held that a railroad company was liable for the sickness of a boy two years old who was forcibly put on board a freight-train by the brakeman, and, after being carried five miles against his will, was allowed to leave the train, and was so alarmed at his situation that he ran nearly all the way home. So also it has been held that where a child passenger has been carried past her destination, she may recover damages for fright and all the consequences of trying to regain the station by walking along the track: *East Tennessee etc. R. R. Co.* v. *Lockhart*, 79 Ala. 315.

25. DEFECT IN HIGHWAY, WHEN DEEMED PROXIMATE CAUSE OF INJURY TO TRAVELER.—See generally note to *Morse* v. *Town of Richmoud*, 98 Am. Dec. 608–612. For later cases see notes to *Horstick* v. *Dunkle*, 27 Am. St. Rep. 685; *North M. Tp.* v. *Arnold*, 4 Am. St. Rep. 650; *Schaeffer* v. *Jackson Tp.*, 30 Am. St. Rep. 792; *Pratt* v. *Weymouth*, 9 Am. St. Rep. 691; *Mahogany* v. *Ward*, 27 Am. St. Rep. 753; *Herr* v. *Lebanon*, 34 Am. St. Rep. 603; *Jackson* v. *Wagner*, 14 Am. St. Rep. 833; *Plymouth* v. *Graver*, 11 Am. St. Rep. 867; *Harris* v. *Clinton*, 8 Am. St. Rep. 842; *Burrell Tp.* v. *Uncapher*, 2 Am. St. Rep. 664; *Chamberlain* v. *Oshkosh, post*, 923; *Joliet* v. *Shufeld, ante* 453. The decisions in the different states are reviewed by Mr. Justice Earl in *Ring* v. *City of Cohoes*, 77 N. Y. 83; 33 Am. Rep. 574, and the general principles upon which the liability of municipalities depends are expounded with great clearness. The learned judge shows that the rule applied by those courts, which are not controlled by statutory provisions may be formulated thus: "When two causes combine to produce an injury to a traveler on a highway, both of which are in their nature proximate, the one being a culpable defect in the highway and the other some occurrence for which neither party is responsible —the municipality is liable, provided the injury would not have happened but for such defect." The Massachusetts doctrine, which imposes a more qualified description of liability, is admitted to be irreconcilable with general principles of law, and to depend entirely upon provisions of the highway statutes: *McDonald* v. *Snelling*, 14 Allen, 290; 92 Am. Dec. 768. The manner in which the stricter and the more qualified standards of responsibility have been applied under the various combinations of facts will be readily understood by referring to the cases cited in the notes above mentioned. A detailed examination of the subject scarcely falls within the limits of the present note.

26. INTERVENING CAUSES—IRRESPONSIBLE AGENCIES—(a) *Generally.*—In the foregoing sections a large number of cases have been cited which tend to establish the proposition that, so long as the intervention of an intelligent will is not perceptible in a series of causes and effects, the person who put the first of the causes in operation is to be held legally responsible for any injury to another person which ultimately results. Logically, only one exception to this rule should be recognized, viz: the case in which that abnormal exhibition of physical energy which is known as an act of God is interposed between the original act and the final wrong. To the scientist the so-called act of God is a phenomenon not less inevitably foreordained to occur than the more common every-day events which the play of natural forces presents to the observation of mankind. But the law, taking as its standard the ordinary ideas of the average member of the community as to such matters, very properly declares that such extraordinary phenomena are

not included among those natural and 'probable consequences of an act, for which the doer of the act must answer.

At the same time it must be admitted, that some courts assume in their rulings that the liability of a wrongdoer stops far short of this point, and have rendered decisions which can only be justified on the hypothesis that "natural and probable" are to be regarded as synonymous with "usual," or "more likely than not to happen under the circumstances." This doctrine is especially noticeable in some of the cases dealing with the spread of fires, but it has been applied consistently in other connections also by the courts of several states. It seems to us that the inevitable result of such a doctrine must be to render it virtually impossible to refer the liability of wrongdoers to any fixed principles, and to make the "personal equation" of judges and jurors the controlling factor in each case.

To show the extent to which these two doctrines clash with one another it will be sufficient to supplement the cases already given with three others. In *South Side Pass. Ry. Co.* v. *Trich,* 117 Pa. St. 390, 2 Am. St. Rep. 672, the defendant was held not liable for an injury to one who, while getting on a car, was thrown off by the sudden starting of the horses, and, after falling safely on his feet, was run over by a runaway team. Might it not be fairly argued that, in such a case, the possibility that a team might pass just at that moment was sufficiently strong to raise a question for the jury at least? The accident might have happened just as readily if the team had been under control, and the driver, assuming that the passenger was already safely mounted on the car, had taken no measures to meet the emergency. In *Ransier* v. *Minneapolis etc. R. R. Co.*, 32 Minn. 331, a defective brake caused a train to separate, and the after section subsequently ran into the forward part, and killed the conductor who was in the caboose, knowing nothing of what had happened. It was held that the event was one which, under the circumstances, was not unlikely to happen, and that a verdict against the company could not be disturbed. That a defective brake should cause a train to separate is certainly at least as uncommon an occurrence as that a passenger suddenly thrown off a street-car would be run over by a passing team. Both cases seem to fall under the rule already referred to that if mischief of some sort is likely to result from the defendant's act it is not necessary that the precise form of it should not have been foreseen. *Sharp* v. *Powell,* L. R. 7 Com. P. 253, the facts of which have been already stated (section 8), is a still stronger case, for if a person cannot be charged with a knowledge of such an ordinary result of the operation of physical laws as that water which is set flowing in a street during the prevalence of a hard frost will be likely to accumulate somewhere and harden into ice, it is difficult to see upon what principle the boundary line between excusable and nonexcusable ignorance in such matters is to be drawn. In that case, it is true, the formation of the dangerous sheet of ice happened in a somewhat unexpected fashion; but if there is one rule more firmly established than another in regard to this perplexing subject, it is that a wrongdoer is not to be excused merely because the final injury comes in a shape which would beforehand have seemed somewhat unlikely: Sec. 3 (*d*), *ante.* The court seems to have been principally influenced by the fact that the defendant's servant was not aware of the existence of the obstruction in the grating which caused the mischief, and had no reasonable means of acquiring the necessary knowledge. But this qualification of responsibility is quite opposed to the general current of authority in this country, as will be seen from the cases cited in the section of this note just referred to.

(b) *Accident.*—Nor is it easy to see how such decisions as these just referred to can be reconciled with that line of cases in which it has been held
that, even if an event of the unusual kind which is commonly termed accident concurs with the negligence of the defendant to produce the injury, he is
still liable. A leading case on this point is *The Lords Bailiff-Jurats of Romney
Marsh* v. *Corporation of Trinity House*, L. R. 5 Ex. 204; 7 Ex. 247; Thompson
on Negligence, 1063. There the defendant's ship, owing to the negligence of
the crew, foundered on a sandbank, and, becoming unmanageable, was driven
by a strong wind and a flool tide upon the seawall of the plaintiffs. It was
held that the interposition of the unusual natural forces which caused the
injury did not absolve the defendant. To the same effect see *Wakeman* v.
Robinson, 1 Bing. 213; *Austin* v. *New Jersey Steamboat Co.*, 43 N. Y. 75; 3
Am. Rep. 663; *The George and Richard*, L. R. 3 Adm. 466. In *Deming*
v. *Merchants' Cotton Press Co.*, 90 Tenn. 306; it was held that if a carrier
delays the forwarding of goods, which are subsequently lost by a fire
not due to his negligence, is liable, though there is a fire clause exemption in the bill of lading; but under similar circumstances, in *Hoadley* v.
Northern Transp. Co., 115 Mass. 304, 15 Am. Rep. 106, the carrier was absolved. And it should be noticed that the conflict of authority upon which
we have been commenting is traceable, where an intervening accident is in
terms alleged: *Schaeffer* v. *Jackson Tp.*, 150 Pa. St. 145; 30 Am. St. Rep.
792; *McGrew* v. *Stone*, 53 Pa. St. 436; *Lewis* v. *Flint etc. Ry. Co.*, 54 Mich.
55; 52 Am. Rep. 790. In the last case there was held to be no liability
where the plaintiff was carried past a station at night, and, being put off,
undertook to find his way to the road, but, owing to a "visual deception,"
mistook his distance from a cattle-guard, and fell into it. But here it might
be fairly said that the plaintiff undertook the responsibility for all that
occurred after leaving the train, and the defendant to be not liable for that
reason.

(c) *Act of God, When Deemed Proximate Cause of Injury.*—There is no dispute as to the proposition that, if the defendant is not in fault in his management of the thing which causes an injury, it is a complete defense that
such injury resulted from the act of God, or some extraordinary operation
of natural forces amounting to *vis major: Blyth* v. *Birmingham W. W. Co.*,
11 Ex. 781 (overflow caused by the bursting of water-pipes in an exceptionally severe frost); *Blythe* v. *Denver etc. Ry. Co.*, 15 Col. 333; 22 Am. St.
Rep. 403 (railway car upset by tornado and ignited by the fire in the stove);
Baltimore etc. R. R. Co. v. *Sulphur Springs Dist.*, 96 Pa. St. 65; 42 Am. Rep.
529 (culvert burst by flood); *Flori* v. *City of St. Louis*, 69 Mo. 341; 33 Am.
Rep. 504 (building overthrown by tempest and causing injury); *Knoll* v.
Light, 76 Pa. St. 268 (growth of grass in millpond caused water to back
up and overflow land above). For other cases of flooding, *Borchardt* v.
Wausau Boom Co., 54 Wis. 107; 41 Am. Rep. 12; *Nichols* v. *Marshland*, L.
R. 2 Ex. D. 1; *Nitro-Phosphate etc. Co.* v. *London etc. Docks*, L. R. 9 Ch. Div.
503, may be consulted. Similar rules are applied where there is irresistible
force used by a body of soldiers belonging to the United States Army: *Watkins*
v. *Roberts*, 28 Ind. 167 (bailee excused for not returning hired property); or
where a great public calamity has occurred, such as the Chicago fire: *Michigan
Cent. R. R. Co.* v. *Burrows*, 33 Mich. 5, or the Johnstown flood: *Long* v. *Pennsylvania R. R. Co.*, 147 Pa. St. 343; 30 Am. St. Rep. 732, and note. See also
note to *Chicago etc. Ry. Co.* v. *Sawyer*, 18 Am. Rep. 618–621.

But in regard to cases in which there has been negligence also on the part
of the defendant, a notable conflict of opinion exists between the courts.

The matter has been discussed almost entirely in connection with the con. tract of carriage, and where the negligence consists merely in a delay in the forwarding of the goods, the larger number of authorities sustain the prin. ciple that the carrier cannot be held liable, if the goods thus delayed are de. stroyed by the act of God, though but for the delay they would have reached a place of safety, the ground assigned being that the delay becomes a remote cause of the loss, when a calamity which could not have been anticipated intervenes: *Morrison* v. *Davis*, 20 Pa. St. 171; 57 Am. Dec. 695; *Denny* v. *New York Cent. Ry. Co.*, 13 Gray, 48; 74 Am. Dec. 645; *McClary* v. *Sioux City etc. R. R. Co.*, 3 Neb. 44; 19 Am. Rep. 631; *Michigan Cent. R. R. Co.* v. *Burrows*, 33 Mich. 5; *Daniels* v. *Ballentine*, 23 Ohio St. 532; 13 Am. Rep. 264; *Clark* v. *Pacific R. R. Co.*, 39 Mo. 184; 90 Am. Dec. 456; *Railroad Co.* v. *Reeves*, 10 Wall. 176.

On the other hand some cases hold that, under such circumstances, the carrier is liable: *Michaels* v. *New York Cent. R. R. Co.*, 30 N. Y. 564; 86 Am. Dec. 415; *Read* v. *Spaulding*, 30 N. Y. 630; 86 Am. Dec. 426; *Merritt* v. *Earle*, 29 N. Y. 115; 86 Am. Dec. 292; *Bostwick* v. *Baltimore etc. R. R. Co.*, 45 N. Y. 712; *Condict* v. *Grand Trunk R. R. Co.*, 54 N. Y. 500; *Pruitt* v. *Hannibal etc. R. R. Co.*, 62 Mo. 527; *Rodgers* v. *Central Pac. R. R. Co.*, 67 Cal. 607; *McGraw* v. *Baltimore etc. R. R. Co.*, 18 W. Va. 361; 41 Am. Rep. 696. These decisions are based upon the supposition that the rule which disables a carrier from excusing himself for a loss by the plea of an act of God applies to cases of negligence consisting merely in delay. But it can scarcely be said that the authorities relied on justify any larger doctrine, than that such a plea will not avail, if the carrier has been guilty of negli- gence or misconduct in the active duties of forwarding the goods—as by furnishing defective instrumentalities for that purpose, or placing the goods in a position in which they are exposed to some ascertainable danger—or if the external agency which causes the loss is only partially due to the act of God. See especially *Smith* v. *Shephard* (cited in Abbott on Shipping, part 3, chapter 4, sec. 1, and summarized in *Michaels* v. *New York Cent. R. R. Co.*, 30 N. Y. 564; 86 Am. Dec. 415); *Trent Navigation Co.* v. *Wood*, 3 Esp. 127; *McArthur* v. *Sears*, 21 Wend. 190; *Backhouse* v. *Sneed*, 1 Murph. 173. See also the later case of *New Brunswick S. Co.* v. *Tiers*, 24 N. J. L. 697; 64 Am. Dec. 394. But it is going very far to hold a carrier liable where his only fault consists in leaving the goods in a depot or on a siding for an undue period; for such a position is ordinarily secure, and remains so until the act of God supervenes. The acceptance of such a principle involves the rather remarkable result that the carrier's measure of liability for various parcels of goods destroyed at the same place by the same act of God may depend upon the length of time each parcel has been there. Cases like *Hand* v. *Brynes*, 4 Whart. 204, 33 Am. Dec. 54, and *Davis* v. *Garret*, 6 Bing. 716, though also relied on by the New York court, are distinguishable as being cases of deviation, which makes a carrier absolutely liable, as for a conversion: *Railroad Co.* v. *O'Donnell*, 49 Ohio St. 489; 34 Am. St. Rep. 579. (See sec. 8, *ante*.) *Williams* v. *Grant*, 1 Conn. 492, 7 Am. Rep. 235, where the master of a ship took no pilot in a dangerous channel, may be rested on similar grounds, as such conduct amounted to a positive misfeasance. *Bell* v. *Reed*, 4 Binn. 127, 5 Am. Dec. 398, and *Hart* v. *Allen*, 2 Watts, 114, depend on an analogous principle, viz: that a carrier has no defense, where a loss is partly caused by the unseaworthiness of his ship. In all these cases the essence of the decisions is that the danger was increased before any act of God supervened, and they are obviously not a proper parallel to cases of negligent delay, which does not increase the danger in any way. On the whole, therefore, we venture to think that the New York doctrine is not warranted by the authorities cited in its support, and can only be justified, if at all, by considerations of public policy.

The above controversy does not appear to have come up in England, but it may be noticed that, after *Rylands* v. *Fletcher*, L. R. 3 H. L. Cas. 330, had made a person who collects water in a reservoir absolutely liable for damages caused by its escape, thus creating an accountability somewhat resembling that of a carrier, it was held in *Nichols* v. *Marsland*, L. R. 2 Ex. D. 1, that the defendant was nevertheless excused if the bursting of the reservoir was caused by an act of God.

Of course negligence which occurs after the act of God has operated is the proximate cause of any damage that may ensue, as where a locomotive engineer might, by observing the high-water marks of a flood, have determined whether to proceed with a train, and the train was derailed at a place where the flood had made the track unsafe: *Ellet* v. *St. Louis etc. Ry. Co.*, 76 Mo. 518. Compare *Lambkin* v. *South-Eastern Ry. Co.*, L. R. 5 App. C. 352, involving similar facts, and assuming the rule to be as stated above.

27. RESPONSIBLE AGENCIES, INTERVENTION OF.—In the foregoing subdivisions we have discussed the operation of natural laws in the case of inorganic matter, of animals, and of children. We have now to consider the principles upon which the responsibility of human beings who have arrived at years of discretion, and are therefore presumed by the law to possess an average measure of intelligence and prudence, as well as fully developed reasoning powers, is determined. It will be observed, in the first place, that the law takes notice of the fact that men are under the domination of various feelings, instincts, and impulses, which they have in common with the lower animals, and tort-feasors are charged with a knowledge that, if their wrongful act operates upon any of those feelings, instincts, or impulses in another person, he will probably pursue a certain course of conduct. They are also charged with a knowledge of the ordinary influence of certain classes of acts upon the behavior of men living in a civilized country, and occupying with regard to one another certain relations for business or other social purposes; or, in other words, with the knowledge of the existence of those acquired feelings, instincts, and impulses, which distinguish savages from the members of highly organized communities. But the extent to which the law recognizes the operation either of the natural or the artificial qualities of men, as a consequence of a wrongful act, can scarcely be regarded as settled by the decided cases. The principal source of the uncertainty is, that persons of full age are presumed to possess the power of distinguishing right from wrong, and the courts are apparently divided between a reluctance to base the responsibility of a tort-feasor upon the hypothesis that another person will be influenced by a tort to commit a wrong, and the consciousness that in actual every-day life such a result frequently follows. The whole position cannot be better summed up than in the following words of one of the greatest of modern English judges, Lord Justice Brett, who thus comments upon the case of *Lumley* v. *Gye*, 2 El. & B. 216: "The decision of the majority of the court will be seen, on a careful consideration of their judgments, to have been founded on two chains of reasoning. First, that wherever a man does an act which in law and in fact is a wrongful act, and such an act may, as a natural and probable consequence, produce injury to another, and which in the particular case does produce injury, an action on the case will lie. This is the proposition to be

deduced from the case of *Ashby* v. *White*, Ld. Raym. 938; 1 Smith L. C. 464. If these conditions are satisfied, the action does not the less lie because the natural and probable consequence of the act complained of is an act done by a third person; or, because such act so done by the third person is a breach of duty or contract by him, or an act illegal on his part, or an act otherwise imposing an actionable liability on him. It has been said that the law implies that the act of the third party, being one which he has free will and power to do or not to do, is his own willful act, and therefore is not the natural or probable result of the defendant's act. In many cases that may be so, but, if the law is so to imply in every case, it will be an implication contrary to manifest truth and fact. It has been said that, if the act of the third person is a breach of duty or contract by him, or is an act which it is illegal for him to do, the law will not recognize that it is a natural or probable consequence of the defendant's act. Again, if that were so held in all cases, the law would in some refuse to recognize what is manifestly true in fact": *Bowen* v. *Hall*, L. R. 6 Q. B. D. 333. The cases which will be referred to in the following sections exhibit in a very striking light the unsatisfactory practical results of the conflict of judicial opinion on this vexed question. Upon the whole, it may be said that the American judges have been decidedly more cautious than their English brethren in applying the test of natural and probable consequences to ascertain the liability of a *tortfeasor* for the subsequent wrongful act of another.

28. RESPONSIBLE AGENCIES, INTERVENTION OF—GENERAL PRINCIPLES.—It is universally agreed that the mere fact that the intervention of a responsible human being can be traced between the defendant's wrongful act and the injury complained of will not absolve him: *Hayes* v. *Hyde Park*, 153 Mass. 514; *Quigley* v. *Delaware Canal*, 142 Pa. St. 388; 24 Am. St. Rep. 504; *Weick* v. *Lander*, 75 Ill. 93; *Binford* v. *Johnston*, 82 Ind. 426; 42 Am. Rep. 508; *Stover* v. *Bluehill*, 51 Me. 439; *State* v. *Rankin*, 3 S. C. 438; 16 Am. Rep. 737; *Hughes* v. *MacDonough*, 43 N. J. L. 459; 39 Am. Rep. 603; *McDonald* v. *Snelling*, 14 Allen, 292; 92 Am. Dec. 768; *Powell* v. *Deveney*, 3 Cush. 300; 50 Am. Dec. 738; *Mahogany* v. *Ward*, 16 R. I. 479; 27 Am. St. Rep. 753; *Congreve* v. *Morgan*, 18 N. Y. 84; 72 Am. Dec. 495; *Fitzjohn* v. *Mackender*, 9 Com. B., N. S., 505; Wharton on Negligence, 138–141; Thompson on Negligence, 1089. The intervention must be of such a character that without its having occurred the injury complained of would, in all likelihood, not have happened: *Mire* v. *East Louisiana R. R. Co.*, 42 La. Ann. 385. Such a superseding cause, therefore, cannot be predicated of acts which do not affect the final result, although they cause a temporary diversion, and somewhat retard its occurrence: *Collins* v. *Middle Level Commrs.*, L. R. 4 Com. P. 279. Nor where the subsequent act is merely induced, not caused, by the prior one, as in *Marqueze* v. *Southeimer*, 59 Miss. 430, where it was held that one who had wrongfully attached the plaintiff's property was not liable for the subsequent levying of executions on that property by judgment creditors. The court said: "That another independent agent, acting on his own responsibility, does something, because one has done a particular thing does not make such a one responsible for the act of the other. They are independent actors, and each is answerable for his own acts, because of the want of causal connection between them."

One of the most instructive cases on the subject of intervening agencies is *Clark* v. *Chambers*, L. R. 3 Q. B. D. 327. There the defendant had placed on a private road an unlawful and dangerous obstruction, consisting of a barrier of iron hurdles armed with spikes, commonly called *chevaux-de-frise*, and one of these was removed and placed on the footpath near a gap in the middle of the barrier, which was ordinarily left open for vehicles. The plaintiff, who was lawfully using the road on a dark night, passed through the gap, and, in turning to get on to the footpath, came into collision with one of the spikes of the hurdle which had been moved, and put his eye out. The court adopted the theory of the plaintiff's counsel, that "as the act of the defendant in placing a dangerous instrument on the road had been the primary cause of the evil, by affording the occasion for its being removed, and thus causing the injury to the plaintiff, he was responsible in law for the consequences," and the case, taking it as being an authority merely for the principles upon which it was decided, really belongs to that numerous class which sustain the doctrine that an intermediate act, unless amounting to an independent and willful misfeasance, is entirely disregarded in determining the liability for an injury caused by carelessly dealing with an inherently dangerous article. Here there was at most negligence on the part of the person who moved the hurdle, for he was, as was admitted, acting within his rights in clearing away an unlawful obstruction. Assuming such negligence, the case seems to bear some analogy to another class of cases, viz: those in which the subsequent negligence of a third person will not purge the guilt of the original negligence, if it merely operates upon a dangerous condition of things, for which the defendant is primarily responsible: See sec. 32, *post*.

29. TEST OF NATURAL AND PROBABLE CONSEQUENCE IN CASES OF RE-SPONSIBLE INTERVENTION.—In *Clark* v. *Chambers*, L. R. 3 Q. B. D. 327, Chief Justice Cockburn thought the circumstances would also stand the test of natural and probable consequence, and that the decision might be placed upon that ground as well. "A man who unlawfully places an obstruction across either a public or private way may anticipate the removal of the obstruction by some one entitled to use the way, as a thing likely to happen; and if this should be done, the probability is that the obstruction so removed will, instead of being carried away altogether, be placed somewhere near; thus, if the obstruction be in the carriageway, it will very likely be placed, as was the case here, in the footpath." If we accept as correct the comprehensive doctrine propounded by Lord Justice Brett (see sec. 27, *ante*), there should clearly be no difficulty about the conclusion here drawn from the circumstances under review. But it is extremely difficult, if not impossible, to formulate any rule which will enable us to apply the test with precision to the infinite variations of facts which may occur. If it were applied with something like logical consistency by the courts, we should arrive at this doctrine: That the act of a responsible agent is not a natural and probable consequence, and therefore breaks the causal connection, whenever it tends to produce an injury of a character different from that which the original tort-feasor must, according to the usual theory of accountability, be deemed to have contemplated. In other words, the hypothetical intention, which, by a legal fiction, he entertains at the time the first act is done, should always be considered in determining whether the subsequent act is to be treated as furthering or disappointing his presumed purpose. This principle is regularly applied in all cases where the intervening act is merely negligent (see sec. 32), but, as will be seen from the cases cited in the following paragraph, the courts, at least in this country, refuse to hold a tort-feasor liable for the results of a subsequent act which is willfully wrong, unless

that act was actually intended by him. Presumed intention is not enough, whatever the character of the act.

30. INTERVENTION OF WILLFUL TORTS.—A very eminent judge thus states the principle governing these cases: "Wrongful acts of independent third persons (not actually intended by the defendant), are not regarded by the law as natural consequences of his wrong, and he is not bound to anticipate the general probability of such acts, any more than a particular act by this or that individual": *Burt* v. *Advertiser etc. Co.*, 154 Mass. 238 (per Holmes, J.). This principle is illustrated in *Barton* v. *Pepin Co. etc. Soc.*, 83 Wis. 19; *Burton* v. *Pinkerton*, L. R. 2 Ex. 340; *Washington* v. *Baltimore etc. R. R. Co.*, 17 W. Va. 190; *Cuff* v. *Newark etc. R. R. Co.*, 35 N. J. L. 17; 10 Am. Rep. 205; *Bosworth* v. *Brand*, 1 Dana, 377; *Royston* v. *Illinois Cent. R. R. Co.*, 67 Miss. 376; *Hullinger* v. *Worrell*, 83 Ill. 220; *Congreve* v. *Morgan*, 18 N. Y. 84; 72 Am. Dec. 495; *Cahill* v. *Dawson*, 3 Com. B., N. S., 106; *Burrows* v. *Wright*, 1 East, 615; *Alexander* v. *Newcastle*, 115 Ind. 51; *Blagrave* v. *Bristol W. W. Co.*, 1 Hurl. & N. 369; *Marsden* v. *Assurance Co.*, 1 Com. B. 240; *White* v. *Conly*, 14 Lea, 51; 52 Am. Rep. 154, *Clark* v. *Chambers*, L. R. 3 Q. B. D. 327, was cited in *Binford* v. *Johnston*, 82 Ind. 426; 42 Am. Rep. 508, as sustaining the opposite doctrine, but the statement of that case given above shows that no such point was involved. *Heney* v. *Dennis*, 93 Ind. 452, 47 Am. Rep. 378, goes further than any case we have found in extending a defendant's liability in this direction. There the defendant left a barrel of fish-brine in the street of a town, and a passerby noticing that a cow (lawfully running at large), had her head in the barrel trying to get at the liquid, tried to drive her away, and finding he could not succeed in this he poured out the brine, and left the spot. The cow then licked up from the ground as much of the brine as she could, and died from the effects. The defendant was held liable, the court thinking the case fell within the principle of *Binford* v. *Johnston*, 82 Ind. 426; 42 Am. Rep. 508. The latter, however, was merely a case of supplying a dangerous firearm to a child who, being too young to know how to use it, injured another child in handling it. There was no question of an intervening responsible agency, in the proper sense of the term. *Heney* v. *Dennis*, 93 Ind. 452; 47 Am. Rep. 378, therefore, fairly presents the issue whether the intervention of a willfully wrong act, such as intermeddling with another's property, may still leave the chain of causation unbroken, not because the act was actually intended by the original tort-feasor, but by reason of an implied intention. The remarks of Lord Justice Brett, quoted in section 27, *ante*, do, if taken literally, countenance even that extension of a defendant's liability, and some other remarks of English judges pointing in the same direction are referred to below. But we doubt if any decided case, except this Indiana one, has really affirmed the point, that an implied intention is sufficient. The remark of Judge Holmes, cited above, shows that, in his opinion, the defendant is not liable unless he actually intended the intervening willful wrong, and the English cases have in practice gone no further than to maintain the existence of a liability under such circumstances: See *Lumley* v. *Gye*, 2 El. & B. 216; *Bowen* v. *Hall*, 6 Q. B. Div. 333. The extract from the opinion in the latter case given above (sec. 27) shows that the court laid down an unnecessarily broad principle, and in America several courts have refused to follow these cases even to the extent of admitting a responsibility to exist under circumstances which show that the intervening act was actually intended by the defendant: See *Chambers* v. *Baldwin*, 91 Ky. 121; 34

Am. St. Rep. 165; *Bourlier* v. *Macauley,* 91 Ky. 135; 34 Am. St. Rep. 171, and the notes in this series.

31. REPETITION OF SLANDER.—The general rule as to the interposition of a willfully wrong act has frequently been illustrated in the case of unauthorized repetitions of slanderous words. For the consequences of such repetitions the original utterer of the words has uniformly been held not responsible: *Ward* v. *Weeks,* 7 Bing. 211; *Dixon* v. *Smith,* 5 Hurl & N. 450; *Pilmore* v. *Hood,* 5 Bing. N. C. 97; *Parkins* v. *Scott,* 1 Hurl. & C. 153; *Stevens* v. *Hartwell,* 11 Met. 542; *Prime* v. *Eastwood,* 45 Iowa, 640; *Hastings* v. *Stetson,* 126 Mass. 329; 30 Am. Rep. 683; *Burt* v. *Advertiser etc. Co.,* 154 Mass. 238; *Shurtleff* v. *Parker,* 130 Mass. 293; 39 Am. Rep. 454; *Elmer* v. *Fessenden,* 151 Mass. 359. As this nonliability is based on the fact that the repetition is a willfully wrong act, it was suggested in *Keenholts* v. *Becker,* 3 Denio, 346, that a liability arises if the repetition was innocent. ·Nor has the rule ever been extended in favor of the publisher of a printed libel: *King* v. *Patterson,* 49 N. J. L. 417; 60 Am. Rep. 622. It has, however, been felt by more than one judge that the accepted rule is based rather upon the analogy of other cases of intervening willful torts than upon a fair regard to the ordinary ways of men. If the test of "natural and probable consequence" is to be applied, there should certainly be no difficulty in holding that the original slanderer must be taken to have intended all the damages that the widest possible spread of the slander could produce, for it is the most threadbare of truisms to say that nine persons out of every ten to whom a slander is spoken are certain to repeat it: See further the significant remarks of Martin, B., in *Parkins* v. *Scott,* 1 Hurl. & C. 153, and of Kelly, C. B., in *Riding* v. *Smith,* L. R. 1 Ex. D. 91.

Wrongful Acts of Third Party Induced by Slander.—How far a slandered person may hold the slanderer for damages arising from the conduct of a third party who has been induced by the defamatory words to break a contract or do an illegal act to the injury of the slandered person has been much discussed in England since the case of *Vicars* v. *Wilcocks,* 8 East, 1; Smith's Leading Cases, 1805, was decided. There Lord Ellenborough held that no recovery could be had on the ground that the plaintiff's employer had dismissed him from his service, when he heard the slander, and this ruling was followed in *Kelly* v. *Partington,* 5 Barn. & Adol. 645, and *Knight* v. *Gibbs,* 1 Ad. & E. 43. But in the latter case, some doubts were expressed as to the correctness of the decision, and its soundness has also been impugned in *Green* v. *Button,* 2 Cromp. M. & R. 707; *Lynch* v. *Knight,* 9 H. L. Cas. 577; *Bowen* v. *Hall,* L. R. 6 Q. B. D. 333. In the last case Brett, L. J., used these words: "It has been said that, if the act of third person is a breach of duty or contract by him, or is an act which it is illegal for him to do, the law will not recognize that it is a natural or probable consequence of the defendant's act. If that were so in all cases, the law would in some refuse to recognize what is manifestly true in fact. If the judgment in *Vicars* v. *Wilcocks* requires that doctrine for its support it is, in our opinion, wrong." In *Lynch* v. *Knight,* 9 H. L. Cas. 577, also, Lord Wensleydale takes the case put by Lord Ellenborough as an absurd one—that, if damages could be recovered under the circumstances before the court in *Vicars* v. *Wilcocks,* 8 East, 1, damages could also be recovered if, in consequence of the words spoken, the plaintiff had been thrown into a horse-pond—and said that he could conceive of a case when such a result might be very natural, as if the public mind was greatly excited on the subject of some disgraceful crime, and a person was accused of it in the presence of a mob. It would seem then that, so far as defamation is concerned, the leaning of judicial opinion in England is setting strongly in the direction of the doctrine that the mere fact that the injury to the plaintiff consists in a wrongful act by a third person is no defense.   How far the courts have been influenced by the peculiar facility with which men are induced to do wrongful acts to one who has been slandered is not apparent, nor can it reasonably be argued that such a concession to human weakness would necessarily involve the conclusion, that this liability exists wherever the willful act of the intervening wrongdoer was natural and probable: See the preceding section.

32. INTERVENING NEGLIGENT ACTS.—When the intervening act is merely negligent, the courts hold, on principles analogous to those discussed in the two preceding sections, that an independent act of negligence by a third party is an occurrence which the defendant is not, as a general rule, bound to anticipate: *Daniel* v. *Metropolitan Ry. Co.*, L. R. 3 Com. P. 216; *Tutein* v. *Hurley*, 98 Mass. 211; 93 Am. Dec. 154; *De Camp* v. *Sioux City*, 74 Iowa, 392; *Cuff* v. *Newark etc. R. R. Co.*, 35 N. J. L. 18; 10 Am. Rep. 205; *Gilkey* v. *Beta*, 44 Fed. Rep. 389.   But exceptions to this rule are admitted with much greater freedom than where the intervening act is a willful tort, since no distinction is made between actual and implied intention on the part of the original tort-feasor.   The most frequent illustration of this liability based on an implied intention is to be found in that numerous class of cases in which a person by his negligence produces a dangerous condition of things, which does not become active for mischief, until another person has operated upon it by the commission of another negligent act, which might not unreasonably be anticipated to occur.   The original act of negligence is then regarded as the proximate cause of the injury which finally results.   The principle is, that the first act is regarded as being continuous in its operation up to the time of the second, and therefore, for the purposes of fixing the defendant's liability, the two acts are treated as contemporaneous: *Chicago etc. Ry. Co.* v. *Goss*, 17 Wis. 428; 84 Am. Dec. 755; *Kellow* v. *Central Iowa Ry. Co.*, 68 Iowa, 470; 56 Am. Rep. 858; *Joliet* v. *Shufeldt*, 144 Ill. 403; ante, 453; *Johnson* v. *Northwestern Telephone Co.*, 48 Minn. 433; *Martin* v. *North Star Iron Works*, 31 Minn. 407; *Hunt* v. *Missouri Pac. Ry. Co.*, 14 Mo. App. 160; *Byrne* v. *Wilson*, 15 I. R. C. L. 332; *Pastene* v. *Adams*, 49 Cal. 87; *Campbell* v. *Stillwater*, 32 Minn. 308; 50 Am. Rep. 567; *Cline* v. *Crescent City Ry. Co.*, 43 La. Ann. 327; 26 Am. St. Rep. 187; *Gulf etc. Ry. Co.* v. *McWhirter*, 77 Tex. 356; 19 Am. St. Rep. 755; *Electric Ry. Co.* v. *Shelton*, 89 Tenn. 423; 24 Am. St. Rep. 614; *Consolidated Ice Machine Co.* v. *Keifer*, 134 Ill. 481; 23 Am. St. Rep. 688; *Burrows* v. *March Gas etc. Co.*, L. R. 5 Ex. 67; L. R. 7 Ex. 96; *Harrison* v. *Great Northern Ry. Co.*, 3 Hurl. & C. 231; *Bartlett* v. *Boston Gas Co.*, 117 Mass. 533; 19 Am. Rep. 421; *Hill* v. *Port Royal etc. Ry. Co.*, 31 S. C. 393; *State* v. *Rankin*, 3 S. C. 438; 16 Am. Rep. 737; *Sheridan* v. *Brooklyn etc. R. R. Co.*, 36 N. Y. 39; 93 Am. Dec. 490; *Illidge* v. *Goodwin*, 5 Car. & P. 190; *Abbott* v. *Macfie*, 2 Hurl. & C. 744.   See also the extended note to *Village of Carterville* v. *Cook*, 16 Am. St. Rep. 250–263.

Upon this principle one who has received personal injuries by the negligence of the defendant, and used reasonable care in selecting a medical attendant, may recover from the defendant enhanced damages, if the effect of his injuries is aggravated by unskillful treatment: *Pullman Palace Car Co.* v. *Bluhm*, 109 Ill. 20; 50 Am. Rep. 601; *Stover* v. *Inhabitants of Bluehill*, 51 Me. 439; *Tuttle* v. *Farmington*, 58 N. H. 13; *Lyons* v. *Erie Ry.*, 57 N. Y.

489; *Loeser* v. *Humphrey*, 41 Ohio St. 378; 52 Am. Rep. 86; *Sauter* v. *New York Cent. etc. R. R. Co.*, 66 N. Y. 50; 23 Am. Rep. 18; *Rice* v. *Des Moines*, 40 Iowa, 638; *Collins* v. *Council Bluffs*, 32 Iowa, 324; 7 Am. Rep. 200. A like rule prevails where a horse has been injured by the negligence of one to whom it has been hired, and dies under the treatment of the veterinary surgeon: *Eastman* v. *Sanborn*, 3 Allen, 594; 81 Am. Dec. 667.

It may be observed also that the cases in which a servant is allowed to recover damages for the negligence of a co-servant rest upon the theory that the master has created the dangerous state of things by which the injury was finally produced: See, for example, *Pullman Palace Car Co.* v. *Laack*, 143 Ill. 242; *McMahon* v. *Davidson*, 12 Minn. 357; *Cayzer* v. *Taylor*, 10 Gray, 274; 69 Am. Dec. 317; *Grand Trunk Ry. Co.* v. *Cummings*, 106 U. S. 700; *Rogers* v. *Leyden*, 127 Ind. 50 (citing many cases); *Hawkesworth* v. *Thompson*, 98 Mass. 77; 93 Am. Dec. 137; *Phelps* v. *Wait*, 30 N. Y. 78; *Pfau* v. *Williamson*, 63 Ill. 16; *Paulmier* v. *Erie R. R. Co.*, 34 N. J. L. 151; *Boyce* v. *Fitzpatrick*, 80 Ind. 526; *Crutchfield* v. *Richmond etc. R. R. Co.*, 76 N. C. 320; *Booth* v. *Boston etc. R. R. Co.*, 73 N. Y. 38; *Stringham* v. *Stewart*, 100 N. Y. 516.

33. PROXIMATE AND REMOTE CAUSE, DOCTRINE OF CONTRIBUTORY NEGLIGENCE AN ILLUSTRATION OF.—The rule that, if the plaintiff has contributed by his own negligence to the injury complained of, he cannot recover rests upon the ground that, by the interposition of his independent will the causal connection is broken: Wharton on Negligence, sec. 300; Pollock on Torts, 380. A large number of cases to the point that contributory negligence will not bar the plaintiff's action unless it is the proximate cause of the injury will be found in the extended note on contributory negligence appended to *Freer* v. *Cameron*, 55 Am. Dec. 668-670. See, also, Thompson on Negligence, 1151-1155.

34. NEGLIGENT OR WILLFUL MISSTATEMENTS, LIABILITY FOR.—The extent to which a defendant may be held liable for the natural consequences of the tendency of men to rely, under ordinary circumstances, upon the statements of others belongs, so far as willful misstatements are concerned, to the subject of fraud, and is therefore quite beyond the scope of the present note, but it may be noted that negligence in representing a certain state of facts to exist will render the defendant liable on the same principles as he is held responsible for any other negligence. Thus where a drover, traveling with horses, was told by the conductor of the train that it would not start for several minutes, and proceeded to get into a car to tie one of his horses, it was held that the company was liable for the injuries he received by being thrown off through the sudden starting of the train: *Olson* v. *St. Paul etc. R. R. Co.*, 45 Minn. 536; 22 Am. St. Rep. 749. So, also, the ejection of a passenger is a natural consequence of a representation by a railroad company's authorized agent that a stopover ticket, which the conductor refuses to accept, is good: *New York etc. Co.* v. *Winter*, 143 U. S. 60. In *Chicago etc. Ry. Co.* v. *Elliott*, 55 Fed. Rep. 949, it was attempted to show that a statement made by the conductor of a cattle-train to a drover, that the caboose would not be changed at a certain point, and that there would be no time to examine the stock, was the proximate cause of injuries received by the drover who, in spite of the above statement, got off and examined several cars, and, finding that the train was beginning to move, climbed on one of the cars and walked back towards the caboose along the top of the train. The train stopped and began to back before he reached the caboose. Just as he was stepping on to it, it was kicked off for the purpose of changing it, and he fell on the track

and had his foot crushed by a wheel. The court held that no one could have anticipated such an effect from such a cause.

35. Liability for Acts Prompted by More or Less Uncontrollable Impulses—(a) *Instinct of Self-preservation.*—We have already shown that, if a person terrifies animals so that they become uncontrollable by their owners, or rush into dangers which they would otherwise have avoided, he must answer for the consequences. In the case of human beings the instinct of self-preservation must also be reckoned with, though the extent to which the operation of that instinct will excuse or charge with liability must depend, in some degree, upon whether the occasion was one which permitted in any degree the exercise of the reason—a consideration which, in the nature of the case, is not applicable where animals are concerned. If the effect of the danger is such as to deprive the person exposed to it of all power of reasoning, he is regarded as an entirely irresponsible agent, for the purpose both of charging an original tort-feasor with any damage that he may do to others, while in such a condition, and of retaining his own right to recover compensation from such tort-feasor for such injuries as he or his property may suffer as the result of the tort.

Thus, as an illustration of the first branch of the rule, the old case of *Bessey* v. *Olliot*, T. Raym. 467 (cited in *Brown* v. *Collins*, 53 N. H. 443, 16 Am. Rep. 372, may be referred to). It was there said that one who lifts a stick to defend himself and strikes a bystander unintentionally is not liable to the latter for the hurt thereby inflicted. The same principle is illustrated in *Vandenburgh* v. *Truax*, 4 Denio, 464, 47 Am. Dec. 268, where a boy while fleeing from an assailant damaged the plaintiffs' property in his efforts to escape. The assailant in that case was deemed the nearest responsible agent to the injury. Such also is the ground of the decision in the well-known "Squib case." *Scott* v. *Shepherd*, 3 Wils. 403. A somewhat similar case was *Ricker* v. *Freeman*, 50 N. H. 420; 9 Am. Rep. 267. There A caught B by the arm and swung him violently round, and let him go; the impetus carried him against C, who immediately pushed him off so that he struck a hook and was injured. *Held*, That B could recover damages from A, C not being a responsible agent. So, also, if A by working on B's fears so that, out of regard for his own safety, the latter breaks off a business relation profitable to C, A is liable to an action by C, as in *Tarleton* v. *McGauley*, Peake, 205, where the defendant fired on some negroes who were trading with the plaintiff on the coast of Africa, and thereby deterred them from continuing the trade.

Choice Between Dangerous Alternatives.—The second branch of the general rule has been frequently illustrated by that line of cases which have followed the authority of *Jones* v. *Boyce*, 1 Stark. 493, where it was said by Lord Ellenborough that one who places a man " in such a situation that he must adopt a perilous alternative is responsible for all the consequences." Since that decision the courts have uniformly held that an act done instinctively to avoid an impending danger is not contributory negligence: *Ingalls* v. *Bills*, 9 Met. 1; 43 Am. Dec. 346; *Spicer* v. *Chicago etc. Ry. Co.*, 29 Wis. 580; *Smith* v. *St. Paul etc. Ry. Co.*, 30 Minn. 169; *Lund* v. *Tyngsboro*, 11 Cush. 563; 59 Am. Dec. 159; *Turner* v. *Buchanan*, 82 Ind. 147; 42 Am. Rep. 485; *Twomley* v. *Central Park R. R. Co.*, 69 N. Y. 158; 25 Am. Rep. 162, and note; *Vallo* v. *United States Exp. Co.*, 147 Pa. St. 404; 30 Am. St. Rep. 741; *Frink* v. *Potter*, 17 Ill. 406; *Buel* v. *New York etc. R. R. Co.*, 31 N. Y. 314; 88 Am. Dec. 271; *Coulter* v. *American etc. Exp. Co.*, 56 N. Y. 585; *Moore* v. *Central R. R. of Iowa*, 47 Iowa, 688; *Sears* v. *Dennis*, 105 Mass. 310; *Baltimore etc. R. R. Co.* v. *McKenzie*, 81 Va. 71; *Stokes* v. *Saltonstall*, 13 Pet.

181; *Dyer* v. *Erie Ry. Co.*, 71 N. Y. 228; *Voak* v. *Northern Cent. Ry. Co.*, 75 N. Y. 320; *Mark* v. *St. Paul etc. Ry. Co.*, 30 Minn. 493. And if the ultimate injury results, not to the person trying to save himself, but to his property, the connection of cause and effect still remains intact. Thus in *Quigley* v. *Delaware etc. Canal Co.*, 142 Pa. St. 388; 24 Am. St. Rep. 504, a locomotive engineer omitted to give the proper signal while approaching a crossing. The driver of a team alarmed by the sudden appearance of the train, and fearing that he would be run over, jumped from his wagon. The horses ran away, and one of them fell and was so injured by the others that he had to be killed. *Held,* That the negligence of the engineer was the proximate cause of the loss. That one whose wrongful act has forced another to make an effort to save himself and thereby to cause an injury to another from the same source as that from which the primary danger emanated, seems to be denied in *Kistner* v. *Indianapolis etc. R. R. Co.*, 100 Ind. 210. There the defendant backed a train over a crossing which he had not made secure, as it was his duty to do. The plaintiff was in the act of crossing, when the driver of a wagon, to save himself from the train, suddenly pulled his team to one side, and threw the plaintiff under the wheels of the cars. The court said that "the intervening agency here was so direct and positive in its nature and effect, that the death of the plaintiff cannot be attributed to the alleged negligence of the railroad company." This case, it is submitted cannot be sustained on principle or authority. Under the facts given, there was plainly as complete an absence of an intervening responsible agency as in any of the cases cited above. The case was merely a modified form of *Vandenburgh* v. *Truax*, 4 Denio, 464; 47 Am. Dec. 268; and *Scott* v. *Shepherd*, 3 Wils. 403. Certainly the fact that the very person whose negligence caused the driver to swerve so suddenly also supplied the agency by which the injury to the plaintiff was ultimately inflicted was not such as to make the case a stronger one for the defendant.

(b) *Choice Between Disagreeable Alternatives.*—To this head may also be referred those cases in which, although the danger is not so extreme as to deprive the person alarmed of his reasoning powers, he may be held justified in pursuing a course of conduct involving risks of a modified kind. Such seems to be the principle underlying *I. & G. N. Ry. Co.* v. *Gilbert*, 64 Tex. 536, in which a female passenger was wrongfully ejected at a place where there was no suitable accommodation, and, being seriously alarmed at her situation and having reason to believe herself in danger of bodily harm, returned on foot to the nearest safe and comfortable place of which she had any knowledge, and contracted a sickness from the exertion. The company, under these circumstances was held liable for the sickness. Possibly, however, the element of alarm was not necessary in such a state of facts to raise a right of action, for since *Hobbs* v. *London etc. Ry. Co.*, L. R. 10 Q. B. 111, was discredited in *Macmahon* v. *Field*, L. R. 7 Q. B. D. 591, there seems to be no doubt that the instinct of self-preservation, operating in the qualified form of a desire to avoid discomfort and hardship, will justify an injured person in adopting an unpleasant alternative, and, if sickness results therefrom, the person who compelled this choice of evils will be responsible therefor: *Schumaker* v. *St. Paul etc. Ry. Co.*, 46 Minn. 39; *Houston etc. Ry. Co.* v. *Sympkins*, 54 Tex. 615; 38 Am. Rep. 632, but this principle is subject to the qualification that the course pursued must be reasonably necessary, and that the alternative risk confronted must not be out of all proportion to the one against which it has to be weighed: *Texas & Pac. Ry. Co.* v. *Cole*, 66 Tex. 562; *Indianapolis etc. Ry. Co.* v. *Birney*, 71 Ill. 391. Nor is mere inconvenience of a slight character any excuse for plaintiff's doing something ob-viously dangerous, as where a person fell out in trying to shut the door of a railway car which would not stay fastened. Such an accident is not a natural or probable consequence of a defective condition of the door: *Adams* v. *Lancashire etc. Ry. Co.*, L. R. 4 Com. P. 739, 885. So, too, where one was wrongfully imprisoned by the captain of a ship and procured a passage in another vessel at the first stopping place, rather than remain in the same ship with the captain, it was held that he could not recover the passage money thus paid: *Boyce* v. *Bayliffe*, 1 Camp. 58.

(c) *Desire to Save Life—Curiosity.*—It is now well settled that the law has so high a regard for human life that it will not impute negligence to an effort to preserve life unless made under circumstances which, in the judgment of prudent persons, constitute rashness: *Eckert* v. *Long Island R. R. Co.*, 43 N. Y. 502; 3 Am. Rep. 721; *Linnehan* v. *Sampson*, 126 Mass. 506; 30 Am. Rep. 692; *Harris* v. *Clinton*, 64 Mich. 447; 8 Am. St. Rep. 842; *Donahoe* v. *Wabash etc. Ry. Co.*, 83 Mo. 560; 53 Am. Rep. 594; *Pennsylvania Co.* v. *Langendorf*, 48 Ohio St. 316; 29 Am. St. Rep. 553; *Gibney* v. *State*, 137 N. Y. 1; 33 Am. St. Rep. 690. The general principle here involved is that obedi-ence to such an impulse is not blamable from any point of view. In the well-known case of *Guille* v. *Swan*, 19 John. 381, 10 Am. Dec. 234, this prin-ciple was applied to charge a wrongdoer with the damage done to a garden resulting from the assembling of a crowd in response to the cries for help uttered by the defendant, whose balloon had descended in the garden. At least this seems to be the only ground upon which the case can be sustained, although Judge Spencer, in his opinion, leaves us to suppose that the same ruling would have been made if the trespass of the crowd had been prompted by mere curiosity. This doctrine, that curiosity, however singular the cir-cumstances which may excite it, is a sufficient justification for damaging the property of others, seems more than questionable, and was in fact directly repudiated in *Scholes* v. *North London Ry. Co.*, 21 L. T., N. S., 835, where it was held that a railroad company was not answerable for the damage done by a crowd which gathered in a garden to look at a locomotive which had fallen there. In *Fairbanks* v. *Kerr*, 70 Pa. St. 86, 10 Am. Rep. 664, the de-fendant began to make a speech in a public street, and thereby attracted a crowd, which mounted on a pile of flagstones, and his liability was held to be a question for the jury. The court said: "It cannot be said with judicial certainty that when he stopped to make his speech in the street, he must have foreseen, as the natural and probable consequences of his act, that the persons collecting together to listen to him would mount the pile of stones, and even if some of them would, that so many would as by their collected weight might break some of the stones." To us it seems to be going very far to admit the possibility of a person's being liable in such a case. The crowd, under such circumstances, must surely have been presumed to know that in mounting the pile of flagstones they were meddling with private property just as inexcusably as if they had entered a garden, as in the Eng-lish case just cited. The speaker might well be held responsible in such a case for the ordinary consequences of collecting a crowd, such as obstructing the free use of the highway: See *Rex* v. *Carlile*, 6 Car. & P. 636; but the climbing of the heap of stones appears to be an independent and spontaneous act entirely disconnected from the defendant's tort.

(d) *Desire to Preserve Property Endangered by Defendant's Negligence.*—In *Pike* v. *Grand Trunk Ry. Co.*, 39 Fed. Rep. 255, the court refused to hold the defendant liable for the death of a woman whose clothes caught fire while she was helping to extinguish a fire on a neighbor's property, the evidence showing that she had no interest in the premises imperiled, and that she was not acting under the fear of any immediate danger to herself. In *Liming v. Illinois Cent. R. R. Co.*, 81 Iowa, 246, it was held that whether the plaintiff's conduct under similar circumstances was negligent or not was a question for the jury. On the other hand, where the plaintiff's horse broke through a defective bridge, and the plaintiff, while endeavoring to extricate the animal, was injured by it, the defect was held to be the proximate cause of the injury: *Page v. Bucksport*, 64 Me. 53; 18 Am. Rep. 239.

36. INJURIES TO BUSINESS, WHEN PROXIMATE RESULT OF A TORT.—The liability of a defendant for injuring the plaintiff's business has been illustrated in several of the foregoing sections. That liability may be said to rest partly on a knowledge of physical laws and of the natural instincts and impulses of men and animals, and partly upon the circumstance that civilization has given rise to a number of complex relations between man and man, with reference to which every member of the community must be presumed to act. A few cases in which a damage to the pecuniary interests of the plaintiff was the controlling fact will now be cited. A secretly loosed the nails in a horse's shoe for the purpose of inducing the owner to believe that B had done the shoeing unskillfully, and of injuring him in his trade. B consequently lost the owner's custom. *Held*, a natural result of the misfeasance: *Hughes v. McDonogh*, 43 N. J. L., 459; 39 Am. Rep. 603. Where a charter party gives the charterers the option of canceling it after a certain date, if the vessel is not ready, and she is prevented by a collision from leaving the port where she lies in time to begin the loading, according to the agreement, the vessel responsible for the collision is answerable for the loss of profits caused by the charter party, subject to all reasonable deductions, such as the wear and tear of the vessel and the uncertainties and perils of sea voyages: *Star of India*, L. R. 1 P. D. 466. The net earnings of a mill during the past and present may be shown as a basis for estimating the damages caused by an overflow which stopped its operation of the mill: *Terre Haute v. Hudnut*, 112 Ind. 542. In an action for wrongful attachment, the general loss of credit, the stoppage of business, and the prevention of sales, are the proximate results of the act: *Donnell v. Jones*, 17 Ala. 689; 52 Am. Dec. 194; *Contra: Loewenstein v. Monroe*, 55 Iowa, 82, following *Campbell v. Chamberlain*, 10 Iowa, 337; but in the same state compensation for the deterioration of the goods while attached may be recovered: *Knapp v. Barnard*, 78 Iowa, 347. In an action for personal injuries the plaintiff may prove his losses through not being able to attend to his business: *Bradshaw v. Lancashire etc. Ry. Co.*, 31 L. T., N. S., 847; *Masterton v. Mayor*, 7 Hill, 61; 42 Am. Dec. 38; *Bierbach v. Goodyear etc. Co.*, 54 Wis. 208; 41 Am. Rep. 19; but special damages for an assault, claimed on the ground that by reason thereof the plaintiff had been driven away from the place where he carried on business, cannot be recovered: *Moore v. Adam*, 2 Chit. 198; nor can a person wrongfully ejected from a train, and thereby delayed in his journey, recover the loss caused by failing to secure a job which he would have obtained if he had arrived by the train from which he was ejected: *Carsten v. Northern Pac. Ry. Co.*, 44 Minn. 454; 20 Am. St. Rep. 589, citing *Brown v. Cummings*, 7 Allen, 507. The same point was ruled in regard to a similar consequence of false imprisonment in *Hoey v. Felton*, 11 Com. B., N. S., 142. But in *People v. Musical etc. Union*, 118 N. Y. 101, it was held that the plaintiff might recover damages for the loss of an appointment in consequence of his wrongful discharge from a benevolent society.

The loss sustained by plaintiff in being unable to improve his property owing to the enticing away of his servant may be recovered in an action for such misfeasance: *Smith* v. *Goodman*, 75 Ga. 198. So, also, one who maliciously arrests a locomotive engineer is liable for the loss caused by the stoppage of the train: *St. Johnsbury etc. R. R. Co.* v. *Hunt*, 55 Vt. 570; 45 Am. Rep. 639. Compare *McAfee* v. *Crofford*, 13 How. 447, cited in section 9, *ante*. On the other hand it was held in *Sledge* v. *Reid*, 73 N. C. 440, that a trespass in killing two mules was not the proximate cause of the loss of a crop, caused by want of work animals.

For the unskillful management of his logs by the defendant, which injures the rafts of the plaintiff, and thus prevents him from moving them as rapidly as under normal circumstances, the loss by depreciation of market during the delay may be recovered: *Dubois* v. *Glaub*, 52 Pa. St. 238; and the same rule prevails with regard to increased expenses which the plaintiff has to sustain owing to the presence of an unlawful obstruction in the stream, which prevents his moving his logs until the season of low water: *Gates* v. *Northern Pacific R. R. Co.*, 64 Wis. 64, following *Brown* v. *Chicago etc. R. R. Co.*, 54 Wis. 342; 41 Am. Rep. 41. Compare for the general principle here involved: *Buffalo Bayou etc. Co.* v. *Milby*, 63 Tex. 492, 51 Am. Rep. 668, where the wrongful act alleged was that one controlling a public waterway, for the use of which ships were required to pay a toll, refused to allow a ship to pass on the ground that the shipowner was in arrears with his tolls. This refusal was held to be the proximate cause of the damage incurred by the freighters in being thus forced to resort to a more expensive method of unloading. On the other hand the loss by depreciation in the market value of a cargo is not an element of damages in an action by the shipper against the owners of a ship which had negligently run into and damaged the one on which the cargo was: *The Nottinghill*, L. R. 9 P. D. 105.

37. FUNCTIONS OF COURT AND JURY IN THE DETERMINATION OF PROXIMATE AND REMOTE CAUSE.—There appears to be no dispute as to the proposition that the question of causal connection between the wrongful act and the injury complained of is ordinarily for the jury, under proper instructions from the court: *Pennsylvania etc. Ry. Co.* v. *Hope*, 80 Pa. St. 373; 21 Am. Rep. 100; *Hoag* v. *Lake Shore etc. R. R. Co.*, 85 Pa. St. 293; 27 Am. Rep. 653; *Milwaukee etc. Ry. Co.* v. *Kellogg*, 94 U. S. 469; *Hartvig* v. *Northern Pac. L. Co.*, 19 Or. 522; *Patten* v. *Chicago etc. Ry. Co.*, 32 Wis. 524; *Drake* v. *Kiely*, 93 Pa. St. 492; *Lange* v. *Wagner*, 52 Md. 310; 36 Am. Rep. 380; *Railroad Co.* v. *Stout*, 17 Wall. 657; *Hayes* v. *Michigan Cent. R. R. Co.*, 111 U. S. 228; *Shumaker* v. *St. Paul etc. R. R. Co.*, 46 Minn. 39; *Blythe* v. *Denver etc. R. R. Co.*, 15 Col. 333; 22 Am. St. Rep. 403; *Atkinson* v. *Goodrich Transp. Co.*, 60 Wis. 141; 50 Am. Rep. 352; *Scott* v. *Hunter*, 46 Pa. St. 192; 84 Am. Dec. 542; *Tice* v. *Munn*, 94 N. Y. 621; *Lake* v. *Milliken*, 62 Me. 240; 16 Am. Rep. 456; *Ehrgott* v. *Mayor etc. of New York*, 96 N. Y. 264; 48 Am. Rep. 622; *Baltimore etc. R. R. Co.* v. *Kemp*, 61 Md. 619; 48 Am. Rep. 134; *Pittsburgh etc. R. R. Co.* v. *Staley*, 41 Ohio St. 118; 52 Am. Rep. 74; *Fairbanks* v. *Kerr*, 70 Pa. St. 86; 10 Am. Rep. 664; *Clemens* v. *Hannibal etc. R. R. Co.*, 53 Mo. 366; 14 Am. Rep. 460. To justify the court in taking a case from the jury, it must be able to say with judicial certainty that the injury is or is not the natural and probable consequence of the act complained of: *Fairbanks* v. *Kerr*, 70 Pa. St. 86; 10 Am. Rep. 664. To the same effect, see *Lake* v. *Milliken*, 62 Me. 240; 16 Am. Rep. 456; *Delaware etc. R. R. Co.* v. *Salmon*, 39 N. J. L. 299; 23 Am. Rep. 214. In other cases it is said to be a question for the court whenever the facts are undisputed: *Bunting* v. *Hoggsett*, 139

Pa. St. 363; 23 Am. St. Rep. 192: *West Mahanoy Tp.* v. *Watson*, 116 Pa.
St. 344; 2 Am. St. Rep. 604; *Henry* v. *St. Louis etc. Co.*, 76 Mo. 288; 43 Am.
Rep. 762; *Ahern* v. *Oregon Telegraph Co.* (Or. Sup. Ct., June 19, 1893).
But, so far as the action of the appellate courts is concerned, a perusal of
the cases leaves the impression that this nominal division of functions is of
very small practical importance.

Proximate and Remote Causes in Insurance Cases.

38. GENERAL PRINCIPLES.—The maxim, *In jure non remota causa sed proxima spectatur,* is applied in a much more literal sense to cases in which the
liability of an insurer is to be ascertained than to those involving a breach
of contract or a tort. If the nearest efficient cause of the loss is one of the
perils insured against, the courts look no further: *General Mut. Ins. Co.* v.
Sherwood, 14 How. 351; *Howard Fire Ins. Co.* v. *Norwich etc. Transportation
Co.*, 12 Wall. 194. In the latter case Mr. Justice Strong said: "There is,
undoubtedly, difficulty in many cases attending the application of the maxim,
but none when the causes succeed each other in order of time. In such
cases the rule is plain. When one of several successive causes is sufficient to produce the effect (for example, to cause a loss), the law will never
regard an antecedent cause of that cause, or the *causa causans.* In such a
case there is no doubt which cause is the proximate one within the meaning
of the maxim. But when there is no order of succession in time—when
there are two concurrent causes of a loss, the predominating efficient one
must be regarded as the proximate, when the damage done by each cannot
be distinguished." The learned judge then proceeds to express his approval
of Mr. Phillips' rule as to strictly concurrent and contemporaneous causes:
Phillips' Law of Insurance, secs. 1136, 1137. This writer has expressed
his opinion that on the whole the maxim "seems to have served to divert
attention from the proper inquiry and to becloud instead of elucidating
the subject," and in *Brady* v. *Northwestern Ins. Co.*, 11 Mich. 425, we find a
similar unfavorable criticism. But it will, we think, be found that any
difficulty which has arisen in the application of the maxim is due to the
failure to bear in mind the fundamental distinction between those cases in
which the causes operate successively and those in which they operate contemporaneously: See the remarks of Mr. Justice Strong just quoted.

**39. EFFECT OF NEGLIGENCE OR MISCONDUCT OF THE ASSURED OR HIS
SERVANTS.**—In no respect is the difference between the application of the
maxim to cases of breach of contract or tort and to those of insurance
more strikingly indicated than by the circumstance that the well-established rule that "when an efficient cause nearest the loss is a peril expressly
insured against the insurer is not to be relieved against responsibility by
his showing that the property was brought within that peril by a cause
not mentioned in the contract" (*Howard F. Ins. Co.* v. *Norwich etc. Transp.
Co.*, 12 Wall. 194; *St. John* v. *American Mut. Ins. Co.*, 11 N. Y. 516),
is extended to cases in which the precedent cause was the negligence of
the insured or his servant: *Busk* v. *Royal Ex. Ins. Co.*, 2 Barn. & Ald.
73; *Walker* v. *Maitland*, 5 Barn. & Ald. 171; *Bishop* v. *Pentland*, 7 Barn.
& C. 219; *Dixon* v. *Sadler*, 5 Mees. & W. 405; *Waters* v. *Merchants' etc. Ins.
Co.*, 11 Pet. 213; *Columbia Ins. Co.* v. *Lawrence*, 10 Pet. 507; *Patapsco Ins.
Co.* v. *Coulter*, 3 Pet. 222; *General Mut. Ins. Co.* v. *Sherwood*, 14 How. 352;
Phoenix Ins. Co. v. *Erie Transp. Co.*, 117 U. S. 312; *Orient Ins. Co.* v. *Adams*,
123 U. S. 67; *Copeland* v. *New England Ins. Co.*, 2 Met. 432; *Perrin* v.
Protection Ins. Co., 11 Ohio, 147; 38 Am. Dec. 728; *Mathews* v. *Howard*

Ins. Co., 11 N. Y. 9; *Franklin Ins. Co.* v. *Humphrey*, 65 Ind. 549; 32 Am. Rep. 78; *Mississippi Valley Ins. Co.* v. *Humphrey*, 66 Ind. 600; *National Ins. Co.* v. *Webster*, 83 Ill. 470; *Sturm* v. *Atlantic Mut. Ins. Co.*, 63 N. Y. 77; *Hume* v. *Providence etc. Ins. Co.*, 23 S. C. 190; *Sperry* v. *Delaware Ins. Co.*, 2 Wash. C. C. 243; *American Ins. Co.* v. *Insley*, 7 Pa. St. 223; 47 Am. Dec. 509; *Phœnix F. Ins. Co.* v. *Cochran*, 51 Pa. St. 143; *Williams* v. *New England etc. Ins. Co.*, 31 Me. 219; *Georgia Ins. Co.* v. *Dawson*, 2 Gill, 365; *Gates* v. *Madison County M. Ins. Co.*, 5 N. Y. 469; 55 Am. Dec. 360; *Aurora F. Ins. Co.* v. *Johnson*, 46 Ind. 315; *Kansas Ins. Co.* v. *Berry*, 8 Kan. 159; *Shaw* v. *Roberts*, 6 Ad. & E. 75; *Enterprise Ins. Co.* v. *Parisot*, 35 Ohio St. 35; 35 Am. Rep. 589; *Levi* v. *New Orleans Ins. Assn.*, 2 Woods, 63; *Redman* v. *Wilson*, 14 Mees. & W. 476; *Johnson* v. *Berkshire Fire Ins. Co.*, 4 Allen, 388.

But this liberal construction of the policy cannot be extended to cases in which it would contravene the fundamental rule of insurance law that the assurers are not liable for a loss occasioned by the wrongful act of the assured. To absolve the assurers the misconduct need not be the *causa causans*. It is enough if it be the *causa sine qua non:* *Thompson* v. *Hopper*, 6 El. & B. 938, where a vessel was sent to sea in an unseaworthy state. But the unseaworthiness only bars an action, if it was known to the assured: *Dudgeon* v. *Pembroke*, L. R. 2 App. C. 284. So also a deviation, if voluntary, will discharge the underwriters: *Natchez Ins. Co.* v. *Stanton*, 2 Smedes & M. 340; 41 Am. Dec. 592. So, too, negligence showing fraud or design will discharge the insurer: *Lebanon Mut. Ins. Co.* v. *Kepler*, 106 Pa. St. 28; *Cumberland Valley etc. Co.* v. *Douglas*, 58 Pa. St. 419; 98 Am. Dec. 298; *Huckins* v. *People's Mut. F. Ins. Co.*, 31 N. H. 238; *Orient Ins. Co.* v. *Adams*, 123 U. S. 67. The same ruling has been made where the negligence was gross: *Whitehurst* v. *Fayetteville Mut. Ins. Co.*, 6 Jones, 352. So also the fact that the negligence was that of the owner himself, while in command of his ship, has been held to be a bar to recovery: *Schultz* v. *Pacific Ins. Co.*, 14 Fla. 73; but this decision seems to introduce a very doubtful qualification of the general rule. Barratry, unless expressly assured against, will discharge the underwriter: *Waters* v. *Merchants' etc. Ins. Co.*, 11 Pet. 213; *Firemen's Ins. Co.* v. *Powell*, 13 B. Mon. 311; *St. Louis Ins. Co.* v. *Glasgow*, 8 Mo. 713; 41 Am. Dec. 661; *Cory* v. *Burr*, L. R. 8 App. C. 393; *Citizen's Ins. Co.* v. *Marsh*, 41 Pa. St. 386. The same effect will follow if the master of a ship resists search: *Robinson* v. *Jones*, 8 Mass. 536; 5 Am. Dec. 114; or the owner fails to comply with the statutory provisions as to the ship's manifest, provided the loss actually arises from his omission: *Carruthers* v. *Gray*, 15 East, 35; or the master of a neutral ship negligently leaves the ship's register on shore: *Cleveland* v. *Union Ins. Co.*, 8 Mass. 308; or does not adopt certain stipulated precautions to mask the ownership of the goods, so as to prevent capture by privateers: *Himely* v. *Stewart*, 1 Brev. 209. These last four cases might perhaps be placed also on the ground of an increase of risk.

Of course if the negligence of the master is the proximate cause of the loss the insurer is discharged. Thus where a vessel was lost, but the cargo saved, and the master took no steps to tranship the goods or repair the vessel, it was held that the insurer of the cargo was not liable: *Schieffelin* v. *New York Ins. Co.*, 9 Johns. 21. Compare *Bradhurst* v. *Columbian Ins. Co.*, 9 Johns. 17; *American Ins. Co.* v. *Centre*, 4 Wend. 45; 7 Cow. 564; *McGaw* v. *Ocean Ins. Co.*, 23 Pick. 405; *General Mut. Ins. Co.* v. *Sherwood*, 14 How.

351, 365; *Copeland* v. *New England Mar. Ins. Co.*, 2 Met. 432; *Hazard* v. *New England Mar. Ins. Co.*, 1 Sum. 218.

40. MARINE INSURANCE.—(a) *Loss by Perils of the Sea, What Is.*—The general rule is settled beyond all controversy, that "any loss caused immediately by the perils of the sea is within the policy, though it would not have occurred but for the concurrent action of some cause which is not within it": *Dudgeon* v. *Pembroke*, L. R. 9 Q. B. 581; 1 Q. B. Div. 96. 2 App. Cas. 284 (per Lord Penzance). In that case it was held that the mere fact that the vessel became unseaworthy during the voyage did not excuse the underwriters, where the loss ultimately occurred through stormy weather. But the unseaworthiness will be regarded as the proximate cause of the loss, if the owner of the vessel neglects to make repairs, when it is in his power to do so: *Paddock* v. *Franklin Ins. Co.*, 11 Pick. 234; *Copeland* v. *New England M. Ins. Co.*, 2 Met. 437. The latter case also holds that the omission of the mate to take charge when the master is incapacitated is not to be placed on the same footing as an omission to make repairs, and that such inaction will not discharge the insurers (Wilde, J., dissenting).

There has been a good deal of discussion in regard to the question, What losses arising from the effect of the voyage upon the cargo are losses by perils of the sea? The general principle is stated by Pollock, C. B., to be that "where mischief arises from perils of the sea and the natural inevitable consequence of that mischief is to create further mischievous results, the underwriters are responsible for the further mischief so occasioned": *Montoya* v. *London Assur. Co.*, 6 Ex. 451. There some of the cargo became putrid by contact with sea-water, and this putrefaction spoilt another portion. *Held*, To be a loss by perils of the seas. To the same effect see *Baker* v. *Manufacturer's Ins. Co.*, 12 Gray, 603. Owing to these decisions, the wording of policies was changed in England and the United States so as to make the liability in such cases depend upon "actual contact with sea-water," and the effect of this alteration was stated by Mr. Justice Gray in *Cory* v. *Boylston Ins. Co.*, 107 Mass. 140, 9 Am. Rep. 14, to be that "it was not enough to bring a case within this clause that perils of the sea should be the efficient, and, within the rules laid down in the previous decisions, proximate, cause by which the sea-water was shipped, which, more or less directly, operates on and injures the goods; or that the sea-water should come in contact with part of the cargo; but it must come in actual contact with the articles, for the damage to which the underwriters are sought to be charged." To the same effect is *Neidlinger* v. *Insurance Co. of North America*, 10 Ben. 254; affirmed 18 Blatchf. 297; 11 Fed. Rep. 514.

An insurance against loss by perils of the sea does not cover the deterioration of the cargo caused by a prolonged voyage in stormy weather *Taylor* v. *Dunbar*, L. R. 4 Com. P. 206 (meat putrified); nor the loss of goods which are spoilt by the climate of a place where they are temporarily unladen for the purpose of making repairs rendered necessary by sea perils: *Goold* v. *Shaw*, 1 Johns. Cas. 293; nor the death of slaves owing to deficiency of provisions on a passage unusually protracted by bad weather: *Tathan* v. *Hodgson*, 6 Term Rep. 656. On the other hand, such insurance covers the loss of animals caused by the violent motion of the ship: *Lawrence* v. *Aberdein*, 5 Barn. & Ald. 107; *Snowden* v. *Guion*, 101 N. Y. 458; even though the damage is occasioned by the breaking of partitions which allows the animals to get at and injure one another by kicking: *Gabay* v. *Lloyd*, 3 Barn. & C. 793.

Measures taken to obviate the consequences of damage from sea perils do not break the causal connection between the operation of the sea peril and a loss which occurs as the result of or in spite of such measures: *Swift* v. *Union Mut. Ins. Co.*, 122 Mass. 573. Compare section 40 (*f*), *post*. But the insurer is not liable for the value of goods sold to defray the expense of making repairs in the ship after she has been damaged by a sea peril: *Dyer* v. *Piscataqua etc. Ins. Co.*, 53 Me. 118, the court saying that the sale was not the "necessary result of the peril at sea, but rather of the want of funds or credit in port": Compare *Greer* v. *Poole*, L. R. 5 Q. B. D. 272; *Powell* v. *Gudgeon*, 5 Maule & S. 431; *Sarguy* v. *Hobson*, 2 Barn. & C. 7.

A different rule, however, prevails where "the thing insured becomes by law directly chargeable with any expense, contribution, or loss, in consequence of a particular peril." In such a case the law treats that peril, for all practical purposes, as the proximate cause of such expense, contribution, or loss: *Peters* v. *Warren Ins. Co.*, 14 Pet. 99, per Story, J., disapproving *De Vaux* v. *Salvador*, 4 Ad. & E. 420, which involved the same facts, viz., a collision in which neither party was in fault, and they were each condemned, according to the usual admiralty practice, to pay one-half of the damages. Mr. Justice Story in *Hall* v. *Washington Ins. Co.*, 2 Story, 176, extended the liability to a case in which the collision was caused by the negligence of the crew of the insured ship. This ruling was disapproved in *General Mut. Ins. Co.* v. *Sherwood*, 14 How. 351, but followed in *Nelson* v. *Suffolk Ins. Co.*, 8 Cush. 476; 54 Am. Dec. 770. In *Berens* v. *Rucker*, 1 W. Black, 313, recovery was allowed of the money paid for a *bona fide* compromise, made to prevent a ship from being condemned as lawful prize, and in *Dent* v. *Smith*, L. R. 4 Q. B. 414, and *Pike* v. *Merchants' Mut. Ins. Co.*, 26 La. Ann. 392, the underwriters were held liable for salvage payments.

(*b*) *Consequences of Hostilities—Capture When Proximate Cause of Loss.—* In *Dean* v. *Hornby*, 3 El. & B. 180, the cases were said to establish the principle that "if once there has been a total loss by capture, that is construed to be a permanent total loss unless something afterwards happens by which the assured either has the possession restored, or has the means of obtaining such restoration, and reference was made to *Holdsworth* v. *Wise*, 7 Barn. & C. 794; *Parry* v. *Aberdeen*, 9 Barn. & C. 411; *MacIver* v. *Henderson*, 4 Maule & S. 576. To the same effect is *Magoun* v. *New England Mar. Ins. Co.*, 1 Story, 157; *Bondrett* v. *Hentigg*, Holt, N. P. C. 149. On the other hand, if there has been a total loss by a peril of the sea, the fact that the cargo is afterwards seized by the enemy will not turn it into a loss by capture: *Hahn* v. *Corbett*, 2 Bing. 205. Where there is a partial loss by perils of the sea, followed by a capture, the doctrine of some of the earlier cases is that the previous loss is disregarded, and the underwriters are discharged: *Livie* v. *Jansen*, 12 East, 648; *Rice* v. *Homer*, 12 Mass, 230: *Patrick* v. *Commercial Ins. Co.*, 11 Johns. 9; the last two rulings being made on the authority of the first. But considerable doubt has been thrown on the soundness of *Livie* v. *Jansen*, as by Best, C. J., in` *Hahn* v. *Corbett*, 2 Bing. 205, and Willes, J., in *Ionides* v. *Universal Mar. Ins. Co.*, 14 Com. B., N. S., 259; and Mr. Phillips, with much reason, contends that the true rule is that if the damage by the perils respectively insured against can be discriminated, each party must bear his proportion: 1 Phillips' Law of Insurance, sec. 673. This principle is assumed to be the true one in the well-known case of *Ionides* v. *Universal Mar. Ins. Co.*, 14 Com. B., N. S., 259. There the policy contained the warranty "free from all consequences of hostilities": The ship on which the cargo was loaded being on a voyage between New

Orleans and New York during the war between the northern and southern states, the captain lost his reckoning, and supposing that he had passed the dangerous headland, Cape Hatteras, took a course which led to the stranding of the ship, which was seized by the confederate troops. A portion of the cargo was saved, and the remainder lost by a storm which ensued. It appeared that until recently a light had always been kept burning on Cape Hatteras, but that it had been extinguished by the confederates for the purpose of harassing the federal shipping. Under these circumstances it was held, after a very elaborate discussion, that the portion of the cargo which had not been saved was a loss by the perils of the sea, and not a consequence of hostilities, the efficient and proximate cause of the mishap being the fact that the master had lost his reckoning. The absence of the light was merely a condition of the loss, or as Byles, J., expressed it, "the absence of an extrinsic saving power." The insurers were therefore adjudged to pay only for that portion of the cargo, and the goods that were landed were held to be covered by the warranty against "the consequences of hostilities."

(c) *Acts of Princes, etc.*—In *Rice* v. *Homer*, 12 Mass. 230, seizure was held to be the proximate cause of a loss where a ship was driven into a port of necessity, and there taken possession of by the authorities, but this ruling has been questioned: See (b), *ante*. If the crew of a ship is sent ashore to attend to the mooring of the ship, and is imprisoned by a press gang, in consequence of which the ship drifts ashore, the loss is one by the perils of the sea: *Hodgson* v. *Malcolm*, 2 Bos. & P. 336. So also where a vessel is driven ashore during detention, the underwriter is liable for a loss by perils of the sea: *Bailey* v. *South Carolina Ins. Co.*, 3 Brev. 354. In *Forster* v. *Christie*, 11 East, 205, a vessel was detained by the officer commanding a convoy, and an embargo afterwards laid on the ships of the owner's country at the port of destination. The embargo was held to be the proximate cause of the loss of the voyage.

(d) *Piracy—Insurrection.*—In *Palmer* v. *Naylor*, 10 Ex. 382, coolies made a piratical seizure of a vessel, the motive being their unwillingness to proceed on the voyage. *Held,* That the act of piracy, not the unwillingness to proceed, was the proximate cause of the loss of the voyage. So also where the slaves on board an American ship rose against the crew and took her to a British port, where they ran away, and thus became free so long as they remained in British territory, it was held that the insurrection was the proximate cause of the loss, on the ground that consequences naturally flowing from a peril are properly attributable to it: *McCargo* v. *New Orleans Ins. Co.*, 10 Rob. (La.) 202; 43 Am. Dec. 180.

(e) *Bursting of Boilers.*—A policy excepting loss by "bursting of boilers," but covering that, "occurring subsequent to and in consequence of a bursting, does not cover a loss by an explosion so violent as to tear out the sides of the vessel, so that she sinks in five or ten minutes": *Evans* v. *Columbian Ins. Co.*, 44 N. Y. 146; 4 Am. Rep. 650. Hunt, C., dissented on the ground that the sinking was the proximate cause of the loss. If the policy merely exempts the insurers from liability for "the bursting of boilers," they are not liable for a total loss caused by the ship's sinking after the explosion: *Strong* v. *Sun Mut. Ins. Co.*, 31 N. Y. 103; 88 Am. Dec. 242. In *Western Ins. Co.* v. *Cropper*, 32 Pa. St. 351, 75 Am. Dec. 561, a different conclusion was reached, but principally on the ground that the wording of the policy in question required that inference. If a boiler has been weakened by the growth of a scale due to the action of sea-water, the loss is still one by explosion, and not by the perils of the sea: *West India Tel. Co.* v. *Home etc. Ins. Co.*, L. R. 6 Q. B. D. 51.

(*f*) *Ice Clause.*—In *Brown* v. *St. Nicholas Ins. Co.*, 61 N. Y. 332, the effect of a condition that "if a boat is prevented or detained by ice or the closing of navigation, the policy should cease to attach on the cargo," was discussed, and held not to be applicable to a case where a tow was separated from its tug by a storm, and driven on shore, and while in that position blockaded by the sudden formation of ice, while the main channel still remained open. The storm was said to be the efficient predominating cause of the loss of the boat, which sank while in that position. In *Allison* v. *Corn Exch. Ins. Co.*, 57 N. Y. 87, damage from ice was excepted from the policy. A vessel was moored during the winter in a canal basin separated from a river by a wall. When spring came the ice broke up and created an ice-jam at a bridge which crossed the river above. In consequence of this, the flood-water rose rapidly and flowed over the wall, loosening the stern of the boat, while the bow was still fast on the ice, and thereby twisting the framework. *Held*, That the ice was the proximate cause of the damage, on the ground that, if the ice had not caused the ice-jam, the stern of the boat would not have been disturbed, and that, if the ice had not imprisoned the bow, the excess of water would not have twisted the boat. Two of the commissioners of appeal dissented on the ground that the freshet was the active, efficient, and direct cause of the damage, since without it the boat would have been safe.

(*g*) *Collision.*—The cases in which a fire has followed a collision have raised some embarrassing questions. If a steamboat is insured against "loss by fire only," and there is no exception of fire caused by collision, the insurer is liable, where that contingency arises: *Germania Ins. Co.* v. *Sherlock*, 25 Ohio St. 33. A similar policy makes the underwriters responsible, where, but for the breaking out of a fire, the collision would not have caused the boat to sink: *Howard F. Ins. Co.* v. *Norwich etc. Transp. Co.*, 12 Wall. 194; and a like ruling was made in *New York Exp. Co.* v. *Traders' etc. Ins. Co.*, 132 Mass. 377, 42 Am. Rep. 440, where goods were insured against "immediate loss by fire," and a fire having broken out after a collision, the vessel sank before the flames reached the goods insured. In *Norwich etc. Transp. Co.* v. *Western Mass. Ins. Co.*, 34 Conn. 561, a steamer was injured by a collision. The water rushed in, and forced the boiler fires out upon the woodwork. She took fire, and a part of her promenade deck was burnt. It was shown that, but for the burning of the deck, she would merely have sunk as far as that deck, and might have been towed to a place of safety. Under these circumstances the insurer was held liable for all the damage except that received by the collision alone.

41. FIRE INSURANCE—(*a*) *What Is a Loss by Fire, Generally.*—In *Everett* v. *London Ass. Co.*, 19 Com. B. N. S. 126, it was said that the expression "loss or damage occasioned by fire" is to be, construed as ordinary people would construe it, and that those words mean "loss or damage either by ignition of the article consumed, or by ignition of part of the premises where the article is." It was held accordingly that damage caused by the atmospheric concussion accompanying the explosion of a powder magazine half a mile distant was not an injury caused by fire. To the same effect see *Caballero* v. *Home Mut. Ins. Co.*, 15 La. Ann. 217. In *Providence Wash. Ins. Co.* v. *Adler*, 65 Md. 162; 57 Am. Rep. 314, a fire arising from spontaneous combustion was not covered by an ordinary marine insurance policy, that being the result of an inherent defect. But this case rests rather on the peculiar effect of the rule of marine insurance law exempting the insurer from lia-

bility for damage caused by inherent defects of the cargo than on general principles, and we agree with Mr. May (Insurance, sec. 413) that, in the absence of some such consideration as the above, there is no valid reason why a fire arising from spontaneous combustion should not be covered by an ordinary policy.

(b) *Fire Accompanied by Explosion.*—The maxim has been applied, in fire insurance cases, principally to those in which it is necessary to determine how far the ordinary clause exempting the insurer from liability for explosions constitutes a defense in an action by the insured. The authorities hold that, where there is no exception against loss by explosion, the fire producing the explosion, although of an innocent character, like the flame of a gas-jet or candle, is a cause of the whole loss, within the meaning of the policy: *Waters* v. *Merchants' etc. Ins. Co.*, 11 Pet. 213; *City Fire Ins. Co.* v. *Corlies*, 21 Wend. 367; 34 Am. Dec. 258; *Renshaw* v. *Firemen's Ins. Co.*, 33 Mo. App. 394; *Scripture* v. *Fire Ins. Co.*, 10 Cush. 356; 57 Am. Dec. 111; *Heuer* v. *Northwestern Nat. Ins. Co.*, 144 Ill. 393; *Briggs* v. *N. A. & M. Ins. Co.*, 53 N. Y. 446. The opposite doctrine, however, was laid down in *Millandon* v. *New Orleans Ins. Co.*, 4 La. Ann. 15; 50 Am. Dec. 550, on the ground that the chances of loss from explosion are not the same as those from fire. So, also, when that exception is inserted in the policy, most of the cases seem to sustain the proposition that, if there is a destructive fire in progress when the explosion occurs, that is, when the explosion is an incident of the fire, the insurer is liable for the loss caused by the explosion as well as that caused by the fire: *Heuer* v. *Northwestern Nat. Ins. Co.*, 144 Ill. 393; *Transatlantic Fire Ins. Co.* v. *Dorsey*, 56 Md. 70; 40 Am. Rep. 403; *Washburn* v. *Miami etc. Ins. Co.*, 2 Fed. Rep. 633; *Washburn* v. *Farmers' Ins. Co.*, 2 Fed. Rep. 304. But in England it is held that the loss caused by an explosion under such circumstances is not covered, and that, if the plaintiff cannot distinguish the one loss from the other, the damage must be borne by him and not by the insurers: *Stanley* v. *Western Ins. Co.*, L. R. 3 Ex. 71.

If on the other hand, there is no fire antecedent to the explosion, except such as is of an entirely innocent kind, until it becomes the agency for producing the explosion, it is held that, under a clause exempting the insurer from liability for explosions, he cannot be held either for the damage produced immediately by the explosion of any kind, or for that resulting from a fire which is started by the explosion: *United Life etc. Ins. Co.* v. *Foot*, 22 Ohio St. 340; 10 Am. Rep. 735; *Briggs* v. *N. A. & M. Ins. Co.*, 53 N. Y. 446; *St. John* v. *Am. Mut. Fire Ins. Co.*, 11 N. Y. 516; *Strong* v. *Sun Mut. Ins. Co.*, 31 N. Y. 103; 88 Am. Dec. 242; *Mutual Ins. Co.* v. *Tweed*, 7 Wall. 44; *Stanley* v. *Western Ins. Co.*, L. R. 3 Ex. 71; *Roe* v. *Columbus Ins. Co.*, 17 Mo. 301; *Montgomery* v. *Firemen's Ins. Co.*, 16 B. Mon. 427; *Transatlantic Fire Ins. Co.* v. *Dorsey*, 56 Md. 70; 40 Am. Rep. 403; *Tanneret* v. *Merchants' Mut. Ins. Co.*, 34 La. Ann. 249; *McAllister* v. *Tenn. Ins. Co.*, 17 Mo. 306; *Hayward* v. *Liverpool etc. Ins. Co.*, 3 Keyes, 456; *Commercial Ins. Co.* v. *Robinson*, 64 Ill. 265; 16 Am. Rep. 557, and *Dows* v. *Faneuil Hall etc. Ins. Co.*, 127 Mass. 346; 34 Am. Rep. 384, are *contra*, but were decided rather upon a construction of the policies than upon general principles.

(c) *Fall of Building.*—Under the clause providing for the determination of the risk if the building falls, it is held that the insured cannot recover where a fire breaks out in the debris after the collapse of the structure: *Liverpool etc. Ins. Co.* v. *Ende*, 65 Tex. 118; *Nave* v. *Home Mut. Ins. Co.*, 37 Mo. 430; 90 Am. Dec. 394; *Huck* v. *Globe Ins. Co.*, 127 Mass. 306; 34 Am. Rep. 373. The building must fall as the result of fire to make the insurers liable:

Transatlantic F. Ins. Co. v. *Dorsey*, 56 Md. 70; 40 Am. Rep. 403. But the insurer is not exempted if the building is merely a good deal damaged, and even rendered unfit for occupancy by a storm: *Fireman's F. Ins. Co.* v. *Congregation etc. Sholom*, 80 Ill. 558, or where only .about three-fourths of the building falls, and it is afterwards destroyed by fire communicated from an adjoining building: *Breuner* v. *Liverpool etc. Ins. Co.*, 51 Cal. 101; 21 Am. Rep. 703.

(d) *Invasion—Military or Usurped Power, etc., Exception Against.*—In *Barton* v. *Home Ins. Co.*, 42 Mo. 156, 97 Am. Dec. 326, where the national soldiers were compelled to surrender to a force of confederate soldiers, who burned the property insured, the insurers were held exempt under the above clause, although it was not proved that any order to destroy the property was given by the officer in command. "The real question," said the court, "is, Did the fire happen or the loss occur by reason of or in consequence of the military and usurped power of the rebels, ... and were they the proximate cause of the burning and destruction of the property?" A similar ruling was made as to the loss of buildings by fire communicated from buildings which a union officer had ordered to be burned to prevent their falling into the hands of the confederates: *Insurance Co.* v. *Boon*, 95 U. S. 117. But see *Portsmouth Ins. Co.* v. *Reynolds*, 32 Gratt. 613, where it was held, under similar circumstances, that as the order of secession was not in force when the fire took place, the loss was not within such an exception.

(e) *Acts of Municipal Authorities Preventing Rebuilding.*—In two cases it has been held that where a wooden building is only partially destroyed, but a fire-limits ordinance prevents its being restored to its former condition, the fire becomes the proximate cause of the total loss thus incurred, and that the insured may claim accordingly: *Hamburg-Bremen F. Ins. Co.* v. *Garlington.* 66 Tex. 103; 59 Am. Rep. 613; *Brady* v. *Northwestern Ins. Co.*, 11 Mich. 425.

(f) *Acts Done to Save Goods.*—It is well established that, for the purposes of fixing the underwriters' liability, a fire is regarded as the proximate cause of damage to or loss of goods, which is suffered in the process of removing them to save them from the fire: *Balestracci* v. *Firemen's Ins. Co.*, 34 La. Ann. 844; or of injuries received by the water used to extinguish the fire: *Lewis* v. *Springfield etc. Ins. Co.*, 10 Gray, 159; but not of injuries received by goods which are merely being removed from a neighboring building under a reasonable apprehension of the spread of the fire: *Hillier* v. *Allegheny Ins. Co.*, 3 Pa. St. 470; 45 Am. Dec. 656. So, too, the underwriter is liable, where the captain of a ship burns it to prevent its falling into the hands of the enemy: *Gordon* v. *Rimmington*, 1 Camp. 123, or where the municipal authorities blow up a building to stop the progress of a conflagration: *City F. Ins. Co.* v. *Corlies*, 21 Wend. 367; 34 Am. Dec. 258; *Greenwald* v. *Insurance Co.*, 3 Phila. 323.

42. Accident and Life Insurance—(a) *Excepted Peril Incurred by Mistake.*—Under an ordinary accident policy which excepts injuries, "happening directly or indirectly by the taking of poison," the fact that poison is taken as the result of a mistake will not render the poison any the less the proximate cause of the death which ensues therefrom, and the insurer will in such case be discharged: *Pollock* v. *United States Mut. Acc. Assn.*, 102 Pa. St. 230; 48 Am. Rep. 204.

(b) *Secondary Results of an Accident Do Not Break the Causal Connection.*—This rule was applied in *Baylies* v. *Travelers' Ins. Co.*, 14 Blatchf. 143, where an accident to an internal organ, which produced a disordered state of the injured part, and so incapacitated other organs from performing their natural functions, was held the proximate cause of death. The same ruling was made where a wound in the abdomen received in using a hay-fork resulted in peritonitis: *North American L. Ins. Co.* v. *Burroughs*, 69 Pa. St. 43; 8 Am. Rep. 212. In some policies the companies have guarded themselves by exceptions of certain secondary results, and the question then becomes one of construction rather than of causal connection. For two cases involving such a point see *Fitton* v. *Accidental Death Ins. Co.*, 17 Com. B., N. S., 122, where the company was held liable, and *Smith* v. *Accident Ins. Co.*, L. R., 5 Ex. 302, where it was discharged from liability.

(c) *Drowning.*—The general rule is that where death occurs in the water it is covered by an ordinary accident policy, if it arises from suffocation caused by the ordinary action of the water, and not as the result of some bodily affection, such as apoplexy, and in case of doubt the question is to be left to the jury: *Trew* v. *Railway Passengers' Assur. Co.*, 6 Hurl. & N. 839. This rule was applied in *Reynolds* v. *Accidental Ins. Co.*, 22 L. T., N. S., 820, to a case where the insured went to bathe, and, while in a pool one foot deep, became insensible from some internal cause, and fell face downwards. The evidence showing that he had breathed after so falling, it was held that the proximate cause of his death was suffocation by water, though he would not have been suffocated, if he had been able to take care of himself. In *Mallory* v. *Travelers' Ins. Co.*, 47 N. Y. 52, 7 Am. Rep. 410 it was ruled that, where the insurer was to be liable in case the insured "should have sustained personal injury caused by an accident within the meaning of the policy, a death was not the less accidental because the deceased had received a wound which was not sufficient to cause death, but which caused him to fall into the water, where he was drowned.

(d) *Fits.*—Where there is an exception of death by "fits" the company is liable, when the deceased is merely placed by the occurrence of the fit in a dangerous position, and the death is then caused by some other agency. Thus in *Winspear* v. *Accident Ins. Co.*, L. R. 6 Q. B. D. 42, the deceased, while in a fit, fell into the water, and was drowned, and in *Lawrence* v. *Accidental Ins. Co.*, L. R. 7 Q. B. D. 522, fell upon a railway track and was run over by a train. In both cases the company was held liable upon a strict application of the maxim as to proximate and remote cause.

(e) *Intemperance.*—If the policy is to be void in case "the insured dies by reason of intemperance and the use of intoxicating liquors," intemperance which merely shortens life will not discharge the insurer, unless it is the sole cause of the death—the *onus* of proving this being on the insurer—but this exception covers a case where the insured, while in a fit of *delirium tremens*, escaped from his keepers, ran into the street, and from the exposure contracted a fatal disease: *Miller* v. *Mutual Benefit L. Ins. Co.*, 31 Iowa, 216; 7 Am. Rep. 122.

(f) *Death in Violation of Law.*—If the insurer is to be discharged when the insured dies, "in consequence of the violation of the law" of the state, it is sufficient to bring a case within the condition, "if there is such a relation between the act and the death that the latter would not have occurred at the time if the deceased had not been engaged in the violation of the law": *Murray* v. *New York Life Ins. Co.*, 96 N. Y. 614; 48 Am. Rep. 658. There A the insured and his brother B planned an assault on C. During the scuffle C succeeded in drawing a pistol, and A tried to make his escape, but was shot. *Held*, That whether the discharge of the pistol was accidental or not, the death of A occurred in the violation of law. So also a policy is avoided where the assured assaults a married woman, with justifiable cause, and her husband, while defending her, kills him: *Bloom* v. *Franklin Ins. Co.*, 97 Ind. 478; 49 Am. Rep. 469; or, where the insured, while engaged in driving unlawfully in a race, comes into collision with another sulky, leaps out to avoid the peril, and is killed: *Insurance Co.* v. *Seaver*, 19 Wall. 531; or where the insured, a pregnant woman, dies as the result of an operation undergone for the purpose of producing an abortion without medical necessity: *Hatch* v. *Mutual Life Ins. Co.*, 120 Mass. 550; 21 Am. Rep. 541. If death occurs during an affray the essential question is, whether the person to whose act the death is due was acting in self-defense: *Bradley* v. *Mutual Benefit Life Ins. Co.*, 45 N. Y. 422; 6 Am. Rep. 115; *Overton* v. *St. Louis Mut. L. Ins. Co.*, 39 Mo. 122; 90 Am. Dec. 455; *Murray* v. *New York Life Ins. Co*, 96 N. Y. 614; 48 Am. Rep. 658. Therefore, if the deceased has abandoned the conflict before he is killed, the death is not deemed to have occurred in violation of law: *Harper* v. *Phœnix Mut. Life Ins. Co.*, 19 Mo. 506. The general principle here involved, that, if the unlawful act is no longer in progress at the time of the death, the insurer is liable, is also the foundation of the decision in *Goetzman* v. *Connecticut Mut. Life Ins. Co.*, 3 Hun, 515, where the insured, who was killed by B, immediately after committing adultery with B's wife, was held not have been killed while in violation of the law: Compare also *Griffin* v. *Western Mut. Assn.*, 20 Neb. 620; 57 Am. Rep. 648. With the above cases it will be instructive to compare these cited *ante*, section 7, in regard to the necessary connection that must exist between an illegal act and the injury sustained in order to enable the injured person to hold the doer of the act responsible. As to the cases in which suicide by the deceased precludes recovery: See note to *Breasted* v. *Farmers' etc. Ins. Co.*, 59 Am. Dec. 487–497.

HOLMAN *v.* BOYCE.

[65 VERMONT, 318.]

ESTOPPEL BY ADMISSIONS, EXTENT OF.—A party to a suit is not precluded from proving that his admissions, whether express or implied from his conduct, were mistaken or untrue, unless another person has been induced by them to alter his conduct. In that case he and all claiming under him are estopped from disputing the truth of the admissions so far as that person is concerned, but are not bound as to third persons.

ESTOPPEL OF DEBTOR BY REPRESENTATIONS AS TO AMOUNT DUE ON A NOTE.—When one takes an assignment of a chose in action by the debtor's procurement or with his assent, and on the faith of representations made by him at the time, the debtor is estopped to impeach the chose by a defense inconsistent with his representations, even though such defense is usury.

FORECLOSURE SUIT. The defendant Boyce was the administrator of Bates the purchaser of the mortgaged premises.

J. D. Denison, for the orator.

Dillingham, Huse, and Howland, for the defendants.

820 ROWELL, J.   The orator's letter of March 29, 1888, in
reply to one from the defendant Boyce, in which the orator
denied the existence of the agreement of February 14, 1878,
found by the master, and on which the orator now seeks to
stand, did not estop the orator from claiming before the master the untruth of his denial, if he did so claim; nor does it
disentitle him to the benefit of that agreement now that it is
found, it not appearing that Boyce or any of the other defendants was thereby induced to alter their conduct.   The
rule applicable here is thus stated in *Heane* v. *Rogers,* 9 Barn.
& C. 577: "There is no doubt that the express admissions of
a party to the suit, or admissions implied from his conduct,
are evidence, and strong evidence, against him; but we think
that he is at liberty to prove that such admissions were mistaken, or were untrue, and is not estopped or concluded by
them, unless another person has been induced by them to
alter his conduct, in which case the party is estopped from
disputing their truth with respect to that person and those
claiming under him and that transaction, but as to third persons he is not bound." This rule is approved in *Newton* v.
Liddiard, 12 Q. B. 925: See also 2 Wharton's Evidence, sec.
1077, and *Stowe* v. *Bishop,* 58 Vt. 498; 56 Am. Rep. 569.

321 Gordon held the mortgage in question against Church
and Mattoon.   Bates bought the mortgaged premises, and assumed and agreed to pay the mortgage debt as a part of the
purchase money.   Disagreement arose between Bates and
Gordon about extra interest that the former claimed to have
paid the latter, whereupon Gordon left the notes with a lawyer for collection, and the lawyer notified Bates that they
must be paid.   Thereupon Bates arranged with the orator to
buy and hold the notes, and, for the purpose of ascertaining
the amount due on them, Bates and Gordon, with their attorneys and the orator, met on February 14, 1878, when such
proceedings were had that Bates and Gordon agreed that
the amount then due was four hundred and sixteen dollars
and sixty-five cents, and an indorsement to that effect was
then made thereon.   In a few days after, the orator, relying
on said agreement, paid Gordon the amount thus found due,
and took an assignment of the notes and the mortgage, and
now seeks to foreclose the mortgage and to stand on the
amount thus agreed upon as a basis for ascertaining the sum
due in equity.   The defendants seek to compute the notes
anew, claiming that, by reason of the payment of extra in-

tercst and otherwise, there was much less due on them on February 14, 1888, than was then agreed.

We think that Bates, if living, would be estopped to deny that there were four hundred and sixteen dollars and sixty-five cents due on the notes when the orator took them, and that therefore the administrators of his estate are estopped, and the other defendants, who claim under the administrators. The rule is, that when one takes an assignment of a chose in action by the debtor's procurement or with his assent, and on the faith of representations made by him at the time, the debtor is estopped to impeach the chose by a defense inconsistent with his representations, even though the defense is usury: *Payne* v. *Burnham*, 62 N. Y. 69; *Smyth* v. *Munroe*, 84 N. Y. 359. *Union Dime Sav. Inst.* v. *Wilmot*, 94 N. Y. 221, 46 Am. Rep. 137, was an [322] action to foreclose a mortgage, and the defense was that the mortgage was void for usury. The mortgagor and the mortgagee represented to the plaintiff that the mortgage was a purchase-money mortgage, without defense, and that the full amount named therein was due thereon. Relying on this the plaintiff bought the mortgage at a discount of seven per cent from its face, and took an assignment of it. It was held that the mortgagee and the mortgagor were estopped to deny the validity of the mortgage, and precluded from interposing the defense of usury, and that Wilmot, who was alone defendant, was bound by the same estoppel, as he had bought the premises subject to the mortgage.

Decree affirmed and cause remanded.

ESTOPPEL BY ADMISSION.—One is estopped to deny his admissions which were designed to influence the conduct of another, and which did so influence it, where such denial would operate to the injury of the latter: *Thompson* v. *Simpson*, 128 N. Y. 270; *Humphreys* v. *Finch*, 97 N. C. 303; 2 Am. St. Rep. 293; *Taylor* v. *Zepp*, 14 Mo. 482; 55 Am. Dec. 113; *Simpson* v. *Pearson*, 31 Ind. 1; 99 Am. Dec. 577, and note; *Rudd* v. *Matthews*, 79 Ky. 479; 42 Am. Rep. 231, and note; *Hefner* v. *Dawson*, 63 Ill. 403; 14 Am. Rep. 123; *Hefner* v. *Vandolah*, 62 Ill. 483; 14 Am. Rep. 106, and note; *Brown* v. *Bowen*, 30 N. Y. 519; 86 Am. Dec. 406, and note; *Phillipsburgh Bank* v. *Fulmer*, 31 N. J. L. 52; 86 Am. Dec. 193; *Davis* v. *Davis*, 26 Cal. 23; 85 Am. Dec. 157, and note, with the cases collected; *Brooks* v. *Martin*, 43 Ala. 360; 94 Am. Dec. 686, and note.

KINNEY *v.* HOOKER.

[65 VERMONT, 333.]

DEEDS, EXTRANEOUS EVIDENCE TO EXPLAIN AMBIGUITIES IN.—If the language of a grant is uncertain and ambiguous, the circumstances surrounding it and the situation of the parties are to be considered in ascertaining their true intent.

DEEDS—EXTRANEOUS EVIDENCE TO SHOW INTENT OF PARTIES, HOW FAR ADMISSIBLE.—In construing a grant, the courts will give effect to the intention of the parties as disclosed by their situation and by the surrounding circumstances, unless the intention thus disclosed is inconsistent with the language of the grant.

DEEDS—LOCATION OF RIGHT OF WAY BY PAROL AGREEMENT.—When a right of way is granted by a deed, but the location of the way is not described therein, the parties may locate it by a parol agreement, and evidence of such agreement is admissible, and does not vary or contradict the deed, provided the way is located within the boundaries of the land over which the right was granted.

PRIVATE WAYS, PAROL AGREEMENT FIXING POSITION OF, EFFECT OF.—If a landowner and his vendee, by a parol agreement entered into after the execution of a deed which grants a right of way over other lands belonging to the vendor, locate the precise position of the way, that agreement will limit and define the right of way which will pass to a sub-purchaser of the same premises as appurtenant thereto, and he cannot maintain the privilege of passing in a different direction over the servient tenement.

SUIT for the establishment of a right of way.

Wing and Fay, for the oratrix.

W. A. and O. B. Boyce, for the defendant.

334 START, J.   The oratrix is the owner of two pieces of land in the village of Barre.   One, called the "flat," is situated north of the defendant's land; the other, the "Kinney homestead," is situated north of a piece of land called the "Batchelder lot."   All the above-mentioned land was formerly owned by W. C. French and wife, who first conveyed the "Kinney homestead" to Ira Trow, and subsequently, on the thirtieth day of April, 1870, conveyed the "flat" to said Trow by their deed of warranty, containing the following provision: "Said Trow has the privilege of going onto our land at the south end of the piece as above set forth in the description."   On the twenty-third day of November, 1870, French and wife conveyed to the defendant the land now owned by him, by their deed of warranty, without reservation except as to certain water rights.   On the twenty-third day of September, 1881, French conveyed the "Batchelder lot," with the following reservation: "I reserve the right to cross the above-described land at the northwesterly corner as is conveyed by deed, H. W. and E. C. French to Ira Trow, dated April 30, 1870." The conveyance referred to [335] in this reservation is the deed of the "flat" from French and wife to Trow.

The "flat" is some nine feet higher than the "Kinney homestead" and is practically inaccessible by team there. from without going upon the "Batchelder lot." Ira Trow occupied the "flat" and the "Kinney homestead," under his deeds from French and wife, until September 11, 1872, and during this time he exercised his right of way over the north. west corner of the "Bachelder lot," entering the "flat" at its southeast corner, and, in so doing, passing over the corner of the defendant's land. Trow was called as witness, and testi- fied that at the time he took his deed of the "flat" he and French agreed by parol that his right should be exercised in this place; and if this testimony was admissible, the master so finds the fact. The oratrix claims that, under the deed from French and wife to Trow, she has a right of way across the defendant's land to Prospect street. The defendant claims that the right of way granted is at the southeast corner of the "flat" and northwest corner of the "Batchelder lot," where Trow exercised the right.

We will first consider what was intended by the words, "our land at the south end of the piece as above set forth in the description," found in the deed of the "flat." At the time this deed was executed the defendant's land and the "Batchelder lot" were one lot, owned by French and wife. The words, "our land at the south end of the piece as above set forth in the description," do not limit the way to any par- ticular portion of the lot south of the "flat." They are so general that the exercise of the right of way over any por- tion of the lot, as then owned and situated, could be fairly said to be an exercise of the right granted; and the right granted could be exercised over what is now called the "Batchelder lot," if such was the intent of the parties to the grant. If the language of a grant is uncertain and ambigu- ous, the circumstances surrounding it and the situation of [336] the parties are to be considered in arriving at the true intent of the parties.

In determining the intent of the parties to the grant in question, it is important that we consider the situation and relation of the respective lots to each other and the purpose for which they were used. The "flat" was used for a pasture

and joined the "Kinney homestead," which, at the time of
the grant, was owned and occupied by Trow. He could not
pass directly from the "Kinney homestead" to the "flat,"
because of an embankment, but it was necessary to go around
the embankment over a corner of the "Batchelder lot," and
the northeast corner of the defendant's land. This was the
most convenient and direct way of reaching the "flat." In
order to reach the "flat" without going upon the "Batchelder
lot," it was necessary to go by the highway around the "Batchelder lot" and across the defendant's land, where the oratrix
now claims a right of way. From the surrounding circumstances, the situation of the lots and the parties at the time
of the grant, we think that the parties intended that the
grantee should exercise his right of way over such portions of
the entire lot owned by the grantors and situated south of the
"flat" as was necessary to enable him to conveniently reach
the "flat"; and if the convenient, reasonable, and proper exercise of the right granted required that he go upon what is now
the "Batchelder lot," the right to do so was granted. In construing a grant of a right of way, courts will give effect to
the intention of the parties as disclosed by the surrounding
circumstances and the situation of the parties, provided the
intention thus disclosed is not inconsistent with the language
of the grant: *Herman* v. *Roberts*, 119 N. Y. 37; 16 Am. St.
Rep. 800; *Bakeman* v. *Talbot*, 31 N. Y. 370; 88 Am. Dec. 275;
Burnham v. *Nevins*, 144 Mass. 93; 59 Am. Rep. 61; *Atkins* v.
Bordman, 2 Met. 457; 37 Am. Dec. 100.

When a way is not located by the grant, the parties may
[337] locate it by parol agreement at any point on the premises over which the right is granted, and evidence of such
agreement is admissible, and does not contradict or vary the
deed, provided the way is located within the boundaries of
the land over which the right is granted. The deed, in this
case, did not locate the way. It granted the right, but did
not limit or define it. The grantee was entitled to a convenient, reasonable, and accessible way, and such a way could
be located by the agreement of the parties: *George* v. *Cox*, 114
Mass. 382; *Johnson* v. *Kinnicutt*, 2 Cush. 153; *Bannon* v. *An-
gier*, 2 Allen, 128; 2 Washburn on Real Property, 53; *Wyn-
koop* v. *Burger*, 12 Johns. 222; *Onthank* v. *Lake Shore etc. R. R.
Co.*, 71 N. Y. 194; 27 Am. Rep. 35; Gale and Whortley on
Easements, 344; *French* v. *Hayes*, 43 N. H. 30; 80 Am. Dec.
127; *Cheswell* v. *Chapman*, 38 N. H. 14; 75 Am. Dec. 158.

It does not appear that a right of way was mentioned in the deed from Trow, under which the oratrix claims, or that Trow undertook to convey a right of way over any land. If, at the time of this conveyance, there was a right of way over the defendant's land appurtenant to the "flat," it was the way used by Trow, and located by him and French; and if the oratrix now has a right of way over the defendant's land, it is the way then located, and is passed to her as an appurtenance to the "flat," and her right is limited to the way that was appurtenant to the "flat" at the time it was conveyed by Trow: *George* v. *Cox*, 114 Mass. 382; *Onthank* v. *Lake Shore etc. R. R. Co.*, 71 N. Y. 194; 27 Am. Rep. 35; *Jennison* v. *Walker*, 11 Gray, 423; *French* v. *Marstin*, 24 N. H. 440; 57 Am. Dec. 294; *Cheswell* v. *Chapman*, 38 N. H. 14; 75 Am. Dec. 158; *Kent* v. *Waite*, 10 Pick. 138.

It not appearing that the oratrix ever claimed any right over the way agreed upon and used by Trow, or that such [338] right has been denied her by the defendant, the bill was properly dismissed.

The *pro forma* decree of the court of chancery is affirmed, and cause remanded.

DEEDS—EXTRINSIC EVIDENCE TO SHOW INTENT OF PARTIES.—Where the intent of the parties in making a conveyance is doubtful on the face of the instrument, light may be shed upon it by the attending circumstances: *Bortz* v. *Bortz*, 48 Pa. St. 382; 86 Am. Dec. 603, and note; *Soye* v. *McCallister*, 18 Tex. 80; 67 Am. Dec. 689; *Bartholomew* v. *Muzzy*, 61 Conn. 387; 29 Am. St. Rep. 206.

DEEDS—EXTRINSIC EVIDENCE TO EXPLAIN AMBIGUITIES IN.—Where the language of a grant is uncertain or ambiguous, it must be interpreted with regard to the surrounding circumstances: *Herman* v. *Roberts*, 119 N. Y. 37; 16 Am. St. Rep. 800; *Atkins* v. *Bordman*, 2 Met. 457; 37 Am. Dec. 100. Evidence of extrinsic facts and circumstances is admissible to identify the premises sold or to apply the description thereto: *Herrick* v. *Morrill*, 37 Minn. 250; 5 Am. St. Rep. 841; *French* v. *Hayes*, 43 N. H. 30; 80 Am. Dec. 127, and note. See the extended note to *Blossom* v. *Griffin*, 67 Am. Dec. 80.

PRIVATE WAYS—PAROL AGREEMENTS TO ESTABLISH.—Verbal promises to establish a passway through land cannot be enforced, because there is no specific contract entered into by any person or persons, and because such promises are not obligatory under the statute of frauds: *Hall* v. *McLeod*, 2 Met. (Ky.) 98; 74 Am. Dec. 400; but see *Rhea* v. *Forsyth*, 37 Pa. St. 503; 78 Am. Dec. 441.

RUTLAND ELECTRIC LIGHT COMPANY *v.* MARBLE CITY ELECTRIC LIGHT COMPANY.

[65 VERMONT, 377.]

ELECTRIC LIGHT COMPANIES—IMPAIRMENT OF FRANCHISE TO USE STREETS.
When a city has conferred upon an electric light company the right to erect its poles on certain streets, and the company, relying upon the license thus given, expends money in establishing its plant and appliances, the city cannot, by a subsequent ordinance, infringe the rights thus vested or bestow upon another the authority to infringe them.

ELECTRIC LIGHT COMPANIES—EXTENT OF THE RIGHTS OF COMPANIES USING THE SAME STREETS.—An electric light company which receives from a municipal corporation a license to erect its poles on certain streets, and expends money on the faith of such license, does not obtain thereby an exclusive privilege. A second company upon which a similar privilege is conferred acquires merely subordinate rights, and any interference of its wires with those of the prior licensee may be restrained by injunction.

PETITION for an injunction to restrain an electric light company from maintaining its wires so as to interfere with those of the orator.

George E. Lawrence and C. H. Joyce, for the orator.

J. C. Baker, for the respondent.

378 TYLER, J. The orator and defendant are rival corporations organized under the general laws of this state for the purpose of carrying on, respectively, the business of electric lighting in the village of Rutland.

In May, 1886, the orator entered into a written contract with the trustees of the village for lighting the village streets, and acting upon and in compliance with that contract it established a plant, erected poles, strung wires, and commenced doing business. It was stipulated that where wires crossed streets they should not be within thirty feet of the ground and that line wires should be at least twenty feet above the ground. The poles were erected at points indicated by the trustees.

Some three years later the defendant, by permission of the trustees, erected poles, strung wires, and commenced the business of electric lighting in competition with the orator. Its poles were also placed under direction of the trustees. In some of the principal streets the poles were set on the same side as the orator's poles and quite near to them. The orator employs a system for lighting buildings with incandescent lamps with a current of electricity used on its wires of only

one hundred and ten volts, which is so low a current that
the wires when charged can be handled with safety.   **379** The
defendant uses for its incandescent lamps an alternating current of one thousand volts on its wires in the streets.   By
means of what are called converters a current of fifty volts is
taken into buildings.

When the defendant's wires were first strung upon the poles
they did not touch the wires and poles of the orator, but from
the effect of storms, from stretching or some other cause, they
now sometimes come in contact with the orator's poles and
wires and injure them.   The wires should not be nearer each
other than twelve inches, and the cross-pieces upon which
they are strung should be at least two feet apart, so that when
the wires are loaded with snow and ice, or when swayed by
the wind, they will not come in contact.   When the wire
carrying a heavy current comes in contact with one carrying
a lighter current, the heavy current is liable to be inducted
into the other wire, which endangers the orator's wires, lamps,
and plant, and is liable to set fire to buildings, for which the
orator would be answerable in damages.

The defendant's poles are not as high as those of the orator;
the cross-pieces to which its wires are attached are nearer the
ground than those of the orator, so that in places the defendant's wires are under the orator's, which renders it difficult
and dangerous for the orator's employees to reach their wires
for repairs and other purposes.   No accident has thus far
happened.   The defendant's wires are not usually charged
with electricity in the daytime, but the two plants are entirely independent of each other, and the orator's employees
have no means of knowing when the defendant's wires are
charged.

Where the wires of the parties cross Centre street the orator's is only twenty-one feet above the ground; the defendant's is strung above it, and, having sagged, rests upon it.
At other places where the respective wires enter buildings
they interfere with each other.   These are the material
380 facts found by the master.   It is conceded that the village trustees had authority to make the contract with the
orator.

The defendant virtually concedes that the orator's contract
with the trustees is the measure of its rights.   The village,
by its trustees, invested the orator with certain rights, and
after the orator, relying upon the contract, had expended

money in establishing its plant and appliances, the village could not by an ordinance have infringed these rights, and clearly it could not confer upon the defendant authority to infringe them.

On the other hand it is not claimed that the orator obtained a privilege of the streets to the exclusion of the defendant, but that the defendant's rights were subordinate to the orator's, and must be exercised in such a manner as not to interfere with them. If authorities were required to sustain so plain a proposition, those cited upon the orator's brief are pertinent.

In *Hudson Tel. Co. v. Jersey City*, 49 N. J. L. 303, 60 Am. Rep. 619, it was held that where the city by an ordinance, under statutory authority, had designated certain public streets in which the company might place its telegraph poles, and the company had expended money in placing its poles upon such streets, the city could not by subsequent ordinances revoke such designation; that the company had an irrevocable vested right to use the streets for the designated purpose.

Thompson's Law of Electricity lays down the general rule that when a municipal corporation under a statutory provision has, by ordinance or other lawful mode, authorized a telephone company to erect its posts or poles in certain designated streets, and the company proceeds so to erect them and to expend money on the faith of the license so granted, it thereby acquires a vested right to the use of the designated streets so long as it conforms to the conditions of the license; and the license cannot thereafter be revoked by the municipality. So an ordinance authorizing a telephone [381] company to maintain lines on its streets, without limitation as to time, for a stipulated consideration, when accepted and acted upon by the grantee, by a compliance with its conditions, becomes a contract which the city cannot abolish or alter without consent of the grantees.

It appears that the orator has suffered some damage in consequence of its wires coming in contact with the defendant's; that it is constantly exposed to danger from such contact, and that its men cannot conveniently and without danger reach its wires for the purpose of making repairs and of connecting lines therewith to buildings. We therefore think that the orator is entitled to relief according to the prayer of the bill.

The *pro forma* decree dismissing the bill is reversed and

the cause remanded; an accounting is ordered for the damages already suffered by the orator, and the orator may have a perpetual injunction restraining the defendant from maintaining its wires so as to interfere with those of the orator.

MUNICIPAL CORPORATIONS—RIGHT TO USE STREET CANNOT BE IMPAIRED, WHEN.—Where a right to use a street is acquired pursuant to a statute and under a license from the municipality, it is in the nature of a contract right, and the municipality itself cannot destroy or materially impair it: *Williams v. Citizen's Ry. Co.*, 130 Ind. 71; 30 Am. St. Rep. 201, and note; *People v. O'Brien*, 111 N. Y. 1; 7 Am. St. Rep. 684. A grant of a franchise to a street railway is a vested right, and cannot be impaired by the authorities that made it: *Mayor etc. v. Houston etc. Ry. Co.*, 83 Tex. 548; 29 Am. St. Rep. 679, and note.

MUNICIPAL CORPORATIONS.—A GRANT OF A FRANCHISE TO A STREET RAILWAY COMPANY by a city to maintain its tracks along and upon its streets does not confer an exclusive privilege nor prevent the city from extending similar privileges to other companies: *Mayor etc. v. Houston etc. Ry. Co.*, 83 Tex. 548; 29 Am. St. Rep. 679, and note with the cases collected.

BEDELL *v.* WILDER.

[65 VERMONT, 406.]

MISTAKE, WHEN AVOIDS CONTRACT.—A contract induced by a mutual mistake in respect to the subject matter is inoperative, and void.

CONTRACTS—EXTRINSIC EVIDENCE AS TO MUTUAL MISTAKE.—Parol evidence may be adduced to show that a lease was taken with the understanding, on the part of both the lessor and the lessee, that the premises were to be used for a certain purpose, and that this understanding was based on a mistake as to the true facts of the case. Such evidence is properly admitted, not to vary the effect of the contract, but to show that it never had any valid existence.

ASSUMPSIT—CONSTRUCTIVE NOTICE OF MATERIAL FACT, WHEN NOT AN ESTOPPEL.—If a landowner has taken water to a mill, and leased it in connection therewith, the lessee is entitled, in the absence of actual notice, to infer that there is no restriction upon the water rights, and mere constructive notice from the record of a deed limiting those rights will not estop him from recovering rent which he has paid to the lessor in the belief that no such limitations existed.

ASSUMPSIT—RECOVERY OF RENT BY LESSEE UPON FAILURE OF LESSOR'S TITLE.—Where a lessee, after accepting a lease of land and water rights, discovers that another person lays claim to the water rights, and the lessor thereupon insists that he is entitled to the rent, but promises to do "whatever his contract calls upon him to do," and, if the contract requires it, "to stand between the lessee and the other claimant," the rent which the lessee is afterwards forced to pay to such claimant, when the proprietorship of the water rights has been established, may be recovered from the lessor.

ASSUMPSIT by a lessee to recover moneys paid to his lessor
as rent of water rights. The parties to the lease understood
that a building then on the leased premises was to be used
for the manufacture of pulp, and, as a matter of fact, that
was the sole purpose for which the premises could be used,
and for which they were actually used. The evidence as to
the understanding of the parties, and as to the limited uses
to which the premises could be put, was parol evidence, and
on that ground excepted to by the defendant. Previous to
the payment of any rent, the lessee received notice from one
Clement that he claimed the water rights which had been
leased, and would hold him liable for the use thereof. The
lessee reported the claim to his lessor, who denied that it
was a valid one, and insisted that the rent should be paid
to him. The report of the master as to what was said at
the time, is as follows: " I do not find this claim established
by the evidence. I find that the facts are that Wilder told
Bedell that he should look to him for the rent, and should
expect him to fulfill his part of the contract, and he should
his, that whatever his contract called upon him to do, he
should do, and if it called upon him to stand between him and
the Clements, he should do so; that he must go on and pay
the rent to him, and fulfill the contract on his part. Wilder
knew that Bedell was using the mill for the manufacture of
pulp, and expected him to control and use it for that purpose.
Wilder further told Bedell that if his contract required him
to pay what he paid Clement, he should do so. He also
claimed to Bedell that the Clements had no right to the water.
Plaintiff claims that after he paid Clement, Wilder promised
to fix the matter up with him. I do not find any absolute
promise upon the part of Wilder to pay Bedell what he paid
Clement, but that the talk in regard to fixing up was dependent upon his liability under his lease. I find that Wilder
recognized Bedell as his lessee, and received rent of him as
a lessee, and that he did agree that if his lease made him
liable to any one as a lessor, he was liable to him, and would
pay him what he paid Clement." In consequence of what
was said, the lessee paid the lessor the full amount of the
rent for the time during which the premises were occupied
by him. A decision of the supreme court afterwards settled
that the water could not be used for the purpose contemplated
by the parties, and the plaintiff, being forced to pay the same
amount of rent to Clement also, now brought suit to recover it.

W. P. Stafford, for the defendant.

Smith and Sloane, for the plaintiff.

[409] TAFT, J. When the lease in question was executed by the defendant, and when the plaintiff took the assignment of it, the parties to both instruments understood that the water power which was the subject of the lease could be used in manufacturing pulp. With this understanding, the lease and assignment were made, and without it, it is apparent that no lease nor assignment would have been executed. The water could not be used for such purpose: *Clement* v. *Gould,* 61 Vt. 573. The lease was made and assigned in ignorance of this fact; an instance of a mistake as to the subject matter of the thing contracted for, a common mistake as to the rights conveyed by the lease. It is clear that the defendant supposed he was selling and the plaintiff that he was buying a right to water which could be used in making pulp. The plaintiff secured by the contracts no such rights, for the defendant had none to convey. It is analogous in principle to those cases of sale in which the subject of the sale has ceased to exist, and the parties are ignorant of the fact, like the destruction of a building by fire before the sale, or the death of an animal, or the sale of an annuity when the annuitant is dead. An error of fact takes place [410] when some fact is supposed to exist which does not exist. The parties in entering into the contracts in question, supposed the water could be used by them in making pulp; it could not be so used. Clearly an error of fact. In respect of such a state of facts the law is this: If an agreement is induced by a mistake common to both parties, without which mistake the agreement would not have been made, and the mistake was in respect of the subject matter of the contract, the agreement is inoperative and void. Such was the civil law: Domat's Civil Law, part 1, book 1, title 18, section 1, article 7. The same rule has been adopted as a part of the common law, and is based upon the idea that in such cases no contract has been consummated, that the minds of the parties have never met in respect of the real subject matter of the contract. It is not a case of a mere failure of consideration, for that implies the existence of a contract, while a mutual mistake prevents the existence of one.

The law in this state in such cases was announced in *Ketchum* v. *Catlin,* 21 Vt. 191. The defendant sold produce

which both parties supposed was in Whitehall; in fact it was
in Boston. By reason of this mutual mistake, the plaintiff
was permitted to recover what he had paid defendant on
account of it, and that vigorous master of the common law,
the late Bennett, J., says, "if a contract is made in mutual
error of material facts which have induced the contract, it is
invalid and may be set aside. This is upon the principle,
mainly, that when the parties are under a mutual mistake as
to material facts, affecting the subject matter of the contract,
there is a want of a binding assent; and we think a contract
so made may be avoided in a court of law": And see *Kelley*
v. *Solari*, 9 Mees. & W. 59; *Wheadon* v. *Olds*, 20 Wend. 174;
Fleetwood v. *Brown*, 109 Ind. 567; *Newell* v. *Smith*, 53 Conn.
72, in which case a compromise was set aside for that the
parties mutually supposed a cow was [411] not in calf, when
in fact she was. The effect of a mistake, when it has any
operation at all, is to avoid the contract, and if the contract
is avoided, an action lies to recover money paid under it.

The parol evidence was properly admitted, not to vary the
terms nor the effect of the contract, but to show that it never
took effect as a valid agreement. The claim was not based
upon the lease, but upon a fact back of it, the mutual mistake of the parties, which led to the execution of it and the
assignment. The plaintiff is not estopped from asserting this
claim against the defendant. It is true he had constructive
notice of the limitation upon the water rights, as the deed
limiting them was upon record; but the defendant had taken
the water to the pulp mill and had leased it in connection
with the mill, and the plaintiff might well infer, without actual notice, that there was no limit nor restriction upon the
water rights.

The mistake was discovered before the payment, which
the plaintiff is seeking to recover, was made. After it was
discovered that Clement made claim to the water rights, the
defendant insisted that he, Clement, had no title to the water
and that the plaintiff must pay him, the defendant, the rent,
and the effect of the report is that he did agree that if in
respect of the lease he was liable to any one, it was to the
plaintiff, and that he would pay him what he was compelled
to pay Clement.

We do not think a technical, narrow construction should
be given to the terms of the defendant's agreement. He
promised the plaintiff that he would pay "if his lease made

him liable": he would do "whatever his contract called upon him to do." It is true he cannot be made liable in an action upon the lease, but he is liable in respect of it, and the lease being inoperative and void, the law calls upon him to refund whatever he has received upon it. The agreement although conditional has become absolute, the plaintiff is entitled to [412] its performance, and the defendant should "pay him what he paid Clement," and thus "stand between him and all harm" as he agreed to do.

Judgment affirmed.

Mistake—When Avoids Contract.—A contract entered into through the mutual mistake of the parties thereto respecting its contents is not binding upon them: *Rowland* v. *New York etc. R. R. Co.*, 61 Conn. 103; 29 Am. St. Rep. 175, and note with the cases collected. This question is thoroughly discussed in the monographic note to *Miles* v. *Stevens*, 45 Am. Dec. 631.

Contracts—Parol Evidence Showing Attendant Circumstances.— Conversations and negotiations preliminary to a written agreement although merged in it, may still be admissible, not to explain its terms, but to throw light upon the question of its execution or other questions connected therewith: *Wilbur* v. *Stoepel*, 82 Mich. 344; 21 Am, St. Rep. 568, and note. Parol evidence is admissible to show that at the time of the execution of a written contract, a parol agreement was entered into by the parties and made a part of it: *Redfield* v. *Gleason*, 61 Vt. 220; 15 Am. St. Rep. 889, and note; *Real Estate etc. Trust Co's Appeal*, 125 Pa. St. 549; 11 Am. St. Rep. 920, and note. See also *Schmittler* v. *Simon*, 114 N. Y. 176; 11 Am. St. Rep. 621, and note, and the extended note to *Sullivan* v. *Lear*, 11 Am. St. Rep. 393.

Rents—Failure of Landlord's Title as a Defense in an Action for.—Eviction of a tenant by a paramount title is a good defense in an action of covenant for rent: *Smith* v. *Shepherd*, 15 Pick. 147; 25 Am. Dec. 432, and note; *Halligan* v. *Wade*, 21 Ill. 470; 74 Am. Dec. 108, and note; *Poston* v. *Jones*, 2 Ired. Eq. 350; 38 Am. Dec. 683; *Manville* v. *Gay*, 1 Wis. 250; 60 Am. Dec. 379, and note. A failure of the lessor to deliver possession of the leased premises to his lessee justifies the latter in abandoning the premises and discharges him from the liability to pay rent: *Dengler* v. *Michelssen*, 76 Cal. 125. For a further discussion of this question, see the notes to the following cases: *George* v. *Putney*, 50 Am. Dec. 791, and *Giles* v. *Comstock*, 53 Am. Dec. 378.

BARRETT *v.* CARDEN.

[65 VERMONT, 431.]

PLEADING—A SEAL IMPORTS CONSIDERATION, and, in declaring upon a bond, the consideration that induced its execution need not be stated.

PLEADING—THE DECLARATION IN AN ACTION FOR A BREACH OF A BOND, by which the defendant had obligated himself to accept the provisions of a certain will, and not to claim under the statute of distribution, need not aver that the plaintiff is a beneficiary under the will, and that the defendant had a right to waive it. The breach of such a bond is sufficiently shown by allegations setting forth the decease of the testator, the regular probate of the will, and the waiver by the defendant of his rights under the will, and his acquisition of the same interests as if such will had not been probated.

CONTRACTS CONTRAVENING PUBLIC POLICY, AVOIDANCE OF, WHEN PROPER.—The power of the courts to declare contracts void because in contravention of a sound public policy should be exercised only in cases free from doubt.

CONTRACTS NOT TO CONTEST WILLS nor to claim under the statute of distributions are not contrary to public policy.

ACTION of debt upon a bond not to contest a will. A general demurrer to the declaration was overruled, and the defendant excepted. The declaration set forth the execution of the bond, and proceeded thus: " Which said writing obligatory is subject to the following conditions, that the said defendant shall abide by and accept the provisions of the last will and testament of one Abigail L. Carden, of said Dummerston, made on the 30th of April, 1891, and make no opposition to the probate and establishment thereof as the last will of said Abigail L., and shall not waive the same or make or cause to be made any trouble or expense to the said plaintiff in respect to any bequest or legacy made or given to him, then said obligation to be void, otherwise to remain in full force and effect. And the plaintiff avers that said defendant has broken and disregarded his said obligations. That the said Abigail L. Carden deceased in the summer of 1891; that said will was duly probated by the probate court for the district of Marlboro on, to wit, the 25th of July, A. D. 1891, and that on, to wit, the eleventh day of February, A. D. 1892, the said defendant waived the provisions of said will and filed on the day and year last aforesaid, in the probate court aforesaid, a waiver in writing of said will, and asserted a claim to his interest and rights in the estate of said Abigail L., the same as if said will had not been made and probated, whereby the devise and legacy in said will to said plaintiff became of no value to him, the said plaintiff."

Waterman, Martin, and Hitt, for the defendant.

Haskins and Stoddard, for the plaintiff.

[432] START, J. It is claimed that the declaration does not show a cause of action. It sets forth a bond with its condition and a breach thereof. The bond is under seal and imports [433] a consideration, and it is not necessary to state the consideration that induced its execution. The defendant cannot be heard to say that it is without consideration. 1 Chitty on Pleadings, p. 366; Chitty on contracts, p. 4.

It was not necessary to allege that a will was made by Abigail L. Carden, or that the plaintiff was a beneficiary under it, or that the defendant had a right to waive it. The defendant obligated himself to abide by, accept of, and not waive the provisions of the last will of Abigail L. Carden, made on the thirtieth day of April, 1891. The declaration alleges that Abigail L. Carden deceased in the summer of 1891; that her said will was duly probated on the twenty-fifth day of July, 1891; and that on the eleventh day of February, 1892, the defendant waived its provisions. From these allegations the condition and breach of the bond sufficiently appear without setting forth the defendant's right to waive the provisions of the will, or the plaintiff's rights under it. The defendant's undertaking was to accept of, and not waive, its provisions. The question of whether he had a right to waive it is immaterial. He has done so, and thereby subjected himself to an action on the bond, for a breach of its express condition. The extent of the plaintiff's interest in the estate under the will or otherwise is material only upon the measure of damages, and this question is not now before us. The defendant had a right to give and the plaintiff to take the bond; the performance of its condition is in no way dependent upon the plaintiff's interest in the estate, and for a breach thereof the plaintiff is entitled to recover at least nominal damages.

The defendant insists that the alleged undertaking of the defendant is contrary to public policy, and that for this reason the bond should be declared void. Courts will not declare contracts void on grounds of public policy, except in cases free from doubt, and prejudice to the public interest must clearly appear before the court is justified in pronouncing [434] an instrument void on this account. In *Richmond* v. *Dubuque etc. R. R. Co.,* 26 Iowa, 191, it is said, "that the

power of courts to declare a contract void for being in contravention of sound public policy is a very delicate and
undefined power, and, like the power to declare a statute unconstitutional, should be exercised only in cases free from
doubt." In *Kellogg* v. *Larkin*, 3 Pinn. 123, 56 Am. Dec. 164,
Howe, J., said: "He is the safest magistrate who is more
watchful over the rights of the individual than over the convenience of the public, as that is the best government which
guards more vigilantly the freedom of the subject than the
rights of the state." In *Richardson* v. *Mellish*, 2 Bing. 229; 9
Eng. Com. L. 557, Sir James Burrough said: "I protest, as
my lord has done, against urging too strongly upon public
policy; it is a very unruly horse, and when once you get
astride it you never know where it will carry you. It may
lead you from the sound law. It is never urged at all but
when other points fail." In *Walsh* v. *Fussell*, 6 Bing. 169, 19
Eng. Com. L. 83, Lord Chief Justice Tindale, in pronouncing
judgment, said: "It is not contended that the covenant was
illegal on the ground of the breach of any direct rule of law,
or the direct violation of any statute, and we think to hold it
to be void on the ground of its impolicy or inconvenience, we
ought to be clearly satisfied that the performance of it would
be necessarily attended with injury or inconvenience to the
public."

This case is distinguishable from those where bonds are
given, or other agreements made, as a reward for using influence and power over another person to induce him to make a
will in favor of the obligor, for all such contracts tend to deceive and injure third persons, and encourage artifice and
improper attempts to control the exercise of free judgment.
In this case there was no intent to defraud, deceive, or influence any one. The defendant did not undertake to do an act
prohibited by the common law or by statute. ⁴³⁵ On the
contrary his undertaking is in accord with our statute relating to the disposition of property by will, and the universal
rule by which courts seek for and give effect to the intention
of the testator. It was not an undertaking to control the exercise of the testatrix's wish and judgment in the disposition
of her property. The acts to be done and omitted by the defendant were not calculated to thwart the plans of the testatrix or disappoint her intentions. The undertaking was to
abide by the provisions of the will and not waive them,
thereby giving effect to and carrying out the testatrix's

wishes. Such agreements are calculated to avoid or settle family controversies, to adjust doubtful rights, to preserve the harmony, affections, or honor of the family, to promote justice, and enable one to provide for the natural objects of his bounty; they are not in contravention of public policy: 1 Story's Equity Jurisprudence, sec. 625; *Johnson v. Hubbell*, 10 N. J. Eq. 332; 66 Am. Dec. 773; *Fulton v. Smith*, 27 Ga. 413; *Carmichael v. Carmichael*, 72 Mich. 76; 16 Am. St. Rep. 528; *Huguley v. Lanier*, 86 Ga. 636; 22 Am. St. Rep. 487; *Hobson v. Trevor*, 2 P. Wms. 191.

Judgment affirmed, and cause remanded.

A SEAL IMPORTS À CONSIDERATION, or, more accurately, estops the covenantor from denying a consideration, except for fraud: *Smith* v. *Smith*, 36 Ga. 184; 91 Am. Dec. 761. For a full discussion of this subject, see the extended note to *Garden* v. *Derrickson*, 95 Am. Dec. 287-290.

WILLS—VALIDITY OF CONDITION NOT TO CONTEST.—A condition in a will excluding from a share in the estate any heir or testator who "goes to law to break his will" is valid: *Bradford* v. *Bradford*, 19 Ohio St. 546; 2 Am. Rep. 419; extended note to *Hoit* v. *Hoit*, 59 Am. Rep. 46-48.

CONTRACTS AGAINST PUBLIC POLICY—WHEN SHOULD BE AVOIDED.— Courts will not declare contracts void on the ground of public policy, except in cases free from doubt: *Smith* v. *Du Bose*, 78 Ga. 413; 6 Am. St. Rep. 260, and note; *Kellogg* v. *Larkin*, 3 Pinn. 123; 3 Chand. 133; 56 Am. Dec. 164, and note. For a full discussion of contracts void as being in contravention of public policy, see the following line of cases: *Brooks* v. *Cooper*, 50 N. J. Eq. 761; 35 Am. St. Rep. 793, and note; *Harvey* v. *Merrill*, 150 Mass. 1; 15 Am. St. Rep. 159; *McNamara* v. *Gargett*, 68 Mich. 454; 13 Am. St. Rep. 355, and note; *Tatum* v. *Kelley*, 25 Ark. 209; 94 Am. Dec. 717; *Bowman* v. *Gonegal*, 19 La. Ann. 328; 92 Am. Dec. 537, and note; *City Bank* v. *Perkins*, 29 N. Y. 554; 86 Am. Dec. 332, and note; *Ohio Life Ins. etc. Co.* v. *Merchants' Ins etc. Co.*, 11 Humph. 1; 53 Am. Dec. 742, and note, and the extended note to *Parsons* v. *Trask*, 66 Am. Dec. 505-514.

CASWELL *v.* JONES.

[65 VERMONT, 457.]

SALES—CHANGE OF POSSESSION.—The fact that a husband has in his possession a chattel received by his wife in exchange for another which was sold to her by one of her husband's creditors, to whom it had been transferred in payment of a debt, will not invalidate her title to the chattel thus acquired by her as against an attachment thereof by the other creditors of her husband. Under such circumstances her title is derived, not from her husband, but from the person with whom the exchange is made.

EXECUTION SALES—OFFICER ACTING AS AGENT FOR PURCHASER.—An officer conducting an execution sale cannot act as the agent of an absent purchaser.

880   CASWELL *v.* JONES.   [Vermont,

EXECUTION SALES, HOW FAR MAY BE IMPEACHED.—An execution sale, regular on its face, is presumed to be a *bona fide* sale. It may be impeached for fraud and collusion between the execution creditor and debtor, and, if assailed on that ground, its *bona fides* should be submitted to the jury.

REPLEVIN for two cows attached as the property of the plaintiff's husband.

Norman Paul, for the defendant.

W. C. French and J. C. Enright, for the plaintiff.

458 THOMPSON, J. Albee took of the plaintiff's husband, **459** Joseph C. Caswell, a cow in payment of a debt due him from the husband, and sold the cow to the plaintiff for twenty dollars, giving her a bill of sale of the same. This cow remained with the other cows of Joseph C. Caswell and in his possession from the time the plaintiff made this purchase until she exchanged her with Keniston for one of the cows replevied. As between the parties, the purchase of the cow by Albee and the sale by him to the plaintiff was valid without any change of possession. The plaintiff acquired title to the Keniston cow from Keniston and not from her husband. The latter was never the owner of this cow, and hence his possession would not affect the rights of the plaintiff in case of an attachment by the husband's creditors while in his possession. To make a change of possession of personal property necessary in order to protect it from the alleged vendor's creditors there must have been some time when, as against the vendee, the alleged vendor owned it and had it in his possession: *Fitch* v. *Burk*, 38 Vt. 683; *Leavitt* v. *Jones*, 54 Vt. 423; 41 Am. Rep. 849; *Walworth* v. *Jenness*, 58 Vt. 670. Upon the facts stated in respect to the manner in which the plaintiff acquired title to the Keniston cow, it was not error for the court below to refuse to charge, as requested, that "the transaction in regard to the sale and exchange of said cows was a fraud on the creditors of Joseph C. Caswell, and wholly void." As against his creditors, the plaintiff's title to the Keniston cow was good. The case at bar is distinguishable from *Mills* v. *Warner*, 19 Vt. 609; 47 Am. Dec. 711. In this case the plaintiff herself made the exchange; in that case the former owner, who then had possession of the property, made it "for the convenience and advantage of his own business, and for aught that appears, in his own name and ostensibly on his own account."

It is conceded that prior to January 8, 1891, Joseph C. Caswell was the owner of the other cow replevied. In May, 1891, he rented her to Chamberlain, who retained possession **460** of her as lessee, until she was attached on a writ against Joseph C. Caswell by the defendant as deputy sheriff. Chamberlain was never notified of a sale of this cow, but during all the time he kept her he paid the rent for her to Joseph C. Caswell. The plaintiff claims that this cow was sold on execution at sheriff's sale, January 8, 1891, to George E. Smith, and that she subsequently purchased her of Smith, and that by reason of Smith's having purchased the cow at sheriff's sale, no change of possession was necessary to protect her from attachment by the creditors of Joseph C. Caswell. The plaintiff has no title to this cow unless she derived it from Smith in the manner claimed. Smith never had title to her unless he acquired it by virtue of his alleged purchase at the sale on execution. If that was a valid sheriff's sale, without fraud or collusion, and Smith acquired title to the cow by virtue of such sale, it is well settled in this state that no change of possession was necessary to protect the property of the purchaser: *Fitzpatrick* v. *Peabody*, 51 Vt. 195, and cases there cited. The execution was in favor of Smith and against Joseph C. Caswell, and was committed to the officer, Hudson, to levy and collect, and who conducted and made the alleged sale of the cow on the execution. Smith was not present at the sale, but he had given Hudson instructions, with full discretionary power, to bid off all the property sold on the execution for him, and Hudson, acting under these instructions and power, bid off the cow for Smith at the sale on the execution.

The defendant requested the court below to hold that Hudson, as the officer conducting the execution sale, had no right to bid off the cow for Smith, but it refused to so hold, and instructed the jury that the sale on the execution was "in law sufficient to pass the title to Smith," to which refusal and charge the defendant excepted. Assuming that the other proceedings connected with this sale were such as to make good the title of a purchaser of property at it, but in regard to **461** which we make no decision, the question is presented whether an officer at a sale on execution, conducted by himself, can act as the agent with full discretionary power of an absent person in the purchase of property.

Such officer cannot make a valid purchase **for** himself at

such sale: *Woodbury* v. *Parker*, 19 Vt. 353; 47 Am. Dec. 695;
Downing v. *Lyford*, 57 Vt. 508. In *Woodbury* v. *Parker*, 19
Vt. 353, 47 Am. Dec. 695, Royce, C. J., says: "According to
all the authorities such an officer, in addition to his character
as a minister of the law, is regarded as a sort of a trustee and
agent both for the creditor and debtor. The two characters
place him on higher and more responsible ground than a mere
private trustee or agent." In *Harrison* v. *McHenry*, 9 Ga.
164, 52 Am. Dec. 435, where this question is discussed, Nes-
bit, J., says: "If the policy of the law prohibits a sheriff from
buying on his own account, I do not see how it is competent
for him to purchase as the agent of another. He can do
nothing for himself or for another which is incompatible with
his duties as sheriff. We have seen what they are. His skill,
diligence and fidelity belong to the defendant in execution.
He may not be in this latter case subject to the same temptations to do wrong that he is subject to when he buys for himself. This is true, but still the duty which he assumes as
agent for the buyer is incompatible with the duty which he
has assumed as agent for the seller. If acting under a general
and unrestricted power to buy at auction, he must be understood as charged with the duty of buying as low as possible,
whilst, at the same time, it is his duty as agent for the seller
to make the property bring as much as possible. Here is a
direct antagonism of position and duty, and involves, almost
necessarily, infidelity to one or the other of his principals.
His first obligation is to the seller, and the law will not permit him to place himself in a position which subjects him to
the chances of violating that obligation—its policy will not
allow it."

462 This reasoning seems unanswerable. Human nature is
such that it is as true now as ever that "no man can serve
two masters."

Freeman on Executions, section 292, says: "Nor can the
officer making the sale act as the agent of a person desirous
of bidding. He can neither bid for himself nor for another."
We think this is the true doctrine and the only rule consistent with a safe and sound public policy in respect to this
class of sales. We therefore hold on the facts stated in the
exceptions, that Hudson could not act as the agent for Smith
to purchase the cow for him at the execution sale, and that
as an attempted sheriff's sale of the cow it was void, and
passed no title to Smith. Hence the county court erred in

refusing to hold as requested and in charging the jury as it did on this subject.

From this view of the matter it follows that this cow was still liable to be taken by attachment on writs against Joseph C. Caswell in favor of his creditors: *Wheeler* v. *Selden,* 63 Vt. 430; 25 Am. St. Rep. 771.

This holding renders it unnecessary for us to consider the other points urged by the defendant against the validity of this sale to so pass title to the cow that change of possession was unnecessary.

Were the attempted sale to Smith apparently regular as a sheriff's sale on execution, it was error for the court to instruct the jury, as it did without qualification, that it was valid to pass title to the cow without change of possession. This assumed as a matter of law that the sale was without collusion and fraud as between the execution creditor and debtor. When the execution sale is regular on its face, the *prima facie* presumption is that it was a *bona fide* sale, but it may be impeached for fraud and collusion between the execution creditor and debtor, and when assailed on that ground, it is a question of fact for the jury to determine whether it was a *bona fide* sale on execution, giving such [463] *prima facie* presumption its due weight. The charge of the court did not submit that question to the jury: *Judevine* v. *Weaks,* 57 Vt. 278; *Boardman* v. *Keeler,* 1 Aiken, 158; 15 Am. Dec. 670; *Batchelder* v. *Carter,* 2 Vt. 168; 19 Am. Dec. 707; *Austin* v. *Soule,* 36 Vt. 645. So far as we can discover from the exceptions and that part of the charge furnished us, the only question of fact submitted to the jury in respect to this cow was whether the plaintiff purchased her of Smith as she claimed. The question being thus limited, what the court said in relation to Joseph C. Caswell's preferring to have Smith attach this property " and cover it and protect it for him, rather than to have some of his other creditors," could have no possible bearing or effect upon the jury in their determination of the question of the alleged purchase of the cow by the plaintiff from Smith. Had the question of the alleged execution sale being *bona fide* or not been submitted to the jury, then the language used would have been clearly misleading and error.

Judgment reversed and cause remanded.

SALES—CHANGE OF POSSESSION.—Retention of possession by a seller is *prima facie* evidence of fraud: *Hopkins* v. *Bishop,* 91 Mich. 328; 30 Am. St. Rep. 480, and note with the cases collected; *Brown* v. *O'Neal,* 95 Cal. 282;

29 Am. St. Rep. 111, and note; notes to *Wheeler* v. *Selden*, 25 Am. St. Rep. 773; and *Etchepare* v. *Aguirre*, 25 Am. St. Rep. 185.

EXECUTION SALE—OFFICER ACTING AS AGENT FOR PURCHASER.—A ministerial officer cannot buy at an execution sale, either for himself or as agent for another. If he does the sale passes no property: *Robinson* v. *Clark*, 7 Jones, 562; 78 Am. Dec. 265, and note; see *Farr* v. *Sims*, Rich. Eq. 122; 24 Am. Dec. 396. A sheriff cannot act as a discretionary agent to purchase at his own sale: *Harrison* v. *McHenry*, 9 Ga. 164; 52 Am. Dec. 435, and note with cases collected.

STATE v. KELLEY.

[65 VERMONT, 531.]

EVIDENCE IN CRIMINAL TRIALS—PROOF OF OTHER OFFENSES.—The charge upon which a defendant is being tried cannot be supported by proof of other offenses. But evidence which legitimately tends to support the charge is not to be excluded on the ground that it shows other offenses.

EVIDENCE—CHARACTER OF AMBIGUOUS TRANSACTION, WHEN MAY BE SHOWN BY PROOF OF OTHER CRIMES.—On a trial for larceny, in which the only direct evidence for the state consists of the narrative of an accomplice, which, as regards the act set forth in the indictment, leaves room for a reasonable doubt as to the felonious participation of the defendant, such participation may be established by other portions of the same narrative showing that, on the same expedition during which the larceny is alleged to have been committed, the defendant had actively engaged in abstracting other personal property from various places, and by the testimony of the owners of the stolen articles that they were in the places from which the accomplice asserts them to have been taken, were missed about the time at which the accomplice said the expedition took place, and were afterwards found and identified on the defendant's premises. But evidence of a larceny committed by the defendant and his accomplice during a second expedition, undertaken upon the renewal of a purpose entertained before the first expedition, has no legitimate tendency to support the charge, and should be excluded.

THE defendant was indicted for the larceny of two lap-robes. One Howe, the only witness for the state, was working on the defendant's farm at the time of the alleged crime, and testified that on the night named in the indictment the defendant proposed that they should go into a neighboring town and steal some phosphate from a certain storehouse. They accordingly started with Howe's team, and broke open the storehouse. Not finding any phosphate there, they abstracted some other articles. They then drove to several other places in the neighborhood, and stole a number of articles, some of which were handled by the defendant and

some by Howe. During this expedition they stopped at a
house near which was a shed. The defendant remained in
the wagon, and Howe went into the shed, and brought out
and laid in the wagon the two lap-robes specified in the indictment. They then returned home and ate some food,
after which the defendant proposed that, as they were still
without their phosphate, they should go out again and steal
some. This was accordingly done. The state had no witness except Howe to testify that the expedition had been
made, that the articles had been taken, or that the defendant
and Howe were together in the town on the night in question, a fact which was denied by the defendant; but the
owners of the various articles were permitted to testify that
they were stolen by some one about that time, and that, at a
subsequent date, several of those articles were found on the
defendant's premises. The admission of evidence concerning any other larceny than the one specified in the indictment was excepted to by the defendant.

J. A. Wing and J. G. Wing, for the defendant.

Z. S. Stanton, state's attorney, and *J. H. Senter,* for the state.

[533] MUNSON, J. It is a general rule that the charge upon
which a respondent is being tried cannot be supported by
proof of his having committed other offenses: Roscoe's Criminal Evidence, 81; *Shaffner v. Commonwealth,* 72 Pa. St. 60; 13
Am. Rep. 649. But evidence which legitimately tends to
support the charge is not to be excluded on the ground that
it [534] will show other offenses: 1 Wharton's Criminal Law,
sec. 649; *Commonwealth v. Choate,* 105 Mass. 451. The numerous cases in which evidence of this nature has been received have been classified with more or less particularity by
different textwriters: Stephen's Digest of Evidence, arts. 11,
12; 1 Greenleaf on Evidence, sec. 53 n.; 1 Bishop's Criminal
Procedure, secs. 1125–1129; *Strong v. State,* 44 Am. Rep. 299,
note.

Evidence tending to show that the respondent has been
guilty of other like offenses is received in cases where it is
necessary to prove a knowledge of the character of the thing
in respect of which the act was done. Thus, upon the trial of
one charged with passing counterfeit money, it may be shown
that he has, upon other occasions, passed money of that character: *Regina v. Forster,* Dears. C. C. 456; *Commonwealth v.
Bigelow,* 8 Met. 235. See *Wood v. United States,* 16 Pet. 342.

So, on an indictment for receiving stolen goods, it may be shown that the respondent has at different times received from the same individual other goods known to have been stolen from the same person or place: *Rex* v. *Dunn*, 1 Moody, 146; *Copperman* v. *People*, 56 N. Y. 591.

Evidence of this description has also been received to establish the felonious use of certain destructive agencies, which may be so obscurely employed as to leave their results naturally referable to accident. Thus, upon the charge of burning a building with intent to defraud the insurers, evidence that other insured buildings owned by the respondent had burned from unexplained causes has been received: *Regina* v. *Gray*, 4 Fost. & F. 1102; but see *State* v. *Raymond*, 53 N. J. L. 260. And it has been held that when a murder is alleged to have been committed by administering poison to the deceased, it may be shown that others who had previously received food or medicine from the respondent had died of the same poison: *Regina* v. *Geering*, 18 L. J. M. C. 215; *Goersen* v. *Commonwealth*, 99 Pa. St. 388; 106 Pa. St. 477; 51 Am. Rep. 534.

Evidence covering the commission of another offense is [535] also admissible when two crimes are so linked together in point of time or circumstances that one cannot be fully shown without proving the other. It is doubtless true that the criminal acts shown in many of the cases referred to this rule would come within some phase of the two comprehensive rules hereafter stated; but it is evident that the circumstantial connection between transactions of a criminal nature may be so intimate as to require proof of them all, independently of other grounds of admission: *Mason* v. *State*, 42 Ala. 532; *State* v. *Folwell*, 14 Kan. 105; *State* v. *Wentworth*, 37 N. H. 196; *Heath* v. *Commonwealth*, 1 Rob. (Va.) 735; *Brown* v. *Commonwealth*, 76 Pa. St. 319; *Rex* v. *Ellis*, 6 Barn. & C. 145.

Such evidence is also received to show identity of person, local proximity, or other facts calculated to connect the respondent with the commission of the offense: *Halleck* v. *State*, 65 Wis. 147; *Commonwealth* v. *Choate*, 105 Mass. 451. In the case last cited, there was evidence tending to show that the building which the respondent was charged with burning had been fired by means of an ingeniously constructed box, adapted to incendiary purposes only; and the prosecution was permitted to show that the respondent had the skill, materials, and tools requisite for the construction of this box, by evidence which tended to prove that he had constructed and made felonious use of another box of the same description.

Again, the prosecutor may show motive, purpose, preparation, or concealment, even though it involve proof of a distinct crime. On a trial for murder the prosecution may show an adulterous intimacy between the respondent and the wife of the deceased, not broken off before the commission of the offense charged: *Commonwealth* v. *Ferrigan*, 44 Pa. St. 386. An intention to do the violence alleged may be established, not only by showing threats of injury, but by showing indictable attempts to do the injury: *Williams* v. [536] *State*, 8 Humph. 585; *Lamb* v. *State*, 66 Md. 285. It may be shown upon the trial of one charged with burning an outbuilding that he had previously poisoned the occupant's house dog: *Halleck* v. *State*, 65 Wis. 147. On an indictment for murder it may be shown that the deceased had taken the life of another on the respondent's procurement, and had been seen in the act: *Rex* v. *Clewes*, 4 Car. & P. 221.

It is also held that in establishing certain offenses involving sexual intimacy, the prosecution may show other instances of like criminal conduct between the respondent and the one with whom the offense is claimed to have been committed. This is upon the ground that it is proper to show the existence of a continuing adulterous disposition of the two persons toward each other, and that there can be no better evidence of such a disposition than commissions of the act itself: *State* v. *Bridgman*, 49 Vt. 202; 24 Am. Rep. 124. But it will be noticed that this evidence touches only the respondent's relations to the particular individual concerned in the offense charged. Evidence of other offenses is never received to establish a criminal disposition in the broad sense of the term, or a tendency to commit generally offenses like the one alleged.

The admissibility of the evidence received under objection in this case must be tested by the rules above stated. The evidence covered fifteen larcenies other than the one charged in the indictment. These larcenies were all committed on the same night, and all but one on the same expedition. They were committed at different buildings located on a section of road several miles in length. They were not committed in the execution of any settled plan, but were severally undertaken as occasion offered. They were all accomplished with the aid of the same person. Neither the respondent nor his accomplice was seen by any one during the time in question. The evidence of the state consisted [537] of the narrative of the accomplice, and the testimony of all but one of the owners of the stolen property that the several articles were in the places from which the accomplice said they were taken, and that they were missed about the time the accomplice said the expedition took place, together with evidence of an identification of some of the articles by their owners as being the same found some months after upon the respondent's premises.

The mere fact that certain larcenies were committed on the same night, or the same expedition, did not entitle the state to show all in proof of one. The fact that both the respondent and the witness were concerned in them all did not so link them together as to make evidence of all admissible. Evidence of the larcenies not embraced in the charge was received upon the ground that the fact of such larcenies having been committed, when connected with the testimony as to the time when, and places from which the articles were missed, and of the subsequent discovery of some of them on the respondent's premises, tended to corroborate the testimony of the accomplice as to the commission of the theft in question. But such evidence could have no legitimate corroborative force unless there was some sufficient connection between these offenses and the one for which the respondent was being tried. Testimony that on the previous night the witness and the respondent had gone together to a certain place and stolen a harness, accompanied with evidence of a harness having been missed at that time, would have had no tendency to corroborate the witness in his account of this theft. The question is whether the fact that the articles shown to have been missed and in part found were taken on the same night or the same expedition afforded the necessary connection. If the evidence was admissible in this view, it must have been upon the ground that the fundamental assertion of the principal witness was that such an expedition did occur on the night and over the road stated, and [538] that evidence of these other articles having been left at, and afterwards missed from, the places stated, and of some of them being finally found on the respondent's premises, was corroborative of the fact upon which the testimony concerning the taking of the lap-robes rested. But it is urged with some force that evidence that certain articles were missed along

the line of this road soon after the night in question in no
way corroborated the statements of the witness connecting
the respondent with the expedition. The same objection
might, perhaps, be urged to the evidence relating to such of
the articles as were afterwards found on the respondent's
premises, in view of the fact that the accomplice lived and
kept his team at the same place. If, however, it were to be
held that other offenses might be shown on the ground above
stated, this would not sustain the admission of so much of
the testimony of the principal witness as related to the larceny concerning which there was no other evidence.

But without passing upon the admissibility of the evidence
on this ground, or considering other grounds upon which evidence of some of the larcenies might be held admissible, we
think evidence of all the larcenies committed on the same
expedition was, in the circumstances of this case as presented by the exceptions, fairly within the reason of the rule
first above stated. It does not appear that the respondent's
defense had been limited by any previous statement, and the
admissibility of the evidence must be tested upon the case
presented by the state, without regard to the respondent's
subsequent testimony that he did not accompany the state's
witness on any such trip. The expedition was with a team
which belonged to the witness. The lap-robes were not taken
by the respondent personally, nor in his presence. It does
not appear that there had been any conference or understanding in regard to them. The respondent remained in the
wagon which stood in the road, while [539] the witness went
away, and afterwards returned with the lap-robes and placed
them in the wagon. If the evidence of the state had been
confined to this single occurrence, the jury, even if satisfied
that the occurrence took place as stated, might have considered
that there was room for a reasonable doubt as to whether the
respondent was cognizant of the nature of the transaction.
But when the evidence disclosed the gathering from different
places of a miscellaneous assortment of personal property, in
taking some of which the respondent was actively engaged,
and a return with the load thus made up to the respondent's
house, it might no longer be doubted that the respondent had
participated in the removal of the lap-robes with full knowledge that they were stolen.

But testimony received on this ground could not properly
be extended beyond the history of the load which contained

the lap-robes. We find no ground upon which evidence of the subsequent larceny could be received. After the respondent and his accomplice had returned with the load made up as above stated and stowed the articles away, it was suggested that they go in another direction and steal some phosphate; and this was accordingly done. It cannot be said that this was made admissible by the evidence of the state as to the inception of the first expedition. It had appeared that that expedition was suggested and undertaken by the respondent for the purpose of stealing some phosphate which he expected to find at a certain shed, and that the expedition failed of its original purpose because no phosphate was found there. But the respondent's desire to steal some phosphate cannot be held to have entitled the state to prove everything that occurred until that desire was satisfied. Evidence of a second expedition, undertaken upon a renewal of the original purpose, had no legitimate tendency to support the other statements of the witness. It was not needed to relieve his main narrative of an inherent [540] improbability. Any discrepancy which might otherwise have been suggested between the alleged purpose of the expedition and their return without phosphate was sufficiently explained by their failure to find any; and evidence that the respondent persisted in his purpose until it was accomplished had no explanatory effect beyond this. The argument by which it is sought to sustain the admissibility of this evidence would have justified proof of the successful termination of the respondent's attempt to steal phosphate if it had occurred a week or a month later. We find no such connection between the larceny charged, and the theft of phosphate on another expedition and in a different locality, as would make evidence of the latter admissible in proof of the former. It was effective only as it appealed to the tendency to believe that a man who has committed a larceny at one time may very likely have been guilty of the same offense at another.

Sentence vacated, judgment reversed, and cause remanded.

EVIDENCE OF OTHER CRIMES: See the notes to *Thayer* v. *Thayer*, 100 Am. Dec. 113; *Barkly* v. *Copeland*, 5 Am. St. Rep. 418; and the extended note to *Strong* v. *State*, 44 Am. Rep. 299–308. Evidence of a prior crime can have no legitimate place in an investigation as to whether a subsequent crime was committed by the same person: *People* v. *Sharp*, 107 N. Y. 427; 1 Am. St. Rep. 851; *People* v. *Corbin*, 56 N. Y. 363; 15 Am. Rep. 427, and note; *Farris* v. *People*, 129 Ill. 521; 16 Am. St. Rep. 283, and note. Evidence of a crime different from the one charged is never admissible except for the purpose of showing motive, interest, or guilty knowledge: *People* v. *Greenwall,* 108 N. Y. 296; 2 Am. St. Rep. 415, and note; *Dunn* v. *State,* 2 Ark. 229; 35 Am. Dee. 54; *Ingram* v. *State,* 39 Ala. 247; 84 Am. Dec. 782, and note.

BARRE WATER COMPANY *v.* CARNES.

[65 VERMONT, 626.]

WATERS AND WATERCOURSES—RIPARIAN RIGHTS OF MUNICIPALITIES.— Dwellers in towns and villages, through which a stream passes, may use the water thereof to the same extent as any other riparian proprietors, provided they can reach the stream by a public highway, or secure a right of way over the lands of others.

WATERS AND WATERCOURSES—USE OF STREAM FOR SUPPLY OF MUNICIPALITY, WHEN NOT ENJOINED.—A riparian municipality which has obtained legislative authority to build a dam and lay pipes, with a view to obtaining, for domestic, fire, and sanitary purposes, a reasonable supply of water from a stream on which it is situated, cannot be enjoined from so using the water at the suit of a municipality lower down the same stream, which has never acquired, by purchase or otherwise, the rights of the riparian proprietors above it.

BILL for an injunction to restrain the defendant from constructing water-works for the supply of a riparian municipality. The opinion states the facts.

E. W. Bisbee and George W. Wing, for the orator.

Barney and Hoar, and S. C. Shurtleff, for the defendant.

628 START, J. This cause was heard on bill and answer, and the facts stated in the answer are to be taken as true. A stream of water, called Jail branch, runs through the town of Barre, flowing through the villages of East Barre and Barre, the former village being about four miles above the latter on said stream. Under No. 171 of the Acts of 1886, the orator has erected a dam across Jail branch three miles above the village of Barre and one below East Barre, and the village of Barre is being supplied therefrom. There is also a stream of water called Nichol's brook, which flows through East Barre and empties into Jail branch about one mile above the orator's dam. The inhabitants of East Barre have always taken water from Jail branch, its feeders and tributaries, for their necessary use, and must always do so, as they have no other source of supply. The orator has never obtained, by purchase or by the right of eminent domain, any right in the waters of the Jail branch or its tributaries

above its reservoir. The defendants, under No. 186 of the
Acts of 1892, have, by purchase, acquired the right to construct a dam across Nichol's brook and to build a reservoir
at a point three-fourths of a mile southerly from Jail branch,
and have purchased the rights of the riparian owners in and
to the waters of said stream flowing over and through their
respective lands, from the site of their proposed dam and
reservoir to the main stream; and they have constructed an
aqueduct from the site of said proposed dam to East Barre
for the purpose of supplying the inhabitants of [629] East
Barre with water for domestic, sanitary, and fire purposes.

The waters of Jail branch flow over the orator's dam and
along its proper channel, notwithstanding the amount of water
taken from the stream by the orator's aqueduct. Jail branch
is the natural outlet for the water in East Barre, and all water
taken from said stream, its feeders, and tributaries, and not
consumed, must flow into Jail branch about one mile above
the orator's dam. The defendants deny that there will be
any sensible diminution of the water, or the free flowing of
the same, at the orator's reservoir, except the natural waste.
The orator claims it is entitled to have all the waters of
Nichol's brook flow into Jail branch and from thence into its
aqueduct, and seeks to enjoin the defendants from taking any
of the water in Nichol's brook for the purposes aforesaid. The
inhabitants of East Barre have always obtained water for their
use from Jail branch and its tributaries, and all such inhabitants as can reach this stream and its tributaries without trespassing upon the lands of others can lawfully use the water
flowing therein for domestic purposes. In *Philadelphia* v.
Collins, 68 Pa. St. 115, it is said: " Every individual residing
upon the banks of a stream has a right to the use of the water
to drink, and for the ordinary uses of domestic life; and where
large bodies of people live upon the banks of a stream, as they
do in large cities, the collective body of the citizens has the
same right, but of course in a greatly exaggerated degree."

A riparian owner may conduct water by means of pipes to
any part of his premises, where he thinks it will be most convenient and advantageous to him, and may use the part so
diverted for the same purposes and to the same extent that
he could if it flowed there through a natural channel: *Chat-
field* v. *Wilson*, 31 Vt. 358; *Wheatley* v. *Chrisman*, 24 Pa. St.
298; 64 Am. Dec. 657. Dwellers in towns and villages watered
by a stream may use the water for domestic purposes to the

same [630] extent that a riparian owner can, provided they can
reach the stream by a public highway, or secure a right of
way over the lands of others. It is immaterial how the dwellers
on the stream take the water for the purposes for which they
may lawfully use it. They can drive their cattle to the stream
and allow them to quench their thirst, and can carry water
in pails to their homes; or each individual can carry the
water in a pipe to his dwelling for such use, provided he can
secure a right of way for that purpose; or the dwellers on the
stream may combine their funds to procure cheaper and better
transportation by means of a pipe, and may use the water for
their several necessities to the same extent that they could if
it flowed past their dwellings in a natural channel: *Mayor of
Philadelphia* v. *Commissoners etc.*, 7 Pa. St. 363.

The orator has not by purchase or otherwise acquired the
water rights of the inhabitants of East Barre. It has not
purchased or exercised the right of eminent domain in respect
to any water rights above its reservoir, nor is it alleged in the
bill that it has acquired a right to have the waters of Nichol's
brook flow into its reservoir. The rights acquired by the
orator as against the inhabitants of East Barre are no greater
than those of any riparian owner lower down the stream. By
acquiring the right to construct a dam at a point one mile
below East Barre and take water from that point by means
of an acqueduct to the village of Barre, the orator acquired no
greater rights, as against those using water above this dam,
than the riparian owners of whom it procured such rights.
The rights of these riparian owners in and to the waters of
Jail branch and its tributaries were subject to a reasonable
use by the inhabitants of East Barre and the riparian owners
above for domestic purposes; and if all the water is required
and taken by such reasonable use the riparian owners below
have no remedy. The water first reaches the inhabitants of
East Barre and they can lawfully [631] use so much of it as is
necessary for domestic, fire, and sanitary purposes: *Evans* v.
Merriweather, 3 Scam. 492; 38 Am. Dec. 106; *Spence* v. *Mc-
Donough*, 77 Iowa, 460.

The legislature has granted the defendants the right to
supply the inhabitants of East Barre with water in the same
manner that they could, individually or collectively, supply
themselves. Acting under the authority thus given, the defendants have acquired by purchase the rights of the riparian
owners on Nichol's brook from the site of their proposed

reservoir to the main stream, and have constructed an aqueduct from this point to East Barre; and they intend, without materially diminishing the flow of water to the orator's reservoir, or doing any unnecessary injury to the orator, to supply the inhabitants of East Barre with water for their reasonable use from the same source they have been accustomed to take it, and in the same manner that the orator, under legislative authority, is supplying the inhabitants of the village of Barre. We see no reason why they may not lawfully do so, as against the orator, who has never acquired, by purchase or otherwise, the water rights of the inhabitants of East Barre, or the rights of the riparian owners of Nichol's brook. To prevent them by injunction from so doing would, in our judgment, be inequitable, and this is a sufficient reason for denying the injunction prayed for: *Ottaquechee Woolen Co.* v. *Newton*, 57 Vt. 451.

Decree affirmed, and cause remanded.

MUNSON, J., concurs in the result.

WATERS—RIPARIAN RIGHTS GENERALLY.—A riparian owner may use the water of a stream for domestic and other useful purposes: *Clark* v. *Pennsylvania R. R. Co.*, 145 Pa. St. 438; 27 Am. St. Rep. 710, and note with the cases collected; *Wadsworth* v. *Tillotson*, 15 Conn. 366; 39 Am. Dec. 391, and note; *Society etc.* v. *Morris Canal etc. Co.*, 1 N. J. Eq. 157; 21 Am. Dec. 41, and note; *Plumleigh* v. *Dawson*, 1 Gilm. 544; 41 Am. Dec. 199, and note; *Tillotson* v. *Smith*, 32 N. H. 90; 64 Am. Dec. 355, and note; *Stein* v. *Burden*, 29 Ala. 127; 65 Am. Dec. 394, and note; extended note to *Davis* v. *Getchell*, 79 Am. Dec. 639; note to *Jones* v. *Adams*, 3 Am. St. Rep. 797. See also *Ulbricht* v. *Eufaula Water Co.*, 86 Ala. 587; 11 Am. St. Rep. 72, and note.

CASES

IN THE

SUPREME COURT

OF

WISCONSIN.

CREAM CITY GLASS COMPANY *v.* FRIEDLANDER.

[84 WISCONSIN, 53.]

CONTRACTS, PAROL EVIDENCE, WHEN INADMISSIBLE TO VARY.—The legal effect of a written contract cannot be varied by evidence of the previous negotiations between the contracting parties.

AGENT, CONTRACTING IN HIS OWN NAME.—One who executes a written contract of sale, which upon its face binds him personally, cannot relieve himself of responsibility thereunder by showing that he was acting simply as agent or broker for a principal. Whether such principal was disclosed or undisclosed is immaterial.

SALES—VENDEE'S RIGHT TO TEST THE QUALITY OF ARTICLES PURCHASED. A vendee, after having determined by inspection alone that the subject matter of the sale does not conform to the contract, and thereupon notified the vendor that it has been rejected, cannot, if he intends to insist upon his right to reject, deal with it in any manner inconsistent with the rejection, as by using up a quantity of it for the purpose of making a practical test of its quality, and thus providing evidence of its unfitness, to be used upon the trial of an action brought to rescind the contract, and recover from the vendor the purchase price of the goods.

ACTION for money had and received. The plaintiffs, a company engaged in the manufacture of glass at Milwaukee, entered into a contract with the defendant, the memorandum of which was as follows:

"CHICAGO, SEPTEMBER 4, 1890.

"CREAM CITY GLASS COMPANY: Sold to you about one hundred and fifty (150) tons Muspratt Bros. & Huntley's 48 per cent carbonated soda ash for shipment by steamers from Liverpool, monthly, in about equal parts, during the months of October, November, and December of the current year (about fifty tons monthly), at $1.65 per 100 net, invoice weights, cash on arrival, against delivery of documents, less one per cent accidents to factory, in transit, or *force majeure* excepted. Subject also to changes, if any, in United States tariff laws during pendency of this contract.

"L. M. FRIEDLANDER.

"No change in tariff impending.   L. M. F."

The defendant had the goods duly shipped from Liverpool, and they arrived at the plaintiff's side-track about December 13, 1890. The plaintiff unloaded the goods, and finding, upon an examination, that they appeared to have been injured by water, sent to the defendant the following letter:

"DEAR SIR: The railroad has just delivered your soda to us. On opening it, we find it absolutely unfit for use. The casks have evidently been under water until over half of the soda has soaked away. We wish you would come up and see it at once.   Very truly yours,

"CREAM CITY GLASS CO."

On December 19th the following notice was also sent:

"DEAR SIR: Please take notice that the shipment of soda ash made by you and received by us on or about the tenth day of December, 1890, under your contract of September 4, 1890, amounting to about sixty-three casks, was found to be wholly unfit for the uses and purposes for which it was purchased. We therefore notify you that we hereby rescind the said sale, and hereby offer to return to you the said soda ash. We further notify you that said soda ash is now at our factory, subject to your order, and that we hereby demand immediate repayment to us of the purchase price paid by us therefor.   Respectfully yours,

"CREAM CITY GLASS CO.

"RICHARD OGDEN, Sec."

Friedlander refused to take back the goods, and about six weeks afterwards the plaintiff made a practical test of the material by trying to make glass therefrom. He asserted that this test showed its unfitness for that purpose. From the evidence it appeared that the quantity used was no more than was necessary to make a proper test. As to the effect of this partial use of the material upon the plaintiff's right to rescind the contract, the jury was instructed as follows: "If you find from the evidence that the plaintiff, in making such test, used more of the soda ash in question than was absolutely necessary to determine its merchantable quality, or whether it was fit and proper for the uses for which it was bought and sold, or whether it was in accordance with the contract, or if you find that it was unnecessary to make such test, then such act is inconsistent with such rescission, and you will find for the defendant; or, if you find from all the facts and circumstances in the case that the plaintiff, after such election to rescind, did any act inconsistent with the ownership of the defendant, then you will find for the defendant." The defendant excepted to this charge. The plaintiff had a verdict and judgment for the full amount of the purchase money, and also for the freight and duty paid. The defendant appealed.

Williams, Friend and Bright, and Williams and Robinson, for the appellant.

Ogden, Hunter and Bottun, for the respondent.

[57] WINSLOW, J. The defendant claimed that he only acted as a broker between the plaintiff and the Liverpool firm for the sale of the soda ash in question, and upon the trial offered much testimony, consisting of letters and telegrams which passed between himself and the plaintiff, and which led up to and finally culminated in the written contract of sale which is set forth in the statement of the case. This testimony was offered for the purpose of showing that defendant acted simply as a broker, and that the contract should be construed simply as a broker's sold note. This testimony was all rejected by the trial court, upon the ground that it tended to vary and contradict the terms of a written contract. This ruling was strictly right. The contract which defendant executed, and under which the goods were delivered, was a plain and unambiguous contract of sale, and upon familiar rules previous negotiations could not change its legal effect. There was nothing to [58] prevent the defendant from making a contract binding himself personally if he chose to do so, notwithstanding his ordinary business may have been simply that of a broker, and notwithstanding also the fact that he may have preliminarily negotiated in the capacity of a broker in this very transaction. Having made such a contract, he cannot now relieve himself from responsibility thereunder by showing that he was acting simply as agent or broker for a principal whether such principal was disclosed or undisclosed: *Weston* v. *McMillan,* 42 Wis. 567.

We shall consider but one other question upon this appeal, and that is the question of the effect upon the rights of the parties of the use of six tierces of the soda ash by the plaintiff in January or February following the sale, for the purpose of testing its fitness for the manufacture of glass. Assuming that the evidence is sufficient to establish an implied warranty that the soda ash in question was of a quality reasonably fit to be used in the manufacture of glass, the question is, Could the plaintiff, after having decided that the material was wholly unfit, and notified the defendant of its decision and its rejection of the material, proceed to use three quarters of a ton of the material in making a practical test, and still insist on its right of rejection? It seems clear that the plaintiff was entitled to a reasonable time after actual receipt of the material to exercise the right of rejection in case the goods did not conform to the contract: Benjamin on Sales, 6th ed., section 703. If this fact could only be ascertained by a practical test, the plaintiff also had the right, within such reasonable time, to make such practical test, using only so much of the material as was reasonably necessary for the purpose, without thereby losing the right of rejection: Benjamin on Sales, 6th ed., section 896; *Philadelphia Whiting Co.* v. *Detroit White Lead Works*, 58 Mich. 29. But this test is plainly for the purpose only of enabling the purchaser to decide whether the material conforms [59] to the contract. If the fact can be determined by inspection alone, the test is not necessary, and the use of the material, therefore, clearly unjustifiable. Now in this case the plaintiff's officers determined at once, and upon inspection alone, that the material was unfit for their purposes, and so notified the defendant, and rejected the entire lot. They did not claim to need any test. They took their position definitely. After that act they could not deal with the property in any way inconsistent with the rejection, if they proposed to insist upon their right to reject: *Churchill* v. *Price*, 44 Wis. 540. They must do no act which they would have no right to do unless they were owners of the goods: Benjamin on Sales, 6th ed., section 703. Under these rules it is evident the plaintiff had no right to use up a quantity of the material several weeks after the rejection. By the rejection it became defendant's property, if such rejection was rightful. Plaintiff had no right to use any part of it. It is claimed that the use was simply for the purpose of providing evidence of unfitness for the purposes of the trial of this case; but one has no right to use his opponent's property for the purpose of making evidence. The act was an unmistakable act of ownership, and entirely inconsistent with the claim that the material had been rejected and was owned by defendant. It follows that the judgment must be reversed.

By the COURT. Judgment reversed, and cause remanded for a new trial.

CONTRACTS—PAROL EVIDENCE OF PRIOR NEGOTIATIONS.—Parol evidence is not admissible to vary a written contract by showing that it does not accord with the previous agreement of the parties: La Farge v. Rickert, 5 Wend. 187; 21 Am. Dec. 209, and note; McLean v. Nicol, 43 Minn. 169; Smith v. Deere, 48 Kan. 416; Aultman v. Falkum, 47 Minn. 414; Spann v. Baltzell, 1 Fla. 301; 46 Am. Dec. 346; Rockmore v. Davenport, 14 Tex. 602; 65 Am. Dec. 132, and note; notes to Appeal of Cornwall etc. R. R. Co., 11 Am. St. Rep. 894, and Sullivan v. Lear, 11 Am. St. Rep. 394. While negotiations preliminary to a written agreement may not be admissible to explain its terms, still they may be admitted to throw light on the question of its execution and other questions connected therewith: Wilbur v. Stoepel, 82 Mich. 344; 21 Am. St. Rep. 568, and note.

AGENCY—LIABILITY OF AGENT CONTRACTING IN HIS OWN NAME.—An agent who contracts in his own name and fails to disclose his principal's name at the time of making a contract, is personally liable for whatever obligation may arise out of the contract: Argersinger v. Macnaughton, 114 N. Y. 535; 11 Am. St. Rep. 687, and note; Bank of Rochester v. Monteath, 1 Denio, 402; 43 Am. Dec. 681, and note; Newhall v. Dunlap, 14 Me. 180; 31 Am. Dec. 45, and note; Stone v. Wood, 7 Cow. 453; 17 Am. Dec. 529, and note; Hobson v. Hassett, 76 Cal. 203; 9 Am. St. Rep. 193, and note. This question will be found fully discussed in the notes to the following cases: Wallace v. Bentley, 11 Am. St. Rep. 234; Tarver v. Garlington, 13 Am. St. Rep. 632; Knight v. Clark, 57 Am. Rep. 536; Burlingame v. Brewster, 22 Am. Rep. 179; Davis v. Henderson, 59 Am. Dec. 231; Bayley v. Onondaga County etc. Ins. Co., 41 Am. Dec. 761, and Andrews v. Estes, 26 Am. Dec. 524.

GILMAN v. KETCHAM.

[84 WISCONSIN, 60.]

INTERSTATE COMITY—GARNISHMENT OF DEBTOR OF DISSOLVED CORPORATION IN SISTER STATE, WHEN RECEIVER MAY AVOID.—After a receiver has been duly appointed for a dissolved corporation, in accordance with the laws of the state in which it was organized, and the creditors of such corporation have been regularly enjoined from commencing any suits to enforce the collection of their debts, the claim of such receiver to the assets of the corporation will be sustained in a sister state, as against a garnishment proceeding instituted by one of the creditors so enjoined against a debtor of the corporation residing in the latter state.

THE plaintiff, a resident of New York, as administrator of the estate of W. W. Gilman, deceased, a creditor of the Hudson River Boot and Shoe Manufacturing Co., a corporation organized under the laws of New York, instituted an action in Wisconsin, in which Hubbard and Baker, residents of that state, were garnished as debtors to the corporation. After the commencement of the action, W. M. Ketcham was allowed to interplead as a claimant to the money thus garnished. His answer stated, that by virtue of proceedings regularly taken in New York for the dissolution of the corporation he had become the qualified receiver of such corporation, and being thus vested with the right to all its property and credits, was entitled to receive the money owed by the garnishees. This sum having been admitted by the said garnishees to be due, and being in the custody of the court, the receiver demanded judgment that the clerk pay it over to him. A demurrer to the petition, on the ground that it did not state facts sufficient to constitute a cause of action, and that the receiver had no legal capacity to maintain the suit, was struck out as frivolous, and the order asked for was granted. From this order the plaintiff appealed.

Rietbrock and Halsey, for the appellant.

Williams and Robinson, for the respondent.

[65] PINNEY, J. It is not disputed but that the proceedings in the supreme court of New York were properly instituted and conducted, and the dissolution of the corporation regularly adjudged, upon the voluntary application of its trustees, and the respondent appointed receiver of all its property, assets, and estate, according to the statute of that state, with a view of applying the proceeds equally to the payment of all its creditors, and the distribution of any residue equally to and among its stockholders. The plaintiff in this action was at the time, and still is, a resident and citizen of the state of New York, of which state the corporation was a citizen, and he was served with an injunction in that proceeding restraining him, as a creditor of the corporation, from commencing any suit against it to enforce the collection of his debt, in order that the property and assets of the corporation might be properly and judiciously administered and applied by the receiver under the authority of the court appointing him, and in the regular and orderly administration of its estate. The proceeding did not contemplate a discharge of the debtor as

upon the surrender and application of his property under insolvent laws, but the property of the corporation was passed and vested, pursuant to the statute, in the respondent as its receiver, and the corporation was dissolved, so that no other than the receiver had a right to assert or maintain any title to it thereafter, and he could do so only for the purpose of its equal and just application to the payment of its creditors, and the just division of any residue to and among its stockholders. The effect of such voluntary dissolution was to place all its property and assets *in custodia legis* to be collected and applied by the receiver. There is nothing in the statute of New York, or in this proceeding under it, in conflict with or in contravention of the laws or public policy of this state, as declared by its statutes and the decisions of its courts, nor does the present proceeding interfere, or [66] tend to interfere, with or prejudice the rights of any citizen of this state. The case concerns citizens of New York alone, the garnishees having paid the fund into court and been discharged. The case is therefore free from all objections, which by the general current of authority, might prevent or induce the courts of Wisconsin to refrain from giving, in a spirit of just interstate comity, the same force and effect here to the proceedings in the supreme court of the state of New York in question as would be accorded to them there. There are many cogent reasons, in our judgment, why we should accord to them such effect upon principles of comity.

The situation, in brief, is that after the plaintiff had been enjoined, by a competent court of the jurisdiction in which he resided, from bringing any action against the corporation, his debtor, for the recovery of any sum of money, so that he should not obtain any undue preference over its other creditors; in violation of the purpose and policy of the law of New York and the proceeding thus instituted, and after an adjudication absolutely dissolving the corporation had been made, and after the title to its property, effects, and credits had been vested in the claimant as such receiver, the plaintiff came into the circuit court of this state, and commenced an action to recover his demand against a dissolved corporation. The question is one wholly between parties residing in New York and bound by the proceedings in question, neither of whom is in any position to invoke the assistance of the courts of this state to defeat or deny full effect to the proceeding in New York, or the title resulting from it. It is clear that the

adjudication of dissolution, and the appointment of the receiver vesting in him the title to the chose in action in question, were binding on these parties, and the courts of New
York would have enforced the receiver's title had this controversy originated there. The plaintiff asks us to aid him
in violating [67] the law of his own state and evading the
process of its courts.

Our own citizens, in a proper case, would no doubt be protected against the effect of such extraterritorial act and
adjudication, if injurious to their interests or in conflict with
the laws and public policy of Wisconsin, and effect would
not be given to it at the expense of injustice to our own citizens. The transfer of this debt, valid in New York, must,
we think, be held valid on principles of comity here. When,
therefore, the garnishee process was served, there was no
debt due to the corporation upon which it could act, and the
money that has been paid into court belongs to the receiver
claimant; and, no principle of public policy or rights of
citizens of Wisconsin intervening, by a fair and liberal spirit
of comity our courts ought to give the same force and effect
to the proceedings in question as they would have in the
courts of New York.

The tendency of modern adjudications is in favor of a liberal extension of interstate comity, and against a narrow and
provincial policy, which would deny proper effect to judicial
proceedings of sister states under their statutes and rights
claimed under them, simply because, technically, they are
foreign and not domestic. In the recent case of *Cole* v. *Cunningham*, 133 U. S. 107, the subject was very fully considered,
and the various cases were cited; and it was there held that
a creditor who is a citizen and resident of the same state
with his debtor, against whom insolvent proceedings have
been instituted in said state, is bound by the assignment of
the debtor's property in such proceedings, and if he attempts
to attach or seize the personal property of the debtor, situated
in another state and embraced in the assignment, he may be
restrained by injunction by the courts of the state in which
he and his debtor reside; that every state exercises, to a
greater or less extent, as it deems expedient, the comity of
giving effect to the insolvent proceedings of other states, and
where the [68] transfer of the debtor's property is the result of
a judicial proceeding, as a general rule, no state will carry it
into effect to the predjudice of its own citizens: *Reynolds* v.

Adden, 136 U. S. 353, 354. In *Bagby* v. *Atlantic etc. R. R. Co.*, 86 Pa. St. 291, it was held that, where a receiver of a corporation has been appointed by a court of competent jurisdiction in another state, a creditor who resides in that state and is bound by the decree of its court appointing the receiver cannot, in an attachment or execution, recover the assets of the corporation in another state, which the receiver claims. In *Bacon* v. *Horne*, 123 Pa. St. 452, 453, speaking to this point, the court said: "As before observed, both of these parties, plaintiffs and defendant, are residents of New York. They come into this state to obtain an advantage by our law which they could not obtain by their own. They are seeking to nullify the law of their own state, and ask the aid of our court to do so. This they cannot have. If for no other reason, it is forbidden by public policy and the comity which exists between the states. This comity will always be enforced when it does not conflict with the rights of our own citizens." To the same effect is the case of *In re Waite*, 99 N. Y. 433, 439, 448, and also *Phelps* v. *McCann*, 123 N. Y. 641. In *Toronto General Trust Co.* v. *Chicago etc. R. R. Co.*, 123 N. Y. 37, 47, it was said that "foreign receivers and assignees, taking their title to property by virtue of foreign laws, or legal proceedings in foreign courts, may come here and maintain suits in our courts when they do not come in conflict with the rights or interests of domestic creditors"; and the general rule laid down in *Hibernia Nat. Bank* v. *Lacombe*, 84 N. Y. 367, 38 Am. Rep. 518, must be considered as qualified by these cases. The same doctrine is laid down in *Woodward* v. *Brooks*, 128 Ill. 222, 15 Am. St. Rep. 104, where it is held that if an assignment is valid in the state where made it will be enforced in another state as a matter of comity, but not to the predjudiee of the citizens [69] of the latter, who may have demands against the assignor; that while it is contrary to public policy to allow the property of a nonresident debtor to be withdrawn from the state, and thus compel creditors to seek redress in a foreign jurisdiction, yet for all other purposes between the citizens of the state where the assignment is made, if valid by the *lex loci*, it will be carried into effect by the courts of Illinois; and this rule is held not to be in conflict with *Rhawn* v. *Pearce*, 110 Ill. 350; 51 Am. Rep. 691.

The assignment in this case was voluntary, it is true, and not by proceedings *in invitum*. We are unable to see upon what substantial ground it can be maintained that the title of the

receiver in this case, founded upon the voluntary dissolution
of the corporation, does not stand on equally as favorable
ground as that of an assignee for the benefit of creditors: *Parsons* v. *Charter Oak L. Ins.Co.*, 31 Fed. Rep. 305; *Relfe* v. *Run-
dle*, 103 U. S. 222, 225; *Williams* v. *Hintermeister*, 26 Fed. Rep.
889. In *Merchants' Nat. Bank* v. *McLeod*, 38 Ohio St. 174, it
was held that a receiver appointed under the authority of the
court of one state, and vested with the title to property temporarily in another, might, under the comity between states,
by an action brought in the latter state in his own name,
assert his right to the possession of it, where such right was
not in conflict with the rights of the citizens of the latter state,
nor against the policy of its laws; nor is there anything in the
case of *McClure* v. *Campbell*, 71 Wis. 350, 5 Am. St. Rep. 220,
in conflict with this conclusion. Mr. Justice Lyon had in view
in that case the question of giving effect to foreign insolvency
proceedings resulting in a discharge of the debtor prejudicially
to the interests of citizens of the state wherein the assignee
attempted to enforce the assignment. In *Filkins* v. *Nunne-
macher*, 81 Wis. 91, the question was whether judicial comity
would allow a receiver, appointed in a creditor's suit in another
state, to maintain a suit in Wisconsin to set aside an alleged
fraudulent conveyance, from the debtor to [70] the defendant
of property within the latter state, and presented an entirely
different question from the one in this case, which is whether
a foreign receiver can be heard to assert in the courts of this
state a title to property which he claims by an assignment
valid and binding against all the parties to the litigation, and
is more nearly analogous to the question involved and decided
in *Cook* v. *Van Horn*, 81 Wis. 291. The question is not materially different from that involved in *Smith* v. *Chicago etc. Ry.
Co.*, 23 Wis. 267, where it was determined that effect would
be given by the courts of this state, subject to the qualifications here stated, to an assignment made in another state by
a party in order to avoid imprisonment in proceedings supplemental to execution for refusal to apply rights in action—corporate stocks—to the payment of a judgment; and it is evident
that if the title depended wholly upon the coercive power of the
court the result would have been the same. The principle is
universal that the assets of insolvent corporations are to be
regarded as a trust fund for the benefit of all the creditors,
and "that kind of diligence by which one creditor of an insolvent corporation secures to himself a prior right to its

property, and an unequal advantage over the other creditors, is without merit, and more selfish than just ": *Ballin* v. *Loeb*, 78 Wis. 404. The public policy of Wisconsin and New York in this respect are in accord.

For these reasons we are of the opinion that the claim of the receiver, as stated in his intervening petition, to the fund in court, must be sustained, and that the circuit court properly overruled the plaintiff's demurrer thereto.

By the COURT. The order of the circuit court is affirmed.

STATES—COMITY BETWEEN.—The comity of one state will enforce the laws of another, when such enforcement neither violates its own laws nor infringes the rights of its citizens: *Deringer* v. *Deringer*, 5 Houst. 416; 1 Am. St. Rep. 151, and note; note to *Forepaugh* v. *Delaware etc. R. R. Co.*, 15 Am. St. Rep. 679. See also *Herrick* v. *Minneapolis etc. Ry. Co.*, 31 Minn. 11; 47 Am. Rep. 771, and note.

BURR *v.* GERMAN INSURANCE COMPANY.

[84 WISCONSIN, 76.]

INSURANCE, CONTRACT OF, WHEN ENTIRE.—A policy of insurance covering several lots of personal property in the same building, and distributing the risk to each item, but providing for the payment of a gross sum as premium, creates an entire, indivisible contract. If such policy is conditioned to be no longer binding upon the insurer in case the property is levied upon or taken into possession under any legal process, a levy upon a part of the property insured renders the policy inoperative as to the whole.

ACTION upon a policy of fire insurance. The opinion states the material facts.

Sylvester and Scheiber, for the appellant.

John J. Wood and Gabe Bouck, for the respondent.

⁷⁸ CASSODAY, J. It is undisputed that the policy was issued to James Carey; that after the fire, and before the commencement of this action, the claim for the loss was assigned to the plaintiff by Carey; that September 14, 1889, and five days prior to the fire, upon an attachment issued in an action in favor of one Stanley and against said Carey and another, the sheriff levied upon and seized, under said writ, all the cranberries, cranberry boxes, and barrels then in the warehouse mentioned in said policy, except the east fifteen hundred boxes of berries, and except the west three hundred boxes of berries, which he did not levy upon, for the reason

that they had previously been conveyed or mortgaged to
W. D. Williams. For the reasons given in the opinion of Mr.
Justice Orton in *Carey* v. *German American Ins. Co.*, 84 Wis.
80, *post*, p. 907, we must hold that the policy was rendered
inoperative and void by such levy, seizure, and change of
possession, under the clause of the policy on that subject contained in the foregoing statement, and that the same was not
waived or revived by the defendant's adjuster and state agent,
the provisions of the two policies in these respects being substantially the same.

The question recurs whether the policy was thereby rendered inoperative and void as to the property thereby insured
and not so levied upon nor seized by the sheriff. In *Loomis*
v. *Rockford Ins. Co.*, 77 Wis. 87, 20 Am. St. Rep. 96, and 81
Wis. 366, three buildings and certain personal property, situated on three different farms, were insured, each for a separate amount, by a policy stating the premium as a gross sum;
[79] and it was held that the contract was divisible, and that
the sale of one of the buildings, in violation of a stipulation
against changing the title of the insured property without
the consent of the insurer, did not avoid the policy as to
the other property, situated several miles from the building
sold.

In that case the present chief justice discusses the questions of divisibility and indivisibility of such contracts at
length, and upon authority and reason; and there is no purpose here of renewing the discussion. In so deciding, the
court expressly adhered to the former adjudications of this
court there cited. In each of those cases the property insured
consisted of buildings and personal property contained therein,
with the risk distributed to the different items covered by the
policy, and it was held that the contract of insurance, as to
each building and the personal property therein, was indivisible: *Schumitsch* v. *American Ins. Co.*, 48 Wis. 26; *Hinman* v.
Hartford F. Ins. Co., 36 Wis. 159. In the case at bar the
property covered by the policy was all personal, and situated
in the same warehouse. The premium paid was a gross sum.
The provision avoiding the policy in case of such levy, seizure, or change of possession was designed to protect the company against any increase of risk by virtue of such levy,
seizure, or change of possession. The property insured being so situated that any increase in the risk, as to any portion
thereof, necessarily increased the risk as to the whole, it is very

obvious that the whole risk was a unit, and the contract of insurance an entire, indivisible contract. It follows that the avoidance of the policy by virtue of the levy, seizure, and change of possession went to the whole contract, and rendered it wholly inoperative and void. This makes it unnecessary to consider the question whether the action was commenced within the time limited by the policy.

By the COURT. The judgment of the circuit court is reversed, and the cause is remanded for a new trial.

INSURANCE—WHEN CONTRACT ENTIRE AND WHEN SEVERABLE.—This question was discussed in the following recent cases in this series: *Coleman* v. *Insurance Co.*, 49 Ohio St. 310; 34 Am. St. Rep. 565, and note; *German Ins. Co.* v. *York*, 48 Kan. 488; 30 Am. St. Rep. 313, and note; *German Ins. Co.* v. *Fairbank*, 32 Neb. 750; 29 Am. St. Rep. 459, and note; *Stephens* v. *Queen Ins. Co.*, 81 Wis. 335; 29 Am. St. Rep. 905; *Pioneer Mfg. Co.* v. *Phœnix Assur. Co.*, 110 N. C. 176; 28 Am. St. Rep. 673.

CAREY *v.* GERMAN-AMERICAN INSURANCE COMPANY OF NEW YORK.

[84 WISCONSIN, 80.]

INSURANCE—CONDITION AGAINST "CHANGE OF POSSESSION BY LEGAL PROCESS."—A writ of attachment is a "process," and therefore a policy conditioned to be void in case "any change takes place in the title or possession of the property, whether by sale, etc., legal process, or judicial decree," becomes inoperative when an attachment is levied on such property.

INSURANCE—CHANGE OF POSSESSION OF PROPERTY, SEIZURE BY OFFICER, WHEN AMOUNTS TO.—A seizure of property by an officer in the regular course of attachment proceedings, as prescribed by the statute, works a change in the possession of such property sufficient to avoid an insurance policy thereon, which is conditioned to become inoperative in case "any change of possession takes place by legal process."

INSURANCE—NOTICE ON FORFEITURE OF POLICY, WHEN NOT NECESSARY.—If a clause in a policy provides that "it shall be void" upon the breach of a specified condition, the insurer's exemption from liability becomes absolutely fixed as soon as that condition is broken, and does not depend upon whether he notifies, or omits to notify, the insured, after such breach, what action he intends to take in regard to the continuance or forfeiture of the policy.

INSURANCE—ORAL WAIVER OF FORFEITURE, WHEN INEFFECTUAL.—If it is expressly stipulated by the parties to a contract of insurance that "no officer of the company shall be held to have waived any of the terms and conditions of the policy, unless such waiver shall be indorsed thereon in writing," an oral waiver of a forfeiture is a nullity.

INSURANCE—CONDITION AGAINST CHANGE OF POSSESSION, WHEN BROKEN.
If a policy which, so far as the risk is concerned, creates an indivisible contract is condititioned to be void when a change takes place in
the possession of the property insured, that condition is deemed to be
broken if there is a change in the possession of a large or considerable
portion of such property.

INSURANCE.—A CONDITION AGAINST CHANGE OF POSSESSION applies to an
involuntary change of possession by legal process as well as to a voluntary change resulting from the action of the insured himself.

INSURANCE.—A CONDITION AGAINST CHANGE OF POSSESSION BY LEGAL
PROCESS is broken when an officer takes possession of the property by
virtue of a writ of attachment issued according to law, even though it
afterwards appears that there was no ground for issuing such writ.

ACTION on a fire insurance policy.

H. W. Chynoweth, for the appellant.

John. J Wood and *Gabe Bouck,* for the respondent.

[82] ORTON, J.   On the fourteenth day of September, 1889,
the appellant company issued to the respondent a policy of
insurance for two thousand five hundred dollars on his cranberries stored in his frame shingle-roof warehouse, and in
boxes piled next to said [83] warehouse covered with canvas,
situated in Waushara county, in this state.   The policy
provided that a part of the loss should be paid to one W. D.
Williams, as his interest might appear.   The insured property was nearly totally destroyed by fire on the nineteenth
day of the same month.   The plaintiff recovered a judgment
for two thousand eight hundred and twelve dollars and forty-
six cents as damages, besides costs   In said judgment it is
ordered that seven hundred dollars of the said damages be
paid to the said Williams as the mortgagee of a part of the
property.   The defendant company has appealed from said
judgment.

In said policy of insurance there is the following condition
of forfeiture, viz: "Or if any change takes place in the title
or possession of the property (except in case of succession by
reason of the death of the assured), whether by sale, transfer,
conveyance, legal process, or judicial decree, ... then and
in every such case this policy shall be void."   The main defense was that a change in the possession of the insured property took place by legal process according to this condition,
and that thereby the policy was forfeited and became void.

On the said fourteenth day of September, but after said policy was delivered and in force, one Frank W. Stanley, on the
proper affidavit and bond, procured a writ of attachment
against the property of said James Carey, the assured, and of

one Richard Carey, to be sued out of the circuit court of Green Lake county; and on the same day the writ was duly served by a deputy sheriff, by attaching and seizing nearly all of said insured property, or except that part of it which had been conveyed to said W. D. Williams, consisting of three hundred boxes of berries and the boxes containing them. The deputy sheriff made return on said writ that he had levied upon and seized said property on that day, and that he delivered to each of said defendants in the attachment copies of said writ, affidavit, and undertaking, and that before he could make a full inventory and appraisement [84] of said property taken by the writ, all of it, except fourteen boxes of cranberries and the boxes containing them, was destroyed and consumed by fire on the nineteenth day of September, 1889; and that he afterwards made an inventory of the part thereof not so destroyed, and had the same duly appraised, and delivered to the defendants therein copies of such inventory and appraisement. This brings us to the main questions in the case. The learned counsel of the respondent contends: 1. That the said writ of attachment was not a "legal process," mentioned in said condition; 2. That a change of possession of the property did not take place by such pretended levy of attachment; 3. That, upon the company having notice of such change in the possession, it should have exercised its option to continue the policy or to declare it forfeited and void; and 4. That there was a waiver of the condition and forfeiture by the local agent of the company, who negotiated the insurance.

1. Was the writ of attachment process? The statute would seem to settle this question beyond dispute. Section 2421 of the Revised Statutes, provides how "process" may issue. It shall be tested in the name of the judge, signed by the clerk, and sealed with the seal of the court. Section 2591 provides that the clerk may deliver to any attorney "blank process and seals." Section 2420 provides that circuit courts may issue "writs, process, and commissions." Sec. 725: The sheriff, undersheriff, and deputy may execute all processes, writs, precepts, and orders. Sec. 2730: The writ of attachment is issued by the clerk at request. It is directed to the sheriff by the state, attested in the name of the judge, and sealed by the seal of the court; and before executed an affidavit must be made and an undertaking given. Sec. 2736: The officer having the writ of attachment shall execute it by

seizing the property of the defendant to satisfy the demand.
This writ has all the requisites of any [85] writ or process
named in the statutes. All writs are called "process" in the
statutes. A writ is process, and process is a writ, interchange-
ably. If this writ of attachment is not process, then we have
no process in this state. This writ was issued strictly according to law, and has all the requisites of a process anywhere.

2. Did the sheriff in serving the writ take possession of the
property, or did he dispossess the insured? 1. The sheriff
returns "that he seized the property on the writ"; 2. James
Carey, the plaintiff, testified on the trial " that he told Tucker,
the agent, that Stanley had attached their berries, and that
he was going to try and fix it up, and pay Stanley"; 3. The
plaintiff, long after the fire that destroyed the property, tra-
versed the affidavit in the attachment in order to have it dismissed. If it had not been fully served, it could do no harm;
4. The questions and answers in the special verdict on the
traverse assume a full service of the writ and levy on the property: 1. "What were the number of boxes of cranberries levied
upon under the writ of attachment?   Answer, 1,658." "7.
What other property of defendants was seized under the attachment and destroyed by the fire"?   Answered by the court. "8.
The value thereof when seized "?   " 10. At the time of the seizure how many berries remained unpicked "?   " 12. Were the
berries that remained unpicked lost and injured by reason of
such levy and seizure under said writ of attachment"?   5.
The special verdict in this case finds that a levy of the attachment had been made. The first question is: " On the Monday next after the levy under the Stanley attachment did A.
L. Tucker, the local agent of the defendant at Berlin, Wisconsin, have knowledge that the levy proved under the Stanley
attachment had been made"?   Answered by the court, " Yes."
This question assumes that the levy had been proved. The
second question is: " Did such local agent, on said Monday
[86] after the levy under said Stanley attachment, and after he
had knowledge of such levy, agree with the plaintiff that the
defendant's policy should remain in force upon the property
insured "?   Answer, " Yes."   There is not only a specific
finding of the fact that a levy had been made, but the finding that the company waived the forfeiture is based upon
such fact. The statute requires the officer having the writ
of attachment to seize the property of the defendant, and the
officer returns that he did seize the property; and the fact

that he levied upon the property or seized it is found by the jury and by the court, and is a conclusive matter of record, and really not open for argument. D. C. Evans, the deputy sheriff who served the writ, testified on the trial that "he made a levy by taking possession of the berries, and continued in possession until they were burned." It may be said that there may be evidence of record that the officer seized or levied on the property, but that that is no proof that he took exclusive possession of the berries. The legal definition of the word "seizure" is: "The taking possession of the property by an officer." "They are seized when the goods are within the power of the officer": Bouvier's Law Dictionary, tit. Seizure. And so the legal definition of "levy" is: "To have the property within the power and control of the officer"; and the first definition is "seizure": Bouvier's Law Dictionary, tit. Levy. "When an officer seizes and possesses himself of chattels under a writ, in such manner as to enable him to maintain trespass or replevin against a wrongful taker thereof (*Buckwheat* v. *St. Croix L. Co.*, 75 Wis. 194), then it is a sufficient levy and service of the writ. There can be no doubt that the officer here stood precisely in that relation to the property. There can be no question but that Evans, the deputy sheriff, took exclusive possession of the property under the writ, and that a change of the possession of the property took place "by legal process," in the language of the condition.

[87] 3. Ought the company to have declared the policy void or continued it, on notice of the breach of this condition? This was the ground on which the circuit court refused to grant a new trial in this case. This condition is clear, explicit, positive, and of but one possible meaning. If any such change in the possession of the property takes place, "this policy shall be void"—that is, *ipso facto* void. It is void when or as soon as this takes place, and is no longer a policy of insurance. There is no room for construction here. The learned judge bases his decision on that question on the case of *Wakefield* v. *Orient Ins. Co.*, 50 Wis. 532. It will be seen that that case has no possible application to this. The condition in that case is: "If the premises insured shall at any time during the life of this policy become vacant by the removal of the owner or occupant, without immediate notice to the company and indorsement made on the policy, this instrument shall be void and of no effect." The circuit court

held that this language conveyed a doubtful meaning, and was subject to construction; and that it meant, when the premises became vacant, without notice to the company, the policy became void, subject, however, to the action of the company. The company must indorse on the policy either the forfeiture of the policy on account of such vacancy, or its consent to its continuance. When the insured has given notice of the vacancy, as in that case, he has done all he can do or is required to do. Then the company must act, and make the indorsement on the policy of the forfeiture or continuance of the policy. The company must notify the insured what action it intends to take. The company did not do this, and therefore there was no forfeiture. This view was adopted by this court, and such a construction of the condition was approved. Keeping in view the principle that a forfeiture is not favored and should not be declared unless compelled by the clear and positive terms of the condition, [88] we are yet compelled to hold that this condition cannot possibly mean anything different from what its language clearly imports, and that there is no chance for a more favorable construction on behalf of the assured.

4. Was such forfeiture waived by the local agent of the company who negotiated the insurance, or could it be waived by him? The local agent, Tucker, had very early knowledge of the levy of the attachment, and, after such knowledge, according to the testimony of the plaintiff, consented to a continuance of the policy, and the jury so found in their special verdict. This brings us to consider the following stipulation or covenant of the policy: "And it is further expressly covenanted by the parties hereto that no officer, agent, or representative of the company shall be held to have waived any of the terms and conditions of this policy, unless such waiver shall be indorsed hereon in writing." The evidence of such pretended waiver was oral. It was objected to by the learned counsel of the appellant on that account, and the objection overruled. This we must hold was error. We know of no good reason, and are aware of no authority by the decisions of this court, that should cause us to declare the above covenant or stipulation void. It is a plain and explicit stipulation of the contract upon which the minds of the parties met, and is as binding on the assured as any stipulation in the policy. When the assured sought to have Tucker, the local agent, waive the forfeiture which he virtually admitted had

tàken place by a change of possession of the property insured by legal process, he knew that by the terms of his policy he had no power or authority to waive it, unless it was indorsed on the policy in writing. This provision was a clear restriction and limitation of his power. It was his own fault that he failed or omitted to have such waiver so indorsed. The courts cannot relieve a party from the legal consequences of such an omission to abide by the plain [89] stipulations of his contract, or make a new contract for him different from the one made by himself.

But this question has already been decided by this court in recent cases. In *Knudson* v. *Hekla F. Ins. Co.*, 75 Wis. 198, the stipulation of the policy was that "agents have no authority to make any verbal agreement whatsoever for or on behalf of this company; and this company will not be liable for any agreement except such as shall be indorsed, signed, and dated in writing on this policy." The pretended waiver by the local agent was of the proofs of loss in verbal conversation. It was held that the agent had no power to waive conditions in the policy in that way, or not indorsed on the policy; and therefore such testimony was improper, and should have been excluded. The chief justice, who wrote the opinion, cites *Hankins* v. *Rockford Ins. Co.*, 70 Wis. 1. The stipulation in the policy in that case was: "No local agent can in any manner waive any condition of this policy." The agent had consented that the assured might put a mortgage on the property. Mr. Justice Cassoday said in the opinion: "It has been frequently held by this and other courts, in effect, that where a person was authorized by an insurance company to make a contract of insurance, he thereby had implied authority in doing so to waive stipulations as to the condition of the property or other facts then existing, and it may be as to subsequent conditions, if such waiver is made at the time of effecting the insurance. But those cases have no bearing upon the question here presented. The contract of insurance was completed in all its terms, and binding upon both parties. The plaintiff accepted it with all its conditions and limitations. In the absence of any fraud or mistake, he was, on general principles, conclusively presumed to know its conditions." I may say further that if the agent had knowledge of certain conditions of the property when the contract was being made, such knowledge entered into and became a part of the contract, and modified it to that extent; but if

such conditions, or a knowledge of them, occur subsequently,
his power to waive them or to change the contract in any respect is governed strictly by the provisions of the contract.
If he can waive any condition, he must do so only in the
manner provided by the contract. In that case the attempted
waiver was held a nullity. There is no difference in principle
between that case and this. Numerous cases in other courts
are cited in the opinion to sustain this doctrine, which need
not be recited in this opinion.

The learned counsel of the respondent, with considerable
plausibility, contends that the agent in the above case was
prohibited from waiving any of the conditions in the policy,
while here the agent is permited to waive in writing, indorsed
on the policy. But the stipulation here is both prohibitory
and permissive. It, in effect, prohibits any agent from waiving any of the terms and conditions of the policy, unless in
writing, indorsed on the policy, and permits the agent to do
so in that way only. But in *Knudson* v. *Hekla F. Ins. Co.*, 75
Wis. 198, the provision is nearly the same as in this case, and
is both prohibitory and permissive, and yet no such distinction is made.

Cases in this court are cited by the learned counsel as being
adverse to such a doctrine, such as *Renier* v. *Dwelling House
Ins. Co.*, 74 Wis. 89. In that case the agent knew of the
mortgage on the property when he issued the policy, and. as
said above in relation to such cases, he had the power to
waive the condition. In *Gans* v. *St. Paul etc. Ins. Co.*, 43
Wis. 108, 28 Am. Rep. 535, the agent knew that the house
was unoccupied before it was burned. This knowledge of the
agent was held to be that of the company, and the company
afterwards required further proofs of loss at considerable expense to the insured, and that waived the condition. These
cases, together with others cited as being adverse to this doctrine, are materially different and inapplicable.[91] We must
therefore hold that the provision of the policy was binding on
the assured, and that the agent neither did or could waive it,
or the forfeiture of the policy under it, verbally or by parol,
and that the pretended waiver by the agent was a nullity.

There are three subordinate questions raised by the learned
counsel of the respondent to be considered.

1. The possession of all the insured property was not
changed or taken away from the insured by the writ of attachment or " by legal process." Seven hundred dollars'

worth of the insured cranberries covered by the mortgage of
W. D. Williams were not taken by the writ. The property
insured was indivisible and an entirety, so far as the risk was
concerned. This condition, that the possession shall not be
changed, was inserted in the policy to secure proper care of
the property and protection from fire. The company knew
the assured, and was willing to trust its possession to him,
but not willing to trust it to unknown strangers and their
questionable care. The possession of a large portion of the
property by others would equally endanger the whole and
expose it to loss. This question, however, is decided in a
similar case on this calendar, of *Burr* v. *German Ins. Co.*, 84
Wis. 76, *ante*, 905, and the question treated in the opinion
of Mr. Justice Cassoday by reference to previous cases in
this court. It is therefore held that it made no difference
whether the possession of all the property was changed or
not, if the possession of a large or considerable portion of it
had been so changed.

2. That it was not intended that such an involuntary
change of possession by a writ of process should forfeit the
policy, but it must be by some act of omission or commission
of the assured, or by a process by his order or under his control. It is held that, when an attachment is issued against a
fraudulent debtor, he suffers it to issue and is responsible for
it, because he could have prevented it by paying [92] the debt
when due and by not committing the fraud which is the
ground or cause of it. But the company had the undoubted right to make such an event, voluntary or involuntary,
endangering the property or increasing the risk, a condition
of forfeiture. The insured voluntarily consented to the condition, and he cannot complain.

3. Long after the fire the attachment was dissolved. It
was held on a traverse of the affidavit that the writ never
ought to have issued, and that there was no ground for it.
Does such fact make the writ any less a "legal process"
when served? It was a legal process when issued. It was
issued by the authority of and according to law. It was
based on a sufficient affidavit. The dismissal of the attachment on the trial of the traverse did not make the writ void
when it issued. It was a protection to the officer and a valid
process. It did not issue on the truth of the affidavit, although it was dismissed on its falsity. The law presumed
the affidavit to be true, and authorized the writ. It was a

legal process when it was served, and changed the possession
of the property. That was sufficient. The possession of
the property was changed by it at the time lawfully, and it
put the officer in possession of it lawfully. It was this
change of the possession that enhanced the risk and avoided
the policy.

I have thus disposed of all the contentions of the distinguished counsel of the respondent. I have cited but few of
the authorities found in the able brief of the learned counsel
of the appellant. They will be in the case for reference.
Our own adjudicated cases seemed to be sufficient on every
question, and, when they are so, I seldom go abroad for authority. The case was very ably presented by the learned
counsel on both sides. The exceptions are not specially considered. The main questions upon which the case depends
only have been considered. The defendant company proved
a good defense to the action, and the [93] court should have
rejected the testimony tending to show a waiver of the condition of forfeiture, because such waiver was not indorsed on
the policy in writing. The defendant was entitled to a judgment in its favor.

By the COURT. The judgment of the circuit court is reversed, and the cause remanded for a new trial.

INSURANCE.—EFFECT OF CHANGE OF POSSESSION BY LEGAL PROCESS: See
the extended note to Lane v. Maine etc. Ins. Co., 28 Am. Dec. 158.

INSURANCE—WAIVER OF FORFEITURE, WHEN MUST BE IN WRITING.—
When a policy of insurance declares that there can be no waiver except in
writing indorsed on the policy, conditions in the policy cannot be waived by
an agent to whom the provision as to written indorsement relates, except in
the manner in the contract provided: Wheaton v. North British etc. Ins. Co.,
76 Cal. 415; 9 Am. St. Rep. 216, and extended note fully discussing this subject; note to Burlington Ins. Co. v. Gibbons, 19 Am. St. Rep. 124. The contrary doctrine is maintained in Phœnix Ins. Co. v. Munger, 49 Kan. 178; 33
Am. St. Rep. 360; while in Viele v. Germania Ins. Co., 26 Iowa, 9; 96 Am. Dec.
83, the rule is stated to be, that an insurance company may waive a forfeiture
arising from a breach of condition in its policy, by parol, in a case where the
policy is not attested by the corporate seal of the company.

INSURANCE—CONDITION AGAINST A CHANGE OF POSSESSION is not broken
where the sale was voidable and was afterwards set aside: Commercial etc.
Assur. Co. v. Scammon, 126 Ill. 355; 9 Am. St. Rep. 607, and note.

Dowd *v.* Chicago, Milwaukee, and St. Paul Railway Company.

[84 Wisconsin, 105.]

Railroad Companies—Duty to Maintain Safe Platforms, to Whom Owing.—A railroad company is bound to provide reasonably safe platforms for the use not only of persons who intend to travel by ordinary passenger trains, but also of persons who come to a station with such intending passengers to see them off; but no such duty can be implied in favor of persons who accompany to a station for that purpose one who is an intending passenger merely in the restricted sense of having contracted for the privilege of riding on a freight train, to take care of some stock conveyed thereon. Such persons are bare licensees, and the company owes them no duty except in that capacity.

Action to recover damages for personal injuries alleged to have been received by reason of the defendant's negligence in failing to provide a proper platform. The plaintiff's husband had received permission to load some horses on a freight train at the high platform ordinarily used for the loading of freight instead of at the stockyard, and, as a part of the contract for the carriage of the horses, had been granted the privilege of riding on the same train with them, so as to be able to take care of them while in transit. On the night on which the train was to start the plaintiff, accompanied by some friends, went with her husband to the station to see him off. Having bidden him good-bye, while standing on the high platform, she turned and proceeded to leave it by a flight of steps with the position of which she was well acquainted. The night was very dark, but she found the steps and had placed her right foot upon the upper one, when she was startled by the approach of a train, and in a hasty effort to finish the descent missed the step with her left foot and fell to the ground, receiving the injuries complained of. The train by which the plaintiff's husband was to travel was strictly a freight train. The agent was not allowed to sell passenger tickets for it, and the only persons allowed to ride upon it were the company's employees and persons who were in charge of livestock. A verdict for three thousand five hundred dollars was rendered for the plaintiff, and a motion for a new trial on the ground that it was contrary to law and to the evidence was denied.

John T. Fish, Jackson and Jackson, and Burton Hanson, for the appellant.

Fethers, Jeffris, and Fifield, for the respondent.

[1] Pinney, J. There is no conflict in the evidence in relation to the duty, if any, which the defendant owed the plaintiff, or as to the facts relied on to show that the defendant was guilty of negligence causing the injury which she sustained. All the evidence is embraced in the bill of exceptions, and the court having refused to direct a verdict for defendant, and to set aside the verdict on the ground that it was contrary to law and the evidence, the question to be determined is wholly one of law.

The transaction in question between the plaintiff's husband and the railway company is relied on, in virtue of which it is alleged that the company owed the plaintiff a duty; but it could arise only, if at all, by virtue of her privity or legal relation, under the circumstances, with her husband. The particular business in hand had no relation to or connection with the passenger business or traffic of the company, but concerned only the method of conducting its freight traffic and business, and the rights and duties [2] arising out of it in the carriage of livestock. The fact that the plaintiff's husband was allowed to accompany the train, and ride in the car or on the train to take care of the horses, without charge for it other than the sum paid for the car, was a mere incident of the carriage of the stock, and did not give him all the rights of an intending passenger on a passenger train, though he would not be chargeable, if injured on the trip by the neglect of the company, with contributory negligence because riding in a freight car and exposed to greater peril than if he rode in a passenger car: *Lawson* v. *Chicago etc. Ry. Co.*, 64 Wis. 447; 54 Am. Rep. 634. We consider it misleading to treat the rights of the plaintiff and her husband, and the duties the company owed them, or either of them, upon the basis or from the standpoint that the husband was an intending passenger in the ordinary passenger traffic of the company. The real nature of the transaction and attending circumstances must be considered, with a view of ascertaining what, if any, duty the company owed the plaintiff.

The company owes certain duties, no doubt, in regard to the safety of its platform, to those who come upon it in pursuit of a matter of common interest to both. "The principle appears to be that invitation is inferred where there is a common interest or mutual advantage, while a license is inferred where the object is the mere pleasure or benefit of the person using it": Campbell on Negligence, sec. 33; *Bennett* v. *Rail-road Co.*, 102 U. S. 585. A licensee who enters upon or uses premises by permission only, without any enticement, allure-ment, or inducement being held out to him by the owner or occupant, cannot recover damages for injuries caused by ob-structions or insufficiency. He goes there at his own risk, and enjoys the license subject to its concomitant perils, and no duty is imposed by law on the owner or occupant to keep his premises in a suitable condition for those who come there or use them solely for their own convenience [114] or pleasure. He must use the premises in the condition in which he finds them: *Vanderbeck* v. *Hendry*, 34 N. J. L. 472; *Gallagher* v. *Humphrey*, 6 L. T., N. S., 684; *Ivay* v. *Hedges*, 9 Q. B. Div. 80; *Reardon* v. *Thompson*, 149 Mass. 267. As to a licensee, so long as there is no active misconduct towards him, no lia-bility is incurred by the occupier of the premises by reason of injury sustained by a visitor thereon: *Sweeny* v. *Old Colony etc. R. R. Co.*, 10 Allen, 368; 87 Am. Dec. 644. If the presence of the plaintiff on the platform had any necessary or proper con-nection with any business or traffic she had or designed to have with the company, or she was an intending pasenger on a train about to depart, then an invitation would no doubt be implied on the part of the company for her to come upon and use the platform for such purposes, and a consequent duty devolved on it to use due care to have the platform reasonably safe, both as to access, use, and departure from it. This view is not only a reasonable one, but is sustained by numerous ad-judications: Smith on Negligence, 59, 60, and cases cited; *Heaven* v. *Pender*, 9 Q. B. Div. 302, 305; *Indermauer* v. *Dames*, L. R. 2 Com. P. 311, *Smith* v. *London etc. Docks Co.*, L. R. 3 Com. P. 326. And we think it equally well settled that where an intending passenger is about to take a train in the course of regular passenger traffic, the implied invitation extends also to those who go upon the platform to see him off, and as well to those who go there to meet a friend expected to arrive. In *Watkins* v. *Great Western Ry. Co.*, 46 L. J. Com. P. Div. 817, 821, Denman, J., said: "I re-gard the passenger's friend so permitted to go along . . . . as not being in the nature of a person barely licensed to be there, but as being invited to the same extent as the pas-senger he accompanies, and who is there on lawful business in which the passenger and the company have both an inter-est." And many cases in this country sustain the same view:

Tobin v. *Portland etc. R. R. Co.*, 59 Me. 183; 8 Am. Rep. 415; *Hamilton* v. *Texas etc. Ry. Co.*, 64 Tex. [115] 251; 53 Am. Rep. 756; *McKone* v. *Michigan Cent. R. R. Co.*, 51 Mich. 601; 47 Am. Rep. 596; *Atchison etc. R. R. Co.* v. *Johns*, 36 Kan. 769; 59 Am. Rep. 609; *Toledo etc. Ry. Co.* v. *Grush*, 67 Ill. 263; 16 Am. Rep. 618; *Central R. & B. Co.* v. *Smith*, 80 Ga. 526.

The duty of railroad companies to maintain sufficient and proper platforms for the use and accommodation of passengers, and to properly light them, is fully set forth in *Patten* v. *Chicago etc. Ry. Co.*, 32 Wis. 524. No duty will arise on the part of the company in guarding or lighting its platform as to a particular person, unless there has been an implied invitation on its part, at least, for him to enter in respect to some matter of common interest between them, or in which the party is in some proper way connected. There is no universal rule applicable alike to all cases, and the difficulty of determining whether a mere license or an invitation to enter and use the platform will be implied has been found, in the practical application of these rules of liability, to be very embarrassing. All the cases cited, or which have come under our observation, are those where an invitation has been implied in favor of one or more friends of an intending or arriving passenger, between whom and the company the relation of carrier and passenger existed in the course of regular passenger traffic; and the implication of invitation and consequent duty to those who go to welcome the coming and speed the parting guest seems to be founded on the amenities and social observances which are an inseparable concomitant of modern railway passenger traffic and travel. We think that the rule is limited to the usages in which it had its origin. We do **not** think any such invitation or implication of duty arises, in a matter relating to freight traffic, as to one having no interest in, or duty to perform, in relation to the matter in hand, and that it ought not to be so extended without some strong reason for it.

Negligence consists in the violation of some duty, having [116] regard to the relation between the parties, to time, place, and circumstances; and whether a duty arises that may be violated or neglected, there being, as here, no dispute as to the facts, is a question of law to be determined by the court. As was said in *Cahill* v. *Layton*, 57 Wis. 614, 46 Am. Rep. 46, "It is true that fault and negligence in keeping and maintaining the platform is alleged; but in the language of Willes,

J., in *Gautret* v. *Egerton*, L. R. 2 Com. P., 375, 'to bring the case within the category of actionable negligence, some wrongful act must be shown, or a breach of some positive duty. . . . . It is not enough to show that the defendant has been guilty of negligence, without showing in what respect he was negligent, and how he became bound to use care to prevent injury to others.'" And so in *Cole* v. *McKey*, 66 Wis. 510, 57 Am. Rep. 293: "To constitute actionable negligence, the defendant must be guilty of some wrongful act or breach of positive duty to the plaintiff." The duty of the company in such a case is relative, and not absolute; and this is well illustrated in *Griswold* v. *Chicago etc. Ry. Co.*, 64 Wis. 657; *Gillis* v. *Pennsylvania R. R. Co.*, 59 Pa. St. 143; 98 Am. Dec. 317; and *Baltimore etc. R. R. Co.* v. *Schwindling*, 101 Pa. St. 261; 47 Am. Rep. 706. A railway company has a right to expect that an arriving passenger or an intending one may be met or accompanied by friends, and so it may be said that, in virtue of the relation between the passenger and the company, there is an implied invitation in their case, and that it owes them a corresponding duty. Not so, however, in the exceptional case, in freight traffic, where ladies, or others even, attend one who is about to leave in a freight-car, riding in charge of livestock—one who cannot be said to be a passenger except in a very limited and restricted sense. Such cars, in the usual course of business, have no business to transact at platforms, save as the one in charge of stock may enter across it to go to the office, and the company is not expected to provide a platform and have it, or the steps leading [117] to it, protected by rails or lights at stock chutes, for the use of such so-called passengers, or those who may come to see them off. The court must take notice of the general methods of transacting such business and of matters of common knowledge. To hold that the company owes such duties in these exceptional cases, where, from motives of mere curiosity or of friendship, or even of affection, persons come to see off one in charge of livestock, would unduly burden and embarrass the freight traffic of the company, and establish a rule which has not heretefore been supposed to obtain. Lights are not maintained in or about such places as upon passenger platforms, and railings around them would be a great hindrance, and on the sides of a few steps or stairs unusual or unnecessary.

The facts and circumstances in this case were not such as to give rise to any implied invitation to the plaintiff to come

or be on the platform on the evening in question, and wholly
fail, in our judgment, to show that the company owed her any
duty except that of a mere licensee, to come or go as others
might, with the attendant risk. It is material to note the
undisputed facts. This station was one where but little business was transacted, and but two shipments of stock had been
made by the train in question within two years. The plaintiff was familiar with the platform, and had been upon it often
as a passenger, both going and coming, and knew all about
the steps, and had been up and down them a dozen times.
The high platform in question was never lighted except when
excursion trains were run to the fair, etc. Evidently she and
her husband understood this, for they and their party brought
lanterns with them. The plaintiff brought her lantern, and
there were at least three lanterns at one time there, and at no
time less than two. Such lights as these are the ones used in
and around freight trains and stations, and in loading stock-
cars. The company was not bound to allow the [118] plaintiff's
husband to load his horses from the high platform, nor to embark or take the train from that point, any more than, in the
case of an arriving train, it would be bound to allow him to
disembark or get off there. In *Hemmingway* v. *Chicago etc.
Ry. Co.*, 67 Wis. 676, it was said: "If the company carries
passengers upon its freight trains, we are aware of no rule of
law which makes it the duty of the company to give such
passengers an opportunity to disembark on the depot platform. In many, perhaps in most, cases this would be impracticable; and it is common knowledge that it is not usually done.
The company fulfills all its legal requirements if it affords
such passengers sufficient opportunity to leave the train at a
reasonably safe and convenient place upon the depot grounds
of the station, although not at the depot or platform."

The plaintiff's rights, whatever they were in this case, were
no greater than those of her husband, in privity with whom
she derived them. The plaintiff's husband had solicited the
privilege of loading the horses into the car at the high platform, undoubtedly so as to have it coupled in from that point.
This privilege was granted him, for otherwise the horses would
have been loaded in, and the car would have started from,
the stockyard, some distance west of the depot. Neither the
plaintiff nor her husband was in any just sense invited to the
platform, so as to devolve on the company any duty in respect
to the plaintiff's presence there. They were licensees; cer-

tainly so as to the plaintiff. Conceding that her husband was invited, in a legal sense, to the office to sign the contract, the plaintiff had no duty to perform and no interest to care for in that respect. In no fair or legal sense can it be said that the plaintiff was invited there by the defendant. Whatever right she had was as a mere licensee, and the company did not owe her any duty except in that capacity. When the horses had been put in the car, and the freight contract [119] signed, the agent gave over to the plaintiff's husband and his party, consisting in all of some seven persons, the entire control of the depot, requesting them, when they left, to put out the lights in the waiting-room and close the door. While they occupied the waiting-room until the train came, not by virtue of any implied invitation arising out of the business in hand, but by the permission or license to load the horses and have the car start from the high platform instead of the stockyards, the party took, in addition to the knowledge of the situation, the risks and dangers incident to it. They had the lights ordinarily used in such business to avoid danger or injury, and, had a reasonably prudent use been made of the means at hand, there is no reason to suppose that the plaintiff would have suffered any injury. The reason for not doing so is that she did not think of it. It was her duty to think of it, and not the duty of the company. We think that upon the whole case it may be properly said the plaintiff has wholly failed to show the breach by the defendant of any duty it owed to her. For these reasons we think that the verdict should have been set aside, and a new trial granted.

By the Court. The judgment of the circuit court is reversed, and the cause is remanded for a new trial.

RAILROADS—DUTY TO KEEP PLATFORMS SAFE.—The rule is well settled that railroad companies are bound to make and keep their stations, station platforms, and approaches thereto safe for persons going there to assist passengers, or to receive or part with them: Extended note to *Little Rock etc. Ry. Co. v. Lawton,* 29 Am. St. Rep. 55, where the cases discussing this subject will be found collected.

McClure v. City of Sparta.

[84 Wisconsin, 269.]

Municipal Corporations—Liability for Defects in Sidewalks.—It is the duty of a city which allows a house-owner to maintain a hatchway in a sidewalk to see to it that such hatchway is so located and constructed as not to be unnecessarily insecure for persons passing when it is open, and it is therefore not error in an action for injuries caused by falling into a hatchway, to submit to the jury the question whether the sidewalk was defective by reason of the improper location of such hatchway.

Negligence, Concurrent of Third Person, No Defense, When.—A city is liable for the injuries received by a traveler, who falls into a hatchway, which a house-owner has been allowed to locate and maintain in a dangerous position, although the immediate cause of the accident was the negligence of such house-owner in not guarding the opening.

Action to recover damages for personal injuries. For the purpose of convenient access to a cellar, one Baldwin, a storekeeper in Sparta, had constructed a hatchway near the middle of a plank sidewalk. Having occasion to use it one evening he opened it, and stationed his wife with a lantern beside it to warn passersby. After a while she left her post for some reason and went into the store, placing the lantern on a box near the opening. During her absence the plaintiff passed along the sidewalk with her mother, and not seeing the open hatchway stepped into it and was injured. The defendant appealed from the denial of a motion asking for a new trial.

Morrow and Masters, for the appellant.

C. J. Smith and O. B. Wyman, for the respondent.

[272] Lyon, C. J. The hatchway through which the plaintiff fell was inserted in the sidewalk by Mr. Baldwin, with the knowledge and consent of the city authorities, and with their implied license that the same should be opened and used from time to time as the exigencies of his business might require. While it was probably lawful for the city to allow Mr. Baldwin to make an outside hatchway in the sidewalk leading to his cellar, it was the duty of the city to see to it that the same was so located and constructed as not to render the walk unnecessarily unsafe to persons passing along the same when the hatchway should be open. If not thus located and constructed, the walk was defective, and a failure of duty on the part of the city in respect thereto is negligence.

Water street seems to be one of the principal thoroughfares in the city of Sparta, and large numbers of people travel the same, and the sidewalks thereof, daily and nightly. The hatchway in question was located nearly in the center of the walk (the center line thereof crossing it), and directly in the line of most of the travel over the walk. The danger that persons passing along such walk when the hatchway was open would fall into the opening was much greater than it would have been had the hatchway been located close to the store, or even close to the curb, thus leaving seven feet of the walk, extending from one side thereof two feet past the center, unobstructed. This is manifest. It was the duty of the city to direct the location of the hatchway with due regard to the safety of travelers upon the [273] walk. It is obvious that this was not done, but the hatchway was located by Baldwin with sole reference to the convenient transaction of his own business. Under these circumstances, had the court held it conclusively proved that the sidewalk was defective because of the improper location of the hatchway, it would be difficult to say that the ruling was erroneous. However, the court did not so hold, but (what is more favorable to the city) submitted to the jury the question whether the sidewalk was defective because of the improper location of the hatchway and the consequent negligence of the city in respect to its location. The jury must have resolved the question against the city, else they could not have found for plaintiff, under the charge of the court. We think the city cannot be heard to allege that the submission of the above question to the jury was error.

But it is maintained by the learned counsel for the city that Baldwin was negligent in not properly guarding the opening, which negligence was an independent, proximate cause of the injury complained of, and that for this reason the city is not liable in this action. Assuming, for the purposes of the case, that the negligence of Baldwin is conclusively proved, there are adjudications, notably in Massachusetts, which sustain the above contention. Among these are the cases of *Rowell* v. *Lowell*, 7 Gray, 100; 66 Am. Dec. 464; *Kidder* v. *Dunstable*, 7 Gray, 104; *Shepherd* v. *Chelsea*, 4 Allen, 113. It is held in those cases that if the injury is the combined result of a defect in the highway and the negligence or unlawful act of a third person, the town or city is not liable for such injury.

Whether, in order to render a town or city liable in an action founded upon an alleged defect in a highway, the defect must be the sole cause of the injury complained of, was discussed by the late Chief Justice Dixon in *Houfe* v. *Fulton*, 29 Wis. 296; 9 Am. Rep. 568. The conclusion reached by the court [274] in that case was, that "if, besides the defect in the way, there is another proximate cause of the injury, contributing directly to the result, but which cause is not attributable to the fault or negligence of the plaintiff, nor of any third person, ... the town is liable, provided the jury shall determine that the damage would not have been sustained but for the defect in the way." The writer of this opinion presided at the trial of that case, and granted a nonsuit, in accordance with certain adjudications in Massachusetts, which are cited by the chief justice in his opinion. This court repudiated the doctrine of those cases, and reversed the judgment of nonsuit. The plaintiff, Houfe, afterwards recovered for his injuries, and the judgment in his favor was affirmed by this court: *Houfe* v. *Fulton*, 34 Wis. 608; 17 Am. Rep. 463. But the question here presented, whether the city can be held liable where, as in this case, the other proximate cause of the injury is the negligence of a third person, was not decided in *Houfe* v. *Fulton.*

The above question, however, has been decided in several later adjudications of this court against the doctrine of the cases in 7 Gray and 4 Allen, first above cited. Thus, in *Stetler* v. *Chicago etc. Ry. Co.*, 46 Wis. 497, it was held that where the negligence of the railroad company directly contributed to the injury of one of its employees, the company is liable therefor, though it also appears that the negligence of a co-employee contributed directly to the injury. It is there said the rule is universal that contributory negligence, to defeat an action, must be the negligence of the plaintiff, or of some other person for whose acts he is responsible.

In *Atkinson* v. *Goodrich Transp. Co.*, 60 Wis. 141, 50 Am. Rep. 352, Mr. Justice Taylor discussed this subject quite elaborately, and cited numerous cases elsewhere in support of the rule of *Stetler* v. *Chicago etc. Ry. Co.*, 46 Wis. 497, which was there reaffirmed by this court. The rule there adopted is correctly stated in a headnote as [275] follows: "In an action for an injury from negligence, the fact that another person contributed, either before the defendant's interposition or concurrently therewith, in producing the damage, is no defense." The same rule has since been applied in *Papworth* v. *Milwaukee*, 64 Wis. 389, and *Sherman* v. *Menominee R. L. Co.*, 72 Wis. 122. It is now too firmly established in our jurispru- dence to be repealed or disturbed by judicial decision.

The charge of the learned circuit judge to the jury is, we think, in strict accordance with the foregoing views. Many exceptions were taken thereto, but it seems hardly necessary to set out the charge in full or to state such exceptions in detail, for we think none of the exceptions are well taken. Brief reference will be made, however, to two of them: 1. One sentence of the charge is as follows: "Whenever any one has occasion to travel along a sidewalk of any city, he has a right to a sidewalk that is safe to travel over. It is the duty of a city to make a sidewalk in that condition." Standing alone, it might well be claimed that this instruction imposed upon the city the obligation to make its sidewalks absolutely safe to travelers upon them. But the instruction is preceded and followed by other instructions to the effect that the city is only required to make its sidewalks reasonably safe, which is the true rule. Hence, if the defective condition of the side- walk was not conclusively proved (and for that reason was a question for the jury), we do not think the jury could possi- bly have been misled by the instruction excepted to. 2. The court said to the jury: "If it [the sidewalk] was not reason- ably safe and sufficient, then the plaintiff is entitled to recover in this action." This instruction was equivalent to one that there was no evidence of contributory negligence on the part of the plaintiff. The question of contributory negligence does not seem to have been raised on the trial, and we think there is nothing in the [276] testimony which would warrant its sub- mission to the jury. Hence the instruction was not erroneous.

At the commencement of the trial counsel for the city ob- jected to the admission of any testimony under the complaint, for the alleged reason that no cause of action is stated therein. In the view we have taken of the liability of the city the complaint clearly states a cause of action.

By the COURT. The judgment of the circuit court is affirmed.

MUNICIPAL CORPORATIONS—LIABILITY FOR DEFECTS IN SIDEWALKS.—A city must keep its sidewalks in good repair, and if a person is injured, with- out fault on his part, by its failure so to do, the city will be liable: *Cline* v. *Crescent City R. R. Co.*, 43 La. Ann. 327; 26 Am. St. Rep. 187; *City of Den- ver* v. *Dean*, 10 Col. 375; 3 Am. St. Rep. 594, and note. See also the notes to *McArthur* v. *City of Saginaw,* 55 Am. Rep. 692, and *Goddard, Petitioner,* 28 Am. Dec. 264.

NEGLIGENCE—CONCURRENT OF THIRD PERSON WHETHER A DEFENSE.— When it is negligence on the part of a city at the time of an injury to have failed to remove a lumber-pile from a street, and this failure and the act of a drayman both concur in causing the injury, without contributory negligence on the part of the person injured, the city is liable, no matter whether the act of the drayman was negligent or not: *Gonzales* v. *Galveston,* 84 Tex. 3; 31 Am. St. Rep. 17, and note. The subject of concurrent negligence will be found fully treated in the monographic note to *Village of Cartersville* v. *Cook,* 16 Am. St. Rep. 250–257.

CHAMBERLAIN *v.* CITY OF OSHKOSH.

[84 WISCONSIN, 289.]

MUNICIPAL CORPORATIONS—LIABILITY FOR SLIPPERY SIDEWALKS.—To render a city liable for injuries resulting from a fall upon a sidewalk which has become dangerous to travelers through the formation of a smooth and slippery surface of ice thereon, it is necessary that some other defect should have combined with the ice to cause the injury.

NEGLIGENCE—PROXIMATE AND REMOTE CAUSE.—Where water accumulates in a hole in a sidewalk and forms a sheet of ice on which a traveler falls, the ice, and not the hole, is the proximate cause of the accident, and the city is not liable for the injuries thereby sustained.

ACTION to recover damages for personal injuries.

H. I. Weed, for the appellant.

Finch and Barber, for the respondent.

[290] ORTON, J. This action is to recover damages for a personal injury to the plaintiff, occasioned by the want of repair and defective condition of a walk in Merritt street, in the city of Oshkosh. The defect is thus described in the complaint: "The said street, known as Merritt street, at a certain place in said street, to wit, on the south side of said Merritt street, on the southeast corner thereof where said Merritt street intersects with Ford street of said city, was [on the twenty-first day of February, 1889] and for a period of four weeks or more had been, unsafe, insufficient, defective, and badly out of repair, in this, to wit, that at the point of junction between the stone crossing on the south side of said Merritt street, where said Merritt street intersects with Ford street, and the sidewalk on the south side of said Merritt street, where said stone crossing ends, the authorities [291] of the city of Oshkosh, to wit, this defendant, negligently permitted a large hole to exist

within the usual line and course of travel over said stone crossing and sidewalk, and negligently permitted and allowed said hole to exist and remain without placing any guard over or around the same, and negligently allowed said hole to become filled with water, and to become frozen over with a large surface of smooth ice, and negligently failed to place any protection, guard, or cover over or around said surface of ice, and failed to take any precaution to prevent or warn travelers over said crossing or sidewalk from walking upon and over said surface of ice; that persons traveling over and upon said crossing and sidewalk were compelled to walk upon and over said surface of ice, and that the aforesaid city authorities, to wit, the defendant, negligently failed to provide a safe and sufficient crossing or passage over or around said large surface of smooth ice."

The plaintiff's injury, and the manner of it, are substantially described as follows: The plaintiff, while traveling upon said Merritt street and over said stone crossing, "did by necessity and in the ordinary course of travel walk upon and over said large surface of ice, and without any fault on her part she fell upon said surface of ice with great force," and received great bodily injuries therefrom.

After the plaintiff was sworn as a witness in her own behalf, the defendant city interposed a demurrer *ore tenus*, on the ground that the complaint did not state a cause of action, and the objection to any evidence under it was overruled, and exception taken. The plaintiff testified that when she came to that point "her feet came from under her, and she came down on her back." "She did not notice any barriers or guards around this place, or any ashes upon the sidewalk where she slipped." According to the evidence, the depression in the street, where the water had accumulated which made the ice on which the plaintiff [292] slipped down and was injured, was made by the junction of a sidewalk coming down Ford street with the stone cross-walk over Merritt street. It would seem that the slight difference of the grade of the two streets made the depression. The slope of the plank sidewalk down to its junction with the stone cross-walk was only four inches, and the depression in the stone cross-walk where the ice accumulated was from an inch to an inch and a half. The plank walk was over the gutter on Merritt street. This defect, if any, appears to have been in the plan of the work and its construction.

At the conclusion of the testimony the defendant's motion **for a** nonsuit was overruled. The jury found a special verdict "that the cross-walk was in a defective and dangerous condition," and "that such condition caused the plaintiff's injury," and assessed her damages at eleven hundred dollars.

It will be observed that the complaint does not charge that the plaintiff's injury was caused by a hole or depression in the cross-walk, but that it was caused wholly by the smooth surface of the ice at that place, and such was the evidence. The plaintiff slipped and fell on the smooth surface of the ice. The ice was the proximate cause of the injury. The depression in the walk where the ice formed, if a defect and a cause of the injury in any sense, was a remote, and not the proximate cause of the injury. But at this time there was no hole or even depression at that place. It was filled up by the ice. It is too plain for argument that the cause of the plaintiff's injury, both by the complaint and testimony, was the smooth surface of the ice on the cross-walk. The special verdict is careful not to state the defect or dangerous condition. It will be observed, also, that the negligence of the city consists "in failing to provide a safe crossing or passage over and around said large surface of smooth ice," and that it "allowed and permitted said crossing to remain in such insufficient, [293] unsafe, and defective condition for a period of four weeks, and failed to take any precaution to prevent or warn travelers over said crossing or sidewalk from walking upon and over said surface of ice."

The existence and continuance of said ice for four weeks was the presumptive notice to the city of the defect complained of. The plaintiff does not complain of being injured by the hole or depression, but by the "large surface of smooth ice." The depression was the cause of ice accumulating there, and the water, combined with a low temperature, caused the ice to form which injured the plaintiff. The depression was a remote cause or cause of causes. The proximate or direct cause was the ice, and this must be the cause of action. *Causa proxima non remota spectatur.* The proximate and not the remote cause must be considered. The cause nearest in order of causation, which is adequate to produce the result, is the direct cause. In law, only the direct **cause is** considered. These are familiar maxims: "The proximate cause is the cause which leads to, and is instrumental in producing the result": 3 Am & Eng. Ency. of

Law, 45; *State* v. *Manchester etc. R. R. Co.*, 52 N. H. 528. In this case the hole or depression is not the cause of the injury for which an action may be brought. It is too remote. There is a direct cause of the injury, and that is the ice on which she slipped down, and that is the only one which can be considered. The defect in the street or walk is the ice, and the negligence of the city consists in allowing it to remain. This was dangerous to the traveling public, and the cause of the plaintiff's injury in the law and by the complaint and testimony. This ice was smooth and level, and accumulated through the sole agency of the elements and in the order of nature. No argument, speculation or casuistry can make this case any different from this. The main and important question which first presents itself on the demurrer to the complaint, and again on the [294] motion for a nonsuit, is, Is such a condition of the walk an actionable defect? This question is settled by this court in the negative in many cases, after a very full examination of the authorities elsewhere, which we need not cite. "When the walk is slippery because of the smooth surface of the snow and ice which had accumulated upon it," such a defect is not actionable: *Cook* v. *Milwaukee*, 24 Wis. 270; 1 Am. Rep. 183; 27 Wis. 191. In *Perkins* v. *Fond du Lac*, 34 Wis. 435, "the walk was entirely covered with packed snow and ice, and the whole surface of the walk was very smooth and slippery." It was held that such a condition of the walk did not alone constitute an actionable defect; and so in *Grossenbach* v. *Milwaukee*, 65 Wis. 31; 56 Am. Rep. 614. This holding is most reasonable. Such a defect in a walk or street is common and natural everywhere in the winter season, and such actions would be numberless, unreasonable, and oppressive. The municipalities are powerless to prevent or remove such a common and natural condition. The authorities cited by the learned counsel of the respondent are not applicable to this case. They are cases where other defects combine with the ice to cause the injury. Such defects must be present with the ice, and they together constitute a cause of action; as, where the ice is formed on a steep declivity or descending grade, or there is some other condition of the walk, which, together with the ice, makes the walk dangerous, as in *Grossenbach* v. *Milwaukee*, 65 Wis. 31, 56 Am. Rep. 614, and *Perkins* v. *Fond du Lac*, 34 Wis. 435, and other cases in this court. But here the hole or depression does not combine with the ice, and is not present with it. There is no hole at the time, as it is filled with ice and the surface is made level as ice can be anywhere. The plaintiff was not injured by stepping into the hole, but by slipping on the ice. But I have said enough of this. The hole was only the remote cause or cause of causes, which produced the result, and was not the direct, efficient, or adequate cause, which alone is actionable. [295] The court should have sustained the demurrer *ore tenus*, or, failing in that, ought to have ordered a nonsuit on the evidence.

By the COURT. The judgment of the circuit court is reversed, and the cause is remanded for a new trial.

MUNICIPAL CORPORATIONS—LIABILITY FOR SLIPPERY SIDEWALKS.—Mere slipperiness arising from a smooth surface of snow or ice on a sidewalk is not such a defect as will render a city liable for damages for injuries caused by a fall thereon: *Cook* v. *Milwaukee*, 24 Wis. 270; 1 Am. Rep. 183; *Chase* v. *Cleveland*, 44 Ohio St. 504; 58 Am. Rep. 843; *Mauch Chunk* v. *Kline*, 100 Pa. St. 119; 45 Am. Rep. 364; *Grossenbach* v. *Milwaukee*, 65 Wis. 31; 56 Am. Rep. 614. But a defective construction of a street in conjunction with an accumulation of ice thereon casts upon the city the duty of removing the obstruction on notice, and a failure to perform such duty is negligence: *Decker* v. *Scranton City*, 151 Pa. St. 241; 31 Am. St. Rep. 757, and note where the cases discussing this subject will be found collected.

NEGLIGENCE—PROXIMATE AND REMOTE CAUSE.—This question will be found extensively treated in *Gilson* v. *Delaware etc. Canal Co.*, 65 Vt. 213; 36 Am. St. Rep. 802, and the lengthy monographic note thereto.

BROTHERS *v.* BANK OF KAUKAUNA.

[84 WISCONSIN, 381.]

AGENT, NOTICE TO, HOW FAR DEEMED NOTICE TO PRINCIPAL.—If an agent has acquired knowledge of a fact so recently as to make it incredible that he should have forgotten it, his principal will be bound, although he did not acquire such knowledge, while transacting his principal's business. Hence, if the cashier of a bank has been present at the execution of a mortgage and promissory note by one whose visible condition at the time was such as to put a reasonably observant person upon inquiry as to his capacity to contract, and it appears that immediately after the execution of the instruments the bank acquired possession of them as collateral security for the debt of a third party, the bank is chargeable with notice of all the material facts of which its cashier had notice, and cannot be regarded as a *bona fide* purchaser of those instruments.

HUSBAND AND WIFE—WIFE'S PARTICIPATION IN EXECUTION OF MORTGAGE AFTERWARDS AVOIDED, EFFECT OF.—A married woman who signs a mortgage at the same time as her husband is not bound thereby, if the instrument is subsequently declared invalid, on the ground that he was mentally incompetent at the time it was executed.

ESTOPPEL IN PAIS—FACTS NOT SUFFICIENT TO RAISE.—Where the widow and son of a mortgagor are seeking, on the ground of his mental incapacity, to set aside a mortgage after it has passed into the possession of a bank as collateral security for the debt of a third party, and it appears that the bank had, through its cashier, notice of all the material facts surrounding the execution of the mortgage, such bank is in no position to insist upon an equitable estoppel based merely on the facts, that the widow signed the mortgage with her husband, that the son attested it, that various small checks drawn by the mortgagor before the execution of the mortgage and one drawn after it were paid by the bank, and that a payment of interest was made by the mortgagor's son for the mortgagor's estate upon the indebtedness for which the mortgage was collateral security.

ACTION brought to cancel a note and mortgage executed by George W. Kelso, on the ground that he was, at the time it was executed, incompetent to transact any business. The defendants denied all knowledge of such incompetency, and insisted that the plaintiffs were estopped to contest the validity of the instruments by reason of the fact that the mortgagor's widow and one of his sons, who, with the mortgagor's administrator, were joined as plaintiffs in the action, had been present at, and assisted in, the execution and delivery of those instruments. The evidence showed that the mortgagee, another of the mortgagor's sons, was, at the time of the execution of the note and mortgage in a very embarrassed position financially, and that, very soon after such execution, the defendant bank, to whom he was in debt, acquired possession of the instruments as collateral security for the money owed by him. The rest of the material facts appear sufficiently from the opinion of the court. The trial court made no finding as to the competency of the mortgagor, but found for the defendant on all the other questions involved.

John Bottensek, for the appellants.

H. D. Ryan, G. H. Dawson, and Humphrey Pierce, for the respondent.

393 PINNEY, J. 1. The evidence establishes beyond doubt or question that George W. Kelso, at the time he signed the note and mortgage in question, was of unsound mind and wholly incapable of conducting the business transaction in question. Extended comment is unnecessary to establish a conclusion so manifest, and against which respondent's counsel were unable to offer serious argument. We have collected the evidence as to the condition of George W. Kelso, and as to what took place at the time the note and mortgage were

signed, with the manner of its execution and alleged delivery,
because of its important bearing upon the question of notice
of his incompetency to the bank defendant. Mr. Towsley,
who certified to the acknowledgment of the mortgage, and
signed it as a subscribing witness, was, and for some two or
three years had been, cashier and general manager of the
bank, and it is fair to assume that he possessed the intelligence, quickness of perception, experience, and sound judgment necessary to fit him for his position, and which similar
bank officers usually possess.   George F. Kelso owned and
carried on a pulp mill, and had had dealings with the bank,
and was then owing it a considerable sum of money, and in
almost desperate financial straits.   This note and mortgage
were devised as a means of relief, either by selling it, or, it would
seem, by using it at the bank; and the claim was made, ao-
quiesced in by [394] him, as appears from his testimony, that,
having been deposited in the bank immediately after its execution, it at once became collateral security for his indebtedness to the bank.   Mr. Towsley testifies to going with George
F. Kelso to the house of his father, George W. Kelso, with the
note and mortgage already prepared, to get them executed,
when it appears that George F. Kelso had never exchanged a
word with his father in relation to them, and had never talked
with him on the subject at all; that he went solely at the request of George F. Kelso, and that it was not a matter in
which he personally or the bank had any interest.   But the
fact is that the bank within less than two weeks advanced, as
it is said, $1,500 in money on account of the note and mort-
gage, and followed it with other sums at short intervals, until
the entire advances within about sixty days reached $3,800.
The condition of George W. Kelso at the time these papers
were signed was quite enough to admonish any intelligent
person not to undertake any business transaction with him,
for he was a total wreck, mentally as well as physically, and
had not as much business capacity as a mere child.   It is
difficult to understand how, as an acknowledging officer, Mr.
Towsley could fairly certify to the acknowledgment of the
mortgage.   It was for a large sum, and upon the farm and
homestead of one deplorably mentally incompetent.   Mr.
Towsley's testimony in respect to what occurred is in some
material points at variance with that of three others who
were present, and the fact that he asked William A. Kelso,
then present, if he understood the transaction, shows at least

a consciousness that there was some propriety at least that some one connected with the family, aside from George F. Kelso, should comprehend it. He denies that he then knew or understood that George W. Kelso was mentally incompetent, but he testifies on cross-examination that beyond a slight inclination of his head, and saying "yes" twice, George **395** W. Kelso did not say anything; and that he spoke or could speak at all was denied by the others.

The situation and the transaction just as it appeared spoke for themselves in a manner not to be misunderstood, and if Mr. Towsley is now able to say that he did not know or understand that George W. Kelso was a mere imbecile it is evident that the fault is his own. The facts and circumstances within his knowledge were such as to require him to stay his hand and make that inquiry which would have dispelled any doubt. The testimony of Freeman in this connection is not without weight or consequence, and is corroborated in part by the bank stamp of payment on his check. In view of all the facts and circumstances which could not fail to have been in Towsley's mind, as they were of such recent occurrence, as cashier of the bank he made the subsequent advances, now amounting, with interest, to over five thousand dollars, for which the bank claims to hold and enforce the mortgage, for which no consideration whatever was ever paid, or agreed to be paid, to George W. Kelso or his wife.

2. Notice to an agent is notice to his principal, and it is conceded that the principal is bound and affected by such knowledge or notice as his agent obtains in negotiating or attending to the particular transaction. But if the agent acquires his information so recently as to make it incredible that he should have forgotten it, his principal will be bound, although not acquired while transacting the business of the principal. The case of *Walker* v. *Grand Rapids F. M. Co.*, 70 Wis. 92, is a strong case in point to show that the bank, when it acquired its interest in the note and mortgage, became affected with the notice Towsley had then so recently acquired at the time the papers were executed. This conclusion is supported by *Dresser* v. *Norwood*, 17 Com. B., N. S., 466; *The Distilled Spirits*, 11 Wall. 366; *Hovey* v. *Blanchard*, 13 N. H. 145; *Patten* v. *Merchants' etc. Ins. Co.*, 40 N. H. 375; *Hart* v. *Farmers' etc. Bank*, 33 Vt. 252; *Holden* v. **396** *New York etc. Bank*, 72 N. Y. 286; *Fulton Bank* v. *New York etc. Canal*

Co., 4 Paige, 127. Besides Towsley was the principal financial officer, the real and constant controller and manager of
the affairs of the bank. Indeed, it is not easy to separate
him from it, or to consider him other than the bank itself, so
fully were the affairs under his management and control.
It seems, in view of the particular circumstances, but proper
to regard the case in the same manner as if a natural person,
as Towsley himself, had acquired the note and mortgage
with the knowledge he possessed; and in this connection it is
material to observe that it was claimed, supported by George
F. Kelso's testimony, that the note and mortgage became
immediately, on execution, collateral security for the debt he
then owed the bank. We are therefore of the opinion that
the bank is chargeable with notice of all the material facts
of which Towsley had notice, and cannot be regarded as a
bona fide purchaser of the note and mortgage.

3. It is contended that the plaintiffs are estopped from
disputing the validity of the note and mortgage in the hands
of the bank, and the judgment of the circuit court proceeds
upon this ground. There is no ground for saying that either
of them is estopped by the mortgage. William A. Kelso was
was not a party to it, and Margaret Kelso, the wife of the
mortgagor, was not bound by it, either as to her dower or
homestead right. If the mortgage did not bind her husband
it did not bind her, and if avoided as to him it would be
avoided as to her as well. Separate and apart from her husband she could not convey or bind by deed or mortgage her
dower or homestead right: *Munger* v. *Perkins*, 62 Wis. 499;
Godfrey v. *Thornton*, 46 Wis. 677. As the bank is affected
with notice through Towsley, its cashier, of all the material
facts, it is in no position to insist upon an estoppel by matter
in pais, or an equitable estoppel as against the plaintiffs. It
cannot say that it has [397] been misled.

In order that such an estoppel shall exist there must generally be some intended deception in the conduct or declaration of the party to be estopped, or such gross negligence on
his part as to amount to constructive fraud, by which another
has been misled to his injury: *Kingman* v. *Graham*, 51 Wis.
233; *McLean* v. *Dow*, 42 Wis. 610; *Brant* v. *Virginia C. & I.
Co.*, 93 U. S. 326. The fact that prior to the 1st of October,
1885, George W. Kelso signed various small checks ranging
from ten dollars to fifty dollars, drawn on the bank, which
were paid by it, is a circumstance of little or no weight as

against the plaintiffs on the question of estoppel. It is not claimed that but one of these checks was so signed after the execution of the note and mortgage, and the cashier then had notice of facts and circumstances which would have justified him in refusing payment of it. The payment of sixty-eight dollars and sixty-seven cents interest on the indebtedness to which the note and mortgage were collateral, by William A. Kelso, for George W. Kelso's estate, as appears to have been the fact, was doubtless a payment made for the guardian, Hood, George W. Kelso being then alive. The facts relied on furnish, we think, no ground for holding that the plaintiffs are estopped from disputing the note and mortgage.

For these reasons the judgment of the circuit court is erroneous, and should have been in favor of the plaintiffs and against the defendants.

By the COURT. The judgment of the circuit court is reversed, and the cause remanded, with directions to enter judgment declaring the note and mortgage in question void, and canceling the same as against the plaintiffs and their right, title, and interest in the lands described.

AGENCY—NOTICE TO, WHEN NOTICE TO PRINCIPAL.—The knowledge of a fact acquired by an agent at a time when he is not acting as such, if actually had in mind by him when afterwards acting for his principal, will, as respects that transaction, be imputed to the principal: *Wilson* v. *Minnesota Farmers' etc. Ins. Assn.*, 36 Minn. 112; 1 Am. St. Rep. 659; *Constant* v. *University*, 111 N. Y. 604; 7 Am. St. Rep. 769, and note; *Snyder* v. *Partridge*, 138 Ill. 173; 32 Am. St. Rep. 130, and note. See also the extended notes to *Trentor* v. *Pothen*, 24 Am. St. Rep. 228, and *Fairfield Sav. Bank* v. *Chase*, 39 Am. Rep. 323.

CASE v. HOFFMAN.

[84 WISCONSIN, 438.]

WATERS AND WATERCOURSES—SURFACE WATERS, WHAT ARE.—Surface waters are such as lie upon or spread over the surface, or percolate the soil, as in swamps, and do not flow in a particular direction.

WATERCOURSES, WHAT ARE.—To constitute a watercourse, it is not necessary that there should be a continual flow of water, but there must be a stream, which usually flows in a particular direction, in a well-defined channel, having a bed and sides or banks. Such a stream, so long as it can be traced by the existence of such a channel, wherever the ground is suitable for cutting one, and does not lose its identity as the same stream, does not cease to be a watercourse because it spreads out at some points into marshes and swamps.

WATERS AND WATERCOURSES—SUFFICIENCY OF COMPLAINT IN ACTION TO

ESTABLISH RIGHTS IN A WATERCOURSE.—A complaint in an action to establish certain rights in a watercourse, alleged to have been diverted, is not demurrable on the ground that the stream described is not a watercourse, when it alleges that "there were always, and are yet, living springs, which continuously flow and discharge their waters by a well-defined stream into a natural lake of about sixty acres in extent, known as 'Big lake'"; that "the waters so gathered flowed, under natural conditions, upon the surface and beneath the surface of the lands lying to the southeast of said lake to and across the said lands of the plaintiff, and thence easterly, until they discharged themselves and were again collected in a stream known as 'Beaver creek'"; that "the said natural flow or stream of water from the lake was well defined and established, and, in places, one of which was upon the land of the plaintiff, had made for itself a distinct and plainly marked channel, pointing and showing the natural flow of the water" and that "said stream was known and commonly called by the name of the 'West branch' of 'Beaver creek.'" The fact that such complaint also shows that the stream spread over wide reaches of marsh and swamp lands, and percolated the soil in many or most places between the 'Big lake' and 'Beaver creek,' therein referred to, does not affect its sufficiency.

WATERS AND WATERCOURSES—ACTION TO ENJOIN DIVERSION—PLEADING. A complaint in an action to establish rights in an alleged watercourse, and to enjoin the diversion thereof, is not demurrable on the ground of misjoinder of causes of action, when it also asks for the specific performance of a contract made by the plaintiff with the defendant's grantors, by virtue of which it is averred that, even if the waters in question do not technically constitute a watercourse, the plaintiff is entitled to have the use of them for irrigating his land.

WATERS AND WATERCOURSES—ACTION TO ESTABLISH RIGHTS IN WATER-COURSE, OF EQUITABLE COGNIZANCE, WHEN.—An action to enjoin the diversion of a watercourse, and to enforce the specific performance of a contract, by which the plaintiff was to have the use of the waters in such watercourse for irrigating his land, is of equitable cognizance.

SUIT to establish rights in a watercourse.

La Follette, Harper, Roe, and Zimmerman, and H. W. Chynoweth, for the appellants.

Bushnell, Rogers, and Hall, and Gardner and Gaynor, for the respondents.

440 ORTON, J. This is an appeal from the order of the circuit court sustaining a demurrer to the complaint on the ground that it did not state a cause of action. The facts stated in the complaint are substantially as follows:

The plaintiff is the owner of 440 acres of land in sections 21 and 22, town 20, range 1 east, purchased and suitable for the cultivation of cranberries. "There is a natural stream of water known as 'Beaver creek,' with clearly defined banks and a fixed channel, varying in depth, but always with a steady flow of the waters in an easterly direction, bearing south, through the northern portion of [441] said town 20, at a distance of about two miles from the plaintiff's said lands, and, after passing the eastern line of the town, bends its course so as to flow in a southerly and southwesterly direction for a considerable distance below the south line of said town. There were always and still are in the northwestern portion of said town living springs, which continuously flow and discharge their waters by a well-defined stream into a natural lake of about sixty acres in extent, situated in section 8 of said town, known as 'Big lake.' From said lake the waters so gathered flowed, under natural conditions, upon the surface and beneath the surface of the lands lying to the southeast of said lake to and across the said lands of the plaintiff, and thence easterly, until they discharged themselves and were again collected in said Beaver creek. The said natural flow or stream of water from said lake in section 8 was well defined and established, and in places, one of which was upon the land of the plaintiff, had made for itself a distinct and plainly marked channel, pointing and showing the natural flow of the water; and said stream was known and called by the name of the 'West branch' of Beaver creek. At the time of the purchase by the plaintiff of his said lands in section 22, the actual flow and source of the water above described from said Big lake still continued as in a state of nature across the lands of the plaintiff as aforesaid, discharging to and upon the lands lying to the east of the plaintiff, and to some extent to the south of the lands of the plaintiff, and were to a considerable extent dispersed over a large area of land drained by Beaver creek. The plaintiff's lands were also supplied with water from surface springs, northward therefrom, in large numbers, constant in their supply, furnishing a large quantity of living water, moving in a southeasterly direction through and across the lands lying between said springs and plaintiff's land, and over, through, and across said lands, though not usually in [442] perfectly defined channels. At the time of the purchase of said lands in section 22 by the plaintiff as aforesaid, immemorially theretofore, and thereafter continuously until about the year 1883, the waters of said West branch, together with the other waters last aforesaid, were sufficient in volume adequately to irrigate and supply waters sufficient to moisten said lands and make them suitable to the cultivation of cranberries." Immediately after the purchase of the lands in section 22, the plaintiff began the cultivation of cranberries on said land, and cut ditches across the same to make available the natural flow of said waters, and has continued to improve said lands for such purpose by an expenditure of a large sum of money; and the improvements so made are of the value of $12,000, and the lands, with said improvements, are now of the value of $20,000.

The complaint then states, in substance, as follows: About 1883, D. A. and C. A. Goodyear built a sawmill about a mile south of plaintiff's land, and, for the purpose of getting logs from near said Big lake to their mill, they obtained an act of the legislature, chapter 271, Laws of 1883, and claimed to act in accordance with the same, and made a ditch or canal from six to twelve feet wide, and four feet deep, from Big lake along the general course of the West branch aforesaid, down through a portion of the plaintiff's lands, and to said sawmill, and floated logs to said mill; but they so conducted their business and managed their ditch as to greatly injure the lands of the plaintiff and others. They then entered into a contract with the plaintiff to make such ditches on his land with supply gates, so that he could make the same use of the waters of said West branch as before said large ditch was made. The cutting of this ditch not only used all the waters of said West branch along their natural channel and bed, but diverted the same, as it left the plaintiff's land into another direction [443] to said mill, and southeastwardly to a stream called "Silver creek," a long distance from Beaver creek, into which it formerly ran and was a tributary thereof. A branch ditch was also cut into Beaver creek northwardly, which diverted a portion of its waters also to the said mill and into Silver creek. The plaintiff continued to enjoy the advantages of said contract until the said mill and the floating of logs to it through said big ditch were abandoned, and the Goodyears sold out all their interest in the same to the defendants in 1889. The defendants then closed up the plaintiff's gates by which he was wont to obtain sufficient water for his cranberry culture, and cut ditches from the main ditch outside of plaintiff's lands and around the same, and diverted all the water of said West branch and of said main ditch around and away from the same to said mill and Silver creek, and thereby nearly destroyed the use of the lands and improvements of the plaintiff. But some water escaped through the east banks out of repair and beneath the broken gates, which he used to irrigate his lands to a limited extent. The defendants then constructed ditches, dams, and embankments, solely for the purpose of removing and diverting said watercourse wholly from and off the plaintiff's lands, intending thereby to deprive the plaintiff from receiving a supply of living water from any source whatever for his lands. The plaintiff's cranberry crop is now liable to destruction from the want of water.

The plaintiff prays that his rights may be established to said water; that the Goodyear contract be specifically performed; that the defendants be enjoined from diverting said waters, and be required to remove said obstructions to the natural flow thereof; and that the plaintiff be permitted by the order of the court to cut through said dam, and allow the waters to pass through the plaintiff's land; and, finally, for damages of three thousand five hundred dollars, and for other relief.

The principal contention of the learned counsel of the [444] respondents in support of the demurrer is that the waters coming to the plaintiff's lands, and for the diversion of which the plaintiff complains, are mere surface waters, which the defendants had their right to deal with on their own land and for their own benefit as they saw fit, and that their alleged diversion thereof from the plaintiff's lands does not give him any right of action therefor. The learned counsel of the appellant contend that such waters are of a natural watercourse and living stream, in which he has the rights of a riparian proprietor, and that therefore he has in this action the right to recover for the diversion thereof by the defendants.

The distinction between mere surface waters and a natural watercourse is wide enough to be readily discerned, and to determine which the complaint describes is not difficult. We will first briefly examine the law and the authorities as to the peculiar and indispensable elements, and characteristics of each, and then make application of them to the complaint.

1. Surface water is such as its name indicates. It spreads over the surface of the ground. It has its origin most commonly in rains and melted snow. It may stand in swamps, or it may percolate through or under the soil. It is as well defined, and the law applicable to it stated as well, in *Hoyt* v. *Hudson*, 27 Wis. 656, 9 Am. Rep. 473, as in any case in the books. "The doctrine of the common law," say Chief Justice Dixon, "is that there exists no such natural easement or serv-

itude in favor of the owner of the superior or higher ground
or fields as to mere surface water, or such as falls or accumulates by rain or the melting of snow; and that the proprietor
of the inferior or lower tenement or estate may, if he choose,
lawfully obstruct or hinder the natural flow of such water
thereon, and in so doing may turn the same back upon or off
onto or over the lands of other proprietors, without liability
for injuries ensuing from such [445] obstruction or diversion."
Nearly the same language is used by the same learned chief
justice in *Pettigrew* v. *Evansville*, 25 Wis. 223; 3 Am. Rep. 50.

It is further described as "waters flowing in hollows or
ravines, from rain or melting snow"; or "drainage over the
land occasioned by unusual freshets or other extraordinary
causes," and are not permanent, but soon pass off or dry up
when the cause ceases: *Fryer* v. *Warne*, 29 Wis. 511; *Eulrich*
v. *Richter*, 37 Wis. 226; *Allen* v. *Chippewa Falls*, 52 Wis. 434;
38 Am. Rep. 748; *O'Connor* v. *Fond du Lac. etc. R. R. Co.*,
52 Wis. 530; 38 Am. Rep. 753; *Hanlin* v. *Chicago etc. Ry. Co.*,
61 Wis. 515; *Lessard* v. *Stram*, 62 Wis. 112; 51 Am. Rep. 715.
"Surface water lies upon or spreads over the surface, or percolates the soil, as in swamps, and does not flow in a particular channel." "The owner may expel surface water from
his own land to that of another without wrong": Gould on
Waters, sec. 263. "But one may do so only to protect himself, or to benefit his own land, but no further." "But even
surface water becomes a natural watercourse at the point
where it begins to form a reasonably well-defined channel,
with bed and banks or sides, and current with nearly constant flow": Gould on Waters, sec. 263.

2. A natural watercourse is also as well defined and the
law that governs it stated in our own cases as anywhere.
Says Chief Justice Dixon, in *Hoyt* v. *Hudson*, 27 Wis. 656; 9
Am. Rep. 473: "The term 'watercourse' is well defined.
There must be a stream usually flowing in a particular direction, though it need not flow continually. It may sometimes
be dry. It must flow in a definite channel, having a bed,
sides, or banks, and usually discharge itself into some other
stream or body of water." The following streams are held
to come within this definition. In *Spelman* v. *Portage*, 41
Wis. 144, the streams held to be watercourses were across the
low grounds of considerable extent between said rivers, which
had their origin in the overflow of the Wisconsin river to the
Baraboo river, caused by unusual freshets. [446] They had no

well-defined channels or banks, but spread widely over the
intervening ground. They came from one unquestionable
watercourse, and passed. into another one, and did not lose
their character as watercourses by passing and spreading
over the intervening low ground. In *Gillett* v. *Johnson*, 30
Conn. 392, there was a living spring about sixteen rods from
the dividing line on the land of the defendant. It ran off in
a stream that would fill a half-inch pipe. The supply was
constant, except in a very dry time. For six or eight rods it
ran rapidly between abrupt banks and in a well-defined channel. It then came to marshy ground, where it spread out, so
that its flow was slight, in a sluggish current, but in a natural bed or depression to a watering place on the plaintiff's
land. The defendant diverted the stream on his own land
from the watering place of the plaintiff. It was held to be a
watercourse, and the defendant liable. In *Macomber* v. *Godfrey*, 108 Mass. 219, 11 Am. Rep. 349, the stream came across
a road onto the defendant's land, in a well-defined channel,
but when within five rods of the plaintiff's land, below it,
spread out several rods in width, and so it ran upon the plaintiff's land, which was a flat and level meadow, where it irrigated it in a valuable manner, and there was no defined
channel on the plaintiff's land; but a short distance below
his land it again formed into a brook, with a channel and
current, and so ran on and emptied into a river. Held to be
a watercourse, which the defendant could not divert from the
plaintiff's land. In *Miller* v. *Laubach*, 47 Pa. St. 154, 86 Am.
Dec. 521, the waters came from winter springs on defendant's
land, and soon spread out and made his land wet and boggy,
and they were wont to pass onto the plaintiff's land, and there
soon dry up by evaporation. The defendant cut a ditch on
his own land, which gathered the waters together and discharged them on the plaintiff's land in such a manner as
to cause him great injury, by making his land wet and useless. The defendant [447] was held liable.

In *Kauffman* v. *Griesemer*, 26 Pa. St. 407, 67 Am. Dec. 437,
the stream came from springs on the plaintiff's land, which,
increased by rains and snow, ran down on and through the
defendant's land and emptied into a creek. They ran in a
general channel, but their flow was not continuous. The
defendant made a sod dam at his line, and thereby turned the
waters back onto the plaintiff's land, to his injury. It was
held that this stream was a watercourse, and governed by

the maxim of the common law, "*aqua currit et debet currere,*" and the plaintiff recovered. In *Rhoads* v. *Davidheiser,* 133 Pa. St. 226, 19 Am. St. Rep. 630, it is held that even surface water, if it run in a channel with banks and current and in a certain direction when there is water, although not continuously, is a watercourse and governed by the same law. In *Earl* v. *De Hart*, 12 N. J. Eq. 280, 72 Am. Dec. 395, it is held that when the country is such that the water from rains and melting snow is necessarily collected into one body, so large as to require an outlet, and is discharged through it in a well-defined channel, where it is accustomed to flow and has flowed from time immemorial, such channel is an ancient natural watercourse. The common-law doctrine prevails in New Jersey. A spring without an outlet or inlet is not a watercourse, but if it have an outlet through a well-defined channel it is a watercourse: *Delhi* v. *Youmans*, 50 Barb. 316. Where a spring rises on one man's land, and from it a stream runs with a current and in a well-defined channel onto the land of another below, although it furnished no more water than the superior proprietor could use for domestic purposes and to water his land, he cannot divert or wholly consume it to the detriment of the inferior owner: *Arnold* v. *Foot*, 12 Wend. 330; *Smith* v. *Adams*, 6 Paige, 435, is to the same effect. "A spring, to be protected by the law, must be one which issues out of the earth by natural forces": Gould on Waters, sec. 286. A spring becomes a watercourse at [448] the point where the water comes to the surface and flows off in a defined channel or bed, with banks or shores which confine the water and cause it to run in a certain direction: Gould on Waters, sec. 41. It must have a current, or it cannot be obstructed or diverted to any one's injury. If a watercourse is lost in a swamp or lake, it is still a watercourse if it emerges therefrom in a well-defined channel; or if it spreads over a meadow, and it can be identified or traced as the same stream, it is still a watercourse: Gould on Waters, sec. 264; *Briscoe* v. *Drought*, 11 I. C. L. R. 250; *Munkres* v. *Kansas City etc. R. R. Co.*, 72 Mo. 514; *Hebron G. R. Co.* v. *Harvey*, 90 Ind. 192; 46 Am. Rep. 199; *Robinson* v. *Shanks*, 118 Ind. 125. "If the channel and banks formed by running water present to the eye at a casual glance the unmistakable evidence of the frequent action of running water, then it is a natural watercourse": Gould on Waters, sec. 264.

I will close these citations by a very strong case in favor of the plaintiff's right, in this court. The plaintiffs owned a mill at Cross Plains, on Black Earth creek. The creek had its rise in Mud lake in another town, which lake was partially fed by springs, but mainly by rains and surface waters, and out of it the waters flowed through an outlet into Black Earth creek, but the outlet had been considerably filled up. The defendant sought to excavate an outlet on the opposite side of said lake, and draw off the water into a big marsh, and so eastwardly by Pheasant branch into Lake Mendota, and wholly divert them from Black Earth creek, to the injury of the plaintiffs' mill-power. In *Mohr v. Gault*, 10 Wis. 513, 78 Am. Dec. 687, Chief Justice Dixon said, in passing upon the above facts: "The owners along the creek have a legal right to the natural and usual flow of the waters of the lake through it." It is said also in the opinion, as it was also found by the trial court, "that there was no perceptible fall or difference in the height of the surface of the lake from one end to the other." "The [449] depth of this lake was from two to seven feet, and the main body was covered by vegetation." "The waters had been raised one and a half feet by the filling up of this outlet, and more than that by surface waters running into it from the adjacent country." The defendant sought to divert the waters of the lake in the proposed direction, in order to drain his own land covered by its waters to the depth of from a few inches to three feet. From this it appears that this lake is protected as a natural watercourse.

Application may now readily be made of these principles and authorities to the waters described in the complaint.

1. North of the plaintiff's land "there were always, and are yet, living springs, which continuously flow and discharge their waters by a well-defined stream into a natural lake of about sixty acres in extent, known as 'Big lake.'" This being the source of the waters, it is material to inquire whether, so far as described, they constitute a natural watercourse. "A well-defined stream," that has flowed continuously forever from everlasting springs, and made a lake of such extent, must have had a well-defined "channel," strong "current," and "bed and banks"—all the characteristics of a watercourse. From the words of description used, common reason supplies every element of such a natural stream as to make it a watercourse in law and in fact. The springs had been gathered into one stream, which made a watercourse to all intents and purposes; and "Big lake" was certainly a

watercourse, according to the above decision. What becomes
of it afterwards?

2. From the lake the waters so gathered flowed, under
natural conditions, upon and beneath the surface of the lands
lying to the southeast of said lake, to and across the land of
the plaintiff, and thence easterly, until they discharged themselves and were again collected in the "Beaver creek." This
distance is but a few miles. Did this natural watercourse
lose its essential character by its course ⁴⁵⁰ from Big lake to
Beaver creek? Did it become mere surface waters? There
is not one word descriptive of "surface waters" in the complaint. The waters all go in the same direction, and are
tributary to Beaver creek.

3. "The said natural flow or stream of water from the lake
was well defined and established, and in places, one of which
was upon the land of this plaintiff, had made for itself a distinct and plainly marked channel, pointing and showing the
natural flow of the water; and said stream was known and
commonly called by the name of the 'West branch' of Beaver
creek." Would it not be idle and hypercritical to say: "But
this description does not use the words 'bed and banks' and
'current'—the language of the books in describing a watercourse"? These waters in such volume could not flow continuously, always in a distinct and plainly marked channel,
well defined and established, without making for themselves
a bed and banks or sides to the stream in the places mentioned, one of which is on the land of the plaintiff. It is a
most reasonable, necessary, and inevitable consequence by
the laws of nature. Such a body of water, gathered into a
stream and flowing in one channel continuously, could not
help from cutting for itself in suitable soil or high ground a
watercourse, with banks, bed, and current, any more than it
could help from running down an inclined plane. Admit
that the complaint shows that this stream spreads over wide
reaches of marsh and swamp lands, and percolates the soil
in many and most places between Big lake and Beaver creek,
or in all places except those mentioned, where the ground was
suitable for cutting a well-defined channel, as above described;
according to the above authorities, such spreading of a stream
through marshes and swamps, on or below the surface, does
not militate against its being a watercourse in every essential
particular, if it can be traced or identified as the same stream;
and its identity is alleged in ⁴⁵¹ the complaint in this case,

and it is a fact to be proved and established on the trial. A stream that can be utilized by confining its waters in a ditch or canal, wide and deep enough for floating logs down from Big lake past the plaintiff's land is not small or inconsiderable. Even where it widely spreads over or under intervening marshes, it must have considerable current and a constant flow towards Beaver creek, across the lands of the plaintiff.

In view of the above authorities, and on well-established principles, there would seem to be no question but that these waters constitute a watercourse over the lands of the plaintiff, and that he has an "equal right, inseparably annexed to the soil, to their use for every useful purpose to which they can be applied as they are wont to run, without diversion, alteration, or diminution"; *Wadsworth* v. *Tillotson*, 15 Conn. 366; 39 Am. Dec. 391; *Perkins* v. *Dow*, 1 Root, 535.

This stream being so clearly and unquestionably a watercourse in which the plaintiff's rights are protected by the law, and this being the main and material ground of the plaintiff's complaint and cause of action, and sufficient to sustain the complaint as against the demurrer, other matters alleged therein as grounds of the action, such as the plaintiff's rights under the Goodyear contract, and his rights in these waters upon his land, even if they do not technically constitute a watercourse, will not be considered any further than to say that they do not constitute several and inconsistent causes of action, but are different grounds of the same action.

The jurisdiction of a court of equity to take cognizance of the matters of the complaint, and to grant the relief demanded, has been sustained by this court in many cases: *Sheldon* v. *Rockwell*, 9 Wis. 166; 76 Am. Dec. 265; *Patten* v. *Marden*, 14 Wis. 473; *Pioneer W. P. Co.* v. *Bensley*, 70 Wis. 477; *Patten Paper Co.* v. *Kaukauna W. P. Co.*, 70 Wis. 659; *Cedar Lake Hotel Co.* v. *Cedar Creek Hydraulic Co.*, 79 Wis. 302; *Kimberly etc. Co.* v. *Hewitt*, 75 Wis. 371.

By the COURT. The order of the circuit court is reversed, and the cause remanded for further proceedings according to law.

WINSLOW, J., and BINNEY, J., dissent.

WATERCOURSES—SURFACE WATERS, WHAT ARE.—Waters composed partly of seepage water escaping through a levee by percolation and partly of rainfall are subject to the rules in regard to surface waters: *Gray* v. *McWil-*

liams, 98 Cal. 157; 35 Am. St. Rep. 163, and note with the cases collected. But mere overflow is not surface water: *Johnson* v. *Chicago etc. R. R. Co.,* 80 Wis. 641; 27 Am. St. Rep. 76.

WATERCOURSES, WHAT ARE.—A watercourse is a channel for the conveyance of water, and may be natural or artificial. It consists of bed, banks, and water, though the water need not flow continuously. There must be a distinct channel with well-defined banks cut into the soil by the flow of the water, presenting at a casual glance to every eye the unmistakable evidence of the frequent action of running water, and not a mere depression: *Hawley* v. *Sheldon,* 64 Vt. 491; 33 Am. St. Rep. 941, and note; *Simmons* v. *Winters,* 21 Or. 35; 28 Am. St. Rep. 727, and note with the cases collected.

STATE EX REL. GARRABAD *v.* DERING.

[84 WISCONSIN, 585.]

CONSTITUTIONAL LAW—ORDINANCE REGULATING STREET PARADES, WHEN VOID.—A municipal ordinance which declares that "it shall be unlawful for any person or persons, society, association, or organization, to march or parade" upon certain streets of a city, "shouting, singing, or beating drums or tambourines, or playing upon any other musical instrument, for the purpose of advertising or attracting the attention of the public, or to the disturbance of the public peace or quiet, without first having obtained a permission to so march or parade, signed by the mayor of said city," or, "in case of the mayor's illness or absence," by other specified officials, and which further provides that "this section shall not apply to funerals, fire companies, nor regularly organized companies of the state militia," and that "permission to march or parade shall at no time be refused to any political party having a regular organization," not only creates by its express terms unjust discriminations between the persons and organizations referred to, but also vests the mayor or his substitutes with arbitrary power to create other equally unjust discriminations in carrying out its provisions, and is therefore void, as being an enactment which contravenes the fourteenth amendment of the constitution of the United States.

CERTIORARI to review the decision of C. L. Dering, court commissioner of Columbia county, who had refused to discharge from custody the petitioner, Joseph Garrabad. The sheriff's return to the writ of *habeas corpus* issued by the said commissioner showed that the petitioner was being held in custody by virtue of a "commitment," issued by a justice of the peace of the city of Portage in Columbia county, reciting that the city had recovered judgment against said petitioner for a fine imposed in accordance with the provisions of a certain ordinance of that city, and commanding the sheriff, or any constable of the county, if the petitioner had no goods or chattels to be levied upon, to deliver him to the keeper of the

county jail, there to be imprisoned for twenty days, unless
the fine and costs were sooner paid, or he should be discharged
by due process of law.   The nature of the ordinance in question sufficiently appears from the head-note and the opinion
of the court.   The petitioner having demurred to the return,
the commissioner overruled the demurrer, and ordered him to
be kept in custody, as the commitment required.

Rogers and'Hall, for the relator.

W. S. Stroud, for the respondent.

588 PINNEY, J.   The city charter of the city of Portage
(Laws of 1882, c. 132, sec. 31) confers upon the common
council of the city power to pass ordinances and by-laws on
certain subjects, under and by virtue of the delegation of the
police powers of the state to the common council and city
officers for the government of the city and the preservation of
order and public safety.   In respect to such ordinances or by-
laws it has long been the established doctrine that they must
be reasonable, not inconsistent with the charter, nor with any
statute, nor with the general principles of the common law of
the land, particularly those having relation to the liberty of
the subject or the rights of private property: Dillon on Municipal Corporations, section 319, and cases cited in notes.
The particular objections urged to the validity of the ordinance in question fall within the scope of the fourteenth
amendment to the constitution of the United States, which
provides that "no state shall make or enforce any law which
shall abridge the privileges or immunities of citizens of
the United States, nor shall any state deprive any person
of life, liberty, or property, without due process of law, nor
deny to any person within its jurisdiction the equal protection
of the laws."   These provisions apply equally to all persons
within the territorial jurisdiction of the United States, without regard to any differences of color or nationality; and the
equal protection of the laws is a pledge, it is held, "of the
protection of equal laws": *Yick Wo v. Hopkins*, 118 U. S. 369.

589 It is objected that the ordinance is void on its face, by
reason of its operating unequally and creating an unjust and
illegal discrimination, not only: 1. By the express terms of
the ordinance itself, but 2. It is so framed as to punish the
petitioner for what is permitted to others as lawful, without
any distinction of circumstances, whereby an unjust and
illegal discrimination occurs in its execution, and which,

though not made by the ordinance in express terms, is made
possible by it; and 3. In that it vests in the mayor, or other
officers of the city named in it, power to arbitrarily deny persons and other societies or organizations the right secured by
it to others to march and parade on the streets named. The
general subject and scope of the ordinance is marching or
parading by "any person or persons, society, association or
organization" over the streets named, "shouting, singing,
or beating drums or tambourines, or playing upon any musical instrument or instruments, for the purpose of advertising
or attracting the attention of the public, or to the disturbance
of the public peace or quiet," without having obtained permission as prescribed in the ordinance. It provides, among
other things, that the ordinance shall not apply to fire companies, nor to regularly organized companies of the state
militia, and that permission to march or parade shall at no
time be refused to any political party having a regular state
organization. The permission, it will be seen, is required
absolutely to be granted to political parties having a regular
state organization, so they are practically excepted out of the
ordinance. Whether permission shall be granted to any
other society, civic, religious, or otherwise, depends not upon
the character of the organization, or upon the particular circumstances of the case, but upon the arbitrary discretion of
the mayor or other officers named in the ordinance, acting in
his absence. It is therefore argued that, as between different
persons, societies, associations, or organizations, the ordinance
operates [590] unequally and creates unjust and illegal discriminations by its express terms, and makes such discriminations not only possible but necessary in its administration,
and therefore that the ordinance is void upon common-law
principles, as heretofore recognized and administered .in the
courts of the country

The rights of persons, societies, and organizations to parade
and have processions on the streets with music, banners,
songs, and shouting, is a well-established right, and, indeed,
the ordinance upon its face recognizes to a certain extent the
legality of such processions and parades, and provides for
permitting them, in the discretion of the mayor, in all cases
except those named, and as to those the right is practically
secured. The ordinance, as framed, and as it is to be executed under the arbitrary discretion of the mayor or other
officer, is clearly an abridgment of the rights of the people;

and in many cases it practically prevents those public demonstrations that are the most natural product of common aims and kindred purposes. "It discourages united effort to attract public attention and challenge public examination and criticism of the associated purposes": *Anderson* v. *Wellington*, 40 Kan. 173, 10 Am. St. Rep. 175, contains a careful discussion and examination of a similar ordinance, which was there held to be void as contravening common right. In *In re Frazee*, 63 Mich. 396, 6 Am. St. Rep. 310, after a full discussion by Campbell, C. J., a similar ordinance was also held void, and that it is not in the power of the legislature to deprive any of the people of the enjoyment of equal privileges under the law, or to give cities any tyrannical powers; that charters, laws, and regulations, to be valid, must be capable of construction, and must be construed, in conformity to constitutional principles and in harmony with the general laws of the land; and that any by-law which violates any of the recognized principles of lawful and equal rights is necessarily void so far as it does so, and void entirely if it [591] cannot be reasonably applied according to its terms; and no grant of absolute discretion to suppress lawful action can be sustained at all; that it is a fundamental condition of all liberty, and necessary to civil society, that men must exercise their rights in harmony with and yield to such restrictions as are necessary to produce peace and good order; and it is not competent to make any exceptions for or against the so-called "Salvation Army" because of its theories concerning practical work; that in law it has the same right, and is subject to the same restrictions, in its public demonstrations, as any secular body or society which uses similar means for drawing attention or creating interest. Hence the by-law there in question, because it suppressed what was in general perfectly lawful, and left the power of permitting or restraining processions and their courses to an unlawful official discretion, was held void; and that any regulation, to be valid, must be by permanent legal provisions, operating generally and impartially.

The return of the sheriff utterly fails to show of what specific offense the petitioner was convicted, that is to say, in what particular respect he violated the ordinance. We may infer, however, for the purpose of argument and illustration, from the fact that the petition for the writ addressed to this court states that the petitioner is a member of the Salvation Army, that he was convicted of parading the streets in that capacity.

It cannot be maintained that any person or persons or society have any right, for religious purposes or as religious bodies, to use the streets for purposes of public parade because the purpose in view is purely religious and not secular, but they certainly have the same right to equal protection of the laws as secular organizations. The objections urged against this ordinance are, we think, fatal to any conviction which might take place under it, by reason of its unreasonable and unjust discriminations and of the arbitrary power conferred upon [592] the mayor or other officer of the city to make others in its administration and execution; so that it is impossible to sustain the conviction in any aspect in which the question may be viewed.

A careful examination of the decisions in various states, and the considerations upon which they are founded, is not material to the determination of the case, for the whole subject is governed and controlled by the provisions of the fourteenth amendment to the constitution of the United States already referred to. In construing and applying this amendment the supreme court of the United States have said, in *Barbier* v. *Connolly*, 113 U. S. 27, that it "undoubtedly intended not only that there should be no arbitrary deprivation of life or liberty, or arbitrary spoliation of property, but that equal protection and security should be given to all under like circumstances in the enjoyment of their personal and civil rights; that all persons should be equally entitled to pursue their happiness and acquire and enjoy property; that they should have like access to the courts of the country for the protection of their persons and property, the prevention and redress of wrongs, and the enforcement of contracts; that no impediment should be interposed to the pursuits of anyone except as applied to the same pursuits by others under like circumstances; that no greater burdens should be laid upon one than are laid upon others in the same calling and condition. . . . . Class legislation discriminating against some and favoring others is prohibited, but legislation which, in carrying out a public purpose, is limited in its application, if within the sphere of its operation it affects alike all persons similarly situated, is not within the amendment." The entire subject underwent careful examination in the case of *Yick Wo* v. *Hopkins*, 118 U. S. 356, where the subject of city ordinances and the principles regulating their validity were considered. The objections to the validity of the ordinances in that [593] case were, in substance, the same that are urged in this, and the ordinances in question were held void.

The objections urged in the case of *Mayor of Baltimore* v. *Radecke*, 49 Md. 217, 33 Am. Rep. 239, were also in substance the same, for the ordinance in that case upon its face committed to the unrestrained will of a single public officer the power to determine the rights of parties under it, when there was nothing in the ordinance to guide or control his action, and it was held void because "it lays down no rules by which its impartial execution can be secured, or partiality and oppression prevented," and that "when we remember that action or nonaction may proceed from enmity or prejudice, from partisan zeal or animosity, from favoritism, and other improper influences and motives easy of concealment and difficult to be detected and exposed, it becomes unnecessary to suggest or to comment upon the injustice capable of being wrought under cover of such a power, for that becomes apparent to every one who gives to the subject a moment's consideration. In fact, an ordinance which clothes a single individual with such power hardly falls within the domain of law, and we are constrained to pronounce it inoperative and void." The doctrine of this case was approved in *Yick Wo* v. *Hopkins*, 118 U. S. 356, and the court in the latter case observed: "We are not obliged to reason from the probable to the actual, and pass upon the validity of the ordinances complained of as tried merely by the opportunities which their terms afford of unequal and unjust discrimination in their administration"; and proceeded to show that in the case there presented the ordinances in actual operation established "an administration directed so exclusively against a particular class of persons as to warrant and require the conclusion that whatever may have been the intent of the ordinances as adopted, they were applied by the public authorities charged with their administration, and thus representing the state itself, with a mind so unequal and oppressive [594] as to amount to a practical denial by the state of that equal protection of the laws which is secured to the petitioners, as to all other persons, by the broad and benign provisions of the fourteenth amendment to the constitution of the United States"; and the court added: "Though the law itself be fair on its face and impartial in appearance, yet if it is applied and administered by public authority with an evil eye and with an unequal hand, so as to practically make unjust and illegal discriminations between persons in similar circumstances, material to their rights, the denial of equal justice is still within the prohibition of the constitution."

Nearly all the processions, parades, etc., that ordinarily occur are excepted from the ordinance in question, followed by a provision that permission to march or parade shall at no time "be refused to any political party having a regular state organization." It is difficult to see how this can be considered municipal legislation, dictated by a fair and equal mind, which takes care to protect and provide for the parades and processions with trumpets, drums, banners, and all the accompaniments of political turnouts and processions, and at the same time provides, in effect, that the Salvation Army, or a Sunday-school, or a temperance organization, with music, banners, and devices, or a lodge of Odd Fellows or Masons, shall not in like manner parade or march in procession on the streets named without getting permission of the mayor, and that it shall rest within the arbitrary, uncontrolled discretion of this officer whether they shall have it at all. The ordinance resembles more nearly the means and instrumentalities frequently resorted to in practising against and upon persons, societies, and organizations a petty tyranny, the result of prejudice, bigotry, and intolerance, than any fair or legitimate provision in the exercise of the police power of the state to protect the public peace and safety. It is entirely un-American and [595] in conflict with the principles of our institutions and all modern ideas of civil liberty.

It is susceptible of being applied to offensive and improper uses, made subversive of the rights of private citizens, and it interferes with and abridges their privileges and immunities, and denies them the equal protection of the laws in the exercise and enjoyment of their undoubted rights. In the exercise of the police power the common council may, in its discretion, regulate the exercise of such rights in a reasonable manner, but cannot suppress them, directly or indirectly, by attempting to commit the power of doing so to the mayor or any other officer. The discretion with which the council is vested is a legal discretion, to be exercised within the limits of the law, and not a discretion to transcend it or to confer upon any city officer an arbitrary authority, making him in its exercise a petty tyrant. Such ordinances or regulations, to be valid, must have an equal and uniform application to all persons, societies, or organizations similarly circumstanced

and not be susceptible of unjust discriminations, which may
be arbitrarily practiced to the hurt, prejudice, or annoyance
of any. An ordinance which expressly secures to political
parties having state organizations the absolute right to street
parades and processions, with all their usual accompaniments,
and denies it to the societies and other like organizations
already mentioned, except by permission of the mayor, who
may arbitrarily refuse it, is not valid, and offends against all
well-established ideas of civil and religious liberty. The
people do not hold rights as important and well-settled as the
right to assemble and have public parades and processions
with music and banners, and shoutings and songs, in support
of any laudable or lawful cause, subject to the power of any
public officer to interdict or prevent them. Our government
is "a government of laws, and not of men," and these principles, well established by the courts, by the fourteenth [596]
amendment to the constitution of the United States, have become a part of the supreme law of the land, so that no officer,
body, or lawful authority can "deny to any person the equal
protection of the laws." It is plain that the ordinance in
question is illegal, and void, and for this reason the order of
the commissioner must be reversed.

By the COURT. The order of the court commissioner is reversed, and the petitioner ordered discharged.

MUNICIPAL CORPORATIONS.—CONSTITUTIONALITY OF ORDINANCES REGU-
LATING STREET PARADES will be found discussed in the following cases:
Commonwealth v. *Plaisted,* 148 Mass. 375; 12 Am. St. Rep. 566, and note;
Anderson v. *City of Wellington,* 40 Kan. 173; 10 Am. St. Rep. 175, and *Mat-
ter of Frazee,* 63 Mich. 396; 6 Am. St. Rep. 310, and note.

GOULD *v.* SULLIVAN.

[84 WISCONSIN, 659.]

TAX SALES—STATEMENT BY TOWN TREASURER THAT NOTHING IS DUE, EFFECT
OF.—It is the duty of a town treasurer to furnish taxpayers with information as to the amount of taxes payable upon their lands in the
township; and, as they have a right to rely upon that information, they
cannot be prejudiced by its incorrectness. Hence if a landowner,
through his agent, attempts and offers to pay, in due season, all the
taxes due upon his property within a township, and the treasurer erroneously states that there is nothing assessed upon the roll against
a certain tract, a tax deed issued upon a subsequent sale of that tract
for nonpayment of taxes thereon is void, and its invalidity may be

made available in a legal action of ejectment as well as in an equitable suit for its cancellation.

TAX SALES—STATUTE OF LIMITATIONS, WHEN NOT A BAR TO RECOVERY OF LAND.—The statute of limitations fixing a period within which lands sold for nonpayment of taxes may be redeemed does not apply to a case where all the taxes due upon such lands have been regularly tendered, and the proper amount has not been paid merely because the officer to or through whom such payment could alone be made has negligently made a misstatement as to the sum actually due.

EJECTMENT to recover lands sold for nonpayment of taxes. The defendant made title under a tax deed regularly issued upon a sale held as prescribed by law, and relied on the bar of the statute of limitations fixing the period for redemption of lands so sold. The facts were found by the trial court to be substantially as follows: An agent of the plaintiff had furnished the town treasurer with a list of all the plaintiff's lands within the township upon which he desired to pay taxes for the year 1884; that on the tax receipt given by such treasurer the lands which it was sought to recover in this action were entered and marked, "Not on the roll," and no tax was carried out against them; and that the said agent, relying upon the treasurer's statement that the amount in the receipt was the whole amount due, paid the taxes mentioned in the receipt, and no more. As a conclusion of law it was found that the defendant acquired no title by the tax deed. From the judgment entered on these findings the defendant appealed.

Alban and Barnes, for the appellant.

Hume and Oellerich, for the respondent.

663 PINNEY, J. 1. The lands in question in this case were regularly taxed for the year 1884, and were returned as delinquent, sold for nonpayment of the taxes, etc., and, no redemption having been made, a tax deed thereof was executed to the defendant, and recorded May 29, 1888. The lands were then unoccupied, and so remained for the period necessary to bar an action for their recovery under sections **664** 1188, 1189 of Sanborn and Berryman's Annotated Statutes. It is plain that the plaintiff,. the former owner, had in good faith attempted and offered to pay to the proper town treasurer, in due season, the taxes for which the lands were sold together with the taxes on his other lands in the same town, and was informed that there were no taxes on the roll against them. The town treasurer, whose official duty it was to furnish the information applied for, and who represented the state in the exercise of the taxing power *pro hac vice*, was mistaken; and no fault, upon the facts found, can be imputed to the plaintiff. He had a right to regard the information as true, and there is nothing to show that he had any reason to distrust it. There was no occasion for him to consult the sale list, or the notice of redemption of lands sold, and he had no occasion to pursue the matter further. Shall he lose his lands by reason of the tax deed, and for no fault of his own?

Here is a clear case of mutual mistake, which would certainly be ground for relief in a court of equity under its original jurisdiction in cases of fraud, accident, and mistake—a mistake which, if not corrected, carries with it all the injurious consequences of a fraudulent misrepresentation. Equity has jurisdiction not only to arrest tax proceedings, but to set aside tax deeds founded on or resulting from fraudulent conduct of taxing officers: *Lefferts* v. *Board of Supervisors*, 21 Wis. 688; *Slater* v. *Maxwell*, 6 Wall. 268, 277. And the first question presented is, assuming that sufficient ground exists for avoiding the tax deed after the lapse of the statutory bar of three years, whether it can be made available in a legal action of ejectment, or resort must be had to an equitable action to cancel the tax deed. The statute, section 1188, is, that "no action shall be maintained by the former owner, or any person claiming under him, to recover the possession of any land, or any interest therein, which shall have been conveyed by deed for the [665] nonpayment of taxes, or to avoid such deed against any person claiming under such deed, unless such action shall be brought within three years next after the recording of such deed."

This statute does not apply: 1. When the tax has been paid before sale; and 2. When the land has been redeemed after sale. Under our system of pleading no formal reply is allowed to new matter set up as a defense, but the plaintiff is allowed to reply in evidence at the trial. Had the taxes in this case been actually paid to the treasurer, there can be no doubt the plaintiff would be allowed to show that fact to defeat the tax deed, because in such case, by the statute, it would be absolutely void and of no avail.

In *Morgan* v. *Bishop*, 56 Wis. 284, it was held that the plaintiff in ejectment might, without having pleaded them, show any facts affecting the validity of the tax deed, or which would render it unavailable to the defendant. We hold,

therefore, that the question raised can be litigated in this
action, under the present pleadings.

2. It cannot be maintained, we think, that the taxes in
this case were actually paid. The order providing for the
payment of the amount of such taxes, interest, etc., into court,
before judgment was entered for the plaintiff, sets that question at rest; but the question still remains whether what took
place by way of offer to pay, and mistaken information by the
officer whose duty it was to state the amount of taxes, if any,
on plaintiff's land, does not place him substantially, for all
purposes of protecting his rights, in the same position as if he
had actually paid his money, and so that the lien of the taxes
was removed in like manner as that of a mortgage by tender,
though not kept good, which discharges the lien of a mortgage: *Breitenbach* v. *Turner*, 18 Wis. 147; *Kortright* v. *Cady*, 21
N. Y. 343; 78 Am. Dec. 145; *Loomis* v. *Pingree*, 43 Me. 312;
and therefore the power of the taxing officer to proceed further
was suspended or defeated. In *Breisch* v. *Coxe*, 81 Pa. St. 346,
it [666] is said: "It is an almost universal rule which substitutes a tender for performance when the tender is frustrated
by the act of the party entitled to performance." In *Randall*,
v. *Dailey*, 66 Wis. 285, it was held, in respect to paying taxes
after they had been returned as delinquent—a similar question—that a landowner making such payment to the county
treasurer is entitled to rely upon the statement of the officer
as to the amount due, and cannot be prejudiced by a mistake
of the officer as to the amount, and the tax deed issued upon
a subsequent sale was held void, although the sum paid was
twenty-five cents less than the amount actually due; and in
many other like cases the same ruling has been made, to the
effect that the mistake of the officer in stating the amount
due will not affect the redemption made in reliance thereon:
Dietrick v. *Mason*, 57 Pa. St. 40; *Price* v. *Mott*, 52 Pa. St. 315;
Baird v. *Cahoon*, 5 Watts. & S. 540. In *Bubb* v. *Tompkins*, 47
Pa. St. 359, a redemption was held not defeated by the failure
to pay another tax on the lands, necessary to make the redemption good, caused by the mistake of the county treasurer; and *Forrest* v. *Henry*, 33 Minn. 434, was a like case to
the last, where a subsequent sale and deed for the omitted
tax were held void.

In *Van Benthuysen* v. *Sawyer*, 36 N. Y. 150, it was held
that, if redemption of lands sold for taxes is prevented by
the fault or misconduct of the officer through whom such

redemption is to be made, the title will not pass by a subsequent deed to the purchaser.

These decisions are founded on the ground that the treasurer is the legal custodian of the books, and possesses full and authentic information, and it is his official duty to furnish it; that the landowner cannot get the necessary information in any other way, and is not bound to search the books for himself, and that landowners almost always do, and rightfully may, depend on information thus received; and that the party cannot be involved in the loss of his land [667] by the mistake of the officer.

The same reasons ought to be followed with like consequences in a case like this, where the landowner applies to pay, and offers, and is ready to pay, the taxes on his lands, and is informed by the treasurer, as in this case, that there are none to pay; and courts of the highest respectability and authority have so held. In *People* v. *Registrar of Arrears*, 114 N. Y. 19, it was held that where a taxpayer calls upon the proper officer for a statement of all the taxes due from him, receives a statement, and pays accordingly, and afterwards the land is sold for nonpayment of taxes in arrear when such statement was furnished, and not included by mistake of the officer, the title of the taxpayer is not divested by the sale. To the same effect is the case of *Martin* v. *Barbour*, 34 Fed. Rep. 701-710, where the question was elaborately considered. *Kinsworthy* v. *Austin*, 23 Ark. 375, is to the same effect; and in the case of *Breisch* v. *Coxe*, 81 Pa. St. 336, 345-348, the authorities are reviewed, and it is there held that if the owner pays all the taxes stated by the treasurer he has done his whole duty; that "his claim to be protected against a sale of his lands for taxes he stood ready to pay, but which the proper officer has failed to present to him on demand, is quite as great as that of the purchaser to be protected against the act of the same officer in making a sale for taxes actually paid"; and that "it is but just that a *bona fide* attempt to pay all the taxes, frustrated by the fault of the treasurer, should stand as the equivalent of actual payment": *Loomis* v. *Pingree*, 43 Me. 312.

In *Breisch* v. *Coxe*, 81 Pa. St. 336, it was held that the five years statute of limitations contained in the third section of the Act of April 3, 1804, that no action should lie for the recovery of lands sold for taxes, "unless the same be brought within five years after the sale thereof for taxes, as aforesaid,"

would not bar the plaintiff's right of recovery as against a
sale for taxes under such circumstances, [668] and it was said
by the court: "If then, a *bona fide* offer to pay all the taxes,
. . . . frustrated by the negligence of the treasurer to give information of all the taxes charged against the land, is the
legal equivalent of actual payment of taxes in taking away
the jurisdiction, as we have seen it is, the conclusion follows
that the limitation of five years in the Act of 1804 does not
apply to such a case. The want of authority to sell is as
clear as when the taxes have been actually paid, and the
owner is not bound to presume a sale, and follow up its consequences within five years. All the hardship attributed to
the purchaser's want of knowledge is as fairly imputable to a
case of actual payment as it is to one of tendered payment.
In neither does the fact appear so as to challenge his notice."

As to all such defects or want of authority to sell and convey, the doctrine of *caveat emptor* applies, and the purchaser
who takes a title depending upon the exercise of special statutory authority cannot be considered a *bona fide* purchaser without notice. He must see to it, at his peril, that the title he takes
is a valid one. Besides, he never pays a full or fair price,
but gets, rather, "acres for cents": Cooley on Taxation, 2d
ed., 475–553; 2 Desty on Taxation, 850; *Curts* v. *Cisna*, 7
Biss. 260, 268; *Martin* v. *Barbour*, 34 Fed. Rep. 711. And
this is true even after the three years statute of limitations
has run in favor of the deed, to the extent that a purchaser
for full value and without notice from the grantee in the tax
deed will not be protected from a secret and unofficial redemption from the sale: *Warren* v *Putnam*, 63 Wis. 410; *Cornell University* v. *Mead*, 80 Wis. 387. It was not within the
plan or purpose of the statute of limitations in respect to tax
deeds that the lapse of the statutory period should be conclusive as against the question of payment or redemption or *bona
fide* attempts to make payment or redemption which have
been frustrated by the fault of the officer to or through whom
[669] such payment could alone be made: *McMahon* v. *McGraw*,
26 Wis. 615; *Fox* v. *Zimmermann*, 77 Wis. 415. This special
limitation applies only to actions in which the validity or
regularity of the tax proceedings are questioned for want of
conformity with the provisions of law. Questions of payment
and redemption, and matters which put the landowner in a
position where he may claim that, as to him, the taxes have
been so far paid, or the land redeemed, as to make further

proceedings illegal, are not within the statute or concluded by it. This is no hardship, as against the purchaser at the tax sale, who purchases for such a small consideration, and who stands in privity with the tax officers who are alone at fault in the premises, and is, in law, affected with notice of that fact. We therefore hold that the recovery in this case was right.

By the COURT. The judgment of the circuit court is affirmed.

TAX SALES—HOW DEFEATED.—The operation of a tax deed may be defeated by showing that the taxes were paid before the sale: *Bank of Utica* v. *Mersereau*, 3 Barb. Ch. 528; 49 Am. Dec. 189, and note; *Wallace* v. *Brown*, 22 Ark. 118; 76 Am. Dec. 421, and note; *Lefebre* v. *Negrotto*, 44 La. Ann. 792. Tax sales of lands on which no taxes were due conveys no title: *Blight* v. *Banks*, 6 T. B. Mon. 192, 17 Am. Dec. 136.

The principal case is in harmony with *Pottsville L. Co.* v. *Wells*, 157 Pa. St. 512, where the court quoted and approved the following from the opinion in *Breisch* v. *Coxe*, 81 Pa. St. 336: "It must be conceded that the payment of taxes is a duty, and a failure to perform it is the fault of the owner. But payment is one thing, and the steps leading to it are another. For the latter the owner is not responsible. He cannot assess himself or know what is charged against him. He must await the action of the agents of the law. He cannot pay until he is informed what he is to pay. To perform the duty of payment he must apply to the treasurer for the taxes charged against his land. If this officer fail to give him the information on demand, on what just principle shall it be said he has not performed his duty? It is said, there are the tax books open to inspection, let him search them. But this is neither his business nor his duty. As was said in *Dietrick* v. *Mason*, 7 P. F. Smith, 40, the treasurer is the legal custodian of the books and entries of the taxes necessary to show the sum to be tendered. This information it is his duty to give, and he cannot lay the books before the owner, and compel him to search for himself. The knowledge of the latter may be inadequate to find what he needs. If then the owner pays all the taxes stated by the treasurer, he has done his whole duty. He can do no more. . . . . It is but just, then, that a *bona fide* attempt to pay all taxes, frustrated by the fault of the treasurer, should stand as the equivalent of an actual payment. It is an almost universal rule, which substitutes a tender for performance, when the tender is frustrated by the act of the party entitled to performance."

INDEX TO THE NOTES.

PROXIMATE CAUSE, personal injuries, unskillful treatment by physician may enhance damages for, 845.

persons who cannot recover for damages resulting from, 813.

physical laws, liability for results of, 821.

possible consequence of, wrongdoer when liable for, 811.

presumption as to laws of inorganic matter, 812.

presumption as to nature and habits of animals, 812.

property, acts induced by desire and effort to save, 849.

property of another, intermeddling with, liability for consequences resulting from, 821.

railway corporations, omission to give signals, 817.

railway corporations, unlawful speed of trains of, what deemed to be, 818.

responsible human agency, intervention of, when does not relieve wrongdoer from liability, 841.

results which all persons must regard as natural consequences, 812.

sickness, liability for causing, 829, 830.

slander, acts of third persons caused by, 844.

slander, repetition of by third persons is not deemed a probable result, 844.

statutory duty, breach of what deemed to be the, 817, 818.

statutory duty, breach of when subjects person to liability, 817.

statutory duty, plaintiff's breach of, when precludes his recovery, 818.

tests of, 810.

time and distance, when make the result remote, 811.

time is not a test of, 811.

torts, business, injuries to resulting from, 850.

uncontrollable impulses, acts resulting from, 847.

unlawful acts, whether render wrongdoer liable for remote consequences, 819, 820.

unlawful assumption of dominion over the property of another, liability for, 821.

vagueness of rules and definitions concerning, 811.

vegetation, growth of, all persons must take notice of, 823.

water, liability for results of action of, 821, 822.

water, what action by must be compensated for by the wrongdoer, 822.

willful and malignant torts, whether there is a difference between liability for, 821.

wrongdoer, whether answerable for remote consequences, 820.

PUBLIC OFFICE, acceptance of second office cannot be compelled, 524.

compensation must be provided before party can be compelled to accept, 524.

duty of accepting, 523.

mandamus to compel acceptance of, 503.

penalty against person refusing to qualify for, 523.

refusal to accept is a public offense, 523.

resignation, acceptance of, what is, 526.

resignation, cannot be tendered until officer has qualified, 524.

resignation, effect of without acceptance, 525.

resignation, form in which may be tendered, 524.

resignation, mandamus to compel performance of duties after, 526.

resignation, may be by parol, 524.

resignation, may be tendered at pleasure, 526.

INDEX.

ABANDONMENT.
See LANDLORD AND TENANT, 7.

ACCEPTANCE.
See CHECK; GUARANTY, 7, 11; MANDAMUS.

ACKNOWLEDGMENT.
See HOMESTEAD, 4, 5.

ACQUIESCENCE.
See ATTORNEY AND CLIENT, 14; CORPORATIONS, 10.

ACTIONS.

PROCESS—SERVICE AS COMMENCEMENT OF ACTION.—As to each defendant in any action it is commenced and pending against him only from the time of service of summons on him, or of his appearance without service, and, when each may object that the action was not commenced within the time limited by statute, its commencement as against his objection is to be determined solely by the time of service on him, and not by the time of service on some other defendant. *Smith* v. *Hurd*, 661.

See AWARD, 2; MECHANIC'S LIEN, 14, 15; NEGLIGENCE, 11.

ADMISSIONS.
See AGENCY, 8; ESTOPPEL, 3; PARTNERSHIP, 6.

ADVANCEMENTS.

1. AN ADVANCEMENT Is a gift by an ancestor of property which, but for the gift, would pass to an heir or distributee on the ancestor's death, or it is something purchased with his funds in the name or for the benefit of the heir. *Cazassa* v. *Cazassa*, 112.

2. THE PROCEEDS OF AN INSURANCE POLICY taken on his life by a parent in the name of his child, or taken in his name and afterwards transferred to the child, are presumed to be advancements for which the child must account in the settlement of his claims as an heir from his parent's estate. *Cazassa* v. *Cazassa*, 112.

ADVERTISEMENT.

See ATTORNEY AND CLIENT, 2, 3.

AGENCY.

1. No AUTHORITY WILL BE IMPLIED FROM AN EXPRESS AUTHORITY. *Jackson* v. *Bank*, 81.

2. AUTHORITY TO INDORSE COMMERCIAL PAPER AS AGENT OF THE OWNER will not be implied from some other express authority unless shown to be strictly necessary to the complete execution of the express power. *Jackson* v. *Bank*, 81.

3. A DRUMMER OR COMMERCIAL TRAVELER employed to sell and take orders for goods, to collect accounts, and to receive moneys and checks payable to the order of his principal, is not by implication authorized to indorse such principal's name to such checks. *Jackson* v. *Bank*, 81.

4. POWER TO INDORSE AND COLLECT A NEGOTIABLE INSTRUMENT is not implied from the possession of such instrument by one claiming to be agent of the payee. *Jackson* v. *Bank*, 81.

5. AUTHORITY TO RECEIVE CHECKS IN LIEU OF CASH, in payment of bills in the hands of an agent for collection, does not authorize the agent to indorse and collect the checks. *Jackson* v. *Bank*, 81.

6. IF FALSE REPRESENTATIONS ARE MADE BY AN AGENT employed to sell property as to the price paid for it by his principal, they must be regarded as made by the principal if he accepts their fruits. He cannot accept the property secured by means of such representations and then disclaim responsibility for the fraud through which the property was procured. *Fairchild* v. *McMahon*, 701.

7. NOTICE TO, HOW FAR DEEMED NOTICE TO PRINCIPAL.—If an agent has acquired knowledge of a fact so recently as to make it incredible that he should have forgotten it, his principal will be bound, although he did not acquire such knowledge, while transacting his principal's business. Hence, if the cashier of a bank has been present at the execution of a mortgage and promissory note by one whose visible condition at the time was such as to put a reasonably observant person upon inquiry as to his capacity to contract, and it appears that immediately after the execution of the instruments the bank acquired possession of them as collateral security for the debt of a third party, the bank is chargeable with notice of all the material facts of which its cashier had notice, and cannot be regarded as a *bona fide* purchaser of those instruments. *Brothers* v. *Bank*, 932.

8. CORPORATIONS—EVIDENCE.—ADMISSIONS AND DECLARATIONS OF THE OFFICERS of a corporation made after it has discounted a note are not admissible to prove knowledge on the part of the bank that such note, though apparently the note of the signers thereof, was intended to be the note of a corporation of which they were officers. An agent has no authority to bind his principal by statements as to bygone transactions. *Merchants' Nat. Bank* v. *Clark*, 710.

9. AGENT, CONTRACTING IN HIS OWN NAME.—One who executes a written contract of sale, which upon its face binds him personally, cannot relieve himself of responsibility thereunder by showing that he was acting simply as agent or broker for a principal. Whether such principal was disclosed or undisclosed is immaterial. *Cream City Glass Co.* v. *Friedlander*, 895.

10. On the Death of a Principal the power of his agent to collect and receive rents terminates, unless the agent had a power coupled with an interest. A payment made to the agent after such death does not bind the estate of the principal, though neither the agent nor the person making the payment had notice of such death. *Farmers' Loan etc. Co.* v. *Wilson*, 696.

11. Statute of Frauds.—An Oral Approval by a Principal of a sale of lands made by an agent who had written authority to make the sale, but on different terms than those upon which it was made, is unavailing. To sell upon different terms requires a new and further authority, and such authority, to be valid under the statute of frauds, must itself have been in writing, signed by the principal. *Kozel* v. *Dearlove*, 416.

See Attachment, 4; Brokers; Contracts, 8; Corporations, 4–11; Custom, 2, 3; Execution, 4; Powers.

ALIENS.
See Descent; Partition; Treaties, 2, 3.

ALIMONY.
See Marriage and Divorce, 1.

ALTERATION OF INSTRUMENTS.
Negotiable Instruments.—An Alteration as to the Date of Payment in a note, in the absence of proof of fraud on the part of the payee or holder, does not prevent a recovery thereon in its original form. *Wolferman* v. *Bell*, 126.

APPEAL.
1. Evidence—Objection to When Waived.—A specific objection to the admissibility of evidence not presented to the trial court cannot be presented on appeal, but must be deemed to have been waived. *Cronfeldt* v. *Arrol*, 648.

2. Erroneous When Will Not Reverse.—A tendency or capacity of instructions to mislead, while it will justify their refusal, is no ground for reversal after they are given, if they in fact assert the law correctly. *Eastis* v. *Montgomery*, 227.

3. Evidence Showing a Motive of a Witness to Testify Falsely Should Not Be Excluded.—Hence in a trial for larceny, it is error to refuse to permit the defendant to prove that an important witness for the prosecution has himself been arrested on a charge of stealing the property named in the indictment. *State* v. *Burpee*, 775.

4. Appellate Practice—Evidence Not Prejudicial Not Ground for Reversal.—The admission of immaterial evidence, when not prejudicial, is not reversible error. *Cronfeldt* v. *Arrol*, 648.

5. A Judgment Will Not Be Reversed because an improper question is asked, if the witness refuses to answer the question, and it is not insisted upon. *State* v. *Burpee*, 775.

6. Res Judicata—Decision of Motion.—An order discharging a writ of attachment after a full hearing is appealable either before or after judgment upon the main issue in the case. Such order is conclusive of all matters adjudicated thereby. *Hall* v. *Harris*, 730.

7. Judgment of Dismissal May Be Upheld on appeal, though the ground stated in the judgment order does not warrant it, if the record discloses other grounds which, as matter of law, show that plaintiff is not entitled to recover in any event. *Wadsworth* v. *Union Pac. Ry. Co.*, 309.

See BILLS OF REVIEW; JURISDICTION, 1, 3; NEW TRIAL, 2; RECEIVERS, 1, 3; REPLEVIN; TRIAL.

APPEARANCE.

See ACTIONS.

APPROPRIATION.

See WATERS, 9-12.

ARCHITECTS.

See AWARD; BUILDING CONTRACTS; MECHANIC'S LIEN, 11.

ASSIGNMENT.

See MORTGAGES, 7; SETOFF.

ASSIGNMENT FOR THE BENEFIT OF CREDITORS.

1. ASSIGNMENT OF MORTGAGED PREMISES FOR BENEFIT OF CREDITORS—FORE-CLOSURE OF MORTGAGE—RIGHTS OF ASSIGNEE.—If mortgaged premises are assigned by the mortgagor in trust for the benefit of creditors, the assignee is a necessary party defendant in a suit to foreclose the mortgage, because the legal title to the property is in him, and it is his duty on behalf of creditors to protect their rights in the foreclosure suit. If he represents any creditor, who, if the assignment had not been made, would have had a standing in court to question the validity of the mortgage, the assignee may, as the representative of that creditor, assail such conveyance. *Hutchinson* v. *First Nat. Bank*, 537.

2. ASSIGNMENT OF MORTGAGE FOR BENEFIT OF CREDITORS—FORECLOSURE OF MORTGAGE—DUTY OF ASSIGNEE.—If the creditors of a mortgagor, who has assigned the mortgage in trust for the benefit of his creditors, are not in a position to successfully assail its validity on foreclosure, it is not the duty of the assignee to assail it. *Hutchinson* v. *First Nat. Bank*, 537.

3. AN INDORSER for an insolvent debtor is, before the payment of the debt, entitled to prove his claim as such indorser against the estate of the insolvent. *Citizens' Bank* v. *Kendrick*, 96.

See NEGOTIABLE INSTRUMENTS, 4.

ASSOCIATIONS.

1. CORPORATIONS—RIGHT TO BE ADMITTED TO MEMBERSHIP.—If the by-laws of a corporation, not for pecuniary profit, provide for admission to membership on the written application of an applicant indorsed by two members, approved by seven votes by the board of directors, and upon payment of an initiation fee, or on presentation of a certificate of un-impaired or unforfeited membership, duly transferred, and by signing an agreement to abide by the rules, regulations, by-laws, and amend-ments thereto of the association, the ownership of such certificate does not constitute the holder a member nor entitle him to any rights as such, and the only way in which he can avail himself of such certificate is, by tendering it in lieu of the prescribed initiation fee in case he is admitted

to membership, or in case his application is rejected, then by selling it for a consideration to some person who may desire to become a member. *American Live Stock etc. Co.* v. *Chicago Live Stock Exchange*, 385.

2. CORPORATIONS—RIGHT TO REGULATE ADMISSION TO MEMBERSHIP.—A corporation, not for pecuniary profit, has a right to adopt rules prescribing the only mode in which membership therein can be maintained; and no one can justly claim to be a member who has not been admitted in the mode thus prescribed, nor has a court of equity any power to compel the corporation to issue a certificate of membership to an applicant who has not complied with such prescribed mode. *American Live Stock etc. Co.* v. *Chicago Live Stock Exchange*, 385.

3. CORPORATIONS—STRANGER CANNOT COMPLAIN OF RULES GOVERNING MEMBERSHIP.—A person who is not a member of a corporation, nor entitled, either directly or indirectly, to any of the rights arising from membership therein, cannot complain of any of the rules adopted by it for the government of the conduct of its members, or invoke the aid of a court of equity to restrain their enforcement. *American Live Stock etc. Co.* v. *Chicago Live Stock Exchange*, 385.

4. CORPORATIONS—BY-LAWS RELATING TO MEMBERSHIP—RIGHT OF STRANGER TO COMPLAIN OF.—A voluntary association, whether incorporated or not, has, within certain well-defined limits, power to make and enforce by-laws for the government of its members, and such by-laws are ordinarily matters between the association and its members alone, with which strangers have no concern. If it passes by-laws, which are unreasonable, or contrary to law or public policy, and attempts to enforce them against a dissenting or unwilling minority, the latter may, in proper cases, appeal to the courts for relief against their enforcement, but strangers have no right to interfere, as they do not apply to, nor bind, them. *American Live Stock Co.* v. *Chicago Live Stock Exchange*, 385.

ATTACHMENT.

1. RIGHT OF SURETIES TO REQUIRE ACTION ON BOND.—If the principal in an attachment bond is a nonresident, and has no property in the state liable to attachment, his sureties cannot require the obligee, by notice in writing, to forthwith institute an action against the principal. *Seattle Crockery Co.* v. *Haley*, 156.

2. ACTION ON BOND—SUFFICIENCY OF COMPLAINT.—A complaint in an action against sureties in an attachment bond which alleges the execution of the bond by the principal, and sets out a copy thereof with the names of the sureties appended, but fails to allege that they joined in its execution, is insufficient on demurrer. *Seattle Crockery Co.* v. *Haley*, 156.

3. LIABILITY ON BOND—ESTOPPEL.—Persons who have joined in giving a bond for the attachment of the property of a corporation cannot deny its corporate existence. *Seattle Crockery Co.* v. *Haley*, 156.

4. LIABILITY ON BOND FOR WRONGFUL LEVY BY AGENT.—Liability upon an attachment bond for a malicious levy accrues if the person whose direct act caused the writ to be issued was actuated by malicious motives, although the principal for whom he acted as agent knew nothing of the transaction, unless it is shown that the agent had no authority to attach under any circumstances, and that his act in attaching was affirmatively repudiated as soon as knowledge of it was received. *Seattle Crockery Co.* v. *Haley*, 156.

15. EXEMPTIONS—TOOLS.—TWO SEWING-MACHINES KEPT AND PERSONALLY USED BY A TAILOR for the purpose of carrying on his trade, if reasonably necessary therefor, are exempt from attachment or execution as tools and instruments used in carrying on a trade. *Cronfeldt v. Arrol*, 648.

16. EXEMPTIONS—TOOLS.—GENERAL EXEMPTION OF ONE SEWING-MACHINE from attachment or execution has no reference to the occupation of the owner, and in no way qualifies or restricts a specific exemption of the tools and instruments of a person used in carrying on his trade. A tailor who necessarily uses two sewing-machines in carrying on his trade is entitled to the exemption as to both of them. *Cronfeldt v. Arrol*, 648.

17. EXEMPTIONS—EXEMPLARY DAMAGES FOR WRONGFUL SEIZURE.—Exemplary damages may be recovered for a seizure of exempt property under attachment with knowledge of the exemption, and in culpable disregard of the debtor's rights. *Cronfeldt v. Arrol*, 648.

See APPEAL, 6; CORPORATIONS, 1; INSURANCE, 2–4, 7; SALES, 2; SHERIFFS, 1.

ATTORNEY AND CLIENT.

1. ATTORNEYS—PRACTICE OF LAW.—EXECUTION OF TRUSTS, such as accepting appointments as executor or administrator, and acting as such, is not part of the duties peculiarly pertaining to the legal profession, and does not constitute what is ordinarily understood as the practice of law. *Metcalfe v. Bradshaw*, 478.

2. ADVERTISEMENT FOR DIVORCE BUSINESS—DISBARMENT.—An advertisement published by an attorney at law to the effect that divorces can be legally obtained very quietly which shall be good everywhere is only the more mischievous because anonymous. Such an advertisement is against good morals, public and private, and as it is a false representation and a libel upon the courts of justice, it is ground for the disbarment or suspension from practice of the attorney publishing it. *People v. MacCabe*, 270.

3. RIGHT TO ADVERTISE.—The ethics of the legal profession forbid that an attorney should advertise his talents or his skill as a shopkeeper advertises his wares. *People MacCabe*, 270.

4. RIGHT TO RECOVER COMPENSATION.—When the amount of compensation is not fixed by any contract under which an attorney is employed, he is entitled to recover such reasonable fee under an implied contract as his services are worth, or as has been usually paid to others for similar services. *Elmore v. Johnson*, 401.

5. RETAINER IN DIVORCE.—An attorney at law may properly accept a retainer for the prosecution or defense of an action for divorce when convinced that his client has a good cause, but to invite or encourage such litigation is most reprehensible. *People v. MacCabe*, 270.

6. MORAL CHARACTER—DISBARMENT.—A good moral character is one of the essential requisites to admission to the bar, and the tenure of office thereby conferred is during good behavior; and when it appears upon full investigation that an attorney has forfeited his good moral character, and has by his conduct shown himself unworthy of his office, it becomes the duty of the court to revoke the authority it gave him upon his admission. *People v. Keegan*, 274.

7. DISBARMENT OF.—A court intrusted with the power to admit and disbar attorneys should be considerate and careful in exercising its jurisdiction; the interests of the attorney must in every case be weighed in the

balance against the rights of the public, and the court should endeavor to
guard and protect both with fairness and impartiality. *People* v. *Mac-
Cabe*, 270.

8. MISCONDUCT—DISBARMENT.—A conspiracy entered into by an attorney
at law to cheat and defraud a third person by which a sum of money is
obtained is such misconduct as will authorize his disbarment. *People*
v. *Keegan*, 274.

9. TRANSACTIONS BETWEEN, HOW REGARDED.—In view of the confidential
relations existing between attorney and client, transactions between
them are often declared to be voidable which would be deemed to be
unobjectionable between other parties. *Elmore* v. *Johnson*, 401.

10. CONTRACTS BETWEEN AS TO FEES.—Before an attorney undertakes the
business of a client he may contract with reference to compensation for
his services, as no confidential relation then exists and the parties deal
with each other at arm's length. The same rule applies with regard to
dealings between them after the relation of attorney and client has been
dissolved. *Elmore* v. *Johnson*, 401.

11. CONTRACTS BETWEEN, WHEN VOIDABLE.—If the title to property is so
involved in litigation that the value of the property depends upon the
decision as to such title, a contract between attorney and client made
during the pendency of the litigation to compensate the attorney for his
legal services with part of the property involved, is voidable at the election of the client, irrespective of the fairness or unfairness of the contract,
provided such election is exercised within a reasonable time. *Elmore* v.
Johnson, 401.

12. CONTRACT AND DEED BETWEEN—WHEN MAY BE AVOIDED.—A contract
for compensation between attorney and client and a deed made in pursuance thereof, executed during the existence or the relation of attorney
and client securing a larger compensation to the former for his legal
services than those services are really worth, may be set aside by the
client by a suit commenced within a reasonable time. What is such
reasonable time is to be determined by the court under all the circumstances of the case. *Elmore* v. *Johnson*, 401.

13. PURCHASE BY ATTORNEY—PRESUMPTION—BURDEN OF PROOF.—In case
of a purchase of all or a part of the subject matter in litigation during
the pendency of the suit by an attorney from his client, the transaction
is presumably fraudulent, and the burden is on the attorney to show
affirmatively the most perfect good faith, the absence of undue influence, a fair price, knowledge, intention, and freedom of action by the
client, and also that he gave him full information and disinterested
advice. *Elmore* v. *Johnson*, 401.

14. VOIDABLE CONVEYANCE BETWEEN—LACHES.—In case of a voidable conveyance of land between attorney and client, the latter who is entitled
to set the transaction aside, cannot be charged with delay, or with
acquiescence, or confirmation, unless there has been full knowledge on
his part of all the facts, and perfect freedom of action. Acts which
might appear to be acts of acquiescence, are not deemed to be such if
the client is ignorant of the circumstances, or under the control of the
original influence, or otherwise so situated as not to be free to enforce
his rights. *Elmore* v. *Johnson*, 401.

15. LACHES IN AVOIDING DEED BETWEEN.—When a client, during the
pendency of his suit, conveys to his attorney part of the property in
litigation as payment for his legal services, with full knowledge that

the part conveyed is of greater value than such services, a delay of seven years before seeking to set the deed aside, during all of which time both parties treated the land as belonging to the attorney, is such laches on the part of the client as will bar his right of action. *Elmore v. Johnson*, 401.

See JUDGMENTS, 10.

AWARD.

1. AN AWARD IS IN THE NATURE OF A JUDGMENT from the obligation of which nothing can release the defendant but payment or discharge. *Hynes v. Wright*, 344.

2. REPUDIATION OF.—Though after the making of an award, the party in whose favor it is, declares that he repudiates and will not be bound by it, and his adversary also thereafter gives notice that he will also repudiate and not be bound by it, it is neither paid nor discharged, and may be enforced by action. *Hynes v. Wright*, 344.

BAILMENT,
See FALSE PRETENSES, 3.

BANKS.

1. BANK PAYING A CHECK TO PERSON OTHER THAN THE PERSON to whose order it is made payable does so at its peril. It must see that the check is paid to him upon his genuine indorsement. *Jackson v. Bank*, 81.

2. A BANK PAYING A CHECK ON A FORGED INDORSEMENT of the names of the payees is answerable to them for the amount thereof. *Jackson v. Bank*, 81.

3. NEGOTIABLE INSTRUMENTS—DISCOUNTING BEFORE MATURITY—DUTY TO MAKE INQUIRY.—When a note payable one year after date has been discounted by a bank one month before maturity, it can make no possible difference as affecting the right of the bank to recover, whether or not it is customary for it to make inquiry as to the *bona fides* of all such paper so discounted by it. *Washington Nat. Bank v. Pierce*, 174.

4. CORPORATIONS—NOTICE TO AGENT AS NOTICE TO.—Notice to the president of a bank by the maker of a note that it was procured by fraud and without consideration, and will not be paid, is not notice to the bank, and will not make it liable for subsequently discounting the note, when such notice was not given to the president in his official capacity, nor at the bank, nor with any reference to the bank's business. *Washington Nat. Bank v. Pierce*, 174.

See AGENCY, 7; CHECKS; CORPORATIONS, 6, 7; DISCOUNT, 1; ESTOPPEL, 2; FALSE PRETENSES; USURY.

BEQUESTS.
See CHARITIES, 2, 5; WILLS, 3.

BILLS OF EXCHANGE.
See NEGOTIABLE INSTRUMENTS; NEW TRIAL, 1.

BLANKS.
See SURETYSHIP, 5, 6.

BILLS OF REVIEW.

1. If there has been an erroneous application of facts found by a decree, a court of equity may revise or reverse the decree by a bill of review. *Jackson* v. *Jackson,* 427.

2. BILLS OF REVIEW MUST BE PROSECUTED WITHIN THE TIME FOR PROSECUT-ING WRITS OF ERROR where there is no statute specifying the time within which such bills may be prosecuted. *Jackson* v. *Jackson,* 427.

3. FINAL DECREE—TIME FOR PROSECUTING.—If a decree of partition deter-mines the interests of the respective parties and directs partition to be made accordingly, the time within 'which a bill of review may be prose-cuted must be computed from the date of such decree and not from the date of a subsequent order or decree dismissing the action. *Jack-son* v. *Jackson,* 427.

BONDS.

See PLEADING, 2, 3; SHERIFFS, 3.

BOUNDARIES.

See DEEDS, 2.

BRIDGES.

See RAILROADS, 8, 9.

BROKERS.

1. CONTRACT FOR COMMISSIONS EARNED IN VIOLATION OF LAW.—When a city ordinance duly enacted prohibits unlicensed real estate brokers from transacting business within the city limits, a real estate agent negotiat-ing a sale or exchange of city real estate without procuring a license cannot recover commissions for his services. *Buckley* v. *Humason,* 637.

2. AGENCY—VOID AGREEMENT AS TO COMMISSIONS.—An agreement between real estate agents by which each is to share in commissions paid by their principals, contingent upon the sale or exchange of the latter's property, is opposed to public policy and void, even though a price is fixed by the principals upon their respective properties. *Levy* v. *Spencer,* 303.

3. AGENCY—DUTY OF AGENT TO PRINCIPAL.—Upon an exchange of property, each principal is entitled to the benefit of the unbiased judgment of his agent as to the value to be placed upon the other's property, and to a reasonable effort on the part of such agent to obtain a reduction of the value to be allowed therefor in the exchange. The agents cannot act in each other's interest and antagonistic to the interests of their princi-pals by sharing commissions received upon the completion of the ex-change. *Levy* v. *Spencer,* 303.

See AGENCY, 9.

BUILDING CONTRACTS.

1. ARCHITECT'S CERTIFICATE.—If, by the terms of a building contract, it is provided that payment shall be only upon the certificate of the archi-tect, such certificate is a condition precedent to payment, and no action can be sustained upon the contract in the absence of such certificate, unless it has been demanded from the architect and fraudulently with-held. *Arnold* v. *Bournique,* 419.

2. PRESENTATION OF ARCHITECT'S CERTIFICATE, WHEN EXCUSED.—If, by the terms of a contract, the builders were to be paid on the presenta-

tion of a certificate signed by the architect, and such architect adjusts the account between the parties and gives the builders a certificate showing the amount found due them, which by them is handed back to the architect because not satisfactory, after which he refuses either to return the certificate or to make any other, the builders may recover the amount specified in such certificate, though they have not presented and cannot present it to the defendant. Presentation of the certificate is not one of the substantial requirements of the contract. *Arnold* v. *Bournique*, 419.

BURDEN OF PROOF.

See ATTORNEY AND CLIENT, 13; JUDGMENTS, 8; SEDUCTION, 1; WILLS, 3, 6, 11.

BY-LAWS.

See ASSOCIATIONS, 1, 4; CORPORATIONS, 18.

CARRIERS.

1. RAILROAD CORPORATIONS—DISCRIMINATION, WHEN A QUESTION OF LAW. If the facts of an alleged unlawful discrimination are conceded, or are established by undisputed testimony, whether an unreasonable discrimination was made, such as is forbidden by statute, is a question of law for the court. *Hoover* v. *Pennsylvania R. R.*, 43.
2. RAILROAD CORPORATIONS.—A DISCRIMINATION MADE BETWEEN MANUFACTURERS and dealers in coal in charges made for the transportation of such coal is not forbidden by a statute prohibiting discrimination between persons in like conditions and under similar circumstances, if, by reason of the coal so transported for the manufacturers, they produce a larger amount of freight for the carrier, while such a result does not follow the coal carried for the dealers. *Hoover* v. *Pennsylvania R. R.*, 43.

See NEGLIGENCE, 5–8.

CASHIER.

See AGENCY, 7.

CEMETERY.

See EMINENT DOMAIN.

CERTIFICATE.

See ASSOCIATIONS, 1, 2; BUILDING CONTRACTS, 2.

CHANCERY.

See EQUITY.

CHARACTER.

See ATTORNEY AND CLIENT, 7.

CHARITIES.

1. CHARITABLE USES ARE FAVORED IN EQUITY and will be supported when a trust would fail for uncertainty were it not for the charity. *Johnson* v. *Johnson*, 104.
2. A CHARITABLE DEVISE OR BEQUEST WILL BE UPHELD where it is created in favor of a person having sufficient capacity to take as donee, or if it

be not direct to such person, where it is definite in its object, lawful in its creation, and to be executed by trustees. *Johnson v. Johnson,* 104.

3. CHARITABLE BEQUEST.—DESIGATION OF A TRUSTEE OF A CHARITABLE TRUST is sufficient if the will devises property to the wife and daughter in trust with power to nominate their successors and other associates in trust from the testator's descendants or their Protestant husbands or wives, not exceeding five, who may in turn elect their successors from his descendants, and if there should at any time be not as many as two of his descendants able and willing to take charge of the trust, then it shall revert to a board consisting of the elders of the several Presbyterian churches of the city of M., who shall, with the assistance of the Presbyterian pastors, nominate from the bankers and business men of their body an executive committee, who shall have full power and control to manage the trust. *Johnson v. Johnson,* 104.

4. CHARITABLE TRUSTS.—THE DOCTRINES OF CY PRES AND PARENS PATRIÆ, as recognized in the English law, have never obtained in Tennessee. Only those powers which in England were exercised by the chancellor by virtue of his extraordinary, as distinguished from his specially delegated, jurisdiction exist in the chancery courts of that state. *Johnson v. Johnson,* 104.

5. CHARITABLE TRUSTS—VOID FOR WANT OF BENEFICIARY.—A devise and bequest of property to trustees with power to control and manage the trust so that it shall be productive of the most good to the greatest number, in a will in which the testator expressed his desire that the proceeds of the trust should be devoted to a free female college, but in case the way is not clear to that end, that they should be used for some charitable purpose, preference always being given to something of an educational nature, is void, because under the provisions of the trust there can be no one who can demand of the trustees the benefit of the trust on the ground that he is one of a class for whose benefit it was intended. *Johnson v. Johnson,* 104.

CHASTITY.

See SEDUCTION.

CHATTEL MORTGAGES.

1. FRAUDULENT IN PART.—A lease which is in legal effect a chattel mortgage, if presumptively fraudulent as to part of the goods therein described, is presumptively fraudulent as to all. *Greeley v. Winsor,* 720.

2. MORTGAGE OR CONDITIONAL SALE.—An agreement for the conditional sale of chattels whereby the vendor reserves the right, on default in the payment of a note given for the purchase price, to retake the property and to regard all money paid as being paid for its use, and stipulates that, on his doing so, the note shall be canceled, is not a mortgage, and does not invest the vendor with the rights of a mortgagee. *Crompton v. Beach,* 323.

3. CHATTEL MORTGAGE IN LEASE—VALIDITY OF.—A lease executed and recorded as required by the law relating to chattel mortgages, providing that the "rents, whether due or to become due, shall be a perpetual lien on any and all goods, merchandise, furniture, and fixtures now contained, or which may at any time during the continuance of the lease be contained in the building, except such goods as are sold in the usual course of retail trade," must be treated as a chattel mortgage, and because it gives permission to the mortgagor to sell part of the mortgaged property for his own benefit, is presumptively fraudulent as to his other creditors. *Greeley v. Winsor*, 720.

CHECKS.

BANKING.—ACCEPTANCE BY A BANK OF A CHECK and a promise to pay it according to its terms should be inferred from the receipt and the retention of the check and charging its amount to the account of the drawer, who has sufficient funds on deposit to meet it, if he subsequently recognizes the check in a settlement with the bank, though it was presented to the bank by an unauthorized person and paid to him on his unauthorized indorsement. *Jackson v. Bank*, 81.

See AGENCY, 3, 5; BANKS, 1, 2.

CODICIL.

See WILLS, 1.

COLLATERAL ATTACK.

See HIGHWAYS, 7.

COLLATERAL SECURITY.

See ESTOPPEL, 2; JUDGMENTS, 11.

COMITY.

See STATES.

COMMERCE.

See INTERSTATE COMMERCE.

COMMISSIONERS.

See HIGHWAYS, 5–7.

COMMISSIONS.

See BROKERS; PARTNERSHIP, 1–3; POWERS; WAREHOUSEMEN.

COMMUNITY PROPERTY.

See HUSBAND AND WIFE, 6, 7.

COMPROMISE.

1. DEATH, COMPROMISE OF CAUSE OF ACTION ARISING OUT OF.—A statute creating a cause of action in favor of a widow, and in case there is no widow, of the children or personal representative of a decedent, for the benefit of his widow and children, against one through whose negligence his death resulted, gives the widow the power to compromise her suit against the objection of the children and without let or hinderance from any one, and such compromise as she may make, either before or after the bringing of the suit, binds all parties having any interest in the cause of action. *Holder v. Railroad*, 77.

2. WIDOW'S RIGHT TO COMPROMISE CLAIM FOR DAMAGES resulting from the death of her husband includes authority to receive the sum agreed upon, and its payment is a full and complete satisfaction of the claim, and is binding on the children and next of kin of the decedent. *Holder v. Railroad*, 77.

CONCEALMENT.
See SURETYSHIP, 13.

CONDITIONS.
See COVENANTS; DEEDS, 5-7; DEVISE, 2; EMINENT DOMAIN.

CONFLICT OF LAWS.
See CONTRACTS, 20; INSURANCE, 2.

CONGRESS.
See INTERSTATE COMMERCE, 1, 8.

CONSIDERATION.
See CONTRACTS, 6, 12; FRAUDULENT CONVEYANCES, 1, 2; JOINT LIABILITY; LOTTERIES, 1, 4; PLEADING, 3, TRUSTS, 9, 10.

CONSPIRACY.

1. WHAT IS.—To constitute a criminal conspiracy there must not only be an agreement to co-operate to do a certain act, but that act must also be unlawful. *Connor* v. *People*, 295.
2. CONSPIRACIES INJURIOUS TO TRADE AND COMMERCE.—An agreement between dealers, made for the purpose of controlling the price and managing the business of the sale of coal, so as to prevent competition in price between the parties to the agreement, is illegal, and if the price of coal was raised in pursuance of the agreement and to effect its objects the crime of conspiracy was committed, and is punishable, under a statute making it a misdemeanor for two or more persons to conspire to commit any act injurious to trade and commerce; nor can the guilty parties escape conviction by proving that the object of the agreement was to prevent ruinous rivalry between dealers in the same commodity, and that it had not resulted in raising the price beyond its nominal and reasonable value. *People* v. *Sheldon*, 690.
3. OVERT ACT.—If an unlawful agreement to raise the price of coal was entered into between dealers therein, the raising of the price in pursuance of such agreement, and to accomplish its purpose, is an overact sufficient to sustain a conviction for conspiracy. *People* v. *Sheldon*, 690.

CONSTITUTIONAL LAW.
See CONSTITUTIONS; LEGISLATURE; REFORM SCHOOLS; STATUTES.

CONSTITUTIONS.

1. CONSTITUTIONAL LAW.—A STATUTE DECLARING THAT ANY PERSONS, FIRMS, OR CORPORATIONS REFUSING TO CASH ANY CHECK OR SCRIP presented to them within thirty days of its date of issuance shall be deemed guilty of a misdemeanor is in conflict with the provisions of the constitution prohibiting the legislature from passing any law authorizing imprisonment for debt, and is therefore void. *State* v. *Paint Rock Coal etc. Co.*, 68.
2. CONSTITUTIONAL LAW—EQUAL PROTECTION AND DUE PROCESS OF LAW.—A statute making a railroad company unconditionally liable for damages for any animal killed by it, and fixing a schedule of arbitrary prices for certain animals killed, without allowing proof of their value, though

allowing the owner to resort to his common-law action if he so desires, while the company has no alternative if the owner resorts to his statutory action, is unconstitutional, as denying the company the equal protection of the laws, and as depriving it of its property without due process of law. *Wadsworth* v. *Union Pac. Ry. Co.,* 309.

See LEGISLATURE; MUNICIPAL CORPORATIONS, 5; REFORM SCHOOLS, 1; STATUTES; WATERS, 8.

CONSTRUCTION.

See CONTRACTS, 1-5; GUARANTY, 1-3; DEEDS, 4; MECHANIC'S LIEN, 4, 5; TREATIES, 1; WILLS, 2.

CONTRA BONOS MORES.

See CONTRACTS, 12.

CONTRACTS.

1. CONSTRUCTION.—If a contract admits of two meanings, one of which will render it unlawful and the other lawful, the latter construction must be adopted, and all doubtful words or provisions must be taken most strongly against the grantor. *Wyatt* v. *Larimer etc. Irr. Co.,* 280.

2. CONSTRUCTION WHEN TERMS DOUBTFUL.—When doubt exists as to the construction of a contract prepared by one party, upon the faith of which the other party has incurred obligations, or parted with property, that construction most favorable to the latter party will be adopted; and when the contract is susceptible of two constructions, one involving injustice and the other consistent with right, the latter must be adopted. *Wyatt* v. *Larimer etc. Irr. Co.,* 280.

3. CONSTRUCTION WHEN AMBIGUOUS.—When the language used by parties to a contract is indefinite and ambiguous, the practical interpretation by the parties themselves is entitled to great, if not controlling, influence, in ascertaining their understanding of its terms. *Wyatt* v. *Larimer etc. Irr. Co.,* 280.

4. WATERS—CONSTRUCTION OF CONTRACT FOR.—When an irrigation company, by the terms of its contract with water-takers, having the right to dispose of definite water rights by ambiguous expressions in subsequent provisions of the contract reserves the power to render such rights indefinite and uncertain as to quantity by disposing of water rights in excess of its ability to furnish water, the contract is not only inequitable and unjust, but also illegal, and cannot be enforced. *Wyatt* v. *Larimer etc. Irr. Co.,* 280.

5. WATERS—CONSTRUCTION OF CONTRACT FOR.—The true intent and meaning of a contract between an irrigation company and water-takers must be determined from the terms used, read in the light of surrounding circumstances at the time of its execution, from the subject matter, and the purposes and objects to be accomplished by it. *Wyatt* v. *Larimer etc. Irr. Co.,* 280.

6. PROMISE TO FORBEAR SUIT—CONSIDERATION.—An order upon a third person for the payment of a debt not due, if accepted, is sufficient consideration for a promise to forbear to sue upon an obligation already due. *Staver* v. *Missimer,* 142.

CONVEYANCE.

CORPORATIONS.

COVENANTS.

CONDITIONS SUBSEQUENT.—If a grant of property to be used as a cemetery contains a condition that a good fence shall be erected and maintained around it, the grantor being then the owner of adjacent lands, the stipulation will be construed to be a covenant and not a condition subsequent, and the grantor is not entitled to re-enter for failure to erect the fence. *Scovill* v. *McMahon,* 350.

See DEEDS, 5.

CREDITOR'S SUIT.

LIEN UNDER.—A judgment creditor may have land fraudulently conveyed by his debtor before the rendition of the judgment, sold under a decree establishing an equitable lien thereon in an action to set the conveyance aside, although at the time of the decree and sale the judgment at law had ceased to be a lien on the land under the statute. *Davidson* v. *Burke,* 367.

See LIENS.

CRIMINAL LAW.

RIGHT TO DECOY INTO CRIME.—Officers or detectives have no right to suggest the commission of a crime, and instigate others to take part in its commission, in order to arrest them while in the act, although the purpose may be to capture old offenders. Such conduct on their part is not only reprehensible but criminal, and will not be justified or encouraged by the courts. *Connor* v. *People,* 295.

See CONSPIRACY, 3; FALSE PRETENSES; LARCENY; LOTTERIES; MANDAMUS; REFORM SCHOOLS, 1, 2; OFFICERS, 1; SEDUCTION, 1; STATUTES, 3, 4; TRIAL, 1; USURY.

CULVERTS.

See RAILROADS, 2–9.

CURTESY.

AN ESTATE AS TENANT BY THE CURTESY VESTS IN a husband if his wife dies seised of an estate of inheritance, having had issue born alive and which might have inherited it as her heir, and she thereafter dies in the lifetime of her husband. *Jackson* v. *Jackson,* 427.

See STATUTES, 6, 12.

CUSTOM.

1. A PERSON CANNOT BY PROOF establish a usage or custom which, in his own interest, contravenes an established rule of commercial law. *Jackson* v. *Bank,* 81.

2. WHEN UNREASONABLE AS BETWEEN PRINCIPAL AND AGENT.—A custom that an agent, as soon as his agency is terminated, may at once for his own advantage undo, so far as it can be undone, all the business that he has done for his principal, is unreasonable, opposed to the policy of the law, and void. *Merchants' Ins. Co.* v. *Prince,* 626.

3. CUSTOM AS TO INSURANCE—WHEN UNREASONABLE.—A local custom that insurance agents, after their agency has terminated, may cancel policies issued through them within a certain period, so that they may turn over the insurance represented by such policies to some other company

of which they may have the agency, is unreasonable and void as being opposed to established rules of law governing the relation of principal and agent. *Merchants' Ins. Co.* v. *Prince*, 626.

CY PRES.

See TRUSTS, 4.

DAMAGES.

1. NEGLIGENCE.—EVIDENCE that the plaintiff in an action to recover damages for personal injuries has a wife and child should not be admitted. *Standard Oil Co.* v. *Tierney*, 595.

2. THE DAMAGES TO A SHIPPER FOR UNJUST DISCRIMINATION between him and other shippers is not necessarily the difference between the prices charged him and them, under a statute giving him treble the amount of injury suffered. The railway corporation has a right to clear and definite proof as to what the actual damage was. *Hoover* v. *Pennsylvania R. R.*, 43.

3. DAMAGES FOR PERSONAL INJURIES, WHEN DEEMED EXCESSIVE.—Where the conductor of a train, a vigorous man of about thirty years of age, and a laborious and useful employee, is so badly burnt about the face, as to be disfigured for life, suffers much pain and anguish for several months, and loses the use of his left arm, and to some extent of his right also, a verdict for twenty-five thousand dollars is excessive. *Standard Oil Co.* v. *Tierney*, 595.

4. MEASURE OF.—A plaintiff prevailing in an action to recover damages for personal injuries is entitled to be awarded such an amount as, in the opinion of the jury, will fairly compensate him for any suffering, mental or physical, theretofore experienced by him, directly resulting from the injury, and for any suffering or disability that may be believed from the testimony to be reasonably certain to be experienced by him in the future, and for any reduction in his power to earn money during the remainder of his life, if such reduction there be directly resulting from the injury. *Standard Oil Co.* v. *Tierney*, 595.

See ATTACHMENT, 5–9, 17; COMPROMISE, 2; FRAUD, 4; INJUNCTIONS, 3, 4; RAILROADS, 4–6; REAL PROPERTY, 1.

DEATH.

See COMPROMISE, 1; ELECTIONS.

DEBTOR AND CREDITOR.

See ASSIGNMENT FOR THE BENEFIT OF CREDITORS; ATTACHMENT, 10; CORPORATIONS. 11–13; EXECUTION, 2; FRAUDULENT CONVEYANCES; GUARANTY; HOMESTEADS, 6; LIENS; MORTGAGES, 3–5; NOTICE; SALES, 2.

DECLARATIONS.

See AGENCY, 8; EVIDENCE, 2; PARTNERSHIP, 5, 6.

DECOYING.

See CRIMINAL LAW; LARCENY, 2.

DEEDS.

1. DELIVERY OF.—A conveyance from a father to his minor child is inoperative for want of delivery when, though signed and acknowledged

by him, it always remained in his possession and was never filed for record, and he never mentioned the fact of making it to his wife or any of his friends, and always during the balance of his life treated as his own the property therein described. *Cazassa* v. *Cazassa*, 112.

2. LOCATION OF RIGHT OF WAY BY PAROL AGREEMENT.—When a right of way is granted by a deed, but the location of the way is not described therein, the parties may locate it by a parol agreement, and evidence of such agreement is admissible, and does not vary or contradict the deed, provided the way is located within the boundaries of the land over which the right was granted. *Kinney* v. *Hooker*, 864.

3. EXTRANEOUS EVIDENCE TO EXPLAIN AMBIGUITIES IN.—If the language of a grant is uncertain and ambiguous, the circumstances surrounding it and the situation of the parties are to be considered in ascertaining their true intent. *Kinney* v. *Hooker*, 864.

4. EXTRANEOUS EVIDENCE TO SHOW INTENT OF PARTIES, HOW FAR ADMISSIBLE.—In construing a grant, the courts will give effect to the intention of the parties as disclosed by their situation and by the surrounding circumstances, unless the intention thus disclosed is inconsistent with the language of the grant. *Kinney* v. *Hooker*, 864.

5. CONDITIONS SUBSEQUENT ARE NOT FAVORED and may be created only by express terms or clear implication. The courts will always construe clauses in deeds as covenants rather than as conditions, if they can reasonably do so. Though apt words for the creation of a condition subsequent are employed, yet, in the absence of an express provision for re-entry and forfeiture, the courts, from the nature of the acts to be performed, or prohibited, from the relation and situation of the parties, and from the entire instrument, will determine the real intention of the parties. *Scovill* v. *McMahon*, 350.

6. CONDITIONS SUBSEQUENT—WAIVER OF.—The right of entry for breach of a condition subsequent may be waived or lost by laches. Therefore, where land was granted on the condition that it should be used as a burying-ground, and that the grantee should build and keep a good and sufficient fence around it, and it was used for a burying-ground for more than forty-five years, but no fence was ever erected around it, and no complaint was ever made of the absence of such fence, it is then too late for the successor in interest of the grantor to enter for condition broken. *Scovill* v. *McMahon*, 350.

7. CONDITIONS SUBSEQUENT—PERFORMANCE PROHIBITED BY LAW.—If the further performance of a condition subsequent that premises should be used as a cemetery is rendered unlawful by a valid act of the legislature, the condition is thereby discharged and the title of the grantee freed therefrom. *Scovill* v. *McMahon*, 350.

See ATTORNEY AND CLIENT, 12, 15; INFANTS; NOTICE, 2; PRIVATE WAYS.

DEFAULT.

See JUDGMENTS, 10–15; MORTGAGES, 9, 10, 12.

DEFINITIONS.

Advancements *Cazassa* v. *Cazassa*, 112.
Award. *Hynes* v. *Wright*, 344.
Conspiracy. *Connor* v. *People*, 295.
Discount. *Youngblood* v. *Bermingham Trust etc. Co.*, 243.

DELIVERY.

See DEEDS, 1.

DEMURRER.

See PLEADING, 5, 9.

DEPUTIES.

See SHERIFFS, 2.

DESCENT.

IF THE NEXT OF KIN OF A DECEDENT IS A NONRESIDENT ALIEN, NOT CAPABLE OF INHERITING under the laws of the state, but there are other kindred who are residents of the state, the property does not escheat, but vests in the kindred who have capacity to inherit in the same manner as if the person incapable of inheriting by the laws of the state had never existed. *Schultze* v. *Schultze*, 432.

DEVISE.

1. A DEVISE OF THE RENTS, PROFITS, AND INCOME OF PROPERTY is in effect a devise of the property itself. *Johnson* v. *Johnson*, 104.

2. WILLS—CONDITION SUBSEQUENT—NONCOMPLIANCE WITH WITHOUT FAULT.—A devisee who takes a vested remainder subject to the performance of a condition subsequent does not forfeit his interest by noncompliance with that condition, if such noncompliance is not the result of his own fault. *Bryant* v. *Dungan*, 618.

See CHARITIES, 2, 5; ESTATES, 2, 3; WILLS, 2.

DIRECTORS.

See CORPORATIONS, 5, 8–11.

DISBARMENT.

See ATTORNEY AND CLIENT, 2, 6–8.

DISCOUNT.

1. DEFINITION OF.—A discount by a bank means a deduction or drawback made upon its advances or loans of money upon negotiable paper, or other evidences of debt payable at a future day which are transferred to the bank. In other words, discount is the interest reserved from the amount loaned at the time the loan is made. *Youngblood* v. *Birmingham Trust etc. Co.*, 245.

2. WHAT IS.—Every loan made upon evidences of debt when compensation for the use of the money till the maturity of the debt is deducted from the principal and retained by the lender at the time of making the loan is a discount in the absence of statute to the contrary. *Youngblood* v. *Birmingham Trust etc. Co.*, 245.

See BANKS, 3, 4; USURY.

DISCRIMINATION.

DISMISSAL.

DISQUALIFICATION.

DISTRIBUTION.

DIVERSION.

DITCH COMPANIES.

DITCHES.

DOMICILE.

DOWER.

1. A DECREE OF DIVORCE BARS ALL CLAIM TO DOWER. *Carr* v. *Carr,* 614.
2. DOWER RIGHTS, AGREEMENT IN FRAUD OF.—An agreement between the parties to a mortgage that it shall be foreclosed and a sale made for the purpose of cutting off the dower rights of the wife of the mortgagor in a part of the premises, and that the balance shall be reconveyed to him, is not a fraud upon her, depriving a court of equity of the power to enforce the agreement, if the result of the agreement and of the sale is to free the part left to the mortgagor of a servitude thereon, and to give to the residue a greater value than was possessed by the whole tract before the agreement was made. It is not material that the wife was applied to and refused to release her dower, and that the foreclosure scheme was necessary to counteract her unreasonable obstinacy, if the result contemplated and realized by her husband was to increase the value of the property subject to her dower interest. *Fellows* v. *Loomis,* 17.

DRAFTS.

DUE PROCESS OF LAW.

DURESS.

PAYMENT FOR WATER UNDER.—Payment under protest by a property owner employing a large number of persons of an excessive charge for necessary water in order to prevent the threatened shutting off of the only available water supply is compulsory and made under duress, and an action lies to recover the excess so paid. *Panton* v. *Duluth Gas etc. Co.*, 635.

EARNINGS.

See HUSBAND AND WIFE, 8.

EASEMENTS.

See PRIVATE WAYS.

EJECTMENT.

See MORTGAGES, 1.

ELECTION.

See SALES, 3.

ELECTIONS.

1. OFFICES—REQUISITES OF A VALID ELECTION.—No person can be regarded as duly elected to an office unless he receives a majority of the votes, when there are two candidates, or a plurality of the votes, when there are more than two. *Howes* v. *Perry*, 591.
2. OFFICES—DEATH OF ONE OF TWO CANDIDATES BEFORE THE CLOSE OF THE POLL, EFFECT OF.—A candidate for an elective office who receives a smaller number of votes than the only other competitor therefor, is not entitled to be declared elected because it appears that the latter died before all the votes were cast. Such a candidate cannot show that he was the choice of a majority or a plurality of those voting at the election, and is therefore incapable of establishing his right to be installed in the office which he claims. *Howes* v. *Perry*, 591.

See CORPORATIONS, 10.

ELECTRIC LIGHT COMPANIES.

1. IMPAIRMENT OF FRANCHISE TO USE STREETS.—When a city has conferred upon an electric light company the right to erect its poles on certain streets, and the company, relying upon the license thus given, expends money in establishing its plant and appliances, the city cannot, by a subsequent ordinance, infringe the rights thus vested or bestow upon another the authority to infringe them. *Rutland Electric Light Co.* v. *Marble City Electric Light Co.*, 868.
2. EXTENT OF THE RIGHTS OF COMPANIES USING THE SAME STREETS. An electric lightcompany which receives from a municipal corporation a license to erect its poles on certain streets, and expends money on the faith of such license, does not obtain thereby an exclusive privilege. A second company upon which a similar privilege is conferred acquires merely subordinate rights, and any interference of its wires with those of the prior licensee may be restrained by injunction. *Rutland Electric Light Co.* v. *Marble City Electric Light Co.*, 868.

ELEVATORS.

See NEGLIGENCE, 9; REAL PROPERTY, 4.

EMINENT DOMAIN.

Property Is Not Taken for a public use within the meaning of the constitution by the enactment and enforcement of a statute forbidding its use in a manner hurtful to the health and comfort of the community. Therefore, though a party had a right entry of for breach of a condition subsequent that lands should be used for a public cemetery, and the land is freed from that condition under a valid act of the legislature forbidding any further interment therein, and requiring the removal therefrom of all bodies and monuments, and authorizing the taking of the property, after such removal, for a public park, upon payment to its owners of the sums decreed by the court, he has no right to any part of the money awarded for such property. *Scovill* v. *McMahon*, 350.

ENTIRETIES.

See HUSBAND AND WIFE, 1-5; LIMITATIONS OF ACTIONS, 3.

EQUITY.

1. **MUNICIPAL CORPORATIONS.**—COURTS OF EQUITY will not attempt to control discretionary or legislative powers vested by law in municipl corporations. *Stevens* v. *St. Mary's Training School*, 438.

2. **WATERS AND WATERCOURSES**—ACTION TO ESTABLISH RIGHTS IN WATERCOURSE, OF EQUITABLE COGNIZANCE, WHEN.—An action to enjoin the diversion of a watercourse, and to enforce the specific performance of a contract, by which the plaintiff was to have the use of the waters in such watercourse for irrigating his land, is of equitable cognizance. *Case* v. *Hoffman*, 937.

See ASSOCIATIONS, 3; BILLS OF REVIEW, 1; CHARITIES, 1; FRAUD, 2; IMPROVEMENTS, 3; INJUNCTIONS; JUDGMENTS, 5; MARRIAGE AND DIVORCE; MORTGAGES, 1; PLEADING, 6, 9.

ERROR.

See APPEAL.

ESCHEAT.

See TAXES, 2.

ESTATES.

1. **FREEHOLD IS ANY ESTATE OF INHERITANCE** or for life in either a corporeal or incorporeal hereditament existing in or arising from real property of free tenure. *Wyatt* v. *Larimer etc. Irr. Co.*, 280.

2. **WILLS**—DEVISE TO WIFE AND CHILDREN.—Under a devise by a husband directly to his wife and children the wife takes a life estate only, unless there is some other provision in the will showing a contrary intention. *Weaver* v. *Weaver*, 604.

3. **WILLS**—DEVISE TO WIFE WITH DIRECTIONS TO MANAGE FOR BENEFIT OF CHILDREN.—Where a testator directs his executor to "take possession of his estate, both real and personal," and, after paying his debts, "deliver the remainder to his wife, who is requested and expected to manage the same to the best advantage in caring for and educating the children and supporting herself," the will is to be construed as giving to the widow a life estate in all the property, both real and personal, and the

children take merely an estate in remainder expectant upon the decease
of their mother. *Weaver v. Weaver*, 604.

4. DEEDS CONSTRUCTION OF.—A CONVEYANCE TO A MARRIED WOMAN AND
THE HEIRS OF HER BODY by a specified husband, from whom the consideration moves, passes only a life estate to the woman herself, and
her children, whether born before or after the execution of the deed,
take a vested estate in the remainder. *Fletcher v. Tyler*, 584.

See CURTESY; TREATIES, 3.

ESTOPPEL.

1. REPUGNANT DEFENSES.—A defendant in an action who has obtained a
substantial advantage by taking and successfully maintaining the position that the land in controversy is a homestead, is thereby estopped
from claiming on the same evidence, and in the same action, that it is
not a homestead. *Hodges v. Winston*, 241.

2. ESTOPPEL IN PAIS—FACTS NOT SUFFICIENT TO RAISE.—Where the widow
and son of a mortgagor are seeking, on the ground of his mental incapacity, to set aside a mortgage after it has passed into the possession
of a bank as collateral security for the debt of a third party, and it appears that the bank had, through its cashier, notice of all the material
facts surrounding the execution of the mortgage, such bank is in no
position to insist upon an equitable estoppel based merely on the facts,
that the widow signed the mortgage with her husband, that the son attested it, that various small checks drawn by the mortgagor before the
execution of the mortgage and one drawn after it were paid by the
bank, and that a payment of interest was made by the mortgagor's son
for the mortgagor's estate upon the indebtedness for which the mortgage was collateral security. *Brothers v. Bank*, 932.

3. ESTOPPEL BY ADMISSIONS, EXTENT OF.—A party to a suit is not precluded
from proving that his admissions, whether express or implied from his
conduct, were mistaken or untrue, unless another person has been induced by them to alter his conduct. In that case he and all
claiming under him are estopped from disputing the truth of the admissions so far as that person is concerned, but are not bound as to
third persons. *Holman v. Boyce*, 861.

**4. ESTOPPEL OF DEBTOR BY REPRESENTATIONS AS TO AMOUNT DUE ON A
NOTE.**—When one takes an assignment of a chose in action by the
debtor's procurement or with his assent, and on the faith of representations made by him at the time, the debtor is estopped to impeach the
chose by a defense inconsistent with his representations, even though
such defense is usury. *Holman v. Boyce*, 861.

See CORPORATIONS, 4; INFANTS, 2; LANDLORD AND TENANT, 9; MORTGAGES,
8; MUNICIPAL CORPORATIONS, 7; SURETYSHIP, 4.

EVIDENCE.

1. SALES OF REAL ESTATE—EVIDENCE OF VALUE.—Actual sales of property in
the vicinity and near the time are competent, and the most satisfactory,
evidence of value as far as they go, yet, they are only one of the modes
of proving value, and not the only mode. Sales made in one year are
not an exact criterion of values in the same vicinity five years later.
Elmore v. Johnson, 401.

2. WILLS—DECLARATIONS AS EVIDENCE.—Declarations by an executor and
beneficiary, under a will not made in the presence of the testator, as to

the disposition to be made of property, are not admissible either to support or invalidate the will, whether they were made before or after its execution. *Eastis* v. *Montgomery*, 227.

3. EVIDENCE THAT A WITNESS HAS ON OTHER OCCASIONS made statements similar to those to which he has testified is inadmissible. What he has said out of court, and when not under oath, cannot be received to fortify his testimony. *Connor* v. *People*, 295.

4. NEGOTIABLE INSTRUMENTS—ALTERATIONS.—IT IS PRESUMED that a note was in the same condition when signed as when offered in evidence, and such presumption is not changed by the fact that the note shows upon its face that the orignal draft thereof has been changed. *Wolferman* v. *Bell*, 126.

5. LAWS OF SISTER STATE—PRESUMPTION.—In the absence of allegation and proof, the laws of another state are presumed to be the same as the laws of the state in which action is brought. *Thomas* v. *Pendleton*, 726.

6. NEGOTIABLE INSTRUMENTS.—PAROL EVIDENCE IS ADMISSIBLE to prove that persons whose names appear on a note as indorsers signed their names thereon before it was delivered, and are therefore liable as makers. *Bank of Jamaica* v. *Jefferson*, 100.

7. CONTRACTS—EXTRINSIC EVIDENCE AS TO MUTUAL MISTAKE.—Parol evidence may be adduced to show that a lease was taken with the understanding, on the part of both the lessor and the lessee, that the premises were to be used for a certain purpose, and that this understanding was based on a mistake as to the true facts of the case. Such evidence is properly admitted, not to vary the effect of the contract, but to show that it never had any valid existence. *Bedell* v. *Wilder*, 871.

8. CONTRACTS, PAROL EVIDENCE, WHEN INADMISSIBLE TO VARY.—The legal effect of a written contract cannot be varied by evidence of the previous negotiations between the contracting parties. *Cream City Glass Co.* v. *Friedlander*, 895.

9. CONTENTS OF TELEGRAM.—When one commences correspondence with another by telegraph he makes the telegraph company his agent for the transmission and delivery of his communication, and the transmitted message actually delivered is primary evidence of the transaction. If such message is lost or destroyed, its contents may be proved by parol. *Magie* v. *Herman*, 660.

See APPEAL, 1, 3, 4; DAMAGES, 1; DEEDS, 2–4; FILING INSTRUMENTS, 3; JUDGMENTS, 15; LARCENY, 3; NEGLIGENCE, 3, 8; SEDUCTION; SHERIFFS, 3; STATUTES, 1; TRIAL, 1, 2; TRUSTS, 6; WILLS, 8–10, 14; WITNESSES.

EXECUTION.

1. EXECUTION SALE, CHANGE OF POSSESSION.—If personal property taken upon execution is sold at public auction *bona fide* and after compliance with all lawful formalities, the rule imperatively requiring a change in the possession of such property as between vendor and vendee and raising, as a matter of law in favor of attaching creditors, from the failure of such change, a conclusive presumption of fraud does not arise. *Huebler* v. *Smith*, 337.

2. EXECUTION SALE—RETENTION OF POSSESSION.—If an execution sale is made, and the judgment creditor permits the debtor to remain in possession after the sale, such conduct raises an inference against the validity of the transaction which it is incumbent on such creditor to overcome by proof that his judgment was for an honest debt and that there was no collusion between him and his debtor to cheat or defraud other creditors. *Huebler v. Smith,* 337.

3. EXECUTION SALES, HOW FAR MAY BE IMPEACHED.—An execution sale, regular on its face, is presumed to be a *bona fide* sale. It may be impeached for fraud and collusion between the execution creditor and debtor, and, if assailed on that ground, its *bona fides* should be submitted to the jury. *Caswell v. Jones,* 879.

4. EXECUTION SALES—OFFICER ACTING AS AGENT FOR PURCHASER.—An officer conducting an execution sale cannot act as the agent of an absent purchaser. *Caswell v. Jones,* 879.

5. EXEMPTIONS.—STOCK IN DITCH COMPANY is personal property, and not exempt from execution. *Struby-Estabrook Mercantile Co. v. Davis,* 266.

6. HOMESTEAD ENTRY—WHEN SUBJECT TO EXECUTION.—Lands entered under the United States homestead laws are liable to the satisfaction of debts contracted by the homestead claimant between the date of the final certificate of entry and the date of the patent. *Struby-Estabrook Mercantile Co.* v. *Davis,* 266.

7. EXEMPTIONS.—CAPITAL STOCK OF DITCH COMPANY is not exempt from levy and sale on the ground that the ditch is used to convey water to land entered under homestead laws. *Struby-Estabrook Mercantile Co.* v. *Davis,* 266.

See HOMESTEADS, 3, 5.

EXECUTORS AND ADMINISTRATORS.
See ATTORNEY AND CLIENT, 1; PARTNERSHIP, 1-3.

EXEMPTIONS.
See ATTACHMENT, 15-17; EXECUTIONS, 5-7.

EXPECTANCIES.

1. CONVEYANCE OF—WHAT NECESSARY TO SUSTAIN—INSANITY OF TESTATOR.—A contract for the conveyance of an expectant interest in an ancestor's estate cannot be enforced until it is shown that there was neither fraud nor oppression, and that the ancestor had knowledge of and consented to such contract; and the fact that he was incapable of consenting because of his insanity does not constitute an exception to the rule requiring his assent. *McClure v. Raben,* 558.

2. CONVEYANCE OF AGAINST PUBLIC POLICY.—Contracts for the conveyance of expectant interests in ancestor's estates, without the knowledge and consent of the latter, are illegal as being contrary to public policy. *McClure v. Raben,* 558.

EXPRESS COMPANIES.
See INTERSTATE COMMERCE, 6.

FALSE PRETENSES.

1. WHAT CONSTITUTE.—If a person obtains a loan of money by a false pretense of an existing fact, although he intends to repay such money, he is guilty of the crime of obtaining money by false pretenses. *Commonwealth v. Schwartz,* 609.

3. **DELIVERY OF PROPERTY, HOW FAR ESSENTIAL.**—If the possession of goods has been delivered to the defendant, but the right of property has not passed, and after such delivery he obtains the title by false pretenses, he is guilty under the statute of obtaining the goods by false pretenses. *Commonwealth* v. *Schwartz*, 609.

4. **DELIVERY—BAILEE, WHEN GUILTY OF CRIME.**—If a banker collects money on commercial paper, and has possession of it as agent, and when the owner demands it induces him by false representations as to the solvency of the bank, to part with his title and lend the money to the bank, there is a complete transfer of property without delivery, and therefore it is not necessary in order to make out the offense against the statute to prove false pretenses relating to the delivery of the money. *Commonwealth* v. *Schwartz*, 609.

FALSE REPRESENTATIONS.
See AGENCY, 6; FRAUD, 5; SALES, 5.

FEES.
See ATTORNEY AND CLIENT, 4, 10–12.

FELLOW-SERVANTS.
See RAILROADS, 21.

FILING INSTRUMENTS.

1. **WHAT CONSTITUTES.**—The duty of a party required to file a paper, in the absence of any question as to fees, is discharged when he has placed it in the hands of the proper custodian at the proper time and in the proper place. *Hook* v. *Fenner*, 277.

2. **WHAT SUFFICIENT.**—The placing of a paper in a case as a permanent record in the office of a justice of the peace is a sufficient filing, no matter if he fails to perform the mere clerical act of indorsing it as filed. His failure to so indorse it cannot operate to the prejudice of either party. *Hook* v. *Fenner*, 277.

3. **FILING INSTRUMENT IN COURT—WHEN COMPLETE.**—Filing a paper in court may be complete without the indorsement of such filing. The indorsement is only evidence of the filing, but it is not the exclusive evidence. *Hook* v. *Fenner*, 277.

FIRES.
See LICENSE.

FIREWORKS.
See MUNICIPAL CORPORATIONS, 13, 14; NUISANCE.

FLOODS.
See MUNICIPAL CORPORATIONS, 10; RAILROADS, 7, 8.

FORBEARANCE.
See CONTRACTS, 6; PLEADING, 7.

FORECLOSURE.

See ASSIGNMENT FOR THE BENEFIT OF CREDITORS, 1, 2; DOWER, 2; ME-
CHANIC'S LIEN, 15; MORTGAGES, 1, 6–12; RECEIVERS, 2.

FORFEITURE.

See INSURANCE, 8, 9; LANDLORD AND TENANT, 2, 3, 5; MECHANIC'S LIEN, 9;
MORTGAGES, 8, 12.

FORGERY.

See BANKS, 2.

FRAUD.

1. WHEN MUST BE FOUND AS FACT.—If by statute the question of fraud
is made one of fact, and fraud is essential to the cause of action, it must
be found as a fact, and not left to be inferred as matter of law. *Hutchinson* v. *First Nat. Bank*, 537.

2. INNOCENT MISREPRESENTATION NO ONE PERMITTED TO RETAIN FRUITS
OF.—Though one who brings about a contract by misrepresentation
commits no fraud, because his representation was, when made, innocent
in the ordinary sense, yet if, after ascertaining its falsity, he refuses to
relinquish the advantage derived therefrom, upon receiving an offer of
reciprocal relinquishment from the injured party, he is guilty of constructive fraud, and the contract is subject to rescission by a court of
equity. *Prewitt* v. *Trimble*, 586.

3. ACTUAL KNOWLEDGE OF FALSITY OF STATEMENT, WHEN NOT ESSEN-
TIAL.—When a person is in a situation to know, and it is his duty to
know, whether a statement, upon the faith of which another has been
induced to enter into a contract, is true or false, the law imputes such
knowledge to him, and the statement, if untrue, is held to be fraudulent as regards the person who relied upon it. *Prewitt* v. *Trimble*,
586.

4. FALSE STATEMENT AS TO CONDITION OF BANK—PRESIDENT CANNOT
PROFIT BY.—A statement signed by the president and directors of a
bank, which is circulated with and refers with approval to a statement
in which the cashier sets forth the resources and liabilities of the bank,
is a deliberate affirmation of the truth of the latter statement, and
equivalent to a report of the affairs of the bank made by the president
and directors themselves. Under such circumstances, if the cashier's
statement proves to be false, one who has been induced by it to purchase bank shares from the president at a price exceeding their real
value may maintain an action against his vendor to recover damages for
misrepresentation or to procure the recission of the sale. *Prewitt* v.
Trimble, 586.

5. FALSE REPRESENTATIONS AS TO THE PRICE WHICH HAD BEEN PAID FOR
THE PROPERTY when bought about a month previously is a sufficient
basis to predicate a finding of fraud upon, when such representation is
deliberately made by the holder of such property or his agent then seeking to sell it, and is relied upon by the party to whom it was made, and
was intended to influence him. *Fairchild* v. *McMahon*, 701.

See AGENCY, 6; ALTERATION OF INSTRUMENTS; DOWER, 2; EXECUTION, 1;
IMPROVEMENTS, 2; MORTGAGES, 3, 4; TRUSTS, 1, 2, 4, 5, 7, 8, 11;
WILLS, 7.

FRAUDULENT CONVEYANCES.

1. LIFE SUPPORT AS CONSIDERATION.—One cannot transfer all his property in consideration of support for life without first satisfying his existing debts; and without this a fraudulent intent to hinder and delay creditors follows necessarily as a conclusion of law, regardless of what the parties to the transaction in fact intended. *Davidson* v. *Burke*, 367.

2. LIFE SUPPORT AS CONSIDERATION.—A conveyance by a debtor of all his property in consideration of support for life is fraudulent in law, although he acts in good faith under the erroneous supposition that a note for which he is jointly liable has been paid. *Davidson* v. *Burke*, 367.

3. FRAUDULENT INTENT MUST BE ALLEGED.—In an action brought by, or for the benefit of, subsequent creditors, the complaint must aver that the instrument to be avoided was executed with intent to defraud subsequent as well as existing creditors. *Hutchinson* v. *First Nat. Bank*, 537.

4. FRAUD MUST BE ALLEGED AND FOUND.—Not only must fraud be found as an ultimate fact, in order to avoid a conveyance as being fraudulently executed to hinder and delay creditors, when the statute makes fraud a question of fact, but the complaint in such action must also expressly allege that the instrument was executed with a fraudulent intent. *Hutchinson* v. *First Nat. Bank*, 537.

See CHATTEL MORTGAGES, 1–3; CORPORATIONS, 12, 13; JUDGMENTS, 4; LIENS; MORTGAGES, 2.

FREEHOLD.
See ESTATES, 1; JURISDICTION, 6; WATERS, 4.

GAME LAWS.

OYSTERS AND OYSTER-BEDS—STATE PROPERTY RIGHTS IN AND CONTROL OF. A state has an absolute property right in its oysters and oyster-beds, and, through its legislature, has the absolute right to dispose of them to its people, and may adopt all precautions and regulations deemed desirable or necessary for the preservation and increased production of its oysters so far as this may be done without obstructing the paramount right of navigation. *State* v. *Harrub*, 195.

GARNISHMENT.
See ATTACHMENT, 11–13.

GIFT ENTERPRISES.
See LOTTERIES.

GIFTS.
See ADVANCEMENTS, 1; HUSBAND AND WIFE, 7.

GUARANTY.

1. LIABILITY WHEN ATTACHES.—Under a guaranty that the purchaser will promptly pay for them at maturity, the liability of the guarantor does not attach until the expiration of the term of credit given the principal debtor. *Taussig* v. *Reid*, 504.

2. CONSTRUCTION OF CONTRACT.—A collateral continuing guaranty is to be construed as favorably in favor of the creditor, and as strongly against the guarantor, as the sense of the words of the contract will permit. *Taussig* v. *Reid*, 504.

3. COLLATERAL AND CONTINUING CONSTRUCTION.—A written guaranty for the prompt payment of the price of goods purchased, or to be thereafter purchased, to the amount of a certain sum named, is a collateral continuing guaranty, and the amount stated is a limitation upon the liability of the guarantor, and not upon the credit to be extended to the principal debtor, *Taussig* v. *Reid*, 504.

4. LIABILITY OF GUARANTOR IS NOT AFFECTED by the previous condition of the debtor's account with that of the creditor as to any sum from the payment of which the guarantor is not discharged by the failure of the creditor to give notice within a reasonable time of nonpayment by the principal debtor. *Taussig* v. *Reid*, 504.

5. DEMAND AND NOTICE OF NONPERFORMANCE.—In case of an absolute guaranty, the guarantor is not entitled to demand or notice of nonperformance, but when the undertaking is collateral, notice must be given within a reasonable time, unless circumstances exist which excuse want of notice or the guarantor is not prejudiced thereby. If the principal is insolvent when the debt becomes due, or default is made, so that no benefit could be derived by the guarantor from the receipt of notice, none is required. *Taussig* v. *Reid*, 504.

6. NEGOTIABLE INSTRUMENTS—DEMAND AND NOTICE OF NONPAYMENT.— When the payee of an unconditional promissory note, or a third party, executes a contract on the back thereof for the payment of the money at a specified time, in which he guarantees the payment of the note at maturity, the holder thereof is under no obligation to demand payment of the maker, and, on default of payment, notify the guarantor. *Taussig* v. *Reid*, 504.

7. NECESSITY FOR NOTICE OF ACCEPTANCE.—In case of a written guarantee for a debt yet to be created and uncertain in amount, the guarantor must be given notice within a reasonable time that the guaranty is accepted, and that credit has been given upon the faith of it. *Taussig* v. *Reid*, 504.

8. NOTICE OF DEFAULT IN PAYMENT.—In case of a collateral continuing guaranty, as for the payment of goods to be thereafter purchased, reasonable notice of the default of payment on the part of the principal debtor must be given to the guarantor, and he will be discharged from payment, so far as he has sustained loss or damage resulting from a failure of the creditor to give him notice. *Taussig* v. *Reid*, 504.

9. NOTICE OF DEFAULT BY DEBTOR.—Reasonable time is allowed to the creditor in which to give notice to a guarantor of the default of the principal debtor to make payment, and what is such reasonable time depends upon the circumstances of each particular case. *Taussig* v. *Reid*, 504.

10. INSOLVENCY OF PRINCIPAL—EFFECT OF FAILURE TO NOTIFY GUARANTOR OF DEFAULT.—When notice of default by the principal debtor can result in no benefit to the guarantor, as when the principal is insolvent when the guaranty is made, and so remains, a failure to give notice of his default in payment is not a defense to an action on the guaranty. *Taussig* v. *Reid*, 504.

11. RIGHT TO REVOKE.—An undertaking of guaranty is primarily an offer, and does not become a binding obligation until it is accepted, and notice of acceptance has been given to the guarantor. Such offer may be recalled at any time before notice of acceptance. *Saint v. Wheeler etc. Mfg. Co.*, 210.

See SURETYSHIP, 1, 7, 8.

GUARDIAN AND WARD.

See REFORM SCHOOLS, 4, 5.

HEREDITAMENTS.

See ESTATES, 1; WATERS, 4.

HIGHWAYS.

1. OPENING, AND LAYING OUT—FAILURE TO COMPLY WITH STATUTE.—When a statute provides that if the board of supervisors does not file an order describing a highway within twenty days after an application for the establishment thereof, it shall be deemed to have decided against the application, any proceeding by the board thereafter, and after a failure to file such order for record, is of no force and effect, and the parties thereto stand in the same position as if no application had been made. *Town of Wayne v. Caldwell*, 750.

2. LAYING OUT, ALTERING, OR DISCONTINUING a public highway is an exercise of arbitrary power conferred upon supervisors or road officers for the good and necessity of the general public, and the exercise of this power must be made a matter of public record by them, so that private and public rights may be clearly defined. *Town of Wayne v. Caldwell*, 750.

3. COMPLIANCE WITH STATUTE IN ALTERING OR LAYING OUT.—The altering and laying out of roads for the use of the public is a taking of private property for a public use, and every substantial requirement of the statute must be complied with by the supervisors or road officers. Otherwise their proceedings are void. *Town of Wayne v. Caldwell*, 750.

4. WAIVER OF STATUTORY PROVISIONS CONCERNING.—In proceedings to lay out or alter a public highway statutory requirements relating solely to private persons may be waived by the parties interested, but provisions in which the public have a general interest must be strictly followed or the proceedings are void. *Town of Wayne v. Caldwell*, 750.

5. FALSE INDUCEMENTS TO SIGN PETITION FOR—REMEDY.—When a free gravel highway is sought to be established, and certain petitioners therefor are harmed by false inducements held out to influence them to sign the petition, their remedy is by objection made before the sufficiency of the petition is established by the board of commissioners, and failing to do so they are precluded by the judgment if the latter is regular and effectual. *Board of Commissioners v. Justice*, 528.

6. MINISTERIAL ACT IN APPROVING BOND FOR COSTS OF ESTABLISHING.—The act of a board of commissioners in approving a bond to secure the expense of a preliminary survey and report in establishing a free gravel road, is merely ministerial and the fact that one of the commissioners is an interested party does not affect the action of the board. *Board of Commissioners v. Justice*, 528.

7. JUDGMENT BY DISQUALIFIED JUDGE—COLLATERAL ATTACK.—The act of a board of commissioners in passing upon the sufficiency of a petition and appointing viewers and a surveyor for the establishment of a free gravel road is judicial in its nature, and the participation therein by a

commissioner disqualified to act by reason of interest or otherwise renders the judgment of the board voidable by appropriate proceeding, but when the board has acquired jurisdiction of the subject matter and of the person by giving the required statutory notice, and an opportunity by appeal is given of having a trial by an impartial tribunal, such voidable act by the board is not subject to collateral attack by injunction or otherwise. *Board of Commissioners* v. *Justice*, 528.

See JURISDICTION, 3.

HOMESTEAD.

1. CONDITIONS ESSENTIAL TO ENJOYMENT OF.—A homestead right cannot be acquired by one who has no family, but after the right has once vested, the loss of the family by death or marriage will not divest it. *Stults* v. *Sale*, 575.

2. HOMESTEADS IN SEPARATE TRACTS OF LAND.—Two parcels of land, though not contiguous, if occupied and cultivated in connection with each other, and used as a common source of family support, may together constitute a homestead. *Hodges* v. *Winston*, 241.

3. CONVEYANCE OF HOMESTEAD BY HUSBAND TO WIFE, accepted by her, is an alienation of the premises in the sense of passing the legal title to her, but is not an alienation of the homestead exemption, since that does not thereby pass from the husband, the wife, or the family, but the land still remains their homestead in every essential quality and attribute, and cannot be taken under execution, nor again conveyed without the voluntary consent and signature of both husband and wife. *Turner* v. *Bernheimer*, 207.

4. CONVEYANCE OF CERTIFICATE OF ACKNOWLEDGMENT.—A conveyance of a homestead by a husband and wife, without the separate acknowledgment of the wife and certificate thereof as required by the statute is a mere nullity. When such conveyance has been completely executed by delivery and acceptance for record, the officer before whom it was acknowledged has no power to alter or add to the certificate, or make a new one, without a reacknowledgment. *Hodges* v. *Winston*, 241.

5. CONVEYANCE OF DEFECTIVE ACKNOWLEDGMENT—LIEN OF EXECUTION.—A conveyance of a homestead by husband and wife, to which the certificate of separate acknowledgment of the wife is not made until after the conveyance has been delivered and recorded, and then without a reacknowledgment and after the lien of an execution has attached, is a mere nullity, and the execution purchaser acquires a good title if the levy and sale were made after the land ceased to be a homestead. *Hodges* v. *Winston*, 241.

6. CONVEYANCE OF—VALIDITY AS AGAINST CREDITORS.—Simple money judgment creditors and those claiming under them have no right to complain of the conveyance of his homestead by their debtor. *Hodges* v. *Winston*, 241.

See ESTOPPEL, 1; EXECUTION, 6, 7.

HUSBAND AND WIFE.

1. A TENANCY BY THE ENTIRETIES, ON THE DIVORCE OF THE HUSBAND AND WIFE, is destroyed, and the property which was subject thereto vests in them as tenants in common. *Hopson* v. *Fowlkes*, 120.

ICE.

IMPROVEMENTS.

2. IMPROVEMENTS ON LAND—EQUITABLE LIEN FOR REIMBURSEMENT.—In equity when one has made improvements innocently, or through mistake, upon the land of another, he will not ordinarily be allowed to enforce a claim for reimbursement as an actor; but when the true owner seeks relief in equity he may be required to make compensation for the improvements. Even in such case compensation is not allowed for the increased value caused by the improvements, nor will the courts sustain a bill to recover for such enhanced value after the true owner has recovered the premises at law. *Williams* v. *Vanderbilt*, 486.

See INFANTS, 3, 4; LANDLORD AND TENANT. 4.

IMPRISONMENT.
See CONSTITUTIONS, 1; REFORM SCHOOLS, 3.

INDORSEMENT.
See AGENCY, 2–5; ASSIGNMENT FOR THE BENEFIT OF CREDITORS, 3; EVIDENCE, 6; FILING INSTRUMENTS, 2, 3; NEGOTIABLE INSTRUMENTS, 1–4; PAYMENT, 2.

INFANTS.

1. AN INFANT'S DEED does not bind him, if, upon coming of age, he decides to disaffirm it. It is not void but voidable, and the right to disaffirm it is personal to himself. *Dolph* v. *Hand*, 25.

2. AVOIDANCE OF DEEDS BY—ESTOPPEL.—The mere fact that a married woman who executed a deed while still a minor appeared to be of full age, and that the grantee, when he made his purchase, believed her to be of full age, will not estop her to avoid the deed, after she reaches her majority. *Sewell* v. *Sewell*, 606.

3. AN INFANT'S RIGHT TO DISAFFIRM HIS DEED MUST BE EXERCISED WITHIN A REASONABLE TIME after his coming of age. If, for fifteen years after attaining his majority, he resides near the property he has conveyed, and knows of improvements being made upon it and of its use for mining purposes, without objecting and without indicating any intention of disaffirming his deed, he thereby irrevocably ratifies it. *Dolph* v. *Hand*, 25.

4. POWER OF TO SELL LAND—WHEN NOT IMPLIED.—A conveyance of land to an infant, in which no power to sell such land during his minority is conferred in express terms, implies merely the right to sell, when the disability of infancy is removed, and the law enables him to make a good title to the property. The existence of such a power cannot be inferred where a deed, by which a father conveys land to an infant married daughter, contains a clause which provides that "nothing is to prevent her selling the land, if she so desire, by her husband uniting with her." *Sewell* v. *Sewell*, 606.

5. DECREE CANCELING DEED OF INFANT MARRIED WOMAN—PROPER FORM OF.—When a married woman, during her minority, executed a deed of her land, by uniting with her husband, who had a contingent estate therein, dependent upon his surviving his wife, and brought suit, after becoming of full age, to avoid the conveyance, and it appeared that the grantee had made valuable improvements on the land, but not exceeding the value of the rent, no account should be taken of the rents and improvements, and the decree should merely require the petitioner to account for whatever part of the purchase money she may have received, with interest from the date of the deed, and leave to the grantee such title as her husband has. *Sewell* v. *Sewell,* 606.

INHERITANCE.

See DESCENT; ESTATES, 1.

INJUNCTIONS.

1. MUNICIPAL CORPORATIONS.—A COURT OF EQUITY, at the instance of a taxpayer, may restrain municipal corporations and their officers from making unauthorized appropriations of the corporate funds, and from making payments of illegal claims. *Stevens* v. *St. Mary's Training School,* 438.

2. MUNICIPAL CORPORATIONS—VOID ORDINANCES—RESTRAINING ENACTMENT OF.—The enactment of void ordinances will not ordinarily be enjoined. The restrictive powers of the courts should be directed against the enforcement rather than against the passage of such ordinances. Therefore, an injunction will not issue to prevent county commissioners from entering into a contract with a corporation controlled by the Roman Catholic Church for the payment to it of moneys for the instruction of boys committed to its care, though such contract is prohibited by the state constitution, and will be void if made. A court of chancery cannot assume in advance that the commissioners will ignore the real facts and violate the fundamental law of the state by making an illegal contract, and, if they should make such contract, the county will not be estopped from taking advantage of its incapacity to make it. *Stevens* v. *St. Mary's Training School,* 438.

3. INJUNCTION TO RESTRAIN THE BREACH OF A CONTRACT will not be granted unless the injury to be apprehended is not susceptible of adequate damages at law. *Dills* v. *Doebler,* 345.

4. IF THE PARTIES TO A CONTRACT STIPULATE FOR THE PAYMENT IN CASE OF ITS BREACH of a specified sum, which is truly liquidated damages, equity will not interfere to prevent such breach, though the party guilty thereof is insolvent. *Dills* v. *Doebler,* 345.

5. INJUNCTION WILL NOT ISSUE TO COMPEL THE DEFENDANT NOT TO EXERCISE HIS TRADE OR BUSINESS in a city, or within fifteen miles thereof, he having agreed that he would not so exercise it, and that if he did, he would pay complainant one thousand dollars, and it further appearing that he has not paid such sum, and is insolvent. *Dills* v. *Doebler,* 345.

See ELECTRIC LIGHT COMPANIES, 2; PLEADING, 1, 9; WATERS, 3, 6.

INSANITY.

See EXPECTANCIES, 1; WILLS, 6.

INSOLVENCY.

See ASSIGNMENT FOR THE BENEFIT OF CREDITORS, 3; GUARANTY, 5, 10; INJUNCTIONS, 4, 5; MORTGAGES, 4; NEGOTIABLE INSTRUMENTS, 4; SETOFF.

INSTRUCTIONS.

See APPEAL, 2; TRIAL, 4; WILLS, 12, 14.

INSURANCE.

1. CONTRACT OF, WHEN ENTIRE.—A policy of insurance covering several lots of personal property in the same building, and distributing the

risk to each item, but providing for the payment of a gross sum as premium, creates an entire, indivisible contract. If such policy is conditioned to be no longer binding upon the insurer in case the property is levied upon or taken into possession under any legal process, a levy upon a part of the property insured renders the policy inoperative as to the whole. *Burr* v. *German Ins. Co.*, 905.

2. INSURANCE POLICY—WHERE ENFORCEABLE.—It is no part or ingredient of a contract of insurance that it shall be enforced only in conformity to the law of the place where it is executed. On the contrary it can generally be enforced in any state where the company issuing it can be legally served with process. *Neufelder* v. *German-American Ins. Co.*, 166.

3. CONDITION AGAINST "CHANGE OF POSSESSION BY LEGAL PROCESS."— A writ of attachment is a "process," and therefore a policy conditioned to be void in case "any change takes place in the title or possession of the property, whether by sale, etc., legal process, or judicial decree," becomes inoperative when an attachment is levied on such property. *Carey* v. *German-American Ins. Co.*, 907.

4. CHANGE OF POSSESSION OF PROPERTY, SEIZURE BY OFFICER, WHEN AMOUNTS TO.—A seizure of property by an officer in the regular course of attachment proceedings, as prescribed by the statute, works a change in the possession of such property sufficient to avoid an insurance policy thereon, which is conditioned to become inoperative in case "any change of possession takes place by legal process." *Carey* v. *German-American Ins. Co.*, 907.

5. CONDITION AGAINST CHANGE OF POSSESSION, WHEN BROKEN.—If a policy which, so far as the risk is concerned, creates an indivisible contract is conditioned to be void when a change takes place in the possession of the property insured, that condition is deemed to be broken if there is a change in the possession of a large or considerable portion of such property. *Carey* v. *German-American Ins. Co.*, 907.

6. A CONDITION AGAINST CHANGE OF POSSESSION applies to an involuntary change of possession by legal process as well as to a voluntary change resulting from the action of the insured himself. *Carey* v. *German-American Ins. Co.*, 907.

7. A CONDITION AGAINST CHANGE OF POSSESSION BY LEGAL PROCESS is broken when an officer takes possession of the property by virtue of a writ of attachment issued according to law, even though it afterwards appears that there was no ground for issuing such writ. *Carey* v. *German-American Ins. Co.*, 907.

8. ORAL WAIVER OF FORFEITURE, WHEN INEFFECTUAL.—If it is expressly stipulated by the parties to a contract of insurance that "no officer of the company shall be held to have waived any of the terms and conditions of the policy, unless such waiver shall be indorsed thereon in writing," an oral waiver of a forfeiture is a nullity. *Carey* v. *German-American Ins. Co.*, 907.

9. NOTICE ON FORFEITURE OF POLICY, WHEN NOT NECESSARY.—If a clause in a policy provides that "it shall be void" upon the breach of a specified condition, the insurer's exemption from liability becomes absolutely fixed as soon as that condition is broken, and does not depend upon whether he notifies, or omits to notify, the insured, after such breach, what action he intends to take in regard to the continuance or forfeiture of the policy. *Carey v. German-American Ins. Co.*, 907.

See ADVANCEMENTS, 2; ATTACHMENT, 12; CUSTOM, 3; VENDOR AND PUR-
CHASER.

INTEREST.

See DISCOUNT; STATUTES, 5; USURY.

INTERSTATE COMMERCE.

1. INTERSTATE AND DOMESTIC COMMERCE—RIGHT TO REGULATE.—To constitute interstate commerce there must be traffic and interstate intercourse between different states, and the power vested in Congress to
regulate interstate commerce does not authorize it to regulate the
domestic commerce between the citizens of the same state or different
parts thereof. This latter power belongs to the several states alone,
exclusive of the power of Congress. *State v. Harrub*, 195.

2. WHAT IS NOT.—One who maintains a store for the purpose of carrying on
business in this state is not entitled to immunity as being engaged in interstate commerce on the ground that he is the agent of a nonresident
manufacturer of the goods which are kept for sale. *Commonwealth v.
Schollenberger*, 32.

3. WHAT IS NOT.—If a nonresident comes into the state to embark in
business, his situation is like that of any other resident, and his business
done at his store is state, not interstate. It does not matter where he
obtains his goods. Men who buy and sell foreign merchandise are not
necessarily engaged in interstate commerce. *Commonwealth v. Schollenberger*, 32.

4. AN ORIGINAL PACKAGE IS SUCH FORM AND SIZE OF PACKAGE as is used
by producers or shippers for the purpose of securing both convenience in
handling and security of transportation of merchandise between dealers
in the ordinary course of actual commerce. *Commonwealth v. Schollenberger*, 32.

5. OLEOMARGARINE—ORIGINAL PACKAGES.—A sale of oleomargarine, otherwise in violation of a state law, is not protected as a part of interstate
commerce by proof that it was made, stamped, and printed in another
state for use as an article of food, weighed eighty pounds, and was sold
in the form in which the maker put it up at his factory in such other
state, and that the person making the sale was his agent in this state,
having and maintaining a store here for the purpose of effecting such
sales. *Commonwealth v. Schollenberger*, 32.

6. LICENSE TAX, WHEN DEEMED ATTEMPTED REGULATION OF.—A statute
providing that "all express companies doing business in this state shall
be required to pay a license-tax of five hundred dollars per annum where
the distance over which the lines of such companies operate or extend
in this state is less than one hundred miles, and the annual sum of one
thousand dollars where the distance is more than one hundred miles,"
imposes a tax upon the privilege of transacting business within the state,
and, as regards express companies operating between this and other
states, is invalid as an attempt to regulate interstate commerce. *Commonwealth v. Smith*, 578.

7. INVALIDITY OF TAX ON AGENCIES OF.—A tax may be levied by a state
upon the property of a foreign corporation within its boundaries,
although that corporation is an agency of interstate commerce, but a

statute imposing a tax which is essentially a burden upon the business
of such a corporation, is an attempted exercise of a power belonging to
the national government, and must be held invalid. *Commonwealth* v.
Smith, 578.

**8. Tax on Property of Telegraph Companies, When Deemed an
Attempted Regulation of.**—A revenue law providing that, at a
certain time in each year, the managing officer of "any telegraph company, working, operating, or controlling any telegraph line in this
state," shall "pay into the treasury a tax equal to one dollar per mile
for the line of poles and first wire, and fifty cents per mile for each
additional wire," imposes a tax on the business, not on the property, of
the companies affected, and if those companies are agencies of interstate commerce, the law is invalid as being an attempted exercise of a
power belonging exclusively to the federal legislature. *Commonwealth*
v. *Smith*, 578.

9. Oysters—State Control Over.—A state, through its legislature, may
confine the taking and use of its oysters to its own citizens, and regulate
their shipment and disposition within its borders for the use of such
citizens so as to prevent such oysters from becoming an article of interstate commerce. *State* v. *Harrub*, 195.

10. Oysters—State Control Over.—A state has the right by statute to
license its own citizens to catch and take the oysters within its borders,
and to deny to citizens of another state the right to take and transport
them, and to absolutely prohibit their shipment beyond its borders,
and to regulate their sale therein, not imposing any conditions, burdens,
or restrictions upon the oyster as a commodity after it has entered
another state or after it is legally delivered in the home state for
exportation by any of the means by which interstate commerce is
effected. *State* v. *Harrub*, 195.

**11. Oysters—State Control Over—When Become Article of Inter-
state Commerce.**—A state has the right by statute to limit the exportation of oysters taken within its borders to such as may have been
shelled before shipment, and when the statute so provides the oyster
cannot become an article of interstate commerce while in the shell.
State v. *Harrub*, 195.

INVENTIONS.

See Receivers, 3.

IRRIGATION COMPANIES.

1. Waters—Status of Irrigation Company.—An irrigation or canal company is not the proprietor of the water diverted by it, but is only an intermediate agency, existing for the purpose of aiding consumers in the
exercise of their constitutional rights, as well as a private enterprise prosecuted for the benefit of its owners. *Wyatt* v. *Larimer etc. Irr. Co.*,
280.

2. Waters—Construction of Contract for.—Under a contract between
an irrigation ditch company and water-takers by which each taker has the
right to a definite amount of water, and providing that the sale of water
rights shall terminate when the outstanding rights shall equal the estimated capacity of the ditch, and giving the company the power to distribute the waters flowing through its ditch *pro rata*, among existing
water-takers, if from any cause the supply shall become inadequate to
furnish an amount equal to then outstanding rights, the company's

power to dispose of water rights is limited by the furnishing capacity of the ditch as dependent upon the source of supply or other circumstances and not by its carrying capacity. *Wyatt v. Larimer etc. Irr. Co.*, 280.

See CONTRACTS, 4, 5; WATERS, 3, 4, 9.

JOINT LIABILITY.

JOINT DEBTORS—RELEASE OF ONE OF SEVERAL—CONSIDERATION.—An agreement between the holder of a note and one of the joint makers thereof that upon payment of one-half of the note by such maker the holder will probate it against the estate of the other maker to recover the remaining half is void for want of consideration; and a failure to so probate the note is no defense to a suit on a judgment for the balance of the note recovered against such joint maker. *Davidson v. Burke*, 367.

JOINT TENANCY.

See HUSBAND AND WIFE, 4.

JUDGES.

See JUDGMENTS, 1.

JUDGMENTS.

1. **JUDGMENT BY DISQUALIFIED JUDGE.**—In an action to declare a judgment participated in by a disqualified and interested judge a nullity, the fact that the major portion of the members of the court were disinterested, and that a large number of parties litigant, other than such disqualified judge, were interested in, and would be affected by, such judgment is not without weight. *Board of Commissioners v. Justice*, 528.

2. **JUDGMENTS UPON CONSTRUCTIVE SERVICE OF PROCESS—WARNING ORDER, REQUISITES OF.**—The omission of the name of the defendant's postoffice in the affidavit upon which the warning order is made will not invalidate a judgment rendered upon constructive service of process. *Carr v. Carr*, 614.

3. **JUDGMENTS UPON CONSTRUCTIVE SERVICE OF PROCESS.—THE PREMATURE HEARING** of an action commenced by publication of summons will not invalidate the judgment rendered therein. *Carr v. Carr*, 614.

4. **JUDGMENT LIENS—WHETHER ATTACH TO LANDS FRAUDULENTLY CONVEYED.**—When a debtor conveys his property in fraud of creditors, before the rendition of judgment against him, by a conveyance valid between the parties to it, such judgment does not create a lien on such property by operation of law. *Davidson v. Burke*, 367.

5. **JUDGMENT LIENS—WHEN LOST BY NEGLECT.**—When statutes prescribe the time during which judgment shall have the force of liens on the land of judgment debtors, one who has neglected to enforce his judgment lien in proper time will not in equity be relieved from the consequences of his neglect. *Davidson v. Burke*, 367.

6. **FORMER DECISION WHEN NOT RES JUDICATA.**—It will not be presumed that the supreme court adjudicated a question not before it in a former case, not affecting the rights of the same parties, and collateral thereto, so as to make that decision a rule of the case upon new questions thereafter arising between other parties. *O'Brien v. Moffitt*, 566.

7. **RES JUDICATA—WHERE SEVERAL DEFENSES ARE PLEADED**, upon all of which evidence is given, a general verdict in favor of the defendant fol-

lowed by a judgment thereon, is at least *prima facie* evidence that all
the issues were found in his favor. Therefore if in an action of trespass
quare clausum fregit against a city for removing soil from an alleged
street, the defendant pleaded 1, that the *locus in quo* is a public highway;
2, the statute of limitations; 3, that the *locus in quo* is the property of
the defendant, and evidence was offered by both parties on all the issues,
and a general verdict entered in favor of the defendant, such verdict
is in a subsequent action between the same parties, *prima facie* evidence
that all the issues were found in favor of the defendant. *Rhoads* v.
Metropolis, 468.

8. JUDGMENTS OF SISTER SATES—BURDEN OF PROOF IN ACTION ON.—If a
judgment of another state is offered in evidence, the burden of proof is
upon the party who relies upon it, to show that it is valid according
to the laws of the state within whose jurisdiction it was pronounced.
Thomas v. *Pendleton*, 726.

9. JUDGMENTS OF SISTER STATES—COMPLAINT IN ACTION ON.—A complaint
upon a judgment recovered in another state containing a copy of a note
and power of attorney upon which the judgment was rendered before
the maturity of the note is insufficient in the absence of any allegation
of law authorizing the rendition of such judgment, to sustain an attachment issued upon an affidavit stating no ground of claim except by
reference to such complaint. *Thomas* v. *Pendleton*, 726.

10. VACATING FOR—ATTORNEY'S MISTAKE.—If a defendant having a meritorious defense, relying upon the erroneous advice of his attorney,
allows a judgment by default to be rendered against him, his failure
to answer in time may be excused, and the judgment set aside so as to
allow him to answer, when he acts promptly, and none of the parties
are prejudiced by reopening the judgment. *Baxter* v. *Chute*, 633.

11. VACATING DEFAULTS—IMPOSING TERMS.—A court can modify a default
judgment by depriving it of its ordinary character as *res judicata* and
leave it in full force as a lien, or collateral security, for any judgment
finally recovered. *Griswold Linseed Oil Co.* v. *Lee*, 761.

12. VACATING DEFAULTS—IMPOSING TERMS.—A court may, upon opening a judgment rendered by default, impose, in addition to costs as
terms, that the judgment stand as security for any judgment finally
recovered, in the absence of a good and sufficient bond for the payment
of such final judgment. *Griswold Linseed Oil Co.* v. *Lee*, 761.

13. VACATING DEFAULTS—DISCRETION OF COURT.—The granting of applications for relief from judgments by default is entirely within the discretion of the court to which application is made. *Griswold Linseed Oil
Co.* v. *Lee*, 761.

14. VACATING DEFAULTS—RELIEF WHEN GRANTED.—A judgment by default
should be opened and leave given to answer upon prompt application
therefor, and a good and sufficient showing of mistake, inadvertence,
surprise, or excusable neglect, together with an affidavit of merits stating that the applicant *prima facie* has a good defense and makes the
application in good faith. *Griswold Linseed Oil Co.* v. *Lee*, 761.

15. VACATING DEFAULTS—EVIDENCE.—On the hearing of an application
to set aside a judgment rendered by default, and for leave to answer, the evidence is confined to the question whether or not the
judgment has been taken through the inadvertence, mistake, surprise,
or excusable neglect of the defendant. He is not required to make
more than such a *prima facie* showing on the merits as arises from his

own affidavits; and evidence to controvert the merits of his defense is irrelevant to the issue, and inadmissible. *Griswold Linseed Oil Co. v. Lee*, 761.

See APPEAL, 5; AWARD, 1; COURTS; CREDITOR'S SUIT; HOMESTEADS, 6; JURISDICTION, 4–6; MARRIAGE AND DIVORCE, 2; MORTGAGES, 9.

JURISDICTION.

1. JURISDICTION OF SUPREME COURT may be invoked upon an appeal from a judgment of the district court or of the court of appeals in actions that relate to a freehold. *Wyatt v. Larimer etc. Irr. Co.*, 280.

2. EFFECT OF.—When judicial tribunals have no jurisdiction of the subject matter on which they assume to act, their proceedings are absolutely void, but when they have jurisdiction of the subject matter, irregularity, or illegality in their proceedings does not render them void, but merely voidable. *Town of Wayne v. Caldwell*, 750.

3. WHEN NOT ACQUIRED.—An appellate court acquires no jurisdiction of a question of damages to be awarded in laying out a public highway, when such highway is illegally laid out, on the ground that the proceeding of the lower tribunal in establishing such road are void for a failure to comply with statutory requirements. *Town of Wayne v. Caldwell*, 750.

4. RIGHT OF COURT TO DETERMINE.—A court which is competent to decide on its own jurisdiction in a given case can determine that question at any time in the proceedings, whenever that fact is made to appear to its satisfaction, either before or after judgment. *Town of Wayne v. Caldwell*, 750.

5. ATTACHMENT—SERVICE BY PUBLICATION.—If property is attached and the defendant served by publication only the court has jurisdiction to render a judgment personal in form, but affecting only the property attached. *Neufelder v. German American Ins. Co.*, 166.

6. WATERS—FREEHOLD IN—JURISDICTION.—An action to enjoin a permanent diminution of a perpetual right to have a certain quantity of water flow through an irrigation ditch involves a freehold, and the supreme court has jurisdiction to review the judgment in such action on appeal. *Wyatt v. Larimer etc. Irr. Co.*, 280.

7. WAIVER OF BY STIPULATION.—Mere irrregularities in judicial proceedings may be waived by stipulation, but no such waiver can confer jurisdiction on any tribunal having no jurisdiction of the subject matter of the action. *Town of Wayne v. Caldwell*, 750.

See CHARITIES, 4.

JURY AND JURORS.
See TRIAL, 3.

JURY TRIAL.
See REFORM SCHOOLS, 4.

JUSTICES OF THE PEACE.
See REFORM SCHOOLS, 1–4.

KINDRED.
See DESCENT.

KNOWLEDGE.

See CORPORATIONS, 6; FRAUD, 3; MORTGAGES, 12.

LACHES.

See ATTORNEY AND CLIENT, 15.

LANDLORD AND TENANT.

1. DESTRUCTION OF PREMISES—RECOVERY OF RENT PAID IN ADVANCE.—A tenant in possession of premises for which he pays a monthly rental in advance is entitled to recover the amount paid for that part of the month remaining after the total destruction of the premises by fire or otherwise. *Porter* v. *Tull*, 172.

2. FORFEITURE OF LEASEHOLD INTEREST IN LAND is not implied nor favored in law. *Williams* v. *Vanderbilt*, 486.

3. WAIVER OF FORFEITURE OF LEASE—EFFECT ON MECHANIC'S LIEN. Although generallyy an act done by a landlord knowing of a cause of forfeiture by his tenant, affirming the existence of the lease and recognizing the lessee as his tenant, is a waiver of such forfeiture, yet a landlord with such knowledge and also knowledge that the premises are undergoing repairs under the direction of the lessee, but with no reason to believe that the latter is not able to pay his debts, is not obliged to assume that the employees will not receive their money from the lessee, and declare an immediate forfeiture to save himself from liability under a mechanic's lien. *Williams* v. *Vanderbilt*, 486.

4. IMPROVEMENTS—EQUITABLE LIEN FOR AFTER FORFEITURE OF LEASE.— A party who repairs buildings on leased premises under a contract with the tenant, but without authority or contract express or implied from the landlord to pay therefor, is not entitled to an equitable lien on the premises for the value of the improvements, if the lease is declared forfeited for nonpayment of rent as provided for therein, subsequent to the time when the improvements are completed. *Williams* v. *Vanderbilt*, 486.

5. FORFEITURE OF LEASE—A DEMAND FOR RENT on the day it falls due is not necessary in order to cause a forfeiture of the lease. The lessor may declare a forfeiture on some subsequent day. *Williams* v. *Vanderbilt*, 486.

6. ONE LESSEE CANNOT DESTROY RIGHTS of his co-lessees nor extinguish their title by conveying to his lessor. *Williams* v. *Vanderbilt*, 486.

7. SURRENDER of written lease may be made by parol, by abandonment of the premises by the tenant and entry by the landlord, or by an executed agreement to surrender. *Williams* v. *Vanderbilt*, 486.

8. SURRENDER OF LEASED PREMISES operates from the execution of a new lease with the tenant's consent to another who enters thereunder and pays rent, or from an agreement, either express or implied, to release the original lessee and accept a new tenant, or from an actual and continued change of possession by the mutual consent of the parties *Williams* v. *Vanderbilt*, 486.

9. ASSUMPSIT—CONSTRUCTIVE NOTICE OF MATERIAL FACT, WHEN NOT AN ESTOPPEL.—If a landowner has taken water to a mill, and leased it in connection therewith, the lessee is entitled, in the absence of actual notice, to infer that there is no restriction upon the water rights, and mere constructive notice from the record of a deed limiting those rights

will not estop him from recovering rent which he has paid to the lessor in the belief that no such limitations existed. *Bedell* v. *Wilder*, 871.

10. ASSUMPSIT—RECOVERY OF RENT BY LESSEE UPON FAILURE OF LESSOR'S TITLE.—Where a lessee, after accepting a lease of land and water rights, discovers that another person lays claim to the water rights, and the lessor thereupon insists that he is entitled to the rent, but promises to do "whatever his contract calls upon him to do," and, if the contract requires it, "to stand between the lessee and the other claimant," the rent which the lessee is afterwards forced to pay to such claimant, when the proprietorship of the water rights has been established, may be recovered from the lessor. *Bedell* v. *Wilder*, 871.

See MECHANIC'S LIEN, 7–16.

LARCENY.

1. CONSENT.—To CONSTITUTE LARCENY there must be a trespass, that is, a taking of property without the consent of the owner, coupled with an intent to steal the property so taken; and the crime is not committed, when, with the consent of the owner, his property is taken, however guilty may be the taker's purpose and intent. *Connor* v. *People*, 295.

2. DECOYING INTO CRIME.—Larceny is not committed when property is taken with the consent of the owner, although such consent is given for the purpose of decoying and entrapping the party suspected, and the latter, when taking the property, did not know of the consent which prevented the criminal quality from attaching to the act. *Connor* v. *People*, 295.

3. EVIDENCE—CHARACTER OF AMBIGUOUS TRANSACTION, WHEN MAY BE SHOWN BY PROOF OF OTHER CRIMES.—On a trial for larceny, in which the only direct evidence for the state consists of the narrative of an accomplice, which, as regards the act set forth in the indictment, leaves room for a reasonable doubt as to the felonious participation of the defendant, such participation may be established by other portions of the same narrative showing that, on the same expedition during which the larceny is alleged to have been committed, the defendant had actively engaged in abstracting other personal property from various places, and by the testimony of the owners of the stolen articles that they were in the places from which the accomplice asserts them to have been taken, were missed about the time at which the accomplice said the expedition took place, and were afterwards found and identified on the defendant's premises. But evidence of a larceny committed by the defendant and his accomplice during a second expedition, undertaken upon the renewal of a purpose entertained before the first expedition, has no legitimate tendency to support the charge, and should be excluded. *State* v. *Kelley*, 884.

See APPEAL, 3.

LEASE.

See CHATTEL MORTGAGES, 1, 3; LANDLORD AND TENANT; MECHANIC'S LIEN, 7–10.

LEGISLATURE.

CONSTITUTIONAL LAW.—THE LEGISLATURE POSSESSES THE WHOLE LEGISLATIVE POWER of the people, except so far as such power may be limited by the constitution. *People* v. *Cannon*, 665.

See MECHANIC'S LIEN, 5.

LEVY.

LICENSE.

LICENSE TO ENTER PREMISES IN CASE OF FIRE.—In case of fire in a building the public authorities, fire-patrol men, or private parties may enter upon adjacent premises, as they may find it necessary or convenient, in their efforts to extinguish or to arrest the spread of the flames, and though they have no permission to enter they have an implied license by law to do so in order to save the property. *Gibson* v. *Leonard*, 376.

LIENS.

CREDITOR'S BILL—LIEN CREATED BY.—The filing of a creditor's bill and the service of process creates an equitable lien upon lands fraudulently conveyed by the judgment debtor, and when the creditor has no lien on the property sought to be reached it is the filing of the bill in equity after the return of the execution at law which gives him a specific lien. In such case the *lis pendens* is an equitable levy, and creates an equitable lien on the lands, and it is wholly unimportant that the final decree establishing the lien and ordering a sale is not rendered until long after the judgment at law has ceased to be a lien, by force of the statute upon the real estate of the judgment debtor. *Davidson* v. *Burke*, 367.

LIMITATIONS OF ACTIONS.

1. WHEN WILL RUN AGAINST MUNICIPALITIES.—The statute of limitations runs against municipal corporations such as cities, towns or counties, except as to the property devoted to a public use, or held upon a public trust, and contracts and rights of a public nature. *City of Bedford* v. *Willard*, 563.

2. WHEN RUNS AGAINST LAND OWNED BY MUNICIPALITY.—When land is held by a county in its private capacity, subject to sale by it to private individuals, and is by it conveyed to a city, the statute of limitations runs against both county and city in favor of an adverse holder for the statutory period. *City of Bedford* v. *Willard*, 563.

3. IF AFTER THE DIVORCE OF A HUSBAND AND WIFE lands which they before held as tenants by the entireties are sold under an execution against him, and the purchasers take and maintain possession of the whole thereof, claiming title adversely to the wife, her right to maintain an action for the recovery of such land is barred by the statute of limitations of Tennessee, if she has not brought such action within five years after such adverse possession began. *Hopson* v. *Fowlkes*, 120.

4. RESIDENCE OUT OF STATE.—When one has an established residence within the state he can only "depart from and reside outside the state" by changing his residence and taking up an actual residence elsewhere, as distinguished from a temporary sojourn, and the fact that he departs from and remains out of the state for some considerable time without changing his permanent place of residence does not interrupt the running of the statute of limitations. *Kerwin* v. *Sabin*. 645.

RÉSIDENCE OUT OF STATE.—A Congressman who leaves his home in the occupancy of servants during sessions of Congress and then resides with his family in rented premises at the national capital, returning to and occupying his permanent home during congressional recesses, without intending to change his place of residence, does not at any time reside out of the state so as to interrupt the running of the statute of limitations. *Kerwin v. Sabin*, 645.

See TAXES, 3.

LIS PENDENS.
See LIENS.

LOTTERIES.

1. WHAT IS.—A lottery is a scheme by which, on one's paying money or some other thing of value, he obtains the contingent right to have something of greater value, if an appeal to chance, by lot or otherwise, under the direction of the manager of the scheme, should decide in his favor. A valuable consideration must be paid, directly or indirectly, for a chance to draw a prize by lot, to bring the transaction within the class of lotteries or gift enterprises that the law prohibits as criminal. *Cross v. People*, 292.

2. WHAT DOES NOT CONSTITUTE.—A gratuitous distribution of property by lot or chance, if not resorted to as a device to evade the law, and no consideration is derived directly or indirectly from the party receiving the chance, does not constitute a lottery prohibited by law. *Cross v. People*, 292.

3. WHAT DOES NOT CONSTITUTE.—The gratuitous distribution of business cards to purchasers and nonpurchasers alike which entitle the holders to a chance in a drawing for a piano to be determined as the holders of such chances might elect is not a lottery prohibited by law. *Cross v. People*, 292.

4. CONSIDERATION FOR CHANCE.—The fact that chances in a drawing for a piano are gratuitously and indiscriminately given away to induce people to visit a certain store with the expectation that they may purchase goods and thereby increase trade is a benefit too remote to constitute a consideration for the chances and make it a lottery prohibited by law. *Cross v. People*, 292.

MALICE.
See ATTACHMENT, 4, 6, 8.

MANDAMUS.

1. OFFICE AND OFFICERS—MANDAMUS WILL LIE TO COMPEL ACCEPTANCE of a municipal office by one who, possessing the requisite qualifications, refuses to accept the office after he has been duly elected or appointed thereto. *People v. Williams*, 514.

2. OFFICE AND OFFICERS—MANDAMUS TO COMPEL ACCEPTANCE OF OFFICE. One elected to an office owes a duty to the public to qualify himself therefor, and to enter upon the discharge of his duties, and upon a refusal so to do he may be compelled by *mandamus* to assume the office and take upon himself the duties thereof, although he is also subject to indictment or fine for a failure to do so. *People v. Williams*, 514.

3. MANDAMUS TO COMPEL ACCEPTANCE OF OFFICE.—A person duly elected or appointed to a public municipal office who refuses to qualify and assume the duties of such office upon notice of his election or appointment may be compelled to do so by writ of *mandamus*, without any formal demand upon him to accept the office, notwithstanding the fact that a statute provides a penalty for his refusal to accept. *People* v. *Williams*, 514.

MARKETS.

POWER OF COURTS TO DECLARE THEM TO BE PUBLIC.—If a market has not been established by municipal authority or by virtue of a market franchise by the state such market cannot be deemed, merely because of the magnitude of the business carried on therein, to be impressed with a public use, so as to be held by the courts to be a public market in that sense, and subject to the rules of a public policy peculiar to that class of markets. *American Live Stock Co.* v. *Chicago Live Stock Exchange*, 385.

MARRIAGE AND DIVORCE.

1. DIVORCE—ALIMONY—LEWD LIFE AS BAR TO.—A wife who leads a lewd life, yielding her person to the embraces of different men, has no claim upon her husband for support and maintenance or alimony when divorce is granted to the husband on account of her misconduct. A court abuses its discretion in granting the wife alimony in such a case. *Spaulding* v. *Spaulding*, 534.

2. JUDGMENT OF DIVORCE, WHEN WILL NOT BE VACATED ON PETITION. When a woman who has been divorced on the ground of desertion brings suit after her husband's death to recover a widow's part of his estate, averring that the decree of divorce is a nullity for the reason that she had no notice of the proceedings against her, and that, although she abandoned her husband, she was forced to do so by his cruel treatment, and, issue having been joined on these averments, it appears not only that she had actual knowledge of the pendency of the proceedings, but that, if she had made her defense, her husband would have been entitled to a decree in his favor, the equity of the case is against her, and the judgment of divorce, even if erroneous, cannot be reopened and vacated upon a petition in a court of chancery. *Carr* v. *Carr*, 614.

See DOWER, 1; HUSBAND AND WIFE, 1.

MARRIED WOMEN.

See INFANTS, 4, 5.

MASTER AND SERVANT.

See DAMAGES, 3; NEGLIGENCE, 5–8; RAILROADS, 15; SURETYSHIP, 13.

MECHANIC'S LIEN.

1. NOTICE OF CLAIM.—A notice of a mechanic's lien, describing the property as all of a certain lot except the west twenty feet thereof, is insufficient when the building also occupies a portion of another lot, although it is also described by a certain name and as being located at the northwest corner of two streets. *Whittier* v. *Stetson etc. Mill Co.*, 149.

2. NOTICE OF CLAIM—MISTAKE IN.—A mechanic's lien for material used in a building constructed by owners of adjoining lots, under one contract, the material being furnished under the supposition that it is for the entire building as the property of the owner against whom the claim is filed, is not void because it covers some material not used in the part of the building described, but used in the part belonging to the other owner. The claimant has a valid lien for the material furnished for and used in the part of the building described, and may recover therefor against the party named in the claim by remitting for the remainder not used in his part of the building. *Whittier* v. *Stetson etc. Mill Co.*, 149.

3. NOTICE OF CLAIM—INSUFFICIENCY OF DESCRIPTION of property in one part of a mechanic's lien claim is cured by a description in correct form in a subsequent part of such claim. *Whittier* v. *Stetson etc. Mill Co.*, 149.

4. MECHANIC'S LIEN LAW, CONSTRUCTION OF.—While a mechanic's lien law is favored and the remedial laws for its enforcement should be liberally construed, they should not be so construed as to include persons not enumerated in the statute. *Thompson* v. *Baxter*, 85.

5. CONSTRUCTION OF.—A statute creating a right to a mechanic's lien is in derogation of the common law, and must receive a strict construction. It must not be applied to cases which do not fall within its provisions. If they are not broad enough, it is the province of the legislature to extend them. *Williams* v. *Vanderbilt*, 486.

6. TO WHAT INTEREST ATTACHES.—The party with whom the contract is made by a person furnishing labor or materials, is regarded as the owner of the premises only to the extent of his interest, and that interest only is subject to a mechanic's lien. Hence a tenant for life or years cannot, by contract, create a lien upon the fee, on the contrary he can create a lien only to the extent of his right and interest in the premises. *Williams* v. *Vanderbilt*, 486.

7. MECHANIC'S LIEN ON LEASEHOLD.—A material-man's lien for making, altering, or repairing a building under a contract made with the lessee of the premises extends to the leasehold interest only. *Williams* v. *Vanderbilt*, 486.

8. MECHANIC'S LIEN ON LEASEHOLD—REPAIRS—CONSTRUCTION OF STATUTE. A statute conferring a mechanic's lien upon a leasehold interest in land, must be construed with reference to the common-law rule, that the burden of repairs is cast upon the tenant, and that the landlord is under no implied obligation to make them. *Williams* v. *Vanderbilt*, 486.

9. MECHANIC'S LIEN ATTACHING TO LEASEHOLD ESTATE is subject to all conditions of the lease, and may be defeated by a forfeiture under the express conditions thereof. *Williams* v. *Vanderbilt*, 486.

10. MECHANIC'S LIEN ON LEASEHOLD—SUBJECT TO ARREARS OF RENT.—When a lease for years has been forfeited for nonpayment of rent under the express conditions of the lease, a holder of a mechanic's lien upon the premises must pay all arrears of rent to the lessor before he can acquire the rights of the lessee thereunder, even by purchase. *Williams* v. *Vanderbilt*, 486.

11. A SUPERVISING ARCHITECT employed to draw plans and specifications, solicit bids for, and to supervise the construction of, a building is not entitled to a lien thereon under the statute conferring a right to a lien on all persons doing any portion of the work, or furnishing any portion of the material, in the construction of a house or other building. *Thompson* v. *Baxter*, 85.

12. A SUBCONTRACTOR'S RIGHT TO FILE A LIEN CANNOT BE DESTROYED except by an express covenant against liens by either the contractor or

subcontractor, or such a covenant so clearly implied that a mechanic or material-man cannot fail to understand it. *Cresswell Iron Works v. O'Brien,* 30.

12. A SUBCONTRACTOR IS NOT PRECLUDED FROM OBTAINING A LIEN by a provision in the principal contract that the contractor will not suffer or permit any lien by any person to be put and remain upon the building, and that any such lien, until it is removed, shall preclude any and all claim and demand for any payment under this contract, and that the last installment shall not be payable unless, in addition to the architect's certificate, a full release of all claims and liens for all work done and all materials furnished has been delivered by the contractor. *Cress. well Iron Works v, O'Brien,* 30.

14. PROCESS—SERVICE AS COMMENCEMENT OF ACTION TO PRESERVE LIEN.— In an action to enforce a mechanic's lien service of summons on the owner of the premises within two years, as prescribed by statute, will not preserve the lien as against other defendant lienholders, not served with summons until after the expiration of the two years. *Smith v. Hurd,* 661.

15. PROCESS—SERVICE AS COMMENCEMENT OF ACTION TO FORECLOSE MECHANIC'S LIEN.—One entitled to defend against a mechanic's lien may show that it is not a lien against his interest because the lien has expired or the remedy upon it has been lost by lapse of time before the action was commenced as to him. *Smith v. Hurd,* 661.

See LANDLORD AND TENANT, 3.

MINORS.

See INFANTS; REFORM SCHOOLS.

MISDEMEANOR.

See CONSPIRACY, 2; STATUTES, 5; USURY.

MISREPRESENTATION.

See FRAUD, 2, 4; MORTGAGES, 4.

MISTAKE.

WHEN AVOIDS CONTRACT.—A contract induced by a mutual mistake in respect to the subject matter is inoperative, and void. *Bedell v. Wilder,* 871.

See EVIDENCE, 7; IMPROVEMENTS, 2; JUDGMENTS, 10, 14, 15; MECHANIC'S LIEN, 2.

MORTGAGES.

1. MORTGAGEE IN POSSESSION.—One who enters into the possession of property under a mortgage foreclosure, defective in not making the owner of the fee a party thereto, is entitled to the rights of a mortgagee in possession, and cannot be ousted by an action of ejectment brought by the owner of the fee whose title is subject to such mortgage. His remedy is by a suit to foreclose his equity of redemption by an equitable action to redeem from the mortgage. *Croner v. Cowdrey,* 716.

2. UNRECORDED MORTGAGES—EFFECT OF ON CREDITORS.—When by statute unrecorded mortgages are to be deemed, as an inference of law, fraudu-

MUNICIPAL CORPORATIONS.

similar vaults, and that the vault will not be removed unless public convenience or necessity requires it, and under a bond executed by himself that he will keep such street or alley forever in repair, and save and keep the city harmless from all loss or damage by reason of its being out of repair, the permit and bond together constitute a contract between the parties founded upon a sufficient consideration, securing rights mutually advantageous to both, and is not revocable by the city unless the public interest or convenience demands it, or the holder of the permit fails to perform his covenants, or some one of them, and the city cannot at will revoke such permit for the benefit of some other person who is sought to be invested with a similar permit. *Gregsten* v. *Chicago*, 496.

5. CONSTITUTIONAL LAW—ORDINANCE REGULATING STREET PARADES, WHEN VOID.—A municipal ordinance which declares that "it shall be unlawful for any person or persons, society, association, or organization, to march or parade" upon certain streets of a city, "shouting, singing, or beating drums or tambourines, or playing upon any other musical instrument, for the purpose of advertising or attracting the attention of the public, or to the disturbance of the public peace or quiet, without first having obtained a permission to so march or parade, signed by the mayor of said city," or, "in case of the mayor's illness or absence," by other specified officials, and which further provides that "this section shall not apply to funerals, fire companies, nor regularly organized companies of the state militia," and that "permission to march or parade shall at no time be refused to any political party having a regular organization," not only creates by its express terms unjust discriminations between the persons and organizations referred to, but also vests the mayor or his substitutes with arbitrary power to create other equally unjust discriminations in carrying out its provisions, and is therefore void, as being an enactment which contravenes the fourteenth amendment of the constitution of the United States. *State* v. *Dering*, 948.

6. WHEN BOUND BY CONTRACT.—A city, when acting in its private capacity as contradistinguished from its governmental capacity, is bound by its contracts, and may be estopped by the conduct of its proper officers when acting within the lawful scope of their powers. *Gresten* v. *Chicago*, 496.

7. IF A MUNICIPAL CORPORATION ENTERS IN A CONTRACT WHICH IS ULTRA VIRES such contract is void. *Nashville* v. *Sutherland*, 88.

8. MUNICIPAL CORPORATION CANNOT ASSUME LIABILITY FOR NEGLIGENCE where none is imposed by law. *Nashville* v. *Sutherland*, 88.

9. MUNICIPAL CORPORATIONS ARE LIABLE ONLY FOR THE ABSENCE OF REASONABLE CAUTION AND SKILL in the execution of work, and their officers cannot lawfully contract to bind them beyond this without express charter authority. Therefore, so much of a contract purporting to be executed by a city as stipulates that it will have a sewer so constructed with a suitable valve as will prevent, in case of high floods, the flowing back of water from the river through such sewer, is *ultra vires*, and void, because its effect is to make the city answerable as insurer against any damage to result by reason of overflow through this valve and pipe. *Nashville* v. *Sutherland*, 88.

10. NEGLIGENCE—PROXIMATE AND REMOTE CAUSE.—Where water accumulates in a hole in a sidewalk and forms a sheet of ice on which a traveler falls, the ice, and not the hole, is the proximate cause of the accident, and the city is not liable for the injuries thereby sustained. *Chamberlain* v. *Oshkosh,* 928.

11. LIABILITY FOR SLIPPERY SIDEWALKS.—To render a city liable for injuries resulting from a fall upon a sidewalk which has become dangerous to travelers through the formation of a smooth and slippery surface of ice thereon, it is necessary that some other defect should have combined with the ice to cause the injury. *Chamberlain* v. *Oskhosh,* 928.

12. LIABILITY FOR DEFECTS IN SIDEWALKS.—It is the duty of a city which allows a house-owner to maintain a hatchway in a sidewalk to see to it that such hatchway is so located and constructed as not to be unnecessarily insecure for persons passing when it is open, and it is therefore not error in an action for injuries caused by falling into a hatchway, to submit to the jury the question whether the sidewalk was defective by reason of the improper location of such hatchway. *McClure* v. *Sparta,* 924.

13. A MUNICIPAL CORPORATION IS ANSWERABLE FOR INJURIES TO PROPERTY FROM A DISPLAY OF FIREWORKS in the public streets of a densely populated part of the city, if such display was sanctioned by permit from the mayor, purporting to be authorized by one of its ordinances, though the ordinance may have transcended the powers of the common council, or may not have sanctioned the permit granted, if it had been generally understood and acted upon as if authorizing such permit. *Spier* v. *Brooklyn,* 664.

14. A MUNICIPAL CORPORATION DIRECTING OR AUTHORIZING THE DISCHARGE OF FIREWORKS in the public streets under such circumstances as to create a public nuisance is liable to any person who, without any fault on his part, is injured thereby. *Speir* v. *Brooklyn,* 664.

15. A MUNICIPAL CORPORATION MAY COMMIT AN ACTIONABLE WRONG and become liable for a tort. *Speir* v. *Brooklyn,* 664.

16. A MUNICIPAL CORPORATION FOR A MISTAKE IN THE EXERCISE OF ITS POWERS, OR FOR ACTING IN EXCESS of its powers upon any subject within its jurisdiction, is answerable to a third person injured thereby. *Speir* v. *Brooklyn,* 664.

See COUNTIES; ELECTRIC LIGHT COMPANIES; EQUITY, 1; INJUNCTIONS, 1, 2; LIMITATIONS OF ACTIONS, 1, 2; MANDAMUS; MARKETS; NEGLIGENCE, 4; WATERS, 6.

NAVIGATION.
See GAME LAWS; WHARVES, 1.

NEGLIGENCE.

1. WHEN ACTIONABLE.—Actionable negligence grows only out of a want of ordinary care and skill in respect to a person to whom the defendant is under obligation or duty to exercise such care and skill. *Gibson* v. *Leonard,* 376.

2. NEGLIGENCE MUST BE CAUSE OF INJURY.—When negligence in the breach of a city ordinance does not cause, or contribute to cause, the injury complained of no action will lie on account of such breach. *Gibson* v. *Leonard,* 376.

3. EVIDENCE that the defendant in an action to recover damages for personal injuries has adopted, since the occurrence of the accident, certain precautions calculated to prevent a repetition thereof is not admissible. *Standard Oil Co.* v. *Tierney,* 595.

4. Proximate Cause.—If a Person Is Injured by the Conjoint Result of an accident and of the negligence of a city, and but for such negligence the injury would not have occurred, the city is liable. Therefore, if, without the fault of the driver of a horse attached to a buggy, the bridle broke, and the horse became unmanageable, and ran away, and turned into a public street, and there, because of the defective condition and want of repair of the street, the buggy was thrown against a wall, and an injury inflicted on the driver, which he would not have suffered had the street been in proper repair, the municipality is answerable. *City of Joilet* v. *Shufeldt*, 453.

5. Duty of Shipper of Dangerous Goods.—If the shipper of an explosive or dangerous substance fails to notify the carrier or his agent of the danger which attends the handling of it, while in course of transportation, and an injury results to the employees of the carrier, the shipper is liable for the injury thus sustained; but when the carrier is notified whether by a mark upon the parcel or otherwise, that the article shipped is of a dangerous character, and one of the carrier's employee's is injured by handling the article, the mere fact that no knowledge of its real nature was brought home to the employee will not render the shipper liable. *Standard Oil Co.* v. *Tierney*, 595.

6. Carriage of Dangerous Articles—Duty of Shipper and Carrier. Where a dangerous article is delivered to a carrier for transportation, it is the duty both of the shipper and the carrier to notify those who handle it of its dangerous character, and no arrangement between the shipper and the carrier, though made in the best of faith, by which the article is to be shipped under a name which does not indicate its true nature, will excuse the shipper for the nonperformance of that duty on his part. *Standard Oil Co.* v. *Tierney*, 595.

7. The Shipper's Duty to Mark Dangerous Articles delivered to a carrier for transportation in such a way that the carrier's employees may have due notice of the real character of those articles is not sufficiently performed when a substance so extremely dangerous as naphtha is described on the freight-bill as carbon oil, and merely branded, "unsafe for illuminating purposes." *Standard Oil Co.* v. *Tierney*, 595.

8. Dangerous Article Shipped Under a Fictitious Name.—Where the employee of a carrier is suing a shipper to recover damages for injuries sustained by an explosion of naphtha which was described in the bill of lading as carbon oil, it is not error to refuse evidence going to show that the carrier had been informed of the real meaning of the words used in the bill of lading. *Standard Oil Co.* v. *Tierney*, 595.

9. Duty of Owner of Elevator to Licensee.—A city ordinance providing that in every structure where machinery is used, and so located as to endanger the lives and limbs of employees, it "shall, so far as practicable, be so covered and guarded as to insure against injury to such employees" protects only the latter and cannot be extended so as to protect or give a right of action to a mere licensee who is injured through the negligence of the owner of an elevator in failing to have it properly guarded. *Gibson* v. *Leonard*, 376.

10. Concurrent of Third Person, No Defense, When.—A city is liable for the injuries received by a traveler, who falls into a hatchway, which a house-owner has been allowed to locate and maintain in a dangerous position, although the immediate cause of the accident was the negligence of such house-owner in not guarding the opening. *McClure* v. *Sparta*, 924.

11. REMEDY UNDER STATUTE—TO WHOM AVAILABLE.—When a statute gives a remedy for negligence in its violation to a certain class of persons only such persons as are intended to be benefited or protected by it can rely upon its violation as giving a cause of action. *Gibson* v. *Leonard*, 376.

See COMPROMISE, 1; DAMAGES, 1, 3, 4; MUNICIPAL CORPORATIONS, 8, 10; RAILROADS, 1, 2, 5, 15, 17–20; REAL PROPERTY, 1; TAXES, 3.

NEGOTIABLE INSTRUMENTS.

1. INDORSER'S LIABILITY.—One who indorses commercial paper thereby becomes responsible for its genuineness and that of all previous indorsements. *Rhodes* v. *Jenkins*, 263.

2. PERSONS INDORSING A NEGOTIABLE INSTRUMENT BEFORE ITS DELIVERY must be regarded as joint makers, and liable as such without any demand, protest, or notice of nonpayment. *Bank of Jamaica* v. *Jefferson*, 100.

3. INDORSER'S RIGHT TO EQUITABLE SETOFF.—Indorser for insolvent maker, being indebted to such maker, may bring the holder of the paper indorsed and the maker before a court of equity and have the indorser's debt to the maker applied to the debt of the holder. *Citizens' Bank* v. *Kendrick*, 96.

4. INSOLVENCY OF MAKER AND INDORSER.—If both the maker and indorser of a negotiable instrument become insolvent and assign their property for the benefit of creditors, the holder of such paper may prove the whole amount thereof against both parties at the same time, and receive from each estate the full *pro rata* of that amount, provided only that the two sums so received shall in no case exceed the true amount of the debt. *Citizens' Bank* v. *Kendrick*, 96.

5. NEGOTIABLE INSTRUMENTS SIGNED BY OFFICERS OF A CORPORATION.—If a negotiable promissory note is given in payment of the debt of a corporation but the language of the promise does not disclose a corporate obligation, and the signatures are the names of individuals, a holder taking *bona fide* and without notice of the circumstances of the making of the note is entitled to hold and enforce it as the personal obligation of the signers, though they affixed to their names the titles of their offices. Unless the note creates, or fairly implies, an undertaking of the corporation, if the purpose is equivocal the obligation is that of the apparent makers. *Casco Nat. Bank* v. *Clark*, 705.

6. APPEARANCE ON THE MARGIN OF A NEGOTIABLE INSTRUMENT OF THE NAME "RIDGEWOOD ICE CO." does not create any presumption that such paper was, or was intended to be, the paper of that company. *Casco Nat. Bank* v. *Clark*, 705.

See AGENCY, 2–4; ALTERATION OF INSTRUMENTS; BANKS, 3; CORPORATIONS, 4–6; EVIDENCE, 4, 6; FALSE PRETENSES, 3; GUARANTY, 6; JOINT LIABILITY; PARTNERSHIP, 4; PAYMENT, 2; USURY.

NEW TRIAL.

1. NOTICE OF INTENTION to move for a new trial is not rendered uncertain by a statement that the motion will be made on the minutes of the court and a bill of exceptions. *Hall* v. *Harris*, 730.

2. EFFECT OF DENIAL OF.—When a new trial is denied and plaintiff thereupon elects to stand by his case as made, whereupon the court

dismisses the action, an appeal from the judgment of dismissal will be treated as showing an intention on the part of the parties to treat the case as though a nonsuit had been granted because of the plaintiff's failure to establish a sufficient case for the jury. *Wadsworth* v. *Union Pac. Ry. Co.*, 309.

NONRESIDENTS.

See ATTACHMENT, 1, 11; INTERSTATE COMMERCE, 2, 3; PARTITION; STATUTES, 7; TREATIES, 2, 3.

NONSUIT.
NEW TRIAL, 2.

NOTICE.

1. NOTICE FROM POSSESSION—CREDITORS MAY BE POSTPONED OR DEFEATED by notice of claims of third parties to property, the record and title of which is in their debtor, and possession may be notice to them, as well as to a purchaser, so as to preclude them from obtaining a lien on the estate or interest of the occupant. *Groff* v. *State Bank.* 640.

2. NOTICE FROM POSSESSION OF GRANTOR.—Possession by a grantor after the delivery of his deed is as effectual as notice of his interest in the granted premises as against the creditors of the grantee, as is the possession by a stranger to the record title. *Groff* v. *State Bank,* 640.

NUISANCE.

THE DISCHARGE OF FIREWORKS at the junction of two narrow streets of a large city, completely built upon, and where any misadventure is likely to result in injury to persons or property when the display is of considerable magnitude, and the explosives heavily charged, and the discharge is managed by private persons, not under any official responsibility, is an unreasonable and unlawful use of the streets, and constitutes a public nuisance. *Spier* v. *Brooklyn,* 664.

See AGENCY, 7, 10; BANKS, 4; CORPORATIONS, 7; GUARANTY, 4–11; INSURANCE, 9; LANDLORD AND TENANT, 9; MECHANIC'S LIEN, 1–3; MUNICIPAL CORPORATIONS, 14; NEW TRIAL, 1; TRUSTS, 5, 7, 9.

OFFICERS.

1. DUTY TO ACCEPT OFFICE.—It is the duty of every person having the requisite qualifications, when elected or appointed to a public municipal office, to accept it. The refusal to do so is a crime, punishable as such under the principles of the common law. *People* v. *Williams,* 514.

2. POWER TO RESIGN.—A person holding a public office has no power of his own motion to resign it, and his resignation does not become effective to discharge him from the performance of the duties of such office, until accepted by lawful and competent authority. *People* v. *Williams,* 514.

See BANKS, 4; ELECTIONS; EXECUTION, 4; FRAUD, 4; MANDAMUS; MUNICIPAL CORPORATIONS, 6, 9; NEGOTIABLE INSTRUMENTS, 5, 6; SHERIFFS; SURETYSHIP, 3; TRUSTS, 9; CORPORATIONS, 4–11.

OPTIONS.
See COURTS; VENDOR AND PURCHASER.

ORDINANCES.

See Brokers, 1; Injunctions, 2; Municipal Corporations, 5, 13; Negligence, 2, 9.

ORIGINAL PACKAGES.
See Interstate Commerce, 4, 5.

OYSTERS.
See Game Laws; Interstate Commerce, 9–11; Wharves.

PARENT AND CHILD.
See Advancements, 2; Deeds, 1; Estates, 2, 4; Wills, 10.

PAROL.
See Evidence, 6–9.

PARTIES.
See Assignment for the Benefit of Creditors, 1; Reform Schools, 5.

PARTITION.

Who May Sue for.—A nonresident alien, whose interests in the property will terminate unless he exercises, within three years, his power to sell it, can maintain a suit in partition to have his interest set aside in severalty. *Schultze v. Schultze*, 432.

PARTNERSHIP.

1. Partnership to Practice Law—Firm Profits, What Are Not.—Commissions received by one member of a law firm while acting as an executor or administrator for the estate of a third person, without objection or with the assent of the other members of the partnership, are not firm profits or earnings for which he must account to the partnership. *Metcalfe v. Bradshaw*, 478.

2. Partnership to Practice Law—Firm Profits.—If a partner in a law firm carries on a business not connected with nor competing with that of the firm, such as acting as an executor or administrator, his partners have no right to the profits he thereby makes, though he has agreed not to carry on any separate business. *Metcalfe v. Bradshaw*, 478.

3. Partnership to Practice Law—Firm Profits, What Are Not.— Though a partner in a law firm has agreed only to give his time, talents and strength to the prosecution of the firm business, he does not by becoming an executor or administrator with the consent and approval of his copartners, engage in a business or enterprise in competition with his firm, or which involves the use, for his own advantage, of anything belonging thereto. The commissions received by him as such executor or administrator are not firm assets, and he is entitled to retain them as his own. *Metcalfe v. Bradshaw*, 478.

4. Indorsement by Member of Firm—Who Bound by.—When notes are indorsed by a member of a firm, not on account of any partnership liability or transaction, but solely for accommodation purposes, a substitute note given to take up the prior notes, in the hands of a third person having knowledge of the facts is not enforceable against the firm, nor the members thereof, except as against the one so

indorsing without affirmative evidence of prior authority to execute, or
subsequent ratification of such execution by the other partners. *Slipp*
v. *Hartley*, 629.

5. DECLARATIONS OF PARTNER WHEN NOT EVIDENCE AGAINST FIRM.—A
partner's declarations or admissions do not bind his associates in
concerns and transactions foreign to the partnership, and he cannot, by such declarations or admissions, bring a transaction within the
scope of the partnership business, when in fact it had no connection
therewith. *Slipp* v. *Hartley*, 629.

6. DECLARATIONS OF PARTNER WHEN EVIDENCE AGAINST FIRM.—Admissions or declarations of a partner made during the existence of the
partnership while engaged in transacting its legitimate business, or relating to matters within the scope of the partnership, are admissible
against the firm. *Slipp* v. *Hartley*, 629.

7. STATUTE OF FRAUDS—A PARTNERSHIP FOR BUYING AND SELLING LANDS
FOR PROFIT may be created by parol. The existence of such partnership
and the respective interests of the several parties therein may also be
established by parol. *Speyer* v. *Desjardins*, 473.

8. CONTINUATION AFTER EXPIRATION OF TERM.—If a partnership is continued after the expiration of the term fixed by the articles of copartnership, without the adoption of new articles or new arrangements,
it is continued in all respects subject to the original articles, except
that either partner may terminate it at pleasure. *Metcalfe* v. *Bradshaw*, 478.

PAYMENT.

1. PAYMENT MADE WITH FUNDS NOT BELONGING TO THE PAYER.—The payment of money to a creditor who receives it in discharge of an existing
debt innocently and without knowledge, or means of knowledge, that
the debtor had no rightful ownership in the funds received, is good and
effectual, and does not subject the creditor to a recovery by the true
owner of such funds. *Newhall* v. *Wyatt*, 712.

2. PAYMENT BY TAKING NOTE OF THIRD PERSON.—Whether or not the taking of the note of a third person from a debtor without the latter's indorsement is conclusive evidence of payment, depends upon the intent
of the parties, and if it appears that at the time such note was taken it
was not the intent of the parties that it should be received as an absolute
payment, then upon nonpayment of the note, the original indebtedness
can be enforced. *Duggan* v. *Pacific Boom Co.*, 182.

See AGENCY, 10; DURESS; GUARANTY; TRUSTS, 5, 10.

PERSONAL PROPERTY.
See ATTACHMENT, 10; EXECUTION, 5; HUSBAND AND WIFE, 3; SALES.

PLATFORMS.
See RAILROADS, 13.

PLEADING.

1. WATERS—VIOLATION OF CONTRACT FOR—SUFFICIENCY OF COMPLAINT FOR
INJUNCTION.—A complaint by water-takers from an irrigation ditch to
enjoin the ditch company from selling additional water rights, in violation of its contract obligations with them, is sufficient, although it does
not allege the cubical dimensions of the ditch, nor the adjudicated

priorities in its waters, provided it states the contract, and alleges that the ditch company is violating, or intends to violate, its contract obligations with such water-takers. *Wyatt v. Larimer etc. Irr. Co.*, 280.

2. The Declaration in an Action for a Breach of a Bond, by which the defendant had obligated himself to accept the provisions of a certain will, and not to claim under the statute of distribution, need not aver that the plaintiff is a beneficiary under the will, and that the defendant had a right to waive it. The breach of such a bond is sufficiently shown by allegations setting forth the decease of the testator, the regular probate of the will, and the waiver by the defendant of his rights under the will, and his acquisition of the same interests as if such will had not been probated. *Barrett v. Carden*, 876.

3. A Seal Imports Consideration, and, in declaring upon a bond, the consideration that induced its execution need not be stated. *Barrett v. Carden*, 876.

4. Statute of Frauds.—Compliance with the statute of frauds need not be pleaded either at law or in equity, because it is presumed. *Speyer v. Desjardins*, 473.

5. Statute of Frauds—The Benefit of the Statute of Frauds as a Defense cannot be taken by demurrer, unless when it affirmatively appears by the bill and complaint that the demurrer relied upon was not evidenced by a writing duly signed. If the agreement is alleged to have been made between the parties, it will be presumed to have been in writing and signed, when such signature and writing are necessary to its validity. *Speyer v. Desjardins*, 473.

6. Pleading in Chancery.—Relief Under General Prayer.—Any relief consistent with, and justified by, facts alleged in a bill in equity, may be decreed under the prayer for general relief, although not specially prayed for. *Davidson v. Burke*, 367.

7. Contracts.—A Promise to Forbear to Sue May be Pleaded in Bar to an action upon the original indebtedness. *Staver v. Missimer*, 142.

8. Repugnant Defenses.—One who for the purpose of maintaining a defense deliberately represents a thing in one aspect is not permitted to contradict his own representation by giving the same thing another aspect in the same case. *Hodges v. Winston*, 241.

9. Dismissal of Bill on Motion to Dissolve Injunction.—When a bill in chancery is in effect a prayer for an injunction only, a motion to dissolve the injunction has the same effect as a demurrer to the bill, and the court on sustaining such motion may properly dismiss the bill. *American Live Stock Co. v. Chicago Live Stock Exchange*, 385.

See Attachment, 2; Corporations, 19; Fraudulent Conveyances, 3, 4; Judgments, 9; Trusts, 4, 5; Waters, 3, 7.

POLICE POWER.

See Statutes, 13.

POSSESSION.

See Execution, 1, 2; Mortgages, 1; Notice; Sales, 3.

POWERS.

Principal and Agent—Power Coupled With an Interest, What Is Not.—The fact that an agent is entitled to commission on moneys collected by him does not give him a power coupled with an interest so as to support a payment made to him after the death of his principal. The interest which can protect the power from the death of the person by whom it was created must be an interest in the thing itself. *Farmers' Loan etc. Co.* v. *Wilson*, 696.

See AGENCY, 2, 10.

POWER OF ATTORNEY.
See JUDGMENTS, 9.

PRESUMPTIONS.
See ATTORNEY AND CLIENT, 13; EVIDENCE, 4, 5; EXECUTION, 1, 3; NEGOTIABLE INSTRUMENTS, 6; STATUTES, 2; WILLS, 3, 6.

PRINCIPAL AND AGENT.
See AGENCY.

PRIVATE WAYS.
PRIVATE WAYS, PAROL AGREEMENT FIXING POSITION OF, EFFECT OF.—If a landowner and his vendee, by a parol agreement entered into after the execution of a deed which grants a right of way over other lands belonging to the vendor, locate the precise position of the way, that agreement will limit and define the right of way which will pass to a sub-purchaser of the same premises as appurtenant thereto, and he cannot maintain the privilege of passing in a different direction over the servient tenement. *Kinney* v. *Hooker*, 864.

PROCESS.
SERVICE ON OWNER AS SERVICE ON LIENHOLDER.—There is no unity of interest between the legal owner of real estate and one claiming a lien on it through him, either by mortgage, mechanic's lien, or otherwise, such as makes either the representative of the other in an action, so that service of summons on one is equivalent to service on the other. *Smith* v. *Hurd*, 661.

See ACTIONS; INSURANCE, 3, 6, 7; JUDGMENTS. 2, 3; JURISDICTION, 5; MECHANIC'S LIEN, 14, 15; STATUTES, 7.

PROTEST.
See NEGOTIABLE INSTRUMENTS, 2.

PUBLICATION OF SUMMONS.
See JUDGMENTS, 2, 3; JURISDICTION, 5; STATUTES, 7.

PUBLIC LANDS.
See EXECUTION, 6.

PUBLIC POLICY.
See ASSOCIATIONS, 4; CONTRACTS, 11, 13; CORPORATIONS, 2; EXPECTANCIES, 2.

RAILROADS.

might have been foreseen, such as ordinary periodical freshets, the railroad company whose superstructure is the immediate cause of the mischief is liable for the damage; but if the injury is occasioned by an act of Providence, such as an extraordinary flood, which could not have been anticipated, it cannot be held liable. The company is not liable for remote and uncertain consequences, but only for the necessary and proximate effects of the structure. *Ohio etc. Ry. Co.* v. *Thillman,* 359.

8. WATERCOURSES—OBSTRUCTION BY RAILROAD.—DEGREE OF CARE REQUIRED to be used by a railroad company in constructing a bridge across a natural watercourse is to bring such engineering skill to bear as is ordinarily applied to works of that kind, in view of the size and habits of the stream, the character of its channel, and the declivity of the circumjacent territory forming the watershed. *Ohio etc. Ry. Co.* v. *Thillman,* 359.

9. WATERCOURSES—OBSTRUCTION BY RAILROAD—DEGREE OF CARE REQUIRED QUESTION FOR JURY.—A railroad company, in bridging a natural watercourse or building an embankment across it, is bound to exercise such ordinary care in providing for the free passage of the water as is usually exercised by men of ordinary prudence in their own affairs; and in the exercise of such care the company must guard against such freshets or floods as men of ordinary prudence can foresee, but not against such extraordinary floods and accidental casualties as cannot reasonably be anticipated; and whether the flood causing the injury is such as should have been anticipated and provided against is a question for the jury to decide. *Ohio etc. Ry. Co.* v. *Thillman,* 359.

10. A DISCRIMINATION IN FAVOR OF A MANUFACTURING CORPORATION, and against a dealer in coal arising from the railway corporation making an agreement in advance of the establishment of the manufacturing corporation to ship coal to it for a specific time and at specified rates, in order to induce such establishment, and increase the railroad's freight and earnings thereby, is not a discrimination between persons in like conditions and under similar circumstances. The railway corporation is not obliged to abandon its agreement, nor, while maintaining it, to carry freight for other shippers on the terms therein stipulated. *Hoover* v. *Pennsylvania R. R.,* 43.

11. DISCRIMINATION.—UNDER A STATUTE PROHIBITING UNREASONABLE PREFERENCE OR ADVANTAGE a railway corporation may lawfully enter into a contract for the carriage of goods for a particular individual or corporation at a lower rate in respect to large quantities of goods and for longer distances than for one who sends them in small quantities or short distances. *Hoover* v. *Pennsylvania R. R.,* 43.

12. DISCRIMINATION IN FAVOR OF A MANUFACTURING CORPORATION, and against retail dealers, in the price charged for shipping coal, though justified on the ground that such corporation is engaged in a business necessarily resulting in an increase of the business of the carrier, must be discontinued if such manufacturer engages in the business of selling coal, and thus becomes a competitor with other dealers in that commodity. *Hoover* v. *Pennsylvania R. R.,* 43.

13. RAILROAD COMPANIES—DUTY TO MAINTAIN SAFE PLATFORMS, TO WHOM OWING.—A railroad company is bound to provide reasonably safe platforms for the use not only of persons who intend to travel by ordinary passenger trains, but also of persons who come to a station with such intending passengers to see them off; but no such duty can be implied

men employed by the railway company. *Cleveland etc. Ry. Co. v. Ketcham*, 550.

See CONSTITUTIONS, 2; DAMAGES, 2, 3.

RATIFICATION.

See PARTNERSHIP, 4.

REAL PROPERTY.

1. NEGLIGENCE—OWNER'S DUTY TO LICENSEE.—The owner of lands and buildings assumes no duty to one who is on his premises by permission only as a mere licensee, except that he will refrain from willful or affirmative injurious acts. Hence a mere licensee who enters without any enticement, allurement, or inducement being held out to him by the owner or occupant, cannot recover damages caused by obstructions or pitfalls. *Gibson v. Leonard*, 376.

2. LICENSE—DUTY OF OWNER TO LICENSEE.—When an entry on premises is by naked license the fact that the licensor has knowledge that the licensee may at some time enter, imposes no duty upon the former in favor of the latter, except to refrain from affirmative or willful acts that work an injury. *Gibson v. Leonard*, 376.

3. LICENSEE—DUTY OF OWNER TO.—A mere naked license or permission to enter premises, whether implied by law or given by the owner or occupant, does not impose upon the latter any obligation to provide against the dangers of accident to such licensee. *Gibson v. Leonard*, 376.

4. NEGLIGENCE—DUTY OF OWNER TO FIRE PATROLMAN AS LICENSEE.—The members of an underwriter's fire patrol who force open and enter a building to save property from fire, without invitation, permission, or license express or implied, from the owner or occupant, are not trespassers, as they enter and remain under a license implied by law; but such owner or occupant is not liable to one of their number injured by using a defective elevator and its appliances, especially when such elevator is intended for freight, and not for passengers. *Gibson v. Leonard*, 376.

See IMPROVEMENTS; LICENSE; NEGLIGENCE, 10; PROCESS; VENDOR AND PURCHASER.

RECEIVERS.

1. APPOINTMENT—DISCRETION OF COURT.—Appointing or refusing a receiver is within the sound judicial discretion of the court to which application is made. The exercise of such discretion will not be interfered with on appeal when the evidence is conflicting unless such discretion has been clearly abused, but when such abuse is shown and the evidence is not conflicting the judgment of the lower court will be reversed or modified. *Simmons Hardware Co. v. Waibel*, 755.

2. WHEN SHOULD NOT BE APPOINTED IN ACTION TO FORECLOSE MORTGAGE.—When, in an action to foreclose a mortgage against a mortgagor and his assignee, the mortgagee asks that a receiver be appointed without notice, for the reason, as he alleges, that his security will be impaired because such assignee will not prevent a sale of buildings and machinery on the mortgaged premises under a pretended chattel mortgage, the application for the appointment of the receiver should be denied, when the assignee avers in his answer that he has refused to allow, and has obtained an injunction against, such sale and has instituted suit to have the chattel mortgage declared void. *Hutchinson* v. *First Nat. Bank,* 537.

3. TRADE SECRETS—INJUNCTION AND RECEIVER TO PROTECT.—The inventor and owner of a secret code or system of letters, figures, or characters showing the cost and selling price of goods for the use of himself and his traveling salesmen has a property therein which, when the remedy at law is inadequate, will be protected in equity by granting a temporary injunction and appointing a receiver in order to prevent irreparable injury *pendente lite.* If a copy of such code and of the key thereto is wrongfully and fraudulently in the possession of a third person the court should, upon proper application, take such copy into its possession through a receiver and retain it during the pendency of the action. The refusal of the court to do so is an abuse of discretion which will be corrected on appeal. *Simmons Hardware Co.* v. *Waibel,* 755.

RECORDS.
See FILING INSTRUMENTS; HIGHWAYS, 2; MORTGAGES, 2–5.

REDEMPTION.
See MORTGAGES, 1, 7, 10, 11.

REFORM SCHOOLS.

1. CONSTITUTIONAL LAW.—A statute authorizing and empowering justices of the peace to commit infants to the care and guardianship of the board of managers of a reform school in consequence of incorrigibly vicious conduct, though for a time exceeding the criminal jurisdiction of such justices, is a valid exercise of legislative power. *State* v. *Brown,* 651.

2. CONSTITUTIONAL LAW.—A person committed by a justice of the peace to the care and custody of a board of managers of a reform school is not punished or imprisoned in the ordinary meaning of those words. Hence a constitutional provision regulating and limiting the jurisdiction of justices of the peace in criminal matters has no application in the premises. *State* v. *Brown,* 651.

3. JURISDICTION TO COMMIT TO—CONSTITUTIONAL LAW.—An infant committed by a justice of the peace to a reform school is not punished or imprisoned in the ordinary meaning of those words, hence he is not deprived of his constitutional right to a jury trial. *State* v. *Brown,* 651.

4. JURISDICTION OF COMMITTING MAGISTRATE—CONSTITUTIONAL LAW.— When committing an infant to the care and custody of the board of managers of a reform school, a justice of the peace is not appointing a guardian for him, nor does such magistrate or the board of managers assume any control over his estate. Hence the committing magistrate does not violate a constitutional provision conferring jurisdiction in matters of guardianship solely upon probate courts. *State* v. *Brown,* 651.

5. PROCEEDING TO COMMIT TO—PARTIES.—In a proceeding to commit a minor to a reform school his natural or legal guardian should be made a party. *State* v. *Brown,* 651.

REGISTRATION.
See FILING INSTRUMENTS.

SALES.
WHAT IS.—If a person engaged in the manufacture and sale of soda waters delivers them in bottles to a customer, and takes a deposit from

him, with the understanding that he may return the bottles and take back his deposit, or keep the bottles and regard it as payment, as he may elect, such transaction constitutes a sale of the bottles at the election of the customer, and a prosecution against a dealer in second-hand bottles for having such bottles unlawfully in his possession without the consent of such manufacturer cannot be sustained. *People v. Cannon,* 668.

2. CHANGE OF POSSESSION.—The fact that a husband has in his possession a chattel received by his wife in exchange for another which was sold to her by one of her husband's creditors, to whom it had been transferred in payment of a debt, will not invalidate her title to the chattel thus acquired by her as against an attachment thereof by the other creditors of her husband. Under such circumstances her title is derived, not from her husband, but from the person with whom the exchange is made. *Caswell v. Jones,* 879.

3. IF BY THE TERMS OF A CONDITIONAL SALE OF CHATTELS, the vendor, on the nonpayment of a note given for the purchase price, is entitled to resume possession of the property sold and to consider all payments made as for the use of the property while in the hands of the vendee, and agrees that the note shall be surrendered and canceled, he cannot, after maintaining a proceeding to collect his note and receiving a dividend by virtue of such proceeding, sustain an action of replevin to recover the property. The vendor has an option either to resume possession of the property and terminate the contract of sale, or to consider it as still subsisting and pursue his remedy on the note, but, having elected to pursue the latter remedy, his election is irrevocable, and precludes any subsequent resort to another. *Crompton v. Beach,* 323.

4. VENDEE'S RIGHT TO TEST THE QUALITY OF ARTICLES PURCHASED.— A vendee, after having determined by inspection alone that the subject matter of the sale does not conform to the contract, and thereupon notified the vendor that it has been rejected, cannot, if he intends to insist upon his right to reject, deal with it in any manner inconsistent with the rejection, as by using up a quantity of it for the purpose of making a practical test of its quality, and thus providing evidence of its unfitness, to be used upon the trial of an action brought to rescind the contract, and recover from the vendor the purchase price of the goods. *Cream City Glass Co. v. Friedlander,* 895.

5. FAILURE OF TITLE AS DEFENSE.—The purchaser of peronal property in undisturbed possession cannot recover damages in an action on an implied warranty of title, nor set up want of title in his vendor as a defense to an action for the purchase money, although he offers to rescind, in the absence of fraudulent representations made by the vendor in regard to the title. *Johnson v. Oehmig,* 204.

See AGENCY, 9; CHATTEL MORTGAGES, 2; CORPORATIONS, 1; EVIDENCE, 1; EXECUTION, 1–4; STATUTES, 13: TAXES; VENDOR AND PURCHASER.

SEAL.

See PLEADING, 3.

SEDUCTION.

1. BURDEN OF PROOF AS TO CHASTITY—CORROBORATION OF PROSECU-TRIX.—In a prosecution for seduction under promise of marriage the burden of proof is upon the prosecution to prove the previous chaste character of the prosecutrix, and her testimony must be corroborated by other evidence, but only such corroborative evidence is required as, in the nature of the case, is obtainable, and when produced, though circumstantial and slight in its character, a case is made for the jury to determine. *State* v. *Lockerby*, 656.

2. EVIDENCE OF GENERAL REPUTATION FOR CHASTITY.—In a prosecution for seduction under promise of marriage, evidence of the general reputation of the prosecutrix for chastity is admissible in corroboration of her own testimony. *State* v. *Lockerby*, 656.

SEPARATE PROPERTY.
See HUSBAND AND WIFE, 6–8.

SETOFF.

EQUITABLE SETOFF.—The right of an equitable setoff already existing by reason of the insolvency of the creditor cannot be affected by his assignment of his assets. *Citizens' Bank* v. *Kendrick*, 96.
See NEGOTIABLE INSTRUMENTS, 3.

SEWERS.
See MUNICIPAL CORPORATIONS, 9.

SHERIFFS.

1. LIABILITY FOR FAILURE TO MAKE LEVY—BURDEN OF PROOF.—When a writ of attachment is placed in the hands of a sheriff to be levied, a bond of indemnity given, and property in the possession of defendant apparently subject to levy is pointed out, the sheriff is *prima facie* liable for a failure to make the levy. *Mathis* v. *Carpenter*, 187.

2. LIABILITY FOR ACTS OF DEPUTY.—A sheriff is liable for the wrongful official acts of a person who, representing himself as a deputy sheriff, acts as such in the presence of, and with the knowledge, consent, and approbation of, such sheriff, although the latter denies the appointment of such deputy, and it appears that his oath of office was irregularly filed. *Mathis* v. *Carpenter*, 187.

3. OFFICIAL BONDS OF AS EVIDENCE.—If, in an action against a sheriff and his sureties on two bonds given by him, pleas are filed by the sheriff and his sureties jointly, such bonds are admissible in evidence, although some of the sureties on one bond are not upon the other. *Mathis* v. *Carpenter*, 187.

SIDEWALKS.
See MUNICIPAL CORPORATIONS, 10–12.

SPECIFIC PERFORMANCE.
See CONTRACTS, 14, 15; EQUITY, 2; WATERS, 3.

STATES.

INTERSTATE COMITY—GARNISHMENT OF DEBTOR OF DISSOLVED CORPORATION IN SISTER STATE, WHEN RECEIVER MAY AVOID.—After a receiver has been duly appointed for a dissolved corporation, in accordance with the laws of the state in which it was organized, and the creditors of such corporation have been regularly enjoined from commencing any

suits to enforce the collection of their debts, the claim of such receiver
to the assets of the corporation will be sustained in a sister state, as
against a garnishment proceeding instituted by one of the creditors so
enjoined against a debtor of the corporation residing in the latter state.
Gilman v. *Ketcham,* 899.

See EVIDENCE; GAME LAWS; INTERSTATE COMMERCE.

STATUTE OF FRAUDS.
See AGENCY, 11; CONTRACTS, 7-9; PARTNERSHIP, 7; PLEADING, 4, 5.

STATUTE OF LIMITATIONS.
See LIMITATIONS OF ACTIONS.

STATUTES.

1. SUBJECT EXPRESSED IN TITLE.—A statute is not open to the objection
that it contains subjects not "clearly" expressed in its title when such
subjects are all "referable and cognate" to the subjects expressed in
such title. *State* v. *Harrub,* 195.

2. EVIDENCE.—STATUTE MAY MAKE THE EXISTENCE OF CERTAIN FACTS PRIMA
FACIE EVIDENCE OF THE COMMISSION OF A CRIME, though the explanation of the facts from which the presumption arises is not peculiarly
within the knowledge of the person accused. *People* v. *Cannon,* 668.

3. CONSTRUCTION AND CONSTITUTIONALITY OF.—A STATUTE FOR THE
PROTECTION OF OWNERS OF BOTTLES used in the sale of soda waters
and like beverages, making it unlawful for anyone to fill any bottle
marked by a trademark, or to deface or obliterate such mark, or to sell
or otherwise dispose of such bottles, unless purchased from the person
whose mark is on the bottle, or sanctioned by his written consent, does
not prohibit one who has purchased the beverage in such bottles from
reselling it while in the same bottles in which he bought it, nor does the
statute unnecessarily destroy or unlawfully decrease the trade in empty
bottles; therefore it is not unconstitutional. One purchasing or coming
into the possession of a bottle with such a mark upon it is charged with
the duty of ascertaining, at his peril, whether the person whose name
or mark is upon it has parted with his ownership in it or given written
permission to any one to refill it. *People* v. *Cannon,* 668.

4. CONSTITUTIONAL LAW—EVIDENCE.—A statute providing that any junk-
dealer or dealer in second-hand articles, having possession of certain
kinds of bottles having on them the mark or name of a person, without
his written consent, shall be presumed to be in the unlawful use, purchase, or traffic in such bottles, is not unconstitutional. Such presumption may be made applicable to criminal prosecutions. Notwithstanding
the presumption, the jury should refuse to convict unless satisfied from
the whole evidence, beyond a reasonable doubt, of the guilt of the accused. *People* v. *Cannon,* 668.

5. CONSTITUTIONAL LAW—VALIDITY OF STATUTE RELATING TO INTEREST.
A statute making it a misdemeanor for any banker to discount any note,
bill, or draft at a higher rate of interest than eight per cent per annum
not including the difference of exchange applies to all kinds of bankers,
and is not invalid as an unlawful exercise of class legislation. *Youngblood* v. *Birmingham Trust etc. Co.,* 245.

See CARRIERS; COMPROMISE, 1; CONSTITUTIONS, 1; CONTRACTS, 12, 19; EMINENT DOMAIN; GAME LAWS; HIGHWAYS, 1, 3; INTERSTATE COMMERCE; JURISDICTION, 3; MECHANIC'S LIEN, 4, 5, 11, 14; MORTGAGES, 2; NEGLIGENCE, 11; REFORM SCHOOLS, 1; USURY.

STOCK.
See CORPORATIONS, 1-3, 14,. 15, 17; EXECUTION, 5, 7.

STOCKHOLDERS.
See CORPORATIONS, 9-11.

STREET PARADES.
See MUNICIPAL CORPORATIONS, 5.

STREETS.
See ELECTRIC LIGHT COMPANIES; MUNICIPAL CORPORATIONS, 1-4; NEGLIGENCE, 5; NUISANCE.

SUBCONTRACTOR.
See MECHANIC'S LIEN, 12, 13.

SUBROGATION.
See ATTACHMENT, 13.

SUBSCRIBERS.
See CORPORATIONS, 14, 15.

SUMMONS.
See PROCESS.

SUPREME COURT.
See JURISDICTION, 1, 6.

SUPERVISORS.
See HIGHWAYS, 1-3.

SURETYSHIP.

1. CONTRACT OF WHAT CONSTITUTES.—A contract under seal signed jointly by several persons by which they "guarantee" and directly obligate themselves, along with one of their number, to pay, absolutely and wholly, irrespective of his solvency or insolvency, all damages which may result to the obligee from his default, and by which they expressly stipulate that the obligee need not exhaust his remedies against their principal before proceeding against them, is a contract of suretyship and not of guaranty. *Saint v. Wheeler etc. Mfg. Co.*, 210.

2. CONTRACT OF WHEN BECOMES BINDING.—A contract of suretyship does not require notice of acceptance, but is complete and binding on delivery. After delivery one of the obligors cannot revoke it unless he has expressly reserved the right of revocation. *Saint v. Wheeler etc. Mfg. Co.*, 210.

3. OFFICIAL BONDS—LIABILITY OF SURETY.—An official bond in which the officer is named as principal, but which is not executed by him, is *prima facie* invalid, and not binding upon the sureties named therein. *Board of Education* v. *Sweeney,* 767.

4. UNDERTAKING—AUTHORITY TO FILL BLANKS IN—ESTOPPEL.—A surety who signs an incomplete undertaking and places it in the hands of another to use for a particular purpose, and with ostensible authority to fill in any needed matter to make it effective, is estopped from controverting its validity to the prejudice of the obligee, after it is accepted by him in its completed form, without negligence on his part. *Palacios* v. *Brasher,* 305.

5. UNDERTAKING—BLANKS IN—LIABILITY OF OBLIGOR.—Sureties who sign an undertaking in blank are bound to know its contents, and that the blanks must be filled to make it accomplish the purpose for which it is intended. They cannot evade liability after it has been completed by filling such blanks, by pleading a want of such knowledge, unless prevented from reading it by some trick or artifice of the obligee. *Palacios* v. *Brasher,* 305.

6. UNDERTAKING.—AUTHORITY TO COMPLETE AN UNDERTAKING, BY FILLING BLANKS THEREIN after the obligors have signed it, may be implied. *Palacios* v. *Brasher,* 305.

7. SURETY AND GUARANTOR—DIFFERENCE BETWEEN.—A surety is one who undertakes to pay at all events if the principal does not; a guarantor undertakes to pay only if the debtor cannot. The first is an insurer of the debt; the latter an insurer only of the solvency or ability of the debtor to pay. A contract of suretyship is the joint and several contract of the principal and surety, while the contract of a guarantor is his own separate undertaking in which the principal does not join. *Saint* v. *Wheeler etc. Mfg. Co.,* 210.

8. JOINT CONTRACT INDICATES.—The joint execution of a contract by a principal and another operates to exclude the idea of a guaranty, and is an index pointing to a contract of suretyship. *Saint* v. *Wheeler etc. Mfg. Co.,* 210.

9. RELEASE OF ONE SURETY OPERATES TO RELEASE OTHER SURETIES on the same contract or undertaking only to the extent of his aliquot share of the whole liability. *Saint* v. *Wheeler etc. Mfg. Co.,* 210.

10. DISCHARGE OF SURETY BY CHANGE IN CONTRACT WITHOUT HIS CONSENT.—Sureties under a contract for the faithful performance of certain duties by their principal are not discharged from all liability by reason of certain parol changes made in the original contract by the obligee and the principal imposing new and additional duties upon the latter after the obligors have become sureties, and without their knowledge, consent, or ratification, unless the imposition of these new duties and their performance by the principal render impossible or materially hinder, delay or impede the proper and faithful performance of the service originally undertaken. *Saint* v. *Wheeler etc. Mfg. Co.,* 210.

11. DISCHARGE OF SURETY BY CHANGE IN CONTRACT WITHOUT HIS CONSENT.—Sureties are not discharged by a change in the contract between the principal and the obligee as to the amount of compensation of the former, made without the consent or knowledge of the sureties, when the settlement between the parties on which the default of the principal is ascertained is based on the original contract, nor are such sureties discharged by reason of a subsequent parol agreement between principal and obligee, without their knowledge or consent, by which the principal is allowed to retain his compensation out of collections without remitting them to the obligee as required by the original contract. *Saint* v. *Wheeler etc. Mfg. Co.*, 210.

12. INDULGENCE TO PRINCIPAL AS DISCHARGE OF SURETY.—Mere indulgence by a creditor or employer to the principal in a contract, or a new agreement to give him further time to pay his debt or make good a default, if not supported by any new consideration, does not discharge the sureties on the original contract. *Saint* v. *Wheeler etc. Mfg. Co.*, 210.

13. CONCEALMENT OF PRINCIPAL'S DISHONESTY AS DISCHARGE OF SURETY.—In case of a continuing suretyship for the honesty of a servant, if the master discovers that the servant has been guilty of dishonesty in the service, and if, instead of dismissing him, he continues him in his employ without the consent of the surety, express or implied, the latter is not liable for any loss arising from the dishonesty of the servant during the subsequent service. This rule applies as well to a private corporation as an employer as to an individual, when its agent, in the discharge of his duties, discovers the dishonesty of the servant, and, having authority, fails to give notice of such dishonesty to the surety, and the corporation thereafter retains the servant in its employ. *Saint* v. *Wheeler etc. Mfg. Co.*, 210.

See ATTACHMENT, 1–3, 6, 9; GUARANTY; SHERIFFS, 3.

SURRENDER.
See LANDLORD AND TENANT, 7, 8.

SURVIVORSHIP.
See HUSBAND AND WIFE.

TAX DEEDS.
See TAXES, 1

TAXES.

1. TAX SALES—STATEMENT BY TOWN TREASURER THAT NOTHING IS DUE, EFFECT OF.—It is the duty of a town treasurer to furnish taxpayers with information as to the amount of taxes payable upon their lands in the township; and, as they have a right to rely upon that information, they cannot be prejudiced by its incorrectness. Hence if a landowner, through his agent, attempts and offers to pay, in due season, all the taxes due upon his property within a township, and the treasurer erroneously states that there is nothing assessed upon the roll against a certain tract, a tax deed issued upon a subsequent sale of that tract for nonpayment of taxes thereon is void, and its invalidity may be made available in a legal action of ejectment as well as in an equitable suit for its cancellation. *Gould* v. *Sullivan*, 955.

2. TAX SALE OF PROPERTY ESCHEATED TO THE STATE.—If persons are in possession of land claiming to own it, and having the rights of mortgagees in possession, and it is assessed to them for delinquent taxes, they cannot defeat an action of ejectment by the purchaser by proving that the property had escheated to the state, and was therefore not subject to taxation. They are not in a position to dispute the plaintiff's title. The state, because it cannot do so without paying off the mortgage, may choose never to enforce its right to escheat. *Croner* v. *Cowdrey*, 716.

3. TAX SALES—STATUTE OF LIMITATIONS, WHEN NOT A BAR TO RECOVERY OF LAND.—The statute of limitations fixing a period within which lands sold for nonpayment of taxes may be redeemed does not apply to a case where all the taxes due upon such lands have been regularly tendered, and the proper amount has not been paid merely because the officer to or through whom such payment could alone be made has negligently made a misstatement as to the sum actually due. *Gould* v. *Sullivan*, 955.

See INTERSTATE COMMERCE, 6-8.

TELEGRAMS.
See EVIDENCE, 9; INTERSTATE COMMERCE, 8.

TENDER.
See MORTGAGES, 13.

TICKETS.
See RAILROADS, 16.

TOOLS.
See ATTACHMENT, 15, 16.

TORTS.
See MUNICIPAL CORPORATIONS, 15.

TRADEMARKS.
See STATUTES, 3.

TREATIES.

1. CONSTRUCTION OF.—IF A TREATY ADMITS OF TWO CONSTRUCTIONS, one restrictive of the rights that may be claimed under it and the other liberal, the latter is to prevail. *Schultze* v. *Schultze*, 432.

2. IF A NONRESIDENT ALIEN DOES NOT SELL PROPERTY INHERITED BY HIM within the time stipulated in the treaty between the United States and the sovereignty of which he is a subject, the state law comes into force, and controls the disposition to be made of such property. *Schultze* v. *Schultze*, 432.

3. INHERITANCE BY NONRESIDENT ALIENS.—A treaty stipulating that the citizens of the contracting parties shall have power to dispose of their personal goods by testament or otherwise, and their representatives, being citizens of either party, shall succeed to such goods, and if in the case of real estate, the said heirs would be prevented from entering into the possession of the inheritance on account of their character as aliens, there shall be granted to them three years to dispose of the same, gives nonresident aliens who would be heirs but for their alienage, three years within which to dispose of their share of the lands of their ancestor, and to remove the proceeds. The estate which they acquire is a fee, determinable by the nonexercise of the power of sale within the three years. *Schultz* v. *Schultze*, 432.

TRESPASSERS.

TRIAL.

1. EVIDENCE IN CRIMINAL TRIALS—PROOF OF OTHER OFFENSES.—The charge upon which a defendant is being tried cannot be supported by proof of other offenses. But evidence which legitimately tends to support the charge is not to be excluded on the ground that it shows other offenses. *State* v. *Kelley*, 884.

2. EVIDENCE.—CONFLICT ON A QUESTION OF FACT is presented for the jury under proper instructions when the evidence is conflicting, or of such character that different conclusions may be reasonably drawn therefrom. *Wadsworth* v. *Union Pac. Ry. Co.*, 309.

3. FUNCTIONS OF COURT AND JURY.—In criminal cases the jury are not judges of the law as well as of the facts. *State* v. *Burpee*, 775.

4. INSTRUCTIONS—REFUSAL TO GIVE WHEN NOT ERROR.—A party is entitled to have an instruction given for the purpose of making more definite another instruction given by the court, but when a requested instruction embodies improper matter, the court may properly refuse to give it as a whole. *Duggan* v. *Pacific Boom Co.*, 182.

See APPEAL; ESTOPPEL, 1.

TRUSTS.

1. CONSTRUCTIVE TRUST—WHAT CONSTITUTES.—When one takes a conveyance secretly, contrary to the wishes of and in violation of his duty to the beneficiary, and in fraud of his rights, the trust is not resulting, but constructive or involuntary. *Farmers' etc. Bank* v. *Kimball Milling Co.*, 739.

2. INVOLUNTARY OR CONSTRUCTIVE TRUSTS INCLUDE all instances in which a trust is raised by the doctrines of equity for the purpose of working out justice when there is no intention of the parties to create a trust relation, and a contrary intent exists on the part of the holder of the legal title. These trusts may usually be referred to fraud, either actual or constructive, as an essential element. *Farmers' etc. Bank* v. *Kimball Milling Co.*, 739.

3. CONSTRUCTIVE TRUSTS.—GAINS AND PROFITS arising from property impressed with a constructive trust inure to the benefit of the real owner, and should be impressed with a like trust in his favor. *Farmers' etc. Bank* v. *Kimball Milling Co.*, 739.

4. CONSTRUCTIVE TRUSTS—PLEADING—COMPLAINT IN AN ACTION TO ENFORCE.—A constructive trust which alleges that a specific amount of funds has been fraudulently diverted and invested in corporation property, and that the entire property sought to be charged has been created from the funds fraudulently obtained, except a specified amount thereof, is sufficient on general demurrer as a definite statement of amount. *Farmers' etc. Bank* v. *Kimball Milling Co.*, 739.

5. CONSTRUCTIVE TRUSTS—PLEADING TO ENFORCE.—NOTICE OF FRAUD need not be alleged in a complaint in an original action to enforce a constructive trust in property acquired from funds fraudulently diverted and invested. Want of notice, payment of a valuable consideration, and good faith are affirmative matters to be pleaded and proved by the defendant. *Farmers' etc. Bank* v. *Kimball Milling Co.*, 739.

USAGE,
See CUSTOM.

USES.
See CHARITIES, 1.

USURY.

BANKS AND BANKING—DISCOUNT OF NEGOTIABLE PAPER.—A bank which discounts a draft at a rate of interest equal to twelve per cent per annum in violation of a statute providing that "any banker who discounts any note, bill of exchange, or draft at a higher rate of interest than eight per cent per annum, not including the difference of exchange, is guilty of a misdemeanor," and cannot recover on the draft, as it is void in its hands as being acquired under an unlawful and criminal contract. *Youngblood v. Birmingham Trust etc. Co.*, 245.

VENDOR AND PURCHASER.

1. AN OPTION TO PURCHASE REAL PROPERTY IS A SUBSTANTIAL INTEREST IN LAND, and when the option is exercised the purchaser is considered as the owner *ab initio*. *Peoples etc. Ry. Co.* v. *Spencer*, 22.
2. IF AN OPTION IS GIVEN TO PURCHASE REAL PROPERTY UPON WHICH AN INSURANCE AGAINST LOSS BY FIRE exists or is subsequently effected, and the loss occurs, after which the option is exercised and a conveyance of the property made, the purchaser is entitled to the moneys due upon such insurance. *Peoples etc. Ry. Co.* v. *Spencer*, 22.

See AGENCY, 11; CONTRACTS, 8, 9; DEEDS; EVIDENCE, 1; PRIVATE WAYS.

VESTED RIGHTS.
See ELECTRIC LIGHT COMPANIES; STATUTES, 13.

WAIVER.
See APPEAL, 1; DEEDS, 6; HIGHWAYS, 4; INSURANCE, 8; JURISDICTION, 7; LANDLORD AND TENANT, 3; PLEADING, 2; REPLEVIN.

WAREHOUSEMEN.

SELLING GOODS ON COMMISSION, LIABILITY OF.—A mortgagee of goods cannot maintain an action for conversion against a public warehouseman who receives a portion of those goods from the apparent owner, in the usual way and without any notice, either actual or constructive, of an adverse claim, and sells them on commission at a public sale in the regular course of business, without asserting any interest or right hostile to such mortgagee. *Abernathy* v. *Wheeler*, 593.

WARRANTY.
See SALES.

WATERS.

1. WHAT ARE.—To constitute a watercourse, it is not necessary that there should be a continual flow of water, but there must be a stream, which usually flows in a particular direction, in a well-defined channel, having a bed and sides or banks. Such a stream, so long as it can be traced by the existence of such a channel, wherever the ground is suitable for

cutting one, and does not lose its identity as the same stream, does not cease to be a watercourse because it spreads out at some points into marshes and swamps. *Case* v. *Hoffman*, 937.

2. SURFACE WATERS, WHAT ARE.—Surface waters are such as lie upon or spread over the surface, or percolate the soil, as in swamps, and do not flow in a particular direction. *Case* v. *Hoffman*, 937.

3. ACTION TO ENJOIN DIVERSION—PLEADING.—A complaint in an action to establish rights in an alleged watercourse, and to enjoin the diversion thereof, is not demurrable on the ground of misjoinder of causes of action, when it also asks for the specific performance of a contract made by the plaintiff with the defendant's grantors, by virtue of which it is averred that, even if the waters in question do not technically constitute a watercourse, the plaintiff is entitled to have the use of them for irrigating his land. *Case* v. *Hoffman*, 937.

4. RIGHT TO WHEN A FREEHOLD.—A perpetual right to have a certain quantity of water flow through an irrigation ditch is an easement therein, and an incorporeal hereditament descendible by inheritance, hence a freehold estate. *Wyatt* v. *Larimer Irr. Co.*, 280.

5. RIPARIAN RIGHTS OF MUNICIPALITIES.—Dwellers in towns and villages, through which a stream passes, may use the water thereof to the same extent as any other riparian proprietors, provided they can reach the stream by a public highway, or secure a right of way over the lands of others. *Barre Water Co.* v. *Carnes*, 891.

6. USE OF STREAM FOR SUPPLY OF MUNICPALITY, WHEN NOT ENJOINED.—A riparian municipality which has obtained legislative authority to build a a dam and lay pipes, with a view to obtaining, for domestic, fire, and sanitary purposes, a reasonable supply of water from a stream on which it is situated, cannot be enjoined from so using the water at the suit of a municipality lower down the same stream, which has never acquired, by purchase or otherwise, the rights of the riparian proprietors above it. *Barre Water Co.* v. *Carnes*, 891.

7. SUFFICIENCY OF COMPLAINT IN ACTION TO ESTABLISH RIGHTS IN A WATERCOURSE.—A complaint in an action to establish certain rights in a watercourse, alleged to have been diverted, is not demurrable on the ground that the stream described is not a watercourse, when it alleges that "there were always, and are yet, living springs, which continuously flow and discharge their waters by a well-defined stream into a natural lake of about sixty acres in extent, known as 'Big lake'"; that "the waters so gathered flowed, under natural conditions, upon the surface and beneath the surface of the lands lying to the southeast of said lake to and across the said lands of the plaintiff, and thence easterly, until they discharged themselves and were again collected in a stream known as 'Beaver creek'"; that "the said natural flow or stream of water from the lake was well defined and established, and, in places, one of which was upon the land of the plaintiff, had made for itself a distinct and plainly marked channel, pointing and showing the natural flow of the water" and that "said stream was known and commonly called by the name of the 'West branch' of 'Beaver creek.'" The fact that such complaint also shows that the stream spread over wide reaches of marsh and swamp lands, and percolated the soil in many or most places between the 'Big lake' and 'Beaver creek,' therein referred to, does not affect its sufficiency. *Case* v. *Hoffman*, 937.

8. PROPERTY RIGHTS IN.—The water of every natural stream in Colorado is the property of the public. Private ownership therein is not recognized, but the right to divert water therefrom and apply it to beneficial uses is expressly guaranteed by the constitution. *Fort Morgan Land etc. Co. v. South Platte Ditch Co.*, 259.

9. APPROPRIATION, WHAT CONSTITUTES.—A priority of right to the water of a natural stream can be legally acquired only by the application of such water to a beneficial use. Hence, there must not only be a diversion of the water from the stream, but an actual application of it to the soil, to constitute a constitutional appropriation for irrigation. *Fort Morgan Land etc. Co. v. South Platte Ditch Co.*, 259.

10. APPROPRIATION OF.—By the diversion and use of the waters of a natural stream, a priority of right to such use may be acquired, and, when so acquired, such priority is a property right, subject to sale and transfer. *Fort Morgan Land etc. Co. v. South Platte Ditch Co.*, 259.

11. APPROPRIATION, WHEN COMPLETE.—An appropriation of the water of a natural stream is complete only when some open, physical demonstration indicates an intent to take, for a valuable or beneficial use, and such intent is followed by taking and applying the water to the use designed. *Fort Morgan Land etc. Co. v. South Platte Ditch Co.*, 259.

12. APPROPRIATION — PRIORITIES.—Awarding priorities to several ditches in excess of the amount of water actually appropriated at the time the decree is rendered is error. A prior diversion and promised future use do not support such decree. *Fort Morgan Land etc. Co. v. South Platte Ditch Co.*, 259.

See CONTRACTS, 4, 5; EQUITY, 2; IRRIGATION COMPANIES; JURISDICTION, 6; LANDLORD AND TENANT, 8-10; PLEADING, 1; RAILROADS, 1-9; WHARVES.

WAYS.
See PRIVATE WAYS.

WHARVES.

1. RIPARIAN PROPRIETOR'S RIGHT TO WHARFAGE.—A proprietor of lands fronting upon navigable waters has the right to connect himself therewith by means of wharves or channels extending from his uplands out to navigable water, so long as he does nothing to interfere with the free navigation of such water. *Prior v. Swartz*, 333.

2. NAVIGABLE WATERS—CONFLICT BETWEEN RIGHT TO PLANT OYSTERS AND THE RIGHT TO CONSTRUCT WHARVES.—The right of a riparian proprietor, by wharves and channels, to connect his upland with the navigable water in front thereof is paramount to any right in others to plant or cultivate oysters on the land covered by such wharves or channels. *Prior v. Swartz*, 333.

WILLS.

1. DIFFERENT PAPERS EXECUTED AT DIFFERENT DATES AS ONE WILL.— A testamentary paper executed by a testatrix in execution of a testamentary power conferred on her by her deceased husband is not revoked by the execution of a later will and codicil containing substantially the same provisions as the first paper, but without referring to it, and the two instruments, when taken together, constitute the last will of the testatrix. *Knox v. Knox*, 235.